LAW OF

FEDERAL COURTS

By

CHARLES ALAN WRIGHT

William B. Bates Chair for the Administration of Justice
The University of Texas

FIFTH EDITION

HORNBOOK SERIES

ST. PAUL, MINN.
WEST PUBLISHING CO.
1994

Hornbook Series, WESTLAW, the West Publishing Co. Logo, and the key symbol appearing on the front cover are registered trademarks of West Publishing Co. Registered in the U.S. Patent and Trademark Office.

COPYRIGHT © 1963, 1970, 1976, 1983 WEST PUBLISHING CO.
COPYRIGHT © 1994 By WEST PUBLISHING CO.

610 Opperman Drive
P.O. Box 64526
St. Paul, MN 55164–0526
1–800–328–9352

All rights reserved
Printed in the United States of America

Library of Congress Cataloging-in-Publication Data

Wright, Charles Alan.
    The law of federal courts / by Charles Alan Wright. — 5th ed.
      p. cm. — (Hornbook series)
    Includes index.
    ISBN 0–314–04022–6
    1. Jurisdiction—United States. 2. Procedure (Law)—United
States. I. Title. II. Series.
KF8840.W7 1994
347.73'2—dc20
   [347.3072]

                                                       94–19498
                                                           CIP

ISBN 0–314–04022–6

1st Reprint–1995

Preface to Fifth Edition

It has been a long time between books. Indeed it has been far too long. The Fourth Edition of this book was published in March, 1983, but the manuscript was actually sent to the publisher in August, 1982, so that—save for a few last-minute additions that were made when the Fourth Edition was in proof—the Fourth Edition speaks of the federal courts as they were 12 years ago.

The Supreme Court, as always, has been busy. A trilogy of decisions—Franchise Tax Board of California v. Construction Laborers Vacation Trust for Southern California, 103 S.Ct. 2841 (1983), Merrell Dow Pharmaceuticals Inc. v. Thompson, 106 S.Ct. 3229 (1986), and Metropolitan Life Insurance Co. v. Taylor, 107 S.Ct. 1542 (1987)—have reaffirmed some principles that had been under attack about original jurisdiction and removal of federal-question cases, but those cases have also created some new rules of their own. The law of standing continues to fluctuate, with Lujan v. Defenders of Wildlife, 112 S.Ct. 2130 (1992), and Northeastern Florida Contractors v. Jacksonville, 113 S.Ct. 2297 (1993), perhaps the most striking examples of movements both to restrict and to expand standing. There has been no expansion of habeas-corpus jurisdiction. The final traces of Fay v. Noia, 83 S.Ct. 822 (1963), have been obliterated and the cause-and-prejudice standard now applies across the board, greatly sharpened by the decision in Teague v. Lane, 109 S.Ct. 1060 (1989), and its progeny to bar relief to a state defendant who relies on a "new rule".

The proper application of the Eleventh Amendment divided the Court in a number of cases, of which Pennhurst State School & Hospital v. Halderman, 104 S.Ct. 900 (1984), is perhaps the most notable. The use of "Colorado River" abstention was cut back in Moses H. Cone Memorial Hospital v. Mercury Construction Corp., 103 S.Ct. 927 (1983), and there was a major pronouncement in Pennzoil Co. v. Texaco, Inc., 107 S.Ct. 1519 (1987), on the application of the Younger doctrine in civil cases. Michigan v. Long, 103 S.Ct. 3469 (1983), made a considerable change in the Supreme Court's treatment of cases in which it is unclear whether a state-court decision rested on state or federal grounds.

The decisions in the two preceding paragraphs show how busy the Court has been in this rapidly changing field. But Congress also has been busy—and a good case can be made that it has been the more important actor in the years just past. Three statutes are of particular significance. The Judicial Improvements and Access to Justice Act of 1988, Pub.L. 100–702, 102 Stat. 4642, made changes in the statutes on diversity, jurisdictional amount, removal, and venue. Even more important is the Judicial Improvements Act of 1990, Pub.L. 101–650, 104 Stat. 5089.

Title III of that Act, itself known as the "Federal Courts Study Committee Implementation Act of 1990", codified the doctrines of pendent jurisdiction and ancillary jurisdiction under a new name, "supplemental jurisdiction". It rewrote the rules on venue in a well-intended but ineptly executed fashion, which has been only partly repaired by an amendatory statute in 1992. The 1990 statute also made major changes on removal and on appealability. Finally, the Civil Justice Reform Act of 1990, Pub.L. 101–416, 104 Stat. 5089, has brought anarchy into federal procedure by, in effect, allowing each district to decide in large measure what procedures it will use.

Nor have the rulemakers been idle. When the Fourth Edition was published Civil Rule 11 merited only a single paragraph. Amendments to that rule that took effect later in 1983 became extremely controversial and led to equally controversial amendments, effective December 1, 1993, cutting back on the 1983 revisions. Rule 4 on service of process was completely rewritten in 1993. And the rules on discovery were changed in several respects in 1993, with the most notable change—which became law after narrowly escaping a Congressional veto—being the new provisions of Rule 26(a) calling for required disclosures by the parties.

All of these developments, and many others that have not been detailed here, have been incorporated into this new volume. Four completely new sections have been added. These are: § 6A, Supporting Services for the Courts; § 63A, The Civil Justice Reform Act of 1990; § 69A, Sanctions; and § 83A, Required Disclosures. Even on aspects that have not significantly changed since 1983, what was said then has been reexamined, later cases noted where they add to or alter what earlier cases had said, and later scholarly commentary cited.

As in the past, this book makes frequent references to the multi-volume Treatise on Federal Practice and Procedure, which I have been writing in collaboration with Professors Arthur R. Miller, Edward H. Cooper, Kenneth W. Graham, Mary Kay Kane, Victor J. Gold, and Richard L. Marcus. Those who wish more detail on matters discussed here will find it by going to the cited portions of the Treatise. The citations to the Treatise omit its full title, and show only volume number, the authors of the volume in question, the unit of the Treatise to which the citation is being made—Criminal, Civil, Jurisdiction, or Evidence—and then the particular reference within the volume. (The designation "2d" following the name of the unit shows that the citation is to a volume for which a Second Edition is now in print.) In addition, so many references are made in this book to the American Law Institute Study of Division of Jurisdiction between State and Federal Courts (Official Draft, 1969) that a short form of reference, "ALI Study," has been used.

At a number of places throughout the book I acknowledge my indebtedness to persons who have helped me on a particular section or issue. But there are some persons who have given me the benefit of their wisdom on a wide variety of subjects and whose assistance cannot be acknowledged in a single footnote. For valuable help of this kind I must particularly thank Professors Ronald J. Mann of the Washington University Law School, John B. Oakley of the University of California at Davis Law School, and David J. Sharpe of the National Law Center of George Washington University.

Although I have written many books, I have never felt it necessary to acknowledge publicly the assistance I have had from my secretaries. But this is the first time I have ever written a book on a computer. I found this an interesting and effective way to do a new edition of an old book, but it worked only because Colleen D. Kieke became so expert on these mysteries of technology that she was able to get me through this new process. And while we were laboring over a hot computer, my other secretary, Kathryn R. Bartsch, was fending off telephone calls and other distractions and doing the countless other things that gave me time to work on the Fifth Edition. To them—and to David L. Gunn, the reference librarian at the Tarlton Law Library who professes to enjoy hunting out answers to my unusual questions—my warm thanks.

In the Preface to the First Edition I suggested that the needs of law students are far different from those of lawyers and judges and I said that this work was intended for students. It was and is. But I underestimated the extent to which all of us in the legal profession remain students throughout our lives, and it has been highly gratifying to me to see the extent to which courts and lawyers have found the earlier editions of the book useful.

The Preface to the First Edition is not retained in this edition simply as a monument to my own failure to appreciate the needs of lawyers and judges. A more important reason is to preserve what I said then about my dear friends and mentors, Charles E. Clark and Charles T. McCormick. The First Edition of this book was published in September, 1963. Before the end of that year both Judge Clark and Dean McCormick were dead. The Fourth Edition was dedicated to my dear friend and colleague, Bernard J. Ward, who died in 1982 at much too young an age but who still has an important place in the minds and the hearts of all those who care about what he called "the Judges of the Third Article". See the memorial tributes to him at 61 Texas L.Rev. 1 (1982). Judge Clark, Dean McCormick, and Bernie Ward are all long dead, but I remember them fondly and miss them greatly.

CHARLES ALAN WRIGHT

Austin, Texas
April, 1994

*

Preface to First Edition

This book is intended to provide for law students a comprehensive textual discussion of the jurisdiction and procedure of the federal courts. I have been greatly aided in preparing the book by my recent reexamination of these subjects in the course of doing my revision of the Barron & Holtzoff Treatise. The availability of the Treatise has been helpful, too, since it has made it possible to confine case citations to the more important precedents, while referring the reader interested in exhaustive citation to the Treatise. This book, however, is not a mere abridgement of the Treatise. The needs, as I conceive them, of the law student are so far different from those of the lawyer and the judge, for whom the Treatise was written, that it has been necessary to write for the student an entirely new book. The Treatise endeavors to state accurately and completely what the law is. This book, written for a student audience, is more concerned with why the law is as it is, and whether existing doctrine works as satisfactorily as it should. Thus, though there are occasional passages where I have borrowed what I have already said in the Treatise, the great bulk of the book is freshly written and based on fresh research.

The organization of the book is generally similar to that of the casebooks on this subject by Forrester and Currier, and by McCormick, Chadbourn, and Wright, though the subject of procedure in the federal courts is given more attention here than in those casebooks, and is intended to be useful by students taking courses which emphasize federal procedure, or procedure in a state with rules modelled on the Federal Rules. Necessarily the discussion here is primarily about civil cases, though I have endeavored to suggest a few of the problems which arise in criminal cases, and to indicate that not all of the business of the federal courts is civil. Like everyone who has worked in this field in the last decade, I have been influenced by the great work of scholarship produced by Professors Hart and Wechsler. Their insistence that the problems of federal jurisdiction be considered in terms of their effect on our system of federalism, rather than as purely technical exercises, is especially congenial to one whose professional concerns are with the federal courts and with constitutional law, and I am hopeful that some of that emphasis appears in the pages which follow.

My debts are many. I have acquired many valuable insights into the working of the federal courts from my brilliant and experienced colleagues on the Advisory Committee on Civil Rules. Dean W. Page Keeton has been a source of great encouragement, and has provided facilities and teaching arrangements conducive to scholarship. Three of my former students, Bert B. Adkins, Jr., Buford P. Berry, and Thomas S. Terrell, have kindly read the manuscript, and pointed out many places where revision was necessary if the book was to meet the needs and the understanding of law students.

But to two men I owe an overwhelming debt. Each has been my friend and my collaborator. Each, through his scholarly work and his effort for reform, has done much to shape the federal court system as we know it. From each I have learned much. As an inadequate token of my gratitude to, and admiration for, these great men, this book is respectfully dedicated to Charles E. Clark and Charles T. McCormick, with the hope that they will not find it unworthy.

CHARLES ALAN WRIGHT

Austin, Texas
June, 1963

WESTLAW® Overview

Law of Federal Courts offers a detailed and comprehensive treatment of legal principles and issues relating to federal court jurisdiction. To obtain supplemental information to the information contained in this book, you can access WESTLAW, a computer-assisted legal research service of West Publishing Company. WESTLAW contains a broad library of legal research resources, including case law, statutes, current developments and many information databases.

Learning how to use these materials effectively will enhance your legal research. To help you coordinate your book and WESTLAW research, this volume contains an appendix listing WESTLAW databases, search techniques and sample problems.

THE PUBLISHER

*

Summary of Contents

*

Table of Contents

CHAPTER 4. DIVERSITY OF CITIZENSHIP

CHAPTER 5. JURISDICTIONAL AMOUNT

CHAPTER 6. REMOVAL JURISDICTION AND PROCEDURE

CHAPTER 7. VENUE

CHAPTER 8. THE RELATIONS OF STATE AND FEDERAL COURTS

CHAPTER 9.   THE LAW APPLIED BY
THE FEDERAL COURTS

CHAPTER 10.   PROCEDURE IN THE DISTRICT COURTS

A.   INTRODUCTION

B.   PROCESS

C.   PLEADINGS

D.   JOINDER OF CLAIMS AND PARTIES

E.   DISCOVERY

*

LAW OF
FEDERAL COURTS

*

Chapter 1

THE FEDERAL JUDICIAL SYSTEM

Analysis

---

§ 1. The Historical Bases [1]

Any study of the federal courts in the latter part of the 20th century necessarily must begin with two 18th-century landmarks—Article III of the Constitution and the Judiciary Act of 1789. Changes, indeed important changes, there surely have been, but the decisions made at the very beginning of the republic as to the nature of the federal judicial system have a marked imprint on even the most routine case to this day.

The necessity for constant resort to the Constitution in understanding the federal judicial system is obvious. The federal courts cannot be given authority beyond that conferred by the Constitution. This was recognized in the first case to hold an Act of Congress unconstitutional, the landmark decision in Marbury v. Madison,[2] where the Supreme

§ 1

1. The classic study of the history of the federal judiciary, somewhat misleadingly titled, is Frankfurter & Landis, The Business of the Supreme Court, 1928. Warren, New Light on the History of the Federal Judiciary Act of 1789, 1923, 37 Harv.L.Rev. 49, has long been thought definitive on the subject it treats, and has been extremely influential. Both Mr. Warren's scholarship and his conclusions are sharply challenged, however, in Ritz, Rewriting the History of the Judiciary Act of 1789, Holt & LaRue eds. 1990. See also Origins of the Federal Judiciary: Essays on the Judiciary Act of 1789, Marcus ed. 1992; Hart & Wechsler, The Federal Courts and the Federal System, Bator, Meltzer, Mishkin, & Shapiro ed.

1988, pp. 1–64; Borchers, The Origins of Diversity Jurisdiction, the Rise of Legal Positivism, and a Brave New World for Erie and Klaxon, 1993, 72 Texas L.Rev. 79, 86–110; Holt, "To Establish Justice": Politics, the Judiciary Act of 1789, and the Invention of the Federal Courts, 1989 Duke L.J. 1421; Casto, The First Congress's Understanding of Its Authority Over the Federal Court's Jurisdiction, 1985, 26 B.C.L.Rev. 1101; Frank, Historical Bases of the Federal Judicial System, 1948, 13 Law & Contemp.Probs. 3. The deliberations of the Constitutional Convention will be found in Farrand, The Records of the Federal Convention, rev. ed. 1937.

2. 1803, 1 Cranch 137, 2 L.Ed. 60.

1

Court held invalid a statute that purported to grant to it original jurisdiction beyond that defined in the Constitution. Although there is dispute as to which provisions of the Constitution are to be looked to in determining the power of the federal courts,[3] it is beyond challenge that the Constitution does mark the limits.[4]

In a more far-reaching sense, questions of federal jurisdiction are questions of constitutional law. In 1864 former Justice Benjamin Curtis made the still-timely reminder: "Let it be remembered, also, for just now we may be in some danger of forgetting it, that questions of jurisdiction were questions of power as between the United States and the several States."[5] There is a recurring temptation to view questions of federal jurisdiction as if they were simple procedural questions, to be resolved in whatever fashion will best serve the desirable goal of efficient judicial administration. Settled doctrine does give some play to such considerations.[6] But when it is remembered that the delicate balance of a federal system is at stake, and that expansion of the jurisdiction of the federal courts diminishes the power of the states, it is apparent that efficiency cannot be the sole or the controlling consideration.

The Constitutional Convention had no difficulty in agreeing to the novel proposal of a federal judiciary. Randolph's resolution "that a National Judiciary be established" was unanimously adopted early in the convention.[7] There was more disagreement as to the form such a judiciary should take. Though the Committee of the Whole had at first approved the proposition that such a judiciary should consist of one supreme tribunal and of inferior tribunals,[8] this came under attack from those who argued that an additional set of courts was an unnecessary expense, and that it would be sufficient to have all cases decided in the state courts in the first instance, with appeal to the supreme national court. A motion to strike out the provision for inferior tribunals prevailed by a vote of five states to four, with two states divided.[9] Wilson and Madison then put forward a compromise. They moved that the national legislature be empowered to institute inferior tribunals, and noted the distinction between establishing such tribunals absolutely and giving a discretion to the legislature to establish or not establish them. This motion prevailed, by a vote of eight states to two, with one divided,[10] and this compromise formed the basis for the language later used in the Constitution itself.

The decisions of the convention about appointment, tenure, and compensation of judges were of importance—and with regard to the first, quite controversial—but the other principal decision that had to be made

---

3. See §§ 11, 20 below.

4. See § 8 below.

5. Curtis, Notice of the Death of Chief Justice Taney, Proceedings in Circuit Court of the United States for the First Circuit, 1864, p. 9.

6. See §§ 9, 19 below. And see 28 U.S.C.A. § 1367.

7. 1 Farrand, The Records of the Federal Convention, rev. ed. 1937, p. 104.

8. Id. at pp. 104–105, 119.

9. Id. at pp. 124–125.

10. Id. at p. 125.

in the Constitution was the scope of the judicial power to be granted to the national courts. On this subject, unfortunately, the records of the convention are unilluminating, and it is not possible to say what motivated the Framers in including particular grants of jurisdiction in § 2 of Article III. Perhaps most easily explained are the grants of admiralty jurisdiction and of jurisdiction over cases between two or more states. Maritime commerce was at that time the principal business activity of the states. The need for uniformity in such cases was deeply felt, and it was recognized also that admiralty cases normally arise outside the borders of any state and that they may involve relations with other nations. For all these reasons, in Hamilton's phrase, even "the most bigoted idolizers of State authority have not thus far shown a disposition to deny the national judiciary the cognizance of maritime causes."[11] Similarly the grant of jurisdiction over controversies between states was responsive to experience. There had been such disputes, principally over borders, and there was a felt need for a tribunal to resolve them. The jurisdiction thus granted may perhaps be thought of as a transfer to the national judiciary of a power exercised by the Privy Council prior to the revolution.

A number of the other jurisdictional clauses can be justified by the need of the national government to enforce its laws and to collect its revenues—thus, the jurisdiction over cases arising under the Constitution or laws of the United States and over cases to which the United States shall be a party—and to speak for all the nation in dealings with foreign governments and peoples—thus, the jurisdiction over cases arising under treaties, or affecting ambassadors, other public ministers or consuls, or between states, or their citizens, and foreign states, citizens, or subjects.

The greatest mystery, and the most heated controversy, surrounds the diversity jurisdiction, permitting the national courts to hear suits between citizens of different states, and between a state and citizens of another state. As will be seen later,[12] there is to this day no consensus as to the historical justification or the contemporary need for diversity jurisdiction, though it was accepted without question at the Constitutional Convention.

The judicial article of the Constitution was the center of much argument in the ratification debates. Five of the Federalists Papers, Nos. 78–82, are devoted to the judiciary. Though the basic idea of a national judiciary did not come under attack, many of the state ratifying conventions proposed amendments regarding the courts. The proposals that trial by jury be guaranteed in civil as well as in criminal cases, and that appellate review be limited to questions of law, were incorporated by the First Congress in the Seventh Amendment. Attempts to do away

---

11. The Federalist No. 80, at 502, Wright ed. 1961 (Hamilton). See also Casto, The Origins of Federal Admiralty Juris-diction in an Age of Privateers, Smugglers, and Pirates, 1993, 37 Am.J.Legal Hist. 117.

12. See § 23 below.

with diversity jurisdiction, and to take away the authority to establish inferior federal courts, were unsuccessful.

The other great landmark, the Judiciary Act of 1789 [13]—or the First Judiciary Act as it is often called—has acquired a status almost as exalted as the Constitution itself. The act itself, primarily drafted by Oliver Ellsworth, was much criticized in the early days of the Republic, but it is now universally regarded as "a great law." [14] The act has a special authority of its own, not only because of its intrinsic merit, but because of the circumstances of its enactment. The Supreme Court has noted that the act "was passed by the first congress assembled under the constitution, many of whose members had taken part in framing that instrument, and is contemporaneous and weighty evidence of its true meaning." [15] The most significant aspect of the First Judiciary Act is that the power to create inferior federal courts was immediately exercised. As it had in the Constitutional Convention and in the ratification debates, the necessity for such courts aroused warm controversy, but in the end Congress proceeded to create not one set of inferior courts but two. It created for each state at least one district court. Finally it created three circuit courts. Judges were provided for the Supreme Court and for the district courts, but the circuit courts were given no judges of their own. Instead the circuit court was to hold two sessions each year at each district within the circuit, with the court made up of two justices of the Supreme Court, and the district judge for the district.

The district courts were entirely courts of original jurisdiction, authorized to entertain admiralty cases, minor criminal cases, and some other rather limited classes of cases. The circuit courts had both original and appellate jurisdiction. They were the court of original jurisdiction in diversity cases, most criminal cases, and larger cases to which the United States was a party. They had appellate jurisdiction over the district courts in civil cases where the amount in controversy exceeded $50 and in admiralty cases where the amount in controversy exceeded $300. The Supreme Court had some original jurisdiction, as the Constitution provided, and had appellate jurisdiction over the circuit courts in civil cases where the amount in controversy exceeded $2,000, and over the state courts in cases raising a federal question. There was no review in the Supreme Court of federal criminal cases.

Certain features of the First Judiciary Act deserve special comment. It was argued in Congress that there was a duty to confer on the federal courts the full judicial power granted by the Constitution. This view was rejected by Congress, and indeed at no time in history has the entire judicial power been vested in the federal courts.

13. Act of Sept. 24, 1789, 1 Stat. 73. "The phrase, 'Judiciary Act,' is modern usage; the term was not used then by either Congress or the public, so far as we can determine." Ritz, note 1 above, at p. 3.

14. Frankfurter & Landis, note 1 above, at p. 4.

15. Wisconsin v. Pelican Ins. Co., 1888, 8 S.Ct. 1370, 1378, 127 U.S. 265, 297, 32 L.Ed. 239.

It is interesting that Congress proceeded immediately to give the circuit courts jurisdiction in diversity cases, but that no jurisdiction was conferred on the lower courts in cases arising under the Constitution or laws of the United States. Except for a grant in 1801 that lasted little more than a year, not until 1875 was there a general grant of federal-question jurisdiction; such cases could only be brought in the state courts.

The First Judiciary Act introduced the device of removal from state to federal courts, a device not mentioned in the Constitution. Subject to a jurisdictional amount of $500, the privilege of removing to the circuit court a case commenced in state court was given to alien defendants, defendants in diversity cases where the plaintiff was a citizen of the state in which suit was brought, and to either party in cases involving title to land where the parties were relying on grants from different states.

Section 34 of the act is well known as the Rules of Decision Act. It provided that, except as otherwise required by federal law, "the laws of the several states" should be regarded as rules of decision in trials at common law in the federal courts in cases where they applied. Probably no statute regarding the federal courts has led to such difficulty.[16]

Finally, section 25 of the First Judiciary Act gave the Supreme Court appellate jurisdiction over final judgments of the highest state courts in certain cases involving federal questions.

The least satisfactory feature of the First Judiciary Act was the requirement that the Supreme Court justices "ride circuit" and participate in the proceedings of the circuit courts. As early as 1792 Chief Justice Jay and his associates joined in a memorial to the President in which they protested that the task of circuit riding was "too burdensome." Congress gave some relief in 1793 by providing that only one justice, rather than two, need attend each session of a circuit court,[17] but more than a century was to go by before the Supreme Court justices were entirely relieved of this burden.

There was, indeed, an earlier attempt to give complete relief. In the dying days of the Adams administration Congress passed the short-lived "Midnight Judges Act,"[18] which, so we are told on high authority, "combined thoughtful concern for the federal judiciary with selfish concern for the Federalist party."[19]

The 1801 Act put an end to circuit riding by the Supreme Court justices, and authorized the appointment of sixteen new circuit judges, so that each circuit court thereafter would consist of three judges appointed to that court. In addition the act purported to give the circuit courts jurisdiction in all cases to which the judicial power of the United States

---

16. See §§ 54–60 below.

17. Act of March 2, 1793, 1 Stat. 333.

18. Act of Feb. 13, 1801, 2 Stat. 89. See Turner, Midnight Judges, 1961, 109 U.Pa. L.Rev. 494; Surrency, The Judiciary Act of 1801, 1958, 2 Am.J.Leg.Hist. 53.

19. Frankfurter & Landis, note 1 above, at p. 25.

extended, subject in some cases to a jurisdictional amount of $400. Adams, before leaving office, promptly appointed deserving Federalists to the sixteen judicial posts thus created. The new administration and Congress lost little time in repealing the 1801 Act,[20] despite the argument, never judicially tested, that it was unconstitutional to abolish judgeships to which the Constitution gives life tenure. The 1802 legislation repealing the "Midnight Judges Act" did expand the number of circuits, and it contained a provision that circuit court might be held by a single judge. Thus, while the justices of the Supreme Court were not relieved directly of the burden of circuit riding, the pressure of their other duties was such that increasingly the circuit court was held by a single district judge.

Though changes were constantly being made in details of the organization and jurisdiction of the federal courts, only a few developments need be noticed here. In 1869 Congress authorized the appointment of one circuit judge for each of the circuits, and provided that a Supreme Court justice need sit with the circuit court only once every two years in each district within his circuit.[21] Legislation in 1875 finally gave the federal courts original jurisdiction, in terms very nearly as broad as the constitutional grant, to cases arising under the Constitution, laws, or treaties of the United States.[22] Thus, for the first time general federal-question jurisdiction was conferred, though in prior years particular statutes had authorized jurisdiction in some classes of federal-question cases. The same statute also broadened diversity jurisdiction. The expanded jurisdiction naturally caused increased congestion in the courts, which an increase of the jurisdictional amount to $2,000 in 1887 failed to check. The time had come for a more drastic reshaping of the judicial structure.

Such a reshaping came with the adoption in 1891 of the Evarts Act.[23] This statute created for each circuit a circuit court of appeals, and authorized the appointment of an additional circuit judge for each circuit. The new circuit court of appeals was to consist of three judges, the two circuit judges and either a justice of the Supreme Court or one of the district judges from within the circuit. An important change, however, was the provision that no judge was to sit on an appeal in a case that he had heard below. Prior to 1891 it happened not infrequently that on appeal from the district court to the circuit court the district judge who had decided against appellant in the district court would be found hearing the appeal.

The Evarts Act retained both the district courts and the circuit courts as nisi prius courts, but it did abolish the appellate jurisdiction of the circuit courts. Thus, there were still to be two baseline courts, with varying jurisdiction, but appeal from each was either to the circuit court of appeals or to the Supreme Court. The act provided for direct review

---

20. Act of March 8, 1802, 2 Stat. 132.

21. Act of April 10, 1869, 16 Stat. 44.

22. Act of March 3, 1875, 18 Stat. 470. See § 22 below.

23. Act of March 3, 1891, 26 Stat. 826.

in the Supreme Court of certain cases of an important nature. Other cases were to be appealed to the circuit court of appeals. In some classes of cases, notably diversity and admiralty, the decision of the circuit court of appeals was final, unless that court certified a question to the Supreme Court or the Supreme Court granted the discretionary writ of certiorari to bring the case up for further review. In other cases there was appeal as of right to the Supreme Court from the decision of the circuit court of appeals.

With the adoption in 1911 of a Judicial Code,[24] the circuit courts were finally abolished. A source of complaint and controversy from their establishment in 1789, they had been quite unnecessary since the adoption of the Evarts Act in 1891. In 1911 their jurisdiction was transferred to the district courts. The Judicial Code of that year also increased the jurisdictional amount for most cases in the district court, this time to $3,000.

One last landmark must be mentioned. This was the "Judges' Bill," so-called because it was drafted by a committee of Supreme Court justices, adopted by Congress in 1925.[25] This act was intended to reduce the burden on the Supreme Court. It did this in two ways. Direct review in the Supreme Court of decisions of the district courts was eliminated, except in a very few classes of cases of particular importance and urgency. The principle of discretionary review in the Supreme Court by use of the writ of certiorari, first introduced by the Evarts Act, was greatly expanded. With regard both to the circuit courts of appeals and the state appellate courts, the Supreme Court was given discretion whether to hear the case, except in compelling instances where a state court has rejected a claim based on the supremacy of federal law, or where a federal court has held unconstitutional a state statute.

Changes continue to be made at virtually every session of Congress in the laws regulating the federal judiciary. The Judicial Code was recodified in 1948, while 1958 produced important enactments increasing the jurisdictional amount to $10,000, redefining corporate citizenship, and allowing for discretionary interlocutory appeals from the district courts to the courts of appeals. The requirement of an amount in controversy for federal-question cases, always largely illusory, was greatly reduced in application in 1976 and abolished entirely in 1980. Another 1980 statute provides for the first time a means other than impeachment for investigating and resolving allegations that a federal judge has been unable to discharge efficiently all the duties of the office or has engaged in conduct inconsistent with the effective and expeditious administration of the courts.[26] The Court of Appeals for the Federal Circuit was created in 1982; it differs from the other courts of appeals in

24. Act of March 3, 1911, 36 Stat. 1087.

25. Act of Feb. 13, 1925, 43 Stat. 936.

26. 28 U.S.C.A. § 372(c). See Symposium, Disciplining the Federal Judiciary, 1993, 142 U.Pa.L.Rev. 1; Symposium on Judicial Discipline and Impeachment, 1988, 76 Ky. L.J. 633; Rieger, the Judicial Councils Reform and Judicial Conduct and Disability Act: Will Judges Judge Judges?, 1988, 37 Emory L.J. 45; Burbank, Politics and Progress in Implementing the Federal Judicial Discipline Act, 1987, 71 Judicature 13.

that it hears cases in specified kinds of cases from district courts around the country, rather than hearing appeals from district courts within the borders of the circuit.[27] Other significant changes were made by legislation in 1988 and 1990.[28] But with the passage of the Judges' Bill in 1925, the federal-court structure took on essentially the form that it has to this day. Its resemblance to the structure originally provided in 1789 is quite clear.

The pressures of docket congestion have caused many thoughtful persons and groups to think that the time has come for reexamination of the organization of the federal courts and for restructuring similar to the changes that occurred in the Evarts Act of 1891 and the Judges' Bill in 1925. Although there have been numerous provocative proposals to this end,[29] there is not yet agreement on whether fundamental changes are needed or what they should be.

§ 2. The District Courts [1]

The general court of original jurisdiction in the federal system is the United States District Court. The statutes divide the nation, including the District of Columbia and Puerto Rico, into 91 districts, in each of which there is established a district court. Other courts similarly named are created for the Canal Zone, Guam, the Virgin Islands, and the Northern Mariana Islands. The statutes specify with great particularity the borders of a district, and the places within the district at which court is to be held.[2]

Following the example set in the First Judiciary Act and consistently adhered to since, districts do not—with one insignificant exception [3]— extend across state lines. Thus, a state will constitute at least one

27. Act of April 2, 1982, Pub.L. 97–164, 96 Stat. 25. See § 5 below.

28. Oakley, Recent Statutory Changes in the Law of Federal Jurisdiction and Venue: The Judicial Improvements Acts of 1988 and 1990, 1991, 24 U.C.Davis L.Rev. 735

29. E.g., ALI Study; Commission on Revision of the Federal Court Appellate System, Structure and Internal Procedures: Recommendations for Change, June 1975, reprinted 67 F.R.D. 195; Hruska, The National Court of Appeals: An Analysis of Viewpoints, 1975, 9 Creighton L.Rev. 286; Report of the Study Group on the Caseload of the Supreme Court, 1972, reprinted 57 F.R.D. 573; Friendly, Federal Jurisdiction: A General View, 1973; Haworth & Meador, A Proposed New Federal Intermediate Appellate Court, 1979, 12 U.Mich.J.L.Ref. 201; Hufstedler, Comity and the Constitution: The Changing Role of the Federal Judiciary, 1972, 47 N.Y.U.L.Rev. 841. Other materials on this subject are collected in 13 Wright, Miller & Cooper, Jurisdiction § 3510.

A comprehensive examination of the federal court system, but one that did not propose fundamental structural change, is Report of the Federal Courts Study Committee, April 2, 1990.

§ 2

1. Marshall, Some Reflections on the Quality of Life of a United States District Judge, 1985, 27 Ariz.L.Rev. 593; Clark, Adjudication to Administration: A Statistical Analysis of Federal District Courts in the Twentieth Century, 1981, 55 S.Cal.L.Rev. 65; Steckler, The Future of the Federal District Courts, 1978, 11 Ind.L.Rev. 523; Surrency, Federal District Court Judges and the History of Their Courts, 1966, 40 F.R.D. 139. The latter article has a history, as of that time, of each district and of the judges who have served in it.

2. 28 U.S.C.A. §§ 81–131.

3. The District Court for the District of Wyoming includes all of that state and such portions of Yellowstone National Park as are within Montana and Idaho.

judicial district, and many states are divided into two, three, or even, in the case of California, New York, and Texas, four districts. Many districts are further subdivided into divisions, but the divisions are of very little importance. Since 1988 there has been no statutory requirement that an action be commenced in a particular division within a district.

The formation within a state of districts, and of divisions within districts, has not been an entirely rational process. There is no immediately apparent reason, for example, why Mississippi should be divided into two districts, which in turn are subdivided into four and five divisions, while the entire state of Massachusetts, with almost as many district judges, constitutes a single district and single division.

The statute authorizes 581 district judges to sit in the 91 district courts.[4] There were once many districts with only a single judge, but there are no longer any such districts. All districts now have two or more judges, ranging up to the 28 judges authorized for the Southern District of New York. Normally a single judge will sit in a case pending before the district court,[5] and it is the function of the chief judge of the district to apportion the business of the court among the judges in accordance with such rules and orders as the court may have made.[6] There are certain exceptional cases, dealt with elsewhere,[7] that call for the creation of a statutory three-judge court, made up of at least one circuit judge and the remainder district judges.

In addition, the statutes do not forbid, and some districts follow, the practice of having all the judges of the court sit en banc in important matters.[8] Finally in some districts, on procedural questions and others where a uniform practice within the district is especially desirable, the judge hearing the case will state in his opinion that he has shown the opinion to the other judges and they concur therein.[9]

The Federal Magistrates Act of 1968 created United States magistrates to assist the district courts.[10] The statute specifies some of the functions that magistrates can perform and allows a district court to assign to the magistrate "such additional duties as are not inconsistent with the Constitution and laws of the United States."[11] The statute has

---

4. 28 U.S.C.A. § 133.

5. 28 U.S.C.A. § 132(c).

6. 28 U.S.C.A. § 137.

7. See § 50 below.

8. E.g., Ainsworth v. Vasquez, D.C.Cal. 1991, 759 F.Supp. 1467; Greer v. Skilcraft, D.C.Ala.1989, 704 F.Supp. 1570; Hickman v. Taylor, D.C.Pa.1945, 4 F.R.D. 479; Bartels, United States District Courts En Banc—Resolving the Ambiguities, 1989, 73 Judicature 40.

In other cases a panel of judges, but not all of the judges of the district, may be named in order to establish uniformity within the district on recurring questions.

E.g., U.S. v. Johnson, D.C.Mo.1988, 682 F.Supp. 1033, affirmed 1989, 109 S.Ct. 647, 488 U.S. 361, 102 L.Ed.2d 714; Close v. Calmar S.S. Corp., D.C.Pa.1968, 44 F.R.D. 398, 401 n. 3.

9. E.g., Slomberg v. Pennabaker, D.C.Pa.1967, 42 F.R.D. 8, 12; Dziwanoski v. Ocean Carriers Corp., D.C.Md.1960, 26 F.R.D. 595, 599; U.S. v. Napela, D.C.N.Y. 1928, 28 F.2d 898, 904.

10. 28 U.S.C.A. §§ 631–639.

11. 28 U.S.C.A. § 636(a), (b). See U.S. v. Raddatz, 1980, 100 S.Ct. 2406, 447 U.S. 667, 65 L.Ed.2d 424; Mathews v. Weber, 1976, 96 S.Ct. 549, 423 U.S. 261, 46 L.Ed.2d 483.

been amended several times since adoption to broaden the duties that can be entrusted to magistrates,[12] and in 1990 the title of these officers was changed to "United States magistrate judge."[13]

§ 3. The Courts of Appeals[1]

The creation of the circuit courts of appeals in 1891, after a century of discontent with the prior structure of the courts, was described above.[2] These courts were renamed by the 1948 Judicial Code, and are now properly known as the United States Court of Appeals for the _____ Circuit.

The work of the courts of appeals is principally appellate, reviewing cases from the district courts, although the courts also have jurisdiction to review orders of many administrative agencies, and to issue original writs in appropriate cases.[3] In the year ended September 30, 1992, 41,543 appeals were filed with the courts of appeals from decisions of the district courts, 1,637 appeals were filed from bankruptcy courts, 598 original proceedings were commenced, and 3,235 applications were filed for review of orders of administrative agencies, for a total of 47,013 cases of all types.[4]

There are now 13 courts of appeals, one for the District of Columbia, 11 for numbered circuits that include anywhere from three to ten states and territories, and, created in 1982, the Court of Appeals for the Federal Circuit.[5] Normally cases are heard by a division of the court constituting three judges.[6] The number of judges appointed for each

---

12. 28 U.S.C.A. § 636. See Report on Magistrates by the Committee on the Federal Courts of the New York County Lawyers' Association, 1990, 136 F.R.D. 193; Silberman, Judicial Adjuncts Revisited: The Proliferation of Ad Hoc Procedure, 1989, 137 U.Pa.L.Rev. 2131; Seron, Magistrates and the Work of Federal Courts: A New Division of Labor, 1986, 69 Judicature 353; Puro, Goldman & Padawer–Singer, The Evolving Role of U.S. Magistrates in the District Courts, 1981, 64 Judicature 436; Comment, The Boundaries of Article III: Delegation of Final Decisionmaking Authority to Magistrates, 1985, 52 U.Chi.L.Rev. 1032; Note, Article III Constraints and the Expanding Civil Jurisdiction of Federal Magistrates: A Dissenting View, 1979, 88 Yale L.J. 1023.

13. Act of Dec. 1, 1990, Pub.L. 101–650, § 321, 104 Stat. 5117. See Smith, Judicial Lobbying and Court Reform: U.S. Magistrate Judges and the Judicial Improvements Act of 1990, 1992, 14 U.Ark.-L.R.L.J. 163; Smith, From U.S. Magistrates to U.S. Magistrate Judges; Developments Affecting the Federal District Courts' Lower Tier of Judicial Officers, 1991, 75 Judicature 210.

§ 3

1. See Howard, Courts of Appeals in the Federal Judicial System, 1981; Starr, The Courts of Appeals and the Future of the Federal Judiciary, 1991 Wis.L.Rev. 1; Lay, The Federal Appeals Process: Whither We Goest? The Next Fifty Years, 1989, 15 Wm.Mitchell L.Rev. 515; Hellman, Jumboism and Jurisprudence: The Theory and Practice of Precedent in the Large Appellate Court, 1989, 56 U.Chi.L.Rev. 541; Friendly, The "Law of the Circuit" and All That, 1972, 46 St. John's L.Rev. 406.

For an excellent history of a particular circuit, see Frederick, Rugged Justice: The Ninth Circuit Court of Appeals and the American West, 1891–1941, 1994.

2. See § 1 above.

3. As to the jurisdiction of the courts of appeals, see §§ 101–104 below, and see 15A Wright, Miller & Cooper, Jurisdiction 2d §§ 3901–3914.14, 15B id. §§ 3914.15–3919.- 10, 16 id. §§ 3920–3944.

4. Ann.Rep., Director of the Administrative Office of the United States Courts, 1992, Table B–3.

5. 28 U.S.C.A. § 41.

6. 28 U.S.C.A. § 46(c).

court of appeals ranges from six to 28,[7] and in addition the Supreme Court justice allotted as circuit justice for the circuit, and other judges or justices designated or assigned, are competent to sit on the court.[8] In particular, the chief judge of the court of appeals may designate and assign a district judge within the circuit to sit as a member of the court of appeals at a specific time,[9] and this power is frequently utilized.

The statute specifies the places within the circuit where the court is to sit during the year, but there is an increasing tendency, with improved methods of transportation, to centralize the work of a particular circuit at one place, and to hold most, or all, of the sessions of the court at that place.

By statute, a majority of the circuit judges of the circuit who are in active service may order a hearing or a rehearing before the court en banc.[10] Prior to 1953 this power was exercised in some circuits, but ignored in others. In that year the Supreme Court held that each circuit should establish a clear procedure for determining when en banc hearings would be had, and cautioned against indiscriminate refusal to order such hearings.[11] That decision has led to more frequent use of the en banc procedure,[12] which has the advantage, in the unusual case to which it is suited, of avoiding conflicts of view within a circuit and promoting finality of decision in the courts of appeals.[13]

---

7. 28 U.S.C.A. § 44(a).

8. 28 U.S.C.A. § 43(b). See Oberman, Coping with Rising Caseload: A New Model of Appellate Review, 1980, 46 Brooklyn L.Rev. 841; Green & Atkins, Designated Judges: How Well Do They Perform?, 1978, 61 Judicature 358.

9. 28 U.S.C.A. § 292(a).

10. 28 U.S.C.A. § 46(c). The statute codified the decision in Textile Mills Securities Corp. v. Commissioner, 1943, 62 S.Ct. 272, 314 U.S. 326, 86 L.Ed. 249, that the courts of appeals had power to hold rehearings en banc.

See also Appellate Rule 35. The spelling "en banc" is far more common in the cases and the literature, and is "certainly the predominant form in English-speaking countries," Garner, Dictionary of Modern Legal Usage, 1987, p. 213, but the Supreme Court has noted that both the statute and the rule say "in banc." Missouri v. Jenkins, 1990, 110 S.Ct. 1651, 1661 n. 15, 495 U.S. 33, 47 n. 15, 109 L.Ed.2d 31.

11. Western Pac. R. Corp. v. Western Pac. R. Co., 1953, 73 S.Ct. 656, 345 U.S. 247, 97 L.Ed. 986.

See also Shenker v. Baltimore & O. Co., 1963, 83 S.Ct. 1667, 1670, 374 U.S. 1, 4–5, 10 L.Ed.2d 709, emphasizing the discretion each circuit has in fashioning its own administrative machinery for determining when to hear a matter en banc. But there is no discretion to ignore clear requirements of the statute. Moody v. Albemarle Paper Co., 1974, 94 S.Ct. 2513, 417 U.S. 622, 41 L.Ed.2d 358.

An en banc court consists of all the circuit judges in regular active service and a senior circuit judge of the circuit if the judge has been a member of panel whose decision is under review and chooses to participate. A circuit with more than 15 active judges may determine by rule the number of members of its en banc courts. Pub.L. 95–486, § 6, 92 Stat. 1633. To date only the Ninth Circuit has taken advantage of this provision. 9th Cir. R. 35–3. The practice in the Ninth Circuit is examined in Hellman, Breaking the Banc: The Common–Law Process in the Large Appellate Court, 1991, 23 Ariz.St.L.J. 915. The conclusion reached there is that the Ninth Circuit practice has led to the maintenance and development of a consistent body of precedent.

12. See Louisell & Degnan, Rehearing in American Appellate Courts, 1960, 25 F.R.D. 143, 160–163. See also Stein, Uniformity in the Federal Courts: A Proposal for Increasing the Use of En Banc Appellate Review, 1993, 54 U.Pitt.L.Rev. 805.

13. Maris, Hearing and Rehearing Cases in Banc, 1954, 14 F.R.D. 91, 96. See generally Stein, Uniformity in the Federal Courts: A Proposal for Increasing the Use

The problem of conflicts among circuits is a persistent one. The Supreme Court cannot resolve every conflict between circuits, but it is not even clear how many of these conflicts are so serious that they require resolution and proposals to have some tribunal other than the Supreme Court resolve conflicts have met with strong opposition.[14] Government agencies often refuse to acquiesce in a decision of a court of appeals and will continue to take a position that one, or even many, court of appeals has rejected.[15] There is now a considerable literature on the wisdom, and even the constitutionality, of both intercircuit and intracircuit nonacquiescence.[16]

A statute, which seems to state an obvious truth but which changed the prior practice when it was first adopted in 1891, provides that no judge shall hear or determine an appeal from the decision of a case or issue tried by him.[17]

The Federal Rules of Appellate Procedure were adopted in 1968 and have been amended several times since. These had the salutary purpose of making procedures in the various courts of appeals largely uniform, rather than leaving appellate procedure, as in the past, to be regulated by rules of each of the courts of appeals.[18] That goal has been made largely illusory by the subsequent adoption of lengthy and inconsistent local rules in each circuit.[19]

The last three decades have seen a sudden and sharp increase in the workload of the courts of appeals that poses a major crisis in judicial administration. The number of cases commenced in all of the courts of appeals increased moderately from 2830 in 1950 to 3899 in 1960. By 1970, it was 11,662 and there was a further increase to 26,362 by 1981. By 1992, as has been seen, the total was 47,013. Congress has provided for additional judgeships, so that there are now 167 judgeships on the 13

of En Banc Appellate Review, 1993, 54 U.Pitt.L.Rev. 805; Solimine, Ideology and En Banc Review, 1988, 67 N.C.L.Rev. 29; McFeeley, En Banc Proceedings in the United States Courts of Appeals, 1988, 24 Idaho L.Rev. 255; Kaufman, Do the Costs of the En Banc Proceeding Outweigh Its Advantages?, 1985, 69 Judicature 7; 16 Wright, Miller & Cooper, Jurisdiction § 3981.

14. The Federal Courts Study Committee recommends that the Federal Judicial Center study the problem, that there be an experimental pilot project by which the Supreme Court could refer selected cases to an en banc court of appeals for disposition and creation of a nationally binding precedent, and that a court of appeals give "considerable respect" to a decision on the point by another court of appeals. Report of the Federal Courts Study Committee, April 2, 1990, pp. 124–130.

15. The United States is not bound by nonmutual issue preclusion in these cir-

cumstances. U.S. v. Mendoza, 1984, 104 S.Ct. 568, 464 U.S. 154, 78 L.Ed.2d 379.

16. See Coenen, The Constitutional Case Against Intracircuit Nonacquiescence, 1991, 75 Minn.L.Rev. 1339, citing, at 1340 n. 1, other writing on the subject. See also the doubts expressed about nonacquiescence, on both constitutional and statutory grounds, in Johnson v. U.S. Railroad Retirement Board, C.A.D.C.1992, 969 F.2d 1082, 1090–1093, certiorari denied 113 S.Ct. 1842, ___ U.S. ___, 123 L.Ed.2d 467.

17. 28 U.S.C.A. § 47. There is an interesting discussion of the statute in Swann v. Charlotte–Mecklenburg Bd. of Educ., C.A.4th, 1970, 431 F.2d 135 (Craven, J.). See also 13 Wright, Miller & Cooper, Jurisdiction § 3545.

18. See Ward, The Federal Rules of Appellate Procedure, 1968, 54 A.B.A.J. 661.

19. See 16 Wright, Miller & Cooper, Jurisdiction § 3945.

courts of appeals compared with 68 in 1960. The Fifth Circuit, which had grown to 26 judgeships, was split in 1981 after years of discussion, and a new Eleventh Circuit created in the three easternmost states of the former Fifth Circuit.[20] The Ninth Circuit, with 28 judgeships, is now an obvious candidate for a split, but with 49% of its business coming from California it is hard to know how it can be split without taking on a local rather than a national character.[21]

Even without counting the 12 judges who have become judges of the newly-formed Court of Appeals for the Federal Circuit, the number of court-of-appeals judges has increased 128% since 1960, but the number of filings in the courts of appeals has multiplied more than ten times in the same period. In 1960 57.3 cases were filed for each authorized judgeship. In 1991 the number was 234.8.[22] To cope with this vast volume of business the courts have had to restrict or eliminate oral argument in many cases, limit publication of opinions, and adopt other innovations to dispose of more cases more quickly.[23]

§ 4. The Supreme Court [1]

The Supreme Court, alone among the federal courts, is created directly by the Constitution, rather than by choice of Congress. It

---

20. Act of Oct. 14, 1980, Pub.L. 96–452, 94 Stat. 1994. See Barrow & Walker, A Court Divided: The Fifth Circuit Court of Appeals and the Politics of Judicial Reform, 1988; Godbold, The Eleventh Circuit Court of Appeals—The First Ten Years, 1992, 43 Mercer L.Rev. 961; Reavley, The Split of the Fifth Circuit: Update and Finis, 1981, 12 Texas Tech L.Rev. 1; Wisdom, Requiem for a Great Court, 1980, 26 Loy.L.Rev. 787; Wright, The Overloaded Fifth Circuit: A Crisis in Judicial Administration, 1964, 42 Texas L.Rev. 949.

21. Hellman, Legal Problems of Dividing a State between Federal Judicial Circuits, 1974, 122 U.Pa.L.Rev. 1188.

See also the Report of the Federal Courts Study Committee, April 2, 1990, pp. 123–124; the two reports of the Commission on Revision of the Federal Court Appellate System: The Geographical Boundaries of the Several Judicial Circuits: Recommendations for Change, December 1973, reprinted 62 F.R.D. 223; and Structure and Internal Procedures: Recommendations for Change, June 1975, reprinted 67 F.R.D. 195; and Baker, A Compendium of Proposals to Reform the United States Courts of Appeals, 1985, 37 U.Fla.L.Rev. 225.

22. Judge King has pointed out that in 1992 the judges of the Fifth Circuit were required to turn out one opinion almost every working day, based on a six-day work week, and to carefully review two other opinions. Each judge also had to consider

motions and petitions for rehearing averaging 1.4 per calendar day. King, A Matter of Conscience, 1991, 28 Hous.L.Rev. 955, 957.

23. See § 104 below. See also Carrington, Ceremony and Realism: Demise of Appellate Procedure, 1980, 66 A.B.A.J. 863; Godbold, Improvements in Appellate Procedure: Better Use of Available Facilities, 1980, 66 A.B.A.J. 863.

§ 4

1. The literature about the Supreme Court is vast—and fascinating. See, e.g., Warren, The Supreme Court in United States History, 1922; Hughes, The Supreme Court of the United States, 1928; Frankfurter & Landis, The Business of the Supreme Court, 1928; Rodell, Nine Men, 1955 (reprinted 1988); Westin, The Anatomy of a Constitutional Law Case, 1958; Frank, Marble Palace, 1958; Freund, The Supreme Court of the United States, 1961; Schwartz, Super Chief, 1983; Rehnquist, The Supreme Court: How It Was; How It Is, 1987.

A good feel for how the Supreme Court functions may be obtained from four extremely readable books about particular cases and groups of cases: Westin, The Supreme Court—Views from Inside, 1961; Prettyman, Death and the Supreme Court, 1961; Lewis, Gideon's Trumpet, 1964; Kluger, Simple Justice, 1975; and Friendly, Minnesota Rag, 1981.

Even to cite a select bibliography of law-review articles about the Court would be an consists at the present time of the Chief Justice of the United States and eight associate justices.[2]

The Court has not always had a total membership of nine. The First Judiciary Act created a Court with six members. This was increased to seven in 1807, to nine in 1837, and to ten in 1864. An 1866 statute, enacted to prevent Andrew Johnson from making any appointments to the Court, provided that no vacancy should be filled until the number of associate justices was reduced to six, but before enough deaths had occurred to accomplish this object, an 1869 statute was passed setting the size of the Court at nine, where it has since remained. In 1937 President Roosevelt proposed a bill that would have authorized the appointment of an additional justice for each sitting justice over 70 years of age, up to a maximum of 15 justices. The bitter fight that led to the defeat of this "court-packing" plan, as it was regarded, has given the notion of a nine-judge Court such sanctity that it is unlikely that the size will again be changed.

The Supreme Court sits in Washington, D.C., in an annual term that begins on the first Monday in October and in recent years has normally risen in the last week of June or the first week of July.[3] Six justices constitute a quorum, and there have been cases in which the Court has been unable to act because of inability to muster six justices who were not, for some reason, disqualified or unwilling to sit on a case. In one such situation Congress has given relief. Where a case comes to the Court on direct appeal from a district court, and there is no quorum, the case may be remitted to the court of appeals for the circuit including the district in which the case arose, and that court may make a final decision.[4] The provision for a quorum of six has led to some criticism in another direction. It means that in some cases a majority of only four justices may reverse a court below, and indeed even hold a statute unconstitutional. There has been a suggestion, never adopted, to prevent such situations by providing for summoning lower court judges to

impossible task. One article, however, though its conclusions are extremely controversial, deserves mention because of the detailed picture it gives of the work of the Court. Hart, The Time Chart of the Justices, 1959, 73 Harv.L.Rev. 84. Other recent articles of interest include: Rehnquist, The Supreme Court: Past and Present, 1973, 59 A.B.A.J. 361; Cannon, Administrative Change and the Supreme Court, 1974, 57 Judicature 334; New York University Supreme Court Project, 1984, 59 N.Y.U.L.Rev. 677; Symposium on Supreme Court Advocacy, 1984, 33 Cath.U.L.Rev. 525.

2. 28 U.S.C.A. § 1.

3. Since 1979 the Court has recessed when it has finished its work for the year, rather than adjourning as it had done previously, so that it now has a 12–month term. Stern, Gressman, Shapiro & Geller, Supreme Court Practice, 7th ed. 1993, pp. 3–4.

4. 28 U.S.C.A. § 2109. Apparently the statute has only been utilized in one case. U.S. v. Aluminum Co. of America, 1944, 64 S.Ct. 1281, 322 U.S. 716, 88 L.Ed. 1557.

If a case comes to the Supreme Court other than by direct review of a district court, and a quorum cannot be mustered, the same statute provides that the judgment of the court below is affirmed with the same effect as affirmance by an equally-divided court. Haig v. Bissonette, 1988, 108 S.Ct. 1253, 485 U.S. 264, 99 L.Ed.2d 288; Sloan v. Nixon, 1974, 95 S.Ct. 218, 419 U.S. 958, 42 L.Ed.2d 174.

sit with the Supreme Court to make a full bench of nine.[5] The Supreme Court is not authorized to sit in divisions. All the qualified justices participate in each decision of the Court.

The Supreme Court has a limited original jurisdiction, and also exercises appellate jurisdiction, now almost always exercised by the discretionary writ of certiorari, over the district courts, the courts of appeals, and the highest courts of the states.[6] In the 1992–1993 Term, the Court disposed of 6,336 cases. Of these 6,110 were disposed of by denial or dismissal of appeals and petitions for review, while 226 cases were determined on the merits. In 119 cases the Court disposed of a matter with a full opinion. Of these 77 were civil actions from inferior federal courts, 11 were federal criminal cases, ten were federal habeas corpus cases, four were civil actions from state courts, 9 were state criminal cases, and three were cases in the Court's original jurisdiction.[7]

There is, of course, no direct review of decisions of the Supreme Court. The late Justice Jackson observed: "We are not final because we are infallible, but we are infallible only because we are final."[8] In some instances, however, decisions of the Supreme Court do not finally resolve a controversy, though they dispose of the particular case. Decisions turning on statutory construction are subject to change in the statute by Congress, while in five instances the Constitution has been amended to overcome Supreme Court decisions.[9]

§ 5. Specialized Courts

Although the Supreme Court, the courts of appeals, and the district courts are from any standpoint the most important federal courts, and the courts to which the balance of this book is almost exclusively devoted, there are certain specialized courts that deserve brief mention. The exact status of these courts, and of the judges thereof, has been a troublesome matter, and will be considered in a later section.[1]

In geographical areas governed by Congress, and not a part of a state, there is a need for tribunals to exercise local jurisdiction, of the sort usually performed by state courts, as well as jurisdiction of a federal nature. In the District of Columbia, under the District of Columbia Court Reform and Criminal Procedure Act of 1970,[2] what formerly were

---

5. See Carrington, The Problem of Minority Decision, 1958, 44 A.B.A.J. 137.

6. See §§ 105–110 below.

A 1988 statute, adopting a reform that had long been urged, largely eliminated the former distinction between appeal and certiorari and gave the Court almost complete discretion over what cases it will hear. Act of June 27, 1988, Pub.L. 100–332, 102 Stat. 662. See Boskey & Gressman, The Supreme Court Bids Farewell to Mandatory Appeals, 1988, 121 F.R.D. 81.

7. The Supreme Court—1992 Term, 1993, 107 Harv.L.Rev. 77, 476–378. In 1980–1981, by way of contrast, the Court disposed of only 4,280 cases, but 159 of these were with a full opinion.

8. Brown v. Allen, 1953, 73 S.Ct. 397, 427, 344 U.S. 443, 540, 97 L.Ed. 469.

9. 13 Wright, Miller & Cooper, Jurisdiction 2d § 3507 n. 14.

§ 5

1. See § 11 below.

2. Pub.L. 91–358, 84 Stat. 473; D.C.Code, tit. 11. See Symposium, The Modernization of Justice in the District of Columbia, 1971, 20 Amer.U.L.Rev. 237, the Court of General Session, the Juvenile Court, and the District of Columbia Tax Court were consolidated into a single court known as the Superior Court, with jurisdiction of civil and criminal matters of a local nature similar to the state court systems in the 50 states. The District of Columbia Court of Appeals—not to be confused with the United States Court of Appeals for the District of Columbia Circuit—is the appellate court for the local system of courts and its decisions are reviewable in the Supreme Court in the same manner as decisions of the highest court of a state.[3] The District Court for the District of Columbia and the United States Court of Appeals for the District of Columbia Circuit hear only federal matters of the kind heard by federal courts in the states.

The District Courts of the Canal Zone, the Virgin Islands, Guam, and the Northern Mariana Islands and the High Court of American Samoa have a dual jurisdiction. In addition to federal jurisdiction they have practically the same scope as state courts of general jurisdiction.[4] The District Court for the District of Puerto Rico is rather different. It is defined by statute as a "court of the United States" and its jurisdiction is the same as that of district courts generally.[5] Puerto Rico has a system of courts of its own, and decisions of the Supreme Court of Puerto Rico are reviewed by the United States Supreme Court in a fashion similar to review of a state court.[6]

The other specialized courts have traditionally been limited to particular subject matters. The oldest of these, the Court of Claims, was established in 1855. Until 1982, when it was merged with the Court of Customs and Patent Appeals to form the new Court of Appeals for the Federal Circuit, it was a court of seven judges, sitting in divisions of three. It had nationwide jurisdiction and sat in Washington.[7] It had jurisdiction, in some instances concurrent with the district courts, to hear such claims against the United States as the Constitution or

621; 14 Wright, Miller & Cooper, Jurisdiction 2d § 3681.

3. 28 U.S.C.A. § 1257.

4. Canal Zone: 7 C.Z.Code § 23–26; Virgin Islands: 48 U.S.C.A. § 1612; Guam: 48 U.S.C.A. § 1424; Northern Marianas, 48 U.S.C.A. § 1694; American Samoa, Am. Samoa Code § 3–1001. See Barnard v. Thorstenn, 1989, 109 S.Ct. 1294, 489 U.S. 546, 103 L.Ed.2d 559 (Virgin Islands); Laughlin, The Constitutional Structure of the Courts of the United States Territories: The Case of American Samoa, 1991, 13 U.Haw.L.Rev. 379.

There is also a United States Court for Berlin, an extraordinary creation that apparently has heard only one case. See Lowenfeld, Hijacking, Freedom, and the "American Law", 1985, 83 Mich.L.Rev. 1000.

5. 28 U.S.C.A. § 451; 48 U.S.C.A. § 863. The statutes were amended in 1966 to give life tenure to judges subsequently appointed to that court. 28 U.S.C.A. § 134(a). See generally U.S. v. Montanez, C.A.2d, 1967, 371 F.2d 79, certiorari denied 88 S.Ct. 147, 389 U.S. 884, 19 L.Ed.2d 181. See 17 Wright, Miller & Cooper, Jurisdiction 2d § 4106.

6. 28 U.S.C.A. § 1258.

7. Ellison, United States Court of Claims: Keeper of the Nation's Conscience for One Hundred Years, 1956, 24 Geo. Wash.L.Rev. 251; McNamara, The Court of Claims: Its Development and Present Role in the Unified Court System, 1965, 40 St. John's L.Rev. 1; Symposium, The United States Court of Claims, 1967, 55 Geo.L.J. 573.

statutes permit to be maintained.[8] Initially it was held that decisions of the Court of Claims could not be reviewed by the Supreme Court, since the earliest statutes permitted the Secretary of the Treasury to revise the court's judgment.[9] The provision for revision of the judgment was stricken in 1866, and it became established that, so long as the Court of Claims was performing a judicial function, its decisions were reviewable by the Supreme Court.[10] In the court year ending September 30, 1980, the Court of Claims disposed of 571 petitions in which nearly $1.3 billion was claimed.[11]

The Court of Customs and Patent Appeals was created in 1909 to take over specialized litigation that at that time was swamping the Second Circuit, into which most imports come.[12] At the time of its merger with the Court of Claims in 1982 into the new Court of Appeals for the Federal Circuit, the Court of Customs and Patent Appeals consisted of five judges. The judges had their official station in Washington, D.C., but the jurisdiction ran throughout the nation and the court could sit at such times and places as it fixed by rule.[13] It had jurisdiction to review certain determinations of the Court of International Trade (formerly known as the Customs Court), decisions of the Board of Appeals and the Board of Patent Interferences of the Patent Office as to patent applications and interferences, decisions of the Commissioner of Patents as to trademark applications, the findings of the United States International Trade Commission as to unfair practices in import trade, certain findings of the Secretary of Commerce about tariffs, and certain appeals under the Plant Variety Protection Act.[14] In the year ended June 30, 1980, the court disposed of 41 cases involving customs and international trade and 128 patents cases.[15]

A change in the structure of these two courts was made in 1982. A new court, the United States Court of Appeals for the Federal Circuit, was given the appellate jurisdiction of the Court of Claims and the Court of Customs and Patent Appeals. Another new court, the United States Claims Court (which since 1992 has been the United States Court of

---

8. See 17 Wright, Miller & Cooper, Jurisdiction 2d § 4101.

9. Gordon v. U.S., 1865, 2 Wall. 561, 17 L.Ed. 921 (the important opinion of Chief Justice Taney, who died before the decision was handed down, appears only in 117 U.S. 697. See § 11 n. 12 below).

10. Pope v. U.S., 1944, 65 S.Ct. 16, 23, 323 U.S. 1, 12–14, 89 L.Ed. 3.

11. Ann.Rep., Director of the Administrative Office of the United States Courts, 1980, pp. 568–569.

12. Frankfurter and Landis, The Business of the Supreme Court, 1928, pp. 148.–152.

As created in 1909 it was the Court of Customs Appeals. Its jurisdiction was enlarged and its name changed in 1929.

13. Graham, Court of Customs and Patent Appeals: Its History, Functions and Jurisdiction, 1932, 1 Fed.B.A.J. 33.

14. 28 U.S.C.A. §§ 1541–1545. The constitutionality of the jurisdiction to review decisions of the International Trade Commission, purportedly granted by 28 U.S.C.A. § 1543, was highly doubtful. See Glidden Co. v. Zdanok, 1962, 82 S.Ct. 1459, 1488–1490, 1492–1493, 370 U.S. 530, 579–583, 587–589, 8 L.Ed.2d 671; 17 Wright, Miller & Cooper, Jurisdiction 2d § 4104.

15. Ann.Rep., Director of the Administrative Office of the United States Courts, 1980, p. 567.

Federal Claims), was created to assume the trial jurisdiction of the Court of Claims.[16] In the year ended September 30, 1992, the Federal Circuit disposed of 1,563 cases and the United States Court of Federal Claims disposed of 1,652 cases.[17]

The Customs Court was established as such in 1926, replacing the former Board of General Appraisers. Its name was changed again in 1980 to the Court of International Trade, and its jurisdiction redefined to create a comprehensive system of judicial review of civil actions arising from import transactions and to avoid jurisdictional conflicts that had been caused previously by the ill-defined division of jurisdiction between the former Customs Court and the federal district courts.[18] The court has nine judges, and its offices are in New York, but it may sit at any place within the jurisdiction of the United States.[19] During the year ended September 30, 1991, the Court of International Trade disposed of 1,487 cases.[20]

For many years the Tax Court of the United States was not a court at all, despite its name, but was an administrative agency and a part of the executive branch of the government. Its name and status were changed by a 1969 statute. It is now the United States Tax Court and is a court of record under Article I of the Constitution rather than an executive agency.[21] But the Court of Military Appeals, and the courts-

---

16. Act of April 2, 1982, Pub.L. 97–164, 96 Stat. 25, tit. I. See Schwartz, Two New Federal Courts, 1982, 68 A.B.A.J. 1091; Meador, Origin of the Federal Circuit: A Personal Account, 1992, 41 Am.U.L.Rev. 581.

In addition to the jurisdiction previously exercised by the two courts it succeeded, the Court of Appeals for the Federal Circuit was given exclusive jurisdiction of appeals from district courts throughout the country in cases arising under the laws relating to patents or plant variety protection and in cases against the United States, except for Tort Claims Act cases and internal revenue cases. 28 U.S.C.A. § 1295. Since 1989 it has also had jurisdiction to review decisions of the newly created United States Court of Veterans Appeals. 38 U.S.C.A. § 7292. See Dreyfuss, The Federal Circuit: A Case Study in Specialized Courts, 1989, 64 N.Y.U.L.Rev. 1; Note, Subject Matter Jurisdiction in the Federal Circuit: A Lesson on the Effects of a Poorly Drafted Statute, 1987, 36 Am.U.L.Rev. 943.

The United States Claims Court, an Article I court, was given the trial jurisdiction of the former Court of Claims, which had largely been exercised by commissioners of that court, but it is also given jurisdiction, which the Court of Claims never had, to grant declaratory judgments and give equitable relief in controversies within its jurisdiction. 28 U.S.C.A. § 1491(a)(2), (3). In

1992 the court was changed to the United States Court of Federal Claims. 28 U.S.C.A. § 171(a). See 17 Wright, Miller & Cooper, Jurisdiction 2d § 4101. The United States Claims Court was held not to be a "court of the United States", within the meaning of the statute authorizing waiver of filing fees, Cofield v. U.S., 1992, 25 Cl.Ct. 465, and presumably this will be equally true of the new Court of Federal Claims.

17. Ann.Rep., Director of the Administrative Office of the United States Courts, 1992, Tables B–8, G–2A.

18. 28 U.S.C.A. §§ 1581–1585; See Cohen, The New United States Court of International Trade, 1981, 20 Col.J. Transnational L. 277; Comment, Customs Court Act of 1980: An Evaluation and Analysis, 1981, 4 Hamline L.Rev. 537; 17 Wright, Miller & Cooper, Jurisdiction 2d § 4103.

19. 28 U.S.C.A. §§ 251–257.

20. Ann.Rep., Director of the Administrative Office of the United States Courts, 1992, Table G–1.

21. 26 U.S.C.A. (I.R.C.1954) § 7441, as amended by Act of Dec. 30, 1969, Pub.L. 91–172, § 951, 83 Stat. 487; 17 Wright, Miller & Cooper, Jurisdiction § 4102. The Tax Court is a "Court of Law" within the meaning of the Appointments Clause of Art. II, § 2, of the Constitution, and the statute, 26 U.S.C.A. § 7443A(a), authorizing the martial it reviews, remain a part of the government of the armed forces, and are largely separate from the judiciary,[22] although a 1983 statute for the first time gives the Supreme Court jurisdiction to review by certiorari decisions of the Court of Military Appeals.[23]

Some specialized courts that existed in the past have been abolished. The Commerce Court, with jurisdiction to review decisions of the Interstate Commerce Commission, was established in 1910, over strong congressional opposition. It was saved from extinction only by a presidential veto in 1912, and in 1913, with a new administration in power, was abolished. A number of cases in which the court was reversed by the Supreme Court, and a fear, widely voiced before its creation and never quieted, that it would incline too much in favor of the railroads and against the public interest, led to abolition of the court.[24]

There is in each district a unit of the district court known as the bankruptcy court, with judges appointed for a 14–year term by the court of appeals for the circuit. These new courts took over duties that had previously been performed by "referees in bankruptcy" acting for the district court, but the 1978 statute that created these new bankruptcy courts gave them more sweeping jurisdiction. Giving Article I judges such broad jurisdiction was held to go beyond constitutional bounds by the Supreme Court in 1982.[25] Congress responded with a 1984 statute that restructured the bankruptcy court system and limited their jurisdiction to those "core proceedings" that it is thought Article I judges may properly decide.[26] Bankruptcy judges' judgments may be appealed either to the district court or to the court of appeals, and the statute also allows a court of appeals to establish a "bankruptcy appellate panel" of three

chief judge of the Tax Court to appoint special trial judges, is constitutional. Freytag v. C.I.R., 1991, 111 S.Ct. 2631, 501 U.S. 868, 115 L.Ed.2d 764.

The Federal Courts Study Committee has proposed creating an Article III appellate division of the Tax Court and vesting nearly exclusive jurisdiction of tax cases in the Tax Court. Report of the Federal Courts Study Committee, April 2, 1990, pp. 69–72. See Geier, The Tax Court, Article III, and the Proposal Advanced by the Federal Courts Study Commission: A Study in Applied Constitutional Theory, 1991, 76 Cornell L.Rev. 985.

22. 10 U.S.C.A. § 867; Dynes v. Hoover, 1857, 20 How. 65, 79, 15 L.Ed. 838; O'Callahan v. Parker, 1969, 89 S.Ct. 1683, 1686–1687, 395 U.S. 258, 265, 23 L.Ed.2d 291; Willis, The United States Court of Military Appeals: Its Origin, Operation and Future, 1972, 55 Military L.Rev. 39; Willis, The Constitution, The United States Court of Military Appeals and the Future, 1972, 57 Military L.Rev. 27.

The appointment of military judges by Judge Advocates General, and with no fixed term of office, does not violate the Appointments Clause or the Due Process Clause. Weiss v. U.S., 1994, 114 S.Ct. 752, ___ U.S. ___, 127 L.Ed.2d 1.

23. 28 U.S.C.A. § 1259. See Boskey & Gressman, The Supreme Court's New Certiorari Jurisdiction Over Military Appeals, 1984, 102 F.R.D. 329.

24. Frankfurter & Landis, The Business of the Supreme Court, 1928, pp. 153–174; Dix, The Death of the Commerce Court: A Study in Institutional Weakness, 1964, 8 Am.J.Leg.Hist. 238.

25. Northern Pipeline Construction Co. v. Marathon Pipe Line Company, 1982, 102 S.Ct. 2858, 458 U.S. 50, 73 L.Ed.2d 598. See § 11 below.

26. 28 U.S.C.A. § 151–158, as amended by Act of July 10, 1984, Pub.L. 98–353, Title I, § 104(a). 98 Stat. 336. See 17 Wright, Miller & Cooper, Jurisdiction 2d § 4106.

bankruptcy judges.[27]

The Emergency Court of Appeals was created during the Second World War to review orders of the Price Control Administrator. With the end of price control, there was no continued need for such a court, and it was abolished, except for concluding pending cases, in 1953.[28] However, in 1971 Congress created a Temporary Emergency Court of Appeals, staffed by judges of the existing federal courts, to hear all appeals in cases arising out of the then-current price-wage regulation.[29] That court was finally abolished in 1992.[30] Another special court is created by § 209 of the Regional Rail Reorganization Act of 1973. That court, composed of three designated federal judges, has exclusive jurisdiction to review the final system plan called for by that statute.[31]

In 1988 Congress created, as an Article I court, the United States Court of Veterans Appeals. It has exclusive jurisdiction to review decisions of the Board of Veterans' Appeals and the decisions of the new courts are reviewable by the Court of Appeals for the Federal Circuit.[32]

There are other instances in which Congress has made special provision for the designation of existing judges as a "court" to perform particular functions. Seven district judges from seven district circuits are designated by the Chief Justice of the United States as the Foreign Intelligence Surveillance Court to grant orders approving electronic surveillance anywhere within the United States and three other judges are designated as a court of review to review the denial of any application for a surveillance order.[33] Similarly the Chief Justice was authorized in 1978 to appoint a court of three judges of courts of appeals or justices as the Special Division. This court, which is a "division of the United States Court of Appeals for the District of Columbia," considers and acts upon applications by the Attorney General for appointment of an independent counsel to investigate and, if appropriate, prosecute certain high-ranking government officials for violation of federal crimi-

27. 28 U.S.C.A. § 158. The provision for a "bankruptcy appellate panel" is 28 U.S.C.A. § 158. Decisions of a bankruptcy appellate panel may be appealed to the court of appeals. In 1990 only the Ninth Circuit had such a panel, but it was said to be so successful there that it has been recommended that Congress require that every circuit have a panel of this kind. Report of the Federal Courts Study Committee, April 2, 1990, pp. 74–76.

28. 50 App.U.S.C.A. § 2166.

29. Act of Dec. 22, 1971, Pub.L. 92–210, § 211(b), 85 Stat. 743. The program of controls was ended in 1974. See 12 U.S.C.A. § 1904 note. However, the court has been given jurisdiction under other statutes. See 17 Wright, Miller & Cooper, Jurisdiction 2d § 4105. The Federal

Courts Study Committee recommended abolition of the court. Report of the Federal Courts Study Committee, April 2, 1990, p. 73.

30. Act of Oct. 29, 1992, Pub.L. 102–572, § 103, 106 Stat. 4506.

31. 45 U.S.C.A. § 719. See 17 Wright, Miller & Cooper, Jurisdiction § 4106. The constitutionality of the statute creating the court was upheld in Blanchette v. Connecticut Gen. Ins. Corp., 1974, 95 S.Ct. 335, 419 U.S. 102, 42 L.Ed.2d 320.

32. 38 U.S.C.A. §§ 7004, 7241–7256, 7292. See Helfer, The Politics of Judicial Structure: Creating the United States Court of Veterans Appeals, 1992, 25 Conn. L.Rev. 155.

33. 50 U.S.C.A. § 1803.

nal statutes.[34]

Neither the two Emergency Courts of Appeals nor the special railroad court nor the courts to approve surveillance applications or appoint "independent counsel" have had judges of their own, but were made up of sitting judges designated for part-time duty on those courts. There may be some significance to this beyond the history of these particular courts. Very few specialized courts have been created since the demise of the Commerce Court in 1913. The Court of Appeals for the Federal Circuit and the United States Court of Federal Claims assumed jurisdiction that had already been vested in specialized courts. The Customs Court, now known as the Court of International Trade, was a formalization of an agency that had a long history. The bankruptcy courts build on what district courts had long done through referees in bankruptcy and are still closely related to the district courts.[35] The Emergency Court of Appeals, and its 1971 successor, merely centralized in one place litigation of a type that otherwise could have been brought anywhere in the country, and it was made up of judges who were not appointed solely for that purpose. The same things may be said of the court created by the Regional Rail Reorganization Act.

Since 1913 Congress has resisted the many pressures, which continue to this day,[36] for creation of new courts with specialized subject-matter jurisdiction. The history of the Commerce Court may have given rise to a feeling, whether or not justified, that it is more desirable to use judges who hear all types of cases than to create a special tribunal with judges who hear only that kind of case.

§ 6.   The Judicial Code

In 1911, after 12 years' work, the first Judicial Code was adopted, as an attempt to unify the previously scattered provisions relating to the business of the federal courts.[1] With the passage of time frequent amendments to these provisions suggested the desirability of a new code. The Judicial Code of 1948, which appears as Title 28 in the United States Code, is the product of this labor.[2] The Code has been warmly praised on eminent authority. The Supreme Court has said: "This was

---

34. 28 U.S.C.A. § 49. The substantive provisions concerning appointment of an "independent counsel"—popularly known as a "special prosecutor"—are set out in 28 U.S.C.A. §§ 591–599. The constitutionality of the creation and means of appointment of this court was upheld in Morrison v. Olson, 1988, 108 S.Ct. 2597, 487 U.S. 654, 101 L.Ed.2d 569.

35. But see Report of the Federal Courts Study Committee, April 2, 1990, p. 74: "The system for adjudicating bankruptcy cases is an example of successful specialized adjudication."

36. See 13 Wright, Miller & Cooper, Jurisdiction 2d § 3508.

See generally Jordan, Specialized Courts: A Choice?, 1981, 76 Nw.U.L.Rev. 745.

§ 6

1. Frankfurter & Landis, The Business of the Supreme Court, 1928, pp. 130–145.

2. See Barron, The Judicial Code—1948 Revision, 1949, 8 F.R.D. 439; Holtzoff, The New Federal Judicial Code, 1949, 8 F.R.D. 343; Maris, New Federal Judicial Code, 1948, 34 A.B.A.J. 863.

The legislative history of the 1948 Code is collected in Legislative History of Title 28, United States Code "Judiciary and Judicial Procedure," Mersky & Jacobstein eds. 1971.

scarcely hasty, ill-considered legislation. To the contrary, it received close and prolonged study. Five years of Congressional attention supports the Code. And from the start, Congress obtained the most eminent expert assistance available. The spadework was entrusted to two lawbook-publishing firms, the staffs of which had unique experience in statutory codification and revision. They formed an advisory committee, including distinguished judges and members of the bar, and obtained the services of special consultants. Furthermore, an advisory committee was appointed by the Judicial Conference. And to assist with matters relating to the jurisdiction of this Court, Chief Justice Stone appointed an advisory committee, consisting of himself and Justices Frankfurter and Douglas." [3]

The 1948 Code is accompanied by Reviser's Notes,[4] which have been given great weight by the Supreme Court in determining the meaning of the Code.[5]

Despite the praise that the 1948 Code has received, there is no unanimity of professional opinion on this subject. Indeed it has been called everything from "a masterpiece of legislative draftsmanship" [6] to "one of the worst pieces of draftsmanship in all history." [7] An Amendatory Act in 1949 corrected numerous errors in the original Code.

In 1959 in an address to the American Law Institute Chief Justice Warren said that it "is essential that we achieve a proper jurisdictional balance between the Federal and State Court systems, assigning to each system those cases most appropriate in the light of the basic principles of federalism." He suggested that it would be desirable if the Institute would undertake such a study. Work was begun in 1960 and the task was completed in 1968.[8] It proposed to repeal the chapters of the

---

3. Ex parte Collett, 1949, 69 S.Ct. 944, 949–950, 337 U.S. 55, 65–66, 93 L.Ed. 1207.

4. The Historical Notes in 28 U.S.C.A. contain the Reviser's Notes to the 1948 Code.

5. Ex parte Collett, note 3 above; Fourco Glass Co. v. Transmirra Products Corp., 1957, 77 S.Ct. 787, 353 U.S. 222, 1 L.Ed.2d 786. In the latter case Justice Harlan protested that the "Notes have been given undue weight." 77 S.Ct. at 792, 353 U.S. at 229.

6. Holtzoff, The New Federal Judicial Code, 1949, 8 F.R.D. 343, 344.

7. Book Note, 1951, 36 Minn.L.Rev. 117, 118; Wright, Foreword, in Legislative History of Title 28, United States Code "Judiciary and Judicial Procedure," Mersky & Jacobstein eds., 1971, p. iii. There are substantive criticisms of the 1948 Code in Wechsler, Federal Jurisdiction and the Revision of the Judicial Code, 1948, 13 Law & Contemp.Probs. 216, and in Keeffe et al., Venue and Removal Jokers in the New Federal Judicial Code, 1952, 38 Va.L.Rev. 569.

See also Keeffe, Twenty–Nine Distinct Damnations of the Federal Practice—And a National Ministry of Justice, 1954, 7 Vand. L.Rev. 636.

8. American Law Institute, Study of the Division of Jurisdiction between State and Federal Courts, Official Draft, 1969 (cited hereafter as ALI Study). See Field, Jurisdiction of Federal Courts—A Summary of American Law Institute Proposals, 1969, 46 F.R.D. 141. There is a critical examination of the proposals in Currie, The Federal Courts and the American Law Institute, 1968–1969, 36 U.Chi.L.Rev. 1, 268. They are defended in Wright, Restructuring Federal Jurisdiction: The American Law Institute Proposals, 1969, 26 Wash. & Lee L.Rev. 185.

See generally Symposium, An Analysis of the ALI's Approach to the State–Federal Jurisdiction Dilemma, 1972, 21 Am. U.L.Rev. 287; Fraser, Proposed Revision of the Jurisdiction of the Federal District Courts, 1974, 8 Valp.U.L.Rev. 189.

Judicial Code dealing with jurisdiction of the district courts, venue, and removal, and to substitute new statutory provisions. In addition changes in other portions of the Judicial Code were proposed. Although the ALI Study continues to influence thinking about the federal courts, and some of the specifics of its proposals have borne legislative fruit, time and increasing dockets have made many of its recommendations no longer appropriate, and it would not now be desirable, even if it were possible, to have it adopted in its entirety by Congress.

The Judicial Code of 1911 lasted for 37 years. The 1948 Judicial Code has already been on the books for 48 years. It was not well drafted to begin with and it has been amended many times, often not skillfully.[9] The time is surely ripe for the careful preparation of a new Judicial Code.

Though the Judicial Codes, both of 1911 and 1948, have largely been responsive to professional suggestions and drafted for the legal profession, statutes regulating the judiciary can hardly avoid political and sectional pressures. This was true of the Midnight Judges Act of 1801, and the repeal of that act a year later.[10] It continues to be true today, and explains much that otherwise would be obscure in the Code.

§ 6A. Supporting Services for the Courts [1]

With the growth of the federal judiciary, and the increased burdens on it, it has been necessary to provide additional staff support for individual judges and to create organizations that assist, and speak to or for, the judiciary generally. This carries risks as well as benefits.[2] It is difficult to see, however, how the courts could meet the demands now made on them without the supporting services they have been given.

The Judicial Conference of the United States is the primary policy-making body for the federal judiciary. It comprises the Chief Justice of the United States, the chief judges of each circuit and of the Court of International Trade, and a district judge from each circuit elected by the circuit and district judges of that circuit. It is to make a comprehensive

---

9. There is much awkwardness and ambiguity in the important 1990 statute, 28 U.S.C.A. § 1367, creating "supplemental jurisdiction." See § 9 below. A 1988 amendment of the remand statute, 28 U.S.C.A. § 1447(c), does not clearly state what Congress said it intended and has led to a split among the circuits. See § 41 below at notes 3 to 6. And although a 1992 amendment has corrected the most serious mistake in the 1990 revision of the general venue statutes, 28 U.S.C.A. § 1391, it still has drafting errors that ought to be corrected. See § 42 n. 35 below.

10. See § 1 above.

§ 6A

1. The author is grateful to Professor George K. Walker of the Wake Forest University Law School for suggesting the need for a section on this subject and to Professor Douglas D. McFarland of Hamline University School of Law and Joseph P. Spaniol, formerly of the Administrative Office of the United States Courts, for commenting on a draft.

2. See Rubin, Bureaucratization of the Federal Courts: The Tension between Justice and Efficiency, 1980, 55 Notre Dame L.Rev. 648. See also Report of the Study Group on the Caseload of the Supreme Court, 1972, 57 F.R.D. 573, 582–583: "The Court is an institution of nine Justices, who bear non-delegable responsibilities of judgment and exposition; it must not become a federation of nine corporate aggregates or chambers."

survey of the condition of business in the courts of the United States, to prepare plans for assignments of judges to and from particular courts where necessary, to make suggestions and recommendations to the various courts to promote uniformity of management procedures and the expeditious conduct of court business, and to submit to Congress its recommendations for legislation.[3] It has responsibility to carry on the rulemaking process for the federal courts generally and to recommend to the Supreme Court such changes in and additions to the various sets of rules that apply nationwide.[4] It also must review all rules particular courts, other than the Supreme Court and the district courts, have made for themselves to be sure that those rules are consistent with federal law.[5] The Conference, which meets twice a year, operates largely through committees.

The Chief Justice of the United States is the chief administrative officer of the federal-court system. He is chairman of the Judicial Conference of the United States[6] and of the Board of the Federal Judicial Center[7] and he appoints the Director of the Administrative Office of the United States.[8] Since 1972 the Chief Justice has had an Administrative Assistant, who performs "such duties as may be assigned to him by the Chief Justice."[9] The Administrative Assistant has supervised the Supreme Court's nonjudicial employees and assisted the Chief Justice in such matters as seeking legislation, writing speeches, and dealing with other judges.

The Administrative Office of the United States was created by statute in 1939 to compile statistical data on the operation of the courts and to provide support services of a logistical nature. The Director of the Administrative Office is "the administrative officer of the courts" and, as amended over the years, the statute sets out a long list of duties the Director is to perform under the supervision and direction of the Judicial Conference.[10] The annual reports of the Director, which are bound in a volume with the reports of the proceedings of the Judicial Conference, contain detailed statistics on every aspect of the operation of the federal courts. The Director is responsible for fixing the salaries for the support staff of federal courts other than the Supreme Court, purchasing and paying the expenses associated with lawbooks, and equipment, and supplies needed by the courts, and for disbursing the funds necessary for the maintenance and operation of the courts.[11]

3. 28 U.S.C.A. § 331.

4. See §§ 63, 64 below.

5. This primarily refers to the local rules the courts of appeals have adopted. Local rules made by district courts are reviewed by the judicial council of the circuit. 28 U.S.C.A. §§ 331, 332(d)(4), 2071(c).

6. 28 U.S.C.A. § 331.

7. 28 U.S.C.A. § 621(a)(1).

8. 28 U.S.C.A. § 601.

9. 28 U.S.C.A. § 677(a).

10. 28 U.S.C.A. § 604.

11. 28 U.S.C.A. § 604. In fiscal 1992 the total appropriations for the Judiciary (exclusive of the Supreme Court and the U.S. Sentencing Commission) were $2,337,-402. Ann.Rep., Director of the Administrative Office of the United States Courts, 1992, Table 27.

The Federal Judicial Center was created in 1967. Its purpose is "to further the development and adoption of improved judicial administration in the courts of the United States."[12] It is heavily engaged in research and study of the operation of the courts and conducts programs of continuing education for judges and others associated with the judiciary.[13] The activities of the Center are supervised by a Board of which the Chief Justice of the United States is chairman and the members include the Director of the Administrative Office, two judges from courts of appeals, three district-court judges, and a bankruptcy judge.[14] The Board appoints the Director of the Federal Judicial Center, who supervises and appoints the professional personnel and staff of the Center and performs other duties assigned by the Board.[15]

Each circuit has a judicial council, which is authorized by statute to make all necessary and appropriate orders for the effective and expeditious administration of justice within its circuit. The judicial council consists of the chief judge of the circuit and an equal number of circuit judges and district judges.[16] The judicial councils have no traditional judicial powers. They have been described by the Supreme Court as "an administrative body functioning in a narrow sense as a 'board of directors' for the circuit."[17] The judicial council is authorized to appoint a circuit executive to exercise administrative control of all nonjudicial activities of the court of appeals for the circuit.[18] The judicial councils have recently been given power to review, and modify or abrogate, local rules prescribed by district courts within the circuit[19] and to deal with problems arising from the disability or misconduct of any judge within the circuit.[20]

Each circuit also has a judicial conference, at which the judges within the circuit and selected members of the bar meet "for the purpose of considering the business of the courts and advising means of improving the administration of justice within such circuit."[21] These circuit

---

12. 28 U.S.C.A. § 620(a).

13. The work of the Center's Division of Continuing Education and Training has been so successful that it has been called a "school of judges." Clark, The Federal Judicial Center, 1974 Ariz.St.L.J. 537, 539.

14. 28 U.S.C.A. § 621(a). The other members of the Board are the Director of the Administrative Office and six active judges elected by the members of the Judicial Conference of the United States.

15. 28 U.S.C.A. §§ 624, 625. The Directors have been either federal judges or law professors.

16. 28 U.S.C.A. § 332(a). See generally 16 Wright, Miller & Cooper, Jurisdiction § 3939; Oliver, Reflections on the History of Circuit Judicial Councils and Circuit Judicial Conferences, 1974, 64 F.R.D. 201.

17. Chandler v. Judicial Council of the Tenth Circuit, 1970, 90 S.Ct. 1648, 1654 n.

7, 398 U.S. 74, 86 n. 7, 26 L.Ed.2d 100. The history of judicial councils and of what they were expected to do is set out in Justice Harlan's concurring opinion in that case. 90 S.Ct. at 1660–1664, 398 U.S. at 96–105. See also Oliver, Reflections on the History of Circuit Judicial Council and Circuit Judicial Conferences, 1974, 64 F.R.D. 201.

18. 28 U.S.C.A. § 332(e). See Federal Judicial Center, The Impact of the Circuit Executive Act, 1979.

19. 28 U.S.C.A. § 332(d)(4).

20. 28 U.S.C.A. § 372(c), added by the Judicial Councils Reform and Judicial Conduct and Disability Act of 1980, Pub.L. 96–458, § 3(a), (b), 94 Stat. 2036. See § 1 n. 26 above.

21. 28 U.S.C.A. § 333. These had been held annually, but a 1990 amendment of the statute allows the chief judge of the judicial conferences are purely advisory. They are "intended to provide an opportunity for friendly interchange among judges and between bench and bar, out of which might grow increased understanding of problems of judicial administration and enhanced cooperation toward their solution." [22]

The principal administrator of each district court is its clerk, appointed by the judges of the district.[23] The district court also appoints court reporters and each district judge may appoint a crier, who performs also the duties of bailiff and messenger.[24]

United States Marshals provide for the security and enforce the orders of the district courts, the courts of appeals, and the Court of International Trade.[25] The Marshals Service is a bureau within the Department of Justice and each United States Marshal is appointed by the President.[26]

Each judge and justice is authorized to appoint necessary law clerks and secretaries.[27] Today law clerks are almost always recent law school graduates. In addition to the personal law clerks each judge has, the courts of appeals have "staff law clerks" who are often supervised by a staff attorney.[28] The function of staff law clerks varies from circuit to circuit.[29]

circuit to decide whether to have the conference every year or every two years.

22. Chandler v. Judicial Council of the Tenth Circuit, 1970, 90 S.Ct. 1648, 1660, 398 U.S. 74, 98, 26 L.Ed.2d 100 (Harlan, J., concurring). See also the article by Judge Oliver, note 16 above; Fish, The Circuit Councils: Rusty Hinges of Federal Judicial Administration, 1970, 37 U.Chi.L.Rev. 203.

23. 28 U.S.C.A. § 751. Other statutes authorize the appointment of a clerk for the Supreme Court, each of the courts of appeals, and other courts. The Federal Courts Study Committee has recommended that districts be permitted to use the title "district court administrator" rather than "clerk of court." Report of the Federal Courts Study Committee, April 2, 1990, p. 153.

24. 28 U.S.C.A. §§ 753, 755.

25. 28 U.S.C.A. § 566.

26. 28 U.S.C.A. § 561.

27. 28 U.S.C.A. §§ 675, 712, 752, 755. See Federal Judicial Center, Law Clerk Handbook, 1989; Oakley & Thompson, Law Clerks and the Judicial Process, 1980; Boley, Pretrial Motions in a U.S. District Court: The Role of the Law Clerk, 1990, 74 Judicature 44.

28. See 28 U.S.C.A. § 715.

29. Ubell, Report of Central Staff Attorneys' Offices in the United States Courts of Appeals, 1980, 87 F.R.D. 253.

Chapter 2

THE JUDICIAL POWER OF
THE UNITED STATES

Analysis

---

§ 7.   Courts of Limited Jurisdiction [1]

It is a principle of first importance that the federal courts are courts of limited jurisdiction. Most state courts are courts of general jurisdiction, and the presumption is that they have jurisdiction over a particular controversy unless a showing is made to the contrary. The federal courts, on the other hand, cannot be courts of general jurisdiction. They are empowered to hear only such cases as are within the judicial power of the United States, as defined in the Constitution, and have been entrusted to them by a jurisdictional grant by Congress.[2]

Because of this unusual nature of the federal courts, and because it would be not simply wrong but indeed an unconstitutional invasion of the powers reserved to the states if those courts were to entertain cases not within their jurisdiction, the rule is well settled that the party seeking to invoke the jurisdiction of a federal court must demonstrate that the case is within the competence of such a court. The presumption is that the court lacks jurisdiction in a particular case until it has been demonstrated that jurisdiction over the subject matter exists.[3]

§ 7

1. 13 Wright, Miller & Cooper, Jurisdiction 2d § 3522.

2. Bender v. Williamsport Area School Dist., 1988, 106 S.Ct. 1326, 1331, 475 U.S. 534, 541, 89 L.Ed.2d 501.

3. Turner v. Bank of North America, 1799, 4 Dall. 8, 1 L.Ed. 718.

To rebut this presumption against jurisdiction, the facts that disclose the existence of jurisdiction must be affirmatively alleged.[4] If these facts are challenged, the burden is on the party claiming jurisdiction to demonstrate that jurisdiction of the subject matter exists.[5] But what if the parties fail to raise any jurisdictional question? The rule is that the parties cannot confer on a federal court jurisdiction that has not been vested in the court by the Constitution and Congress. The parties cannot waive lack of jurisdiction, whether by express consent,[6] or by conduct,[7] or even by estoppel.[8] The court, whether trial or appellate, is obliged to notice want of jurisdiction on its own motion,[9] and it may well happen that the party who has invoked the jurisdiction of the federal court will be unhappy with the result it achieves there and will challenge the jurisdiction at a late stage of the proceedings after it has lost on the merits.[10] Such a harsh rule could hardly be defended as a sensible regulation of procedure, and can only be justified by the delicate problems of federal-state relations that are involved.[11]

4. Bingham v. Cabot, 1798, 3 Dall. 382, 1 L.Ed. 646. As to how jurisdiction is pleaded, see § 69 below.

5. McNutt v. General Motors Acceptance Corp., 1935, 56 S.Ct. 780, 298 U.S. 178, 80 L.Ed. 1135.

6. Jackson v. Ashton, 1834, 8 Pet. 148, 8 L.Ed. 898; Sosna v. Iowa, 1975, 95 S.Ct. 553, 556–557, 419 U.S. 393, 398, 42 L.Ed.2d 532. The rule has been said to be "[g]raven in stone" and "enforced with draconian zeal." Reale International, Inc. v. Federal Republic of Nigeria, C.A.2d, 1981, 647 F.2d 330, 331–332.

7. Dred Scott v. Sandford, 1857, 19 How. 393, 15 L.Ed. 691 (defendant pleaded over after his plea in abatement, challenging jurisdiction, had been overruled); Mitchell v. Maurer, 1934, 55 S.Ct. 162, 293 U.S. 237, 79 L.Ed. 338 (party never raised lack of jurisdiction in any court); Goldstone v. Payne, C.C.A.2d, 1938, 94 F.2d 855 (party who counterclaimed in federal court allowed to assert lack of jurisdiction after losing on merits).

8. Mansfield, C. & L.M. Ry. v. Swan, 1884, 4 S.Ct. 510, 111 U.S. 379, 28 L.Ed. 462; Richardson v. U.S., C.A.9th, 1991, 943 F.2d 1107, 1113, certiorari denied 112 S.Ct. 1473, ___ U.S. ___, 117 L.Ed.2d 617.

9. Mansfield, C. & L.M. Ry. v. Swan, 1884, 4 S.Ct. 510, 111 U.S. 379, 28 L.Ed. 462; Cameron v. Hodges, 1888, 8 S.Ct. 1154, 127 U.S. 322, 32 L.Ed. 132; Louisville & N.R. Co. v. Mottley, 1908, 29 S.Ct. 42, 211 U.S. 149, 53 L.Ed. 126; Sumner v. Mata, 1981, 101 S.Ct. 764, 769 n. 2, 449 U.S. 539, 547 n. 2, 66 L.Ed.2d 722.

10. E.g., American Fire & Cas. Co. v. Finn, 1951, 71 S.Ct. 534, 341 U.S. 6, 95 L.Ed. 702 (party who removed case to federal court, and successfully resisted plaintiff's attempts to have it remanded, can raise want of jurisdiction after verdict for plaintiff). See also Santos v. Alaska Bar Assn., C.A.9th, 1980, 618 F.2d 575; Sadat v. Mertes, C.A.7th, 1980, 615 F.2d 1176, 1188–1189.

But a final judgment has res judicata effect even though there was a jurisdictional defect that the parties did not raise. See § 16 below.

11. The doctrine is criticized in the provocative article, Morse, Judicial Self–Denial and Judicial Activism: The Personality of the Original Jurisdiction of the District Courts, 1954, 3 Clev.–Mar.L.Rev. 101, 1955, 4 Clev.–Mar.L.Rev. 7. See also Note, 1960, 7 Utah L.Rev. 258.

Professor Dobbs also is critical of the rule that jurisdiction over the subject matter cannot be obtained by consent. His penetrating study of the history of the rule demonstrates that it was not until the middle of the 19th century, when textwriters began to generalize broadly from more limited views dating back to Bracton and Lord Coke, that such a rule become thoroughly settled in the common law. Dobbs, The Decline of Jurisdiction by Consent, 1961, 40 N.C.L.Rev. 49. See also Dobbs, Beyond Bootstrap: Foreclosing the Issue of Subject–Matter Jurisdiction Before Final Judgment, 1967, 51 Minn.L.Rev. 491. It is clear, however, that this has long been accepted as the rule for the federal courts.

Another extreme application of this doctrine is in the Supreme Court's announcement that "by definition, a jurisdictional ruling may never be made prospective only." [12] If constitutional decisions can be made prospective only, so that even those whose cases are on direct appeal do not get the benefit of a new constitutional rule,[13] it is difficult to see why a different standard should be applied to jurisdictional rulings.[14]

The doctrine that the courts are of limited jurisdiction is embodied in the Federal Rules of Civil Procedure. Most defects are waived if the party fails to assert them at the time specified by the rules, but it is specifically provided that "whenever it appears by suggestion of the parties or otherwise that the court lacks jurisdiction of the subject matter, the court shall dismiss the action." [15]

A well-known case, if sound, would have made serious inroads on the doctrine just described. In a diversity case defendant challenged the existence of diversity, and the case was set for a preliminary hearing on this issue. Before the date set for the hearing, the parties filed a stipulation that the court had jurisdiction, and so the hearing was not held. Twenty-three months later, after the parties had made extensive preparation for trial, and after the statute of limitations had run on plaintiff's claim, defendant, at the pretrial conference, once more asserted lack of jurisdiction, and presented facts that showed conclusively that there was a want of diversity. The trial court dismissed the action, but the Third Circuit reversed.[16] The basis of the decision is not entirely clear. The court relied on cases that have held that after jurisdiction has been challenged, and the court on inquiry has held that jurisdiction exists, the issue cannot be relitigated.[17] Though the Third Circuit said

---

12. Firestone Tire & Rubber Co. v. Risjord, 1981, 101 S.Ct. 669, 676, 449 U.S. 368, 379, 66 L.Ed.2d 571.

13. The classic example is Johnson v. New Jersey, 1966, 86 S.Ct. 1772, 384 U.S. 719, 16 L.Ed.2d 882. The Court there affirmed death sentences on two prisoners, holding that the Miranda rules, which had been announced one week earlier, applied only to those whose trials began after the date of the Miranda decision.

14. The Court has applied a jurisdictional ruling prospectively. In Northern Pipeline Const. Co. v. Marathon Pipe Line Co., 1982, 102 S.Ct. 2858, 458 U.S. 50, 73 L.Ed.2d 598, the Court held that a provision of the Bankruptcy Act of 1978 was unconstitutional insofar as it purported to give bankruptcy judges jurisdiction to hear a state-created claim for damages for breach of contract brought on behalf of a company that had filed a petition for reorganization. But the Court held that this ruling would be applied prospectively only. Indeed it stayed its judgment for more than three months, until October 4, 1982, to give

Congress time to act. 102 S.Ct. at 2880, 458 U.S. at 87–89. On October 4th the stay was further extended until December 24th. 103 S.Ct. 199, 459 U.S. 813, 74 L.Ed.2d 160. On December 28th the Court denied the Solicitor General's motion for a further extension of the stay. 103 S.Ct. 992, 459 U.S. 1094, 74 L.Ed.2d 942. If a fundamental violation of Article III can be limited to prospective effect, surely a matter of the etiquette of final-judgment appeals can be treated in the same way.

15. Fed.R.Civ.P. 12(h)(3).

16. Di Frischia v. New York Central R. Co., C.A.3d, 1960, 279 F.2d 141, noted 1960, 7 Utah L.Rev. 258, 1961, 15 U.Miami L.Q. 315. The result of the case is supported in Stephens, Estoppel to Deny Federal Jurisdiction—Klee and Di Frischia Break Ground, 1963, 68 Dick.L.Rev. 47.

17. Price v. Greenway, C.A.3d, 1948, 167 F.2d 196; Murphy v. Sun Oil Co., C.C.A.5th, 1936, 86 F.2d 895, certiorari denied 57 S.Ct. 754, 300 U.S. 683, 81 L.Ed. 886.

that defendant's stipulation that jurisdiction existed was equivalent to inquiry and a finding by the court, it may be questioned whether the action of the parties can be so readily equated to a determination by the court.[18] The Third Circuit also argued that the belated assertion of lack of jurisdiction amounted in effect to an attempt to amend the answer. It is discretionary whether to accept amendments to the pleadings, and the court said it would be an abuse of discretion to permit such an amendment in the circumstances before it. This argument seems to assume that the court has discretion to hear a case where jurisdiction is not present, a very doubtful assumption. Finally it was said that "a defendant may not play fast and loose with the judicial machinery and deceive the courts." [19] The argument is appealing, but the answer to it may lie in the suggestion of the Seventh Circuit, sustaining a similarly belated challenge to jurisdiction, that while an intentional failure to raise the jurisdictional question in the beginning would be reprehensible, the remedy for such conduct would be disciplinary action by the court rather than an assumption of jurisdiction that the court does not have.[20]

The matter seems to be settled, contrary to the view of the Third Circuit, by a later Supreme Court decision. On the third day of trial in a wrongful death action the party being sued, which had admitted the jurisdictional allegations in the complaint, disclosed for the first time that its principal place of business was in Iowa, not in Nebraska as alleged in the complaint, and that diversity did not exist. The district court thought it had discretion to finish the trial, and a substantial verdict was returned for plaintiff. The Eighth Circuit affirmed, saying that "the most elementary considerations of judicial fairness" precluded the belated challenge to jurisdiction, particularly since there seemed a good possibility that the statute of limitations would now bar action in state court.[21] The Supreme Court reversed. In a curt footnote it said: "Our holding is that the District Court lacked power to entertain the

---

18. See also Ferguson v. Neighborhood Housing Services of Cleveland, Inc., C.A.6th, 1986, 780 F.2d 549, 550–551. The court, in a lengthy dictum, says that while a party cannot consent to jurisdiction, it can admit a fact and that fact creates federal subject-matter jurisdiction. A similar view is advocated in Marshall, The "Facts" of Federal Subject–Matter Jurisdiction, 1985, 35 DePaul L.Rev. 23.

19. 279 F.2d at 144.

20. Page v. Wright, C.C.A.7th, 1940, 116 F.2d 449, 455. See also Basso v. Utah Power & Light Co., C.A.10th, 1974, 495 F.2d 906; Knee v. Chemical Leaman Tank Lines, Inc., D.C.Pa.1968, 293 F.Supp. 1094. Sanctions against the party or its attorneys were suggested also in Tuck v. United Services Automobile Assn., C.A.10th, 1988, 859 F.2d 842, 846. A fine of $5,000 was imposed in Itel Containers Intern. v. Puerto Rico Marine Management, Inc., D.C.N.J.

1985, 108 F.R.D. 96, for actively concealing from plaintiff and the court the lack of jurisdiction, but in Wojan v. General Motors Corp., C.A.7th, 1988, 851 F.2d 969, defendant's failure to make a timely denial of diversity was held not to warrant imposition of sanctions. On sanctions generally, see § 69A below.

"The Di Frischia decision has received considerable attention from the commentators * * *, but has been ignored, criticized, or limited to its facts and distinguished by the federal courts." Sadat v. Mertes, C.A.7th, 1980, 615 F.2d 1176, 1189; To the same effect, see Von Dunser v. Aronoff, C.A.6th, 1990, 915 F.2d 1071, 1074. "Di Frischia can no longer be regarded as the law of this circuit." Rubin v. Buckman, C.A.3d, 1984, 727 F.2d 71, 72.

21. Kroger v. Owen Equipment & Erection Co., C.A.8th, 1977, 558 F.2d 417, 427.

respondent's lawsuit against the petitioner. Thus, the asserted inequity in the respondent's alleged concealment of its citizenship is irrelevant. Federal judicial power does not depend upon 'prior action or conduct of the parties.' " [22]

Undoubtedly Congress has power to ameliorate, if not to abolish altogether, the doctrine that a jurisdictional defect must be noticed at any time. If the defect is that the case is not within the statutory grant of jurisdiction, as where the jurisdictional amount is not satisfied, Congress, having created the statutory limitation, may determine at what stage of the case it can be asserted. The matter is more difficult if the defect is that the case does not fall within the constitutional grant of judicial power. Even here, however, a tenable argument may be made that the "necessary and proper" clause of the Constitution gives Congress power to avoid wasteful burdens on the courts by setting a time limit for raising jurisdictional questions. This is the view of the American Law Institute. It proposed a statute providing that no federal court shall consider a jurisdictional defect, except in certain specified circumstances, after the trial on the merits has begun or the district court has made a decision dispositive of the merits.[23]

It is important to understand that the present section is concerned solely with jurisdiction over the subject matter. Jurisdiction over the person is a waivable defect, which must be asserted by the party who would take advantage of it.[24] And a distinction must be drawn between lack of jurisdiction and want of merits. A court may have jurisdiction over a case even though the case is one to which there is no merit.[25] "Jurisdiction is authority to decide the case either way." [26] The jurisdiction of the federal courts is dependent on the subject matter of the action or the status of the parties to it; it is not dependent on the merits of the case.

§ 8. Constitutional Basis of the Judicial Power

Article III, § 2 of the Constitution provides in part: "The judicial Power shall extend to all Cases, in Law and Equity, arising under this Constitution, the Laws of the United States, and Treaties made, or which shall be made, under their Authority;—to all Cases affecting Ambassadors, other public Ministers and Consuls;—to all Cases of admi-

22. Owen Equipment & Erection Co. v. Kroger, 1978, 98 S.Ct. 2396, 2404 n. 21, 437 U.S. 365, 377 n. 21, 57 L.Ed.2d 274.

23. ALI Study, § 1386. The proposal is criticized as both "too broad and too narrow" by Dobbs, Beyond Bootstrap: Foreclosing the Issue of Subject–Matter Jurisdiction Before Final Judgment, 1967, 51 Minn.L.Rev. 491, 527. See Note, Second Bites at the Jurisdictional Apple: A Proposal for Preventing False Assertions of Diversity of Citizenship, 1990, 41 Hastings L.J. 1417. The Note proposes a provision similar to that suggested by the ALI, but would

do this by the questionable device of an amendment of Civil Rule 12(h)(3).

24. Fed.R.Civ.P. 12(h)(1); Petrowski v. Hawkeye–Sec. Ins. Co., 1956, 76 S.Ct. 490, 350 U.S. 495, 100 L.Ed. 639.

25. Venner v. Great Northern Ry. Co., 1908, 28 S.Ct. 328, 209 U.S. 24, 52 L.Ed. 666; Duke Power Co. v. Carolina Environmental Study Group, Inc., 1978, 98 S.Ct. 2620, 2629, 438 U.S. 59, 70–72, 57 L.Ed.2d 595.

26. The Fair v. Kohler Die & Specialty Co., 1913, 33 S.Ct. 410, 411, 228 U.S. 22, 25, 57 L.Ed. 716.

ralty and maritime jurisdiction;—to Controversies to which the United States shall be a party;—to Controversies between two or more States;—between a State and Citizens of another State;—between Citizens of different States;—between Citizens of the same State claiming Lands under Grants of different States, and between a State, or the Citizens thereof, and foreign States, Citizens or Subjects.

"In all Cases affecting Ambassadors, other public Ministers and Consuls, and those in which a State shall be a party, the Supreme Court shall have original Jurisdiction. In all the other Cases before mentioned, the Supreme Court shall have appellate Jurisdiction, both as to Law and Fact, with such Exceptions, and under such Regulations as the Congress shall make."

The quoted provision is the primary, if not the exclusive, source of power for the federal courts. In 1809 the Supreme Court decided the case of Hodgson v. Bowerbank.[1] In that case the record showed that the plaintiffs were English citizens, and thus aliens, but did not show the citizenship of the defendants. The First Judiciary Act provided for jurisdiction in all suits in which an alien was a party, and it was argued accordingly that since the plaintiffs were aliens, the citizenship of the defendants was immaterial. Not so, said Chief Justice Marshall, for the Court. "Turn to the article of the Constitution of the United States, for the statute cannot extend the jurisdiction beyond the limits of the Constitution." Since the Constitution does not authorize jurisdiction in all cases to which an alien is a party, but only to cases "between a State, or the citizens thereof, and foreign States, citizens, or subjects," there was no jurisdiction, where the citizenship of the defendants was not shown, even though the statute purported to confer jurisdiction.

The Court cited no authority for this proposition, nor did it need to do so. The landmark case of Marbury v. Madison,[2] decided six years before, had held unconstitutional so much of a section of the First Judiciary Act as purported to give the Supreme Court original jurisdiction in a case admittedly within the judicial power of the United States but not within the definition of original jurisdiction in the second paragraph of Article III, § 2. If, as there held, Congress cannot distribute the judicial power of the federal courts among the various federal courts except as provided by the Constitution, then it appears to be an a fortiori proposition that Congress cannot give federal courts jurisdiction in cases not within the constitutional definition of the judicial power.[3]

§ 8

1. 1809, 5 Cranch 303, 3 L.Ed. 108.

2. 1803, 1 Cranch 137, 2 L.Ed. 60.

3. It has recently been argued that Hodgson represented merely a narrow interpretation of § 11 of the Judiciary Act of 1789, rather than a holding that § 11 was unconstitutional insofar as it purported to give the federal courts jurisdiction of all suits to which an alien was a party. Maho-ney, A Historical Note on Hodgson v. Bowerbank, 1982, 49 U.Chi.L.Rev. 725. The latter view is described, at 733, as "[t]he Hart–Wechsler–Wright revisionist interpretation of Hodgson's significance * * *." The important point of Hodgson, however, is its recognition that a statute cannot extend the jurisdiction beyond the limits of the Constitution. Whether the Court then interpreted the statute narrowly, because it would be unconstitutional if construed liter-

This principle, that the jurisdiction of the federal courts cannot extend beyond that given by the Constitution, would seem to be fundamental. It has, however, been subject to some inroads. Thus, the Constitution does not in terms permit the removal of cases from state court to federal court. Yet the First Judiciary Act, and all since, have authorized this in particular circumstances, and where the case is one within the judicial power of the United States, the provision for removal has been held to be an appropriate exercise of the congressional power to make laws "necessary and proper" for carrying out the tasks delegated to the national government.[4] There are some matters that cannot be independently asserted in a federal court, because they do not come within the judicial power of the United States, but that may, as a matter of procedural convenience, be raised as "ancillary" or "supplemental" to a matter that is properly being heard by the federal court.[5] Finally there has been some recent contention that Congress is not confined to Article Three in conferring jurisdiction on the federal courts, but may also give to those courts jurisdiction as to any matter within the legislative powers of Congress, set out in Article One. This contention is discussed later.[6]

§ 9. Ancillary or "Supplemental" Jurisdiction [1]

In 1990 Congress gave the district courts what the statute calls "supplemental jurisdiction" over certain claims that are part of the same case or controversy as other claims of which the district courts have original jurisdiction.[2] This brings together two related judge-made doc-

ally, or whether it held the statute pro tanto unconstitutional, seems to the present author a question of semantics.

4. Tennessee v. Davis, 1880, 100 U.S. 257, 25 L.Ed. 648.

5. See § 2 below.

6. See § 11 below. See also § 20 below.

§ 9

1. 13 Wright, Miller & Cooper, Jurisdiction 2d § 3523; 13B id. § 3567.3; McLaughlin, The Federal Supplemental Jurisdiction Statute—A Constitutional and Statutory Analysis, 1992, 24 Ariz.St.L.J. 849.

2. 28 U.S.C.A. § 1367, added by Act of Dec. 1, 1990, Pub.L. 101–650, Title III, § 310(a), 104 Stat. 5113.

There is already extensive commentary on the statute. For an excellent brief treatment, see Oakley, Recent Statutory Changes in the Law of Federal Jurisdiction and Venue: The Judicial Improvements Acts of 1988 and 1990, 1991, 24 U.C.Davis L.Rev. 735, 757–769. See also Note, The Congressional Resurrection of Supplemental Jurisdiction in the Post–Finley Era, 1991, 42 Hastings L.J. 1611. The legislative process that led to the enactment of

§ 1367 is described in detail in Wolf, Codification of Supplemental Jurisdiction: Anatomy of a Legislative Proposal, 1992, 14 W.New Eng.L.Rev. 1. For a spirited—and sometimes intemperate—debate in detail about the new statute, see Freer, Compounding Confusion and Hampering Diversity: Life After Finley and the Supplemental Jurisdiction Statute, 1991, 40 Emory L.J. 445; Rowe, Burbank & Mengler, Compounding or Creating Confusion about Supplemental Jurisdiction? A Reply to Professor Freer, 1991, 40 Emory L.J. 943; Arthur & Freer, Grasping at Burnt Straws: The Disaster of the Supplemental Jurisdiction Statute, 1991, 40 Emory L.J. 963; Rowe, Burbank & Mengler, A Code on Supplemental Jurisdiction, 1991, 40 Emory L.J. 993; Arthur & Freer, Close Enough for Government Work: What Happens When Congress Doesn't Do Its Job, 1991, 40 Emory L.J. 1007. This in turn provoked an interesting Colloquy, Perspectives on Supplemental Jurisdiction, 1992, 41 Emory L.J. 1, in which five other scholars give their reflections on the subject. Another scholar has said: "Beyond the important beneficial impact of statutory recognition of pendent party jurisdiction, the new § 1367 is plagued with problems, ambiguity, and contrines, ancillary jurisdiction and pendent jurisdiction. The former is discussed here and the latter in a later section.[3]

The most important instance in which the federal courts heard cases, prior to 1990, over which no jurisdiction is conferred on them, in terms, by the Constitution, or by the statutes, has been where the ill-defined concept of "ancillary jurisdiction" could be brought into play. By this concept it was held that a district court acquires jurisdiction of a case or controversy as an entirety, and may, as an incident to disposition of a matter properly before it, possess jurisdiction to decide other matters raised by the case of which it could not take cognizance were they independently presented. Thus, if the court had jurisdiction of the principal action, it could hear also any ancillary proceeding therein, regardless of the citizenship of the parties, the amount in controversy, or any other factor that would normally determine jurisdiction.[4]

That there should be such an ancillary jurisdiction is, in some instances, virtually a matter of necessity. This is illustrated by the leading case of Freeman v. Howe.[5] In an action properly in federal court on the basis of diversity, Freeman, the United States marshal, seized certain railroad cars under writs of attachment. The mortgagees of the railroad then brought an action of replevin against Freeman in a state court, and had judgment there. On review of the state court decision, the Supreme Court held that a state court has no authority to interfere with property that is under control of the federal court. Such a holding is inevitable, if an unseemly conflict between courts is to be avoided and if the federal court is indeed to function as a court. But the mortgagees argued that to bar their action in state court would be to leave them remediless, since, as to them, there was no diversity and they could not proceed to assert their claim against the property in federal court. The Supreme Court said that this was a misapprehension. It said that any party whose interests are affected by the action in federal court in which that court has taken control of the property may assert his claim to the property in federal court, and that such a claim would be ancillary and dependent, supplementary merely to the original suit out of which it had arisen, and maintained without reference to the citizenship or residence of the parties.

Once it is agreed that a state court cannot interfere with property in the control of the federal court, the notion of ancillary jurisdiction put forward in Freeman v. Howe cannot be avoided. Unless the federal court has ancillary jurisdiction to hear the claims of all persons to the property, regardless of their citizenship, some persons, with a valid claim

troversy." Redish, Reassessing the Allocation of Judicial Business between State and Federal Courts: Federal Jurisdiction and "The Martian Chronicles", 1992, 78 Va. L.Rev. 1769, 1817.

3. See § 19 below.

4. Krippendorf v. Hyde, 1884, 4 S.Ct. 27, 110 U.S. 276, 28 L.Ed. 145; Sandlin v. Corporate Interiors, Inc., C.A.10th, 1992,

972 F.2d 1212, 1216; Compton v. Jesup, C.C.A.6th, 1895, 68 F. 263; and cases cited 13 Wright, Miller & Cooper, Jurisdiction 2d § 3523 n. 2.

5. 1860, 24 How. 450, 16 L.Ed. 749. See the discussion of this case in Aldinger v. Howard, 1976, 96 S.Ct. 2413, 2418–2419, 427 U.S. 1, 10–11, 49 L.Ed.2d 276.

to the property, would be deprived of any forum in which to press that claim.[6] Most of the early cases of ancillary jurisdiction were of this type.

In addition to the cases in which property was under the control of the court, there was a group of cases holding that the federal court has jurisdiction to do those acts that it must do in order properly to effectuate its judgment on a matter as to which it has jurisdiction. Thus it may enjoin relitigation in state courts of issues already determined in a federal action, and issue such other writs as are needed to make its judgment effective.[7] This jurisdiction, too, is required if the federal court is to make effective disposition of cases properly before it.

If this were the total extent of ancillary jurisdiction, it would be a concept of importance but of limited usefulness. As late as 1925 the Supreme Court said "no controversy can be regarded as dependent or ancillary unless it has direct relation to property or assets actually or constructively drawn into the court's possession or control by the principal suit."[8] Literally this was not true. There were obscure earlier cases in which ancillary jurisdiction had been exercised though it did not involve property controlled by the court, nor was it needed to effectuate the judgment.[9] But it is significant that the Supreme Court thought that ancillary jurisdiction was so limited.

The major expansion of ancillary jurisdiction rests on a case decided in 1926. In Moore v. New York Cotton Exchange[10] there was no diversity. Plaintiff's claim was properly in federal court, since it alleged a violation of the Sherman Act. Defendant asserted a counterclaim, compulsory under the Equity Rules of 1912 since it arose out of the same transaction as did plaintiff's claim, asking for an injunction. The counterclaim did not involve a federal question. It was held, nevertheless, that after the plaintiff's claim had been dismissed on the merits, the court could go ahead and award the injunction sought by the counterclaim. The Moore case did not use the term "ancillary jurisdiction" nor did it cite to the earlier cases in which that concept had been applied. Indeed the Court cited no cases, and gave very little explanation of why the federal court had jurisdiction to hear the counterclaim. It said only: "So close is the connection between the case sought to be stated in the bill and that set up in the counterclaim that it only needs the failure of the former to establish a foundation for the latter; but the relief afforded by the dismissal of the bill is not complete without an injunction restraining appellant from continuing to obtain by stealthy appro-

---

6. Aldinger v. Howard, 1976, 96 S.Ct. 2413, 2419 n. 7, 427 U.S. 1, 11 n. 7, 49 L.Ed.2d 276.

7. Supreme Tribe of Ben–Hur v. Cauble, 1921, 41 S.Ct. 338, 255 U.S. 356, 65 L.Ed. 673. See § 47 below. See also Board of County Commrs. v. U.S. ex rel. Moulton, 1884, 5 S.Ct. 108, 112 U.S. 217, 28 L.Ed. 698; Note, Federal Supplemental Enforcement Jurisdiction, 1991, 42 S.C.L.Rev. 469.

8. Fulton Nat. Bank of Atlanta v. Hozier, 1925, 45 S.Ct. 261, 262, 267 U.S. 276, 280, 69 L.Ed. 609.

9. Dewey v. West Fairmont Gas Coal Co., 1887, 8 S.Ct. 148, 123 U.S. 329, 31 L.Ed. 179; Partridge v. Phoenix Mut. Life Ins. Co., 1872, 15 Wall. 573, 580, 21 L.Ed. 229. See also Barney v. Latham, 1881, 103 U.S. 205, 26 L.Ed. 514.

10. 1926, 46 S.Ct. 367, 270 U.S. 593, 70 L.Ed. 750.

priation what the court had held it could not have by judicial compulsion." [11] The result is a convenient one. When parties have conflicting claims arising from a single transaction, it is undesirable to require that the litigation be divided between state and federal court. But there is a difference between allowing ancillary jurisdiction to do those things that are a necessity if the court is to function as a court, as the earlier cases had permitted, and allowing ancillary jurisdiction to do those things that are merely procedurally convenient.

The Federal Rules of Civil Procedure, adopted in 1938, broadened prior provisions for joinder of claims and joinder of parties. Many of these joinder rules would be of limited utility if they were subject to the ordinary rules of jurisdiction and venue, yet the rules themselves cannot extend jurisdiction or venue. Following the lead of the Moore case, the federal courts have employed the concept of ancillary jurisdiction in an effort to balance federal jurisdictional requirements with the liberal provisions of the rules as to joinder. [12] Since it was not until 1978 that the Supreme Court spoke significantly on the permissible scope of ancillary jurisdiction under the rules, there was disagreement on how far it extended.

The 1978 decision was in Owen Equipment & Erection Co. v. Kroger. [13] The Court there rejected the notion that a "common nucleus of operative fact" is enough for the exercise of ancillary jurisdiction. [14] The test, the Court said, is "not mere factual similarity but logical dependence." [15] It went on to emphasize that "ancillary jurisdiction typically involves claims by a defending party haled into court against his will, or by another person whose rights might be irretrievably lost unless he could assert them in an ongoing action in a federal court." [16]

The 1990 statute is the outgrowth of a recommendation by the Federal Courts Study Committee earlier that year. The Committee had expressed concern that "[r]ecent decisions of the Supreme Court raise doubts about the scope of pendent party and ancillary jurisdiction under existing federal statutes" and recommended that Congress expressly authorize federal courts to assert jurisdiction over claims that require the joinder of additional parties so long as they arise out of the same "transaction or occurrence" as a claim within federal jurisdiction. [17] Six months later Congress had acted. [18] The statute made major changes in

11. 46 S.Ct. at 371, 270 U.S. at 610.

12. Revere Copper & Brass Inc. v. Aetna Cas. & Sur. Co., C.A.5th, 1970, 426 F.2d 709, 716–717; Brandt v. Olson, D.C.Iowa 1959, 179 F.Supp. 363, 370; Miller, Ancillary and Pendent Jurisdiction, 1985, 26 S.Texas L.J. 1.

13. 1978, 98 S.Ct. 2396, 437 U.S. 365, 57 L.Ed.2d 274.

14. 98 S.Ct. at 2403, 437 U.S. at 374–375.

15. 98 S.Ct. at 2404, 437 U.S. at 376.

16. 98 S.Ct. at 2404, 437 U.S. at 376.

17. Report of the Federal Courts Study Committee, April 2, 1990, p. 47.

18. 28 U.S.C.A. § 1367. As pointed out by Oakley, note 2 above, at 736 n. 2, the statute was passed in the middle of the busy final night of the 101st Congress and had little public or professional attention prior to its passage. The statute applies only to civil actions commenced after its enactment, i.e., December 1, 1990. Pub.L. 101–650, Title III, § 310(c), 104 Stat. 5114. The legislative history of the statute is examined in detail in Wolf, note 2 above.

the law as it then stood on pendent jurisdiction, and it is discussed in that context in § 19. It made very little change, other than a new name, in the rules about ancillary jurisdiction. This was quite deliberate; the House Judiciary Committee Report says that it was intended "to implement the principal rationale" of the Owen Equipment case.[19]

Section 1367(a) is a broad—though awkwardly phrased—grant of supplemental jurisdiction. In any civil action of which a district court has original jurisdiction it is given "supplemental jurisdiction over all other claims that are so related to claims in the action within such original jurisdiction that they form part of the same case or controversy under Article III of the United States Constitution."[20] This includes claims that involve the joinder or intervention of additional parties. Subsection (c) tempers that broad grant of jurisdiction by a narrow recognition of discretion not to exercise supplemental jurisdiction over a claim. This may be done only if the claim raises a novel or complex issue of state law, or it substantially predominates over the claim of which the court has original jurisdiction, or all claims of which the court has original jurisdiction have been dismissed, or "in exceptional circumstances, there are other compelling reasons for declining jurisdiction."[21]

The statute is explicit that supplemental jurisdiction includes claims that involve the joinder or intervention of additional parties. Thus it allows what are known as "pendent parties," as where plaintiff has a federal claim against one defendant and a state claim against a second defendant.[22] The Supreme Court in Finley v. United States[23] had appeared to disapprove joinder of pendent parties, but the stated purpose

---

19. H.R.Rep. No. 734, 101st Cong., 2d Sess., 1990, at 29 n. 16, reprinted in 1990 U.S. Code Cong. & Adm. News 6860, 6875. In the articles by Rowe, Burbank, and Mengler, and by Arthur and Freer, note 2 above, there is much debate about the wisdom of codifying Owen Equipment and about what the undefined "principal rationale" of that case was. See also Perdue, The New Supplemental Jurisdiction Statute—Flawed But Fixable, 1992, 41 Emory L.J. 69, 71–77.

20. Although the statute speaks in terms of constitutional limits, and does not use the "transaction or occurrence" language that the Federal Courts Study Committee had used, see note 17 above, it is clear that Congress thought it was codifying what the Committee had recommended, and either the "common nucleus of operative fact" test of Gibbs or the "transaction or occurrence" test and § 1367(a) ought to be so construed. See Teply & Whitten, Civil Procedure, 1991, pp. 106–112; McLaughlin, note 1 above, at 907–913.

21. See Oakley, note 2 above, at 766–768; Executive Software North America, Inc. v. United States Dist. Court, C.A.9th 1994, 15 F.3d 1484.

Section 1367(d) tolls the statute of limitations for any claim asserted under supplemental jurisdiction that is dismissed by the court until 30 days after the claim is dismissed "unless State law provides a longer tolling period." In addition, if a party chooses voluntarily to dismiss other claims when the claim within supplemental jurisdiction is dismissed, the tolling provision applies to those other claims also. Thus, if the supplemental claim is dismissed a party can dismiss its other claims and refile the entire suit in a state court free of limitations problems.

Subsection (d) applies only if a "claim asserted under subsection (a)" has been dismissed. The statute of limitations would not be tolled in a case such as Owen Equipment itself, since plaintiff's claim against the third-party defendant in that case is a claim by plaintiff "against persons made parties under Rule 14" and, by virtue of § 1367(b), is excluded from the grant of supplemental jurisdiction in § 1367(a).

22. See § 19 below.

23. 1989, 109 S.Ct. 2003, 490 U.S. 545, 104 L.Ed.2d 593.

of § 1367 was to overrule Finley.[24] It is equally clear, however, that the statute does not allow joinder of additional parties if to do so would defeat the rule of complete diversity. In diversity cases supplemental jurisdiction will usually have no application to joinder of parties under Rule 20; no matter how closely related the matters may be, a party whose citizenship is wrong or whose claim is for less than the jurisdictional amount cannot be joined in a suit with a party who satisfies federal jurisdictional requirements.[25]

It is subsection (b) of § 1367 that purports to codify Owen Equipment. In a case in which jurisdiction is based solely on diversity of citizenship or alienage, supplemental jurisdiction cannot support assertion by the plaintiff of claims against persons made parties under Rules 14, 19, 20, or 24, or over claims by persons proposed to be joined as plaintiffs under Rule 19, or by persons seeking to intervene as plaintiffs under Rule 14. This limitation applies only "when exercising supplemental jurisdiction over such claims would be inconsistent with the jurisdictional requirements of section 1332." 28 U.S.C.A. § 1332 is the general diversity statute and the jurisdictional requirements referred to must be the rule of complete diversity [26] and the requirement of a jurisdictional amount.

The permissibility of supplemental jurisdiction will be considered with regard to particular rules in later sections. The following statements probably represent a consensus of the results that the courts had worked out on their own, under the guise of ancillary jurisdiction. For the most part, the statute codifies those past results. The occasions where this is less certain will be pointed out.

Supplemental jurisdiction permits courts to hear compulsory counterclaims, under Rule 13(a), but permissive counterclaims, under Rule 13(b), require independent jurisdictional grounds.[27] Cross-claims, under Rule 13(g), are ancillary and within supplemental jurisdiction.[28] Impleader of a third party defendant under Rule 14 falls within supplemen-

---

24. "This section would authorize jurisdiction in a case like Finley, as well as essentially restore the pre-Finley understandings of the authorization for and limits on other forms of supplemental jurisdiction." H.R.Rep. No. 101–734, 101st Cong., 2d Sess., 1990, at 28, reprinted in 1991 U.S. Code Cong. & Adm. News 6860, 6874.

25. See §§ 24, 71 below. It is unclear how the statute will apply if there is complete diversity in the action as originally filed and it is then proposed to amend to add a nondiverse coplaintiff under Rule 20. The drafters of the statute hope that the courts will cure this oversight in the statute. Rowe, Burbank & Mengler, note 2 above, 40 Emory L.J. at 961 n. 91. Their critics think this will be difficult for the courts to do. Arthur & Freer, note 2 above, 40 Emory L.J. at 982–983.

26. The rule, which is a construction of the general diversity statute rather than a constitutional requirement, was first laid down in 1806. See § 24 below. According to the three law professors who were active in the drafting of § 1367, the phraseology of the statute leaves it open for the courts to decide whether the rule of complete diversity applies to alienage cases. Rowe, Burbank & Mengler, note 2 above, 40 Emory L.J. at 954–955. Their critics think the statute can only be read as requiring complete diversity in alienage cases and believe that this was an unfortunate oversight. Arthur & Freer, note 2 above, 40 Emory L.J. at 954–957. For the drafters' rebuttal, see 40 Emory L.J. at 998–999.

27. See § 79 below.

28. See § 80 below.

tal jurisdiction, but the assertion by plaintiff of a claim against a third-party defendant does not.[29] Joinder of claims under Rule 18 is not within supplemental jurisdiction except in nondiversity cases where the federal and nonfederal claims are so closely related as to amount to part of the same case or controversy under Article III.[30] Supplemental jurisdiction is available in interpleader, under Rule 22.[31] The previous learning had been that intervention as of right, under Rule 24(a), came within the court's ancillary jurisdiction, but that permissive intervention, under Rule 24(b), did not. The statute excludes from supplemental jurisdiction claims by persons seeking to intervene as plaintiffs under Rule 24, but the implications of that are not yet clear.[32]

The rule in class actions had been that only the citizenship of the named parties was considered, but that each member of the class, whether named or unnamed, must satisfy the jurisdictional-amount requirement.[33] The new statute was "not intended to affect the jurisdictional requirements of 28 U.S.C. § 1332 in diversity-only class actions, as those requirements were interpreted prior to Finley." [34] Unless the legislative history is to prevail over the plain language of the statute, however, the broad grant of supplemental jurisdiction in § 1367(a) and the failure to include Rule 23 in the limitations on supplemental jurisdiction in § 1367(b) must mean that if one member of a class has a claim that satisfies the jurisdictional-amount requirement, other persons with smaller claims can be included in the class.[35]

It was usually held that where ancillary jurisdiction sufficed to allow a claim or a party without independent jurisdictional grounds, it was also unnecessary to satisfy the venue statutes with regard to that claim or party. The new statute has done nothing to change this, and the result seems right. Though there have been cases to the contrary,[36] if procedural convenience is enough to avoid the constitutional limitations on the jurisdiction of the federal court, it should suffice also to dispense with the purely statutory requirements as to venue.[37]

In general the ancillary concept does not avoid the requirement that the party to be brought in must be served with process within the territorial limits set out in Rule 4(f).[38] One interesting problem in this

---

29. See § 76 below.

30. See §§ 19, 78 below.

31. See § 74 below.

32. See § 75 below.

33. See § 72 below.

34. H.R.Rep. No. 101–734, 91st Cong., 2d Sess., 1991, at 29, reprinted in 1991 U.S. Code Cong. & Adm. News 6860, 6875.

35. Compare Rowe, Burbank & Mengler, note 2 above, 40 Emory L.J. at 960 n. 90, with Arthur & Freer, note 2 above, 40 Emory L.J. at 981.

36. Lewis v. United Air Lines Transport Corp., D.C.Conn.1939, 29 F.Supp. 112; King v. Shepherd, D.C.Ark.1938, 26 F.Supp.

357; Habina v. M.A. Henry Co., D.C.N.Y. 1948, 8 F.R.D. 52.

37. Haile v. Henderson Nat. Bank, C.A.6th, 1981, 657 F.2d 816, 822 n. 6; Lesnik v. Public Industrials Corp., C.C.A.2d, 1944, 144 F.2d 968, 974–977; Herndon v. Herndon, D.C.Tex.1980, 491 F.Supp. 53; 6 Wright & Miller, Civil 2d § 1445. But see Note, Ancillary Process and Venue in the Federal Courts, 1960, 73 Harv.L.Rev. 1164.

38. Pecarsky v. Marina Associates, D.C.N.J.1985, 107 F.R.D. 107; Donnely v. Copeland Intra Lenses, Inc., D.C.N.Y.1980, 87 F.R.D. 80.

area, however, has not yet been resolved by the courts. Where out-of-state service is possible under a federal statute allowing such service for particular claims, does the process also bring the party into court to respond to a claim, joined with the statutory claim, as to which, if sued on independently, out-of-state service would be improper? Though the matter is not settled,[39] it would seem that where the claims are sufficiently related to come within the ancillary or supplemental jurisdiction concept, the process should be regarded as sufficient to bring the party into court to respond to both claims.[40]

§ 10. Congressional Control of Jurisdiction [1]

In § 8 it was seen that, in general, the jurisdiction of the federal courts must find its basis in Article III of the Constitution. The present

39. See 4 Wright & Miller, Civil § 1125.

40. E.g., International Controls Corp. v. Vesco, C.A.2d, 1979, 593 F.2d 166, 175 n. 5, certiorari denied 99 S.Ct. 2884, 442 U.S. 941, 61 L.Ed.2d 311; Robinson v. Penn Central Co., C.A.3d, 1973, 484 F.2d 553; Mills, Pendent Jurisdiction and Extraterritorial Service Under the Federal Securities Law, 1970, 70 Col.L.Rev. 423; Note, Pendent Personal Jurisdiction and Nationwide Service of Process, 1989, 64 N.Y.U.L.Rev. 113; ALI Study, § 1313(a). But see, e.g., Wilensky v. Standard Beryllium Corp., D.C.Mass.1964, 228 F.Supp. 703, 705–706; Ferguson, Pendent Personal Jurisdiction in the Federal Courts, 1965, 11 Vill.L.Rev. 56.

§ 10

1. 13 Wright, Miller & Cooper, Jurisdiction 2d §§ 3525, 3526; Redish, Federal Jurisdiction: Tensions in the Allocation of Judicial Power, 1980, pp. 7–34; Hart, The Power of Congress to Limit the Jurisdiction of Federal Courts: An Exercise in Dialectic, 1953, 66 Harv.L.Rev. 1362; Ratner, Congressional Power over the Appellate Jurisdiction of the Supreme Court, 1960, 109 U.Pa.L.Rev. 157; Merry, Scope of the Supreme Court's Appellate Jurisdiction: Historical Basis, 1962, 47 Minn.L.Rev. 53; Strong, Rx for a Nagging Constitutional Headache, 1971, 8 San Diego L.Rev. 246; Keeffe & Warlick, Article III: Where Are You Now that We Need You?, 1976, 62 A.B.A.J. 246; Redish & Woods, Congressional Power to Control the Jurisdiction of Lower Federal Courts: A Critical Review and a New Synthesis, 1975, 124 U.Pa. L.Rev. 45; McGowan, Federal Jurisdiction: Legislative and Judicial Change, 1978, 28 Case W.Res.L.Rev. 517; Symposium, Limiting Federal Court Jurisdiction, 1981, 65 Judicature 177; Sager, Foreword: Constitutional Limitations on Congress' Authority to Regulate the Jurisdiction of the Federal Courts, 1981, 95 Harv.L.Rev. 17; Young,

Congressional Regulation of Federal Courts' Jurisdiction and Processes: United States v. Klein Revisited, 1981 Wis.L.Rev. 1189; Redish, Constitutional Limitations on Congressional Power to Control Federal Jurisdiction: A Reaction to Professor Sager, 1982, 77 Nw.U.L.Rev. 143; Auerbach, The Unconstitutionality of Congressional Proposals to Limit the Jurisdiction of Federal Courts, 1982, 47 Mo.L.Rev. 47; Meserve, Limiting Jurisdiction and Remedies of Federal Courts, 1982, 68 A.B.A.J. 159; Anderson, The Government of Courts: The Power of Congress under Article III, 1982, 68 A.B.A.J. 686; Brilmayer & Underhill, Congressional Obligation to Provide a Forum for Constitutional Claims: Discriminatory Jurisdictional Rules and the Conflict of Laws, 1983, 69 Va.L.Rev. 819; Tushnet & Jaff, Why the Debate Over Congress' Power to Restrict the Jurisdiction of the Federal Courts is Unending, 1984, 72 Geo.L.J. 1311; Gunther, Congressional Power to Curtail Federal Court Jurisdiction: An Opinionated Guide to the Ongoing Debate, 1984, 36 Stan.L.Rev. 895; Casto, The First Congress's Understanding of Its Authority Over the Federal Courts' Jurisdiction, 1985, 26 B.C.L.Rev. 205; Amar, A Neo–Federalist View of Article III: Separating the Two Tiers of Federal Jurisdiction, 1985, 65 B.U.L.Rev. 205; Clinton, A Mandatory View of Federal Court Jurisdiction: Early Implementation of and Departures from the Constitutional Plan, 1986, 86 Col.L.Rev. 1515; Casto, An Orthodox View of the Two–Tier Analysis of Congressional Control Over Federal Jurisdiction, 1990, 7 Const.Commentary 89; Friedman, A Different Dialogue: The Supreme Court, Congress and Federal Jurisdiction, 1990, 85 Nw.U.L.Rev. 1; Amar, Taking Article III Seriously: A Reply to Professor Friedman, 1990, 85 Nw.U.L.Rev. 442 (1991); Friedman, Federal Jurisdiction and Legal Scholsection is concerned with the extent to which the judicial power granted by the Constitution is subject to control by Congress.

The question is most readily answered with regard to the original jurisdiction of the Supreme Court. Although the First Congress, in the Judiciary Act of 1789, undertook to set forth that jurisdiction, it has always been understood that the constitutional language is, in this regard, self-executing, and that Congress cannot take that jurisdiction away from the Supreme Court.[2] Congress cannot expand the original jurisdiction of the Supreme Court, even to cases otherwise within the judicial power of the United States,[3] nor can it deny such jurisdiction. It can, however, provide that the jurisdiction of the Supreme Court, in cases within the grant of original jurisdiction, be concurrent with the district courts,[4] and can give appellate jurisdiction in cases that might also fall within the original jurisdiction of the Supreme Court.[5]

The extent of congressional control of the appellate jurisdiction of the Supreme Court and of the lower federal courts has not been the subject of many court decisions. It has, however, aroused much debate and scholarly writing when legislation has been proposed that would limit jurisdiction as a means of depriving the federal courts of authority in fields in which their decisions have been controversial. In the 1950s the issue was subversion; in the 1980s and 1990s it is such matters as abortion, school prayer, and busing.

The Constitution, after defining the original jurisdiction of the Supreme Court, provides that in all other cases within the judicial power of the United States, "the supreme Court shall have appellate Jurisdiction, both as to Law and Fact, with such Exceptions, and under such Regulations as the Congress shall make." The power to make exceptions in this jurisdiction was tested in the famous case of Ex parte McCardle.[6] An Act of 1867 gave the Supreme Court appellate jurisdiction in habeas-corpus cases. Prior to that time there was no such jurisdiction on appeal, though the Supreme Court could issue original writs of habeas corpus and certiorari, and review a denial of habeas corpus below by this means. McCardle was a civilian, held for trial by a military commission in Mississippi pursuant to Reconstruction statutes. The circuit court denied his application for habeas corpus, and he

arship: A (Dialogic) Reply, 1991, 85 Nw. U.L.Rev. 478.

2. Chisholm v. Georgia, 1793, 2 Dall. 419, 1 L.Ed. 440; Florida v. Georgia, 1854, 17 How. 478, 15 L.Ed. 181; Kentucky v. Dennison, 1860, 24 How. 66, 16 L.Ed. 717; California v. Arizona, 1979, 99 S.Ct. 919, 440 U.S. 59, 59 L.Ed.2d 144; 17 Wright, Miller & Cooper, Jurisdiction 2d § 4043.

3. Marbury v. Madison, 1803, 1 Cranch 137, 2 L.Ed. 60; Wisconsin v. Pelican Ins. Co. of New Orleans, 1888, 8 S.Ct. 1370, 1379, 127 U.S. 265, 300, 32 L.Ed. 239.

4. Ohio v. Wyandotte Chemicals Corp., 1971, 91 S.Ct. 1005, 401 U.S. 493, 28

L.Ed.2d 256; Ames v. Kansas ex rel. Johnston, 1884, 4 S.Ct. 437, 111 U.S. 449, 28 L.Ed. 482; U.S. v. California, C.A.9th, 1964, 328 F.2d 729, certiorari denied 85 S.Ct. 34, 379 U.S. 817, 13 L.Ed.2d 29. Congress has in fact done this ever since 1789. See 28 U.S.C.A. §§ 1251, 1351. See §§ 109, 110 below.

5. Cohens v. Virginia, 1821, 6 Wheat. 264, 5 L.Ed. 257.

6. 1868, 7 Wall. 506, 19 L.Ed. 264. See Van Alstyne, A Critical Guide to Ex Parte McCardle, 1973, 15 Ariz.L.Rev. 229.

appealed. In 1868, while the case was pending before the Supreme Court, Congress, apprehensive lest the Supreme Court would grant the writ and thus invalidate much of the Reconstruction legislation, passed an amendatory statute taking away the appellate jurisdiction of the Supreme Court in habeas corpus cases. The Supreme Court held that the 1868 legislation deprived it of jurisdiction. It considered that this was a legitimate exercise of the congressional power to make exceptions to appellate jurisdiction, and that it was immaterial that the act was passed after the Supreme Court had already taken jurisdiction of the case. This case has long been read as giving Congress full control over the Supreme Court's appellate jurisdiction, but of late there has been some suggestion that this is reading too much into the McCardle decision, and that Congress does not have power to make such exceptions as will destroy the essential role of the Supreme Court in the constitutional plan.[7] This reading, for which there is little or no direct authority, is fortified by the fact that shortly after the McCardle case it was held that the Supreme Court could still issue original writs of habeas corpus and certiorari, and thus review in a case like McCardle's.[8] The argument is that the essential role of the Supreme Court is not destroyed when, as in 1868, one means of approach is taken away but another is left open. To deprive litigants altogether of access to the Supreme Court in cases involving the supremacy of federal law would, on this approach, be invalid.

The orthodox view, however, is that Congress possesses plenary power to confer or withhold appellate jurisdiction.[9] Even those who subscribe to this traditional view of congressional power may still conclude, however, that Congress may not violate other provisions of the Constitution in controlling appellate jurisdiction.[10] Thus, it can be argued that a jurisdictional statute that acted as an arbitrary or invidious exclusion of a class of litigants or that purported to prevent Supreme Court review of a class of cases involving constitutional rights because of dissatisfaction with the Court's past decisions in that field of law would be unconstitutional.[11]

7. Sager, note 1 above, at 42–68. Brant, Appellate Jurisdiction: Congressional Abuse of the Exceptions Clause, 1973 Ore. L.Rev. 3; Ratner, note 1 above; Hart, note 1 above, at 1365. See also Merry, note 1 above, arguing that congressional control of the Supreme Court's appellate jurisdiction was intended to extend only to questions of fact, not questions of law.

In a dissenting opinion in Glidden Co. v. Zdanok, 1962, 82 S.Ct. 1459, 1501 n. 11, 370 U.S. 530, 605, 8 L.Ed.2d 671, Justices Douglas and Black say "there is a serious question whether the McCardle case could command a majority view today."

8. Ex parte Yerger, 1869, 8 Wall. 85, 19 L.Ed. 332.

9. Abraham, A "Self–Inflicted Wound?", 1981, 65 Judicature 179; Rice, The Consti-

tutional Basis for the Proposals in Congress Today, 1981, 65 Judicature 190; Anderson, The Power of Congress to Limit the Appellate Jurisdiction of the Supreme Court, 1981 Det.C.L.L.Rev. 753; Van Alstyne, note 6 above; Wechsler, The Courts and the Constitution, 1965, 65 Col.L.Rev. 1001, 1005.

10. Meserve, note 1 above, Taylor, The Unconstitutionality of Current Legislative Proposals, 1981, 65 Judicature 199; Van Alstyne, note 6 above.

11. See Taylor, note 10 above; Sager, note 1 above, at 68–80.

The case of U.S. v. Klein, 1872, 13 Wall. 128, 20 L.Ed. 519, lends some support to this thesis, but the decision is cryptic, and there is much argument on how far it goes.

Congress has a considerable discretion in dealing with the jurisdiction of the lower federal courts. It can provide a particular court for hearing certain questions and deny all other courts the power to consider that question,[12] even to the point of precluding raising the invalidity of a regulation as a defense in a criminal action, where there was a court provided in which the invalidity of the regulation might have been asserted.[13] Congress can provide that cases within the judicial power shall come to the federal courts by removal, rather than in their original jurisdiction.[14] It can take away from the courts power to grant a particular remedy or to enforce a particular kind of contract.[15]

From the First Judiciary Act to the present, Congress has provided that in certain instances the jurisdiction of the federal courts shall be exclusive of the courts of the several states,[16] though federal jurisdiction is not exclusive unless Congress chooses to make it so, either expressly or by fair implication.[17] At present the most significant areas in which Congress has made federal jurisdiction exclusive are bankruptcy proceedings,[18] patent and copyright cases,[19] cases involving fines, penalties, forfeitures, or seizures, under laws of the United States,[20] and crimes against the United States,[21] though there are some others.[22] The statute

See Young, Congressional Regulation of Federal Courts' Jurisdiction and Processes: United States v. Klein Revisited, 1981 Wis. L.Rev. 1189.

12. Lockerty v. Phillips, 1943, 63 S.Ct. 1019, 319 U.S. 182, 87 L.Ed. 1339.

13. Yakus v. U.S., 1944, 64 S.Ct. 660, 321 U.S. 414, 88 L.Ed. 834.

14. Tennessee v. Davis, 1880, 100 U.S. 257, 25 L.Ed. 648; Martin v. Wyzanski, D.C.Mass.1967, 262 F.Supp. 925.

15. Lauf v. E.G. Shinner & Co., 1938, 58 S.Ct. 578, 303 U.S. 323, 82 L.Ed. 872; Chrisman v. Sisters of St. Joseph of Peace, C.A.9th, 1974, 506 F.2d 308.

But see Meserve, note 1 above, Sager, note 1 above at 80–88; Rotunda, Congressional Power to Restrict the Jurisdiction of the Lower Federal Courts and the Problem of School Busing, 1976, 64 Geo.L.J. 839.

16. 13 Wright, Miller & Cooper, Jurisdiction 2d § 3527. The constitutionality of this practice was thought beyond serious question in The Moses Taylor, 1867, 4 Wall. 411, 18 L.Ed. 397.

17. Claflin v. Houseman, 1876, 93 U.S. 130, 23 L.Ed. 833. The Court presumes that there is state-court jurisdiction over claims arising under federal law, and this presumption can be rebutted only by "an explicit statutory directive, by unmistakable implication from legislative history, or by a clear incompatibility between state-court jurisdiction and federal interests." Tafflin v. Levitt, 1990, 110 S.Ct. 792, 795, 493 U.S.

455, 460, 107 L.Ed.2d 887. See Solimine, Rethinking Exclusive Federal Jurisdiction, 1991, 62 U.Pitt.L.Rev. 383; Redish & Muench, Adjudication of Federal Causes of Action in State Court, 1976, 75 Mich.L.Rev. 311. Professor Redish thinks that the only area in which federal courts should have exclusive jurisdiction is cases seeking directly to control the official actions of federal officers through injunction, mandamus, or habeas corpus. Redish, Reassessing the Allocation of Judicial Business between State and Federal Courts: Federal Jurisdiction and "The Martian Chronicles", 1992, 78 Va.L.Rev. 1769, 1811–1814. Professor Shapiro disagrees. Shapiro, Reflections on the Allocation of Jurisdiction between State and Federal Courts, 1992, 78 Va.L.Rev. 1839, 1843–1844.

18. 28 U.S.C.A. § 1334; 13A Wright, Miller & Cooper, Jurisdiction 2d § 3570.

19. 28 U.S.C.A. § 1338(a); 13 Wright, Miller & Cooper, Jurisdiction 2d § 3582; Cooper, State Law of Patent Exploitation, 1972, 56 Minn.L.Rev. 313; Chisum, The Allocation of Jurisdiction between State and Federal Courts in Patent Litigation, 1971, 46 Wash.L.Rev. 633.

20. 28 U.S.C.A. §§ 1355, 1356; 13 Wright, Miller & Cooper, Jurisdiction 2d § 3578. The ALI Study, pp. 184–186, proposed repeal of these provisions.

21. 18 U.S.C.A. § 3231.

22. 28 U.S.C.A. §§ 1351 (consuls and vice-consuls as defendants), 1583 (review of purports to give the federal courts exclusive jurisdiction of cases of admiralty and maritime jurisdiction,[23] but by virtue of the "saving to suitors" clause in the statute, in fact federal jurisdiction is exclusive only in some eight kinds of maritime actions.[24]

Though a wide power in Congress to regulate the jurisdiction of the federal courts has never been challenged, there has been discussion ever since 1789 about whether Congress is required to vest all of the judicial power defined in Article III, § 2, in some federal court. On this question at least four positions are possible: (1) the constitutional grant is self-executing, and if there is some part of the judicial power not vested by Congress, the courts can hear such cases on the basis of the Constitution alone; (2) the constitutional language is mandatory, and Congress should vest the whole of the judicial power, but the duty is not enforceable if Congress should fail to act; (3) Congress has discretion in deciding whether or not to give to the federal courts any part of the constitutional judicial power, save that the grant of original jurisdiction to the Supreme Court is self-executing; (4) though Congress has a wide discretion in granting or refusing to grant jurisdiction, there are due-process limitations on this discretion. Scholarly and judicial support can be found for each of these views.

The difficulty on this point was felt in the first Congress. "The crucial contest in the enactment of the Judiciary Act," Charles Warren tells us, was between the broad pro-Constitution men who believed that Congress had no power to withhold from the federal courts any of the judicial power granted by the Constitution, and the narrow pro-Constitution men who were anxious to give the federal courts as little jurisdiction as possible.[25] Though the jurisdictional grants that were made in the First Judiciary Act are patently a compromise between these two positions, the fact is that Congress did not grant to the federal courts the full

---

decisions of collectors of customs); 1346 (United States as defendant). In the last of these categories it is only by implication that federal jurisdiction is exclusive.

It has been held that federal courts do not have exclusive jurisdiction over honorary consuls. Foxgord v. Hischemoeller, C.A.9th, 1987, 820 F.2d 1030, noted 1988, 12 Suffolk Transnatl.L.J. 243.

Some provisions for exclusive federal jurisdiction appear outside the Judicial Code. See, e.g., 15 U.S.C.A. §§ 15, 26 (antitrust actions), 15 U.S.C.A. § 78aa (cases under the Securities Exchange act), 15 U.S.C.A. § 717u (violations of the Natural Gas Act), and 40 U.S.C.A. § 270(b) (suits on bonds under the Miller Act).

See Dickinson, Exclusive Federal Jurisdiction and the Role of the States in Securities Regulation, 1980, 65 Iowa L.Rev. 1201; Note, The Securities Exchange Act and the Rule of Exclusive Federal Jurisdiction, 1979, 89 Yale L.J. 95.

23. 28 U.S.C.A. § 1333.

24. See 14 Wright, Miller & Cooper, Jurisdiction 2d § 3672; ALI Study, pp. 234–239; Black, Admiralty Jurisdiction: Critique and Suggestions, 1950, 50 Col. L.Rev. 259, 266–267. In private actions there is exclusive federal jurisdiction of: arrest (Supplement Rule C); maritime attachment and garnishment (Supplemental Rule B); possessory, petitory, and partition actions (Supplemental Rule D); exoneration from or limitations of shipowners' liability (46 U.S.C.A. § 183 et seq. and Supplemental Rule F); and foreclosure of ship mortgages (46 U.S.C.A. § 31325). Public actions of which there is exclusive federal jurisdiction are: Suits in Admiralty Act (46 U.S.C.A. App. § 741 et seq.); Public Vessels Act (46 U.S.C.A. § 781 et seq.); and prize cases (28 U.S.C.A. § 1333(2)).

25. Warren, New Light on the History of the Federal Judiciary Act of 1789, 1923, 37 Harv.L.Rev. 49, 65–70.

judicial power of the United States.   There was no general grant of federal-question jurisdiction, jurisdictional-amount requirements barred access to federal court for small cases otherwise within the judicial power, and the troublesome "assignee clause" denied jurisdiction, though there was diversity between the parties of record, in some cases where the plaintiff was an assignee of a claim originally owned by a person who, for want of diversity, could not have sued in federal court.[26]

The constitutionality of the decision of the first Congress might have been thought settled in 1799.[27]   A case came to the Supreme Court in which the indorsee of a note had sued, and diversity existed between him and the defendants, but the record did not show the citizenship of the indorsers of the note.   At the oral argument it was asserted that the citizenship of the indorsers was immaterial; since there was citizenship between the parties of record, the constitutional requirement was satisfied, and Congress lacked power to limit that jurisdiction by the assignee clause.   Chief Justice Ellsworth expressed his doubt as to how far the argument could be carried, and Justice Chase expressed his view more strongly: "The notion has frequently been entertained, that the federal courts derive their judicial power immediately from the constitution; but the political truth is, that the disposal of the judicial power (except in a few specified instances) belongs to Congress.   If Congress has given the power to this court, we possess it, not otherwise; and if Congress has not given the power to us, or to any other court, it still remains at the legislative disposal.   Besides, Congress is not bound, and it would, perhaps, be inexpedient, to enlarge the jurisdiction of the federal courts, to every subject, in every form, which the constitution might warrant." [28] Though the opinion of the Court, holding the suit must fail for want of allegations as to the citizenship of the indorsers, does not discuss the constitutional question, it was necessarily present in the case, and, in view of the oral argument, cannot be thought to have been overlooked.

A different answer was given, however, by Justice Story, speaking for the Court in 1816, in the supremely important case of Martin v. Hunter's Lessee.[29]   The language of Article III, he said, "is manifestly designed to be mandatory upon the legislature.   Its obligatory force is so imperative that Congress could not, without a violation of its duty, have refused to carry it into operation.   The judicial power of the United States shall be vested (not may be vested) in one supreme court, and in such inferior courts as Congress may, from time to time, ordain and establish.   * * * The judicial power must, therefore, be vested in some court, by Congress; and to suppose that it was not an obligation binding on them, but might, at their pleasure, be omitted or declined, is to suppose that, under the sanction of the constitution they might defeat

---

26. A contrary view is taken by Professor Amar, note 1 above, who argues that substantially all of the judicial power was vested in one federal court or another.

27. Turner v. The President, Directors, and Co. of the Bank of North America, 1799, 4 Dall. 8, 1 L.Ed. 718.

28. 4 Dall. at 10.

29. 1816, 1 Wheat. 304, 4 L.Ed. 97.

the constitution itself; a construction which would lead to such a result cannot be sound. * * * If, then, it is the duty of Congress to vest the judicial power of the United States, it is a duty to vest the whole judicial power. The language, if imperative as to one part, is imperative as to all." [30]

Despite this strong statement, Justice Story apparently believed that the Constitution, though mandatory, was not self-executing. Sitting at circuit two years later, he marveled at the fact that the jurisdiction conferred by Congress fell so far short of the constitutional extent, but held nevertheless that the court had no jurisdiction not given by some statute.[31]

Justice Story's view was not to prevail. At least since 1845 it has been frequently stated by the Supreme Court that "the judicial power of the United States, although it has its origin in the Constitution, is (except in enumerated instances, applicable exclusively to this court) dependent for its distribution and organization, and for the modes of its exercise, entirely upon the action of Congress, who possess the sole power of creating the tribunals (inferior to the Supreme Court), for the exercise of the judicial power, and of investing them with jurisdiction either limited, concurrent, or exclusive, and of withholding jurisdiction from them in the exact degrees and character which to Congress may seem proper for the public good." [32]

There is so much authority for the proposition that Congress is free to grant or withhold the judicial power that it might seem unnecessary to belabor the point. Yet lingering doubts remain. In 1949 the Court of Appeals for the District of Columbia asserted that it is compulsory upon Congress to confer the whole of the judicial power upon some federal court, and that if a case arises under the Constitution, laws, or treaties of the United States, jurisdiction to entertain it is in some district court by compulsion of the Constitution itself.[33] That decision was reversed, though on other grounds,[34] but it is interesting that a court at so late a date was willing to take a position which went even beyond Story's. Yet the position is supported by some modern writers.[35] Further there are other writers who recognize the general authority of Congress in this area, but who suggest that there are due-process limits on the congres-

---

30. 1 Wheat. at 328–330.

31. White v. Fenner, C.C.D.R.I.1818, 29 F.Cas. 1015 (No. 17,547).

32. Cary v. Curtis, 1845, 3 How. 236, 245, 11 L.Ed. 576. To the same effect, see Sheldon v. Sill, 1850, 8 How. 441, 12 L.Ed. 1147; Plaquemines Tropical Fruit Co. v. Henderson, 1898, 18 S.Ct. 685, 170 U.S. 511, 42 L.Ed. 1126; Kline v. Burke Constr. Co., 1922, 43 S.Ct. 79, 260 U.S. 226, 67 L.Ed. 226; Lockerty v. Phillips, 1943, 63 S.Ct. 1019, 319 U.S. 182, 87 L.Ed. 1339;

Palmore v. U.S., 1973, 93 S.Ct. 1670, 1678, 411 U.S. 389, 400–402, 36 L.Ed.2d 342.

33. Eisentrager v. Forrestal, D.C.Cir. 1949, 174 F.2d 961, 966.

34. Johnson v. Eisentrager, 1950, 70 S.Ct. 936, 339 U.S. 763, 94 L.Ed. 1255.

35. 1 Crosskey, Politics and the Constitution in the History of the United States, 1953, pp. 610–620; Howland, Shall Federal Jurisdiction of Controversies Between Citizens of Different States be Preserved?, 1932, 18 A.B.A.J. 499; Eisenberg, Congressional power.[36] A decision of the Second Circuit lends support to this thesis, saying that "while Congress has the undoubted power to give, withhold, and restrict the jurisdiction of the courts other than the Supreme Court, it must not so exercise that power as to deprive any person of life, liberty, or property without due process of law or take private property without just compensation." [37] If there is any limit on Congress, this is probably the maximum limit. Nearly two centuries of history stand in the way of those who would claim that Congress must vest the entire judicial power.

§ 11. "Constitutional" and "Legislative" Courts [1]

Article III, § 1, of the Constitution provides: "The judicial Power of the United States, shall be vested in one supreme Court, and in such inferior Courts as the Congress may from time to time ordain and establish. The Judges, both of the supreme and inferior Courts, shall hold their Offices during good Behaviour, and shall, at stated Times, receive for their Services a Compensation which shall not be diminished during their Continuance in Office." This would seem to be a very clear declaration that the judicial power of the United States, as defined in the following section of Article III, can only be conferred on courts where the judges enjoy tenure for good behavior and assurance against diminution of salary, protections that the Framers, and all succeeding generations,[2] have thought of vital importance in preserving judicial independence. It would seem also to follow that the holding of the Court, through

sional Authority to Restrict Lower Federal Court Jurisdiction, 1974, 83 Yale L.J. 498.

36. Pritchett, The Political Offender and the Warren Court, 1958, pp. 65–69; Taylor, note 10 above; Sager, note 1 above; Redish, note 1 above.

37. Battaglia v. General Motors Corp., C.A.2d, 1948, 169 F.2d 254, 257, certiorari denied 69 S.Ct. 236, 335 U.S. 887, 93 L.Ed. 425.

Several district courts held that Congress could not constitutionally require that more than $10,000 be in controversy if the effect was to bar any judicial review of a constitutional claim. Cortright v. Resor, D.C.N.Y. 1971, 325 F.Supp. 797, 808–811; West End Neighborhood Corp. v. Stans, D.C.D.C.1970, 312 F.Supp. 1066, 1068; Murray v. Vaughn, D.C.R.I.1969, 300 F.Supp. 688, 695–696. The courts of appeals held to the contrary. Goldsmith v. Sutherland, C.A.6th, 1970, 426 F.2d 1395, certiorari denied 91 S.Ct. 353, 400 U.S. 960, 27 L.Ed.2d 270; Spock v. David, C.A.3d, 1972, 469 F.2d 1047; McGaw v. Farrow, C.A.4th, 1973, 472 F.2d 952.

§ 11

1. 13 Wright, Miller & Cooper, Jurisdiction 2d § 3528; Redish, Federal Jurisdiction: Tensions in the Allocation of Judicial Power, 1980, pp. 35–51; Cross, Congressional Power to Extend Federal Jurisdiction to Disputes Outside Article III: A Critical Analysis from the Perspective of Bankruptcy, 1993, 87 Nw.U.L.Rev. 1188; Whitten, Consent, Caseload, and Other Justifications for Non–Article III Courts and Judges: A Comment on Commodities Futures Trading Commission v. Schor, 1987, 20 Creighton L.Rev. 11; Resnik, The Mythic Meaning of Article III Courts, 1985, 56 U.Colo.L.Rev. 581; Gallagher & Kutcher, Quis Custodiet Custodes? The Case Against Article I Courts, 1976, 22 Loy.L.Rev. 301.

2. The Federalist No. 78, at 494–496, No. 79, at 497, Wright ed. 1961 (Hamilton).

The meaning of the tenure provision is considered in the symposia and articles cited § 1 n. 26 above.

"The very point of the tenure guarantee of Article III is to release federal judges from any debts of gratitude running to the President who appointed them. As one Justice told a new colleague worried about pressures from former associates, 'Yes, but you are here now.' " Hobson v. Hansen, D.C.D.C.1967, 265 F.Supp. 902, 931 n. 50 (Wright, J., dissenting).

Marshall, in Hodgson v. Bowerbank,[3] is applicable to all courts created by Congress, and that such courts cannot hear a case that is beyond the judicial power of the United States.[4] The historical development, however, has been much more complicated than these seemingly obvious propositions would suggest.

Difficulty began in 1828, in the case of American Insurance Co. v. Canter.[5] The case came from the territory of Florida. Acts of Congress had created for that territory two Superior Courts, with judges to serve for four-year terms, and had authorized the territorial legislature to create courts inferior to the Superior Courts. One such inferior court, created by the territorial legislature, was the "wreckers court" at Key West, consisting of a notary and five temporary members. This court had jurisdiction over salvage matters, and the members of the court were paid a fee dependent on the value of the salvage. A certain ship was wrecked on the coast of Florida, part of the cargo was salvaged, and a judicial sale of the cargo was had on the order of the wreckers court. At that sale, David Canter purchased 356 bales of cotton. Subsequently he shipped the cotton to Charleston, where suit was brought claiming it by the insurance company, which had succeeded to the claims of the owners of the cargo. If the sale in Key West was lawful, Canter had good title to the cotton. If the sale was invalid, the insurance company's claim to the cotton had to be sustained.

In attacking the sale at Key West, the insurance company argued that a sale of salvaged cargo was within admiralty jurisdiction, that the judicial power of the United States extended to all cases of admiralty and maritime jurisdiction, and that accordingly this portion of the judicial power could only be conferred on the Superior Courts, which Congress had established, and not on the wreckers court, which was not a court established by Congress. To this argument Chief Justice Marshall made a famous answer: "We have only to pursue this subject one step further, to perceive that this provision of the Constitution does not apply to it. The next sentence declares that 'the judges both of the supreme and inferior courts, shall hold their offices during good behavior.' The judges of the Superior Courts of Florida hold their offices for four years. These courts, then, are not Constitutional courts, in which the judicial power conferred by the Constitution on the general government can be deposited. They are incapable of receiving it. They are legislative courts, created in virtue of the general right of sovereignty which exists in the government, or in virtue of that clause which enables Congress to make all needful rules and regulations, respecting the territory belonging to the United States. The jurisdiction with which they are invested, is not a part of that judicial power which is defined in the 3d article of the Constitution, but is conferred by Congress, in the execution of those general powers which that body possesses over the territories of the United States. Although admiralty jurisdiction can be exercised in the

---

3. 1809, 5 Cranch 303, 3 L.Ed. 108. See § 8 above at notes 1 to 3.

4. See § 8 above.

5. 1828, 1 Pet. 511, 7 L.Ed. 242.

States in those courts only which are established in pursuance of the 3d article of the Constitution, the same limitation does not extend to the territories. In legislating for them, Congress exercises the combined powers of the general and of a State government." [6]

Thus, David Canter was allowed to keep the cotton he had purchased at Key West, a result that seems quite just, but it was settled that territorial courts are not created pursuant to Article III of the Constitution, a doctrine of doubtful soundness. Accordingly it was later held that the salary of a territorial judge may be reduced,[7] and that he may be removed from office regardless of good behavior before the expiration of his statutory term.[8] In some of the territories Congress had provided that the judges were to hold office during good behavior, but even this was not enough to alter the status of the court. The grant of tenure was thought to be a matter of legislative grace rather than constitutional compulsion.[9]

Although Marshall had said that the jurisdiction of the territorial courts is not a part of the judicial power of the United States, it has been held from the earliest times that the Supreme Court may review decisions of a territorial court.[10] How the same case can involve the judicial power of the United States when it reaches the Supreme Court, but not be within the judicial power when it is tried in the territorial court, is only one of the conceptual problems to which the "legislative court" fiction gives rise.

From 1828 to 1923, the notion of a "legislative court" was confined to territorial courts and other courts beyond the limits of the United States.[11] There was a brief flurry with regard to the Court of Claims. When it was created in 1855, it had no power to enter judgments, but only to report its findings to Congress. In 1863, however, it was empowered to render final judgment, with a right of appeal to the Supreme Court in certain cases. Nevertheless the Supreme Court construed one section of the 1863 act as leaving it in the discretion of the Secretary of the Treasury whether to pay judgments that the Court of Claims had entered. The Supreme Court refused to hear appeals from the Court of Claims, on the ground that the authority in the Secretary of the Treasury to revise decisions of the court denied to the Court of Claims judicial power.[12] The offensive section was quickly repealed, and

---

6. 1 Pet. at 546.

7. U.S. v. Fisher, 1883, 3 S.Ct. 154, 109 U.S. 143, 27 L.Ed. 885.

8. McAllister v. U.S., 1891, 11 S.Ct. 949, 141 U.S. 174, 35 L.Ed. 693.

9. Ibid., 11 S.Ct. at 953, 141 U.S. at 186; see Glidden Co. v. Zdanok, 1962, 82 S.Ct. 1459, 1471, 370 U.S. 530, 548, 8 L.Ed.2d 671.

10. E.g., Durousseau v. U.S., 1810, 6 Cranch 307, 3 L.Ed. 232.

11. E.g., In re Ross, 1891, 11 S.Ct. 897, 140 U.S. 453, 35 L.Ed. 581 (consular court).

12. Gordon v. U.S., 1864, 2 Wall. 561, 17 L.Ed. 921. The draft opinion of Chief Justice Taney, prepared before his death and before reargument of the Gordon case, was ordered published many years later, 117 U.S. 697, and has been much cited, but cannot be regarded as the opinion of the Court in that case. Indeed in U.S. v. Jones, 1886, 7 S.Ct. 283, 119 U.S. 477, 30 L.Ed. 440, the Court found in its records the opinion of Chief Justice Chase in Gordon, which differs from that published in 1864.

thereafter the Supreme Court took jurisdiction on appeals from the Court of Claims.[13] In later years the Supreme Court seemed to have no doubt but that the Court of Claims was a "constitutional" court, created under Article III.[14]

The modern expansion of the "legislative court" concept began in 1923, when the Supreme Court refused to hear an appeal from the Court of Appeals of the District of Columbia in a case involving utility rates. The Court held that the relevant statute required the District of Columbia courts to assume legislative or administrative duties in these cases.[15] Such duties could be imposed on the District of Columbia courts, it was held, since they were created pursuant to the power of Congress over the District under Article I, § 8, of the Constitution, but the Supreme Court, created as it is under Article III, could not review a matter that was not judicial in nature.[16] A similar result was reached seven years later with regard to review of decisions of the District of Columbia courts involving orders of the Federal Radio Commission.[17]

The whole question of "legislative courts" was fully discussed in 1929 by Justice Van Devanter, for a unanimous Court, in Ex parte Bakelite Corporation.[18] The case involved the status of the Court of Customs Appeals—later known as the Court of Customs and Patent Appeals and in 1982 merged into the Court of Appeals for the Federal Circuit. This Court had been created in 1909 to hear appeals from the Board of General Appraisers—later known as the Customs Court and, since 1980, as the Court of International Trade—in cases involving duty, which had previously been heard by the circuit courts. The statute creating the court set no limit on the tenure of the judges. In 1922, however, it was given further jurisdiction to review findings of the Tariff Commission on certain matters that must ultimately be decided by the President, and that are fairly clearly not "cases or controversies" in the Article III sense.[19] When one such case came before the Court of Customs Appeals, a writ of prohibition was sought in the Supreme Court to restrain it from hearing it, on the ground that as a constitutional court it could not give what was, in effect, an advisory opinion. The Court held, however, that the Court of Customs Appeals was not a "constitutional court," and thus that it could hear the matter before it whether or not it was within the judicial power of the United States. Justice Van Devanter reviewed all the special courts, and declared in extended dicta that the courts in the District of Columbia and the Court

---

13. De Groot v. U.S., 1866, 5 Wall. 419, 18 L.Ed. 700; U.S. v. Jones, 1886, 7 S.Ct. 283, 119 U.S. 477, 30 L.Ed. 440; Pope v. U.S., 1944, 65 S.Ct. 16, 323 U.S. 1, 89 L.Ed. 3.

14. U.S. v. Union Pac. R. Co., 1878, 98 U.S. 569, 603, 25 L.Ed. 143; Miles v. Graham, 1925, 45 S.Ct. 601, 268 U.S. 501, 1067.

15. See § 15 below.

16. Keller v. Potomac Elec. Power Co., 1923, 43 S.Ct. 445, 261 U.S. 428, 67 L.Ed. 731.

17. Federal Radio Comm. v. General Elec. Co., 1930, 50 S.Ct. 389, 281 U.S. 464, 74 L.Ed. 969.

18. 1929, 49 S.Ct. 411, 279 U.S. 438, 73 L.Ed. 789.

19. See § 12 below.

of Claims were all "legislative courts." [20] He found that the Court of Customs Appeals was a "legislative court" because its jurisdiction included "nothing which inherently or necessarily requires judicial determination, but only matters the determination of which may be, and at times has been, committed exclusively to executive officers." [21] He refused to ascribe any importance to the fact that the statute creating the Court of Customs Appeals apparently gave life tenure to the judges, saying that that argument "mistakenly assumes that whether a court is of one class or the other depends on the intention of Congress, whereas the true test lies in the power under which the court was created and in the jurisdiction conferred." [22]

The next step came in companion cases decided in 1933. A year earlier Congress had purported to reduce the salaries of judges, but had excepted from the reduction "judges whose compensation may not, under the Constitution, be diminished during their continuance in office." Suit was brought by judges of the Court of Appeals and the Supreme Court of the District of Columbia, and by judges of the Court of Claims, contending that the act did not apply to them since their salaries were constitutionally protected. In O'Donoghue v. United States [23] it was held, over three dissents, that this was true as to the District of Columbia judges. The statement four years before in the Bakelite case, that those courts were "legislative," was dismissed by Justice Sutherland as "made incidentally, by way of illustration merely and without discussion or elaboration, * * * [and] not necessary to the decision." [24] Instead a new theology was announced by which the courts in the District were "hybrid." They were "constitutional courts," created under Article III of the Constitution and endowed with the judicial power of the United States, and accordingly their judges enjoyed the protections of Article III. But at the same time "the clause giving plenary power of legislation over the District enables Congress to confer such jurisdiction in addition to the federal jurisdiction which the District courts exercise under article 3." [25]

In the companion case, Williams v. United States,[26] Justice Sutherland spoke for a unanimous Court in holding that the Court of Claims was a "legislative court" and that the salary of its judges could be diminished. The result was not unexpected, but the reasoning, in the phrase of two distinguished scholars, "introduced intellectual chaos." [27] The dictum in the Bakelite case about the Court of Claims was given much weight. Though it was conceded that the views there expressed were "not strictly necessary to the decision, * * * they are elucidated and fortified by reasoning and illustration, and, moreover, are the result

20. 49 S.Ct. at 413–415, 279 U.S. at 450–455.

21. 49 S.Ct. at 416, 279 U.S. at 458.

22. 49 S.Ct. at 416, 279 U.S. at 459.

23. 1933, 53 S.Ct. 740, 289 U.S. 516, 77 L.Ed. 1356.

24. 53 S.Ct. at 750, 289 U.S. at 550.

25. 53 S.Ct. at 748, 289 U.S. at 546.

26. 1933, 53 S.Ct. 751, 289 U.S. 553, 77 L.Ed. 1372.

27. Hart & Wechsler, The Federal Courts and the Federal System, 1953, p. 237.

of a careful review of the entire matter." [28]   The numerous earlier expressions that the Court of Claims was a "constitutional" court were rejected as "clearly obiter dicta." [29]

The principal difficulty in the way of Justice Sutherland's conclusion that the Court of Claims does not exercise the judicial power of the United States was the provision in Article III, § 2, that that judicial power extends to "Controversies to which the United States shall be a party." The United States is a party to every case in the Court of Claims. Justice Sutherland was equal to this difficulty. He argued, on dubious historical grounds, that in 1787 suit against the sovereign was unknown, and that the Framers therefore must have meant to extend the judicial power only to "controversies to which the United States shall be a party plaintiff or petitioner." [30] Thus, suits against the United States were not within the constitutionally defined judicial power, and the Court of Claims, hearing such suits, must necessarily be a "legislative," not a "constitutional," court.

On this construction, it may well be asked how the Supreme Court was able to entertain in its original jurisdiction a suit by a state against the United States, to which the latter had consented. [31] It is also not clear why a suit against the United States, authorized by federal statute, is not a case arising under the Constitution, laws, or treaties of the United States. [32]

At this stage in the development of the "legislative court" doctrine, confusion reigned. There were no dependable criteria for identifying the nature of a particular court, [33] and the conceptual basis of the doctrine led inevitably to contradictions. As an example, the Tucker Act of 1887 gave the Court of Claims and the district courts concurrent jurisdiction over actions against the United States in particular situations, provided the amount sued for was not in excess of $10,000. [34] Logically it would seem that such a suit either is or is not an exercise of the judicial power of the United States. If it is, then the Court of Claims—held in the Williams case to be a "legislative court"—should not be able to hear it, for Marshall had declared in the Canter case that "legislative courts" are "incapable of receiving" the judicial power. On the other hand, if a Tucker Act case does not involve the judicial power of the United States,

28. 53 S.Ct. at 756, 289 U.S. at 571.

29. 53 S.Ct. at 756, 289 U.S. at 568.

30. 53 S.Ct. at 759, 289 U.S. at 577.

31. Minnesota v. Hitchcock, 1902, 22 S.Ct. 650, 654, 655, 185 U.S. 373, 384, 386, 46 L.Ed. 954; cf. U.S. v. Louisiana, 1887, 8 S.Ct. 17, 18, 123 U.S. 32, 35, 31 L.Ed. 69.

32. Justice Jackson was later to offer this explanation: "Moreover, the Tucker Act simply opens those courts to plaintiffs already possessed of a cause of action. If that is sufficient to make the case one arising under the laws of the United States, the same is true of this suit and all others like it." National Mut. Ins. Co. v. Tidewater

Transfer Co., Inc., 1949, 69 S.Ct. 1173, 1178 n. 22, 337 U.S. 582, 594 n. 22, 93 L.Ed. 1556. In the same case, however, Justice Rutledge took the position that the cases in question do "arise under" the laws of the United States. 69 S.Ct. at 1187, 337 U.S. at 610.

33. The best article on the subject in this period, fully developing the difficulties, is Watson, Concept of the Legislative Court: A Constitutional Fiction, 1942, 10 Geo. Wash.L.Rev. 799.

34. See 28 U.S.C.A. § 1346(a)(2).

a district court should not be able to hear it, for Marshall had declared in Hodgson v. Bowerbank that a court created under Article III could not be given jurisdiction beyond the judicial power as there defined. Perhaps it is possible for a particular case to be either within or without the judicial power, depending on the court it is in. This would escape the dilemma just posed, and would be consistent with the decisions permitting review in the Supreme Court of cases coming from the territorial courts or other "legislative courts." But if the analysis of the Williams case is accepted, cases under the Tucker Act, the Federal Tort Claims Act, or other suits to which the United States has consented, are not within the Article III judicial power, and it is very unclear how they may be heard in the district courts.

Three justices thought they had an answer to the problem last stated, which they put forward in 1949 in the remarkable case of National Mutual Insurance Co. of District of Columbia v. Tidewater Transfer Co., Inc.[35] The case is more fully considered in a later section.[36] For present purposes it is enough to note that Justice Jackson, in an opinion concurred in by Justices Black and Burton, was willing to extend the logic of the O'Donoghue case and make all of the courts created under Article III into "hybrid" courts. He concluded that "where Congress in the exercise of its powers under Art. I finds it necessary to provide those on whom its power is exerted with access to some kind of court or tribunal for determination of controversies that are within the traditional concept of the justiciable, it may open the regular federal courts to them regardless of lack of diversity of citizenship." [37] So long as the regular federal courts were not asked to participate in any legislative, administrative, political, or other nonjudicial function or to render any advisory opinion,[38] Congress could give them, on this view, jurisdiction in any case in which Congress has legislative power under Article I.[39]

In the National Mutual Insurance case the other six justices rejected Jackson's argument that the district courts could be made into "hybrid" courts. The statute in question, which treated citizens of the District of Columbia as if they were citizens of a state for purposes of diversity,[40] was upheld, however. Two other justices, though disagreeing with Jackson's argument, voted to uphold the statute on a different line of reasoning, rejected by their seven brethren.

During the 1950s statutes were passed in which Congress declared the Court of Claims, the Customs Court, and the Court of Customs and Patent Appeals to be courts "established under Article III of the Consti-

35. 1949, 69 S.Ct. 1173, 337 U.S. 582, 93 L.Ed. 1556.

36. See § 24 below.

37. 69 S.Ct. at 1182, 337 U.S. at 600.

38. See 69 S.Ct. at 1177, 337 U.S. at 591.

39. Compare the similar, but more sophisticated, argument for "protective jurisdiction," discussed in § 20 below.

40. The present form of the statute is 28 U.S.C.A. § 1332(d).

tution of the United States." [41] The effect of these declarations was not free from doubt. In the Bakelite case Justice Van Devanter had said that whether a court is "constitutional" or "legislative" does not depend on the intention of Congress. Further, the Court of Claims and the Court of Customs and Patent Appeals, at least, continued to have jurisdiction to give what amounted to advisory opinions in some cases, [42] and such jurisdiction was difficult to reconcile with the concept of a "constitutional" court.

The status of the Court of Claims and the Court of Customs and Patent Appeals came before the Supreme Court in 1962 in two cases decided under the name of Glidden Company v. Zdanok. [43] The cases arose because of the statutory power to assign judges of one court to sit with another. [44] Under these statutes a retired judge of the Court of Customs and Patent Appeals had been designated by the Chief Justice to sit in the District Court for the District of Columbia, and, while there, had presided over a criminal trial in which the defendant was convicted. Similarly a judge of the Court of Claims had been designated to sit with the Court of Appeals for the Second Circuit, and had cast the deciding vote in an important case. Though there was no suggestion that either of these judges had in any way shown a lack of the judicial independence that Article III, § 1, is intended to secure, it was argued that as judges of "legislative" courts they could not be assigned temporarily for service with a "constitutional" court.

In the Glidden case the Supreme Court held that the Court of Claims and the Court of Customs and Patent Appeals are "constitutional" courts and that the assignment of judges or retired judges of these courts to sit with courts that are clearly "constitutional" is valid. Unfortunately the justices in the majority reached this result on varying grounds, so that there is no authoritative answer as to why this is so. Seven justices participated in the decision in Glidden. Justice Harlan, speaking for himself and Justices Brennan and Stewart, concluded that the Bakelite and Williams decisions were erroneous and should be overruled, and thus held that the courts in question have always been "constitutional" courts. The other four justices participating, however, declared expressly that Bakelite and Williams should not be overruled. Justice Clark, for himself and Chief Justice Warren, reached the same result as did Justice Harlan by relying on the recent statutes declaring the congressional intention to treat these as "constitutional" courts. In this view, the Court of Claims became a "constitutional" court in 1953, and the Court of Customs and Patent Appeals achieved this status in

41. 28 U.S.C.A. § 171, as amended by Act of July 28, 1953, c. 253, § 1, 67 Stat. 226 (Court of Claims); 28 U.S.C.A. § 251, as amended by Act of July 14, 1956, c. 589, § 1, 70 Stat. 532 (Customs Court); 28 U.S.C.A. § 211, as amended by Act of Aug. 25, 1958, Pub.L. 85–755, § 1, 72 Stat. 848 (Court of Customs and Patent Appeals). These citations are to the former statutes. As discussed later in this section, the Court of Claims and the Court of Customs and Patent Appeals were abolished in 1982.

42. Note, The Constitutional Status of the Court of Claims, 1955, 68 Harv.L.Rev. 527.

43. 1962, 82 S.Ct. 1459, 370 U.S. 530, 8 L.Ed.2d 671.

44. 28 U.S.C.A. § 293(a).

1958.[45] Justice Harlan recognized these congressional declarations as "persuasive evidence"[46] but did not rest his opinion on them. Justice Douglas, in a dissenting opinion for himself and Justice Black, rejected both of these lines of argument, and would have held that the courts in question were still "legislative" in nature.

Both of the opinions for the justices in the majority recognized that the jurisdiction of the Court of Claims to hear matters on reference from Congress and report to that body[47] and the jurisdiction of the Court of Customs and Patent Appeals to review Tariff Commission findings in proceedings relating to unfair practices in the import trade[48] might well go beyond the judicial power that can be given to a "constitutional" court. Justice Clark's opinion asserted flatly that such matters are not within the judicial power, while Justice Harlan noted the doubt but put off definitive decision until such a case should arise. In any event, both opinions regarded this as a very small portion of the business of the courts in question, insufficient to alter the basic character of the courts as "constitutional," and indicated that if such jurisdiction is not within the judicial power, then the courts should refuse to entertain such cases.[49]

Even if the varying opinions in Glidden meant that there was still no clear analytical answer as to when a court is "legislative," the result in the case apparently restored the situation that existed prior to 1923. The Court of Claims and the Court of Customs and Patent Appeals were definitely "constitutional" courts, as is the Court of Appeals for the Federal Circuit, into which they have now been merged. The same seems true of what is now the Court of International Trade and was formerly the Customs Court.[50] The 1956 statute declaring it to have been established under Article III, together with the composition and jurisdiction of the court, satisfied the tests applied by Justice Black, while it also meets Justice Harlan's stated test that "whether a tribunal is to be recognized as one created under Article III depends basically upon whether its establishing legislation complies with the limitations of that article; whether, in other words, its business is the federal business

---

45. 82 S.Ct. at 1491–1492, 370 U.S. at 586–587.

46. 82 S.Ct. at 1469, 370 U.S. at 542.

47. 28 U.S.C.A. §§ 1492, 2509. These statutes were amended in 1966 to provide that congressional-reference cases be heard by the chief commissioner of the Court of Claims rather than by the court itself. Act of Oct. 15, 1966, Pub.L. 89–681, 80 Stat. 958.

48. 28 U.S.C.A. § 1543. The relevant statutes were amended in 1975 to provide for review of what has been redesignated as the International Trade Commission only after the possibility of presidential revision of the determinations of the Commission

has passed. See 19 U.S.C.A. § 1337(c). This should obviate the difficulties noted in the Glidden case.

49. After the Glidden decision, and prior to the 1966 legislation described note 47 above, the Court of Claims refused to accept jurisdiction of new congressional-reference cases, but it passed on those that had been referred prior to Glidden. Armiger et al. Estates v. U.S., 1964, 339 F.2d 625, 627 n. 1, 168 Ct.Cl. 379. See Note, The Court of Claims and Congressional Referrals, 1965, 51 Va.L.Rev. 486.

50. See Eastern States Petroleum Corp. v. Rogers, D.C.Cir.1960, 280 F.2d 611, 614.

there specified and its judges and judgments are allowed the independence there expressly or impliedly made requisite." [51]

There was nothing said in the Glidden case altering the decision in O'Donoghue that the courts in the District of Columbia are "hybrid," but the statutes giving "administrative" jurisdiction to those courts, which led to this classification of them, have long since been repealed,[52] and the 1970 reorganization of the court system in the District of Columbia has given jurisdiction of local matters to a local system of courts.[53] These local courts are "legislative" courts,[54] but the United States District Court for the District of Columbia and the United States Court of Appeals for the District of Columbia Circuit are now "constitutional."

Since 1969 the United States Tax Court has been a "legislative" court, created under Article 1 of the Constitution.[55] The United States Court of Federal Claims is declared by statute to be an Article I court [56] as is the Court of Veterans Appeals.[57] The Court of Military Appeals is not a part of the judiciary at all, but is a military tribunal, created pursuant to the Article I power to make rules for the government and regulation of the land and naval forces.[58]

The other remaining "legislative" courts are the district courts for Guam, the Virgin Islands, the Northern Mariana Islands, and American Samoa.[59] Whether the necessity that is thought to have required the development in 1828 of the concept of "legislative" courts for the territories still exists may well be questioned.[60] If judicial independence is of vital importance in the states, it is hard to see why it is not equally valuable in the territories.[61] The district judges there try persons for

---

51.   82 S.Ct. at 1474, 370 U.S. at 552.

52.   82 S.Ct. at 1488 n. 53, 370 U.S. at 580 n. 53.

A statute authorizing the judges of the District Court for the District of Columbia to appoint members of the board of education was sustained, over a strong dissent, in Hobson v. Hansen, D.C.D.C.1967, 265 F.Supp. 902, with the majority relying on the "hybrid" nature of the court. The statute was amended the following year to take this power away from the judges and provide for election of the school board. D.C.Code, 31–101(a), as amended by Act of April 22, 1968, Pub.L. 90–292, 82 Stat. 101.

53.   See § 5 n. 2 above.

54.   Palmore v. U.S., 1973, 93 S.Ct. 1670, 411 U.S. 389, 36 L.Ed.2d 342. See Keeffe & Warlick, Article III: Where Are You Now That We Need You?, 1976, 62 A.B.A.J. 240; Comment, Palmore v. United States: The Interrelationship of Article I and Article III of the Constitution 1973, 23 Amer.U.L.Rev. 119.

55.   26 U.S.C.A. (I.R.C.1954) § 7441, as amended by Act of Dec. 30, 1969, Pub.L.

91–172, § 951, 83 Stat. 487. See § 5 n. 21 above.

56.   28 U.S.C.A. § 171.

57.   38 U.S.C.A. § 7251.

58.   See § 5 n. 22 above.

59.   That "legislative" courts are still possible in the territories is held in Barnard v. Thorstenn, 1989, 109 S.Ct. 1294, 489 U.S. 546, 103 L.Ed.2d 559 (Virgin Islands); Corporation of the Presiding Bishop of the Church of Jesus Christ of the Latter–Day Saints v. Hodel, C.A.D.C.1987, 830 F.2d 374, certiorari denied 108 S.Ct. 1752, 486 U.S. 1015, 100 L.Ed.2d 214 (American Samoa).

60.   The question is left open in Justice Harlan's opinion in the Glidden case. See 82 S.Ct. at 1472 n. 19, 370 U.S. at 548 n. 19.

61.   Loring, Judicial Power and Territorial Judges, 1955, 7 Hastings L.J. 62. See U.S. v. Montanez, C.A.2d, 1967, 371 F.2d 79, 84, certiorari denied 88 S.Ct. 147, 389 U.S. 884, 19 L.Ed.2d 181.

crimes against the United States. They hear civil cases in which the United States is a party. They should be able to decide such cases fearlessly and impartially, without being dependent upon the Department of Justice for their continued tenure. Unfortunately instances are not unknown of territorial judges who have not been reappointed, under circumstances where it appears that they have been denied reappointment because of decisions displeasing to the appointing authority.[62] So long as these judges have limited tenure, the possibility of such abuse, or apparent abuse, will persist. The granting to these judges of tenure during good behavior, as was done in 1966 for Puerto Rico,[63] would be desirable.

There have been questions of the extent to which the judicial power of the United States may validly be exercised by United States magistrates—since 1990 called "United States magistrate judges"—who serve for an eight-year term,[64] and these questions have been sharpened by 1979 amendments to the Magistrates' Act enlarging the powers of magistrates.[65] These questions will now have to be examined in the light of the Court's 1982 decision in Northern Pipeline Construction Co. v. Marathon Pipe Line Co.,[66] in which the Court again struggled with the metaphysics of "constitutional" and "legislative" courts, this time in the context of bankruptcy courts.

Until 1978 the district courts acted as bankruptcy courts. Although proceedings were generally conducted before referees in bankruptcy, the district court could withdraw a case from a referee and the final order of a referee was appealable to the district court. The Bankruptcy Act of 1978 made drastic changes in that scheme. It established "in each judicial district, as an adjunct to the district court for such district, a bankruptcy court which shall be a court of record known as the United States Bankruptcy Court for the district."[67] The judges of the new courts were to serve 14–year terms, they were removable by the judicial council of the circuit, and salaries were not protected against diminution.[68] By any test these were not Article III courts. Their jurisdiction, however, was sweeping. They were authorized to hear all civil proceedings arising under Title 11, the bankruptcy title, "or arising in or related to cases under title 11."[69] The Northern Pipeline case itself was a state-

---

62. See Metzger, Why I Am No Longer A Judge, 1953, 177 The Nation 52.

63. 28 U.S.C.A. § 134(a), as amended by Act of Sept. 12, 1966, Pub.L. 89–571, 80 Stat. 764.

64. 28 U.S.C.A. § 631(e). See § 2 n. 11.

65. Comment, The Boundaries of Article III: Delegation of Final Decisionmaking Authority to Magistrates, 1985, 52 U.Chi. L.Rev. 1032; Note, Federal Magistrates and the Principles of Article III, 1984, 97 Harv. L.Rev. 1947.

A magistrate judge may not preside over selection of a jury in a felony trial. Gomez v. U.S., 1989, 109 S.Ct. 2237, 490 U.S. 858,

104 L.Ed.2d 923. But he may do so if the parties consent. Peretz v. U.S., 1991, 111 S.Ct. 2661, 501 U.S. 923, 115 L.Ed.2d 808.

66. 1982, 102 S.Ct. 2858, 458 U.S. 50, 73 L.Ed.2d 598. See generally Cross, note 1 above; Chemerinsky, Ending the Marathon: It is Time To Overrule Northern Pipeline, 1991, 65 Am.Bankr.L.J. 311.

67. 28 U.S.C.A. § 151(a).

68. 28 U.S.C.A. §§ 152–154.

69. Former 28 U.S.C.A. § 1471(b). The bankruptcy judges were also given power to hold jury trials, former 28 U.S.C.A. § 1480, and to issue writs of habeas corpus under created claim for damages for breach of contract and warranty, brought in a bankruptcy court because Northern Pipeline had earlier filed a petition for reorganization.

Although it was held that an Article I court could not hear a claim such as Northern Pipeline's claim against Marathon, the Court was as badly fragmented in reaching this result as it had been in the National Mutual Insurance case and the Glidden case. Justice Brennan wrote the lead opinion, but he spoke for a plurality of the Court, since only Justices Marshall, Blackmun, and Stevens joined his opinion. Justice Brennan undertook to rationalize the earlier cases as establishing a "constitutional command that the judicial power of the United States must be vested in Art. III courts," except for "three narrow situations not subject to the command, each recognizing a circumstance in which the grant of power to the Legislative and Executive Branches was historically and constitutionally so exceptional that the congressional assertion of a power to create legislative courts was consistent with, rather than threatening to, the constitutional mandate of separation of powers." [70]

The first of these three exceptions involved the courts in the territories and in the District of Columbia. In these geographical areas, in which no state operated as sovereign, Congress was to exercise the general powers of government.[71] Next were the cases upholding the military system of courts-martial. "It too involves a constitutional grant of power that has been historically understood as giving the political branches of Government extraordinary control over the precise subject matter at issue." [72]

Finally Justice Brennan considered a group of cases in which the Court had upheld the constitutionality of legislative courts and administrative agencies created by Congress to adjudicate cases involving "public rights." [73] This "public rights" doctrine, he said, may be explained in part by reference to the principle of sovereign immunity, but it also draws upon the principle of separation of powers, and an historical understanding that certain prerogatives were reserved to the political branches of government. "The understanding of these cases is that the Framers expected that Congress would be free to commit such matters completely to non-judicial executive determination, and that as a result there can be no constitutional objection to Congress' employing the less drastic expedient of committing their determination to a legislative court

certain circumstances, former 28 U.S.C.A. § 2256.

70. 102 S.Ct. at 2867–2868, 458 U.S. at 64.

71. 102 S.Ct. at 2868, 458 U.S. at 64–65.

72. 102 S.Ct. at 2869, 458 U.S. at 66.

73. 102 S.Ct. at 2869–2871, 458 U.S. 67–70.

The "public rights" doctrine has its origin in Murray's Lessee v. Hoboken Land & Improvement Co., 1855, 18 How. 272, 284, 15 L.Ed. 372. Limitations on the distinction between private rights and public rights were emphasized by the Court in Thomas v. Union Carbide Agricultural Products Co., 1985, 105 S.Ct. 3325, 473 U.S. 568, 87 L.Ed.2d 409, though that case upheld giving decisionmaking authority to tribunals that lack the attributes of Article III courts.

or an administrative agency." [74] The "public rights" doctrine, he said, is limited to matters arising between the government and others and cannot extend to a case such as the Northern Pipeline case, involving the liability of one individual to another.[75]

To Justice Brennan, and the three others who joined him, none of the three exceptions to the command of Article III were present in the case before them. They rejected also the argument that Congress is free to use "legislative" courts whenever it thinks this expedient in exercising its Article I powers. Language in an earlier case that the requirements of Article III must "give way to accommodate plenary grants of power to Congress to legislate with respect to specialized areas having particularized needs and warranting distinctive treatment" [76] was read by them as referring only to geographic areas, rather than to specialized subject matter.[77] The plurality opinion also rejected the argument that the bankruptcy court was merely an "adjunct" to the district court and that the delegation of certain adjudicative functions to the bankruptcy court was accordingly consistent with the principle that the judicial power of the United States must be vested in Article III courts.[78]

Justices Rehnquist and O'Connor concurred in the judgment only. In an opinion by Justice Rehnquist, they agreed that Marathon could not constitutionally be compelled to defend a state-created claim for damages by a private plaintiff before a court whose judges do not have the tenure and salary protection of Article III. They thought that was all that it was necessary to decide in the case before them, and that in this area of law, "with its frequently arcane distinctions and confusing precedents," [79] it was especially important that the Court not decide more of a constitutional question than is absolutely necessary. They found it unnecessary to decide whether the Court's earlier decisions on "constitutional" and "legislative" courts "support a general proposition and three tidy exceptions, as the plurality believes, or whether instead they are but landmarks on a judicial 'darkling plain' where ignorant armies have clashed by night, as Justice White apparently believes them to be." [80] Thus, the concurring opinion left open the possibility that the bankruptcy courts could be given jurisdiction to hear private lawsuits on federally-created claims.

74. 102 S.Ct. at 2870, 458 U.S. at 68.

75. 102 S.Ct. at 2870–2871, 458 U.S. at 69–70.

76. Palmore v. U.S., 1973, 93 S.Ct. 1670, 1681, 411 U.S. 389, 407–408, 36 L.Ed.2d 342. It has been said that the Northern Pipeline case "must realistically be read as a disavowal by the majority of some of the more expansive statements in Justice White's Palmore opinion respecting congressional power to dispense with Article III judges in sanctioning contexts." U.S. v. Canel, C.A.3d, 1983, 708 F.2d 894, 896, certiorari denied 104 S.Ct. 165, 464 U.S. 852, 78 L.Ed.2d 151.

77. 102 S.Ct. at 2872–2874, 458 U.S. at 72–76.

78. 102 S.Ct. at 2874–2880, 458 U.S. at 76–80.

79. 102 S.Ct. at 2881, 458 U.S. at 90.

80. 102 S.Ct. at 2882, 458 U.S. at 91.

Justice White dissented at length, joined by Chief Justice Burger and Justice Powell.[81]   He concluded that "[t]here is no difference in principle between the work that Congress may assign to an Article I court and that which the Constitution assigns to Article III courts. * * * Article III is not to be read out of the Constitution; rather, it should be read as expressing one value that must be balanced against competing constitutional values and legislative responsibilities.   This Court retains the final word on how that balance is to be struck."[82]   In the case of the bankruptcy courts he would have held that the reform of the bankruptcy system Congress was attempting was important enough, and the safeguard provided by allowing appellate review in Article III courts was sufficient, to justify striking the balance in favor of allowing use of Article I courts.[83]

That is the present status of the question of "constitutional" and "legislative" courts.   A new Bankruptcy Act was adopted in 1984.   The bankruptcy courts were made elements of the district courts.   The bankruptcy judges have jurisdiction only over core bankruptcy matters, while jurisdiction over plenary matters, such as state-based tort and contract claims, is left to the district judges.[84]

In his plurality opinion in Glidden Justice Harlan wrote that the distinction "between 'constitutional' and 'legislative' courts has been productive of much confusion and controversy."[85]   Neither the confusion nor the controversy has ended in the ensuing 30 years.

§ 12.   "Case or Controversy"—In General [1]

The judicial power of the United States, according to the Constitution, extends to "all Cases" of three designated types and to "Controversies" of six other types.   The courts of the United States do not sit to decide questions of law presented in a vacuum, but only such questions as arise in a "case or controversy."   The two terms can be used interchangeably, for, we are authoritatively told, a "controversy," if distinguishable at all from a "case," is distinguishable only in that it is a less comprehensive term, and includes only suits of a civil nature.[2]

What is a "case or controversy" that is justiciable in the federal courts?   The answer of Chief Justice Hughes is classic if cryptic.   He

---

81.   There is also a brief separate dissent by Chief Justice Burger.

82.   102 S.Ct. at 2893, 458 U.S. at 113.

83.   102 S.Ct. at 2894–2896, 458 U.S. at 116–118.

84.   Act of July 10, 1984, Pub.L. 98–353, 98 Stat. 333.   See 17 Wright, Miller & Cooper, Jurisdiction 2d § 4106.

85.   82 S.Ct. at 1464, 370 U.S. at 534.

§ 12

1.   13 Wright, Miller & Cooper, Jurisdiction 2d § 3529; Radcliffe, The Case–or–Controversy Provision, 1978; Lee, Deconstitutionalizing Justiciability: The Example

of Mootness, 1992, 105 Harv.L.Rev. 605; Varat, Variable Justiciability and the Duke Power Case, 1980, 58 Texas L.Rev. 273.

On "ripeness" as an element of justiciability, see 13A Wright, Miller & Cooper, Jurisdiction 2d §§ 3532–3532.6; Mansfield, Standing and Ripeness Revisited: The Supreme Court's "Hypothetical" Barriers, 1992, 68 N.D.L.Rev. 1; Nichol, Ripeness and the Constitution, 1987, 54 U.Chi.L.Rev. 153.

2.   Aetna Life Ins. Co. v. Haworth, 1937, 57 S.Ct. 461, 463, 300 U.S. 227, 239, 81 L.Ed. 617, quoting from Re Pacific Ry. Commn., C.C.D.Cal.1887, 32 F. 241, 255.

said: "A 'controversy' in this sense must be one that is appropriate for judicial determination. A justiciable controversy is thus distinguished from a difference or dispute of a hypothetical character; from one that is academic or moot. The controversy must be definite and concrete, touching the legal relations of parties having adverse legal interests. It must be a real and substantial controversy admitting of specific relief through a decree of a conclusive character, as distinguished from an opinion advising what the law would be upon a hypothetical state of facts." [3] Unfortunately this definition, though often quoted, turns upon labels that the Court had used in the past to describe cases before it, and the labels themselves are "elastic, inconstant and imprecise." [4]

In a later case, Chief Justice Warren said of the "case or controversy" requirement that "those two words have an iceberg quality, containing beneath their surface simplicity submerged complexities which go to the very heart of our constitutional form of government. Embodied in the words 'cases' and 'controversies' are two complementary but somewhat different limitations. In part those words limit the business of federal courts to questions presented in an adversary context and in a form historically viewed as capable of resolution through the judicial process. And in part those words define the role assigned to the judiciary in a tripartite allocation of power to assure that the federal courts will not intrude into areas committed to the other branches of government. Justiciability is the term of art employed to give expression to this dual limitation placed upon federal courts by the case and controversy doctrine." [5]

It should also be noted that the limitation to "case or controversy" is intimately related to the doctrine of judicial review. In Marbury v. Madison [6] it was central to Chief Justice Marshall's argument that a court has power to declare a statute unconstitutional only as a consequence of the power of the court to decide a case properly before it. Unconstitutional statutes there may be, but unless they are involved in a case properly susceptible of judicial determination, the courts have no power to pronounce that they are unconstitutional. The reluctance of courts to pass on constitutional issues unless absolutely necessary has

---

3. Aetna Life Ins. Co. v. Haworth, 1937, 57 S.Ct. 461, 464, 300 U.S. 227, 240–241, 81 L.Ed. 617 (citations omitted).

4. Public Serv. Commn. of Utah v. Wycoff Co., 1952, 73 S.Ct. 236, 239–240, 344 U.S. 237, 242, 97 L.Ed. 291.

"[T]he standards by which cases and controversies are distinguished from claims premature or insufficiently adverse are not susceptible of ready application to a particular case. The considerations, while catholic, are not concrete." McCahill v. Borough of Fox Chapel, C.A.3d, 1971, 438 F.2d 213, 215.

5. Flast v. Cohen, 1968, 88 S.Ct. 1942, 1949–1950, 392 U.S. 83, 94, 95, 20 L.Ed.2d 947.

"All of the doctrines that cluster about Article III—not only standing but mootness, ripeness, political question, and the like—relate in part, and in different though overlapping ways, to an idea, which is more than an intuition but less than a rigorous and explicit theory, about the constitutional and prudential limits to the powers of an unelected, unrepresentative judiciary in our kind of government." Vander Jagt v. O'Neill, C.A.D.C.1984, 699 F.2d 1166, 1178–1179 (Bork, J., concurring), quoted with approval in Allen v. Wright, 1984, 104 S.Ct. 3315, 3324, 468 U.S. 737, 750, 82 L.Ed.2d 556.

6. 1803, 1 Cranch 137, 2 L.Ed. 60.

led to a rigorous set of rules about what constitutes a justiciable "case or controversy."

"Concerns of justiciability go to the power of the federal courts to entertain disputes, and to the wisdom of their doing so." [7] Expansion of the categories of justiciable controversies has underscored the nearly ineffable nature of the judgments involved.[8] Whether the decisions on justiciability are cast in terms of Article III limitations on judicial power or in terms of wise refusal to exercise acknowledged power, there are few clear rules. The precedents are sufficiently malleable to afford ample opportunity for courts to avoid decision on justiciability grounds simply because decision is thought inconvenient. This has led to continuing debate on the extent to which courts should in fact be free to avoid awkward decisions on grounds of "prudence" falling somewhere between implementation of strict principle and mere caprice.[9]

In private litigation there is, in fact, very little difficulty. Now that the dispute over whether the federal courts can render declaratory judgments has been satisfactorily resolved, most private litigation is of a nature clearly meeting the tests of justiciability. The main body of law on "case or controversy" comes from cases raising questions of constitutionality of statutes, or cases seeking judicial review of administrative action. For this reason this subject is usually treated with care in courses and treatises on constitutional law and administrative law, and may be more summarily considered here.

It is easy to understand, for example, why moot cases are held to be beyond the judicial power.[10] There is no case or controversy once the

---

7. Renne v. Geary, 1991, 111 S.Ct. 2331, 2336, 501 U.S. 312, ___, 115 L.Ed.2d 288.

8. "[T]he fact that justiciability is not precisely definable does not make it ineffable." Poe v. Ullman, 1961, 81 S.Ct. 1752, 1767, 367 U.S. 497, 524, 6 L.Ed.2d 989 (Harlan, J., dissenting).

9. Compare Bickel, The Supreme Court 1960 Term: Foreword: The Passive Virtues, 1961, 75 Harv.L.Rev. 40, with Redish, The Federal Courts in the Political Order, 1991, pp. 87–109; Wechsler, Toward Neutral Principles of Constitutional Law, 1959, 73 Harv.L.Rev. 1; Gunther, The Subtle Vices of the "Passive Virtues"—A Comment on Principle and Expediency in Judicial Review, 1964, 64 Col.L.Rev. 1, and Varat, note 1 above.

See also Brilmayer, The Jurisprudence of Article III: Perspectives on the "Case or Controversy" Requirement, 1979, 93 Harv. L.Rev. 297; Tushnet, The Sociology of Article III: A Response to Professor Brilmayer, 1980, 93 Harv.L.Rev. 1698; Brilmayer, A Reply, 1980, 93 Harv.L.Rev. 1727.

10. E.g., California v. San Pablo & T.R. Co., 1893, 13 S.Ct. 876, 149 U.S. 308, 37

L.Ed. 747; A.L. Mechling Barge Lines, Inc. v. U.S., 1961, 82 S.Ct. 337, 368 U.S. 324, 7 L.Ed.2d 317.

A party's emotional involvement in knowing whether conduct was wrongful is not enough to save a case from mootness. Ashcroft v. Mattis, 1977, 97 S.Ct. 1739, 431 U.S. 171, 52 L.Ed.2d 219.

A case may be dismissed as moot even though the parties are agreed that it is not moot. Lake Coal Co. v. Roberts & Schaefer Co., 1985, 106 S.Ct. 553, 554, 474 U.S. 120, 88 L.Ed.2d 418; DeFunis v. Odegaard, 1974, 94 S.Ct. 1704, 416 U.S. 312, 40 L.Ed.2d 164.

Whether an appellate court should routinely vacate a final judgment when cases were settled while on appeal remains an open question. Kaisha v. U.S. Philips Corp., 1993, 114 S.Ct. 425, ___ U.S. ___, 126 L.Ed.2d 396. See Manufacturers Hanover Trust Co. v. Yanakas, C.A.2d, 1993, 11 F.3d 381.

See generally 13A Wright, Miller & Cooper, Jurisdiction 2d § 3533–3533.10; Kates & Barber, Mootness in Judicial Proceedings: Toward a Coherent Theory, 1974, 62 matter has been resolved.[11] The Court, particularly in recent years, has had considerable difficulty in deciding when a case is moot. The easiest cases are those in which the plaintiff abandons the quest for relief or obtains relief by settlement.[12] Other cases involve intervening events, often beyond the control of either party, that raise the question whether relief that once seemed possible and useful remains so.[13] And legislative enactments by statute or administrative regulation are changed in ways that satisfy claims of illegality or supersede them.[14]

There is a useful escape from the mootness rule in the doctrine that if an issue is "capable of repetition, yet evading review" the courts may decide the case though the particular circumstances that gave rise to it have come to an end.[15] The stated doctrine is that this escape can be used only if two elements are combined: the challenged action was in its duration too short to be fully litigated prior to its cessation or expiration; and there was a reasonable expectation that the same complaining party would be subjected to the same action again.[16] In applying this principle, however, the Court has drawn distinctions too subtle for many observers,[17] and it has not yet clearly defined the extent to which an even

---

Calif.L.Rev. 1385; Comment, A Search for Principles of Mootness in the Federal Courts, 1976, 54 Texas L.Rev. 1289; Note, The Mootness Doctrine in the Supreme Court, 1974, 88 Harv.L.Rev. 373.

11. Although mootness determinations are repeatedly grounded in Article III, and this must be regarded as the major foundation of current doctrine, other cases reflect flexible doctrines of remedy and judicial administration. 13A Wright, Miller & Cooper, Jurisdiction 2d § 3533.1. Chief Justice Rehnquist, arguing that mootness doctrine has at most an "attenuated connection" to Article III, has said that once the Supreme Court has accepted a case for review, it should hear the case on the merits even if supervening events have rendered the case moot. Honig v. Doe, 1988, 108 S.Ct. 592, 607–609, 484 U.S. 305, 329–332, 98 L.Ed.2d 686 (concurring opinion). This view is supported in Nichol, Moot Cases, Chief Justice Rehnquist, and the Supreme Court, 1990, 22 U.Conn.L.Rev. 703. See also Lee, note 1 above.

12. 13A Wright, Miller & Cooper, Jurisdiction 2d § 3533.2.

13. 13A Wright, Miller & Cooper, Jurisdiction 2d § 3533.3. A very common variation occurs when a private defendant simply asserts that challenged behavior has been discontinued voluntarily and will not be resumed. Id., § 3533.5.

14. 13A Wright, Miller & Cooper, Jurisdiction 2d § 3533.6. And public officials, just as private defendants, may assert that they have changed their behavior and that

there is no need for judicial review. Id., § 3533.7.

15. Southern Pac. Terminal Co. v. ICC, 1911, 31 S.Ct. 279, 283, 219 U.S. 498, 515, 55 L.Ed. 310; 13A Wright, Miller & Cooper, Jurisdiction 2d § 3533.8. See Roe v. Wade, 1973, 93 S.Ct. 705, 712–713, 410 U.S. 113, 124–125, 35 L.Ed.2d 147, holding that the natural termination of a pregnancy did not moot an action challenging the restrictions on abortions. See also Press–Enterprise Co. v. Superior Court, 1986, 106 S.Ct. 2735, 2739, 478 U.S. 1, 5, 92 L.Ed.2d 1.

16. City of Los Angeles v. Lyons, 1983, 103 S.Ct. 1660, 1669, 461 U.S. 95, 109, 75 L.Ed.2d 675; Murphy v. Hunt, 1982, 102 S.Ct. 1181, 455 U.S. 478, 71 L.Ed.2d 353.

17. Compare, for example, the 5–4 decisions one week apart, reaching opposite results though the later case does not cite the earlier, in Super Tire Engineering Co. v. McCorkle, 1974, 94 S.Ct. 1694, 416 U.S. 115, 40 L.Ed.2d 1, and DeFunis v. Odegaard, 1974, 94 S.Ct. 1704, 416 U.S. 312, 40 L.Ed.2d 164. And in Honig v. Doe, 1988, 108 S.Ct. 592, 601–604, 484 U.S. 305, 318–323, 98 L.Ed.2d 686, the Court relaxed to the point of virtual abolition the requirement that plaintiff be able to show that he is likely to be affected again by the challenged conduct. It said that only a "reasonable likelihood" need be shown, rather than a "demonstrated probability", and it relied on a tenuous chain of predictions to find even that reasonable likelihood, but it may well be that this shows only that the requirement is flexible and not that it will be discarded as a general matter.

broader escape from the usual rules of mootness may be available if a suit was brought as a class action.[18]

It is held also that the courts will not hear collusive cases.[19] Though the rule is not in terms so confined, it is principally applied in constitutional cases, on the notion that "it never was the thought that, by means of a friendly suit, a party beaten in the legislature could transfer to the courts an inquiry as to the constitutionality of the legislative act." [20] Even here application of the rule has not always been rigid—some of the most famous constitutional decisions have come in what now seem to have been collusive cases.[21] Nor is it fatal to the existence of a case or controversy that a party has deliberately provoked a test case.[22]

The rule against collusive litigation does not mean—though it is sometimes stated as if it meant—that the parties must actually disagree. A court has jurisdiction to render judgment by default or on a plea of guilty.[23] It may order naturalization of an alien though no one challenges the alien's petition.[24] But if one party is financing and controlling both sides of the litigation, the court should deem the suit collusive. If both litigants desire precisely the same result there is no case or controversy within the meaning of Article III.[25] The same result is reached if one party refuses to take a position on the merits and merely asks that a matter be resolved.[26] But there is adverseness in the Article III sense, even though the parties agree to the correct answer to the question presented, if they disagree on what the result should be after that question is resolved.[27]

When the authors of the Constitution restricted the federal courts to determination of cases and controversies, presumably they had in mind that the business of the courts should be the kind of judicial business with which they were familiar in the English courts. Indeed a member of the Court has observed that "a court will not decide a question unless the nature of the action challenged, the kind of injury inflicted, and the

---

18. Compare Deposit Guar. Nat. Bank v. Roper, 1980, 100 S.Ct. 1166, 445 U.S. 326, 63 L.Ed.2d 427, with Sosna v. Iowa, 1975, 95 S.Ct. 553, 419 U.S. 393, 42 L.Ed.2d 532. See 13A Wright, Miller & Cooper, Jurisdiction 2d § 3533.9.

19. Lord v. Veazie, 1850, 8 How. 251, 12 L.Ed. 1067; 13 Wright, Miller & Cooper, Jurisdiction 2d § 3530.

20. Chicago & G.T. Ry. Co. v. Wellman, 1892, 12 S.Ct. 400, 402, 143 U.S. 339, 345, 36 L.Ed. 176. See also U.S. v. Johnson, 1943, 63 S.Ct. 1075, 319 U.S. 302, 87 L.Ed. 1413.

21. E.g., Fletcher v. Peck, 1810, 6 Cranch 87, 3 L.Ed. 162; Dred Scott v. Sandford, 1857, 19 How. 393, 15 L.Ed. 691.

22. Havens Realty Corp. v. Coleman, 1982, 102 S.Ct. 1114, 455 U.S. 363, 71 L.Ed.2d 214; Evers v. Dwyer, 1958, 79 S.Ct. 178, 358 U.S. 202, 3 L.Ed.2d 222.

23. See In re Metropolitan Ry. Receivership, 1907, 28 S.Ct. 219, 208 U.S. 90, 52 L.Ed. 403.

24. Tutun v. U.S., 1926, 46 S.Ct. 425, 270 U.S. 568, 70 L.Ed. 738. See Note, Judicial Determinations in Nonadversary Proceedings, 1959, 72 Harv.L.Rev. 723.

25. Moore v. Charlotte–Mecklenburg Bd. of Educ., 1971, 91 S.Ct. 1292, 402 U.S. 47, 28 L.Ed.2d 590. But cf. GTE Sylvania, Inc. v. Consumers Union, 1980, 100 S.Ct. 1194, 445 U.S. 375, 63 L.Ed.2d 467.

26. Princeton Univ. v. Schmid, 1982, 102 S.Ct. 867, 455 U.S. 100, 70 L.Ed.2d 855.

27. Cardinal Chemical Co. v. Morton Intern., Inc., 1993, 113 S.Ct. 1967, 1971 n. 9, ___ U.S. ___, ___ n. 9, 124 L.Ed.2d 1; INS v. Chadha, 1983, 103 S.Ct. 2764, 2778, 462 U.S. 919, 939–940, 77 L.Ed.2d 317.

relationship between the parties are such that judicial determination is consonant with what was, generally speaking, the business of the Colonial courts and the courts of Westminster when the Constitution was framed." [28] Yet the oldest and most consistent thread in the federal law of justiciability is that the federal courts will not give advisory opinions, though at least by 1770 the power of the English judges to give advisory opinions was well recognized.[29] Thus, the refusal to give advisory opinions must be based on "the implicit policies embodied in Article III, and not history alone." [30] It recognizes the risk that comes from passing on abstract questions rather than limiting decisions to concrete cases in which a question is precisely framed by a clash of genuine adversary argument exploring every aspect of the issue.[31]

The rule against advisory opinions was first enunciated in 1793. Secretary of State Jefferson submitted to the Supreme Court 29 questions dealing with international law, neutrality, and the construction of the French and British treaties. In its reply to President Washington, the Court said that the separation of powers contemplated by the Constitution, and the fact that the Supreme Court is a court of last resort, afforded strong arguments against the propriety of an extrajudicial decision of the questions.[32] Very shortly thereafter a similar rule was established for the trial courts. A 1792 statute provided that disabled veterans of the Revolutionary War wishing to be put on the pension list should apply to the circuit court, which would determine whether the applicant was in fact a veteran and disabled, and then would certify to the Secretary of War that the applicant should be put on the pension lists at a stated amount. The Secretary of War on receiving such a certificate was to put the applicant on the pension list unless he had cause to suspect imposition or mistake. The circuit courts to which such petitions were presented, on which five of the Supreme Court justices sat, uniformly refused to entertain such petitions, on the grounds that the business was not properly judicial in nature and that the power of the Secretary of War to suspend the decision deprived the proceeding of the finality requisite to a judgment of a court.[33]

28. Frankfurter, J., concurring in Joint Anti–Fascist Refugee Committee v. McGrath, 1951, 71 S.Ct. 624, 637, 341 U.S. 123, 150, 95 L.Ed. 817. See also Coleman v. Miller, 1939, 59 S.Ct. 972, 985, 307 U.S. 433, 460, 83 L.Ed. 1385 (separate opinion of Frankfurter, J.).

29. Frankfurter, 1 Encyc. of the Social Sciences, 1937, p. 476.

30. Flast v. Cohen, 1968, 88 S.Ct. 1942, 1950, 392 U.S. 83, 95, 20 L.Ed.2d 947.

31. U.S. v. Fruehauf, 1961, 81 S.Ct. 547, 554, 365 U.S. 146, 157, 5 L.Ed.2d 476. See also Golden v. Zwickler, 1969, 89 S.Ct. 956, 394 U.S. 103, 22 L.Ed.2d 113. For a recent example of a case dismissed because it sought merely an advisory opinion, see Dix-

ie Elec. Co-op. v. Citizens of Alabama, C.A.11th, 1986, 789 F.2d 852.

See 13 Wright, Miller & Cooper, Jurisdiction 2d § 3529.1; Weinstein, Rendering Advisory Opinions—Do We, Should We?, 1970, 54 Judicature 140; Frankfurter, A Note on Advisory Opinions, 1924, 37 Harv.L.Rev. 1002; Note, The Case for an Advisory Function in the Federal Judiciary, 1962, 50 Geo.L.J. 785.

32. 3 Correspondence and Public Papers of John Jay, 1890, pp. 488–489.

33. Hayburn's Case, 1796, 2 Dall. 408, 1 L.Ed. 436. For a similar ruling in a different context, see U.S. v. Ferreira, 1852, 13 How. 40, 14 L.Ed. 40.

The rule against advisory opinions has had modern importance in casting doubt, now resolved, on the power of the federal judiciary to give declaratory judgments. Muskrat v. United States,[34] decided in 1911, involved a statute authorizing certain named Indians to bring a test suit against the United States to determine whether a 1906 statute, broadening the class of Indians who were to be allotted certain lands, was an unconstitutional modification of a 1902 statute allotting the lands. Suit was to be brought in the Court of Claims with review in the Supreme Court. The Supreme Court held that there was no case or controversy in the constitutional sense, relying on the debatable assertion that the United States, the named defendant, had no interest adverse to the plaintiffs, and on the notion that since in a legal sense the judgment could not be executed, it amounted in fact to no more than an expression of opinion upon the validity of the statutes in question.[35]

The case of Willing v. Chicago Auditorium Association[36] in 1928 purported to be a suit in the nature of a bill to remove a cloud upon title by the lessee of real estate. The lessee desired to tear down an unprofitable auditorium on the land and erect an office building in its stead. The lessor had indicated informally that to do so would violate the lease, and the lessee desired to determine this question before demolishing the auditorium. The Supreme Court held that this was not a proper case for a bill to remove a cloud on title, but added the dictum that "what the plaintiff seeks is simply a declaratory judgment. To grant that relief is beyond the power conferred upon the federal judiciary."[37]

When the issue was finally presented squarely to the Supreme Court, it ignored its past doubts and recognized that where there is an actual controversy between real parties, the constitutional requisites of jurisdiction are met even though the judgment is declaratory and cannot be executed. Thus, in 1933 it held that review of an action brought under a state declaratory judgment statute was within the judicial power, saying that "the Constitution does not require that the case or controversy should be presented by traditional forms of procedure, invoking only traditional remedies. The judiciary clause of the Constitu-

34. 1911, 31 S.Ct. 250, 219 U.S. 346, 55 L.Ed. 246.

35. 31 S.Ct. at 256, 219 U.S. at 362. The merits of the Indians' claim were decided the following year in Gritts v. Fisher, 1912, 32 S.Ct. 580, 224 U.S. 640, 56 L.Ed. 928, an action for an injunction against the Secretary of the Interior. In 1976 the Court decided on the merits a case that seems very similar to Muskrat without commenting on the obvious parallels to that case. Northern Cheyenne Tribe v. Hollowbreast, 1976, 96 S.Ct. 1793, 425 U.S. 649, 48 L.Ed.2d 274.

36. 1928, 48 S.Ct. 507, 277 U.S. 274, 72 L.Ed. 880.

37. 48 S.Ct. at 509, 277 U.S. at 289. Justice Stone concurred in the result but objected to the quoted dictum as "very similar itself to a declaratory judgment to the effect that we could not constitutionally be authorized to give such judgments—but is, in addition, prospective, unasked, and unauthorized under any statute." 48 S.Ct. at 510, 277 U.S. at 291.

A similarly hostile attitude toward declaratory judgments was shown in Liberty Warehouse Co. v. Grannis, 1927, 47 S.Ct. 282, 273 U.S. 70, 71 L.Ed. 541. But cf. Fidelity Nat. Bank & Trust Co. v. Swope, 1927, 47 S.Ct. 511, 274 U.S. 123, 71 L.Ed. 959.

tion defined and limited judicial power, not the particular method by which that power might be invoked. It did not crystallize into changeless form the procedure of 1789 as the only possible means for presenting a case or controversy otherwise cognizable by the federal courts." [38] This decision led to the enactment of a federal statute authorizing declaratory judgments in the following year, and the validity of this statute too was upheld.[39] There are sometimes still difficulties in determining whether a particular controversy is appropriate for issuance of a declaratory judgment, and the Court is particularly loath to allow important constitutional questions to be litigated by this procedure,[40] but the declaratory judgment is now a familiar and often-used tool of the federal courts.[41]

§ 13. "Case or Controversy"—Standing to Litigate [1]

The law of standing, the Supreme Court says, is a "complicated specialty of federal jurisdiction, the solution of whose problems is in any event more or less determined by the specific circumstances of individual situations * * *." [2] The description of this problem as a "specialty of federal jurisdiction" has caused difficulty. State courts must and do have a body of law determining who has standing to litigate particular matters. One leading writer has taken the view that standing is a specialty of federal jurisdiction only in the sense that the federal law of standing involves artificialities that the states have wisely refused to follow.[3] The phrase can, however, be understood in a different sense. Since standing to sue is an element of the federal constitutional concept

---

38. Nashville, C. & St. L. Ry. Co. v. Wallace, 1933, 53 S.Ct. 345, 348, 288 U.S. 249, 264, 77 L.Ed. 730.

39. Aetna Life Ins. Co. v. Haworth, 1937, 57 S.Ct. 461, 300 U.S. 227, 81 L.Ed. 617.

40. See, e.g., Electric Bond & Share Co. v. S.E.C., 1938, 58 S.Ct. 678, 303 U.S. 419, 82 L.Ed. 936; United Public Workers v. Mitchell, 1947, 67 S.Ct. 556, 330 U.S. 75, 91 L.Ed. 754; International Longshoremen's and Warehousemen's Union Local 37 v. Boyd, 1954, 74 S.Ct. 447, 347 U.S. 222, 98 L.Ed. 650; Steffel v. Thompson, 1974, 94 S.Ct. 1209, 1216 n. 10, 415 U.S. 452, 459 n. 10, 39 L.Ed.2d 505; Ellis v. Dyson, 1975, 95 S.Ct. 1691, 421 U.S. 426, 44 L.Ed.2d 274.

A declaratory judgment action by a doctor and several of his patients, challenging a state statute that prohibited him from giving them needed advice as to contraceptives, was held not justiciable where past history led the Court to believe there was no likelihood that the statute would be enforced. Poe v. Ullman, 1961, 81 S.Ct. 1752, 367 U.S. 497, 6 L.Ed.2d 989. See Comment, Threat of Enforcement—Prerequisite of a Justiciable Controversy, 1962, 62 Col.

L.Rev. 106. Subsequently the state brought a criminal action against the doctor and another who had openly violated the statute, and the law was held unconstitutional. Griswold v. Connecticut, 1965, 85 S.Ct. 1678, 381 U.S. 479, 14 L.Ed.2d 510.

41. See § 100 below.

§ 13

1. 13 Wright, Miller, & Cooper, Jurisdiction 2d § 3531–3531.10; 13A id. §§ 3531.-11–3531.16; Fletcher, The Structure of Standing, 1988, 98 Yale L.J. 221; Winter, The Metaphor of Standing and the Problem of Self–Governance, 1988, 40 Stan.L.Rev. 1371.

2. U.S. ex rel. Chapman v. FPC, 1953, 73 S.Ct. 609, 612, 345 U.S. 153, 156, 97 L.Ed. 918.

"Generalizations about standing to sue are largely worthless as such." Association of Data Processing Serv. Organizations, Inc. v. Camp, 1970, 90 S.Ct. 827, 829, 397 U.S. 150, 151, 25 L.Ed.2d 184.

3. 4 Davis, Administrative Law Treatise, 1983, § 24:2, at p. 210. See also Scanwell Laboratories, Inc. v. Shaffer, C.A.D.C. 1970, 424 F.2d 859, 861–862.

of "case or controversy," [4] perhaps the Supreme Court meant to say only that on such questions the federal courts must reach their own decisions without regard to what the state law in point may be.[5]

The law of standing is almost exclusively concerned with such public-law questions as determinations of constitutionality and review of administrative or other governmental action. In theory, of course, it is not so limited. The person suing for breach of contract or for a tort must satisfy the court that he or she is the real party in interest, but in practice such suits are brought only by a person harmed by the supposed wrong, and standing to sue is self-evident. It is only where the question is of a public nature that the interested bystander is likely to attempt suit.[6]

The law of standing has experienced rapid and repeated change in the years since 1968. The Court has vacillated on whether it is desirable to relax the requirement of standing, although in general the recent cases have been more restrictive than those earlier in that period. About all that is certain on the subject is that the last word has not yet been written. In a 1982 decision, Valley Forge Christian College v. Americans United for Separation of Church and State, Inc.,[7] almost the only noncontroversial statement the Court made was: "We need not mince words when we say that the concept of 'Art. III standing' has not been defined with complete consistency in all of the various cases decided by this Court which have discussed it, nor when we say that this very fact is probable proof that the concept cannot be reduced to a one-sentence or one-paragraph definition." [8]

The best-known Supreme Court decision on standing, prior to 1968, was Frothingham v. Mellon,[9] often referred to as Massachusetts v.

4. "But of one thing we may be sure: Those who do not possess Art. III standing may not litigate as suitors in the courts of the United States." Valley Forge Christian College v. Americans United for Separation of Church and State, Inc., 1982, 102 S.Ct. 752, 760, 454 U.S. 464, 475–476, 70 L.Ed.2d 700. Of course this would not be true if the rule of standing in issue is a prudential rule, rather than one grounded in Article III.

5. New York State Club Assn., Inc. v. City of New York, 1988, 108 S.Ct. 2225, 2231 n. 2, 487 U.S. 1, 8 n. 2, 101 L.Ed.2d 1; 13A Wright, Miller & Cooper, Jurisdiction 2d § 3531.14.

But the Supreme Court can review a state-court decision resting on an interpretation of federal law if the decision causes concrete injury to the party seeking review, even though the state-court plaintiff lacked standing by federal principles. ASARCO Inc. v. Kadish, 1989, 109 S.Ct. 2037, 490 U.S. 605, 104 L.Ed.2d 696.

6. Although questions of standing generally are concerned with who can bring

suit, they can arise also in connection with whether someone has standing to take an appeal. See § 104 n. 16 below.

7. 1982, 102 S.Ct. 752, 454 U.S. 464, 70 L.Ed.2d 700.

8. 102 S.Ct. at 760, 454 U.S. at 475.

9. 1923, 43 S.Ct. 597, 262 U.S. 447, 67 L.Ed. 1078.

As was common in the earlier standing cases, the term "standing" is not used in the opinion. "The word *standing* is rather recent in the basic judicial vocabulary and does not appear to have been commonly used until the middle of our own century. No authority that I have found introduces the term with proper explanations and apologies and announces that henceforth *standing* should be used to describe who may be heard by a judge. Nor was there any sudden adoption by tacit consent. The word appears here and there, spreading very gradually with no discernible pattern. Judges and lawyers found themselves using the term and did not ask why they did so or

Mellon, a related case that the Court decided in the same opinion. Mrs. Frothingham, alleging that she was a taxpayer of the United States, sued to restrain payments from the Treasury to the several states that chose to participate in a program created by the Maternity Act of 1921. Her claim was that the federal government lacked power to appropriate money for the reduction of maternal and infant mortality, and that such appropriations would cause an unconstitutional increase in her future taxes. The Court never reached the merits of her attack on the statute, for it held that she lacked what is now called standing to make such a challenge. The Court recognized that it had entertained suits by a municipal taxpayer, but held that the case of a federal taxpayer is far different, since her interest in the federal revenue is shared with millions of others, is comparatively minute and indeterminable, and the effect on future taxation of any particular payment is remote, fluctuating, and uncertain. The Court also was alarmed at the prospect that to allow such a suit would mean that any federal taxpayer could challenge the validity of any federal expenditure. Finally the Court stated that its power to declare statutes unconstitutional exists only where the statute is involved in a justiciable case, and that to present such a case the plaintiff "must be able to show, not only that the statute is invalid, but that he has sustained or is immediately in danger of sustaining some direct injury as the result of its enforcement, and not merely that he suffers in some indefinite way in common with people generally." [10]

The Frothingham decision, taken together with the decision in the companion case that a state cannot challenge the constitutionality of a federal expenditure,[11] had the effect of taking the spending power beyond the scope of judicial review. Though the case was thus of the first importance, and perhaps at the time salutary in result, neither its reasoning nor its result found much favor with later commentators. They noted that states almost universally permit review of governmental spending at the instance of local or state taxpayers.[12] The distinction drawn in Frothingham between federal and municipal taxpayers, based on the size of their interest, seemed unrealistic at a time when certain large corporations pay in taxes as much as 2% of the entire federal revenue, and thus have an interest of twenty million dollars in, for example, a billion-dollar spending program. Sums of this nature, far exceeding the amount likely to be at stake in a suit by a municipal taxpayer, did not seem to fit the Court's description of "comparatively

where it came from." Vining, Legal Identity, 1978, p. 55.

10. 43 S.Ct. at 601, 262 U.S. at 488.

11. See § 14 below.

On the standing of a state to sue parens patriae, see also Pennsylvania v. New Jersey, 1976, 96 S.Ct. 2333, 426 U.S. 660, 49 L.Ed.2d 124; Hawaii v. Standard Oil Co. of California, 1972, 92 S.Ct. 885, 405 U.S. 251, 31 L.Ed.2d 184; Pennsylvania by Shapp v. Kleppe, C.A.D.C.1976, 533 F.2d 668; Strausberg, The Standing of a State as Par-

ens Patriae To Sue the Federal Government, 1976, 35 Fed.Bar J. 1; Comment, State Standing to Challenge Federal Administrative Action: A Re–Examination of the Parens Patriae Doctrine, 1977, 125 U.Pa.L.Rev. 1069. On that and other aspects of standing for governments and public officials, see 13A Wright, Miller & Cooper, Jurisdiction 2d § 3531.11.

12. See Comment, Taxpayers' Suits—A Survey and Summary, 1960, 69 Yale L.J. 895.

minute." Further it was argued that it would be better to permit a suit, and have the constitutionality of a particular expenditure determined on its merits, than to have the matter go by default.

The heaviest pressure on the Frothingham rule, however, was based on wholly practical rather than theoretical considerations. There was considerable uncertainty about the extent to which the First Amendment permits Congress to provide financial aid to educational institutions operated in the interest of a particular religious group. Both those who favored such aid and those who opposed it were eager to have some means by which the constitutionality of this kind of aid might be tested, since each side thought its constitutional arguments would be vindicated, and a resolution of the matter would affect the willingness of Congress to make such appropriations. Several times bills passed the Senate that purported to grant standing to a variety of interested persons and institutions to challenge grants of this kind, but these bills never became law.

The Supreme Court resolved the problem in 1968 in Flast v. Cohen.[13] A taxpayers' action challenged the allegedly unconstitutional expenditure of federal funds under the Elementary and Secondary Education Act of 1965. The appropriations involved under that act were used to finance instruction in reading, arithmetic, and other subjects in religious schools, and to purchase textbooks for use in those schools. The district court dismissed the action on the authority of Frothingham, but the Supreme Court reversed. The Court did not overrule Frothingham, as the commentators had urged. Instead it distinguished Frothingham by recognizing a qualification on what had seemed to be a broad ban against suits by federal taxpayers to challenge federal appropriations.

The Court drew a distinction that had not always been clearly made in earlier cases between whether a plaintiff is a proper party to request an adjudication of a particular issue and whether the issue itself is justiciable.[14] In terms of constitutional limitation, "the question of standing is related only to whether the dispute sought to be adjudicated will be presented in an adversary context and in a form historically viewed as capable of judicial resolution."[15] On this analysis there is no absolute bar to suits by federal taxpayers, and the question is whether the circumstances are such that a federal taxpayer has the personal

13. 1968, 88 S.Ct. 1942, 392 U.S. 83, 20 L.Ed.2d 947. The decision, and the vagaries that it left in the law of standing generally, were criticized by Professor Davis in a typically thoughtful and thought-provoking article. Davis, Standing: Taxpayers and Others, 1968, 35 U.Chi.L.Rev. 601. See also the witty exchange: Bittker, The Case of the Fictitious Taxpayer: The Federal Taxpayer's Suit Twenty Years After Flast v. Cohen, 1969, 36 U.Chi.L.Rev. 364; Davis, The Case of the Real Taxpayer: A Reply to Professor Bittker, 1969, 36 U.Chi.L.Rev. 375.

14. 88 S.Ct. at 1952, 392 U.S. at 99. At the same time, the focus on the party may take account of the relationship between the party and the particular claim being advanced. Intern. Primate Protection League v. Administrators of Tulane Educ. Fund, 1991, 111 S.Ct. 1700, 1704, 500 U.S. 72, ___, 144 L.Ed.2d 134; Fletcher, note 1 above, at 229.

15. 88 S.Ct. at 1953, 392 U.S. at 101.

stake and interest necessary to give the litigation the concreteness required by Article III. This, Chief Justice Warren wrote for the Court, depends on "whether there is a logical nexus between the status asserted and the claim sought to be adjudicated." [16]

To establish the required nexus between his status and his claim, a taxpayer challenging a federal appropriation must show two things. "First, the taxpayer must establish a logical link between that status and the type of legislative enactment attacked. Thus, a taxpayer will be a proper party to allege the unconstitutionality only of exercises of congressional power under the taxing and spending clause of Art. I, § 8, of the Constitution. It will not be sufficient to allege an incidental expenditure of tax funds in the administration of an essentially regulatory statute. * * * Secondly, the taxpayer must establish a nexus between that status and the precise nature of the constitutional infringement alleged. Under this requirement, the taxpayer must show that the challenged enactment exceeds specific constitutional limitations imposed upon the exercise of the congressional taxing and spending power and not simply that the enactment is generally beyond the powers delegated to Congress by Art. I, § 8." [17]

Both the plaintiffs in the Flast case and Mrs. Frothingham met the first test, since both were attacking a federal spending program rather than a regulatory statute. The Flast plaintiffs met the second test as well, since the Establishment Clause of the First Amendment "operates as a specific constitutional limitation upon the exercise by Congress of the taxing and spending power * * *." [18] Mrs. Frothingham failed the second test since the constitutional provisions on which she relied, the Tenth Amendment and the Due Process Clause of the Fifth Amendment, are not specific limitations on the taxing and spending power. The

---

16. 88 S.Ct. at 1953, 392 U.S. at 101. The Court here cited McGowan v. Maryland, 1961, 81 S.Ct. 1101, 1107–1108, 366 U.S. 420, 429–430, 6 L.Ed.2d 393, in which it was held that merchants attacking a Sunday-closing law on the ground that it caused them economic injury had standing to claim that the law violated the Establishment Clause of the First Amendment but could not press a claim under the Free Exercise Clause.

Although the reference in Flast to McGowan would have suggested that the nexus requirement is of general applicability, the court has since said it applies only in taxpayer cases. Duke Power Co. v. Carolina Environmental Study Group, Inc., 1978, 98 S.Ct. 2620, 2633, 438 U.S. 59, 78–79, 57 L.Ed.2d 595.

17. 88 S.Ct. at 1954, 392 U.S. at 102.

18. 88 S.Ct. at 1954–1955, 392 U.S. at 102–106.

The Flast tests were satisfied and taxpayers had standing to mount an Establishment Clause challenge to specific grants to individual grantees under the Adolescent Family Life Act. Bowen v. Kendrick, 1988, 108 S.Ct. 2562, 2579–2580, 487 U.S. 589, 618–622, 101 L.Ed.2d 520.

In Richardson v. Kennedy, D.C.Pa.1970, 313 F.Supp. 1282, affirmed 1971, 91 S.Ct. 868, 401 U.S. 901, 27 L.Ed.2d 800, it was held that a taxpayer does not have standing to challenge increase of congressional salaries by a commission, since the authority for the payment of congressional salaries comes from Article I, § 6, rather than Article I, § 8, of the Constitution, and Article I, § 6 is not a specific limitation on the taxing and spending power.

The Flast tests were also held not satisfied in U.S. v. Richardson, 1974, 94 S.Ct. 2940, 418 U.S. 166, 41 L.Ed.2d 678, Schlesinger v. Reservists Committee to Stop the War, 1974, 94 S.Ct. 2925, 418 U.S. 208, 41 L.Ed.2d 706, and the Valley Forge Christian College case, all discussed in the text below.

Court did not decide whether any provision of the Constitution other than the Establishment Clause is a specific limitation on the taxing and spending power. That was left to be "determined only in the context of future cases." [19]

In general the Court has remained true to the other aspect of the rule recognized in Frothingham, and has entertained suits by local taxpayers challenging local expenditures.[20] There was an important qualification announced, however, in the Doremus case in 1952.[21] This was an attack by state and municipal taxpayers on a state statute requiring the reading of a portion of the Old Testament at the beginning of each school day. The state court entertained the suit and held the statute valid, but the Supreme Court dismissed an appeal on the ground that the plaintiffs lacked standing. It held that a taxpayer's suit could be heard only if it was a good-faith pocketbook action, and that in the case before it, where there was no measurable disbursement of school funds because of the activity complained of, the plaintiff was not seeking to litigate a direct dollars-and-cents injury but only a religious difference.

A case decided the same day as Doremus illustrates strikingly the vagaries in the law of standing. In Adler v. Board of Education [22] the challenge was to a New York statute directing the state board of regents to make regulations looking to the elimination of subversive teachers from the public schools. The plaintiffs in the suit attacking the statute included variously taxpayers, parents of school children, and teachers. The teachers did not show that they were in the class sought to be reached by the statute, and, on precedent,[23] probably lacked standing. The standing of the parents seems even more problematical. Parents may well have standing to challenge school activities that injure their children in an unconstitutional way,[24] but in the vivid phrase of one

19. 88 S.Ct. at 1955, 392 U.S. at 105.

20. E.g., Everson v. Board of Educ., 1947, 67 S.Ct. 504, 330 U.S. 1, 91 L.Ed. 711, (taxpayer had standing to challenge use of public funds for transportation to parochial schools). The Court has also accepted, without comment on the standing question, suit by a state taxpayer challenging a state statute. Wieman v. Updegraff, 1952, 73 S.Ct. 215, 344 U.S. 183, 97 L.Ed. 216.

21. Doremus v. Board of Educ., 1952, 72 S.Ct. 394, 342 U.S. 429, 96 L.Ed. 475.

22. 1952, 72 S.Ct. 380, 342 U.S. 485, 96 L.Ed. 517.

23. See United Public Workers v. Mitchell, 1947, 67 S.Ct. 556, 330 U.S. 75, 91 L.Ed. 754 (federal employees who alleged that they wished to participate in political activities, but had been advised that this would cause them to lose their jobs under the Hatch Act, lacked standing to challenge that act since they had not yet in fact violated it).

24. The Court has listened to attacks on school released-time programs brought by plaintiffs who sued as parents and as taxpayers. McCollum v. Board of Educ., 1948, 68 S.Ct. 461, 333 U.S. 203, 92 L.Ed. 649; Zorach v. Clauson, 1952, 72 S.Ct. 679, 343 U.S. 306, 96 L.Ed. 954. This was the basis for standing in Engel v. Vitale, 1962, 82 S.Ct. 1261, 370 U.S. 421, 8 L.Ed.2d 601, but that decision has been criticized for holding that the parents had standing. Sutherland, Establishment According to Engel, 1962, 76 Harv.L.Rev. 25. See also School Dist. of Abington Tp., Pa. v. Schempp, 1963, 83 S.Ct. 1560, 1572 n. 9, 374 U.S. 203, 224 n. 9, 10 L.Ed.2d 844. In the Valley Forge Christian College case the Court says: "The plaintiffs in Schempp had standing not because their complaint rested on the Establishment Clause—for as Doremus demonstrated, that is insufficient—but because impressionable schoolchildren were subjected to unwelcome religious exercises or were forced to assume special burdens to justice, "it is like catching butterflies without a net to try to find a legal interest" in the parent's desire to have his child educated in a school where the teachers are free from unconstitutional restraint.[25] Finally the taxpayers would seem barred by the doctrine announced that day in the Doremus case, for as in that case, they could show no measurable pocketbook injury.

The striking thing about the Adler decision is not that the Court decided the case on its merits; the standing of each of the classes of plaintiffs is at least arguable. But the Court never made the argument. It upheld the law on the merits, over a strong dissent on grounds of standing and ripeness, without ever discussing standing or even stating who the plaintiffs were.

As the Doremus and Adler cases show, the decisions on standing are not easy to reconcile on their facts. Nor has the theory on standing questions been much more satisfactory. It used to be said that to have standing the plaintiff must be able to demonstrate injury to a legally protected interest.[26] Such an approach is demonstrably circular: if the plaintiff is given standing to assert his claims, his interest is legally protected; if he is denied standing, his interest is not legally protected.

The requirement of a legal interest was rejected by the Supreme Court in 1970 in Association of Data Processing Service Organizations, Inc. v. Camp.[27] The Court held that sellers of data-processing services have standing to challenge a ruling of the Comptroller of the Currency allowing national banks to provide services of that kind. The lower courts had denied standing on the ground that competitors had no legally protected interest. Although that view was based on an earlier Supreme Court decision,[28] the Court rejected it, saying: "The 'legal interest' test goes to the merits. The question of standing is different."[29] It announced a two-part test for standing. Standing exists if "the plaintiff alleges that the challenged action has caused him injury in fact, economic or otherwise,"[30] and if "the interest sought to be protected by the complainant is arguably within the zone of interest to be protected or regulated by the statute or constitutional guarantee in question."[31]

avoid them." 102 S.Ct. at 766 n. 22, 454 U.S. at 492 n. 22.

25. 72 S.Ct. at 390, 342 U.S. at 502 (Frankfurter, J., dissenting).

26. Tennessee Elec. Power Co. v. Tennessee Val. Auth., 1938, 59 S.Ct. 366, 306 U.S. 118, 83 L.Ed. 543 (competing corporations lack standing to assert unconstitutionality of TVA); Alabama Power Co. v. Ickes, 1938, 58 S.Ct. 300, 302 U.S. 464, 82 L.Ed. 374 (competitors lack standing to challenge loans and grants to municipal corporations because "no violation of a right"); Perkins v. Lukens Steel Co., 1940, 60 S.Ct. 869, 310 U.S. 113, 84 L.Ed. 1108 (seller of goods to

government has no legal right and cannot challenge administrative determination of wages government suppliers must pay).

27. 1970, 90 S.Ct. 827, 397 U.S. 150, 25 L.Ed.2d 184.

28. Tennessee Elec. Power Co. v. TVA, 1938, 59 S.Ct. 366, 369, 306 U.S. 118, 137–138, 83 L.Ed. 543. See also the other cases cited in n. 26 above.

29. 90 S.Ct. at 830, 397 U.S. at 153.

30. 90 S.Ct. at 829, 397 U.S. at 152.

31. 90 S.Ct. at 830, 397 U.S. at 153.

In a companion case this test was applied to hold that tenant farmers receiving benefits under the upland cotton program had standing to challenge a regulation that, so they alleged, gave their landlord an opportunity to require them to assign their benefits to the landlord in advance as a condition to obtaining a lease to work the land.[32] Justices Brennan and White concurred in the result in both cases but dissented from the test that the Court announced for standing. They argued that the first part of the Court's test, injury in fact, is all that ought to be required and that the second part of the test, showing that the interest sought to be protected is arguably within the zone of interests protected or regulated by the statute, invites an inquiry into the merits that is unnecessary and inappropriate on the question of standing.[33]

The Court has continued to write frequently about standing. Though the later decisions go both ways, on the whole they suggest that the movement to broaden the standing concept has slowed down, though it has not stopped. In Sierra Club v. Morton [34] in 1972, the Court ruled explicitly that noneconomic injury, such as recreational use or aesthetic appreciation, was enough for standing but held that the Sierra Club lacked standing, despite its longstanding interest and concern in the protection of natural resources and its great litigating experience, since it failed to allege that either it or its members would be in any way affected by the challenged action in their use of the area they sought to protect.[35]

The major change in the direction of denying standing came in

32. Barlow v. Collins, 1970, 90 S.Ct. 832, 397 U.S. 159, 25 L.Ed.2d 192. In that case the Court said that "the tenant farmers are clearly within the zone of interests protected by the Act." 90 S.Ct. at 836, 397 U.S. at 164. The Court never discussed, as the Data Processing test seems to require, why or how the particular "interest sought to be protected by the" tenant farmers was within the zone protected by the statute. See Davis, The Liberalized Law of Standing, 1970, 37 U.Chi.L.Rev. 450, 454–456.

See also Arnold Tours, Inc. v. Camp, 1970, 91 S.Ct. 158, 400 U.S. 45, 27 L.Ed.2d 179, holding that travel agents have standing to challenge a ruling by the Comptroller of Currency that national banks may provide travel services for their customers. The court of appeals, applying the Data Processing standard, thought that the travel agents lacked standing because there was no evidence that Congress was specifically concerned with the competitive interests of travel agencies. C.A.1st, 1970, 428 F.2d 359. The Supreme Court said that Data Processing gives standing to businessmen who compete with national banks in any field other than the performance of bank services.

33. 90 S.Ct. at 838, 397 U.S. at 159.

34. 1972, 92 S.Ct. 1361, 405 U.S. 727, 31 L.Ed.2d 636. See Baude, Sierra Club v. Morton: Standing Trees in a Thicket of Justiciability, 1973, 48 Ind.L.Rev. 197; Sax, Standing to Sue: A Critical Review of the Mineral King Decisions, 1973, 13 Nat.Res.J. 76. In the Sierra Club case Justice Douglas, dissenting, argued that inanimate objects should have standing in their own right and that the case should have been in the name of Mineral King. 92 S.Ct. at 1361, 1369–1375, 405 U.S. at 741–752. The Court of Appeal in England has recently held that a ruined Hindu temple and a stone phallus have legal personality and can sue (and be sued) if they are juristic entities under their own law. Bumper Development Corp. Ltd. v. Commissioner of Police of the Metropolis, [1991] 1 W.L.R. 1362 (C.A.), noted 1992, 51 Camb.L.J. 39

See also U.S. v. S.C.R.A.P., 1973, 93 S.Ct. 2405, 412 U.S. 669, 37 L.Ed.2d 254.

35. As the Supreme Court had indicated, the remedy was easily found in amendment of the complaint on remand. Sierra Club v. Morton, D.C.Cal.1972, 348 F.Supp. 219.

companion 1974 decisions in United States v. Richardson [36] and Schlesinger v. Reservists Committee to Stop the War.[37]   Those cases, building heavily on a renewed emphasis on separation of powers principles, make it clear that a direct injury, and not merely a general interest common to all members of the public, is required for standing.   Neither as a citizen nor as a taxpayer may one invoke judicial review simply to vindicate a belief in the need for lawful conduct by Congress or public officials.[38]   Finally, the fact that if the present plaintiff is not allowed to litigate, no one can do so, is not regarded as an argument for finding that the present plaintiff has standing.   Instead that fact supports the view that the issue is one to be resolved through the political processes rather than in the courts.[39]

The 1976 decision in Simon v. Eastern Kentucky Welfare Rights Organization [40] built on two earlier cases [41] in giving new emphasis to the causal connection between plaintiff's asserted injury and defendant's challenged action.[42]   Suit was brought against the Secretary of the Treasury challenging a new IRS regulation that allowed hospitals to qualify as charitable, and thus for contributions to them to be deductible, although they did not furnish service except in emergencies to indigents.   The plaintiffs were low-income individuals and organizations representing them who claimed that they had been refused treatment, because of their indigency, at hospitals enjoying favorable tax treatment under the new regulation.   A plaintiff, the Court thought, has standing only if he "has shown an injury to himself that is likely to be redressed by a favorable decision." [43]   That test was not met in this case because

36.   1974, 94 S.Ct. 2940, 418 U.S. 166, 41 L.Ed.2d 678.

37.   1974, 94 S.Ct. 2925, 418 U.S. 208, 41 L.Ed.2d 706.

38.   See also Whitmore v. Arkansas, 1990, 110 S.Ct. 1717, 1725–1726, 495 U.S. 149, 160, 109 L.Ed.2d 135; Diamond v. Charles, 1986, 106 S.Ct. 1697, 1705, 476 U.S. 54, 65, 90 L.Ed.2d 48; 13 Wright, Miller & Cooper, Jurisdiction 2d § 3531.10.

39.   The Richardson and Schlesinger cases are discussed in 13 Wright, Miller & Cooper, Jurisdiction 2d §§ 3531.1, 3531.10.

The Valley Forge Christian College case again rejects the argument that plaintiffs must have standing because if they do not, no one does.   "This view would convert standing into a requirement that must be observed only when satisfied."   102 S.Ct. at 767, 454 U.S. at 489.

40.   1976, 96 S.Ct. 1917, 426 U.S. 26, 48 L.Ed.2d 450, noted 1977, 13 Wake Forest L.Rev. 602.   The decision is severely criticized in Davis, Standing, 1976, 1977, 72 Nw.U.L.Rev. 69.

One question inevitably raised by Simon is the extent to which the pleadings are determinative of standing or whether this preliminary issue of standing can be contested by motion for summary judgment. See 96 S.Ct. at 1927 n. 25, 426 U.S. at 45 n. 25; Havens Realty Corp. v. Coleman, 1982, 102 S.Ct. 1114, 1123–1124, 455 U.S. 363, 377–378, 71 L.Ed.2d 214, and the concurring opinion of Powell, J., 102 S.Ct. at 1126–1127, 455 U.S. at 382–384; Gwaltney of Smithfield v. Chesapeake Bay Foundation, Inc., 1987, 108 S.Ct. 376, 385–386, 484 U.S. 49, 98 L.Ed.2d 306; Roberts, Fact Pleading, Notice Pleading, and Standing, 1980, 65 Cornell L.Rev. 390; Garvey, A Litigation Primer for Standing Dismissals, 1980, 55 N.Y.U.L.Rev. 545; 13A Wright, Miller & Cooper, Jurisdiction 2d § 3531.15.

41.   Linda R.S. v. Richard D., 1973, 93 S.Ct. 1146, 410 U.S. 614, 35 L.Ed.2d 536; Warth v. Seldin, 1975, 95 S.Ct. 2197, 422 U.S. 490, 45 L.Ed.2d 343.

42.   On the causation requirement, see Wright, Miller & Cooper, Jurisdiction 2d § 3531.5; Nichol, Causation as a Standing Requirement: The Unprincipled Use of Judicial Restraint, 1981, 69 Ky.L.J. 185.

43.   96 S.Ct. at 1924, 426 U.S. at 38.

the Court found it purely speculative whether the injury to the plaintiffs in not receiving free medical care could be traced to the IRS regulation and whether, if the regulation were changed, hospitals would not do without charitable contributions rather than take on the burden of caring for the indigent.[44] "Speculative inferences are necessary to connect their injury to the challenged actions of petitioners. Moreover, the complaint suggests no substantial likelihood that victory in this suit would result in respondents' receiving the hospital treatment they desire." [45]

In Simon, as in the earlier cases from which it took the requirements that the injury be traceable to defendant's conduct and that the injury was likely to be redressed by a favorable decision, these requirements led to holdings that standing did not exist. In subsequent cases the Court has found these requirements satisfied and upheld standing [46] or it has simply ignored these requirements.[47] Even so the requirements have been mentioned so often in the cases that by 1982 in the Valley Forge Christian College case the Court was able to announce as settled law that "at an irreducible minimum, Art. III requires the party who invokes the court's authority to 'show that he personally has suffered some actual or threatened injury as a result of the putatively illegal conduct of the defendant,' and that the injury 'fairly can be traced to the challenged action' and 'is likely to be redressed by a favorable decision.' " [48]

---

44. Nationwide private philanthropy accounts for only 4% of private hospital revenues. 96 S.Ct. at 1927, 426 U.S. at 43.

45. 96 S.Ct. at 1927–1928, 426 U.S. at 45–46. On the requirement of redressability—that some personal benefit will result to plaintiff from a remedy that the court is prepared to give—see 13 Wright, Miller & Cooper, Jurisdiction 2d § 3531.6.

46. Village of Arlington Heights v. Metropolitan Housing Development Corp., 1977, 97 S.Ct. 555, 429 U.S. 252, 50 L.Ed.2d 450; Duke Power Co. v. Carolina Environmental Study Group, Inc., 1978, 98 S.Ct. 2620, 438 U.S. 59, 57 L.Ed.2d 595; Watt v. Energy Action Educational Foundation, 1981, 102 S.Ct. 205, 454 U.S. 151, 70 L.Ed.2d 309; Larson v. Valente, 1982, 102 S.Ct. 1673, 456 U.S. 228, 72 L.Ed.2d 33; Heckler v. Mathews, 1984, 104 S.Ct. 1387, 465 U.S. 728, 79 L.Ed.2d 646; Metropolitan Washington Airports Auth. v. Citizens for the Abatement of Aircraft Noise, Inc., 1991, 111 S.Ct. 2298, 501 U.S. 252, 115 L.Ed.2d 236.

47. Orr v. Orr, 1979, 99 S.Ct. 1102, 440 U.S. 268, 59 L.Ed.2d 306; Hooper v. Bernalillo County Assessor, 1985, 105 S.Ct. 2862, 472 U.S. 612, 86 L.Ed.2d 487. See also Arkansas Writers' Project, Inc. v. Rag-

land, 1987, 107 S.Ct. 1722, 1726, 481 U.S. 221, 227, 95 L.Ed.2d 209.

48. 102 S.Ct. at 758, 454 U.S. at 472 (citations omitted).

The quoted passage seems to suggest that ability to trace the injury to the challenged action and the likelihood of redress are but two facets of a single causation requirement. Indeed in Duke Power Co. v. Carolina Environmental Study Group, Inc., 1978, 98 S.Ct. 2620, 2631, 438 U.S. 59, 74, 57 L.Ed.2d 595, the Court says that these are but two ways of putting the same thing. But in Allen v. Wright, 1984, 104 S.Ct. 3315, 3325 n. 19, 468 U.S. 737, 753 n. 19, 82 L.Ed.2d 556, the Court, while acknowledging that these were initially articulated as two facets of one requirement, said: "To the extent there is a difference, it is that the former examines the causal connection between the assertedly unlawful conduct and the alleged injury, whereas the latter examines the causal connection between the alleged injury and the judicial relief requested. Cases such as this, in which the relief requested goes well beyond the violation of law alleged, illustrate why it is important to keep the inquiries separate if the 'redressability' component is to focus on the requested relief."

In the Valley Forge Christian College case it was the requirement of injury in fact, rather than the causation requirements, that was held fatal to standing. A statute allows a cabinet member to dispose of surplus government property without charge to tax exempt educational institutions. What had been a military hospital was turned over under that statute to a sectarian college. An organization dedicated to separation of church and state, along with several of its employees, challenged the conveyance on the ground that it was aid to religion in violation of the Establishment Clause.

The Supreme Court held that plaintiffs lacked standing. After a lengthy exposition of the principles concerning standing that have developed from the time of Frothingham, and of the reasons for rules of standing, the Court first rejected plaintiffs' argument that they had standing as taxpayers. Flast, it said, had created only a limited exception to the Frothingham principle that taxpayers do not have standing. That exception, under the first test of Flast, applies only where the challenge is to an exercise of the taxing and spending powers of Article I, § 8 of the Constitution. Here the property transfer challenged was an exercise of the power of Congress under Article IV, § 3, to dispose of property of the United States, and Flast had no application.

Nor could plaintiffs claim standing as citizens. Their claim that they had suffered a particular and concrete injury to a personal constitutional right was not enough for standing. "Although they claim that the Constitution has been violated, they claim nothing else. They fail to identify any personal injury suffered by the plaintiffs *as a consequence* of the alleged constitutional error, other than the psychological consequence presumably produced by observation of conduct with which one disagrees."[49] The Court reiterated its prior holdings that standing may be predicated on noneconomic injury,[50] but said that these plaintiffs had not alleged any injury of any kind, economic or otherwise, sufficient to confer standing. The Court, rejecting the views of four dissenters, could find no principled basis for a special judicial role, and thus a lesser

---

49. 102 S.Ct. at 765, 454 U.S. at 485 (emphasis in original). The requirement of injury in fact is examined in 13 Wright, Miller & Cooper, Jurisdiction 2d § 3531.4.

In Northeastern Florida Contractors v. Jacksonville, 1993, 113 S.Ct. 2297, ___ U.S. ___, 124 L.Ed.2d 586, the Court held that the "injury in fact" constitutionally required for standing to challenge on equal-protection grounds a racially discriminatory procedure for distributing a scarce governmental benefit, such as public-works contracts, is "the inability to compete on an equal footing" for the rationed benefit, not the deprivation of the benefit itself. 113 S.Ct. at 2203, ___ U.S. at ___. Thus, a plaintiff disadvantaged by the discriminato-

ry-allocation procedure has standing to challenge the procedure without showing that, but for the discrimination, the plaintiff would have been awarded the benefit in question.

50. Duke Power Co. v. Carolina Environmental Study Group, Inc., 1978, 98 S.Ct. 2620, 2630, 438 U.S. 59, 73–74, 57 L.Ed.2d 595 ("environmental and aesthetic consequences"); U.S. v. S.C.R.A.P., 1973, 93 S.Ct. 2405, 2415–2416, 412 U.S. 669, 686–688, 37 L.Ed.2d 254. The Court has since said that the analysis of standing in the S.C.R.A.P. case "surely went to the very outer limit of the law." Whitmore v. Arkansas, 1990, 110 S.Ct. 1717, 1725, 495 U.S. 149, 159, 109 L.Ed.2d 135.

requirement of standing, in enforcing the Establishment Clause than for other provisions of the Constitution.[51]

In recent years almost no discussion of standing by the Supreme Court has been complete without its reference to the observation in Baker v. Carr that "the gist of the question of standing" is whether the plaintiffs have alleged "such a personal stake in the outcome of the controversy as to assure that concrete adverseness which sharpens the presentation of issues upon which the court so largely depends for illumination of difficult constitutional questions."[52] Despite the frequent reiteration of this language, the rules the Court has announced have little relation to that stated test. It is as unrealistic to place emphasis on a plaintiff's status as taxpayer, when the amount of that person's dollars going to finance a challenged program is minute and will be exacted by the government in any event, as it is to suppose that the Sierra Club will not bring concrete adverseness to its presentation of issues whether or not any of its members have ever used a particular area.[53] That concrete adverseness is not itself a test of standing was clearly stated in the Valley Forge Christian College case, where the Court said that "standing is not measured by the intensity of the litigant's interest or the fervor of his advocacy."[54] Concrete adverseness, on this view, is the anticipated consequence of proceedings commenced by one who has been injured in fact, and is not a permissible substitute for the showing of injury itself. A more useful key than "concrete adverseness" is Justice O'Connor's observation that "the law of Art. III standing is built on a single basic idea—the idea of separation of powers."[55]

51. 102 S.Ct. at 764–768, 454 U.S. at 482–490. See Nichol, Standing on the Constitution: The Supreme Court and Valley Forge, 1983, 61 N.C.L.Rev. 798; Marshall & Flood, Establishment Clause Standing: The Not Very Revolutionary Decision at Valley Forge, 1982, 11 Hofstra L.Rev. 63.

52. 1962, 82 S.Ct. 691, 703, 369 U.S. 186, 204, 7 L.Ed.2d 663.

53. An organization may sue in its own right if it shows concrete and demonstrable injury to its activities, and a consequent drain on its resources, rather than merely, as in Sierra Club, a setback to the organization's abstract social interests. Havens Realty Corp. v. Coleman, 1982, 102 S.Ct. 1114, 1124–1125, 455 U.S. 363, 71 L.Ed.2d 214.

To have standing to sue on behalf of its members it must show that: "(a) its members would otherwise have standing to sue in their own right; (b) the interests it seeks to protect are germane to the organization's purpose; and (c) neither the claim asserted nor the relief requested requires the participation of individual members in the lawsuit." Hunt v. Washington State Apple Advertising Comm., 1977, 97 S.Ct. 2434, 2441, 432 U.S. 333, 343, 53 L.Ed.2d 383, noted 1978, 64 Iowa L.Rev. 121.

Environmental organizations were denied standing where they failed to show that any of their members would be directly affected apart from the members' special interest in the subject. Lujan v. Defenders of Wildlife, 1992, 112 S.Ct. 2130, ___ U.S. ___, 119 L.Ed.2d 351. The decision is criticized in 3 Davis & Pierce, Administrative Law Treatise, 3d ed. 1994, § 16.16; Meeks, Justice Scalia and the Demise of Environmental Law Standing, 1993, 8 J.Land Use & Envtl.L. 343; Nichol, Justice Scalia, Standing, and Public Law Litigation, 1993, 42 Duke L.J. 1141, and Sustein, What's Standing After Lujan? Of Citizen Suits, "Injuries," and Article III, 1992, 91 Mich.L.Rev. 163, but discussed more favorably in Breger, Defending Defenders: Remarks on Nichol and Pierce, 1993, 42 Duke L.J. 1202.

54. 102 S.Ct. at 766, 454 U.S. at 486.

55. Allen v. Wright, 1984, 104 S.Ct. 3315, 3325, 468 U.S. 737, 752, 82 L.Ed.2d 556. The holding of the Allen case is that parents of black school children lack standing to sue the Internal Revenue Service contending that it had not adopted sufficient standards and procedures to deny tax-exempt status to racially discriminatory private schools. The case is fully described in

What has been said thus far has concerned the Article III limitations on standing. Even when the Article III requirements are met, "a plaintiff may still lack standing under the prudential principles by which the judiciary seeks to avoid deciding questions of broad social import where no individual rights would be vindicated and to limit access to the federal courts to those litigants best suited to assert a particular claim." [56] Three such prudential rules have been identified.[57] These are that the plaintiff's interest must come within the "zone of interests" arguably protected or regulated by the law in question,[58] that the courts will not hear "generalized grievances" shared in substantially equal measure by all or a large class of citizens,[59] and that plaintiff must assert its own legal interests rather than those of third parties.[60]

A well-known example of the third of these limitations is Tileston v. Ullman,[61] holding that a physician, seeking a declaratory judgment that a statute preventing him from giving advice as to contraceptives was

13 Wright, Miller & Cooper, Jurisdiction 2d § 3531.2 and criticized in Nichol, Abusing Standing: A Comment on Allen v. Wright, 1985, 133 U.Pa.L.Rev. 635. The separation-of-powers arguments for strict views of standing are appraised in 13 Wright, Miller & Cooper, Jurisdiction 2d § 3531.3.

56. Gladstone, Realtors v. Village of Bellwood, 1979, 99 S.Ct. 1601, 1608, 441 U.S. 91, 99–100, 60 L.Ed.2d 66.

57. Ibid. See also Valley Forge Christian College, 102 S.Ct. at 760, 454 U.S. at 474–475.

A lower court has now recognized a fourth prudential rule in a situation that has not yet come to the Supreme Court. It was held in Riegle v. Federal Open Market Committee, C.A.D.C.1981, 656 F.2d 873, that ordinary rules of standing will determine whether a member of Congress can attack the constitutionality of a federal statute or the legitimacy of executive action, but that separation of powers considerations would be taken into account as a matter of equitable discretion in determining whether to decide the merits of the case. See also 13A Wright, Miller & Cooper, Jurisdiction 2d § 3531.11; McGowan, Congressmen in Courts: The New Plaintiffs, 1981, 15 Ga.L.Rev. 241. Because the case was moot, the Supreme Court found it unnecessary to decide in Burke v. Barnes, 1987, 107 S.Ct. 734, 479 U.S. 361, 93 L.Ed.2d 732, whether any special rules of standing apply to members of Congress. See also the several opinions in Moore v. U.S. House of Representatives, C.A.D.C. 1984, 733 F.2d 946.

58. See the discussion in the text above, and in note 32, of Association of Data Processing Serv. Organizations v. Camp, and of

cases in which the "zone of interests" test has been applied.

The failure of the Supreme Court to refer to "zone of interests" in Duke Power Co. v. Carolina Environmental Study Group, Inc., 1978, 98 S.Ct. 2620, 438 U.S. 59, 57 L.Ed.2d 595, caused some speculation that the limitation had been abandoned, but it was referred to as one of the prudential limitations in the cases cited in notes 50 and 51 above. It was put in eclipse again in Clarke v. Securities Industry Assn., 1987, 107 S.Ct. 750, 754–759, 479 U.S. 388, 393–402, 93 L.Ed.2d 757, where it was said to be "most usefully understood as a gloss" on § 10 of the Administrative Procedure Act and that it is "not a test of universal application." 107 S.Ct. at 758 n. 16, 479 U.S. at 400 n. 16. But in Air Courier Conference of America v. American Postal Workers Union, 1991, 111 S.Ct. 913, 498 U.S. 517, 112 L.Ed.2d 1125, the test was relied on to hold that a postal workers' union lacked standing where the statute involved was intended to protect citizens generally rather than postal workers. See 13 Wright, Miller & Cooper, Jurisdiction 2d § 3531.7.

59. See the discussion in the text above of the Schlesinger and Richardson cases. See also 13 Wright, Miller & Cooper, Jurisdiction 2d § 3531.10; 13A id. § 3531.11.

60. Phillips Petroleum Co. v. Shutts, 1985, 105 S.Ct. 2965, 2970, 472 U.S. 797, 804, 86 L.Ed.2d 628.

61. 1943, 63 S.Ct. 493, 318 U.S. 44, 87 L.Ed. 603.

See also Whitmore v. Arkansas, 1990, 110 S.Ct. 1717, 495 U.S. 149, 109 L.Ed.2d 135; Laird v. Tatum, 1972, 92 S.Ct. 2318, 408 U.S. 1, 33 L.Ed.2d 154; Moose Lodge No. 107 v. Irvis, 1972, 92 S.Ct. 1965, 1968, 407 U.S. 163, 166, 32 L.Ed.2d 627.

unconstitutional, could not rely on his patients' right to life, which the statute supposedly threatened. Many other cases announce a similar rule. Nevertheless "this rule has not been imposed uniformly as a firm constitutional restriction on federal court jurisdiction." [62] Indeed when the statute involving contraceptives came before the Court in a criminal prosecution of a doctor, he was allowed to assert the constitutional rights of his patients. The Court distinguished Tileston v. Ullman, on the ground that it was a declaratory judgment action in which the requirements of standing should be strict, while the case before it was a criminal prosecution, and the doctor, charged as an accessory, should have standing to assert that the offense he was charged with assisting cannot constitutionally be made a crime. [63]

In one striking case, a white person was suing for specific performance of his contract to sell real estate to a black person. The defense was that a city ordinance barred black persons from the area in question. Such an ordinance violates the Equal Protection Clause of the Fourteenth Amendment but here the black defendant, whose constitutional rights were violated by the ordinance, was relying on it as a defense, while the white person, whose constitutional rights were not hurt by the ordinance, was claiming it to be unconstitutional. The challenge was permitted, however. [64] Similar cases are well known. A parochial school was allowed to attack a statute that would have required public education for all children, though the constitutional rights involved were those of children and their parents. [65] Organizations have been allowed to put forward the constitutional rights of their members. [66] A school board was allowed to obtain an injunction barring conduct that would have interfered with the right of school children to be free from segregation. [67] A white defendant has been allowed to assert, as a defense in an action for damages for breach of a racially restrictive covenant, that to enforce the covenant would be unconstitutional state action, although it was clearly recognized that the constitutional right involved was not that of the defendant, but of unidentified nonwhites who, in the future, would find it more difficult to buy property if their vendor would be required to respond in damages. [68] These cases were all explainable on the ground, made explicit in the restrictive-covenant case, that the rule against relying on the rights of others is merely a rule of self-restraint, not part of the constitutional requirement of standing, and should not be applied

62. Flast v. Cohen, 1968, 88 S.Ct. 1942, 1952, n. 20, 392 U.S. 83, 90 n. 20, 20 L.Ed.2d 947.

63. Griswold v. Connecticut, 1965, 85 S.Ct. 1678, 1679–1680, 381 U.S. 479, 481, 14 L.Ed.2d 510.

See also Eisenstadt v. Baird, 1972, 92 S.Ct. 1029, 405 U.S. 438, 31 L.Ed.2d 349.

64. Buchanan v. Warley, 1917, 38 S.Ct. 16, 245 U.S. 60, 62 L.Ed. 149.

65. Pierce v. Society of Sisters, 1925, 45 S.Ct. 571, 268 U.S. 510, 69 L.Ed. 1070.

66. Joint Anti–Fascist Refugee Committee v. McGrath, 1951, 71 S.Ct. 624, 341 U.S. 123, 95 L.Ed. 817; National Assn. for the Advancement of Colored People v. Alabama ex rel. Patterson, 1958, 78 S.Ct. 1163, 1170, 357 U.S. 449, 458–460, 2 L.Ed.2d 1488.

See also note 53 above.

67. Brewer v. Hoxie Sch. Dist. No. 46, C.A.8th, 1956, 238 F.2d 91, 104–105.

68. Barrows v. Jackson, 1953, 73 S.Ct. 1031, 346 U.S. 249, 97 L.Ed. 1586.

where, as in those cases, it would be difficult if not impossible for the persons whose rights were asserted to present their grievance before any court.[69] Because the rule is not constitutionally required, and because it is concerned with the arguments a litigant can make rather than with his right to be in court at all, the Supreme Court has now followed the lead of commentators in referring to this rule as one of "jus tertii" rather than of standing.[70]

The rule against relying on jus tertii has been markedly relaxed in recent years. Physicians have been allowed to assert the rights of their patients in challenging a statute to limit abortions.[71] A seller of 3.2% beer has been allowed to assert that men aged 18 to 20 have the same right to purchase that beverage as do women in the same age group.[72] A mail-order seller of contraceptives has been allowed to raise the privacy rights of potential customers.[73] Booksellers were allowed to raise the First Amendment rights of bookbuyers.[74] A lawyer may argue that a rule limiting the fees he or she can receive deprives clients of a due-process right to obtain legal representation.[75] The Court seems to have moved close to a general rule that either party to a relationship that is regulated or prohibited by statute will be allowed to raise the rights of the other, at least if there is some hindrance to the other party asserting his or her own rights.[76] As the Court recently put it: "We have recognized the right of litigants to bring actions on behalf of third parties, provided three important criteria are satisfied: the litigant must have suffered an 'injury-in-fact,' thus giving him or her a 'sufficiently concrete interest' in the outcome of the issue in dispute * * *; the litigant must have a close relation to the third party * * *; and there must exist some hindrance to the third party's ability to protect his or her own interests."[77]

Closely related to the rule that one may not, save in exceptional cases, assert the rights of another is the rule that a defendant cannot

69. 73 S.Ct. at 1034–1035, 346 U.S. at 255–257.

70. Secretary of State of Md. v. Joseph H. Munson Co., 1984, 104 S.Ct. 2839, 2846, 467 U.S. 947, 956, 81 L.Ed.2d 786; Craig v. Boren, 1976, 97 S.Ct. 451, 455, 429 U.S. 190, 193, 50 L.Ed.2d 397. See Sedler, Standing to Assert Constitutional Jus Tertii in the Supreme Court, 1962, 71 Yale L.J. 599; Note, Standing to Assert Constitutional Jus Tertii, 1974, 88 Harv.L.Rev. 423.

71. Singleton v. Wulff, 1976, 96 S.Ct. 2868, 428 U.S. 106, 49 L.Ed.2d 826.

72. Craig v. Boren, 1976, 97 S.Ct. 451, 429 U.S. 190, 50 L.Ed.2d 397.

73. Carey v. Population Services Intl., 1977, 97 S.Ct. 2010, 431 U.S. 678, 52 L.Ed.2d 675.

74. Virginia v. American Booksellers Assn., Inc., 1988, 108 S.Ct. 636, 484 U.S. 383, 98 L.Ed.2d 782.

75. U.S. Dept. of Labor v. Triplett, 1990, 110 S.Ct. 1428, 494 U.S. 715, 108 L.Ed.2d 701.

76. "When * * * enforcement of a restriction against the litigant prevents a third party from entering into a relationship with the litigant (typically a contractual relationship) to which relationship the third party has a legal entitlement (typically a constitutional entitlement), third-party standing has been held to exist." U.S. Dept. of Labor v. Triplett, 1990, 110 S.Ct. 1428, 1432, 494 U.S. 715, 720, 108 L.Ed.2d 701. See generally 13 Wright, Miller & Cooper, Jurisdiction 2d § 3531.9; Monaghan, Third Party Standing, 1984, 84 Col. L.Rev. 277; Sedler, The Assertion of Constitutional Jus Tertii, 1982, 70 Calif.L.Rev. 1308.

77. Powers v. Ohio, 1991, 111 S.Ct. 1364, 1370–1371, 499 U.S. 400, 410, 113 L.Ed.2d 411.

claim a statute is unconstitutional in some of its reaches if the statute is constitutional as applied to him.[78] Nor, if he is required by the statute to do some particular act, can he defend on the ground that if he does so, he will in the future be exposed to some sanction that cannot validly be imposed.[79] The court in these cases will treat the present requirement as separable, and will leave to a later day the validity of the provisions not immediately in question.

To the propositions just stated there are, however, either limits or exceptions, depending on how they are viewed. The statute may be so broad in its scope that defendant will be allowed to assert that it is void for vagueness, even though it may clearly and constitutionally reach his case.[80] Particularly in the First Amendment area, there has been an inclination to consider the validity of the statute on its face, rather than as applied to the particular case, probably because of the threat a broad statute is thought to pose of inhibiting free expression.[81] The Court will entertain challenges to a statute as overbroad if the statute regulates pure speech.[82] It is more reluctant to hear this kind of challenge to a statute that primarily regulates conduct and not merely speech, even if the First Amendment may protect some of the activity condemned by the statute.[83]

There are two important respects in which the prudential rules about standing differ from the Article III limitations on standing. First, the Court itself is free to disregard one of the prudential rules when it

78. Yazoo & M.V.R.R. v. Jackson Vinegar Co., 1912, 33 S.Ct. 40, 226 U.S. 217, 57 L.Ed. 193; U.S. v. Raines, 1960, 80 S.Ct. 519, 522–524, 362 U.S. 17, 21–24, 4 L.Ed.2d 524.

79. Communist Party of the U.S. v. Subversive Activities Control Bd., 1961, 81 S.Ct. 1357, 1396–1402, 367 U.S. 1, 69–81, 6 L.Ed.2d 625; Electric Bond & Share Co. v. SEC, 1938, 58 S.Ct. 678, 303 U.S. 419, 82 L.Ed. 936.

80. See Lanzetta v. New Jersey, 1939, 59 S.Ct. 618, 306 U.S. 451, 83 L.Ed. 888; U.S. v. L. Cohen Grocery Co., 1921, 41 S.Ct. 298, 255 U.S. 81, 65 L.Ed. 516; U.S. v. Reese, 1876, 92 U.S. 214, 23 L.Ed. 563; Amsterdam, The Void for Vagueness Doctrine in the Supreme Court, 1960, 109 U.Pa.L.Rev. 67.

81. Thornhill v. Alabama, 1940, 60 S.Ct. 736, 310 U.S. 88, 84 L.Ed. 1093; Winters v. New York, 1948, 68 S.Ct. 665, 333 U.S. 507, 92 L.Ed. 840; National Assn. for Advancement of Colored People v. Button, 1963, 83 S.Ct. 328, 371 U.S. 415, 9 L.Ed.2d 405; FW/PBS, Inc. v. City of Dallas, 1990, 110 S.Ct. 596, 493 U.S. 215, 107 L.Ed.2d 603.

The farthest extension of this doctrine came in Dombrowski v. Pfister, 1965, 85 S.Ct. 1116, 1121, 380 U.S. 479, 487, 14 L.Ed.2d 22. The Court seemed to withdraw substantially from this aspect of Dombrowski, as from others, in Younger v. Harris, 1971, 91 S.Ct. 746, 753–755, 401 U.S. 37, 50–53, 27 L.Ed.2d 669. But those cases involved special considerations of federalism, and the rules stated in the text seem well accepted when the problem of federal interference with state proceedings is not present.

82. Massachusetts v. Oakes, 1989, 109 S.Ct. 2633, 491 U.S. 576, 105 L.Ed.2d 493; Board of Airport Commrs. v. Jews for Jesus, Inc., 1987, 107 S.Ct. 2568, 482 U.S. 569, 96 L.Ed.2d 500; Bigelow v. Virginia, 1975, 95 S.Ct. 2222, 421 U.S. 809, 44 L.Ed.2d 600; Lewis v. City of New Orleans, 1974, 94 S.Ct. 970, 415 U.S. 130, 39 L.Ed.2d 214. Even if a statute regulates pure speech, a statute can be struck down only if there is substantial overbreadth. Brockett v. Spokane Arcades, Inc., 1985, 105 S.Ct. 2794, 2802 n. 12, 472 U.S. 491, 503 n. 12, 86 L.Ed.2d 394.

83. Broadrick v. Oklahoma, 1973, 93 S.Ct. 2908, 413 U.S. 601, 37 L.Ed.2d 830. The distinction drawn in Broadrick was applied in, e.g., New York State Club Assn. v. City of New York, 1988, 108 S.Ct. 2225, 2232–2235, 487 U.S. 1, 9–16, 101 L.Ed.2d 1.

thinks it appropriate to do so. The jus tertii rule, in particular, has often been disregarded by the Court in cases that seemed to it proper.[84] Second, Congress is free to grant standing, if it chooses, to the full limits of Article III. If Congress has done so, the courts lack authority to create prudential barriers to standing in suits brought under a statute in which Congress has done this.[85]

§ 14. "Case or Controversy"—Political Questions [1]

No branch of the law of justiciability is in such disarray as the doctrine of the "political question." Judge Carl McGowan has said that "the recent history of the doctrine has been one of judicial indifference and scathing scholarly attack." [2] Professor Louis Henkin has asked the heretical question whether there is any such doctrine,[3] while Professor Martin Redish has written that there is indeed a political-question doctrine, but that there should not be.[4] Even those who accept the existence of the doctrine recognize that there is no workable definition of characteristics that distinguish political questions from justiciable questions, and that the category of political questions is "more amenable to description by infinite itemization than by generalization." [5]

Yet the notion that there are political questions that courts are not to decide has ancient roots in American law, and the Supreme Court still seems to take that notion seriously, even if today it does not often find cases that fit within the category. In the happy figure of speech Zechariah Chafee, Jr., devised in another context, it may be said of

84. E.g., Duke Power Co. v. Carolina Environmental Study Group, Inc., 1978, 98 S.Ct. 2620, 2634–2635, 438 U.S. 59, 80–82, 57 L.Ed.2d 595. See also text above at notes 60–77.

85. It has been held that Congress did this in §§ 810 and 812 of the Fair Housing Act of 1968, 42 U.S.C.A. §§ 3610, 3612. Havens Realty Corp. v. Coleman, 1982, 102 S.Ct. 1114, 455 U.S. 363, 71 L.Ed.2d 214; Gladstone, Realtors v. Village of Bellwood, 1979, 99 S.Ct. 1601, 441 U.S. 91, 60 L.Ed.2d 66; Trafficante v. Metropolitan Life Ins. Co., 1972, 93 S.Ct. 364, 409 U.S. 205, 34 L.Ed.2d 415.

Many other Acts of Congress appear on their face to contain very broad grants of standing. See 13A Wright, Miller & Cooper, Jurisdiction 2d § 3513.13.

§ 14

1. 13A Wright, Miller & Cooper, Jurisdiction 2d §§ 3534–3534.3; Franck, Political Questions Judicial Answers, Does the Rule of Law Apply to Foreign Affairs?, 1992; Strum, The Supreme Court and "Political Questions": A Study in Judicial Evasion, 1974; Nagel, Political Law, Legalistic Politics: A Recent History of the Political Question Doctrine, 1989, 56 U.Chi.L.Rev. 643; Mulhern, In Defense of the Political Question Doctrine, 1988, 137 U.Pa.L.Rev. 97; Redish, Judicial Review and the "Political Question," 1985, 79 Nw.U.L.Rev. 1031; Henkin, Is There a "Political Question" Doctrine?, 1976, 85 Yale L.J. 597; Jackson, The Political Question Doctrine: Where Does It Stand after Powell v. McCormack, O'Brien v. Brown, and Gilligan v. Morgan?, 1973, 44 U.Colo.L.Rev. 477; Tigar, Judicial Power, The "Political Question Doctrine," and Foreign Relations, 1970, 17 U.C.L.A.L.Rev. 1135; Scharpf, Judicial Review and the Political Question: A Functional Analysis, 1966, 75 Yale L.J. 517.

2. McGowan, Congressmen in Court: The New Plaintiffs, 1981, 15 Ga.L.Rev. 241, 256.

3. Henkin, note 1 above. See also Tigar, note 1 above, at 1163; Cox, The Role of Congress in Constitutional Determinations, 1971, 40 U.Cin.L.Rev. 199, 201.

4. Redish, note 1 above, at 1059–1060.

5. Frank, Political Questions, in Supreme Court & Supreme Law, Cahn ed. 1954, p. 36.

political questions: "They are at least as real as Santa Clauses in department stores before Christmas. We have to know what to do about them even if we believe they ought not to be there." [6]

The political-question doctrine goes back to the great case of Marbury v. Madison.[7] Chief Justice Marshall there expressed the view that the courts will not entertain political questions even though such questions involve actual controversies. Unlike the rules of standing,[8] ripeness,[9] and mootness,[10] political-question doctrine purports to establish that a particular question is beyond judicial competence no matter who raises it, how immediate the interests it affects, or how burning the controversy. Judicial incompetence to decide is in effect found to be beyond the help or needs of any adversaries. Courts are held incompetent to decide either because of a conclusion that a particular matter has been confided to the superior authority of another branch or because of a belief that judicial procedures and abilities are not adequate to the task of decision. Whichever perspective is chosen, the focus is on separation of powers. The relationship between the judiciary and the other branches of the federal government gives rise to the political question, and whether a matter has been committed by the Constitution to another branch of the government or is beyond judicial capability is decided by the Court.

Modern political-question analysis derives from the classic legislative-apportionment decision in 1962 in Baker v. Carr.[11] Justice Brennan there repeatedly emphasized that the concern underlying the doctrine is that of separating the proper sphere of federal judicial power from the appropriate spheres of federal executive and legislative power. After examining several categories of matters that had been regarded as political questions, he summarized the relevant considerations: "Prominent on the surface of any case held to involve a political question is found a textually demonstrable constitutional commitment of the issue to a coordinate political department; or a lack of judicially discoverable and manageable standards for resolving it; or the impossibility of deciding without an initial policy determination of a kind clearly for nonjudicial discretion; or the impossibility of a court's undertaking independent resolution without expressing lack of the respect due coordinate branches of government; or an unusual need for unquestioning adherence to a political decision already made; or the potentiality of embarrassment from multifarious pronouncements by various departments on one question." [12]

6. Chafee, Some Problems of Equity, 1950, p. 374.

7. 1803, 1 Cranch 137, 164–166, 2 L.Ed. 60. And see 1 Cranch at 170: "Questions, in their nature political, or which are by the constitution and laws, submitted to the executive, can never be made in this court."

8. See § 13 above.

9. See § 12 n. 1.

10. See § 12 above.

11. 1962, 82 S.Ct. 691, 369 U.S. 186, 7 L.Ed.2d 663.

12. 82 S.Ct. at 710, 369 U.S. at 217.

As has been pointed out by several commentators, the doctrine, as summarized by Justice Brennan, contains at least three theoretical strands.[13] The Baker formulation lists six factors, at least one of which must be unmistakably present in a case before it is dismissed as a political question. The first factor—a textually demonstrable commitment to another branch—is the classical view that the Court must decide all cases and issues before it unless, as a matter of constitutional interpretation, the Constitution itself has committed the determination of the issue to another branch of government.[14] The second and third factors—lack of judicially discoverable standards and involvement of the judiciary in nonjudicial policy determinations—suggest a functional approach.[15] The final three factors—lack of respect for other branches, need for adherence to a political decision already made, and possibility of embarrassment—all seem to be prudential considerations.[16] These six factors, and these three possible approaches, have been mingled in various proportions in the uses that have been made of the political-question doctrine over the years.

The clearest example of a nonjusticiable political question is a claim resting on the provision in Article IV, § 4, that the United States shall guarantee every state a republican form of government. Either because this is a textually demonstrable constitutional commitment of the issue to a coordinate political department,[17] or, as suggested in Baker v. Carr, for lack of judicially manageable standards,[18] it is accepted that such claims are nonjusticiable. In Luther v. Borden[19] the Court refused to decide which group was the legitimate government of Rhode Island, relying on this ground, and since then the Court has consistently refused to resort to the Guaranty Clause as a constitutional source for invalidating state action.[20] It has also held that a challenge to congressional

---

13. Tribe, American Constitutional Law, 2d ed. 1988, p. 96; Gunther, Constitutional Law—Cases and Materials, 12th ed. 1991, pp. 389–450, 1688–1690; Thomas & Thomas, Presidential War–Making Power: A Political Question?, 1981, 35 Sw.L.J. 879, 882.

14. Wechsler, Toward Neutral Principles of Constitutional Law, 1959, 73 Harv. L.Rev. 1, 7–9; Weston, Political Questions, 1925, 38 Harv.L.Rev. 296.

15. Nowak & Rotunda, Constitutional Law, 4th ed. 1991, pp. 113–114; Scharpf, note 1 above.

16. Bickel, The Least Dangerous Branch, 1962, pp. 23–28, 69–71; Bickel, The Supreme Court, 1960 Term: Foreword: The Passive Virtues, 1961, 75 Harv.L.Rev. 40, 46, 75; Finkelstein, Judicial Self–Limitation, 1924, 37 Harv.L.Rev. 338, 361; Finkelstein, Some Further Notes on Judicial Self–Limitation, 1926, 39 Harv.L.Rev. 221.

17. " 'The United States shall guarantee' plausibly refers to the political branches, and it is not implausible to read it as excluding monitoring and enforcement by the courts. If so, we may have a unique constitutional clause excluding the courts; but that hardly adds up to a 'political question doctrine.' " Henkin, note 1 above, at 609.

18. 82 S.Ct. at 713, 369 U.S. at 223.

19. 1849, 7 How. 1, 12 L.Ed. 581. See Note, Political Rights as Political Questions: The Paradox of Luther v. Borden, 1987, 100 Harv.L.Rev. 1125.

20. See, e.g., Mountain Timber Co. v. Washington, 1917, 37 S.Ct. 260, 243 U.S. 219, 61 L.Ed. 685; Pacific States Tel. & Tel. Co. v. Oregon, 1911, 32 S.Ct. 224, 223 U.S. 118, 56 L.Ed. 377; Taylor v. Beckham, 1900, 20 S.Ct. 890, 178 U.S. 548, 44 L.Ed. 1187. See 13A Wright, Miller & Cooper, Jurisdiction 2d § 3534.1, at 487–490. But see Note, A Niche for the Guarantee Clause, 1981, 94 Harv.L.Rev. 681.

action on the ground that it is inconsistent with the Guaranty Clause presents no justiciable question.[21]   However, the nonjusticiability of claims resting on the Guaranty Clause does not mean that similar questions will not be heard if other provisions of the Constitution, such as the Equal Protection Clause, are in issue.[22]

A great many questions involving political rights are not political questions.   The objection that a suit charging racial discrimination in conducting Democratic party primary elections in Texas involved a political question, for instance, was curtly rejected as "little more than a play on words." [23]   But in Colegrove v. Green [24] three of the seven justices who sat agreed that malapportionment of congressional districts in a state was political and thus nonjusticiable.   The concurring justice disagreed with this reasoning, but concurred in the result on the ground that it would be inequitable to issue an injunction.   For the next 16 years other attacks on apportionments and similar state laws were, with one exception, unsuccessful, though a variety of grounds were used by the Court to reach such results.[25]   This was changed in 1962 by the decision in Baker v. Carr. In that case plaintiffs, qualified voters from populous counties in Tennessee, sued in federal court, claiming that the existing apportionment of the state legislature provided inequality of representation, and that the resulting discrimination was a violation of equal protection of the laws.   The district court dismissed the complaint for lack of jurisdiction of the subject matter and for want of a justiciable issue.   The Supreme Court reversed, holding that the district court had jurisdiction of the subject matter and that a claim that the apportionment of a state legislature denied equal protection presented a justiciable issue.

Since Baker v. Carr the Court has passed on a variety of issues that previously would have been thought not to be justiciable: the choice by Congress of a mathematical formula to allot seats in the House of Representatives to the states after a census; [26] the standard for apportioning seats in Congress,[27] a state legislature,[28] or a local governing

21.   Georgia v. Stanton, 1867, 6 Wall. 50, 18 L.Ed. 721.

22.   Baker, 82 S.Ct. at 716, 369 U.S. at 228.

23.   Nixon v. Herndon, 1927, 47 S.Ct. 446, 447, 273 U.S. 536, 540, 71 L.Ed. 759.

24.   1946, 66 S.Ct. 1198, 328 U.S. 549, 90 L.Ed. 1432.

25.   E.g., Cox v. Peters, 1952, 72 S.Ct. 559, 342 U.S. 936, 96 L.Ed. 697 (per curiam) (want of a substantial federal question); South v. Peters, 1950, 70 S.Ct. 641, 339 U.S. 276, 94 L.Ed. 834 (want of equity); Colegrove v. Barrett, 1947, 67 S.Ct. 973, 330 U.S. 804, 91 L.Ed. 1262 (per curiam) (want of equity).   Only in Gomillion v.

Lightfoot, 1960, 81 S.Ct. 125, 364 U.S. 339, 5 L.Ed.2d 110, was relief granted.   In Gomillion the plaintiffs complained of affirmative legislative action that deprived them of their vote.   The decision was based on discriminatory treatment of a racial minority which violated the Fifteenth Amendment.

26.   U.S. Dept. of Commerce v. Montana, 1992, 112 S.Ct. 1415, ___ U.S. ___, 110 L.Ed.2d 87.

27.   Wesberry v. Sanders, 1964, 84 S.Ct. 526, 376 U.S. 1, 11 L.Ed.2d 481.

28.   Reynolds v. Sims, 1964, 84 S.Ct. 1362, 377 U.S. 533, 12 L.Ed.2d 506; Lucas v. Forty–Fourth Gen. Assembly, 1964, 84 S.Ct. 1459, 377 U.S. 713, 12 L.Ed.2d 632.

board; [29] claims of partisan gerrymandering; [30] the method by which a state chooses a governor if no candidate has a majority of the popular vote; [31] the refusal by the House of Representatives or by a state legislature to seat a person elected to that body; [32] the hurdles a state may properly impose on an attempt by a new political party to win a place on the ballot; [33] the validity of state procedures for recounting votes in an election for the United States Senate; [34] the use of government jobs for political patronage; [35] and whether majorities of both city voters and county voters can be required in approving amendments to a county charter.[36] The Court has left open, however, the possibility that decisions of the national political parties about representation in their national conventions are political questions.[37]

Possibly the most difficult and important of these cases is the decision in Powell v. McCormack,[38] in which it was held that the House of Representatives had erred in refusing to seat Congressman-elect Adam Clayton Powell. It was strongly argued that there was a "textually demonstrable commitment of the issue to a coordinate political department" in Article I, § 5, of the Constitution, providing that "Each House shall be the Judge of the * * * Qualifications of its own Members." The Court concluded, however, that this was "at most a 'textually demonstrable commitment' to Congress to judge only the qualifications expressly set forth in the Constitution." [39] Since it was conceded that Powell met the qualifications expressly set forth, and was not excluded for failure to meet those, the Court held that this exclusion on other purported grounds of disqualification was justiciable.

In Baker v. Carr the Court said "it is error to suppose that every case or controversy which touches foreign relations lies beyond judicial cognizance." [40] At the same time it recognized that many such cases are

29. Davis v. Bandemer, 1986, 106 S.Ct. 2797, 478 U.S. 109, 92 L.Ed.2d 85.

30. Board of Estimate of City of New York v. Morris, 1989, 109 S.Ct. 1433, 489 U.S. 688, 103 L.Ed.2d 717; Avery v. Midland County, Texas, 1968, 88 S.Ct. 1114, 390 U.S. 474, 20 L.Ed.2d 45.

31. Fortson v. Morris, 1966, 87 S.Ct. 446, 385 U.S. 231, 17 L.Ed.2d 330.

32. Powell v. McCormack, 1969, 89 S.Ct. 1944, 395 U.S. 486, 23 L.Ed.2d 491; Bond v. Floyd, 1966, 87 S.Ct. 339, 385 U.S. 116, 17 L.Ed.2d 235.

33. Williams v. Rhodes, 1968, 89 S.Ct. 5, 393 U.S. 23, 21 L.Ed.2d 24.

34. Roudebush v. Hartke, 1972, 92 S.Ct. 804, 405 U.S. 15, 31 L.Ed.2d 1.

The Court said, however, that which candidate is entitled to be seated in the Senate is a nonjusticiable political question. 92 S.Ct. at 807, 405 U.S. at 19. See also Morgan v. U.S., C.A.D.C.1986, 801 F.2d 445, certiorari denied 107 S.Ct. 1359, 480

U.S. 911, 94 L.Ed.2d 529; McIntyre v. Fallahay, C.A.7th, 1985, 766 F.2d 1078.

35. Elrod v. Burns, 1976, 96 S.Ct. 2673, 427 U.S. 347, 49 L.Ed.2d 547.

36. Town of Lockport v. Citizens for Community Action at the Local Level, Inc., 1977, 97 S.Ct. 1047, 430 U.S. 259, 51 L.Ed.2d 313. See also Quinn v. Millsap, 1989, 109 S.Ct. 2324, 2329, 491 U.S. 95, 102, 105 L.Ed.2d 74.

37. Cousins v. Wigoda, 1975, 95 S.Ct. 541, 419 U.S. 477, 42 L.Ed.2d 595. See 13A Wright, Miller & Cooper, Jurisdiction 2d § 3534.1, at 466–468.

38. 1969, 89 S.Ct. 1944, 395 U.S. 486, 23 L.Ed.2d 491.

39. 89 S.Ct. at 1978, 395 U.S. at 548.

40. 82 S.Ct. at 707, 369 U.S. at 211.

See also 13A Wright, Miller & Cooper, Jurisdiction 2d § 3534.2; Franck, note 1 above; Henkin, Foreign Affairs and the Constitution, 1972, pp. 210–216; Scharpf, note 1 above; Tigar, note 1 above.

political questions because they "turn on standards that defy judicial application, or involve the exercise of a discretion demonstrably committed to the executive or legislature" or "uniquely demand single-voiced statement of the Government's views." [41]

The 1979 case of Goldwater v. Carter [42] is of particular interest. Senator Goldwater and others challenged the power of President Carter to terminate the mutual-defense treaty with Taiwan without either a two-thirds vote of the Senate or a majority vote of each house of Congress. The court of appeals held for the President.[43] The Supreme Court summarily vacated the judgment of the court of appeals and directed that the action be dismissed. Two justices would have set the case down for oral argument, and one concurred in the result without explanation, but the other six all spoke to the application to the case of the political-question doctrine. To Justice Rehnquist, with whom three others joined, the case was a nonjusticiable political question. The Constitution says how a treaty must be ratified, but is silent on how it may be terminated, and since different methods of termination might be appropriate for different treaties, the matter should be settled by political standards rather than by having a rule laid down by the courts. The fact that foreign relations were involved strengthened his conclusion. Justice Powell agreed that the case should be dismissed, but on the ground that it was not yet ripe for decision because neither the Senate nor the House had rejected the President's claim of power to terminate.[44] He rejected the view, however, that it was a political question, arguing that there was no textually demonstrable commitment to another branch, judicially manageable standards could be discovered, and the case touched foreign affairs only at the stage of resolving the constitutional division of power between Congress and the President. Justice Brennan would have affirmed the court of appeals. He thought it already well settled that the Constitution commits to the President alone the power to recognize, and withdraw recognition from, foreign regimes,[45] and that a court could properly decide that abrogation of the defense treaty was a necessary incident to recognition of the Peking government.

An area closely related to foreign relations was involved in Commercial Trust Co. v. Miller.[46] War with Germany was officially ended by a joint resolution of Congress with the approval of the President in July of

---

Interpretation of statutes affecting foreign affairs is not barred by the political-question doctrine. Japan Whaling Assn. v. American Cetacean Socy., 1986, 106 S.Ct. 2860, 478 U.S. 221, 92 L.Ed.2d 166.

41. 82 S.Ct. at 707, 369 U.S. at 211.

See particularly Chicago & Southern Air Lines, Inc. v. Waterman S.S. Corp., 1948, 68 S.Ct. 431, 333 U.S. 103, 92 L.Ed. 568; U.S. v. Curtiss–Wright Export Corp., 1936, 57 S.Ct. 216, 299 U.S. 304, 81 L.Ed. 255.

42. 1979, 100 S.Ct. 533, 444 U.S. 996, 62 L.Ed.2d 428.

43. Goldwater v. Carter, C.A.D.C.1979, 617 F.2d 697, 199. The court of appeals also held that the plaintiffs had standing, an issue not reached by any of the opinions in the Supreme Court. See § 13 n. 57.

44. On ripeness generally, see materials cited in § 12 n. 1 above.

45. See U.S. v. Pink, 1942, 62 S.Ct. 552, 315 U.S. 203, 86 L.Ed. 796.

46. 1923, 43 S.Ct. 486, 262 U.S. 51, 67 L.Ed. 858.

1921. In August a proclamation of peace was issued. Subsequently the Alien Property Custodian sought to seize a trust fund held for the benefit of a German citizen, relying on his powers under the Trading with the Enemy Act. The Act provided that it continued in effect, and all property subject to it should remain under the control of the United States, until the German government had made acceptable provision for the satisfaction of all claims, but it was argued that the end of the war should end the Custodian's power. The Court rejected this argument, saying: "the power which declared the necessity is the power to declare its cessation, and what the cessation requires. The power is legislative." [47] Thus, it appears that the Court will not review the determination of the political departments as to when the exigencies produced by war have ended.

More than 70 lawsuits were brought challenging American military involvement in Viet Nam and Southeast Asia. Reasoning by the courts varied widely, but the striking fact is that in no case was the involvement held unconstitutional and that most of the courts refused to reach the merits of the constitutional issue by finding that the suits raised a political question or were otherwise nonjusticiable. [48]

The processes by which statutes or constitutional amendments are adopted have been thought to be political and nonjusticiable. The leading case is Coleman v. Miller, [49] where it was held that Congress, rather than the Court, can decide how long a proposed amendment to the Constitution remains open for adoption and what effect a prior rejection has on the power of a state to ratify such an amendment. The pendency of the proposed Equal Rights Amendment produced a rich literature on whether Coleman v. Miller remains the law and on what the answers should be to the questions left unresolved in Coleman if they should be found to be justiciable. [50]

A famous case had held that a contention by a state that the federal government has exceeded its powers under the Constitution is political,

47. 43 S.Ct. at 488–489, 262 U.S. at 51. But cf. Chastleton Corp. v. Sinclair, 1924, 44 S.Ct. 405, 264 U.S. 543, 68 L.Ed. 841.

48. See Thomas & Thomas, note 10 above; Firmage, The War Powers and the Political Question Doctrine, 1977, 49 U.Colo.L.Rev. 65.

Courts have similarly refused to pass on challenges to the activities of the United States in El Salvador and Nicaragua. Crockett v. Reagan, C.A.D.C.1983, 720 F.2d 1355, certiorari denied 104 S.Ct. 3533, 467 U.S. 1251, 82 L.Ed.2d 839; Sanchez–Espinoza v. Reagan, C.A.D.C.1985, 770 F.2d 202. See Cole, Challenging Covert War: The Politics of the Political Question Doctrine, 1985, 26 Harv.Intl.L.J. 155.

49. 1939, 59 S.Ct. 972, 307 U.S. 433, 83 L.Ed. 1385. See also Leser v. Garnett, 1922, 42 S.Ct. 217, 258 U.S. 130, 66 L.Ed.

505; Field v. Clark, 1892, 12 S.Ct. 495, 143 U.S. 649, 36 L.Ed. 294. But cf. Gardner v. Collector, 1867, 6 Wall. 499, 18 L.Ed. 890.

50. Dellinger, The Legitimacy of Constitutional Change: Rethinking the Amendment Process, 1983, 97 Harv.L.Rev. 386; Ginsburg, Ratification of the Equal Rights Amendment: A Question of Time, 1979, 57 Texas L.Rev. 919; Note, Article V: Political Questions and Sensible Answers, 1979, 57 Texas L.Rev. 1259; 13A Wright, Miller & Cooper, Jurisdiction 2d § 3534.1, at 480–485.

Coleman v. Miller, at least by way of dictum, supported the view that a state, once having ratified, cannot later rescind its ratification. That question too was mooted in the materials just cited.

not judicial, in character.[51]   The Court, without any reasoned explanation, has since departed from this rule and heard challenges by states to Acts of Congress dealing with the right to vote.[52]

To a distinguished commentator one of the few issues committed by the constitutional text to another branch of government, and thus wholly excluded from judicial review, was the impeachment process.[53] The Constitution gives the House of Representatives "the sole Power of Impeachment" and the Senate "the sole Power to try all impeachments."[54] The events of 1972 to 1974 caused some to doubt even this, and to assert that the courts could intervene in at least some aspects of the impeachment process.[55] Most commentators adhered to the orthodox view that the courts have no role to play with regard to impeachment,[56] and the Court has now confirmed that this is true.[57]

In two recent cases the Supreme Court has rejected arguments by the United States that particular issues should be held nonjusticiable as political questions.   One case involved a statute imposing a special assessment on persons convicted of misdemeanors.   The statute was challenged on the ground that it had not originated in the House of Representatives, as the Constitution requires for revenue measures.[58] The government argued that this was a political question because inquiry into the Origination Clause question would express a lack of respect for the ability of the House to protect its own interests.   The Court responded that determination of this question of constitutionality showed no more lack of respect than determination of the many other questions of constitutionality that are routinely confronted by federal courts.[59]   In another case Montana challenged the mathematical method by which Congress apportioned seats in the House of Representatives among the several states "according to their respective Numbers."[60] The United States agreed that the Constitution places substantive limitations on Congress's apportionment power, but argued that it leaves it entirely to Congress to determine which mathematical method to use.

51. Massachusetts v. Mellon, 1923, 43 S.Ct. 597, 262 U.S. 447, 67 L.Ed. 1078.

See the discussion of this question in the dissent in Massachusetts v. Laird, 1970, 91 S.Ct. 128, 129–135, 400 U.S. 886, 887–900, 27 L.Ed.2d 140.

52. South Carolina v. Katzenbach, 1966, 86 S.Ct. 803, 383 U.S. 301, 15 L.Ed.2d 769. See Bickel, The Voting Rights Cases, 1966, Sup.Ct.Rev. 79, 80–92. A similar case was heard in Oregon v. Mitchell, 1970, 91 S.Ct. 260, 400 U.S. 112, 27 L.Ed.2d 272.

53. Wechsler, note 14 above, at 8.

54. Const., Art. I, §§ 2, 3.

55. Berger, Impeachment: The Constitutional Problem, 1973; Gerhardt, The Constitutional Limits to Impeachment and Its Alternatives, 1989, 68 Texas L.Rev. 1, 99–100.

56. Black, Impeachment: A Handbook, 1974; Nowak & Rotunda, Constitutional Law, 4th ed. 1991, p. 112; Rotunda, An Essay on the Constitutional Parameters of Federal Impeachment, 1988, 76 Ky.L.J. 707, 728–732; Gunther, Judicial Hegemony and Legislative Autonomy: The Nixon Case and the Impeachment Process, 1974, 22 U.C.L.A.L.Rev. 30.

57. Nixon v. U.S., 1993, 113 S.Ct. 732, ___ U.S. ___, 122 L.Ed.2d 1.

58. Const., Art. I, § 7, cl. 1.

59. U.S. v. Munoz–Flores, 1990, 110 S.Ct. 1964, 1968–1971, 495 U.S. 385, 390–396, 109 L.Ed.2d 384. On the merits the Court found that the statute was not one raising revenue.

60. Const., Art. I, § 2, cl. 3.

That was not enough, the Court said, to make the issue nonjusticiable. The controversy between Montana and the United States turnèd on the proper interpretation of the relevant constitutional provisions and that is an issue well within the competence of the judiciary. Respect for a coordinate branch of the federal government raises special concerns, but those concerns relate to the merits of the controversy rather than to the Court's power to resolve it.[61]

Clearly the political-question doctrine has shrunken in scope since Baker v. Carr and Powell v. McCormack. It is not yet dead. In one case a lower court referred to "the diminished vitality of the political question doctrine" and entertained a suit requiring judicial surveillance over the training and weaponry of the National Guard. The Supreme Court tartly responded that "because this doctrine has been held inapplicable to certain carefully delineated situations, it is no reason for federal courts to assume its demise."[62] It found in the constitutional language that states are to train the militia "according to the discipline prescribed by Congress"[63] a textual commitment of the question to a coordinate branch of the federal government.[64]

§ 15. "Case or Controversy"—Administrative Questions[1]

Another limitation on the jurisdiction of the federal courts is that they cannot exercise administrative, or legislative, power. This limitation is a requirement of Article III, since it extends the judicial power only to "cases or controversies."[2] The necessity for distinguishing judicial from legislative or administrative power usually arises when a court is called upon to review action taken by agencies or lower courts. Where the scope of review could be unlimited, the early cases indicated that the nature of the power the court would exercise on review was determined by the nature of the function performed by the lower tribunal. It was established that the nature of the function depends not on the character of the tribunal but on the character of the proceedings before it.[3] If the lower tribunal is a court, but has performed a

---

61. U.S. Dept. of Commerce v. Montana, 1992, 112 S.Ct. 1415, 1424–1426, ___ U.S. ___, ___-___, 118 L.Ed.2d 87. On the merits the Court found that Congress had ample power to choose the method of apportionment it did.

62. Gilligan v. Morgan, 1973, 93 S.Ct. 2440, 2446, 413 U.S. 1, 11, 37 L.Ed.2d 407.

63. Const., Art. I, § 8, cl. 16.

64. See also Goldwater v. Carter, note 43 above, where, as discussed in the text above, four of the six justices who addressed the issue were prepared to dismiss the case as a nonjusticiable political question, and Nixon v. U.S., note 57 above, where the Court held that the Senate's method of trying an impeachment is a political question.

§ 15

1. 13A Wright, Miller & Cooper, Jurisdiction 2d § 3535.

2. An Article III court, however, may appoint independent counsel since Article II specifically provides authority independent of Article III when it empowers Congress to vest the appointment of inferior officers in the courts of law. The court's authority to define the jurisdiction of counsel and to terminate the office of counsel are properly incident to the power to appoint. Morrison v. Olson, 1988, 108 S.Ct. 2597, 2608–2615, 487 U.S. 654, 670, 101 L.Ed.2d 569.

3. Prentis v. Atlantic Coast Line Co., 1908, 29 S.Ct. 67, 211 U.S. 210, 53 L.Ed. 150.

legislative function, no review can be had in a "constitutional" court.[4]

There is no established formula for deciding whether a certain proceeding or function is, by its nature, judicial or administrative.[5] The distinction has been determined case by case in terms of traditional concepts of judicial and administrative or legislative matters,[6] and is not easy to trace. It is often said that if a tribunal has discretion whether to issue an order or grant a privilege its function is administrative.[7] There is no exercise of discretion, however, when a court applies the standards of a statute.[8] Naturalization proceedings in a district court are similar to licensing proceedings in administrative agencies: a petition for citizenship is submitted to the court, and the court then decides whether the petitioner has complied with the terms of the statute. Yet naturalization proceedings are held to be judicial.[9] Similarly an order of a state court denying a license to practice law has been held reviewable in the United States Supreme Court, despite the state court's view that it was not engaged in a judicial proceeding.[10] It may well be that it is easier to find "judicial" action where the proceedings involve important human rights.

4. Federal Radio Comm. v. General Elec. Co., 1930, 50 S.Ct. 389, 281 U.S. 464, 74 L.Ed. 969. For the meaning of a "constitutional" court, see § 11 above.

In Chandler v. Judicial Council of the Tenth Circuit, 1970, 90 S.Ct. 1648, 398 U.S. 74, 26 L.Ed.2d 100, noted 1971, 51 B.U.L.Rev. 106, the Court considered, but did not decide, whether action by a circuit Judicial Council limiting the cases that a district judge could hear was "judicial" action, reviewable on mandamus from the Supreme Court, or was "administrative," and not reviewable in an original proceeding in the Supreme Court.

5. In Prentis v. Atlantic Coast Line Co., 1908, 29 S.Ct. 67, 69, 211 U.S. 210, 226, 53 L.Ed. 150, Justice Holmes wrote that judicial matters involve the application of laws supposed already to exist to present or past facts, while legislation looks to the future and changes existing conditions. That formula is often still quoted. E.g., New Orleans Pub. Serv., Inc. v. Council of City of New Orleans, 1989, 109 S.Ct. 2506, 2519–2520, 491 U.S. 350, 369–371, 105 L.Ed.2d 298. It is impossible to reconcile it, however, with cases such as United Steelworkers of America v. U.S., 1959, 80 S.Ct. 1, 361 U.S. 39, 4 L.Ed.2d 12, upholding the validity of the 80–day strike-injunction provisions of the Taft–Hartley Act. This was found to pose issues suitable for judicial, rather than merely legislative, determination, even though in issuing an injunction the court

need not find that anything unlawful has been done. It is enough that the court establish a standard of conduct for the future that it believes will avoid a peril to the national health or safety. The Prentis formula also cannot be reconciled with the many cases holding that courts may make even constitutional decisions prospective only. See § 7 above at notes 12–14.

6. See United Steelworkers of America v. U.S., 1959, 80 S.Ct. 1, 4, 185, 361 U.S. 39, 43, 60, 4 L.Ed.2d 12.

7. E.g., R.C., 1949, 62 Harv.L.Rev. 1067, 1069.

8. Ullmann v. U.S., 1956, 76 S.Ct. 497, 350 U.S. 422, 100 L.Ed. 511; U.S. v. First City Nat. Bank of Houston, 1967, 87 S.Ct. 1088, 1093–1094, 386 U.S. 361, 369–370, 18 L.Ed.2d 151.

9. Tutun v. U.S., 1926, 46 S.Ct. 425, 270 U.S. 568, 70 L.Ed. 738.

10. In re Summers, 1945, 65 S.Ct. 1307, 325 U.S. 561, 89 L.Ed. 1795. See also Willner v. Committee on Character & Fitness, 1963, 83 S.Ct. 1175, 1179, 373 U.S. 96, 102, 10 L.Ed.2d 224.

Denial by the District of Columbia Court of Appeals of a petition that it waive one of its requirements for admission to the bar was held to be judicial. District of Columbia Court of Appeals v. Feldman, 1983, 103 S.Ct. 1303, 460 U.S. 462, 75 L.Ed.2d 206.

In Keller v. Potomac Electric Power Co.[11] it was held that the Supreme Court could not review a decision of the Court of Appeals for the District of Columbia involving public-utility rates, since the court of appeals had, by statute, such broad power in cases coming to it from the Public Utilities Commission that its action was thought administrative rather than judicial. Again in the first Federal Radio Commission case,[12] review was refused by the Supreme Court since the court below was authorized by statute to revise or alter licensing orders of the Commission as the court might deem just. This made the proceedings in the Court of Appeals for the District of Columbia "administrative." Later Congress amended the statute so that review of orders of the Radio Commission was confined to questions of law, with findings of fact by the Commission to be upheld if supported by substantial evidence. In the second Federal Radio Commission case[13] the Supreme Court held that it could now hear cases in which the court below had passed on orders of the commission, since the proceedings below were now "judicial." Application of the substantial evidence test was considered a legal question on the theory that a capricious order of the Commission would be outside the authority conferred on it by statute. This is the reasoning on which all review of administrative determinations[14] is now justified. Although the proceedings before the agency may be "administrative," the courts can review "judicial" questions.

A 1966 statute allows the Comptroller of the Currency to permit certain bank mergers if he finds them justified by standards set out in the statute. If an antitrust proceeding is later brought attacking the merger, the court is to apply these same standards but it is to "review de novo the issues presented."[15] The Supreme Court held that this did not require the courts to perform nonjudicial tasks, and that it is valid, on the ground that "the courts are not left at large as planning agencies" and that the standards to be applied are familiar ones and within "the area of judicial competence."[16] After this decision, it is hard to see what vitality, if any, is left in the first Federal Radio case. But the case just described, like its predecessors, fails to provide any concrete method of determining whether a particular grant of power to the courts should be found to involve matters beyond judicial competence, suitable only for planning agencies.

---

11. 1923, 43 S.Ct. 445, 261 U.S. 428, 67 L.Ed. 731.

12. 1930, 50 S.Ct. 389, 281 U.S. 464, 74 L.Ed. 969.

13. 1933, 53 S.Ct. 627, 289 U.S. 266, 77 L.Ed. 1166.

14. See § 103 below.

15. 12 U.S.C.A. § 1828(c)(7).

16. U.S. v. First City Nat. Bank of Houston, 1967, 87 S.Ct. 1088, 1094, 386 U.S. 361, 369–370, 18 L.Ed.2d 251.

See also Chandler v. Roudebush, 1976, 96 S.Ct. 1949, 425 U.S. 840, 48 L.Ed.2d 416.

§ 16. Jurisdiction to Determine Jurisdiction [1]

"Jurisdiction to determine jurisdiction" refers to the power of a court to determine whether it has jurisdiction over the parties to and subject matter of a suit. If the jurisdiction of a federal court is questioned, the court has the power, subject to review, to determine the jurisdictional issue.[2] Questions have arisen, however, about the effect of a court's finding that it has jurisdiction in a particular case.

It used to be said that a judgment or order entered by a court is open to direct or collateral attack upon the ground that the court entering the judgment lacked jurisdiction of either the parties or the subject matter.[3] However, it is now held that if a party appears before a court to contest its jurisdiction in personam, a finding that jurisdiction exists will bind the party, and it cannot later collaterally attack that court's judgment upon the basis of lack of personal jurisdiction.[4] The finding of jurisdiction is considered to be res judicata of the issue.

More difficult theoretical problems are encountered when the question is of a court's jurisdiction of the subject matter of a suit. The rule has been that a court's determination that it has subject-matter jurisdiction is res judicata of the issue, if the jurisdictional question was actually litigated and expressly decided.[5] This rule was expanded in Chicot County Drainage District v. Baxter State Bank.[6] There the parties collaterally attacking the judgment had not contested the jurisdiction in the original suit. Jurisdiction had been founded upon a federal statute later held unconstitutional. The Supreme Court held that the judgment was not subject to collateral attack. The later holding of unconstitution-

§ 16

1. 13A Wright, Miller & Cooper, Jurisdiction 2d §§ 3536, 3537; Moore, Collateral Attack on Subject Matter Jurisdiction: A Critique of the Restatement (Second) of Judgments, 1981, 66 Cornell L.Rev. 534; Dobbs, The Validation of Void Judgments: The Bootstrap Principle, 1967, 53 Va.L.Rev. 1003; Dobbs, The Scope of Bootstrap, 1967, 53 Va.L.Rev. 1241; Dobbs, The Decline of Jurisdiction by Consent, 1961, 40 N.C.L.Rev. 49; Boskey & Braucher, Jurisdiction and Collateral Attack, 1940, 40 Col. L.Rev. 1006; Note, Filling the Void: Judicial Power and Jurisdictional Attacks on Judgments, 1977, 87 Yale L.J. 164.

2. U.S. v. United Mine Workers of America, 1947, 67 S.Ct. 677, 330 U.S. 258, 91 L.Ed. 884.

3. See § 7 above; Comment, 1939, 39 Col.L.Rev. 274. For criticism of the unhistorical basis of the orthodox rule, see Dobbs, The Decline of Jurisdiction by Consent, 1961, 40 N.C.L.Rev. 49.

4. Restatement Second of Judgments, 1982, § 10(2); American Sur. Co. v. Baldwin, 1932, 53 S.Ct. 98, 287 U.S. 156, 77

L.Ed. 231; Baldwin v. Iowa State Traveling Men's Assn., 1931, 51 S.Ct. 517, 283 U.S. 522, 75 L.Ed. 1244. See 18 Wright, Miller & Cooper, Jurisdiction § 4430.

5. Stoll v. Gottlieb, 1938, 59 S.Ct. 134, 305 U.S. 165, 83 L.Ed. 104. For Professor Chafee's comments on the case, see Chafee, Some Problems of Equity, 1950, p. 319 n. 42. See also Davis v. Davis, 1938, 59 S.Ct. 3, 305 U.S. 32, 83 L.Ed. 26; Durfee v. Duke, 1963, 84 S.Ct. 242, 375 U.S. 106, 11 L.Ed.2d 186.

6. 1940, 60 S.Ct. 317, 308 U.S. 371, 84 L.Ed. 329. See also Boskey & Braucher, Jurisdiction and Collateral Attack, 1940, 40 Col.L.Rev. 1006; Comment, The Applicability of Res Judicata to Determinations of "Subject Matter" Jurisdiction in Conflict of Laws Cases, 1963, 11 Kan.L.Rev. 544.

This rule may have been expanded in Honneus v. Donovan, C.A.1st, 1982, 691 F.2d 1, where it was held that a default judgment could not later be challenged for lack of diversity.

ality would not operate retroactively so as to render the judgment void,[7] and the judgment would be deemed to include a finding of jurisdiction. The result of the decision appears to be that a party who does not actually contest the jurisdiction will be bound by the judgment.[8]

The rule that a finding of jurisdiction is res judicata of the issue is subject to exception when the policy in favor of finality of judgments is outweighed by other factors.[9] Thus, when a federal statute has vested exclusive jurisdiction of a particular type of case in the federal courts, the finding by a state court that it has jurisdiction over such a case will not preclude collateral attack upon the judgment rendered in the state court.[10] Similarly collateral attack is permitted on a judgment that violates the government's immunity from suit.[11]

Before it has determined whether it has jurisdiction of an action, a federal court may issue various orders, such as temporary restraining orders or preliminary injunctions. In the 19th century there was no speedy means for review of such orders, and no review at all of contempt convictions for violation of such orders except by habeas corpus. To fill this gap, the Supreme Court developed the notion that a decree issued by a court that lacked jurisdiction was void, permitting the person found guilty of contempt to go free on habeas corpus.[12] This notion that the orders of a court lacking jurisdiction of the merits were not binding was applied whether the order granted substantive relief[13] or merely aimed to preserve the status quo pending determination of the jurisdictional question.[14] One who violated such an order could be punished for

---

7. In so holding the Court, 60 S.Ct. at 318, 308 U.S. at 374, expressly limited statements in Norton v. Shelby County, 1886, 6 S.Ct. 1121, 1125, 118 U.S. 425, 442, 30 L.Ed. 178, and Chicago, I. & L.R. Co. v. Hackett, 1913, 33 S.Ct. 581, 584, 228 U.S. 559, 566, 57 L.Ed. 966, that had indicated that a law held unconstitutional is inoperative and confers neither rights nor duties.

8. This is in accord with the general principle that res judicata applies not only to matters actually litigated but to all other matters that might have been presented to sustain or defeat the right asserted in the earlier proceeding. Cromwell v. County of Sac, 1877, 94 U.S. 351, 24 L.Ed. 195; Grubb v. Public Utilities Comm., 1930, 50 S.Ct. 374, 281 U.S. 470, 74 L.Ed. 972; Underwriters Nat. Assur. Co. v. North Carolina Life & Accident & Health Ins. Guar. Assn., 1982, 102 S.Ct. 1357, 455 U.S. 691, 71 L.Ed.2d 558. See Restatement Second of Judgments, 1982, § 12 comm. d, 18 Wright, Miller & Cooper, Jurisdiction § 4428; § 100A below.

9. Restatement Second of Judgments, 1982, § 12. See Moore, note 1 above, at 544–547, 554–560.

10. Kalb v. Feuerstein, 1940, 60 S.Ct. 343, 308 U.S. 433, 84 L.Ed. 370; Consolidated Rail Corp. v. Illinois, Spec.Ct.R.R.R.A. 1976, 423 F.Supp. 941, 947–950, certiorari denied 1977, 97 S.Ct. 1111, 429 U.S. 1095, 51 L.Ed.2d 542.

11. U.S. v. U.S. Fidelity & Guar. Co., 1940, 60 S.Ct. 653, 309 U.S. 506, 84 L.Ed. 894.

The Supreme Court, however, has said of this case, and the Kalb case, note 10 above, that "in neither of these cases had the jurisdictional issues actually been litigated in the first forum." Durfee v. Duke, 1963, 84 S.Ct. 242, 247 n. 12, 375 U.S. 106, 114 n. 12, 11 L.Ed.2d 186.

12. See Chafee, note 5 above, at pp. 337–363.

13. Ex parte Fisk, 1884, 5 S.Ct. 724, 113 U.S. 713, 28 L.Ed. 1117; Ex parte Rowland, 1881, 104 U.S. 604, 26 L.Ed. 861. See Thomas v. Collins, 1945, 65 S.Ct. 315, 323 U.S. 516, 89 L.Ed. 430.

14. Ex parte Sawyer, 1887, 8 S.Ct. 482, 124 U.S. 200, 31 L.Ed. 402, discussed by Chafee, note 5 above, at pp. 337–343; Ex parte Ayers, 1887, 8 S.Ct. 164, 123 U.S. 443, 31 L.Ed. 216.

contempt only if the court were ultimately found to possess jurisdiction of the merits. The only exception to that test existed where the violation of the order operated in itself to defeat the jurisdiction of the court, such as by making the case moot.[15]

The law on this point was apparently changed in United States v. United Mine Workers of America.[16] The United States sued to restrain a strike in mines that had earlier been seized by the government. There was a serious question whether the Norris–LaGuardia Act deprived the district court of jurisdiction to issue a temporary restraining order in such a labor dispute. The defendants permitted the strike notice to remain in effect and the strike to occur. The district court held the defendants to be in civil and criminal contempt of court. As an alternative ground for affirmance of the conviction of criminal contempt, the Supreme Court held that orders issued by the district court must be obeyed until they are set aside, and their violation is punishable as criminal contempt, even if it is ultimately determined that the district court lacked jurisdiction to make the order.

The view of the majority of the Supreme Court in the United Mine Workers case appeared to be that every court has the power to determine if it has the capacity to hear and decide the merits of the case before it. That power, or jurisdiction to determine jurisdiction, is of itself sufficient to give binding effect to the orders of the court issued to preserve the status quo, even though the court is ultimately found to lack jurisdiction of the merits. A party is bound to obey such orders until the jurisdictional question is determined. The only limitation to the binding effect of such orders is that the assertion of jurisdiction must possess some merit; the order need not be obeyed if the assertion of jurisdiction is only "frivolous."

The impact of the United Mine Workers decision was unclear. The order violated was one intended to preserve the status quo, and it could

---

15. U.S. v. Shipp, 1906, 27 S.Ct. 165, 203 U.S. 563, 51 L.Ed. 319. In that case the Supreme Court had allowed an appeal from denial of habeas corpus in a state court and had stayed all proceedings pending appeal. While the appeal was pending, the prisoner was taken from jail and lynched. Shipp, the sheriff who was charged with contempt for conspiring with others to permit the lynching, sought unsuccessfully to defend on the ground that the Supreme Court had no jurisdiction to issue a stay since the federal questions on which relief was sought were frivolous and a mere pretense.

See also Griffin v. County Sch. Bd. of Prince Edward Co., Va., C.A.4th, 1966, 363 F.2d 206, certiorari denied 87 S.Ct. 395, 385 U.S. 960, 17 L.Ed.2d 305, noted 1966, 52 Va.L.Rev. 1556, 1967, 24 Wash. & Lee L.Rev. 119. It is there held that it is civil contempt to disburse a fund at a time when the appellate court has before it an application to prevent such disbursement, although no injunction has yet issued. There is an interesting discussion of the case in Rendleman, Compensatory Contempt to Collect Money, 1980, 41 Ohio St.L.J. 625, 631–635.

16. 1947, 67 S.Ct. 677, 330 U.S. 258, 91 L.Ed. 884. See Chafee, note 5 above, at pp. 364–380; Watt, Divine Right of Government by Judiciary, 1947, 14 U.Chi.L.Rev. 409; Cox, The Void Order and the Duty to Obey, 1948, 16 U.Chi.L.Rev. 86; Rendleman, More on Void Orders, 1973, 7 Ga. L.Rev. 246; Notes, 1947, 60 Harv.L.Rev. 811, 35 Ill.B.J. 414.

have been that the decision was limited to orders of that kind.[17]   There were suggestions, however, that the decision might apply also to orders granting substantive relief.[18]

The authoritative effect of the United Mine Workers decision was also unclear.   Only five of the nine justices thought there was a duty to obey an order if the court that issued it lacked jurisdiction, and since three of these five thought that the court below had jurisdiction of the case, there was, in Professor Chafee's phrase, "a lack of impressive solidity on this point." [19]

Subsequent decisions of the Supreme Court did not dispel all questions.   In one case, In re Green,[20] a state-court contempt conviction was set aside on finding that the state court lacked jurisdiction because the question involved was exclusively of federal concern.   The United Mine Workers case was brushed aside in a footnote on the ground that it "involved a restraining order of a federal court and presented no question of pre-emption of a field by Congress where, if the federal policy is to prevail, federal power must be complete." [21]   It is hard to see why the determination by Congress in the Norris–LaGuardia Act that federal courts are not to act is less puissant than its determination in the preemption area that state courts are not to act.

In Walker v. City of Birmingham [22] a bare majority of the Court upheld contempt convictions against Dr. Martin Luther King and a number of others for parading in violation of a temporary injunction issued by an Alabama state court.   They had felt free to defy the injunction on the ground that it was unconstitutional.   The Court agreed that "the breadth and vagueness of the injunction itself would * * * unquestionably be subject to substantial constitutional question," [23] and that the same was true of the city ordinance on parades that underlay the injunction.   It held, however, that the state court undoubtedly had jurisdiction of the parties and the subject matter, and that the constitutional claims should have been presented to that court.   The United Mine Workers case was cited once, at the end of a long string of

---

17.   Stewart v. Dunn, C.A.5th, 1966, 363 F.2d 591, 598; U.S. v. Thompson, C.A.2d, 1963, 319 F.2d 665, 668; James, Book Review, 1965, 78 Harv.L.Rev. 1296, 1298.

As Professor James points out in the cited book review, this may well explain the cases in which an appellate court, without reference to the United Mine Workers case, has reversed contempt convictions of persons who have refused to comply with discovery orders, when the appellate court found issuance of the order was an abuse of discretion.   E.g., Guilford Nat. Bank of Greensboro v. Southern Ry. Co., C.A.4th, 1962, 297 F.2d 921; Hauger v. Chicago, R.I. & P.R. Co., C.A.7th, 1954, 216 F.2d 501; cf. Appeal of U.S. Securities & Exchange

Comm., C.A.6th, 1955, 226 F.2d 501.   But see Southern Ry. Co. v. Lanham, C.A.5th, 1969, 408 F.2d 348, 349–350 (Brown, J., dissenting).

18.   Giancana v. Johnson, C.A.7th, 1964, 335 F.2d 372; Note, 1947, 35 Ill.B.J. 414.

19.   Chafee, note 5 above, at p. 367.

20.   1962, 82 S.Ct. 1114, 369 U.S. 689, 8 L.Ed.2d 198, noted 1962, 57 Nw.U.L.Rev. 609.

21.   82 S.Ct. at 1117 n. 1, 369 U.S. at 692 n. 1.

22.   1967, 87 S.Ct. 1824, 388 U.S. 307, 18 L.Ed.2d 1210.

23.   87 S.Ct. at 1830, 388 U.S. at 317.

cases.[24] The case of In re Green was distinguished on the ground that there the claim was that the state court was "without jurisdiction," and that: "The petitioner in Green, unlike the petitioners here, had attempted to challenge the validity of the injunction *before* violating it by promptly applying to the issuing court for an order vacating the injunction. The petitioner in Green had further offered to prove that the court issuing the injunction had agreed to its violation as an appropriate means of testing its validity." [25]

Finally in yet another case the Supreme Court recognized the possibility that a court may not wish to punish a person for violating an order subsequently held to be invalid.[26]

In fact, however, a sensible reconciliation of the Supreme Court cases on this point is possible. It would be that the validity of an order can be challenged in a contempt proceeding for violation of the order only if there was no opportunity for effective review of the order before it was violated. This view is suggested by the quoted passage from the Walker case. It emerges even more clearly from the decision in United States v. Ryan.[27] The holding in Ryan was that an order denying a motion to quash a grand jury subpoena duces tecum was not appealable. It was said that if the subpoena was unduly burdensome or otherwise unlawful, the party on whom it was served "may refuse to comply and litigate those questions in the event that contempt or similar proceedings are brought against him. Should his contentions be rejected at that time by the trial court they will then be ripe for appellate review." [28] In a footnote at that point in the opinion the Court said: "Walker v. Birmingham * * * is not to the contrary. Our holding that the claims there sought to be asserted were not open on review of petitioners' contempt convictions was based upon the availability of review of those claims at an earlier stage." [29] This is a clearer explanation of the Walker decision than the opinion in that case itself provides.

It should be noted that it is only a realistic opportunity for effective review that bars later challenge in a contempt proceeding. In the Walker case the Court said that the matter would be in a different posture if the defendants had challenged the injunction in the Alabama courts "and had been met with delay or frustration of their constitutional claims." [30] The Court pointed out that the injunction had issued ex parte, that if the court had been presented with defendant's contentions it might well have dissolved or modified the order, and that under Alabama procedure there was an expedited process of appellate review.[31]

24. 87 S.Ct. at 1828 n. 5, 388 U.S. at 314 n. 5.

25. 87 S.Ct. at 1829, n. 6, 388 U.S. at 315 n. 6 (emphasis by the Court).

26. Donovan v. City of Dallas, 1964, 84 S.Ct. 1579, 1583, 377 U.S. 408, 414, 12 L.Ed.2d 409, on remand Tex.Civ.App.1964, 384 S.W.2d 724. Dunn v. U.S., C.A.10th, 1968, 388 F.2d 511, is to the same effect.

27. 1971, 91 S.Ct. 1580, 402 U.S. 530, 29 L.Ed.2d 85.

28. 91 S.Ct. at 1582, 402 U.S. at 532.

29. 91 S.Ct. at 1582 n. 4, 402 U.S. at 532 n. 4.

30. 87 S.Ct. at 1831, 388 U.S. at 318.

31. 91 S.Ct. at 1831, 388 U.S. at 319.

By way of contrast, in the earlier case of In re Green, in which a contempt conviction was set aside because the temporary injunction that was violated should not have issued, the party held in contempt had sought unsuccessfully to have the trial court vacate the temporary injunction and, though the Supreme Court did not mention this in its opinion, it appears from the briefs in the case that state law did not permit appellate review of a temporary injunction.

That the key is the effectiveness of appellate review is also made clear by Maness v. Meyers,[32] where a contempt conviction was set aside because there was no effective way to test an order requiring a party to produce material that he thought would incriminate him except by refusing compliance and raising the issue on appeal of the conviction.

This interpretation of the United Mine Workers rule reconciles it also with the 19th-century cases allowing challenge to an injunctive order by appeal from a contempt conviction. As has been pointed out,[33] at the time they were decided there was no speedy or effective means for review of such orders.

In the Walker case the Court left open the possibility of an exception to the rule that an order must be obeyed even if it may later prove to be unconstitutional. It said that "this is not a case where the injunction was transparently invalid or had only a frivolous pretense to validity."[34] A lower court has found this "transparently invalid" exception applicable to a gag order that was viewed as a prior restraint on pure speech.[35]

The rule announced in the United Mine Workers case, and refined in the later cases, applies only to criminal contempt. Civil contempt is designed to coerce compliance with the court's decree and the civil-contempt order falls with a showing that the court was without authority to enter the decree.[36] The rule is otherwise with sanctions imposed under Civil Rule 11. Their purpose is to punish a party who has already violated the court's rules and sanctions can be imposed even though the court lacked subject-matter jurisdiction of the case.[37]

---

32. 1975, 95 S.Ct. 584, 419 U.S. 449, 42 L.Ed.2d 574.

See also U.S. v. Dickinson, C.A.5th, 1972, 465 F.2d 496, 509–514, adhered to as law of the case C.A.5th, 1973, 476 F.2d 373, certiorari denied 94 S.Ct. 270, 414 U.S. 979, 38 L.Ed.2d 223.

33. See text at notes 12–15 above.

34. 87 S.Ct. at 1829, 388 U.S. at 315.

35. In Matter of Providence Journal Co., C.A.1st, 1986, 820 F.2d 1342, modified on rehearing C.A.1st, 1987, 820 F.2d 1354, certiorari dismissed 108 S.Ct. 1502, 485 U.S. 693, 99 L.Ed.2d 785.

36. U.S. Catholic Conference v. Abortion Rights Mobilization, Inc., 1988, 108 S.Ct. 2268, 487 U.S. 72, 101 L.Ed.2d 69.

37. Willy v. Coastal Corp., 1992, 112 S.Ct. 1076, ___ U.S. ___, 117 L.Ed.2d 280.

Chapter 3

FEDERAL QUESTION

Analysis

---

§ 17. The Meaning of "Arising Under" [1]

The Constitution provides that federal courts may be given jurisdiction over "Cases, in Law and Equity, arising under this Constitution, the Laws of the United States, and Treaties made, or which shall be made, under their authority." Cases that fall under this head of jurisdiction are usually spoken of as involving a "federal question." This jurisdiction was one of the principal reasons that the Constitution authorized Congress to create a system of inferior federal courts, but it was not until 1875 that Congress gave the federal courts general original jurisdic-

§ 17

1. 13B Wright, Miller & Cooper, Jurisdiction 2d §§ 3561–3563; ALI Study, § 1311 and Commentary thereto. The following articles and commentaries are cited in chronological order for they represent something of a dialogue, in which each writer draws on and discusses the writings that have been published earlier: Forrester, The Nature of a Federal Question, 1942, 16 Tul. L.Rev. 363; Chadbourn & Levin, Original Jurisdiction of Federal Questions, 1942, 90 U.Pa.L.Rev. 639; Forrester, Federal Question Jurisdiction and Section 5, 1943, 18 Tul.L.Rev. 263; Note, Proposed Revision of Federal Question Jurisdiction, 1945, 40 Ill. L.Rev. 387; Bergman, Reappraisal of Federal Question Jurisdiction, 1946, 46 Mich. L.Rev. 17; Fraser, Some Problems in Federal Question Jurisdiction, 1950, 49 Mich. L.Rev. 73; Mishkin, The Federal "Question" in the District Courts, 1953, 53 Col. L.Rev. 157; London, "Federal Question" Jurisdiction—A Snare and a Delusion, 1959, 57 Mich.L.Rev. 835; Cohen, The Broken Compass: the Requirement that a Case Arise "Directly" Under Federal Law, 1967, 115 U.Pa.L.Rev. 890; Aycock, Introduction to Certain Members of the Federal Question Family, 1970, 49 N.C.L.Rev. 1; Note, The Outer Limits of "Arising Under," 1979, 54 N.Y.U.L.Rev. 978; Hirshman, Whose Law Is It Anyway? A Reconsideration of Federal Question Jurisdiction Over Cases of Mixed State and Federal Law, 60 Ind.L.J. 17 (1985); Doernberg, There's No Reason for It: It's Just Our Policy: Why the Well–Pleaded Complaint Rule Sabotages the Purposes of Federal Question Jurisdiction, 1987, 38 Hastings L.J. 597.

tion over such cases.[2] The statute, first passed in that year and preserved substantially unchanged to the present, confers original jurisdiction on the federal courts over federal-question cases in language virtually the same as the Constitution.[3] The key phrase, both in the Constitution and in the statute, is "arises under." Though the meaning of this phrase has attracted the interest of such giants of the bench as Marshall, Waite, Bradley, the first Harlan, Holmes, Cardozo, Frankfurter, and Brennan, and has been the subject of voluminous scholarly writing, it cannot be said that any clear test has yet been developed to determine which cases "arise under" the Constitution, laws, or treaties of the United States.[4]

Analysis must begin with Marshall's opinion in Osborn v. Bank of the United States.[5] The congressional act chartering the bank authorized it "to sue and be sued * * * in any Circuit Court of the United States." The bank brought suit to enjoin the state auditor of Ohio from collecting from it a tax alleged to be unconstitutional. In considering the jurisdictional question, Chief Justice Marshall first held that the authorization to "sue and be sued" was a grant by Congress to the federal courts of jurisdiction in all cases to which the bank was a party. Even this conclusion is debatable.[6] Assuming that conclusion, the question then occurred whether Congress had constitutional power to confer jurisdiction of such cases. Surely the power existed in the case actually before the Court, for the bank was asserting a claim under the federal Constitution, which would suffice for jurisdiction by any test.

2. Act of March 3, 1875, § 1, 18 Stat. 470. The history of the constitutional provision, and of the 1875 Act, are set out in the two articles by Dean Forrester cited note 1 above. The situation under the 1789 Act is discussed in Engdahl, Federal Question Jurisdiction Under the 1789 Judiciary Act, 14 Okla.City U.L.Rev. 521 (1989).

There had been a short-lived grant of this jurisdiction in the Midnight Judges Act of 1801, but this was promptly repealed a year later. See § 1 above.

3. 28 U.S.C.A. § 1331: "The district courts shall have original jurisdiction of all civil actions arising under the Constitution, laws, or treaties of the United States."

There are also many statutes granting jurisdiction in particular federal-question cases. From 1875 to 1980 the general federal-question statute had required a jurisdictional amount, most recently $10,000, and these other statutes were significant since they granted jurisdiction without regard to amount. See § 32 below. With the abolition in 1980 of the amount requirement in § 1331, the special statutes, which are scattered in chapter 85 of title 28, have lost their significance. It is clear, in any event, that "arising under" has the same

meaning in these statutes as in § 1331. Christianson v. Colt Industries Operating Corp., 1988, 108 S.Ct. 2166, 2173, 486 U.S. 800, 808–809, 100 L.Ed.2d 811.

In the year ended September 30, 1992, 118,180 of the 230,509 cases brought in the district courts were private "federal question" cases. Ann.Rep. of the Director of the Administrative Office of the U.S. Courts, 1992, Table C–2.

4. Franchise Tax Board v. Construction Laborers Vacation Trust, 1983, 103 S.Ct. 2841, 2846, 463 U.S. 1, 8, 77 L.Ed.2d 420.

One court has referred to the problem as "the Serbonian bog." Amoco Production Co. v. Sea Robin Pipeline Co., C.A.5th, 1988, 844 F.2d 1202, 1205 (per John R. Brown, J.).

5. 1824, 9 Wheat. 738, 6 L.Ed. 204.

6. A more natural interpretation might have been that the charter gave the bank capacity to be a party to a suit but did not in itself create jurisdiction. This is the construction now usually placed on such language in charters. Bankers' Trust Co. v. Texas & P. Ry. Co., 1916, 36 S.Ct. 569, 241 U.S. 295, 60 L.Ed. 1010. But see American Natl. Red Cross v. S.G., 1992, 112 S.Ct. 2465, ___ U.S. ___, 120 L.Ed.2d 201.

Marshall's opinion, however, undertakes to support the validity of the jurisdictional grant in all cases to which the bank might be a party, and discusses in detail the situation that would be presented if the bank were asserting a claim under the state law arising out of a contract.[7] Even here, it was held, federal-question jurisdiction would exist. Since the bank is a mere creature of federal law, in every case the first question that presents itself must be whether this legal entity has a right to sue. Once this question is settled, it is of course unlikely that it would be raised in subsequent cases, but this, in Marshall's view, was immaterial. "The question forms an original ingredient in every cause. Whether it be in fact relied on or not, in the defence, it is still a part of the cause, and may be relied on." [8] Earlier in the opinion Marshall, in language heavily relied on by later judges, had seemed to say that federal-question jurisdiction existed only when the title or right set up by the party might be defeated by one construction of the Constitution or law of the United States and sustained by the opposite construction,[9] but his later analysis, just described, demonstrates that this was not his position, and that jurisdiction would be present even in a case where no question of federal law is ever raised.

The Osborn decision took on importance after the 1875 statute gave the federal courts general original jurisdiction of federal-question cases. At least until comparatively recent years, no decision construing the statute was complete without its reference to the Osborn case and its praise for Marshall's analysis there. What was not clearly perceived in the early cases construing the 1875 act, and until very recently had not always been kept in mind even in the later cases, is that there is a difference between construing the Constitution, as Marshall was obliged to do in Osborn, and construing a statute. The very expansive reading Marshall gave to the "cases arising under" language of the Constitution is appropriate in dealing with a constitution. It leaves room for Congress to grant such particular jurisdiction as may in the future be seen to be necessary. But to hold that the 1875 statute gives federal jurisdiction wherever some element of federal law is an "ingredient" of the cause of action would mean, for example, that virtually every case involving the title to land in the western states, where title descends from a grant from the United States, could be litigated in federal court. If Congress in fact meant to open the door of the federal courthouse to such a flood of litigation, the Osborn case shows that it had power to do so. Actually both the language of the 1875 statute, following so closely the constitu-

---

7. Such a situation was in fact presented by the companion case of Bank of the U.S. v. Planter's Bank of Georgia, 1824, 9 Wheat. 904, 6 L.Ed. 244, decided on the authority of Osborn.

8. 9 Wheat. at 824, 6 L.Ed. at 224.

9. 9 Wheat. at 822, 6 L.Ed. at 224. In the earlier case of Cohens v. Virginia, 1821, 6 Wheat. 264, 379, 5 L.Ed. 257, 285, Marshall had written: "A case in law or equity consists of the right of the one party, as well as of the other, and may truly be said to arise under the constitution or a law of the United States, whenever its correct decision depends on the construction of either." In Cohens, however, Marshall was considering the appellate jurisdiction of the Supreme Court over state courts, which involves different considerations than does the original jurisdiction of the federal trial courts.

tional language, and such skimpy legislative history as exists,[10] do support the view that Congress meant to give all the jurisdiction it could constitutionally confer, but this is not an inevitable conclusion, and the courts acted understandably in giving a restrictive reading to the statute. Regrettably, from the standpoint of clear analysis, they did so by a distortion of the Osborn opinion, rather than by an overt recognition that their problem of statutory construction was not the same as Marshall's problem of interpreting the Constitution.

The point emerges most clearly in the Pacific Railroad Removal Cases,[11] decided in 1885, where the Court, through Justice Bradley, held that ordinary tort actions against railroads with federal charters were within the scope of the 1875 statute. Chief Justice Waite, dissenting, stated that "in my opinion congress did not intend to give the words 'arising under the constitution or laws of the United States,' in the act of 1875, the broad meaning they have when used by Chief Justice Marshall in the argument of the opinion in Osborn v. Bank of U.S." [12] The case itself is now regarded by the Supreme Court as an "unfortunate decision" [13] and has long since been effectively overruled by Congress.[14] But Waite himself, in decisions before and after the Pacific Railroad Removal Cases, was able to give a restrictive reading to the 1875 statute while purporting to apply the Osborn rule,[15] and later judges have done the same thing.[16]

When courts are unclear in formulating the question before them, it is not surprising if the answers are also wanting in clarity. The Osborn theory, that when federal law is an ingredient of the claim there is a federal question, has been rejected in construing the statute. It is not easy to state what has been substituted in its stead. One line of

10. See Forrester, Federal Question Jurisdiction and Section 5, 1943, 18 Tul. L.Rev. 263, 276–280.

11. 1885, 5 S.Ct. 1113, 115 U.S. 1, 29 L.Ed. 319.

12. 5 S.Ct. at 1124, 115 U.S. at 24.

13. Romero v. International Terminal Operating Co., 1959, 79 S.Ct. 468, 484 n. 50, 358 U.S. 354, 379 n. 50, 3 L.Ed.2d 368.

14. 28 U.S.C.A. § 1349 provides that the district courts shall not have jurisdiction on the ground that a corporation was incorporated by Congress unless the United States owns more than half the capital stock of the corporation. See also 28 U.S.C.A. § 1348 (national banks). But there is federal-question jurisdiction of all cases in which Amtrak is a defendant since the United States owns more than 50% of its stock. Estate of Wright v. Illinois Cent. R. Co., D.C.Miss.1993, 831 F.Supp. 574.

15. E.g., Gold–Washing & Water Co. v. Keyes, 1877, 96 U.S. 199, 24 L.Ed. 656;

Starin v. New York, 1885, 6 S.Ct. 28, 115 U.S. 248, 29 L.Ed. 388.

16. Thus, Justice Stone, in People of Puerto Rico v. Russell & Co., 1933, 53 S.Ct. 447, 288 U.S. 476, 77 L.Ed. 903, and Justice Cardozo, in Gully v. First Nat. Bank in Meridian, 1936, 57 S.Ct. 96, 299 U.S. 109, 81 L.Ed. 70, felt obliged to express misgivings about the Osborn decision, rather than distinguishing it as involving a different question.

The distinction between the constitutional question and the statutory question is recognized in Shoshone Mining Co. v. Rutter, 1900, 20 S.Ct. 726, 177 U.S. 505, 44 L.Ed. 864, Romero v. International Terminal Operating Co., 1959, 79 S.Ct. 468, 484 n. 51, 358 U.S. 354, 379 n. 51, 3 L.Ed.2d 368, and in Verlinden B.V. v. Central Bank of Nigeria, 1983, 103 S.Ct. 1962, 1972, 461 U.S. 480, 494–495, 76 L.Ed.2d 81, and subsequent cases.

decisions is symbolized by Justice Holmes' statement that "a suit arises under the law that creates the action."[17]   Many cases can be explained by—or at least are consistent with—this test,[18] though of late it has been thought that the "Holmes' formula is more useful for inclusion than for the exclusion for which it was intended."[19]   There are surely other cases that cannot be reconciled with the test proposed by Holmes, cases in which federal-question jurisdiction has been upheld although the action was created by state law,[20] and in which jurisdiction has been denied although federal law created the action.[21]

Other cases have said that "a suit to enforce a right which takes its origin in the laws of the United States is not necessarily, or for that reason alone, one arising under those laws, for a suit does not so arise unless it really and substantially involves a dispute or controversy respecting the validity, construction or effect of such a law, upon the determination of which the result depends."[22]   Such a test would be difficult, if not impossible, to apply, in view of the rule that jurisdiction must be determined from plaintiff's well-pleaded complaint.[23]   The complaint by itself can hardly disclose on what aspects of the case there will be dispute or controversy.   Such a test would be inconsistent, also, with those cases that hold that federal jurisdiction exists though defendant

---

17. American Well Works Co. v. Layne & Bowler Co., 1916, 36 S.Ct. 585, 586, 241 U.S. 257, 260, 60 L.Ed. 987 (no jurisdiction over suit for damages to business from defendant's statements that plaintiff was infringing defendant's patents).

18. E.g., no jurisdiction: Albright v. Teas, 1883, 1 S.Ct. 550, 106 U.S. 613, 27 L.Ed. 295 (suit on a contract involving a patent); People of Puerto Rico v. Russell & Co., 1933, 53 S.Ct. 447, 288 U.S. 476, 77 L.Ed. 903 (federal law gave authority to bring suit but suit itself was under local law); Gully v. First Nat. Bank in Meridian, 1936, 57 S.Ct. 96, 299 U.S. 109, 81 L.Ed. 70 (suit to collect state taxes that could not be brought unless federal law granted permission).

Jurisdiction: Feibelman v. Packard, 1883, 3 S.Ct. 289, 109 U.S. 421, 27 L.Ed. 984 (suit on bond required by federal law); The Fair v. Kohler Die & Specialty Co., 1913, 33 S.Ct. 410, 228 U.S. 22, 57 L.Ed. 716 (suit for patent infringement); Thurston Motor Lines, Inc. v. Jordan K. Rand, Ltd., 1983, 103 S.Ct. 1343, 460 U.S. 533, 75 L.Ed.2d 260 (suit to recover money due under ICC tariffs).

19. T.B. Harms Co. v. Eliscu, C.A.2d 1964, 339 F.2d 823, 827 (per Friendly, J.), certiorari denied 85 S.Ct. 1534, 381 U.S. 915, 14 L.Ed.2d 435. Judge Friendly's insight was accepted by the Supreme Court in Franchise Tax Board v. Construction La-

borers Vacation Trust, 1983, 103 S.Ct. 2841, 2846, 463 U.S. 1, 8–9, 77 L.Ed.2d 420 (per Brennan, J.).

The formula of Justice Holmes is sharply attacked in Note, The Outer Limits of "Arising Under," 1979, 54 N.Y.U.L.Rev. 978. But another commentator argues that "the courts should turn, or return, to the straightforward analysis set forth by Justice Holmes." Hirshman, note 1 above, at 72.

20. Smith v. Kansas City Title & Trust Co., 1921, 41 S.Ct. 243, 255 U.S. 180, 65 L.Ed. 577 (suit to enjoin bank from investing in particular government bonds, on ground that Act of Congress authorizing the bonds was unconstitutional).

21. Shoshone Mining Co. v. Rutter, 1900, 20 S.Ct. 726, 177 U.S. 505, 44 L.Ed. 864 (federal statute authorized suit to determine adverse claims to mining right, but no jurisdiction since local rules or customs were to govern result). See also Roecker v. U.S., C.A.5th, 1967, 379 F.2d 400, 407–408, certiorari denied 88 S.Ct. 563, 389 U.S. 1005, 19 L.Ed.2d 600.

22. Shulthis v. McDougal, 1912, 32 S.Ct. 704, 706, 225 U.S. 561, 569, 56 L.Ed. 1205. See also Gold–Washing & Water Co. v. Keyes, 1877, 96 U.S. 199, 203, 24 L.Ed. 656; Gully v. First Nat. Bank in Meridian, 1936, 57 S.Ct. 96, 98, 299 U.S. 109, 114, 81 L.Ed. 70.

23. See § 18 below.

defaults, and thus controverts nothing,[24] or that it exists though the only questions are fact questions and the application of the federal law is not in issue.[25]

In Gully v. First National Bank in Meridian,[26] Justice Cardozo, after repeating most of the earlier definitions of a federal question, cautioned against broad and abstract definitions and called for a common-sense accommodation of judgment to kaleidoscopic situations. "If we follow the ascent far enough, countless claims of right can be discovered to have their source or their operative limits in the provisions of a federal statute or in the Constitution itself with its circumambient restrictions upon legislative power. To set bounds to the pursuit, the courts have formulated the distinction between controversies that are basic and those that are collateral, between disputes that are necessary and those that are merely possible. We shall be lost in a maze if we put that compass by." [27]

Professor Mishkin had distilled the course of decision here described into the succinct test that for original federal jurisdiction there must be "a substantial claim founded 'directly' upon federal law." [28] As definitions go—having in mind Cardozo's warning against their hazards—this seemed as good as any, but it had to be recognized that the books contained some results, and a good deal more language, inconsistent with it. Others thought that rather than attempting a test it might be wiser simply to recognize that "the existing doctrines as to when a case raises a federal question are neither analytical nor entirely logical," [29] and that in the unusual case in which there is a debatable issue about federal-question jurisdiction, pragmatic considerations must be taken into account.[30]

---

24. E.g., The Fair v. Kohler Die & Specialty Co., 1913, 33 S.Ct. 410, 228 U.S. 22, 57 L.Ed. 716. See ALI Study, pp. 486–487.

25. E.g., Thurston Motor Lines, Inc. v. Jordan K. Rand, Ltd., 1983, 103 S.Ct. 1343, 460 U.S. 533, 75 L.Ed.2d 260.

26. 1936, 57 S.Ct. 96, 299 U.S. 109, 81 L.Ed. 70.

27. 57 S.Ct. at 100, 299 U.S. at 118. "This is prose so beautiful that it seems almost profane to analyze it. Yet, committing the sacrilege will make it clear that as long as we are forbidden to look at both sides of the pleadings the distinction between 'controversies that are basic and those that are collateral, between disputes that are necessary and those that are merely possible' still have us without compass—lost in a maze." Chadbourn & Levin, Original Jurisdiction of Federal Questions, 1942, 90 U.Pa.L.Rev. 639, 671.

28. Mishkin, The Federal "Question" in the District Courts, 1953, 53 Col.L.Rev. 157, 165, 168.

29. ALI Study, p. 179. See also Currie, The Federal Courts and the American Law Institute (Part II), 1969, 36 U.Chi.L.Rev. 268, 276–279.

30. Cohen, The Broken Compass: The Requirement that a Case Arise "Directly" Under Federal Law, 1967, 115 U.Pa.L.Rev. 890. Professor Cohen suggests, at 916, that the relevant pragmatic considerations include such matters as: "the extent of the caseload increase for federal trial courts if jurisdiction is recognized; the extent to which cases of this class will, in practice, turn on issues of state or federal law; the extent of the necessity for an expert federal tribunal to handle issues of state law that do arise; the extent of the necessity for a sympathetic federal tribunal in cases of this class." See also Redish, Federal Jurisdiction: Tensions in the Allocation of Judicial Power, 1980, p. 71.

But the Note cited note 19 above says, at 980–981: "The jurisdictional grants do not invite ad hoc assessments of 'pragmatic need.' "

In 1964 Judge Henry J. Friendly suggested that there may be some room for finding federal jurisdiction, though both the right and the remedy are state-created, if an important question is an essential element in the case.[31] Two important Supreme Court cases have built on that insight and provided additional guidelines—though still no clear answers—on what is a federal-question case. They are Franchise Tax Board v. Construction Laborers Vacation Trust,[32] decided in 1983, and a 1986 decision, Merrell Dow Pharmaceuticals Inc. v. Thompson.[33]

The Franchise Tax Board must surely be one of the most complicated decisions the Supreme Court has handed down in this area of law, but its complications mainly go to the application of the well-pleaded complaint rule, which is discussed in the next section.[34] For present purposes it is enough to note that, in a unanimous opinion by Justice Brennan the Court, as has been noted above, held that the Holmes test that a suit arises under the law that creates the cause of action is more useful as a description of the vast majority of cases that come within the federal-question jurisdiction than for defining those that are beyond the jurisdiction of the district courts.[35] The Court found that there was no federal jurisdiction of the case before it, saying that Congress has given the district courts jurisdiction to hear, either originally or by removal, "only those cases in which a well-pleaded complaint establishes either that federal law creates the cause of action or that the plaintiff's right to relief necessarily depends on resolution of a substantial question of federal law." [36]

The Merrell Dow case was a state-court suit against the manufacturer of Bendectin, alleging that use of that drug had caused birth defects. The complaint alleged a variety of claims under state law, but also alleged that the promotion of Bendectin violated the Federal Food, Drug, and Cosmetic Act (FDCA). On the basis of this allegation defendant removed the case to federal court, but the propriety of removal turned on whether the case could have been brought in federal court as a federal-question case.[37] The parties agreed, and the Supreme Court assumed, that there is no federal cause of action for FDCA violations. A bare majority of the Court held that there is no federal-question jurisdiction of a suit alleging a violation of a federal statute as an element of a state cause of action when Congress has determined that there should be no private federal cause of action. Plaintiffs had argued that their allegation about FDCA meant that the case presented a "substantial" question of federal law, within the meaning of the Franchise Board test. Five justices, speaking through Justice Stevens, disagreed. "[T]he con-

31. T.B. Harms Co. v. Eliscu, C.A.2d, 1964, 339 F.2d 823, 827, certiorari denied 85 S.Ct. 1534, 381 U.S. 915, 14 L.Ed.2d 435.

32. 1983, 103 S.Ct. 2841, 463 U.S. 1, 77 L.Ed.2d 420.

33. 1986, 106 S.Ct. 3229, 478 U.S. 804, 92 L.Ed.2d 650, noted 1987, 39 Baylor L.Rev. 543.

34. See § 18 below. The best exploration of the complexities of the decision is in Note, Federal Jurisdiction over Preemption Claims: A Post–Franchise Tax Board Analysis, 1984, 62 Texas L.Rev. 895.

35. 103 S.Ct. at 2846, 463 U.S. at 9. See note 19 above.

36. 103 S.Ct. at 2856, 463 U.S. at 27–28.

37. See § 38 below.

gressional determination that there should be no federal remedy for the violation of this federal statute is tantamount to a congressional conclusion that the presence of a claimed violation of the statute as an element of a state cause of action is insufficiently 'substantial' to confer federal-question jurisdiction." [38]

The federal law that will support federal-question jurisdiction may be the Constitution, a statute of the United States, an administrative regulation, or a treaty.[39] There was once a contention that federal admiralty law is a "law of the United States" within the meaning of the jurisdictional statute, and thus that admiralty suits could be brought on the "law side" of the court, where trial is to a jury, rather than on the "admiralty side," where admittedly they can be brought [40] but where there is no jury. After conflicting decisions in the courts of appeals, the Supreme Court rejected this argument.[41] The decision is of general significance because of the clear recognition that the problem was to determine the intent of the draftsmen of the 1875 act, rather than to rely on constitutional conceptions. The decisions construing the statute would be more coherent if this distinction had always been observed.

Beyond this, however, the decision just mentioned states a rule confined to the esoteric area of admiralty and maritime jurisdiction. As had been anticipated,[42] it has now been held that "federal common law," when it exists,[43] is among the "laws of the United States" referred to in the jurisdictional statute, and that, except in the admiralty field, there is

38. 106 S.Ct. at 3235, 478 U.S. at 814. Justice Brennan dissented, in an opinion joined by Justices White, Marshall, and Blackmun. There is an excellent discussion of the implications of the case in Alleva, Prerogative Lost: The Trouble with Statutory Federal Question Doctrine After Merrell Dow, 1991, 52 Ohio St.L.J. 1477.

The Merrell Dow test is applied, and jurisdiction found not to exist, in Smith v. Industrial Valley Title Ins. Co., C.A.3d, 1992, 957 F.2d 90, and Clark v. Velsicol Chemical Corp., C.A.4th, 1991, 944 F.2d 196, certiorari denied 112 S.Ct. 1173, — U.S. —, 117 L.Ed.2d 418.

39. 13A Wright, Miller & Cooper, Jurisdiction 2d § 3563.

40. On the admiralty jurisdiction of the federal courts, see 28 U.S.C.A. § 1333; 14 Wright, Miller & Cooper, Jurisdiction 2d §§ 3671–3678; ALI Study, pp. 225–245; Robertson, Admiralty Procedure and Jurisdiction After the 1966 Unification, 1976, 74 Mich.L.Rev. 1627; Landers, by Sleight of Rule: Admiralty Unification and Ancillary and Pendent Jurisdiction, 1972, 51 Texas L.Rev. 50; Black, Admiralty Jurisdiction: Critique and Suggestions, 1950, 50 Col. L.Rev. 259; Symposium, 1969, 5 Willamette L.Rev. 367.

Admiralty jurisdiction extends to a collision between two recreational boats on navigable waters even though no commercial activity was involved. Foremost Ins. Co. v. Richardson, 1982, 102 S.Ct. 2654, 457 U.S. 668, 73 L.Ed.2d 300. And admiralty jurisdiction exists over a limitation-of-liability suit by the owner of a boat that caught fire while it was docked at a marina, since there was a potential hazard to maritime commerce, and the fire had a substantial relationship to a traditional maritime activity. Sisson v. Ruby, 1990, 110 S.Ct. 2892, 497 U.S. 358, 111 L.Ed.2d 292.

41. Romero v. International Terminal Operating Co., 1959, 79 S.Ct. 468, 358 U.S. 354, 3 L.Ed.2d 368. See Currie, The Silver Oar and All That: A Study of the Romero Case, 1959, 27 U.Chi.L.Rev. 1; Kurland, The Romero Case and Some Problems of Federal Jurisdiction, 1960, 73 Harv.L.Rev. 817; 14 Wright, Miller & Cooper, Jurisdiction 2d § 3673.

42. See ALI Study, pp. 180–182; Kurland, note 41 above, at 829–833; Comment, 1964, 74 Yale L.J. 325.

43. See § 60 below.

federal-question jurisdiction of claims based on federal common law.[44]

Laws that are applicable exclusively to the District of Columbia are not "laws * * * of the United States" for purposes of federal-question jurisdiction.[45] Although there has been uncertainty on the matter, it seems probable that a claim based on an interstate compact is within federal-question jurisdiction,[46] and that the same is true of claims based on customary international law.[47]

It is not enough for federal-question jurisdiction that federal law has been incorporated by reference in a state statute.[48] In the converse situation, in which an Act of Congress incorporates state law, the state law becomes federal law for purposes of federal-question jurisdiction.[49]

§ 18. Determination From the Pleadings [1]

In the preceding section it was seen that the scope of the 1875 statute, conferring general original jurisdiction of federal-question cases, was narrowed considerably from what the words of the statute might seem to suggest by restrictive definitions of what is a "case arising under" federal law. The scope of the jurisdiction was further narrowed by application of a rigid pleading rule that the federal question must appear on the face of the well-pleaded complaint.

The first Supreme Court decision to construe the 1875 statute applied such a rule, citing Chitty to determine what allegations are proper,[2] and the rule has been insisted upon ever since. Its continuing vitality was firmly endorsed by a unanimous Court in the extremely important—and extremely complicated—1983 decision of Franchise Tax Board v. Construction Laborers Vacation Trust.[3] The rule severely

---

44. Illinois v. City of Milwaukee, 1972, 92 S.Ct. 1385, 406 U.S. 91, 31 L.Ed.2d 712, noted 1973, 49 Denv.L.J. 609; Nat. Farmers Union Ins. Co. v. Crow Tribe of Indians, 1985, 105 S.Ct. 2447, 2451, 471 U.S. 845, 850, 85 L.Ed.2d 818.

45. 28 U.S.C.A. § 1366.

46. Jurisdiction was upheld in League to Save Lake Tahoe v. Tahoe Regional Planning Agency, C.A.9th, 1974, 507 F.2d 517, certiorari denied 95 S.Ct. 1398, 420 U.S. 974, 43 L.Ed.2d 654. This result is supported in Comment, Federal Question Jurisdiction to Interpret Interstate Compacts, 1975, 64 Geo.L.J. 87. See also Engdahl, Construction of Interstate Compacts: A Questionable Federal Question, 1965, 51 Va.L.Rev. 987, 1025.

47. ALI Study, p. 181; Filartiga v. Pena–Irala, C.A.2d, 1980, 630 F.2d 876; Forti v. Suarez–Mason, D.C.Cal.1987, 672 F.Supp. 1531; Note, Enforcement of International Human Rights in the Federal Courts After Filartiga v. Pena–Irala, 1981, 67 Va.L.Rev. 1379.

48. Buethe v. Britt Airlines, Inc., C.A.7th, 1984, 749 F.2d 1235; Nuclear En-

gineering Co. v. Scott, C.A.7th, 1981, 660 F.2d 241; United Air Lines v. Division of Indus. Safety, C.A.9th, 1980, 633 F.2d 814, certiorari denied 102 S.Ct. 485, 454 U.S. 944, 70 L.Ed.2d 255; Greene, Hybrid State Law in the Federal Courts, 1969, 83 Harv. L.Rev. 289, 322–325.

49. Willis v. Craig, C.A.9th, 1977, 555 F.2d 724; Haas v. Pittsburgh Nat. Bank, D.C.Pa.1973, 60 F.R.D. 604. But cf. Sylvane v. Whelan, D.C.N.Y.1981, 506 F.Supp. 1355.

§ 18

1. 13B Wright, Miller & Cooper, Jurisdiction 2d § 3566; ALI Study, pp. 169–172.

2. Gold–Washing & Water Co. v. Keyes, 1877, 96 U.S. 199, 203, 24 L.Ed. 656.

3. 1983, 103 S.Ct. 2841, 463 U.S. 1, 77 L.Ed.2d 420. The legal propositions for which the case stands can be stated without too much difficulty, but the fact situation, the issues, and the holding of the case itself defy summarization in any manageable space. To borrow a phrase Professor John B. Oakley of the Davis Law School used in limits the number of cases that may be initiated in or removed to federal district court, and it sometimes produces "awkward results,"[4] but the Court adheres to it because it "makes sense as a quick rule of thumb."[5]

Because of this rule, it does not suffice for jurisdiction that the answer raises a federal question. If the basis for original federal-question jurisdiction is that the federal courts have a special expertness in applying federal law, and that assertions of federal law will be received more hospitably in a federal court, it would seem that the courts should have jurisdiction where there is some federal issue regardless of which pleading raises it. The rule to the contrary probably stems from the conceptual notion that unless the initial pleading is sufficient to invoke the jurisdiction of the court, the court lacks power to require responsive pleadings or take any other act in the case. The rule is an inconvenient one, especially when, as seen in section 17, the existence of a federal question is said to depend on a genuine and present controversy. How a controversy can be found in plaintiff's pleading alone "still remains a mystery of the judicial process."[6]

Plaintiff's expectation that its opponent will raise a federal question cannot serve to bring the case to federal court. In 1871 the Louisville & Nashville Railroad settled a claim for damages that a Mr. and Mrs. Mottley had against it by agreeing to give the Mottleys free passes each year for the remainder of their lives. In 1906 an Act of Congress became law prohibiting free transportation by railroads, and the following year the railroad did not give the Mottleys their pass. They sued in federal court for specific performance, alleging that the statute did not apply in the circumstances of their case, and that if it did it was unconstitutional. The Mottleys won in the trial court, but on appeal the Supreme Court held that the trial court had no jurisdiction.[7] "It is not enough," the Court said, "that the plaintiff alleges some anticipated defense to his cause of action, and asserts that the defense is invalidated by some provision of the Constitution of the United States. Although such allegations show that very likely, in the course of the litigation, a question under the Constitution would arise, they do not show that the

---

another connection, it is "the Exam Question from Hell masquerading as a federal lawsuit." The case is analyzed in detail in 13B Wright, Miller & Cooper, Jurisdiction 2d § 3566, at pp. 90–106. The most valuable commentary on the case itself is Note, Federal Jurisdiction over Preemption Claims: A Post–Franchise Tax Board Analysis, 1984, 62 Texas L.Rev. 893.

4. 103 S.Ct. at 2847, 463 U.S. at 12.

5. 103 S.Ct. at 2847, 463 U.S. at 11.

The rule is sharply criticized in Doernberg, There's No Reason for It: It's Just Our Policy: Why the Well–Pleaded Complaint Rule Sabotages the Purposes of Federal Question Jurisdiction, 1987, 38 Hastings L.J. 597.

6. Chadbourn & Levin, Original Jurisdiction of Federal Questions, 1942, 90 U.Pa. L.Rev. 639, 671.

In the Franchise Tax Board case Justice Brennan says it is "possible to conceive of a rational jurisdictional system in which the answer as well as the complaint would be consulted" before a determination was made whether the case was properly commenced in federal court or removed there, and he describes proposals, in ALI Study § 1312 and elsewhere, to that effect, but notes that "those proposals have not been adopted." 103 S.Ct. 2847 n. 9, 463 U.S. 10 n. 9.

7. Louisville & N.R. Co. v. Mottley, 1908, 29 S.Ct. 42, 211 U.S. 149, 53 L.Ed. 126.

suit, that is, the plaintiff's original cause of action, arises under the Constitution." [8]   Thus, the Mottleys were forced to begin anew in the state courts. Again they were successful below but the question as to the meaning and validity of the 1906 Act, though insufficient as a basis for original jurisdiction, did suffice to support appeal from the Kentucky courts to the United States Supreme Court, where, three years after their first appearance, they finally lost on the merits. [9]   The case illustrates strikingly the proposition that original federal-question jurisdiction is not coextensive with the constitutional grant of jurisdiction, [10] but it also shows the practical inconvenience of the "well-pleaded complaint" rule.

The plaintiff is not permitted to anticipate defenses in his complaint. [11]   Nor can it win admission to federal court by allegations to support its own case that are not required by nice pleading rules. If title to land is in doubt because of some matter of federal law, there is federal jurisdiction to entertain a bill to remove a cloud on title [12] but not a suit to quiet title, [13] since allegations about the nature of the cloud are proper in the first kind of action but improper in the second. An action to enjoin another from using land that, by federal law, is asserted to be plaintiff's raises a proper federal question, [14] but if plaintiff is out of possession, it has an adequate legal remedy in an action for ejectment, in which allegations as to the title of land are not proper, and it cannot invoke federal-question jurisdiction. [15]

The well-pleaded complaint rule focuses on claims, not theories. A single claim supported by alternative theories in the complaint is not the basis for federal-question jurisdiction unless federal law is essential to each of the theories. [16]

These subtle distinctions, dependent on long-forgotten lore as to the forms of action, are hard enough to apply in conventional law suits.

---

8.   29 S.Ct. at 43, 211 U.S. at 152.

9.   Louisville & N.R. Co. v. Mottley, 1911, 31 S.Ct. 265, 219 U.S. 467, 55 L.Ed. 297.

10.   See § 17 n. 16 above.

11.   Phillips Petroleum Co. v. Texaco, Inc., 1974, 94 S.Ct. 1002, 415 U.S. 125, 39 L.Ed.2d 209.

12.   Hopkins v. Walker, 1917, 37 S.Ct. 711, 244 U.S. 486, 61 L.Ed. 1270; New York v. White, C.A.2d 1975, 528 F.2d 336.

13.   Shulthis v. McDougal, 1912, 32 S.Ct. 704, 225 U.S. 561, 56 L.Ed. 1205; Marshall v. Desert Properties Co., C.C.A.9th, 1939, 103 F.2d 551, certiorari denied 60 S.Ct. 74, 308 U.S. 563, 84 L.Ed. 473.

14.   Lancaster v. Kathleen Oil Co., 1916, 36 S.Ct. 711, 241 U.S. 551, 60 L.Ed. 1161.

15.   White v. Sparkill Realty Corp., 1930, 50 S.Ct. 186, 280 U.S. 500, 74 L.Ed. 578; Taylor v. Anderson, 1914, 34 S.Ct. 724, 234

U.S. 74, 58 L.Ed. 1218; Joy v. St. Louis, 1906, 26 S.Ct. 478, 201 U.S. 332, 50 L.Ed. 776; Heirs of Burat v. Board of Levee Commrs., C.A.5th, 1974, 496 F.2d 1336, certiorari denied 95 S.Ct. 625, 419 U.S. 1049, 42 L.Ed.2d 644.

The Supreme Court recognized this as the general rule but was able to create an exception where Indian tribes are claiming title. Oneida Indian Nation of New York State v. County of Oneida, 1974, 94 S.Ct. 772, 414 U.S. 661, 39 L.Ed.2d 73.

16.   Christianson v. Colt Industries Operating Corp., 1988, 108 S.Ct. 2166, 2174–2175, 486 U.S. 800, 810–811, 100 L.Ed.2d 811. (Although this case involved § 1338 rather than § 1331, the Court made it clear that "arising under" has the same meaning in both statutes. 108 S.Ct. at 2174, 486 U.S. at 808–809.

There has been added uncertainty about how the the well-pleaded complaint rule is to be applied in the new statutory action for a declaratory judgment.[17] There are two possibilities. The complaint in a declaratory judgment action may be judged on its own merits; if it reveals a federal claim, then jurisdiction will exist. But this, as will be seen, would permit some cases to be brought in federal court that could not be so brought absent the Declaratory Judgment Act. The alternative is to say that the declaratory action may be entertained in federal court only if the coercive action that would have been necessary, absent declaratory-judgment procedure, might have been so brought.

There is no difficulty in an action to establish that plaintiff has an affirmative federal right. If the Jones Company brings an action for a declaratory judgment that its patent is valid and being infringed by a device manufactured by Smith, the federal claim necessarily appears on the face of the complaint, and if there were no declaratory-judgment procedure, Jones Company could have brought a coercive action for damages or injunction.

The matter is somewhat more difficult where the suit is for a declaratory judgment that the other party does *not* have a federal right. If Jones Company does not sue, but merely threatens Smith, he will have a lively interest in determining whether the patent is valid and whether his device is infringing. Prior to the Declaratory Judgment Act, his action to resolve this question would not, absent diversity, have been within federal jurisdiction.[18] Nevertheless it is settled that Smith can sue for a declaratory judgment of invalidity or noninfringement.[19] Again the federal nature of the claim appears on the complaint for declaratory judgment. Here the precise issue could have been litigated in federal court in a coercive action brought by Jones Company, and this is thought to suffice, even though Smith could not have brought a coercive action. As the Court put it in Franchise Tax Board: "Federal courts have regularly taken original jurisdiction over declaratory judgment suits in which, if the declaratory judgment defendant brought a coercive action to enforce its rights, that suit would necessarily present a federal question." [20]

17. 10A Wright, Miller & Kane, Civil 2d § 2767; Trautman, Federal Right Jurisdiction and the Declaratory Remedy, 1954, 7 Vand.L.Rev. 445; Mishkin, The Federal "Question" in the District Courts, 1953, 53 Col.L.Rev. 157, 177–184.

18. American Well Works Co. v. Layne & Bowler Co., 1916, 36 S.Ct. 585, 241 U.S. 257, 60 L.Ed. 987.

19. Hanes Corp. v. Millard, C.A.1976, 531 F.2d 585, 594 n. 8, 174 U.S.App.D.C. 253; E. Edelmann & Co. v. Triple–A Specialty Co., C.C.A.7th, 1937, 88 F.2d 852, certiorari denied 57 S.Ct. 673, 300 U.S. 680, 81 L.Ed. 884.

20. 103 S.Ct. at 2851, 463 U.S. at 19. The E. Edelmann case, note 19 above, was cited with approval. But in Franchise Tax Board itself the Court found an exception to the principle stated in the text. There is no federal jurisdiction of an action brought by a state or a state agency for a declaratory judgment, even though the party sued by the state could have brought a coercive action arising under federal law. The Court found "good reasons why the federal courts should not entertain suits by the States to declare the validity of their regulations despite possibly conflicting federal law." 103 S.Ct. at 2852, 463 U.S. at 21.

The hardest situation had been thought to be where a party seeks a declaration that it is immune, by virtue of federal law, from a nonfederal claim that the other party may have. Suppose the controversy between the Louisville & Nashville Railroad and the Mottleys had arisen after passage of the Declaratory Judgment Act. Could the railroad sue in federal court for a declaratory judgment that the statute relieved it from its obligation to give Mr. and Mrs. Mottley a pass? On the narrow view it could not, for, absent the declaratory procedure, the federal claim would arise only as a defense to the passholders' common-law action for breach of contract, and the only possible coercive action, that by the Mottleys for specific performance, would raise no federal question.[21] The broader view would permit the declaratory action since in that suit the railroad's federal claim of an immunity to the common-law action would appear on the face of the railroad's complaint. Though this would mean that the federal courts were entertaining a suit not within their jurisdiction prior to passage of the Declaratory Judgment Act, this broad view would have the merit of being far simpler to apply than the narrow view and would be a sensible departure from the use of the old forms of action as tests for federal jurisdiction. Some early decisions from lower courts had apparently adopted the broader view,[22] but in the Skelly Oil case there was strong language from the Supreme Court that it would "distort the limited procedural purpose of the Declaratory Judgment Act" to permit a party by "artful pleading" to anticipate a defense based on federal law and thus to bring a suit within federal jurisdiction that could not otherwise be heard in federal court.[23]

In Franchise Tax Board the Supreme Court expressly accepted the narrower view.[24] It endorsed the Skelly Oil case, which it described as standing for the proposition that "if, but for the availability of the declaratory judgment procedure, the federal claim would arise only as a defense to a state created action, jurisdiction is lacking."[25] It noted strong criticism of the Skelly Oil doctrine, but said any change in it must come from Congress.[26]

21. Louisville & N.R. Co. v. Mottley, 1908, 29 S.Ct. 42, 211 U.S. 149, 53 L.Ed. 126.

22. 10A Wright, Miller & Kane, Civil 2d § 2767 n. 12.

23. Skelly Oil Co. v. Phillips Petroleum Co., 1950, 70 S.Ct. 876, 880, 339 U.S. 667, 673–674, 94 L.Ed. 1194. See dicta to the same effect in Public Serv. Comm. of Utah v. Wycoff Co., 1952, 73 S.Ct. 236, 242–243, 344 U.S. 237, 248–249, 97 L.Ed. 291.

This proposition is attacked in Doernberg & Mushlin, The Trojan Horse: How the Declaratory Judgment Act Created a Cause of Action and Expanded Federal Jurisdiction While the Supreme Court Wasn't Looking, 1989, 36 UCLA L.Rev. 529; Doernberg & Mushlin, History Comes Calling: Dean Griswold Offers New Evidence about the Jurisdictional Debate Surrounding the Enactment of the Declaratory Judgment Act, 1989, 37 UCLA L.Rev. 139.

24. 103 S.Ct. at 2848–2853, 463 U.S. at 14–22.

25. 103 S.Ct. at 2850, 463 U.S. at 16.

26. 103 S.Ct. at 2851 n. 17, 463 U.S. at 18 n. 17. The Court quoted the criticism of the Skelly Oil rule in ALI Study § 1311, at pp. 170–171.

The application of the Skelly Oil principle to cases in which it is asserted that a state-law claim has been preempted by federal law occurs primarily where it is sought to remove such a case from state court to federal court and is discussed elsewhere.[27] But a party may also go to federal court for an injunction against state officers from enforcing a state statute or for a declaratory judgment that they cannot enforce the statute because it is preempted by federal law. There is federal-question jurisdiction of a suit of this kind.[28] As the great case of Ex parte Young[29] shows, the Supremacy Clause creates an implied right of action for injunctive relief against state officers who are threatening to violate the federal Constitution or laws,[30] and this right of action is equally available though the party seeks only a declaratory judgment.[31] This right of action can be asserted only where a state official is the defendant, so that there is no federal jurisdiction if a private party sues another private party, contending that federal law has preempted a duty he would otherwise owe to the defendant.[32]

It has been seen that the federal question must appear in the complaint. A corollary rule is that federal jurisdiction exists if the complaint states a case arising under federal law, even though on the merits the party may have no federal right. If its claim is bad, then judgment is to be given against it on the merits, and even if the court is persuaded that federal law does not give the right the party claims, it is to dismiss for failure to state a claim on which relief can be granted rather than for want of jurisdiction.[33] Dismissal for want of jurisdiction is appropriate only if the federal claim is not "substantial", i.e., it is frivolous or a mere matter of form.[34]

---

27. See § 21 below.

28. Shaw v. Delta Air Lines, Inc., 1983, 103 S.Ct. 2890, 2899 n. 14, 463 U.S. 85, 96 n. 14, 77 L.Ed.2d 490; Lawrence County v. Lead–Deadwood School Dist., 1985, 105 S.Ct. 695, 697 n. 6, 469 U.S. 256, 259 n. 6, 83 L.Ed.2d 635.

29. 1908, 28 S.Ct. 441, 209 U.S. 123, 52 L.Ed. 714. See § 48 below.

30. Guaranty Nat. Ins. Co. v. Gates, C.A.9th, 1990, 916 F.2d 508, 511–512.

31. First Nat. Bank of Eastern Arkansas v. Taylor, C.A.8th, 1990, 907 F.2d 775, 777 n. 3, certiorari denied 111 S.Ct. 442, 498 U.S. 972, 112 L.Ed.2d 425; 13B Wright, Miller & Cooper, Federal Practice & Procedure: Jurisdiction 2d § 3566, at pp. 98–99.

32. Colonial Penn Group, Inc. v. Colonial Deposit Co., C.A.1st, 1987, 834 F.2d 229, 237; Lowe v. Ingalls Shipbuilding, C.A.5th, 1984, 723 F.2d 1173, 1180 n. 7; Note, note 3 above, at 895–896.

33. Bell v. Hood, 1946, 66 S.Ct. 773, 327 U.S. 678, 90 L.Ed. 939. To the same effect see The Fair v. Kohler Die & Specialty Co.,

1913, 33 S.Ct. 410, 228 U.S. 22, 57 L.Ed. 716; Montana–Dakota Utilities Co. v. Northwestern Public Serv. Co., 1951, 71 S.Ct. 692, 341 U.S. 246, 95 L.Ed. 912; Duke Power Co. v. Carolina Environmental Study Group, 1978, 98 S.Ct. 2620, 2629, 438 U.S. 59, 69, 57 L.Ed.2d 595; Jackson Transit Auth. v. Local Div. 1285, Amalgamated Transit Union, 1982, 102 S.Ct. 2202, 2206 n. 6, 457 U.S. 15, 21 n. 6, 72 L.Ed.2d 639.

Dissenting from the denial of certiorari in Yazoo County Indus. Development Corp. v. Suthoff, 1982, 102 S.Ct. 1032, 454 U.S. 1157, 71 L.Ed.2d 316, Justice Rehnquist has questioned the soundness of Bell v. Hood and whether its doctrine, described in the text, can be reconciled with Rule 12.

34. 13B Wright, Miller & Cooper, Jurisdiction 2d § 3564; Hagans v. Lavine, 1974, 94 S.Ct. 1372, 1378–1379, 415 U.S. 528, 536–538, 39 L.Ed.2d 577; Bell v. Hood, 1946, 66 S.Ct. 773, 327 U.S. 678, 90 L.Ed. 939; Levering & Garrigues Co. v. Morrin, 1933, 53 S.Ct. 549, 550, 289 U.S. 103, 105, 77 L.Ed. 1062. See Seid, The Tail Wags the Dog: Hagans v. Lavine and Pendent Jurisdiction, 1975, 53 J.Urban Law 1.

§ 19. Scope of the Jurisdiction [1]

Under a 1990 statute, 28 U.S.C.A. § 1367(a), if a federal court has original jurisdiction of a case because of a federal question, it also has "supplemental jurisdiction over all other claims that are so related to claims in the action within such original jurisdiction that they form part of the same case or controversy under Article III of the United States Constitution. Such supplemental jurisdiction shall include claims that involve the joinder or intervention of additional parties." Behind this statute lies a long, and sometimes erratic, history.

In the Osborn case, Chief Justice Marshall observed that "when a question to which the judicial power of the Union is extended by the constitution, forms an ingredient of the original cause, it is in the power of congress to give the circuit courts jurisdiction of that cause, although other questions of fact or of law may be involved in it." [2] There could hardly be any other rule. When the Supreme Court is reviewing a state-court decision it can and does confine its review to the federal question in the case,[3] but a court of original jurisdiction could not function, as Marshall recognized, unless it had power to decide all the questions that the case presents. This functional justification of the Osborn rule finds support also in the constitutional language, which grants jurisdiction over "cases" rather than over "questions."

The Osborn doctrine was expanded in Siler v. Louisville & Nashville R. Co.[4] A state order regulating rates was attacked as unauthorized by state law and as unconstitutional by federal law. The Supreme Court said: "The Federal questions as to the invalidity of the state statute because, as alleged, it was in violation of the Federal Constitution, gave the circuit court jurisdiction, and, having properly obtained it, that court had the right to decide all the questions in the case, even though it decided the Federal questions adversely to the party raising them, or even if it omitted to decide them at all, but decided the case on local or state questions only." [5] In fact the state regulation was held invalid on state grounds, and the Court declared this preferable to an unnecessary determination of federal constitutional questions. This rule, that the

---

§ 19

1. 13B Wright, Miller & Cooper, Jurisdiction 2d §§ 3567–3567.3; ALI Study, § 1313 and Commentary thereto; Note, The Res Judicata Implications of Pendent Jurisdiction, 1981, 66 Cornell L.Rev. 608.

2. Osborn v. Bank of United States, 1824, 9 Wheat. 738, 823, 6 L.Ed. 204.

3. See § 107 below.

4. 1909, 29 S.Ct. 451, 213 U.S. 175, 53 L.Ed. 753.

5. 29 S.Ct. at 454–455, 213 U.S. at 191.

In Schmidt v. Oakland Unified Sch. Dist., 1982, 102 S.Ct. 2612, 457 U.S. 594, 73 L.Ed.2d 245, it was held to have been an abuse of discretion to decide a case on federal constitutional grounds when it might

have been decided on a pendent state ground.

But pendent jurisdiction, and the doctrine of the Siler case, have a different scope when applied to suits against a state. Those doctrines cannot displace the Eleventh Amendment. A claim that state officials violated state law in carrying out their official responsibilities is a claim against the state that is prohibited by the Eleventh Amendment, see § 48 below, and this principle applies as well to state-law claims brought into federal court under pendent jurisdiction. Pennhurst State School & Hospital v. Halderman, 1984, 104 S.Ct. 900, 917–919, 465 U.S. 89, 117–121, 79 L.Ed.2d 67.

federal court need not, and perhaps should not, decide the federal issues but may resolve the case entirely on state grounds is not, as the Osborn rule was, a rule of necessity. It is, however, a useful rule. It avoids decision of constitutional questions where possible, and it permits one lawsuit, rather than two, to resolve the entire controversy.

Finally in Hurn v. Oursler [6] the Court extended this rule of "pendent jurisdiction," as until recently it was usually known, to situations where decision of state issues must be justified solely on the ground of procedural convenience. In that case plaintiffs were claiming that defendants had incorporated an idea from a play written by plaintiffs and shown to defendants in a play that defendants later wrote. Plaintiffs sought to enjoin infringement of their copyrighted play, unfair competition in unauthorized use of the copyrighted play, and unfair competition through interference with plaintiffs' rights in an uncopyrighted version of the play. The trial court, finding no copyright infringement, dismissed the first claim on its merits and then dismissed the other two claims, which raised no federal question, for want of jurisdiction. The Supreme Court considered that the Siler rule applied. It measured the scope of federal jurisdiction in terms of the elusive concept of a "cause of action." If a plaintiff presented "two distinct grounds," one state and one federal, "in support of a single cause of action," the federal court had jurisdiction of the entire claim, but if plaintiff's assertions amounted to "two separate and distinct causes of action," there was jurisdiction only over the federal "cause of action." [7]

Applying this test, the Court held that the claim of unfair competition with regard to the copyrighted play arose from the same cause of action as the claim of infringement of the copyrighted play, and thus was within the pendent federal jurisdiction. The claim with regard to the uncopyrighted version of the play was held to involve a separate and distinct cause of action not within the pendent jurisdiction principle. This illustrates the difficulty of a test centering on so elastic a yardstick as the extent of a "cause of action." It could be reasonably argued that a single cause of action encompassed the right to protection of the play in all its versions.

The indefiniteness of the Hurn v. Oursler test created difficulties, and uncertainty in application, among the lower courts. A test based on the concept of "cause of action" inevitably became "the source of considerable confusion" [8] and the application it received in many lower court cases was, as the Court later said, "unnecessarily grudging." [9] Although the Hurn doctrine was purportedly codified in the 1948 Judi-

---

6. 1933, 53 S.Ct. 586, 289 U.S. 238, 77 L.Ed. 1148.

7. 53 S.Ct. at 589, 289 U.S. at 245–246.

8. United Mine Workers v. Gibbs, 1966, 86 S.Ct. 1130, 1138, 383 U.S. 715, 724, 16 L.Ed.2d 218.

9. United Mine Workers v. Gibbs, 1966, 86 S.Ct. 1130, 1139, 383 U.S. 715, 725, 16 L.Ed.2d 218.

cial Code, the statute created problems of its own rather than solving old problems.[10]

Thus, the Court returned to the subject in 1966 in the case of United Mine Workers v. Gibbs.[11] Gibbs sued the union in federal court, alleging that the union had brought improper pressure on his employer to discharge him. He asserted both a federal claim of violation of the Taft–Hartley Act and a state claim of unlawful conspiracy to interfere with his contract of employment. After verdict for Gibbs, the trial court held that he had failed to establish his federal claim, but entered judgment for him on the basis of the state claim. The union argued that the court lacked jurisdiction to give judgment on the state claim, but the Supreme Court, though holding for the union on the merits, expressly decided that there was pendent jurisdiction to decide the state claim.

The Court discarded the test of Hurn v. Oursler, cast in terms of "cause of action", and held that as a matter of constitutional power pendent jurisdiction exists whenever the state and federal claims "derive from a common nucleus of operative fact" and are such that a plaintiff "would ordinarily be expected to try them all in one judicial proceeding." [12]

The Court distinguished sharply, however, between constitutional power and discretionary exercise of that power. Even before Gibbs, some lower courts had recognized a discretion in the trial judge to refuse to hear a pendent state claim after dismissal of the federal claim if judicial economy would not be served by hearing the state claim.[13] The Court in Gibbs broadened the discretion to refuse to hear the pendent claim. The trial court, it said, should look to "considerations of judicial economy, convenience and fairness of litigants" in exercising its discretion, and should avoid needless decisions of state law.[14] It appeared to require dismissal of the state claim if the federal claim, though substantial enough to confer jurisdiction, were dismissed before trial.[15] Even if

10. 28 U.S.C.A. § 1338(b): "The district court shall have original jurisdiction of any civil action asserting a claim of unfair competition when joined with a substantial and related claim under the copyright, patent or trade-mark laws." See Note, The Doctrine of Hurn v. Oursler and the New Judicial Code, 1952, 37 Iowa L.Rev. 406.

11. 1966, 86 S.Ct. 1130, 383 U.S. 715, 16 L.Ed.2d 218.

12. 86 S.Ct. at 1138, 383 U.S. at 725.

One commentator read the requirements of a common nucleus of fact and that the claims would ordinarily be expected to be tried in a single proceeding as alternatives, either of which creates power to hear the claim. Baker, Toward a Relaxed View of Federal Ancillary and Pendent Jurisdiction, 1972, 33 U.Pitt.L.Rev. 759, 764–765. The courts and the other commentators have always regarded them as cumulative re-

quirements, both of which must be satisfied. E.g., ALI Study, p. 210; Mason v. Richmond Motor Co., D.C.Va.1986, 625 F.Supp. 883, 887, affirmed C.A.4th, 1987, 825 F.2d 407.

13. "Where the federal element which is the basis for jurisdiction is disposed of early in the case, as on the pleadings, it smacks of the tail wagging the dog to continue with a federal hearing of the state claim." McFaddin Exp., Inc. v. Adley Corp., C.A.2d, 1965, 346 F.2d 424, 427, certiorari denied 86 S.Ct. 643, 382 U.S. 1026, 15 L.Ed.2d 539.

14. 86 S.Ct. at 1139, 383 U.S. at 726.

15. 86 S.Ct. at 1139, 383 U.S. at 726.

If a case was removed to federal court from state court, and the federal claims that were the basis for removal have been eliminated from the case, the district court has discretion to remand the pendent state-this were not the case, the state claim should be dismissed without prejudice if the state issues substantially predominate,[16] or if the possibility of jury confusion would justify separating the state and federal claims for trial.[17] The argument is stronger for retaining the state claim if it is closely tied to questions of federal policy,[18] as was true in Gibbs itself where the scope of the state claim was limited by the federal doctrine of preemption.[19] The question of power to hear the pendent claim, the Court said, should ordinarily be resolved on the pleadings, but the discretion whether to dismiss the state claim exists throughout the case.[20]

In 1974, however, in Hagans v. Lavine [21] the court seemed to encourage hearing pendent claims. It said that "it is evident from Gibbs that pendent state law claims are not always, or even almost always, to be dismissed and not adjudicated. On the contrary, given advantages of economy and convenience and no unfairness to litigants, Gibbs contemplates adjudication of these claims." [22] The Court also indicated that the argument for hearing the pendent claim is much stronger where, instead of being a state-created claim, the pendent claim is a federal claim that is not independently within federal jurisdiction because the amount in controversy is insufficient.[23] Finally the Court held that if the federal claim that gives jurisdiction raises a significant constitutional issue, the interest in avoiding unnecessary decision of constitutional questions suggests that ordinarily it is preferable to dispose of the case, if possible, by deciding the pendent claim, whether state or federal, rather than resolving the constitutional issue.[24]

Gibbs had presented a classic illustration of pendent jurisdiction. There was one plaintiff, one defendant, and a federal claim joined with a state-created claim. Hagans, as has been seen, broadened the applica-

---

law claims to state court rather than dismissing them. Carnegie–Mellon University v. Cohill, 1988, 108 S.Ct. 614, 484 U.S. 343, 98 L.Ed.2d 720. See the discussion of the case in § 41 at notes 18–20.

But in Rosado v. Wyman, 1970, 90 S.Ct. 1207, 1212–1214, 397 U.S. 397, 402–405, 25 L.Ed.2d 442, it was held that a federal court has discretion to decide a claim within its pendent jurisdiction after the claim that gives it jurisdiction has become moot. In that case the Court said that pendent jurisdiction is based on "the commonsense policy" of "the conservation of judicial energy and the avoidance of multiplicity of litigation." 90 S.Ct. at 1214, 397 U.S. at 405.

Cases in which jurisdiction of pendent claims was retained although the federal claim was dismissed without trial are cited in 13B Wright, Miller & Cooper, Jurisdiction 2d § 3567.1 n. 20.

16. 86 S.Ct. at 1139, 383 U.S. at 726–727.

The state claim can also be left undecided if it is not pressed until too late in the proceeding. Mayor of City of Philadelphia v. Educational Equality League, 1974, 94 S.Ct. 1323, 1336, 415 U.S. 605, 627, 39 L.Ed.2d 630.

17. 86 S.Ct. at 1139, 383 U.S. at 727.

See also Moor v. County of Alameda, 1973, 93 S.Ct. 1785, 1799, 411 U.S. 693, 716–717, 36 L.Ed.2d 596.

18. 86 S.Ct. at 1139, 383 U.S. at 727.

19. 86 S.Ct. at 1140, 383 U.S. at 729.

20. 86 S.Ct. at 1139, 383 U.S. at 727.

21. 1974, 94 S.Ct. 1372, 415 U.S. 528, 39 L.Ed.2d 577. The decision was scathingly criticized in Seid, The Tail Wags the Dog: Hagans v. Lavine and Pendent Jurisdiction, 1975, 53 J.Urban Law 1.

22. 94 S.Ct. at 1383, 415 U.S. at 545–546.

23. 94 S.Ct. at 1385, 415 U.S. at 548.

24. 94 S.Ct. at 1383–1384, 415 U.S. at 546–547.

tion of pendent jurisdiction to include a federal claim for which no amount in controversy was required joined with a second federal claim that did not satisfy the amount requirement. Presumably that kind of pendent jurisdiction will now fade away again, since a 1980 amendment removed the amount requirement from the general federal-question statute.[25]

There was another, more surprising and more controversial, expansion of pendent jurisdiction after Gibbs. It had always been understood that the same parties must be involved for pendent jurisdiction to be used.[26] In 1971, however, Judge Henry J. Friendly, writing for the Second Circuit, led the way in holding that pendent jurisdiction would allow taking jurisdiction of a state claim against one party if it were related closely enough to a federal claim against another party, even though there was no independent jurisdictional base for the state claim.[27]

This concept of "pendent parties," as it quickly came to be called, found favor with other lower courts and with the commentators.[28] The Supreme Court seemed to give cautious approval to the concept in 1976 in Aldinger v. Howard.[29] That was a suit in which a civil-rights claim against county officials was joined with a state-law claim against the county itself. There was no independent basis of jurisdiction against the county, since there was no diversity between it and the plaintiff and a municipal corporation, such as a county, was not then regarded as a "person" against whom an action would lie under the Civil Rights Act of 1871, 42 U.S.C.A. § 1983.[30] Thus, the county could be retained as a defendant only if the concept of "pendent parties" was valid.

The Supreme Court approached the issue guardedly and refused to "formulate any general, all-encompassing jurisdictional rule."[31] It discerned important differences between the traditional pendent-jurisdiction situation and that in which it is sought to add a completely new party, but believed that ultimately the question must be decided "upon the deductions which may be drawn from congressional statutes as to whether Congress wanted to grant this sort of jurisdiction to federal

---

25. See § 32 below.

26. E.g., Wojtas v. Village of Niles, C.A.7th, 1964, 334 F.2d 797, certiorari denied 1965, 85 S.Ct. 655, 379 U.S. 964, 13 L.Ed.2d 558; Note, 1968, 81 Harv.L.Rev. 657, 662–664.

27. Astor–Honor, Inc. v. Grosset & Dunlap, Inc., C.A.2d, 1971, 441 F.2d 627; Leather's Best, Inc. v. S.S. Mormaclynx, C.A.2d, 1971, 451 F.2d 800.

28. See cases and commentaries cited in 13B Wright, Miller & Cooper, Jurisdiction 2d § 3567.2 nn. 2, 13.

29. 1976, 96 S.Ct. 2413, 427 U.S. 1, 49 L.Ed.2d 276.

See Currie, Pendent Parties, 1978, 45 U.Chi.L.Rev. 753.

30. In Monell v. New York City Dept. of Social Services, 1978, 98 S.Ct. 2018, 436 U.S. 658, 56 L.Ed.2d 611, the Court overruled an earlier decision and held that a municipal corporation could be a "person" and suable under 42 U.S.C.A. § 1983. "But Monell in no way qualifies the holding of Aldinger that the jurisdictional questions presented in a case such as this one are statutory as well as constitutional, a point on which the dissenters in Aldinger agreed with the Court." Owen Equipment & Erection Co. v. Kroger, 1978, 98 S.Ct. 2396, 2402 n. 12, 437 U.S. 365, 372 n. 12, 57 L.Ed.2d 274.

31. 96 S.Ct. at 2419, 427 U.S. at 13.

courts." [32]   Since the Court then thought that Congress had clearly excluded counties from liability in § 1983, the general jurisdictional statutes should not be read as bringing a county back in as a "pendent party."   The Court recognized that other statutory grants and other alignments of parties and claims might call for a different result, and it concluded with two observations: "If the new party sought to be impleaded is not otherwise subject to federal jurisdiction, there is a more serious obstacle to the exercise of pendent jurisdiction than if parties already before the court are required to litigate a state law claim. Before it can be concluded that such jurisdiction exists, a federal court must satisfy itself not only that Art. III permits it, but that Congress in the statutes conferring jurisdiction has not expressly or by implication negated its existence." [33]   The Court also hinted that the pendent-party concept might well be proper where the federal claim is one of which the federal courts have exclusive jurisdiction, so that "the argument of judicial economy and convenience can be coupled with the additional argument that *only* in a federal court may all of the claims be tried together." [34]

That was where things stood until 1989, when the Supreme Court handed down its surprising decision in Finley v. United States.[35]   By a 5–4 vote, the Court held that in a suit against the United States under the Federal Tort Claims Act, two private parties, whose negligence allegedly also was involved, could not be joined as defendants when there was no independent basis for jurisdiction against them.   Even if the decision were read narrowly, as a construction of the particular federal statute, it would have been contrary to the strong hint in Aldinger that pendent-party jurisdiction would be proper where, as is true of the Federal Tort Claims Act, federal jurisdiction is exclusive and a refusal to allow joinder of pendent parties would require separate suits in state and federal court.[36]   But it seemed clear that this reading would have been much too narrow.   Although the Court was at pains to say that it was not limiting Gibbs and the other cases allowing pendent-claim jurisdiction, it was effectively putting an end to pendent-party jurisdiction.   Justice Scalia, writing for the majority, assumed, without deciding that pendent-party jurisdiction would be within the constitutional grant of judicial power, but held that "an affirmative grant of pendent-party jurisdiction" must be found in a statute.[37]   This was quite different from Aldinger, where it had been said that pendent-party jurisdiction, if within the constitutional grant of judicial power, may be exercised so long as "Congress in the statutes conferring jurisdiction has not expressly or by implication negated its existence." [38]   Indeed there was reason for concern over

32. 96 S.Ct. at 2421, 427 U.S. at 17.

33. 96 S.Ct. at 2422, 427 U.S. at 18.

34. 96 S.Ct. at 2422, 427 U.S. at 18.

35. 1989, 109 S.Ct. 2003, 490 U.S. 545, 104 L.Ed.2d 593.

36. The Finley Court recognized this. "We acknowledged this potential consider-

ation in Aldinger, * * * but now conclude that the present statute permits no other result." 109 S.Ct. at 2010, 490 U.S. at 555.

37. 109 S.Ct. at 2009, 490 U.S. at 553.

38. 96 S.Ct. at 2422, 427 U.S. at 18.

whether the accepted rules about ancillary jurisdiction had survived Finley.[39]

At the end of the Finley opinion the Court said: "Whatever we say regarding the scope of jurisdiction conferred by a particular statute can of course be changed by Congress."[40] Congress responded with unusual alacrity. The following year it adopted a new statute[41] that codifies the doctrines of "pendent jurisdiction" and "ancillary jurisdiction" under a new name, "supplemental jurisdiction."[42] There is much room for justifiable criticism of § 1367 insofar as it applies to diversity cases and to what used to be called ancillary jurisdiction.[43] Its codification of pendent jurisdiction, however, has caused no problems. Its purpose was to overrule Finley and it has done that.[44] The statute specifically reaches joinder of additional parties and pendent-party jurisdiction may now be exercised except "as expressly provided otherwise by Federal statute."[45] Supplemental jurisdiction extends to all claims that "form part of the same case or controversy under Article III of the United States Constitution." Since the discussion in Gibbs of the power to exercise pendent jurisdiction was expressly put in constitutional terms,[46] the Gibbs tests—that the claims arise from a common nucleus of operative facts and that they be such that a plaintiff would ordinarily be expected to try them in one judicial proceeding—are the appropriate tests in applying the statute to pendent claims and pendent parties.[47] Subsection (c) defines the circumstances in which the court may decline to exercise supplemental jurisdiction. The statutory language seems to

---

39. See § 9 above.

40. 109 S.Ct. at 2010, 490 U.S. at 556.

41. 28 U.S.C.A. § 1367, added by Act of Dec. 1, 1990, Pub.L. 101–650, § 310. The new statute applies only to actions commenced after December 1, 1990.

The 1990 statute responds to a recommendation earlier that year by the Federal Courts Study Committee, a distinguished group created by Act of Congress. Its Recommendation 2.B.2.b was: "Congress should expressly authorize federal courts to assert pendent jurisdiction over parties without an independent federal jurisdictional basis." Report of the Federal Courts Study Committee, April 2, 1990, p. 47.

See Oakley, Recent Statutory Changes in the Law of Federal Jurisdiction and Venue: The Judicial Improvements Acts of 1988 and 1990, 1991, 24 U.C.Davis L.Rev. 735, 757–769; Wolf, Codification of Supplemental Jurisdiction: Anatomy of a Legislative Proposal, 1992, 14 W.New Eng.L.Rev. 1; Note, The Congressional Resurrection of Supplemental Jurisdiction in the Post–Finley Era, 1991, 42 Hastings L.J. 1611.

42. The Supreme Court had twice found it unnecessary to decide whether there were any principled differences between "pendent jurisdiction," discussed in this section, and "ancillary jurisdiction," discussed in

§ 9 above. Aldinger v. Howard, 1976, 96 S.Ct. 2413, 2420, 427 U.S. 1, 13, 49 L.Ed.2d 276; Owen Equipment & Erection Co. v. Kroger, 1978, 98 S.Ct. 2396, 2401 n. 8, 437 U.S. 365, 370, n. 8, 57 L.Ed.2d 274. Yet it seemed convenient to keep the terms separate, with pendent jurisdiction referring to those claims asserted by plaintiffs in their complaints, while ancillary jurisdiction was used to refer to the joinder, ordinarily by a party other than the plaintiff, of additional claims and parties after the complaint has been filed. The new name used in § 1367 blurs that useful distinction.

43. See § 9 above.

44. E.g., Hollman v. U.S., D.C.Pa.1992, 783 F.Supp. 221 (allowing pendent-party jurisdiction in a Federal Tort Claims Act case); McCray v. Holt, D.C.Fla.1991, 777 F.Supp. 945, 948.

45. 28 U.S.C.A. § 1367(a).

46. 86 S.Ct. at 1138, 383 U.S. at 735.

47. E.g., Corporate Resources, Inc. v. Southeast Suburban Ambulatory Surgical Center, Inc., D.C.Ill.1991, 774 F.Supp. 503, 505; Arnold v. Kimberly Quality Care Nursing Service, D.C.Pa.1991, 762 F.Supp. 1182, 1186.

confine that discretion quite narrowly, but the legislative history says that the statute "codifies the factors that the Supreme Court has recognized as providing legitimate bases upon which a district court may decline jurisdiction over a supplemental claim,"[48] and many courts have been exercising their discretion to exercise or to decline jurisdiction just as they did under Gibbs.[49]

If a pendent state claim is properly within the supplemental jurisdiction of the federal court, it should not be ground for objection that venue would not be proper if that claim were sued on alone, or that personal jurisdiction has been obtained only by virtue of a federal statute allowing nationwide service on the federal claim. As was seen earlier, however,[50] to date the cases are divided on this point.

If a court determines to exercise supplemental jurisdiction over a state-created claim, state substantive law is controlling on the state claim.[51] Evidence Rule 501 seems to state very clearly that the state rules of privilege are to apply on the pendent state claim, but there is disagreement on this point.[52]

§ 20. "Protective Jurisdiction"[1]

As is seen elsewhere, in one well-known case three members of the Supreme Court took the view, rejected however by the other six, that Article I of the Constitution empowers Congress to confer on "constitutional" federal courts powers beyond those defined in Article III.[2] Since the rejection of that theory, commentators have put forward, and some judges have endorsed, a more subtle theory that would reach the same result while purporting to respect the limits of Article III. The theory, popularly known as "protective jurisdiction," is that, with regard to subjects where Congress has legislative power, it can pass a statute granting federal jurisdiction and that the jurisdictional statute is itself a

48. H.R. Rep. No. 734, 101st Cong., 2d Sess., 1990, at 2. See Oakley, note 41 above, at 766–768.

49. But see Executive Software North America, Inc. v. United States Dist. Court, C.A.9th, 1994, 15 F.3d 1484, where § 1367(c) is narrowly construed.

The statute also includes a tolling provision to preserve litigants' rights to effective relief in state court in the event a federal court declines, as permitted by subsection (c), to exercise its supplemental jurisdiction. 28 U.S.C.A. § 1367(d).

50. See § 9 above.

51. Gibbs, 86 S.Ct. at 1139, 383 U.S. at 726.

52. See § 93 below.

§ 20

1. 13B Wright, Miller & Cooper. Jurisdiction 2d § 3565; Goldberg–Ambrose, The Protective Jurisdiction of the Federal Courts, 1983, 30 UCLA L.Rev. 542; Cross, Congressional Power to Extend Federal Jurisdiction to Disputes Outside Article III: A Critical Analysis from the Perspective of Bankruptcy, 1993, 87 Nw.U.L.Rev. 1188, 1210–1224; Comment, A Comprehensive Theory of Protective Jurisdiction: The Missing "Ingredient" of "Arising Under" Jurisdiction, 1993, 61 Fordham L.Rev. 1235; Note, Over–Protective Jurisdiction: A State Sovereignty Theory of Federal Questions, 1989, 102 Harv.L.Rev. 1948; Note, The Theory of Protective Jurisdiction, 1982 57 N.Y.U.L.Rev. 933.

2. National Mut. Ins. Co. of Dist. of Columbia v. Tidewater Transfer Co., 1949, 69 S.Ct. 1173, 337 U.S. 582, 93 L.Ed. 1556, discussed § 11 above and § 24 below.

"law of the United States" within Article III, even though Congress has not enacted any substantive rule of decision and thus state law is to be applied.[3] The argument had been of particular consequence with regard to § 301 of the Taft–Hartley Act,[4] which grants jurisdiction of suits for violation of labor-management contracts in industries affecting interstate commerce, but does not set out any rules of decisions for such suits. That particular controversy has now been resolved. In the Lincoln Mills case[5] a majority of the Supreme Court read § 301 as requiring the federal courts, in such cases, to fashion and apply a federal common law of labor-management contracts. Though this interpretation poses its own difficulties,[6] it obviates any jurisdictional problem, since federal law then provides both the right and the remedy, and the case is one of true federal-question jurisdiction. Prior to the Lincoln Mills decision, however, the First Circuit, assuming that state law was to govern at least some of the issues in a § 301 case, found the statute nevertheless to be a valid exercise of "protective jurisdiction."[7] In the Lincoln Mills case itself, two members of the Court rejected the view that federal law was to be applied, but concurred in the result upholding § 301 on the "protective jurisdiction" theory.[8] Justice Frankfurter, on the other hand, in a dissenting opinion that considered the precedents and the arguments at great length, asserted that " 'protective jurisdiction,' once the label is discarded, cannot be justified under any view of the allowable scope to be given to Article III. * * * The theory must have as its sole justification a belief in the inadequacy of state tribunals in determining state law. The Constitution reflects such a belief in the specific situation within which the Diversity Clause was confined. The intention to remedy such supposed defects was exhausted in this provision of Article III."[9] Thus, the case gave no definitive answer about the validity of the "protective jurisdiction" theory and it remained in the realm of speculation.

The argument for "protective jurisdiction" rests on Chief Justice

3. Wechsler, Federal Jurisdiction and the Revision of the Judicial Code, 1948, 13 Law & Contemp.Probs. 216, 224–225; Mishkin, The Federal "Question" Jurisdiction of the District Courts, 1953, 53 Col. L.Rev. 157, 184–196. Professor Wechsler apparently would allow a grant of such "protective jurisdiction" wherever Congress has substantive legislative power, while Professor Mishkin would limit such jurisdiction to those areas of the law where Congress has an articulated and active policy regulating a field. See also Casto, The Federal Court's Protective Jurisdiction Over Torts Committed in Violation of the Law of Nations, 1986, 18 Conn.L.Rev. 467.

This concept is the basis for proposed legislation that would allow the federal courts to hear consumer class actions that are governed by state law. The jurisdictional implications are discussed in Note, Protective Jurisdiction and Adoption as Alternative Techniques for Conferring Jurisdiction on Federal Courts in Consumer Class Actions, 1971, 69 Mich.L.Rev. 710.

4. 29 U.S.C.A. § 185.

5. Textile Workers Union of America v. Lincoln Mills of Alabama, 1957, 77 S.Ct. 912, 353 U.S. 448, 1 L.Ed.2d 972.

6. See Bickel & Wellington, Legislative Purpose and the Judicial Process: The Lincoln Mills Case, 1957, 71 Harv.L.Rev. 1.

7. International Broth. of Teamsters v. W.L. Mead, Inc., C.A.1st, 1956, 230 F.2d 576, 580–581.

8. Justices Harlan and Burton, concurring in the result, 77 S.Ct. at 920, 353 U.S. at 460.

9. 77 S.Ct. at 930, 353 U.S. at 474–475.

Marshall's opinion in the Osborn case,[10] where he said that Congress could authorize a bank chartered by it to sue in federal court though only state issues were involved, and on the line of cases permitting a trustee in bankruptcy to pursue in federal court a private cause of action arising under and wholly governed by state law.[11] It is true that in those cases there is, in the background at least, some federal right, other than the bare right to sue in federal court. The bank's very existence was as a creature of federal law; in the bankruptcy cases the trustee is an officer of a federal court, and his ancillary suit is a part of the whole bankruptcy process, itself governed by federal law. Nevertheless attempts to distinguish Osborn and the bankruptcy cases do not seem entirely successful.[12] Despite this, it is difficult to believe that the Court, if clearly confronted with the question, would accept the commentators' proposals for "protective jurisdiction" when to do so would have such drastic consequences on the accepted understanding of Article III as a limitation on the federal courts.[13]

It now seems quite probable that the validity of "protective jurisdiction" is an intellectually interesting question that fortunately will never need to be resolved.[14] The key case is Verlinden B.V. v. Central Bank of Nigeria.[15] The Foreign Sovereign Immunities Act of 1976 grants federal jurisdiction of, among other things, a suit by an alien against a foreign state.[16] The governing law is either international law or state law; in any event, it is not federal law. The Second Circuit found that the case did not come within the "arising under" language of Article III, § 2, and it rejected the notion of "protective jurisdiction". The Supreme Court reversed. It held that the Act is much more than merely a jurisdictional statute. In it, the Court said, Congress had exercised its power to regulate foreign commerce by setting forth comprehensive rules governing sovereign immunity. "The Act codifies the standards governing

10. Osborn v. Bank of the United States, 1824, 9 Wheat. 738, 6 L.Ed. 204. See § 17 above.

11. Schumacher v. Beeler, 1934, 55 S.Ct. 230, 293 U.S. 367, 79 L.Ed. 433; Williams v. Austrian, 1947, 67 S.Ct. 1443, 331 U.S. 642, 91 L.Ed. 1718.

12. In his Lincoln Mills dissent, where he makes an extended effort to distinguish the cases, Justice Frankfurter is forced to conclude that there are "some elements of analytical similarity" between the Osborn case and the case before him, and that the bankruptcy cases do show at least "a superficial analogy." 77 S.Ct. at 934, 353 U.S. at 481–482. See also his dissent in National Mut. Ins. Co. of Dist. of Columbia v. Tidewater Transfer Co., 1949, 69 S.Ct. 1173, 1198 n. 3, 337 U.S. 582, 652 n. 3, 93 L.Ed. 1556, where he offers what seems a somewhat different distinction of the bankruptcy cases.

13. "[P]rotective jurisdiction, in each of its variants, is fundamentally unsound and should be rejected." Cross, note 1 above, at 1224; "There is, however, a technical problem with the protective-jurisdiction theory: What is the federal law under which the case arises? The only federal law in the picture is the federal law creating federal jurisdiction. To say that a case arises under federal law whenever a federal statute gives jurisdiction is to destroy all limitations on federal jurisdiction." Currie, Federal Jurisdiction in a Nutshell, 3d ed. 1990, p. 94. See also Redish, Federal Jurisdiction: Tensions in the Allocation of Judicial Power, 1980, pp. 59–63.

14. See Chemerinsky, Federal Jurisdiction, 1989, p. 230.

15. 1983, 103 S.Ct. 1962, 461 U.S. 480, 76 L.Ed.2d 81.

16. 28 U.S.C.A. § 1330(a). See 14A Wright, Miller & Cooper, Jurisdiction 2d § 3662.

foreign sovereign immunity as an aspect of substantive federal law * * *; and applying those standards will generally require interpretation of numerous points of federal law." [17]

On this view of the statute it provides "true" federal-question jurisdiction. It is immaterial that the 1976 statute comes into the case by negating a defense of sovereign immunity that the defendant might otherwise have, since the rule that the federal question must appear in the well-pleaded complaint and may not enter in anticipation of a defense [18] is a construction of the statute for general federal-question jurisdiction and is not a limit on the constitutional grant of jurisdiction in Article III.[19] On this analysis it became unnecessary to consider the "protective jurisdiction" theory.[20]

The Court again found that it need not adopt a theory of "protective jurisdiction" in a 1989 decision, Mesa v. California.[21] Section 1442(a) of Title 28 allows a federal officer to remove from state court to federal court any civil or criminal prosecution commenced against him for any act done under color of office. The Court held that this allows removal only if the officer alleges a colorable federal defense. "[I]t is the raising of a federal question in the officer's removal petition that constitutes the federal law under which the action against the federal officer arises for Art. III purposes. The removal statute itself merely serves to overcome the 'well-pleaded complaint' rule which would otherwise preclude removal even if a federal defense were alleged. * * * Adopting the Government's view would eliminate the substantive Art. III foundation of § 1442(a)(1) and unnecessarily present grave constitutional problems." [22] The statement about "grave constitutional problems" is about as close as the Court is likely ever to come to passing on the validity of "protective jurisdiction."

§ 21. Criminal Prosecutions

The federal district courts are given by statute original jurisdiction, exclusive of the courts of the states, of all offenses against the laws of the United States.[1] Thus, they always have jurisdiction where a federal

---

17. 103 S.Ct. at 1973, 461 U.S. at 496–497.

18. See § 18 above.

19. 103 S.Ct. at 1972, 461 U.S. at 494–495.

20. 103 S.Ct. at 1970 n. 17, 461 U.S. at 491 n. 17.

On similar reasoning a lower court found it unnecessary to resort to "protective jurisdiction" to uphold the Price–Anderson Amendments Act. That statute establishes federal jurisdiction over "public liability actions" relating to nuclear incidents though the rules of decision are to be derived from state law. 42 U.S.C.A. §§ 2014(hh), 2210(n)(2). The court found that there are important federal questions that are indispensable incidents of those actions. In re TMI Litigation Cases Consolidated II, C.A.3d, 1991, 940 F.2d 832, certiorari denied 112 S.Ct. 1262, ___ U.S. ___, 117 L.Ed.2d 491.

21. 1989, 109 S.Ct. 959, 489 U.S. 121, 103 L.Ed.2d 99.

22. 109 S.Ct. at 969–969, 489 U.S. at 136–137.

§ 21

1. 18 U.S.C.A. § 3231.

offense is charged, and in some few instances have jurisdiction, by removal from state court, of state criminal prosecutions.[2]

In 1812 the Supreme Court held that there are no federal common-law crimes.[3] Recent scholarly research suggests considerable doubt about whether this holding was in accord with the intent of Congress when it passed the Judiciary Act of 1789,[4] but sound or unsound, the principle of no common-law crimes is now well settled.[5] Since federal criminal prosecutions must, therefore, rest on an Act of Congress defining the crime, it is clear that all such cases "arise under" the laws of the United States, within the meaning of the constitutional grant of jurisdiction, and the state criminal prosecutions that come to the federal courts on removal do so because the circumstances under which the statutes provide for removal are enough to raise a federal question, within the meaning of the constitutional language even if not within the usual original federal-question jurisdiction.[6]

Although the federal courts have exclusive jurisdiction of federal criminal prosecutions, the same act may constitute a federal crime and a state crime. In such a situation the offender may be prosecuted by both sovereigns, at least under the decisions to date.[7]

The federal statutes, notably in Title 18 of the United States Code, define a great many offenses that are crimes against the United States,[8] and criminal cases occupy much of the attention of the district courts.[9] Special provision is made in the statutes for crimes committed on the high seas or in territories that are under the exclusive jurisdiction of the United States and where, therefore, there is no state criminal code to cover ordinary offenses.[10] A special District of Columbia Code performs the same function for that area. Further the so-called Assimilative Crimes Act, first adopted in 1825, provides that in areas within a state subject to federal jurisdiction, if an act is committed that would be a

2. 28 U.S.C.A. §§ 1441, 1442a, 1443. In the year ended June 30, 1991, there were 12 criminal cases removed from state court to federal court. Ann.Rep. of the Director of the Administrative Office of the United States Courts, 1991, Table D–2.

3. U.S. v. Hudson & Goodwin, 1812, 7 Cranch 32, 3 L.Ed. 259. See also U.S. v. Coolidge, 1816, 1 Wheat. 415, 4 L.Ed. 124.

4. Warren, New Light on the History of the Federal Judiciary Act of 1789, 1923, 37 Harv.L.Rev. 49, 73; 2 Crosskey, Politics and the Constitution in the History of the United States, 1953, pp. 763–784; Ritz, Rewriting the History of the Judiciary Act of 1789, 1990, pp. 126–148.

5. E.g., U.S. v. Eaton, 1892, 12 S.Ct. 764, 144 U.S. 677, 36 L.Ed. 591; U.S. v. George, 1913, 33 S.Ct. 412, 228 U.S. 14, 57 L.Ed. 712.

6. Tennessee v. Davis, 1879, 100 U.S. 257, 25 L.Ed. 648; Mesa v. California, 1989, 109 S.Ct.959, 489 U.S. 121, 103 L.Ed.2d 99.

7. Bartkus v. Illinois, 1959, 79 S.Ct. 676, 359 U.S. 121, 3 L.Ed.2d 684; Abbate v. U.S., 1959, 79 S.Ct. 666, 359 U.S. 187, 3 L.Ed.2d 729; U.S. v. Logan, C.A.5th, 1991, 949 F.2d 1370, 1380 n. 16.

8. See Schwartz, Federal Criminal Jurisdiction and Prosecutors' Discretion, 1948, 13 Law & Contemp.Probs. 64.

9. In the year ended Sept. 30, 1992, there were 47,472 criminal cases commenced in the district courts, as against 230,509 civil cases. Ann.Rep. of the Director of the Administrative Office of the United States Courts, 1992, Tables C–2, D–2.

10. 18 U.S.C.A. § 7.

crime by state law it is also a crime by federal law.[11]

§ 22.   Civil Actions to Which the United States Is a Party [1]

The most frequent litigant in the courts of the United States is the United States. It is a party in more than one-fourth of the civil cases in the district courts.[2]

If the United States is plaintiff to an action, there are no jurisdictional difficulties. The Constitution defines the judicial power as extending to "Controversies to which the United States shall be a Party," and a statute grants jurisdiction, except as otherwise provided, in "all civil actions, suits or proceedings commenced by the United States, or by any agency or officer thereof expressly authorized to sue by Act of Congress." [3]

The United States Code is filled with sections authorizing federal litigation in various kinds of cases, but the government can sue even if there is no specific authorization. In such cases, however, it must have some interest to be vindicated sufficient to give it standing. It cannot lend its name to a suit merely for the benefit of some private individual.[4] It is not required, however, that the government's interest be pecuniary or proprietary. "The obligations which it is under to promote the interest of all, and to prevent the wrongdoing of one resulting in injury to the general welfare, is often of itself sufficient to give it a standing in court." [5] If suit by the United States is expressly authorized by Act of

---

11. 18 U.S.C.A. § 13. See U.S. v. Sharpnack, 1958, 78 S.Ct. 291, 355 U.S. 286, 2 L.Ed.2d 282, upholding the 1948 revision of this statute by which a continuing conformity to state law, rather than the assimilation of state law as of the date of enactment of the federal statute, is provided.

§ 22

1. 14 Wright, Miller & Cooper, Jurisdiction 2d §§ 3651–3659.

2. In the year ended September 30, 1992, 230,509 civil cases were commenced in the district courts. The United States was a party plaintiff in 35,453 of these cases and defendant in 27,147 cases. Ann. Rep. of the Director of the Administrative Office of the U.S. Courts, 1992, Table C–2. Rather surprisingly, the percentage of civil cases in which the United States is a party has dropped from 34% in 1981 to 27% in 1991.

3. 28 U.S.C.A. § 1345. It was once argued that the United States could not sue for damages for wrongs done to it, and was confined to criminal proceedings against the wrongdoer, but this view was rejected in Cotton v. U.S., 1850, 11 How. 229, 13 L.Ed. 675.

4. U.S. v. San Jacinto Tin Co., 1888, 8 S.Ct. 850, 125 U.S. 273, 31 L.Ed. 747; U.S. v. Kuehn, C.A.7th, 1977, 562 F.2d 427.

5. In re Debs, 1894, 15 S.Ct. 900, 906, 158 U.S. 564, 584, 39 L.Ed. 1092. See also Wyandotte Transp. Co. v. U.S., 1967, 88 S.Ct. 379, 389 U.S. 191, 19 L.Ed.2d 407; Sanitary Dist. of Chicago v. U.S., 1925, 45 S.Ct. 176, 266 U.S. 405, 69 L.Ed. 352; U.S. v. American Bell Tel. Co., 1888, 9 S.Ct. 90, 97, 128 U.S. 315, 367–368, 32 L.Ed. 450; Note, Nonstatutory Executive Authority to Bring Suit, 1972, 85 Harv.L.Rev. 1566.

It has been held that the United States has standing to seek to enjoin the practice of "sewer service," by which defendants bring state court actions against delinquent debtors and obtain default judgments on the basis of affidavits falsely reciting that service has been made. U.S. v. Brand Jewelers, Inc., D.C.N.Y.1970, 318 F.Supp. 1293, noted 1971, 37 Brook. L.Rev. 426, 84 Harv. L.Rev. 1930, 46 N.Y.U.L.Rev. 367, 20 J.Pub.L. 337, 24 Vand.L.Rev. 829, 17 Wayne L.Rev. 1287, 1971 Wis.L.Rev. 665. The court based standing on the authority of the United States to remove large-scale burdens on interstate commerce and on the authority to correct widespread deprivations, by what amounts to state action, of

Congress, there is no problem of standing; Congress has power to authorize the United States to be guardian of the public interest by bringing suit.[6]

The jurisdiction of the district courts in cases instituted by the United States is generally concurrent with the state courts, though if such actions are commenced in state court they may be removed by a nonresident defendant to federal court.[7] Suits involving seizures, or to recover fines, penalties, or forfeitures incurred under any Act of Congress, are exclusively in the jurisdiction of the district courts.[8]

Although it is commonly said that when the United States sues, it comes into court on an equality with private litigants,[9] in fact it enjoys a number of advantages, both statutory and court-made,[10] of which perhaps the most important is that it is not bound by statutes of limitations save as Congress may have imposed them.[11] In 1966 a statute was enacted for the first time providing a general statute of limitations applicable to most actions brought by the United States or by a federal

the right not to be deprived of property without due process of law.

It has also been held that the United States has standing to seek invalidation of state miscegenation statutes, U.S. v. Brittain, D.C.Ala.1970, 319 F.Supp. 1058, to prevent a city from taxing property owned by a foreign government when the tax would violate a treaty obligation of the United States. U.S. v. City of Glen Cove, D.C.N.Y.1971, 322 F.Supp. 149, affirmed C.A.2d, 1971, 450 F.2d 884, and to protect national security, U.S. v. Marchetti, C.A.4th, 1972, 466 F.2d 1309, certiorari denied 93 S.Ct. 553, 409 U.S. 1063, 34 L.Ed.2d 516.

A more restrictive view has been taken in recent cases holding that in the absence of statutory authorization the United States lacks standing to sue to protect the constitutional rights of mentally retarded individuals in state mental hospitals. U.S. v. Mattson, C.A.9th, 1979, 600 F.2d 1295; U.S. v. Solomon, C.A.4th, 1977, 563 F.2d 1121. This result was changed by statute in 1980. 42 U.S.C.A. § 1997. It has been held also that the United States lacks standing to challenge allegedly unconstitutional practices of a city police department. U.S. v. City of Philadelphia, C.A.3d, 1980, 644 F.2d 187.

See generally Note, Fourteenth Amendment Rights of Action in Favor of the United States, 1981, 61 B.U.L.Rev. 1159.

6. U.S. v. Raines, 1960, 80 S.Ct. 519, 526, 362 U.S. 17, 27, 4 L.Ed.2d 524 (civil rights action); U.S. Fidelity & Guar. Co. v. U.S., for Benefit of Kenyon, 1907, 27 S.Ct. 381, 204 U.S. 349, 51 L.Ed. 516 (suit in the name of the United States by a materialman on the bond of a contractor for public works).

7. 28 U.S.C.A. § 1441. See § 38 below.

The American Law Institute proposed not to allow removal of actions commenced by the United States in a state court. ALI Study, p. 257.

8. 28 U.S.C.A. §§ 1355, 1356.

9. E.g., Brent v. Bank of Washington, 1836, 10 Pet. 596, 614, 9 L.Ed. 547; U.S. v. Stinson, 1905, 25 S.Ct. 426, 426–427, 197 U.S. 200, 205, 49 L.Ed. 724.

10. 14 Wright, Miller & Cooper, Jurisdiction 2d § 3652. For example, the United States is given extra time to file an answer, Fed.R.Civ.Proc. 12(a), and to take an appeal, Fed.R.App.Proc. 4(a)(1). Only recently was provision made for taxation of costs against the United States and the statute limits the taxable costs. 28 U.S.C.A. § 2412; 10 Wright, Miller & Kane, Civil 2d § 2672. The United States enjoys special evidentiary privileges. 8 Wright, Miller & Marcus, Civil 2d § 2019. In a rescission action the United States is not required to make tender. Causey v. U.S., 1916, 36 S.Ct. 365, 240 U.S. 399, 60 L.Ed. 711. Fees and mileage need not be tendered to a witness subpoenaed on behalf of the United States or an officer or agency thereof. 28 U.S.C.A. § 1825; Fed.R.Civ. Proc. 45(b); Fed.R.Crim.Proc. 17(d).

11. U.S. v. Summerlin, 1940, 60 S.Ct. 1019, 310 U.S. 414, 84 L.Ed. 1283; Guaranty Trust Co. of New York v. U.S., 1938, 58 S.Ct. 785, 304 U.S. 126, 82 L.Ed. 1224.

officer or agency.[12] Other statutory restrictions that would bar suit by a private litigant are held not to apply if suit is by the United States.[13]

More difficult problems arise when the United States is named as a party defendant, for such litigation is involved with the mysteries of sovereign immunity and with a curiously conceptual approach to the nature of the jurisdiction.

It is now well settled—though for a century the rule was stated only in dicta—that the United States may not be sued without its consent.[14] Want of consent is a fundamental defect that may be asserted at any time and that is not subject to estoppel.[15] If Congress has in fact consented to a particular kind of suit, the stated rule long has been that the consent is to be strictly interpreted,[16] but in recent years the Court has regarded the defense of sovereign immunity with "disfavor," [17] and has viewed more liberally waivers of such immunity.[18]

Over the years Congress has successively broadened the consent of the United States to be sued. The Court of Claims was created in 1855 to determine money claims against the government founded on Acts of Congress, or regulations of executive departments, or express or implied contracts with the government.[19] This jurisdiction was expanded in 1887 by the passage of the Tucker Act, which grants jurisdiction additionally in cases founded upon the Constitution, and in cases for damages, not sounding in tort, in respect of which the plaintiff would be entitled to redress in a civil action or in admiralty if the United States were suable.[20] Jurisdiction under the Tucker Act is now in the United

12. 28 U.S.C.A. §§ 2415, 2416.

13. Department of Employment v. U.S., 1966, 87 S.Ct. 464, 466–467, 385 U.S. 355, 357–358, 17 L.Ed.2d 414 (Tax Injunction Act, 28 U.S.C.A. § 1341, inapplicable); Leiter Minerals, Inc. v. U.S., 1957, 77 S.Ct. 287, 352 U.S. 220, 1 L.Ed.2d 267 (Anti-Injunction Act, 28 U.S.C.A. § 2283, inapplicable).

14. U.S. v. Clarke, 1834, 8 Pet. 436, 444, 8 L.Ed. 1001; U.S. v. Eckford, 1867, 6 Wall. 484, 18 L.Ed. 920; U.S. v. Lee, 1882, 1 S.Ct. 240, 106 U.S. 196, 27 L.Ed. 171; Cunningham v. Macon & B. Ry. Co., 1883, 3 S.Ct. 292, 109 U.S. 446, 27 L.Ed. 992; Kansas v. U.S., 1907, 27 S.Ct. 388, 204 U.S. 331, 51 L.Ed. 510; Ickes v. Fox, 1937, 57 S.Ct. 412, 300 U.S. 82, 81 L.Ed. 525; Larson v. Domestic & Foreign Commerce Corp., 1949, 69 S.Ct. 1457, 337 U.S. 682, 93 L.Ed. 1628; Block v. North Dakota ex rel. Bd. of Univ. & School Lands, 1983, 103 S.Ct. 1811, 1816, 461 U.S. 273, 280, 75 L.Ed.2d 840.

Only Congress can consent. A district court's plenary power to see that its orders are obeyed does not allow it to reach into the coffers of the United States. Merrill Lynch, Pierce, Fenner & Smith, Inc. v. Jacks, C.A.10th, 1992, 960 F.2d 911.

15. Minnesota v. U.S., 1939, 59 S.Ct. 292, 305 U.S. 382, 83 L.Ed. 235; People of Enewetak v. U.S., C.A.Fed.1988, 864 F.2d 134, certiorari denied 109 S.Ct. 3198, 491 U.S. 909, 105 L.Ed.2d 706; U.S. v. Rochelle, C.A.5th, 1966, 363 F.2d 225.

16. E.g., Library of Congress v. Shaw, 1986, 106 S.Ct. 2957, 2963, 478 U.S. 310, 317, 92 L.Ed.2d 250; U.S. v. Sherwood, 1941, 61 S.Ct. 767, 771, 312 U.S. 584, 590, 85 L.Ed. 1058.

17. National City Bank of New York v. Republic of China, 1955, 75 S.Ct. 423, 426, 348 U.S. 356, 359, 99 L.Ed. 389; FHA v. Burr, 1940, 60 S.Ct. 488, 490, 309 U.S. 242, 245, 84 L.Ed. 724.

18. U.S. v. Yellow Cab Co., 1951, 71 S.Ct. 399, 404, 340 U.S. 543, 550, 95 L.Ed. 523. But see McMahon v. U.S., 1951, 72 S.Ct. 17, 19, 342 U.S. 25, 27, 96 L.Ed. 26.

19. Act of Feb. 24, 1855, 10 Stat. 612. See 17 Wright, Miller & Cooper, Jurisdiction 2d § 4101.

20. Act of Mar. 3, 1887, 24 Stat. 505. For the present provisions of the Tucker Act, see 28 U.S.C.A. §§ 1346(a)(2), 1491. See 14 Wright, Miller & Cooper, Jurisdiction 2d § 3657.

States Claims Court or, if the claim does not exceed a certain amount, now $10,000, in the district court.

In 1946 the Federal Tort Claims Act was adopted.[21] Though it contains many exceptions, it recognizes the general principle that the United States should be liable for the negligence of government employees if a private person would be liable under the same circumstances.[22] Jurisdiction under this act is exclusively in the district courts.

In addition to the three statutes discussed, there are a great many other statutes, of less general import, by which the United States has consented to be sued.[23]

There is some authority holding that if the United States has brought an action, defendant may not assert a counterclaim, even though the counterclaim is such that an independent action on it could be brought against the United States.[24] The better view, supported by recent cases, is that if the government has waived immunity, it should make no difference whether the claim is brought as an independent action or asserted as a counterclaim.[25]

It would seem that there ought to be no jurisdictional difficulties if the United States has consented to be sued, since such cases appear to be within the constitutional definition, "Controversies to which the United States shall be a Party." So indeed the Court had said.[26] But in

The Tucker Act is a jurisdictional statute only, and does not create any substantive right enforceable against the United States for money damages. U.S. v. Mitchell, 1980, 100 S.Ct. 1349, 1351, 445 U.S. 535, 538, 63 L.Ed.2d 607.

21. Act of Aug. 2, 1946, Title IV, 60 Stat. 812, 842. The substantive grant of jurisdiction is now found in 28 U.S.C.A. § 1346(b). See also 28 U.S.C.A. §§ 1402(b), 2401, 2402, 2411, 2412, 2671–2680.

22. 14 Wright, Miller & Cooper, Jurisdiction 2d § 3658.

23. 28 U.S.C.A. § 1346(a)(1) (suits to recover taxes); 46 U.S.C.A. § 741 et seq. (Suits in Admiralty Act); 46 U.S.C.A. §§ 781 et seq. (Public Vessels Act); 28 U.S.C.A. §§ 1347, 2409 (partition actions where United States is a tenant in common or joint tenant); 5 U.S.C.A. § 552(b) (Freedom of Information Act); 5 U.S.C.A. § 552(a)(1) (Privacy Act); 41 U.S.C.A. § 113(b) (suits on contracts); 28 U.S.C.A. § 1353 (rights to Indian lands); 42 U.S.C.A. § 405(c)(5)(g) (actions under Social Security Act). See 14 Wright, Miller & Cooper, Jurisdiction 2d § 3656.

The United States has consented to be named as a party in actions affecting property on which it has a lien, 28 U.S.C.A. § 2410, but the statute is not a grant of jurisdiction and suit must be in state court unless there is some other basis of federal jurisdiction. See cases cited 14 Wright, Miller & Cooper, Jurisdiction 2d § 3656 nn. 25–27.

24. E.g., U.S. v. Patterson, C.A.5th, 1953, 206 F.2d 345; In re Greenstreet, Inc., C.A.7th, 1954, 209 F.2d 660; and cases cited 6 Wright, Miller & Kane, Civil 2d § 1427 n. 17.

25. E.g., Frederick v. U.S., C.A.5th, 1967, 386 F.2d 481; U.S. v. Springfield, C.A.5th, 1960, 276 F.2d 798, 803–804; U.S. v. Silverton, C.A.1st, 1952, 200 F.2d 824; City of Newark v. U.S., C.A.3d, 1958, 254 F.2d 93; Thompson v. U.S., C.A.4th, 1957, 250 F.2d 43, 44; U.S. v. Summ, D.C.N.J. 1968, 282 F.Supp. 628; U.S. v. Southern Pac. Co., D.C.Cal.1962, 210 F.Supp. 760; U.S. v. Capital Transit Co., D.C.D.C.1952, 108 F.Supp. 348; and see 6 Wright, Miller & Kane, Civil 2d § 1427, pp. 202–205.

See also § 79 below, discussing whether a claim otherwise barred by sovereign immunity, the statute of limitations, or some other reason can be used defensively in an action by the United States.

26. Minnesota v. Hitchcock, 1902, 22 S.Ct. 650, 654, 185 U.S. 373, 384, 46 L.Ed. 954.

This was also the view of Justice Harlan in the plurality opinion in Glidden Co. v. Zdanok, 1962, 82 S.Ct. 1459, 1480, 370 U.S. 530, 564, 8 L.Ed.2d 671.

Williams v. United States [27] this natural reading was rejected, the judicial power was said to extend only to cases to which the United States is a party plaintiff, and suits against the government were regarded as not exercises of the constitutional judicial power at all. Some of the difficulties of this position have already been explored.[28] In particular, even if it be accepted that the clause of the Judiciary Article dealing with cases to which the United States is a party is inapplicable, cases under the Tucker Act, the Tort Claims Act, and similar legislation would seem to be cases "arising under" the laws of the United States, and thus within the constitutional judicial power.[29] Despite the conceptual difficulties introduced by the Williams opinion, the courts have not hesitated to accept jurisdiction of suits against the United States if consent has been given.[30]

There is no statute granting jurisdiction generally over actions against federal officers and agencies, and such actions must find independent grounds for jurisdiction.[31] Section 10 of the Administrative Procedure Act [32] was held not to be a grant of subject-matter jurisdiction.[33] A suit against an officer in his official capacity will ordinarily arise under the Constitution or laws of the United States, but until 1976 28 U.S.C.A. § 1331 required that more than $10,000 be in controversy.[34] Even if that requirement were satisfied, suit would often be barred by sovereign immunity. When property rights of the government are challenged, the Court, despite strong scholarly criticism,[35] has been firmly committed to the doctrine that suits, though in form against the officer, are in reality against the United States and thus barred by sovereign immunity,[36] except in the unlikely circumstance that the

---

27. 1933, 53 S.Ct. 751, 289 U.S. 553, 77 L.Ed. 1372.

28. See § 11 above.

29. The Court did not consider this possibility in the Williams case. Justice Jackson attempted to meet this argument in National Mut. Ins. Co. of Dist. of Columbia v. Tidewater Transfer Co., 1949, 69 S.Ct. 1173, 1178 n. 22, 337 U.S. 582, 93 L.Ed. 1556. See the contrary view of Justice Rutledge in the same case, 69 S.Ct. at 1187, 337 U.S. at 610.

30. See ALI Study, pp. 260–261.

31. 14 Wright, Miller & Cooper, Jurisdiction 2d § 3655.

32. 5 U.S.C.A. §§ 701–706.

33. Califano v. Sanders, 1977, 97 S.Ct. 980, 430 U.S. 99, 51 L.Ed.2d 192.

34. See § 32 below.

35. Cramton, Nonstatutory Review of Federal Administrative Action: The Need for Statutory Reform of Sovereign Immunity, Subject Matter Jurisdiction, and Parties Defendant, 1970, 68 Mich.L.Rev. 387; Byse,

Proposed Reforms in Federal "Nonstatutory" Judicial Review: Sovereign Immunity, Indispensable Parties, Mandamus, 1962, 75 Harv.L.Rev. 1479; Davis, Suing the Government by Falsely Pretending to Sue an Officer, 1962, 29 U.Chi.L.Rev. 435; Jaffe, Suits Against Governments and Officers, 1963, 77 Harv.L.Rev. 1, 209.

36. Larson v. Domestic & Foreign Commerce Corp., 1949, 69 S.Ct. 1457, 337 U.S. 682, 93 L.Ed. 1628; Malone v. Bowdoin, 1962, 82 S.Ct. 980, 369 U.S. 643, 8 L.Ed.2d 168; Dugan v. Rank, 1963, 83 S.Ct. 999, 372 U.S. 609, 10 L.Ed.2d 15; Hawaii v. Gordon, 1963, 83 S.Ct. 1052, 373 U.S. 57, 10 L.Ed.2d 191. Since the passage of the Tucker Act in 1887, compensation is now available if the officer has taken property that belongs to the plaintiff, and thus it is held that he is not acting unconstitutionally in holding the property. On this ground the once-leading case of U.S. v. Lee, 1882, 1 S.Ct. 240, 106 U.S. 196, 27 L.Ed. 171, which permitted an action of ejectment against the officer, is of no current relevance, since it was decided prior to enactment of the Tucker Act.

officer named as defendant is exceeding his statutory powers in holding the property or that his statutory powers are constitutionally void.

A 1962 statute eased the situation somewhat by granting the district courts original jurisdiction of any action in the nature of mandamus to compel an officer or employee of the United States or any agency thereof to perform a duty owed to the plaintiff.[37] Jurisdiction under the statute is "intricate, if not mazelike." [38] Although the statute led to decentralization of some kinds of litigation, including suits involving water rights, mineral rights, and grazing permits, most courts allowed what has been called "mandamus medievalism" [39] to limit its application and it did not make significant inroads on sovereign immunity.[40] "The common-law writ of mandamus, as codified in 28 U.S.C. § 1361, is intended to provide a remedy for a plaintiff only if he has exhausted all other avenues of relief and only if the defendant owes him a clear nondiscretionary duty." [41]

Important changes were made, however, in 1976. Since that year no amount in controversy has been required in actions brought under 28 U.S.C.A. § 1331 against the United States, any agency thereof, or any officer or employee sued in his official capacity.[42] The same act amended 5 U.S.C.A. § 702 to provide that an action "seeking relief other than money damages and stating a claim that an agency or officer or employee thereof acted or failed to act in an official capacity or under color of legal authority shall not be dismissed nor relief therein be denied on the ground that it is against the United States or that the United States is an indispensable party." This is a waiver of sovereign immunity for nonstatutory review in suits brought under 28 U.S.C.A. § 1331.[43] The waiver does not apply to suits for money damages,[44] nor does it confer authority to grant relief if any other statute that grants consent to suit expressly or impliedly forbids the relief that is sought.[45]

---

37. 28 U.S.C.A. § 1361, added by Act of Oct. 5, 1962, Pub.L. 87–748, § 1(a), 76 Stat. 744. The same act made liberal provisions for venue and service of process in actions against federal agencies, officers, and employees. 28 U.S.C.A. § 1391(e).

38. Estate of Watson v. Blumenthal, C.A.2d, 1978, 586 F.2d 925, 934.

39. Davis, Administrative Law of the Seventies, 1976, p. 543.

40. See 14 Wright, Miller & Cooper, Jurisdiction 2d § 3655, pp. 232–249; Brill, The Citizen's Relief Against Inactive Federal Officials: Case Studies in Mandamus, Actions "In the Nature of Mandamus," and Mandatory Injunctions, 1983, 16 Akron L.Rev. 308; French, The Frontiers of the Federal Mandamus Statute, 1976, 21 Vill. L.Rev. 637.

41. Heckler v. Ringer, 1984, 104 S.Ct. 2013, 2022, 466 U.S. 602, 615, 80 L.Ed.2d 622. See also Pittston Coal Group v. Seb-

ben, 1988, 109 S.Ct. 414, 424, 488 U.S. 105, 121, 102 L.Ed.2d 408.

42. 28 U.S.C.A. § 1331(a), as amended by Act of Oct. 21, 1976, Pub.L. 94–574, 90 Stat. 2721. Section 1331 was amended again in 1980 to remove the requirement of amount in controversy in all cases brought under the section. See § 32 below.

43. Presbyterian Church (U.S.A.) v. U.S., C.A.9th, 1989, 870 F.2d 518, 524–526; B. K. Instrument, Inc. v. U.S., C.A.2d, 1983, 715 F.2d 713, 724–725; Webster, Beyond Federal Sovereign Immunity: 5 U.S.C. § 702 Spells Relief, 1988, 49 Ohio St.L.J. 725.

44. Drake v. Panama Canal Commn., C.A.5th, 1990, 907 F.2d 532; 14 Wright, Miller & Cooper, Jurisdiction 2d § 3659, pp. 355–358.

45. 5 U.S.C.A. § 702.

Thus, the statute cannot be used to avoid the limitation in the Tucker Act that the

§ 22A.　Civil–Rights Cases [1]

Almost all of this book is immediately relevant to civil-rights cases. However they have become such an important, controversial, and distinctively federal class of cases that some of their major features will be pointed out here, with more detailed discussion, when it is appropriate, in other sections.

Although the principal civil-rights statutes go back to the Reconstruction period, for many years they were rarely used.[2] This situation has changed dramatically in the last three decades. In 1961 there were 296 civil-rights cases filed in federal courts, or barely half of one percent of all the civil cases commenced in that year.[3] In the year ended September 30, 1992, by contrast, there were 30,556 civil-rights cases filed by federal and state prisoners (not including habeas corpus, motions to vacate, and similar attacks on a criminal conviction itself), and 24,233 civil-rights cases by persons other than prisoners. Taken together these were nearly 24% of the civil cases commenced in that year.[4]

This tremendous increase in civil-rights litigation is the result of several factors. In the first place, the time was ripe for it. The Supreme Court in interpreting the Constitution and Congress in legislating were broadening the categories of civil rights to which all persons are entitled, and, through holdings that various portions of the Bill of Rights are applicable to the states by virtue of the Fourteenth Amendment, the Court was expanding the rights enforceable against the states.[5]

The other principal factor is a series of Supreme Court decisions removing what had been thought to be barriers against litigation under the Reconstruction civil-rights statutes. The key case was Monroe v. Pape,[6] decided in 1961. It held that persons were acting "under color

United States Claims Court (now the United States Court of Federal Claims) has exclusive jurisdiction of contract claims for more than $10,000. Rogers v. Ink, C.A.10th, 1985, 766 F.2d 430, 433–435.

§ 22A

1. 13B Wright, Miller & Cooper, Jurisdiction 2d § 3573–3573.4; Lewis & Blumoff, Reshaping Section 1983's Assymetry, 1992, 140 U.Pa.L.Rev. 755; Blackmun, Section 1983 and Federal Protection of Individual Rights—Will the Statute Remain Alive or Fade Away?, 1985, 60 N.Y.U.L.Rev. 1; Eisenberg, Section 1983: Doctrinal Foundations and An Empirical Study, 1982, 67 Cornell L.Rev. 482.

2. Of the most important of the civil-rights statutes, 42 U.S.C.A. § 1983, it has been said: "United States Code Annotated notes only 19 decisions under the section in its first 65 years on the statute books." Note, Limiting the Section 1983 Action in the Wake of Monroe v. Pape, 1969, 82 Harv. L.Rev. 1486 n. 4.

3. Ann.Rep. of the Director of the Administrative Office of the U.S. Courts, 1961, Table C–2.

4. Ann.Rep. of the Director of the Administrative Office of the U.S. Courts, 1992, Table C–2.

5. Professor Weinberg argues that this, rather than Monroe v. Pape, caused the explosion of civil-rights litigation. Weinberg, The Monroe Mystery Solved: Beyond the "Unhappy History" Theory of Civil Rights Litigation, 1991 B.Y.U.L.Rev. 737.

6. 1961, 81 S.Ct. 473, 365 U.S. 167, 5 L.Ed.2d 492. In a memorial tribute to the late Professor Bernard J. Ward, Justice Powell said: "Once, in describing the revolution in the role of the federal courts that has taken place since Monroe v. Pape was decided in 1961, Bernie quipped that prior to that decision the work of the federal courts had as much importance in the life of the average American citizen as did the poetry of Algernon Swinburne." Powell, Bernard J. Ward, 1982, 61 Texas L.Rev. 1, 2.

of" state law, and could be sued under 42 U.S.C.A. § 1983, although their acts were not authorized by the state and indeed were forbidden by the state. The net effect of Monroe, and of other important cases that have followed it, is that the door to the federal court is now open to those who think they have been denied federally secured rights by persons acting under state law.[7] During the same period the Court has also been willing to imply a remedy for those denied constitutional rights under color of federal law.[8]

Other statutes with origins in Reconstruction have recently been revitalized and have significant uses today.[9] There are also important modern provisions, most of which come from the Civil Rights Act of 1964 and later statutes. Vital as these other statutes are, however, they take second place to 42 U.S.C.A. § 1983, the text of which is set out in the margin.[10] It and its jurisdictional counterpart, 28 U.S.C.A. § 1343(a),

7. Although the Supreme Court has referred to § 1983 as providing "a uniquely federal remedy," Mitchum v. Foster, 1972, 92 S.Ct. 2151, 2160, 407 U.S. 225, 239, 32 L.Ed.2d 705, it is settled that a § 1983 action can be brought in state court. Martinez v. California, 1980, 100 S.Ct. 553, 558 n. 7, 444 U.S. 277, 283 n. 7, 62 L.Ed.2d 481. See Steinglass, Section 1983 Litigation in State Courts, 1988. A state court is required to assume jurisdiction over § 1983 cases if it entertains similar state-law actions against state defendants. Howlett by Howlett v. Rose, 1990, 110 S.Ct. 2430, 496 U.S. 356, 110 L.Ed.2d 332.

8. The leading case is Bivens v. Six Unknown Named Agents of Federal Bureau of Narcotics, 1971, 91 S.Ct. 1999, 403 U.S. 388, 29 L.Ed.2d 619, on remand C.A.2d, 1972, 456 F.2d 1339, implying a right of action for damages against federal officers for violation of the Fourth Amendment. A 1974 statute made the Federal Tort Claims Act applicable to such torts by federal investigative or law enforcement officers. 28 U.S.C.A. § 2680(h).

A victim of sex discrimination has a right of action for damages implied from the equal-protection component of the Due Process Clause of the Fifth Amendment. Davis v. Passman, 1979, 99 S.Ct. 2264, 442 U.S. 228, 60 L.Ed.2d 846.

An implied remedy is available for an alleged violation of Eighth Amendment rights even though the Federal Tort Claims Act provides a statutory remedy. Carlson v. Green, 1980, 100 S.Ct. 1468, 446 U.S. 14, 64 L.Ed.2d 15.

9. 42 U.S.C.A. § 1981 (equal rights under the law). See Runyon v. McCrary, 1976, 96 S.Ct. 2586, 427 U.S. 160, 49 L.Ed.2d 415. In Patterson v. McLean Credit Union, 1989, 109 S.Ct. 2363, 491 U.S.

164, 105 L.Ed.2d 132, the Court reaffirmed the holding in Runyon that § 1981 prohibits racial discrimination in the making and enforcement of private contracts, though it also held in Patterson that racial harassment in the course of employment is not actionable under § 1981.

42 U.S.C.A. § 1982 (property rights of citizens). See Jones v. Alfred H. Mayer Co., 1968, 88 S.Ct. 2186, 392 U.S. 409, 20 L.Ed.2d 1189. Arabs and Jews are protected from racial discrimination under both § 1981 and § 1982. St. Francis College v. Al–Khazraji, 1987, 107 S.Ct. 2022, 481 U.S. 604, 95 L.Ed.2d 582; Shaare Tefila Congregation v. Cobb, 1987, 107 S.Ct. 2019, 481 U.S. 615, 95 L.Ed.2d 594.

42 U.S.C.A. § 1985 (conspiracy to interfere with civil rights). See Griffin v. Breckenridge, 1971, 91 S.Ct. 1790, 403 U.S. 88, 29 L.Ed.2d 338; Note, The Scope of Section 1985(3) Since Griffin v. Breckenridge, 1977, 45 Geo.Wash.L.Rev. 239.

10. "Every person who, under color of any statute, ordinance, regulation, custom, or usage, of any State or Territory or the District of Columbia, subjects, or causes to be subjected, any citizen of the United States or other person within the jurisdiction thereof to the deprivation of any rights, privileges, or immunities secured by the Constitution and laws, shall be liable to the party injured in an action at law, suit in equity, or other proper proceeding for redress. For the purposes of this section, any Act of Congress applicable exclusively to the District of Columbia shall be considered to be a statute of the District of Columbia." This is 42 U.S.C.A. § 1983 as it was amended in 1979 by the addition of the second sentence and the reference to the District of Columbia in what is now the first sentence.

are derived from § 1 of the Ku Klux Klan Act of 1871.[11]   Although Professor Chafee thought § 1983 an "unintelligible statute" and considered it "very queer to try to protect human rights in the middle of the Twentieth Century by a left-over from the days of General Grant," [12] endless pages of United States Reports have been filled with examination of the legislative history of the 1871 statute and of its codification in the Revised Statutes in 1874, and the answers that various majorities of the Court have found in these sources define the application today of the principal statute for the protection of civil rights.

Section 1983 provides a remedy for "any citizen of the United States or other person within the jurisdiction thereof."   Thus, it is available to all persons, whether they are citizens or not.[13]

The defendant in a § 1983 action must be a "person," and this has been construed as a term of art. In Monroe v. Pape it was first held, on the basis of the 1871 enactment, that a municipal corporation is not a "person" in this sense.[14]   In 1978, however, in Monell v. Department of Social Services,[15] the Court reexamined the legislative history of the 1871 law and concluded that its previous reading of that history had been erroneous.

Under Monell a local government can be sued for monetary, declaratory, or injunctive relief, but only if the action that is alleged to be unconstitutional implements or executes "a policy statement, ordinance, regulation, or decision officially adopted and promulgated" by the officers of the corporation or has been taken "pursuant to governmental 'custom' even though such a custom has not received formal approval through the body's official decisionmaking channels." [16]   A municipality "cannot be held liable *solely* because it employs a tortfeasor—or, in other words, a municipality cannot be held liable under § 1983 on a *respondeat superior* theory." [17]

"[N]either a State nor its officials sued in their official capacity are

---

11. Act of April 20, 1871, § 1, 17 Stat. 13. The 1871 statute was in turn derived from § 2 of the Civil Rights Act of 1866, 14 Stat. 27.

12. Chafee, Safeguarding Fundamental Human Rights, 1959, 27 Geo.Wash.L.Rev. 519, 526, 529.

13. Hague v. CIO, 1939, 59 S.Ct. 954, 307 U.S. 496, 83 L.Ed. 1423.

14. 81 S.Ct. at 484–486, 365 U.S. at 187–192.

15. 1978, 98 S.Ct. 2018, 436 U.S. 658, 56 L.Ed.2d 611. See Gerhardt, The Monell Legacy: Balancing Federalism Concerns and Municipal Accountability Under Section 1983, 1989, 62 S.Cal.L.Rev. 539; Mead, 42 USC § 1983 Municipal Liability: The Monell Sketch Becomes a Distorted Picture, 1987, 65 N.C.L.Rev. 517.

16. 98 S.Ct. at 2036, 436 U.S. at 690–691. See Peppler, Policy, Custom, or Practice: The Contours of Proof of Section 1983 Municipal Liability, 1987, 10 Am.J.Trial Advoc. 477; Bandes, Monell, Parratt, Daniels, and Davidson: Distinguishing a Custom or Policy from a Random, Unauthorized Act, 1986, 72 Iowa L.Rev. 101.

A decision by a municipal policymaker on a single occasion may in some circumstances be regarded as "official municipal policy." Pembaur v. City of Cincinnati, 1986, 106 S.Ct. 1292, 475 U.S. 469, 89 L.Ed.2d 452.

17. 98 S.Ct. at 2036, 436 U.S. at 691 (emphasis in original). See Comment, Section 1983 Municipal Liability and the Doctrine of Respondeat Superior, 1979, 46 U.Chi.L.Rev. 935.

'persons' under § 1983." [18] Even if a state were a "person," it would be protected by the Eleventh Amendment.[19] But the result is different in suits against state officials in their personal capacity. They have no Eleventh Amendment protection and they may be held personally liable for damages under § 1983 for actions taken in their official capacities.[20]

For a person to be liable under § 1983 he or she must have acted under color of state law, or, in the more precise statutory term, "under color of any statute, ordinance, regulation, custom, or usage" of a state, territory, or the District of Columbia. It has been held that "custom, or usage" requires state involvement and is not simply a practice that reflects long-standing social habits, generally observed by the people in a locality. The custom or usage "must have the force of law by virtue of the persistent practices of state officials." [21]

Commonly the defendants in § 1983 actions will be municipal corporations or state or local officials exercising the authority of the state, but the statute is not limited to these bodies or functionaries. A private person who is a willful participant in a joint activity with the state is acting under color of state law.[22] As pointed out earlier, the major turning point in the construction of § 1983 came when Monroe v. Pape held that an action is "under color of" law even though it has not been authorized by the state and is indeed prohibited by the state. Section 1983 reaches those "who carry a badge of authority of a State and represent it in some capacity, whether they act in accordance with their authority or misuse it." [23]

Section 1983 provides a remedy for deprivation of "any rights, privileges, or immunities secured by the Constitution and the laws

---

18. Will v. Michigan Dept. of State Police, 1989, 109 S.Ct. 2304, 2311, 491 U.S. 58, 71, 105 L.Ed.2d 45.

19. Quern v. Jordan, 1979, 99 S.Ct. 1139, 440 U.S. 332, 59 L.Ed.2d 358.

Local government units that are considered part of the state for Eleventh Amendment purposes also are protected. Monell, 98 S.Ct. at 2035 n. 54, 436 U.S. at 690, n. 54.

20. Hafer v. Melo, 1991, 112 S.Ct. 358, ___ U.S. ___, 116 L.Ed.2d 301.

21. Adickes v. S.H. Kress & Co., 1970, 90 S.Ct. 1598, 1613, 398 U.S. 144, 167, 26 L.Ed.2d 142.

See generally 13B Wright, Miller & Cooper, Jurisdiction 2d § 3573.2, pp. 207–214; Zagrans, "Under Color of" *What* Law: A Reconstructed Model of Section 1983 Liability, 1985, 71 Va.L.Rev. 499.

22. Lugar v. Edmondson Oil Co., 1982, 102 S.Ct. 2744, 2756, 457 U.S. 922, 941, 73 L.Ed.2d 482.

This is so even if the state official with whom private persons have conspired is a judge who is protected by judicial immuni-

ty. Dennis v. Sparks, 1980, 101 S.Ct. 183, 449 U.S. 24, 66 L.Ed.2d 185. See Note, Section 1983 Liability of Private Actors Who Conspire With Immune State Officials, 1980, 80 Col.L.Rev. 802.

But a warehouseman's proposed private sale of goods entrusted to him for storage, as permitted by the self-help provisions of the New York Uniform Commercial Code, was not "state action" as required for a federal civil-rights action, absent any allegation of the participation of public officials. Flagg Bros., Inc. v. Brooks, 1978, 98 S.Ct. 1729, 436 U.S. 149, 56 L.Ed.2d 185.

23. 81 S.Ct. at 476, 365 U.S. at 172. See Winter, The Meaning of "Under Color of" Law, 1992, 91 Mich.L.Rev. 323.

A bare majority of the Court has said: "If the challenged conduct of respondents constitutes state action as delimited by our prior decisions, then that conduct was also action under color of state law and will support a suit under § 1983." Lugar v. Edmondson Oil Co., 1982, 102 S.Ct. 2744, 2752, 457 U.S. 922, 935, 73 L.Ed.2d 482.

* * *." [24] Of course not every right is a product of the federal Constitution or laws, and those rights that come from the states, rather than from the federal government, are not properly the subject of a § 1983 action.[25]

The jurisdictional counterpart of § 1983, 28 U.S.C.A. § 1343(a)(3), does not use the broad term, "the laws," used in the substantive statute. It speaks instead of "any Act of Congress providing for equal rights of citizens or of all persons within the jurisdiction of the United States." Thus, it was held that the Social Security Act is not a statute "providing for equal rights of citizens" and that § 1343(a)(3) did not grant jurisdiction of a claim of deprivation of rights under the Act.[26] One year later, however, it was held that "the laws" in § 1983 is to be interpreted according to its plain language and that the substantive statute includes all federal statutes, rather than merely civil-rights or equal-protection laws. On this reasoning it was held that a claim under the Social Security Act comes within § 1983 although not within the jurisdictional statute, 28 U.S.C.A. § 1343(3).[27]

The significance of this was that § 1343(3) grants jurisdiction without regard to amount in controversy.[28] A suit under the Social Security Act itself, or under the Act as one of "the laws" referred to in § 1983, could have been brought in federal court under the general federal question statute, 28 U.S.C.A. § 1331, but until 1980 that statute required that more than $10,000 be in controversy, and this would rarely be true of social-security claims. Now that an amount in controversy is

24. The Supreme Clause does not by itself confer any rights, privileges, or immunities enforceable under § 1983. Chapman v. Houston Welfare Rights Organization, 1979, 99 S.Ct. 1905, 1915, 441 U.S. 600, 615, 60 L.Ed.2d 508. But the Commerce Clause by its own force imposes limitations on state regulations of commerce and these may be enforced by a § 1983 action. Dennis v. Higgins, 1991, 111 S.Ct. 865, 872, 498 U.S. 439, 450, 112 L.Ed.2d 969.

25. Collins v. City of Harker Heights, 1992, 112 S.Ct. 1061, ___ U.S. ___, 117 L.Ed.2d 261 (failure to warn city employees of known hazards in workplace); DeShaney v. Winnebago County Dept. of Social Services, 1989, 109 S.Ct. 998, 489 U.S. 189, 103 L.Ed.2d 249 (child abuse); Baker v. McCollan, 1979, 99 S.Ct. 2689, 443 U.S. 137, 61 L.Ed.2d 433, (false arrest); Paul v. Davis, 1976, 96 S.Ct. 1155, 424 U.S. 693, 47 L.Ed.2d 405 (defamation).

In some of those cases the Court was unwilling to convert a state-created right into a federal right under the guise of substantive due process. As the Court put it in the Collins case: "[T]he Court has always been reluctant to expand the concept of substantive due process because the guideposts for responsible decisionmaking in this

uncharted area are scarce and open-ended." 112 S.Ct. at 1068, ___ U.S. at ___. See Fallon, Some Confusions About Due Process, Judicial Review, and Constitutional Remedies, 1993, 93 Col.L.Rev. 309.

26. Chapman v. Houston Welfare Rights Organization, 1979, 99 S.Ct. 1905, 441 U.S. 600, 60 L.Ed.2d 508. How the language in the two statutes came to differ is elaborately discussed in several opinions in this case.

27. Maine v. Thiboutot, 1980, 100 S.Ct. 2502, 448 U.S. 1, 65 L.Ed.2d 555.

28. For many years the conventional wisdom, derived from a separate opinion of Justice Stone in Hague v. CIO, 1939, 59 S.Ct. 954, 965–971, 307 U.S. 496, 518–532, 83 L.Ed. 1423, had been that § 1343(a)(3) could be used only for personal rights, such as the right to vote and the rights of free expression, that could not be valued in dollars, and that § 1331 must be used, and the amount requirement satisfied, if the party were claiming a property right that could be given a dollars-and-cents value. This distinction was rejected, and § 1343(a)(3) held applicable to property rights as well as personal rights, in Lynch v. Household Fin. Corp., 1972, 92 S.Ct. 1113, 405 U.S. 538, 31 L.Ed.2d 424. See § 37 below.

no longer required under § 1331, the difference in language between the substantive and jurisdictional statutes on civil rights is not of importance.[29]

The basic purpose of a damages award under § 1983 is to compensate persons for injuries caused by the deprivation of constitutional rights. Thus, the common-law rules of damages are to be adapted as needed to provide fair compensation for injuries.[30] The Civil Rights Attorneys' Fees Awards Act of 1976 allows the court, in its discretion, to award a reasonable attorney's fee to the prevailing party in civil-rights actions.[31]

Under another Reconstruction statute, 42 U.S.C.A. § 1988, whenever the civil-rights statutes "are deficient in the provisions necessary to furnish suitable remedies," the courts are to look to state law "so far as the same is not inconsistent with the Constitution and laws of the United States." Thus, state law is looked to in determining the applicable period of limitations for a § 1983 action [32] and in determining whether the action abates on the death of the plaintiff.[33]

In Monroe v. Pape the Court held that state judicial remedies need not be exhausted before bringing a § 1983 action,[34] and two years later it seemed to say that there is also no need to exhaust state administrative remedies.[35] Although the Court subsequently made flat statements that exhaustion of administrative remedies is not required, there was much

29. The holding that § 1983 includes all federal statutes might have ended the much litigated question whether a remedy can be implied from a federal statute that does not give one in terms, since it could have been said that § 1983 is an express congressional authorization of private suits under all federal laws. But it was subsequently held that if the remedial devices provided in a particular statute are sufficiently comprehensive, they may suffice to demonstrate congressional intent to preclude the remedy of suits under § 1983. Middlesex County Sewerage Authority v. National Sea Clammers Assn., 1981, 101 S.Ct. 2615, 2625–2627, 453 U.S. 1, 19–21, 69 L.Ed.2d 435. See also Jackson Transit Auth. v. Local Div. 1285, Amalgamated Transit Union, 1982, 102 S.Ct. 2202, 2210 n. 12, 457 U.S. 15, 28 n. 12, 72 L.Ed.2d 639; Note, Comprehensive Remedies and Statutory Section 1983 Actions: Context as a Guide to Procedural Fairness, 1989, 67 Texas L.Rev. 627.

30. Carey v. Piphus, 1978, 98 S.Ct. 1042, 435 U.S. 247, 55 L.Ed.2d 252. See Note, Damage Awards for Constitutional Torts: A Reconsideration After Carey v. Piphus, 1980, 93 Harv.L.Rev. 966.

Punitive damages can be recovered in a § 1983 case, but cannot be awarded against a municipality. City of Newport v. Fact Concerts, Inc., 1981, 101 S.Ct. 2748, 453 U.S. 247, 69 L.Ed.2d 616.

31. 42 U.S.C.A. § 1988. See cases cited 13B Wright, Miller & Cooper, Jurisdiction 2d § 3573.4 n. 21.

An attorney's fee can be awarded against a state, Hutto v. Finney, 1978, 98 S.Ct. 2565, 437 U.S. 678, 57 L.Ed.2d 522, and can be awarded in state court litigation. Maine v. Thiboutot, 1980, 100 S.Ct. 2502, 448 U.S. 1, 65 L.Ed.2d 555.

32. Board of Regents v. Tomanio, 1980, 100 S.Ct. 1790, 446 U.S. 478, 64 L.Ed.2d 440. A § 1983 action is considered a personal-injury action for this purpose. Wilson v. Garcia, 1985, 105 S.Ct. 1938, 471 U.S. 261, 85 L.Ed.2d 254. If a state has more than one statute of limitations for personal-injury actions, a § 1983 action is governed by the residual or general personal-injury statute of limitations rather than the statute of limitations for enumerated intentional torts. Owens v. Okure, 1989, 109 S.Ct. 573, 488 U.S. 235, 102 L.Ed.2d 594.

33. Robertson v. Wegmann, 1978, 98 S.Ct. 1991, 436 U.S. 584, 56 L.Ed.2d 554.

34. 81 S.Ct. at 482, 365 U.S. at 183.

35. McNeese v. Board of Educ., 1963, 83 S.Ct. 1433, 373 U.S. 668, 10 L.Ed.2d 622.

voiced dissatisfaction with this rule both on the Court itself and in the lower courts.[36] The Court gave full consideration to the question in 1982 in Patsy v. Board of Regents of State of Florida,[37] and there reaffirmed the rule that exhaustion is not required. There is however a statutory scheme that requires exhaustion of administrative remedies in suits filed by prisoners if the court believes exhaustion would be "appropriate and in the interests of justice" and if the Attorney General or the court has determined that there exist prison-grievance procedures that are in substantial compliance with federal standards established by the Attorney General.[38] And if a prisoner is challenging the very fact or duration of his physical imprisonment, habeas corpus is the only remedy available and state remedies must first be exhausted.[39] But a federal prisoner need not resort to the internal grievance procedure promulgated by the Federal Bureau of Prisons before he may initiate a suit for money damages for violation of his constitutional rights.[40]

Even state judicial remedies may be significant in another way. There are circumstances in which the remedy that a state provides for a deprivation of liberty or property is sufficient to satisfy the requirements of due process, so that the deprivation is not a violation of the Fourteenth Amendment and thus is not cognizable under § 1983.[41]

Many civil-rights cases either arise out of or are related to prior litigation in state court. Some commentators had argued, and some lower courts had held, that the usual rules about the preclusive effect of state-court judgments did not apply to § 1983 suits.[42] In 1980, in Allen v. McCurry,[43] the Court found that the legislative history of § 1983 "does not in any clear way suggest that Congress intended to repeal or restrict the traditional doctrines of preclusion."[44] All that Allen actually holds is that issue preclusion—or collateral estoppel, as it used to be called—applies if an issue actually decided after a full and fair hearing in state court is raised subsequently in a § 1983 action. That holding, as well as some of the questions about preclusion left open by Allen, is explored elsewhere.[45]

36. 17 Wright, Miller & Cooper, Jurisdiction 2d § 4233.

37. 1982, 102 S.Ct. 2557, 457 U.S. 496, 73 L.Ed.2d 172.

38. 42 U.S.C.A. § 1997(e). See Doumar, Prisoners' Civil Rights Suits: A Pompous Delusion, 1988, 11 Geo.Mason L.Rev. 1; Lay, Exhaustion of Grievance Procedures for State Prisoners Under Section 1997e of the Civil Rights Act, 1986, 71 Iowa L.Rev. 935.

39. Preiser v. Rodriguez, 1973, 93 S.Ct. 1827, 411 U.S. 475, 36 L.Ed.2d 439.

40. McCarthy v. Madigan, 1992, 112 S.Ct. 1081, ___ U.S. ___, 117 L.Ed.2d 291.

41. Hudson v. Palmer, 1984, 104 S.Ct. 3194, 468 U.S. 517, 82 L.Ed.2d 393; Parratt v. Taylor, 1981, 101 S.Ct. 1908, 451

U.S. 527, 68 L.Ed.2d 420; Ingraham v. Wright, 1977, 97 S.Ct. 1401, 430 U.S. 651, 51 L.Ed.2d 711. See Blum, Defining the Parratt/Hudson Doctrine: Defining the Scope of the Long Established State Procedure Exception and Determining the Adequacy of State Postconviction Remedies, 1986, 13 Hastings Const.L.Q. 732; Kirby, Demoting 14th Amendment Claims to State Torts, 1982, 68 A.B.A.J. 166.

42. See 18 Wright, Miller & Cooper, Jurisdiction § 4471.

43. 1980, 101 S.Ct. 411, 449 U.S. 90, 66 L.Ed.2d 308.

44. 101 S.Ct. at 417, 449 U.S. at 98–99.

45. See § 100A below.

A judge is immune from civil liability for acts done in the course of the judicial function, and this rule is not changed by the civil-rights statutes.[46] Prosecutors also are absolutely immune from damages, though not from injunctive or declaratory relief,[47] and a public defender does not act under color of state law, so that the question of immunity does not arise.[48] Members of a legislative body are absolutely immune so long as they are acting in a legislative capacity.[49] With regard to officers of the executive branch, a qualified immunity is available in varying scope, the variation being dependent upon the scope of discretion and responsibilities of the office and all the circumstances as they reasonably appear at the time of the action on which liability is sought to be based.[50] In those situations, however, in which Monell allows suit against a municipal corporation, it cannot defend on the ground that the good faith of its officers would have given them a qualified immunity if suit had been against them.[51]

The Anti–Injunction Act provides that a federal court may not grant an injunction to stay proceedings in a state court "except as expressly authorized by Act of Congress."[52] It has been held that § 1983 actions come within that exception,[53] but in so holding the Court made it clear that "we do not question or qualify in any way the principles of equity, comity, and federalism that must restrain a federal court when asked to enjoin a state court proceeding."[54] Lower courts had held that the more

---

46. Mireles v. Waco, 1991, 112 S.Ct. 286, ___ U.S. ___, 116 L.Ed.2d 9; Stump v. Sparkman, 1978, 98 S.Ct. 1099, 435 U.S. 349, 55 L.Ed.2d 331. But there is no absolute immunity if the judge's action is administrative, rather than judicial or adjudicative. Forrester v. White, 1988, 108 S.Ct. 538, 484 U.S. 219, 98 L.Ed.2d 555.

See Maher, Federally–Defined Judicial Immunity: Some Quixotic Reflections on an Unwarranted Imposition, 1984, 88 Dick. L.Rev. 326; Block, Stump v. Sparkman and the History of Judicial Immunity, 1980 Duke L.J. 879.

47. Imbler v. Pachtman, 1976, 96 S.Ct. 984, 424 U.S. 409, 47 L.Ed.2d 128. See Note, Delimiting the Scope of Prosecutorial Immunity from Section 1983 Damage Suits, 1977, 52 N.Y.U.L.Rev. 173.

But a prosecutor has only qualified immunity for giving legal advice to the police. Burns v. Reed, 1991, 111 S.Ct. 1934, 500 U.S. 478, 114 L.Ed.2d 547. There is also only qualified immunity for a prosecutor's out-of-court statements to the press and for actions by a prosecutor who is acting as an investigator rather than as an advocate. Buckley v. Fitzsimmons, 1993, 113 S.Ct. 2606, ___ U.S. ___, 125 L.Ed.2d 209.

48. Polk County v. Dodson, 1981, 102 S.Ct. 445, 454 U.S. 312, 70 L.Ed.2d 509.

But an appointed defense attorney in a federal criminal prosecution has no immu-

nity from a malpractice suit. Ferri v. Ackerman, 1979, 100 S.Ct. 402, 444 U.S. 193, 62 L.Ed.2d 355.

49. Lake Country Estates, Inc. v. Tahoe Regional Planning Agency, 1979, 99 S.Ct. 1171, 440 U.S. 391, 59 L.Ed.2d 401.

50. Hunter v. Bryant, 1991, 112 S.Ct. 534, ___ U.S. ___, 116 L.Ed.2d 589; Anderson v. Creighton, 1987, 107 S.Ct. 3034, 483 U.S. 635, 97 L.Ed.2d 523; Harlow v. Fitzgerald, 1982, 102 S.Ct. 2727, 457 U.S. 800, 73 L.Ed.2d 396.

See Freed, Executive Official Immunity for Constitutional Violations: An Analysis and a Critique, 1977, 72 Nw.U.L.Rev. 526; Comment, Harlow v. Fitzgerald: The Lower Courts Implement the New Standard for Qualified Immunity Under Section 1983, 1984, 132 U.Pa.L.Rev. 901.

51. Owen v. City of Independence, 1980, 100 S.Ct. 1398, 445 U.S. 622, 63 L.Ed.2d 673. See Levinson, Suing Political Subdivisions in Federal Court: From Edelman to Owen, 1980, 11 U.Tol.L.Rev. 829.

52. 28 U.S.C.A. § 2283. See § 47 below.

53. Mitchum v. Foster, 1972, 92 S.Ct. 2151, 407 U.S. 225, 32 L.Ed.2d 705.

54. 92 S.Ct. at 2162, 407 U.S. at 243.

See the discussion of the abstention doctrines, in § 52 below, and of "Our Federalism," in § 52A below.

specific statutory prohibitions against enjoining state tax collections or state rate proceedings [55] are applicable even to actions brought under § 1983, but the Supreme Court found it unnecessary to decide that question, holding instead that the principle of comity barred a civil-rights suit against state tax officials.[56]

---

55. 28 U.S.C.A. §§ 1341, 1342. See § 51 below.

56. Fair Assessment in Real Estate Assn., Inc. v. McNary, 1981, 102 S.Ct. 177, 454 U.S. 100, 70 L.Ed.2d 271.

Chapter 4

DIVERSITY OF CITIZENSHIP

Analysis

---

§ 23. Justifications of Diversity Jurisdiction

Ever since the First Judiciary Act, the federal courts have had original jurisdiction of so-called diversity cases, those involving a controversy between citizens of different states or between a citizen of a state and an alien.[1] This jurisdiction is retained today, subject to a jurisdic-

§ 23

1. See generally 13B Wright, Miller & Cooper, Jurisdiction 2d § 3601.

A distinction may be drawn between cases involving citizens of different states, properly referred to as diversity cases, and cases between a citizen of a state and an alien, properly referred to as alienage cases. It has been argued that historically alienage jurisdiction was the single most important grant of jurisdiction to the federal courts in the 1789 Judiciary Act. Holt, The Origins of Alienage Jurisdiction, 1989, 14 Okla.City U.L.Rev. 547. But for most purposes the distinction is unimportant, and in this book, as in the literature generally, the two classes of cases will usually be dealt with under the general head of diversity. Under a 1988 amendment of 28 U.S.C.A. § 1332(a) "an alien admitted to the United States for permanent residence shall be deemed a citizen of the State in which such alien is domiciled."

The Foreign Sovereign Immunities Act of 1976, Pub.L. 94–583, 90 Stat. 2891, is based

in part on the constitutional grant of jurisdiction of suits between citizens of a state and foreign states. 28 U.S.C.A. § 1332(a)(4) grants jurisdiction of suits by a foreign state as plaintiff against citizens of a state or of different states. 28 U.S.C.A. § 1330 grants jurisdiction of cases against foreign states. Other provisions added to Title 28 by the 1976 Act are § 1391(f) (venue in suits against foreign states), § 1441(d) (removal of suits against foreign states), and §§ 1602–1611 (defining "foreign state" and specifying when a foreign state is immune from jurisdiction). See Kane, Suing Foreign Sovereigns, A Procedural Compass, 1982, 34 Stan.L.Rev. 385; 14 Wright, Miller & Cooper, Jurisdiction 2d § 3662.

In the year ended September 30, 1992, of 230,509 civil cases commenced in district courts, 49,432 were based on diversity. Nearly half of these, 23,905, were automobile accident or similar personal-injury cases. Ann.Rep. of the Director of the Administrative Office of the U.S. Courts, 1992, Table C–2.

141

tional amount of $50,000, in 28 U.S.C.A. § 1332. As was seen in section 1, neither the debates of the Constitutional Convention nor the records of the First Congress shed any substantial light on why such jurisdiction was granted by the Constitution or why the First Congress exercised its option to vest such jurisdiction. The diversity jurisdiction was the object of attack during the ratification debates, and, in the view of one historian, "the most astounding thing * * * is not the vigor of the attack but the apathy of the defense." [2]

The traditional explanation of the diversity jurisdiction is a fear that state courts would be prejudiced against those litigants from out of state. This explanation has the weighty support of Marshall: "However true the fact may be, that the tribunals of the states will administer justice as impartially as those of the nation, to parties of every description, it is not less true that the Constitution itself either entertains apprehensions on this subject, or views with such indulgence the possible fears and apprehensions of suitors, that it has established national tribunals for the decision of controversies between aliens and a citizen, or between citizens of different states." [3] This explanation for the grant of diversity jurisdiction has been disputed. One scholar concludes that in the period prior to the drafting of the Constitution there is no evidence of such prejudice by state courts,[4] while others, surveying the same period, conclude that it cannot be said that local prejudice was inconsequential.[5]

It might be thought that the historical origins of a jurisdiction that has been employed steadily for almost two centuries would be a subject of interest only to antiquarians. With regard to diversity, however, time has only exacerbated the controversy stirred at the time of the ratification debates. Thus, the late Justice Jackson declared shortly before his death that "in my judgment the greatest contribution that Congress could make to the orderly administration of justice in the United States would be to abolish the jurisdiction of the federal courts which is based solely on the ground that the litigants are citizens of different states." [6] Justice Frankfurter, a long-time foe of diversity,[7] referred to "the mounting mischief inflicted on the federal judicial system by the unjustifiable continuance of diversity litigation." [8] For at least the last 65 years

---

2. Friendly, The Historic Basis of Diversity Jurisdiction, 1928, 41 Harv.L.Rev. 483, 487.

There is an excellent discussion of the history in Borchers, The Origins of Diversity Jurisdiction, the Rise of Legal Positivism, and a Brave New World for Erie and Klaxon, 1993, 72 Texas L.Rev. 79, 82–110.

3. Bank of the United States v. Deveaux, 1809, 5 Cranch 61, 87, 3 L.Ed. 38.

4. Friendly, note 2 above.

5. Yntema & Jaffin, Preliminary Analysis of Concurrent Jurisdiction, 1931, 79 U.Pa.L.Rev. 869, 876. See also Frank, His-

torical Bases of the Federal Judicial System, 1948, 13 Law & Contemp.Probs. 1.

6. Jackson, The Supreme Court in the American System of Government, 1955, p. 38.

7. Frankfurter, Distribution of Judicial Power Between United States and State Courts, 1928, 13 Corn.L.Q. 499; Frankfurter, A Note on Diversity Jurisdiction—In Reply to Professor Yntema, 1931, 79 U.Pa. L.Rev. 1097.

8. Lumbermen's Mut. Cas. Co. v. Elbert, 1954, 75 S.Ct. 151, 155, 348 U.S. 48, 54, 99 L.Ed. 59 (concurring opinion).

the desirability of diversity jurisdiction has stirred continuing debate in the law reviews and in the halls of Congress.

The conditions that existed, or were feared to exist, in 1789 are irrelevant in determining the continued necessity for diversity jurisdiction. As the protagonists in this continuing controversy have recognized, the decision to retain or abolish such jurisdiction today must depend on the utility of the jurisdiction in today's society.

There are limits to the area of debate, though they are not always made explicit by the debaters. Even those who call for the complete abolition of diversity jurisdiction would hardly support its abandonment where, as with the Federal Interpleader Act,[9] it is a convenient means of providing a federal forum for cases of which no state court could obtain jurisdiction. Again the abolitionists probably would agree to removal of a diversity case where there is an actual showing of prejudice or local influence against the litigant from out of state,[10] though experience under earlier statutes containing such a provision suggests that such a showing is nearly impossible to make.[11]

On the other hand, even the strongest supporters of the retention of diversity recognize that the statutory scheme may require revision to prevent abuses. The fact that a corporation could carry on most or all of its business in a particular state, but still resort to the federal courts for litigation simply because it was incorporated elsewhere, was recognized by all as an abuse,[12] and has been ended by the definition of corporate citizenship that Congress adopted in 1958.[13] The supporters of diversity are divided, however, on other reforms that seem clearly required. They do not agree on the desirability of closing the doors of the federal court to a suit by a citizen of the forum state against a nonresident.[14] There

---

9. 28 U.S.C.A. § 1335. See § 74 below.

There have also been many proposals to use diversity as a basis for providing a federal forum in cases involving many parties in many different states, cases that otherwise could not be heard in any court. E.g., Report of the Federal Courts Study Committee, April 2, 1990, pp. 44–45. See Mullenix, Complex Litigation Reform and Article III Jurisdiction, 1990, 59 Fordham L.Rev. 169.

10. See Ball, Revision of Federal Diversity Jurisdiction, 1933, 28 Ill.L.Rev. 356; Coffin, Judicial Gridlock, 10 Brookings Rev., Winter 1992, pp. 34, 37; Wechsler, Federal Jurisdiction and the Revision of the Judicial Code, 1948, 13 Law & Contemp.Probs. 216, 234–240.

11. Such provisions, dating back to the Act of March 2, 1867, 14 Stat. 558, were eliminated as unnecessary in the 1948 revision of the Judicial Code. The removal because of local prejudice in City of Detroit v. Detroit City Ry., C.C.Mich.1893, 54 F. 1, was on highly unusual facts.

12. The abuse was dramatized by Black & White Taxicab & Transfer Co. v. Brown & Yellow Taxicab & Transfer Co., 1928, 48 S.Ct. 404, 276 U.S. 518, 72 L.Ed. 681, where a Kentucky corporation, simply by reincorporating in Tennessee, was able to gain access to federal court and thus, under the Swift v. Tyson rule, avoid Kentucky decisions that would have been unfavorable to its monopolistic designs.

13. 28 U.S.C.A. § 1332(c), as amended by Act of July 25, 1958, § 2, 72 Stat. 415. See § 27 below. For the purpose of the statute, see 13B Wright, Miller & Cooper, Jurisdiction 2d § 3624. But see Phillips & Christensen, Should Corporations Be Regarded as Citizens Within the Diversity Jurisdiction Provisions?, 1962, 48 A.B.A.J. 435, which expresses some skepticism as to the 1958 amendment and argues against any further limitation on diversity with regard to corporations.

14. This is favored by Marbury, Why Should We Limit Federal Jurisdiction?, 1960, 46 A.B.A.J. 379, and Marsh, Diversity was not even unanimity on the need to abolish the rule by which diversity was artificially created through the appointment of an out-of-state administrator or guardian to bring suit on behalf of one local person against another local person,[15] but Congress made that change in 1988.[16]

Within the limits thus defined, the battle rages furiously. Some say diversity must go,[17] others argue for its retention,[18] while a third group

Jurisdiction: Scapegoat of Overcrowded Federal Courts, 1982, 48 Brook.L.Rev. 197, 221–222, but opposed by Farage, Proposed Code Will Emasculate Diversity Jurisdiction, April/May 1966, Trial Magazine, p. 30, and Moore & Weckstein, Diversity Jurisdiction: Past, Present and Future, 1964, 43 Texas L.Rev. 1, 33–34, among others. Senator Charles E. Grassley, while dissenting from the recommendation of the Federal Courts Study Committee that diversity be abolished, supported barring the in-state plaintiff from invoking diversity. Report of the Federal Courts Study Committee, April 2, 1990, p. 42.

Chief Justice Rehnquist, while not taking sides in the controversy about abolition of diversity, has argued strongly that the in-state plaintiff ought not to be able to invoke diversity. Rehnquist, Reforming Diversity Jurisdiction and Civil RICO, 1989, 21 St. Mary's L.J. 5, 7–9.

15. Abolition of this rule was favored by Moore & Weckstein, note 14 above, at 35, but strongly opposed by Farage, note 14 above, at p. 20.

The former rule is discussed in §§ 29, 31 below.

16. 28 U.S.C.A. § 1332(c)(2).

17. Ball, Revision of Federal Diversity Jurisdiction, 1933, 28 Ill.L.Rev. 356; Bork, Dealing with the Overload in Article III Courts, 1976, 70 F.R.D. 231, 236–237; Bratton, Diversity Jurisdiction: An Idea Whose Time Has Passed, 1976, 51 Ind.L.J. 347; Butler & Eure, Diversity in the Court System: Let's Abolish It, 11 Va.B.J., Winter 1985, p. 4; Coffin, Judicial Gridlock: The Case for Abolishing Diversity Jurisdiction, 10 Brookings Rev., Winter 1992, p. 34; Currie, The Federal Courts and the American Law Institute, 1968, 36 U.Chi.L.Rev. 1, 4–49; Feinberg, Is Diversity Jurisdiction An Idea Whose Time Has Passed?, N.Y.St.B.J., July 1989, p. 14; Frankfurter, Distribution of Judicial Power Between United States and State Courts, 1928, 13 Corn.L.Q. 499; Frankfurter, A Note on Diversity Jurisdiction—In Reply to Professor Yntema, 1931, 79 U.Pa.L.Rev. 1097; Haynsworth, Book Review, 1974, 87 Harv.L.Rev. 1082, 1089–1091; Hunter, Federal Diversity Jurisdic-

tion: The Unnecessary Precaution, 1978, 46 UMKC L.Rev. 347; Jackson, The Supreme Court in the American System of Government, 1955, p. 38; Kastenmeier & Remington, Court Reform and Access to Justice: A Legislative Perspective, 1979, 16 Harv.J.Legis. 301, 311–318; Kramer, Diversity Jurisdiction, 1990 B.Y.U.L.Rev. 97; Kurland, The Distribution of Judicial Power Between National and State Courts, 1958, 8 U.Chi.Law School Record 145; Miner, The Tensions of a Dual Court System and Some Prescriptions for Relief, 1987, 51 Alb.L.Rev. 151, 153–158; Rowe, Abolishing Diversity Jurisdiction: Positive Side Effects and Potential for Further Reforms, 1979, 92 Harv.L.Rev. 963; Rubin, An Idea Whose Time Has Come, 70 A.B.A.J., July 1984, p. 16; Sheran & Isaacman, State Cases Belong In State Courts, 1978, 12 Creighton L.Rev. 1; Sloviter, A Federal Judge Views Diversity Jurisdiction Through the Lens of Federalism, 1992, 78 Va.L.Rev. 1671; Wechsler, Federal Jurisdiction and the Revision of the Judicial Code, 1948, 13 Law & Contemp.Probs. 216, 234–240.

18. Brieant, Diversity Jurisdiction: Why Does the Bar Talk One Way But Vote the Other Way With Its Feet, N.Y.St.B.J., July 1989, p. 20; Brown, The Jurisdiction of the Federal Courts Based on Diversity of Citizenship, 1929, 78 U.Pa.L.Rev. 179; Farage, Proposed Code Will Emasculate Diversity Jurisdiction, April/May 1966, Trial Magazine, p. 30; Frank, An Idea Whose Time Is Still Here, 70 A.B.A.J., June 1984, p. 17; Frank, The Case for Diversity Jurisdiction, 1979, 16 Harv.J.Legis. 403; Frank, For Maintaining Diversity Jurisdiction, 1963, 73 Yale L.J. 7; Howland, Shall Federal Jurisdiction of Controversies Between Citizens of Different States Be Preserved?, 1932, 18 A.B.A.J. 499; McGugin, Let's Keep Diversity Jurisdiction, 1988, 55 Def. Coun.J. 363; Marbury, Why Should We Limit Federal Diversity Jurisdiction?, 1960, 46 A.B.A.J. 379; Moore & Weckstein, Diversity Jurisdiction: Past, Present and Future, 1964, 43 Texas L.Rev. 1; Parker, The Federal Jurisdiction and Recent Attacks Upon It, 1932, 18 A.B.A.J. 433; Parker, Dual Sovereignty and the Federal Courts, says that it must be severely limited. The limitation usually proposed in the past has been that jurisdiction be denied where a citizen of a state is suing a corporation doing business in that state on a claim arising out of the corporation's activity in the state,[19] but one writer suggests barring from federal court all personal-injury cases that arise solely under state law,[20] others would limit the jurisdiction to controversies between citizens and foreign states or foreign nations—alienage cases—and statutory interpleader actions,[21] and still another would allow each district to decide by local rule whether to eliminate or restrict diversity jurisdiction in that district.[22]

For a time the focus of the recent debate had been the recommendations made by the American Law Institute in its Study of Division of Jurisdiction between State and Federal Courts. These were a rather complex series of proposals that would have expanded jurisdiction in some respects but curtailed it in many more; the net effect would have been to reduce the volume of diversity litigation by about half. In particular, an individual who resided in a state or had his principal place of business there would not have been permitted to invoke diversity jurisdiction in that state, nor would a corporation or partnership with a "local establishment" in the state have been allowed to invoke diversity jurisdiction in an action arising out of activities of that establishment. These recommendations were based on the principle that "the function of the jurisdiction is to assure a high level of justice to the traveler or

1956, 51 Nw.U.L.Rev. 407; Phillips & Christensen, Should Corporations Be Regarded as Citizens Within the Diversity Jurisdiction Provisions?, 1962, 48 A.B.A.J. 435; Wright, The Federal Courts and the Nature and Quality of State Law, 1967, 13 Wayne L.Rev. 317; Yntema, The Jurisdiction of the Federal Courts in Controversies Between Citizens of Different States, 1933, 19 A.B.A.J. 71, 149, 265.

19. Clark, Diversity of Citizenship Jurisdiction of the Federal Courts, 1933, 19 A.B.A.J. 499; Joiner, Corporations as Citizens of Every State Where They Do Business: A Needed Change for Diversity Jurisdiction, 1987, 70 Judicature 291; Marsh, note 14 above, at 225–226; Comment, Limiting Jurisdiction of Federal Courts—Comment by Members of Chicago University Law Faculty, 1932, 31 Mich.L.Rev. 59. This is apparently also the view of George Cochran Doub, though, after rejecting the conventional justifications of diversity, he is not explicit as to how much of the jurisdiction he would retain. See Doub, Time for Re–Evaluation: Shall We Curtail Diversity Jurisdiction?, 1958, 44 A.B.A.J. 243; Doub, The Federal Diversity Jurisdiction, 1959, 45 A.B.A.J. 1273.

The proposal with regard to corporations was originally put forward by Attorney General William D. Mitchell, in the early '30s, as an alternative to the bill then sponsored by Senator Norris to abolish diversity jurisdiction entirely.

20. Meador, A New Approach to Limiting Diversity Jurisdiction, 1960, 46 A.B.A.J. 383.

21. Report of the Federal Courts Study Committee, April 2, 1990, pp. 38–43; Friendly, Federal Jurisdiction: A General View, 1973, pp. 139–152.

22. Shapiro, Federal Diversity Jurisdiction: A Survey and a Proposal, 1977, 91 Harv.L.Rev. 317. See also Bumiller, Choice of Forum in Diversity Cases: Analysis of a Survey and Implications for Reform, 1980, p. 29.

One district took a long step in this direction. It announced that its judges were not able to try promptly all cases filed, and had divided cases into priority groups. The fourth and lowest priority was for cases that can be brought in either state or federal court, in which the court identified FELA cases, diversity cases, and general federal-question cases, "particularly civil rights cases brought under 42 U.S.C. § 1983." The court then spoke favorably of the willingness and ability of the state judges to try diversity cases. District of Minnesota, Policy Statement, Aug. 19, 1977.

visitor from another state; when a person's involvement with a state is such as to eliminate any real risk of prejudice against him as a stranger and to make it unreasonable to heed any objection he might have to the quality of its judicial system, he should not be permitted to choose a federal forum, but should be required to litigate in the courts of the state."[23]   This rationale, and the detailed recommendations based on it, were heavily attacked and no longer figure significantly in the diversity debate.[24]

The arguments against diversity are not in themselves of great force. They rest primarily on the congestion that diversity cases are thought to cause for the federal courts,[25] and on the inappropriateness of asking federal judges to decide these cases when, under the rule of Erie Railroad Co. v. Tompkins,[26] they are obliged to apply state law and thus are plunged into difficult questions on which only the state courts can speak authoritatively.[27]   It is thought, too, that judicial and legislative

---

23. ALI Study, p. 2.

Since the present author was one of the Reporters for the ALI Study, it is proper to note that he joined the Study after its work on diversity was virtually completed, and that he did not participate in the formulation of the diversity proposals. See Wright, Restructuring Federal Jurisdiction: The American Law Institute Proposals, 1969, 25 Wash. & Lee L.Rev. 185, 204.

24. The ALI proposals are criticized in the articles cited note 17 above by Currie and note 18 above by Farage, Frank, Moore & Weckstein, and Judge Wright. They are defended by Professor Richard H. Field, the Chief Reporter for the ALI Study, in Field, Diversity of Citizenship: A Response to Judge Wright, 1967, 13 Wayne L.Rev. 489. There is also an interesting debate between Professor Field and John P. Frank in 1965, 17 S.C.L.Rev. 669. The present author, though having reservations about some aspects of the proposals, had urged their adoption. See Wright, note 23 above. However, the passage of time persuaded him that a more complete abolition of diversity is needed.

See generally Burdick, Diversity Jurisdiction under the American Law Institute Proposals: Its Purpose and Its Effect on State and Federal Courts, 1971, 48 N.D.L.Rev. 1.

For the view that time has passed the ALI proposals by, see Note, Eliminating Diversity Jurisdiction: A Short–Term Solution to a Long–Term Problem, 1978, 8 U.Tol.L.Rev. 896, 911–912.

25. "The impact of diversity litigation on federal courts is of jolting dimensions. Since the early 1970s diversity cases have accounted for one-fourth of the district courts' civil docket, one-fifth of their total

docket, and 10–14 percent of the dockets of the courts of appeal * * *. Even these statistics understate the real time and effort invested in diversity cases. A better measure is the number of trials, particularly jury trials, in district courts. In fiscal year 1990, diversity cases accounted for 40 percent of all trials, jury and nonjury, and more than half—53 percent—of all jury trials * * *. In addition, more than half of all cases that have been pending for more than three years are diversity cases * * *." Coffin, note 10 above, at 34–35.

26. 1938, 58 S.Ct. 817, 304 U.S. 64, 82 L.Ed. 1188.

On this particular phase of the argument, each side has sought to have it both ways. Prior to the Erie decision in 1938, the federal courts were free to apply "federal common law", see § 54 below, and this in itself was thought an argument against diversity jurisdiction. On the other hand, prior to 1938 the defenders of diversity argued that this very freedom of the federal courts led to a desirable uniformity of law, while since 1938 they have been saying that diversity is harmless since state law is applied.

27. Judge J. Skelly Wright, in the article cited note 18 above, recognizes the difficulties that the Erie doctrine creates for diversity litigation. He suggests that this might be avoided by having Congress enact "if constitutionally permissible, a unitary federal substantive rule to govern every transaction and lawsuit, no matter where it arises or in what court, state or federal." 13 Wayne L.Rev. at 334.

Judge Henry J. Friendly, in the book cited note 21 above at p. 143 n. 17, points to a case—Holt v. Seversky Electronatom Corp., C.A.2d, 1971, 452 F.2d 31—in which authority should be coextensive, and that for federal courts to decide cases arising under state law is an undesirable interference with state autonomy.[28] Finally it is said that the continuation of diversity jurisdiction diminishes the incentives and energies for reforming state courts of those influential groups who, by virtue of the diversity litigation, are able to avoid the state courts.[29] Though each of these arguments has force, they would not, singly or together, make a case for the abolition of diversity jurisdiction if that jurisdiction in fact serves some useful purpose in a federal system. Here is the crux of the controversy. Is there any continuing justification for diversity?

It is remarkable how little justification is offered in the literature, even by those who are friendly to diversity jurisdiction. This jurisdiction "is at least as traditionally federal as the Flag and the 4th of July,"[30] and many of the writers who support diversity content themselves with asserting that the burden of proof is on those who would limit or abolish the jurisdiction.[31] This, of course, avoids, if indeed it does not beg, the key question of what utility diversity has today. Others of the defenders of diversity do undertake to justify its present value, but their arguments to this effect rarely rise beyond the level of mere assertion. Professor Yntema, himself friendly to diversity, wrote 30 years ago: "The theoretical arguments in favor of the maintenance of the federal diverse-citizenship jurisdiction, like the theories to the contrary which have just been considered, suffer from incomplete analysis of the problem and are in large part based upon general assumptions which have not been sufficiently verified."[32] This observation remains true today. It is

---

the Second Circuit "had to predict how the New York Court of Appeals would choose between the conflicting views of Corbin and Williston on a point of contract law."

See Hertz, Misreading the Erie Signs: The Downfall of Diversity, 1973, 61 Ky.L.J. 861, arguing that federal courts often misread or misapply state law. "Therefore, in crucial cases, the litigant may indeed hope to gain something by 'forum-shopping.'" Id. at 878.

28. ALI Study, p. 99; Sloviter, note 17 above.

A study of decisions in one circuit concludes that diversity jurisdiction is not in fact an intrusion on state autonomy because the state courts pay little heed, one way or the other, to federal decisions about state law. Note, The Effect of Diversity Jurisdiction on State Litigation, 1965, 40 Ind.L.J. 566.

But see the related argument in Landes & Posner, Legal Change, Judicial Behavior, and the Diversity Jurisdiction, 1980, 9 J.Leg.Studies 367, 386: "Our results cast doubt on the wisdom of proposals to abolish the federal diversity jurisdiction. Contrary to the conventional view, we find that fed-

eral courts in diversity cases appear to make a significant contribution to continuing development of the common law." But a comment on that paper takes issue with that conclusion, arguing that the empirical results it relies on are ambiguous and that there are many other explanations for the results. Komesar, Comment, 1980, 9 J.Leg.Studies 387, 396–397.

29. See Frankfurter, J., concurring in Lumbermen's Mut. Cas. Co. v. Elbert, 1954, 75 S.Ct. 151, 158, 348 U.S. 48, 60, 99 L.Ed. 59.

See also ALI Study, pp. 458–459.

30. Frank, Federal Diversity Jurisdiction—An Opposing View, 1965, 17 S.C.L.Rev. 677, 682.

31. This position is explicitly taken in the articles by Howland and by Marbury, cited note 18 above. It is also put forward by Frank, and by Moore & Weckstein, in their articles cited note 18 above, but those writers do not rest their case on this argument alone.

32. Yntema, The Jurisdiction of the Federal Courts in Controversies Between Citizens of Different States, 1933, 19 A.B.A.J. 71, 75.

necessary, therefore, to make an independent examination of the arguments that may justify retention of diversity jurisdiction.

The traditional explanation for the creation of diversity jurisdiction is, as has been seen, a fear that state courts would be prejudiced against those from out-of-state. Some of the defenders of diversity assert that such prejudice continues to be a danger.[33] But in a society infinitely more mobile than that of 1789, it is difficult to believe that prejudice against a litigant, merely because he is a citizen of a different state, is a significant factor. Juries may, regrettably, be subject to many kinds of prejudice. Race, religion, appearance, wealth, city as against country, home town as against another part of the state—all these are factors that may sway a jury. If litigants subject to any or all of these prejudices must take their chances with a state court, it is hard to defend provision of a federal forum to protect a person against such prejudice as may still be felt merely because the litigant is a citizen of another state.

Another argument, with respectable historical antecedents,[34] is that diversity jurisdiction is necessary in order to implement the constitutional guarantee that "the citizens of each State shall be entitled to all the privileges and immunities of citizens of the several States."[35] This argument was long ago characterized as "specious,"[36] and the Supreme Court has summarily rejected it.[37]

33. See the articles by Brown and by Parker, cited note 18 above. A more sophisticated statement of the bias argument is advanced in ALI Study, pp. 105–110, to justify so much of the jurisdiction as it is there proposed to retain.

The scanty empirical evidence is inconclusive on the extent to which fear of prejudice is a factor in the decision to seek a federal forum. One study finds that it is a factor in only 4.3% of cases taken to federal court. Summers, Analysis of Factors that Influence Choice of Forum in Diversity Cases, 1962, 47 Iowa L.Rev. 933, 937–938. In another survey, however, 60.3% of the attorneys responding indicated that local prejudice against an out-of-state plaintiff is a factor leading to preference for a federal court when representing a plaintiff. Note, The Choice between State and Federal Court in Diversity Cases in Virginia, 1965, 51 Va.L.Rev. 178, 179. See also Miller, An Empirical Study of Forum Choices in Removal Cases under Diversity and Federal Question Jurisdiction, 1992, 41 Am. U.L.Rev. 369; Goldman & Marks, Diversity Jurisdiction and Local Bias: A Preliminary Empirical Inquiry, 1980, 9 J.Leg.Studies 93. A recent study suggests that "the state residence of the client may be less important than the rural or urban location *within* the state." Flango, Attorneys' Perspectives on Choice of Forum in Diversity Cases, 1991, 25 Akron L.Rev. 41, 64. The same

study also says: "Of the various reasons attorneys give for choosing one forum over the other, three stood out: quality of judges, client characteristics, and convenience." Id. at 105.

34. See Hamilton in The Federalist No. 80, at 502, Wright ed. 1961. Perhaps this is the argument Justice Wayne had in mind when he wrote, in Dodge v. Woolsey, 1855, 18 How. 331, 354, 15 L.Ed. 401: "The foundation of the right of citizens of different states to sue each other in the courts of the United States, is not an unworthy jealousy of the impartiality of the state tribunals. It has a higher aim and purpose. It is to make the people think and feel, though residing in different states of the Union, that their relations to each other were protected by the strictest justice, administered in courts independent of all local control or connection with the subject matter of the controversy between the parties to a suit."

35. The argument is made today by Marbury, in the article cited note 18 above.

36. Friendly, The Historic Basis of Diversity Jurisdiction, 1928, 41 Harv.L.Rev. 483, 492 n. 44.

37. Chase Manhattan Bank (Nat. Assn.) v. South Acres Dev. Co., 98 S.Ct. 544, 546, 434 U.S. 236, 238, 54 L.Ed.2d 501.

Another argument, again going back to Hamilton,[38] is that the federal courts are so much better than the state courts that it is desirable to channel as many cases as possible to federal court, or at least that those from out-of-state, who have no opportunity to work for the improvement of the state courts, should be spared from exposure to them.[39] There are reasons why this might be true. Federal judges enjoy life tenure, they are free to comment on the evidence, and they sit with juries selected from a broader geographical area.[40] Not all lawyers would agree, however, that these differences lead to better justice, and though the prestige of the federal courts has generally been high, there have been long periods when these very procedural differences have led to suspicion of the federal courts as rich men's courts or defendants' courts. Further, arguments stemming from a supposed inferiority of state justice are insusceptible of proof and hardly politic to advance. There is, however, a somewhat related argument that the existence of concurrent state and federal jurisdiction acts as a spur to higher standards of justice in each system of courts.[41] It is hard to believe that already-crowded state courts will feel a strong incentive to improve in order to attract the comparative handful of cases where diversity exists and where, therefore, the litigants have a choice of forum. In addition, concurrent jurisdiction exists in any event over most federal-question cases, and whatever benefits it may be thought to confer can be had from that phase of jurisdiction. Undoubtedly, so long as diversity exists, the choice of forum will be utilized for tactical purposes by particular litigants in particular cases, who think they may obtain an advantage from one forum or the other, but to the extent this exists, as it surely does,[42] it

38. The Federalist No. 81, at 510, Wright ed. 1961 (Hamilton): "[E]very man may discover, that courts constituted like those of some of the States would be improper channels of the judicial authority of the Union."

39. This argument is made by Professors Moore & Weckstein, and by Judge Parker and by Judge Wright, in the articles cited note 18 above. The ALI Study, pp. 107–108, seems to accept so much of the argument as concerns persons from out-of-state.

See also the query in Currie, Federal Courts: Cases and Materials, 4th ed. 1990, p. 228, whether this is "any more a perversion of constitutional authority than the common use of the commerce and tax powers to combat prostitution or child labor?"

40. It is argued that a federal court can better protect against bias because of "the advantages of federal procedure, Article III judges less exposed to local pressures than their state court counterparts, juries selected from wider geographical areas, review in appellate courts reflecting a multistate perspective, and more effective review by this Court." United Steelworkers of America,

AFL–CIO v. R.H. Bouligny, Inc., 1965, 86 S.Ct. 272, 275, 382 U.S. 145, 150, 15 L.Ed.2d 217. The Court was listing the advantages claimed by a party arguing before it and did not indicate whether it agreed with these arguments.

A new trial must be ordered by the appellate court if the verdict is found in any degree to have been reached as a result of appeals to regional or other prejudice. Pappas v. Middle Earth Condominium Assn., C.A.2d, 1992, 963 F.2d 534.

41. Such an argument seems implicit in Hart, The Relations between State and Federal Law, 1954, 54 Col.L.Rev. 489. See especially pp. 513, 540.

It is stated explicitly by Judge Wright and Mr. Frank in their articles cited note 18 above.

42. The choice is clearly recognized as a purely tactical one in Kennedy, Federal Diversity Jurisdiction, 1961, 10 Kans.L.Rev. 47, 54. See also Summers, Analysis of Factors that Influence Choice of Forum in Diversity Cases, 1962, 47 Iowa L.Rev. 933; Note, The Choice between State and Federal Court in Diversity Cases in Virginia, 1965, 51 Va.L.Rev. 178.

would seem more an abuse of concurrent jurisdiction than an argument for its retention.[43]

It is argued also that there is no merit in transferring cases from congested federal courts to congested state courts, and that the practical consequence of abolition would be "to tell thousands upon thousands of American citizens to wait twice as long as before to have their suits disposed of, when it was already taking far too long." [44]   Careful studies have shown, however, that because there are many more state judges than federal judges, abolition of diversity would have only a minimal impact on state-court workloads.[45]   The argument also fails to consider that the cases would take less judicial time to resolve in state courts of general jurisdiction than in federal courts, where preliminary determinations regarding the existence of diversity and of amount in controversy are often difficult and time-consuming without advancing decision on the merits of the case.[46]

Finally there is a comparatively new argument for diversity—though it may have been in the minds of the Framers [47]—that deserves consideration.   As articulated by Chief Justice Taft, the argument is that "no single element in our governmental system has done so much to secure capital for the legitimate development of enterprises throughout the West and South as the existence of federal courts there, with a jurisdiction to hear diverse citizenship cases." [48]   This argument at one time was endorsed by the Judicial Conference of the United States [49] and by

43.   "Why the federal system should offer forum shopping as a service [Mr. Frank] does not make clear, for it is an option denied to all non-diverse fellow citizens whose claims are in all other aspects identical.   In fact, what diversity jurisdiction provides is 'convenience' for a small number of lawyers."   Rubin, note 17 above.

44.   Frank, The Case for Diversity Jurisdiction, 1979, 16 Harv.J.Legis. 403, 413.

45.   Sheran & Isaacman, note 17 above, at 55–68.   The same authors quote also at 51 n. 255 the 1977 resolution of the Conference of Chief Justices saying that the state courts "are able and willing" to assume all or part of the diversity jurisdiction now exercised by the federal courts.

"A National Center for State Courts study concludes * * * that total abolition of diversity jurisdiction would, on average, generate about eleven more cases for each state court judge of general jurisdiction, and, most important, suggests that these cases would generally be evenly distributed and so would not overwhelm courts in a few areas.   In short, what is a heavy burden to the federal system would represent an insignificant addition to the work of most state courts because the state court system is so much larger in the aggregate than the

federal court system."   Report of the Federal Courts Study Committee, note 21 above, at p. 41.

For other statistical studies of this question, see Flango & Blair, The Relative Impact of Diversity Cases on State Trial Courts, 1978, 2 St.Court J. 20; Flango & Boersema, Changes in Federal Diversity Jurisdiction: Effects on State Court Caseloads, 1990, 15 U.Dayton L.Rev. 405, 423.

46.   See the articles by Coffin and Rowe, note 17 above.   A shorter version of the Rowe article appears as Rowe, Abolishing Diversity Jurisdiction: The Silver Lining, 1980, 66 A.B.A.J. 177.

47.   See Frank, Historical Bases of the Federal Judicial System, 1948, 13 Law & Contemp.Probs. 1.

48.   Taft, Possible and Needed Reforms in the Administration of Justice in the Federal Courts, 1922, 47 A.B.A.Rep. 250, 258–259.

49.   Report of the Judicial Conference of the United States, 1951, p. 27.

In recent years the Judicial Conference has repeatedly endorsed the complete abolition of general diversity jurisdiction.   E.g., Reports of the Judicial Conference of the United States, 1979, p. 66; 1986, p. 17;

many of the writers who support the retention of diversity.[50] If indeed diversity jurisdiction is an indispensable condition to the free flow of capital from one part of the nation to another, then diversity should be retained. It might seem at first glance that the merit of this argument is dependent on the other arguments—which have been seen to be of doubtful validity—for diversity. If, in fact, local prejudice will not be a significant factor, if state courts are as good as federal courts, then there is no apparent reason why the decisions of entrepreneurs to invest their funds in other parts of the country should be affected by the existence of recourse to the federal courts. On reflection, however, it will be apparent that this answer is insufficient, as most of those who have put forward the flow-of-capital argument recognize. The key question is not whether out-of-state investors will in fact receive fair treatment from state courts, but whether they think they will.[51] If abolition, or significant curtailment, of diversity jurisdiction would give rise to irrational fears by investors, and inhibit their willingness to invest in different parts of the country, then diversity serves a useful purpose and should be retained. It is true that this proposition can never be proved short of "the heroic experiment of its abolition." [52] Nevertheless there is reason to believe that investors are now sufficiently national-minded, and that they are accustomed enough to investing abroad where they enjoy no protection from the federal courts, that it is no longer necessary to preserve diversity jurisdiction to comfort investors.[53]

It is unfortunate that the future of diversity jurisdiction is not likely to be resolved by objective consideration of the arguments for and against this head of jurisdiction. Any proposal to modify diversity meets

1987, p. 72; 1988, p. 22. Most recently, while repeating its endorsement of complete abolition of diversity jurisdiction, it separately endorsed repeal of jurisdiction in cases involving an instate plaintiff. Report of the Judicial Conference of the United States, Sept. 1993, p. 48.

50. See the articles by Brieant, Brown, Marbury, Moore & Weckstein, and Parker, cited note 18 above. See also Frank, note 18 above, at 410, and Marsh, note 14 above, at 205–210. The argument is most fully developed by Marbury, who says, at 380, that there is "value to our present-day economy in a system which guarantees to the citizen who moves beyond the borders of his own community the protecting mantle of the federal judiciary * * * enterprise is definitely encouraged by the fact that the federal courts are available under such circumstances."

51. Thus, Chief Justice Taft, in the speech cited note 40 above, recognizes that "the material question is not so much whether the justice administered is actually impartial and fair, as it is whether it is thought to be so by those who are consider-

ing the wisdom of investing their capital in states where that capital is needed for the promotion of enterprises and industrial and commercial progress." Marbury, in the article cited note 18 above, says that his clients would be hesitant to invest in distant states without the assurance diversity jurisdiction provides, and then says, at 380: "I grant that if put to it to demonstrate a rational basis for that feeling, they might flounder a bit * * *. Perhaps what we are dealing with here is something that cannot be rationalized, but it is not for that reason less entitled to recognition." See also the article by Brown, cited note 18 above.

52. Yntema, The Jurisdiction of the Federal Courts in Controversies Between Citizens of Different States, 1933, 19 A.B.A.J. 71, 75.

53. It is worthy of note that the Reporters for the American Law Institute dismiss this argument for diversity without extended discussion—see ALI Study, pp. 105–106—and that their proposals for curtailment of diversity would deny its benefits in large measure to corporations that operate in many states.

immediate organized opposition from those who believe that they have a vested interest in preserving, for their own advantage, the widest possible choice of forum.[54]

In 1978 the House of Representatives twice voted by large margins to abolish general diversity jurisdiction. Neither bill reached a vote in the Senate.[55] And in 1990 the Federal Courts Study Committee, a distinguished body created by Act of Congress, called for abolition,[56] but Congress has not acted on that recommendation.

§ 24. Kinds of Diversity That Give Jurisdiction[1]

The constitutional grant of diversity jurisdiction extends "to Controversies * * * between Citizens of different states * * * and between a State, or the Citizens thereof, and foreign States, Citizens or Subjects."[2] This jurisdiction is conferred, subject to some important changes, by § 1332 of the Judicial Code. In all cases in which that section of the code is relied on as the basis of jurisdiction, the amount in controversy must exceed $50,000.[3]

The typical case is that in which a citizen of Texas sues a citizen of New York. Here there is plainly diversity, but it is not clear that these facts in themselves should be enough for jurisdiction. Section 11 of the Judiciary Act of 1789 granted jurisdiction only where "the suit is between a citizen of the State where the suit is brought, and a citizen of

---

54. See the articles by Coffin, note 17 above; Kastenmeier & Remington, note 17 above, at 317–318; Wright, Procedural Reform: Its Limitations and Its Future, 1967, 1 Ga.L.Rev. 563, 576–577; Wright, note 22 above, at 185, 204–207; Wright, Lawyers and Their Pocketbooks, 10 Brookings Rev., Spring 1992, p. 3.

"The only groups who still argue strongly for diversity jurisdiction are the Association of Trial Lawyers of America, whose members specialize in personal injury litigation, and corporate lawyers whose clients prefer the federal courts." Sheran & Isaacman, note 17 above, at 52.

A poll of lawyers showed that they opposed abolition of diversity by a 69–26% margin, with 5% undecided. On a more modest proposal to retain diversity for a nonresident defendant but eliminate it for a resident plaintiff, 58% were opposed, 33% in favor, and 9% undecided. Law Poll, 1980, 66 A.B.A.J. 148, 149.

55. 124 Cong.Rec. 5009, Feb. 28, 1978; 124 Cong.Rec. 33546, Oct. 4, 1978. See Kastenmeier & Remington, note 17 above, at 312.

56. "We believe that diversity jurisdiction should be virtually eliminated for two simple reasons: On the one hand, no other class of cases has a weaker claim on federal

judicial resources. On the other hand, no other step will do anywhere nearly as much to reduce federal caseload pressures and contain the growth of the federal judiciary. Given all the demands on the federal courts, there is little reason to use them for contract disputes or automobile accident suits simply because the parties live across state boundaries—especially where litigants who do not live in different states must bring otherwise identical suits in state courts." Report of the Federal Courts Study Committee, note 21 above, at p. 39.

§ 24

1. 13B Wright, Miller & Cooper, Jurisdiction 2d §§ 3602–3605.

2. The Constitution also extends the judicial power to controversies "between Citizens of the same State claiming Lands under Grants of different States." It has been proposed that the statute implementing this grant of jurisdiction, 28 U.S.C.A. § 1354, be repealed on the ground that it is now obsolete. ALI Study, p. 411. Jurisdiction was based on conflicting grants of land from different states in Port of Portland v. Island in the Columbia River, D.C.Or.1971, 326 F.Supp. 291, reversed on other grounds C.A.9th, 1973, 479 F.2d 549.

3. See §§ 32–37 below.

another State." [4] Thus, in the example given, if suit were brought in the federal court in Pennsylvania, there would have been no jurisdiction under the 1789 statute, since neither of the parties would be a citizen of the state where the suit is brought. If the basis for diversity jurisdiction is fear of prejudice against the litigant from out of state,[5] there would seem no danger of such prejudice, and thus no reason for federal jurisdiction, where neither of the parties is a citizen of the forum state. This restriction was removed, however, in 1875, and ever since then jurisdiction has been granted where the suit is between "citizens of different States," regardless of where it is brought.[6] This leads to the further anomaly—which was true also under the 1789 formulation—that the Texas plaintiff can, if he or she is able to obtain service of process, bring suit against the New York citizen in the federal court in Texas. If the local-prejudice rationalization for diversity jurisdiction is accepted, it is difficult to understand why a plaintiff who is a citizen of the forum state is able to resort to federal court.[7]

State citizenship is necessary for diversity jurisdiction. A person may be a citizen of the United States but domiciled abroad. Such a person is not a citizen of any state, and cannot sue or be sued in federal court on that basis, and since the person is not an alien, the alienage jurisdiction also cannot be invoked.[8] Nor can a person who has dual nationality, and who is a citizen of the United States but is regarded as a citizen also by another country, take advantage of alienage jurisdiction. A litigant in this position will be treated as though he or she possesses only United States citizenship.[9]

4. The requirement that one of the parties must be a citizen of the state where suit was brought was added to the bill in the Senate. See Holt, "To Establish Justice": Politics, the Judiciary Act of 1789, and the Invention of the Federal Courts, 1989 Duke L.J. 1421, 1503.

5. See § 23 above.

6. 28 U.S.C.A. § 1332(a)(1), carrying forward language that originally appeared in the Act of March 3, 1875, § 1, 18 Stat. 470.

In Poulos v. Naas Foods, Inc., C.A.7th, 1992, 959 F.2d 69, 71 n. 2, this is referred to as "one of the anomalies of federal diversity jurisdiction. Since none of the parties is from Wisconsin, there is no prima facie reason to suspect that a Wisconsin state court would be any more partial than a federal court."

7. The heart of the American Law Institute's proposals about diversity was to deny jurisdiction if the plaintiff was a citizen of the forum or otherwise closely associated with the forum. ALI Study, § 1302.

8. Newman–Green, Inc. v. Alfonzo–Lorrain, 1989, 109 S.Ct. 2218, 2221, 490 U.S. 826, 828, 104 L.Ed.2d 893; Cresswell v.

Sullivan & Cromwell, C.A.2d, 1990, 922 F.2d 60; Hammerstein v. Lyne, D.C.Mo. 1912, 200 F. 165; 13B Wright, Miller & Cooper, Jurisdiction 2d § 3621.

The converse situation cannot arise. A state may confer the benefits of state citizenship on anyone it thinks fit, but the power of naturalization is exclusively vested in Congress, and it is not possible for one who is not a citizen of the United States to be a citizen of a state for purposes of diversity. City of Minneapolis v. Reum, C.C.A.8th, 1893, 56 F. 576; Frick v. Lewis, C.C.A.6th, 1912, 195 F. 693, affirmed 1914, 34 S.Ct. 488, 233 U.S. 291, 58 L.Ed. 967.

9. Sadat v. Mertes, C.A.7th, 1980, 615 F.2d 1176, 1182–1188; Las Vistas Villas, S.A. v. Petersen, D.C.Fla.1991, 778 F.Supp. 1202; Risk v. Kingdom of Norway, D.C.Cal. 1989, 707 F.Supp. 1159, 1162–1163, affirmed C.A.9th, 1991, 936 F.2d 393, certiorari denied 112 S.Ct. 880, ___ U.S.___, 116 L.Ed.2d 784; Currie, The Federal Courts and the American Law Institute, 1968, 36 U.Chi.L.Rev. 1, 10 n. 50.

But cf. Aguirre v. Nagel, D.C.Mich.1967, 270 F.Supp. 535, holding that plaintiff who was a citizen of Michigan and also of Mexico could sue a citizen of Michigan in federal

Jurisdiction is granted also where there is a suit between a citizen of a state and foreign states or citizens or subjects thereof.[10] Here it has never made any difference where the suit is brought, and probably should not, since there may be a real danger of prejudice, in any forum, against the alien.[11] The 1789 Judiciary Act purported to extend jurisdiction to all suits in which an alien is a party. The Court at a very early date held that this was unconstitutional insofar as it might permit suit in federal courts between two aliens, while the Constitution only authorizes jurisdiction of suits between a citizen of a state and an alien.[12] The alien must be a citizen or subject of a foreign state; there is no jurisdiction if the suit is between a citizen of one of the United States and a person who is not a citizen either of the United States or of any other country.[13]

In 1988 Congress amended the general diversity statute by adding a sentence saying that for the purposes of that statute, the interpleader statute, and the removal statute, "an alien admitted to the United States for permanent residence shall be deemed a citizen of the State in which such alien is domiciled." [14] The legislative history is exceptionally skimpy, but the purpose was to eliminate jurisdiction in a suit between a citizen of a state and an alien permanently resident in that state.[15]

court. The Aguirre case was purportedly followed in Robinson v. Anastasiou, D.C.Tex.1972, 339 F.Supp. 472, though that precedent was in fact irrelevant. The Robinson case was a suit by a citizen of Texas against a defendant who was a citizen of Greece—and perhaps also of Great Britain—and who was domiciled in Texas. The domicile of a party who is not a United States citizen is irrelevant and this was a simple case of a suit by a citizen of a state against an alien.

10. 28 U.S.C.A. § 1332(a)(2).

There is also jurisdiction of a suit between citizens of different states in which foreign countries or their citizens are additional parties. 28 U.S.C.A. § 1332(a)(3). See 13B Wright, Miller & Cooper, Jurisdiction 2d § 3604; Transure, Inc. v. Marsh and McLennan, Inc., C.A.9th, 1985, 766 F.2d 1297. But this does not permit suit by an alien against a citizen of a state and a citizen of some other foreign country. Ed & Fred, Inc. v. Puritan Marine Ins. Underwriters Corp., C.A.5th, 1975, 506 F.2d 757.

The Foreign Sovereign Immunities Act grants jurisdiction of actions by a foreign state against citizens of a state or of different states. 28 U.S.C.A. § 1332(a)(4).

11. "Alienage jurisdiction, as embodied in the Constitution and as put into action in the Judiciary Act of 1789, was thus an attempted solution to a major political problem of international dimensions." Holt, The Origins of Alienage Jurisdiction, 1989, 14 Okla.City U.L.Rev. 547, 564.

12. Hodgson v. Bowerbank, 1809, 5 Cranch 303, 3 L.Ed. 108. For the significance of this case, see § 8 above.

13. This at least is the holding of Blair Holdings Corp. v. Rubinstein, D.C.N.Y. 1955, 133 F.Supp. 496, and if there can actually be such a "man without a country," the decision appears sound. The Supreme Court may simply have overlooked this possibility in Sun Printing & Pub. Assn. v. Edwards, 1904, 24 S.Ct. 696, 194 U.S. 377, 48 L.Ed. 1027, where, in sustaining jurisdiction, it asserted that a person domiciled in Delaware must either be a citizen of Delaware or a citizen or subject of a foreign state.

14. 28 U.S.C.A. § 1332(a), as amended by Act of Nov. 19, 1988, Pub.L. 100–702, § 203, 102 Stat. 4646.

The meaning of permanent residence, for purposes of this statute, is considered in Miller v. Thermarite Pty. Ltd., D.C.Ala. 1992, 793 F.Supp. 306.

15. Oakley, Recent Statutory Changes in the Law of Federal Jurisdiction and Venue: The Judicial Improvements Acts of 1988 and 1990, 1991, 24 U.C.Davis L.Rev. 735, 741–742; Linn, Diversity Jurisdiction

Whether it was wise to restrict jurisdiction in this way is debatable,[16] but Congress had undoubted power to do so and the statute clearly achieves that purpose. Unfortunately the plain language of the statute equally clearly purports to give jurisdiction of a suit by an alien permanently resident in one state against an alien permanently resident in another state. The constitutional power of Congress to open the federal courthouse door to such a suit is extremely doubtful.[17] Courts will have to decide whether to construe the statute, despite its words, in a way that will accomplish its stated purpose and will avoid a constitutional question[18] or to apply it literally and confront "one of the most perplexing and confusing questions in constitutional law."[19]

In an early decision the Court, speaking through Chief Justice Marshall, held that a citizen of the District of Columbia is not a citizen of a state, for purposes of diversity jurisdiction,[20] and the same result was later reached with regard to citizens of territories.[21] Marshall's opinion was unfortunately cryptic, for, after commenting on how extraordinary it was that the courts of the United States should be open to aliens but not to those who resided in the District of Columbia, he said that "this is a subject for legislative, not for judicial consideration."[22] This would seem to suggest that only the statute, rather than the Constitution, precluded diversity jurisdiction in suits between a citizen of the District of Columbia and a citizen of a state. This is a strange suggestion, since there was no significant difference between the language of the statute and that of the Constitution, but the alternative explanation of Marshall's statement is the strained argument that "constitutional amendment as well as statutory revision is for legislative, not judicial, consideration."[23]

Against this background Congress, in 1940, undertook to provide that citizens of the District of Columbia, and of the territories, should be

and Permanent Resident Aliens, 1991, 38 Fed.B.News & J. 284, 287.

16. It is strongly argued that it was unwise in Linn, note 15 above.

17. See Hodgson v. Bowerbank, 1809, 5 Cranch 303, 3 L.Ed. 108, discussed in § 8 above; Oakley, note 15 above, at 741–745; Linn, note 15 above, at 284–286; Kramer, Diversity Jurisdiction, 1990 B.Y.U.L.Rev. 97, 122. But see VanDercreek, From the Judiciary Act of 1789 to the Judicial Improvements Act of 1988, 1989, 14 Okla.City U.L.Rev. 565, 595–597.

18. As was done in Arai v. Tachibana, D.C.Hawaii 1991, 778 F.Supp. 1535, and in Lloyds Bank PLC v. Norkin, D.C.N.Y.1993, 817 F.Supp. 414.

19. Linn, note 15 above, at 286.

The statute was applied literally in Singh v. Daimler–Benz, AG, C.A.3d, 1993, 9 F.3d 303. In Singh plaintiff was a citizen of India permanently resident in Virginia. He sued Daimler–Benz, a German corporation, and its American distributor, a Delaware corporation with its principal place of business in New Jersey. The court thought this was within the power of Congress to vest jurisdiction when there is minimal diversity. The court felt that it could leave "to another day" the constitutional question that would be presented if Singh had sued only Daimler–Benz, so that the suit would have been entirely between two aliens.

20. Hepburn & Dundas v. Ellzey, 1804, 2 Cranch 445, 2 L.Ed. 332.

21. Corporation of New Orleans v. Winter, 1816, 1 Wheat. 91, 4 L.Ed. 44.

22. Hepburn & Dundas v. Ellzey, 1804, 2 Cranch 445, 453, 2 L.Ed. 332.

23. Jackson, J., in National Mut. Ins. Co. of Dist. of Columbia v. Tidewater Transfer Co., 1949, 69 S.Ct. 1173, 1175, 337 U.S. 582, 587, 93 L.Ed. 1556.

regarded as citizens of a state for purposes of diversity jurisdiction.[24] Most of the lower courts thought this provision unconstitutional, but the Supreme Court, in the very unusual case of National Mutual Insurance Co. of District of Columbia v. Tidewater Transfer Co.[25] upheld the statute. Two justices thought that the older decisions should be over-ruled, and that citizens of the District of Columbia were citizens of a state within Article III of the Constitution. The other seven justices disagreed. Three justices, while of the view that these persons were not citizens of a state, voted to uphold the statute on the basis of the power of Congress, under Article I of the Constitution, to enact legislation for the inhabitants of the District of Columbia and the territories.[26] The other six justices rejected this line of argument. Nevertheless five justices altogether voted to uphold the statute, and it must now be regarded as valid,[27] even though seven and six justices respectively rejected the two lines of argument offered to support the statute.

The problems of diversity become more complex when there are multiple parties. Suppose that a citizen of Texas and a citizen of Oklahoma join as plaintiffs in a suit against a citizen of New York. Here it is settled that diversity exists, and that neither the statute nor the Constitution require that all the parties on one side be citizens of the same state.[28] But if the Texan and the Oklahoman join to bring suit against two defendants, one of whom is a citizen of New York but the other a citizen of Texas (or Oklahoma), there is no diversity jurisdiction. This is the rule of "complete diversity," first laid down by Chief Justice Marshall in the famous case of Strawbridge v. Curtiss.[29] A later justice was to write that, to the knowledge of several members of the Court, Marshall had repeatedly expressed regret that the decision in the Straw-bridge case had been made, and had said that if the point of jurisdiction was an original one, the conclusion would be different.[30] Nevertheless, with one important exception, the complete diversity rule has since been

24. The 1940 statute conferred jurisdiction where suit "is between citizens of different States, or citizens of the District of Columbia, the Territory of Hawaii, or Alaska, and any State or Territory." Act of April 20, 1940, 54 Stat. 143. In its present form, as revised in the 1948 Judicial Code and subsequently amended, the provision is: "The word 'States', as used in this section, includes the Territories, the District of Columbia, and the Commonwealth of Puerto Rico." 28 U.S.C.A. § 1332(d).

25. 1949, 69 S.Ct. 1173, 337 U.S. 582, 93 L.Ed. 1556.

26. See § 11 above.

27. In Americana of Puerto Rico, Inc. v. Kaplus, C.A.3d, 1966, 368 F.2d 431, so much of 28 U.S.C.A. § 1332(d) as provides that the Commonwealth of Puerto Rico is a "state" for purposes of diversity jurisdiction was upheld as a valid exercise of the power of Congress under Article IV, § 3, of

the Constitution to make rules and regulations for United States territories.

See generally 13B Wright, Miller & Cooper, Jurisdiction 2d § 3603.

28. Sweeney v. Carter Oil Co., 1905, 26 S.Ct. 55, 199 U.S. 252, 50 L.Ed. 178; Great Northern Ry. Co. v. Galbereath Cattle Co., 1926, 46 S.Ct. 439, 271 U.S. 99, 70 L.Ed. 854.

Prior to 1948 there was a question, never resolved, whether jurisdiction existed if an alien and a citizen of a state joined in a suit against a citizen of another state. See Ryan v. Ohmer, D.C.N.Y.1916, 233 F. 165. The question was of purely statutory dimension, and was settled in the 1948 Code by an express grant of jurisdiction in such a situation. 28 U.S.C.A. § 1332(a)(3). See note 10 above.

29. 1806, 3 Cranch 267, 2 L.Ed. 435.

30. Louisville, C. & C.R. Co. v. Letson, 1844, 2 How. 497, 555, 11 L.Ed. 353.

consistently followed.[31] The exception was in interpleader cases, where the statute calls only for "two or more adverse claimants, of diverse citizenship." [32] The lower courts had held that "minimal diversity" was enough, and that jurisdiction existed if there were a claimant on each side from different states, even though all the other claimants on each side might be citizens of a single state.[33]

This application of the interpleader statute was valid only if Strawbridge v. Curtiss could be regarded as merely a construction of the diversity statute then in effect rather than a construction of the Constitution.[34] On its face the decision purported merely to construe the statute; though it is hard to find any significant difference between the language of the statute and that of the Constitution, there are other instances where statutory language, seemingly taken directly from Article III, has been given a narrower construction than the similar words in the Constitution itself.[35] To have held that the Constitution requires complete diversity would have had a debilitating effect on the interpleader act, and would have largely precluded the possibilities of using the diversity jurisdiction as a basis for providing a federal forum for other cases in which no state court could grant effective relief.[36] Even those most critical of diversity generally have recognized and supported the potentialities of diversity for situations of the sort described,[37] and a construction barring this use of diversity would have been most unfortunate.

Fortunately when the Supreme Court finally decided this matter, it held that minimal diversity is enough to meet the requirement of the Constitution and that the rule of Strawbridge v. Curtiss is merely a construction of the general-diversity statute. In 1967, in the case of State Farm Fire & Casualty Co. v. Tashire,[38] the Court, in an interpleader situation, raised the question of jurisdiction on its own motion. The Court had no difficulty in finding that Congress had intended to let minimal diversity suffice in interpleader, and in three sentences the Court resolved more than 150 years of controversy by holding that neither Article III nor the Strawbridge case barred Congress from doing so. " * * * Chief Justice Marshall there purported to construe only 'The words of the act of congress,' not the Constitution itself. And in a variety of contexts this Court and the lower courts have concluded that Article III poses no obstacle to the legislative extension of federal jurisdiction, founded on diversity, so long as any two adverse parties are

---

31. See 13B Wright, Miller & Cooper, Jurisdiction 2d § 3605.

32. 28 U.S.C.A. § 1335(a)(1).

33. Haynes v. Felder, C.A.5th, 1957, 239 F.2d 868, and cases there cited. See § 74 below.

34. The question was specifically left open in Treinies v. Sunshine Mining Co., 1939, 60 S.Ct. 44, 47, 308 U.S. 66, 71–72, 84 L.Ed. 85. In Shields v. Barrow, 1855, 17 How. 130, 145, 15 L.Ed. 158, the Court talked as if complete diversity were consti-

tutionally required, but the remark was not necessary to decision.

35. This is notably true with regard to federal-question jurisdiction. See § 17 n. 16 above.

36. See § 23 n. 9 above and ALI Study, §§ 2371–2376.

37. See § 23 above.

38. 1967, 87 S.Ct. 1199, 1203–1204, 386 U.S. 523, 530–531, 18 L.Ed.2d 270.

not co-citizens. Accordingly, we conclude that the present case is properly in the federal courts." [39]

It must be kept clearly in mind that the Tashire case holds only that complete diversity is not required by the Constitution, and that Congress can permit less. It does not alter the established construction of the general diversity statute, and except where Congress, as in the interpleader statute, has authorized something less than complete diversity, Strawbridge v. Curtiss remains the controlling rule. [40]

A few district-court cases relied on the then-evolving concept of "pendent parties" to entertain suits in which diversity was not complete. [41] Most courts recognized that whatever the merits, or lack thereof, of that concept to bring in additional parties in cases in which there is a federal question [42] or to overcome problems of amount in controversy, [43] it was not properly used to avoid the longstanding requirement of complete diversity. [44] The 1990 statute codifying a concept of "supplemental jurisdiction" and allowing the bringing in of "pendent parties" is limited so that it cannot be used to thwart the requirement of complete diversity. [45]

§ 25. Exceptions From the Diversity Jurisdiction [1]

The diversity statute, 28 U.S.C.A. § 1332, purports to speak in very broad terms. If a suit is between citizens of different states, and the jurisdictional amount is satisfied, the district court has original jurisdiction. There are, however, limitations on the breadth of the jurisdiction thus seemingly conferred.

Thus, it is provided by statute that there is no jurisdiction if a party, by assignment or otherwise, is improperly or collusively joined to invoke federal jurisdiction. [2] The rule is also well settled that a federal court cannot entertain an in-rem action if the property is already in the

---

39. 87 S.Ct. at 1203–1204, 386 U.S. at 531. The Court indicated, id. at n. 7, that "full-dress arguments for the constitutionality of 'minimal diversity' " might be found in several cited lower-court opinions and in scholarly writings. See particularly Supporting Memorandum A in ALI Study, pp. 426–436, one of the sources cited by the Court.

40. Professor Currie believes that Strawbridge was wrongly decided and should be overruled by statute. Currie, note 9 above, at 18–34.

41. Wittersheim v. General Transp. Services, Inc., D.C.Va.1974, 378 F.Supp. 762; Campbell v. Triangle Corp., D.C.Pa.1972, 336 F.Supp. 1002. Both of these cases relied on Borror v. Sharon Steel Co., C.A.3d, 1964, 327 F.2d 165, but that case was easily distinguishable, as the Third Circuit itself recognized in the Seyler case, note 44 below.

42. See § 19 above.

43. See § 36 below.

44. Parker v. W.W. Moore & Sons, Inc., C.A.4th, 1975, 528 F.2d 764; Seyler v. Steuben Motors, Inc., C.A.3d, 1972, 462 F.2d 181; 13B Wright, Miller & Cooper, Jurisdiction 2d § 3605. This view was confirmed by the Supreme Court, though in a somewhat different context. Owen Equipment & Erection Co. v. Kroger, 1978, 98 S.Ct. 2396, 2404–2405, 437 U.S. 365, 377, 57 L.Ed.2d 274.

45. 28 U.S.C.A. § 1367(b). See § 9 above.

§ 25

1. 13B Wright, Miller & Cooper, Jurisdiction 2d §§ 3609, 3610; Vestal & Foster, Implied Limitations on the Diversity Jurisdiction of Federal Courts, 1956, 41 Minn. L.Rev. 1.

2. 28 U.S.C.A. § 1359. See § 31 below.

custody of a state court of competent jurisdiction;[3] the rule is based on considerations of comity, but it is cast in terms of a limitation on the jurisdiction of the federal court.[4] The rapidly burgeoning abstention doctrines permit, and in some circumstances may require, a federal court to decline jurisdiction, or to postpone its exercise, even though the requirements of the diversity statute are satisfied.[5]

Finally there are two important areas, domestic-relations cases and probate matters, where, by a judge-made exception to the statute, the federal courts will not act though diversity is present.[6] These two exceptions were first developed at a time when the diversity statute granted jurisdiction of "suits of a civil nature in law or in equity," and it was thought that the domestic-relations and probate cases, being matters that would have been heard in the ecclesiastical courts, did not fit this description. The 1948 Judicial Code substituted the term "civil action" for the phrase used in the older statutes, but the exceptions have persisted. Today the exceptions may more rationally be defended on the ground that these are areas of the law in which the states have an especially strong interest and a well-developed competence for dealing with them.[7]

The exception with regard to domestic-relations cases dates back to a dictum in an 1859 case. There the Court held that a wife could sue, on the basis of diversity, in a federal court in Wisconsin to enforce the decree of a New York state court that granted her a divorce and alimony, but it added: "We disclaim altogether any jurisdiction in the courts of the United States upon the subject of divorce, or for the allowance of alimony, either as an original proceeding in chancery or as an incident to divorce *a vinculo,* or to one from bed and board."[8] In a later case the Supreme Court announced that federal courts cannot hear child-custody cases, making the sweeping statement that "the whole subject of the domestic relations of husband and wife, parent and child, belongs to the laws of the States and not to the laws of the United States."[9]

3. Princess Lida of Thurn and Taxis v. Thompson, 1939, 59 S.Ct. 275, 305 U.S. 456, 83 L.Ed. 285; 14 Wright, Miller & Cooper, Jurisdiction 2d § 3631.

4. Princess Lida of Thurn and Taxis v. Thompson, 1939, 59 S.Ct. 275, 281, 305 U.S. 456, 467–468, 83 L.Ed. 285. See also Porter v. Sabin, 1893, 13 S.Ct. 1008, 1010, 149 U.S. 473, 480, 37 L.Ed. 815; Wabash R. Co. v. Adelbert College, 1908, 28 S.Ct. 182, 187, 208 U.S. 38, 54, 52 L.Ed. 379; Lion Bonding & Sur. Co. v. Karatz, 1923, 43 S.Ct. 480, 484, 262 U.S. 77, 88–89, 67 L.Ed. 871.

5. See §§ 52, 52A below.

6. These limitations are inapplicable in the territories, and prior to the 1970 reorganization of the District of Columbia courts—see § 5 above—they were inapplicable there, but the basis of jurisdiction is not diversity in those places.

7. Ankenbrandt v. Richards, 1992, 112 S.Ct. 2206, 2215, ___ U.S. ___, ___, 119 L.Ed.2d 468; Phillips, Nizer, Benjamin, Krim & Ballon v. Rosenstiel, C.A.2d, 1973, 490 F.2d 509, 512.

8. Barber v. Barber, 1858, 21 How. 582, 584, 16 L.Ed. 226.

See generally 13B Wright, Miller & Cooper, Jurisdiction 2d § 3609.

9. Ex parte Burrus, 1890, 10 S.Ct. 850, 853, 136 U.S. 586, 593–594, 34 L.Ed. 500 (federal court order granting habeas corpus to obtain custody of a child was absolutely void, and could be disregarded with impunity).

One extreme case held that a state court had jurisdiction of an action for divorce against the consul of a foreign country, though normally the federal courts have exclusive jurisdiction of actions against con-

It was not until 1992, in Ankenbrandt v. Richards,[10] that the Supreme Court spoke clearly on the rationale and the present vitality of this exception. It explained there that domestic-relations matters are within the judicial power of the United States, as defined in Article III, and that the 1859 decision must have been based on a belief that the language of the diversity statute, as it then stood, did not extend to matters that would have been beyond the jurisdiction of the court of chancery in England. Although the language of the diversity statute was changed in 1948, the Ankenbrandt case reasoned that Congress did not intend to make any change in this long-standing interpretation of the statute. But in Ankenbrandt the Court was at pains to put limits on the exception. It "encompasses only cases involving the issuance of a divorce, alimony, or child custody decree,"[11] and does not apply to an action such as the Ankenbrandt case itself, in which a woman was suing her former husband and his female companion for torts allegedly committed against the plaintiff's children. The Court said that there may be circumstances in which Burford-type abstention[12] would be relevant in other kinds of cases involving elements of the domestic relationship,[13] but this was not true in Ankenbrandt where the status of the domestic relationship had been determined as a matter of state law and in any event had no bearing on the underlying torts involved.

The exception from the diversity jurisdiction for probate matters[14] is far from absolute. It turns, instead, on unclear distinctions of the utmost subtlety. A federal court may not probate a will nor undertake the administration of an estate.[15] But if diversity or some other basis for jurisdiction is present, the federal court can entertain actions against administrators, executors, and other claimants in which plaintiffs seek to establish their claims against an estate so long as the federal court does not interfere with the probate proceedings or assume general jurisdiction of the probate or control of the property in the custody of the state court.[16] The federal action in such a case will establish the claimant's

---

suls, 28 U.S.C.A. § 1351, on the ground that a federal court could not entertain the divorce action. Ohio ex rel. Popovici v. Agler, 1930, 50 S.Ct. 154, 280 U.S. 379, 74 L.Ed. 489.

10. 1992, 112 S.Ct. 2206, ___ U.S. ___, 119 L.Ed.2d 468, noted 1993, 28 Wake Forest L.Rev. 1137.

11. 112 S.Ct. at 2215, ___ U.S. at ___.

12. See § 52A below.

13. "Such might well be the case if a federal suit were filed prior to effectuation of a divorce, alimony, or child custody decree, and the suit depended on a determination of the status of the parties." 112 S.Ct. at 2216, ___ U.S. at ___.

14. See 13B Wright, Miller & Cooper, Jurisdiction 2d § 3610; Vestal & Foster, note 1 above, at 13–23; Comment, Federal Court Probate Proceedings, 1970, 45 Ind.

L.J. 387. In Dragan v. Miller, C.A.7th, 1982, 679 F.2d 712, certiorari denied 103 S.Ct. 378, 459 U.S. 1017, 74 L.Ed.2d 511, there is an interesting discussion by Judge Posner of what he calls "one of the most mysterious and esoteric branches of the law of federal jurisdiction."

15. In re Broderick's Will, 1875, 21 Wall. 503, 22 L.Ed. 599; Hook v. Payne, 1872, 14 Wall. 252, 20 L.Ed. 887; Byers v. McAuley, 1893, 13 S.Ct. 906, 149 U.S. 608, 37 L.Ed. 867; Turton v. Turton, C.A.5th, 1981, 644 F.2d 344.

16. Markham v. Allen, 1946, 66 S.Ct. 296, 326 U.S. 490, 90 L.Ed. 256; Waterman v. Canal–Louisiana Bank & Trust Co., 1909, 30 S.Ct. 10, 215 U.S. 33, 54 L.Ed. 80; Georges v. Glick, C.A.7th, 1988, 856 F.2d 971, certiorari denied 109 S.Ct. 1570, 489 U.S. 1097, 103 L.Ed.2d 936; Lee v. Hunt, D.C.La.1977, 431 F.Supp. 371.

right in a fashion that will be binding in the state proceedings, but the federal court cannot order actual distribution of property in the custody of the state court nor give execution on its judgment.[17]

The state practice is controlling as to will contests. If the state permits an independent action to annul a will or to set aside a probate, such an action may be brought in federal court if jurisdictional requisites are met, but the federal court will not take jurisdiction if the state regards such contests as ancillary to the probate proceedings.[18] Federal courts will also entertain actions to construe wills or trusts,[19] and will hear suits seeking a personal judgment against an executor or administrator for fraud, but only if a final accounting has been made in the state probate proceeding.[20] A federal court has power to appoint or to remove a trustee,[21] but it may not interfere with property in the custody of a state court.[22]

§ 26. The Meaning of Citizenship [1]

Diversity jurisdiction is dependent upon the citizenship of the parties. Though the Fourteenth Amendment declares that citizens of the United States are citizens "of the State wherein they reside," it is quite settled that mere residence in a state is not enough for purposes of diversity,[2] and that the more elusive concept of "domicile" is controlling.[3] A person's domicile is that place where he has his true, fixed, and permanent home and principal establishment, and to which he has the intention of returning whenever he is absent therefrom.[4] A person may

17. Byers v. McAuley, 1893, 13 S.Ct. 906, 149 U.S. 608, 37 L.Ed. 867; Yonley v. Lavender, 1874, 21 Wall. 276, 22 L.Ed. 536.

18. Sutton v. English, 1918, 38 S.Ct. 254, 246 U.S. 199, 62 L.Ed. 664; McKibben v. Chubb, C.A.10th, 1988, 840 F.2d 1525, 1529–1530.

19. Colton v. Colton, 1888, 8 S.Ct. 1164, 127 U.S. 300, 32 L.Ed. 138; Fontain v. Ravenel, 1854, 17 How. 369, 15 L.Ed. 80.

20. Compare Lathan v. Edwards, C.C.A.5th, 1941, 121 F.2d 183, with Kittredge v. Stevens, C.C.A.1st, 1942, 126 F.2d 263, certiorari denied 63 S.Ct. 34, 317 U.S. 642, 87 L.Ed. 517. See 13B Wright, Miller & Cooper, Jurisdiction 2d § 3610.

21. Burgess v. Murray, C.A.5th, 1952, 194 F.2d 131, 133.

22. Bedo v. McGuire, C.A.6th, 1985, 767 F.2d 305; Kenney v. Kenney, C.A.D.C.1963, 314 F.2d 268; Beach v. Rome Trust Co., C.A.2d, 1959, 269 F.2d 367; In re Butler's Trust, D.C.Minn.1962, 201 F.Supp. 316.

§ 26

1. 13B Wright, Miller & Cooper, Jurisdiction 2d §§ 3611–3613; Weckstein, Citizenship for Purposes of Diversity Jurisdiction, 1972, 26 Sw.L.J. 360.

2. Sun Printing & Pub. Assn. v. Edwards, 1904, 24 S.Ct. 696, 194 U.S. 377, 48 L.Ed. 1027. It had been held in Robertson v. Cease, 1878, 97 U.S. 646, 24 L.Ed. 1057, that the prior rule to this effect had not been changed by the Fourteenth Amendment. See also Poulos v. Naas Foods, Inc., C.A.7th, 1992, 959 F.2d 69, 70 n. 1.

3. 13 Wright, Miller & Cooper, Jurisdiction § 3612. Chicago & N.W.R. Co. v. Ohle, 1886, 6 S.Ct. 632, 117 U.S. 123, 29 L.Ed. 837; Reynolds v. Adden, 1890, 10 S.Ct. 843, 136 U.S. 348, 34 L.Ed. 360; Rodriguez–Diaz v. Sierra–Martinez, C.A.1st 1988, 853 F.2d 1027.

A federal test is applied in determining domicile for purposes of diversity. Kantor v. Wellesley Galleries, Ltd., C.A.9th, 1983, 704 F.2d 1088; Sadat v. Mertes, C.A.7th, 1980, 615 F.2d 1176; Ziady v. Curley, C.A.4th, 1968, 396 F.2d 873.

4. Stine v. Moore, C.A.5th, 1954, 213 F.2d 446, 448, paraphrasing the much-quoted definition in Story, Conflict of Laws, 8th ed. 1883, § 41. See also 13B Wright, Miller & Cooper, Jurisdiction 2d § 3612.

The definition of "domicile" in Restatement, Conflict of Laws, 1934, § 9, is rather more vague than that set forth in the text.

have a number of residences, but it is impossible for him to have more than one domicile.[5] The domicile of a child, at least until it is emancipated, has been thought to be that of its parents.[6] Traditionally a married woman acquired the domicile of her husband, but the modern tendency is to allow a married woman to acquire a separate domicile and to determine her domicile through the same objective examination of the circumstances that is made for other persons.[7]

A citizen of the United States can change his domicile instantly. To do so, two elements are necessary. He must take up residence at the new domicile, and he must intend to remain there indefinitely. Neither the physical presence nor the intention to remain is alone sufficient.[8] He need not intend to remain permanently at the new domicile;[9] it is enough that he intends to make the new state his home and that he has no present intention of going elsewhere.[10] If these two elements are

See also Restatement Second of Conflict of Laws, 1971, §§ 11–23. One difficulty with this subject is the tendency to use cases and texts dealing with "domicile" in the law of conflicts as applicable to "domicile" for purposes of federal jurisdiction. The problem of what law to apply is surely a different problem from that of whether a litigant should have access to federal court, and it does not conduce to clarity of analysis to suppose that the same answers will suffice for different questions. The notion that conflicts-of-laws principles are determinative of "domicile" for purposes of diversity is rejected in Stifel v. Hopkins, C.A.6th, 1973, 477 F.2d 1116, 1124. And see Krasnov v. Dinan, C.A.3d, 1972, 465 F.2d 1298, 1300 n. 1. Instead those cases, and such other cases as Galva Foundry Co. v. Heiden, C.A.7th, 1991, 924 F.2d 729, 730, Ziady v. Curley, C.A.4th, 1968, 396 F.2d 873, and Elliott v. Krear, D.C.Va.1979, 466 F.Supp. 444, give attention to the policy of diversity jurisdiction to protect out-of-state litigants from bias, and look to whether a party is a stranger to a state who might be the victim of bias.

5. Harding v. Standard Oil Co., C.C.D.Ill.1910, 182 F. 421; Restatement Second of Conflict of Laws, 1971, § 11.

6. Rodriguez–Diaz v. Sierra–Martinez, C.A.1st, 1988, 853 F.2d 1027; Delaware, L. & W.R. Co. v. Petrowsky, C.C.A.2d, 1918, 250 F. 554, 558–559, certiorari denied 38 S.Ct. 427, 247 U.S. 508, 62 L.Ed. 1241. See Beale, The Domicile of an Infant, 1923, 8 Cornell L.Q. 103.

But see Ziady v. Curley, C.A.4th, 1968, 396 F.2d 873; Elliott v. Krear, D.C.Va.1979, 466 F.Supp. 444; Restatement Second of Conflict of Laws, 1971, § 22; 13B Wright, Miller & Cooper, Jurisdiction 2d § 3615.

7. 13B Wright, Miller & Cooper, Jurisdiction 2d § 3614. Williamson v. Osenton, 1914, 34 S.Ct. 442, 232 U.S. 619, 58 L.Ed. 758; Napletana v. Hillsdale College, C.A.6th, 1967, 385 F.2d 871; Knapp v. State Farm Ins., D.C.La.1984, 584 F.Supp. 905.

8. 13B Wright, Miller & Cooper, Jurisdiction 2d § 3613; Mitchell v. U.S., 1874, 21 Wall. 350, 22 L.Ed. 584; Sun Printing & Pub. Assn. v. Edwards, 1904, 24 S.Ct. 696, 194 U.S. 377, 48 L.Ed. 1027; Lew v. Moss, C.A.9th, 1986, 797 F.2d 747, 749–750.

9. Hawes v. Club Ecuestre El Comandante, C.A.1st, 1979, 598 F.2d 698; Hardin v. McAvoy, C.A.5th, 1954, 216 F.2d 399; Gallagher v. Philadelphia Transp. Co., C.A.3d, 1950, 185 F.2d 543; Brookley v. Ranson, D.C.Iowa 1974, 376 F.Supp. 195; 13B Wright, Miller & Cooper, Jurisdiction 2d § 3613.

10. Chicago & N.W.R. Co. v. Ohle, 1886, 6 S.Ct. 632, 117 U.S. 123, 29 L.Ed. 837; Gilbert v. David, 1915, 35 S.Ct. 164, 235 U.S. 561, 59 L.Ed. 360; Milliken v. Tri–County Elec. Co-op., Inc., D.C.S.C.1966, 254 F.Supp. 302, 305, noted 1966, 18 S.C.L.Rev. 847; Anderson v. Splint Coal Corp., D.C.Ky.1937, 20 F.Supp. 233. Compare Morris v. Gilmer, 1889, 9 S.Ct. 289, 129 U.S. 315, 32 L.Ed. 690, where a move to another state was ineffective to change domicile in view of the party's testimony that whether he would return to the original state "depends altogether upon circumstances."

A citizen of Missouri who was studying at Ohio State and intended to remain in Ohio only as long as his studies required did not acquire an Ohio domicile. Holmes v. Sopuch, C.A.8th, 1981, 639 F.2d 431. See also Mas v. Perry, C.A.5th, 1974, 489 F.2d 1396, certiorari denied 95 S.Ct. 74, 419 U.S. 842, satisfied, it is immaterial that the motive for the change of domicile was to create diversity and gain access to federal court.[11]

The determination of whether a party has in fact made a bona fide change of domicile may, in the discretion of the court, be made either by the judge or by the jury.[12] The "normal and usual course" is for the judge to determine this question,[13] and it is said that the judge cannot be charged with abuse of discretion in doing so.[14] In determining whether a party has intended to establish a domicile in the state to which he or she has moved, the factfinder will look to such circumstances as the party's declarations, exercise of political rights, payment of personal taxes, house of residence, and place of business.[15]

§ 27. Corporations and Other Associations [1]

When the Constitution was adopted, the private corporation was virtually unknown. One of the most interesting chapters in constitutional history has been the effort, frequently successful, to obtain for corporations the benefits extended by the Constitution to natural persons.[2] Among the benefits thus sought has been the right to invoke the diversity jurisdiction of the federal courts.[3]

In 1809, when the Court was first faced with the problem in the Deveaux case, Chief Justice Marshall referred to the corporation as an "invisible, intangible, and artificial being," a "mere legal entity" which is "certainly not a citizen." [4] In his view the citizenship of the members of the corporation would control.

This view did not long prevail. The increased use of the corporate device as a means of doing business and the desire of these corporations

42 L.Ed.2d 70; Scoggins v. Pollock, C.A.11th, 1984, 727 F.2d 1025; Las Vistas Villas, S.A. v. Petersen, D.C.Fla.1991, 778 F.Supp. 1202. But see Bair v. Peck, D.C.Kan.1990, 738 F.Supp. 1354. See 13B Wright, Miller & Cooper, Jurisdiction 2d § 3619.

11. Williamson v. Osenton, 1914, 34 S.Ct. 442, 232 U.S. 619, 58 L.Ed. 758; Roorda v. Volkswagenwerk, A.G., D.C.S.C. 1979, 481 F.Supp. 868.

12. Gilbert v. David, 1915, 35 S.Ct. 164, 235 U.S. 561, 59 L.Ed. 360. On pleading and proof as to jurisdictional questions generally, see § 69 below.

13. Hardin v. McAvoy, C.A.5th, 1954, 216 F.2d 399, 403. See also Galva Foundry Co. v. Heiden, C.A.7th, 1991, 924 F.2d 729, and Lew v. Moss, C.A.9th, 1986, 797 F.2d 747, holding that the determination of domicile by the district judge is to be upheld unless clearly erroneous.

14. Seideman v. Hamilton, C.A.3d, 1960, 275 F.2d 224, certiorari denied 80 S.Ct. 1258, 363 U.S. 820, 4 L.Ed.2d 1517.

15. Mitchell v. U.S., 1874, 21 Wall. 350, 353, 22 L.Ed. 584. Illustrative cases hold-

ing that particular circumstances were or were not sufficient to establish a new domicile are cited in 13 Wright, Miller & Cooper, Jurisdiction § 3612.

§ 27

1. 13B Wright, Miller & Cooper, Jurisdiction 2d §§ 3623–3630.

2. The classic work is Henderson, The Position of Foreign Corporations in American Constitutional Law, 1918.

3. See Warren, Corporations and Diversity of Citizenship, 1933, 19 Va.L.Rev. 661; McGovney, A Supreme Court Fiction: Corporations in the Diverse Citizenship Jurisdiction of the Federal Courts, 1943, 56 Harv.L.Rev. 853, 1090, 1225; Green, Corporations as Persons, Citizens, and Possessors of Liberty, 1945, 94 U.Pa.L.Rev. 202; Moore & Weckstein, Corporations and Diversity of Citizenship Jurisdiction: A Supreme Court Fiction Revisited, 1964, 77 Harv.L.Rev. 1426.

4. Bank of the United States v. Deveaux, 1809, 5 Cranch 61, 86, 3 L.Ed. 38.

to resort to federal court proved irresistible. Thus, in 1844, in the Letson case, the Court declared that a corporation chartered by a state is "entitled, for the purpose of suing and being sued, to be deemed a citizen of that state."[5] Pressure from dissenting judges forced reexamination of this position ten years later, but while the rationale changed, the practical result remained the same. In Marshall v. Baltimore & Ohio R. Co.[6] the Court returned to Chief Justice Marshall's view that a corporation is an artificial being, that it cannot be a citizen and that the citizenship of the stockholders must control, but it then created a conclusive presumption that all of the stockholders of a corporation are citizens of the state of incorporation. Except as modified by a 1958 statute, to be discussed below, this proposition remains settled law.[7] Indeed it may have been extended, or at least carried to its logical limits. There is a similar presumption that all of the stockholders of a corporation chartered by a foreign country are citizens of that country, and the corporation may come into federal court under the alienage jurisdiction.[8] Municipal corporations are regarded as citizens of the state in which they are located,[9] though the state itself is not a citizen for purposes of diversity.[10] National banks, not chartered by any state, are, by statute, to be "deemed citizens" of the states in which they are located,[11] and some courts have reached the same result with regard to other corporations chartered by the federal government with activity localized in a particular state.[12]

The conclusive presumption that all the stockholders of a corporation are citizens of the state of incorporation was dubious in 1854.

---

5. Louisville, C. & C.R. Co. v. Letson, 1844, 2 How. 497, 555, 11 L.Ed. 353.

6. 1853, 16 How. 314, 14 L.Ed. 953.

7. The Court has said that the rule laid down in the Marshall case was "a compromise destined to endure for over a century," United Steelworkers of America v. R.H. Bouligny, Inc., 1965, 86 S.Ct. 272, 273, 382 U.S. 145, 148, 15 L.Ed.2d 217, and that "the rule regarding the treatment of corporations as 'citizens' has become firmly established * * *." Carden v. Arkoma Associates, 1990, 110 S.Ct. 1015, 1018, 494 U.S. 185, 189, 108 L.Ed.2d 157.

8. National S.S. Co. v. Tugman, 1882, 1 S.Ct. 58, 106 U.S. 118, 27 L.Ed. 87; Barrow S.S. Co. v. Kane, 1898, 18 S.Ct. 526, 170 U.S. 100, 42 L.Ed. 964.

9. Moor v. County of Alameda, 1973, 93 S.Ct. 1785, 1800–1802, 411 U.S. 693, 717–721, 36 L.Ed.2d 596; Illinois v. City of Milwaukee, 1972, 92 S.Ct. 1385, 1390, 406 U.S. 91, 97, 31 L.Ed.2d 712; Cowles v. Mercer County, 1868, 7 Wall. 118, 74 U.S. 118, 19 L.Ed. 86.

If suit against a governmental unit is in reality a suit against the state itself, the Eleventh Amendment deprives the court of jurisdiction. See § 46 below.

10. Postal Telegraph Cable Co. v. Alabama, 1894, 15 S.Ct. 192, 155 U.S. 482, 39 L.Ed. 231; Nuclear Engineering Co. v. Scott, C.A.7th, 1981, 660 F.2d 241, 250, certiorari denied 102 S.Ct. 1622, 455 U.S. 993, 71 L.Ed.2d 855; 13B Wright, Miller & Cooper, Jurisdiction 2d § 3602 n. 13.

11. 28 U.S.C.A. § 1348; Walker v. Bank of America Nat. Trust & Sav. Assn., C.A.9th, 1959, 268 F.2d 16, certiorari denied 80 S.Ct. 211, 361 U.S. 903, 4 L.Ed.2d 158.

12. Feuchtwanger Corp. v. Lake Hiawatha Federal Credit Union, C.A.3d, 1959, 272 F.2d 453; Provident Nat. Bank v. California Fed. Sav. & Loan Assn., D.C.Pa.1985, 624 F.Supp. 858, affirmed C.A.3d, 1987, 819 F.2d 434; Elwert v. Pacific First Federal Sav. & Loan Assn., D.C.Or.1956, 138 F.Supp. 395. See Moore & Weckstein, note 3 above, at 1436–1438. Contra: Hancock Financial Corp. v. Federal Sav. & Loan Ins. Corp., C.A.9th, 1974, 492 F.2d 1325; Rice v. Disabled American Veterans, D.C.D.C.1968, 295 F.Supp. 131.

See generally 13B Wright, Miller & Cooper, Jurisdiction 2d § 3627.

Today it is clear that it is purest fiction. Marshall v. Baltimore & Ohio R. Co., and the doctrine that is based on it, have been severely criticized, as an expansion of federal jurisdiction by means of fiction.[13] It may be argued, however, that it is the Deveaux case, not the Marshall case, that is wrong. A corporation is an entity quite apart from its stockholders, an out-of-state corporation is as likely to be the object of local prejudice as is an out-of-state individual, and arguably should have whatever protection a federal court can provide.[14] One's view on this question is very likely to be determined by his or her position as to the utility of diversity jurisdiction generally.[15]

Even those who favor permitting corporations to avail themselves of diversity jurisdiction have recognized that it is an abuse of this jurisdiction when "a local institution, engaged in a local business and in many cases locally owned, is enabled to bring its litigation into the Federal courts simply because it has obtained a corporate charter from another State."[16] To prevent such abuse, and as part of a general purpose to limit diversity jurisdiction,[17] a 1958 statute provided that a corporation shall be deemed a citizen of any state in which it has been incorporated and of the state in which it has its principal place of business.[18] Arguments that the statute was unconstitutional were properly rejected by the courts as insubstantial.[19] The statute does not give the pleader an option to allege the corporation's citizenship as being either that of the state of incorporation or that of the state where the principal place of business is located. Instead the corporation must be regarded as a citizen of both states. Thus, where a corporation incorporated in Delaware and with its principal place of business in Ohio is a party to the suit, diversity is lacking if any adverse party is a citizen either of Delaware or of Ohio.[20]

---

13. See the articles by Warren and by McGovney cited note 3 above. A contrary view is expressed in Phillips & Christensen, Should Corporations Be Regarded as Citizens Within the Diversity Jurisdiction Provisions?, 1962, 48 A.B.A.J. 435.

The American Law Institute proposed to bar a corporation or other business association from invoking diversity jurisdiction in a state in which it has had, for two years, a "local establishment," as elaborately defined, in any action arising out of the activities of the local establishment. ALI Study, § 1302(b). One court has said that this proposal "makes a good deal of sense and is much more compatible with what little basis there is for diversity jurisdiction." Asher v. Pacific Power & Light Co., D.C.Cal. 1965, 249 F.Supp. 671, 678. But Professors Moore & Weckstein, in the article cited note 3 above, say, at 1451, that the proposal is "not only unnecessary but unwise."

14. See the articles by Green and by Moore & Weckstein, note 3 above.

15. See § 23 above.

16. Sen.Rep. No. 1830, 85th Cong., 2d Sess., 1958, U.S.Code Cong. & Adm.News, pp. 3099, 3101–3102.

17. See 13B Wright, Miller & Cooper, Jurisdiction 2d § 3624.

18. 28 U.S.C.A. § 1332(c), as amended by Act of July 25, 1958, § 2, 72 Stat. 415. For the legislative history of the Act, see the Senate Report cited note 16 above.

19. E.g., Eldridge v. Richfield Oil Corp., D.C.Cal.1965, 247 F.Supp. 407, affirmed C.A.9th, 1966, 364 F.2d 909, certiorari denied 87 S.Ct. 750, 385 U.S. 1020, 17 L.Ed.2d 556.

20. Canton v. Angelina Cas. Co., C.A.5th, 1960, 279 F.2d 553; Bender v. Hilton Riviera Corp., D.C.Puerto Rico 1973, 367 F.Supp. 380; Jaconski v. McCloskey & Co., D.C.Pa.1958, 167 F.Supp. 537.

Prior to the adoption of the 1958 statute, there was a vexing question in determining the citizenship of corporations incorporated in more than one state. The general rule was that if such a corporation were a party to a lawsuit in one of the states in which it was incorporated, it would be considered solely a citizen of that state. Thus, if a citizen of Massachusetts sued a corporation incorporated both in New York and Massachusetts, diversity existed if the suit was brought in federal court in New York, where the corporation would be regarded as a citizen of New York, but if the suit was brought in federal court in Massachusetts, the corporation would be regarded as a Massachusetts citizen, and the suit dismissed for want of diversity.[21] Several courts and writers thought that this artificial rule had survived the 1958 reform,[22] but the sounder view is to the contrary. The matter would be clearcut if the 1958 statute had said that the corporation is to be deemed a citizen of "every" state in which it has been incorporated,[23] but this is the most logical, and surely the most desirable, meaning to ascribe to the phrase "any state" that Congress actually used.[24]

The legislative history of the 1958 statute indicates that the "principal place of business" of a corporation is to be determined by tests developed for the similar phrase in the Bankruptcy Act.[25] The determi-

21. Seavey v. Boston & M.R. Co., C.A.1st, 1952, 197 F.2d 485; Jacobson v. New York, N.H. & H.R. Co., C.A.1st, 1953, 206 F.2d 153, affirmed per curiam, 1954, 74 S.Ct. 474, 347 U.S. 909, 98 L.Ed. 1067; cf. Patch v. Wabash R. Co., 1907, 28 S.Ct. 80, 207 U.S. 277, 52 L.Ed. 204. Contra: Gavin v. Hudson & M.R. Co., C.A.3d, 1950, 185 F.2d 104 (in the example given in the text, the Massachusetts plaintiff could treat the corporation as a New York citizen in whichever state he brought suit).

Professor Weckstein's exhaustive examination of the question recognizes that the Supreme Court had taken "seemingly irreconcilable positions," but concludes that the proposition stated in the text "may be accepted as the law as it existed prior to the 1958 Amendment." Weckstein, Multi-State Corporations and Diversity of Citizenship: A Field Day for Fictions, 1964, 31 Tenn.L.Rev. 195, 198, 202. To Professor Currie this is "less certain." Currie, Federal Courts: Cases and Materials, 4th ed. 1990, p. 286. See also Currie, The Federal Courts and the American Law Institute, 1968, 36 U.Chi.L.Rev. 1, 39–43.

Under the former rule, a corporation was not considered as incorporated in a second state where the second state compelled the reincorporation as a condition of doing business. Southern R. Co. v. Allison, 1903, 23 S.Ct. 713, 190 U.S. 326, 47 L.Ed. 1078.

22. Hudak v. Port Auth. Trans–Hudson Corp., D.C.N.Y.1965, 238 F.Supp. 790; Ma-

jewski v. New York Central R. Co., D.C.Mich.1964, 227 F.Supp. 950; see Jaconski v. McCloskey & Co., D.C.Pa.1958, 167 F.Supp. 537, 540; Friedenthal, New Limitations on Federal Jurisdiction, 1959, 11 Stan.L.Rev. 213, 236–241.

23. As in ALI Study, § 1301(b)(1).

24. Yancoskie v. Delaware River Port Auth., C.A.3d, 1975, 528 F.2d 722, 727 n. 17; Smith v. Arundel Co-op., Inc., D.C.D.C. 1987, 660 F.Supp. 912, 913–914; Oslick v. Port Auth. of New York and New Jersey, D.C.N.Y.1979, 83 F.R.D. 494; French v. Clinchfield Coal Co., D.C.Del.1976, 407 F.Supp. 13; Evans–Hailey Co. v. Crane Co., D.C.Tenn.1962, 207 F.Supp. 193, appeal dismissed 1965, 86 S.Ct. 10, 382 U.S. 801, 15 L.Ed.2d 55; 13B Wright, Miller & Cooper, Jurisdiction 2d § 3626; Weckstein, note 21 above, at 210–216.

But cf. Rudisill v. Southern Ry. Co., D.C.N.C.1976, 424 F.Supp. 1102, affirmed C.A.4th, 1977, 548 F.2d 488, holding that a corporation is not to be regarded as a citizen of a state in which it was compelled to reincorporate as a condition of doing business in that state.

25. Moesser v. Crucible Steel Co. of America, D.C.Pa.1959, 173 F.Supp. 953. For the legislative history see the Senate Report cited note 16 above, and see Inland Rubber Corp. v. Triple A Tire Serv., Inc., D.C.N.Y.1963, 220 F.Supp. 490, 492–495. The phrase appears in the Bankruptcy Act at former 11 U.S.C.A. § 11 (11 U.S.C.A.

nation of the principal place of business has not been as simple a matter as this might suggest. It is, in each case, a question of fact, and the court must consider such factors as the character of the corporation, its purposes, the kind of business in which it is engaged, and the situs of its operations.[26]

The early cases seemed to divide between two different views on how to determine the principal place of business of a corporation with significant activities in several states. On one view, the principal place of business was the place where a corporation's home office was located, since this was "the nerve center from which it radiates out to its constituent parts and from which its officers direct, control and coordinate all activities without regard to locale, in the furtherance of the corporate objective."[27] The other principal view looked to the place where day-to-day control of the business is exercised.[28] Indeed there were also cases that held that the principal place of business was the place where the corporation carried on the bulk of its activity, even though the home office, in either of the senses described above, was elsewhere.[29]

The essential difficulty is that the 1958 amendment is read, rightly so it seems, as meaning that every corporation must have one, but only one, "principal place of business."[30] This is highly unrealistic when applied to a far-flung corporate enterprise,[31] and the unreality of the process has given new vigor to those who urge that a corporation should be deemed a citizen of every state in which it has substantial local

§ 109(a)). Cases construing the phrase in that Act are collected in the Appendix to Kelly v. U.S. Steel Corp., C.A.3d, 1960, 284 F.2d 850, 855. As the Kelly case points out, at 852, though the question is one of fact, the relative significance of different facts is a question of law. Moore & Weckstein, in the article cited note 3 above, at 1439, are critical of the suggestion that the bankruptcy cases could be used as precedent since "ample precedent there was, but consistent precedent there was not."

26. The cases collected in 13B Wright, Miller & Cooper, Jurisdiction 2d § 3625, illustrate the welter of views courts have taken and the variety of factors that have been considered.

27. Scot Typewriter Co. v. Underwood Corp., D.C.N.Y.1959, 170 F.Supp. 862, 865. See also Wisconsin Knife Works v. National Metal Crafters, C.A.7th, 1986, 781 F.2d 1280–1282. For the factors to be considered in a circuit that continues to adhere to the "nerve center" test, see Chamberlain Mfg. Corp. v. Maremont Corp., D.C.Ill.1993, 828 F.Supp. 589.

28. Kelly v. U.S. Steel Corp., C.A.3d, 1960, 284 F.2d 850.

29. Anniston Soil Pipe Co. v. Central Foundry Co., C.A.5th, 1964, 329 F.2d 313; Lurie v. Loew's San Francisco Hotel Corp., D.C.Cal.1970, 315 F.Supp. 405; Inland Rubber Corp. v. Triple A Tire Serv., Inc., D.C.N.Y.1963, 220 F.Supp. 490.

30. J.A. Olson Co. v. City of Winona, C.A.5th, 1987, 818 F.2d 401, 406; Campbell v. Associated Press, D.C.Pa.1963, 223 F.Supp. 151, 153–154; Kaufman v. General Ins. Co. of America, D.C.Cal.1961, 192 F.Supp. 238, 240–242.

31. "The concept may get artificial in some cases as indeed it is in the case before us. This great corporation has fourteen divisions of the parent corporation and eleven principal subordinate companies. Its various manufacturing activities are spread over practically all the United States and extend to foreign countries. It has literally dozens of important places of business one of which we must pick out as the principal one because the statute says so." Kelly v. U.S. Steel Corp., C.A.3d, 1960, 284 F.2d 850, 853 (per Goodrich, J.).

activity.[32] So long as the present statutory test is to be employed, reliance on the location of the home office simply on the ground that it is the "nerve center" gives too much weight to "a pleasant and alluring figure of speech." [33]

The courts have increasingly come to recognize that the earlier cases can be reconciled, in the light of their particular facts, and that a single rule can be applied. This rule—which is now usually called the "total activity" test—looks to the place where the bulk of the corporate activity takes place, if there is any one state in which this is true, while resorting to the location of the home office only if the corporation's activities are dispersed among several states and no one state clearly predominates.[34]

The draftsmen of the 1958 amendment did not consider how it would apply to corporations incorporated in a foreign country or to domestic corporations with their principal place of business abroad. Some cases have held that § 1332(c) has no application to corporations chartered in foreign countries, and that such a corporation, as was true prior to 1958, is deemed to be a citizen only of the foreign country, regardless of where it has its principal place of business.[35] This result is defensible as a matter of statutory construction, but it is an unappealing result if it permits a corporation with its principal place of business in New York to invoke diversity in litigation with a New York citizen simply because the corporation is incorporated in Liberia rather than in Delaware.[36] More recent cases have avoided this result by holding that a foreign corporation is considered a citizen of the state or foreign state in which it has its principal place of business.[37] It also has been held that a

32. See § 23 above. See also the proposal of the American Law Institute, described note 13 above.

33. Kelly v. U.S. Steel Corp., C.A.3d, 1960, 284 F.2d 850, 853.

34. Industrial Tectonics, Inc. v. Aero Alloy, C.A.9th, 1990, 912 F.2d 1090, 1092–1094; J.A. Olson Co. v. City of Winona, C.A.5th, 1987, 818 F.2d 401, 404–412 (discussing fully the caselaw and the factors to be considered); Vareka Invs., N.V. v. American Inv. Properties, Inc., C.A.11th, 1984, 724 F.2d 907, 909, certiorari denied 105 S.Ct. 107, 469 U.S. 826, 83 L.Ed.2d 51; White v. Halstead Industries, Inc., D.C.Ark. 1990, 750 F.Supp. 395, 397; North Star Hotels Inc. v. Mid–City Hotel Associates, D.C.Minn.1988, 696 F.Supp. 1265, 1270; Mahoney v. Northwestern Bell Tel. Co., D.C.Neb.1966, 258 F.Supp. 500, affirmed C.A.8th, 1967, 377 F.2d 549; 13B Wright, Miller & Cooper, Jurisdiction 2d § 3625.

35. E.g., Clarkson Co. v. Shaheen, C.A.2d, 1976, 544 F.2d 624, 628 n. 5; Weight v. Kawasaki Heavy Industries, Ltd., D.C.Va.1984, 597 F.Supp. 1082; Salomon Englander y Cia, Ltd. v. Israel Discount Bank, Ltd., D.C.N.Y.1980, 494 F.Supp. 914;

cf. Eisenberg v. Commercial Union Assur. Co., D.C.N.Y.1960, 189 F.Supp. 500.

36. ALI Study, § 1301(b)(1); Moore & Weckstein, note 3 above, at 1435–1436.

The result described in the text, which the ALI proposal was specifically intended to avoid, was reached in Chemical Transp. Corp. v. Metropolitan Petroleum Corp., D.C.N.Y.1964, 246 F.Supp. 563.

37. Danjaq, S.A. v. Pathe Communications Corp., C.A.9th, 1992, 979 F.2d 772; Cabalceta v. Standard Fruit Co., C.A.11th, 1989, 883 F.2d 1553; Jerguson v. Blue Dot Investment, Inc., C.A.5th, 1981, 659 F.2d 31, certiorari denied 102 S.Ct. 2013, 456 U.S. 946, 72 L.Ed.2d 469; Rouhi v. Harza Engineering Co., D.C.Ill.1992, 785 F.Supp. 1290; Danjaq, S.A. v. MGM/UA Communications, Co., D.C.Cal.1991, 773 F.Supp. 194; Southeast Guar. Trust Co. v. Rodman & Renshaw, Inc., D.C.Ill.1973, 358 F.Supp. 1001. See 13B Wright, Miller & Cooper, Jurisdiction 2d § 3628.

There is also authority, however, for treating the corporation as a citizen of the state in which it has its principal place of business, but not of the country of its incorporation. Trans World Hospital Supplies, domestic corporation is a citizen of the state of its incorporation, but that it is not to be regarded as a citizen of a foreign country even though it has its principal place of business in that country.[38]

The statutory definition of corporate citizenship was further amended in 1964 to provide that in a direct action against a liability insurer, to which the insured is not a party, the insurer shall be deemed to be a citizen of the state of which the insured is a citizen, as well as of its state of incorporation and of the state where it has its principal place of business.[39] This statute grew out of a problem that had led to clogged dockets in the federal courts in Louisiana. Because of the broad review of jury verdicts that the Louisiana practice permits, lawyers for plaintiffs in that state greatly preferred to be in federal court rather than in state court. They were able to convert what otherwise would have been a routine automobile-accident case between two Louisiana citizens into a diversity action by taking advantage of the state statute permitting suit directly against the insurer without joinder of the insured.[40] If the defendant's insurer was incorporated and had its principal place of business in a state other than Louisiana, diversity was held to exist.[41] The statute has cured that problem, but it has raised many problems of construction of its own.[42] The Supreme Court has held that in view of the unambiguous language of the statute, it does not apply to a suit by an insurer.[43]

The settled rule has long been that unincorporated associations do not enjoy the same fiction that is applied to corporations, and that when a partnership, a joint stock company, a labor union, the governing board of an institution, or some similar association is a party, the actual citizenship of each of its members must be considered in determining whether diversity exists.[44] This rule was followed even where local law

Ltd. v. Hospital Corp. of America, D.C.Tenn.1982, 542 F.Supp. 869; Note, Alien Corporations and Federal Diversity Jurisdiction, 1984, 84 Col.L.Rev. 177.

The principal place of business within the United States will not be looked to if the foreign corporation has a more important place of business in some other country. Roby v. General Tire & Rubber Co., D.C.Md.1980, 500 F.Supp. 480; Arab Intl. Bank & Trust Co. v. National Westminster Bank Ltd., D.C.N.Y.1979, 463 F.Supp. 1145.

38. Cabalceta v. Standard Fruit Co., C.A.11th, 1989, 883 F.2d 1553.

39. 28 U.S.C.A. § 1332(c), as amended by Act of Aug. 14, 1964, Pub.L. 88–439, 78 Stat. 445. The statute is criticized by Weckstein, The 1964 Diversity Amendment: Congressional Indirect Action against State "Direct Action" Laws, 1965 Wis.L.Rev. 268.

40. Only Louisiana and Wisconsin have such statutes. Wisconsin does not have the peculiarly broad scope of review that is had in Louisiana, and there is no indication that

in Wisconsin the direct-action statute was often used as a means of creating diversity. See Weckstein, note 39 above.

41. Lumbermen's Mut. Cas. Co. v. Elbert, 1954, 75 S.Ct. 151, 348 U.S. 48, 99 L.Ed. 59.

42. See 13B Wright, Miller & Cooper, Jurisdiction 2d § 3629.

43. Northbrook Nat. Ins. Co. v. Brewer, 1989, 110 S.Ct. 297, 493 U.S. 6, 107 L.Ed.2d 223. The Court recognized the "seeming incongruity" of denying a federal forum when the action is against the insurer, but allowing it when the action is by the insurer, despite the fact that "it is difficult to see how the nonresident insurer's interest in a federal forum is any greater when it brings the action." 110 S.Ct. at 300, 493 U.S. at 12.

44. 13B Wright, Miller & Cooper, Jurisdiction 2d § 3630; Great Southern Fire Proof Hotel Co. v. Jones, 1900, 20 S.Ct. 690, 177 U.S. 449, 44 L.Ed. 842 (partnership); Chapman v. Barney, 1889, 9 S.Ct. 426, 129 permitted the association to sue or be sued as an entity and declared that it was to be treated as if it were a corporation.[45] Some lower court cases evinced a willingness to depart from what had been the settled rule, and to treat an association as an entity for diversity purposes.[46] The Supreme Court, however, refused to permit this. It recognized the appealing arguments for giving entity treatment to associations, but held that "pleas for extension of the diversity jurisdiction to hitherto uncovered broad categories of litigants ought to be made to the Congress and not to the courts." [47]

More recently, however, in Navarro Savings Association v. Lee,[48] the Court, rejecting many contrary decisions from the lower courts, held that the individual trustees of a business trust organized under Massachusetts law can invoke diversity jurisdiction on the basis of their own citizenship, without regard to the citizenship of the trust's beneficial shareholders. The Court chose to adhere to the rule, established since 1808, that the trustee of an express trust can sue on the basis of his own citizenship. Although a business trust differs from conventional trusts in some respects, and resembles a business enterprise, the trustees in this case were active trustees whose control over the assets held in their names was real and substantial, and this was thought decisive.

A bare majority of the Court soon made it clear that the Navarro case was not a departure from what had been the rule about unincorporated associations. In Carden v. Arkoma Associates [49] the Court held that in a suit by a limited partnership, the citizenship of each of the limited partners had to be considered in determining whether diversity existed. The Court reviewed the cases involving entities other than corporations and praised what it called "the admirable consistency of our jurisprudence on this matter." [50] The Navarro case was distinguished on

U.S. 677, 32 L.Ed. 800 (joint stock company); Thomas v. Board of Trustees of Ohio State Univ., 1904, 25 S.Ct. 24, 195 U.S. 207, 49 L.Ed. 160 (governing board); United Steelworkers of America v. R.H. Bouligny, Inc., 1965, 86 S.Ct. 272, 382 U.S. 145, 15 L.Ed.2d 217 (labor union); Carden v. Arkoma Associates, 1990, 110 S.Ct. 1015, 494 U.S. 185, 108 L.Ed.2d 157 (limited partnership).

45. Great Southern Fire Proof Hotel Co. v. Jones, 1900, 20 S.Ct. 690, 177 U.S. 449, 44 L.Ed. 842.

46. Mason v. American Exp. Co., C.A.2d, 1964, 334 F.2d 392; Van Sant v. American Exp. Co., C.A.3d, 1947, 169 F.2d 355; Comment, 1965 Duke L.J. 329; Note, 1959, 68 Yale L.J. 1182.

47. United Steelworkers of America v. R.H. Bouligny, Inc., 1965, 86 S.Ct. 272, 275, 382 U.S. 145, 150–151, 15 L.Ed.2d 217.

48. 1980, 100 S.Ct. 1779, 446 U.S. 458, 64 L.Ed.2d 425.

49. 1990, 110 S.Ct. 1015, 494 U.S. 185, 108 L.Ed.2d 157. See Comment, Carden v.

Arkoma Associates: The Citizenship of Limited Partnerships, Associations, and Juridical Entities—A Chilling Future for Diversity Jurisdiction, 1992, 27 N.Eng.L.Rev. 505.

50. 110 S.Ct. at 1018, 494 U.S. at 189.

The only exception the Court could find to this "admirable consistency" was People of Puerto Rico v. Russell & Co., 1933, 53 S.Ct. 447, 288 U.S. 476, 77 L.Ed. 903, where a sociedad en comandita formed under Puerto Rican law was held to have so complete a "personality" under that law as to be treated as a corporation, for purposes of defeating diversity. The Carden Court said that the Russell case involved a problem "of fitting an exotic creation of the civil law * * * into a federal scheme which knew it not," 110 S.Ct. at 1015, 494 U.S. at 190 (quoting Bouligny, note 47 above, 86 S.Ct. at 275, 382 U.S. at 151) and that the result there would not be applied to common-law entities.

the ground that the suit there was brought not by the business trust but the eight individual trustees, suing in their name, and it was their citizenship that was controlling. The majority in Carden admitted that their results in this area "can validly be characterized as technical, precedent-bound, and unresponsive to policy considerations raised by the changing realities of business organization." [51] But it said that "the course we take today does not so much disregard the policy of accommodating our diversity jurisdiction to the changing realities of commercial organization, as it honors the more important policy of leaving that to the people's elected representatives. * * * We have long since decided that, having established special treatment for corporations, we will leave the rest to Congress; we adhere to that decision." [52]

As the dissenters in Carden pointed out, in many cases it is possible to avoid the impact of the rule announced there about unincorporated associations by bringing a class action for or against members of the association, naming as representatives of the class only those whose citizenship will produce diversity.[53]

§ 28. Time of Determination of Diversity [1]

In a 1991 decision, the Court applied once again "the well-established rule that diversity of citizenship is assessed at the time the action is filed. We have consistently held that if jurisdiction exists at the time an action is commenced, such jurisdiction may not be divested by subsequent events." [2] If diversity existed between the parties when the action was filed, it is not defeated because one of the parties later becomes a citizen of the same state as his opponent.[3] Nor will a change of parties, by intervention or substitution, divest the jurisdiction of the federal court.[4] By the same token, if there was no diversity when the action was commenced, it cannot be created by a change of domicile of one of the parties or other subsequent event.[5] It may be, however, that

---

51. 110 S.Ct. at 1021, 494 U.S. at 195.

52. 110 S.Ct. at 1022, 494 U.S. at 197.

53. 110 S.Ct. at 1027, 494 U.S. at 207. See Rule 23.2; § 72 below; Curley v. Brignoli, Curley & Roberts, Associates, C.A.2d, 1990, 915 F.2d 81, certiorari denied 111 S.Ct. 1430, 499 U.S. 955, 113 L.Ed.2d 484. See also 7C Wright, Miller & Kane, Civil 2d § 1861.

§ 28

1. 13B Wright, Miller & Cooper, Jurisdiction 2d § 3608.

2. Freeport–McMoRan, Inc. v. K. N. Energy, Inc., 1991, 111 S.Ct. 858, 860, 498 U.S. 426, 428, 112 L.Ed.2d 951.

3. Morgan's Heirs v. Morgan, 1817, 2 Wheat. 290, 15 U.S. 290, 4 L.Ed. 242; In re Agent Orange Product Liability Litigation, C.A.2d, 1987, 818 F.2d 145, 163, certiorari denied 108 S.Ct. 344, 484 U.S. 953, 98 L.Ed.2d 370.

4. Wichita R. & Light Co. v. Public Utilities Comm. of the State of Kansas, 1922, 43 S.Ct. 51, 260 U.S. 48, 67 L.Ed. 124 (intervention); Hardenbergh v. Ray, 1894, 14 S.Ct. 305, 151 U.S. 112, 38 L.Ed. 93 (substitution). In the Freeport–McMoRan case, note 2 above, the Court said: "A contrary rule could well have the effect of deterring normal business transactions during the pendency of what might be lengthy litigation. Such a rule is not in any way required to accomplish the purposes of diversity jurisdiction." 111 S.Ct. at 860, 498 U.S. at 428–429.

5. Aetna Cas. & Surety Co. v. Hillman, C.A.5th, 1986, 796 F.2d 770 (substitution of party); Field v. Volkswagenwerk AG, C.A.3d, 1980, 626 F.2d 293 (change of administratrix); Kendrick v. Kendrick, C.C.A.5th, 1927, 16 F.2d 744, certiorari denied 47 S.Ct. 472, 273 U.S. 758, 71 L.Ed. 877 (intervention); E.K. Carey Drilling Co.

a new suit can then be commenced, and it is clear that if a party whose citizenship destroys diversity is not indispensable, that party can be dropped, even by an appellate court.[6]

These principles apply only where the nature of the action remains the same. If the change in parties reflects a change in the nature of the action, the test of diversity must be met with regard to the parties to the altered action.[7] And in determining whether realignment of parties is required,[8] the position taken by a party during the litigation may be considered in determining how the party should originally have been aligned.[9]

§ 29. Parties Considered in Determining Diversity [1]

It was seen earlier [2] that under the rule of Strawbridge v. Curtiss [3] complete diversity between the parties opposed in interest is a requisite of diversity jurisdiction, except as Congress has otherwise provided. In determining whether complete diversity exists, nominal or formal parties may be ignored.[4] Thus, there is diversity despite the joinder of a party who has no interest in the controversy,[5] and the fraudulent joinder of a

v. Murphy, D.C.Colo.1953, 113 F.Supp. 226 (change of domicile).

6. Newman–Green, Inc. v. Alfonzo–Larrain, 1989, 109 S.Ct. 2218, 490 U.S. 826, 104 L.Ed.2d 893.

7. Lewis v. Odell, C.A.2d, 1974, 503 F.2d 445; Grady v. Irvine, C.A.4th, 1958, 254 F.2d 224, certiorari denied 79 S.Ct. 30, 358 U.S. 819, 3 L.Ed.2d 60.

8. See § 30 below.

9. Reed v. Robilio, C.A.6th, 1967, 376 F.2d 392, 396; Green v. Green, C.A.7th, 1954, 218 F.2d 130, 144, certiorari denied 75 S.Ct. 606, 349 U.S. 917, 99 L.Ed. 1250; B.J. Van Ingen & Co. v. Burlington County Bridge Comm., D.C.N.J.1949, 83 F.Supp. 778, 788–789; Hellenthal v. John Hancock Mut. Life Ins. Co., D.C.Wash.1929, 31 F.2d 997, 998.

The subsequent events can be looked to, however, only insofar as they shed light on facts in existence at the time the action was commenced. American Motorists Ins. Co. v. Trane Co., C.A.7th, 1981, 657 F.2d 146, 151 n. 3.

§ 29

1. 13B Wright, Miller & Cooper, Jurisdiction 2d § 3606.

2. See § 24 above.

3. 1806, 3 Cranch 267, 2 L.Ed. 435.

4. Carneal v. Banks, 1825, 10 Wheat. 181, 6 L.Ed. 297; Salem Trust Co. v. Manufacturers' Fin. Co., 1924, 44 S.Ct. 266, 264 U.S. 182, 68 L.Ed. 628; Broyles v. Bayless, C.A.11th, 1989, 878 F.2d 1400. See also

Bumberger v. Insurance Co. of North America, C.A.3d, 1991, 952 F.2d 764. On the significance of "John Doe" defendants, see § 31 below.

The removal of a suit by Pete Rose against the Commissioner of Baseball was based on a finding that the Cincinnati Reds and Major League Baseball were "fraudulently" joined in the sense in which that term is used in connection with removal. Rose v. Giamatti, D.C.Ohio 1989, 721 F.Supp. 906. The case is criticized in Note, Maintaining the Home Field Advantage: Rose vs. Federal Court, 1990, 10 Loy.Ent. L.J. 695. In that case, however, the court also characterizes those other parties as merely nominal defendants, and the case may be better explained on the ground that in a suit for injunctive relief the court may disregard nominal resident defendants if complete relief can be afforded against nonresident defendants. Frontier Airlines, Inc. v. United Air Lines, Inc., D.C.Colo.1989, 758 F.Supp. 1399, 1404.

5. Salem Trust Co. v. Manufacturers' Fin. Co., 1924, 44 S.Ct. 266, 264 U.S. 182, 68 L.Ed. 628; Mayor and City Council of Baltimore v. Weinberg, D.C.Md.1961, 190 F.Supp. 140 (mortgagee whose mortgage had been satisfied before commencement of proceedings).

Similarly no diversity exists if the party of record is merely formal, and the real party is a citizen of the same state as his opponent. Miller & Lux v. East Side Canal & Irrigation Co., 1908, 29 S.Ct. 111, 211 U.S. 293, 53 L.Ed. 189.

defendant of the same citizenship as plaintiff will not defeat removal of an action.[6]

It is clear that the court may not disregard the citizenship of "indispensable" parties,[7] and indeed it is sometimes said too loosely that only the citizenship of "indispensable" parties will be considered. This is not the rule. Even though a party is merely proper, as, for example, a joint tortfeasor, if it has in fact been joined its citizenship must be considered,[8] although where the party is not "indispensable" it may be possible for plaintiff to have the action dismissed as to the cocitizen and in this way perfect jurisdiction.[9] Where parties who are merely "proper" are involved, and they are not "needed for just adjudication" by the tests of Rule 19, a large measure of choice in shaping the action is thus left to the plaintiff.

It was noted above that nominal parties will be disregarded. In applying this rule, however, one who has the legal right to sue and to represent those having a beneficial interest in the recovery is not treated as a nominal party, and its citizenship, rather than the citizenship of those whom it represents, is looked to for determining diversity. This rule was so well established in early decisions [10] that by 1824 Chief Justice Marshall could announce as "the universally received construction" that "jurisdiction is neither given nor ousted by the relative situation of the parties concerned in interest, but by the relative situation of the parties named on the record." [11] In order to come within this rule, however, the representative must have actual powers with regard to the matter in litigation. Where the representative cannot prevent the institution or prosecution of the actions, or exercise any control over them, and is thus a mere conduit through whom the law affords a remedy to the persons aggrieved, the representative is treated as a nominal party, and the citizenship of the persons aggrieved is determinative.[12]

Applying these two rules, if some officer is named as the formal obligee of a bond, for the benefit of private individuals, the citizenship of the individuals controls,[13] but the result is otherwise if the obligee has a

---

6.   See § 31 below at notes 50, 51.

7.   Moore v. Ashland Oil, Inc., C.A.7th, 1990, 901 F.2d 1445; and cases cited 13B Wright, Miller & Cooper, Jurisdiction 2d § 3606 n. 8.

On when the conclusory label "indispensable" is appropriate, see § 70 below.

8.   Chicago, R.I. & P.R. Co. v. Dowell, 1913, 33 S.Ct. 684, 229 U.S. 102, 57 L.Ed. 1090 (removal); Carson v. Allied News Co., C.A.7th, 1975, 511 F.2d 22 (original jurisdiction); Iowa Public Serv. Co. v. Medicine Bow Coal Co., C.A.8th, 1977, 556 F.2d 400 (removal); Dollar S.S. Lines v. Merz, C.C.A.9th, 1934, 68 F.2d 594 (original jurisdiction).

9.   See § 69 below.

10.   Chappedelaine v. Dechenaux, 1808, 4 Cranch 306, 307, 2 L.Ed. 629; Childress v. Emory, 1823, 8 Wheat. 642, 5 L.Ed. 705.

11.   Osborn v. Bank of the United States, 1824, 9 Wheat. 738, 856, 6 L.Ed. 204.

12.   The rule set out in the text is taken from Susquehanna & Wyoming Valley R. & Coal Co. v. Blatchford, 1870, 11 Wall. 172, 177, 20 L.Ed. 179.

13.   Browne v. Strode, 1809, 5 Cranch 303, 3 L.Ed. 108; McNutt for Use of Leggett v. Bland, 1844, 2 How. 9, 11 L.Ed. 159; Howard v. U.S., 1902, 22 S.Ct. 543, 184 U.S. 676, 46 L.Ed. 754.

real interest in the suit on the bond.[14] The citizenship of an active trustee, rather than that of the beneficiaries, is decisive,[15] but again a different result is reached with regard to a dry passive trustee who has only a naked legal title to the property.[16] Only the citizenship of the named representative in a class action is considered,[17] and this is the rule also in a suit by a receiver [18] or a subrogee.[19]

It was once accepted as the law that the executor or administrator of the estate of a decedent had control over litigation involving that estate, and it was, therefore, the citizenship of the representative, rather than the state of the representative's appointment, or the citizenship of the deceased, or the citizenship of creditors, next of kin, or legatees that controlled for purposes of jurisdiction.[20] This rule was applied whether the result was to create jurisdiction that would otherwise be absent [21] or to defeat jurisdiction that would otherwise exist.[22] It has also been the rule that if a general guardian was empowered by state law to sue in its own name, its citizenship was controlling,[23] but that a guardian ad litem, whose responsibilities were only for a particular litigation, was merely a nominal party and the citizenship of the ward was looked to.[24]

14. U.S. Fidelity & Guar. Co. v. U.S. for the Benefit of Kenyon, 1907, 27 S.Ct. 381, 204 U.S. 349, 51 L.Ed. 516.

15. Susquehanna & Wyoming Valley R. & Coal Co. v. Blatchford, 1870, 11 Wall. 172, 20 L.Ed. 179 (trustee under mortgage); Bullard v. City of Cisco, 1933, 54 S.Ct. 177, 290 U.S. 179, 78 L.Ed. 254 (bondholders' committee); Navarro Savings Assn. v. Lee, 1980, 100 S.Ct. 1779, 446 U.S. 458, 64 L.Ed.2d 425 (business trust).

16. Boon's Heirs v. Chiles, 1834, 8 Pet. 532, 8 L.Ed. 1034; Bogue v. Chicago, B. & Q.R. Co., D.C.Iowa 1912, 193 F. 728.

17. Snyder v. Harris, 1969, 89 S.Ct. 1053, 1059, 394 U.S. 332, 340, 22 L.Ed.2d 319; In re School Asbestos Litigation, C.A.3d, 1990, 921 F.2d 1310, 1317–1318, certiorari denied 111 S.Ct. 1623, 499 U.S. 976, 113 L.Ed.2d 720; 7A Wright, Miller & Kane, Civil 2d § 1755.

18. Gross v. Hougland, C.A.6th, 1983, 712 F.2d 1034, certiorari denied 104 S.Ct. 1281, 465 U.S. 1025, 79 L.Ed.2d 684; Farlow v. Lea, C.C.D.Ohio, 1877, 8 Fed.Cas. 1017.

19. City of New Orleans v. Whitney, 1891, 11 S.Ct. 428, 138 U.S. 595, 34 L.Ed. 1102.

20. Childress v. Emory, 1823, 8 Wheat. 642, 5 L.Ed. 705. See also notes 21 and 22 below.

21. Rice v. Houston, 1871, 13 Wall. 66, 20 L.Ed. 484; Lang v. Elm City Constr. Co., C.A.2d, 1963, 324 F.2d 235, noted 1964, 48

Minn.L.Rev. 785, 73 Yale L.J. 873; Deposit Guar. Bank & Trust Co. v. Burton, C.A.6th, 1967, 380 F.2d 346; Janzen v. Goos, C.A.8th, 1962, 302 F.2d 421; Erwin v. Barrow, C.A.10th, 1954, 217 F.2d 522.

22. Mecom v. Fitzsimmons Drilling Co., 1931, 52 S.Ct. 84, 284 U.S. 183, 76 L.Ed. 233; Hot Oil Serv., Inc. v. Hall, C.A.9th, 1966, 366 F.2d 295; Seymour v. Johnson, C.A.6th, 1956, 235 F.2d 181; Grady v. Irvine, C.A.4th, 1958, 254 F.2d 224, certiorari denied 79 S.Ct. 30, 358 U.S. 819, 3 L.Ed.2d 60.

23. "If in the state of the forum the general guardian has the right to bring suit in his own name as such guardian, and does so, he is to be treated as the party plaintiff so far as Federal Jurisdiction is concerned, even though suit might have been instituted in the name of the ward by guardian ad litem or next friend." Mexican Central Ry. Co. v. Eckman, 1903, 23 S.Ct. 211, 213, 187 U.S. 429, 434, 47 L.Ed. 245.

Citizenship of the ward controlled where state law did not permit guardian to sue in its own name. Martineau v. City of St. Paul, C.A.8th, 1949, 172 F.2d 777; Ansaldi v. Kennedy, D.C.Mass.1930, 41 F.2d 858.

24. Ziady v. Curley, C.A.4th, 1968, 396 F.2d 873; Appelt v. Whitty, C.A.7th, 1961, 286 F.2d 135; Blumenthal v. Craig, C.C.A.3d, 1897, 81 F. 320; Curry v. Maxson, D.C.Mo.1970, 318 F.Supp. 842; Hernandez v. Lucas, D.C.Tex.1966, 254 F.Supp. 901; Blackwell v. Vance Trucking Co., D.C.S.C.1956, 139 F.Supp. 103.

These propositions are no longer the law. Beginning with the decision of the Third Circuit in 1968 in McSparran v. Weist,[25] the courts of appeals refused to allow creation of jurisdiction by the appointment of an out-of-state representative whose only function was to give the appearance of diversity. Similarly in Miller v. Perry [26] the Fourth Circuit held that diversity was not defeated by the appointment of a resident ancillary administrator, as required by state law, and that jurisdiction existed because of diversity between the resident defendant and beneficiaries who were citizens of another state.

Although the courts were willing to depart from the old rules about representatives and to disregard the citizenship of the representative in some cases, there was much disagreement on when the appointment should be regarded as a sham and whose citizenship should be looked to if that of the representative were disregarded.[27] Fortunately Congress solved the matter by a 1988 statute. It provides that "the legal representative of the estate of a decedent shall be deemed to be a citizen only of the same State as the decedent and the legal representative of an infant or incompetent shall be deemed to be a citizen only of the same State as the infant or incompetent." [28] This statute, which was taken virtually verbatim from the proposal of the American Law Institute 19 years earlier,[29] provides bright-line rules that have brought stability and rationalization to what had been a vexed area of the law.[30]

§ 30. Realignment of Parties [1]

In determining whether diversity jurisdiction exists, the alignment of the parties as plaintiffs and defendants in the pleadings is not conclusive. It is the duty of the court to "look beyond the pleadings, and

---

25. C.A.3d, 1968, 402 F.2d 867, certiorari denied 89 S.Ct. 1739, 395 U.S. 903, 23 L.Ed.2d 217. The McSparran case itself involved an out-of-state guardian but the Third Circuit rejected any distinction between a guardian and the representative of a decedent's estate, 402 F.2d at 872, and overruled two of its earlier cases that had involved administrators.

26. C.A.4th, 1972, 456 F.2d 63, noted 1972, 47 N.Y.U.L.Rev. 801.

27. See, e.g., Pallazola v. Rucker, C.A.1st, 1986, 797 F.2d 1116; Wilsey v. Eddingfield, C.A.7th, 1985, 780 F.2d 614, certiorari denied 106 S.Ct. 1660, 475 U.S. 1130, 90 L.Ed.2d 202; Bianca v. Parke-Davis Pharmaceutical Division, C.A.5th, 1984, 723 F.2d 392; Mullenix, Creative Manipulation of Federal Jurisdiction: Is There Diversity After Death?, 1985, 70 Cornell L.Rev. 1011.

28. 28 U.S.C.A. § 1332(c)(2), added by Act of Nov. 19, 1988, Pub.L. 100–702, 102 Stat. 4642.

Although the statute speaks only of state citizenship, it has sensibly been held that the representative of the estate of an alien should be treated as an alien for purposes of diversity jurisdiction. Geler v. National Westminster Bank USA, D.C.N.Y.1991, 763 F.Supp. 722, 726.

29. ALI Study, § 1301(b)(4).

30. "The name a given state legislature chooses for its 'legal representative of the estate of a decedent' should not govern federal diversity jurisdiction." Green v. Lake of the Woods County, D.C.Minn.1993, 815 F.Supp. 305. Here it was held that the 1988 statute applied, and the citizenship of the decedent controlled in a wrongful-death action, even though in Minnesota the party who brings such an action is a trustee of an express trust.

§ 30

1. 13B Wright, Miller & Cooper, Jurisdiction 2d § 3607.

arrange the parties according to their sides in the dispute."[2]   Usually such realignment of the parties, where required, will have the effect of defeating jurisdiction,[3] but the rule works both ways and jurisdiction will be sustained, if diversity exists when the parties are properly aligned, even though diversity is lacking on the face of the pleadings.[4]

In determining how the parties should be aligned, the courts look usually to the ultimate interests of each of the parties, and align those together who have the same ultimate interest.   Thus, in an action by one of the owners of land against the lessee of the land claiming a fraud upon the owners, the interest of the other owner is the same as the plaintiff, and she must be realigned as a plaintiff.[5]   Where an insured tortfeasor brings an action against his insurer for a declaratory judgment as to his coverage and names the person suing him in tort as a defendant along with the insurer, the tort claimant will be realigned as a plaintiff, since he and the insured have an identical interest in having it held that the insurance covers the accident in question.[6]   A similar analysis of the interests of the parties is made in other cases.[7]   The ultimate interest test is not, however, the exclusive test.   In a stockholders' derivative action where the corporation is alleged to be under control antagonistic to those bringing the suit, the corporation will be aligned as a defendant, even though any recovery in the suit will be for the benefit of the corporation and thus its ultimate interest is the same as the plaintiffs'.[8] This is done, seemingly, on the theory that the antagonism is sufficient to create the "collision of interest" said to be necessary.[9]   The rules

2. City of Dawson v. Columbia Ave. Sav. Fund, Safe Deposit, Title & Trust Co., 1905, 25 S.Ct. 420, 421, 197 U.S. 178, 180, 49 L.Ed. 713.

3. E.g., Lee v. Lehigh Val. Coal Co., 1925, 45 S.Ct. 385, 267 U.S. 542, 69 L.Ed. 782; City of Indianapolis v. Chase Nat. Bank, 1941, 62 S.Ct. 15, 314 U.S. 63, 86 L.Ed. 47.

4. Pacific Ry. Co. v. Ketchum, 1879, 101 U.S. 289, 25 L.Ed. 932; Broidy v. State Mut. Life Assur. Co. of Worcester, Mass., C.A.2d, 1951, 186 F.2d 490; Smotherman v. Caswell, D.C.Kan.1990, 755 F.Supp. 346. Normally, as in the cases cited, realignment to create diversity will occur in a removed action where the removing party asks for realignment to justify the removal. This need not always be the case. When a party who should join as plaintiff refuses to do so, it may be named as defendant, Fed.R.Civ. Proc. 19(a), 7 Wright, Miller & Kane, Civil 2d § 1605, but should then be realigned as a plaintiff for jurisdictional purposes. Eikel v. States Marine Lines, Inc., C.A.5th, 1973, 473 F.2d 959; Standard Oil Co. of California v. Perkins, C.A.9th, 1965, 347 F.2d 379; cf. Perkins v. Standard Oil Co. of California, D.C.Or.1961, 29 F.R.D. 16; Dental Precision Shoulder v. L.D. Caulk Co., D.C.N.Y. 1947, 7 F.R.D. 203.

5. Lee v. Lehigh Val. Coal Co., 1925, 45 S.Ct. 385, 267 U.S. 542, 69 L.Ed. 782; cf. Alexander v. Washington, C.A.5th, 1960, 274 F.2d 349.

6. Bonell v. General Acc. Fire & Life Assur. Corp., D.C.Cal.1958, 167 F.Supp. 384; cf. Farmer's Alliance Mut. Ins. Co. v. Jones, C.A.10th, 1978, 570 F.2d 1384, certiorari denied 99 S.Ct. 97, 439 U.S. 826, 58 L.Ed.2d 119.

7. See the cases set out in 13A Wright, Miller & Cooper, Jurisdiction 2d § 3607 n. 8.

8. Smith v. Sperling, 1957, 77 S.Ct. 1112, 354 U.S. 91, 1 L.Ed.2d 1205; Doctor v. Harrington, 1905, 25 S.Ct. 355, 196 U.S. 579, 49 L.Ed. 606; and see 7C Wright, Miller & Kane, Civil 2d § 1822. See § 73 below. The same rule has been applied to align a limited partnership as a defendant in a derivative action brought by one of the partners. Duke & Benedict, Inc. v. Wolstein, D.C.Fla.1993, 826 F.Supp. 1413.

9. City of Dawson v. Columbia Ave. Sav. Fund, Safe Deposit, Title & Trust Co., 1905, 25 S.Ct. 420, 421, 197 U.S. 178, 181, 49 L.Ed. 713.

But see Lewis v. Odell, C.A.2d, 1974, 503 F.2d 445, where the corporation was applicable to a stockholders' suit apply also to a suit by a beneficiary of a trust or estate seeking to enforce a claim of the trust or estate.[10]

Although questions of alignment are determined initially from the pleadings, the subsequent course of the litigation may reveal more clearly the position of the various parties and cast light on how they should have been originally aligned.[11]

The most difficult questions of realignment occur where the interests of a party are in accord with those of the plaintiffs in some respects and of the defendants in other respects. This was the problem in the well-known case of City of Indianapolis v. Chase National Bank.[12] The summary of the principles that govern in realignment cases set forth there has properly been regarded as definitive, though these principles are neither novel nor disputed by the four dissenting justices. The dispute turned, as is so often true, on the application of agreed principles to the facts at hand.

The bank, deemed a New York citizen, was trustee under a mortgage deed securing certain bonds issued by a gas company. The bank brought an action against the gas company and the city of Indianapolis, both Indiana citizens, for a determination that the city had succeeded to the obligations of lessee on a lease from the gas company and that the lease was valid, and for overdue interest on the bonds. A bare majority of the Court held that in aligning parties it must look to the "primary and controlling matter in dispute,"[13] which in the case before it was whether the city was bound by the lease. Since on this issue the gas company was united in interest with the bank, the majority held that the gas company should be realigned as a plaintiff and ordered dismissal for want of jurisdiction.[14] The four dissenters, observing that the judgment below did hold the gas company liable for more than a million dollars, though it fixed primary liability on the city, objected to "the subtlety by which a judgment debtor is transfigured into a creditor for jurisdictional purposes."[15] They found a real controversy between the bank and the gas company as to the liability for interest, and rejected the notion that jurisdiction should turn on whether the court considers one issue to

aligned as a plaintiff since the pleadings did not disclose any antagonism of the corporation to the derivative action.

10. Hamer v. New York Railways Co., 1917, 37 S.Ct. 511, 244 U.S. 266, 61 L.Ed. 1125; Reed v. Robilio, C.A.6th, 1967, 376 F.2d 392; Hellenthal v. John Hancock Mut. Life Ins. Co., D.C.Wash.1929, 31 F.2d 997; see Goldstein v. Groesbeck, C.C.A.2d, 1944, 142 F.2d 422, 425, certiorari denied 65 S.Ct. 36, 323 U.S. 737, 89 L.Ed. 590.

11. See § 28 n. 9 above.

12. 1941, 62 S.Ct. 15, 314 U.S. 63, 86 L.Ed. 47, noted 1942, 40 Mich.L.Rev. 1109, 7 Mo.L.Rev. 316, 90 U.Pa.L.Rev. 620, 15 So.Cal.L.Rev. 377, 28 Va.L.Rev. 549.

13. 62 S.Ct. at 17, 314 U.S. at 69. The quoted phrase is taken by the Court from Merchants Cotton–Press & Storage Co. v. Insurance Co. of North America, 1894, 14 S.Ct. 367, 373, 151 U.S. 368, 385, 38 L.Ed. 195.

14. The jurisdictional ruling seems the more technical because it came after years of litigation, and because three years earlier the Supreme Court had refused to review a decision of the circuit court of appeals, prior to trial on the merits, holding that diversity jurisdiction existed. Aggravating as this may seem, it is undoubtedly correct that the earlier denial of certiorari could not confer jurisdiction that Congress or the Constitution has denied. See § 7 above.

15. 62 S.Ct. at 21, 314 U.S. at 79.

"dominate" another or to be more "actual" or "substantial" than the other.

Both the majority and the dissenters relied in part on the earlier decision of Sutton v. English,[16] where it was held that in a suit to set aside testamentary dispositions and to distribute the property among the heirs, a defendant, who as a legatee was interested adversely to the plaintiffs, should not be aligned as a plaintiff for jurisdictional purposes, even though, being also an heir, she would share in the relief if the plaintiffs were successful. To the majority the Sutton case was a clear holding that parties must be aligned according to their attitude toward the actual and substantial controversy,[17] while the dissenters found comfort in the fact that in Sutton it was held error to align one of the defendants with the plaintiff where her interest was adverse to the plaintiff on one out of four issues, although with the plaintiff as to three of the four.[18] The majority seem to have the better of it in their reading of the Sutton case. The issue on which the interest of the heir was adverse to that of the plaintiffs was whether she would take 100% of the estate, as residuary legatee, or 5% of the estate, as she would if the will were set aside. That she and the plaintiffs had a common interest on the other three claims, which, if successful, would have increased the size of the estate, was insignificant in comparison.[19]

It is obvious that reasonable arguments can be made either way in the City of Indianapolis situation. There is practicality in the view of the dissent that the alignment in the pleadings should be accepted if there is any real conflict between the parties there set on opposite sides and that the court should not undertake to decide which issue dominates other issues, though the precedents do not support this view. But it is also not clear that there was any conflict, except in the most formal sense, between the bank and the gas company in the actual case.[20] Thus, the case may stand for no more than a fairly arguable difference of view as to application of the law of alignment to a unique factual situation.[21]

16. 1918, 38 S.Ct. 254, 246 U.S. 199, 62 L.Ed. 664.

17. 62 S.Ct. at 19 n. 4, 314 U.S. at 75.

18. 62 S.Ct. at 23, 314 U.S. at 83.

19. See also Green v. Green, C.A.7th, 1954, 218 F.2d 130, certiorari denied 75 S.Ct. 606, 349 U.S. 917, 99 L.Ed. 1250, a suit by trust beneficiaries against the trustee for an accounting. It was held that the trustee's wife was properly aligned as a defendant, although she had a contingent interest in the trust. If the trustee won, upon his death his wife would inherit absolutely the amount he had allegedly misappropriated from the trust. If he lost, his death would give his wife a tenancy until death or remarriage in the income from one-half of that amount. Simple arithmetic shows where the wife's ultimate interest was.

20. "Plainly, therefore, Chase and Indianapolis Gas are, colloquially speaking, partners in litigation. * * * What Chase wants Indianapolis Gas wants and the City does not want." 62 S.Ct. at 19, 314 U.S. at 74.

21. Of the law review commentaries cited in note 12 above, two (Michigan and Southern California) are approving, two (Missouri and Virginia) are critical, and one (Pennsylvania) is doubtful. The case is called "rigorous and debatable" by Hart & Wechsler, The Federal Courts and the Federal System, Bator, Mishkin, Shapiro & Wechsler ed. 1973, p. 1065.

The lower courts continue to regard City of Indianapolis as the leading case, though with great doubt where it leads.[22] A common fact pattern in recent cases has been a suit by an insurance company for a declaratory judgment in which its insured and other insurers with policies covering the insured are named as defendants. Typically there is diversity in these cases as they are brought, but diversity would not exist if all of the insurers were aligned as plaintiffs. What is emerging as the majority view has come to be called the "principal purpose" or "primary issue" tests, since it rests on Justice Frankfurter's language in City of Indianapolis about looking to the "principal purpose of the suit" and the "primary and controlling matter in dispute."[23] When this test is used the insurers are aligned as plaintiffs and diversity is destroyed.[24] Other courts, however, have interpreted City of Indianapolis to mean that realignment is improper if there is any "actual and substantial conflict" between the parties.[25] Courts adopting this test have held, in the situation described, that the mere fact that the defendant insurers share an interest with the plaintiff insurer in avoiding liability to the insured does not require realignment since there are issues among the insurers as to the duty to defend and which insurer is liable for what.[26] One district court has found it unnecessary to choose between these two tests. In its view the cases applying the "actual and substantial conflict" test have been deficient in that they have accepted counsel's assertion of the existence of conflict at face value, without considering whether the conflict is real or hypothetical. Parties must be realigned, this court ruled, if the only conflict between the plaintiff insurer and the defendant insurers is "an adversity that is unlikely to eventuate but is conjured up by counsel in order to achieve a jurisdictional objective."[27]

22. "The teaching of that opinion is, however, far from clear. Despite the passage of more than half a century, courts remain divided on how to apply the test." Travelers Indem. Co. of Ill. v. Metropolitan Life Ins. Co., D.C.N.Y.1992, 798 F.Supp. 156, 158.

23. See note 13 above.

24. United States Fidelity & Guar. Co. v. Thomas Solvent Co., C.A.6th, 1992, 955 F.2d 1085; Employers Insurance of Wausau v. Crown Cork & Seal Co., C.A.3d, 1991, 942 F.2d 862. The "primary purpose" test has also been applied in other factual contexts. Continental Airlines, Inc. v. Goodyear Tire & Rubber Co., C.A.9th, 1987, 819 F.2d 1519, 1523; Lowe v. Ingalls Shipbuilding, C.A.5th, 1984, 723 F.2d 1173, 1178.

25. Although this test resembles the dissent in City of Indianapolis, it looks also to a footnote in the majority opinion in which Justice Frankfurter considered and rejected the argument that "notwithstanding their indissoluble bond on the controlling issue, there are 'sufficient matters in controversy' between Chase and Indianapo-

lis Gas to preclude their alignment on the same side." 62 S.Ct. at 18 n. 3, 314 U.S. at 73 n. 3.

26. American Motorists Ins. Co. v. Trane Co., C.A.7th, 1981, 657 F.2d 146; Universal Underwriters Ins. Co. v. Wagner, C.A.8th, 1966, 367 F.2d 866, 870–871; American Mut. Liab. Ins. Co. v. Flintkote Co., D.C.N.Y.1983, 565 F.Supp. 843, 846. The same test has been applied in a slightly different fact situation in Farmers Alliance Mut. Ins. Co. v. Jones, C.A.10th, 1978, 570 F.2d 1384, certiorari denied 99 S.Ct. 97, 439 U.S. 826, 58 L.Ed.2d 119. Although the Third Circuit adopted the "primary purpose" test in the Employers Insurance of Wausau case, note 24 above, it held that in cases under the Foreign Sovereign Immunities Act, 28 U.S.C.A. §§ 1330, 1441(d), the "substantial controversy" test should be used in determining alignment. In re Texas Eastern Transmission Corp., C.A.3d, 1994, 15 F.3d 1230.

27. Travelers Indem. Co. of Ill. v. Metropolitan Life Ins. Co., D.C.N.Y.1992, 798 F.Supp. 156, 159.

§ 31. Devices to Create or Defeat Diversity [1]

When there is a legitimate choice between a state and a federal forum for a particular action, the lawyer who has the choice quite properly will weigh what he or she conceives to be the tactical advantages and disadvantages of going to one court or the other. Since 1938 there is, at least in theory, no longer any difference in the substantive law applied in the two sets of courts in diversity cases.[2] The reputation the federal courts once had, whether or not deserved, of being unduly hospitable to corporations and to personal-injury defendants is now dissipated. But in choosing between a particular state court and a particular federal court for a particular case, there are still differences that to the lawyer seem significant. In Louisiana tort claimants prefer federal court, because appellate review of jury verdicts is much more restrictive there than in the state courts. In other areas, where the delay in reaching trial is much greater in federal court than in state court, it is the defendants in tort actions who seek to resort to federal court, and benefit from the attrition of delay, while claimants undertake to remain in the courts of the state.[3] Differences between federal and state procedures may attract a litigant to one court or another. The party may wish to resort to federal court because of the liberal discovery techniques available there,[4] or it may prefer the state court if, as in many states, the judge no longer has the common-law power to comment on the evidence, which federal judges still enjoy. The reputation of the judges in the two courts, or folklore about the relative liberality or parsimony of juries in the two systems, may tip the balance one way or the other.

If a choice of forum exists, there is nothing improper in taking such tactical considerations as those mentioned into account in making that choice. But so long as one court or the other provides, or seems to provide, an advantage, it is not unnatural that lawyers attempt to have the case tried in that forum even though the case appears to present no choice. The books are filled with cases involving devices by which a particular party sought to create diversity, and thus get to federal court, or to prevent diversity, and thus keep the case in state court.

The First Congress, in the Judiciary Act of 1789, sought to outlaw one obvious device for manufacturing federal jurisdiction where it would not otherwise exist. A citizen of New Jersey has a claim, for the requisite amount, against another citizen of New Jersey. Seemingly he must sue in state court. But if, for some reason, he prefers to sue in federal court, he may well think of assigning his claim to a citizen of

§ 31

1. 14 Wright, Miller & Cooper, Jurisdiction 2d §§ 3637–3642.

2. See chapter 9 below.

3. Frankfurter, J., in Lumbermen's Mut. Cas. Co. v. Elbert, 1954, 75 S.Ct. 151, 157, 348 U.S. 48, 58, 99 L.Ed. 59.

4. See, e.g., Mottolese v. Kaufman, C.A.2d 1949, 176 F.2d 301; Boggess v. Columbian Rope Co., D.C.N.Y.1958, 167 F.Supp. 854. See Kennedy, Federal Diversity Jurisdiction, 1961, 10 Kan.L.Rev. 47; Summers, Analysis of Factors that Influence Choice of Forum in Diversity Cases, 1962, 47 Iowa L.Rev. 933.

Pennsylvania, who will then sue on the basis of diversity and pay over the proceeds of the suit to his New Jersey friend. To prevent such a result, it was provided in Section 11 of the Judiciary Act of 1789 that the federal court was to have no jurisdiction of a suit on a promissory note, or other chose of action, in favor of an assignee, unless the suit could have been prosecuted in federal court if no assignment had been made.[5] With changes in language, this "assignee clause," as it was known, was a part of the law until 1948. The statute, even with—or perhaps because of—the successive amendments, was not well drafted. One commentator referred to its "obscure phraseology" as a "jumble of legislative jargon."[6] Its difficult language gave rise to a vast, and highly technical, body of decisions.[7] The clause reached some assigned claims but failed to reach others. If a particular assigned claim was within the ban of the assignee clause, suit in federal court was barred, though the assignment may have been entirely bona fide. If, on the other hand, the particular assignment did not fall within the highly artificial lines drawn by the statute and the decisions construing it, the assignee could sue in federal court even though the only purpose of the assignment was to create federal jurisdiction. Thus, the statute no longer served to effectuate the purpose for which it was originally designed.

In the 1948 Judicial Code the assignee clause was dropped. In its stead the Reviser, building in part on § 37 of the 1911 Code,[8] provided, in 28 U.S.C.A. § 1359, that the district court should not have jurisdiction of a civil action "in which any party, by assignment or otherwise, has been improperly or collusively made or joined to invoke the jurisdiction of such court." This would seem a potent barrier against the manufacture of diversity, whether by assignment or by any other device.[9] The construction initially put on § 1359 by the courts, however, made the statute largely ineffective.

The leading case was Corabi v. Auto Racing, Inc.,[10] a unanimous opinion by the Third Circuit sitting en banc. The holding there was that

---

5. The constitutionality of this partial withdrawal of jurisdiction was suggested at the oral argument in Turner v. The President, Directors, and Co. of the Bank of North America, 1799, 4 Dall. 8, 1 L.Ed. 718, and upheld in Sheldon v. Sill, 1850, 8 How. 441, 12 L.Ed. 1147. See § 10 above.

6. Comment, Chaos of Jurisdiction in the Federal District Courts, 1941, 35 Ill. L.Rev. 566, 569, 570. These strictures on the statute were quoted approvingly in the Reviser's Note to § 1359 of the 1948 Judicial Code.

7. See Dobie, Jurisdiction of the United States Courts as Affected by Assignment, 1920, 6 Va.L.Rev. 553; 14 Wright, Miller & Cooper, Jurisdiction 2d § 3639.

8. Section 37, originally adopted as § 5 of the Act of March 3, 1875, 18 Stat. 472, required the court to dismiss or remand a suit whenever it appeared "that such suit does not really and substantially involve a dispute or controversy properly within the jurisdiction of said district court, or that the parties to said suit have been improperly or collusively made or joined, either as plaintiffs or defendants, for the purpose of creating a case cognizable or removable under this chapter * * *."

9. Section 1359 is aimed at "suitors who by sham, pretense, or other fiction acquire a spurious status that would allow them to invoke the limited jurisdiction of the federal courts." Nolan v. Boeing Co., C.A.5th, 1990, 919 F.2d 1058, 1067, certiorari denied 111 S.Ct. 1587, 499 U.S. 962, 113 L.Ed.2d 651.

10. C.A.3d, 1959, 264 F.2d 784.

diversity jurisdiction existed in a suit by a nonresident administrator, representing the estate of a resident, in a suit against a resident defendant. That result was unattractive, but could readily be explained on the basis of precedent [11] and an unwillingness to look into the motives of the state court in appointing the nonresident as administrator. Unfortunately the court, in laying down what was to be for nearly a decade the authoritative construction of § 1359, turned to Webster's New International Dictionary, rather than to the purpose or history of the statute, to determine its meaning.[12] Many other courts followed the Third Circuit in its holding that a party's actions are not "improper" or "collusive" within the meaning of the statute, even though the sole motive was to gain access to federal court, if the actions were lawful in themselves.[13] The appointment of an administrator or general guardian of the proper citizenship to create diversity became very common,[14] and dubious assignments were held not to violate the ban of § 1359.[15]

In 1968 Judge Thornberry, writing for the Fifth Circuit,[16] took a very different view. The holding there was that if an assignment does not divest the assignors of their interests in the lawsuit and was made only to create diversity, the assignment will be regarded as colorable and ineffective to create jurisdiction. Judge Thornberry was willing to accept the result of Corabi, and the other cases looking to the citizenship of a representative appointed by a state court, but he rejected the interpretation the Corabi case had given to § 1359, as well as the process by which that interpretation was reached.[17]

11. See § 29 above.

12. 264 F.2d at 788.

13. Deposit Guar. Bank & Trust Co. v. Burton, C.A.6th, 1967, 380 F.2d 346; Lang v. Elm City Constr. Co., C.A.2d, 1963, 324 F.2d 235; Todd County v. Loegering, C.A.8th, 1961, 297 F.2d 470.

14. In Jamison v. Kammerer, C.A.3d, 1959, 264 F.2d 789, the court noted that the plaintiff administrator had been named administrator in 33 other cases in the court below "in order to create federal diversity jurisdiction," but held that jurisdiction existed nonetheless.

See also Kaufmann's Estate, Phila.Orphans' Ct., 1954, 87 Pa.D. & C. 401, 4 Fiduciary 253, where the court held that since verdicts in personal injury cases are higher in federal than in state court, it was in the interest of the ward for it to appoint a New Jersey resident as guardian in order to create diversity.

Although the situation in the Eastern District of Pennsylvania was clearly abnormal, 20.5% of all the original diversity actions pending in that court when a study was made were suits by out-of-state representatives against Pennsylvania defendants. ALI Study, p. 118.

15. Bradbury v. Dennis, C.A.10th, 1962, 310 F.2d 73, certiorari denied 83 S.Ct. 874, 372 U.S. 928, 9 L.Ed.2d 733, noted 1963, 14 Syracuse L.Rev. 687; City of Eufaula, Ala. v. Pappas, D.C.Ala.1963, 213 F.Supp. 749. But see Amar v. Garnier Enterprises, Inc., D.C.Cal.1966, 41 F.R.D. 211; Steinberg v. Toro, D.C. Puerto Rico 1951, 95 F.Supp. 791.

16. Caribbean Mills, Inc. v. Kramer, C.A.5th, 1968, 392 F.2d 387, affirmed 1969, 89 S.Ct. 1487, 394 U.S. 823, 23 L.Ed.2d 9.

The same result had been reached in Ferrara v. Philadelphia Labs., Inc., D.C.Vt. 1967, 272 F.Supp. 1000, noted 1968, 56 Geo.L.J. 1205, affirmed C.A.2d, 1968, 393 F.2d 934.

17. "By focusing on the literal meanings of the two words, the court virtually emasculated the statute * * *. If the statute is to have any utility, its meaning must be derived from the prerevision statutes and cases, not from dictionary definitions of the individual words." 392 F.2d at 393.

The Supreme Court agreed to review the Fifth Circuit case,[18] presumably to resolve the conflict between the Third and Fifth Circuits. Twelve days before the Court granted certiorari the conflict vanished. In McSparran v. Weist,[19] the Third Circuit, again sitting en banc, voted 4–2 to overrule Corabi. It now read § 1359 as meaning that "a nominal party designated simply for the purpose of creating diversity of citizenship, who has no real or substantial interest in the dispute or controversy, is improperly or collusively named." [20] The Third Circuit went even further than the Fifth Circuit had urged, since it applied its new rule to a court-appointed representative. It held that this did not amount to a collateral attack on the appointment by the state court, since the representative retains his capacity as such, but is merely a refusal to consider the citizenship of "a straw fiduciary" in determining the existence of diversity.

The rule announced by the Third Circuit in McSparran created its own problems both of meaning and of application. The McSparran case involved a guardian, and if the citizenship of the guardian is disregarded, it is easy to look to the citizenship of the ward. The court said, however, that the same rule should apply to "executors and administrators." [21] If it is so applied, should the court then look to the citizenship of the decedent or to that of the beneficiaries? Tenable arguments can be made both ways.[22] The problem of application arose because McSparran did not hold that the citizenship of a representative is always immaterial but only if the appointment of a nonresident was an attempt to "manufacture" diversity. This was said to be a question of fact on which the plaintiff has the burden of proof.[23]

In Kramer v. Caribbean Mills, Inc.,[24] decided a few months after the McSparran case, the Supreme Court agreed with the view the Fifth Circuit had taken about § 1359 and its application to assignees. The Court held that an assignment for collection only and motivated by a desire to make diversity jurisdiction available falls within the "very core" of § 1359.[25] The Court found it unnecessary to reexamine its line of decisions holding that if the transfer of a claim is absolute, with the transferor retaining no interest in the subject matter, it is not "improperly or collusively made" regardless of the motive for the transfer.[26] The

---

18. 1968, 89 S.Ct. 99, 393 U.S. 819, 21 L.Ed.2d 91.

19. C.A.3d, 1968, 402 F.2d 867, certiorari denied 89 S.Ct. 1739, 395 U.S. 903, 23 L.Ed.2d 217.

20. 402 F.2d at 873.

21. 402 F.2d at 875.

22. The American Law Institute proposed looking to the residence of the decedent. ALI Study, § 1301(b)(4). There is force in Professor Farage's objection that "the decedent is the only one in the whole wide world who literally has no interest in the proceedings * * *." Farage, Proposed

Code Will Emasculate Federal Jurisdiction, Trial Magazine, April/May 1966, p. 30, at 32. Any other test, however, would be too difficult to administer. See Currie, The Federal Courts and the American Law Institute, 1968, 36 U.Chi.L.Rev. 1, 16.

23. 402 F.2d at 875–876.

24. 1969, 89 S.Ct. 1487, 394 U.S. 823, 23 L.Ed.2d 9.

25. 89 S.Ct. at 1491, 394 U.S. at 830.

26. 89 S.Ct. at 1490 n. 9, 394 U.S. at 828 n. 9.

Diversity jurisdiction may still be created by a bona-fide assignment. Western Farm

Court took note of McSparran, and of cases reaching a result contrary to McSparran with regard to administrators and guardians, but found it not necessary to consider that situation. It pointed out three respects in which cases involving court-appointed representatives differ from assignments, but said it was "not necessary to decide whether these distinctions amount to a difference for purposes of § 1359." [27]

Subsequent lower court cases have held with one voice that the distinctions about court-appointed representatives that the Court had noted in Kramer did not amount to a difference, and that if the purpose of appointing an out-of-state representative is to create diversity, § 1359 bars federal jurisdiction. There was great variation among the circuits, however, in determining when to invoke § 1359 and whose decision should control if that of the representative did not. [28] That uncertainty has been resolved by a 1988 statute that is taken nearly verbatim from what the American Law Institute had proposed 19 years earlier. [29] It provides that "the legal representative of the estate of a decedent shall be deemed to be a citizen only of the same State as the decedent, and the legal representative of an infant or incompetent shall be deemed to be a citizen only of the same State as the infant or incompetent." [30] This will eliminate all questions of motivation and provide a test in cases involving decedents, infants, and incompetents that is easy to administer.

A party can gain access to federal court by changing his domicile to another state, chosen so that diversity will exist. Such a move will be effective, though it was motivated solely by a desire to sue in federal court, [31] but it must be a bona fide change of domicile and the party will not succeed if he plans to move back to his former home after the lawsuit is over. [32]

A corporation cannot get into federal court merely by transferring its claim to a subsidiary, incorporated in some other state chosen with diversity in mind, [33] but if the corporation in the original state is

Credit Bank v. Hamakua Sugar Co., Inc., D.C.Hawaii 1994, 841 F.Supp. 976.

27. Id.

28. See 14 Wright, Miller & Cooper, Jurisdiction 2d § 3640; Mullenix, Creative Manipulation of Diversity Jurisdiction: Is There Diversity After Death., 1985, 70 Cornell L.Rev. 1011; Storm, A Quest for Diversity: In Search of the Purpose Behind Appointments in Estate Related Cases, 1988, 18 Stetson L.Rev. 87.

29. See note 22 above. Courts had repeatedly praised the ALI proposal, but held that only Congress could adopt it. E.g., Field v. Volkswagenwerk AG, C.A.3d, 1980, 626 F.2d 293, 303; Lester v. McFaddon, C.A.4th, 1969, 415 F.2d 1101, 1106.

30. 28 U.S.C.A. § 1332(c)(2), added by Act of Nov. 19, 1988, Pub.L. 100–702, 102 Stat. 4642.

"Holding the citizenship of the decedent, not the representative, controlling in diversity suits based in wrongful death makes a pre-existing non-manipulable fact determinative for diversity purposes." Liu v. Westchester County Medical Center, D.C.N.Y. 1993, 837 F.Supp. 82, 83.

31. Williamson v. Osenton, 1914, 34 S.Ct. 442, 232 U.S. 619, 58 L.Ed. 758. See § 26 above.

32. Morris v. Gilmer, 1889, 9 S.Ct. 289, 129 U.S. 315, 32 L.Ed. 690; O'Brien v. Delta Gas, Inc., D.C.La.1980, 486 F.Supp. 810. See § 26 above.

33. Miller & Lux v. East Side Canal & Irrigation Co., 1908, 29 S.Ct. 111, 211 U.S. 293, 53 L.Ed. 189; Southern Realty Inv. Co. v. Walker, 1909, 29 S.Ct. 211, 211 U.S. 603, 53 L.Ed. 346; Prudential Oil Corp. v. Phillips Petroleum Co., C.A.2d, 1976, 546 F.2d 469; Green & White Constr. Co. v. Cormat dissolved, and all the assets transferred to a corporation chartered by the new state, apparently this will be effective,[34] although, under the 1958 amendment to the law, the new corporation will also be deemed a citizen of the state in which it has its principal place of business.[35]

In class actions the court looks only to the citizenship of the named representatives of the class.[36] Thus, where there is a large class and some members of the class are of such citizenship as to prevent diversity, a class action may be brought in which only persons of the right citizenship are named as representative of the class.[37] On the same principle, a stockholders' derivative suit may be brought in federal court if there can be found to act as plaintiff a qualified stockholder who is not a citizen of the same state as the corporation or the other named defendants.[38]

A party cannot create diversity where it would not otherwise exist by aligning the parties in the pleadings contrary to their real interests, since the court will realign the parties to determine the jurisdictional question.[39] Nor can the party avoid the requirement of complete diversity by failing to include as a party one whose citizenship would be wrong, if that party is "indispensable" to determination of the litigation.[40] But if the joinder of the party is not required under Rule 19, then it is permissible not to join that party and federal jurisdiction can be obtained.[41]

If the plaintiff's preference is for a state court, rather than a federal court, he or she may simply file the suit in state court. However, if diversity exists, and none of the defendants is a citizen of the state in which the suit is brought, the defendant or defendants may thwart plaintiff's choice by removal of the suit.[42] There are several devices by which plaintiff can avoid this; indeed plaintiffs would seem to have more freedom here than they do when they are seeking to create diversity, since there is at least a statute, however ineffective it may have been in

Constr. Co., D.C.Ill.1973, 361 F.Supp. 125; cf. Cahokia Sportservice, Inc. v. Cahokia Downs, Inc., D.C.Ill.1958, 165 F.Supp. 686 (assignment of lease by defendant to wholly-owned subsidiary corporation of same citizenship as plaintiff does not defeat diversity). But cf. Piermont Heights, Inc. v. Dorfman, D.C.N.Y.1993, 820 F.Supp. 99, finding a bona fide reason for incorporation in a new state.

34. Black & White Taxicab & Transfer Co. v. Brown & Yellow Taxicab & Transfer Co., 1928, 48 S.Ct. 404, 276 U.S. 518, 72 L.Ed. 681. This decision has been the target of universal condemnation, as the worst example of the abuses of diversity possible under the rule of Swift v. Tyson. See § 54 below.

35. See § 27 above.

36. Snyder v. Harris, 1969, 89 S.Ct. 1053, 1059, 394 U.S. 332, 340, 22 L.Ed.2d 319; Supreme Tribe of Ben Hur v. Cauble,

1921, 41 S.Ct. 338, 255 U.S. 356, 65 L.Ed. 673; In re School Asbestos Litigation, C.A.3d, 1990, 921 F.2d 1310, 1317–1318, certiorari denied 111 S.Ct. 1623, 499 U.S. 976, 113 L.Ed.2d 720.

37. See § 72 below.

38. See § 73 below.

39. See § 30 above.

40. See § 70 below.

41. " * * * Congress has so far proscribed only collusive joinder meant to invoke federal jurisdiction, see 28 U.S.C. § 1359; parties may still obtain a federal forum by colluding not to join." Western Maryland Ry. Co. v. Harbor Ins. Co., C.A.D.C.1990, 910 F.2d 960, 964 (per Clarence Thomas, J.).

42. 28 U.S.C.A. § 1441(b); see § 38 below.

the past, purporting to bar collusive joinder to gain access to federal court, while there is no statute barring collusive action to defeat federal jurisdiction.[43] Despite this, the courts are now "injecting a new note of realism into the determination of diversity jurisdiction," [44] and are refusing to allow artificial devices to be as effective as they formerly were in defeating diversity.

The device of choosing a personal representative of proper citizenship had been as effective to defeat diversity as it had been to create it. Indeed the leading case on this subject, Mecom v. Fitzsimmons Drilling Co.,[45] involved appointment of an administrator so chosen as to defeat removal. Smith, a citizen of Oklahoma, was killed, and his wife, also an Oklahoma citizen, was appointed administratrix of his estate by an Oklahoma probate court. She brought suit in an Oklahoma state court against a Louisiana corporation and certain individuals claimed to be liable for Smith's death. The corporation removed the case to federal court. After an unsuccessful motion to remand, Mrs. Smith dismissed her suit. Twice more she sued in state court, twice more the suit was removed, and twice more she dismissed. Thereupon Mrs. Smith resigned as administratrix, and one Mecom, a Louisiana citizen, was appointed administrator of Smith's estate by the probate court. Mecom did not know Mrs. Smith or her late husband, he knew of no assets in Louisiana, and he did not sign his own bond nor did he come to Oklahoma to be appointed. Instead he had agreed to serve as administrator solely as a favor to Mrs. Smith's attorney, and upon his appointment he immediately named Mrs. Smith as his state agent in Oklahoma. Suit was then brought in Mecom's name, for the wrongful death of Smith, in the Oklahoma state court. This suit also was removed, but after trial on the merits, with judgment for defendants, the Supreme Court held that the removal was improper, and that a motion to remand should have been granted. It stated the hitherto-settled rule that the citizenship of a personal representative, rather than those for whom he sues, is decisive; on this test there were Louisiana citizens on both sides of the suit and thus no diversity. The Court held that the rule was not altered by the fact that the administrator was appointed solely to defeat diversity, saying that the Mecom administrator could not be collaterally attacked because of the purposes and motives of the parties, when they practiced no fraud upon the court.

It was seen earlier that from 1968 on the courts became much less tolerant of the appointment of an out-of-state representative to create jurisdiction. In that same period they began to reexamine Mecom and to hold that the appointment of a representative of the same citizenship need not defeat an out-of-state defendant's right to remove to federal

---

43. "Section 1359, as its language clearly shows, expresses a policy against the creation of federal jurisdiction and not against its avoidance." McSparran v. Weist, C.A.3d 1968, 402 F.2d 867, 875, certiorari denied 89 S.Ct. 1739, 395 U.S. 903, 23 L.Ed.2d 217. See also Herrick v. Pioneer Gas Products Co., D.C.Okl.1976, 429 F.Supp. 80, 84.

44. Miller v. Perry, C.A.4th, 1972, 456 F.2d 63, 67.

45. 1931, 52 S.Ct. 84, 284 U.S. 183, 76 L.Ed. 233.

court.[46] The 1988 statute, quoted above, requires the court in all of these cases to look to the citizenship of the decedent, infant, or incompetent and will be as effective in preventing the appointment of a representative to defeat diversity as in using that device to create diversity.

Living litigants cannot defeat diversity by the choice of a personal representative, but a popular technique has been for plaintiff to assign the claim, or part of it, to a person who is a citizen of the same state as the defendant. Occasionally a district court balked, and pointed to the obvious truth that to allow removal to be defeated by this device "would make federal procedure a game in which the statutory rights of parties might be blocked by an adroit and cleverly designed maneuver of his adversary." [47] Much more often, however, the device worked and it seemed to be supported by several Supreme Court decisions.[48] But since 1969 there has been a definite trend in the district courts to hold that a partial assignment, at least, will be disregarded and will not defeat a right to remove that would otherwise exist.[49]

The fraudulent joinder as defendant of a person against whom plaintiff has no bona fide claim, but who is a citizen of the same state as plaintiff, will not defeat removal.[50] The joinder is not fraudulent within this rule, however, where plaintiff does have a claim against the cocitizen thus joined, even though this defendant may have no means with which

46. The leading case was Miller v. Perry, C.A.4th, 1972, 456 F.2d 63.

47. Phoenix Mut. Life Ins. Co. of Hartford, Conn. v. England, D.C.Mo.1938, 22 F.Supp. 284, 286.

48. Provident Sav. Life Assur. Soc. v. Ford, 1885, 5 S.Ct. 1104, 114 U.S. 635, 20 L.Ed. 261; Oakley v. Goodnow, 1886, 6 S.Ct. 944, 118 U.S. 43, 30 L.Ed. 61; Ridgeland Box Mfg. Co. v. Sinclair Ref. Co., D.C.S.C.1949, 82 F.Supp. 274 (assignment of ⅟₁₀₀ of claim); Krenzien v. United Services Life Ins. Co., D.C.Kan.1954, 121 F.Supp. 243, criticized 1954, 40 Va.L.Rev. 803; Hair v. Savannah Steel Drum Corp., D.C.S.C. 1955, 161 F.Supp. 654; Verschell v. Fireman's Fund Ins. Co., D.C.N.Y.1966, 257 F.Supp. 153.

49. The leading case is Gentle v. Lamb–Weston, Inc., D.C.Me.1969, 302 F.Supp. 161, noted 1969, 83 Harv.L.Rev. 465. The same result has been reached in Grassi v. Ciba–Geigy, Ltd., C.A.5th, 1990, 894 F.2d 181; Picquet v. Amoco Production Co., D.C.La.1981, 513 F.Supp. 938; Carter v. Seaboard Coast Line R. Co., D.C.S.C.1970, 318 F.Supp. 368, noted 1971, 23 S.C.L.Q. 463; McClanahan v. Snodgrass, D.C.Miss. 1970, 319 F.Supp. 913. Contra: Arant v. Stover, D.C.S.C.1969, 307 F.Supp. 144.

It also has been held that plaintiff could not defeat diversity jurisdiction by incorporating in defendant's home state only a few days before filing an action for the express purpose of preventing removal. Douglas Energy of New York, Inc. v. Mobil Oil Corp., D.C.Kan.1984, 585 F.Supp. 546. See generally 14 Wright, Miller & Cooper, Jurisdiction 2d § 3641, pp. 131–135.

50. Wecker v. National Enameling & Stamping Co., 1907, 27 S.Ct. 184, 204 U.S. 176, 51 L.Ed. 430; Poulos v. Naas Foods, Inc., C.A.7th, 1992, 959 F.2d 69; Dodd v. Fawcett Publications, Inc., C.A.10th, 1964, 329 F.2d 82; Covington v. Indemnity Ins. Co. of North America, C.A.5th, 1958, 251 F.2d 930, certiorari denied 78 S.Ct. 1362, 357 U.S. 921, 2 L.Ed.2d 1365; Frontier Airlines, Inc. v. United Air Lines, Inc., D.C.Colo.1989, 758 F.Supp. 1399; Tinney v. McClain, D.C.Tex.1948, 76 F.Supp. 694; and cases cited 14 Wright, Miller & Cooper, Jurisdiction 2d § 3641 n. 23.

As held in the Wecker case above, joinder is fraudulent, even though plaintiff had no actual knowledge of the facts which show that it had no bona fide claim against the joined defendant, if it has willfully closed his eyes to information within his reach. Indeed in this context "fraudulent" has become "a term of art" that "in no way reflects on the integrity of plaintiff or her counsel." Newman v. Forward Lands, Inc., D.C.Pa.1976, 418 F.Supp. 134, 136 n. 1. See also Poulos v. Naas Foods, Inc., C.A.7th, 1992, 959 F.2d 69, 73.

to satisfy a judgment and may have been joined solely to prevent removal of the action.[51]

The practice, popular in some states and notably in California, of naming various "John Doe" defendants has created jurisdictional problems. In an action commenced in federal court, it seems reasonably clear that diversity does not exist unless plaintiff both pleads and proves that the John Does are citizens of some state other than plaintiff's state.[52] In a well-known case, the Supreme Court seemed to lay down a converse rule with regard to a case commenced in state court and sought to be removed. Plaintiff asserted a joint claim against the Pullman Company and one of its porters. The porter was named in the complaint as John Doe One, but his relation to the Pullman Company and his negligence as its servant were alleged. The Court held that to justify removal the Pullman Company was bound to show that the porter was a nonresident of plaintiff's state.[53] It would make federal jurisdiction more of a game than ever if removal could be defeated by the simple device of naming as a defendant a fictional John Doe. At one time the rule that the Ninth Circuit, the court principally confronted with the problem, seemed to be working out was that where, so far as can be told from the complaint, the defendant Does were mere nominal and disinterested parties, who "live not and are accused of nothing," they could be disregarded in determining whether a case was removable.[54]

The Ninth Circuit later abandoned that rule, and many other variations for which support could be found in its cases, and adopted a

---

51. Pirie v. Tvedt, 1885, 5 S.Ct. 1034, 1161, 115 U.S. 41, 29 L.Ed. 331; Chicago, R.I. & P.R. Co. v. Schwyhart, 1913, 33 S.Ct. 250, 227 U.S. 184, 57 L.Ed. 473; Chicago, R.I. & P.R. Co. v. Dowell, 1913, 33 S.Ct. 684, 229 U.S. 102, 57 L.Ed. 1090; Bolstad v. Central Sur. & Ins. Corp., C.C.A.8th, 1948, 168 F.2d 927; Smith v. Southern Pac. Co., C.A.9th, 1951, 187 F.2d 397; Parks v. New York Times Co., C.A.5th, 1962, 308 F.2d 474; Frith v. Blazon–Flexible Flyer, Inc., C.A.5th, 1975, 512 F.2d 899; Auto Ins. Agency, Inc. v. Interstate Agency, Inc., D.C.S.C.1981, 525 F.Supp. 1104; Nosonowitz v. Allegheny Beverage Corp., D.C.N.Y. 1978, 463 F.Supp. 162. See also the statement of the test in Bobby Jones Garden Apartments, Inc. v. Suleski, C.A.5th, 1968, 391 F.2d 172.

"If under our dual court system a potential plaintiff has a choice between a state forum and a federal forum, it is his privilege to exercise that choice subject to legal limitations, and if he can avoid the federal forum by the device of properly joining a nondiverse defendant or a nondiverse co-plaintiff he is free to do so." Iowa Public Serv. Co. v. Medicine Bow Coal Co., C.A.8th, 1977, 556 F.2d 400, 406.

An evidentiary hearing on whether joinder is fraudulent is ordinarily improper.

The court must resolve all disputed questions of fact from the pleadings and affidavits in favor of plaintiff and then determine whether there could possibly be a valid claim under state law against the defendant in question. B., Inc. v. Miller Brewing Co., C.A.5th, 1981, 663 F.2d 545. See also Carriere v. Sears, Roebuck & Co., C.A.5th, 1990, 893 F.2d 98.

52. Garter–Bare Co. v. Munsingwear, Inc., C.A.9th, 1980, 650 F.2d 975, 981; Eckert v. Lane, D.C.Ark.1988, 678 F.Supp. 773; Applegate v. Top Associates, Inc., D.C.N.Y.1969, 300 F.Supp. 51, affirmed C.A.2d, 1970, 425 F.2d 92; Johnson v. General Motors Corp., D.C.Va.1965, 242 F.Supp. 778; and cases cited 14 Wright, Miller & Cooper, Jurisdiction 2d § 3642 n. 3.

But see Hannah v. Majors, D.C.Mo.1964, 35 F.R.D. 179. See also Sligh v. Doe, C.A.4th, 1979, 596 F.2d 1169.

53. Pullman Co. v. Jenkins, 1939, 59 S.Ct. 347, 350, 305 U.S. 534, 540, 83 L.Ed. 334.

54. Grigg v. Southern Pac. Co., C.A.9th, 1957, 246 F.2d 613, 620.

flat rule that in all cases the presence of Doe defendants defeated diversity and precluded removal.[55] Congress responded quickly. Before the year was out it amended the removal statute to overcome that Ninth Circuit decision. Under the 1988 statute, for the purposes of removal "the citizenship of defendants sued under fictitious names shall be disregarded." [56]

A final device for defeating removal is to assert a claim for just less than the amount in controversy required for federal jurisdiction. The court will look to the amount actually claimed, not the amount that might have been claimed.[57] If the claim that could be made is for far more than the jurisdictional amount required, this device is a very expensive way of buying whatever tactical advantage there may be in remaining in state court.[58] If the plaintiff is willing to pay this price, it must do so from the beginning. A reduction in the amount claimed after the suit has actually been removed will not defeat jurisdiction.[59]

55. Bryant v. Ford Motor Co., C.A.9th, 1987, 832 F.2d 1080, 1083, certiorari denied 109 S.Ct. 542, 488 U.S. 986, 102 L.Ed.2d 572.

56. 28 U.S.C.A. § 1441(a), as amended by Act of Nov. 19, 1988, Pub.L. 100–702, § 1016(a), 102 Stat. 4669. See Note, Doe Pleading To Be Disregarded In Diversity Jurisdiction: Congressional Response To Bryant v. Ford Motor Co., 1989, 19 Golden Gate U.L.Rev. 127.

57. Iowa Central Ry. Co. v. Bacon, 1915, 35 S.Ct. 357, 236 U.S. 305, 59 L.Ed. 591; Erwin v. Allied Van Lines, Inc., D.C.Ark. 1965, 239 F.Supp. 144; and cases cited 14A Wright, Miller & Cooper, Jurisdiction 2d § 3725 n. 12. Contra: Capps v. New Jellico Coal Co., D.C.Tenn.1950, 87 F.Supp. 369.

58. The device was more practical in the days before Erie R. Co. v. Tompkins, when different rules of law were applied in federal court than in state court. Thus, in Brady v. Indemnity Ins. Co. of North America, C.C.A.6th, 1933, 68 F.2d 302, noted 1934, 12 N.C.L.Rev. 390, it was to the plaintiff's advantage to sue for $2,999.99 in state court, where his claim would be good, rather than to sue for the full $15,000 face value of the insurance policy and have the case removed to federal court where a policy defense, regarded as valid by the federal courts but void by the state courts, would have barred all recovery.

59. St. Paul Mercury Indem. Co. v. Red Cab Co., 1938, 58 S.Ct. 586, 303 U.S. 283, 82 L.Ed. 845, noted 1938, 51 Harv.L.Rev. 1108, 24 Va.L.Rev. 808, 1939, 37 Mich. L.Rev. 482; Albright v. R.J. Reynolds Tobacco Co., C.A.3d, 1976, 531 F.2d 132, certiorari denied 96 S.Ct. 2229, 426 U.S. 907, 48 L.Ed.2d 832; Marsh v. Tillie Lewis Foods, Inc., D.C.S.D.1966, 257 F.Supp. 645; Facella v. Home Fire & Marine Ins. Co. of California, D.C.N.J.1960, 184 F.Supp. 838; and cases cited 14A Wright, Miller & Cooper, Jurisdiction § 3725 n. 49.

Chapter 5

JURISDICTIONAL AMOUNT

Analysis

§ 32. When Jurisdictional Amount Is Necessary [1]

The Constitution makes no requirement that any particular amount be in controversy in order to invoke the jurisdiction of the federal courts. Nevertheless, since the earliest days of the Republic, there has been a requirement, in some classes of actions, that more than a certain minimum amount be in controversy to bring cases to the federal trial courts. The Judiciary Act of 1789 fixed this sum at $500, and it was increased to $2000 in 1887, $3000 in 1911, $10,000 in 1958, and to the present figure of $50,000 in 1988.[2] For jurisdiction to exist, where this requirement is applicable, the amount in controversy, exclusive of interest and costs, must exceed the stated sum.[3]

By these successive figures, as was said at the time of the 1958 increase, Congress has endeavored to require a jurisdictional amount "not so high as to convert the Federal courts into courts of big business nor so low as to fritter away their time in the trial of petty controversies."[4] An increase in the jurisdictional amount is intended to help reduce congestion in the federal courts,[5] but its effect in this regard is problematical, particularly because in actions for unliquidated damages

---

§ 32

1. 14A Wright, Miller & Cooper, Jurisdiction 2d § 3701.

2. Act of Nov. 19, 1988, Pub.L. 100–702, § 201, 102 Stat. 4642, amending 28 U.S.C.A. § 1332.

3. Clark v. National Travelers Life Ins. Co., C.A.6th, 1975, 518 F.2d 1167; Royal Ins. Co. of Liverpool, England v. Stoddard, C.C.A.8th, 1912, 201 F. 915; Bradford Nat.

Life Ins. Co. v. Union State Bank, D.C.Wis. 1992, 794 F.Supp. 296.

4. Sen.Rep. No. 1830, 85th Cong., 2d Sess., 1958, p. 4, reprinted in 1958 U.S. Code Cong. & Admin. News pp. 3099, 3101.

5. Snyder v. Harris, 1969, 89 S.Ct. 1053, 1058–1059, 394 U.S. 332, 339–340, 22 L.Ed.2d 319; Foiles by Foiles v. Merrell National Labs., D.C.Ill.1989, 730 F.Supp. 108, 110.

arising out of a tort, which make up a large part of the business of the courts, there is little to prevent plaintiffs from increasing their demand for judgment to meet the new jurisdictional test. Thus, Chief Justice Warren reported that while the increase from $3000 to $10,000 in 1958 "did result in a temporary reduction in the filing of private civil cases, the net effect on the workload has been very slight."[6] The increase to $50,000 was credited with a drop of 15% between 1989 and 1990 in the number of diversity cases filed,[7] but this is much less than the 40% reduction that the House Judiciary Committee had predicted.[8]

The $50,000 figure applies to diversity cases.[9] Until 1980 it purportedly applied to federal questions, although, as will be seen below, its application to such cases even before recent statutory amendments, was of limited importance. Other jurisdictional amounts apply to certain actions against the United States[10] and to statutory interpleader actions.[11] There are also some statutes that require an amount in controversy for particular federal-question cases and that continue to apply despite the 1980 removal of an amount requirement from the general federal-question statute. From 1789 to 1925 there were varying jurisdictional amounts required for appeal to the Supreme Court in some kinds of cases, but there is no longer any such requirement. It had long been the law that $500 or more had to be in controversy to appeal as of right to a court of appeals in a summary bankruptcy proceeding, but new bankruptcy legislation adopted in 1978 removed that requirement.[12]

From 1875, when the district courts were first given federal-question jurisdiction by what is now 28 U.S.C.A. § 1331, until 1976, the statute purported to make the same requirement of amount in controversy for federal-question cases as was made for diversity cases. There

6. Warren, Address to the American Law Institute, 1960, 25 F.R.D. 213.

The Court has commented to the same effect. See Lynch v. Household Fin. Corp., 1972, 92 S.Ct. 1113, 1121 n. 18, 405 U.S. 538, 550 n. 18, 31 L.Ed.2d 424.

7. Ann.Rep. of the Director of the Administrative Office of the U.S. Courts, 1991, pp. 87–88.

8. H.Rep. No. 100–889, 100th Cong., 2d Sess., 1988, p. 45, reprinted in 1989 U.S. Code Cong. & Admin. News 6004, 6005–6006.

And by fiscal 1992 the number of diversity cases had increased again. Ann.Rep. of the Director of the Administrative Office of the U.S. Courts, 1992, p. 191.

9. 28 U.S.C.A. § 1332.

10. In cases against the United States not arising under the internal revenue laws nor out of a tort, the district courts have jurisdiction only if the amount does not exceed $10,000. 28 U.S.C.A. § 1346(a)(2). Larger cases must go to the Court of Federal Claims. 28 U.S.C.A. § 1491(a)(1). See

ALI Study, § 1322(a)(1), proposing that the limit be raised to $50,000.

There is a $1000 requirement for judicial review of decisions regarding payments for services under the medicare program. 42 U.S.C.A. § 1395ff.

11. Statutory interpleader actions require that the amount in controversy exceed $500. 28 U.S.C.A. § 1335. It will be seen in § 74 below that there are also nonstatutory interpleader actions, where the usual $50,000 figure is applicable if diversity is the basis of jurisdiction.

12. The amount requirement had appeared in § 25a of the former Bankruptcy Act. The 1978 legislation, Pub.L. 95–598, omitted that former section and created a virtually incomprehensible scheme for appeals in bankruptcy. That scheme was modified in 1984, Pub.L. 98–353, and while the new statute is simpler and more straightforward than the provisions adopted in 1978, it leaves unresolved many troubling ambiguities. 16 Wright, Miller & Cooper, Jurisdiction § 3926.

was much less to this than met the eye, since a long series of statutes, in terms otherwise parallel to the general federal-question statute, granted jurisdiction without regard to amount in virtually all the areas that otherwise would have come under the general statute.[13] These statutes covered so much of the general federal-question jurisdiction that in 1958, when the jurisdictional amount was increased to $10,000, it was repeatedly asserted in the committee reports and supporting documents that "the only significant categories of 'Federal question' cases subject to the jurisdictional amount are suits under the Jones Act and suits contesting the constitutionality of State statutes."[14] It is highly doubtful whether the amount requirement extended even so far as that limited statement would suggest.

No case ever held that Jones Act actions had to meet the jurisdictional amount test of 28 U.S.C.A. § 1331. There were decisions that seemed to assume that the general federal-question statute, § 1331, was the only jurisdictional basis for such suits,[15] but these cases did not so hold, and the assumption was a questionable one. The Jones Act,[16]

---

13. The following statutes all appear in 28 U.S.C.A.:

§ 1333 (admiralty, maritime, and prize cases).

§ 1334 (bankruptcy matters).

§ 1336 (review of certain ICC orders).

§ 1337 (cases arising under any Act of Congress regulating commerce).

§ 1338 (patents, plant variety protection, copyrights, trademarks, and unfair competition).

§ 1339 (postal matters).

§ 1340 (internal revenue; customs duties).

§ 1343 (civil rights cases—see discussion in text below).

§ 1344 (election disputes).

§ 1350 (alien's action for tort).

§ 1351 (actions against consuls, vice consuls, and members of a diplomatic mission). See also § 1364.

§ 1352 (actions on bonds executed under federal law).

§ 1353 (cases involving Indian land allotments).

§ 1355 (actions to recover fines, penalties, or forfeitures incurred under federal law).

§ 1356 (seizures not within admiralty jurisdiction).

§ 1357 (injuries under certain federal laws).

§ 1362 (federal-question actions by certain Indian tribes).

§ 1363 (actions to protect juror's employment rights).

A number of sections of 28 U.S.C.A. also grant jurisdiction without regard to amount in controversy of cases to which the United States is a party:

§ 1345 (United States as plaintiff).

§ 1346 (United States as defendant).

§ 1347 (partition actions where United States is joint tenant).

§ 1348 (actions by United States to wind up national banking associations).

§ 1349 (actions by or against corporations where United States owns more than one-half of the stock).

§ 1358 (eminent domain).

§ 1361 (action in nature of mandamus against a government officer or agency).

§ 1365 (certain suits by the Senate or a committee thereof).

14. Sen.Rep. No. 1830, 85th Cong., 2d Sess., 1958, pp. 6, 15, 22, reprinted in 1958 U.S. Code Cong. & Admin. News 3099, 3103, 3112–3113, 3122.

15. E.g., Wade v. Rogala, C.A.3d, 1959, 270 F.2d 280; Branic v. Wheeling Steel Corp., C.C.A.3d, 1945, 152 F.2d 887, certiorari denied 66 S.Ct. 902, 327 U.S. 801, 90 L.Ed. 1026; Turner v. Wilson Line of Massachusetts, Inc., D.C.Mass.1956, 142 F.Supp. 264, affirmed C.A.1st, 1957, 242 F.2d 414; McDonald v. Cape Cod Trawling Corp., D.C.Mass.1947, 71 F.Supp. 888; Rowley v. Sierra S.S. Co., D.C.Ohio 1942, 48 F.Supp. 193.

16. 46 U.S.C.A. § 688.

which makes available to seamen the remedies given to railway employees by the Federal Employers' Liability Act,[17] rested, at least in part, on the power to regulate commerce,[18] and 28 U.S.C.A. § 1337, granting jurisdiction without regard to amount in suits arising under any Act of Congress regulating commerce,[19] should have been held to cover Jones Act cases.[20]

There was equal difficulty in saying that an amount in controversy was required in suits contesting the constitutionality of state statutes. Many such cases come under 28 U.S.C.A. § 1343(a)(3), which gives jurisdiction without regard to amount of actions to redress the deprivation, under color of any state law, of any right, privilege, or immunity secured by the federal Constitution, or by any federal civil-rights statute.[21] In a separate opinion in Hague v. CIO,[22] Justice Stone endeavored to draw the line between those actions that could be brought under § 1343(a)(3), and required no jurisdictional amount, and those that must be brought under § 1331, where the jurisdictional amount was required, by saying that § 1343(a)(3) covered those cases where the right involved was "inherently incapable of pecuniary valuation," such as the right to vote and the rights of free expression, while resort must be had to § 1331, and the amount-in-controversy test satisfied, where the party was claiming a property right that could be given a dollars-and-cents value.

This distinction between property rights and personal rights became increasingly a source of controversy and it was finally rejected in 1972 in Lynch v. Household Finance Corp.[23] The Court, which was unanimous on this point, said that it had never adopted the property rights-personal liberties test for jurisdiction under 28 U.S.C.A. § 1343(a)(3). It found that the distinction was not supported by the legislative history of the statutes that are now §§ 1343(a)(3) and 1331, and noted "the virtual impossibility of applying" the distinction. Finally it said that "the dichotomy between personal liberties and property rights is a false one. Property does not have rights. People have rights. The right to enjoy

17. 45 U.S.C.A. § 51 et seq.

18. O'Donnell v. Great Lakes Dredge & Dock Co., 1943, 63 S.Ct. 488, 490, 318 U.S. 36, 39, 87 L.Ed. 596.

19. "[T]o found jurisdiction upon § 1337, it is not requisite that the commerce clause be the exclusive source of Federal power; it suffices that it be a significant one." Murphy v. Colonial Federal Sav. & Loan Assn., C.A.2d, 1967, 388 F.2d 609, 615.

As a matter of history it is probable that the statute that is now 28 U.S.C.A. § 1337 was intended to apply only to cases under the original Interstate Commerce Act, as it had been amended prior to 1910, but its language is not so confined and it has been applied much more broadly. See 13B Wright, Miller & Cooper, Jurisdiction 2d § 3574.

20. Ballard v. Moore–McCormack Lines, Inc., D.C.N.Y.1968, 285 F.Supp. 290; Richardson v. St. Charles–St. John the Baptist Bridge and Ferry Auth., D.C.La.1967, 274 F.Supp. 764; Brown v. Sinclair Ref. Co., D.C.N.Y.1964, 227 F.Supp. 714.

21. See § 22A above. See also 13B Wright, Miller & Cooper, Jurisdiction 2d § 3573.

22. 1939, 59 S.Ct. 954, 965–971, 307 U.S. 496, 518–532, 83 L.Ed. 1423.

23. 1972, 92 S.Ct. 1113, 405 U.S. 538, 31 L.Ed.2d 424.

property without unlawful deprivation, no less than the right to speak or the right to travel, is, in truth a 'personal' right, whether the 'property' in question be a welfare check, a home or a savings account." [24]

Even so, there were some federal-question cases in which more than the jurisdictional amount was still required. The most important class of cases was those challenging the validity of actions by federal officers.[25] Judge Medina was surely right when he called this "an unfortunate gap in the statutory jurisdiction of our federal courts." [26] This gap was much criticized by the commentators, who urged the courts to close it on their own.[27] Although some courts took a very relaxed view of what was needed to satisfy the statutory requirement in this class of cases,[28] most courts recognized that the gap was one "to be filled in by Congress" and "not by judicial legislation." [29]

A requirement of amount in controversy in federal-question cases made no sense. The requirement was of extremely limited application, and when it did apply its effect was to deny a federal forum for cases in which the amount involved was small but for which the federal courts had a special expertness and a special interest.[30]

Congress took a long step toward ending this anomaly in 1976 when it amended § 1331 to provide that no amount in controversy was required in any action "brought against the United States, any agency thereof, or any officer or employee thereof in his official capacity." [31] This took care of by far the most important class of federal-question cases in which the amount requirement had been an obstacle to suit. It did not do the whole job. More than the then-amount of $10,000 was still required if a suit against defendants other than federal officers was based on federal common law.[32] Challenges to state statutes did not come within § 1343(a)(3), and still required more than the amount in controversy, if the basis of challenge was that a state statute was inconsistent with an Act of Congress other than one "providing for equal

---

24. 92 S.Ct. at 1122, 405 U.S. at 552.

25. E.g., Schlesinger v. Councilman, 1975, 95 S.Ct. 1300, 1306 n. 9, 420 U.S. 738 n. 9, 43 L.Ed.2d 591; Oestereich v. Selective Serv. System Local Bd. No. 11, 1968, 89 S.Ct. 414, 393 U.S. 233, 21 L.Ed.2d 402.

26. Wolff v. Selective Serv. Local Bd. No. 16, C.A.2d, 1967, 372 F.2d 817, 826.

27. See 13B Wright, Miller & Cooper, Jurisdiction 2d § 3561.1 n. 14.

28. E.g., Spock v. David, C.A.3d, 1974, 502 F.2d 953, reversed on other grounds 1976, 96 S.Ct. 1211, 424 U.S. 828, 47 L.Ed.2d 505; Martin v. Schlesinger, D.C.Ala.1974, 371 F.Supp. 637; Schroth v. Warner, D.C.Hawaii 1973, 353 F.Supp. 1032; and see 14A Wright, Miller & Cooper, Jurisdiction 2d § 3709.

The suggestion that a requirement of an amount in controversy is unconstitutional if

its effect is to bar review of a constitutional claim—see § 10 n. 37 above—was consistently rejected by the appellate courts.

29. See McGaw v. Farrow, C.A.4th, 1973, 472 F.2d 952, 954, and cases there cited.

30. See ALI Study § 1311(a), and Commentary at pp. 172–176; Wechsler, Federal Jurisdiction and the Revision of the Judicial Code, 1948, 13 Law & Contemp.Probs. 216, 225; Friedenthal, New Limitations on Federal Jurisdiction, 1959, 11 Stan.L.Rev. 213, 216–218.

31. Act of Oct. 21, 1976, Pub.L. 94–574, 90 Stat. 2721.

32. Illinois v. City of Milwaukee, 1972, 92 S.Ct. 1385, 406 U.S. 91, 31 L.Ed.2d 712. See T.B. Harms Co. v. Eliscu, C.A.2d, 1964, 339 F.2d 823, 828.

rights of citizens,"[33] and this was probably the rule if the state statute were challenged on the basis of a constitutional provision other than the Fourteenth Amendment.[34]

Congress was persuaded that it had not gone far enough in its 1976 action, and in 1980 it amended § 1331 again to remove any requirement of amount from that general statute.[35] In those few instances where there is a special reason for excluding small federal claims from federal courts, an amount requirement has been separately stated.[36]

It has also been argued that the requirement of amount should be abolished in diversity cases, largely because it is sometimes difficult to determine the amount involved.[37] There is enough uneasiness about diversity jurisdiction generally, however,[38] that it is hardly conceivable that Congress would expand the jurisdiction to open the federal court door to a multitude of small cases.

§ 33. Determination of the Amount in Controversy [1]

In the preceding section it was seen that the amount in controversy must exceed a specified sum, now generally $50,000, to give jurisdiction to the district court in diversity cases and a few other kinds of cases. The present section is concerned with the rules by which to determine whether the matter in controversy does exceed that amount. Considered here are the cases where plaintiff is suing defendant on a single claim, and where defendant will lose whatever plaintiff will gain by the judgment. In these simpler cases the problem is one of determining which elements are included in the "matter in controversy," and in valuing those elements. More complicated problems are considered in the remaining sections of this chapter.

33. Social Security Act. Chapman v. Houston Welfare Rights Organization, 1979, 99 S.Ct. 1905, 441 U.S. 600, 60 L.Ed.2d 508.

34. See Hunt v. Washington State Apple Advertising Comm., 1977, 97 S.Ct. 2434, 2443–2444, 432 U.S. 333, 346–348, 53 L.Ed.2d 383.

35. Act of Dec. 1, 1980, Pub.L. 96–486, 94 Stat. 2369.

36. The same law that removed the amount requirement from 28 U.S.C.A. § 1331 amended the Consumer Product Safety Act to require that more than $10,-000 be in controversy in actions for damages under that statute. 15 U.S.C.A. § 2072.

More than $10,000 must now be in controversy in suits under the Carmack Amendment, 49 U.S.C.A. § 11707, for freight damage or loss resulting from shipments in interstate commerce. 28 U.S.C.A. §§ 1337, 1445(b), as amended in 1978.

At least $50,000 must be in controversy in suits under the Moss–Magnuson Consumer Product Warranties Act. 15 U.S.C.A. § 2310(d). There is an interesting application of this requirement in Boelens v. Redman Homes, Inc., C.A.5th, 1984, 748 F.2d 1058, rehearing denied with opinion, C.A.5th, 1985, 759 F.2d 504.

37. Uxa, The Jurisdictional Amount: An Unreasonable Limitation on Diversity Jurisdiction, 1976, 65 Ill.B.J. 78; Currie, The Federal Courts and the American Law Institute (Part II), 1969, 36 U.Chi.L.Rev. 268, 292–298. The Institute proposes to retain the requirement in diversity cases. ALI Study, § 1301(a).

38. See § 23 above.

§ 33

1. 14A Wright, Miller & Cooper, Jurisdiction 2d § 3702.

Even in the simpler situations here discussed, the rules for measurement of the amount in controversy are complex. This is because of the two contradictory goals that the rules seek to achieve. The amount in controversy cannot be made dependent on the amount the plaintiff will ultimately recover. To do so would make jurisdiction turn on a guess by the trial court as to the final outcome, or would require a preliminary trial on jurisdiction that would duplicate the regular trial on the merits, or would demand a wasteful jurisdictional dismissal, after the case has been fully heard on the merits, because the final award was less than the jurisdictional amount. All these considerations argue in favor of looking to the amount claimed, rather than the amount that will be recovered. At the same time, jurisdiction cannot be determined solely by what the plaintiff has asked for. To do so would destroy the jurisdictional-amount requirement, and would permit the party to create jurisdiction by a wholly frivolous claim. In short, the court should not entertain the suit if the claim for the jurisdictional amount is entirely without merit, but the court should not decide the merits of the case in making that determination.

Thus, it is quite settled that jurisdiction is not lost because the award is for less than the jurisdictional amount.[2] Instead the amount in controversy is measured as of the time the action comes to the federal court. Subsequent events, even including a reduction in the amount sought by the plaintiff, cannot destroy jurisdiction that has once been acquired.[3] It is incumbent on plaintiff to allege a claim that satisfies the jurisdictional-amount requirement,[4] and if this is put in issue, as by a motion to dismiss for want of jurisdiction, the burden is on plaintiff to satisfy the court that the requisite amount is in controversy.[5] Determination of the value of the matter in controversy is a federal question to be decided under federal standards, although the federal court must look to state law to determine the nature and extent of the right to be enforced in a diversity case.[6]

How is the determination to be made of the amount in controversy where it has been challenged? If, as will usually be true, the issue of jurisdictional amount is closely tied to the merits of the cause, the court, it is said, should be reluctant to insist on evidence with respect thereto,

2. See Rosado v. Wyman, 1970, 90 S.Ct. 1207, 1214 n. 6, 397 U.S. 397, 405 n. 6, 25 L.Ed.2d 442; 14A Wright, Miller & Cooper, Jurisdiction 2d § 3702 n. 35.

3. St. Paul Mercury Indem. Co. v. Red Cab Co., 1938, 58 S.Ct. 586, 303 U.S. 283, 82 L.Ed. 845, noted 1938, 51 Harv.L.Rev. 1108, 24 Va.L.Rev. 808, 1939, 37 Mich. L.Rev. 482; Klepper v. First American Bank, C.A.6th, 1990, 916 F.2d 337, 340; Core v. Southwestern Bell Tel. Co., C.A.8th, 1988, 847 F.2d 497; Worthams v. Atlanta Life Ins. Co., C.A.6th, 1976, 533 F.2d 994; and cases cited 14A Wright, Miller & Cooper, Jurisdiction 2d § 3702 n. 33.

4. On pleading jurisdiction, see § 69 below.

5. McNutt v. General Motors Acceptance Corp., 1935, 56 S.Ct. 780, 298 U.S. 178, 80 L.Ed. 1135; Department of Recreation & Sports of Puerto Rico v. World Boxing Assn., C.A.1st, 1991, 942 F.2d 84; and cases cited 14A Wright, Miller & Cooper, Jurisdiction 2d § 3702 nn. 10, 11.

In cases removed from state court to federal court, the removing defendant carries the burden with regard to amount in controversy. See § 40 below.

6. Horton v. Liberty Mut. Ins. Co., 1961, 81 S.Ct. 1570, 367 U.S. 348, 6 L.Ed.2d 890.

lest, under the guise of determining jurisdiction, the merits of the controversy between the parties be summarily decided without the ordinary incidents of trial.[7]   Indeed there is occasional support for the view that in actions at law the parties are entitled to demand that issues of jurisdictional fact be submitted to the jury.[8]   This is not, however, the usual procedure.   More commonly the court will look to the pleadings, and to such affidavits as may be submitted, and determine from these whether there is a substantial claim for an amount satisfying the statute.[9]

In making this examination, the court is guided by rules that have been developed to prevent this preliminary jurisdictional determination from depriving the party unfairly of a trial on the merits.   In a leading case, the Supreme Court put the rule this way: "The rule governing dismissal for want of jurisdiction in cases brought in the federal courts is that, unless the law gives a different rule, the sum claimed by the plaintiff controls if the claim is apparently made in good faith.   It must appear to a legal certainty that the claim is really for less than the jurisdictional amount to justify dismissal." [10]   Thus, in general the court looks to the sum demanded by plaintiff.   It does not matter that on the face of the complaint there may appear a defense to part of the claim, since possibly defendant will not assert that defense.[11]   Nor does it matter that defendant admits it is liable for the sum prayed for.   Where there is a justiciable claim for a certain amount, there is a controversy, or dispute, between the parties within the meaning of the statute, even though the defendant does not controvert or dispute the claim.   It is sufficient that it does not satisfy it.[12]

The court may believe it highly unlikely that plaintiff will recover the amount demanded, but this is not enough to defeat jurisdiction, unless it appears to a legal certainty that plaintiff cannot recover the

---

7.   Smithers v. Smith, 1907, 27 S.Ct. 297, 204 U.S. 632, 51 L.Ed. 656; Continental Cas. Co. v. Department of Highways State of Louisiana, C.A.5th, 1967, 379 F.2d 673; Fireman's Fund Ins. Co. v. Railway Exp. Agency, C.A.6th, 1958, 253 F.2d 780; Billings & Co. v. Pine St. Realty Associates, Ltd. Partnership, D.C.R.I.1990, 754 F.Supp. 10.

8.   Shaffer v. Coty, Inc., D.C.Cal.1960, 183 F.Supp. 662, 666–667.   See Note, Trial by Jury of Preliminary Jurisdictional Facts in Federal Courts, 1963, 48 Iowa L.Rev. 471.

9.   Diefenthal v. Civil Aeronautics Bd., C.A.5th, 1982, 681 F.2d 1039, 1051–1053, certiorari denied 103 S.Ct. 732, 459 U.S. 1107, 74 L.Ed.2d 956; Kennard v. Harris Corp., D.C.Mich.1989, 728 F.Supp. 453, 454.

10.   St. Paul Mercury Indem. Co. v. Red Cab Co., 1938, 58 S.Ct. 586, 590, 303 U.S. 283, 288, 82 L.Ed. 845.

11.   Schunk v. Moline, Milburn & Stoddart Co., 1892, 13 S.Ct. 416, 147 U.S. 500, 37 L.Ed. 255; Zacharia v. Harbor Island Spa, Inc., C.A.2d, 1982, 684 F.2d 199; Reddy v. Barclays Bank of N.Y., N.A., D.C.N.Y. 1991, 773 F.Supp. 655.   Guy v. Duff & Phelps, Inc., D.C.Ill.1985, 625 F.Supp. 1380.

12.   In re Metropolitan Ry. Receivership, 1907, 28 S.Ct. 219, 208 U.S. 90, 107–108, 52 L.Ed. 403.   When this case was decided the statutory phrase was "matter in dispute." This was changed to the present language, "matter in controversy," in the Judicial Code of 1911, 36 Stat. 1091, presumably to codify this decision.   See also Wheel Horse Sales, Inc. v. Spence, C.A.10th, 1977, 566 F.2d 679; Peoples Westchester Savings Bank v. Ganc, D.C.N.Y.1989, 705 F.Supp. 164.

amount that it has demanded.[13] Thus, suppose that plaintiff demands actual damages of $5000 and punitive damages of $20,000. If under the applicable rule of law punitive damages are not recoverable, it can be said that there is a legal certainty that plaintiff will not recover the amount demanded, and the action will be dismissed.[14] If the relevant state law permits punitive damages on the facts alleged, the requisite amount is in controversy, even though it may be unlikely that the amount demanded will be had.[15] Cases from the courts of appeals suggest that jurisdiction exists also if the local law is not clear as to whether such damages are recoverable,[16] although it might be argued contrary to this that the court will have to resolve this legal question at some point in the case and might as well do it at the beginning.

Many cases say that jurisdiction is lacking also if the claim is not made in good faith but is fictitious or colorable.[17] Though this is stated as something in addition to the legal-certainty test, in fact it seems a mere variant of it, for unless it appears to a legal certainty that plaintiff cannot recover the sum for which he or she prays, how can it be held that the claim for that sum is not in good faith?[18] The most difficult

13. Barry v. Edmunds, 1886, 6 S.Ct. 501, 116 U.S. 550, 29 L.Ed. 729; Bell v. Preferred Life Assur. Soc'y, 1943, 64 S.Ct. 5, 320 U.S. 238, 88 L.Ed. 15; Weinberger v. Wiesenfeld, 1975, 95 S.Ct. 1225, 1230 n. 10, 420 U.S. 636, 642 n. 10, 43 L.Ed.2d 514; Ochoa v. Interbrew America, INc., C.A.2d,1993, 999 F.2d 626; and cases cited 14A Wright, Miller & Cooper, Jurisdiction 2d § 3702 n. 2.

14. Kahal v. J.W. Wilson & Associates, Inc., C.A.1982, 673 F.2d 547; Wiggins v. North American Equitable Life Assurance Co., C.A.4th, 1981, 644 F.2d 1014; cf. Vance v. W.A. Vandercook Co., 1898, 18 S.Ct. 645, 170 U.S. 468, 42 L.Ed. 1111 (consequential damages not recoverable in claim and delivery action); Kahn v. Hotel Ramada of Nevada, C.A.5th, 1986, 799 F.2d 199 (statute limited hotel's liability to $750 even if hotel was grossly negligent); Parmelee v. Ackerman, C.A.6th, 1958, 252 F.2d 721 (damages for emotional distress not recoverable); Krider Pharmacy & Gifts, Inc. v. Medi–Care Data Systems, Inc., D.C.Wis.1992, 791 F.Supp. 221 (commercial purchaser of a chattel could not recover more than the purchase price); Bishop v. Byrne, D.C.W.Va.1967, 265 F.Supp. 460 (mental pain and suffering not recoverable); Diana v. Canada Dry Corp., D.C.Pa.1960, 189 F.Supp. 280 (loss of consortium not recoverable).

15. Bell v. Preferred Life Assur. Soc'y, 1943, 64 S.Ct. 5, 320 U.S. 238, 88 L.Ed. 15.

But see Singer v. State Farm Mut. Auto. Ins. Co., D.C.Pa.1992, 785 F.Supp. 510, where the court found that the rejection by

an insurance company of a claim for $5,334 could not sustain a punitive-damage award of almost $45,000, as would be necessary to bridge the jurisdictional gap.

16. Calhoun v. Kentucky–West Virginia Gas Co., C.A.6th, 1948, 166 F.2d 530; Columbia Pictures Corp. v. Grengs, C.A.7th, 1958, 257 F.2d 45. Contra: Nixon v. Loyal Order of Moose, Lodge No. 750, C.A.4th, 1960, 285 F.2d 250, criticized 1961, 63 W.Va.L.Rev. 365.

17. See text at note 10 above; and cases cited in 14A Wright, Miller & Cooper, Jurisdiction 2d § 3702 n. 76. Note, Good Faith Pleading of Jurisdictional Amount, 1963, 48 Iowa L.Rev. 426.

18. "Thus, there is but one test: good faith and legal certainty are equivalents rather than two separate tests." Jones v. Landry, C.A.5th, 1967, 387 F.2d 102, 104. See also Work v. U.S. Trade, Inc., D.C.Va. 1990, 747 F.Supp. 1184, 1187.

Conversely plaintiff's good faith will not save it if it does appear to a legal certainty that plaintiff cannot recover the requisite amount. Tongkook America, Inc. v. Shipton Sportswear Co., C.A.2d, 1994, 14 F.3d 781. "This is not to say that plaintiff acted in deliberate bad faith. Plaintiff may have felt that the insult fully warranted the $15,-000 claimed. The question, however, is whether to anyone familiar with the applicable law this claim could objectively have been viewed as worth $10,000. The answer seems clearly in the negative." Jimenz Puig v. Avis Rent–A–Car System, C.A.1st, 1978, 574 F.2d 37. See also American Mut.

cases are those in which plaintiff is suing for unliquidated damages from a tort, and the amount demanded seems far in excess of any reasonable verdict given the injuries alleged. In the past the prevailing view has been that a federal court should be reluctant to insist on a presentation of evidence regarding the jurisdictional question when it was interwoven with the merits, and that the cause should proceed to trial even if it appeared highly unlikely that plaintiff could recover the jurisdictional amount.[19] Recent decisions suggest that concern over the mounting federal caseload is causing a retreat from this position.[20] Although these decisions do not purport to change the legal-certainty standard, they indicate that the courts are more willing than they have been in the past to scrutinize claims for more than the jurisdictional amount when only minor injuries to the plaintiff appear to be involved.[21]

When the jurisdictional amount was increased in 1958, the statutes were also amended to create a procedure apparently intended to meet the problem presented by such cases as those just described. It was provided that if the plaintiff recovers less than $50,000, the court may refuse to allow him costs, and may impose costs against him.[22] The commentators were skeptical about the value of these provisions,[23] and the cases justify their skepticism. The courts have held that if plaintiff could reasonably have expected to recover a verdict for more than $50,000, and acted in good faith in claiming such an amount, it will be allowed costs even though he actually recovered less than $50,000.[24] On this construction, it is difficult to see what the amended statutory provisions add, except perhaps the wisdom of hindsight, since if the claim is not made in good faith, it is subject to dismissal, even after trial,[25] or sanctions can be imposed under Rule 11.[26]

Liab. Ins. Co. v. Campbell Lumber Mfg. Corp., D.C.Ga.1971, 329 F.Supp. 1283. But compare Tising v. Flanagan, D.C.Wis.1973, 360 F.Supp. 283.

19. Zunamon v. Brown, C.A.8th, 1969, 418 F.2d 883; Jones v. Landry, C.A.5th, 1967, 387 F.2d 102; Jaconski v. Avisun Corp., C.A.3d, 1966, 359 F.2d 931; Deutsch v. Hewes St. Realty Corp., C.A.2d, 1966, 359 F.2d 96; Tullos v. Corley, C.A.6th, 1964, 337 F.2d 884; Wade v. Rogala, C.A.3d, 1959, 270 F.2d 280.

20. A leading case in the new direction is Nelson v. Keefer, C.A.3d, 1971, 451 F.2d 289, noted 1972, 47 N.Y.U.L.Rev. 349, 26 Sw.L.J. 461, 45 Temp.L.Q. 305. See also Burns v. Anderson, C.A.5th, 1974, 502 F.2d 970; Sanders v. Hiser, C.A.8th, 1973, 479 F.2d 71; Shumpert v. Amoco Oil Co., D.C.Wis.1991, 782 F.Supp. 77; Ramirez de Arellano v. Eastern Air Lines, Inc., D.C.Puerto Rico 1985, 629 F.Supp. 189.

21. See 14A Wright, Miller & Cooper, Jurisdiction 2d § 3707; Note, Determination of Federal Jurisdictional Amount in Suits on Unliquidated Claims, 1966, 64 Mich.L.Rev. 930.

22. 28 U.S.C.A. § 1332(b). The provision was invoked in McCord v. Moore–McCormack Lines, Inc., D.C.N.Y.1965, 242 F.Supp. 493; cf. Lutz v. McNair, D.C.Va. 1964, 233 F.Supp. 871, affirmed C.A.4th, 1965, 340 F.2d 709.

23. Cowen, Federal Jurisdiction Amended, 1958, 44 Va.L.Rev. 971, 978 ("likely to create more problems than it solves"); comment, 1958 Amendment to the United States Judicial Code Relative to the Denial of Costs to a Plaintiff, 1961, 21 La.L.Rev. 783; Comment, 1958, 58 Col.L.Rev. 1287, 1291–1294.

24. Bochenek v. Germann, D.C.Mich. 1960, 191 F.Supp. 104; Stachon v. Hoxie, D.C.Mich.1960, 190 F.Supp. 185.

25. City of Boulder v. Snyder, C.A.10th, 1968, 396 F.2d 853.

26. "Appropriate use of that rule could provide a needed disincentive for attorneys to wildly overestimate damage claims in order to obtain diversity jurisdiction." Rosenboro v. Kim, C.A.D.C.1993, 994 F.2d 13, 19. See § 69A below.

Plaintiff cannot satisfy the jurisdictional-amount requirement by alleging, as part of the claim, something that is not actually a part of the matter in controversy. Side effects that the decision may have by way of stare decisis or collateral estoppel will not be considered.[27] Thus, in a suit on bond coupons only the amount of the coupons is to be considered, even though the decision will be conclusive as to validity of the bonds themselves.[28] In a suit to restrain collection of a tax the jurisdictional amount must be satisfied by the tax that will be levied during the period of litigation; neither the capitalized value of the tax, nor the value of the right to conduct business free of the tax, is relevant.[29] In so ruling, the Supreme Court distinguished a case in which the matter in controversy was the validity of a permanent exemption by contract from a particular tax,[30] on the ground that the value of a contract providing permanent immunity from taxation is more than a limited number of the annual payments demanded.[31] The distinction has been criticized,[32] but is in accord with the cases, discussed below, involving installment payments. In the tax case, the Court also distinguished an earlier decision that had held, in a suit contesting the validity of an order of a state commission directing a railroad to construct and maintain an unremunerative spur track, that the amount in controversy was not merely the cost of installation of the track, but was the capitalized value of the annual costs that the track would impose on the railroad.[33] Again the distinction appears sound.

On a principle similar to that of the tax cases, it is held that where a taxpayer sues to prevent the issuance of municipal bonds, the tax that would be levied on plaintiff's property were the bonds issued, rather than the value of the bond issue, is the amount in controversy.[34]

Where a business is threatened, either by a regulatory statute or by unfair competition, the stated rule is that the amount in controversy is the difference between the value of the business unregulated, or not subject to the competition, and its value under the regulation, or with

---

27. Healy v. Ratta, 1934, 54 S.Ct. 700, 292 U.S. 263, 78 L.Ed. 1248; Myers v. Long Island Lighting Co., D.C.N.Y.1985, 623 F.Supp. 1076; and cases cited 14A Wright, Miller & Cooper, Jurisdiction 2d § 3702 n. 46.

28. Town of Elgin v. Marshall, 1882, 1 S.Ct. 484, 106 U.S. 578, 27 L.Ed. 249.

29. Healy v. Ratta, 1934, 54 S.Ct. 700, 292 U.S. 263, 78 L.Ed. 1248; Clark v. Paul Gray, Inc., 1939, 59 S.Ct. 744, 306 U.S. 583, 83 L.Ed. 1001; May v. Supreme Court of State of Colorado, C.A.10th, 1974, 508 F.2d 136.

The commuted value of future taxes may not be considered where it is merely "possible" that the taxpayer will suffer future harm in an amount sufficient to satisfy the statutory test. M & M Transp. Co. v. City of New York, C.A.2d 1950, 186 F.2d 157.

30. Berryman v. Board of Trustees of Whitman College, 1912, 32 S.Ct. 147, 222 U.S. 334, 56 L.Ed. 225.

31. Healy v. Ratta, 1934, 54 S.Ct. 700, 704, 292 U.S. 263, 271, 78 L.Ed. 1248.

32. Note, 1934, 45 Harv.L.Rev. 95, 99; Comment, 1937, 25 Calif.L.Rev. 336, 344; Ilsen & Sardell, The Monetary Minimum in Federal Court Jurisdiction, 1955, 29 St. John's L.Rev. 1, 27.

33. Western & A.R.R. v. Railroad Comm. of Georgia, 1923, 43 S.Ct. 252, 261 U.S. 264, 67 L.Ed. 645, distinguished in Healy v. Ratta, 1934, 54 S.Ct. 700, 704, 292 U.S. 263, 271, 78 L.Ed. 1248.

34. Colvin v. City of Jacksonville, 1895, 15 S.Ct. 866, 158 U.S. 456, 39 L.Ed. 1053; Scott v. Frazier, 1920, 40 S.Ct. 503, 253 U.S. 243, 64 L.Ed. 883; Vraney v. Pinellas County, C.A.5th, 1958, 250 F.2d 617.

the competition.[35] In making this determination, merely possible future harm is not to be considered,[36] but probable consequences will be taken into account.[37] If the statute seeks to impose a complete prohibition of the business, rather than mere regulation, then the entire value of the business furnishes the appropriate measure.[38] In determining the difference between the value of a regulated and an unregulated business, the cost of compliance with the regulation may be considered the amount in controversy.[39] In actions for unfair competition, or to restrain violation of "fair trade" prices, the value of the goodwill of the business is thought to be the relevant consideration,[40] and the amount expended in advertising is looked to in determining the value of the goodwill.[41] There is some suggestion in the literature that, as a matter of comity, a stricter standard of amount in controversy should be used where a state statute is challenged than where suit is between private parties,[42] but the Supreme Court has stated no such distinction and cites public and private cases interchangeably.[43]

Contracts calling for installment payments have been a source of particular difficulty. The holder of a policy of disability insurance claims that he or she is permanently disabled and brings suit for the benefits due. Though the cases are divided, the rule apparently is that only the amount of the installments due at the commencement of the suit may be taken into account, even though the judgment will be determinative of liability for future installments as they accrue.[44] The result is different

35. McNutt v. General Motors Acceptance Corp. of Ind., 1936, 56 S.Ct. 780, 298 U.S. 178, 80 L.Ed. 1135; KVOS, Inc. v. Associated Press, 1936, 57 S.Ct. 197, 299 U.S. 269, 81 L.Ed. 183; and cases cited 14A Wright, Miller & Cooper, Jurisdiction 2d § 3708 nn. 5–7.

36. Pure Oil Co. v. Puritan Oil Co., D.C.Conn.1941, 39 F.Supp. 68, reversed on other grounds, C.C.A.2d, 1942, 127 F.2d 6. See also M & M Transp. Co. v. City of New York, C.A.2d, 1950, 186 F.2d 157.

37. Food Fair Stores v. Food Fair, C.A.1st, 1949, 177 F.2d 177, 184. See also Hunt v. New York Cotton Exchange, 1907, 27 S.Ct. 529, 205 U.S. 322, 51 L.Ed. 821; Bitterman v. Louisville & N.R. Co., 1907, 28 S.Ct. 91, 207 U.S. 205, 52 L.Ed. 171.

38. Gibbs v. Buck, 1939, 59 S.Ct. 725, 307 U.S. 66, 83 L.Ed. 1111.

39. Hunt v. Washington State Apple Advertising Comm., 1977, 97 S.Ct. 2434, 2443–2444, 432 U.S. 333, 346–348, 53 L.Ed.2d 383; Buck v. Gallagher, 1939, 59 S.Ct. 740, 307 U.S. 95, 83 L.Ed. 1128; Allway Taxi, Inc. v. City of New York, D.C.N.Y.1972, 340 F.Supp. 1120, affirmed C.A.2d, 1972, 468 F.2d 624.

40. Schering Corp. v. Sun Ray Drug Co., C.A.3d, 1963, 320 F.2d 72; Barrette v. City of Marinette, D.C.Wis.1977, 440 F.Supp. 1277; Murphey v. G.C. Murphy Co., D.C.La.1963, 216 F.Supp. 124; Coca–Cola Co. v. Foods, Inc., D.C.S.D.1963, 220 F.Supp. 101; Parke, Davis & Co. v. Jarvis Drug Co., D.C.N.Y.1962, 208 F.Supp. 350.

41. Schering Corp. v. Sun Ray Drug Co., C.A.3d, 1963, 320 F.2d 72; American Plan Corp. v. State Loan & Fin. Corp., D.C.Del. 1968, 278 F.Supp. 846; Johnson & Johnson v. Wagonfeld, D.C.N.Y.1960, 206 F.Supp. 30.

42. See Food Fair Stores v. Food Fair, C.A.1st, 1949, 177 F.2d 177, 184; Ilsen & Sardell, note 32 above, at 24–25; Comment, 1937, 37 Calif.L.Rev. 336; see Note, 1960, 73 Harv.L.Rev. 1369, 1375.

43. E.g., Hunt v. Washington State Apple Advertising Comm., 1977, 97 S.Ct. 2434, 2443–2444, 432 U.S. 333, 346–348, 53 L.Ed.2d 383.

44. New York Life Ins. Co. v. Viglas, 1936, 56 S.Ct. 615, 297 U.S. 672, 80 L.Ed. 971; Beaman v. Pacific Mut. Life Ins. Co., C.A.4th, 1966, 369 F.2d 653; Keck v. Fidelity & Cas. Co. of New York, C.A.7th, 1966, 359 F.2d 840; White v. North American Acc. Ins. Co., C.A.10th, 1963, 316 F.2d 5; Cate v. Blue Cross & Blue Shield of Alabama, D.C.Tenn.1977, 434 F.Supp. 1187;

where the entire contract is brought into issue, as where the insurer sues to cancel the policy for fraud.[45] By the same token, a declaratory-judgment action about the validity of a contract should bring into controversy the value of the whole contract.[46] Indeed where an insurer sought a declaratory judgment that it was not liable to defend its insured in a tort action, the amount in controversy was held satisfied, although the policy was for only $10,000, since the insurer would also be obliged to expend attorneys' fees in defense of its insured if it were bound under the policy.[47]

The Supreme Court has distinguished between those cases, just discussed, in which the judgment can only be for installments due at the time of suit, even though it has an estoppel effect as to future payments, and cases where the judgment will clearly and finally create an obligation to pay, over the years, a sum in excess of the jurisdictional amount, even though future events may alter or cut off the obligation. On such a distinction, the jurisdictional amount was held present in a suit under a state workmen's compensation statute where the judgment would create an obligation to make installment payments in the future, even though the obligation would be cut off upon the death or remarriage of the widow and the death or attainment of age 18 of the children.[48]

Button v. Mutual Life Ins. Co. of New York, D.C.Ky.1943, 48 F.Supp. 168, noted 1943, 92 U.Pa.L.Rev. 211. Some of the earlier cases to the contrary are cited in the Button case.

In a removed action installments coming due between the filing of the suit and the petition for removal may be considered, Journal Pub. Co. v. General Cas. Co., C.A.9th, 1954, 210 F.2d 202, but the action must be remanded if the amount due on the date of removal was not sufficient, even though additional installments that have accrued after removal make the amount sufficient. Bowman v. Iowa State Travelers Mut. Assur. Co., D.C.Okl.1978, 449 F.Supp. 60; Strickland Transp. Co. v. Navajo Freight Lines, Inc., D.C.Tex.1961, 199 F.Supp. 108.

45. Franklin Life Ins. Co. v. Johnson, C.C.A.10th, 1946, 157 F.2d 653; New York Life Ins. Co. v. Kaufman, C.C.A.9th, 1935, 78 F.2d 398, certiorari denied 56 S.Ct. 149, 296 U.S. 626, 80 L.Ed. 445; cf. Duderwicz v. Sweetwater Sav. Assn., C.A.5th, 1979, 595 F.2d 1008 (forfeiture of interest because of usury); Morris v. Franklin Fire Ins. Co., C.C.A.9th, 1942, 130 F.2d 553 (reformation of policy).

46. Davis v. American Foundry Equipment Co., C.C.A.7th, 1938, 94 F.2d 441; Landers, Frary & Clark v. Vischer Products Co., C.A.7th, 1953, 201 F.2d 319; Aetna Cas. & Sur. Co. v. Yeatts, C.C.A.4th, 1938,

99 F.2d 665; Note, Declaratory Judgments, 1949, 62 Harv.L.Rev. 787, 801.

47. Allstate Ins. Co. v. Dillard, D.C.Pa. 1960, 190 F.Supp. 111.

A different result is reached if the declaratory action is against injured third persons rather than against the insured. Motorists Mut. Ins. Co. v. Simpson, C.A.7th, 1968, 404 F.2d 511.

48. Aetna Cas. & Sur. Co. v. Flowers, 1947, 67 S.Ct. 798, 330 U.S. 464, 91 L.Ed. 1024, noted 1948, 36 Calif.L.Rev. 124. See also Williams v. Aetna Cas. & Sur. Ins. Co., D.C.Md.1980, 487 F.Supp. 44. A similar result was reached where suit was for statutory maintenance similar to alimony, Thompson v. Thompson, 1912, 33 S.Ct. 129, 226 U.S. 551, 57 L.Ed. 347, or to protect a contract providing for a life pension, Brotherhood of Locomotive Firemen & Enginemen v. Pinkston, 1934, 55 S.Ct. 1, 293 U.S. 96, 79 L.Ed. 219, or for social security benefits, Weinberger v. Wiesenfeld, 1975, 95 S.Ct. 1225, 1230 n. 10, 420 U.S. 636, 642 n. 10, 43 L.Ed.2d 514.

In cases in which future payments can be taken into account, they must be discounted to present worth. Burns v. Massachusetts Mut. Life Ins. Co., C.A.8th, 1987, 820 F.2d 246; Sarnoff v. American Home Products Corp., C.A.7th, 1986, 798 F.2d 1075.

On the problem of installment payments, generally, see 14A Wright, Miller & Cooper, Jurisdiction 2d § 3710.

There appears to be a principle operating in the installment-payment cases, though it is not clearly articulated by the courts. The proper rule is that the amount in controversy is the amount involved as a direct legal effect of the judgment; what that will be in a particular case depends on the applicable substantive law. In a suit for breach of a contract of employment, for example, some jurisdictions allow recovery only for the wages due at the time of filing suit, other jurisdictions require a single suit for the total breach, including wages not yet due, and still others give plaintiff an option either to sue for past-due wages or to treat the contract as totally breached. In a jurisdiction in the first group, only the wages due would be part of the amount in controversy. In one in the second group, the entire amount due under the contract, both past and future, would be in controversy. And in the third group the amount in controversy would depend on which of the alternative remedies plaintiff chooses to pursue.

If the right or matter in controversy cannot be translated into terms of money, there is no pecuniary amount in controversy.[49] Absolute certainty as to amount is not essential, however, and it is sufficient that there is a present probability that the value of the matter in controversy will exceed the jurisdictional amount.[50]

In actions seeking declaratory or injunctive relief, the amount in controversy is not the amount that plaintiff might recover at law, but the value of the right to be protected or the extent of the injury to be prevented.[51] In a suit for specific performance of a contract to sell land, it is the fair market value of the land that is in controversy.[52]

Plaintiff is master of his claim, and if he chooses to ask for less than the jurisdictional amount, only the sum he demands is in controversy and jurisdiction is absent, even though his underlying claim was of a value exceeding the statutory minimum.[53] Rule 54(c), and similar provi-

49. Hague v. CIO, 1939, 59 S.Ct. 954, 307 U.S. 496, 83 L.Ed. 1423 (free speech); Kurtz v. Moffitt, 1885, 6 S.Ct. 148, 115 U.S. 487, 29 L.Ed. 458 (release from arrest); Barry v. Mercein, 1847, 5 How. 103, 12 L.Ed. 70 (custody of a child); Lee v. Lee, 1834, 8 Pet. 44, 8 L.Ed. 860 (freedom for a slave); Lister v. Commissioner Court, Navarro County, C.A.5th, 1978, 566 F.2d 490 (dilution of vote through reapportionment); Senate Select Committee on Presidential Campaign Activities v. Nixon, D.C.D.C. 1973, 366 F.Supp. 51 (access to presidential tapes); and cases cited 14A Wright, Miller & Cooper, Jurisdiction 2d § 3702 n. 65.

50. Wiley v. Sinkler, 1900, 21 S.Ct. 17, 179 U.S. 58, 45 L.Ed. 84; Aetna Cas. & Sur. Co. v. Flowers, 1947, 67 S.Ct. 798, 330 U.S. 464, 91 L.Ed. 1024; Anderson v. Beneficial Mortgage Corp., D.C.Del.1988, 699 F.Supp. 1075, 1079. An action is dismissed if its monetary value to plaintiff is pure conjecture. Kheel v. Port of New York Auth.,

C.A.2d, 1972, 457 F.2d 46, certiorari denied 93 S.Ct. 324, 409 U.S. 983, 34 L.Ed.2d 248.

51. Hunt v. Washington State Apple Advertising Comm., 1977, 97 S.Ct. 2434, 2443, 432 U.S. 333, 347, 53 L.Ed.2d 383; Mississippi & M. R. Co. v. Ward, 1862, 2 Black 485, 17 L.Ed. 311; Department of Recreation & Sports of Puerto Rico v. World Boxing Assn., C.A.1st, 1991, 942 F.2d 84; 14A Wright, Miller & Cooper, Jurisdiction 2d § 3708. See § 34 below.

52. Occidental Chem. Corp. v. Bullard, C.A.11th, 1993, 995 F.2d 1046.

53. Brady v. Indemnity Ins. Co. of North America, C.C.A.6th, 1933, 68 F.2d 302, noted 1934, 12 N.Car.L.Rev. 390; Boardwalk Regency Corp. v. Karabell, D.C.N.J.1989, 719 F.Supp. 1254; Video Connection of America, Inc. v. Priority Concepts, Inc., D.C.N.Y.1986, 625 F.Supp. 1549; Standard Acc. Ins. Co. v. Aguirre, D.C.Tex. 1961, 199 F.Supp. 918; see § 31 above.

sions in a majority of the states, make the demand ineffective as a limitation on the amount recoverable in nondefault cases. But to hold, as a few cases suggest,[54] that this puts the requisite amount in controversy even though plaintiff has demanded less would make the requirement of an amount in controversy meaningless.[55]

§ 34. Viewpoint From Which Amount Is Measured [1]

It will sometimes happen, notably in suits for an injunction or to abate a nuisance, that the benefit to plaintiff will have a different value than the loss to defendant if the relief is granted. Which value represents the amount in controversy?

The leading case is so cryptic as to shed little, if any, light on the direction in which it leads. Mississippi & Missouri Railroad Co. v. Ward[2] was a suit by a steamboat owner for abatement of a bridge over the Mississippi River as a nuisance. Justice Catron disposed of the jurisdictional amount argument by saying: "But the want of a sufficient amount of damage having been sustained to give the Federal Courts jurisdiction, will not defeat the remedy, as the removal of the obstruction is the matter of controversy, and the value of the object must govern."[3] It is entirely unclear here whether the "value of the object" means the value of the bridge, the value of the plaintiff's steamboat business, the cost of removing the bridge, or the value of the plaintiff's right to be free of the obstruction.[4]

Dean Armistead M. Dobie, later a judge on the Fourth Circuit, argued forcefully that the courts should look in such situations only to the benefit to the plaintiff, and this has become known as the "plaintiff viewpoint" rule.[5] It has attracted at least verbal support from some

The principle was applied in debatable circumstances in Kansas City Philharmonic Assn. v. Greyhound Lines, Inc., D.C.Mo. 1966, 257 F.Supp. 941. Plaintiff sued for $12,736 for damages caused it in transporting plaintiff's musicians. It admitted in the complaint that it owed defendant $2,784 for the transportation, and prayed for judgment in the amount of $9,952. It was held that the requisite amount was not in controversy, and the action was not removable, despite the argument that plaintiff was really seeking both judgment for $9,952 and discharge from the admitted liability of $2,784.

The Kansas City Philharmonic case was not followed in Savarese v. Edrick Transfer & Storage, Inc., C.A.9th, 1975, 513 F.2d 140, where jurisdiction was held to exist when plaintiff sought recovery of $11,901.83 but asked that he be allowed to apply $2,578.41 he owed defendant against this recovery.

54. Campbell v. Jordan, D.C.S.C.1947, 73 F.Supp. 318; see Capps v. New Jellico Coal Co., D.C.Tenn.1950, 87 F.Supp. 369;

Griffith v. Alabama By–Products Corp., D.C.Ala.1954, 120 F.Supp. 219.

55. Forest Laboratories, Inc. v. La Maur, Inc., D.C.Wis.1965, 236 F.Supp. 575. See ALI Study, pp. 343–348.

§ 34

1. 14A Wright, Miller & Cooper, Jurisdiction 2d § 3703; Kennedy, Valuing Federal Matters in Controversy: Hohfeldian Analysis in Symbolic Logic, 1968, 35 Tenn. L.Rev. 423.

2. 1862, 2 Black 485, 17 L.Ed. 311.

3. 2 Black at 492.

4. See Judge Learned Hand's attempt to fathom the remark in M & M Transp. Co. v. City of New York, C.A.2d, 1950, 186 F.2d 157, 158. And see the article by Kennedy, note 1 above.

5. Dobie, Jurisdictional Amount in the United States District Court, 1925, 38 Harv.L.Rev. 733.

"Dean Dobie, who is now a Judge of the Fourth Circuit Court of Appeals, calls this judges and writers, and indeed one distinguished court had declared that the "plaintiff viewpoint" rule is now "well settled." [6] The matter is not this clear. The principal Supreme Court decision relied on to support this view is Glenwood Light & Water Co. v. Mutual Light, Heat & Power Co.[7] In that case plaintiff sought to restrain the defendant from erecting poles and wires so as to injure the plaintiff's poles, wires, and business. The trial court, finding that the cost to defendant of removing its poles and wires would be less than the jurisdictional amount, dismissed for want of jurisdiction. The Supreme Court reversed, holding that plaintiff's right to operate its plant and conduct its business free from wrongful interference by defendant had a value in excess of the jurisdictional amount, and in strong language the Court said that the value of the protection of that right was determinative of the jurisdiction. Though the language here supports the "plaintiff viewpoint" rule, the holding, as in the other cases relied on by Dean Dobie,[8] is only that jurisdiction is present if the value to plaintiff exceeds the jurisdictional amount. This does not exclude the possibility that jurisdiction will also be present if the value to defendant is greater than the statutory requirement, even where the benefit to plaintiff is a lesser sum. Neither Dean Dobie nor those who have accepted his view have pointed to any Supreme Court decision rejecting jurisdiction where the jurisdictional amount was satisfied from the defendant's viewpoint, but not from the plaintiff's. Only such a case can conclusively establish the "plaintiff viewpoint" rule. There are some such cases from the lower courts. In one case, plaintiff sought to enjoin defendant from breach of a covenant not to compete. The injunction, if granted, would close defendant's business, from which he was making an annual profit far in excess of $10,000. It was not shown, however, that plaintiff would benefit in an amount of more than $10,000 if defendant's business were shut down. The district court, applying the "plaintiff viewpoint" rule, held that plaintiff had not established that more than $10,000 was in controversy, and dismissed the case for want of jurisdiction.[9]

A few lower-court cases have suggested a different rule. These cases view the amount in controversy from the point of view of the party seeking to invoke federal jurisdiction, and thus look to the plaintiff's

---

'the plaintiff-viewpoint rule.' It is not always easy to apply." Associated Press v. Emmett, D.C.Cal.1942, 45 F.Supp. 907, 914.

6. Central Mexico Light & Power Co. v. Munch, C.C.A.2d 1940, 116 F.2d 85, 87 (per Clark, J.). See also Alfonso v. Hillsborough County Aviation Auth., C.A.5th, 1962, 308 F.2d 724, 727; Massachusetts State Pharmaceutical Assn. v. Federal Prescription Serv., Inc., C.A.8th, 1970, 431 F.2d 130; Kheel v. Port of New York Auth., C.A.2d, 1972, 457 F.2d 46, certiorari denied 93 S.Ct. 324, 409 U.S. 983, 34 L.Ed.2d 248; and cases cited 14A Wright, Miller & Cooper, Jurisdiction 2d § 3703 n. 6. See also Ilsen & Sardell, The Monetary Minimum in Federal Court Jurisdiction, 1955, 29 St. John's L.Rev. 1, 183; Comment, 1939, 49 Yale L.J. 274; Note, 1950, 4 Vand.L.Rev. 146.

7. 1915, 36 S.Ct. 30, 239 U.S. 121, 60 L.Ed. 174.

8. Hunt v. New York Cotton Exchange, 1907, 27 S.Ct. 529, 205 U.S. 322, 51 L.Ed. 821; Bitterman v. Louisville & N.R. Co., 1907, 28 S.Ct. 91, 207 U.S. 205, 52 L.Ed. 171; Western & A.R.R. v. Railroad Comm. of Georgia, 1923, 43 S.Ct. 252, 261 U.S. 264, 67 L.Ed. 645. In each of these cases jurisdiction was held to exist.

9. Zep Mfg. Corp. v. Haber, D.C.Tex. 1962, 202 F.Supp. 847.

viewpoint in a case within the original jurisdiction, and to the defendant's viewpoint in a case brought to federal court by removal from state court.[10]   There is an attraction to this rule, in that it would use the viewpoint of the party who has the burden of proof on jurisdiction. Nevertheless it would create the anomaly that a case brought in the original jurisdiction of the federal court could be dismissed for want of the requisite amount, but then removed to federal court by defendant if it were refiled in state court.[11]

There has been a distinct movement among the lower courts in recent years to yet a third rule.   Under this rule jurisdiction is found if from the viewpoint of either plaintiff or defendant more than the statutory amount is involved.   In a leading case to this effect individuals were suing a railroad to quiet title to water rights.   It was stipulated that the rights in question were worth less than the jurisdictional amount to plaintiffs, but worth far more than the jurisdictional amount to the defendant railroad.[12]   The court upheld jurisdiction, saying: "In determining the matter in controversy, we may look to the object sought to be accomplished by the plaintiff's complaint; the test for determining the amount in controversy is the pecuniary result to either party which the judgment would directly produce." [13]   A number of recent lower-court cases are to the same effect,[14] and this seems the desirable rule,

10.   Bedell v. H. R. C. Ltd., D.C.Ky.1981, 522 F.Supp. 732; Thomas v. General Elec. Co., D.C.Ky.1962, 207 F.Supp. 792; Martin v. City Water Co. of Chillicothe, Mo., D.C.Mo.1912, 197 F. 462, 466; Amelia Milling Co. v. Tennessee C., I. & R. Co., C.C.D.Ga.1903, 123 F. 811, 813; cf. Studebaker v. Salina Waterworks Co., D.C.Kan. 1912, 195 F. 164.

11.   See McCarty v. Amoco Pipeline Co., C.A.7th, 1979, 595 F.2d 389, 393.

12.   Professor David Currie asks: "Does the apparent discrepancy in the value of a single right to the two parties result from a misconception of economics? If the water is worth only $1000 to the plaintiff, cannot the defendant buy it from him for $1000.01?" Currie, Federal Courts—Cases and Materials, 4th ed. 1990, pp. 303–304. But the answer to the latter question will not always be "Yes," either because of stubbornness or because a right may have intangible value to a party, not included among the elements used in measuring the value of the right for purposes of amount in controversy.

13.   Ronzio v. Denver & R.G.W.R.R., C.C.A.10th, 1940, 116 F.2d 604, 606.

14.   Justice v. Atchison, T. & S. F. Ry. Co., C.A.10th, 1991, 927 F.2d 503; McCarty v. Amoco Pipeline Co., C.A.7th, 1979, 595 F.2d 389; Smith v. Washington, C.A.D.C. 1978, 593 F.2d 1097; Government Employees Ins. Co. v. Lally, C.A.4th, 1964, 327 F.2d 568; Ridder Bros., Inc. v. Blethen, C.C.A.9th, 1944, 142 F.2d 395; Melkus v. Allstate Ins. Co., D.C.Mich.1980, 503 F.Supp. 842; and cases cited 14A Wright, Miller & Cooper, Jurisdiction 2d § 3703 n. 21.

A rather cryptic remark from the Supreme Court lends some support to this view.   In Illinois v. City of Milwaukee, 1972, 92 S.Ct. 1385, 1390, 406 U.S. 91, 98, 31 L.Ed.2d 712, the Court's entire discussion of jurisdictional amount consisted of the citation of five authorities in support of the statement: "The considerable interests involved in the purity of interstate waters would seem to put beyond question the jurisdictional amount provided in § 1331(a)." The five authorities it cited in support of that sentence were its own decisions in the Mississippi & Missouri Railroad case and the Glenwood Light & Water Co. case, the Ronzio case, this section of this text, and the Harvard Note cited in note 15 below. Since the two Supreme Court decisions raise, but do not answer, the question of viewpoint, and the Ronzio case, this text, and the Harvard Note all take the view that it is enough if the requisite amount is in controversy from either viewpoint, the Court seems to be saying that that is the rule it was applying. Nevertheless, the passage is opaque and probably not too much should be read into it.

since the purpose of a jurisdictional amount, to keep trivial cases away from the court, is satisfied if the case is worth a large sum to either party.[15]

The rule that the court may look to the viewpoint of either party to see if the necessary amount is in controversy seems both sound and workable in the context of a single plaintiff suing a single defendant. The situation is quite different, however, if a number of plaintiffs are making separate and distinct claims against a defendant in a single suit or if suit is brought on behalf of a class of plaintiffs. Here the rules on aggregation of claims [16] come into play, and there is no jurisdiction if the individual claims are for less than the required amount, even though the total detriment to defendant would exceed the sum specified in the statute.[17]

§ 35. Interest and Costs [1]

The present jurisdictional amount statutes, using language that has appeared unchanged in such statutes since 1887,[2] provide that the matter in controversy is to be determined "exclusive of interest and costs." [3] There has not been much difficulty in deciding which costs are to be excluded. The only problem has been whether attorneys' fees, where they are allowed, are within the exclusion, and it is now quite settled that such fees are a part of the matter in controversy where they are provided for by contract,[4] or by state statute,[5] so long as the fee demanded is reasonable.[6] Where there is no legal authority for collection of an attorneys' fee, such a fee cannot be included in the jurisdictional amount.[7] And while the Moss–Magnuson Consumer Product

15. Note, The Jurisdictional Amount in Controversy Requirement: The Seventh Circuit Rejects the Plaintiff Viewpoint Rule, 1980, 29 De Paul L.Rev. 933; Note, The Jurisdictional Amount Requirement—Valuation from the Defendant's Perspective, 1978, 11 Loy.L.A.L.Rev. 637; Note, Federal Jurisdictional Amount: Determination of the Matter in Controversy, 1960, 73 Harv. L.Rev. 1369.

16. See § 36 below.

17. Snow v. Ford Motor Co., C.A.9th, 1977, 561 F.2d 787; Lonnquist v. J.C. Penney Co., C.A.10th, 1970, 421 F.2d 597; Ferris v. General Dynamics Corp., D.C.R.I. 1986, 645 F.Supp. 1354.

§ 35

1. 14A Wright, Miller & Cooper, Jurisdiction 2d § 3712; Baron, The "Amount in Controversy" Controversy: Using Interest, Costs, and Attorneys' Fees in Computing Its Value, 1988, 41 Okla.L.Rev. 257.

2. From 1789 to 1887, the statutes excluded only costs. "Interest" was added by Act of March 3, 1887, 24 Stat. 552.

3. 28 U.S.C.A. §§ 1332(a), 1337(a); 15 U.S.C.A. §§ 2072, 2310(d)(3)(B).

4. Springstead v. Crawfordsville State Bank, 1913, 34 S.Ct. 195, 231 U.S. 541, 58 L.Ed. 354.

5. Missouri State Life Ins. Co. v. Jones, 1933, 54 S.Ct. 133, 290 U.S. 199, 78 L.Ed. 267; Foret v. Southern Farm Bureau Life Ins. Co., C.A.5th, 1990, 918 F.2d 534; and cases cited 14A Wright, Miller & Cooper, Jurisdiction 2d § 3712 n. 7. It is immaterial that the statute may refer to the attorneys' fee as "costs."

6. Department of Recreation & Sports of Puerto Rico v. World Boxing Assn., C.A.1st, 1991, 942 F.2d 84, 88; S.J. Groves & Sons Co. v. American Arbitration Assn., D.C.Minn.1978, 452 F.Supp. 121.

7. Cupples Co. Mfrs. v. Farmers & Merchants State Bank, C.A.5th, 1968, 390 F.2d 184; Jacobs v. Tawes, C.A.4th, 1957, 250 F.2d 611; Martin v. Granite City Steel Corp., D.C.Ill.1984, 596 F.Supp. 293, 296. But cf. Mutual Benefit Health & Acc. Assn. v. Bowman, C.C.A.8th, 1938, 96 F.2d 7, vacated on other grounds, 1938, 58 S.Ct. 1056, 304 U.S. 549, 82 L.Ed. 1521, holding, somewhat dubiously, that a fee claimed in good faith is to be included even though in

Warranties Act authorizes the award of an attorney's fee,[8] lower courts have held that these fees cannot be considered[9] in calculating the $50,000 amount in controversy that that statute requires.[10]

Interest is more complicated. The first case to come to the Supreme Court raising the question was Brown v. Webster.[11] In that case plaintiff sued for damages of $6000 for eviction from land to which defendant had given him a warranty deed. He had paid only $1200 for the land, and defendant claimed that the case did not satisfy the jurisdictional amount requirement of $2000 then in effect. Under the relevant state law, however, the damages in such an action were return of the purchase price with interest, and the purchase price, with interest from the time of purchase, came to more than $2000. On these facts the Court held that jurisdiction existed. It drew a distinction between "interest as such" and interest "as an instrumentality in arriving at the amount of damages to be awarded on the principal demand," and said that where, as in the case before it, the interest is an essential ingredient of the principal claim, rather than a mere accessory demand, it is not within the statutory exclusion of interest.

The apparent purpose of excluding interest in computing jurisdictional amount is to prevent plaintiff from delaying suit on his claim until the claim, with accruing interest, exceeds the statutory minimum.[12] Thus, under the rule of Brown v. Webster, interest is excluded if it is only an incident to the claim plaintiff is asserting[13] or if it arises solely by virtue of a delay in payment.[14] The interest is not excluded, however, if it is itself the basis of the suit. For example, where plaintiff is suing to collect on bond coupons, these coupons are the matter in controversy, even though they represent, in a sense, "interest."[15] Interest on the coupons themselves or on the bond, after maturity of either, is a different matter, and is excluded, as "interest," in computing the amount in controversy.[16] On similar reasoning it has been held that interest on a note prior to maturity, payable by terms of the note, is a part of the amount in controversy, though interest after maturity would not be.[17]

fact state law does not authorize such a fee. Compare § 33 above.

8. 15 U.S.C.A. § 2310(d)(2).

9. Boelens v. Redman Homes, Inc., C.A.5th, 1984, 748 F.2d 1058, 1069, rehearing denied with opinion C.A.5th, 1985, 759 F.2d 504; Saval v. BL Ltd., C.A.4th, 1983, 710 F.2d 1027, 1032–1033; Rose v. A & L Motor Sales, D.C.Pa.1988, 699 F.Supp. 75; Simmons v. Taylor Childre Chevrolet–Pontiac, Inc., D.C.Ga.1986, 629 F.Supp. 1030, 1033.

10. 15 U.S.C.A. § 2310(d)(3)(B).

11. 1895, 15 S.Ct. 377, 156 U.S. 328, 39 L.Ed. 440.

12. Brainin v. Melikian, C.A.3d, 1968, 396 F.2d 153, 155.

13. Athan v. Hartford Fire Ins. Co., C.C.A.2d, 1934, 73 F.2d 66; Gilliland v. Colorado Life Co., D.C.Mo.1936, 15 F.Supp. 367; Moore v. Town Council of Edgefield, C.C.D.S.C.1887, 32 F. 498.

14. Principal Mut. Life Ins. Co. v. Juntunen, C.A.7th, 1988, 838 F.2d 942, 943; Velez v. Crown Life Ins. Co., C.A.1st, 1979, 599 F.2d 471, 473–474.

15. Edwards v. Bates County, 1896, 16 S.Ct. 967, 163 U.S. 269, 41 L.Ed. 155.

16. Greene County v. Kortrecht, C.C.A.5th, 1897, 81 F. 241.

17. Bailey Employment System, Inc. v. Hahn, C.A.2d, 1981, 655 F.2d 473; Brainin v. Melikian, C.A.3d, 1968, 396 F.2d 153. The Brainin court refused to follow deci-

Finally there is the situation, typified by Brown v. Webster itself, where the interest is regarded as merely one of the elements of damage. Here again it is considered a part of the amount in controversy. Thus, in a suit against a surety to recover on a supersedeas bond, by which the surety was bound to pay the judgment, interest, and costs, the amount in controversy is the whole sum due from the surety, since interest was merely an instrument in calculating the obligation of the bond.[18] Where the judgment in one action includes interest, the amount in controversy in a suit on the judgment is measured by the amount of that first judgment, including interest.[19]

The rules as to interest have been criticized by commentators.[20] They find the distinction between interest "as such" and interest as a principal claim unrealistic, and point out, with some justification, that the rule of Brown v. Webster with regard to interest as damages may open the door of federal court to adroit pleading, which asks simply for damages rather than for interest.[21]

§ 36. Aggregation of Separate Claims [1]

The law on aggregation of claims to satisfy the requirement of amount in controversy is in a very unsatisfactory state. The traditional rules in this area evolved haphazardly and with little reasoning. They serve no apparent policy and "turn on a mystifying conceptual test." [2] There had been a strong tendency among the lower courts to liberalize the traditional rules, but this seems to have been met by Supreme Court decisions reemphasizing the old distinctions. The 1990 statute authorizing "supplemental jurisdiction" [3] has made no change in the law on aggregation in diversity cases. Thus, it is not altogether easy to say what the law is in this area, and it is quite hard to say why it is as it seems to be.

sions to the contrary in Alropa Corp. v. Myers, D.C.Del.1944, 55 F.Supp. 936, and Fritchen v. Mueller, D.C.Kan.1928, 27 F.2d 167.

18. Fitchner v. American Sur. Co. of New York, D.C.Fla.1933, 2 F.Supp. 321.

19. PHI Technologies v. New England Sound & Communications, D.C.Mass.1986, 634 F.Supp. 547; San Juan Hotel Corp. v. Greenberg, D.C.N.Y.1980, 502 F.Supp. 34, affirmed C.A.2d, 646 F.2d 562; Phoenix Scotts–Sports v. Kadish, D.C.Alaska 1971, 321 F.Supp. 556.

20. See Note, 1960, 45 Iowa L.Rev. 832; Note, 1946, 94 U.Pa.L.Rev. 401; Comment, 1936, 10 Tul.L.Rev. 289.

21. Thus, in similar cases where plaintiff was suing on an insurance policy, jurisdiction was denied where his demand was for "$3,000 with interest thereon,"—the jurisdictional amount then being $3000—in

Voorhees v. Aetna Life Ins. Co., D.C.N.J. 1918, 250 F. 484, but sustained where plaintiff simply sued for damages, in the amount of the policy plus interest, for breach of the duty to pay. Continental Cas. Co. v. Spradlin, C.C.A.4th, 1909, 170 Fed. 322.

§ 36

1. 14A Wright, Miller & Cooper, Jurisdiction 2d § 3704; Riddell & Davis, Ancillary Jurisdiction and the Jurisdictional Amount Requirement, 1974, 50 Notre Dame Law. 346; Note, The Federal Jurisdictional Amount and Rule 20 Joinder of Parties: Aggregation of Claims, 1968, 53 Minn.L.Rev. 94.

2. Aetna Cas. & Sur. Co. v. Graves, D.C.La.1974, 381 F.Supp. 1159, 1162.

3. 28 U.S.C.A. § 1367. See § 9 above.

If a single plaintiff has two entirely unrelated claims against a single diverse defendant, each for $30,000, he or she may sue in federal court since the aggregate of the claims exceeds the $50,000 now required. If two plaintiffs each have a $30,000 claim against a single defendant, they may not aggregate their claims, and may not sue in federal court, no matter how similar the claims may be, so long as the claims are regarded as "separate and distinct." Finally if one plaintiff has a claim for $51,000 and another plaintiff has a similar claim against the defendant for $30,000, the traditional rule—which had been under attack in the lower courts but has now been reaffirmed by the Supreme Court—is that the second plaintiff cannot join in the federal-court suit of the first plaintiff but must litigate the matter all over again in state court. A good argument could be made that in each of these situations the result should be precisely opposite what it has traditionally been.

If a single plaintiff is suing a single defendant, Rule 18 permits the plaintiff to join as many claims as he or she may have against the defendant, regardless of their nature, and the value of all the claims is added together in determining whether the jurisdictional amount is met.[4] Ordinarily the claims are in fact closely related, but the statement of the rule in a multitude of decisions has never treated this as relevant to whether aggregation should be permissible. There is no apparent reason why plaintiff should be able to sue on two unrelated claims in federal court when neither claim would in itself be cognizable in federal court. The only virtue of the traditional rule is that it avoids "the cumbersome inquiry into the necessary relationship between the claims."[5]

Thus, a produce company converts apples that belong to three different apple growers. No one of the growers has a claim that meets the jurisdictional-amount requirement, although the three taken together would do so. They cannot sue, individually or together, in federal court. But if a particular bank held a crop mortgage on the crops of each of the three growers, and has standing to sue by virtue of its lien, it can bring action against the produce company in federal court, since the claims it has under the three crop mortgages are aggregated where suit is brought by the single plaintiff.[6] Whether the apples were converted at one time or at different times and whether the issues are the same with regard to all three thefts are treated as immaterial.

---

4. Crawford v. Neal, 1892, 12 S.Ct. 759, 144 U.S. 585, 36 L.Ed. 552; Klepper v. First American Bank, C.A.6th, 1990, 916 F.2d 337; Griffin v. Red Run Lodge, Inc., C.A.4th, 1979, 610 F.2d 1198; Davis H. Elliott Co. v. Caribbean Utilities Co., C.A.6th, 1975, 513 F.2d 1176; Lynch v. Porter, C.A.8th, 1971, 446 F.2d 225, certiorari denied 92 S.Ct. 711, 404 U.S. 1047, 30 L.Ed.2d 739; and cases cited 14A Wright, Miller & Cooper, Jurisdiction 2d § 3704 n. 6.

The same result is reached if a single plaintiff has two claims, each of which is asserted jointly against multiple defendants. Litvak Meat Co. v. Baker, C.A.10th, 1971, 446 F.2d 329; Siegerist v. Blaw–Knox Co., C.A.8th, 1969, 414 F.2d 375, 381.

5. Currie, Federal Courts: Cases and Materials, 4th ed. 1990, p. 309.

6. Cashmere Val. Bank v. Pacific Fruit & Produce Co., Inc., D.C.Wash.1940, 33 F.Supp. 946. Cf. Bank of California Nat. Assn. v. Twin Harbors Lumber Co., C.A.9th, 1972, 465 F.2d 489.

The rule that if there are several parties their claims cannot be aggregated had its origin more than 160 years ago, at a time when joinder of parties was far less understood than it is today, and it was a construction of a statute regulating the appellate jurisdiction of the Supreme Court, rather than the original jurisdiction of the district courts.[7] The rule in its various ramifications was applied much later to determine whether there is original federal jurisdiction without any apparent realization that different policies might well be appropriate for original jurisdiction than for appellate jurisdiction.[8]

To the rule against aggregation of claims for or against multiple parties, there is a single exception: if the several parties have a common undivided interest and a single title or right is involved, the interests of coparties may be added together in determining the amount in controversy.[9] Aggregation is not permitted if the claims for or against the various parties are considered several and distinct, and they may be so considered even though the claims arise from a single instrument or the parties have a community of interest.[10]

7. Oliver v. Alexander, 1832, 6 Pet. 143, 8 L.Ed. 349.

8. Walter v. Northeastern R. Co., 1893, 13 S.Ct. 348, 147 U.S. 370, 37 L.Ed. 206; Wheless v. City of St. Louis, C.C.D.Mo.1899, 96 F. 865, 868–869, affirmed 1901, 21 S.Ct. 402, 180 U.S. 379, 45 L.Ed. 583. See Note, 1968, 53 Minn.L.Rev. 94, 102–105.

9. Troy Bank of Troy, Ind. v. G.A. Whitehead & Co., 1911, 32 S.Ct. 9, 222 U.S. 39, 56 L.Ed. 81 (holders of two notes, secured by a single vendor's lien, suing to assert the lien); Shields v. Thomas, 1854, 17 How. 3, 15 L.Ed. 93 (distributees of an estate against converter of estate); Texas & P. Ry. Co. v. Gentry, 1896, 16 S.Ct. 1104, 163 U.S. 353, 41 L.Ed. 186 (action under wrongful-death act by beneficiaries); Eagle v. American Tel. & Tel. Co., C.A.9th, 1985, 769 F.2d 541, certiorari denied 106 S.Ct. 1465, 475 U.S. 1084, 89 L.Ed.2d 721 (minority-stockholders' claims for wrongful depletion of corporation's assets); Black v. Beame, C.A.2d, 1977, 550 F.2d 815 (right of family members to family services); Berman v. Narragansett Racing Assn., Inc., C.A.1st, 1969, 414 F.2d 311 (suit to require a fund to be created for benefit of a class); Phoenix Ins. Co. v. Woosley, C.A.10th, 1961, 287 F.2d 531 (creditors suing to collect fire insurance payable to their debtor); Lailhengue v. Mobil Oil Corp., D.C.La.1991, 775 F.Supp. 908, 910–914 (plaintiffs' claims for punitive damages); and see cases cited 14A Wright, Miller & Cooper, Jurisdiction 2d § 3704 nn. 24–33.

The same rule applies where suit is against multiple defendants. McDaniel v.

Traylor, 1905, 25 S.Ct. 369, 196 U.S. 415, 49 L.Ed. 533 (suit to set aside lien of judgments obtained fraudulently by defendants acting in concert); Sovereign Camp, Woodmen of the World v. O'Neill, 1924, 45 S.Ct. 49, 266 U.S. 292, 69 L.Ed. 293 (conspiracy by defendants).

10. Thomson v. Gaskill, 1942, 62 S.Ct. 673, 315 U.S. 442, 86 L.Ed. 951 (employees of a single defendant claiming employer had denied them rights under a collective bargaining contract); Pinel v. Pinel, 1916, 36 S.Ct. 416, 240 U.S. 594, 60 L.Ed. 817 (suit by two children claiming to have been omitted from father's will by mistake); Wheless v. City of St. Louis, 1901, 21 S.Ct. 402, 180 U.S. 379, 45 L.Ed. 583 (several owners of land suing to enjoin assessment for street improvements); Lion Bonding & Sur. Co. v. Karatz, 1923, 43 S.Ct. 480, 262 U.S. 77, 67 L.Ed. 871 (bill for appointment of receiver by several small creditors); Apicella v. Valley Forge Military Academy, D.C.Pa.1985, 630 F.Supp. 20 (claim for personal injuries to minor joined with parents' claim for medical expenses incurred for minor's injuries); and see cases cited 14A Wright, Miller & Cooper, Jurisdiction 2d § 3704 nn. 11–13, 16–23.

The rule is the same where suit is against multiple defendants. Walter v. Northeastern Ry. Co., 1893, 13 S.Ct. 348, 147 U.S. 370, 37 L.Ed. 206 (suit to enjoin several counties from collecting taxes); Davis v. Schwartz, 1895, 15 S.Ct. 237, 155 U.S. 631, 39 L.Ed. 289 (suit to set aside separate chattel mortgages executed to different mortgagees to secure different debts).

As the cases in the two preceding footnotes suggest, the distinction between a common undivided interest and several and distinct claims is something less than clear.[11] This is to be expected. Except in property-law contexts, such terms as "common" and "several" are poor words for a test of jurisdiction—or anything else—since they "have little or no clear and ascertainable meaning."[12] It is disappointing that the Supreme Court in Snyder v. Harris[13] should have vigorously endorsed the old test and declared it to be so firmly established that only Congress can change it. In doing so the Court said that "lower courts have developed largely workable standards for determining when claims are joint and common, and therefore entitled to be aggregated, and when they are separate and distinct and therefore not aggregable."[14] It would have been helpful if the Court had indicated what these standards are or where they are to be found.[15]

In recent years there has been particular difficulty in applying this distinction to insurance cases. In one case an insurance company sued for a declaratory judgment of nonliability to a number of persons who had obtained judgments against its insured. The judgments collectively were for far more than the jurisdictional amount but no individual judgment was of that magnitude. The Fourth Circuit found that the defendants had a common or undivided interest as against the insurance company arising out of the single insurance policy, and sustained jurisdiction.[16] In a case shortly thereafter 47 insurance companies, which had joined in issuance of a single policy of insurance to a railroad company, sued for a declaratory judgment that a loss suffered by the railroad was not within the coverage of the policy. The Tenth Circuit held that the claims against the various insurers were common, in the sense of a community of interest in the rights asserted, but not undivided in the sense that they constitute in their totality an integrated right.

---

11. "Difficult it is to draw a general rule or a rationale from the decisions other than the broad rules stated above. Language to support either conclusion in a case such as the present one can be found." Dixon v. Northwestern Nat. Bank, D.C.Minn.1967, 276 F.Supp. 96, 100.

"An identifying characteristic of a common and undivided interest is that if one plaintiff cannot or does not collect his share, the shares of the remaining plaintiffs are increased." Sellers v. O'Connell, C.A.6th, 1983, 701 F.2d 575, 579.

12. Kaplan, Continuing Work of the Civil Committee: 1966 Amendments of the Federal Rules of Civil Procedure, 1967, 81 Harv.L.Rev. 356, 380.

13. 1969, 89 S.Ct. 1053, 394 U.S. 332, 22 L.Ed.2d 319.

14. 89 S.Ct. at 1059, 394 U.S. at 341.

15. "For the Supreme Court in the 1990s—or the 1960s, for that matter—to employ a rule that turns on the 'joint' or 'several' nature of the claims is similar to attempting to drive a Model T on a super-highway. Yet incredibly, the Court in Snyder steadfastly maintained that (1) the rules are not all that difficult to apply, and (2) if a change is to be made it must come from Congress. Both conclusions are simply wrong." Redish, Reassessing the Allocation of Judicial Business between State and Federal Courts: Federal Jurisdiction and "The Martian Chronicles", 1992, 78 Va.L.Rev. 1769, 1808.

16. Manufacturers Cas. Ins. Co. v. Coker, C.A.4th, 1955, 219 F.2d 631. This case is cited in Note, note 1 above, at 108–109, along with Raybould v. Mancini–Fattore Co., D.C.Mich.1960, 186 F.Supp. 235 and Dixon v. Northwestern Nat. Bank, D.C.Minn.1967, 276 F.Supp. 96, as representing an "apparent attempt to expand the 'common and undivided' exception."

It refused to allow aggregation of the claims to measure the amount in controversy.[17]

In the Tenth Circuit case just discussed the potential liability of nine of the 47 insurers was for more than the required amount but this was not held sufficient to support jurisdiction with regard to those insurers with a smaller potential liability.[18] This suggests an additional, and vexing, problem of jurisdictional amount where multiple parties are involved. Suppose that one party has a claim for more than $50,000. Another party has a claim against the same defendant for less than $50,000, and this party's claim is technically "separate and distinct" though it is so closely related to the first party's claim that, as a matter of efficient judicial administration, they should be heard jointly. On these facts can the federal court hear the claim of the second party, when joined with that of the first party? This is a more appealing case for aggregation than the situations, heretofore considered, where no one of the individual claims satisfies the statute. In those other situations refusal to permit aggregation means that all the claims must be brought in state court where, presumably, they can be joined or otherwise conveniently tried. But in the situation now considered, the party with the claim for more than $50,000 has a statutory right to assert that claim in federal court and, if aggregation is not permitted, the party with the smaller claim must bring a wasteful independent suit in state court. The commentators have thought that in these circumstances the two parties should be permitted to join, with the larger claim satisfying the statutory requirement of jurisdictional amount for the entire suit and the smaller claim coming within the court's ancillary jurisdiction.[19] The weight of authority was and is to the contrary[20] but there had been a distinct trend in recent years to apply the ancillary-jurisdiction concept and to hold that the court has discretion to hear the insufficient claim joined with a claim for more than the jurisdictional amount if the claims were closely related and arose for the most part out of the same operative facts.[21] Many of the cases allowing the insufficient claim as

17. Aetna Ins. Co. v. Chicago, R.I. & P.R. Co., C.A.10th, 1956, 229 F.2d 584, noted 1957, 10 Okla.L.Rev. 92. To similar effect, see Niagara Fire Ins. Co. v. Dyess Furniture Co., Inc., C.A.5th, 1961, 292 F.2d 232; Jewell v. Grain Dealers Mut. Ins. Co., C.A.5th, 1961, 290 F.2d 11, criticized 1961, 64 W.Va.L.Rev. 87; cf. Ex parte Phoenix Ins. Co., 1886, 6 S.Ct. 772, 117 U.S. 367, 29 L.Ed. 923.

18. Indeed it did not support jurisdiction even for the nine. Since the action was one for a declaratory judgment, it was held that the court properly exercised its discretion in such an action—see § 100 below—to dismiss the entire suit so that the controversy could be resolved in a state-court action in which all the insurers could be joined.

19. See commentaries cited in 14A Wright, Miller & Cooper, Jurisdiction 2d § 3704 n. 49.

20. Clark v. Paul Gray, Inc., 1939, 59 S.Ct. 744, 306 U.S. 583, 83 L.Ed. 1001; and cases cited 14A Wright, Miller & Cooper, Jurisdiction 2d § 3704 n. 53.

21. Niebuhr v. State Farm Mut. Auto. Ins. Co., C.A.10th, 1973, 486 F.2d 618; Beautytuft, Inc. v. Factory Ins. Assn., C.A.6th, 1970, 431 F.2d 1122; Hatridge v. Aetna Cas. & Sur. Co., C.A.8th, 1969, 415 F.2d 809; Stone v. Stone, C.A.4th, 1968, 405 F.2d 94, 96–99; Jacobson v. Atlantic City Hosp., C.A.3d, 1968, 392 F.2d 149, noted 1968, 30 U.Pitt.L.Rev. 413; Wilson v. American Chain & Cable Co., C.A.3d, 1966, 364 F.2d 558, noted 1967, 16 Cath.U.L.Rev. 336, 66 Mich.L.Rev. 373; and cases cited within the ancillary jurisdiction were cases involving claims by members of a single family arising out of a single accident. This was the strongest case for this result, and the American Law Institute proposed a statutory codification of this approach limited to claims on behalf of members of a single family living in the same household.[22] But if, as is thought, the principle is sound, there seems no reason to limit it to family cases, since they differ from other cases only in degree;[23] the limitation poses serious problems of construction and could give rise to quite fortuitous results.[24]

The Supreme Court's decision in Snyder v. Harris cast grave doubt on this trend toward applying the ancillary jurisdiction principle to questions of aggregation, and its later decision in Zahn v. International Paper Co.[25] was a death blow to that trend. In Snyder the Court had held that a class action cannot be maintained when no member of the class has a claim in the requisite amount. In Zahn it extended this to hold that even when the named plaintiffs have claims for more than the required amount, they cannot represent a class in which many of the members have claims for less than the amount. The Court repeated its dogmatic pronouncement of a "rule that multiple plaintiffs with separate and distinct claims must each satisfy the jurisdictional-amount requirement," and said: "The rule has been applied to forbid aggregation of claims where none of the claimants satisfies the jurisdictional amount * * *. It also requires dismissal of those litigants whose claims do not satisfy the jurisdictional amount, even though other litigants assert claims sufficient to invoke the jurisdiction of the federal court."[26]

Zahn cannot reasonably be read as applying only to class actions. Two of the three cases that the Court cited for the second sentence in the quoted passage are not even arguably class action cases. And it was only after stating these flat and "firmly rooted" rules against aggregation that the Court went on to say that the "same rules were applied to class actions * * *."[27]

Zahn is a puzzling case, particularly because of its failure even to consider the argument of three dissenters that recent principles of ancillary jurisdiction, which had been held to overcome the jurisdictional-amount requirement in other contexts,[28] should do so also in connection with joinder of parties. A few lower courts sought to distinguish Zahn and to apply ancillary jurisdiction in the situation being consid-

14A Wright, Miller & Cooper, Jurisdiction 2d § 3704 n. 54.

22. ALI Study, § 1301(e).

23. R.C., 1967, 81 Harv.L.Rev. 480, 481–482.

24. See Currie, The Federal Courts and the American Law Institute (Part II), 1969, 36 U.Chi.L.Rev. 268, 297.

25. 1973, 94 S.Ct. 505, 414 U.S. 291, 38 L.Ed.2d 511. See Riddell & Davis, note 1 above; Theis, Zahn v. International Paper Co.: The Non–Aggregation Rule in Juris-

dictional Amount Cases, 1974, 35 La.L.Rev. 89.

26. 94 S.Ct. at 508–509, 414 U.S. at 294–295.

27. 94 S.Ct. at 509, 414 U.S. at 296. See also Note, 1975 Wash.U.L.Q. 447, 457–458, agreeing that Zahn states a general rule and is not limited to class actions. But see Note, 1976, 62 Va.L.Rev. 194, 231–236.

28. See § 9 above.

ered[29] but the distinctions seem unsound, as recognized by other lower courts that held that a sufficient claim with regard to one party cannot carry with it jurisdiction of an insufficient claim with regard to another party.[30]

These rules about aggregation have not been changed by the 1990 statute codifying what previously had been known as "ancillary jurisdiction" and "pendent jurisdiction" under the name of "supplemental jurisdiction".[31] Although 28 U.S.C.A. § 1367(a) extends supplemental jurisdiction as far as the Constitution allows, and provides specifically that it includes claims that involve the joinder of additional parties, subsection (b) limits the use of supplemental jurisdiction in diversity cases. It provides, among other things, that in diversity cases "the district courts shall not have supplemental jurisdiction over subsection (a) over claims by plaintiffs against persons made parties under Rule * * * 19, 20" of the Civil Rules "when exercising supplemental jurisdiction over such claims would be inconsistent with the jurisdictional requirements of section 1332." Since Rules 19 and 20 are the rules authorizing joinder of multiple defendants, and since one of the jurisdictional requirements of § 1332 is that more than $50,000 be in controversy, it is quite clear that the established doctrines about aggregation of claims against multiple defendants have not been changed by the new statute.[32] The situation is less clear for multiple plaintiffs. There is nothing in § 1367(b) to except those claims from the general grant of supplemental jurisdiction.[33]

29. In Uniroyal, Inc. v. Heller, D.C.N.Y. 1974, 65 F.R.D. 83, 88, it was held that ancillary jurisdiction can no longer be applied to plaintiffs but it can be applied against defendants. Nothing in Zahn or any prior decision supports such a distinction. In Afton Alps, Inc. v. U.S., D.C.Minn. 1974, 392 F.Supp. 543, 546 n. 2, Zahn was read as applying only to a plaintiff class but not to named plaintiffs. The reasons for rejecting this distinction are stated in the text at note 27 above.

30. Sarnoff v. American Home Products Corp., C.A.7th, 1986, 798 F.2d 1075; National Ins. Underwriters v. Piper Aircraft Corp., C.A.10th, 1979, 595 F.2d 546, noted 1980, 58 Wash.U.L.Q. 497; Hanshew v. U.S. Fidelity & Guar. Co., D.C.Kan.1990, 746 F.Supp. 55; Alco Financial Services, Inc. v. Treasure Island Motor Inn, Inc., D.C.Ill.1979, 82 F.R.D. 735; and cases cited 14A Wright, Miller & Cooper, Jurisdiction 2d § 3704 n. 59.

31. 28 U.S.C.A. § 1367. See § 9 above.

32. Griffin v. Dana Point Condominium Assn., D.C.Ill.1991, 768 F.Supp. 1299, 1301–1302; C.D.S. Diversified, Inc. v. Franchise Finance Corp. of America, D.C.N.Y. 1991, 757 F.Supp. 202. There is a decision to the contrary in Corporate Resources, Inc.

v. Southeast Suburban Ambulatory Surgical Center, Inc., D.C.Ill.1991, 774 F.Supp. 503, but the court does not quote or discuss subsection (b) of § 1367.

33. The draftsmen of the statute hope that it will be construed not to allow the joinder of additional plaintiffs, subsequent to the commencement of the action, if to do so would be inconsistent with the rule of complete diversity, though they concede that this result will not be easy to achieve under the statutory language. See § 9 n. 25 above. The same problem will exist on joinder of additional plaintiffs whose claims do not exceed $50,000. Indeed it would be even harder to avoid the statutory language here, since the legislative history of the 1990 statute shows that the purpose of § 1367(b) was to preserve the rule of complete diversity, but there is nothing to indicate that Congress cared about preserving the existing rules on jurisdictional amount.

The statute was held to apply in this situation and to allow suit where one plaintiff had a claim in excess of $50,000 and other plaintiffs had claims for less than that amount. The court held that it was obliged to reach this result, and to hold that § 1367 has overruled Zahn, "[in light of the literal language of § 1367, and in spite of legisla-

§ 37. Effect of Counterclaims [1]

The extent to which a counterclaim can be considered in determining the amount in controversy has never been satisfactorily answered by the courts, and a baffling 1961 decision of the Supreme Court only added to the difficulty. Here the issue will be examined as it appeared prior to 1961, and then consideration will be given to the 1961 decision and whatever implications it may have for this area of the law.

In approaching the problem it is necessary to distinguish between counterclaims that arise out of the same transaction or occurrence as the plaintiff's claim, and that are, therefore, under Civil Rule 13(a) and similar rules and statutes in many states, compulsory, and counterclaims that do not arise out of the same transaction or occurrence and that are, under Rule 13(b) and corresponding state provisions, permissive.[2] It is also necessary to distinguish between cases brought originally in federal court and those brought in state court where removal to federal court is attempted.

The easiest situation is where plaintiff's claim is for more than the $50,000 now required in diversity cases. It is not necessary here to resort to the counterclaim to make up the jurisdictional amount, and the case can be heard in federal court, if other jurisdictional requirements are met, either originally or by removal. If the counterclaim is compulsory, it falls within what has been called the "ancillary jurisdiction" of the court—and under a 1990 statute is now called "supplemental jurisdiction—and may be heard though it is for less than $50,000 or otherwise does not meet the usual tests for federal jurisdiction; a permissive counterclaim, on the other hand, must have an independent jurisdictional basis.[3]

The problem becomes more difficult where plaintiff sues in federal court on a claim for less than $50,000, and defendant counterclaims for a sum that, either by itself or when added to plaintiff's claim, would make the matter in controversy exceed $50,000. There are virtually no holdings on whether jurisdiction exists in these circumstances.[4] A few

---

tive history which may indicate otherwise * * *." Garza v. National American Ins. Co., D.C.La.1992, 807 F.Supp. 1256, 1258 n. 6. That case is followed in Patterson Enterprises v. Bridgestone/Firestone, Inc., D.C.Kan.1993, 812 F.Supp. 1152, 1154–1155. There is a ruling to the contrary in Chouest v.American Airlines, Inc., D.C.La. 1993, 839 F.Supp. 412.

§ 37

1. 14A Wright, Miller & Cooper, Jurisdiction 2d § 3706.

2. The counterclaim rules are discussed in § 79 below.

3. See § 79 below; 6 Wright, Miller & Kane, Civil 2d §§ 1415, 1423, and cases there cited.

4. Fenton v. Freedman, C.A.9th, 1984, 748 F.2d 1358, upheld jurisdiction of a case in which plaintiff's claims against two of three defendants were less than the $10,000 then required, but defendants' compulsory counterclaims exceeded that amount and defendants did not object to the district court's assumption of jurisdiction over plaintiff's main claim. Roberts Mining and Milling Co. v. Schrader, C.C.A.9th, 1938, 95 F.2d 522, held that jurisdiction existed where the counterclaim by itself is for more than the jurisdictional amount, though the original claim was insufficient. Compare Goldstone v. Payne, C.C.A.2d, 1938, 94 F.2d 855, certiorari denied 58 S.Ct. 1057, 304 U.S. 585, 82 L.Ed. 1547, where it was held that the counterclaim could not be added to the claim to determine the amount in con-cases contain dicta supporting aggregation on such facts,[5] but it is difficult to believe that this can in fact be the rule, at least where the counterclaim is permissive only. The doctrine is well settled in many contexts that the original jurisdiction of the federal court can be invoked only on the basis of what is shown by the plaintiff's complaint, and to depart from that doctrine here would give the defendant the wholly novel privilege of choosing whether the federal court is to have subject-matter jurisdiction of a case originally brought in that court. If the plaintiff's claim is for less than the jurisdictional amount, a motion to dismiss would have to be granted, and a default judgment would be of doubtful validity,[6] and yet if aggregation is permitted here, defendant could breathe life into the defective suit by asserting a counterclaim in the requisite amount.

Removal cases present quite a different problem. If plaintiff sues in state court for less than $50,000, and defendant counterclaims for more than $50,000, it is settled—wisely or not—that plaintiff cannot remove since the statute limits the privilege of removal to defendants.[7] Nor should defendant be able to remove if its counterclaim is permissive by state law. By hypothesis, its counterclaim bears no logical relation to plaintiff's claim against it, and defendant is entirely free to bring its independent action on the counterclaim in federal court. The cases so hold.[8] The cases are divided, however, on whether defendant can

---

troversy; the court left open what the result would be if the counterclaim by itself was for the jurisdictional amount, though strongly suggesting that jurisdiction would be denied even on those facts. In Home Life Ins. Co. v. Sipp, C.C.A.3d, 1926, 11 F.2d 474, there was a dictum that jurisdiction exists if the counterclaim, either by itself or added to the claim, is for the requisite amount, but the holding was against jurisdiction where neither the claim nor the counterclaim was large enough to satisfy the statute, and the counterclaim represented a sum that would be deducted from plaintiff's recovery. Finally, as an alternative ground of decision in Liberty Mut. Ins. Co. v. Horton, C.A.5th, 1960, 275 F.2d 148, 152, the court applied what it termed "the long established rule" that the counterclaim and claim are to be aggregated in measuring the amount in controversy, but the affirmance of this decision by the Supreme Court, 1961, 81 S.Ct. 1570, 367 U.S. 348, 6 L.Ed.2d 890, as will be seen, made no reference to this ground.

Jurisdiction was denied in Motorists Mut. Ins. Co. v. Simpson, C.A.7th, 1968, 404 F.2d 511, in which plaintiff's claim was insufficient but defendant had asserted a counterclaim for more than $10,000. The critical fact there, however, was that defendant had objected to the jurisdiction of the federal court and only asserted the counterclaim, after her jurisdictional objection was over-

ruled, because it was compulsory under Rule 13(a).

5. See Kirby v. American Soda Fountain Co., 1904, 24 S.Ct. 619, 621, 194 U.S. 141, 146, 48 L.Ed. 911; Ginsburg v. Pacific Mut. Life Ins. Co. of California, C.C.A.2d, 1934, 69 F.2d 97, 98; Central Commercial Co. v. Jones–Dusenbury Co., C.C.A.7th, 1918, 251 F. 13, 19; American Sheet & Tin Plate Co. v. Winzeler, D.C.Ohio 1915, 227 F. 321, 324. See also note 4 above.

6. See 18 Wright, Miller & Cooper, Jurisdiction § 4428.

7. Shamrock Oil & Gas Corp. v. Sheets, 1941, 61 S.Ct. 868, 313 U.S. 100, 85 L.Ed. 1214. Nor can the plaintiff remove by claiming that the counterclaim is a separate-and-independent cause of action, under 28 U.S.C.A. § 1441(c). Lee Foods Div. Consol. Grocers Corp. v. Bucy, D.C.Mo.1952, 105 F.Supp. 402, noted 1953, 53 Col.L.Rev. 282. Since 1990 § 1441(c) has applied only in federal-question cases.

The American Law Institute proposed to permit removal on the basis of defendant's counterclaim. ALI Study, §§ 1304(c), (d), 1312(a)(3).

8. Merchants' Heat & Light Co. v. James B. Clow & Sons, 1907, 27 S.Ct. 285, 204 U.S. 286, 51 L.Ed. 488; Bryant Elec. Co. v. Joe Rainero Tile Co., Inc., D.C.Va. 1979, 84 F.R.D. 120.

remove on these facts if the counterclaim is compulsory by state law.[9]

The practical consequence of denying removal in these circumstances is that a party who wins the race to the courthouse by asserting a small claim in state court can compel its opponent to litigate his own claim in that court, even though the opponent's claim is for far more than the amount required for federal jurisdiction. In one such case plaintiff sued in state court for $1,408.72. Defendant's counterclaim, compulsory by state law, was for $78,650.00.[10] Surely to permit plaintiff to force a state forum on defendant in such circumstances is undesirable, as even the judges who have reached this result concede.[11] If this is compelled by statute, then it must be followed, regardless of its desirability, but the courts so holding point to no specific statutory language that requires this result. The removal statutes themselves are silent about amount in controversy. The general diversity statute says only that the courts have jurisdiction "where the matter in controversy exceeds the sum or value of $50,000, exclusive of interest and costs." It would be perfectly consistent with the statute to hold that a claim that arises from the transaction sued on and that, by the relevant state law,[12] must either be asserted in the action or forever barred, is in controversy. There is another curiously conceptual argument in the cases that so to hold would be to permit state law to control removal, contrary to the usual principle that the right to remove is governed solely by federal law. But

9. Removal permitted: Wheatley v. Martin, D.C.Ark.1945, 62 F.Supp. 109 (overruled by the Ingram case below); Lange v. Chicago, R.I. & P.R. Co., D.C.Iowa 1951, 99 F.Supp. 1; McLean Trucking Co. v. Carolina Scenic Stages, D.C.N.C.1951, 95 F.Supp. 437; National Upholstery Co. v. Corley, D.C.N.C.1956, 144 F.Supp. 658; Congaree Broadcasters, Inc. v. TM Programming, Inc., D.C.S.C.1977, 436 F.Supp. 258; Swallow & Associates v. Henry Molded Products, Inc., D.C.Mich.1992, 794 F.Supp. 660.

Removal denied: Collins v. Faucett, D.C.Fla.1949, 87 F.Supp. 254; Barnes v. Parker, D.C.Mo.1954, 126 F.Supp. 649; Trullinger v. Rosenblum, D.C.Ark.1955, 129 F.Supp. 12; Ingram v. Sterling, D.C.Ark. 1956, 141 F.Supp. 786; Continental Carriers, Inc. v. Goodpasture, D.C.Ga.1959, 169 F.Supp. 602, noted 1959, 45 Va.L.Rev. 737; Hall v. Bowman, D.C.Mo.1959, 171 F.Supp. 454; Rudder v. Ohio State Life Ins. Co., D.C.Ky.1962, 208 F.Supp. 577; Burton Lines, Inc. v. Mansky, D.C.N.C.1967, 265 F.Supp. 489; West Virginia State Bar v. Bostic, D.C.W.Va.1972, 351 F.Supp. 1118; Video Connection of America, Inc. v. Priority Concepts, Inc., D.C.N.Y.1986, 625 F.Supp. 1549; Oliver v. Haas, D.C.Puerto Rico 1991, 777 F.Supp. 1040.

10. National Upholstery Co. v. Corley, D.C.N.C.1956, 144 F.Supp. 658. In an even more extreme case the claim was for $4,931.75 and the compulsory counterclaim, by a nonresident defendant, was for $1,050,000. Oliver v. Haas, D.C.Puerto Rico 1991, 777 F.Supp. 1040.

11. See Continental Carriers, Inc. v. Goodpasture, D.C.Ga.1959, 169 F.Supp. 602, 604, calling for remedial legislation to permit a contrary result, and the similar view expressed in the note on that case at 1959, 45 Va.L.Rev. 737. See also Rudder v. Ohio State Life Ins. Co., D.C.Ky.1962, 208 F.Supp. 577, 578.

12. The suggestion of Feinberg, Establishing Jurisdictional Amount by a Counterclaim, 1956, 21 Mo.L.Rev. 243, that the test should be whether the counterclaim is compulsory under the federal rules is unacceptable. It is state law, not the federal rules, that determines whether a speedy plaintiff can compel defendant to litigate in state court a claim for which he otherwise would have a federal forum. This is the evil to which the removal statutes are addressed.

The American Law Institute, however, would have allowed removal if defendant had a claim for more than $10,000 arising out of the same transaction or occurrence as the claim against defendant, without regard to whether the counterclaim is compulsory under state law. ALI Study, § 1304(d).

wherever, in a diversity case, amount in controversy is in question, it is the state law that is controlling, since it defines the elements for which recovery may be had, and prescribes the measure of damages.[13] Again state law is relevant on whether a claim is separate and independent from another claim so as to permit removal under 28 U.S.C.A. § 1441(c).[14] It seems fully in accord with these principles to say that the state law has the effect of putting in controversy defendant's claims arising out of the transaction sued on, and thus to permit removal if the counterclaim is for more than the jurisdictional amount.

Against this background, the surprising decision of the Supreme Court in 1961 in Horton v. Liberty Mutual Insurance Co.[15] can be examined. Horton asserted a claim before the Texas Industrial Accident Board for workers' compensation of $14,035. The Board awarded him $1050. On the day the award was made, the insurer filed suit in federal court to set aside the award to Horton. The complaint alleged diversity, and asserted also that Horton had claimed, was claiming, and would claim $14,035, but that in fact he was not entitled to recover anything at all under Texas law. One week later Horton sued in state court to set aside the Board's award and to recover $14,035. Later he moved to dismiss the insurer's federal-court action on the ground that the value of the "matter in controversy" was only $1050, and also filed, subject to his motion to dismiss, a conditional compulsory counterclaim for the $14,-035. On these facts it was held, five to four, that the amount in controversy exceeded the $10,000 then required, and that federal jurisdiction existed.

The Supreme Court recognized the general rule that the amount in controversy is determined from the complaint, and noted the allegations in the complaint that Horton would claim $14,035. It said: "No denial of these allegations in the complaint has been made, no attempted disclaimer or surrender of any part of the original claim has been made by petitioner, and there has been no other showing, let alone a showing 'to a legal certainty,' of any lack of good faith on the part of the respondent in alleging that a $14,035 claim is in controversy. * * * The claim before the Board was $14,035; the state court suit asked that much; the conditional counterclaim in the federal court claims the same amount. Texas law under which this claim was created and has its being leaves the entire $14,035 claim open for adjudication in a de novo court trial, regardless of the award. Thus the record before us shows beyond a doubt that the award is challenged by both parties and is binding on neither; that petitioner claims more than $10,000 from the respondent and the respondent denies it should have to pay petitioner anything at all. No matter which party brings it into court, the

---

13. See § 33 n. 6 above.

14. See § 39 below.

15. 1961, 81 S.Ct. 1570, 367 U.S. 348, 6 L.Ed.2d 890, noted, usually critically, 1961, 11 DePaul L.Rev. 130, 36 Tul.L.Rev. 148, 1962, 11 Am.U.L.Rev. 102, 1962 Duke L.J. 130, 22 La.L.Rev. 851, 46 Minn.L.Rev. 960, 23 Ohio St.L.J. 777. See the thoughtful Comment, The Effect of the Horton Case on the Determination of the Amount in Controversy Under Statutes Limiting Federal Court Jurisdiction, 1962, 17 Rutgers L.Rev. 200.

controversy remains the same; it involves the same amount of money and is to be adjudicated and determined under the same rules. Unquestionably, therefore, the amount in controversy is in excess of $10,000."[16]

No further light has been shed on this case by later decisions, and it is difficult to the point of impossibility to state for what principle, if any, the decision stands. Is the Court, as its language suggests, really holding that good-faith allegations in the complaint as to what the defendant will claim are to be considered in determining the matter in controversy? Such a holding would be contrary to the rule, developed in other contexts, that plaintiff cannot create federal jurisdiction by anticipating defenses that defendant may assert, but is held to his own well-pleaded claim.[17]

Is the Court saying that since Texas law reopens the entire controversy when court review of a compensation award is sought by either party, the whole amount that might potentially be awarded is the matter in controversy? Such a proposition may be tested by considering what would happen if Horton failed to answer the insurer's federal-court complaint, and judgment went for the insurer by default. The judgment would simply set aside the Board's award of $1050. It is unusual to find the jurisdictional amount satisfied where plaintiff is given a judgment for precisely what he asked, and this judgment awards relief of little more than one-tenth the statutory amount. Yet if the Horton case means anything, surely such a judgment would not be void. Presumably the judgment, on this analysis, would be valid because it would act as a bar against any later claim by Horton for the $14,035. To accept this proposition, however, would have far-reaching effect on the compulsory-counterclaim cases. It would seem to mean that a person who suffers $1000 damage in an automobile accident could sue in federal court for that amount, if his opponent had potential damages from the same accident of more than the $50,000 now required, since the opponent's claim would be barred by Rule 13(a) if he failed to assert it. This goes beyond anything either the cases or the commentators have heretofore suggested. It would permit original jurisdiction, though plaintiff's own claim is for less than $50,000, not only where defendant has asserted a counterclaim for more than the statutory sum but also where it might have asserted a compulsory counterclaim for such amount, notwithstanding that it did not do so. Such an interpretation of Horton would also suggest, contrary to the present case authority,[18] that more than $50,000 is in controversy if plaintiff might have sued for a greater amount but chose to limit its demand to less than $50,000.

Is it decisive in the Horton case that Horton was in fact claiming $14,035, both in his state court action and in his conditional counterclaim in federal court? The Fifth Circuit has thought so, and has held

---

16. 81 S.Ct. at 1573–1574, 367 U.S. at 353–354.

17. Louisville & N.R. Co. v. Mottley, 1908, 29 S.Ct. 42, 211 U.S. 149, 53 L.Ed. 126; Gully v. First Nat. Bank in Meridian,

1936, 57 S.Ct. 96, 299 U.S. 109, 81 L.Ed. 70; see § 18 above.

18. See § 33 n. 53 above.

no jurisdiction in such circumstances where the worker, in federal court, has asked for less than the $10,000 then required, though his original claim before the Board, or even his claim in his own state-court action, was for more than that sum.[19] It is odd to make plaintiff's invocation of federal jurisdiction dependent on what defendant subsequently decides to ask. It is even odder to make jurisdiction turn on the happenstance that the worker files his counterclaim, or brings an action in state court, before the federal court rules on his motion to dismiss. A motion to dismiss for want of jurisdiction can be made in advance of answer, and if it is successful, the defendant is not barred by the compulsory-counterclaim rule from pressing his own claim in an independent suit.[20] If the decisive fact in Horton is that he actually has claimed the $14,035, the result in the case can be avoided simply by moving to dismiss for want of jurisdiction and waiting until that motion has been granted before bringing the state-court action for the full amount,[21] or even by claiming more than the statutory amount in a state-court action while asking for less than that amount in the federal action.[22]

Perhaps the case is no more than a skirmish in the continuing battle between Texas employees, who prefer a state forum for their workers' compensation actions, and insurers, who prefer the federal court.[23] The decision is of little importance if, as now appears, it states a rule confined to Texas workers' compensation cases and motivated by the peculiarities of the Texas law about judicial review of such cases.[24]

19. Hardware Mut. Cas. Co. v. McIntyre, C.A.5th, 1962, 304 F.2d 566, certiorari denied 83 S.Ct. 147, 371 U.S. 878, 9 L.Ed.2d 115, noted 1963, 41 Texas L.Rev. 587; Jekel v. Fireman's Fund Ins. Co., C.A.5th, 1963, 318 F.2d 321, noted 1963, 49 Cornell L.Q. 161; Insurance Co. of North American v. Keeling, C.A.5th, 1966, 360 F.2d 88, certiorari denied 87 S.Ct. 91, 385 U.S. 840, 17 L.Ed.2d 73.

20. Lawhorn v. Atlantic Ref. Co., C.A.5th 1962, 299 F.2d 353; cf. Martino v. McDonald's System, Inc., C.A.7th, 1979, 598 F.2d 1079, 1082, certiorari denied 100 S.Ct. 455, 444 U.S. 966, 62 L.Ed.2d 379; see § 79 below.

21. Jekel v. Fireman's Fund Ins. Co., C.A.5th, 1963, 318 F.2d 321.

22. Insurance Co. of North America v. Keeling, C.A.5th, 1966, 360 F.2d 88, certiorari denied 87 S.Ct. 91, 385 U.S. 840, 17 L.Ed.2d 73.

23. In 1958 Congress prohibited removal of state workmen's compensation cases. 28 U.S.C.A. § 1445(c). Prior to that time the insurers waited for the worker to bring suit, and then they removed. The new statute dictated the new procedure that the dissenters in Horton described as "an unequal race to the courthouse door—a race which the insurers will invariably win, since they have resident counsel in Austin (the location of the Texas Industrial Accident Board) who quickly secure news of Board awards and are thus enabled to 'beat' the workman in the choice of forums." 81 S.Ct. at 1578, 367 U.S. at 362–363.

In Great American Ins. Co. v. Cacciola, D.C.Tex.1963, 213 F.Supp. 303, the insurer won the race to the courthouse by a scant six minutes.

The usual position of the parties was reversed in Kay v. Home Indem. Co., C.A.5th, 1964, 337 F.2d 898. There it was held that the employee's action in federal court to collect compensation should not be heard, though the ordinary requirements of federal jurisdiction were met, since the insurer had earlier sued in state court to set aside the award of compensation. See also Bryan v. Liberty Mut. Ins. Co., C.A.5th, 1969, 415 F.2d 314, certiorari denied 90 S.Ct. 972, 397 U.S. 950, 25 L.Ed.2d 131.

24. One court has said in terms that the holding in Horton was "required by the peculiar provisions of the Compensation Act of the State of Texas" and was not intended to overturn the doctrine of earlier cases about amount in controversy. Gordon v. Daigle, D.C.La.1964, 230 F.Supp. 819, 822.

There is evidence that the lower courts generally regard Horton as being so confined. When the case has been cited it

Nor are any new principles established by the 1990 statute codifying "supplemental jurisdiction".[25] Supplemental jurisdiction is extended by that statute only to "other claims that are so related to claims in the action * * * that they form part of the same controversy under Article III of the United States Constitution." It will undoubtedly be held that the constitutional limits of the controversy include only those claims that arise out of the same transaction or occurrence as the original claim. Thus, it will still be true that compulsory counterclaims require no independent jurisdictional basis and can be heard regardless of the amount sought while a permissive counterclaim can be heard only if there is diversity and more than $50,000 is in controversy.[26]

---

either is in a Texas workmen's compensation case or it is for very familiar propositions relating to the basic principles of subject-matter jurisdiction. A possible exception is Taylor v. Taylor, D.C.Va.1972, 339 F.Supp. 899, in which, as an alternative ground for a decision that was otherwise soundly based, the court did read Horton as establishing a new and general principle.

25. 28 U.S.C.A. § 1367. See § 9 above.

26. Frumkin v. International Business Machines Corp., D.C.N.Y.1992, 801 F.Supp. 1029; Shamblin v. City of Colchester, D.C.Ill.1992, 793 F.Supp. 831. See § 79 below.

Chapter 6

REMOVAL JURISDICTION AND PROCEDURE

Analysis

§ 38.   Scope of the Removal Jurisdiction [1]

The right to remove a case from state to federal court is purely statutory, being dependent on the will of Congress.[2] It is quite an anomalous jurisdiction, giving a defendant, sued in a court of competent jurisdiction, the right to elect a forum of its own choosing. Such a procedure was unknown to the common law, nor is removal mentioned in the Constitution. Nevertheless there has been provision for removal of cases from state courts to federal courts from the First Judiciary Act, in 1789, to the present day, and the constitutionality of removal is entirely settled.[3]

The rather limited right to remove given in 1789 was expanded by a series of particular statutes. A great many such statutes were enacted in the aftermath of the Civil War, and these culminated in 1875 legislation that permitted removal, subject only to the then-required jurisdictional amount of $500, of virtually all cases within the constitu-

---

§ 38

1. 14A Wright, Miller & Cooper, Jurisdiction 2d §§ 3721–3723, 3725–3729; Rich, Current Issues in Removal Jurisdiction, 1991, 57 J.Air L. & Com. 395; Rothfeld, Rationalizing Removal, 1990 B.Y.U.L.Rev. 221.

2. Gold–Washing & Water Co. v. Keyes, 1877, 96 U.S. 199, 24 L.Ed. 656; Finn v. American Fire & Cas. Co., C.A.5th, 1953, 207 F.2d 113, certiorari denied 74 S.Ct. 476, 347 U.S. 912, 98 L.Ed. 1069; and cases cited 14A Wright, Miller & Cooper, Jurisdiction 2d § 3721 n. 2.

Removability is governed by federal law. Grubbs v. General Elec. Credit Corp., 1972, 92 S.Ct. 1344, 405 U.S. 699, 31 L.Ed.2d 612.

3. Chicago & N.W.R. Co. v. Whitton's Admr., 1871, 13 Wall. 270, 20 L.Ed. 571; Tennessee v. Davis, 1879, 100 U.S. 257, 25 L.Ed. 648; Ames v. Kansas ex rel. Johnston, 1884, 4 S.Ct. 437, 111 U.S. 449, 28 L.Ed. 482. See Martin v. Hunter's Lessee, 1816, 1 Wheat. 304, 4 L.Ed. 97.

tional judicial power.[4] This privilege was narrowed in 1887 by a statute that raised the jurisdictional amount to $2000, limited removal to defendants, and was construed as barring removal where defendant relied on federal law as the defense.[5] The present removal statute, 28 U.S.C.A. § 1441, is closely derived from the 1887 legislation.

In general, such actions as might originally have been brought in federal court may be removed thereto, though as will be subsequently seen, there are some respects in which the removal jurisdiction is broader, and some in which it is narrower, than the original jurisdiction of the federal courts. Though original jurisdiction and removal jurisdiction are thus linked, numerically the removal jurisdiction is invoked much less frequently than is the original jurisdiction.[6] Since removability is equated with original jurisdiction, the principles already developed as to existence of a federal question or diversity, and as to jurisdictional amount,[7] are equally relevant here, and need not be restated. There is a surface symmetry in setting out the same tests for removal and for original jurisdiction, but this leads to strange results in the federal-question cases. Defendant can remove a case where the plaintiff relies on federal law for its claim, though the plaintiff is perfectly willing to entrust the federal claim to a state court, but neither party can take the case to federal court if defendant relies on federal law as a defense to a nonfederal claim by plaintiff. This was the construction put on the 1887 statute by the Supreme Court many years ago, over a forceful dissent by the first Justice Harlan, and it is now so firmly entrenched that only a statutory amendment could change it.[8]

---

4. Act of March 3, 1875, c. 137, § 2, 18 Stat. 470.

5. Act of March 3, 1887, c. 373, 24 Stat. 552, corrected by Act of August 13, 1888, 25 Stat. 433. Removal is dealt with in § 2 of that Act. For the construction of the 1887 statute, see Tennessee v. Union & Planters' Bank, 1894, 14 S.Ct. 654, 152 U.S. 454, 38 L.Ed. 511.

6. In fiscal 1992, 27,022 actions were removed from state court to federal court, as against 187,720 civil actions commenced in federal court. Ann.Rep. of the Director of the Administrative Office of the U.S. Courts, 1992, Table S–4.

The reasons attorneys give for choosing to remove are surveyed in Miller, An Empirical Study of Forum Choices in Removal Cases Under Diversity and Federal Question Jurisdiction, 1992, 41 Am.U.L.Rev. 369.

7. See §§ 17–22 (federal question), 23–31 (diversity), and 32–37 (jurisdictional amount), above. Particular reference is made to § 31, which considers devices to create or defeat diversity, since the devices to defeat diversity are primarily employed by plaintiffs who wish to shape their case so that it cannot be removed to federal court.

See also 14A Wright, Miller & Cooper, Jurisdiction 2d §§ 3722, 3723, 3725.

Where defendant seeks to remove on the basis both of diversity and a federal question, the removal will stand if either ground is well taken. Great Northern Ry. Co. v. Galbreath Cattle Co., 1926, 46 S.Ct. 439, 271 U.S. 99, 70 L.Ed. 854.

There are interesting theoretical questions, much discussed in the literature, on whether the limitations on supplemental jurisdiction stated in 28 U.S.C.A. § 1367(b) apply in removed cases. See Steinman, Supplemental Jurisdiction § 1441 Removed Cases: An Unsurveyed Frontier of Congress' Handiwork, 1993, 35 Ariz.L.Rev. 305. The cases, with little or no discussion, assume—rightly it seems—that the limitations do apply. E.g., Lederman v. Marriott Corp., D.C.N.Y.1993, 834 F.Supp. 112; Mayo v. Key Fin. Servs. Inc., D.C.Mass. 1993, 812 F.Supp. 277.

8. The American Law Institute proposed an amendment that would continue to allow defendant to remove if the complaint states a federal claim but that would allow either party to remove, with certain limitations, if defendant asserts a defense or counterclaim based on federal law. ALI

The general removal statute permits removal of "any civil action brought in a State court,"[9] though as will be seen later, special statutes permit certain noncivil proceedings to be removed. Perhaps the limitation to "civil actions" means no more than that criminal actions are not, except as specially provided by statute, removable.[10] Proceedings for garnishment,[11] condemnation,[12] or to compel arbitration or confirm or vacate an arbitration award,[13] are civil actions for this purpose. There is, however, a sensible judge-made limitation that proceedings that are ancillary to an action pending in state court cannot be removed, since it would be wasteful to have the appendage in federal court when the principal claim is being litigated in state court.[14] This has application particularly to garnishment and similar proceedings. The distinction is drawn between supplemental proceedings that are a mere mode of execution or of relief, inseparably connected with the original judgment or decree, and supplemental proceedings that in fact involve an independent controversy with some new and different party.[15] It had been thought that the state law must be looked to in order to determine the nature of the proceedings, and which branch of this rule they fall under. Many cases so held, but the more recent cases show a distinct trend toward regarding this as a question to be decided by federal law, with the state characterization regarded as weighty but not conclusive.[16]

Study, § 1312(a). Rothfeld, note 1 above, at 227–232, is critical of the "curious rule" that bars removal on the basis of a federal defense, but ultimately finds it justified because of concerns about the federal caseload.

9. 28 U.S.C.A. § 1441(a). See Moore & VanDercreek, Federal Removal Jurisdiction—Civil Action Brought in a State Court, 1960, 14 Southwestern L.J. 297; 14A Wright, Miller & Cooper, Jurisdiction § 3721, pp. 200–205.

10. Rand v. Arkansas, D.C.Ark.1961, 191 F.Supp. 20. See also Quinn v. A Book Named "Sixty Erotic Drawings From Juliette," D.C.Mass.1970, 316 F.Supp. 289.

11. Stoll v. Hawkeye Cas. Co. of Des Moines, Iowa, C.A.8th, 1950, 185 F.2d 96, noted 1951, 35 Minn.L.Rev. 675; Graef v. Graef, D.C.Pa.1986, 633 F.Supp. 450.

12. Madisonville Traction Co. v. Saint Bernard Mining Co., 1905, 25 S.Ct. 251, 196 U.S. 239, 49 L.Ed. 462. Nice questions of timing arise in determining the point in a condemnation proceeding at which it becomes a civil action, rather than merely administrative. See Chicago, R.I. & P.R. Co. v. Stude, 1954, 74 S.Ct. 290, 346 U.S. 574, 98 L.Ed. 317, noted 1955, 64 Yale L.J. 600; 12 Wright & Miller, Civil § 3055.

13. Johnson v. England, C.A.9th, 1966, 356 F.2d 44, certiorari denied 86 S.Ct. 1587, 384 U.S. 961, 16 L.Ed.2d 673; Bellow v.

Utica Nat. Ins. Co., D.C.Pa.1988, 701 F.Supp. 1134.

14. See Toney v. Maryland Cas. Co., D.C.Va.1939, 29 F.Supp. 785 (per Dobie, J.); Brucker v. Georgia Cas. Co., D.C.Mo.1926, 14 F.2d 688. The following cases hold particular proceedings to be ancillary, and not removable: Barrow v. Hunton, 1878, 99 U.S. 80, 25 L.Ed. 407 (proceeding to annul a judgment on the ground of irregularities); First Nat. Bank v. Turnbull & Co., 1872, 16 Wall. 190, 21 L.Ed. 296 (petitions of claimants to property seized under execution); Lawrence v. Morgan's L. & T. Ry. & S.S. Co., 1887, 7 S.Ct. 1013, 121 U.S. 634, 30 L.Ed. 1018 (suit to enjoin the sale of land under an execution); Kerbow v. Kerbow, D.C.Tex.1976, 421 F.Supp. 1253 (proceeding involving federal pension plan ancillary to a state divorce action); Buford & Co. v. Strother & Conklin, C.C.D.Iowa, 1881, 10 F. 406 (garnishment after judgment).

15. The rule was so stated by Judge Love in Buford & Co. v. Strother & Conklin, C.C.D.Iowa, 1881, 10 F. 406, 407–408, and since has been much quoted.

16. The following cases allow or refuse removal of garnishment proceedings depending on whether the state law views such proceedings as ancillary or independent: American Auto. Ins. Co. v. Freundt, C.C.A.7th, 1939, 103 F.2d 613 (refused— Illinois law); London & Lancashire Indem. Co. v. Courtney, C.C.A.10th, 1939, 106 F.2d

To be removable, the civil action must be pending in a state "court." This depends on the procedures and functions of the state tribunal rather than the name it is given.[17] A justice-of-the-peace court, or a county board or court that is vested with judicial power, will suffice.[18] An appeal to the courts of a state from an administrative agency may be in the form of a civil action and thus removable.[19]

It was frequently said that jurisdiction on removal is derivative, and that if the state court had no jurisdiction, the federal court acquires none and cannot even remand, but must dismiss for want of jurisdiction.[20] This doctrine may have been justifiable conceptually, but the results to which it led were often absurd. Thus, a suit is brought in state court and removed to federal court. If it is determined that the case was one over which the federal courts have exclusive jurisdiction, the federal court, remarkably enough, could not hear the case. It was required to dismiss a case falling within its exclusive jurisdiction because the court from which the case was removed had no jurisdiction.[21] Fortunately a 1986 statute has put an end to this strange rule. It provides that the court to which a civil action is removed "is not precluded from hearing and determining any claim in such civil action because the State court

277 (allowed—Oklahoma law); Western Medical Properties v. Denver Opportunity, Inc., D.C.Colo.1980, 482 F.Supp. 1205 (refused—Colorado law); Toney v. Maryland Cas. Co., D.C.Va.1939, 29 F.Supp. 785 (refused—Virginia law); Joski v. Short, D.C.Wash.1939, 28 F.Supp. 821 (refused—Washington law); Brucker v. Georgia Cas. Co., D.C.Mo.1926, 14 F.2d 688 (refused—Missouri law); Baker v. Duwamish Mill Co., C.C.D.Wash.1906, 149 F. 612 (allowed—Washington law).

It is held, however, in Stoll v. Hawkeye Cas. Co., C.A.8th, 1950, 185 F.2d 96, criticized 1951, 35 Minn.L.Rev. 675, in Randolph v. Employers Mut. Liab. Ins. Co., C.A.8th, 1958, 260 F.2d 461, in Swanson v. Liberty Nat. Ins. Co., C.A.9th, 1965, 353 F.2d 12, and in Butler v. Polk, C.A.5th, 1979, 592 F.2d 1293, that garnishment is a "civil action" and is removable regardless of how it is characterized under state law. State law is similarly rejected in Reed v. Bloom, D.C.Okl.1936, 15 F.Supp. 7, in Clarise Sportswear Co. v. U & W Mfg. Co., D.C.Pa.1963, 223 F.Supp. 961, and in Graef v. Graef, D.C.Pa.1986, 633 F.Supp. 450. See Note, 1954, 7 Okla.L.Rev. 446.

17. Tool & Die Makers Lodge No. 78 v. General Electric Co., D.C.Wis.1959, 170 F.Supp. 945, 950; Corwin Jeep Sales & Service, Inc. v. American Motors Sales Corp., D.C.Pa.1986, 670 F.Supp. 591.

18. Katz v. Herschel Mfg. Co., C.C.D.Neb.1906, 150 F. 684 (justice of the peace court); Cappetta v. Atlantic Ref. Co., D.C.Conn.1935, 12 F.Supp. 89 (the same); Drainage Dist. No. 19, Caldwell County, Mo. v. Chicago, M. & St. P. Ry. Co., D.C.Mo.1912, 198 F. 253.

A county board without judicial powers is not a court within the removal statute. Fuller v. Colfax County, C.C.D.Neb.1882, 14 F. 177, Gurnee v. Brunswick, C.C.D.Va. 1876, Fed.Cas. 117, No. 5,872.

19. Mississippi & Rum River Boom Co. v. Patterson, 1878, 98 U.S. 403, 25 L.Ed. 206; Floeter v. C.W. Transport, Inc., C.A.7th, 1979, 597 F.2d 1100; and cases cited 14A Wright, Miller & Cooper, Jurisdiction 2d § 3721 n. 65. In such a case the matter may be sufficiently local that the federal court will abstain and leave the parties to their state court remedies. See § 52 below.

20. Lambert Run Coal Co. v. Baltimore & O.R. Co., 1922, 42 S.Ct. 349, 258 U.S. 377, 66 L.Ed. 671; Venner v. Michigan Central R. Co., 1926, 46 S.Ct. 444, 271 U.S. 127, 70 L.Ed. 868; and cases cited 14A Wright, Miller & Cooper, Jurisdiction 2d § 3721 n. 38.

21. General Inv. Co. v. Lake Shore & M.S. Ry. Co., 1922, 43 S.Ct. 106, 260 U.S. 261, 67 L.Ed. 244 (antitrust action); Martinez v. Seaton, C.A.10th, 1961, 285 F.2d 587, certiorari denied 81 S.Ct. 1677, 366 U.S. 946, 6 L.Ed.2d 856 (Tort Claims Act case); and cases cited 14A Wright, Miller & Cooper, Jurisdiction 2d § 3722 n. 66.

from which such civil action is removed did not have jurisdiction over that claim." [22]

It was said at the outset that removal jurisdiction is generally equated with original jurisdiction, but that there are some variations. Thus, in addition to the general removal statute, there are certain other statutes authorizing removal, as where a federal officer is sued or prosecuted in a state court for acts done under color of office [23] or a federal employee is sued for injury caused by a tort the employee is alleged to have committed within the scope of his employment.[24] A foreign state can remove any civil action brought against it in a state court.[25] There are other statutes of less general importance.[26] Either a civil action or a criminal prosecution may be removed by a defendant who cannot secure in state court civil rights guaranteed to him by the Constitution of the United States,[27] but it has been held that this allows removal only in "the rare situations where it can be clearly predicted by reason of the operation of a pervasive and explicit state or federal law that those rights will inevitably be denied by the very act of bringing the defendant to trial in the state court." [28] The fact that removal is

22. 28 U.S.C.A. § 1441(e), added by Act of June 19, 1986, Pub.L. 99–336, § 3(a), 100 Stat. 637. See Brizendine v. Continental Cas. Co., D.C.Ala.1991, 773 F.Supp. 313, 319–320; Foss v. U.S., D.C.N.M.1989, 705 F.Supp. 537, 538. This had been proposed in ALI Study, § 1312(d).

23. 28 U.S.C.A. § 1442; Tennessee v. Davis, 1880, 100 U.S. 257, 25 L.Ed. 648; Willingham v. Morgan, 1969, 89 S.Ct. 1813, 395 U.S. 402, 23 L.Ed.2d 396; and 14A Wright, Miller & Cooper, Jurisdiction 2d § 3727. Section 1442(a)(1) allows removal by "[a]ny officer of the United States or any agency thereof". This allows removal by a federal officer, or an officer of a federal agency, but does not permit a federal agency itself to remove. International Primate Protection League v. Administrators of Tulane Educational Fund, 1991, 111 S.Ct. 1700, 500 U.S. 72, 114 L.Ed.2d 134. This is taken further in a case that holds that a suit against the executive of an agency, solely in her official capacity, is a suit against the agency, not the officer, so that removal is barred. American Policyholders Ins. Co. v. Nyacol Products, Inc., C.A.1st, 1993, 989 F.2d 1256, 1258–1261, certiorari denied 114 S.Ct. 682, ___ U.S. ___, 126 L.Ed.2d 650.

Removal by a federal officer must be predicated on the allegation of a colorable federal defense. Mesa v. California, 1989, 109 S.Ct. 959, 489 U.S. 121, 103 L.Ed.2d 99.

24. 28 U.S.C.A. § 2679(d). See cases cited 14A Wright, Miller & Cooper, Jurisdiction 2d § 3727 n. 15. As originally adopted the statute only applied to injuries caused by the employee's operation of a motor vehicle. It was broadened to cover all torts in 1988.

25. 28 U.S.C.A. § 1441(d), added in 1976. The definition of "foreign state" includes agencies and instrumentalities. 28 U.S.C.A. § 1603(a). The statute generally parallels the grant of original jurisdiction added at the same time as 28 U.S.C.A. § 1330(a).

26. 14A Wright, Miller & Cooper, Jurisdiction 2d § 3729.

27. 28 U.S.C.A. § 1443.

28. City of Greenwood, Miss. v. Peacock, 1966, 86 S.Ct. 1800, 1812, 384 U.S. 808, 828, 16 L.Ed.2d 944. See also Johnson v. Mississippi, 1975, 95 S.Ct. 1591, 421 U.S. 213, 44 L.Ed.2d 121. See 14A Wright, Miller & Cooper, Jurisdiction 2d § 3728; Redish, Revitalizing Civil Rights Removal Jurisdiction, 1980, 64 Minn.L.Rev. 523.

Only a few cases are held to have met this exacting standard. Georgia v. Rachel, 1966, 86 S.Ct. 1783, 384 U.S. 780, 16 L.Ed.2d 925; cf. Sofarelli v. Pinellas County, C.A.11th, 1991, 931 F.2d 718; Achtenberg v. Mississippi, C.A.5th, 1968, 393 F.2d 468; Wyche v. Louisiana, C.A.5th, 1967, 394 F.2d 927; Whatley v. City of Vidalia, C.A.5th, 1968, 399 F.2d 521. White v. Wellington, C.A.2d, 1980, 627 F.2d 582, is one of the very few cases in which removal has been allowed under the second branch of 28 U.S.C.A. § 1443(2).

See ALI Study, §§ 1312(c), 1372(7), and Commentary thereto.

authorized by special statutes of this kind does not of itself permit these actions to be commenced in federal court.[29]

Removal jurisdiction is sometimes narrower than original jurisdiction, in part because of statutes expressly providing that particular actions, principally tort actions in which Congress wishes to give the plaintiff an absolute choice of forum, are not removable.[30] The cases are about equally divided on whether the provision in the Fair Labor Standards Act[31] permitting suit to be "maintained" in any court of competent jurisdiction bars removal of such suits.[32] Maritime actions in state court under the "saving to suitors" clause of 28 U.S.C.A. § 1333 are not removable,[33] but it has long been established that there can be removal if there is an independent basis for federal jurisdiction such as diversity of citizenship and the requisite amount in controversy.[34]

An extremely important limitation on removal is that diversity cases are removable only if none of the parties in interest properly joined and served as defendants is a citizen of the state in which the action is brought.[35] If jurisdiction is based on a federal question, there is no such

29. Martin v. Wyzanski, D.C.Mass.1967, 262 F.Supp. 925; Keppleman v. Upston, D.C.Cal.1949, 84 F.Supp. 478. See also Williams v. Brooks, C.A.5th, 1991, 945 F.2d 1322, 1324 n. 2.

30. 28 U.S.C.A. §§ 1445(a) (Federal Employers' Liability Act and Jones Act cases), 1445(b) (actions against carriers for delay, loss, or damage in shipments, where the matter in controversy is $10,000 or less), 1445(c) (workmen's compensation proceedings). It has been held also that actions under the Securities Act, 15 U.S.C.A. § 77v(a), to recover for misrepresentation are not removable. Wilko v. Swan, 1953, 74 S.Ct. 182, 346 U.S. 427, 98 L.Ed. 168. See generally 14A Wright, Miller & Cooper, Jurisdiction 2d § 3729, and ALI Study, § 1312(b).

31. 29 U.S.C.A. § 216.

32. See ALI Study, § 1312(b)(1), and Commentary thereto. The cases each way are collected in 14A Wright, Miller & Cooper, Jurisdiction 2d § 3729 nn. 56, 57.

33. E.g., Benjamin v.Natural Gas Pipeline Co.of America, D.C.Tex.1992, 793 F.Supp. 729; Coley v. Dragon, Ltd., D.C.Va. 1990, 138 F.R.D. 460. These cases derive support from a dictum in Romero v. International Terminal Operating Co., 1959, 79 S.Ct. 468, 480, 358 U.S. 354, 371–372, 3 L.Ed.2d 368. See Sharpe, Removal to Admiralty Revisited, 1991, 22 J.Mar.L. & Com. 485.

34. E.g., In re Dutile, C.A.5th, 1991, 935 F.2d 61; Poirrier v. Nicklos Drilling Co., C.A.5th, 1981, 648 F.2d 1063; Safir v. Compagnie Generale Transatlantique, D.C.N.Y.

1965, 241 F.Supp. 501. See also ALI Study, pp. 239–243; Currie, The Silver Oar and All That: A Study of the Romero Case, 1959, 27 U.Chi.L.Rev. 1, 16 n. 57; 14 Wright, Miller & Cooper, Jurisdiction 2d § 3674.

Even in the absence of diversity, a case properly brought in state court under the saving-to-suitors clause may be removed if plaintiff fails to make a timely objection. Baris v. Sulpicio Lines, Inc., C.A.5th, 1991, 932 F.2d 1540, certiorari denied 112 S.Ct. 430, ___ U.S. ___, 116 L.Ed.2d 449.

35. 28 U.S.C.A. § 1441(b); Martin v. Snyder, 1893, 13 S.Ct. 706, 148 U.S. 663, 37 L.Ed. 602; and cases cited 14A Wright, Miller & Cooper, Jurisdiction 2d § 3723 n. 10.

A 1990 statute provides that for purposes of, among others, § 1441, "an alien admitted to the United States for permanent residence shall be deemed a citizen of the State in which such alien is domiciled."

It is held, however, that this limitation is not "jurisdictional" and that if plaintiff makes no timely motion to remand after removal by a resident defendant in a diversity case, the objection that the case is not removable is waived. In re Shell Oil Co., C.A.5th, 1991, 932 F.2d 1518; Handley–Mack Co. v. Godchaux Sugar Co., C.C.A.6th, 1924, 2 F.2d 435; Ravens Metal Products, Inc. v. Wilson, D.C.W.Va.1993, 816 F.Supp. 427. See § 41 n. 5 below.

The American Law Institute would permit removal in a diversity case by any defendant who could have removed if sued alone, even though other defendants are joined whose presence, under existing law, limitation, and even a resident defendant may remove.[36] Thus, if a citizen of Utah sues a citizen of Texas in the state court in Texas, defendant cannot remove, if diversity is the only basis for federal jurisdiction. The defendant could remove if suit were brought in any other state. It will be noted in this instance that the plaintiff could have brought the case in federal court, in Texas or in Utah, originally. It is reasonable to deny a resident defendant access to the federal courts by removal, but the same logic would seem to preclude a resident plaintiff from invoking the original jurisdiction of the federal court.[37]

Generally the right of removal is decided by the pleadings, viewed as of the time when the petition for removal is filed.[38] A case not removable when commenced may later become removable under some circumstances, as where the plaintiff has amended its pleadings to change the nature of the claim or has dropped a party whose presence prevented diversity.[39] The plaintiff cannot, however, take action to defeat federal jurisdiction and force remand after the case has been properly removed.[40]

Plaintiff is master of the claim, and if he or she chooses not to assert a federal claim, though one is available, defendant cannot remove on the basis of a federal question.[41] Doubt was cast on this long-established rule, however, by Federated Department Stores, Inc. v. Moitie, in which the Supreme Court, following the lead of a few lower courts, endorsed what it called the "settled principle" that plaintiff cannot use "artful pleading" to avoid removal jurisdiction.[42] This is an area in which the distinctions are extremely subtle, "some courts have not strictly observed the restrictions on removal jurisdiction," [43] and it is likely that the last word has not yet been written.

would prevent removal. ALI Study, § 1304(b).

36. Crawford v. East Asiatic Co., D.C.Cal.1957, 156 F.Supp. 571. See 14A Wright, Miller & Cooper, Jurisdiction 2d § 3722, p. 231.

37. See ALI Study, § 1302(a), and Commentary thereto.

38. American Fire & Cas. Co. v. Finn, 1951, 71 S.Ct. 534, 341 U.S. 6, 95 L.Ed. 702, 19 A.L.R.2d 738; and cases cited 14A Wright, Miller & Cooper, Jurisdiction 2d § 3721 nn. 70–71, § 3723 nn. 11–14, § 3725 n. 8.

The application of this rule to installment payment cases is discussed in § 33 n. 44 above.

39. Great Northern Ry. Co. v. Alexander, 1918, 38 S.Ct. 237, 246 U.S. 276, 62 L.Ed. 713; and cases cited 14A Wright, Miller & Cooper, Jurisdiction 2d § 3721 n. 78, § 3722 nn. 61–63, § 3723 nn. 23–25, § 3725 nn. 47–48.

40. St. Paul Mercury Indem. Co. v. Red Cab Co., 1938, 58 S.Ct. 586, 303 U.S. 283, 82 L.Ed. 845; Hammond v. Terminal R.R.

Assn. of St. Louis, C.A.7th, 1988, 848 F.2d 95, certiorari denied 109 S.Ct. 1170, 489 U.S. 1032, 103 L.Ed.2d 229; and cases cited 14A Wright, Miller & Cooper, Jurisdiction 2d § 3721 n. 80.

41. Caterpillar Inc. v. Williams, 1987, 107 S.Ct. 2425, 2429, 482 U.S. 386, 392, 96 L.Ed.2d 318; Great Northern Ry. Co. v. Alexander, 1918, 38 S.Ct. 237, 239, 246 U.S. 276, 282, 62 L.Ed. 713; and 14A Wright, Miller & Cooper, Jurisdiction 2d § 3722, pp. 266–276.

42. 1981, 101 S.Ct. 2424, 2427 n. 2, 452 U.S. 394, 397 n. 2, 69 L.Ed.2d 103. This is a single footnote on jurisdiction in a case otherwise entirely devoted to the effect of a former judgment. See § 100A below.

The entire artful-pleading doctrine is criticized as "an extreme departure from well-considered law" in Ragazzo, Reconsidering the Artful Pleading Doctrine, 1993, 44 Hastings L.J. 273, 335.

43. 101 S.Ct. at 2433 n. 6, 452 U.S. at 410 n. 6 (Brennan, J., dissenting). Justice Brennan cited as an example In re Carter, C.A.5th, 1980, 618 F.2d 1093, 1101, certio-

The rule that plaintiff is master of the claim works well enough if it is clear that remedies are available under both state and federal law for a particular course of conduct. If plaintiff chooses to pursue only the state remedy, that is its privilege and the case will not be removable as a federal-question case.[44] Often, however, it is contended that the state remedies have been preempted by federal law. The difficulty here is that "preemption" is used in the law in more than one sense. In many instances preexisting state rights of action are cut off by federal law. In these situations preemption is a defense to the state claim, and the rule that jurisdiction must be based on the complaint rather than on defenses[45] is enough to defeat removal.[46] There are other situations, however, of which § 301 of the Taft–Hartley Act[47] is the most conspicuous, in which it is held that federal law has taken over an entire subject matter and made it inherently federal. An action can be brought in state court to enforce rights arising under a collective-bargaining agreement in an industry affecting interstate commerce, but state courts are obliged to follow the decisional law developed by federal courts. Federal law in these labor cases is not merely a defense to a state contract theory, but is the basis of all rights of action under the contract. If state law has been preempted in this sense, so that a state right of action has been replaced by a federal right of action, plaintiff necessarily is stating a federal claim whether he wishes to do so or not, and the case is removable.[48] For 20 years § 301 of Taft–Hartley was the only statute held to have such force, but in Metropolitan Life Insurance Co. v. Taylor[49] a unanimous Court found that the § 502(a)(1)(B)of ERISA[50] has the same "extraordinary" preemptive power as does § 301 so that state-court actions brought under § 502(a)(1)(B) can also be removed.[51]

The preemption cases are difficult enough, but a few cases, including notably the Supreme Court's decision in Moitie, seem to carry the

rari denied 1981, 101 S.Ct. 1410, 450 U.S. 949, 67 L.Ed.2d 378.

44. Pan Am. Petroleum Corp. v. Superior Court, 1961, 81 S.Ct. 1303, 1307, 366 U.S. 656, 662–663, 6 L.Ed.2d 584; Aaron v. National Union Fire Ins. Co. of Pittsburgh, C.A.5th, 1989, 876 F.2d 1157.

45. See § 18 above.

46. Metropolitan Life Ins. Co. v. Taylor, 1987, 107 S.Ct. 1542, 1546, 481 U.S. 58, 63, 95 L.Ed.2d 55.

47. 29 U.S.C.A. § 185. See § 20 above.

48. Avco Corp. v. Aero Lodge No. 735, 1968, 88 S.Ct. 1235, 390 U.S. 557, 20 L.Ed.2d 126.

But see Ragazzo, note 42 above, at 286: "Avco contradicts the well-pleaded complaint and master-of-the-complain rules. Either the Avco decision is misguided or these rules must be abandoned in whole or in part."

49. 1987, 107 S.Ct. 1542, 481 U.S. 58, 95 L.Ed.2d 55.

50. 29 U.S.C.A. § 1132(a)(1)(B). The cited statute is the civil-enforcement provision of ERISA, the popular acronym for the Employee Retirement Income Security Act of 1974.

51. 107 S.Ct. at 1547–1548, 481 U.S. at 64–66. The Court found that the language of the jurisdictional subsection of ERISA's civil-enforcement provisions closely parallels that of § 301 of Taft–Hartley and there were express statements in the legislative history that Congress intended to make these ERISA actions federal-question cases just as are suit under § 301.

"Sometimes, however, federal law so fills every nook and cranny that it is not possible to frame a complaint under state law. An effort to invoke nonexistent state law is no different from a spelling error. * * * Congress has blotted out (almost) all state law on the subject of pensions, so a complaint about pensions rests on federal law no matter what label its author attaches." Bartholet v. Reishauer A.G. (Zürich), C.A.7th, 1992, 953 F.2d 1073, 1075.

"artful pleading" concept even farther. In Moitie the plaintiffs had earlier brought federal antitrust actions, which had been dismissed. They then brought actions in state court in which the allegations were quite similar to those in the earlier case but purported to raise only state-law claims. It was in this context that the Court said that plaintiffs "had attempted to avoid removal jurisdiction by 'artfully' casting their 'essentially federal law claims' as state-law claims." [52] It has never been held that the federal antitrust laws preempt state law. One possible explanation of Moitie is that the "artful pleading" doctrine applies if plaintiff, by his or her own conduct, either by filing originally in federal court and then bringing a second action in state court or by acceding to federal jurisdiction after removal has made the claim a federal one. [53] The lower courts cannot say that there is no "artful pleading" doctrine when the Supreme Court has said that there is, but they are having considerable difficulty trying to define the doctrine. [54]

Despite the usual rule that removability is determined as of the time when the petition for removal is filed, there is a long line of authority that diversity of citizenship, where it is the basis of jurisdiction, must exist at the time of filing the original action as well as at the time of petitioning for removal. [55] The purpose of this limitation is to prevent the defendant from acquiring a new domicile after commencement of the suit and then removing on the basis of diversity. The reason for the limitation is inapplicable where the case has been dropped as to a nondiverse party after its original commencement, since this is action over which defendant has no control, and where such a nondiverse party is formally dropped on the record, the case then becomes removable. [56] Prior to 1949 it was settled that the case did not become removable where the nondiverse party had been eliminated from the case by a directed verdict, [57] a distinction being drawn between subsequent action by a court, which did not make a case removable, and voluntary action by the plaintiff, which did. The distinction had merit, in that it prevented removal where the nondiverse party was eliminated by a court order that might be subject to reversal on appeal. It was not clear, however, that the distinction had survived a 1949 amendment of the

---

52. 101 S.Ct. at 2427 n. 2, 452 U.S. at 397 n. 2.

53. Salveson v. Western States Bankcard Assn., C.A.9th, 1984, 731 F.2d 1423, 1429. Another explanation of the doctrine is that a plaintiff may not artfully omit facts that indicate federal jurisdiction. Burda v. M. Ecker Co., C.A.7th, 1992, 954 F.2d 434, 438 n. 3.

54. E.g., Ultramar America Ltd. v. Dwelle, C.A.9th, 1990, 900 F.2d 1412; Her Majesty the Queen in Right of the Province of Ontario v. City of Detroit, C.A.6th, 1989, 874 F.2d 332, 338–341; United Jersey Banks v. Parell, C.A.3d, 1986, 783 F.2d 360, certiorari denied 106 S.Ct. 2892, 476 U.S. 1170, 90 L.Ed.2d 979.

55. Gibson v. Bruce, 1883, 2 S.Ct. 873, 108 U.S. 561, 27 L.Ed. 825; and cases cited 14A Wright, Miller & Cooper, Jurisdiction 2d § 3723 n. 14.

56. Powers v. Chesapeake & O. Ry. Co., 1898, 18 S.Ct. 264, 169 U.S. 92, 42 L.Ed. 673; Yulee v. Vose, 1878, 99 U.S. 539, 25 L.Ed. 355; and cases cited 14A Wright, Miller & Cooper, Jurisdiction 2d § 3723 n. 15.

57. Whitcomb v. Smithson, 1900, 20 S.Ct. 248, 175 U.S. 635, 44 L.Ed. 303; Great Northern Ry. Co. v. Alexander, 1918, 38 S.Ct. 237, 246 U.S. 276, 62 L.Ed. 713; and cases cited 14A Wright, Miller & Cooper, Jurisdiction 2d § 3723 nn. 16–18.

Judicial Code, which permits removal, if the case was not at first removable, upon "receipt by the defendant, through service or otherwise, of a copy of an amended pleading, motion, order or other paper from which it may first be ascertained that the case is one which is or has become removable." [58] Read literally this would seem to allow removal when the resident defendant was eliminated by court order, and some cases so held.[59] Most cases, however, have held that the old distinction survives.[60]

The right of removal may be lost or waived, but the courts are slow to find such a waiver, even where the defendant had taken action in state court prior to seeking removal.[61] An old case seemed to say that a contract stipulating that the parties would not remove cases to federal court would be invalid,[62] but the modern view is that such a contract is a valid waiver of the right to remove unless the contract is unreasonable or procured by duress.[63] After some vacillation it was finally held by the

---

58. 28 U.S.C.A. § 1446(b). The statute was amended in 1988, and now makes the additional provision that a case may not be removed on the basis of diversity more than one year after commencement of the action. See § 40 below.

59. Lyon v. Illinois Central R. Co., D.C.Miss.1964, 228 F.Supp. 810; cf. Bradley v. Halliburton Oil Well Cementing Co., D.C.Okl.1951, 100 F.Supp. 913. See Comment, Federal Practice: Removal After Resident Defendant is Involuntarily Dismissed, 1964, 17 Okla.L.Rev. 336.

60. Poulos v. Naas Foods, Inc., C.A.7th, 1992, 959 F.2d 69, 71–72; Weems v. Louis Dreyfus Corp., C.A.5th, 1967, 380 F.2d 545; Todd Holding Co. v. Super Valu Stores, Inc., D.C.Colo.1990, 744 F.Supp. 1025; Hearst Corp. v. Shopping Center Network, Inc., D.C.N.Y.1969, 307 F.Supp. 551; and cases cited 14A Wright, Miller & Cooper, Jurisdiction 2d § 3723 n. 20.

In Comment, The Effect of Section 1446(b) on the Nonresident's Right to Remove, 1966, 115 U.Pa.L.Rev. 264, the view that the 1949 amendment changed the law is rejected, but it is argued that the voluntary-involuntary rule should be applied more flexibly and with an eye to considerations of judicial administration. In Jenkins v. National Union Fire Ins. Co. of Pa., D.C.Ga.1986, 650 F.Supp. 609, the court held that the distinction survives, but says that it is not based on the appealability-finality rationale. Instead, the court says, it is based upon the plaintiff's power to determine the removability of her case. See also Insinga v. LaBella, C.A.11th, 1988, 845 F.2d 249.

61. The following conduct has been held not to waive the right to remove: appearance in state court to contest a temporary restraining order and request for appellate review, Rose v. Giamatti, D.C.Ohio 1989, 721 F.Supp. 906; serving interrogatories and filing an answer in state court, Estevez–Gonzalez v. Kraft, Inc., D.C.Fla.1985, 606 F.Supp. 127; filing responsive pleadings, Baldwin v. Perdue, Inc., D.C.Va.1978, 451 F.Supp. 373; requesting an extension of time to answer, Malave v. Sun Life Assur. Co. of Canada, D.C.Puerto Rico 1975, 392 F.Supp. 51; and cases cited 14A Wright, Miller & Cooper, Jurisdiction 2d § 3721 nn. 104, 108.

Voluntary filing of a cross-action in state court has been held to waive the right of removal. Briggs v. Miami Window Corp., D.C.Ga.1956, 158 F.Supp. 229. So too has requesting an injunction and summary judgment, Zbranek v. Hofheinz, D.C.Tex. 1989, 727 F.Supp. 324, or filing a third-party complaint, Knudsen v. Samuels, D.C.Kan.1989, 715 F.Supp. 1505.

A recent case holds that a motion to dismiss in state court waives the right to remove, Scholz v. RDV Sports, Inc., D.C.Fla.1993, 821 F.Supp. 1469, but the opposite result was reached in Bedell v. H.R.C. Ltd., D.C.Ky.1981, 522 F.Supp. 732, 738.

62. Home Ins. Co. of New York v. Morse, 1874, 20 Wall. 445, 22 L.Ed. 365.

63. Foster v. Chesapeake Ins. Co., C.A.3d, 1991, 933 F.2d 1207, certiorari denied 112 S.Ct. 302, ___ U.S. ___, 116 L.Ed.2d 245; Wm. H. Muller & Co., Inc. v. Swedish American Line, Ltd., C.A.2d, 1955, 224 F.2d 806, 808, certiorari denied 76 S.Ct. 182, 350 U.S. 903, 100 L.Ed. 793; Perini Corp. v. Orion Ins. Co., D.C.Cal., 1971, 331 F.Supp. 453, 456.

Supreme Court that a state may not restrict or limit the right to remove, even as a condition to doing business within its borders, and may not penalize a foreign corporation for exercising its removal right.[64]

It is said that the trend of the decisions is to restrict and limit the removal jurisdiction of the federal courts. Certainly there is ample case support for the proposition that removal statutes will be strictly construed.[65]

§ 39. Separate and Independent Claim or Cause of Action[1]

Section 1441(c) is the product of a long and interesting history. The present statute, however, is useless and ought to have been repealed.

From 1789 to 1866 cases could be removed to federal court only where all of the defendants were citizens of states other than the states of which any plaintiff was a citizen. In other words, complete diversity was required, and all cases that were removable could have been brought originally in federal court. The Separable Controversy Act of 1866[2] introduced into the law the notion that where, within the lawsuit, there was "a separable controversy between citizens of different states," this much of the suit could be removed, leaving the balance of the suit, in which citizens of the same state were on opposite sides, in the state court. The statutory language was changed in 1875,[3] and the Court construed the changed language as meaning that where there was a separable controversy, the entire suit was to be removed.[4] The statutory provisions continued in this form substantially unchanged until 1948.

There developed from these statutes a very complex body of law.[5] Kane, a citizen of California, brings suit in a California state court against Meyers, also a citizen of California, and Green, a citizen of Texas. Green wishes to remove. It was necessary, under the pre–1948 law, to decide whether the controversy between Kane and Green was

---

64. Terral v. Burke Constr. Co., 1922, 42 S.Ct. 188, 257 U.S. 529, 66 L.Ed. 352. This result had been indicated by the 1873 decision in the Home Ins. Co. case, note 56 above, but there was an unfortunate decision to the contrary in Security Mut. Life Ins. Co. v. Prewitt, 1906, 26 S.Ct. 619, 202 U.S. 246, 50 L.Ed. 1013, finally overruled in the Terral case.

65. Graves v. Corbin, 1890, 10 S.Ct. 196, 132 U.S. 571, 33 L.Ed. 462; Willy v. Coastal Corp., C.A.5th, 1988, 855 F.2d 1160, 1164; Rezendes v. Dow Corning Corp., D.C.Cal.1989, 717 F.Supp. 1435, 1437; and cases cited 14A Wright, Miller & Cooper, Jurisdiction 2d § 3721 nn. 85–92.

§ 39

1. 14A Wright, Miller & Cooper, Jurisdiction 2d § 3724; Lewin, The Federal Courts' Hospitable Back Door—Removal of "Separate and Independent" Non–Federal Causes of Action, 1953, 66 Harv.L.Rev. 423; Moore & VanDercreek, Multi-party, Multi-claim Removal Problems: The Separate and Independent Claim Under Section 1441(c), 1961, 46 Iowa L.Rev. 489; Cohen, Problems in the Removal of a "Separate and Independent Claim or Cause of Action", 1961, 46 Minn.L.Rev. 1.

2. Act of July 27, 1866, 14 Stat. 306.

3. Act of March 3, 1875, 18 Stat. 470.

4. Barney v. Latham, 1880, 103 U.S. 205, 26 L.Ed. 514.

5. See Texas Employers Ins. Assn. v. Felt, C.C.A.5th, 1945, 150 F.2d 227; Holmes, The Separable Controversy—A Federal Removal Concept, 1939, 12 Miss. L.J. 163; Keeffe & Lacey, The Separable Controversy—A Federal Concept, 1947, 33 Corn.L.Q. 261.

separate, or separable, or nonseparable from the controversy between Kane and Meyers. If, for example, Kane was claiming that Green and Meyers were jointly liable to her, the controversies were deemed non-separable and the case could not be removed.[6] If the claim against Green was entirely separate from the claim against Meyers, as in condemnation actions, Green was permitted to remove the claim against him to federal court while the claim against Meyers stayed in state court.[7] Finally, if the claims were not separate but merely separable, as where Kane claimed that either Green or Meyers was liable to her, but she did not know which, Green could remove the entire case to federal court.[8] The distinctions thus suggested were surely confusing, but were not quite as irrational as they may appear. The notion behind the separable-controversy doctrine was that if the claim against Green was capable of being wholly determined between Kane and Green, then, since diversity existed between those two, Green should be able to resort to federal court; at the same time the claim against Green was not entirely separate from the claim against Meyers, and thus the whole suit should come to federal court to avoid duplicate litigation.

A substantial change was made in this scheme in the 1948 Judicial Code. Section 1441(c) of the Code provided: "Whenever a separate and independent claim or cause of action, which would be removable if sued upon alone, is joined with one or more otherwise non-removable claims or causes of action, the entire case may be removed and the district court may determine all issues therein, or, in its discretion, may remand all matters not otherwise within its original jurisdiction."

As will be seen, the statute was substantially narrowed by amendment in 1990. It is necessary to consider the statute as it stood from 1948 to 1990 before examining the most recent version.

The stated purpose of the change in language embodied in § 1441(c), as adopted in 1948, was simplification and advancement in the interests of justice.[9] This purpose was not achieved. One judge, after reviewing the decisions, declared "it is not an exaggeration to say that at least on the surface the field luxuriates in a riotous uncertainty."[10] The 1948 statute as construed led to at least as much confusion as did the statute it replaced, and it has created additional problems of constitutionality.

The leading case on § 1441(c) is American Fire & Casualty Co. v. Finn.[11] In that case the Supreme Court discerned in the 1948 revision a further purpose, that of reducing the number of cases removable from

---

6. E.g., Pullman Co. v. Jenkins, 1939, 59 S.Ct. 347, 305 U.S. 534, 83 L.Ed. 334.

7. E.g., Pacific R. Removal Cases, 1885, 5 S.Ct. 1113, 115 U.S. 1, 29 L.Ed. 319; Alabama Power Co. v. Gregory Hill Gold Mining Co., D.C.Ala.1925, 5 F.2d 705.

8. E.g., Texas Employers Ins. Assn. v. Felt, C.C.A.5th, 1945, 150 F.2d 227. A leading case, finding a separable controver-sy, is Barney v. Latham, 1880, 103 U.S. 205, 26 L.Ed. 514.

9. H.Rep. No. 308, Apr. 25, 1947, 80th Cong., 1st Sess., p. A. 134.

10. Harper v. Sonnabend, D.C.N.Y. 1960, 182 F.Supp. 594, 595.

11. 1951, 71 S.Ct. 534, 341 U.S. 6, 95 L.Ed. 702.

state courts.[12] This purpose has been achieved. Only a small number of cases have been removed under § 1441(c) since the Supreme Court construed it in the Finn case, and a strong argument can be made that in permitting removal in those cases the district courts applied the statute erroneously, or that the removal was unconstitutional.

The Finn case was a suit by a Texas citizen against two foreign insurance companies and their local agent, also a Texas citizen, claiming in the alternative recovery for fire loss on one or the other of the policies, or that Reiss, the agent, was liable for having failed to keep the property insured. The insurers removed to federal court, relying on § 1441(c). After trial to a jury, judgment was entered for the amount of the loss against one of the insurance companies, while judgment was entered for the other company and the agent. The company against which judgment had been entered then sought to have judgment vacated on the ground that the action had been improperly removed, and that the federal court was without jurisdiction. This contention was upheld in the Supreme Court.[13]

In construing the statute, the Court was forced to plunge into the murky waters of what is a cause of action. After examining some language in its own decisions, and citing with approval Judge Clark's famous discussion of the subject,[14] the Court concluded that "where there is a single wrong to plaintiff, for which relief is sought, arising from an interlocked series of transactions, there is no separate and independent claim or cause of action under § 1441(c)."[15]

Applying that test to the facts before it, the Court found removal improper. "The single wrong for which relief is sought is the failure to pay compensation for the loss on the property. Liability lay among three parties, but it was uncertain which one was responsible. * * * The facts in each portion of the complaint involve Reiss, the damage comes from a single incident. The allegations in which Reiss is a defendant involve substantially the same facts and transactions as do the allegations in the first portion of the complaint against the foreign insurance companies. It cannot be said that there are separate and independent claims for relief as § 1441(c) requires."[16]

12. 71 S.Ct. at 538, 341 U.S. at 9–10.

13. The insurer won the battle, but lost the war. On remand after the Supreme Court decision, plaintiff voluntarily dismissed as to the nondiverse party, Reiss, and the Fifth Circuit held that judgment could again be entered against the insurer on the basis of the former trial. Finn v. American Fire & Cas. Co., C.A.5th, 1953, 207 F.2d 113, certiorari denied 74 S.Ct. 476, 347 U.S. 912, 98 L.Ed. 1069.

14. Clark, Code Pleading, 2d ed. 1947, pp. 137 et seq., cited 71 S.Ct. at 540 n. 12, 341 U.S. at 14 n. 12.

15. 71 S.Ct. at 540, 341 U.S. at 14.

16. 71 S.Ct. at 540–541, 341 U.S. at 14, 16.

Federal law is used to determine whether claims are separate and independent, although state law determines the nature of the claims to which the federal-law test is applied. Justice v. Atchison, T. & S. F. Ry. Co., C.A.10th, 1991, 927 F.2d 503; and 14A Wright, Miller & Cooper, Jurisdiction 2d § 3724, pp. 396–397.

Few, if any, diversity cases could properly have been removed under this statute in the light of the construction placed on it in the Finn case.[17] Writing in 1961, Professor Cohen listed 24 such cases in which removal had been permitted, but noted that there was substantial doubt as to the propriety of removal, evidenced by other cases denying removal in similar circumstances, in many of those cases.[18]

It is not surprising that few diversity cases met the Finn test. Under the most liberal state joinder rules, parties are not properly joined unless there is some question of law or fact common to all of them, and some claim asserted for or against all arising out of a single transaction or occurrence or series of transactions or occurrences.[19] The relation that the joinder-of-parties rules require is just the kind of relation that, according to the Finn case, bars resort to § 1441(c). It is true that, in the example given earlier, if Kane of California has a claim against Meyers of California and Green of Texas on which they are properly joined as defendants, she may then join in the same lawsuit an entirely unrelated claim against Green.[20] This situation would meet the Finn test, and Green could remove under § 1441(c), but such cases appear so rarely in the courts that the utility of having a special and confusing statute to permit their removal may well be doubted. There was some doubt also as to the constitutionality of allowing such removal in the rare case of this type. Removal under § 1441(c) brings the entire case to federal court, including the claim on which California citizens are opposing parties. This occurred for nearly 75 years under the old separable-controversy statute, and its constitutionality was little dis-

---

17. See Spence v. Saunders, D.C.W.Va. 1992, 792 F.Supp. 480, 482; El Dorado Springs R–2 School Dist. v. Moos, D.C.Mo. 1967, 264 F.Supp. 815, 818. But see Climax Chem. Co. v. C.F. Braun & Co., C.A.10th, 1966, 370 F.2d 616, 618–619, certiorari denied 87 S.Ct. 1287, 386 U.S. 981, 18 L.Ed.2d 231, where the court said: "We do not take such a morbid view. If the Court was sounding the death knell of section 1441(c) we believe it would have said so." The Climax Chemical case is noted 1967, 43 Notre Dame Law, 107, 46 Texas L.Rev. 102. And in Herrmann v. Braniff Airways, Inc., D.C.N.Y.1969, 308 F.Supp. 1094, 1097, the court refused to follow what it called the "severely restrictive view" stated in the text.

18. Cohen, note 1 above, at 13 n. 54, 19 n. 76.

Cases permitting removal under § 1441(c) are described in 14A Wright, Miller & Cooper, Jurisdiction 2d § 3724 nn. 43–47. Cases denying such removal are described id. at nn. 37–42.

Some cases showed a greater willingness to find claims separate and independent when multiple plaintiffs had claims against a single defendant. E.g., Pueblo Intl., Inc.

v. DeCardona, C.A.1st, 1984, 725 F.2d 823; Stokes v. Merrill Lynch, Pierce, Fenner & Smith, Inc., C.A.6th, 1975, 523 F.2d 433; Northside Iron & Metal Co. v. Dobson & Johnson, Inc., C.A.5th, 1973, 480 F.2d 798. This seems unsound. The claims of different plaintiffs are certainly "separate" but in the cases cited they were not "independent." Strange v. Arkansas–Oklahoma Gas Corp., D.C.Ark.1981, 534 F.Supp. 138; Schwartz v. Merrill Lynch, Pierce, Fenner & Smith, D.C.Cal.1976, 424 F.Supp. 672; Lavan Petroleum Co. v. Underwriters at Lloyds, D.C.N.Y.1971, 334 F.Supp. 1069; Rosen v. Rozan, D.C.Mont.1959, 179 F.Supp. 829; Note, 1952, 52 Col.L.Rev. 101, 106–107; 14A Wright, Miller & Cooper, Jurisdiction 2d § 3724, pp. 386–388.

19. See § 71 below.

The holding in Leppard v. Jordan's Truck Line, D.C.S.C.1953, 110 F.Supp. 811, permitting removal under § 1441(c) on the basis of misjoined claims, was clearly unsound. See the critical note, 1954, 67 Harv. L.Rev. 519.

20. See § 78 below.

cussed and never denied.[21] Now that it has finally been established that complete diversity is not constitutionally required,[22] federal jurisdiction of Kane's claim against Green and Meyers is defensible on the ground that § 1441(c) is a grant of jurisdiction over cases in which there is only partial diversity.[23]

The cases are quite divided on whether § 1441(c) applies only to claims joined by plaintiff or whether a third-party claim under Rule 14 [24] can be the basis for removal in those rare instances in which it is in fact separate and independent from the main claim.[25] It seems rather drastic to force the plaintiff, whose choice of forum normally should be honored, to litigate in a federal court that it did not choose and one to which its adversary originally could not have removed, and if removal on the basis of a third-party claim is permissible at all, the main action should be remanded if plaintiff desires this.[26]

Prior to 1948, the separable controversy statute applied only to diversity cases. Section 1441(c), on the other hand, reached any separate and independent claim or cause of action that would be removable if sued upon alone, and thus created the possibility for the first time that a case might be removable where a federal question is joined with a separate claim of a nonfederal nature, and diversity is absent. This situation can well arise, since, unlike the diversity cases, it can have reference to joinder of multiple claims by a single plaintiff against a single defendant. State rules on joinder of claims or causes of action would be relevant, and these, in the more liberal jurisdictions, permit such joinder even of completely unrelated claims. Removal of these federal question cases has its own problems, however.[27] It has been well

21. The leading case on constitutionality of separable-controversy removal relied on a theory of ancillary jurisdiction. Texas Employers Ins. Assn. v. Felt, C.C.A.5th, 1945, 150 F.2d 227, noted 1946, 94 U.Pa. L.Rev. 239. This theory was of little help for § 1441(c), since that statute requires that the claims be entirely unrelated.

22. State Farm Fire & Cas. Co. v. Tashire, 1967, 87 S.Ct. 1199, 1203–1204, 386 U.S. 523, 530–531, 18 L.Ed.2d 270. See § 24 above.

23. Gallagher v. Continental Ins. Co., C.A.10th, 1974, 502 F.2d 827; Irving Trust Co. v. Century Export & Import, S.A., D.C.N.Y.1979, 464 F.Supp. 1232, 1237 n. 9; Twentieth Century–Fox Film Corp. v. Taylor, D.C.N.Y.1965, 239 F.Supp. 913, 918–921.

24. See § 76 below.

25. See cases cited 14A Wright, Miller & Cooper, Jurisdiction 2d § 3724 nn. 60–65. There is an excellent discussion of the issue in Patient Care, Inc. v. Freeman, D.C.N.J. 1991, 755 F.Supp. 644.

26. E.g., Carl Heck Engineers v. Lafourche Parish Police Jury, C.A.5th, 1980,

622 F.2d 133; Peturis v. Fendley, D.C.Ala. 1980, 496 F.Supp. 203; Wayrynen Funeral Home, Inc. v. J.G. Link & Co., D.C.Mont. 1968, 279 F.Supp. 803. In Marsh Inv. Corp. v. Langford, D.C.La.1980, 494 F.Supp. 344, affirmed C.A.5th, 1981, 652 F.2d 583, plaintiff did not ask to have the main action remanded.

27. Among them is the unresolved question of what happens when one of the two "separate and independent" claims is, by statute, expressly made nonremovable. Most courts that have considered the matter have concluded that since § 1441(c), unlike § 1441(a), does not have an "except as otherwise provided by law" restriction in it, it takes precedence and allows removal even of claims that by statute are unremovable. See Palser v. Burlington Northern R.R., D.C.Mo.1988, 698 F.Supp. 793 (FELA); Farmers & Merchants Bank v. Hamilton Hotel Partners, D.C.Ark.1988, 702 F.Supp. 1417, 1420 (Securities Act of 1933), and cases there cited.

established for years that federal courts can take jurisdiction of a nonfederal claim if it is so closely related to a federal question as to be within the pendent jurisdiction of the federal court.[28] Such a case would be removable under 28 U.S.C.A. § 1441(a) without regard to separate and independent claims. In the leading case of Hurn v. Oursler,[29] the Supreme Court distinguished between those cases where the federal and nonfederal claims are so closely related that both can come within federal jurisdiction, and cases where there is "a separate and distinct" nonfederal cause of action. Is a "separate and distinct" cause of action the same as the "separate and independent" cause of action for which § 1441(c) calls? If it is, and there are some intimations that it may be,[30] then every case that includes a federal question will be removable. If the federal and the nonfederal claims are separate and independent, the case will be removable under § 1441(c), while if they are not separate and independent, the case will be removable under § 1441(a) with the nonfederal claim heard in the pendent jurisdiction of the federal court.[31]

Such a result would be strange, but an even stranger result is reached if "separate and independent," for purposes of § 1441(c), means something more separate than the concept used as the measure of pendent jurisdiction. This approach would create a tripartite classification. If the two claims are closely enough related, the whole case is removable under § 1441(a). If the two claims are far enough removed, the whole case is removable under § 1441(c). But if the relation is too close for § 1441(c), while yet not close enough for § 1441(a), no part of the case is removable. This seems absurd, but reputable scholars and a court so read the statute.[32]

No matter which view is taken of the preceding question about the interrelation of subsections (a) and (c) of the statute, § 1441(c), if read literally, certainly means that there will be some cases where a federal court will have jurisdiction of a nonfederal claim, though diversity is

---

28. Hurn v. Oursler, 1933, 53 S.Ct. 586, 289 U.S. 238, 77 L.Ed. 1148; United Mine Workers of America v. Gibbs, 1966, 86 S.Ct. 1130, 383 U.S. 715, 16 L.Ed.2d 218. Under a 1990 statute, 28 U.S.C.A. § 1367, this is now referred to as "supplemental jurisdiction" rather than "pendent jurisdiction". See § 19 above.

29. 1933, 53 S.Ct. 586, 589, 289 U.S. 238, 245–246, 77 L.Ed. 1148.

30. The language in American Fire & Cas. Co. v. Finn, 1951, 71 S.Ct. 534, 341 U.S. 6, 95 L.Ed. 702, is similar to that of Hurn v. Oursler, and indeed the Hurn case is cited in footnote 9 of the Finn case. The Finn case in turn was cited when the Court reformulated the pendent-jurisdiction doctrine. United Mine Workers of America v. Gibbs, 1966, 86 S.Ct. 1130, 1137 n. 8, 383 U.S. 715, 723 n. 8, 16 L.Ed.2d 218.

31. This is the holding in Thomas v. Shelton, C.A.7th, 1984, 740 F.2d 478, and in Swift & Co. v. United Packinghouse

Workers, D.C.Colo.1959, 177 F.Supp. 511. The statute is similarly interpreted in Cohen, note 1 above, at 25–34.

32. Lewin, note 1 above, at 441; Moore & VanDercreek, note 1 above, at 506 n. 81; Note, 1952, 52 Col.L.Rev. 101, 111–112.

"What sense does it make, after all, to have a tertium quid of certain state claims—those too distant to be pendent, too close to be 'separate and independent'— that alone, in an 'arising under' case, the federal court would have no power to hear? However, the history of § 1441(c), taken together with Aldinger, suggests that this middle category of cases does exist, and that this case falls within that category." Charles D. Bonanno Linen Service, Inc. v. McCarthy, C.A.1st, 1983, 708 F.2d 1, 9, certiorari denied 104 S.Ct. 346, 464 U.S. 936, 78 L.Ed.2d 312.

absent and though the claim bears no relation to any federal claim in the case. This poses a serious constitutional question. If the cases defining the pendent jurisdiction doctrine do so in terms of constitutional limits,[33] then the statute is unconstitutional when applied to the situation just described.

On the constitutional issues raised by § 1441(c), particularly in nondiversity cases, there has been a good deal of spirited writing by the commentators [34], but very little said by the courts.[35] Even if valid, the statute's utility is greatly outweighed by the confusion it has engendered.[36]

These doubts about the utility of § 1441(c) caused the Federal Courts Study Committee to recommend flatly that the subsection be repealed.[37] Congress was persuaded so far as diversity cases were concerned, but not federal questions. "The reasons for permitting removal of federal question cases applies [sic] with full force." [38] Congress therefore amended the statute so that it now reads: "Whenever a separate and independent claim or cause of action within the jurisdiction conferred by section 1331 of this title, is joined with one or more otherwise non-removable claims or causes of action, the entire case may be removed and the district court may determine all issues therein, or, in its discretion, may remand all matters in which State law predomi-

33. The reformulation in United Mine Workers of America v. Gibbs, 1966, 86 S.Ct. 1130, 1138, 383 U.S. 715, 725, 16 L.Ed.2d 218, appears on its face to be a statement in terms of constitutional limits. Although the Court there abandoned the language in Hurn about "causes of action," and looked instead to see whether the claims "derive from a common nucleus of operative fact" and whether a plaintiff would ordinarily be expected to try them all in one judicial proceeding, this does not seem to affect the analysis of § 1441(c) made in the text.

34. The article by Lewin, note 1 above, concludes that § 1441(c) is unconstitutional in nondiversity cases. See also Rothfeld, Rationalizing Removal, 1990 B.Y.U.L.Rev. 221, 238–239. Professors Moore and VanDercreek, in the article cited note 1 above, reject the attacks on the constitutionality of the statute as completely without substance. See also Ireland, Entire Case Removal Under 1441(c): Toward a Unified Theory of Additional Parties and Claims in Federal Courts, 1978, 11 Ind.L.Rev. 555. Professor Cohen, in the article cited note 1 above, finds the constitutional question difficult, but concludes that in Hurn v. Oursler the Court was merely construing the jurisdictional statutes, and not defining the constitutional limits of ancillary jurisdiction, and thus reasons that the statute is valid. Green, Jurisdiction of United States

District Courts in Multiple–Claim Cases, 1954, 7 Vand.L.Rev. 472, 489–493, makes a similar analysis. All of these discussions, except for the articles by Rothfeld and Ireland, predate the Gibbs case, note 33 above.

35. See Thomas v. Shelton, C.A.7th, 1984, 740 F.2d 478, 483; Samaroo v. Samaroo, D.C.N.J.1990, 743 F.Supp. 309, 316; Stone v. Stone, D.C.Cal.1978, 450 F.Supp. 919, 934, affirmed C.A.9th, 1980, 632 F.2d 740.

36. See Cohen, note 1 above, at 41; Rothfeld, note 34 above, at 239–241; Thomas v. Shelton, C.A.7th, 1984, 740 F.2d 478, 483; Cedillo v. Valcar Enterprises, D.C.Tex. 1991, 773 F.Supp. 932, 935 n. 3.

The American Law Institute would allow removal in diversity cases by any defendant who could have removed if sued upon alone. ALI Study, § 1304(b). For federal-question cases it proposed to define explicitly the reach of pendent jurisdiction, id. at § 1313(a), and to require remand of all claims not within that reach. Id. at § 1313(b). This approach is regarded as preferable to that of § 1441(c) in Comment, 1966, 114 U.Pa.L.Rev. 709.

37. Report of Federal Courts Study Committee, April 2, 1990, p. 94.

38. H.Rep. No. 101–734, 101st Cong., 2d Sess., 1990, p. 23, reprinted in 1990 U.S.Code Cong. & Admin. News 6802, 6869.

nates." [39] Because the statute is now limited to federal-question cases, courts will have to consider more carefully the constitutional issues this raises.[40]

The amended statute also changes the provision for remand. The 1948 version had said that the court "may determine all issues therein, or, in its discretion, may remand all matters not otherwise within its original jurisdiction."[41] As amended in 1990 the discretion is now to "remand all matters in which State law predominates."[42] Surprisingly courts have read this as giving them discretion to remand the entire case, rather than only those claims that would not have been removable if sued on alone.[43]

§ 40. Procedure for Removal [1]

The procedure for removal from state to federal court prior to 1948 was not satisfactory. The petition for removal and bond were filed in state court, and if the state court refused to allow removal, defendant had three courses of action available, none of them very reassuring. He could note his exception, litigate in state court, and on appeal, perhaps to the Supreme Court, contend that removal was erroneously denied. If he was successful in this contention, the case finally would go to federal court to be tried over again. A second possibility was to ignore the state proceedings and go ahead in federal court as if removal had been granted. The risk here was that the state judgment against him would be valid if it were ultimately determined that the state court was right in refusing removal. Finally he could litigate in both state and federal courts at the same time, surely a wasteful procedure.[2]

39. 28 U.S.C.A. § 1441(c), as amended by Act of Dec. 2, 1990, Pub.L. 101–650, § 312, 104 Stat. 5114.

40. Several early cases have expressed serious doubt about the constitutionality of the statute in federal-question cases. Cedillo v. Valcar Enterprises & Darling Delaware Co., D.C.Tex.1991, 773 F.Supp. 932, 935 n. 3; Moore v. DeBiase, D.C.N.J.1991, 766 F.Supp. 1311, 1318 n. 13, 1320 n. 16.

41. 14A Wright, Miller & Cooper, Jurisdiction 2d § 3724, pp. 403–408.

42. The explanation of this change by the House Judiciary Committee is uninformative. "The further amendment to Sec. 1441(c) that would permit remand of all matters in which state law predominates also should simplify administration of the separate and independent claim removal." H.Rep. No. 101–734, note 38 above.

43. Moralez v. Meat Cutter Local 539, D.C.Mich.1991, 778 F.Supp. 368, 370, and cases there cited. The issue is discussed at length, and this result reached, in Moore v. DeBiase, D.C.N.J.1991, 766 F.Supp. 1311, 1319–1321, and the court there did remand the entire case. In the Moore case, however-

er, the removal had not been under § 1441(c). The state and federal claims in that case were closely related and the court expressly noted that the state claims were within its pendent jurisdiction. 766 F.Supp. at 1315. The remand provision of § 1441(c) surely applies only to cases removed under that subsection. This distinction is recognized in Administaff, Inc. v. Kaster, D.C.Tex.1992, 799 F.Supp. 685, 689, but the court there holds that it can remand an entire case, including both a federal claim and pendent state claims, under the discretion recognized in Carnegie–Mellon University v. Cohill, 1988, 108 S.Ct. 614, 484 U.S. 343, 98 L.Ed.2d 720. See § 41 below.

§ 40

1. 14A Wright, Miller & Cooper, Jurisdiction 2d §§ 3730–3738; Rich, Current Issues in Removal Jurisdiction, 1991, 57 J.Air L. & Com. 395, 410–421.

2. These procedures are outlined in Metropolitan Cas. Ins. Co. v. Stevens, 1941, 61 S.Ct. 715, 717–718, 312 U.S. 563, 567–568, 85 L.Ed. 1044.

The 1948 Judicial Code made a substantial improvement in the procedure for removal. It virtually ended the conflicts described between state and federal jurisdiction.[3] Other significant changes in the procedure, for the most part for the better, were made in 1988.

Procedure for removal is now spelled out in 28 U.S.C.A. § 1446. A defendant, wishing to remove, files with the federal district court for the district or division in which the action is pending a notice of removal, containing a short and plain statement of the grounds for removal.[4] The notice must usually be filed within 30 days after defendant receives the complaint. After filing the notice with the federal court, the defendant gives written notice of removal to the plaintiff and files a copy of the notice of removal with the state court. Upon the filing of the copy of the notice with the state court, the state court is prohibited by specific language from proceeding further with the case. Thus, removal does not require leave from either the state or the federal court, although the propriety of removal may later be tested by motion to remand in federal court.[5] Conflict between the two systems of courts is eliminated because of the bar against further state proceedings after removal. So long as the case has not been remanded, any subsequent state action is void,[6] even if the case was removed improperly.[7]

Despite the general simplicity of the procedure for removal, some questions have arisen that require more detailed discussion. Only a

---

3. See Notes, 1949, 98 U.Pa.L.Rev. 80, 1956, 9 Okla.L.Rev. 191.

4. 28 U.S.C.A. § 1446(a). The 1988 amendments—Act of Nov. 19, 1988, Pub.L. 100–702, § 1016, 102 Stat. 4669, changed the name of this document from "petition for removal" to "notice of removal". It no longer need be verified, but it is made subject to Civil Rule 11. See § 69A below. It now must state "the grounds for removal" rather than "the facts which entitle him or them to removal." A bond is no longer required.

5. See § 41 below.

6. 28 U.S.C.A. § 1446(e); National S.S. Co. v. Tugman, 1882, 1 S.Ct. 58, 106 U.S. 118, 27 L.Ed. 87; Kern v. Huidekoper, 1880, 103 U.S. 485, 26 L.Ed. 354; Heniford v. American Motors Sales Corp., D.C.S.C. 1979, 471 F.Supp. 328, appeal dismissed without opinion C.A.4th, 1980, 622 F.2d 584; State v. Francis, 1964, 134 S.E.2d 681, 261 N.C. 358; Garden Homes, Inc. v. District Court of Somerville, 1957, 146 N.E.2d 372, 336 Mass. 432; Fire Assn. of Philadelphia v. General Handkerchief Corp., 1952, 107 N.E.2d 499, 304 N.Y. 382, noted 1953, 53 Col.L.Rev. 287, 66 Harv.L.Rev. 534; and cases cited 14A Wright, Miller & Cooper, Jurisdiction 2d § 3737 nn. 7–10.

7. U.S. v. Ohio, Em.App.1973, 487 F.2d 936, 943, affirmed 1975, 95 S.Ct. 1792, 421

U.S. 542, 44 L.Ed.2d 363; South Carolina v. Moore, C.A.4th, 1971, 447 F.2d 1067; Hopson v. North American Ins. Co., 1951, 233 P.2d 799, 71 Idaho 461; McCauley v. Consolidated Underwriters, Tex.Civ.App.1957, 301 S.W.2d 181, reversed on other grounds 1957, 304 S.W.2d 265, 157 Tex. 475; Artists' Representatives Assn., Inc. v. Haley, 1966, 274 N.Y.S.2d 442, 26 A.D.2d 918. See ALI Study, § 1383(a), and the Commentary thereon at pp. 357–360, proposing a means of escape from the rigidity of this rule. See also Mitchell, Improper Use of Removal and Its Disruptive Effect on State Court Proceedings: A Call to Reform 28 U.S.C.A. § 1446, 1989, 21 St. Mary's L.J. 59.

In a criminal case, however, the filing of a petition for removal—the old name was retained for criminal cases—does not prevent the state court from proceeding further, except that a judgment of conviction shall not be entered unless the petition is denied. 28 U.S.C.A. § 1446(c)(3), as amended in 1977. Removable criminal cases are those against federal officers or members of the armed forces for acts done under color of office, and certain civil rights cases. 28 U.S.C.A. §§ 1442, 1442a, 1443. See § 38 above.

defendant may remove a case. For purposes of removal, federal law determines who is the plaintiff and who is the defendant.[8] All defendants except purely nominal parties must join in the notice of removal,[9] except that defendants not served need not join,[10] and where removal is on the basis of a separate and independent claim or cause of action under § 1441(c)—if there really can be such a case [11]—only the defendants involved in that claim need join.[12]

The venue for removed actions is the district and division in which the state court action is pending.[13] The general venue statutes are irrelevant in removed cases.

8. Mason City & Ft. D.R. Co. v. Boynton, 1907, 27 S.Ct. 321, 204 U.S. 570, 51 L.Ed. 629; Chicago, R.I. & P.R. Co. v. Stude, 1954, 74 S.Ct. 290, 346 U.S. 574, 98 L.Ed. 317; Ballard's Service Center, Inc. v. Transue, C.A.1st, 1989, 865 F.2d 447. See 14A Wright, Miller & Cooper, Jurisdiction 2d § 3731.

The Boynton and Stude cases just cited hold that in a condemnation proceeding the condemnor is the plaintiff for purposes of removal, even though the landowner is denominated as plaintiff by the state statute permitting court review. It is not yet settled who is the plaintiff in an arbitration proceeding. Victorias Milling Co. v. Hugo Neu Corp., D.C.N.Y.1961, 196 F.Supp. 64, approved 1962, 75 Harv.L.Rev. 1438, holds that the party to the arbitration who first invokes judicial intervention is plaintiff for removal purposes.

9. Chicago, R.I. & P. Ry. Co. v. Martin, 1900, 20 S.Ct. 854, 178 U.S. 245, 44 L.Ed. 1055; Padden v. Gallaher, D.C.Wis.1981, 513 F.Supp. 770. As to nominal parties, see Tri–Cities Newspapers, Inc. v. Tri–Cities Pressmen & Assistants' Local 349, C.A.5th, 1970, 427 F.2d 325. See generally cases cited 14A Wright, Miller & Cooper, Jurisdiction 2d § 3731 nn. 7–12.

Each defendant need not sign the original notice of removal, but there must be some timely written indication from each served defendant, or from some representative purporting to have authority to act on the defendant's behalf in this respect, that the defendant has actually consented to removal. Getty Oil Corp. v. Insurance Co. of North America, C.A.5th, 1988, 841 F.2d 1254, 1262 n. 11.

A party named as a defendant who should be realigned as a plaintiff, see § 30 above, need not join in a notice of removal. Sersted v. Midland–Ross Corp., D.C.Wis.1979, 471 F.Supp. 298.

10. Lewis v. Rego Co., C.A.3d, 1985, 757 F.2d 66; Giangola v. Walt Disney World Co., D.C.N.J.1990, 753 F.Supp. 148.

Prior to 1948 it was held that nonresident defendants who had not been served need not join in the petition for removal, but that a resident defendant must join though not served, if there was to be removal. Pullman Co. v. Jenkins, 1939, 59 S.Ct. 347, 305 U.S. 534, 83 L.Ed. 334. The language in § 1441(b) of the 1948 Code, providing that diversity cases "shall be removable only if none of the parties properly joined and served as defendants is a citizen of the State in which such action is brought," seems to imply that a resident defendant who has not been served can be ignored. The cases, however, continue to apply the pre–1948 rule. See Adams v. Lederle Labs., D.C.Mo.1983, 569 F.Supp. 234, 242; and cases cited 14A Wright, Miller & Cooper, Jurisdiction 2d § 3731 n. 16.

11. See the doubts expressed in § 39 above.

12. International Union of Operating Engineers, Local 400 v. Sletten Constr. Co., D.C.Mont.1974, 383 F.Supp. 855; Gratz v. Murchison, D.C.Del.1955, 130 F.Supp. 709.

All defendants need not join if a federal officer named as a defendant seeks removal under 28 U.S.C.A. § 1442. Ely Valley Mines, Inc. v. Hartford Acc. & Indem. Co., C.A.9th, 1981, 644 F.2d 1310, or if removal is under 28 U.S.C.A. § 1443(2). Bridgeport Educ. Assn. v. Zinner, D.C.Conn.1976, 415 F.Supp. 715.

13. 28 U.S.C.A. § 1441(a); Polizzi v. Cowles Magazines, 1953, 73 S.Ct. 900, 902, 345 U.S. 663, 665, 97 L.Ed. 1331; Hartford Fire Ins. Co. v. Westinghouse Elec. Co., D.C.Miss.1989, 725 F.Supp. 317; 14A Wright, Miller & Cooper, Jurisdiction 2d § 3726. But cf. Tanglewood Mall, Inc. v. Chase Manhattan Bank (Nat. Assn.), D.C.Va.1974, 371 F.Supp. 722, affirmed C.A.4th, 1974, 508 F.2d 838, certiorari denied 95 S.Ct. 1954, 421 U.S. 965, 44 L.Ed.2d 452.

In general the notice of removal must be filed within 30 days after the receipt by the defendant, through service or otherwise, of a copy of the initial pleading setting forth the claim for relief upon which such action or proceeding is based, or within 30 days after the service of summons upon the defendant if such initial pleading has then been filed in court, and is not required to be served on the defendant, whichever period is shorter.[14] Time runs from the receipt of the complaint, rather than the date it is filed with the state court.[15] Receipt by a person authorized to accept process for the defendant is sufficient.[16] There was once some question about when the time begins to run if service is on a statutory agent, such as a state officer in a suit against a nonresident motorist. It is now settled that regardless of the niceties of state law as to when service is technically complete, the time for removal begins to run only when the party or his own appointed agent actually receives the process.[17]

There are certain exceptions to the usual 30–day limit on removing.[18] Where defendant claims that a party has been fraudulently joined

---

14. 28 U.S.C.A. § 1446(b); 14A Wright, Miller & Cooper, Jurisdiction § 3732.

Since 1978 a New York statute has required a summons served without a complaint to contain or have appended thereto a notice stating the nature of the action and the relief sought. Receipt of such a notice has been held sufficient to start the time for removal running even though the notice does not state the citizenship of the parties. DiMeglio v. Italia Crociere Internazionale, D.C.N.Y.1980, 502 F.Supp. 316. See also Keller v. Carr, D.C.Ark.1981, 534 F.Supp. 100.

The statutory provision is not entirely appropriate in states in which the initial pleading is not served on defendant but is filed in court after the service of process. See Raymond's, Inc. v. New Amsterdam Cas. Co., D.C.Mass.1956, 159 F.Supp. 212. Cf. ALI Study, § 1382(a).

15. Kulbeth v. Woolnought, D.C.Tex. 1971, 324 F.Supp. 908; and cases cited 14A Wright, Miller & Cooper, Jurisdiction 2d § 3732 n. 7. This gives rise to a potential trap if plaintiff gives defendant a courtesy copy of the complaint before commencement of the action. Since the statute speaks of "receipt," there is a good argument that the 30–day period runs from the time the courtesy copy is given rather than a later time when service is made. Faulkner, The Courtesy Copy Trap: Untimely Removal from State to Federal Courts, 1993, 52 Md.L.Rev. 374.

There is a division on how to calculate the time if multiple defendants receive the complaint on different days. Compare Getty Oil Corp. v. Insurance Co. of North America, C.A.5th, 1988, 841 F.2d 1254

(time begins running when the first defendant is served) with McKinney v. Board of Trustees of Maryland Community College, C.A.4th, 1992, 955 F.2d 924 (time period for each individual defendant to remove begins running when that defendant is served). There is also disagreement on the time for removal by the Federal Deposit Insurance Corporation. See FDIC v. Loyd, C.A.5th, 1992, 955 F.2d 316.

16. York v. Horizon Fed. Sav. & Loan Assn., D.C.La.1989, 712 F.Supp. 85; Davis v. Baer, D.C.Pa.1984, 599 F.Supp. 776. But see Barber v. Willis, D.C.Ga.1965, 246 F.Supp. 814.

17. E.g., Skidaway Associates, Ltd. v. Glen Falls Ins. Co., D.C.S.C.1990, 738 F.Supp. 980; Kurtz v. Harris, D.C.Tex. 1965, 245 F.Supp. 752.

18. Until 1977 28 U.S.C.A. § 1446(c) allowed a criminal case to be removed at any time before trial. This was susceptible of great abuse. South Carolina v. Moore, C.A.4th, 1971, 447 F.2d 1067; Note, Abuse of Procedure in Removal of State Criminal Prosecutions, 1971, 6 U.S.F.L.Rev. 117. As amended in 1977, the statute now requires the petition for removal to be filed not later than 30 days after the arraignment in state court, or before trial, whichever is earlier, although the court may, for good cause, allow it to be filed at a later time.

Foreign banking cases are removable at any time before trial. 12 U.S.C.A. § 632. Manas y Pineiro v. Chase Manhattan Bank, N.A., D.C.N.Y.1978, 443 F.Supp. 418.

The 30–day period may be enlarged for good cause in suits against a foreign state to prevent removal,[19] the petition is timely if it is filed within a reasonable time after defendant should have known that the joinder was fraudulent.[20] In addition, a 1949 amendment to the Code provides that where the case initially was not removable, the petition may be filed within 30 days after receipt by the defendant of an amended pleading, motion, order, or other paper from which it may first be ascertained that the case is one that is or has become removable.[21] As has been pointed out earlier, the better view is that the reference to "order" in the 1949 amendment does not abolish the prior distinction by which voluntary action of the plaintiff would make a case removable, but a court order, dismissing, for example, as to a nondiverse party, would not.[22] In 1988, however, Congress put an important limit on the exception to the usual 30–day rule. A case cannot be removed on the basis of diversity more than one year after commencement of the action.[23] It has been suggested that this provides "a vehicle by which a state court plaintiff may, through innovative litigation tactics, defeat a defendant's right to a federal forum." [24]

Ordinarily the amount demanded by the complaint is regarded as the amount in controversy.[25] This is true even where state law provides

under the Foreign Sovereign Immunities Act of 1976. 28 U.S.C.A. § 1441(d); Gray v. Permanent Mission of the People's Republic of the Congo to the United Nations, D.C.N.Y.1978, 443 F.Supp. 816, affirmed without opinion C.A.2d, 1978, 580 F.2d 1044.

19. See § 31 above.

20. Parks v. New York Times Co., D.C.Ala.1961, 195 F.Supp. 919, reversed on other grounds C.A.5th, 1962, 308 F.2d 474.

21. 28 U.S.C.A. § 1446(b), as amended by the Act of May 24, 1949, c. 139, § 83, 63 Stat. 101. The corresponding section in the 1948 Code made the time run solely from the initial pleading, apparently overlooking the former law to the contrary.

If the case was removable originally, an amendment will not revive the right to remove unless it changes the original complaint so drastically that the purposes of the 30–day limit would not be served by enforcing it. Wilson v. Intercollegiate (Big Ten) Conference Athletic Assn., C.A.7th, 1982, 668 F.2d 962, certiorari denied 103 S.Ct. 70, 459 U.S. 831, 74 L.Ed.2d 70; 14A Wright, Miller & Cooper, Jurisdiction 2d § 3732, pp. 525–527.

22. See § 38 above at n. 60.

23. 28 U.S.C.A. § 1446(b), as amended by Act of Nov. 19, 1988, Pub.L. 100–702, § 1016(b), 102 Stat. 4669, 4670.

24. Billinson, Recent Amendments to the Removal Statute—Judicial Developments and Inaccess, 1989, 40 Syracuse L.Rev. 1145, 1146. The argument is that a plaintiff who wishes to remain in state court need only assert a plausible claim against a resident or nondiverse defendant and then settle with or dismiss that defendant more than one year after the commencement of the action.

There is even a difference of view on whether the one-year limit applies if plaintiff has intentionally withheld service on a nonresident defendant for more than one year in order to defeat removal. Compare Martine v. National Tea Co., D.C.La.1993, 837 F.Supp. 749, with Greer v. Skilcraft, D.C.Ala.1989, 704 F.Supp. 1570. That such an issue should even arise is surprising. The structure of the statute, as amended in 1988, seems clear that the one-year limit applies only to the second paragraph of § 1446(b), removal of a case that was not removable initially but becomes so because of an amended pleading, motion, or order.

25. Hicks v. Universal Housing, Inc., D.C.W.Va.1992, 792 F.Supp. 482. In removal cases "there is a strong presumption that the plaintiff has not claimed a large amount in order to confer jurisdiction on a federal court or that the parties have colluded to that end." St. Paul Mercury Indem. Co. v. Red Cab Co., 1938, 58 S.Ct. 586, 590, 303 U.S. 283, 290, 82 L.Ed. 845; Albright v. R.J. Reynolds Tobacco Co., C.A.3d, 1976, 531 F.2d 132; Morris v. Naugle, D.C.Md.1989, 722 F.Supp. 1285, 1286-1287.

that the relief ultimately given may exceed the demand for judgment.[26] But if the relief demanded is not limited to a money judgment the notice of removal may contain allegations as to the value of the matter in controversy.[27]

Difficult problems are caused for the federal courts and for litigants by the practice in a few states in which no demand for a specific sum is required.[28] Although the cases are far from consistent, courts increasingly hold that while in this situation they can look to the notice of removal,[29] ultimately they must make an independent appraisal of the monetary value of the claim.[30]

The notice of removal must contain a short and plain statement of the grounds of removal.[31] A copy of all process, pleadings, and orders served upon the removing parties must accompany the notice.[32] Prior to the expiration of the 30-day period for removal, the notice of removal may be freely amended, but the cases say that thereafter it can be amended only to state more specifically a ground for removal that is already imperfectly stated.[33] The application of this rule is not yet clearly settled where neither the complaint nor the petition allege the principal place of business of a corporate party, as has been required

26. See § 33 above at nn. 54–55.

27. Davenport v. Procter & Gamble Mfg. Co., C.A.2d, 1957, 241 F.2d 511; Ronzio v. Denver & R.G.W.R. Co., C.A.10th, 1940, 116 F.2d 604; Kennard v. Harris Corp., D.C.Mich.1989, 728 F.Supp. 453; Dri Mark Products, Inc. v. Meyercord Co., D.C.N.Y.1961, 194 F.Supp. 536.

28. Gaitor v. Peninsular & Occidental S.S. Co., C.A.5th, 1961, 287 F.2d 252; Krider Pharmacy & Gifts, Inc. v. Medi–Care Data Systems, Inc., D.C.Wis.1992, 791 F.Supp. 221; Manuel v. Wal–Mart Stores, Inc., D.C.La.1991, 779 F.Supp. 56; Peacock v. American Ins. Co., D.C.Fla.1966, 253 F.Supp. 624; Note, 1961, 15 U.Miami L.Rev. 415. See ALI Study, § 1381(c)(2); 14A Wright, Miller & Cooper, Jurisdiction 2d § 3725, pp. 423–424.

29. See ALI Study, § 1382(d).

30. Marcel v. Pool Co., C.A.5th, 1993, 5 F.3d 81; Atkins v. Harcros Chemicals, Inc., D.C.La.1991, 761 F.Supp. 444; Pakledinaz v. Consolidated Rail Corp., D.C.Mich.1990, 737 F.Supp. 47; Coleman v. Southern Norfolk, D.C.La.1990, 734 F.Supp. 719; Cole v. Great Atl. & Pac. Tea Co., D.C.Ky.1990, 728 F.Supp. 1305; Wagner v. Ohio Bell Tel. Co., D.C.Ohio 1987, 673 F.Supp. 908.

31. 28 U.S.C.A. § 1446(b). Prior to its amendment in 1988, the statute required what was then called the petition for removal to contain "a short and plain statement of the facts" that entitled the parties

to removal. Even then the better view was that "detailed grounds" were not required, Allman v. Hanley, C.A.5th, 1962, 302 F.2d 559, 562, and that the same liberal rules applied in testing the sufficiency of a pleading—see § 68 below—should apply also to a removal petition. Brown v. City of Meridian, C.A.5th, 1966, 356 F.2d 602, 606. See 14A Wright, Miller & Cooper, Jurisdiction 2d § 3733. That result seems clearly required by the amended statute.

The notice of removal need not be verified, but the sanctions of Rule 11 are applicable to it.

32. 28 U.S.C.A. § 1446(a). Failure to attach copies of these papers has been held not to be a jurisdictional defect. Usatorres v. Marina Mercante Nicaraguenses, S.A., C.A.11th, 1985, 768 F.2d 1285; Riehl v. National Mut. Ins. Co., C.A.7th, 1967, 374 F.2d 739.

33. Kinney v. Columbia Sav. & Loan Assn., 1903, 24 S.Ct. 30, 191 U.S. 78, 48 L.Ed. 103; Powers v. Chesapeake & O.R. Co., 1898, 18 S.Ct. 264, 169 U.S. 92, 42 L.Ed. 673; Carson v. Dunham, 1887, 7 S.Ct. 1030, 121 U.S. 421, 30 L.Ed. 992; McGuigan v. Roberts, D.C.N.Y.1959, 170 F.Supp. 372 (amplifying amendment permitted); Gobet v. Intercontinental Hotels Corp. (Ponce), D.C.Puerto Rico, 1960, 184 F.Supp. 171 (amendment inconsistent with original petition not permitted); and cases cited 14A Wright, Miller & Cooper, Jurisdiction 2d § 3733 n. 11.

since 1958 to determine the existence of diversity jurisdiction.[34] Some cases refuse to allow amendment, after expiration of the 30 days, to show the principal place of business, but the cases to the contrary, which allow such an amendment even on appeal,[35] seem consistent with the general rule as to amendment just stated and with the statute permitting defective allegations of jurisdiction to be amended, upon terms, in the trial or appellate courts.[36]

There are cases that say that the grounds for removal must appear on the face of the complaint, unaided by reference to the other pleadings or to the notice of removal.[37] It is entirely clear, however, that this is not the rule. Thus, the statutory provision that removal can be had within 30 days from receipt of the "amended pleading, motion, order or other paper" from which it first appears that the case is removable [38] shows that such papers may be considered in determining the removability of a case, and it is so held.[39] There are many other situations in which the requisite jurisdictional facts will not appear on the face of the complaint. The citizenship of the parties will not normally be set forth in a state-court complaint, and the defendant, seeking to remove on the basis of diversity, must be permitted to show these facts in the notice of removal.[40] In some circumstances the complaint will not sufficiently disclose the jurisdictional amount, and the notice must be used for this purpose.[41] Allegations in the notice may be used to show that parties have been fraudulently joined to defeat removal.[42] These instances can be generalized, and the cases fully support a rule that the court is to consider the facts disclosed on the record as a whole in determining removability,[43] with the one qualification that the existence of a federal

34. 28 U.S.C.A. § 1332(c). See § 27 above.

35. E.g., Barrow Development Co. v. Fulton Ins. Co., C.A.9th, 1969, 418 F.2d 316; Hendrix v. New Amsterdam Cas. Co., C.A.10th, 1968, 390 F.2d 299; Firemen's Ins. Co. of Newark, N.J. v. Robbins Coal Co., C.A.5th, 1961, 288 F.2d 349, certiorari denied 82 S.Ct. 122, 368 U.S. 875, 7 L.Ed.2d 77; Roberts v. Panhandle Eastern Pipeline Co., D.C.Mo.1990, 737 F.Supp. 545; Stanley Elec. Contractors, Inc. v. Darin & Armstrong Co., D.C.Ky.1980, 486 F.Supp. 769. Contra: e.g., Denton v. Wal–Mart Stores, Inc., D.C.Fla.1990, 733 F.Supp. 340; Barnhill v. Insurance Co. of North America, D.C.S.C.1990, 130 F.R.D. 46; Evans–Hailey Co. v. Crane Co., D.C.Tenn.1962, 207 F.Supp. 193, appeal dismissed 1965, 86 S.Ct. 10, 382 U.S. 801, 15 L.Ed.2d 55, criticized 1964, 42 Texas L.Rev. 398. See 14A Wright, Miller & Cooper, Jurisdiction 2d § 3733, pp. 539–541.

36. 28 U.S.C.A. § 1653.

37. Patriot–News Co. v. Harrisburg Printing Pressmen, D.C.Pa.1961, 191 F.Supp. 568; and cases cited 14A Wright,

Miller & Cooper, Jurisdiction 2d § 3734 n. 4.

38. 28 U.S.C.A. § 1446(b).

39. Evangelical Lutheran Church v. Stanolind Oil & Gas Co., C.A.8th, 1958, 251 F.2d 412; Gilardi v. Atchison, T. & S.F. Ry. Co., D.C.Ill.1960, 189 F.Supp. 82.

40. Mattingly v. Northwestern Virginia R. Co., 1895, 15 S.Ct. 725, 158 U.S. 53, 39 L.Ed. 894; Eastern Metals Corp. v. Martin, D.C.N.Y.1960, 191 F.Supp. 245.

41. See notes 28 to 30 above. See also Davenport v. Procter & Gamble Mfg. Co., C.A.2d, 1957, 241 F.2d 511; Steele v. Underwriters Adjusting Co., D.C.Ala.1986, 649 F.Supp. 1414; Studebaker v. Salina Waterworks Co., D.C.Kan.1912, 195 F. 164; and cases cited 14A Wright, Miller & Cooper, Jurisdiction 2d § 3734 n. 6.

42. Chesapeake & O. Ry. v. Cockrell, 1914, 34 S.Ct. 278, 232 U.S. 146, 58 L.Ed. 544; Smoot v. Chicago, R.I. & P.R. Co., C.A.10th, 1967, 378 F.2d 879.

43. Gay v. Ruff, 1934, 54 S.Ct. 608, 292 U.S. 25, 78 L.Ed. 1099; Villarreal v. Brown Exp., Inc., C.A.5th, 1976, 529 F.2d 1219;

question must appear from the well-pleaded complaint, not from the answer.[44]

The notice no longer needs to be accompanied by a bond.[45] Written notice of the removal must be given to the adverse parties "promptly" after the filing of the notice of removal,[46] and a copy of the notice must be filed with the state court as soon thereafter as is practicable.[47] There is a general tendency to regard these steps as modal and formal, and thus to hold that defects with regard to them can be cured and do not defeat the jurisdiction of the federal court.[48] Plaintiff may also waive such defects if he proceeds in federal court with knowledge of the defect.[49] Though there are some cases holding that removal is effective from the time the notice is filed with the federal court, and that the later steps work retroactively to vest jurisdiction in the federal court as of the earlier date,[50] it seems unfair to a state court to hold that it can be stripped of jurisdiction though it has no notice of this fact. Accordingly the sounder rule is that removal is not effective until these later required steps have been taken.[51]

Cook v. Robinson, D.C.Va.1985, 612 F.Supp. 187; and cases cited 14A Wright, Miller & Cooper, Jurisdiction 2d § 3734 n. 10.

44. Tennessee v. Union & Planters' Bank, 1894, 14 S.Ct. 654, 152 U.S. 454, 38 L.Ed. 511. See §§ 18, 38 above.

This limitation is applicable only to removal of a general federal question under 28 U.S.C.A. § 1441. Where removal is sought under § 1442 on the ground that the case is against a federal officer, the notice of removal will establish the defense that makes the case removable. Poss v. Lieberman, D.C.N.Y.1960, 187 F.Supp. 841; Tennessee v. Keenan, D.C.Tenn.1936, 13 F.Supp. 784.

45. Prior to 1988 a bond had been required, and further amendment was needed in 1991 to remove references to a bond that had inadvertently been allowed to remain in the statute. See generally 14A Wright, Miller & Cooper, Jurisdiction 2d § 3735. The American Law Institute had proposed to abolish the requirement of a bond, ALI Study, p. 339.

46. 28 U.S.C.A. § 1446(d). As to what is prompt notice, see Barrett v. Southern Ry. Co., D.C.S.C.1975, 68 F.R.D. 413, 422; Coletti v. Ovaltine Food Products, D.C.Puerto Rico 1967, 274 F.Supp. 719; Kovell v. Pennsylvania R. Co., D.C.Ohio 1954, 129 F.Supp. 906; Jones v. Elliott, D.C.Va.1950, 94 F.Supp. 567; 14A Wright, Miller & Cooper, Jurisdiction 2d § 3736.

47. 28 U.S.C.A. § 1446(d); Patterson v. Refinery Engineering Co., D.C.N.M.1960, 183 F.Supp. 459.

48. Covington v. Indemnity Ins. Co. of North America, C.A.5th, 1958, 251 F.2d 930, certiorari denied 78 S.Ct. 1362, 357 U.S. 921, 2 L.Ed.2d 1365; Rock v. Manthei, D.C.Mo.1955, 129 F.Supp. 769 (bond); Hornung v. Master Tank & Welding Co., D.C.N.D.1957, 151 F.Supp. 169 (filing copy with state court); Heniford v. American Motors Sales Corp., D.C.S.C.1979, 471 F.Supp. 328, appeal dismissed without opinion C.A.4th, 1980, 622 F.2d 584 (notice to plaintiff given prior to filing with federal court). But cf. Merz v. Dixon, D.C.Kan. 1951, 95 F.Supp. 193 (case remanded where notice to plaintiff, and to state court, were given before rather than after federal filing); State v. Butler, La.1981, 405 So.2d 836 (state-court jurisdiction not defeated where notice was given to law clerk of state judge rather than to clerk of state court).

49. Parks v. Montgomery Ward & Co., C.A.10th, 1952, 198 F.2d 772; see Kramer v. Jarvis, D.C.Neb.1948, 81 F.Supp. 360; Note, 1954, 7 Okla.L.Rev. 468.

50. First Nat. Bank in Little Rock v. Johnson & Johnson, D.C.Ark.1978, 455 F.Supp. 361; Barrett v. Southern Ry. Co., D.C.S.C.1975, 68 F.R.D. 413; Marsh v. Tillie Lewis Foods, Inc., D.C.S.D.1966, 257 F.Supp. 645; Corcoran v. Pan American World Airways, D.C.Mass.1961, 194 F.Supp. 840; Patterson v. Refinery Engineering Co., D.C.N.M.1960, 183 F.Supp. 459.

51. Butler v. King, C.A.5th, 1986, 781 F.2d 486; Beleos v. Life & Cas. Ins. Co. of Tennessee, D.C.S.C.1956, 161 F.Supp. 627; Cavanaugh v. Atchison, T. & S.F. Ry. Co., D.C.Mo.1952, 103 F.Supp. 855; see Donlan v. F.H. McGraw & Co., D.C.N.Y.1948, 81

The federal court may protect its jurisdiction by issuing an injunction restraining further proceedings in the state court after removal has been effected.[52]

After removal the federal court may issue all necessary orders and process to bring before it all proper parties whether served by process issued by the state court or otherwise.[53] Process or service may be completed or new process issued in the same manner as in cases originally filed in district court.[54]

A removed case proceeds according to federal procedural rules, as though it had originally been commenced in federal court,[55] and the federal court acquires full and exclusive jurisdiction.[56] The complaint may be amended after removal, even to add a claim that could not have been asserted in the state-court action.[57] If after removal the plaintiff seeks to join additional defendants whose joinder would destroy subject-matter jurisdiction, the court may deem the party indispensable[58] and dismiss the case or it may deny joinder. But if it choose to permit the joinder it must remand the action to the state court.[59] The orders of the state court are not conclusive, but they are binding until set aside.[60]

F.Supp. 599, 600; ALI Study, § 1382(f); 14A Wright, Miller & Cooper, Jurisdiction 2d § 3737.

There also are holdings that both courts have jurisdiction between the filing in federal court and the notice to the state court. Berberian v. Gibney, C.A.1st, 1975, 514 F.2d 790; Howes v. Childers, D.C.Ky.1977, 426 F.Supp. 358.

52. Frith v. Blazon–Flexible Flyer, Inc., C.A.5th, 1975, 512 F.2d 899; Lowe v. Jacobs, C.A.5th, 1957, 243 F.2d 432, certiorari denied 78 S.Ct. 65, 355 U.S. 842, 2 L.Ed.2d 52; Stoll v. Hawkeye Cas. Co. of Des Moines, Iowa, C.A.8th, 1950, 185 F.2d 96; LePore v. Parker-Woodward Corp., D.C.Mich.1993, 823 F.Supp. 432.

But an injunction against further state proceedings has been denied, though authorized by the removal statute, if further litigation will not cause irreparable injury to the plaintiff. Allstate Ins. Co. v. Preston, D.C.Fla.1992, 842 F.Supp. 1441.

53. 28 U.S.C.A. § 1447(a); Gas Serv. Co. v. Hunt, C.A.10th, 1950, 183 F.2d 417; 14A Wright, Miller & Cooper, Jurisdiction 2d § 3738.

54. 28 U.S.C.A. § 1448; Lewis v. Rego Co., C.A.3d, 1985, 757 F.2d 66; Beecher v. Wallace, C.A.9th, 1967, 381 F.2d 372; and cases cited 14A Wright, Miller & Cooper, Jurisdiction 2d § 3738 n. 2.

This does not permit the federal court, however, to breathe life into a case that would be barred in state court for failure to serve process within the time provided by

state law. Witherow v. Firestone Tire & Rubber Co., C.A.3d, 1976, 530 F.2d 160.

55. Granny Goose Foods, Inc. v. Brotherhood of Teamsters & Auto Truck Drivers, 1974, 94 S.Ct. 1113, 1123, 415 U.S. 423, 437, 39 L.Ed.2d 435; and cases cited 14A Wright, Miller & Cooper, Jurisdiction 2d § 3738 n. 6.

56. French v. Hay, 1874, 89 U.S. (22 Wall.) 238, 22 L.Ed. 854; Drainage Dist. No. 17 of Mississippi County, Ark. v. Guardian Trust Co., C.C.A.8th, 1931, 52 F.2d 579, certiorari denied 52 S.Ct. 197, 284 U.S. 680, 76 L.Ed. 575; Texas Pipe Line Co. v. Ware, C.C.A.8th, 1926, 15 F.2d 171, certiorari denied 47 S.Ct. 335, 273 U.S. 742, 71 L.Ed. 869.

57. Freeman v. Bee Machine Co., Inc., 1943, 63 S.Ct. 1146, 319 U.S. 448, 87 L.Ed. 1509.

58. See § 70 below.

59. 28 U.S.C.A. § 1447(e). This provision was added in 1988. See Yniques v. Cabral, C.A.9th, 1993, 985 F.2d 1031; Tillman v. CSX Transportation, Inc., C.A.5th, 1991, 929 F.2d 1023; and cases cited 14A Wright, Miller & Cooper: Jurisdiction 2d § 3739 n. 27.1.

60. 28 U.S.C.A. § 1450; General Inv. Co. v. Lake Shore & M.S. Ry. Co., 1922, 43 S.Ct. 106, 260 U.S. 261, 67 L.Ed. 244; Hinckley v. Gilman, C. & S.R. Co., 1879, 100 U.S. 153, 25 L.Ed. 591; Daniels v. McKay Machine Co., C.A.7th, 1979, 607 F.2d 771; Coyle v. Skirvin, C.C.A.10th, 1942, 124 F.2d 934, certiorari denied 62

Similarly an effective attachment of property in the state court, or a bond given prior to removal, remains effective after removal.[61]

Defendant waives nothing by removal. After removal it may move, in federal court, to dismiss the case, as for improper service, and the fact that it has removed does not act as a general consent to jurisdiction defeating the motion.[62] A party who has made an express demand for jury trial in state court need not repeat the demand after removal, and if the applicable state law in the court from which the case was removed does not require an express demand for jury trial, no demand is needed in federal court unless the court directs the parties after removal to make a demand if they desire trial by jury.[63]

§ 41.   Remand [1]

Although it is no longer the only provision authorizing remand of a case that has been removed to a federal court, easily the most important provision is 28 U.S.C.A. § 1447(c). For many years it had provided that if at any time prior to final judgment it appeared that a case was removed improvidently and without jurisdiction, the federal court must remand the case. As amended in 1988, the language is changed and a distinction is drawn. "If at any time before final judgment it appears that the district court lacks subject matter jurisdiction, the case shall be remanded." But "[a] motion to remand the case on the basis of any defect in removal procedure must be made within 30 days after the filing of the notice of removal under section 1446(a)." [2]

Although the statute could have been more clearly drafted, it seems clear that it means that the 30–day limit applies to all motions to remand except in cases in which the court lacks subject-matter jurisdiction. "[T]he word 'procedural' in section 1447(c) refers to any defect that does not involve the inability of the federal district court to entertain the suit as a matter of its original subject matter jurisdic-

S.Ct. 1044, 316 U.S. 673, 86 L.Ed. 1748; Talley v. American Bakeries Co., D.C.Tenn. 1954, 15 F.R.D. 391; and cases cited 14A Wright, Miller & Cooper, Jurisdiction 2d § 3738 nn. 26–28.

A temporary restraining order issued before removal will not remain in force after removal any longer than it would have remained in effect under state law, and in no event will remain effective longer than the time limitations stated in Civil Rule 65(b), measured from the date of removal. Granny Goose Foods, Inc. v. Brotherhood of Teamsters & Auto Truck Drivers, 1974, 94 S.Ct. 1113, 415 U.S. 423, 39 L.Ed.2d 435.

61. 28 U.S.C.A. § 1450; Clark v. Wells, 1906, 27 S.Ct. 43, 203 U.S. 164, 51 L.Ed. 138; Rorick v. Devon Syndicate, 1939, 59 S.Ct. 877, 307 U.S. 299, 83 L.Ed. 1303; Tanko v. Saperstein, D.C.Ill.1957, 149 F.Supp. 317 (defective attachment perfect-

ed); and cases cited 14A Wright, Miller & Cooper, Jurisdiction 2d § 3738 nn. 35–36.

62. Ditkof v. Owens–Illinois, Inc., D.C.Mich.1987, 114 F.R.D. 104, 105. This was also the rule under the old law. Wabash Western Ry. v. Brow, 1896, 17 S.Ct. 126, 164 U.S. 271, 41 L.Ed. 431. See 14A Wright, Miller & Cooper, Jurisdiction 2d § 3738 nn. 16–18.

63. Civil Rule 81(c); Myers v. U.S. Dist. Court, C.A.9th, 1980, 620 F.2d 741; Cooperman v. R.G. Barry Corp., D.C.Minn. 1992, 141 F.R.D. 132; 9 Wright & Miller, Civil § 2319.

§ 41

1. 14A Wright, Miller & Cooper, Jurisdiction 2d §§ 3739–3740.

2. 28 U.S.C.A. § 1447(c), as amended by Act of Nov. 19, 1988, Pub.L. 100–702, title X, § 1016(a), 102 Stat. 4669.

tion."[3] A few cases have taken a contrary view and have defined "defect in removal procedure" more narrowly.[4] But the construction that the limit applies to all defects other than those going to subject-matter jurisdiction is clearly what Congress intended.[5] other reading would leave a glaring casus omissus. If "defects in removal procedure" does not encompass all nonjurisdictional defects existing at the time of the removal, then there are some nonjurisdictional defects that are not covered by § 1447(c) at all. It is hard to believe that Congress would prescribe by statute a 30–day rule for remand of one class of times and an "at any time" rule for remand of another class of cases, while at the same time remaining silent on when remand may be sought in the large and important class of cases left in the middle.[6]

As has always been true, a motion to remand for lack of subject-matter jurisdiction can be made any time before final judgment.[7] Since parties cannot confer jurisdiction on the federal court by consent, the court may act on its own motion,[8] or on the motion of either party. Indeed even the party who petitioned for removal may move for remand

---

3. Baris v. Sulpicio Lines, Inc., C.A.5th, 1991, 932 F.2d 1540, 1544–1545, certiorari denied 112 S.Ct. 430, ___ U.S. ___, 116 L.Ed.2d 449. In that case the limit was held applicable to the objection that a case was, by statute, not removable to federal court, although it could have been commenced there. To the same effect see Western Securities Co. v. Derwinski, C.A.7th, 1991, 937 F.2d 1276. The 30–day limit applies to a motion to remand based on the fact that some defendants in a diversity case are citizens of the forum state. In re Shell Oil Co., C.A.5th, 1991, 932 F.2d 1523, certiorari denied 112 S.Ct. 914, ___ U.S. ___, 116 L.Ed.2d 814; Ravens Metal Products, Inc. v. Wilson, D.C.W.Va.1993, 816 F.Supp. 427; Veltze v. Bucyrus–Erie Co., D.C.Wis.1992, 791 F.Supp. 1363. It applies to a motion to remand because removal was not within one year of commencement of the original action, as required in a diversity case by 28 U.S.C.A. § 1447(c). Barnes v. Westinghouse Elec. Corp., C.A.5th, 1992, 962 F.2d 513, certiorari denied 113 S.Ct. 600, ___ U.S. ___, 121 L.Ed.2d 536; cf. Maniar v. FDIC, C.A.9th, 1992, 979 F.2d 782. It applies to removal of a workmen's-compensation case, made nonremovable by 28 U.S.C.A. § 1445(c). Williams v. AC Spark Plugs, C.A.5th, 1993, 985 F.2d 783.

4. Foster v. Chesapeake Ins. Co., C.A.3d, 1991, 933 F.2d 1207, certiorari denied 112 S.Ct. 302, ___ U.S. ___, 116 L.Ed.2d 245 (removal in violation of a forum-selection clause); Melahn v. Pennock Ins. Co., C.A.8th, 1992, 965 F.2d 1497, 1502–1503 (motion to remand based on abstention).

5. "So long as the defect in the removal procedure does not involve a lack of federal subject matter jurisdiction, there is no reason why either State or Federal courts, or the parties, should be subject to the burdens of shuttling a case between two courts that each have subject matter jurisdiction. * * * The amendment provides a period of 30 days within which remand must be sought on any ground other than lack of subject matter jurisdiction." H.R.Rep. No. 889, 100th Cong., 2d Sess. 72, reprinted in 1988 U.S.Code Cong. & Admin. News 5981, 6033.

6. Since the author was winning counsel in the Baris case, note 3 above, it seems right to note that the position for which he successfully argued then, and that is expressed here, is one that he and his collaborators have consistently stated since the 1990 Supplement to 14A Wright, Miller & Cooper, Jurisdiction 2d § 3739, long before he had any connection with the Baris case.

7. Ayres v. Wiswall, 1884, 5 S.Ct. 90, 112 U.S. 187, 28 L.Ed. 693; State v. Ivory, C.A.4th, 1990, 906 F.2d 999, 1000 n. 1; Manuel v. Wal–Mart Stores, Inc., D.C.La. 1991, 779 F.Supp. 56; Scott v. Communication Services, Inc., D.C.Tex.1991, 762 F.Supp. 147; Rosciti Const., Inc. v. Lot 10 of East Greenwich Town Assessor's Plat 14, D.C.R.I.1991, 754 F.Supp. 14.

8. Ziegler v. Champion Mortgage Co., C.A.5th, 1990, 913 F.2d 228; Matter of Marriage of Thompson, D.C.Tex.1978, 450 F.Supp. 197; and cases cited 14A Wright, Miller & Cooper, Jurisdiction 2d § 3739 n. 4.

after a verdict unsatisfactory to him.[9] But if at the time of trial or judgment the controversy is one over which the federal court could have entertained original jurisdiction, a removing defendant is estopped from protesting after judgment that there was no right to remove as an initial matter.[10]

As has been seen, under the 1988 statute a motion to remand because of any defect in the removal other than lack of subject-matter jurisdiction must be made within 30 days after the filing of the notice of removal. This means also that a district court cannot remand a case sua sponte after the 30-day period to remand has expired if the defect is such that the 30-day limit would bar a remand motion by a party.[11]

Any issues of fact raised by a motion to remand are for the court alone to decide, with the removing party carrying the burden of proof.[12] Remand can only be to the state court from which the case was removed.[13] The statute has always provided that a remand order may require payment of just costs, and the 1988 amendment also allows the court to order payment of any actual expenses, including attorney fees, incurred as a result of the removal.[14]

There are now three avenues for remand other than § 1447(c). It was pointed out earlier that the statute authorizing removal on the basis of a separate or independent claim or cause of action, which formerly gave the court discretion either to hear the entire case or, in its discretion, to remand all matters not otherwise within its original jurisdiction, was amended in 1990. It now provides that the court may other "determine all issues therein, or, in its discretion, may remand all matters in which state law predominates."[15] This has been read as

---

9. American Fire & Cas. Co. v. Finn, 1951, 71 S.Ct. 534, 341 U.S. 6, 95 L.Ed. 702. For a full discussion of this case, see § 39 above.

10. Grubbs v. General Elec. Credit Corp., 1972, 92 S.Ct. 1344, 405 U.S. 699, 31 L.Ed.2d 612; Baggs v. Martin, 1900, 21 S.Ct. 109, 179 U.S. 206, 45 L.Ed. 155; Smith v. City of Picayune, C.A.5th, 1986, 795 F.2d 482; and cases cited 14A Wright, Miller & Cooper, Jurisdiction 2d § 3739 n. 15. See Comment, Preserving Objections to Jurisdictional Flaws in Removal Cases: The Circuits Disagree, 1991, 21 Cumb. L.Rev. 663.

On this principle removal was upheld although it was plaintiff who removed the case and the amount in controversy was established only by defendant's counterclaim. Lockwood Corp. v. Black, C.A.5th, 1982, 669 F.2d 324.

11. Maniar v. FDIC, C.A.9th, 1992, 979 F.2d 782; FDIC v. Loyd, C.A.5th, 1992, 955 F.2d 316; In re Shell Oil Co., C.A.5th, 1991, 932 F.2d 1523; Air–Shields, Inc. v. Fullam, C.A.3d, 1989, 891 F.2d 63.

The Fifth Circuit has now held that the district court cannot remand sua sponte for a defect in removal procedure even within the 30-day period. In re Allstate Ins. Co., C.A.5th, 1993, 8 F.3d 219.

12. Kansas City, Ft. S. & M.R. Co. v. Daughtry, 1891, 11 S.Ct. 306, 138 U.S. 298, 34 L.Ed. 963; Carson v. Dunham, 1887, 7 S.Ct. 1030, 121 U.S. 421, 30 L.Ed. 992; and cases cited 14A Wright, Miller & Cooper, Jurisdiction 2d § 3739 nn. 22–23.

13. Bloom v. Barry, C.A.3d, 1985, 755 F.2d 356, 358.

14. 28 U.S.C.A. § 1447(c). An award of attorneys' fees does not require a showing of bad faith. Morris v. Bridgestone/Firestone, Inc., C.A.6th, 1993, 985 F.2d 238; Moore v. Permanente Medical Group, Inc., C.A.9th, 1992, 981 F.2d 443; Morgan Guaranty Trust Co. v. Republic of Palau, C.A.2d, 1992, 971 F.2d 917.

15. 28 U.S.C.A. § 1441(c). See § 39 above at notes 41 and 42.

meaning that the court may remand the entire case, rather than only those otherwise nonremovable claims on which state law predominates.[16]

A 1988 statute gives the court discretion whether to allow joinder after removal of additional defendants whose presence destroys subject-matter jurisdiction. If the court permits the joinder, it is required to remand the action to state court.[17]

Finally, a 1988 decision, Carnegie–Mellon University v. Cohill,[18] holds that a federal district court has discretion to remand a properly removed case to state court when all federal-law claims in the action have been eliminated and only pendent state-law claims remain. It has always been true that when a case is in federal court, either originally or by removal, the court has discretion whether to hear or to dismiss any state claims that are pendent to the federal claim that is the basis for jurisdiction. Ordinarily it is to exercise that discretion by dismissing the pendent claims if the federal claim has been dismissed before trial.[19] The Carnegie–Mellon case goes beyond the prior law by recognizing in a removed case a discretion to remand the pendent state claims to state court rather than increase the expense and time involved by dismissing and requiring plaintiff to start over in state court.[20]

Three justices dissented in the Carnegie–Mellon case. It was common ground that the remand that was approved there was not authorized by either § 1441(c) or § 1447(c), the two statutes in which Congress has provided for remand of removed cases and the dissenters thought that it is for Congress to say when or if remand is permissible. The result on the facts of the case itself, however, seems not of great importance. But some lower courts have gone beyond the facts, if perhaps not the language, of Carnegie–Mellon and have found in it discretionary authority to remand an entire case, including the undismissed federal claims that were the basis for removal.[21] They have also read Carnegie–Mellon as allowing remand of cases removed on the basis of diversity, in which no question of pendent claims is involved and the

16. See § 39 n. 43 above.

17. 28 U.S.C.A. § 1447(e). See § 40 n. 59 above.

18. 1988, 108 S.Ct. 614, 484 U.S. 343, 98 L.Ed.2d 720. The case is criticized in Steinman, Removal, Remand and Review in Pendent Claim and Pendent Party Cases, 1988, 41 Vand.L.Rev. 923.

19. See § 19 n. 15 above. See also Carnegie–Mellon, 108 S.Ct. at 619, 484 U.S. at 349–351.

20. "The discretion to remand enables district courts to deal with cases involving pendent claims in the manner that best serves the principles of economy, convenience, fairness, and comity which underlie the pendent jurisdiction doctrine." 108 S.Ct. at 623, 484 U.S. at 357. But the Court cautioned that if it appears that a

plaintiff has dismissed the federal claim that was the basis for removal "to secure a state forum through the use of manipulative tactics," the district court should take this behavior into account in deciding whether to remand. 108 S.Ct. at 622, 623, 484 U.S. at 357.

Manipulation was found, and remand of the pendent claims refused, in Brown v. Southwestern Bell Tel. Co., C.A.5th, 1990, 901 F.2d 1250.

21. Corcoran v. Ardra Ins. Co., Ltd., C.A.2d, 1988, 842 F.2d 31, 36–37 (case remanded on the basis of Burford-type abstention); Administaff, Inc. v. Kaster, D.C.Tex.1992, 799 F.Supp. 685, 690 (case remanded on the basis of Pullman-type abstention).

federal court has no discretion to dismiss.[22] The sounder perception is that of the Fifth Circuit.[23] It holds that in Carnegie–Mellon the Supreme Court established only a narrow exception, based on principles of pendent-claim jurisdiction, to the rule it earlier announced in the Thermtron case that a district court exceeds its authority if it remands a case on grounds not expressly permitted by statute.[24]

If the court orders remand on the grounds specified in § 1447(c), a statute provides that the order is not reviewable on appeal or otherwise.[25] The only exception made in the statute is for civil-rights cases.[26] Even in the Supreme Court on review of a state-court proceeding after remand, the propriety of the remand, if the case is not a civil-rights case, cannot be questioned.[27] This ban on review is intended to spare litigants

22. Foster v. Chesapeake Ins. Co., Ltd., C.A.3d, 1991, 933 F.2d 1207, 1214–1216, certiorari denied 112 S.Ct. 302, ___ U.S. ___, 116 L.Ed.2d 245 (remand based on forum-selection clause); In re Delta America Re Ins. Co., C.A.6th, 1990, 900 F.2d 890, 892 (same), certiorari denied 111 S.Ct. 233, 498 U.S. 890, 112 L.Ed.2d 193; cf. Melahn v. Pennock Ins., Inc., C.A.8th, 1992, 965 F.2d 1497, 1501–1502 (district court had authority to remand what appears to have been a diversity case on the basis of Burford-type abstention, but should not have done so in this case).

23. Buckner v. FDIC, C.A.5th, 1993, 981 F.2d 816, 819–820.

24. Thermtron Products, Inc. v. Hermansdorfer, 1976, 96 S.Ct. 584, 593, 423 U.S. 336, 351, 46 L.Ed.2d 542.

25. 28 U.S.C.A. § 1447(d); Bregman v. Alderman, C.A.11th, 1992, 955 F.2d 660 (no appeal in federal court); Krangel v. General Dynamics Corp., C.A.9th, 1992, 968 F.2d 914 (no interlocutory review under 28 U.S.C.A. § 1292(b) even though important legal issues are raised); Tillman v. CSX Transportation, Inc., C.A.5th, 1991, 929 F.2d 1023 (the words "lacks subject matter jurisdiction" have a "magical effect" and mandamus will not lie if the district court has used those words); Johnson Pub. Co. v. Davis, 1960, 124 So.2d 441, 271 Ala. 474 (not reviewable on appeal in state court); and cases cited 14A Wright, Miller & Cooper, Jurisdiction 2d § 3740 n. 1.

The ban applies to any remand based on § 1447(c) and is not limited to remands for lack of subject-matter jurisdiction. In re Medscope Marine, Ltd., C.A.5th, 1992, 972 F.2d 107; Rich, Current Issues in Removal Jurisdiction, 1991, 57 J.Air L. & Com. 395, 421 (a contrary view "would render section 1447(d)'s prohibitions on review almost meaningless"). Thus, the ban on review applies if remand was on a timely motion raising a procedural defect in removal. In

re Ocean Marine Mut. Protection & Indem. Assn., Ltd., C.A.11th, 1993, 3 F.3d 353; Foster v. Mutual Fire, Marine & Inland Ins. Co., C.A.3d, 1993, 986 F.2d 48; In re Medscope Marine, Ltd., C.A.5th, 1992, 972 F.2d 107. But mandamus will lie if remand because of a defect in removal procedure was ordered on the basis of an untimely motion. Hamilton v. Aetna Life & Cas. Co., C.A.2d, 1993, 5 F.3d 642; In re Digicon Marine, Inc., C.A.5th, 1992, 966 F.2d 158.

The ban on appellate review in § 1447(d) applies to all cases removed from state court to federal court and not merely to those removed under the general provision of § 1441. U.S. v. Rice, 1946, 66 S.Ct. 835, 327 U.S. 742, 90 L.Ed. 982; Mobil Corp. v. Abeille Gen. Ins. Co., C.A.5th, 1993, 984 F.2d 664; In re TMI Litigation Cases Consol. II, C.A.3d, 1991, 940 F.2d 832, 838–839 n. 4. But special statutes, 12 U.S.C.A. § 1819(b)(2)(C) give appellate jurisdiction to review a remand order when the Federal Deposit Insurance Company, 12 U.S.C.A. § 1819(b)(2)(C), or the Resolution Trust Company, 12 U.S.C.A. § 1441a(*l*)(3)(C) appeals such an order.

26. 28 U.S.C.A. § 1447(d), as amended in 1964, permits review "by appeal or otherwise" if removal was sought under the provisions of 28 U.S.C.A. § 1443. Note, 1965, 43 N.C.L.Rev. 628.

27. Missouri Pac. R. Co. v. Fitzgerald, 1896, 16 S.Ct. 389, 396, 160 U.S. 556, 582, 40 L.Ed. 536; Metropolitan Cas. Ins. Co. v. Stevens, 1941, 61 S.Ct. 715, 718, 312 U.S. 563, 568–569, 85 L.Ed. 1044. But see Board of Educ. of City of New York v. City-Wide Committee for Integration of Schools, C.A.2d, 1965, 342 F.2d 284, 286.

delay.[28] If the motion to remand is denied, on the other hand, the propriety of removal is reviewable on appeal from the final judgment in the case.[29] And if, on review from a final judgment, the court of appeals holds the case not removable, and orders remand, this order is not within the statutory ban and may be reviewed by the Supreme Court.[30]

There are exceptions to the usual rule of nonreviewability of remand orders and there has been a distinct tendency in recent years to expand the exceptions.[31] In Thermtron Products, Inc. v. Hermansdorfer [32] it was held that the ban on reviewability in § 1447(d) applies only if the remand is ordered on the grounds stated in § 1447(c). Thus, mandamus will lie to set aside a remand order if the district court has not merely erred in applying the requisite provision for remand but has remanded a case on grounds not specified in § 1447(c).[33] It also is held that if the court orders a party dismissed and the dismissal leads to a remand it is permissible to review the order of dismissal, although not the remand itself.[34] Some courts have expanded on this to hold that whenever a decision to remand is based on a prior determination of substantive law,

28. U.S. v. Rice, 1946, 66 S.Ct. 835, 839, 327 U.S. 742, 751, 90 L.Ed. 982; Herrmann, Thermtron Revisited: When and How Federal Trial Court Remand Orders are Reviewable, 1987, 19 Ariz.St.L.J. 395, 413.

29. American Fire & Cas. Co. v. Finn, 1951, 71 S.Ct. 534, 341 U.S. 6, 95 L.Ed. 702; and cases cited 14A Wright, Miller & Cooper, Jurisdiction 2d § 3740 n. 12.

Denial of remand is not an order from which an immediate appeal will lie, Neal v. Brown, C.A.D.C.1992, 980 F.2d 747, certiorari denied 113 S.Ct. 1945, ___ U.S. ___, 123 L.Ed.2d 650, although on occasion an interlocutory appeal has been allowed under 28 U.S.C.A. § 1292(b). E.g., Dodd v. Fawcett Publications, Inc., C.A.10th, 1964, 329 F.2d 82; and cases cited 14A Wright, Miller & Cooper, Jurisdiction 2d § 3740 n. 13.

30. Gay v. Ruff, 1934, 54 S.Ct. 608, 292 U.S. 25, 78 L.Ed. 1099; Aetna Cas. & Sur. Co. v. Flowers, 1947, 67 S.Ct. 798, 330 U.S. 464, 91 L.Ed. 1024.

31. Comment, Removal Waiver, and the Myth of Unreviewable Remand in the Fifth Circuit, 1993, 45 Baylor L.Rev. 723.

But in Gravitt v. Southwestern Bell Tel. Co., 1977, 97 S.Ct. 1439, 1440, 430 U.S. 723, 724, 52 L.Ed.2d 1, the Supreme Court stressed that Thermtron "did not question but re-emphasized the rule that § 1447(c) remands are not reviewable".

32. 1976, 96 S.Ct. 584, 423 U.S. 336, 46 L.Ed.2d 542.

See Steinman, note 18 above, at 991–1010; Herrmann, note 28 above; Myers, Federal Appellate Review of Remand Orders: Expansion or Eradication?, 1977, 48 Miss.L.J. 741; 15A Wright, Miller & Cooper, Jurisdiction 2d § 3914.11.

The Thermtron exception was held inapplicable in Gravitt v. Southwestern Bell Tel. Co., 1977, 97 S.Ct. 1439, 430 U.S. 723, 52 L.Ed.2d 1.

33. See the cases cited notes 24 and 31 above. See also Executive Software North America, Inc. v. United States Dist. Court, C.A.9th, 1994, 15 F.3d 1484 (district court's application of an incorrect legal standard in ordering remand under 28 U.S.C.A. § 1367(c)); In re Surinam Airways Holding Co., C.A.11th, 1992, 974 F.2d 1255 (district court exercised discretion to remand claims within its supplemental jurisdiction); Hays County Guardian v. Supple, C.A.5th, 1992, 969 F.2d 111 (after dismissing federal claim, district court exercised discretion to remand rather than dismiss pendent state claims); J.O. v. Alton Community Unit School Dist. 11, C.A.7th, 1990, 909 F.2d 267; Bloom v. Barry, C.A.3d, 1985, 755 F.2d 356 (mandamus will lie where "remand" was "not a remand at all, but a transfer to a court which is a stranger to the case").

34. Waco v. United States Fidelity & Guar. Co., 1934, 55 S.Ct. 6, 293 U.S. 140, 79 L.Ed. 244; Gallea v. U.S., C.A.9th, 1986, 779 F.2d 1403. See 15A Wright, Miller & Cooper, Jurisdiction 2d § 3914.11, pp. 710–715.

that substantive question is reviewable on appeal.[35]

A great many cases might be cited for the proposition that if federal jurisdiction is doubtful the case should be remanded. This rule rests on the inexpediency, if not unfairness, of exposing the plaintiff to the possibility that it will win a final judgment in federal court, only to have it determined that the court lacked jurisdiction.[36] The argument to the contrary is that since there is no means for reviewing a remand order, the district court should be cautious about remand, lest it deprive defendant of its right to a federal forum.[37] To this argument, Judge Hutcheson's answer is apposite: "I am not impressed by the assertion that some valuable right which is given him in the federal court will be taken from him by trial in the state court. As I understand the jurisprudence of this state, it operates with an eye to justice, just the same as that of the federal court." [38]

An order of remand ends the jurisdiction of the federal court.[39] The court is required to mail a certified copy of the order to the clerk of the state court, and upon receipt of this copy by the state court, the federal court is without power to vacate the order to remand, even if it be persuaded that the order was erroneous.[40]

35. Bennett v. Liberty Nat. Fire Ins. Co., C.A.9th, 1992, 968 F.2d 969 (claims held not arbitrable); In re TMI Litigation Cases Consol. II, C.A.3d, 1991, 940 F.2d 832, 840–842 (constitutionality of statute providing for removal), certiorari denied 112 S.Ct. 1262, ___ U.S. ___, 117 L.Ed.2d 491; Milk 'N' More, Inc. v. Beavert, C.A.10th, 1992, 963 F.2d 1342; Pelleport Investors, Inc. v. Budco Quality Theatres, Inc., C.A.9th, 1984, 741 F.2d 273 (same).

This exception was held inapplicable in Baldridge v. Kentucky–Ohio Transportation, Inc., C.A.6th, 1993, 983 F.2d 1341.

36. Limbach Co. v. Renaissance Center Partnership, D.C.Pa.1978, 457 F.Supp. 347, 349; and cases cited 14A Wright, Miller & Cooper, Jurisdiction 2d § 3739 n. 30.

37. See Boatmen's Bank of St. Louis, Mo. v. Fritzlen, C.C.A.8th, 1905, 135 F. 650, 653–655, certiorari denied 25 S.Ct. 803, 198 U.S. 586, 49 L.Ed. 1174; Vann v. Jackson, D.C.N.C.1958, 165 F.Supp. 377. There is a thoughtful discussion of the question, with the matter left open, in Minnesota v. Chicago & N.W. Ry. Co., D.C.Minn.1958, 174 F.Supp. 267.

38. Pabst v. Roxana Petroleum Co., D.C.Tex.1929, 30 F.2d 953, 954.

39. U.S. v. Rice, 1946, 66 S.Ct. 835, 327 U.S. 742, 90 L.Ed. 982; New Orleans Public Service, Inc. v. Majoue, C.A.5th, 1986, 802 F.2d 166, 167; Board of Educ. of City of New York v. City–Wide Committee for Integration of Schools, C.A.2d, 1965, 342 F.2d 284, 285.

But if a case was remanded because it was not then removable, it may be removed later if subsequent events make it removable. Kulbeth v. Woolnought, D.C.Tex.1971, 324 F.Supp. 908. See also Dodd v. Fawcett Publications, Inc., C.A.10th, 1964, 329 F.2d 82.

40. Hunt v. Acromed Corp., C.A.3d, 1992, 961 F.2d 1079; Browning v. Navarro, C.A.5th, 1984, 743 F.2d 1069; and cases cited 14A Wright, Miller & Cooper, Jurisdiction 2d § 3739 nn. 41, 42. See Furlow & Kelly, Removal and Remand: When Does a Federal District Court Lose Jurisdiction over a Case Remanded to State Court?, 1987, 41 Sw.L.J. 999.

But if there is a right to appeal a remand order, as in civil-rights cases, see note 26 above, a judge of the appeals court may stay the remand order after it has become effective in order to permit review. Board of Educ. of City of New York v. City–Wide Committee for Integration, C.A.2d, 1965, 342 F.2d 284, 285–286. Cf. ALI Study, § 1384(b).

Chapter 7

VENUE

Analysis

---

§ 42. Civil Cases [1]

Although the concept of venue—that there is a particular court or courts in which an action should be brought—is of ancient common-law lineage,[2] it was not until 1887 that the federal courts had any significant venue requirements for civil actions. Until that time the relevant statute, with origins going back to the First Judiciary Act, permitted suit in any district where the defendant "is an inhabitant, or in which he shall be found * * *."[3] The latter clause meant that venue was proper in ordinary cases wherever service could be made on the defendant. The choice of place to sue was in fact not as broad for much of this period as this statute might indicate, since as has been seen,[4] from 1789 to 1875 the federal courts were given diversity jurisdiction only where one of the parties was a citizen of the state in which suit was brought. In 1887, as part of a general narrowing of access to federal court, the provision that suit might be brought in the district in which the defendant was found

---

§ 42

1. 15 Wright, Miller & Cooper, Jurisdiction 2d §§ 3801–3829; Clermont, Restating Territorial Jurisdiction and Venue for State and Federal Courts, 1981, 66 Cornell L.Rev. 411; Foster, Judicial Economy: Fairness and Convenience of Place of Trial: Long–Arm Jurisdiction in District Courts, 1969, 47 F.R.D. 73; Currie, The Federal Courts and the American Law Institute (Part II), 1969, 36 U.Chi.L.Rev. 268, 299–307; Barrett, Venue and Service of Process in the Federal Courts—Suggestions for Reform, 1954, 7 Vand.L.Rev. 608; Keeffe et al., Venue and Removal Jokers in the New Federal Judicial Code, 1952, 38 Va.L.Rev. 569; Stevens, Venue Statutes: Diagnosis and Proposed Cure, 1951, 49 Mich.L.Rev. 307.

2. Venue gave rise to one of the most famous fictions of the common law. Plaintiff suing for an assault that took place on the island of Minorca, many miles from England, was permitted to allege that the assault occurred "at Minorca, (to wit) at London aforesaid, in the parish of St. Mary le Bow, in the ward of Cheap." Defendant was not permitted to traverse the fictional "to wit" clause, and the allegation permitted suit to be brought in London. Mostyn v. Fabrigas, K.B.1774, 1 Cowp. 161, 98 Eng. Rep. 1021.

3. Act of March 3, 1875, 18 Stat. 470, based on § 11 of the Act of Sept. 24, 1789, 1 Stat. 73, 78.

4. See § 24 above.

was omitted, and it was provided instead that suit should not be brought in "any other district than that whereof he is an inhabitant, but where the jurisdiction is founded only on the fact that the action is between citizens of different states, suit shall be brought only in the district of residence of either the plaintiff or the defendant." [5] Though the present statute speaks of "residence" while the 1887 statute used the term "inhabitant," the main outlines of the general venue statute did not change from 1887 until 1966, and even in the latter year the change was of modest dimension. It was not until 1990 that there was a major overhaul of the venue scheme.

The distinction must be clearly understood between jurisdiction, which is the power to adjudicate, and venue, which relates to the place where judicial authority may be exercised and is intended for the convenience of the litigants.[6] It is possible for jurisdiction to exist though venue in a particular district is improper, and it is possible for a suit to be brought in the appropriate venue though it must be dismissed for lack of jurisdiction. The most important difference between venue and jurisdiction is that a party may consent to be sued in a district that otherwise would be an improper venue,[7] and it e waives his objection to venue if it fails to assert it promptly.[8] This is in striking contrast to subject-matter jurisdiction, which cannot be conferred by the parties, if it has not been granted by Congress, whether by consent, waiver, or estoppel.[9]

It is wholly settled by a long and unbroken line of authority that venue is controlled entirely by Acts of Congress and that the construction of these is a federal question.[10] Although some district courts, construing the 1966 amendment making the district in which the claim arose a proper venue, said that where a claim arises is to be determined by state law, the Supreme Court has now rejected that heresy and made it clear that this, like other questions of federal venue, is to be decided wholly by federal standards.[11]

It is useful to describe the plan of the general venue statutes as they stood prior to 1966 as background for the statutory rules as they now

---

5. Act of March 3, 1887, 24 Stat. 552, as corrected by the Act of August 13, 1888, 25 Stat. 433.

6. Neirbo Co. v. Bethlehem Shipbuilding Corp., 1939, 60 S.Ct. 153, 154, 308 U.S. 165, 167–168, 84 L.Ed. 167; 15 Wright, Miller & Cooper, Jurisdiction 2d § 3801.

7. Consent to be sued in the courts of a state, and designation of an agent for the receipt of process, constitutes consent to venue in the federal courts in that state. Neirbo Co. v. Bethlehem Shipbuilding Corp., 1939, 60 S.Ct. 153, 308 U.S. 165, 84 L.Ed. 167.

8. Fed.R.Civ.Proc. 12(h); 15 Wright, Miller & Cooper, Jurisdiction 2d §§ 3826, 3829.

9. See § 7 above.

10. 15 Wright, Miller & Cooper, Jurisdiction 2d § 3803.

The only possible exception, never clearly resolved, is, as discussed below at notes 75–84, with regard to the concept of a "local action." But on that issue there is no Act of Congress involved, since the whole concept is a judge-made one, and in any event it is not clear that the concept goes to venue.

11. Leroy v. Great Western United Corp., 1979, 99 S.Ct. 2710, 2715 n. 15, 443 U.S. 173, 183 n. 15, 61 L.Ed.2d 464.

exist. If jurisdiction were founded "only" on diversity of citizenship, suit could be brought only in the district "where all plaintiffs or all defendants reside," while if jurisdiction were based in whole or in part on the presence of a federal question, suit had to be brought in the district "where all defendants reside." [12] The word "only" in the statute with regard to diversity cases meant what it said. Even though the stated basis of jurisdiction is diversity and diversity exists, the privilege to sue in the district of plaintiff's residence, which existed until 1990 in diversity cases, was inapplicable if there was a federal question presented in the complaint that would have supported jurisdiction.[13] The requirement that "all" plaintiffs or "all" defendants, as the case may be, must reside in the district was a codification of a result that the Supreme Court, perhaps unnecessarily, had reached under the 1887 statute, which was not explicit on venue for multiple-parties cases.[14]

In addition to satisfying the requirement of the general venue statutes in selection of a district, the suit had to be brought in the division of the district where the party whose residence was being looked to for venue purposes resided.[15] If defendants resided in different divisions of the same district, suit could be brought in any of those divisions,[16] and if they resided in different districts in the same state, suit could be brought in any of those districts.[17] There was no corresponding provision for plaintiffs who resided in different districts in the same state and who were suing on the basis of diversity.

At first glance this scheme might have seemed sensible enough, but on analysis it was difficult to avoid the conclusion that it was entirely irrational. It failed to promote the convenience of the parties, as venue statutes are intended to do, and it overlooked the distinctive functions and opportunities of a federal system of courts. The pre–1966 scheme had three principal weaknesses, and they were not wholly cured by the 1966 amendment.

1. Neither history nor logic explains why a wider choice of venue was available in diversity cases than in federal-question cases. The distinction was the result of a Senate amendment to the House bill that led to the 1887 statute. There is nothing in the legislative history to

---

12. These were the statutes as they existed prior to 1990. 28 U.S.C.A. § 1391(a) (diversity); 28 U.S.C.A. § 1391(b) (federal question). See 15 Wright, Miller & Cooper, Jurisdiction 2d § 3804.

13. Macon Grocery Co. v. Atlantic Coast Line R. Co., 1910, 30 S.Ct. 184, 215 U.S. 501, 54 L.Ed. 300; Bredberg v. Long, C.A.8th, 1985, 778 F.2d 1285.

As will be seen later in this section, the 1990 statutes purport to distinguish between diversity and federal-question cases, but the distinction no longer has any substance.

14. Smith v. Lyon, 1889, 10 S.Ct. 303, 133 U.S. 315, 33 L.Ed. 635 (multiple plaintiffs); Camp v. Gress, 1919, 39 S.Ct. 478, 250 U.S. 308, 63 L.Ed. 997 (multiple defendants). See 15 Wright, Miller & Cooper, Jurisdiction 2d § 3807.

15. Former 28 U.S.C.A. § 1393(a) (repealed in 1988); 15 Wright, Miller & Cooper, Jurisdiction 2d § 3809.

16. Former 28 U.S.C.A. § 1393(b) (repealed in 1988).

17. 28 U.S.C.A. § 1392(a). This was not repealed in 1990, although it is now wholly superfluous in the light of § 1391(a)(1) and (b)(1).

shed light on it, and the probability is that it was entirely fortuitous.[18] Logically one would expect that if there is to be a difference, the wider choice would be in the federal-question cases, since they are the cases for which the federal courts have a special competence. If fear of local prejudice is the basis for diversity jurisdiction, it is quite anomalous to give the diversity plaintiff the privilege of suing in the district where he resides.

2. The statutes frequently precluded suit in the most convenient district. Many times it would serve the convenience of the parties to sue in the district where the claim arose, but until 1966 the venue statutes prohibited this unless this district was also the residence of all the defendants or, in a diversity case, all the plaintiffs.[19]

3. Suppose one defendant resided in New York City while another defendant resided just across the river in Newark. Unless venue objections were waived, there was no way suit against these defendants on a federal question could be brought in a federal court, since there was no district in which all defendants resided. Nor could suit be brought against these two defendants on the basis of diversity if there were two plaintiffs residing in different states, or even in different districts within the same state. These cases involving multiple parties from different states are usually beyond the competence of any state tribunal and seem especially appropriate for a federal forum. Yet the venue statutes, ostensibly for the convenience of litigants, might in some such situations bar the parties from having their day in any court.

In part because these deficiencies in the present scheme of venue had become widely understood, and in part because modern means of transportation had minimized the inconvenience in going to another district to litigate, there has been increasing professional pressure to ease venue requirements, permit nationwide service of process, and provide for easy transfer to the forum that will best serve the convenience of the parties and the court in the particular case.[20]

---

18. The House bill that led to the 1887 statute was intended to limit venue in diversity cases. It continued the authorization for suit wherever the defendant could be found, except in diversity cases, where only the district of residence of the plaintiff or the defendant would be proper. Thus, it was an attempt to restore, through the venue provision, the bar against diversity suits between two noncitizens of the forum that, from 1789 to 1875, appeared in the jurisdictional statute. The Senate struck the language permitting suit where the defendant might be found, and thus confined litigation to the district of which the defendant was an inhabitant except that plaintiff's residence was also proper in diversity cases. It seems most likely that the Senate wished to bar suit in a district merely because plaintiff was able to serve defendant there, and that it failed to see that the effect of this

was to give diversity plaintiffs a wider choice of venue than was given plaintiffs in nondiversity cases. See 18 Cong.Rec. 1887, pp. 613, 2544–2546, 2651, 2672, 2721.

19. Thus, a Wisconsin resident, injured in Florida, could not, prior to 1966, bring suit in the federal court in Florida against two defendants, one a resident of Florida and the other a resident of New Jersey. Dibble v. Cresse, C.A.5th, 1959, 271 F.2d 426.

20. E.g., Barrett, note 1 above, at 627–635; Currie, note 1 above, at 299–307; Keeffe et al., note 1 above, at 586–588. One author would abolish venue requirements entirely in federal-question cases. Seidelson, Jurisdiction of Federal Courts Hearing Federal Cases: An Examination of the Propriety of the Limitations Imposed by

Congress first responded to this pressure in 1966 by amending the general venue statutes to provide that the district "in which the claim arose" is now a permissible alternative venue both in diversity and federal-question cases.[21] This was a significant advance. It did not cure the anomaly that choice of venue was broader in diversity cases than in federal-question cases, but, in theory at least, it should have resolved the second and third of the difficulties just described. Suit would be possible in the district in which the claim arose if that was the most convenient forum and there would be at least one district that is a permissible venue for any federal action.[22] In many cases this will work as intended. Its effectiveness was somewhat limited, however, because even though the district in which the claim arose was made a proper venue, suit could in fact be brought there only if all defendants were subject to process from that district. This, in turn, generally turned on the extent to which the state had an applicable long-arm statute.[23]

In addition, in actions with contacts in several states, there was difficulty in determining that single district "in which the claim rose." The American Law Institute had proposed to allow suit in a district where "a substantial part of the events or omissions giving rise to the claim occurred, or a substantial part of property that is the subject of the action is situated."[24] This would have allowed plaintiff to choose, in the first instance, if a claim had logical ties to more than one district. Some lower courts construed the language Congress actually used as if it meant the same thing as the ALI language, but the Supreme Court firmly rebuffed that view. In Leroy v. Great Western United Corporation,[25] it said: "Without deciding whether this language adopts the occasionally fictive assumption that a claim may arise in only one district, it is absolutely clear that Congress did not intend to provide for venue at the residence of the plaintiff or to give that party an unfettered choice among a host of different districts. * * * [T]he broadest interpretation of the language of § 1391(b) that is even arguably acceptable is that in the unusual case in which it is not clear that the claim arose in only one specific district, a plaintiff may choose between those two (or conceivably even more) districts that with approximately equal plausibility—in terms of the availability of witnesses, the accessibility of other

---

Venue Restrictions, 1968, 37 Geo.Wash. L.Rev. 82.

21. 28 U.S.C.A. § 1391(a), (b), as amended by Act of Nov. 2, 1966, Pub.L. 89–714, 80 Stat. 1111. The amendment repealed a more limited provision, adopted in 1963, applicable only to automobile cases.

22. The 1966 amendment was intended to close "venue gaps" in multiple-party situations. Brunette Machine Works, Ltd. v. Kockum Indus., Inc., 1972, 92 S.Ct. 1936, 1939 n. 8, 406 U.S. 706, 710 n. 8, 32 L.Ed.2d 428.

23. Note, Federal Venue Amendment—Service of Process, Erie and Other Limitations, 1967, 16 Cath.U.L.Rev. 297, 302–317.

This limitation prevented suit in the district in which a collision had occurred in Parham v. Edwards, D.C.Ga.1972, 346 F.Supp. 968, affirmed C.A.5th, 1973, 470 F.2d 1000.

24. ALI Study, §§ 1303(a)(1), 1314(a)(1), and Commentary thereto. Congress used the ALI language in a 1976 statute fixing venue for actions against foreign states. 28 U.S.C.A. § 1391(f)(1).

25. 1979, 99 S.Ct. 2710, 443 U.S. 173, 61 L.Ed.2d 464.

relevant evidence, and the convenience of the defendant (but *not* of the plaintiff)—may be assigned as the locus of the claim."[26]

The Leroy decision raised as many questions as it answered and it led to unnecessary litigation about the place of suit.[27] It is not necessary to go into detail about this because of the changes made in 1990.

The Federal Courts Study Committee was a distinguished group appointed pursuant to an Act of Congress to examine all of the operations of the federal judiciary.[28] In its report, in 1990, it recommended that "Congress should clarify 28 U.S.C. § 1391(a) & (b), the general venue statute." It suggested that the phrase about the district "in which the claim arose" be changed to use the language the ALI had suggested. And it urged Congress to "eliminate the century-old anomaly" allowing venue in a diversity case in the district in which all plaintiffs reside.[29]

Congress responded to this suggestion in the Judicial Improvements Act of 1990.[30] This statute completely rewrote subsections (a) and (b) of § 1391. The amended statute purports to lay down in (a) rules for cases in which jurisdiction is based on diversity only and in (b) for all other cases. Differences in form remain,[31] but there is no longer any difference in substance.

Both in diversity cases, under (a)(1), and in federal-question cases, under (b)(1), suit may be brought in "a judicial district where any defendant resides, if all defendants reside in the same State." There is no longer any provision for laying venue in a district on the ground that all plaintiffs reside there. The century-old anomaly has been ended.

The second possibility, in (a)(2) and (b)(2), uses the language that the American Law Institute had proposed.[32] It replaces the old language about "*the* judicial district in which the claim arose" with "*a* judicial district in which a substantial part of the events or omissions giving rise to the claim occurred, or a substantial part of property that is the subject of the action is situated."[33] This makes it clear that there can be more than one district in which a claim may be thought to have arisen and in which venue will be proper.[34]

26. 99 S.Ct. at 2717–2718, 443 U.S. at 184–185.

27. See the welter of cases, and the absence of any coherent theory, discussed in 15 Wright, Miller & Cooper, Jurisdiction 2d § 3806.

28. See 13 Wright, Miller & Cooper, Jurisdiction 2d § 3510.

29. Report of the Federal Courts Study Committee, April 2, 1990, p. 94.

30. Act of Dec. 1, 1990, Pub.L. 101–650, Tit. III, § 311, 104 Stat. 5114. See Oakley, Recent Statutory Changes in the Law of Federal Jurisdiction and Venue: The Judicial Improvements Acts of 1988 and 1990, 1991, 24 U.C.Davis L.Rev. 735, 769–782.

31. Strangely (a) has three indented subdivisions while the parallel provisions in (b) are set as numbered clauses within a single sentence. There are also verbal differences between (a)(3) and (b)(3).

32. See note 24 above.

33. This language was adopted also in 28 U.S.C.A. § 1391(e), which sets venue for actions against federal officers or agencies.

34. The Federal Courts Study Committee thought that this change would discourage litigation over which of the possibly several districts involved in a multiforum transaction is the one in which the claim arose. Magic Toyota v. Southeast Toyota Distributors, D.C.S.C.1992, 784 F.Supp.

Finally each subdivision has a fallback provision, though there are slight differences in their wording. For diversity cases (a)(3) allows suit in "a judicial district in which the defendants are subject to personal jurisdiction at the time the action is commenced, if there is no district in which the action may be brought." [35] For nondiversity cases (b)(3) permits venue in "a judicial district in which any defendant may be found, if there is no district in which the action may otherwise be brought." It was seen earlier that from 1789 to 1887 the statute allowed suit wherever defendant "shall be found" and this was understood to mean that venue was proper wherever service could be made. Presumably that is the way the 1990 statute will be construed, and "found" in (b)(3) will be read as meaning the same thing as "subject to personal jurisdiction" in (a)(3).[36]

In summary, if all defendants reside in a single state, venue can be laid either in any district in which any defendant resides or in a district in which a substantial part of the events or omissions occurred.[37] If defendants do not all reside in a single state, venue must be put where the events or omissions occurred, and if these were not in the United States, the fallback provision of (3) comes into play and suit can be brought wherever the defendants are subject to personal jurisdiction.

There has been substantial reform, and the 1990 statute has significantly rationalized the tests of venue. It is still possible to conceive of cases in which there will be no federal district in which suit can be brought, but those cases are more likely to arise in classroom hypotheticals than in real life. But it is still necessary to probe some of the

306, 316–317. But it has been said that the new test "hardly comes warranted as less likely to be 'litigation breeding.'" Oakley, note 30 above, at 775.

35. The final clause was added by a corrective amendment in § 504 of the Act of Oct. 29, 1992, Pub. L. 102–572, 106 Stat. 4513. Without that addition (a)(3) seemed to allow suit in any case in any district in which defendants were subject to personal jurisdiction. This would have made (a)(1) and (a)(2) superfluous. As commentators had urged—see Oakley, note 30 above, at 777–782—courts read (a)(3), prior to the 1992 correction, as applying only to cases in which there were multiple defendants. United States Fid. & Guar. Co. v. Mayberry, D.C.Tenn.1992, 789 F.Supp. 901; Harrison Conference Services, Inc. v. Dolce Conference Services, Inc., D.C.N.Y.1991, 768 F.Supp. 405. In this way they avoided making (a)(3) a provision that would apply, and overwhelm (a)(1) and (a)(2), in every case.

The Judicial Conference of the United States has proposed amending 28 U.S.C.A. § 1391(a)(3) to say "any defendant is" rather than "the defendants are". Report of the Judicial Conference of the United States, Sept. 1993, p. 49.

36. It is true that cases interpreting other statutes that speak in terms of where a defendant may be "found" are not in agreement on whether defendant is "found" in a district if it is subject to service there only by use of a "long-arm" statute. See 15 Wright, Miller & Cooper, Jurisdiction 2d § 3818 nn. 17, 26 (Clayton Act), § 3819 nn. 4–12 (copyright cases), § 3820 nn. 4, 5 (fines, penalties, and forfeitures), § 3824 n. 5 (Securities Exchange Act of 1934). But there is nothing in the report of the Federal Courts Study Committee or in the legislative history of the statute itself to suggest any purpose to give a broader application to (3) in diversity cases than in other cases. The statute will best achieve its stated purpose as "a safety net" if "found" is broadly construed.

37. These are alternatives. The contention that the place of the events can be used for venue only if defendants do not reside in the same state has properly been rejected. Merchants Nat. Bank v. Safrabank (California), D.C.Kan.1991, 776 F.Supp. 538, 541.

mysteries that lurk within the easy language of 28 U.S.C.A. § 1391. The principal questions are the meaning of "residence" within the statute, and the determination of the proper venue where corporations or unincorporated associations are parties to a suit. In addition, the exceptions, both statutory and judge-made, to the usual venue rules must be explored.

Quite surprisingly, there is even a little uncertainty whether "residence," within the venue statutes, means the same thing as "citizen," within the diversity statute. Two courts have said that "citizenship" and "residence" are "related or cognate terms," and that the existence of citizenship is cogent evidence of residence, but that they "are not necessarily one and the same thing."[38] Other courts, however, have treated the two concepts as if they are indeed one and the same thing.[39] The question arises in its clearest form where a person maintains two homes. By hypothesis a person may be a citizen of only one state. The courts that treat "citizenship" and "residence" as synonymous have refused to permit venue to be laid in the district where a home is located but where the party is not a citizen.[40] This view finds support in a Supreme Court dictum that equates "residence" and "citizenship" and says that the Code used the former term, in speaking of venue, in order to avoid the anomaly of referring to a "citizen" of a district.[41] This should be regarded as the authoritative view. Although the considerations of convenience that underlie venue might seem to permit suit in the district where the party has his second home, it would be far too confusing to have one body of law on what is "citizenship" for purposes of diversity and a different body of law on what is "residence" for purposes of venue. On the view that the two are synonymous, the court, when venue is challenged, will look to the same factors to determine the party's residence that are considered in determining citizenship for purposes of diversity.[42]

The doctrines just stated with regard to residence do not apply where an alien is a party. An alien may be sued in any district.[43] An alien plaintiff was never allowed to take advantage of the pre–1990 provision allowing diversity cases to be brought in the district in which

---

38. Townsend v. Bucyrus–Erie Co., C.C.A.10th, 1944, 144 F.2d 106, 108. See also Arley v. United Pac. Ins. Co., C.A.9th, 1967, 379 F.2d 183, 185 n. 1.

39. Rosenfeld v. S.F.C. Corp., C.A.1st, 1983, 702 F.2d 282, 283; and cases cited 15 Wright, Miller & Cooper, Jurisdiction 2d § 3805 n. 11. See also note 40 below.

40. MacNeil v. Whittemore, C.A.2d 1958, 254 F.2d 820; King v. Wall & Beaver St. Corp., C.C.A.D.C.1944, 145 F.2d 377; Koons v. Kaiser, D.C.N.Y.1950, 91 F.Supp. 511.

Contra: Arley v. United Pac. Ins. Co., C.A.9th, 1967, 379 F.2d 183, 185 n. 1; Townsend v. Bucyrus–Erie Co., C.C.A.10th, 1944, 144 F.2d 106.

41. Ex parte Shaw, 1892, 12 S.Ct. 935, 936, 145 U.S. 444, 447, 36 L.Ed. 768.

42. As to those factors, see § 26 above.

43. 28 U.S.C.A. § 1391(d). See Berger, Alien Venue: Neither Necessary nor Constitutional, 1976 N.Y.U.J.Intl.L. & Pol. 155.

This rule has been applied also to alien corporations. Brunette Machine Works, Ltd. v. Kockum Indus., Inc., 1972, 92 S.Ct. 1936, 406 U.S. 706, 32 L.Ed.2d 428.

the plaintiff arose. An alien has always had to sue in the district in which all defendants reside or, since 1966, in which the claim arose.[44]

There is also a divergence between the rules for jurisdiction and those for venue with regard to public officials sued in their official capacity. The place where the officer performs his or her official duties is regarded as the officer's residence for purposes of venue, even though the person often will not be a citizen there for purposes of diversity.[45] A federal officer has only one official residence for venue purposes,[46] but this is not necessarily true of a state official.[47]

Corporations have created difficult problems in applying venue rules, as they have in many other areas of the law.[48] For many years it was held that, for purposes of venue, a corporation was a resident only of the state in which it was incorporated, even though it did business or had an agent for service of process in some other state.[49] It was probably inevitable that the expanding economy of the nation and the nationwide activities of great corporations should eventually render intolerable a rule that restricted federal suits to the district of incorporation, especially if that district was remote from the scene of corporate activities. The Supreme Court took the first long step in changing the rule when it held, in the well-known case of Neirbo Co. v. Bethlehem Shipbuilding Corp.,[50] that a corporation that had complied with state law by designating an agent for the service of process had consented to be sued in federal court in that state despite any venue privilege it might otherwise have had. The Neirbo decision left many questions unanswered,[51] but those questions have long since been of only academic interest. In 1958 Congress adopted § 1391(c) of the Judicial Code. From that year until 1988 that section provided: "A corporation may be sued in any judicial district in which it is incorporated or licensed to do

44. Galveston, H. & S.A.R. Co. v. Gonzales, 1894, 14 S.Ct. 401, 151 U.S. 496, 38 L.Ed. 248; 15 Wright, Miller & Cooper, Jurisdiction 2d § 3810. The 1988 amendment of 28 U.S.C.A. § 1332(a) providing that an alien admitted to the United States for permanent residence shall be deemed a citizen of the state in which the alien is located applies only for purposes of three specified jurisdictional statutes. It has no application to the venue statutes.

45. Butterworth v. Hill, 1885, 5 S.Ct. 796, 114 U.S. 128, 29 L.Ed. 119; Neville v. Dearie, D.C.N.Y.1990, 745 F.Supp. 99; and cases cited 15 Wright, Miller & Cooper, Jurisdiction 2d § 3805 nn. 19, 20.

46. Reuben H. Donnelley Corp. v. F.T.C., C.A.7th, 1978, 580 F.2d 264, 266–267; and cases cited 15 Wright, Miller & Cooper, Jurisdiction 2d § 3815 n. 21.

47. St. Regis Mohawk Tribe v. New York, D.C.N.Y.1991, 774 F.Supp. 185, 186 n. 1; Michigan State Chamber of Commerce v. Austin, D.C.Mich.1983, 577 F.Supp. 651, 654–655, reversed on other grounds C.A.6th, 1986, 788 F.2d 1178; Buf-

falo Teachers Federation, Inc. v. Helsby, D.C.N.Y.1976, 426 F.Supp. 828, 829. But see Procario v. Ambach, D.C.N.Y.1979, 466 F.Supp. 452, 454.

48. See § 27 above.

49. Ex parte Shaw, 1892, 12 S.Ct. 935, 145 U.S. 444, 36 L.Ed. 768; In re Keasbey & Mattison Co., 1895, 16 S.Ct. 273, 160 U.S. 221, 40 L.Ed. 402; Southern Pac. Co. v. Denton, 1892, 13 S.Ct. 44, 146 U.S. 202, 36 L.Ed. 942.

Prior to 1887, when venue was proper wherever defendant was "found," it was held, after much vacillation, that a corporation was "found" in a district where it had a designated agent for service of process. Ex parte Schollenberger, 1877, 96 U.S. 369, 24 L.Ed. 853. This construction did not survive the 1887 amendment of the venue statute.

50. 1939, 60 S.Ct. 153, 308 U.S. 165, 84 L.Ed. 167.

51. See Comment, The Aftermath of the Neirbo Case, 1948, 42 Ill.L.Rev. 780.

business or is doing business, and such judicial district shall be regarded as the residence of such corporation for venue purposes." [52] The statute built on the Neirbo principle, but went far beyond that decision in regarding a corporation, for purposes of venue, as a resident of any district in which it is doing business, whether or not it has designated an agent for receipt of process in that district.[53]

The 1958 statute raised its own problems of interpretation. Beneath its deceptively simple language there lurked major ambiguities. Every clause in it raised troublesome questions and was construed in different ways by different courts. Fortunately it is not now necessary to probe all these details,[54] since the statute was significantly rewritten in 1988.

Section 1391(c) as it now stands says: "For purposes of venue under this chapter, a defendant that is a corporation shall be deemed to reside in any judicial district in which it is subject to personal jurisdiction at the time the action is commenced. In a State which has more than one judicial district and in which a defendant that is a corporation is subject to personal jurisdiction at the time an action is commenced, such corporation shall be deemed to reside in any district in that State within which its contacts would be sufficient to subject it to personal jurisdiction if that district were a separate State, and, if there is no such district, the corporation shall be deemed to reside in the district within which it has the most significant contacts." [55]

The 1988 version of § 1391(c) clearly applies only to corporate defendants. This was unclear under the 1958 statute. Read literally it seemed to define the residence for all corporate parties, whether defendants or plaintiffs. The courts, however, resolved the controversy and held that the statute applied only to defendants.[56] This is no longer of

---

52. See generally 15 Wright, Miller & Cooper, Jurisdiction 2d § 3811.

53. In the period between Neirbo and the adoption of § 1391(c), it was held that venue was improper as to a foreign corporation doing business within the state if it had not designated an agent for receipt of process even though state law required such a designation. Moss v. A.C.L.R. Co., C.C.A.2d, 1945, 149 F.2d 701; Donahue v. M.A. Henry Co., D.C.N.Y.1948, 78 F.Supp. 91.

In another respect the statute clearly goes beyond the Neirbo rule. Under Neirbo the Supreme Court had held that though a corporation was amenable to suit where it had qualified to do business in a foreign state, it was not a "resident" of that district for purposes of the statute providing that where defendants resided in two or more districts of a single state, suit might be brought in any such district. Suttle v. Reich Bros. Co., 1948, 68 S.Ct. 587, 333 U.S. 163, 92 L.Ed. 614. Under § 1391(c)

the rule of the Suttle case has been changed. See Robert E. Lee & Co. v. Veatch, C.A.4th, 1961, 301 F.2d 434, 438.

54. They are explored in 15 Wright, Miller & Cooper, Jurisdiction 2d § 3811.

55. Oakley, note 30 above, at 770–774; Siegel, Changes in Federal Jurisdiction and Practice Under the New Judicial Improvements and Access to Justice Act, 1989, 123 F.R.D. 399, 405–408; Welkowitz, Some Thoughts on Corporate Venue and Other Foibles, 1989, 10 Whittier L.Rev. 721; Klein, A Recent Revision to the General Venue Statute Greatly Expands Plaintiff's Venue Choices Against A Corporate Defendant in Federal Suits for Trademark Infringement or Unfair Competition, 1989, 71 J.Pat. & Trademark Office Socy. 886.

56. Wright, Miller & Cooper, Jurisdiction 2d § 3811, pp. 106–109.

The first two editions of this text had taken the contrary view, but the decisions supporting the statement in the text had importance. As subsections (a) and (b) were amended in 1990 the residence of a plaintiff is no longer significant for venue.

The new statute makes no reference to the district in which the corporation is "incorporated" or "licensed to do business." There had been problems of construction with regard to each of these terms under the former statute. The place where the corporation is incorporated is almost certainly a place in which it is subject to jurisdiction, and a place where it is licensed to do business may meet the test of the new statute, but the facts of incorporation or license to do business now merely are factors in determining whether the corporation is subject to personal jurisdiction there and are no longer in themselves a sufficient basis for venue.

Instead of the vague concept of "doing business", which caused immense trouble under the 1958 statute, a corporation is now deemed to reside "in any judicial district in which it is subject to personal jurisdiction at the time the action is commenced." This equating of the tests for personal jurisdiction and for venue had been the better view under the former statute, but had not been adopted by all courts.[57]

In determining whether the corporation is subject to personal jurisdiction in a district, the test is whether its contacts within that district would be sufficient to subject it to personal jurisdiction if the district were a separate state.[58] If this test is satisfied with regard to more than one district in the state, the corporation is regarded as a resident of each of those districts. If a corporation has sufficient contacts with a state to make it subject to personal jurisdiction in the state, but there is no single district in the state where the contacts are sufficient, the corporation is deemed to reside in the district in which it has the most significant contacts.[59]

The law of venue for corporations has been seen not to be simple, even since the adoption of a statute on the subject. The law of venue for unincorporated associations—partnerships, labor unions, and the like—has been even more complex. It must first be determined whether the association has capacity to sue or be sued as such. The question of capacity is resolved in accordance with the law of the state in which the suit is brought, except that such capacity exists, regardless of state law, where the suit involves a claimed right under the federal constitution or laws.[60] Even if the association has capacity to appear in court in its own name, it might still be held that the residences of the individual

become so numerous by the time of the Third Edition that there was no choice save to yield to the weight of authority.

57. Bicicletas Windsor, S.A. v. Bicycle Corp. of America, D.C.N.Y.1992, 783 F.Supp. 781, 786 n. 4. See 15 Wright, Miller & Cooper, Jurisdiction 2d § 3811, pp. 117–130.

58. This is wholly a question of federal law. State law on amenability to process is

irrelevant. See cases cited 15 Wright, Miller & Cooper, Jurisdiction 2d § 3811 n. 64.

It is measured as of "the time the action is commenced." Some courts thought that the earlier version of § 1391(c) looked to the time that the claim arose.

59. Oakley, note 30 above, at 773–774.

60. Fed.R.Civ.Proc. 17(b); 6A Wright, Miller & Kane, Civil 2d §§ 1561, 1564.

members of the association are determinative for venue purposes.[61] This view, once quite commonly accepted, was rejected in several notable cases, and unincorporated associations were assimilated to corporations for purposes of venue.[62] The latter view was finally adopted by the Supreme Court. It concluded that "it most nearly approximates the intent of Congress to recognize the reality of the multi-state, unincorporated association such as a labor union and to permit suit against that entity, like the analogous corporate entity, wherever it is 'doing business.'"[63]

All that has been said so far has been concerned with actions under the general venue statutes. Many actions are governed by other venue provisions. There are numerous special venue statutes, both in the Judicial Code[64] and in other statutes that create particular rights to sue. Usually, though not invariably, these statutes broaden the choice of venue made available by the general venue statutes.[65] One important exception had been the venue statute for patent-infringement actions. It permits suit where the defendant resides or where he has committed acts of infringement and has a regular and established place of business.[66] Since the broad definition of corporate residence set out in the 1958 version of 28 U.S.C.A. § 1391(c) was held inapplicable to this special statute[67]—though not to other such special statutes[68]—a corporation could not be sued for patent infringement in a state other than the

61. Champion Spark Plug Co. v. Karchmar, D.C.N.Y.1960, 180 F.Supp. 727; Harris Mfg. Co. v. Williams, D.C.Ark.1957, 157 F.Supp. 779; cf. Koons v. Kaiser, D.C.N.Y. 1950, 91 F.Supp. 511.

62. The path was broken by Judge Learned Hand in Sperry Products, Inc. v. Association of American Railroads, C.C.A.2d, 1942, 132 F.2d 408, certiorari denied 63 S.Ct. 1031, 319 U.S. 744, 87 L.Ed. 1700, noted 1943, 38 Ill.L.Rev. 208. The principle of that case was further developed in Rutland Ry. Corp. v. Brotherhood of Locomotive Engineers, C.A.2d, 1962, 307 F.2d 21, certiorari denied 83 S.Ct. 949, 372 U.S. 954, 9 L.Ed.2d 978.

63. Denver & R.G.W.R. Co. v. Brotherhood of R.R. Trainmen, 1967, 87 S.Ct. 1746, 1750, 387 U.S. 556, 562, 18 L.Ed.2d 954.

Congress had already provided in 1947 that in suits governed by the Taft–Hartley Act a labor organization may be sued in the district where it maintains its principal office or in the district where its duly authorized officers and agents are engaged in representing or acting for employee members. 29 U.S.C.A. § 185(c).

The Brotherhood of Railroad Trainmen case is to be broadly construed and is not limited to labor unions. It applies also to partnerships, joint ventures, and other forms of unincorporated associations. Penrod Drilling Co. v. Johnson, C.A.5th, 1969,

414 F.2d 1217; Reading Metal Craft Co. v. Hopf Drive Associates, D.C.Pa.1988, 694 F.Supp. 98.

See generally 15 Wright, Miller & Cooper, Jurisdiction 2d § 3812.

64. 28 U.S.C.A. §§ 1394–1403.

65. See 15 Wright, Miller & Cooper, Jurisdiction 2d §§ 3813 (national banks), 3814–3815 (United States or federal officers or agencies), 3816 (administrative matters), 3818 (antitrust), 3819 (copyright), 3820 (fines, penalties, seizures, and forfeitures), 3821 (internal revenue), 3824 (securities regulation), 3825 (miscellaneous cases).

The very restrictive statute on venue in suits against national banks, 12 U.S.C.A. § 94, which had been held to control over broader, more general, venue statutes otherwise applicable, was in effect repealed in 1982. See 15 Wright, Miller & Cooper, Jurisdiction 2d § 3813.

66. 28 U.S.C.A. § 1400(b); 15 Wright, Miller & Cooper, Jurisdiction 2d § 3823.

67. Fourco Glass Co. v. Transmirra Products Corp., 1957, 77 S.Ct. 787, 353 U.S. 222, 1 L.Ed.2d 786.

68. Pure Oil Co. v. Suarez, 1966, 86 S.Ct. 1394, 1396, 384 U.S. 202, 205, 16 L.Ed.2d 474.

state of its incorporation merely because it did business, or was licensed to do business, in that state.[69]   A different result has been reached under § 1391(c) as it was rewritten in 1988.   The new definition of corporate residence says that it is for purposes of venue "under this chapter." Since the venue statute for patent-infringement actions is in Chapter 87 of the Judicial Code, the same chapter as § 1391(c), courts have read the new statute literally and have held that a corporation may now be sued for patent infringement in any district in which it is subject to personal jurisdiction.[70]   But if the language in the new statute that it applies only "under this chapter" is read equally literally, the definition of corporate residence will no longer apply to suits under the Jones Act, the antitrust laws, and many others to which the 1958 version of § 1391(c) had been held applicable.

There are also two important exceptions to the general venue statutes that are judge-made.   Section 1391 applies only to "civil actions."   The Supreme Court has held that the change of venue statute, 28 U.S.C.A. § 1404(a), which also refers to "civil actions," is applicable to actions in admiralty.[71]   Yet there is no sign that the ancient rule that admiralty suits are not subject to the general venue statutes [72] will be altered, and such suits continue to be subject only to the distinctive venue notions long applied in admiralty.[73]   Indeed when admiralty suits were brought under the Rules of Civil Procedure in 1966 a special provision was made so that such suits can remain free from the general venue statutes while remaining subject to the transfer provisions of § 1404(a).[74]

Another judge-made exception, stemming from the common law, is the rule that "local actions" must be brought in the district where the res that is the subject matter of the action is located.[75]   The general venue statutes are broad enough in terms to encompass local actions, but the special rule for such actions is ancient and well settled,[76] and is

---

69. But it was held in that period that an action by the alleged infringer for a declaratory judgment of noninfringement and of invalidity was governed by the general venue statutes rather than by 28 U.S.C.A. § 1400(b).   E.g., Emerson Elec. Co. v. Black & Decker Mfg. Co., C.A.8th, 1979, 606 F.2d 234.

70. VE Holding Corp. v. Johnson Gas Appliance Co., C.A.Fed.1990, 917 F.2d 1574, certiorari denied 111 S.Ct. 1315, 499 U.S. 922, 113 L.Ed.2d 248; O'Rourke, The Modernization of the Patent Venue Statute, 1992, 14 Geo.Mason U.L.Rev. 585.   See also cases and commentaries cited 15 Wright, Miller & Cooper, Jurisdiction 2d § 3823 n. 30.2.

71. Continental Grain Co. v. The FBL–585, 1960, 80 S.Ct. 1470, 364 U.S. 19, 4 L.Ed.2d 1540.   This decision was before the 1966 unification of the General Admiralty Rules with the Civil Rules.

72. Atkins v. Fibre Disintegrating Co., 1873, 18 Wall. 272, 21 L.Ed. 841; In re Louisville Underwriters, 1890, 10 S.Ct. 587, 134 U.S. 488, 33 L.Ed. 991.

73. See 15 Wright, Miller & Cooper, Jurisdiction 2d § 3817.   The American Law Institute, however, proposed to codify the liberal traditions of venue in admiralty. ALI Study, § 1318.   Currie, note 1 supra, at 303, calls this decision by the Institute "wholly unacceptable."

74. Fed.R.Civ.Proc. 82.

75. See 15 Wright, Miller & Cooper, Jurisdiction 2d § 3822; Note, Local Actions in the Federal Courts, 1957, 70 Harv.L.Rev. 708.

76. "The distinction between local and transitory actions is as old as actions themselves, and no one has ever supposed that laws which prescribed generally where one should be sued, included such suits as were recognized by other provisions in the statutes that make reference to local actions.[77] The requirement about local actions leads to some difficulty if the defendant is not subject to process in the state in which the property is located, but the difficulty is obviated in some, but not all, cases by a statute permitting service outside the state in actions to enforce a lien on or claim to, or to remove any incumbrance, lien, or cloud upon the title to property within the district.[78]

Attempts to define the distinction between a local action and a transitory action have been notoriously unsuccessful. A distinction based on the difference between actions in rem and actions in personam would make some sense. Chief Justice Marshall in 1811 said that this is where the line should be drawn, but he felt obliged by precedent to hold that certain in personam actions, such as an action for trespass q.c.f., were local actions, though the Chief Justice confessed the illogic of such a holding.[79] Thus, there is no rationalizing principle that will accommodate the particular rules as to particular actions, and decision rests on the oddities of history and "the tentacles of the common law causes of action" [80] rather than on policy considerations.[81]

It is not even clear whether the local-action concept runs to the jurisdiction or the venue of the federal court. It is usually discussed as a matter of venue, but there are cases holding that the defect that the action was brought in a district other than where the property was

local in their character, either by statute or the common law unless it was expressly so declared." Casey v. Adams, 1880, 102 U.S. 66, 67, 26 L.Ed. 52.

See also Livingston v. Jefferson, C.C.D.Va.1811, 15 Fed.Cas. 660, No. 8411 (per Marshall, C.J.); Greeley v. Lowe, 1894, 15 S.Ct. 24, 155 U.S. 58, 39 L.Ed. 69.

The continuing vitality of the doctrine, as against arguments that it did not survive a 1977 Supreme Court decision or that it is inconsistent with the statutory grant of diversity jurisdiction, was affirmed in Hayes v. Gulf Oil Corp., C.A.5th, 1987, 821 F.2d 285.

77. 28 U.S.C.A. § 1392(b) provides that local actions involving property located in different districts in the same state may be brought in any of such districts and 28 U.S.C.A. § 1392(a) applies to "any civil action, not of a local nature."

78. 28 U.S.C.A. § 1655. See 14 Wright, Miller & Cooper, Jurisdiction 2d §§ 3632–3635 for full discussion of the statute.

The statute does not reach every action of a local nature. Thus, it has been held that a suit to abate a nuisance must be brought in the district where the nuisance is located and that such an action is beyond the scope of § 1655. Ladew v. Tennessee Copper Co.,

C.C.D.Tenn.1910, 179 F. 245, affirmed 31 S.Ct. 81, 218 U.S. 357, 54 L.Ed. 1069.

79. Livingston v. Jefferson, C.C.D.Va. 1811, 15 Fed.Cas. 660, No. 8411. This meant that unless Thomas Jefferson went to Louisiana, where the land was located, Livingston could not have his suit for a money judgment against Jefferson heard.

There is a fascinating account of the Livingston case, with much interesting history about it and the famous persons who were parties to it, and with shrewd analysis of the strategy of the parties and of the court, in Degnan, Livingston v. Jefferson—A Freestanding Footnote, 1987, 75 Calif.L.Rev. 115.

The American Law Institute proposed statutory language to provide that actions for trespass upon or harm to land are subject to the general venue statutes. ALI Study, § 1303(c). It characterized this as a "modest" reform "that is long overdue." Id. at p. 139.

80. Wheatley v. Phillips, D.C.N.C.1964, 228 F.Supp. 439, 442.

81. See Currie, The Constitution and the "Transitory" Cause of Action, 1959, 73 Harv.L.Rev. 36, 66–69. For holdings as to particular cases, see 15 Wright, Miller & Cooper, Jurisdiction 2d § 3822 nn. 28–37.

located is nonwaivable,[82] which would be true only if the defect is a matter of jurisdiction rather than of venue. It is also not clear whether a uniform federal rule applies in determining whether an action is local or transitory, or whether there must be resort to state law. Chief Justice Marshall was "decidedly of opinion" that the federal courts must decide this question for themselves,[83] and this view seems clearly preferable, but other cases, largely relying on later dicta erroneously describing what Marshall had held, have looked to state law in determining the nature of the action.[84]

Since 1979 there has been considerable interest, particularly on the part of some Western senators, in changing the venue laws to shift venue in certain kinds of cases to the locality where the effects of the lawsuit are most directly felt.[85] These senators feel that the 1962 statute, allowing a very broad choice of venue in suits against federal officers and agencies,[86] has been abused "by some litigators, especially public interest law groups focusing on environmental issues and based in Washington,

82. Ellenwood v. Marietta Chair Co., 1895, 15 S.Ct. 771, 158 U.S. 105, 39 L.Ed. 913; Iselin v. Meng, C.A.5th, 1959, 269 F.2d 345, certiorari denied 80 S.Ct. 257, 361 U.S. 913, 4 L.Ed.2d 183; Minichiello Realty Associates, Inc. v. Britt, D.C.N.J.1978, 460 F.Supp. 896, affirmed without opinion C.A.3d, 1979, 605 F.2d 1196. See also Hayes v. Gulf Oil Corp., C.A.5th, 1987, 821 F.2d 285, 287, 290–291. Cases both ways are cited at 15 Wright, Miller & Cooper, Jurisdiction 2d § 3822 nn. 18–19. See also Note, Local Actions in the Federal Courts, 1957, 70 Harv.L.Rev. 708, 712–713.

83. Livingston v. Jefferson, C.C.D.Va. 1811, 15 Fed.Cas. 660, 665, No. 8,411. Accord: Illinois v. City of Milwaukee, C.A.7th, 1979, 599 F.2d 151, 157 n. 5, reversed on other grounds 1981, 101 S.Ct. 1784, 451 U.S. 304, 68 L.Ed.2d 114; Kavouras v. Fernandez, D.C.Ill.1989, 737 F.Supp. 477, 478.

84. The erroneous dicta is in Huntington v. Attrill, 1892, 13 S.Ct. 224, 228, 146 U.S. 657, 669–670, 36 L.Ed. 1123. Among recent cases holding that state law is controlling are: Hayes v. Gulf Oil Corp., C.A.5th, 1987, 821 F.2d 285, 287–288; Still v. Rossville Crushed Stone Co., C.A.6th, 1966, 370 F.2d 324, certiorari denied 87 S.Ct. 2030, 387 U.S. 918, 18 L.Ed.2d 970; General Elec. Cap. Corp. v. East Coast Yacht Sales Inc., D.C.Pa.1991, 757 F.Supp. 19, 20; Landmark Tower Associates v. First Nat. Bank of Chicago, D.C.Fla.1977, 439 F.Supp. 195; Hasburgh v. Executive Aircraft Co., D.C.Mo.1964, 35 F.R.D. 354. In the Hasburgh case the court recognized that applying state law is a "theoretical

error" but it felt bound to do so by the numerical weight of authority.

Fortunately in most cases there is no difference between federal law and the law of the state in which the court is held, and there is no need to distinguish between them. See the comprehensive opinion in Wheatley v. Phillips, D.C.N.C.1964, 228 F.Supp. 439.

85. National Legal Center for the Public Interest, Venue at the Crossroads, 1982. This pamphlet contains articles by Senators DeConcini and Laxalt supporting these changes, and articles by Nicholas Yost and Professor David Currie expressing doubt whether it is possible to achieve the goal of the sponsors without imposing on courts and litigants the wasteful burden of an extensive preliminary trial to determine the appropriate place of trial. The latter view is supported also in Sunstein, Participation, Public Law, and Venue Reform, 1982, 49 U.Chi.L.Rev. 976.

86. 28 U.S.C.A. § 1391(e). See 15 Wright, Miller & Cooper, Jurisdiction 2d § 3815; Cates, Venue in Corporate Suits Against Federal Agencies and Officers, 1975, 60 Minn.L.Rev. 81.

The statute was intended to provide a more convenient forum for individual plaintiffs in actions that are nominally against an individual officer, but are in reality against the government, and does not apply to actions brought against federal officials in their individual capacities. Stafford v. Briggs, 1980, 100 S.Ct. 774, 444 U.S. 527, 63 L.Ed.2d 1, noted 1980, 49 U.Cin.L.Rev. 675.

D.C.'' [87] and that actions have been taken ''by judges in the Federal courts of the District of Columbia in cases which had little or no impact on the residents of Washington, but which deeply affected the lives of citizens living thousands of miles away from the Capital.'' [88] The proposals for change in this respect, some of which are limited to environmental cases while others would reach federal government litigation generally, should not be confused with the common law concept of ''local'' actions that has just been discussed.

Not infrequently a contract will provide that suit on it may only be brought in the courts at a particular place. A provision of this kind will be enforced by the federal court, and venue restricted in this way, unless the provision is thought to be unreasonable in itself or in its possible effect on the rights of litigants.[89]

§ 43. Criminal Cases [1]

In civil cases venue is a matter of convenience for the litigants. In criminal cases venue involves important considerations of policy, with deep historical roots, that are now expressed in a complicated interplay of constitutional provisions, statutes, and rules.

In 1769 Parliament, over the objection of those who said such a course would lead to war, proposed taking Americans to England or to another colony for trial in treason cases. Hearing of this, the Virginia House of Burgesses unanimously adopted the famous Virginia Resolves of May 16, 1769, in which they said that by such a proposal ''the inestimable Privilege of being tried by a Jury from the Vicinage, as well as the Liberty of summoning and producing Witnesses on such Trial, will be taken away from the Party accused.'' [2] One of the grievances asserted against the King in the Declaration of Independence was ''transporting us beyond the Seas for pretended offenses.'' The point was deemed so important by the Founders that the right to be tried for crimes in the state where the crime was committed is protected not once but twice in the Constitution, in Article III, § 2, and in the Sixth Amendment. In an earlier era the place where a crime was committed was usually the place where the defendant lived, and the Supreme Court has spoken eloquently on several occasions about the importance of

---

87. DeConcini, in National Legal Center for the Public Interest, note 85 above, at p. 7.

88. 128 Cong.Rec. S658 (daily ed. Feb. 9, 1982) (remarks of Sen. DeConcini).

89. M/S Bremen v. Zapata Off–Shore Co., 1972, 92 S.Ct. 1907, 407 U.S. 1, 32 L.Ed.2d 513. See 15 Wright, Miller & Cooper, Jurisdiction 2d § 3803.1; Mullenix, Another Choice of Forum, Another Choice of Law: Consensual Adjudicatory Procedure in Federal Court, 1988, 57 Fordham L.Rev. 291.

§ 43

1. 2 Wright, Criminal 2d §§ 301–307; Kershen, Vicinage, 1976, 29 Okla.L.Rev. 801, 1977, 30 Okla.L.Rev. 1; Barber, Venue in Federal Criminal Cases: A Plea for Return to Principle, 1963, 42 Texas L.Rev. 39; Blume, The Place of Trial of Criminal Cases: Constitutional Vicinage and Venue, 1944, 43 Mich.L.Rev. 59.

2. Journals of the House of Burgesses of Virginia, 1766–1769, Kennedy ed. 1906, p. 214. See also Blume, note 1 above, at 63–65; Comment, 1967, 115 U.Pa.L.Rev. 399, 404–414.

trying a criminal defendant in his home district.[3] "Questions of venue in criminal cases, therefore, are not merely matters of formal legal procedure. They raise deep issues of public policy in the light of which legislation must be construed. If an enactment of Congress equally permits the underlying spirit of the constitutional concern for trial in the vicinage to be respected rather than to be disrespected, construction should go in the direction of constitutional policy even though not commanded by it." [4]

The Court, however, has not been consistent in this view. The cases calling for placing venue, where possible, at the defendant's home are intermingled with cases deprecating that consideration and insisting that all that is required is trial at the place of the crime.[5]

Nor has Congress been any more consistent. In 1958 it passed a statute giving defendants in certain income-tax cases an absolute right to trial at their residence, and did so, over objection by the Treasury and Justice Departments, because it recognized the difficulty to defendants required to stand trial away from home.[6] Yet three weeks later it amended the statute on mailing obscene matter to broaden the choice of venue and make it more likely that a defendant would not be tried where he resided.[7]

The constitutional command is reflected in Criminal Rule 18, which says that except as otherwise provided by statute or rule, criminal prosecutions are to be had in the district in which the crime was committed.[8] There are a number of special venue provisions, usually included in particular criminal statutes, but these are largely unnecessary, since Rule 18 and the general venue statutes make ample provision for every type of case. One legitimate purpose of a special venue provision is to narrow the choice of venues that otherwise would be available. Thus, it has always been the rule that the trial of offenses punishable by death shall be in the county where the offense was

---

3. Hyde v. Shine, 1905, 25 S.Ct. 760, 762, 199 U.S. 62, 78, 50 L.Ed. 90; U.S. v. Johnson, 1944, 65 S.Ct. 249, 250–252, 323 U.S. 273, 275–278, 89 L.Ed. 236; U.S. v. Cores, 1958, 78 S.Ct. 875, 877, 356 U.S. 405, 407, 2 L.Ed.2d 873.

4. U.S. v. Johnson, 1944, 65 S.Ct. 249, 251, 323 U.S. 273, 276, 89 L.Ed. 236.

5. Johnston v. U.S., 1956, 76 S.Ct. 739, 742, 351 U.S. 215, 220–221, 100 L.Ed. 1097; Travis v. U.S., 1961, 81 S.Ct. 358, 360–361, 364 U.S. 631, 634, 5 L.Ed.2d 340; Platt v. Minnesota Mining & Mfg. Co., 1964, 84 S.Ct. 769, 772, 376 U.S. 240, 245, 11 L.Ed.2d 674. These inconsistent lines of cases are fully discussed in 2 Wright, Criminal 2d § 301.

6. 18 U.S.C.A. § 3237(b), as amended by Act of Aug. 6, 1958, Pub.L. 85–595, 72 Stat. 512. For the legislative history, see 1958 U.S.Code Cong. & Adm.News 3261.

7. 18 U.S.C.A. § 1461, as amended by Act of Aug. 28, 1958, Pub.L. 85–796, § 1, 72 Stat. 962. See U.S. v. Bagnell, C.A.11th, 1982, 679 F.2d 826, 831 n. 7, certiorari denied 103 S.Ct. 1449, 460 U.S. 1047, 75 L.Ed.2d 803; Comment, Multi–Venue and the Obscenity Statutes, 1967, 115 U.Pa. L.Rev. 399.

8. Until 1966 the rule also required that trial be in the division where the offense is committed. As amended in that year the rule now provides only that the court shall fix the place of trial within the district "with due regard to the convenience of the defendant and the witnesses." See 2 Wright, Criminal 2d § 305; U.S. v. Burns, C.A.11th, 1981, 662 F.2d 1378; U.S. v. Florence, C.A.4th, 1972, 456 F.2d 46.

committed, where that can be done without great inconvenience.[9] Fugitive felons may be prosecuted only in the district where the original offense was committed, though under the general venue statute prosecution would have been possible in any district through which they passed in their flight.[10] Persons charged with using the mails in certain violations of the Internal Revenue Code are given a privilege to be tried in the district where they reside.[11]

The general principle that criminal trials are to be held where the offense was committed leaves three questions open. First, some offenses are committed on the high seas or otherwise not within any district. The Constitution authorized Congress to provide a rule for such cases, and it has provided that such offenses shall be tried in the district where the offender is found or is first brought. Or, if the offender has not been arrested or brought into any district, an indictment or information may be filed either in the district of the offender's last known residence or in the District of Columbia.[12]

Second, in some cases it is not clear where the offense was committed. Statutes set out a rule for particular instances. Thus, in cases of murder or manslaughter, where the injury was inflicted in one district and the victim died in another, the place of injury is declared to be the proper venue.[13] A prosecution for influencing a juror or for tampering with a witness may be brought in the district in which the proceeding was intended to be affected or in the district in which the influencing or tampering occurred.[14] But in most such cases there is no statutory rule, and the courts have had to work out answers for themselves, with the rule being that the locus delicti must be determined from the nature of the crime alleged and the location of the act or acts constituting it.[15] It is now settled, for example, that a prosecution for conspiracy may be had in any district in which any act in furtherance thereof was committed by

---

9. 18 U.S.C.A. § 3235.

10. 18 U.S.C.A. § 1073.

11. 18 U.S.C.A. § 3237(b). The statute was amended in 1984 to make it clear that defendant has the right to have venue changed only when the use of the mails is the basis upon which the United States laid venue in a district other than that of the taxpayer's residence. See U.S. v. Melvan, D.C.Cal.1987, 676 F.Supp. 997, 1001.

12. 18 U.S.C.A. § 3238. See 2 Wright, Criminal 2d § 304; U.S. v. McRary, C.A.5th, 1980, 616 F.2d 181; U.S. v. Kampiles, C.A.7th, 1979, 609 F.2d 1233, certiorari denied 100 S.Ct. 2923, 446 U.S. 954, 64 L.Ed.2d 812.

The two provisions are in the disjunctive. If the defendant is indicted before he is brought into the United States, he may be tried in the district in which he was indicted even if it is not the district in which he is first brought into the United States. U.S. v. Layton, C.A.9th, 1988, 855 F.2d 1388,

1410–1411, certiorari denied 109 S.Ct. 1178, 489 U.S. 1046, 103 L.Ed.2d 244.

13. 18 U.S.C.A. § 3236. Prior to the adoption of the statutory provision to this effect, cases had held that the place where the death occurred was the proper venue. U.S. v. Bladen, C.C.D.C.1809, 24 F.Cas. 1160, No. 14,605; cf. U.S. v. Davis, C.C.D.Mass.1837, 25 F.Cas. 786, No. 14,-932.

14. 18 U.S.C.A. § 1512(h). This 1988 statute resolved a conflict in the cases on this point.

15. U.S. v. Anderson, 1946, 66 S.Ct. 1213, 1216, 328 U.S. 699, 703, 90 L.Ed. 1529. It was held here that refusal to submit to induction into the army was to be prosecuted at the place where the induction center was located, rather than at the place where the draft board was. See also Johnston v. U.S., 1956, 76 S.Ct. 739, 351 U.S. 215, 100 L.Ed. 1097. See 2 Wright, Criminal 2d § 302.

any of the conspirators.[16] The statute under which the prosecution is had must be studied carefully, with particular attention to the verb defining the offense.[17] Thus, where the statute makes it a crime to file a false affidavit, the crime is committed, and prosecution must be had, in the district where the affidavit was filed, even though it was executed in another district and mailed for filing.[18]

A few recent cases, however, reject the traditional view that the Constitution commands a single exclusive venue. These cases employ a "substantial contacts" test that takes into account a number of factors and this may mean that several different districts are proper venues for a particular case.[19]

Finally there are some continuing offenses that are committed in more than one district. Except as otherwise expressly provided by statute, such offenses may be prosecuted in any district in which the offense was begun, continued, or completed.[20] Courts have gone even beyond the statute to hold that one who aids or abets a crime, though he may be prosecuted as a principal, can be tried not only in the district in which the substantive offense was committed, but also in the district in which he performed accessorial acts.[21] And the Second Circuit, in a notable opinion, has held that even where the mailings, which constituted the offense under the Securities Act, were in New York, the case could be tried in Alabama, where the scheme was hatched.[22]

There is obvious danger in those broad provisions and rulings as to venue, in that they make it possible to thwart the purpose of the constitutional requirement of trial in the vicinage. This is especially true as notions of vicarious participation in crime have become more expansive, and use of the mails or other means of interstate communication or transportation has become the touchstone of so many federal

---

16. Hyde v. U.S., 1912, 32 S.Ct. 793, 225 U.S. 347, 56 L.Ed. 1114 (any overt act); Hyde v. Shine, 1905, 25 S.Ct. 760, 199 U.S. 62, 50 L.Ed. 90 (place of agreement); and cases cited 2 Wright, Criminal 2d § 303 nn. 11, 12. See Abrams, Conspiracy and Multi–Venue in Federal Criminal Prosecutions: The Crime Committed Formula, 1962, 9 UCLA L.Rev. 751.

17. Dobie, Venue in Criminal Cases in the United States District Court, 1926, 12 Va.L.Rev. 287, 289; 2 Wright, Criminal 2d § 302.

18. Travis v. U.S., 1961, 81 S.Ct. 358, 364 U.S. 631, 5 L.Ed.2d 340. But see U.S. v. Herberman, C.A.5th, 1978, 583 F.2d 222, 225–227. For similar close analyses of the statutes under which particular prosecutions were brought, see Horner v. U.S., 1892, 12 S.Ct. 407, 143 U.S. 207, 36 L.Ed. 126; Burton v. U.S., 1905, 25 S.Ct. 243, 196 U.S. 283, 49 L.Ed. 482; Burton v. U.S., 1906, 26 S.Ct. 688, 202 U.S. 344, 50 L.Ed. 1057; U.S. v. Lombardo, 1916, 36 S.Ct. 508, 241 U.S. 73, 60 L.Ed. 897; U.S. v. Barsanti,

C.A.4th, 1991, 943 F.2d 428, 434, certiorari denied 112 S.Ct. 1474, ___ U.S. ___. 117 L.Ed.2d 618.

19. U.S. v. Williams, C.A.6th, 1986, 788 F.2d 1213, 1215; U.S. v. Reed, C.A.2d, 1985, 773 F.2d 477, 481.

20. 18 U.S.C.A. § 3237(a). The constitutionality of such provisions was upheld in Armour Packing Co. v. U.S., 1908, 28 S.Ct. 428, 209 U.S. 56, 52 L.Ed. 681.

See 2 Wright, Criminal 2d § 303.

21. U.S. v. Gillette, C.A.2d, 1951, 189 F.2d 449, certiorari denied 72 S.Ct. 49, 342 U.S. 827, 96 L.Ed. 625. See Abrams, note 16 above.

But the fact that an accessory performed acts in a district does not make it a proper venue for prosecution of his principal. U.S. v. Sweig, D.C.N.Y.1970, 316 F.Supp. 1148, 1159–1162.

22. U.S. v. Cashin, C.A.2d, 1960, 281 F.2d 669.

crimes. Thus, suppose that two women in Key West devise a scheme that violates the Securities Act, or that may be used to defraud. The scheme is carried out entirely in the Key West area. One of the women writes a letter to Seattle in connection with the scheme. Not only this woman, but also her associate who had nothing to do with the letter, can, if the government chooses, be prosecuted for their crime in Seattle, though it may be that neither one has ever been in that part of the country. The protection of the Constitution is vastly diluted when this is possible.[23] The remedy, however, is not to narrow criminal venue, but to permit easy transfer, if the government should choose to prosecute in the Western District of Washington, back to the Southern District of Florida, where the defendants reside, and where the witnesses and records are located. Criminal Rule 21(b) was intended to provide just such a procedure, and, as will be seen in the next section, it was amended in 1966 to overcome a strict judicial construction that had prevented it from accomplishing its purpose.

Venue is a fact that must be proved in a criminal case[24] though it need not be proved beyond a reasonable doubt, and the absence of direct proof of venue does not defeat conviction if the fact of venue is properly inferable from all the evidence.[25] Since venue is a privilege of the defendant, it may be waived if the defendant fails to object to an improper venue.[26]

§ 44. Change of Venue [1]

Provisions for change of venue have long been a commonplace in state jurisprudence. In the federal courts they are a novelty of the last three decades. Criminal Rules 21 and 22, effective in 1945, authorized change of venue to avoid prejudice or where the interests of justice so required. For civil cases § 1404(a) of the 1948 Judicial Code permitted

---

23. "Plainly enough, such leeway not only opens the door to needless hardships to an accused by prosecution remote from home and from appropriate facilities for defense. It also leads to the appearance of abuses, if not to abuses, in the selection of what may be deemed a tribunal favorable to the prosecution." U.S. v. Johnson, 1944, 65 S.Ct. 249, 250, 323 U.S. 273, 275, 89 L.Ed. 236.

24. U.S. v. White, C.A.5th, 1980, 611 F.2d 531, certiorari denied 100 S.Ct. 2978, 446 U.S. 992, 64 L.Ed.2d 849; U.S. v. Jones, C.A.7th, 1949, 174 F.2d 746; and cases cited 2 Wright, Criminal 2d § 307 n. 2.

25. U.S. v. Taylor, C.A.10th, 1987, 828 F.2d 630, 633; U.S. v. Rivamonte, C.A.11th, 1982, 666 F.2d 515, 517; and cases cited 2 Wright, Criminal 2d § 307 nn. 4–6.

26. E.g., U.S. v. Roberts, C.A.9th, 1980, 618 F.2d 530; U.S. v. Black Cloud, C.A.8th, 1979, 590 F.2d 270. See 2 Wright, Criminal 2d § 306.

§ 44

1. Civil cases: 15 Wright, Miller & Cooper, Jurisdiction 2d §§ 3841–3855; Kitch, Section 1404(a) of the Judicial Code: In The Interest of Justice or Injustice?, 1965, 40 Ind.L.J. 99; Leathers, Dimensions of the Constitutional Obligation to Provide a Forum, 1974, 62 Ky.L.J. 1; Steinberg, The Motion to Transfer and the Interests of Justice, 1990, 66 Notre Dame L.Rev. 443.

Criminal cases: 2 Wright, Criminal 2d §§ 341–347; Bailey & Golding, Remedies for Prejudicial Publicity—Change of Venue and Continuance in Federal Criminal Procedure, 1958, 18 Fed.B.J. 56; Comment, The Right to Venue and the Right to an Impartial Jury: Resolving the Conflict in the Federal Constitution, 1985, 52 U.Chi. L.Rev. 729; Note, The Efficacy of a Change of Venue in Protecting a Defendant's Right to an Impartial Jury, 1967, 42 Notre Dame Law. 925.

transfer to a more convenient forum, while § 1406(a) provided transfer, as an alternative to dismissal, where the case is brought at an improper venue. Limited provisions for transfer of habeas-corpus cases [2] and for pretrial proceedings in multidistrict litigation [3] have been added more recently. There is also provision allowing transfer of an action or appeal if it is brought in a court that lacks jurisdiction of it.[4] The provisions for criminal cases present fewer problems and will be considered first.

Criminal Rule 21(a) authorizes the court, on motion of a defendant, to transfer the case to another district if the court is satisfied that there exists in the district where the prosecution is pending so great a prejudice against the defendant that he cannot obtain a fair and impartial trial there.[5] Such motions have been granted in very few cases [6] and it is doubtful whether this rule will ever be much used. Given the size of federal judicial districts it is difficult to show that prejudice is so great that an impartial jury cannot be found, and the courts have been strict in demanding such a showing. Further, defendant has a constitutional right to be tried in the state where the offense was committed. Defendant can waive this right by moving to transfer to another state, but he is under no compulsion to do so. Since the Constitution gives a person charged with crime both the right to a fair trial and the right to a trial in the vicinage, defendant may insist upon both rights by moving for a continuance rather than for a transfer.[7]

As amended in 1966, Rule 21(b) provides that, on motion of a defendant, the court may transfer the proceeding as to him or any one or more of the counts therein to any other district [8] "for the convenience of

---

2. 28 U.S.C.A. § 2241(d), as amended in 1966, allows a habeas-corpus action to be brought for a state prisoner either in the district in which he was convicted or the district in which he was confined and permits transfer from one district to the other "in furtherance of justice."

3. 28 U.S.C.A. § 1407, added to the Judicial Code in 1968, allows the temporary transfer of civil actions involving common questions of fact to a single district for purposes of coordinated pretrial proceedings, after which the actions are returned to their original districts for trial. See 15 Wright, Miller & Cooper, Jurisdiction 2d §§ 3861–3868; Herndon & Higginbotham, Complex Multidistrict Litigation—An Overview, 1979, 31 Baylor L.Rev. 33; Comment, The Judicial Panel on Multidistrict Litigation: Time for Rethinking, 1991, 140 U.Pa. L.Rev. 711.

4. 28 U.S.C.A. § 1631. See Tayon, The Federal Transfer Statute: 28 U.S.C. § 1631, 1987, 29 S.Tex.L.J. 189.

5. As amended in 1966, Rule 21(a) permits the court to determine for itself where to transfer a case, and the moving defendant cannot limit this choice. U.S. v. Mar-

cello, D.C.La.1968, 280 F.Supp. 510, 520. See 2 Wright, Criminal 2d § 342 n. 2.

6. Eight reported cases in which a transfer was ordered under Criminal Rule 21(a) are cited in 2 Wright, Criminal 2d § 342 n. 18, while note 19 cites a multitude of cases in which a transfer motion has been denied.

7. Delaney v. U.S., C.A.1st, 1952, 199 F.2d 107. The courts, however, have been very reluctant to grant continuances sought on this ground. See Bailey & Golding, Remedies for Prejudicial Publicity—Change of Venue and Continuance in Federal Criminal Procedure, 1958, 18 Fed.B.J. 56; U.S. v. Marcello, D.C.La.1968, 280 F.Supp. 510, 519.

It is argued in Comment, note 1 above, that if it is not possible to find an impartial jury in the district and the defendant refuses to waive his or her venue right by moving for change of venue, the court has power on its own to order transfer to another district.

8. Unlike Rule 21(a), Rule 21(b) does not provide for transfer to a district "whether or not such district is specified in the defendant's motion." Although the Ad-parties and witnesses, and in the interest of justice." [9] The former rule, which this replaced, was much more restrictive. It allowed transfer only of an offense that could be considered to have been committed in more than one district, and then permitted transfer only to another district in which the offense had been committed.[10] In addition, in a multicount indictment only those counts that charged an offense in more than one district could be transferred,[11] and the courts were naturally reluctant to transfer part of a case while retaining the nontransferable counts.[12] For these reasons the former rule was not much used. The amendment did away with all of these limitations and gave the court ample power in every case to provide for trial in the most convenient forum if requested to do so by the defendant.[13] There is no indication, however, that transfers are being granted more liberally under the amended rule.

Section 1406(a) of the 1948 Code, as amended in 1949, provides that if a civil action is commenced in the wrong district or division, the court shall dismiss, but if it is in the interest of justice, the court may instead transfer the case to any district or division in which it could have been brought.[14] There are some instances in which dismissal will still be ordered,[15] but more commonly transfer will be preferable, since it avoids the need of commencing a new action.[16] Transfer can be ordered only if

visory Committee Note to the amended rule suggests that the court has this power on Rule 21(b) motions, a strong argument can be made that on a 21(b) motion transfer can only be to a district to which defendant has requested transfer. See 2 Wright, Criminal 2d § 345.

9. Although the former Rule 21(b) spoke only of "in the interest of justice," there is no reason to believe that the added reference to the convenience of parties and witnesses makes any substantive change. Jones v. Gasch, C.A.1967, 404 F.2d 1231, 1236–1237, certiorari denied 88 S.Ct. 1414, 390 U.S. 1029, 20 L.Ed.2d 286. Accordingly the factors to be considered listed by the Supreme Court under the old rule in Platt v. Minnesota Mining & Mfg. Co., 1964, 84 S.Ct. 769, 771, 376 U.S. 240, 243–244, 11 L.Ed.2d 674, should continue to be the relevant factors. For discussion of these factors and their application, see 2 Wright, Criminal 2d § 344. For a particular colorful application of these factors, see U.S. v. McDonald, D.C.Alaska 1990, 740 F.Supp. 757.

10. 2 Wright, Criminal 2d § 343 n. 5.

11. U.S. v. Choate, C.A.5th, 1960, 276 F.2d 724.

12. See cases cited 2 Wright, Criminal 2d § 343 nn. 12, 13.

13. See 1 Wright, Criminal 2d § 343. The rule is informatively discussed in Jones v. Gasch, C.A.1967, 404 F.2d 1231, certiorari denied 88 S.Ct. 1414, 390 U.S. 1029, 20

L.Ed.2d 286, in which a refusal to order transfer was upheld.

14. 28 U.S.C.A. § 1406(a); 15 Wright, Miller & Cooper, Jurisdiction 2d § 3827. As adopted in 1948, the statute required transfer whenever a case was brought in the wrong venue. The 1949 amendment authorized dismissal unless the interests of justice required transfer.

Ordinarily it will be a district court that orders transfer under § 1406(a), but if an appellate court is persuaded that venue is wrong and that a transfer would be in the interest of justice, that court may order a transfer. Bolar v. Frank, C.A.2d, 1991, 938 F.2d 377, 379–380; Cox Enterprises, Inc. v. Holt, C.A.11th, 1982, 691 F.2d 989, 990.

15. E.g., Hapaniewski v. City of Chicago Heights, C.A.7th, 1989, 883 F.2d 576, certiorari denied 110 S.Ct. 1116, 493 U.S. 1071, 107 L.Ed.2d 1023; McTyre v. Broward General Medical Center, D.C.N.J. 1990, 749 F.Supp. 102.

In most cases it will be the plaintiff who will wish transfer while the defendant will contend that the suit should be dismissed. See however Stevenson v. U.S., D.C.Tenn. 1961, 197 F.Supp. 355, dismissing the case at plaintiff's request over defendant's motion to transfer.

16. E.g., Corke v. Sameiet M.S. Song of Norway, C.A.2d, 1978, 572 F.2d 77 (statute of limitations had run); Brenner v. Rubin, D.C.Mass.1965, 240 F.Supp. 467 (defendant had misled plaintiff about venue).

the court in which the action was brought has jurisdiction of the subject matter of the action [17] but it is not necessary that it have in personam jurisdiction of the defendant.[18] The action can be transferred, and service made in the transferee district. The suit can only be transferred to a district in which venue is proper [19] and in which defendant is amenable to process.[20]

The most interesting, and most controversial, change-of-venue provision adopted for civil cases is 28 U.S.C.A. § 1404(a). It states: "For the convenience of parties and witnesses, in the interest of justice, a district court [21] may transfer any civil action to any other district or division where it might have been brought." One year earlier the Supreme Court had held that the doctrine of forum non conveniens was available in federal court, and that a court could dismiss a suit, though it had both personal and subject-matter jurisdiction and the venue was properly laid, if there existed another forum so much more convenient for the parties and the courts that plaintiff's privilege of choosing his forum was outweighed.[22] Although the doctrine of forum non conveniens has flourished in the states since 1947,[23] it has largely been superseded in federal courts by the 1948 adoption of § 1404(a).[24] Only in rare instances where the alternative forum is a state court or the court of a foreign country may the federal court now dismiss on grounds of forum non conveniens.[25]

17. N.A.A.C.P.—Special Contribution Fund v. Jones, D.C.Ohio 1990, 732 F.Supp. 791; and cases cited 15 Wright, Miller & Cooper, Jurisdiction 2d § 3827 n. 5.

18. Goldlawr, Inc. v. Heiman, 1962, 82 S.Ct. 913, 369 U.S. 463, 8 L.Ed.2d 39.

19. Manley v. Engram, C.A.11th, 1985, 755 F.2d 1463, 1467; Blackmar v. Guerre, C.A.5th, 1951, 190 F.2d 427, affirmed 1952, 72 S.Ct. 410, 342 U.S. 512, 96 L.Ed. 534.

Except under unusual circumstances the decision by the transferor court that venue is proper and service possible in the transferee court cannot be reconsidered by the transferee court. Hayman Cash Register Co. v. Sarokin, C.A.3d, 1982, 669 F.2d 162.

20. Johnson v. Helicopter & Airplane Services Corp., D.C.Md.1974, 389 F.Supp. 509, 523–525; Smith v. Murchison, D.C.N.Y.1970, 310 F.Supp. 1079, 1089–1090.

21. The language of the statute does not preclude an appellate court from effecting a transfer by direct order if unusual circumstances make this necessary. Koehring Co. v. Hyde Constr. Co., 1966, 86 S.Ct. 522, 382 U.S. 362, 15 L.Ed.2d 416.

22. Gulf Oil Corp. v. Gilbert, 1947, 67 S.Ct. 839, 330 U.S. 501, 91 L.Ed. 1055; Koster v. Lumbermens Mut. Cas. Co., 1947, 67 S.Ct. 828, 330 U.S. 518, 91 L.Ed. 1067.

See 15 Wright, Miller & Cooper, Jurisdiction 2d § 3828; Stewart, Forum Non Conveniens: A Doctrine in Search of a Role, 1986, 74 Calif.L.Rev. 1259.

23. Federal notions of forum non conveniens are not binding on the states, except perhaps in a case governed by federal maritime law. Chick Kam Choo v. Exxon Corp., 1988, 108 S.Ct. 1684, 486 U.S. 140, 100 L.Ed.2d 127. See Robertson & Speck, Access to State Courts in Transnational Personal Injury Cases: Forum Non Conveniens and Antisuit Injunctions, 1990, 68 Texas L.Rev. 937.

24. Collins v. American Auto. Ins. Co. of St. Louis, Missouri, C.A.2d, 1956, 230 F.2d 416, certiorari dismissed 77 S.Ct. 20, 352 U.S. 802, 1 L.Ed.2d 37; Watson v. DeFelice, D.C.D.C.1977, 428 F.Supp. 1276.

25. E.g., Prack v. Weissinger, C.A.4th, 1960, 276 F.2d 446; and cases cited 15 Wright, Miller & Cooper, Jurisdiction 2d § 3828 nn. 6–7.

For the standards to be applied in determining whether to dismiss in favor of a foreign country, see Piper Aircraft Co. v. Reyno, 1981, 102 S.Ct. 252, 454 U.S. 235, 70 L.Ed.2d 419; 15 Wright, Miller & Cooper, Jurisdiction 2d § 3828, pp. 282–308.

In a diversity case a federal court is to apply federal notions of whether to dismiss on the ground of forum non conveniens and

Section 1404(a) has given rise to a veritable flood of litigation. Probably no issue of adjective law gives rise to so many reported decisions, year after year, as does this seemingly simple statute. Most of the decisions merely illustrate how a court has weighed the various factors in determining whether to order transfer in a particular case on particular facts.[26] There are some legal issues posed by the statute, however, that do appear in the cases.

One such issue was swiftly resolved by the Supreme Court. It was contended that § 1404(a) should apply only to actions under the general venue statutes and not to those cases for which there is a special venue statute. The Supreme Court rejected this argument, holding that the broad language "any civil action" meant what it said.[27] Indeed even admiralty suits are subject to § 1404(a),[28] although they are not regarded as civil actions for purposes of the other general venue statutes.[29] There has been disagreement in the cases as to whether an action in rem is transferable under the statute. A Supreme Court decision allowing transfer of an action in which in rem and in personam admiralty proceedings were joined is probably best understood as resting on the Court's refusal to take seriously, in a § 1404(a) context, the archaic admiralty fiction by which an action actually against the ship owner is pretended to be against the ship.[30] The lower courts, however, have read that case as meaning that transfer is possible if in rem and in personam proceedings are joined, and have come to hold that even an action purely

is not to look to state law on this point. In re Air Crash Disaster Near New Orleans, C.A.5th, 1987, 821 F.2d 1147, 1154–1159, noted 1988, 62 Tul.L.Rev. 813; Sibaja v. Dow Chemical Co., C.A.11th, 1985, 757 F.2d 1215. But see Stein, Erie and Court Access, 1991, 100 Yale L.J. 1935.

26. The flood of opinions with little or no precedential value is encouraged by those appellate courts that have urged trial courts to state their reasons for granting or denying a transfer motion: In re Pope, C.A. 1978, 580 F.2d 620, 623; Starnes v. McGuire, C.A.1974, 512 F.2d 918, 934; Plum Tree, Inc. v. Stockment, C.A.3d, 1973, 488 F.2d 754, 756; Solomon v. Continental American Life Ins. Co., C.A.3d, 1973, 472 F.2d 1043, 1048; cf. A.J. Indus., Inc. v. United States Dist. Court, C.A.9th, 1974, 503 F.2d 384, 389; Westinghouse Elec. Corp. v. Weigel, C.A.9th, 1970, 426 F.2d 1356, 1358.

27. Ex parte Collett, 1949, 69 S.Ct. 944, 337 U.S. 55, 93 L.Ed. 1207 (FELA action); U.S. v. National City Lines, Inc., 1949, 69 S.Ct. 955, 337 U.S. 78, 93 L.Ed. 1226; 15 Wright, Miller & Cooper, Jurisdiction 2d § 3843. This result seems especially odd in the FELA cases, since the Code was presented to Congress as containing nothing of

a controversial nature and the same Congress that enacted the Code had refused to adopt proposed legislation that would have limited the plaintiff's choice of forum in FELA cases. See Pope v. Atlantic Coast Line R. Co., 1953, 73 S.Ct. 749, 753, 345 U.S. 379, 386–387, 97 L.Ed. 1094.

28. Continental Grain Co. v. The FBL–585, 1960, 80 S.Ct. 1470, 364 U.S. 19, 4 L.Ed.2d 1540.

29. Fed.R.Civ.Proc. 82, as amended in 1966.

30. Continental Grain Co. v. The FBL–585, 1960, 80 S.Ct. 1470, 364 U.S. 19, 4 L.Ed.2d 1540.

Professor David J. Sharpe, of the National Law Center at George Washington University, has objected to "the rather snide reference" to " 'the archaic admiralty fiction' that an action 'is pretended to be against the ship.' " In a letter of March 30, 1993, to the author, he says: "The bumblebee flies in spite of the aerodynamic improbability; despite the theoretical inconvenience, people today arrest ships quite frequently; and in my discussion with lawyers from other legal cultures, the U.S. procedure is envied abroad for its commercial practicality if not for its jurisprudential elegance."

in rem can be transferred, despite the conceptual argument that there is no other district in which an action in rem can be brought.[31]

The procedure for transfer under § 1404(a) has not given much difficulty. The motion for transfer may be made by any party, including the plaintiff,[32] though other limitations on the statute, discussed below, severely limit the circumstances in which it would be of any use to a plaintiff. The motion may be made at any time, though delay in moving is a factor that will be considered in passing on the motion.[33] Once the motion has been granted and the papers lodged with the transferee court, the transferor court loses all jurisdiction over the case.[34] The case then proceeds in the transferee court as if it had been commenced, and all prior actions had, in that court.[35]

A 1964 Supreme Court decision held that if the transfer was on motion of the defendant, the transferee court must apply the law that would have been applied in the transferor court, so that a change in forum will mean a change in courtrooms, but not a change of law.[36] This means that in passing on a motion to transfer the court must consider, as one of the factors in deciding whether to grant the motion, the effect that retaining the law of the transferor state will have. Thus, if the law is unclear in the state in which the action is commenced, this argues against transfer, since a district judge in that state is presumably better able to fathom its law than is a district judge in the transferee state. Also the fact that the substantive law will not be changed by a transfer

---

31. In re International Marine Towing, Inc., C.A.5th, 1980, 617 F.2d 362. See 15 Wright, Miller & Cooper, Jurisdiction 2d § 3843, pp. 324–326; Comment, Transfer of Quasi in Rem Actions under 28 U.S.C.A. § 1404(a): A Study in the Interpretation of "Civil Action," 1964, 31 U.Chi.L.Rev. 373.

32. E.g., Coffey v. Van Dorn Iron Works, C.A.7th, 1986, 796 F.2d 217, 219; and cases cited 15 Wright, Miller & Cooper, Jurisdiction 2d § 3844 n. 5. Some older cases were to the contrary but that view has no recent support. See also Korbel, Plaintiff's Right to Change of Venue in Federal Courts, 1960, 38 U.Det.L.J. 137.

33. McGraw–Edison Co. v. Van Pelt, C.A.8th, 1965, 350 F.2d 361; Nagle v. Pennsylvania R. Co., D.C.Ohio, 89 F.Supp. 822; and cases cited 15 Wright, Miller & Cooper, Jurisdiction 2d § 3844 n. 18.

34. Starnes v. McGuire, C.A.1974, 512 F.2d 918, 923–925; 15 Wright, Miller & Cooper, Jurisdiction 2d § 3846, pp. 357–358.

But the transferee court may acquire jurisdiction before the papers have physically reached it. Koehring Co. v. Hyde Constr. Co., 1966, 86 S.Ct. 522, 524 n. 4, 382 U.S. 362, 365 n. 4, 15 L.Ed.2d 416.

35. Magnetic Engineering & Mfg. Co. v. Dings Mfg. Co., C.A.2d, 1950, 178 F.2d 866. See 15 Wright, Miller & Cooper, Jurisdiction 2d § 3846.

36. Van Dusen v. Barrack, 1964, 84 S.Ct. 805, 821, 376 U.S. 612, 639, 11 L.Ed.2d 945.

Prior to the Van Dusen decision the courts were divided on this question and the problem was so complex that a leading scholar publicly retracted what he had earlier written on the subject. Compare Currie, Change of Venue and the Conflict of Laws, 1955, 22 U.Chi.L.Rev. 405, with Currie, Change of Venue and the Conflict of Laws: A Retraction, 1960, 27 U.Chi.L.Rev. 341.

It has been held—deciding a question left open in the Van Dusen case, 84 S.Ct. at 821, 376 U.S. at 639–640—that the law of the transferor state will apply even though that state would have dismissed the action on the ground of forum non conveniens. In re Air Crash Disaster at Boston, Mass., D.C.Mass.1975, 399 F.Supp. 1106, 1119–1122.

may cast doubt on the feasibility of consolidating the transferred case with other cases that were commenced in the court to which transfer is proposed, and may have an effect on the witnesses that will be necessary. All of this must be considered by the district court in passing on the transfer motion.[37]

In 1990, in Ferens v. John Deere Co.,[38] it was held that the principle announced in 1964 applied even where it is the plaintiff who moves for a transfer. Pennsylvania plaintiffs brought suit for a Pennsylvania injury in Mississippi, since the statute of limitations would have barred the suit in Pennsylvania. On their motion the district court in Mississippi then transferred the case back to Pennsylvania. Even under those circumstances the Mississippi statute of limitations continued to apply. A bare majority of the Court held that a transferee court must "apply the law of the transferor court, regardless of who initiates the transfer. A transfer under § 1404(a), in other words, does not change the law applicable to a diversity case." [39]

Both in Van Dusen and in Ferens the Court spoke quite explicitly of diversity cases. This suggests that in a federal-question case the transferee court is free to think for itself what federal law is and need not mechanically apply the view of federal law that is taken in the circuit from which the case was transferred.[40]

The statute permits transfer only to another forum where the suit "might have been brought." The meaning of this limitation has caused much disagreement.[41] At a minimum it would seem to preclude transfer to a district that would not have been a proper venue for the action initially, at least in the absence of consent by the defendant. Courts were not agreed, however, as to whether the transferee forum must be one in which process could have been served on defendant. In the leading case of Foster–Milburn Co. v. Knight[42] Judge Learned Hand, speaking for the Second Circuit, held that a case could not be transferred on the motion of plaintiff to a district where defendants were not subject to process. Though the First Circuit rejected the Foster–Milburn rule as

---

37. Van Dusen v. Barrack, 1964, 84 S.Ct. 805, 823–824, 376 U.S. 612, 643–646, 11 L.Ed.2d 945. See cases cited 15 Wright, Miller & Cooper, Jurisdiction 2d § 3854 nn. 28–29.

38. 1990, 110 S.Ct. 1274, 494 U.S. 516, 108 L.Ed.2d 443, noted 1991, 19 N.Ky. L.Rev. 171, 26 Wake Forest L.Rev. 809. See Seidelson, 1 (Wortman) + 1 (Ferens) = 6 (Years): That Can't Be Right—Can It? Statutes of Limitations and Supreme Court Inconsistency, 1991, 57 Brook.L.Rev. 787. See also the comments on the case in Oakley, Recent Statutory Changes in the Law of Federal Jurisdiction and Venue: The Judicial Improvements Acts of 1988 and 1990, 1991, 24 U.C.Davis L.Rev. 735, 781–782 n. 166.

39. 110 S.Ct. at 1280, 494 U.S. at 523.

40. In re Korean Air Lines Disaster of Sept. 1, 1983, C.A.D.C.1987, 829 F.2d 1171, affirmed on other grounds 1989, 109 S.Ct. 1676, 490 U.S. 122, 104 L.Ed.2d 113; Center Cadillac, Inc. v. Bank Leumi Trust Co. of N.Y., D.C.N.Y.1992, 808 F.Supp. 213, 222–224; In re Taxable Municipal Bond Securities Litigation, D.C.La.1992, 796 F.Supp. 954, 962–963; Marcus, Conflicts Among Circuits and Transfers Within the Federal Judicial System, 1984, 93 Yale L.J. 677.

41. 15 Wright, Miller & Cooper, Jurisdiction 2d § 3845.

42. C.A.2d, 1950, 181 F.2d 949, criticized 1951, 60 Yale L.J. 183.

"a gloss" on the statute,[43] and the reasoning of the rule was carefully rebutted by an able district judge,[44] most courts accepted the rule, and the rigid limitation that it placed on the usefulness of § 1404(a).[45]

A doctrine did develop among some courts—though rejected by others—that a defendant could have an action transferred to a district where venue would have been improper or it was not amenable to process since its motion for transfer waived any objection to venue or in personam jurisdiction in the transferee court. The Supreme Court repudiated this doctrine in Hoffman v. Blaski.[46] It held there that the words "might have been brought" direct the attention of the judge to the situation that existed when suit was instituted, and that they permit transfer only to a district where plaintiff would have had the right, independent of the wishes of the defendant, to bring the action. This clearly establishes that consent by the defendant will not permit transfer to a forum where the action could not originally have been commenced.[47] Though a few commentators suggested that Hoffman v. Blaski did not foreclose the Foster–Milburn issue, the rationale and language of the Hoffman opinion is such that any hope that the Foster–Milburn doctrine may yet be overruled seems wishful thinking, and the courts have uniformly so held.[48]

The commentators have been uniformly critical of Hoffman v. Blaski.[49] It is true, as the dissent demonstrates, that the result there is not inevitable from the language of the statute. Any other construction, however, would have converted the statute, intended in part to avoid forum shopping by plaintiffs, into a vehicle for forum shopping by defendants. Under the statute plaintiff must sue in the most convenient forum or he will find his suit transferred there, whether he consents or not. An opposite result in Hoffman would have meant that defendant sued, out of necessity, in a forum not the most convenient for all

---

43. In re Josephson, C.A.1st, 1954, 218 F.2d 174, 185–186.

44. Kaufman, Further Observations on Transfers under Section 1404(a), 1956, 56 Col.L.Rev. 1, 15. See also Note, 1951, 60 Yale L.J. 183.

45. See cases cited 15 Wright, Miller & Cooper, Jurisdiction 2d § 3845 n. 8. Indeed one court that had earlier held to the contrary, Otto v. Hirl, D.C.Iowa 1950, 89 F.Supp. 72, adopted the Foster–Milburn rule in preference to its own former view, Herzog v. Central Steel Tube Co., D.C.Iowa 1951, 98 F.Supp. 607.

46. 1960, 80 S.Ct. 1084, 363 U.S. 335, 4 L.Ed.2d 1254.

47. The reference, however, is only to where the suit "might have been brought" in terms of the federal laws delimiting where actions may be commenced. Neither the law of the transferee state concerning capacity of the plaintiff to sue nor Rule 17(b), defining capacity, are relevant. Van

Dusen v. Barrack, 1964, 84 S.Ct. 805, 813, 376 U.S. 612, 624, 11 L.Ed.2d 945.

48. Relf v. Gasch, C.A.1975, 511 F.2d 804; Shutte v. Armco Steel Corp., C.A.3d, 1970, 431 F.2d 22, certiorari denied 91 S.Ct. 871, 401 U.S. 910, 27 L.Ed.2d 808; Cessna Aircraft Co. v. Brown, C.A.10th, 1965, 348 F.2d 689; and cases cited 15 Wright, Miller & Cooper, Jurisdiction 2d § 3845 n. 20.

49. See Waggoner, Section 1404(a), "Where It Might Have Been Brought: Brought by Whom?," 1988 B.Y.U.L.Rev. 67; Masington, Venue in the Federal Courts— The Problem of the Inconvenient Forum, 1961, U.Miami L.Rev. 237. Student commentaries, cited in 15 Wright, Miller & Cooper, Jurisdiction 2d § 3845 n. 16, were uniformly to the same effect. Some lower courts also did not hide their dislike for the Hoffman rule. See cases cited 15 Wright, Miller & Cooper, Jurisdiction 2d § 3845 n. 17.

concerned would have had a choice either to consent to transfer or to insist that the litigation remain in the inconvenient forum.[50] To the extent that Hoffman and Foster–Milburn prevent some lawsuits from being tried at the most convenient place, the remedy is to strike the words "where it might have been brought" from the statute.[51]

The statute speaks only in the most general terms in setting out the standards to be considered in determining whether to grant or deny a § 1404(a) motion, and the matter is left generally in the discretion of the trial judge.[52] "At best," the Second Circuit said in an early case, "the judge must guess, and we should accept his guess unless it is too wild."[53] One court has endeavored to limit the discretion thus conferred on the trial court, saying "he is limited in his consideration to the three factors specifically mentioned in § 1404(a), and he may not properly be governed in his decision by any other factor or consideration."[54] Paradoxically that court went on to list eight factors, only one of which is mentioned in the statute, that persuaded it that the trial judge had erred in refusing to order transfer.[55] As this illustrates, a limitation to the three factors listed in the statute is unrealistic, except in the most general sense, since the factors mentioned are broad generalities that take on a variety of meanings in specific cases, and the statute gives no hint as to how these vast categories are to be weighed against each

50. See, for example, Gilpin v. Wilson, D.C.Ala.1957, 148 F.Supp. 493. Plaintiff resided in Tennessee, the accident for which suit was brought occurred in Tennessee, and every eyewitness to the accident and all of the doctors and nurses who treated plaintiff were residents of Tennessee. Nevertheless since defendant was not amenable to process in Tennessee and refused to consent to transfer there, the action had to remain in the Middle District of Alabama. This kind of insistence on the least convenient forum would not have been open to plaintiffs had Hoffman v. Blaski been decided the other way.

The problems of forum shopping by defendants were lessened by the 1966 amendment to § 1391(a), making the district "in which the claim arose" a proper venue. But that reform had not been enacted when Hoffman was decided, and the Supreme Court had to consider the consequences of its decision in terms of the venue statutes as they then existed. And even the 1966 amendment would not help in a case like the Gilpin case, discussed above, where the defendant was not amenable to process in the more convenient forum.

51. Thus, a 1958 amendment to 28 U.S.C.A. § 1402, permitting transfer of actions by corporations for the recovery of taxes, does not contain the words "where it might have been brought" and transfer to any other federal court is permitted. See also Rule F(9) of the Supplemental Rules for Certain Admiralty and Maritime Claims

for diversity cases, and Bankruptcy Rule 782.

The proposals of the American Law Institute would permit transfer of a diversity case on motion of the defendant to any district, ALI Study, § 1305(a), but would allow transfer on plaintiff's motion only to a district where venue would have been proper and defendant could have been served. Id. at § 1306(a). Under these proposals a defendant, but not a plaintiff, could continue to insist on trial in an inconvenient forum. No such distinction was made in the proposals for federal-question cases or cases to which the United States is a party. ALI Study, §§ 1315(a), 1327(a).

52. 15 Wright, Miller & Cooper, Jurisdiction 2d § 3847.

53. Ford Motor Co. v. Ryan, C.A.2d 1950, 182 F.2d 329, 331, certiorari denied 71 S.Ct. 79, 340 U.S. 851, 95 L.Ed. 624. Later the same court spoke of the matter as "peculiarly one for the exercise of judgment by those in daily proximity to these delicate problems of trial litigation." Lykes Bros. S.S. Co., Inc. v. Sugarman, C.A.2d, 1959, 272 F.2d 679, 680.

54. Chicago, R.I. & P.R. Co. v. Igoe, C.A.7th, 1955, 220 F.2d 299, 302, certiorari denied 76 S.Ct. 49, 350 U.S. 822, 100 L.Ed. 735.

55. 220 F.2d at 304.

other. "[I]ronclad adherence to abstract rules is generally inappropriate"[56]; instead there must be "individualized, case-by-case determination of convenience and fairness."[57]

Though the Reviser's Notes to § 1404(a), on which the Supreme Court has consistently laid great stress, declare that the statute is drafted "in accordance with the doctrine of forum non conveniens," and in its earliest consideration of the statute the Court referred repeatedly to that doctrine,[58] it later held that § 1404(a) is something more than a mere codification of forum non conveniens and that transfer under the statute can be ordered on a lesser showing of inconvenience than would justify dismissal under forum non conveniens.[59]

The courts have recognized that plaintiff's venue privilege is still a factor to be considered, and that the burden is on the defendant to establish that another forum would be more convenient.[60] In determining where the suit is to be tried, they have looked, as the statute requires, to convenience of the parties,[61] convenience of witnesses,[62] and the interest of justice.[63] Usually the courts have insisted on documents showing that another forum would be more convenient, and have refused to order transfer on the basis of conclusory affidavits that trial where suit was brought would cause great expense and require importation of many witnesses. The courts have demanded that the moving party show what helpful testimony the distant witnesses would provide, and have taken into account that transportation companies, when defendants, have ready means to bring witnesses to the place of trial.[64] Many courts have refused to take into account the convenience of counsel[65] or the availability of expert witnesses,[66] though these factors are relevant

56. Turner & Newall, PLC v. Canadian Universal Ins. Co., D.C.D.C.1987, 652 F.Supp. 1308.

57. Van Dusen v. Barrack, 1964, 84 S.Ct. 805, 812, 376 U.S. 612, 622, 11 L.Ed.2d 945.

58. Ex parte Collett, 1949, 69 S.Ct. 944, 337 U.S. 55, 93 L.Ed. 1207.

59. Norwood v. Kirkpatrick, 1955, 75 S.Ct. 544, 546, 349 U.S. 29, 32, 99 L.Ed. 789. In this rather surprising case, suit in Philadelphia by a black dining-car employee who lived in that city was transferred to South Carolina, where the accident took place. Orthodox forum non conveniens doctrine would not have permitted dismissal where plaintiff sued in the district where he resided.

See also Piper Aircraft Co. v. Reyno, 1981, 102 S.Ct. 252, 264, 454 U.S. 235, 253, 70 L.Ed.2d 419, where it is said that § 1404(a) was "a revision rather than a codification of the common law".

Since a § 1404(a) motion and a motion to dismiss for forum non conveniens require "evaluations of similar, but by no means identical, objective criteria," a prior state-

court dismissal on grounds of forum non conveniens does not require a federal court sitting in the same state to order transfer. Parsons v. Chesapeake & O. Ry. Co., 1963, 84 S.Ct. 185, 375 U.S. 71, 11 L.Ed.2d 137.

60. 15 Wright, Miller & Cooper, Jurisdiction 2d § 3848.

61. 15 Wright, Miller & Cooper, Jurisdiction 2d § 3849.

62. 15 Wright, Miller & Cooper, Jurisdiction 2d §§ 3851, 3853.

63. 15 Wright, Miller & Cooper, Jurisdiction 2d § 3854.

64. E.g., Chicago, R.I. & P.R. Co. v. Hugh Breeding, Inc., C.A.10th, 1956, 232 F.2d 584; General Portland Cement Co. v. Perry, C.A.7th, 1953, 204 F.2d 316; 15 Wright, Miller & Cooper, Jurisdiction 2d § 3851.

65. 15 Wright, Miller & Cooper, Jurisdiction 2d § 3850.

66. Compare Sypert v. Miner, C.A.7th, 1959, 266 F.2d 196 (refusing to consider expert witnesses), with Lykes Bros. S.S. Co., Inc. v. Sugarman, C.A.2d 1959, 272 under forum non conveniens, and some courts have not always viewed realistically racial and other kinds of prejudice where it is claimed to be a factor for or against transfer.[67]

An order granting or denying a § 1404(a) motion is not appealable as a final judgment, and ordinarily will not present a controlling question of law suitable for interlocutory review under 28 U.S.C.A. § 1292(b).[68] It is reviewable on appeal from a final judgment,[69] but by that time the matter will almost always be moot.[70] There have been many efforts to secure review by application for mandamus or prohibition. The use of such writs is proper where it is claimed that there was no power to make a transfer.[71] The circumstances under which the writs will be issued where it is claimed only that the trial court misapplied the statutory standards for transfer is "a thorny thicket" [72] in which the decisions have been correctly said to be in "hopeless conflict." [73] Indeed there is such a variety of views that the decisions can only be considered circuit-by-circuit,[74] and even within a single circuit they are not always consistent. Nevertheless there has been "a growing recognition that 'it will be highly unfortunate if the result of an attempted procedural improvement is to subject parties to two lawsuits: first, prolonged litigation to determine the place where a case is to be tried; and, second, the merits of the alleged cause of action itself.' " [75]

F.2d 679, 681 (taking expert witnesses into account). See 15 Wright, Miller & Cooper, Jurisdiction 2d § 3852.

67. Compare Kirk v. Spur Distributing Co., D.C.Del.1950, 95 F.Supp. 428, and Norwood v. Kirkpatrick, 1955, 75 S.Ct. 544, 349 U.S. 29, 99 L.Ed. 789, with Wilson v. Great Atlantic & Pac. Tea Co., D.C.Mo.1957, 156 F.Supp. 767.

See also Los Angeles Memorial Coliseum Comm. v. National Football League, D.C.Cal.1981, 89 F.R.D. 497. That was an antitrust action against the NFL seeking to make it possible for the Oakland Raiders to move to Los Angeles. A motion to transfer the suit, on the ground that jurors in Los Angeles would be prejudiced in favor of plaintiffs, was denied.

68. Nascone v. Spudnuts, Inc., C.A.3d, 1984, 735 F.2d 763; Garner v. Wolfinbarger, C.A.5th, 1970, 433 F.2d 117; D'Ippolito v. American Oil Co., C.A.2d, 1968, 401 F.2d 764; and cases cited 15 Wright, Miller & Cooper, Jurisdiction 2d § 3855 nn. 1, 17–23.

69. E.g., Chicago, R.I. & P.R. Co. v. Hugh Breeding, Inc., C.A.10th, 1957, 247 F.2d 217, certiorari denied 78 S.Ct. 138, 355 U.S. 880, 2 L.Ed.2d 107. It should be noted that here the appellate court reversed the judgment below on other grounds and also reversed the trial court's refusal to transfer.

70. See In re Josephson, C.A.1st, 1954, 218 F.2d 174, 180; Note, Appealability of

1404(a) Orders: Mandamus Misapplied, 1957, 67 Yale L.J. 122, 124.

71. E.g., Hoffman v. Blaski, 1960, 80 S.Ct. 1084, 363 U.S. 335, 4 L.Ed.2d 1254; Van Dusen v. Barrack, 1964, 84 S.Ct. 805, 809 n. 3, 376 U.S. 612, 615, n. 3, 11 L.Ed.2d 945; and cases cited 15 Wright, Miller & Cooper, Jurisdiction 2d § 3855 n. 24.

72. Hustler Magazine v. U.S. District Court, C.A.10th, 1986, 790 F.2d 69, 70.

73. Clayton v. Warlick, C.A.4th, 1956, 232 F.2d 699, 703. See also Wilkins v. Erickson, C.A.8th, 1973, 484 F.2d 969, 971.

74. As is done in 15 Wright, Miller & Cooper, Jurisdiction 2d § 3855.

75. Ellicott Machine Corp. v. Modern Welding Co., Inc., C.A.4th, 1974, 502 F.2d 178, 181. The internal quotation is from All States Freight v. Modarelli, C.A.3d, 1952, 196 F.2d 1010, 1011–1012.

The American Law Institute accepted the views expressed in Judge Friendly's concurring opinion in A. Olinick & Sons v. Dempster Bros., Inc., C.A.2d, 1966, 365 F.2d 439, 445, and proposed to provide by statute that "the exercise of discretion by the district court on such a motion is not reviewable on appeal or otherwise." ALI Study, §§ 1305(a), 1306(a), 1315(a), 1327(a).

See Comment, Appellate Review of Sect. 1404(a) Orders—Misuse of an Extraordinary Writ, 1968, 1 J.Marsh.J.Prac. & Proc. 297.

Accordingly there is a discernible tendency, despite the differing reasons and formulations by the several courts of appeals, to restrict increasingly the possibility of interlocutory review.[76]

Section 1404(a) is an interesting experiment in judicial administration. It does not permit trial of every suit in the most convenient forum, but it is a step in that direction. The experiment cannot yet be pronounced a complete success.[77]

---

76. Appellate review of forum non conveniens rulings is similar to that of § 1404(a) rulings. Rosenstein v. Merrell Dow Pharmaceuticals, Inc., C.A.6th, 1985, 769 F.2d 352; Castanho v. Jackson Marine, Inc., C.A.5th, 1981, 650 F.2d 546.

77. One critic has formed the harsh judgment that "it is better to bear with the small number of true hardship situations that would arise under a well drawn venue code than with the burdens which will inevitably result from a transfer provision like section 1404(a)." Kitch, note 1 above, at 141–142. Professor Currie says that "the theory is good, but it is practically unworkable." Currie, The Federal Courts and the American Law Institute (Part II), 1969, 36 U.Chi.L.Rev. 268, 307.

See generally 15 Wright, Miller & Cooper, Jurisdiction 2d § 3841.

Chapter 8

THE RELATIONS OF STATE AND FEDERAL COURTS

Analysis

§ 45.   State Enforcement of Federal Law [1]

Congress has, beyond doubt, the power to give the federal courts exclusive jurisdiction of matters falling within the judicial power of the United States.[2] But unless Congress has made federal jurisdiction exclusive, either expressly or by fair implication, the state courts have concurrent jurisdiction with the federal courts, and a state court may entertain an action even though it is entirely based on a federal claim.[3]

§ 45

1. 16 Wright, Miller & Cooper, Jurisdiction § 4024; Gordon & Gross, Justiciability of Federal Claims in State Court, 1984, 59 Notre Dame L.Rev. 1145; Redish & Muench, Adjudication of Federal Causes of Action in State Court, 1977, 75 Mich.L.Rev. 311; Comment, State Court Jurisdiction Over Claims Arising Under Federal Law, 1982, 7 U.Day.L.Rev. 403.

2. See § 10 above; 13 Wright, Miller & Cooper, Jurisdiction 2d § 3527; ALI Study, § 1311(b), and Commentary thereto.

3. "The general principle of state-court jurisdiction over cases arising under federal laws is straightforward: state courts may assume subject matter jurisdiction over a federal cause of action absent provision by Congress to the contrary or disabling in-compatibility between the federal claim and state-court adjudication." Gulf Offshore Co. v. Mobil Oil Corp., 1981, 101 S.Ct. 2870, 2875, 453 U.S. 473, 477–478, 69 L.Ed.2d 784. See also Tafflin v. Levitt, 1990, 110 S.Ct. 792, 795, 493 U.S. 455, 458–460, 107 L.Ed.2d 887. This rule dates back to Claflin v. Houseman, 1876, 93 U.S. 130, 136, 23 L.Ed. 833, where the Court drew heavily on the similar views about concurrent jurisdiction set forth in The Federalist, No. 82 (Hamilton).

In Redish & Muench, note 1 above, at 313–340, it is shown that the Claflin test has often been misunderstood by the courts and Congress, and an alternative test for determining whether federal jurisdiction is exclusive or concurrent is proposed. In the Gulf Offshore case and the Tafflin case,

At the Constitutional Convention, and in the framing of the Judiciary Act of 1789, the states-rights interests were opposed to the creation of inferior federal courts, arguing that the state courts were sufficient to enforce federal law. This view, as has been seen, was rejected at that time.[4] As early as 1815 the states began to shift their ground and to argue that they should not be required to entertain federal claims. For many years, though it was clear that the state courts could hear a federal claim, it was not clear whether they were required to do so. The question was finally resolved in the Second Employers' Liability Cases,[5] where it was held that claims arising under the Federal Employers' Liability Act could be enforced, as of right, in the courts of the states if their jurisdiction, as prescribed by local laws, was adequate to the occasion. The Connecticut court had held that enforcement of an FELA claim in state court was contrary to the policy of that state, but the Supreme Court found such reasoning quite inadmissible, holding that when Congress enacts a law it establishes a policy for all the states, which is as much the policy of Connecticut as if the act had emanated from its own legislature. As the Court stated the matter more recently: "Federal law is enforceable in state courts not because Congress has determined that federal courts would otherwise be burdened or that state courts might provide a more convenient forum—although both might well be true—but because the Constitution and laws passed pursuant to it are as much laws in the States as laws passed by the state legislature."[6]

Some years later New York refused to entertain an FELA claim where the parties were Connecticut residents and the accident occurred in Connecticut, relying on a state statute that permitted dismissal of claims where neither the plaintiff nor defendant was a resident of New York. This refusal was held proper by the Supreme Court, which said "there is nothing in the Act of Congress that purports to force a duty upon such Courts as against an otherwise valid excuse."[7] It is a valid excuse that the action falls within the state's conception of forum non conveniens, so long as the state applies that doctrine in all cases, regardless of their basis.[8] And it is a valid excuse that the claim arose outside of the territorial jurisdiction of the particular state court in which suit is brought.[9] Those cases, all involving neutral state rules regarding the administration of the courts, are the only instances in

however, the Court ignored those criticisms, and was content merely to reaffirm the Claflin test.

4. See § 1 above.

5. 1912, 32 S.Ct. 169, 223 U.S. 1, 56 L.Ed. 327. These cases are also frequently cited under the name Mondou v. New York, N.H. & H.R. Co.

6. Howlett by Howlett v. Rose, 1990, 110 S.Ct. 2430, 2438, 496 U.S. 356, 367, 110 L.Ed.2d 332. The case is discussed in Weinberg, The Federal–State Conflict of Laws: "Actual" Conflicts, 1992, 70 Texas L.Rev. 1744, 1770–1784.

7. Douglas v. New York, N.H. & H.R. Co., 1929, 49 S.Ct. 355, 356, 279 U.S. 377, 388, 73 L.Ed. 747.

8. Missouri ex rel. Southern Ry. v. Mayfield, 1950, 71 S.Ct. 1, 340 U.S. 1, 95 L.Ed. 3.

9. Herb v. Pitcairn, 1945, 65 S.Ct. 459, 324 U.S. 117, 89 L.Ed. 789.

which the Supreme Court has found a valid excuse for a state court's refusal to entertain a federal cause of action.

"An excuse that is inconsistent with or violates federal law is not a valid excuse * * *." [10] For this reason it is not a valid excuse that the statutes granting jurisdiction to the state court do not give it jurisdiction over a particular kind of action if the jurisdictional statutes discriminate against the claim in question because it is created by federal law. This was settled in McKnett v. St. Louis & San Francisco Railway Co.[11] An Alabama statute gave its courts jurisdiction over causes of action arising outside of the state if they were based on "common law or the statutes of another state." An FELA action was brought in Alabama for an injury that had occurred in Tennessee. The Alabama court refused to entertain the action, holding that the federal statute was neither part of the common law nor a statute of another state. A unanimous Supreme Court held that the Alabama statute, as so construed, was unconstitutional and that Alabama was required to entertain the action. Since the Alabama court would have had jurisdiction if the accident had occurred in Alabama, or, although the accident occurred in Tennessee, if the defendant had been an Alabama corporation, the Supreme Court held that the ordinary jurisdiction of the Alabama court was appropriate to enforce the federal claim. "The denial of jurisdiction by the Alabama court is based solely upon the source of law sought to be enforced. The plaintiff is cast out because he is suing to enforce a Federal Act. A state may not discriminate against rights arising under Federal laws." [12]

The cases considered thus far have involved what may be termed remedial federal claims. Most state courts assumed, with support from language in Supreme Court opinions and the writing of eminent scholars, that they were under no duty to enforce federal penal statutes.[13] This was the reaction of the Rhode Island Supreme Court when a case came to it in which a party sought treble damages for sale of an automobile above the ceiling price. The Emergency Price Control Act authorized such a suit for treble damages and provided that the federal courts were to have jurisdiction of this kind of suit "concurrently with

---

10. Howlett by Howlett v. Rose, 1990, 110 S.Ct. 2430, 2440, 496 U.S. 356, 371, 110 L.Ed.2d 332.

11. 1934, 54 S.Ct. 690, 292 U.S. 230, 78 L.Ed. 1227.

12. 54 S.Ct. at 692, 292 U.S. at 234.

The McKnett principle, that there can be no discrimination by the states against federal claims, was applied by a state court in an interesting situation. An Illinois statute barred suit in the courts of that state to recover damages for deaths occurring outside Illinois. As originally enacted the statute was nondiscriminatory. Later Supreme Court decisions laid down the rule, however, that, in view of the Full–Faith–and– Credit Clause, Illinois could not refuse to entertain actions brought under the death

acts of other states. The Illinois Supreme Court held that "by the interplay of judicial decisions, instead of the direct language of the statute," a discrimination against federal law had been created, and that Illinois was constitutionally required to entertain an FELA suit for a death occurring in Indiana. Allendorf v. Elgin, J. & E.R. Co., 1956, 133 N.E.2d 288, 8 Ill.2d 164, certiorari denied 77 S.Ct. 49, 352 U.S. 833, 1 L.Ed.2d 53.

13. See Warren, Federal Criminal Laws and the State Courts, 1925, 38 Harv.L.Rev. 545; Barnett, The Delegation of Federal Jurisdiction to State Courts, 1909, 43 Am. L.Rev. 852, reprinted 1938, 3 Selected Essays on Constitutional Law 1202.

State and Territorial courts." The Rhode Island court reasoned that the treble-damages provision was "a penal statute in the international sense," that a state need not enforce the penal laws of a government that is "foreign in the international sense," and that the United States was "foreign" to Rhode Island in the "private international" sense. From this syllogism, the court held that suits for treble damages under this federal statute could not be maintained in the courts of the state.

The Supreme Court reversed unanimously, in Testa v. Katt.[14] It could have reversed, on the basis of precedent, simply by holding that the Emergency Price Control Act was remedial rather than penal.[15] Justice Black, speaking for the Court, chose instead to assume that the act was penal and to hold that the states have no less duty to enforce federal penal statutes than they do to enforce federal remedial statutes. He relied heavily on the Supremacy Clause of Article VI, § 2, of the Constitution to reject the notion that the United States can be considered "foreign" to Rhode Island in any sense. Since it was conceded that the same type of claim arising under Rhode Island law would be enforced in the courts of that state, he found that they had jurisdiction adequate and appropriate under established local law to hear the action.

The Supreme Court has not yet considered whether Congress can require state courts to entertain federal claims when there is no analogous state-created right enforceable in the state courts. One commentator regards it as fortunate that ultimate questions such as this one do not often have to be faced.[16]

---

14. 1947, 67 S.Ct. 810, 330 U.S. 386, 91 L.Ed. 967. See Note, Utilization of State Courts to Enforce Federal Penal and Criminal Statutes: Development in Judicial Federalism, 1947, 60 Harv.L.Rev. 966.

The doctrine of this case and its predecessors is questioned in Sandalow, Henry v. Mississippi and the Adequate State Ground: Proposals for a Revised Doctrine, 1965 Sup. Ct.Rev. 187, 203–207.

15. See Huntington v. Attrill, 1892, 13 S.Ct. 224, 230, 146 U.S. 657, 673–674, 36 L.Ed. 1123.

16. Hart, The Relations between State and Federal Law, 1954, 54 Col.L.Rev. 489, 507–508.

Note, State Enforcement of Federally Created Rights, 1960, 73 Harv.L.Rev. 1551, 1556, says that "at least in certain circumstances, a proper accommodation of the federal and state interests is not inconsistent with allowing Congress to impose upon state courts the duty to enforce non-analogous federally created rights."

But see Redish & Muench, note 1 above, at 350–351, where it is said that "none of the Supreme Court's state obligation cases explicitly employ the 'analogous state-created' terminology when addressing the valid excuse issue. In fact, there is serious question whether the doctrine is anything more than a product of commentators' unfounded speculation."

In Martinez v. California, 1980, 100 S.Ct. 553, 558 n. 7, 444 U.S. 277, 283 n. 7, 62 L.Ed.2d 481, the Court held that a state court may entertain a civil-rights claim under 42 U.S.C.A. § 1983, and added: "We have never considered, however, the question whether a State *must* entertain a claim under § 1983. We note that where the same type of claim, if arising under state law, would be enforced in the state courts, the state courts are generally not free to refuse enforcement of the federal claim." Whether a state court is free to refuse to hear § 1983 cases was left open also in Arkansas Writers' Project, Inc. v. Ragland, 1987, 107 S.Ct. 1722, 1730 n. 7, 481 U.S. 221, 234 n. 7, 95 L.Ed.2d 209. But if a state court hears such a claim it cannot apply to it a notice-of-claim statute generally applicable to claims against governmental entities. Felder v. Casey, 1988, 108 S.Ct. 2302, 487 U.S. 131, 101 L.Ed.2d 123. Nor can it recognize a defense of "sovereign immunity" that is generally available to state school boards. Howlett by Howlett v. Rose, 1990, 110 S.Ct. 2430, 496 U.S. 356,

As recently as 1944, Justice Frankfurter could declare, in a concurring opinion, that when Congress does provide for enforcement of federal claims in state courts, it must "take the state courts as it finds them, subject to all the conditions for litigation in the state courts that the State has decreed for every other litigant who seeks access to its courts." [17] It is very doubtful whether a similar statement could be made today. Again most of the relevant law has been developed in FELA litigation.[18]

In Minneapolis & St.L.R. Co. v. Bombolis,[19] decided in 1916, the Supreme Court held that a unanimous verdict is not required of a state-court jury hearing an FELA action, even though the Seventh Amendment would require unanimity had suit been brought in federal court. The case was commonly understood as standing for the proposition that a litigant who chooses to assert his federal claim in state court gets the benefit of the federal substantive law but is obliged to accept the usual state procedure. In those earlier days there were opinions that raised doubt as to where to draw the line between substance and procedure, but there was no doubt that there was some area of procedure that the state could continue to regulate for itself even in federal-claim cases. Perhaps this is still true today, but if so this area of procedure has become so shrunken as to fall within the maxim *de minimis*. Thus, it is now held that in an FELA case the state cannot apply its usual rule that pleadings are to be construed strictly against the pleader, but instead must construe the pleading as liberally as possible in favor of the pleader.[20] If this is not procedure, it is hard to know what is. Again the Supreme Court has held that in an FELA case a state cannot follow its usual rule, with respectable equitable antecedents, that it is for the court to decide whether a release is invalid because of fraud, and instead must submit this question to the jury.[21] The Court in this latter case purports

---

110 L.Ed.2d 332. The Howlett case is discussed in Weinberg, note 6 above, at 1773–1784. See generally 16 Wright, Miller & Cooper, Jurisdiction § 4023.

17. Brown v. Gerdes, 1944, 64 S.Ct. 487, 493, 321 U.S. 178, 190, 88 L.Ed. 659 (concurring opinion).

18. Hill, Substance and Procedure in State FELA Actions—The Converse of the Erie Problem?, 1956, 17 Ohio St.L.J. 384; Note, State Enforcement of Federally Created Rights, 1960, 73 Harv.L.Rev. 1551, 1561–1564.

19. 1916, 36 S.Ct. 595, 241 U.S. 211, 60 L.Ed. 961.

20. Brown v. Western Ry. of Alabama, 1949, 70 S.Ct. 105, 338 U.S. 294, 94 L.Ed. 100.

21. Dice v. Akron, C. & Y.R. Co., 1952, 72 S.Ct. 312, 342 U.S. 359, 96 L.Ed. 398.

See also Bowman v. Illinois Central R. Co., 1957, 142 N.E.2d 104, 11 Ill.2d 186, certiorari denied 78 S.Ct. 63, 355 U.S. 837,

2 L.Ed.2d 49, noted 1958, 71 Harv.L.Rev. 730, where the Illinois court held that the appellate courts of that state cannot order a new trial in an FELA case on the ground that the verdict is against the weight of the evidence—though they have the power to do so in common-law actions—since in the federal system only the trial court can order a new trial on this ground.

In Norfolk & W. Ry. Co. v. Liepelt, 1980, 100 S.Ct. 755, 444 U.S. 490, 62 L.Ed.2d 689, it was held that a state court in an FELA action must allow evidence of the income taxes that would have been payable on the decedent's future earnings, which seems clearly to go to the measure of damages and thus to be "substantive," and it was also held that the state court must give a cautionary instruction that the award of damages would not be subject to income taxation, a matter that two dissenters thought to be one of the "ordinary incidents of state procedure," which should be governed by state law. See also St. Louis Sw. Ry. Co. v.

to distinguish the Bombolis case with the surprising suggestion that the state might abolish jury trial in all negligence cases, but that so long as it has not done so it cannot single out the one issue of fraudulent releases and deny the employee jury trial as to that issue. This is such a difficult distinction to defend that it may reasonably be doubted whether the Bombolis decision has any continuing authoritativeness beyond its particular facts.

Some commentators have read the cases just discussed as laying down a rule peculiar to FELA litigation, and have believed that in other types of cases the state courts can still apply state procedure to federal claims. It is certainly true that the Supreme Court has been astute to protect the rights of FELA plaintiffs. But even if the FELA cases are unique, they stand for the proposition that Congress has constitutional power to control the incidents of a state trial of a federal claim.[22]

Usually the federal law that a state court is called upon to enforce is statutory, but this need not always be the case. There is an expanding area of "federal common law," involving matters in which the federal interest is so strong that the federal courts are free to develop substantive rules to protect that interest.[23] When an issue of this nature arises in a state action, the state court must enforce the federal doctrine rather than its own law.[24]

§ 46. State Attempts to Limit Federal Jurisdiction[1]

Article III of the Constitution and the Acts of Congress made pursuant thereto define the jurisdiction of the federal courts. State

Dickerson, 1985, 105 S.Ct. 1347, 470 U.S. 409, 84 L.Ed.2d 303, holding that in an FELA case a state-court jury must be instructed to reduce damages to their present value, and Monessen Sw. Ry. v. Morgan, 1988, 108 S.Ct. 1837, 486 U.S. 330, 100 L.Ed.2d 349, holding that the state court cannot apply a state rule allowing prejudgment interest. The Monessen case is discussed in Weinberg, note 6 above, at 1784–1796.

22. See Note, Procedural Protection for Federal Rights in State Courts, 1961, 30 U.Cin.L.Rev. 184.

See also Gulf Offshore Co. v. Mobil Oil Corp., 1981, 101 S.Ct. 2870, 2879–2880, 453 U.S. 473, 485–488, 69 L.Ed.2d 784.

23. See § 60 below.

24. Free v. Bland, 1962, 82 S.Ct. 1089, 369 U.S. 663, 8 L.Ed.2d 180. See also Local 174, Teamsters, Chauffeurs, Warehousemen & Helpers of America v. Lucas Flour Co., 1962, 82 S.Ct. 571, 576–577, 369 U.S. 95, 102–104, 7 L.Ed.2d 593, holding that the body of federal labor law that § 301(a) of the Taft–Hartley Act, 29 U.S.C.A. § 185(a), requires the federal courts to fashion is binding on the state courts.

See Comment, The State Courts and the Federal Common Law, 1963, 27 Alb.L.Rev. 73, which discusses also the interesting question of the weight state courts should give to decisions of lower federal courts when the state court is applying federal law. On that point, see U.S. ex rel. Lawrence v. Woods, C.A.7th, 1970, 432 F.2d 1072, 1075–1076, certiorari denied 1971, 91 S.Ct. 1658, 402 U.S. 983, 29 L.Ed.2d 148, noted 1971, 25 Sw.L.J. 478, 24 Vand.L.Rev. 627; Thompson v. Village of Hales Corners, 1983, 340 N.W.2d 704, 712–713, 115 Wis.2d 289. Concurring in Lockhart v. Fretwell, 1993, 113 S.Ct. 838, 846, ___ U.S. ___, ___, 122 L.Ed.2d 180, Justice Thomas wrote: "An Arkansas trial court is bound by this Court's (and by the Arkansas Supreme Court's and Arkansas Court of Appeals') interpretation of federal law, but if it follows the Eighth Circuit's interpretation of federal law, it does so only because it chooses to and not because it must."

§ 46

1. 17 Wright, Miller & Cooper, Jurisdiction 2d §§ 4211–4213; Meador, State Law and the Federal Judicial Power, 1963, 49 Va.L.Rev. 1082.

statutes are irrelevant in this connection. The states have not attempted to extend the jurisdiction of the federal courts. Their persistent
attempts to limit federal jurisdiction have been almost uniformly unsuccessful.

A key case is Railway Co. v. Whitton's Administrator.[2] The Wisconsin wrongful-death statute provided that the right it created could be
enforced only in a Wisconsin state court. Despite this limitation, it was
held that a federal court could entertain a suit under the statute where
diversity was present. Justice Field said for the Court: "Whenever a
general rule as to property or personal rights, or injuries to either, is
established by State legislation, its enforcement by a Federal court in a
case between proper parties is a matter of course, and the jurisdiction of
the court, in such case, is not subject to State limitation."[3]

In accord with this principle, the state cannot by statute bar
removal of cases from state to federal court, even as a condition to
permitting a foreign corporation to do business in the state.[4] It cannot
defeat federal jurisdiction of a matter judicial in nature by confiding
jurisdiction to a specialized state court, such as a probate court.[5]

Under the Eleventh Amendment a state is immune from suit in
federal court unless it consents.[6] It can consent to suit in its own courts

2. 1871, 13 Wall. 270, 20 L.Ed. 571.
The case is sometimes cited by the fuller
title Chicago & N.W.R. Co. v. Whitton's
Admr.

See also the earlier case of Suydam v.
Broadnax, 1840, 14 Pet. 67, 10 L.Ed. 357,
holding that a state statute providing that
no suit should be commenced or sustained
against an executor or administrator after
the estate had been declared insolvent
would not abate such a suit instituted in
federal court.

3. 13 Wall. at 286.

4. Home Ins. Co. v. Morse, 1874, 20
Wall. 445, 22 L.Ed. 365; Terral v. Burke
Constr. Co., 1922, 42 S.Ct. 188, 257 U.S.
529, 66 L.Ed. 352. See § 38 above.

5. Payne v. Hook, 1869, 7 Wall. 425, 19
L.Ed. 260; McClellan v. Carland, 1910, 30
S.Ct. 501, 217 U.S. 268, 54 L.Ed. 762;
Greyhound Lines, Inc. v. Lexington State
Bank & Trust Co., C.A.8th, 1979, 604 F.2d
1151; Beach v. Rome Trust Co., C.A.2d,
1959, 269 F.2d 367; 13B Wright, Miller &
Cooper, Jurisdiction 2d § 3610.

A similar result was reached where a
state statute provided that unlawful-detain-
er actions be brought only before a magistrate. Rubel–Jones Agency, Inc. v. Jones,
D.C.Mo.1958, 165 F.Supp. 652.

6. See generally 13 Wright, Miller &
Cooper, Jurisdiction 2d § 3524 and the nu-
merous commentaries on the Eleventh
Amendment cited in § 3524 nn. 1–3, 186.

Consent need not be express. Implied
consent was found where a state acted under an interstate compact that had been
approved by Congress, Petty v. Tennessee–
Missouri Bridge Commn., 1959, 79 S.Ct.
785, 359 U.S. 275, 3 L.Ed.2d 804, and
where a state commenced operation of a
railroad after enactment of the Federal Employers' Liability Act. Parden v. Terminal
Ry., 1964, 84 S.Ct. 1207, 377 U.S. 184, 12
L.Ed.2d 233. More recent cases, however,
have shown the Court reluctant to find an
implied waiver of the Eleventh Amendment
immunity. Edelman v. Jordan, 1974, 94
S.Ct. 1347, 415 U.S. 651, 39 L.Ed.2d 662;
Florida Dept. of Health & Rehabilitative
Servs. v. Florida Nursing Home Assn.,
1981, 101 S.Ct. 1032, 450 U.S. 147, 67
L.Ed.2d 132. The holding of the Parden
case with regard to the Eleventh Amendment has been overruled, Welch v. Texas
Dept. of Highways & Public Transp., 1987,
107 S.Ct. 2941, 483 U.S. 468, 97 L.Ed.2d
389, though it has been reaffirmed to the
extent that it held that an FELA action can
be brought against a state-owned railroad
in a state court, where the Eleventh
Amendment does not apply. Hilton v.
South Carolina Public Railways Commn.,
1991, 112 S.Ct. 560, ___ U.S. ___, 116
L.Ed.2d 560.

Congress can remove a state's Eleventh
Amendment immunity when Congress is
legislating under § 5 of the Fourteenth
Amendment, Fitzpatrick v. Bitzer, 1976, 96

without waiving its Eleventh Amendment immunity.[7] The Eleventh Amendment does not provide immunity for counties and similar municipal corporations. These bodies are suable in federal court, even though the state statutes creating them purport to limit suit to state court.[8]

A few lower courts have held that the conformity to state law required in diversity cases by the Erie doctrine means that the federal court must honor a state statute that limits its waiver of tort immunity for governmental subdivisions only to suits brought in the state courts, or in a specialized state court.[9] The argument is unsound, and was effectively refuted by Judge Haynsworth, speaking for the Fourth Circuit, when he said: "It would be quite foreign to the Erie doctrine, however, to apply a state statute in such a way as to deny all relief in a federal court to a nonresident plaintiff on a cause of action which, clearly, the state courts would recognize and enforce. Erie requires that the federal court grant or withhold relief as the state courts would. It does not require relegation of the diversity jurisdiction to the mercies of the legislatures of fifty separate states." [10]

There is one respect in which the Erie doctrine does give the states a means of limiting indirectly federal jurisdiction. If a state closes its doors to a particular class of litigant or claim, a federal court, exercising diversity jurisdiction, cannot entertain a suit by such a litigant or on such a claim. The rule was to the contrary prior to the Erie case,[11] but Erie is said to have made the earlier decisions obsolete. In two controversial cases the Supreme Court held that a federal court cannot hear a case that the state court would not hear whether the right asserted is

S.Ct. 2666, 427 U.S. 445, 49 L.Ed.2d 614, the Commerce Clause, Pennsylvania v. Union Gas Co., 1989, 109 S.Ct. 2273, 491 U.S. 1, 105 L.Ed.2d 1, and the Bankruptcy Clause, Hoffman v. Connecticut Dept. of Income Maintenance, 1989, 109 S.Ct. 2818, 492 U.S. 96, 106 L.Ed.2d 76. But if Congress intends to overrule a state's Eleventh Amendment immunity, it must do so "with unmistakable clarity." Blatchford v. Native Village of Noatak and Circle Village, 1991, 111 S.Ct. 2578, 2584, 501 U.S. 775, ___, 115 L.Ed.2d 686. See also Dellmuth v. Muth, 1989, 109 S.Ct. 2397, 2401, 491 U.S. 223, 230, 105 L.Ed.2d 181; Note, The Eleventh Amendment's Clear Statement Test After Dellmuth v. Muth and Pennsylvania v. Union Gas Co., 1991, 39 Buff.L.Rev. 1157.

7. Smith v. Reeves, 1900, 20 S.Ct. 919, 178 U.S. 436, 44 L.Ed. 1140; Kennecott Copper Corp. v. State Tax Commn., 1946, 66 S.Ct. 745, 327 U.S. 573, 90 L.Ed. 862; Florida Dept. of Health & Rehabilitative Servs. v. Florida Nursing Home Assn., 1981, 101 S.Ct. 1032, 1034, 450 U.S.147, 150, 67 L.Ed.2d 132.

8. Mount Healthy City Sch. Dist. v. Doyle, 1977, 97 S.Ct. 568, 429 U.S. 274, 50 L.Ed.2d 471; Lincoln County v. Luning, 1890, 10 S.Ct. 363, 133 U.S. 529, 33 L.Ed. 766.

9. Markham v. City of Newport News, D.C.Va.1960, 184 F.Supp. 659, criticized 1961, 109 U.Pa.L.Rev. 428, reversed C.A.4th, 1961, 292 F.2d 711; Zeidner v. Wulforst, D.C.N.Y.1961, 197 F.Supp. 23, criticized 1962, 75 Harv.L.Rev. 1433; Kohlasch v. New York State Thruway Auth., D.C.N.Y.1978, 460 F.Supp. 956.

10. Markham v. City of Newport News, C.A.4th, 1961, 292 F.2d 711, 718, noted approvingly 1962, 48 Corn.L.Q. 192, 75 Harv.L.Rev. 1433, 23 U.Pitts.L.Rev. 800, 36 Tul.L.Rev. 351. To the same effect, see Lamb v. U.S., D.C.Ga.1981, 526 F.Supp. 1117, 1126; Greiner v. Gunnar A. Olsen Corp., D.C.Iowa 1976, 498 F.Supp. 908; S.J. Groves & Sons Co. v. New Jersey Turnpike Auth., D.C.N.J.1967, 268 F.Supp. 568.

11. David Lupton's Sons v. Automobile Club of America, 1912, 32 S.Ct. 711, 225 U.S. 489, 56 L.Ed. 1177.

one created by another state [12] or by the forum state.[13] If the right is created by federal law, however, it can be heard in federal court regardless of whether the state has closed its doors—or validly could close its doors [14]—to such a suit.[15] Even in a diversity case, the continued authoritativeness of the Supreme Court decisions requiring "door-closing" statutes to be followed has been doubted.[16] The Fourth Circuit has held that a district court may entertain a suit by a nonresident against a foreign corporation on a cause of action arising in another state despite a statutory bar to such a suit in the state courts.[17] It held that the state statute did not embody any important policy that would be frustrated by the application of a different rule in federal court, and that the state interest was outweighed by such countervailing federal considerations as the grant of diversity jurisdiction to avoid discrimination against nonresidents, the policy of maximum enforcement in each state of rights created by sister states, and the federal interest in encouraging efficient joinder in multiparty actions.[18]

12. A federal court sitting in North Carolina could not entertain a suit for a deficiency judgment arising out of a Virginia mortgage where a state statute precluded deficiency judgments. Angel v. Bullington, 1947, 67 S.Ct. 657, 330 U.S. 183, 91 L.Ed. 832. See Meador, note 1 above, at 1088–1090; Farinholt, Angel v. Bullington: Twilight of Diversity Jurisdiction?, 1947, 26 N.C.L.Rev. 29; Note, 1947, 33 Va.L.Rev. 739.

13. Where a state statute bars suit in state court by a corporation that has not qualified to do business in that state, the federal court cannot hear a suit by the corporation, even though the state statute does not void the transaction on which suit is brought. Woods v. Interstate Realty Co., 1949, 69 S.Ct. 1235, 337 U.S. 535, 93 L.Ed. 1524. See Stewart, The Federal "Door-Closing" Doctrine, 1954, 11 Wash. & Lee L.Rev. 154.

See also Power City Communications, Inc. v. Calaveras Tel. Co., D.C.Cal.1968, 280 F.Supp. 808. But cf. Avondale Shipyards, Inc. v. Propulsion Systems, Inc., D.C.La. 1971, 53 F.R.D. 341, holding that Rule 13(a) requires assertion of a compulsory counterclaim and that this can be done even though the defendant would be barred from bringing suit, or asserting a counterclaim, on its claim because it has not qualified to do business in the state.

14. See § 45 above.

15. Holmberg v. Ambrecht, 1946, 66 S.Ct. 582, 327 U.S. 392, 90 L.Ed. 743. This distinction is stated, and the Holmberg case cited to support it, in Angel v. Bullington, 1947, 67 S.Ct. 657, 662, 330 U.S. 183, 192, 91 L.Ed. 832.

16. See the article by Dean Meador, note 1 above.

But in Hanna v. Plumer, 1965, 85 S.Ct. 1136, 1143, 380 U.S. 460, 469, 14 L.Ed.2d 8, the Court distinguished the case before it from one in which "application of the state rule would wholly bar recovery," and cited the Woods case, note 13 above, as an example of such a situation.

17. Szantay v. Beech Aircraft Corp., C.A.4th, 1965, 349 F.2d 60, noted 1965, 17 S.C.L.Rev. 631, 1966, 51 Corn.L.Q. 560.

See also Sun Sales Corp. v. Block Land, Inc., C.A.3d, 1972, 456 F.2d 857, holding that a Pennsylvania statute barring suit for services by an unlicensed real estate broker could not bar a New York firm not doing business in Pennsylvania from bringing a diversity action in Pennsylvania, and Foxco Indus., Ltd. v. Fabric World, Inc., C.A.5th, 1979, 595 F.2d 976, holding that a state "door-closing" statute cannot be applied to a corporation if its activities in the state are entirely in the course of interstate commerce.

18. The case described in the text was limited, however, in Bumgarder v. Keene Corp., C.A.4th, 1979, 593 F.2d 572. In the Bumgardner case the plaintiff could have brought suit in North Carolina, where he lived and worked, and thus had an alternate forum in which he could gain full relief. For this reason, it was held that the countervailing federal considerations that justified ignoring the South Carolina statute in the Szantay case, note 17 above, were not present. See also Proctor & Schwartz, Inc. v. Rollins, C.A.4th, 1980, 634 F.2d 738.

See generally cases cited 17 Wright, Miller & Cooper, Jurisdiction 2d § 4211 nn. 21, 22.

Since the states cannot limit the jurisdiction of the federal courts, they cannot enjoin proceedings in federal courts, except to protect the jurisdiction of the state court over property in its custody or under its control.[19] They cannot interfere with the continued prosecution of pending federal actions nor can they bar commencement of a federal suit in the future.[20]

The state courts cannot interfere with the exercise of federal jurisdiction by granting habeas corpus for discharge of a person held in federal custody.[21] On a somewhat related issue, the Supreme Court never decided whether state courts can enjoin federal officers.[22] In the light of 1976 legislation making it always possible for such suits against federal officers to be brought in federal court, the principal argument for allowing state injunctions against federal officers has become moot.[23]

§ 47. Federal Injunctions Against State Proceedings [1]

For almost as long as there have been federal courts, there has been a statutory prohibition against issuance of a writ of injunction "to stay

19. Donovan v. City of Dallas, 1964, 84 S.Ct. 1579, 377 U.S. 408, 12 L.Ed.2d 409. See 17 Wright, Miller & Cooper, Jurisdiction 2d § 4212; Arnold, State Power To Enjoin Federal Court Proceedings, 1965, 51 Va.L.Rev. 59; Comment, State Injunction of Proceedings in Federal Courts, 1965, 75 Yale L.J. 150; Comment, Anti–Suit Injunctions Between State and Federal Courts, 1965, 32 U.Chi.L.Rev. 471.

The American Law Institute adopts the view of the dissenters in the Donovan case and would also allow an injunction "where necessary to protect against vexatious and harassing relitigation of matters determined by an existing judgment of the State court in a civil action." ALI Study, § 1373(2).

Even if a state action is in rem or quasi-in-rem, the state court cannot enjoin a federal in personam action. Meridian Investing & Development Corp. v. Suncoast Highland Corp., C.A.5th, 1980, 628 F.2d 370.

20. General Atomic Co. v. Felter, 1977, 98 S.Ct. 76, 434 U.S. 12, 54 L.Ed.2d 199. See also the same case 1978, 98 S.Ct. 1939, 436 U.S. 493, 56 L.Ed.2d 480.

It is argued in Hornstein & Magle, State Court Power to Enjoin Federal Judicial Proceedings: Donovan v. City of Dallas Revisited, 1982, 60 Wash.U.L.Q. 1, that a state court may enjoin commencement of a suit in federal court if the federal court would lack jurisdiction of the suit. In addition, the authors contend that in such a situation the determination by the state court that the federal courts would lack jurisdiction has preclusive effect and must be followed by the federal court if a party should defy

the state-court injunction and commence suit in federal court. The argument is novel, but ultimately unpersuasive.

21. Ableman v. Booth, 1859, 21 How. 506, 16 L.Ed. 169; In re Tarble, 1872, 13 Wall. 397, 20 L.Ed. 597; Robb v. Connolly, 1884, 4 S.Ct. 544, 111 U.S. 624, 28 L.Ed. 542; see Eisentrager v. Forrestal, C.A.D.C. 1949, 174 F.2d 961, 966.

See also Hagan, Ableman v. Booth, 1931, 17 A.B.A.J. 19; Warren, Federal and State Court Interference, 1930, 43 Harv.L.Rev. 345, 347–359.

If the United States consents, a state court may issue a writ of habeas corpus to bring a federal prisoner before the state court for trial. Ponzi v. Fessenden, 1922, 42 S.Ct. 309, 258 U.S. 254, 66 L.Ed. 607. See Smith v. Hooey, 1969, 89 S.Ct. 575, 393 U.S. 374, 21 L.Ed.2d 607.

22. Compare Arnold, The Power of State Courts to Enjoin Federal Officers, 1964, 73 Yale L.J. 1385, with Warren, Federal and State Court Interference, 1930, 43 Harv.L.Rev. 345, 358. It was held that the state court lacked this power in Pennsylvania Turnpike Comm. v. McGinnes, D.C.Pa. 1959, 179 F.Supp. 578, affirmed C.A.3d, 1960, 278 F.2d 330, certiorari denied 81 S.Ct. 57, 364 U.S. 820, 5 L.Ed.2d 51.

23. See 17 Wright, Miller & Cooper, Jurisdiction 2d § 4213.

§ 47

1. 17 Wright, Miller & Cooper, Jurisdiction 2d §§ 4221–4226; ALI Study § 1372 and Commentary thereto; Wood, Fine–Tuning Judicial Federalism: A Proposal for proceedings in any court of a state." First enacted in 1793,[2] for reasons that are obscure,[3] the statute was not significantly changed in form until the revision of the Judicial Code in 1948.[4] Whatever may have motivated its original adoption, the statute has an important role in a federal system since it is well calculated "to prevent needless friction between state and federal courts"[5] and "represents Congress' considered judgment as to how to balance the tensions inherent in" a dual system of courts.[6]

Until 1941, however, the effectiveness of the statute was diminished by restrictive construction and judge-made exceptions.[7] In that year, in the familiar case of Toucey v. New York Life Insurance Co.,[8] the Court changed its approach to construction of the statute. The precise issue in Toucey was whether an insurance company, which had successfully defended a claim against it in federal court, could enjoin relitigation of the claim in a state court by a person to whom the claimant had assigned his claim in order to defeat diversity and prevent removal. Could the federal courts use their injunctive power, despite the prohibition of the statute, "to save the defendants in the state proceedings the inconvenience of pleading and proving res judicata"?[9] Only seven years earlier

Reform of the Anti–Injunction Act, 1990 B.Y.U.L.Rev. 289; Mayton, Ersatz Federalism Under the Anti–Injunction Statute, 1978, 78 Col.L.Rev. 320; Redish, The Anti–Injunction Statute Reconsidered, 1977, 44 U.Chi.L.Rev. 717; Reaves & Golden, The Federal Anti–Injunction Statute in the Aftermath of Atlantic Coast Line Railroad, 1971, 5 Ga.L.Rev. 294.

2. Act of March 2, 1793, c. 22, § 5, 1 Stat. 334.

3. The possible theories are reviewed in Toucey v. New York Life Ins. Co., 1941, 62 S.Ct. 139, 142–143, 314 U.S. 118, 130–132, 86 L.Ed. 100. It is variously suggested that the statute stems from a 1790 report of Attorney General Edmund Randolph, that it was a response to the unpopular decision two weeks before in Chisholm v. Georgia, 1793, 2 Dall. 419, 1 L.Ed. 440, holding that a state could be sued in federal court by a citizen of another state, or that it reflected the prevailing prejudices against equity jurisdiction. The legislative history is silent.

It has recently been suggested that the purpose of the 1793 statute was to bar injunctions, while allowing the use of common-law certiorari to stay state proceedings, Comment, Federal Court Stays of State Court Proceedings: A Re–Examination of Original Congressional Intent, 1971, 38 U.Chi.L.Rev. 612, or that it was intended to give single justices authority to grant the writ of injunction, with the proviso that this authority not be used to stay a proceeding in state court. Mayton, note 1 above, at

332–338. These arguments are plausible, but it seems unlikely that the Court will abandon its firm perception of the intent of the statute if it should be persuaded that a change from a colon to a semicolon during the legislative process in 1793 was accidental rather than deliberate.

4. An express exception for cases where the bankruptcy laws authorized such an injunction was added in 1874. Rev.Stat. § 720. The provision was carried in this form as § 265 of the Judicial Code of 1911, formerly § 379 of 28 U.S.C.A. The present statute is 28 U.S.C.A. § 2283.

5. Oklahoma Packing Co. v. Oklahoma Gas & Elec. Co., 1940, 60 S.Ct. 215, 218, 309 U.S. 4, 9, 84 L.Ed. 537.

See also Atlantic Coast Line R. Co. v. Brotherhood of Locomotive Engineers, 1970, 90 S.Ct. 1739, 1742–1743, 398 U.S. 281, 285–286, 26 L.Ed.2d 234.

6. Chick Kam Choo v. Exxon Corp., 1988, 108 S.Ct. 1684, 1689, 486 U.S. 140, 146, 100 L.Ed.2d 127.

7. For able discussions of this period in the history of the statute, see Durfee & Sloss, Federal Injunctions against Proceedings in State Courts: The Life History of a Statute, 1932, 30 Mich.L.Rev. 1145; Taylor & Willis, The Power of Federal Courts to Enjoin Proceedings in State Courts, 1933, 42 Yale L.J. 1169.

8. 1941, 62 S.Ct. 139, 314 U.S. 118, 86 L.Ed. 100.

9. 62 S.Ct. at 142, 314 U.S. at 129.

the Court had unanimously held that a federal bankruptcy court could use its injunctive powers to save the bankrupt the inconvenience of pleading and proving discharge in bankruptcy in a later state action.[10] Other cases seemed to support the view that an injunction could issue against relitigation of a matter already decided in federal court.[11] Nevertheless in Toucey the answer was "No."

Justice Frankfurter, speaking for the Court, did not confine himself to the precise issue raised by Toucey but dealt comprehensively with the history and meaning of the statute. He recognized that, in addition to the exception for certain bankruptcy matters specifically written into the statute in 1874, other statutes, dealing with removal of actions, limitation of shipowners' liability, interpleader, and relief for farmers under the Frazier–Lemke Act, authorized injunctions against state proceedings and had to be regarded as implied statutory exceptions to the anti-injunction statute. He was willing to acknowledge, however, only one nonstatutory exception. The rule by this time was quite well settled that while in-personam actions involving the same claim could proceed simultaneously in state and federal court, and the federal court was not to enjoin such a state action even though the federal action had been commenced first,[12] if the action was in rem the court first obtaining jurisdiction over the res could enjoin suits in other courts involving the same res.[13]

All other exceptions not justified by statute Justice Frankfurter rejected. There was a line of cases holding that enforcement of a judgment was not part of the state-court "proceedings" and could be enjoined if the judgment had been obtained by fraud or if its enforcement was otherwise not in accord with equity and good conscience.[14] These cases were said to be "very doubtful," [15] but in any event had no application to the issue presented in Toucey. For the same reason he found it unnecessary to pass on cases holding that the statute did not bar an injunction against commencing a state action.[16] The opinion held

10. Local Loan Co. v. Hunt, 1934, 54 S.Ct. 695, 292 U.S. 234, 78 L.Ed. 1230. Though involving a discharged bankrupt, the case did not come within the statutory exception to the anti-injunction statute dealing with bankruptcy.

11. E.g., Looney v. Eastern Texas Ry. Co., 1918, 38 S.Ct. 460, 247 U.S. 214, 62 L.Ed. 1084; Supreme Tribe of Ben Hur v. Cauble, 1921, 41 S.Ct. 338, 255 U.S. 356, 65 L.Ed. 673.

12. Kline v. Burke Constr. Co., 1922, 43 S.Ct. 79, 260 U.S. 226, 67 L.Ed. 226; Vestal, Repetitive Litigation, 1960, 45 Iowa L.Rev. 525.

13. Hagan v. Lucas, 1836, 10 Pet. 400, 9 L.Ed. 470; Julian v. Central Trust Co., 1903, 24 S.Ct. 399, 193 U.S. 93, 48 L.Ed. 629; Lion Bonding & Surety Co. v. Karatz, 1923, 43 S.Ct. 480, 262 U.S. 77, 67 L.Ed.

871; see Kline v. Burke Constr. Co., 1922, 43 S.Ct. 79, 260 U.S. 226, 67 L.Ed. 226; Warren, Federal and State Court Interference, 1930, 43 Harv.L.Rev. 345, 359–366; 14 Wright, Miller & Cooper, Jurisdiction 2d § 3631.

14. Marshall v. Holmes, 1891, 12 S.Ct. 62, 141 U.S. 589, 35 L.Ed. 870; Ex parte Simon, 1908, 28 S.Ct. 238, 208 U.S. 144, 52 L.Ed. 429; Wells Fargo & Co. v. Taylor, 1920, 41 S.Ct. 93, 254 U.S. 175, 65 L.Ed. 205; Note, Relief against State Judgments Obtained by Fraud, 1945, 54 Yale L.J. 687.

15. 62 S.Ct. at 145, 314 U.S. at 136.

16. Ex parte Young, 1908, 28 S.Ct. 441, 209 U.S. 123, 52 L.Ed. 714; cf. Hale v. Bimco Trading, Inc., 1939, 59 S.Ct. 526, 306 U.S. 375, 83 L.Ed. 771. This exception from the statute had been criticized as illogical in Warren, Federal and State Court clearly, however, that there was no exception for "relitigation" cases. Some of the cases thought to support such an exception were written off as actions in rem.[17] Of the cases that could not be so disposed, the Court said that "loose language and a sporadic, ill-considered decision cannot be held to have imbedded in our law a doctrine which so patently violates the expressed prohibition of Congress." [18] The insurance company was not permitted to escape the inconvenience of pleading and proving res judicata in the state court.

Despite the care and comprehensiveness of the Toucey opinion, it proved unpersuasive to the authors of the 1948 Judicial Code. In the Reviser's Note to § 2283 the dissenting opinion in Toucey was spoken of favorably, and it was said that "the revised section restores the basic law as generally understood and interpreted prior to the Toucey decision." Section 2283, as adopted in 1948, says: "A court of the United States may not grant an injunction to stay proceedings in a State court except as expressly authorized by Act of Congress, or where necessary in aid of its jurisdiction, or to protect or effectuate its judgments."

The revised statute is not a model of clear draftsmanship.[19] The Supreme Court has often been called upon to construe it, and even with these constructions questions remain. In the first such case the issue was whether a federal court could enjoin a state court from restraining peaceful picketing, when the state court lacked jurisdiction to issue such a restraint since Congress had preempted the field and entrusted such matters to the National Labor Relations Board. The Court held that the federal court could not enjoin the state court.[20] With Justice Frankfurter again spokesman for the majority, the Court said that § 2283 "is not a statute conveying a broad general policy for appropriate ad hoc application. Legislative policy is here expressed in a clear-cut prohibi-

---

Interference, 1930, 43 Harv.L.Rev. 345, 372–376.

17. Local Loan Co. v. Hunt, 1934, 54 S.Ct. 695, 292 U.S. 234, 78 L.Ed. 1230, discussed note 10 above, on which the dissenters placed heavy reliance, was thus disposed of by Justice Frankfurter, 62 S.Ct. at 145 n. 6, 314 U.S. at 135 n. 6.

18. 62 S.Ct. at 147, 314 U.S. at 139.

19. "[A]ny amendment should properly solve more questions than it raises. The proposed revision does not appear to have this virtue." Barrett, Federal Injunctions against Proceedings in State Courts, 1947, 35 Calif.L.Rev. 545, 563.

"[T]he anti-injunction statute is rife with inadequacies and ambiguities." Redish, note 1 above, at 760.

Experience has shown that the 1948 revision "has not resolved the problems of interpretation, but rather seems to have generated new confusion." Comment, Anti-Suit Injunctions between State and Federal Courts, 1965, 32 U.Chi.L.Rev. 471, 482. A more recent writer concludes that "the

courts have continued to treat the statutory language like silly putty, stretching and squashing it in an effort to use anti-suit injunctions against state court proceedings when circumstances seemed to justify them." Wood, note 1 above, at 289–290.

20. Amalgamated Clothing Workers v. Richman Bros., 1955, 75 S.Ct. 452, 348 U.S. 511, 99 L.Ed. 600. Such a federal injunction against enforcement of a state-court injunction was held proper when sought by the Labor Board. Capital Serv., Inc. v. NLRB, 1954, 74 S.Ct. 699, 347 U.S. 501, 98 L.Ed. 887. Prior to the 1948 revision it had been held that the anti-injunction statute did not apply where Congress had preempted jurisdiction to the exclusion of state courts. Bowles v. Willingham, 1944, 64 S.Ct. 641, 321 U.S. 503, 88 L.Ed. 892. See also Kochery, Conflict of Jurisdiction: 28 U.S.C.A. § 2283 and Exclusive Jurisdiction, 1955, 4 Buff.L.Rev. 269; Comment, Power of a Federal Court to Enjoin State Court Action in Aid of Its Exclusive Jurisdiction, 1953, 48 Nw.U.L.Rev. 383.

tion qualified only by specifically defined exceptions." [21] Two years later, however, the prohibition was thought to be something less than "clear-cut," and implied exceptions were discovered. The issue was whether § 2283 barred an injunction against state proceedings where the United States sought the injunction. The Court unanimously agreed that it did not. Justice Frankfurter, for the Court, referred to "the severe restrictions" of "an ambiguous statute," and said that "we cannot reasonably impute such a purpose to Congress from the general language of 28 U.S.C.A. § 2283 alone." [22]

This encouraged some lower courts to think that § 2283 was not a limitation on the jurisdiction of the federal court, but only a rule of comity that could be disregarded where necessary to prevent grave and irreparable injury.[23] But with or without § 2283, injunctions cannot issue save to prevent irreparable injury, and there would be no point in the statute if it meant no more than this.[24] Thus, in 1970 the Supreme Court rejected the notion that the statute states only a rule of comity. Speaking through Justice Black, the Court held that the statute is "an absolute prohibition against enjoining state-court proceedings, unless the injunction falls within one of three specifically defined exceptions." [25] It said further that the exceptions are not to be enlarged by loose statutory construction.[26]

Some things are clear under § 2283. It is accepted that the prohibition against enjoining state-court proceedings cannot be avoided by framing an injunction as a restraint on a party rather than directly on the state court.[27] It remains the rule, despite the doubts Toucey might have raised, that the statute does not prohibit an injunction against a state officer who is about to institute proceedings to enforce an unconstitutional statute.[28] The statute does not apply unless the state court is

21. Amalgamated Clothing Workers v. Richman Bros., 1955, 75 S.Ct. 452, 455, 348 U.S. 511, 515–516, 99 L.Ed. 600.

22. Leiter Minerals v. U.S., 1957, 77 S.Ct. 287, 291, 352 U.S. 220, 226, 1 L.Ed.2d 267.

The Leiter Minerals exception was extended in NLRB v. Nash–Finch Co., 1971, 92 S.Ct. 373, 404 U.S. 138, 30 L.Ed.2d 328, where it was held that the Anti–Injunction Act does not bar the NLRB from suing in federal court to enjoin state proceedings on a matter preempted by federal law.

23. Baines v. City of Danville, C.A.4th, 1964, 337 F.2d 579, 593–594, certiorari denied 85 S.Ct. 1772, 381 U.S. 939, 14 L.Ed.2d 702. Machesky v. Bizzell, C.A.5th, 1969, 414 F.2d 283, 287–291; Landry v. Daley, D.C.Ill.1967, 280 F.Supp. 929, 936.

24. Essanay Film Mfg. Co. v. Kane, 1922, 42 S.Ct. 318, 319, 258 U.S. 358, 361, 66 L.Ed. 658; Laker Airways v. Sabena, Belgian World Airlines, C.A.D.C.1984, 731 F.2d 909, 915. See Wood, note 1 above, at

292–293; Comment, note 19 above, at 484; Note, 1964, 50 Va.L.Rev. 1404, 1424–1426.

25. Atlantic Coast Line R. Co. v. Brotherhood of Locomotive Engineers, 1970, 90 S.Ct. 1739, 1743, 398 U.S. 281, 286, 26 L.Ed.2d 234. See also Reaves & Golden, note 1 above.

26. 90 S.Ct. at 1743, 398 U.S. at 287.

27. County of Imperial v. Munoz, 1980, 101 S.Ct. 289, 292, 449 U.S. 54, 58–59, 66 L.Ed.2d 258; Oklahoma Packing Co. v. Oklahoma Gas & Elec. Co., 1940, 60 S.Ct. 215, 218, 309 U.S. 4, 9, 84 L.Ed. 447.

28. Dombrowski v. Pfister, 1965, 85 S.Ct. 1116, 1119 n. 2, 380 U.S. 479, 484 n. 2, 14 L.Ed.2d 22.

The Seventh Circuit, speaking through Judge—now–Justice—Stevens held that an injunction may issue if there was no state action pending when the federal injunction was sought, even though the state action is commenced before the federal court acts on the request for an injunction. Barancik v.

performing a judicial function.[29] Nor does it prevent a federal court from issuing a temporary stay while it determines whether § 2283 is applicable to the case.[30]

The first of the exceptions to § 2283 is "as expressly authorized by Act of Congress." [31] This does not mean that the Act of Congress must refer in terms to § 2283.[32] It is surely enough that it specifically says an injunction may be granted against a proceeding in a state court.[33] Probably it is enough that the Act of Congress permits a federal court to stay any proceeding, though it does not mention states specifically.[34] In Mitchum v. Foster [35] the Supreme Court said that the test is "whether an Act of Congress, clearly creating a federal right or remedy enforceable in a federal court of equity, could be given its intended scope only by the

---

Investors Funding Corp. of New York, C.A.7th, 1973, 489 F.2d 933. The Sixth Circuit, however, has expressly refused to follow that decision. Roth v. Bank of the Com., C.A.6th, 1978, 583 F.2d 527, certiorari dismissed 99 S.Ct. 2852, 442 U.S. 925, 61 L.Ed.2d 292, noted 1980, 64 Minn.L.Rev. 830. The Eighth Circuit, however, has followed the Seventh Circuit, National City Lines, Inc. v. LLC Corp., C.A.8th, 1982, 687 F.2d 1122, 1127, and the First Circuit in a considered dictum has supported that view. Hyde Park Partners, L.P. v. Connolly, C.A.1st, 1988, 839 F.2d 837, 842 n. 6. The Sixth Circuit's view, however, is said to be "much more in line with the statute" in Wood, note 1 above, at 312. That view, that the statute applies if there is a pending state action at the time the federal court acts on the request for the injunction, has been followed more recently by two other circuits. Standard Microsystems Corp. v. Texas Instruments, C.A.2d, 1990, 916 F.2d 58, 61–62, and Royal Ins. Co. of America v. Quinn–L Capital Corp., C.A.5th, 1993, 3 F.3d 877, 884–885.

29. Prentis v. Atlantic Coast Line Co., 1908, 29 S.Ct. 67, 211 U.S. 210, 53 L.Ed. 150; Roudebush v. Hartke, 1972, 92 S.Ct. 804, 405 U.S. 15, 31 L.Ed.2d 1; Lynch v. Household Fin. Corp., 1972, 92 S.Ct. 1113, 405 U.S. 538, 31 L.Ed.2d 424. See 17 Wright, Miller & Cooper, Jurisdiction 2d § 4222 at notes 28–31.

30. See Barancik v. Investors Funding Corp. of New York, C.A.7th, 1973, 489 F.2d 933, 937; ALI Study, p. 307; Note, 1964, 50 Va.L.Rev. 1404, 1426–1427.

31. 17 Wright, Miller & Cooper, Jurisdiction 2d § 4224; Redish, note 1 above, at 726–743.

32. See Amalgamated Clothing Workers of America v. Richman Bros., 1955, 75 S.Ct. 452, 455, 348 U.S. 511, 516, 99 L.Ed. 600.

33. Thus, see the interpleader statute, 28 U.S.C.A. § 2361, Pan American Fire & Cas. Co. v. Revere, D.C.La.1960, 188 F.Supp. 474, and the habeas-corpus statute, 28 U.S.C.A. § 2251.

34. The provision in the Bankruptcy Act, 11 U.S.C.A. § 362, is to this effect, as had been the provision in the Frazier–Lemke Act, 49 Stat. 944.

The limitation-of-liability statute, 46 U.S.C.A. § 185, provides that "all claims and proceedings against the owner with respect to the matter in question shall cease." This is held to meet the "expressly authorized" test. Beal v. Waltz, C.A.5th, 1962, 309 F.2d 721, 724.

The provision of the removal statute that upon removal "the State court shall proceed no further" has always been understood to permit an injunction against further state proceedings. Frith v. Blazon-Flexible Flyer, Inc., C.A.5th, 1975, 512 F.2d 899, 901.

In Studebaker Corp. v. Gittlin, C.A.2d, 1966, 360 F.2d 692, the court was able to bring within the "expressly authorized" language an action by a private person to enjoin violation of Proxy Rules issued by the S.E.C., even though it is only by implication that a private person has any right of action whatever. The case is criticized in Redish, note 1 above, at 727–733. "Many commentators have noted (with glee or despair) that the words 'expressly authorized' actually mean 'implicitly authorized.'" Wood, note 1 above, at 297.

Compare ALI Study, § 1372(1).

35. 1972, 92 S.Ct. 2151, 407 U.S. 225, 32 L.Ed.2d 705.

stay of a state court proceeding." [36] Applying that test the Court held that the legislative history of the civil-rights statute, 42 U.S.C.A. § 1983, was enough to bring its authorization of "suit in equity" within this exception to the Anti–Injunction Act.[37]

Mitchum was not the last word on the application of the "expressly authorized" exception. The Court was sharply divided in 1977 in Vendo Company v. Lektro–Vend Corporation.[38] After the Supreme Court had refused to review a substantial money judgment in a suit for breach of fiduciary duty, the losing defendant successfully moved in federal court for an injunction against collection of the state judgment on the ground that the state litigation had an anticompetitive purpose and violated the federal antitrust laws.

Although the Supreme Court held 5–4 that the injunction should not have issued, it did not agree on the reason. Three justices, in the plurality opinion of Justice Rehnquist, took the position that § 16 of the Clayton Act does not meet the second half of the Mitchum test, and thus is not within the exception to § 2283, since stay of a state action is not necessary to give § 16 its intended scope. The other two majority justices, in a concurring opinion by Justice Blackmun, thought that § 16 is an exception in narrowly limited circumstances, as where the state-court proceedings are part of a pattern of baseless, repetitive claims that are being used as an anticompetitive device. The four dissenters, speaking through Justice Stevens, would have held that § 16 is always an expressly authorized exception and that even a single state-court proceeding can be enjoined. Because the Court was so fragmented, the Vendo case sheds little light on when an injunction of state proceedings is "expressly authorized," and the lower courts continue to take varying views.[39]

The second exception allows a court to enjoin state proceedings "where necessary in aid of its jurisdiction." [40] This means, among other things, that the rule, recognized even in Toucey, remains, and a federal court can enjoin a later state action involving property in the custody of

---

36. 92 S.Ct. at 2160, 407 U.S. at 238.

37. Considerations of comity may bar an injunction even when § 2283 does not apply. See § 52A below.

One court has held that the rule of Mitchum v. Foster applies only when a § 1983 suit is based on a violation of the Constitution and that a suit based on a federal statute, though properly within § 1983, is not within the first exception to § 2283. Hickey v. Duffy, C.A.7th, 1987, 827 F.2d 234, 240–243.

38. 1977, 97 S.Ct. 2881, 433 U.S. 623, 53 L.Ed.2d 1009, noted 1978, 44 Brooklyn L.Rev. 317, 56 N.C.L.Rev. 601. See Mayton, note 1 above, at 355, and Redish, note 1 above, at 739–743.

The Supreme Court had to act twice more before the injunction was finally dissolved. Vendo Co. v. Lektro–Vend Corp., 1978, 98 S.Ct. 702, 434 U.S. 425, 54 L.Ed.2d 659; In re Vendo Co., 1978, 98 S.Ct. 1660, 435 U.S. 994, 56 L.Ed.2d 93. For the final resolution of the case, see Lektro–Vend Corp. v. Vendo Co., C.A.7th, 1981, 660 F.2d 255, certiorari denied 102 S.Ct. 1277, 455 U.S. 921, 71 L.Ed.2d 461.

39. Compare cases cited 17 Wright, Miller & Cooper, Jurisdiction 2d § 4224 nn. 20, 21.

40. 17 Wright, Miller & Cooper, Jurisdiction 2d § 4225.

the federal court.[41] The corollary remains, however, that an injunction cannot issue to restrain a state action in personam involving the same subject matter from going on at the same time. This is true even though the state action raises a question of federal law,[42] or its findings may have an issue-preclusive effect in the federal action,[43] or it raises a claim that should be a compulsory counterclaim in the federal action.[44] The exception does not allow a federal injunction of state proceedings merely because they involve issues presented in a federal in-personam action [45] or because the federal court has exclusive jurisdiction [46] or because the area has been preempted by federal law.[47]

Commentators have urged that the "necessary in aid of its jurisdiction" exception be read more broadly, so that it would encompass more than the in-rem situation.[48] There is a basis for such a broader reading in the Supreme Court's statement that both this and the third exception of § 2283 allow federal injunctive relief where this is "necessary to prevent a state court from so interfering with a federal court's consideration or disposition of a case as to seriously impair the federal court's flexibility and authority to decide that case." [49] There are a few scattered signs of such flexibility in the recent cases. In the school-desegregation area the federal court typically takes a controversy in hand, modifying its orders as need be from time to time, and it has been held that it can enjoin state proceedings that would interfere with the federal court's continuing jurisdiction.[50] There are other cases like this

41. James v. Bellotti, C.A.1st, 1984, 733 F.2d 989; Green v. Green, C.A.7th, 1958, 259 F.2d 229; ALI Study, § 1372(3). See note 13 above.

42. Thiokol Chemical Corp. v. Burlington Indus., Inc., C.A.3d, 1971, 448 F.2d 1328, certiorari denied 1972, 92 S.Ct. 684, 404 U.S. 1019, 30 L.Ed.2d 668.

43. Signal Properties, Inc. v. Farha, C.A.5th, 1973, 482 F.2d 1136; Vernitron Corp. v. Benjamin, C.A.2d, 1971, 440 F.2d 105, certiorari denied 91 S.Ct. 1664, 402 U.S. 987, 29 L.Ed.2d 154.

44. Bruce v. Martin, D.C.N.Y.1989, 724 F.Supp. 124, 131 n. 11; Johnny's Pizza House, Inc. v. G & H Properties, Inc., D.C.La.1981, 524 F.Supp. 495; Carter v. Bedford, D.C.Ark.1976, 420 F.Supp. 927.

45. Phillips v. Chas. Schreiner Bank, C.A.5th, 1990, 894 F.2d 127, 132; In re Federal Skywalk Cases, C.A.8th, 1982, 680 F.2d 1175, certiorari denied 103 S.Ct. 342, 459 U.S. 988, 74 L.Ed.2d 383; Hyde Constr. Co. v. Koehring Co., C.A.10th, 1968, 388 F.2d 501, certiorari denied 88 S.Ct. 1654, 391 U.S. 905, 20 L.Ed.2d 419; Maryland Cas. Co. v. W.R. Grace & Co., D.C.N.Y.1989, 726 F.Supp. 62, 65, affirmed C.A.2d, 1989, 889 F.2d 1231.

46. See note 20 above. See also 1975 Salaried Retirement Plan for Eligible Employees of Crucible, Inc. v. Nobers, C.A.3d, 1992, 968 F.2d 401; Village of Bolingbrook v. Citizens Utilities Co., C.A.7th, 1988, 864 F.2d 481; T. Smith & Sons, Inc. v. Williams, C.A.5th, 1960, 275 F.2d 397, 407.

47. "Rather, when a state proceeding presents a federal issue, even a pre-emptive issue, the proper course is to seek resolution of that issue by the state courts." Chick Kam Choo v. Exxon Corp., 1988, 108 S.Ct. 1684, 1691, 486 U.S. 140, 149–150, 100 L.Ed.2d 127. See also note 20 above.

48. Mayton, note 1 above, at 356–369; Redish, note 1 above, at 743–760.

49. Atlantic Coast Line R. Co. v. Brotherhood of Locomotive Engineers, 1970, 90 S.Ct. 1739, 1747, 398 U.S. 281, 295, 26 L.Ed.2d 234.

50. Swann v. Charlotte–Mecklenburg Bd. of Educ., C.A.4th, 1974, 501 F.2d 383; Oliver v. Kalamazoo Bd. of Educ., D.C.Mich.1981, 510 F.Supp. 1104; Grenchik v. Mandel, D.C.Md.1973, 373 F.Supp. 1298. See also Valley v. Rapides Parish Sch. Bd., C.A.5th, 1981, 646 F.2d 925, 943.

Since in these cases the federal court will typically have already made some orders, they may also be regarded as coming within the third exception to § 2283. E.g., Thomason v. Cooper, C.A.8th, 1958, 254 F.2d 808.

that seem best viewed as analogous to the custody-of-property cases and thus within the second exception.[51]

The third and last exception to § 2283 allows a federal court to stay state proceedings "to protect or effectuate its judgments." This overrules the specific holding of the Toucey case and allows use of an injunction to prevent relitigation that has gone to judgment in the federal court.[52] Although the commentators have thought that a federal injunction should not issue automatically in this situation, and that there should be some showing of irreparable injury and lack of an adequate remedy at law,[53] most cases do not seem to have imposed such a requirement.[54] In determining what is a "judgment" that can be protected under the third exception, Civil Rule 54(a), which defines "judgment" as "any order from which an appeal lies," provides a useful analogy. This would bring within the exception, and allows stays to issue to protect, interlocutory orders that are appealable as of right.[55]

51. Battle v. Liberty Nat. Life Ins. Co., C.A.11th, 1989, 877 F.2d 877, 882; Garcia v. Bauza–Salas, C.A.1st, 1988, 862 F.2d 905, 909; State Water Control Bd. v. Washington Suburban Sanitary Comm., C.A.1981, 654 F.2d 802; Bekoff v. Clinton, D.C.N.Y. 1972, 344 F.Supp. 642; Montgomery County Bd. of Educ. v. Shelton, D.C.Miss.1971, 327 F.Supp. 811; Moss v. Burkhart, D.C.Okl.1963, 220 F.Supp. 149, 162–163, affirmed 1964, 84 S.Ct. 1907, 378 U.S. 558, 12 L.Ed.2d 1026. See also Wood, note 1 above, at 302–304.

This principle would seem to apply to prevent conflicting state actions where many similar suits have been consolidated by the Judicial Panel on Multidistrict Litigation under 28 U.S.C.A. § 1407. The purpose of consolidation is to provide coordinated treatment of these complex cases, and, as in actions in rem and school desegregation cases, it is intolerable to have different orders coming from different courts. An injunction from the multidistrict court was upheld in In re Corrugated Container Antitrust Action Litigation, C.A.5th, 1981, 659 F.2d 1332, but on the basis that settlements that had already been reached were a "judgment" that could be protected under the third exception to § 2283. But see Alton Box Bd. Co. v. Esprit De Corp., C.A.9th, 1982, 682 F.2d 1267.

The issue in In re Federal Skywalk Cases, C.A.8th, 1982, 680 F.2d 1175, certiorari denied 103 S.Ct. 342, 459 U.S. 988, 74 L.Ed.2d 303, was whether a Rule 23(b)(1) class action is barred since it effectively enjoins members of the plaintiff class from pursuing their individual claims in state court. The majority held that the class

action was barred, but there is a strong dissent.

52. 17 Wright, Miller & Cooper, Jurisdiction 2d § 4226.

The relitigation exception to the Anti–Injunction Act does not limit the Full Faith and Credit Act, 28 U.S.C.A. § 1738. If a state court has held, in a judgment entitled to preclusive effect under state law and the Full Faith and Credit Act, that an earlier federal judgment is not binding on it, the federal court must accept that judgment and cannot enjoin the parties from further prosecuting the state action. Parsons Steel, Inc. v. First Alabama Bank, 1986, 106 S.Ct. 768, 474 U.S. 518, 88 L.Ed.2d 877. See the same case on remand, C.A.11th, 1987, 825 F.2d 1475, certiorari denied 108 S.Ct. 1015, 484 U.S. 1060, 98 L.Ed.2d 980. The Parsons Steel case is criticized in Wood, note 1 above, at 305–307.

53. ALI Study, p. 306; Vestal, Protecting A Federal Court Judgment, 1975, 42 Tenn.L.Rev. 635, 661–671; Comment, note 19 above, at 486.

54. See cases cited 17 Wright, Miller & Cooper, Jurisdiction 2d § 4226 nn. 5, 12; Redish, note 1 above, at 723 n. 31.

But see Bechtel Petroleum v. Webster, C.A.9th, 1986, 796 F.2d 252, 253; Southern California Petroleum Corp. v. Harper, C.A.5th, 1960, 273 F.2d 715, 719; Allstate Ins. Co. v. Preston, D.C.Fla.1992, 842 F.Supp. 1441; Texaco, Inc. v. Fiumara, D.C.Pa.1965, 248 F.Supp. 595, 597; and cases cited 17 Wright, Miller & Cooper, Jurisdiction 2d § 4226 n. 34.

55. See § 102 below.

In Chick Kam Choo v. Exxon Corporation [56] the Supreme Court said that the relitigation exception is "founded in the well-recognized concepts of *res judicata* and collateral estoppel." [57] But in the course of that opinion the Court also said that "an essential prerequisite for applying the relitigation exception is that the claims or issues which the federal injunction insulates from litigation in state proceedings actually have been decided by the federal court." [58] A number of circuits have held that this language means that the exception is limited to issues "actually litigated" in a prior court proceeding.[59] But this interpretation would read res judicata—or claim preclusion, as it is now usually called [60]—out of the third exception.[61]

If an injunction would be barred by § 2283, this should also bar the issuance of a declaratory judgment that would have the same effect as an injunction.[62] This problem is now of lessened importance, since most of the cases in which the issue arose involved challenges to official conduct, and most such cases are civil-rights cases that, since 1972, have been held to come within the first exception to § 2283.

The "proceedings" in a state court that cannot be stayed include "execution issued on a judgment" and "any proceeding supplemental or ancillary taken with a view to making the suit or judgment effective." [63] If a state action has ended in a judgment requiring enforcement of a state statute, it may still be the law that this does not bar a federal court from enjoining enforcement of the statute on the suit of "strangers to the state court proceeding." [64] It is almost certainly not still the law that a federal court cannot enjoin the enforcement of a state judgment that has been obtained by fraud or that is otherwise not in accord with equity and good conscience. The early cases that had allowed a federal injunction in these circumstances [65] cannot be comfortably fitted either

---

56. 1988, 108 S.Ct. 1684, 486 U.S. 140, 100 L.Ed.2d 127.

57. 108 S.Ct. at 1690, 486 U.S.at 147.

58. 108 S.Ct. at 1690, 486 U.S. at 148.

59. See Staffer v. Bouchard Transp. Co., C.A.2d, 1989, 878 F.2d 638, 643; and cases cited 17 Wright, Miller & Cooper, Jurisdiction 2d § 4226 n. 12.1.

60. See § 100A below.

61. Western Systems, Inc. v. Ulloa, C.A.9th, 1992, 958 F.2d 864, 869–871, certiorari denied 113 S.Ct. 970, ___ U.S. ___, 122 L.Ed.2d 125.

See Martinez, The Anti-Injunction Act: Fending Off The New Attack on the Relitigation Exception, 1993, 72 Neb.L.Rev. 643.

62. Texas Employers' Ins. Assn. v. Jackson, C.A.5th, 1988, 862 F.2d 491, 496, 504–508, certiorari denied 109 S.Ct. 1932, 490 U.S. 1035, 104 L.Ed.2d 404; Thiokol Chem. Corp. v. Burlington Indus., Inc., C.A.3d, 1971, 448 F.2d 1328, 1332, certiorari denied 1972, 92 S.Ct. 684, 404 U.S. 1019, 30 L.Ed.2d 668; and cases cited 17 Wright, Miller & Cooper, Jurisdiction 2d § 4226 n. 11.

But see Note, The Federal Anti–Injunction Statute and Declaratory Judgments in Constitutional Litigation, 1970, 83 Harv. L.Rev. 1870.

63. Hill v. Martin, 1935, 56 S.Ct. 278, 282, 296 U.S. 393, 403, 80 L.Ed. 293; County of Imperial v. Munoz, 1980, 101 S.Ct. 289, 449 U.S. 54, 66 L.Ed.2d 258.

64. Hale v. Bimco Trading, Inc., 1939, 59 S.Ct. 526, 306 U.S. 375, 83 L.Ed. 771. For the present status of this rule, see County of Imperial v. Munoz, 1980, 101 S.Ct. 289, 449 U.S. 54, 66 L.Ed.2d 258, noted 1981, 8 Ohio N.L.Rev. 419. See also the same case on remand, D.C.Cal.1981, 510 F.Supp. 879, affirmed C.A.9th, 1982, 667 F.2d 811, certiorari denied 103 S.Ct. 58, 459 U.S. 825, 74 L.Ed.2d 62.

65. See notes 14 and 15 above.

with the later definition of "proceedings" that has now been developed or with the language of the exceptions to § 2283 in the 1948 revision.[66]

Even if an injunction against state proceedings is not barred by § 2283, it may still be refused. The various abstention doctrines may counsel that the federal court refrain from exercising its power to issue an injunction.[67] Special considerations of federalism restrict the use of injunctions that will interfere with state law enforcement.[68]

§ 48. Federal Actions to Restrain State Officers [1]

It was pointed out in the first section of this book that questions as to the jurisdiction of the federal courts are not mere details of procedure, but go to the very heart of a federal system and affect the allocation of power between the United States and the several states. This is nowhere more strikingly illustrated than in the famous case of Ex parte Young,[2] and the doctrine that has been generated by that case.

In 1907 the Minnesota legislature passed a law reducing railroad rates and providing severe penalties for any railroad that failed to comply with the law. The day before the law was to take effect stockholders of nine railroads brought suits in federal court to enjoin the companies in which they held stock from complying with the law. They alleged that the rates prescribed by the new law were unjust, unreasonable, and confiscatory, and would deprive the companies of their property without due process of law, contrary to the Fourteenth Amendment, but that the penalties under the law were such that the railroads, if not restrained, would comply with it. Among other defendants plaintiffs included Edward T. Young, the Attorney General of Minnesota, and prayed that he be restrained from seeking to enforce the law. The federal court issued first a temporary restraining order and later a preliminary injunction, granting the relief the plaintiffs sought. This relief was given over Young's objection that the suit was in fact a suit against the state, to which the state had not consented, and thus barred by the Eleventh Amendment. The day after the preliminary injunction was issued Young sued in state court for a writ of mandamus against the

---

66. 17 Wright, Miller & Cooper, Jurisdiction 2d § 4223; ALI Study, pp. 51, 311–312; Warriner v. Fink, C.A.5th, 1962, 307 F.2d 933, certiorari denied 83 S.Ct. 937, 372 U.S. 943, 9 L.Ed.2d 969; Furnish v. Board of Medical Examiners, C.A.9th, 1958, 257 F.2d 520, certiorari denied 79 S.Ct. 123, 358 U.S. 882, 3 L.Ed.2d 111; Norwood v. Parenteau, C.A.8th, 1955, 228 F.2d 148, certiorari denied 76 S.Ct. 852, 351 U.S. 955, 100 L.Ed. 1478; cf. Manufacturers Record Pub. Co. v. Lauer, C.A.5th, 1959, 268 F.2d 187, certiorari denied 80 S.Ct. 258, 361 U.S. 913, 4 L.Ed.2d 184. But see Wood, note 1 above, at 316–317.

Contra: Alleghany Corp. v. Kirby, D.C.N.Y.1963, 218 F.Supp. 164, 169, affirmed C.A.2d, 1964, 333 F.2d 327, affirmed on rehearing C.A.2d, 1965, 340 F.2d 311, certiorari dismissed 86 S.Ct. 1250, 384 U.S. 28, 16 L.Ed.2d 335; Dowd v. Front Range Mines, D.C.Colo.1965, 242 F.Supp. 591; Mayton, note 1 above, at 368–369; Note, 1961, 74 Harv.L.Rev. 726, 728.

67. See § 52 below.

68. See § 52A below.

§ 48

1. 17 Wright, Miller & Cooper, Jurisdiction 2d §§ 4231, 4232; Jacobs, The Eleventh Amendment and Sovereign Immunity, 1972, c. 5.

2. 1908, 28 S.Ct. 441, 209 U.S. 123, 52 L.Ed. 714.

railroads to compel them to comply with the new law. He was adjudged guilty of contempt for this action, fined $100, and ordered to jail until he dismissed the state mandamus proceeding. He then applied to the Supreme Court for a writ of habeas corpus to free him from the custody of the marshal. As the Supreme Court understood the issue, the contempt order was invalid, and habeas corpus should be granted, if the Eleventh Amendment prohibited the injunction against him that he had violated.[3]

The Supreme Court did not write on a clean slate in deciding Young's case. In 1793, in the unpopular decision of Chisholm v. Georgia,[4] it had held that the Constitution permitted a citizen of one state to sue another state in federal court, though the state had not consented to such suit. The Eleventh Amendment was ratified five years later to take away the judicial power of the federal courts in such cases,[5] and though in terms it does not so provide, it was construed as barring suits against a state without its consent even where, as in Young's case, the suit was brought by a citizen of the state and the basis of the jurisdiction was a claim under federal law.[6] In an early decision Chief Justice Marshall had construed the amendment as barring suit only where the state was formally a party of record,[7] but the principle embodied in the Eleventh Amendment was too vital to be restrained by such formalism and Marshall himself later construed the amendment as applying to a suit against the governor of a state where he was being sued in his official capacity.[8] Over the next half-century the decisions were varying and uncertain. The Court undertook to rationalize them, and establish a rule on the subject, in 1887 in the case of In re Ayers.[9] The decision there was that suit against a state officer was not barred where the challenged action, aside from any official authority claimed as its justifi-

---

3. Compare U.S. v. United Mine Workers of America, 1947, 67 S.Ct. 677, 330 U.S. 258, 91 L.Ed. 884, discussed § 16 above.

4. 1793, 2 Dall. 419, 1 L.Ed. 440.

5. See 1 Warren, The Supreme Court in United States History, 2d ed. 1926, pp. 93–102; 13 Wright, Miller & Cooper, Jurisdiction 2d § 3524.

6. Hans v. Louisiana, 1890, 10 S.Ct. 504, 134 U.S. 1, 33 L.Ed. 842. See also Employees of Dept. of Public Health & Welfare v. Department of Public Health & Welfare, 1973, 93 S.Ct. 1614, 1616, 411 U.S. 279, 280, 36 L.Ed.2d 251. This traditional understanding is challenged by Justice Brennan in his dissent in the case just cited. 93 S.Ct. at 1632–1637, 411 U.S. at 313–322. He was later joined by Justices Marshall, Blackmun, and Stevens in this view. See, e.g., Atascadero State Hospital v. Scanlon, 1985, 105 S.Ct. 3142, 3156, 3178, 473 U.S. 234, 247–302, 87 L.Ed.2d 171 (dissenting opinion). On the Eleventh Amendment generally, see § 46 n. 6 above.

7. Osborn v. Bank of the United States, 1824, 9 Wheat. 738, 846, 857, 6 L.Ed. 204.

8. Governor of Georgia v. Madrazo, 1828, 1 Pet. 110, 122–123, 7 L.Ed. 73.

9. 1887, 8 S.Ct. 164, 123 U.S. 443, 31 L.Ed. 216.

In a well-known later case, the Court purported to distinguish the Ayers case and to allow suit against a State Revenue Commissioner to enjoin him from collecting supposedly unconstitutional taxes. Ayers, the Court said, was not in point, because in that case there was no allegation that the challenged tax was a violation of constitutional rights, and thus the suit was directly against the state. Georgia R. & Banking Co. v. Redwine, 1952, 72 S.Ct. 321, 325, 342 U.S. 299, 306, 96 L.Ed. 335. The pleadings in the Ayers case, as well as the Court's opinion in that case, show that plaintiff was explicitly claiming that the tax challenged there impaired the obligation of his contract with the state in violation of Art. I, § 10. See 17 Wright, Miller & Cooper, Jurisdiction 2d § 4231 n. 13.

cation, was a wrong simply as an individual act, such as a trespass, but that if the act of the officer did not constitute an individual wrong and was something that only the state, through its officers, could do, the suit was in substance a suit against the state. The case would seem to be decisive of the Young litigation. Only a state can violate the Fourteenth Amendment. Only a state can compel railroads to charge particular rates. Indeed in the Ayers case the relief unsuccessfully sought was an injunction restraining state attorneys from bringing suits under a supposedly unconstitutional statute. The law was clouded between 1887 and 1908, when Young's case came to the Court, by decisions that, in dicta at least, suggested that the commencement of a suit to enforce an unconstitutional statute could be considered an actionable wrong similar to a trespass.[10]

Against this erratic background, the Court held that the injunction against Young was proper. Justice Peckham, for the Court, announced the rule that has since been repeatedly followed:[11] "The act to be enforced is alleged to be unconstitutional, and, if it be so, the use of the name of the state to enforce an unconstitutional act to the injury of the complainants is a proceeding without the authority of, and one which does not affect, the state in its sovereign or governmental capacity. It is simply an illegal act upon the part of a state official, in attempting by the use of the name of the state to enforce a legislative enactment which is void, because unconstitutional. If the act which the state Attorney General seeks to enforce be a violation of the federal Constitution, the officer in proceeding under such enactment comes into conflict with the superior authority of that Constitution, and he is in that case stripped of his official or representative character and is subject in his person to the consequences of his individual conduct."[12]

Only the first Justice Harlan dissented. In a lengthy opinion he argued: "The suit was, as to the defendant Young, one against him as, and only because he was, Attorney General of Minnesota. No relief was sought against him individually but only in his capacity as Attorney General. And the manifest—indeed, the avowed and admitted—object of seeking such relief was to tie the hands of the state, so that it could not in any manner or by any mode of proceeding in its own courts test the validity of the statutes and orders in question. It would therefore seem clear that within the true meaning of the Eleventh Amendment the suit brought in the federal court was one, in legal effect, against the state."[13]

There is no doubt that the reality is as Justice Harlan stated it, and that everyone knew that the Court was engaging in fiction when it

10. Reagan v. Farmers' Loan & Trust Co., 1894, 14 S.Ct. 1047, 154 U.S. 362, 38 L.Ed. 1014; Scott v. Donald, 1897, 17 S.Ct. 265, 266, 165 U.S. 58, 67, 41 L.Ed. 632; Smyth v. Ames, 1898, 18 S.Ct. 418, 169 U.S. 466, 42 L.Ed. 819; Prout v. Starr, 1903, 23 S.Ct. 398, 188 U.S. 537, 47 L.Ed. 584; Gunter v. Atlantic Coast Line R. Co., 1906, 26 S.Ct. 252, 200 U.S. 273, 50 L.Ed. 477; McNeill v. Southern R. Co., 1906, 26 S.Ct. 722, 202 U.S. 543, 50 L.Ed. 1142.

11. See Duker, Mr. Justice Rufus W. Peckham and the Case of Ex Parte Young: Lochnerizing Munn v. Illinois, 1980 B.Y.U.L.Rev. 539.

12. 28 S.Ct. at 454, 209 U.S. at 159–160.

13. 28 S.Ct. at 459, 209 U.S. at 173–174.

regarded the suit as one against an individual named Young rather than against the state of Minnesota.[14] The fiction has its own illogic. The Fourteenth Amendment runs only to the states; in order to have a right to relief under the amendment the plaintiff must be able to show that state action is involved in the denial of his rights.[15] It would have been possible to hold that the Fourteenth Amendment qualified the immunity from suit granted states by the Eleventh Amendment,[16] but the Court expressly refused to so hold.[17] Instead it created the anomaly that enforcement of the Minnesota statute is state action for purposes of the Fourteenth Amendment but merely the individual wrong of Edward T. Young for purposes of the Eleventh Amendment.[18]

What if the action of the state officer is beyond his authority as a matter of state law? A case prior to Ex parte Young had seemed to hold that an action unauthorized by state law could not be state action for purposes of the Fourteenth Amendment.[19] This decision has no continuing authority. It was settled five years after Ex parte Young that action by a state officer claiming to act under authority of the state can be enjoined, even if the state has not authorized such action.[20]

14. "Of course, the Court well knew that the attorney general was still attorney general while he was enforcing the statute, and the Court well knew that the effect of enjoining the attorney general was to enjoin the state from carrying out the unconstitutional statute. From that day to this the false pretense made by the Court in Ex parte Young has been the mainstay in challenging governmental action through suits for injunctions and declaratory judgments." Davis, Suing the Government by Falsely Pretending to Sue an Officer, 1962, 29 U.Chi.L.Rev. 435, 437.

15. Civil Rights Cases, 1883, 3 S.Ct. 18, 109 U.S. 3, 27 L.Ed. 835. Lewis, The Meaning of State Action, 1960, 60 Calif.L.Rev. 1083. But cf. Williams, The Twilight of State Action, 1963, 41 Texas L.Rev. 347.

16. See Note, 1937, 50 Harv.L.Rev. 956, 961.

17. 28 S.Ct. at 450, 209 U.S. at 150.

If the Fourteenth Amendment does limit the Eleventh Amendment, then many subsequent cases in which a suit against the state itself on Fourteenth Amendment grounds has been held barred by the Eleventh Amendment were wrongly decided. But Justice Marshall, in his dissent in Edelman v. Jordan, 1974, 94 S.Ct. 1347, 1371 n. 2, 415 U.S. 651, 694, 39 L.Ed.2d 662, seemed to regard this as still an open question. Even though the Fourteenth Amendment of its own force does not limit the Eleventh Amendment, Congress, in the exercise of its enforcement powers under § 5 of the Fourteenth Amendment, may take

away a state's Eleventh Amendment immunity. Fitzpatrick v. Bitzer, 1976, 96 S.Ct. 2666, 427 U.S. 445, 49 L.Ed.2d 614. See also § 46 n. 6 above.

18. When the case was decided on the merits, it was discovered that Young had not committed a wrong after all, since the new rates required by the statute were held valid. Minnesota Rate Cases (Simpson v. Shepard), 1913, 33 S.Ct. 729, 230 U.S. 352, 57 L.Ed. 1511. Since he was not acting unconstitutionally in enforcing the rates, Young was not stripped of his state authority and the suit was in fact one against the state. But the ultimate outcome does not defeat the jurisdiction invoked by the complaint. E.g., Bell v. Hood, 1946, 66 S.Ct. 773, 327 U.S. 678, 90 L.Ed. 939; see § 18 nn. 17–18 above.

19. Barney v. City of New York, 1904, 24 S.Ct. 502, 193 U.S. 430, 48 L.Ed. 737. See Isseks, Jurisdiction of the Lower Federal Courts to Enjoin Unauthorized Action of State Officials, 1927, 40 Harv.L.Rev. 969.

20. Home Tel. & Tel. Co. v. City of Los Angeles, 1913, 33 S.Ct. 312, 227 U.S. 278, 57 L.Ed. 510. That case did not specifically overrule the Barney case, and it was possible, as in the article by Isseks cited note 19 above, to suppose that Barney retained some vitality. It was not until U.S. v. Raines, 1960, 80 S.Ct. 519, 525, 362 U.S. 17, 25–26, 4 L.Ed.2d 524, that it was expressly declared that "Barney must be regarded as having 'been worn away by the erosion of time,' * * * and of contrary authority."

The effect of Ex parte Young is to bring within the scope of federal judicial review actions that might otherwise escape such review, and to subject the states to the restrictions of the United States Constitution that they might otherwise be able safely to ignore. If Ex parte Young had been decided the other way, there would have been no practicable means for the railroads to obtain a court determination of the new rates Minnesota wanted them to charge. The state could, of course, consent to suit, either in its own courts or in federal court, simply as a matter of grace, but even today many states have not done so. The railroads could have refused to obey the new law, and asserted its unconstitutionality as a defense to an action against them for its enforcement, but the state might have chosen to enforce the law by the criminal sanctions it supplied, and these were so severe that the railroads could not risk the possibility that they might lose and have to pay crushing fines.[21] In some situations, as where a state has failed to desegregate its schools, affirmative action is required of the state to fulfill its constitutional obligations, and there would not be even the possibility of raising the constitutional issue defensively. A doctrine could have been developed imposing on the states a constitutional obligation to provide some remedy by which constitutional rights could be asserted—indeed a case decided the same day as Ex parte Young hints at such a doctrine [22]—but this would have either the advantage or the disadvantage, depending on how the matter is viewed, that the challenge would come in the first instance in a state court with review by the Supreme Court, rather than initially in the federal court.[23]

The fictional basis of Ex parte Young also limits the relief that can be afforded. A state officer can be enjoined from acting improperly in making welfare payments but he or she cannot be required to make restitution to those who have wrongfully been denied benefits in the past, since such an award would have to be paid from state funds, rather than from the pocket of the officer named as defendant, and would

---

21. Attempts to arrange a friendly test case might have floundered on the requirement of case or controversy. Chicago & G.T. Ry. Co. v. Wellman, 1892, 12 S.Ct. 400, 143 U.S. 339, 36 L.Ed. 176.

22. General Oil Co. v. Crain, 1908, 28 S.Ct. 475, 209 U.S. 211, 52 L.Ed. 754. It was held there that a state court decision denying jurisdiction to hear a federal challenge of a state statute has the effect of upholding the statute, and is reviewable in the United States Supreme Court. The doctrine of the Crain case may have been repudiated by Georgia R. & Banking Co. v. Musgrove, 1949, 69 S.Ct. 407, 335 U.S. 900, 93 L.Ed. 435. See 16 Wright, Miller & Cooper, Jurisdiction § 4024. On the duty of the states to enforce federal law, see generally § 45 above.

23. "If the railroads were required to take no active steps until they could bring a writ of error from this court to the Supreme Court of Appeals after a final judgment, they would come here with the facts already found against them. But the determination as to their rights turns almost wholly upon the facts to be found." Prentis v. Atlantic Coast Line Co., 1908, 29 S.Ct. 67, 70, 211 U.S. 210, 228, 53 L.Ed. 150 (per Holmes, J.).

Limiting the remedy to state courts would also expose litigants to delay if the state court chose not to act promptly. On the potentialities of such delay, see National Assn. for the Advancement of Colored People v. Alabama, 1959, 79 S.Ct. 1001, 360 U.S. 240, 3 L.Ed.2d 1205; National Assn. for the Advancement of Colored People v. Gallion, 1961, 82 S.Ct. 4, 368 U.S. 16, 7 L.Ed.2d 85; National Assn. for the Advancement of Colored People v. Alabama ex rel. Flowers, 1964, 84 S.Ct. 1302, 377 U.S. 288, 12 L.Ed.2d 325.

amount to an action for damages against the state, barred by the Eleventh Amendment. This is the 1974 holding in Edelman v. Jordan.[24] Edelman was reaffirmed five years later, with the Court saying that "[t]he distinction between that relief permissible under the doctrine of Ex parte Young and that found barred in Edelman was the difference between prospective relief on one hand and retrospective relief on the other." [25]

The decision in Ex parte Young rests on purest fiction. It is illogical. It is only doubtfully in accord with the prior decisions. It was greeted with harsh criticism by the country when it was decided and for years thereafter.[26] For half a century Congress and the Court vied in placing restrictions on the doctrine there announced.[27] Yet this case, ostensibly dealing only with the jurisdiction of the federal courts, remains a landmark in constitutional law.[28] In earlier years Ex parte

24. 1974, 94 S.Ct. 1347, 415 U.S. 651, 39 L.Ed.2d 662.

But back payments can be ordered against a state if Congress, in the exercise of its powers under § 5 of the Fourteenth Amendment, has created a statutory remedy against a state. Fitzpatrick v. Bitzer, 1976, 96 S.Ct. 2666, 427 U.S. 445, 49 L.Ed.2d 614.

Lichtenstein, Retroactive Relief in the Federal Courts Since Edelman v. Jordan: A Trip Through the Twilight Zone, 1982, 32 Case W.Res.L.Rev. 364.

25. Quern v. Jordan, 1979, 99 S.Ct. 1139, 1143, 440 U.S. 332, 337, 59 L.Ed.2d 358. The holding in Edelman was affirmed once again in Florida Dept. of Health & Rehabilitative Services v. Florida Nursing Home Assn., 1981, 101 S.Ct. 1032, 450 U.S. 147, 67 L.Ed.2d 132, and in County of Oneida v. Oneida Indian Nation, 1985, 105 S.Ct. 1245, 1260–1261, 470 U.S. 226, 250–253, 84 L.Ed.2d 169.

"However, it is not particularly responsive to argue, as the Court did, that there is a distinction for eleventh amendment purposes between prospective and retroactive relief, even though both may cause significant harm to state treasuries, because one is prospective and the other retroactive. The question before the Court was whether this distinction actually made any practical difference; the Court seemed to concede that often it would not." Redish, Federal Jurisdiction: Tensions in the Allocation of Judicial Power, 1980, p. 158.

The Quern case, above, held that it is permissible for the court to require state officials to send a notice to members of the plaintiff class advising them that their federal suit is at an end, but that there are administrative procedures by which they may receive a determination of eligibility for past benefits. A later case held that the Eleventh Amendment bars "notice relief" of this kind if there is no prospective relief to which notice can be ancillary and that a declaration that the state has violated federal law in the past is barred if it relates only to past violations of federal law. Green v. Mansour, 1985, 106 S.Ct. 423, 474 U.S. 64, 88 L.Ed.2d 371.

Another controversial later case holds that the Eleventh Amendment bars a claim in federal court that the state officers are violating state law, even if the claim is pendent to a claim that the officers are violating the federal Constitution. Pennhurst State School & Hospital v. Halderman, 1984, 104 S.Ct. 900, 465 U.S. 89, 79 L.Ed.2d 67. See Chemerinsky, State Sovereignty and Federal Court Power: The Eleventh Amendment after Pennhurst v. Halderman, 1985, 12 Hast.C.L.Q. 643; Weinberg, The New Judicial Federalism: Where We Are Now, 1985, 19 Ga.L.Rev. 1075; Shapiro, Wrong Turns: The Eleventh Amendment and the Pennhurst Case, 1984, 98 Harv.L.Rev. 61; Dwyer, Pendent Jurisdiction and the Eleventh Amendment, 1987, 75 Calif.L.Rev.129.

26. "[T]he antagonism engendered by suits against officers was intense, verging in one instance, it was said, upon open rebellion. The outcry was reminiscent of that following the decision in Chisholm v. Georgia." Jacobs, note 1 above, at 146.

27. The succeeding five sections examine restrictions on Ex parte Young.

28. "The authority and finality of Ex parte Young can hardly be overestimated." Hutcheson, A Case for Three Judges, 1934, 47 Harv.L.Rev. 795, 799 n. 9.

The Court has refused to overrule Ex parte Young at the request of those who

Young was the foundation from which state utility regulation and welfare legislation were attacked. Today it provides the basis for forcing states to desegregate their schools [29] and reapportion their legislatures. Both lines of cases are highly controversial. Yet in perspective the doctrine of Ex parte Young seems indispensable to the establishment of constitutional government and the rule of law.

§ 49. Exhaustion of State Remedies [1]

The first limitation on the doctrine of Ex parte Young [2] was developed by the Supreme Court in the same year the Young case was decided. In Virginia the State Corporation Commission was authorized to fix railroad rates, with appeal to the Supreme Court of Appeals. The Supreme Court of Appeals was empowered to substitute its decision for that of the Corporation Commission and to fix and determine the rates that might be charged. After a proceeding before the Corporation Commission, resulting in an order lowering rates, the railroads involved sued in federal court to enjoin the members of the Commission from taking any action to enforce the order. The principal contention of the state, on appeal from the injunction that was granted, was that the Commission was a "court" and that the Anti–Injunction Act [3] barred an injunction staying its proceedings. The Supreme Court rejected this argument, finding that the function of the Commission was "legislative," or, as would now be said, "administrative," and thus that it was not functioning as a court. [4] It held, nevertheless, that the injunction action was premature. In view of the powers the Supreme Court of Appeals was granted by the Virginia statute, it was held that the state legislative process did not end until the Supreme Court of Appeals had reviewed the order of the Commission. As a matter of comity and equitable discretion, therefore, rather than as a limitation on jurisdiction, the federal court should not act until the state legislative process was concluded, since it could not lightly be supposed that the Supreme Court of Appeals would approve an unconstitutional order. If the order were finally approved, then an injunction in federal court would lie, and the decision of the Supreme Court of Appeals, since it was here functioning legislatively rather than judicially, would not be res judicata on the constitutional issue. A case a few years later added the limitation that if the review permitted in the state court was "judicial," rather than "legislative," the party need not resort to state court but could bring an action

think it allows too little protection to the states, Ray v. Atlantic Richfield Co., 1978, 98 S.Ct. 988, 994 n. 6, 435 U.S. 151, 156 n. 6, 55 L.Ed.2d 179, and of those who think Young provides too much protection. Alabama v. Pugh, 1978, 98 S.Ct. 3057, 438 U.S. 781, 57 L.Ed.2d 1114.

29. Griffin v. County Sch. Bd. of Prince Edward Co., 1964, 84 S.Ct. 1226, 1232, 377 U.S. 218, 228, 12 L.Ed.2d 256.

§ 49

1. 17 Wright, Miller & Cooper, Jurisdiction 2d § 4233.

2. 1908, 28 S.Ct. 441, 209 U.S. 123, 52 L.Ed. 714, fully discussed § 48 above.

3. See § 47 above.

4. Prentis v. Atlantic Coast Line Co., 1908, 29 S.Ct. 67, 211 U.S. 210, 53 L.Ed. 150.

in federal court upon termination of the state administrative proceedings.[5]

The traditional rule can then be fairly simply stated. A litigant must normally exhaust state "legislative" or "administrative" remedies before challenging the state action in federal court.[6] He or she need not normally exhaust state "judicial" remedies.[7] The rationale for this distinction is that until the administrative process is complete, it cannot be certain that the party will need judicial relief, but when the case becomes appropriate for judicial determination, he or she may choose whether to resort to a state or federal court for that relief. The word "normally" is required in both branches of the rule. Even a state judicial remedy must be exhausted if a federal statute so provides.[8] A state administrative remedy need not be exhausted if the remedy is inadequate.[9]

These rules must now be qualified in the light of cases in the last 30 years announcing different principles for civil-rights actions under 42 U.S.C.A. § 1983. These recent cases are of particular importance since

5. Bacon v. Rutland R. Co., 1914, 34 S.Ct. 283, 232 U.S. 134, 58 L.Ed. 538. This case, like the Prentis case, note 4 above, was written by Justice Holmes.

If the state court in reviewing a commission order acts wholly judicially, its decision is res judicata and bars a subsequent federal court suit. State Corp. Commn. of Kansas v. Wichita Gas Co., 1934, 54 S.Ct. 321, 290 U.S. 561, 78 L.Ed. 500. See also Kremer v. Chemical Constr. Corp., 1982, 102 S.Ct. 1883, 456 U.S. 461, 72 L.Ed.2d 262.

Indeed, under what is now known as "the Rooker–Feldman doctrine", it is now held that if a state court, acting judicially, has decided a matter, a federal court is barred as a matter of jurisdiction, rather than merely res judicata, from reviewing what it has done. Rooker v. Fidelity Trust Co., 1923, 44 S.Ct. 149, 263 U.S. 413, 68 L.Ed. 362; District of Columbia Court of Appeals v. Feldman, 1983, 103 S.Ct. 1303, 460 U.S. 462, 75 L.Ed.2d 206. See 18 Wright, Miller & Cooper, Jurisdiction 2d § 4469. It is argued in Note, The Rooker–Feldman Doctrine and the Subject Matter Jurisdiction of Federal District Courts, 1990, 42 Rutgers L.Rev. 859, that the Rooker–Feldman jurisdictional doctrine is harmful and that res judicata and abstention adequately protect the interests involved.

6. Gilchrist v. Interborough Rapid Transit Co., 1929, 49 S.Ct. 282, 279 U.S. 159, 73 L.Ed. 652; Porter v. Investors' Syndicate, 1931, 52 S.Ct. 617, 286 U.S. 461, 76 L.Ed. 1226, adhered to 1932, 53 S.Ct. 132, 287 U.S. 346, 77 L.Ed. 354; Hunt v. Robeson County Dept. of Social Services, C.A.4th, 1987, 816 F.2d 150.

7. City Bank Farmers' Trust Co. v. Schnader, 1934, 54 S.Ct. 259, 291 U.S. 24, 78 L.Ed. 628; Lane v. Wilson, 1939, 59 S.Ct. 872, 307 U.S. 268, 83 L.Ed. 1281; Amsley v. West Virginia Racing Commn., C.A.4th, 1967, 378 F.2d 815; Dove v. Parham, C.A.8th, 1960, 282 F.2d 256, 262.

8. See 28 U.S.C.A. §§ 1341 (collection of state taxes), 1342 (utility rate orders), 2254 (habeas corpus). These are discussed in § 51 below.

See also 28 U.S.C.A. § 2254 (habeas corpus), discussed in § 53 below.

It may also be that the abstention doctrines or other considerations of federalism will suggest remitting the party to a state judicial remedy. See §§ 52, 52A below.

9. See Gibson v. Berryhill, 1973, 93 S.Ct. 1689, 411 U.S. 564, 36 L.Ed.2d 488 (question of adequacy of remedy identical with merits of suit); Smith v. Illinois Bell Tel. Co., 1926, 46 S.Ct. 408, 270 U.S. 587, 70 L.Ed. 747 (undue delay by agency); Montana Nat. Bank of Billings v. Yellowstone County, 1928, 48 S.Ct. 331, 276 U.S. 499, 72 L.Ed. 673 (agency action controlled by prior state-court decision); Union Pac. R. Co. v. Board of Commrs. of Weld County, 1918, 38 S.Ct. 510, 247 U.S. 282, 62 L.Ed. 1110 (existence of remedy doubtful); Monongahela Connecting R. Co. v. Pennsylvania Public Util. Commn., C.A.3d, 1967, 373 F.2d 142 (inaction by agency); Kelly v. Board of Educ. of City of Nashville, D.C.Tenn.1958, 159 F.Supp. 272 (agency committed in advance to continue segregation).

many of the cases developing the traditional rules were cases in which plaintiffs were claiming that states were unconstitutionally depriving them of their property, and it was not until 1972 that it was held that property rights were protected under § 1983.[10]

The leading case in the revitalization of § 1983, Monroe v. Pape,[11] announced the unexceptionable rule that state judicial remedies need not be exhausted before bringing a federal civil-rights action. Two years later, in McNeese v. Board of Education,[12] the Court seemed to say that there is no need to exhaust state administrative remedies in § 1983 suits. McNeese may not have laid down such a rule,[13] particularly since much of the opinion was devoted to showing that the state administrative remedy in that case was inadequate. But the important fact is that the Supreme Court repeatedly relied on McNeese for the flat statement that exhaustion of administrative remedies is not required in § 1983 actions.[14]

There were cross-currents, however, in the Supreme Court decisions,[15] and members of the Supreme Court, as well as lower-court judges, expressed dissatisfaction with the rule that state administrative remedies need not be exhausted before commencing a federal civil-rights action. Nevertheless, when the Supreme Court was squarely faced with the question in 1982 in Patsy v. Board of Regents of Florida,[16] it held with only two dissents that this continues to be the rule.[17]

In a 1986 case, however, the Supreme Court held that the principles of Younger v. Harris[18] apply to at least some pending administrative proceedings.[19] The Court said that this holding was fully consistent with

10. Lynch v. Household Fin. Corp., 1972, 92 S.Ct. 1113, 405 U.S. 538, 31 L.Ed.2d 424. See § 22A.

11. 1961, 81 S.Ct. 473, 365 U.S. 167, 5 L.Ed.2d 492. Monroe is important because of its holding that state officers were acting under color of state law, within the meaning of § 1983, even though their acts were not authorized by the state and indeed were forbidden by the state.

12. 1963, 83 S.Ct. 1433, 373 U.S. 668, 10 L.Ed.2d 622.

13. See the analysis of McNeese and its progeny by Judge Friendly in Eisen v. Eastman, C.A.2d, 1969, 421 F.2d 560, 567–569.

14. See, e.g., Damico v. California, 1967, 88 S.Ct. 526, 389 U.S. 416, 19 L.Ed.2d 647; Wilwording v. Swenson, 1971, 92 S.Ct. 407, 404 U.S. 249, 30 L.Ed.2d 418; Steffel v. Thompson, 1974, 94 S.Ct. 1209, 1222, 415 U.S. 452, 472–473, 39 L.Ed.2d 505.

15. The statutory requirement of exhaustion for habeas-corpus actions cannot be avoided by casting the suit as a § 1983 action, and a prisoner challenging the very fact or duration of his physical imprisonment, and seeking a determination that he or she is entitled to immediate or more speedy release from imprisonment, must first exhaust all state remedies, both administrative and judicial. Preiser v. Rodriguez, 1973, 93 S.Ct. 1827, 411 U.S. 475, 36 L.Ed.2d 439.

Under the doctrine of "Our Federalism" a litigant who wishes to challenge in federal court a state judgment adverse to him must first exhaust state appellate remedies. Huffman v. Pursue, Ltd., 1975, 95 S.Ct. 1200, 420 U.S. 592, 43 L.Ed.2d 482. See § 52A below.

16. 1982, 102 S.Ct. 2557, 457 U.S. 496, 73 L.Ed.2d 172.

17. Chief Justice Burger and Justice Powell dissented. Justices Rehnquist and O'Connor, concurring, urged Congress to change the rule and require exhaustion.

18. 1971, 91 S.Ct. 746, 401 U.S. 37, 27 L.Ed.2d 669. See § 52A below.

19. Ohio Civil Rights Commn. v. Dayton Christian School, Inc., 1986, 106 S.Ct. 2718, 477 U.S. 619, 91 L.Ed.2d 512.

the Patsy case.[20]

Congress has created one narrow exception to the general rule that exhaustion is not required in a civil-rights case. A 1980 statute, the Civil Rights of Institutionalized Persons Act, requires exhaustion before an adult prisoner can bring a § 1983 action, but establishes procedures to ensure that the administrative remedies that these prisoners must exhaust are adequate and effective.[21]

§ 50. The Three–Judge Court Acts [1]

An interesting, but increasingly unsatisfactory, feature in the federal courts, prior to its virtual abolition in 1976, was the use of special three-judge courts to hear constitutional cases. As a result of the resentment felt by the states to the doctrine of Ex parte Young,[2] there were legislative proposals to strip the federal courts of jurisdiction of suits challenging state laws. Congress chose instead, in 1910, a less drastic remedy. Statutes passed earlier in that decade dealing with certain antitrust actions of general public importance, and with suits to set aside orders of the Interstate Commerce Commission, had created a court of special dignity, composed of three judges, at least one of whom was a judge of the then-Circuit Court of Appeals, with direct appeal to the Supreme Court from the decision of the three-judge court.[3] Congress borrowed this device and made it applicable to suits in which an interlocutory injunction was sought against the enforcement of state statutes by state officers.[4] It was the thought of Congress that there would be less public resentment if enforcement of the state statute were stayed by three judges rather than one, and that the provision for direct appeal to the Supreme Court would provide speedy review.[5]

The 1910 statute was amended in 1913 to include cases in which it was sought to enjoin enforcement of an administrative order made by an

---

20. "Unlike Patsy, the administrative proceedings here are coercive rather than remedial, began before any substantial advancement in the federal action took place, and involved an important state interest." 106 S.Ct. at 2723 n. 2, 477 U.S. at 627 n. 2. This distinction is sharply criticized in Edwards, The Changing Notion of "Our Federalism", 1987, 33 Wayne L.Rev. 1015, 1029.

21. 42 U.S.C.A. § 1997e. The legislative history of the statute is described in the Patsy case, 102 S.Ct. at 2563–2565, 457 U.S. at 507–513. The statute does not apply to federal prisoners. McCarthy v. Madigan, 1992, 112 S.Ct. 1081, ___ U.S. ___, 117 L.Ed.2d 291.

§ 50

1. 17 Wright, Miller & Cooper, Jurisdiction 2d §§ 4234, 4235; Williams, The New Three–Judge Courts of Reapportionment and Continuing Problems of Three–Judge–Court Procedure, 1977, 65 Geo.L.J. 971.

2. 1908, 28 S.Ct. 441, 209 U.S. 123, 52 L.Ed. 714, discussed § 48 above.

3. The use of three-judge courts in these classes of cases was ended by statutes adopted in 1974 and 1975. See Boskey & Gressman, Recent Reforms in the Federal Judicial Structure—Three–Judge District Courts and Appellate Review, 1975, 67 F.R.D. 135.

4. 36 Stat. 557. The statute was codified as § 266 of the 1911 Judicial Code, and until its repeal in 1976, was § 2281 of the 1948 Judicial Code.

5. See 1910, 42 Cong.Rec. 4847, 4853.

administrative board or commission acting under a state statute.[6] Again
it was amended in 1925 to require three judges for the hearing on a
permanent injunction as well as on the application for an interlocutory
injunction, and end the anomaly by which a single judge, on the final
hearing, might overrule the determination of three judges at the hearing
on the interlocutory injunction.[7] Finally, when the statute was codified
as § 2281 of the 1948 Judicial Code it was made applicable to any action
in which either a preliminary injunction or a permanent injunction was
sought.

In the meantime in 1937, as one of the few remnants of President
Roosevelt's court-reform proposals to be enacted, similar provision was
made for a three-judge court and direct review in actions for injunctions
against Acts of Congress claimed to be unconstitutional.[8] This provision
did not reach attacks on federal administrative orders.[9] The procedure
for three-judge court actions was the same whether a state statute or an
Act of Congress was challenged.[10]

The three-judge court statutes placed a heavy burden on the federal
judiciary. It was frequently difficult to summon a second district judge
and a judge of the court of appeals. The direct appeal to the Supreme
Court was contrary to the general scheme giving that Court substantial
control over its own docket. For these reasons the Court had said that
the statute was not "a measure of broad social policy to be construed
with great liberality, but * * * an enactment technical in the strict sense
of the term and to be applied as such." [11] For these reasons also, there
was in recent years a strong movement to abolish three-judge courts,
which succeeded in 1976.

As a result of the 1976 legislation, it is no longer necessary to
examine the enormously complicated body of law that grew up around

---

6. 37 Stat. 1013. It may have been that
this amendment was unnecessary, since the
original statute covered such situations.
See Oklahoma Natural Gas Co. v. Russell,
1923, 43 S.Ct. 353, 354, 261 U.S. 290, 292,
67 L.Ed. 659.

7. 43 Stat. 936. The statute as amended was construed to mean that a three-
judge court was required only where an
application for an interlocutory injunction
had been made and pressed. Smith v. Wilson, 1927, 47 S.Ct. 385, 273 U.S. 388, 71
L.Ed. 699. This was not true under the
1948 revision of the statute. See ALI
Study, p. 322.

The procedural provisions of the statute
were further amended in 1942, 56 Stat. 199,
to define more clearly the powers of a single
judge in an action for a three-judge court.

8. 50 Stat. 752. Until its repeal in
1976, this statute was § 2282 of the 1948
Judicial Code.

9. William Jameson & Co. v. Morgen-
thau, 1939, 59 S.Ct. 804, 307 U.S. 171, 83
L.Ed. 1189.

10. The procedure was and is set out in
28 U.S.C.A. § 2284. The provision for direct appeal to the Supreme Court is 28
U.S.C.A. § 1253. See § 105 below.

11. Phillips v. U.S., 1941, 61 S.Ct. 480,
483, 312 U.S. 246, 251, 85 L.Ed. 800. See
also Ex parte Collins, 1928, 48 S.Ct. 585,
586, 277 U.S. 565, 567, 72 L.Ed. 990; Swift
& Co. v. Wickham, 1965, 86 S.Ct. 258, 267–
268, 382 U.S. 111, 128–129, 15 L.Ed.2d 194.

In recent years there had been a sharp
increase in the number of cases heard by
three-judge courts. The average number of
such cases in the years 1955–1959 was 48.8
per year, and this increased to 95.6 in
1960–1964, 174.8 in 1965–1969, and to
280.4 in 1970–1976. The peak was in 1973,
with 320 of these cases. See ALI Study, pp.
317–318, and Ann.Rep. of the Director of
the Administrative Office of the U.S.
Courts, 1976, p. 208.

"this deceptively simple statute." [12]   There was great confusion on when three judges were required and the rules on appellate review of orders by or about three-judge courts were so complex as to be virtually beyond belief.   Under the 1976 legislation a three-judge court is now required only "when otherwise required by Act of Congress" or "when an action is filed challenging the constitutionality of the apportionment of congressional districts or the apportionment of any statewide legislative body." [13]   The mention of when otherwise required by Act of Congress refers principally to certain provisions of the Civil Rights Act of 1964 and the Voting Rights Act of 1965 that require or permit a three-judge court.[14]   There will be few of these cases, and recent experience demonstrates that the number of three-judge courts that will be needed for reapportionment cases is small.[15]   Thus, the numerical burden of three-judge courts is now virtually ended, and the problems of construction of the opaque provisions of the former statutes should also now be a thing of the past.

The 1976 legislation also clarifies procedural points, for those few three-judge courts that will now be convened, that had previously been unclear.   It is specified that the single judge before whom the action is filed must determine whether three judges are required before notifying the chief judge of the circuit.[16]   The role of the chief judge is the merely ministerial one of designating the other two judges, at least one of whom

---

12.   Sardino v. Federal Reserve Bank of New York, C.A.2d, 1966, 361 F.2d 106, 114, certiorari denied 87 S.Ct. 203, 385 U.S. 898, 17 L.Ed.2d 130.

The Supreme Court had commented on "the opaque terms and prolix syntax" of these "very awkwardly drafted" statutes. Gonzalez v. Automatic Employees Credit Union, 1974, 95 S.Ct. 289, 293–294, 419 U.S. 90, 96–97, 42 L.Ed.2d 249.

13.   28 U.S.C.A. § 2284(a), as amended by Act of Aug. 12, 1976, Pub.L. 94–381, § 3, 90 Stat. 1119.

14.   A three-judge court is mandatory in suits under §§ 4(a), 5, and 10 of the 1965 statute, 42 U.S.C.A. §§ 1973b(a), 1973c, 1973h(c).   The Attorney General may request a three-judge court in actions under the public accommodations and equal employment provisions of the 1964 statute, 42 U.S.C.A. §§ 2000a–5(b), 2000e–6(b).   Either the Attorney General or the defendant may request a three-judge court in actions under the voting provisions of the 1964 statute, 42 U.S.C.A. § 1971g.

A few other statutes requiring a three-judge court are cited in 17 Wright, Miller & Cooper, Jurisdiction 2d § 4235 n. 5.

15.   In the fiscal years 1973–1977 a total of 35 reapportionment cases were heard by three-judge courts, or an average of seven cases per year.   In 1972, however, there were 32 of these cases heard.   Ann.Rep. of the Director of the Administrative Office of the U.S. Courts, 1977, table 36.   In the 11 years 1981–1991 there were hearings by three-judge courts in 81 reapportionment cases, but 42 of these were in 1982, nine in 1983, and 17 in 1984.   Ann.Rep. of the Director of the Administrative Office of the U.S. Courts, 1985, table 52, and 1991, table S–10.   But there is a temporary increase in the number of these suits after decennial census.   In fiscal 1992 there were 32 reapportionment cases heard by three-judge courts, as against only one the preceding year, while the 17 other civil-rights cases heard in 1992 was consistent with the number of those cases in previous years.   Ann. Rep. of the Director of the Administrative Office of the U.S. Courts, 1992, Table S–9.   In the period from 1981–1991, the tables cited from the 1991 report show an average of 16.2 civil-rights cases heard each year by three-judge courts and 1.5 cases in the category described by the Administrative Office as "all other".

16.   Montgomery v. Leflore County Republican Executive Committee, D.C.Miss. 1991, 776 F.Supp. 1142, 1144.

shall be a circuit judge.[17] The single judge can dismiss the action for want of jurisdiction [18] or if the plaintiff lacks standing or the suit is otherwise not justiciable in the federal courts.[19] If irreparable damage will otherwise result, the single judge may grant a temporary restraining order to remain in force until the three-judge court has heard the case, and he may conduct all proceedings except the trial. A single judge, however, may not appoint a master, or order a reference, or hear and determine any application for a preliminary or permanent injunction or motion to vacate such an injunction, or enter judgment on the merits.[20] Nor may a single judge abstain in favor of a state court.[21]

It was formerly the rule that the requirement of three judges was jurisdictional and must be applied even if the parties never raise the point.[22] Section 2284(a) says a three-judge court "shall be convened" in the circumstances there listed, but the procedural provisions of § 2284(b) say that the three-judge court is to be designated "[u]pon the filing of a request for three judges." There is nothing in the legislative history to indicate what Congress intended on this point. The best result would be if the Supreme Court should hold that in all cases under § 2284(a) a request is required and that the three-judge provision is not jurisdictional.[23] But unless and until it does the cautious course for a lower court in a case within § 2284(a) would be to convene a three-judge court even without a request.[24]

The 1976 legislation did not change the statutory provision that any party may appeal to the Supreme Court from an order granting or denying, after notice and hearing, an interlocutory or permanent injunction in an action required by Act of Congress to be heard and determined

17. 28 U.S.C.A. § 2284(b)(1). For the previous uncertainty on the role of the chief judge of the circuit, see ALI Study, pp. 327–329.

18. Ex parte Poresky, 1934, 54 S.Ct. 3, 290 U.S. 30, 78 L.Ed. 152.

19. Gonzalez v. Automatic Employees Credit Union, 1974, 95 S.Ct. 289, 419 U.S. 90, 42 L.Ed.2d 249; Sharrow v. Fish, D.C.N.Y.1980, 501 F.Supp. 202, affirmed C.A.2d, 1981, 659 F.2d 1062.

20. 28 U.S.C.A. § 2284(b)(3). It ought to be held that the rule, first announced in Bailey v. Patterson, 1962, 82 S.Ct. 549, 369 U.S. 31, 7 L.Ed.2d 512 that a single judge can grant an injunction in a case otherwise within the three-judge court statute, where the unconstitutionality of the practice challenged is obvious and patent, has not survived the 1976 revisions in the statute. See 17 Wright, Miller & Cooper, Jurisdiction 2d § 4235, pp. 617–619.

21. Ryan v. State Bd. of Elections, C.A.7th, 1981, 661 F.2d 1130; and cases cited 17 Wright, Miller & Cooper, Jurisdiction 2d § 4235 n. 67.

22. Kennedy v. Mendoza–Martinez, 1963, 83 S.Ct. 554, 559, 372 U.S. 144, 153, 9 L.Ed.2d 644; Goosby v. Osser, 1973, 93 S.Ct. 854, 861, 409 U.S. 512, 522–523, 35 L.Ed.2d 36; see McLucas v. DeChamplain, 1975, 95 S.Ct. 1365, 1370, 421 U.S. 21, 27–29, 43 L.Ed.2d 699.

23. 17 Wright, Miller & Cooper, Jurisdiction 2d § 4235, pp. 608–612; Currie, Federal Jurisdiction in a Nutshell, 3d ed. 1990, pp. 202–203; Williams, note 1 above, at 975. For a contrary view, see Stern, Gressman & Shapiro, Supreme Court Practice, 6th ed. 1986, pp. 91–92.

24. "As attractive as is the proposition that the complexities of the law of three-judge district courts can be ignored if the parties do not raise the issue, we can find nothing in the statute or the case law governing such courts that would support it." Massachusetts v. Mosbacher, D.C.Mass. 1992, 785 F.Supp. 230, 235 n. 2, reversed on other grounds 1992, 112 S.Ct. 2767, ___ U.S. ___, 120 L.Ed.2d 636; Armour v. Ohio, C.A.6th, 1991, 925 F.2d 987, 989.

by a district court of three judges.[25]   In the years immediately prior to 1976 the Court, in an effort to rid itself of as many direct appeals as possible, had developed a bewildering and constantly changing variety of rules on what orders were directly appealable to it and what were reviewable in the courts of appeals.   With three-judge courts now virtually eliminated, it is to be hoped that the provision for direct appeal will be given a straight-forward reading shorn of the complications introduced by the recent cases.[26]

§ 51.   Other   Statutory   Restrictions   on   Injunctions Against State Officers [1]

In addition to the three-judge court acts, there are three other federal statutes that restrict federal injunctions against state officers. As a part of the 1913 amendment of the 1910 three-judge court statute, it was provided that a three-judge court shall, before final hearing, stay any action pending therein to enjoin the enforcement of a state statute or order if it appears that a state court of competent jurisdiction has stayed proceedings under the statute or order pending the determination in the state court of an action to enforce the statute or order.   It was further provided that if the state-court action is not prosecuted diligently and in good faith, the three-judge court may, after notice to the state attorney general, vacate its stay.[2]   The statute was virtually a dead letter,[3] and was repealed when three-judge courts were substantially abolished in 1976.[4]

A statute of much greater importance is the Johnson Act of 1934.[5] This statute deprives the district courts of jurisdiction to enjoin the operation of any order of a state administrative agency or ratemaking body affecting rates chargeable by a public utility.[6]   Four conditions

25.   28 U.S.C.A. § 1253.   This was left intact in 1988 when Congress abolished most of the appeal jurisdiction of the Supreme Court.   See § 105 below.

26.   See 17 Wright, Miller & Cooper, Jurisdiction 2d § 4040.

§ 51

1.   17 Wright, Miller & Cooper, Jurisdiction 2d §§ 4236 (Johnson Act), 4237 (Tax Injunction Act).

2.   Former 28 U.S.C.A. § 2284(5).

3.   Such a stay was granted in Traffic Tel. Workers' Federation v. Driscoll, D.C.N.J.1947, 72 F.Supp. 499, appeal dismissed 1947, 68 S.Ct. 221, 332 U.S. 833, 92 L.Ed. 406, and Judge Hutcheson describes a few unreported cases in which this procedure has been followed.   Hutcheson, A Case for Three Judges, 1934, 47 Harv.L.Rev. 795, 822–825.   On the general disuse of the provision, see Pogue, State Determination of State Law and the Judicial Code, 1928, 41 Harv.L.Rev. 623.

A stay on this ground was refused in Bush v. Orleans Parish Sch. Bd., D.C.La. 1960, 190 F.Supp. 861, affirmed 1961, 81 S.Ct. 754, 365 U.S. 569, 5 L.Ed.2d 806, and in Ramos v. Health and Social Services Bd., D.C.Wis.1967, 276 F.Supp. 474.

4.   See § 50 above.

5.   Act of May 14, 1934, 48 Stat. 775, codified as 28 U.S.C.A. § 1342.   The law takes its name from its sponsor, Senator Hiram W. Johnson of California.

6.   The statute applies to rates fixed by a city ordinance.   East Ohio Gas Co. v. City of Cleveland, D.C.Ohio 1937, 23 F.Supp. 965, affirmed C.C.A.6th, 1938, 94 F.2d 443, certiorari denied 58 S.Ct. 761, 303 U.S. 657, 82 L.Ed. 1116;   Hartford Consumer Activists Assn. v. Hausman, D.C.Conn.1974, 381 F.Supp. 1275.

Since the Johnson Act does not apply only to a "rate" but to "any order affecting rates," it reaches charges for late payment of utility bills.   Tennyson v. Gas Serv. Co., C.A.10th, 1974, 506 F.2d 1135.   It does not must be met for the statute to be applicable. (1) Jurisdiction must be based solely on diversity of citizenship or repugnance to the federal Constitution.[7] (2) The order must not interfere with interstate commerce.[8] (3) The order must have been made after reasonable notice and hearing.[9] (4) There must be "a plain, speedy and efficient remedy" in the courts of the state.[10] Thus, the statute channels normal rate litigation into state courts while leaving the federal courts free to exercise their equity powers where necessary to relieve against arbitrary action.[11]

The other statute, enacted in 1937, prohibits an injunction against the assessment, levy, or collection of any tax under state law where a plain, speedy, and efficient remedy may be had in the state courts.[12]

reach a city ordinance requiring property owners to connect to a new public water system and abandon a private state-approved water supply system. Shrader v. Horton, D.C.Va.1979, 471 F.Supp. 1236, affirmed on opinion below C.A.4th, 1980, 626 F.2d 1163. Nor, since rates are not involved, does it apply to a tariff allowing a telephone company to terminate "dial-it" service to any subscriber who used the service to transmit sexually explicit messages. Carlin Communication, Inc. v. Southern Bell Tel. & Tel. Co., C.A.11th, 1986, 802 F.2d 1352.

The American Law Institute proposed to broaden the Johnson Act to include also orders affecting "the conservation, production, or use of minerals, water, or other like natural resource of the State." ALI Study, § 1371(b)(1).

7. The Act does not apply if suit is brought pursuant to 47 U.S.C.A. § 401(b), which gives jurisdiction of suits brought to enforce FCC orders. Mid–Plains Telephone Co. v. Public Serv. Commn. of Wisconsin, D.C.Wis.1989, 745 F.Supp. 1450, 1452–1453.

8. This condition was not satisfied, and the Johnson Act was held inapplicable, in Public Utilities Commn. of Ohio v. United Fuel Gas Co., 1943, 63 S.Ct. 369, 317 U.S. 456, 87 L.Ed. 396; Charter Limousine Inc. v. Dade County Bd. of Com'rs, C.A.5th, 1982, 678 F.2d 586, 589, and Tri–State Generation & Transmission Assn., Inc. v. Public Serv. Commn. of Wyoming, C.A.10th, 1969, 412 F.2d 115, certiorari denied 1970, 90 S.Ct. 1348, 397 U.S. 1043, 25 L.Ed.2d 654.

The American Law Institute proposed to remove this restriction and to provide instead that the statute applies if "the power of the State to make such order has not been superseded by any Act of Congress or administrative regulation thereunder." ALI Study, § 1371(b)(4).

9. Petroleum Exploration, Inc. v. Public Serv. Commn. of Kentucky, 1938, 58 S.Ct. 834, 304 U.S. 209, 82 L.Ed. 1294; City of El Paso v. Texas Cities Gas Co., C.C.A.5th, 1938, 100 F.2d 501, certiorari denied 59 S.Ct. 592, 306 U.S. 650, 83 L.Ed. 1049. The federal court, rather than the state, determines what is reasonable notice and hearing. Nucor Corp. v. Nebraska Public Power Dist., C.A.8th, 1989, 891 F.2d 1343, 1347–1348, certiorari denied 111 S.Ct. 50, 498 U.S. 813, 112 L.Ed.2d 26.

10. Doubt whether the state remedy is plain, speedy, and efficient will be resolved in favor of federal jurisdiction. Mountain States Power Co. v. Public Serv. Commn. of Montana, 1936, 57 S.Ct. 168, 299 U.S. 167, 81 L.Ed. 99; Driscoll v. Edison Light & Power Co., 1939, 59 S.Ct. 715, 307 U.S. 104, 83 L.Ed. 1134.

11. City of Meridian v. Mississippi Val. Gas Co., C.A.5th, 1954, 214 F.2d 525; Kansas–Nebraska Natural Gas Co. v. City of St. Edward, D.C.Neb.1955, 135 F.Supp. 629.

12. Act of Aug. 21, 1937, 50 Stat. 738, codified as 28 U.S.C.A. § 1341. A similar provision bars injunctions against the collection of federal taxes. 26 U.S.C.A. § 7421(a).

The Tax Injunction Act does not apply to suits challenging tax discrimination against railroad or motor carrier transportation property. 49 U.S.C.A. §§ 11503(c), 11503a(c).

On the meaning of "tax," see Wright v. McClain, C.A.6th, 1987, 835 F.2d 143; and cases cited 17 Wright, Miller & Cooper, Jurisdiction 2d § 4237 n. 17. On the meaning of "assessment, levy, or collection," compare Wells v. Malloy, C.A.2d, 1975, 510 F.2d 74, on remand D.C.Vt., 402 F.Supp. 856, affirmed C.A.2d, 1976, 538 F.2d 317, with Huber Pontiac, Inc. v. Whitler, C.A.7th, 1978, 585 F.2d 817. One court

Although the requirement of a plain, speedy, and efficient remedy does not mean that "every wrinkle of federal equity practice was codified, intact, by Congress,"[13] the Court has not been able to find a significant difference between the equitable requirement of remedies that are "plain, adequate, and complete" and the slightly different list of phrases in the Tax Injunction Act.[14] All that is required is a state-court remedy that meets certain minimal procedural criteria.[15] The state remedy will not bar a federal injunction if it is unduly burdensome, as where the taxpayer would have had to file over 300 separate claims in 14 different counties.[16] A state remedy either in law or in equity will, if otherwise adequate, suffice to defeat jurisdiction.[17] Grave doubt as to the existence of the state remedy will permit the federal court to act.[18] But the state remedy, to satisfy this section, need not necessarily be the best remedy available or even equal to or better than the remedy that might be available in federal court.[19]

Neither statute in terms prohibits the granting of a declaratory judgment. The Supreme Court has not held that the Tax Injunction Act prohibits a declaratory judgment holding state tax laws unconstitutional.[20] In another case taxpayers were suing for damages under the civil-rights statute, 42 U.S.C.A. § 1983, for alleged unconstitutional administration of a state tax system. The Court refrained from deciding whether the Tax Injunction Act, standing alone, barred the suit. In-

---

says that the "classic tax" is one that raises money from any citizens for the benefit of the entire community, as distinguished from fees that are dedicated to provide narrow benefits or to defray the costs of regulation. Trailer Marine Transport Corp. v. Rivera Vazquez, C.A.1st, 1992, 977 F.2d 1, 5.

13. Rosewell v. LaSalle Nat. Bank, 1981, 101 S.Ct. 1221, 1235, 450 U.S. 503, 525, 67 L.Ed.2d 464.

14. Fair Assessment in Real Estate Assn., Inc. v. McNary, 1981, 102 S.Ct. 177, 186 n. 8, 454 U.S. 100, 116 n. 8, 70 L.Ed.2d 271.

15. Rosewell v. LaSalle Nat. Bank, 1981, 101 S.Ct. 1221, 1228–1234, 450 U.S. 503, 512–524, 67 L.Ed.2d 464. The holding there is that a state remedy is plain, speedy, and efficient even though it is long-delayed and makes no provision for interest on refunds.

See also California v. Grace Brethren Church, 1982, 102 S.Ct. 2498, 457 U.S. 393, 73 L.Ed.2d 93.

16. Georgia R.R. & Banking Co. v. Redwine, 1952, 72 S.Ct. 321, 342 U.S. 299, 96 L.Ed. 335.

17. Garrett v. Bamford, C.A.3d, 1978, 582 F.2d 810, 820. This was stated expressly when the statute was adopted in

1937, but the words "at law or in equity" were dropped in the 1948 revision as "unnecessary."

A declaratory judgment can be a sufficient remedy. Tully v. Griffin, 1976, 97 S.Ct. 219, 429 U.S. 68, 50 L.Ed.2d 227.

18. Hillsborough Twp., Somerset County, New Jersey v. Cromwell, 1946, 66 S.Ct. 445, 326 U.S. 620, 90 L.Ed. 358; U.S. v. Livingston, D.C.S.C.1959, 179 F.Supp. 9, affirmed 1961, 80 S.Ct. 1611, 364 U.S. 281, 4 L.Ed.2d 1719.

But if there is a state remedy, it bars relief even though the highest state court has previously rejected the constitutional challenge the taxpayer wishes to raise. Smith v. Travis County Educ. Dist., C.A.5th, 1992, 968 F.2d 453, 456; Cities Service Gas Co. v. Oklahoma Tax Commn., C.A.10th, 1981, 656 F.2d 584, certiorari denied 102 S.Ct. 972, 454 U.S. 1124, 71 L.Ed.2d 111.

19. See Bland v. McHann, C.A.5th, 1972, 463 F.2d 21, 29, 1973, certiorari denied 93 S.Ct. 1438, 410 U.S. 966, 35 L.Ed.2d 700; and cases cited 17 Wright, Miller & Cooper, Jurisdiction 2d § 4237 n. 31.

20. California v. Grace Brethren Church, 1982, 102 S.Ct. 2498, 457 U.S. 393, 73 L.Ed.2d 93.

stead it held that the principle of comity bars taxpayers from asserting § 1983 actions against the validity of state tax systems in federal courts.[21] Similarly the Court, while recognizing that a suit challenging the refusal of a state agency to permit discontinuance of trains is not a rate order and thus not within the Johnson Act, has held that the federal courts should abstain from hearing such a suit where there is an adequate state judicial remedy.[22]

Neither the Johnson Act nor the Tax Injunction Act applies to a suit brought by the United States.[23] Nor does the Tax Injunction Act apply to a suit between states in the original jurisdiction of the Supreme Court.[24]

§ 52. The Abstention Doctrines [1]

In 1824 Chief Justice Marshall said: "It is most true, that this court will not take jurisdiction if it should not; but it is equally true, that it must take jurisdiction, if it should. The judiciary cannot, as the legislature may, avoid a measure, because it approaches the confines of the constitution. * * * With whatever doubts, with whatever difficulties, a case may be attended, we must decide it, if it be brought before us. We have no more right to decline the exercise of jurisdiction which is given, than to usurp that which is not given. The one or the other would be treason to the constitution." [2]

---

21. Fair Assessment in Real Estate Assn., Inc. v. McNary, 1981, 102 S.Ct. 177, 454 U.S. 100, 70 L.Ed.2d 271. Four Justices rejected this use of comity, but agreed with the result because the taxpayers had failed to exhaust their administrative remedies.

It would seem to follow a fortiori that if a case comes within the terms of the Johnson Act or the Tax Injunction Act, the bar of those statutes is not escaped because suit is under § 1983.

22. Alabama Public Serv. Commn. v. Southern Ry. Co., 1951, 71 S.Ct. 762, 341 U.S. 341, 95 L.Ed. 1002.

See also Tennyson v. Gas Serv. Co., C.A.10th, 1974, 506 F.2d 1135.

23. Department of Employment v. U.S., 1966, 87 S.Ct. 464, 385 U.S. 355, 17 L.Ed.2d 414 (Tax Injunction Act); see U.S. v. Public Utilities Commn. of California, D.C.Cal. 1956, 141 F.Supp. 168, affirmed 1958, 78 S.Ct. 446, 355 U.S. 534, 2 L.Ed.2d 470 (Johnson Act); ALI Study, § 1371(g).

Nor does § 1341 apply to a suit by an Indian tribe brought pursuant to 28 U.S.C.A. § 1362. Moe v. Confederated Salish & Kootenai Tribes, 1976, 96 S.Ct. 1634, 425 U.S. 463, 48 L.Ed.2d 96.

24. Maryland v. Louisiana, 1981, 101 S.Ct. 2114, 2128 n. 21, 451 U.S. 725, 745 n. 21, 68 L.Ed.2d 576.

§ 52

1. 17A Wright, Miller & Cooper, Jurisdiction 2d §§ 4241–4248. Only some of the more recent writings on abstention are cited in this footnote. Articles on particular aspects are cited in later notes. For earlier commentary, see 17A id. § 4241 n. 1.

Lee & Wilkins, An Analysis of Supplemental Jurisdiction and Abstention with Recommendations for Legislative Action, 1990 B.Y.U.L.Rev. 321; Friedman, A Revisionist Theory of Abstention, 1989, 88 Mich.L.Rev. 530; Report on the Abstention Doctrine, The Consequence of Federal Court Deference to State Court Proceedings, by the Committee on Federal Courts of the New York State Bar Association, 1988, 122 F.R.D. 89; Davies, Pullman and Burford Abstention: Clarifying the Roles of State and Federal Courts in Constitutional Cases, 1986, 20 U.C.Davis L.Rev. 1; Wells, The Role of Comity in the Law of Federal Courts, 1981, 60 N.C.L.Rev. 59; McMillan, Abstention—The Judiciary's Self–Inflicted Wound, 1978, 56 N.C.L.Rev. 527; Field, The Abstention Doctrine Today, 1977, 125 U.Pa.L.Rev. 590.

2. Cohens v. Virginia, 1821, 6 Wheat. 264, 404, 5 L.Ed. 257. For a more recent expression to similar effect, see Willcox v. Consolidated Gas Co., 1909, 29 S.Ct. 192, 195, 212 U.S. 19, 40, 53 L.Ed. 382.

It may be that there was never such a rule, uniformly applied, in the federal courts. It is clear that there is no such rule today. Since 1941 there has been considerable recognition of circumstances under which a federal court may decline to proceed though it has jurisdiction under the Constitution and the statutes. The cases in which this has been recognized are usually referred to as establishing the "abstention doctrine," but it is more precise to refer to "abstention doctrines" since there are at least four distinguishable lines of cases, involving different factual situations, different procedural consequences, different support in the decisions of the Supreme Court, and different arguments for and against their validity.[3] Abstention is variously recognized: (1) Pullman-type abstention, to avoid decision of a federal constitutional question where the case may be disposed of on questions of state law; (2) Burford-type abstention, to avoid needless conflict with the administration by a state of its own affairs; (3) to leave to the states the resolution of unsettled questions of state law; and (4) to avoid duplicative litigation, now frequently referred to as Colorado River-type abstention.

These various doctrines overlap at times, and the courts have not always distinguished them clearly. Indeed in 1987 the Supreme Court said: "The various types of abstention are not rigid pigeonholes into which federal courts must try to fit cases. Rather, they reflect a complex of considerations designed to soften the tensions inherent in a system

These earlier statements about the duty to exercise jurisdiction are quoted with approval in New Orleans Public Service, Inc. v. Council of City of New Orleans, 1989, 109 S.Ct. 2506, 2512–2513, 491 U.S. 350, 358–359, 105 L.Ed.2d 298. The Court then said: "Underlying these assertions is the undisputed constitutional principle that Congress, and not the judiciary, defines the scope of federal jurisdiction within the constitutionally permissible bounds." But with only a paragraph break the Court went on to say: "That principle does not eliminate, however, and the categorical assertions based upon it do not call into question, the federal courts' discretion in determining whether to grant certain types of relief—a discretion that was part of the common-law background against which the statutes conferring jurisdiction were enacted. See Shapiro, Jurisdiction and Discretion, 60 N.Y.U.L.Rev. 543, 570–577 (1985)." 109 S.Ct. at 2513, 491 U.S. at 359.

The legitimacy of the judge-made abstention doctrines has been attacked, notably by Professor Martin H. Redish. See Redish, The Federal Courts in the Political Order 47–74 (1991). See also Doernberg, "You Can Lead a Horse to Water ..." The Supreme Court's Refusal to Allow the Exercise of Original Jurisdiction Conferred by Congress, 1990, 40 Case W.Res.L.Rev. 999. The propriety of abstention has been defended in: Shapiro, above, at 543–545, 570–577; Wells, Why Professor Redish is Wrong About Abstention, 1985, 19 Ga.L.Rev. 1097; Althouse, The Humble and the Treasonous: Judge–Made Jurisdiction Law, 1990, 40 Case W.Res.L.Rev. 1035; Beerman, "Bad" Judicial Activism and Liberal Federal–Courts Doctrine: A Comment on Professor Doernberg and Professor Redish, 1990, 40 Case W.Res.L.Rev. 1053. One scholar argues that many of the abstention doctrines are constitutionally required. Massey, Abstention and the Constitutional Limits of the Judicial Power of the United States, 1991 B.Y.U.L.Rev. 811. Justice Scalia's citation of Professor David Shapiro's article in the passage quoted in the preceding paragraph suggests the Supreme Court's view of this issue.

3. The Supreme Court, the lower courts, and the commentators differ on how many abstention doctrines there are. Respectable support can be found for classifying the cases into two, three, four, or five categories. The number is of little significance, since the division is a mere organizational convenience. The present author has found the four-part division set forth in the text the most useful. On this view the "Our Federalism" cases, see § 52A below, are regarded as a special case of the second category, while certification is regarded as a procedural device that may be used in cases falling within the first and third categories.

that contemplates parallel judicial processes." [4]   But two years later the Court, after quoting the statement about the various types not being "rigid pigeonholes," went on to say that "the policy considerations supporting Burford and Younger are sufficiently distinct to justify independent analysis." [5]   For similar reasons they are considered separately here.

The first of these doctrines, and the most clearly established, comes in cases where state action is being challenged in federal court as contrary to the federal Constitution, and there are questions of state law that may be dispositive of the case.   This is usually referred to as the Pullman doctrine, from the case of Railroad Commission of Texas v. Pullman Co.,[6] which is probably the first and surely the leading case supporting abstention in such circumstances.   In that case the company was seeking to enjoin enforcement of an order of the Texas Railroad Commission, claiming that the order denied its rights under the Fourteenth Amendment and claiming also that Texas law did not give the Commission authority to make the order in question.   It is settled that a federal court has jurisdiction to decide the ancillary state issues in such a case,[7] but the wisdom of exercising such jurisdiction is doubtful.   A unanimous Court, speaking through Justice Frankfurter, said: "In this situation a federal court of equity is asked to decide an issue by making a tentative answer which may be displaced tomorrow by a state adjudication.   * * * The resources of equity are equal to an adjustment that will avoid the waste of a tentative decision as well as the friction of a premature constitutional adjudication." [8]   The Court ordered the trial court to abstain from deciding the case but to retain jurisdiction until the parties had had an opportunity to obtain from the state court a decision on the state issues involved.   In this way the state court decides the state issues, and the federal court avoids deciding a federal constitutional question prematurely or unnecessarily, since if the state court should hold the order unauthorized as a matter of state law, there will be no need for the federal court to pass on the federal question.

4. Pennzoil Co. v. Texaco, Inc., 1987, 107 S.Ct. 1519, 1526 n. 9, 481 U.S. 1, 11 n. 9, 95 L.Ed.2d 1.

5. New Orleans Public Service, Inc. v. Council of City of New Orleans, 1989, 109 S.Ct. 2506, 2513, 491 U.S. 350, 358, 105 L.Ed.2d 298.

6. 1941, 61 S.Ct. 643, 312 U.S. 496, 85 L.Ed. 971.

Abstention is a "judge-made doctrine * * *, first fashioned in 1941 in Railroad Commission of Texas v. Pullman Co." Zwickler v. Koota, 1967, 88 S.Ct. 391, 395, 389 U.S. 241, 248, 19 L.Ed.2d 444. For the history of the abstention doctrines, and how the Court has vacillated about them, see 17A Wright, Miller & Cooper, Jurisdiction 2d § 4241.

7. Siler v. Louisville & N.R. Co., 1909, 29 S.Ct. 451, 213 U.S. 175, 53 L.Ed. 753. See also Schmidt v. Oakland Unified Sch. Dist., 1982, 102 S.Ct. 2612, 457 U.S. 594, 73 L.Ed.2d 245. There was a considerable retreat from the doctrine of the Siler case in Pennhurst State School & Hospital v. Halderman, 1984, 104 S.Ct. 900, 465 U.S. 89, 79 L.Ed.2d 67. The Court held there that the Siler doctrine can only be applied where the federal court has jurisdiction to decide the state-law issues and is not barred from deciding by the Eleventh Amendment. 104 S.Ct. at 917–919, 465 U.S. at 117–121.

8. 61 S.Ct. at 645, 312 U.S. at 500. This view was anticipated by Isseks, Jurisdiction of the Lower Federal Courts to Enjoin Unauthorized Action of State Officials, 1927, 40 Harv.L.Rev. 969.

Abstention of the Pullman type has been ordered by the Supreme Court in many cases, and usually with substantial unanimity.[9] It will not be ordered if the state law is clear on its face, or if its meaning has already been authoritatively decided by the state courts, or if the constitutional issue would not be avoided or changed no matter how the statute is construed. For abstention to be appropriate, the state law must be "fairly subject to an interpretation which will render unnecessary or substantially modify the federal constitutional question."[10] Abstention is not proper merely to give a state court the opportunity to hold that the statute violates the federal Constitution.[11] The issue is somewhat more complicated if the state statute is clear but there is a fair possibility that the state court may hold that the statute violates the state constitution. In these cases abstention is in order if the case may turn on the interpretation of some specialized state constitutional provision,[12] but not if "the state constitutional provision is the mirror of the federal one."[13]

The price of Pullman-type abstention is not cheap. In a number of well-known cases it has led to delays of many years before the case was finally decided on its merits[14] or limped to an inconclusive end.[15] This delay and expense can only be justified as the price that must be paid to satisfy the exigent demands of federalism and the vital policy of judicial review that dictates against unnecessary resolution of a federal constitu-

9. 17A Wright, Miller & Cooper, Jurisdiction 2d § 4242; Field, Abstention in Constitutional Cases: The Scope of the Pullman Abstention Doctrine, 1974, 122 U.Pa.L.Rev. 1071.

See ALI Study, § 1371(c), where it is proposed to put this type of abstention, with some modifications, into statutory form.

10. Harman v. Forssenius, 1965, 85 S.Ct. 1177, 1182, 380 U.S. 528, 534–535, 14 L.Ed.2d 50, quoted in Babbitt v. United Farm Workers Nat. Union, 1979, 99 S.Ct. 2301, 2313, 442 U.S. 289, 306, 60 L.Ed.2d 895. See 17A Wright, Miller & Cooper, Jurisdiction 2d § 4242, pp. 35–44.

A claim that a state statute is unconstitutionally vague may call for abstention if the question is whether the statute applies to a particular person or a defined course of conduct, but abstention is not required if the claim is that persons to whom the statute plainly applies simply cannot understand what is required of them. Procunier v. Martinez, 1974, 94 S.Ct. 1800, 1805 n. 5, 416 U.S. 396, 401 n. 5, 40 L.Ed.2d 224.

11. The leading case is Wisconsin v. Constantineau, 1971, 91 S.Ct. 507, 400 U.S. 433, 27 L.Ed.2d 515. See also Zablocki v. Redhail, 1978, 98 S.Ct. 673, 677 n. 5, 434 U.S. 374, 379 n. 5, 54 L.Ed.2d 618; Douglas v. Seacoast Products, Inc., 1977, 97 S.Ct.

1740, 1744 n. 4, 431 U.S. 265, 271 n. 4, 52 L.Ed.2d 304.

12. Harris County Commrs. Court v. Moore, 1975, 95 S.Ct. 870, 420 U.S. 77, 43 L.Ed.2d 32; Reetz v. Bozanich, 1970, 90 S.Ct. 788, 397 U.S. 82, 25 L.Ed.2d 68.

13. Herald Co. v. McNeal, C.A.8th, 1977, 553 F.2d 1125, 1130 n. 8. See Hawaii Housing Authority v. Midkiff, 1984, 104 S.Ct. 2321, 2327 n. 4, 467 U.S. 229, 237 n. 4, 81 L.Ed.2d 186; Examining Bd. of Engineers, Architects & Surveyors v. Flores de Otero, 1976, 96 S.Ct. 2264, 2279, 426 U.S. 572, 598, 49 L.Ed.2d 65; White v. Edgar, Me.1974, 320 A.2d 668.

14. E.g., Spector Motor Serv., Inc. v. O'Connor, 1951, 71 S.Ct. 508, 340 U.S. 602, 95 L.Ed. 573 (seven years); England v. Louisiana State Bd. of Medical Examiners, 1966, 86 S.Ct. 1924, 384 U.S. 885, 16 L.Ed.2d 998 (nine years).

15. U.S. v. Leiter Minerals, Inc., 1965, 85 S.Ct. 1575, 381 U.S. 413, 14 L.Ed.2d 692 (dismissed as moot eight years after abstention ordered). See also the Government and Civic Employees case, described at ALI Study, p. 283, in which plaintiff abandoned the fight when five years of litigation, including two trips to the United States Supreme Court and two to the Alabama Supreme Court, had failed to produce a decision on the merits.

tional issue. Experience with abstention has caused some to conclude that this is "an unnecessary price to pay for our federalism." [16] The Supreme Court itself has showed occasional signs of disenchantment with the practice it created in the Pullman case. In one case it said that "we also cannot ignore that abstention operates to require piecemeal adjudication in many courts * * * thereby delaying ultimate adjudication on the merits for an undue length of time," and held that "special circumstances" must exist to justify abstention.[17] In another case it held abstention unwarranted where neither party had requested it and the litigation had already been long delayed.[18]

In the Pullman case the Supreme Court ordered the trial court to retain jurisdiction while the parties sought a state ruling on the state issues. Since retention of jurisdiction is usually [19] ordered in Pullman-type cases, the Court has defended abstention, saying "this principle does not, of course, involve the abdication of federal jurisdiction but only the postponement of its exercise * * *." [20] The implementation of this,

16. England v. Louisiana State Bd. of Medical Examiners, 1964, 84 S.Ct. 461, 470, 375 U.S. 411, 426, 11 L.Ed.2d 440 (Douglas, J., concurring). See also the view of a commentator that abstention has "a Bleak House aspect that in my mind is too high a price to pay for the gains in avoiding error, friction, and constitutional questions." Currie, The Federal Courts and the American Law Institute (Part II), 1969, 36 U.Chi. L.Rev. 268, 317.

17. Baggett v. Bullitt, 1964, 84 S.Ct. 1316, 1324–1326, 377 U.S. 360, 375–379, 12 L.Ed.2d 377.

Other cases say that "special circumstances" are needed to justify abstention, Kusper v. Pontikes, 1973, 94 S.Ct. 303, 306, 414 U.S. 51, 54, 38 L.Ed.2d 260, but the Court is not reluctant to order abstention when it finds those circumstances present. E.g., Lake Carriers' Assn. v. MacMullan, 1972, 92 S.Ct. 1749, 406 U.S. 498, 32 L.Ed.2d 257; Harris County Commrs. Court v. Moore, 1975, 95 S.Ct. 870, 420 U.S. 77, 43 L.Ed.2d 32; Bellotti v. Baird, 1976, 96 S.Ct. 2857, 428 U.S. 132, 49 L.Ed.2d 844.

The delay that abstention will cause is a factor to be weighed against abstention if important interests will be harmed by the delay. Anderson v. Babb, C.A.4th, 1980, 632 F.2d 300; Lister v. Lucey, C.A.7th, 1978, 575 F.2d 1325, 1333, certiorari denied 99 S.Ct. 190, 439 U.S. 865, 58 L.Ed.2d 175; Field, note 7 above, at 1129–1134.

18. Hostetter v. Idlewild Bon Voyage Liquor Corp., 1964, 84 S.Ct. 1293, 1296, 377 U.S. 324, 329, 12 L.Ed.2d 350. See also Mayor of City of Philadelphia v. Educational Equality League, 1974, 94 S.Ct. 1323, 1337, 415 U.S. 605, 628, 39 L.Ed.2d 630.

But a request from a party is not required and abstention may be raised by the court sua sponte. Bellotti v. Baird, 1976, 96 S.Ct. 2857, 2864 n. 10, 428 U.S. 132, 143 n. 10, 49 L.Ed.2d 844.

19. This is said to be the "proper course" in American Trial Lawyers Assn. v. New Jersey Supreme Court, 1973, 93 S.Ct. 627, 629, 409 U.S. 467, 469, 34 L.Ed.2d 651. Dismissal without prejudice may be ordered where retention of jurisdiction would interfere with obtaining a state-court decision. Harris County Commrs. Court v. Moore, 1975, 95 S.Ct. 870, 878 n. 14, 420 U.S. 77, 88 n. 14, 43 L.Ed.2d 32.

20. Harrison v. National Assn. for the Advancement of Colored People, 1959, 79 S.Ct. 1025, 1030, 360 U.S. 167, 175, 3 L.Ed.2d 1152. See Allen v. McCurry, 1980, 101 S.Ct. 411, 418 n. 17, 449 U.S. 90, 101 n. 17, 66 L.Ed.2d 308.

On the procedural consequences of Pullman-type abstention generally, see 17A Wright, Miller & Cooper, Jurisdiction 2d § 4243.

The Supreme Court has recently acknowledged that it speaks of the Pullman doctrine as a form of abstention, but it went on to question that terminology. "To bring out more clearly, however, the distinction between those circumstances that require dismissal of a suit and those that require postponing consideration of its merits, it would be preferable to speak of Pullman 'deferral.'" Growe v. Emison, 1993, 113 S.Ct. 1075, 1080 n. 1, ___ U.S. ___, ___ n. 1, 122 L.Ed.2d 388. Even if this might have been desirable originally, to change the name after more than a half-century of usage would be confusing rather than clarifying.

however, has led to a complicated procedure. The Court first held that the federal constitutional objections must be presented to the state court, so that it may consider the issues of state law in the light of the constitutional claims.[21] But if the state court should decide the federal issues, on ordinary principles of res judicata—or issue preclusion, as it is now called—this would be a binding determination, subject to review only in the Supreme Court, and there would be nothing left for the federal court to decide in the exercise of the jurisdiction it had retained. Since the Supreme Court cannot hear every case tendered to it, this would mean that many litigants would never have a hearing in a federal court though they were asserting claims based on federal law. As the Court said in England v. Louisiana State Board of Medical Examiners,[22] the possibility of review in the Supreme Court is an inadequate substitute for the determination by a district court to which the litigant has a statutory right. "This is true as to issues of law; it is especially true as to issues of fact. Limiting the litigant to review here would deny him the benefit of a federal trial court's role in constructing a record and making fact findings. How the facts are found will often dictate the decision of federal claims."[23] Thus, in the England case the Court announced that though a litigant may submit all aspects of the case for a binding adjudication by the state court,[24] it is not required to do so. Any party may make on the state record a reservation to the disposition of the entire case by the state courts, by informing them that it is exposing its federal contentions only as a matter of information and that it intends to return to the federal court for disposition of the federal contentions.[25]

There are two difficulties with the procedure announced in England. Many state courts will consider that if such a reservation is made, they are disabled from deciding the state issues since their decision would be a mere advisory opinion.[26] Even where the England procedure is accept-

---

21. Government and Civic Employees Organizing Committee, CIO v. Windsor, 1957, 77 S.Ct. 838, 839, 353 U.S. 364, 366, 1 L.Ed.2d 894.

22. 1964, 84 S.Ct. 461, 375 U.S. 411, 11 L.Ed.2d 440.

23. 84 S.Ct. at 465, 375 U.S. at 416.

24. National Assn. for the Advancement of Colored People v. Button, 1963, 83 S.Ct. 328, 335, 371 U.S. 415, 427, 9 L.Ed.2d 405.

25. 84 S.Ct. at 468, 375 U.S. at 421–422. See Liebenthal, A Dialogue on England: The England Case, Its Effect on the Abstention Doctrine, and Some Suggested Solutions, 1966, 18 W.Res.L.Rev. 157; 17A Wright, Miller & Cooper, Jurisdiction 2d § 4243, pp. 72–79.

Strictly speaking the England procedure applies only if a case was begun in federal court and if abstention was on Pullman grounds. Schuster v. Martin, C.A.2d, 1988,

861 F.2d 1369, 1373–1374; Fuller Co. v. Ramon I. Gil, Inc., C.A.1st, 1986, 782 F.2d 306, 311; and cases cited 17A Wright, Miller & Cooper, Jurisdiction 2d § 4243 nn. 27, 40.1 and 18 id. § 4471 nn. 38–40. But if a district court mistakenly orders Pullman abstention where Younger abstention would have been appropriate, the parties may use the England procedure. Ivy Club v. Edwards, C.A.3d, 1991, 943 F.2d 270, certiorari denied 112 S.Ct. 1282, ___ U.S. ___, 117 L.Ed.2d 507.

26. Cf. United Services Life Ins. Co. v. Delaney, Tex.1965, 396 S.W.2d 855, noted 1966, 20 Sw.L.J. 402, 44 Texas L.Rev. 1394; In re Richards, Me.1966, 223 A.2d 827. See Leiter Minerals, Inc. v. California Co., 1961, 132 So.2d 845, 241 La. 915, where the court said it was being asked to give an advisory opinion, but gave it anyhow as a matter of courtesy to, and respect for, the United States Supreme Court. Of course some able to the state court, it invites the kind of shuttling back and forth between judicial systems that aggravates the delay inherently involved in abstention.[27] Given the state of the precedents at the time England was decided, the rule it announces was probably the best possible reconciliation of conflicting interests. If it were possible to start fresh, however, it would seem wiser to provide that, barring some unusual turn of events, a case should not return to the federal court after abstention has been ordered but should be fully and finally adjudicated by the state court with review possible in the Supreme Court. For this to be workable, it would be necessary also to provide that the federal court is not to abstain if the federal claims, and the issues of fact material to them, cannot be adequately protected by Supreme Court review of the state-court decision.[28]

There are cases in which abstention is indicated under the Pullman doctrine, but in which the federal plaintiff will be seriously harmed if the state law is enforced while the state questions are being tested in the state court. Since the federal court is to retain jurisdiction rather than dismiss in these cases, it may give whatever interim relief is needed to protect the party during the period of abstention.[29]

A second type of abstention, which takes its name from the leading case of Burford v. Sun Oil Co.,[30] is Burford-type abstention. Its general thrust can be well captured by saying that abstention is ordered to avoid needless conflict with the administration by a state of its own affairs, though neither this nor any other attempt at defining the class of cases in which this type of abstention is proper is very precise. In Burford a sharply divided Court held that the federal court should have dismissed the complaint in a case involving proration orders in Texas oil fields, on the ground that the issues involved a specialized aspect of a complicated regulatory system of local law, which should be left to the local administrative bodies and courts. Later the Court divided again in saying that a federal court should have declined jurisdiction of an action by a railroad challenging the order of a state regulatory commission refusing to permit discontinuance of certain trains. The railroad could have appealed from the commission's order to a state court, but had come instead to the federal court on the basis both of diversity of citizenship and of a federal

state courts are free to give advisory opinions. See Sun Ins. Office, Ltd. v. Clay, Fla.1961, 133 So.2d 735. For discussion of the problems of justiciability that abstention poses for the state court, see Note, 1962, 40 Tex.L.Rev. 1041.

27. See notes 14 and 15 above.

28. The proposal in the text is that made by the American Law Institute. ALI Study, § 1371(c), (d). It is criticized in Redish, Federal Jurisdiction: Tensions in the Allocation of Judicial Power, 1980, pp. 255–256.

29. Babbitt v. United Farm Workers Nat. Union, 1979, 99 S.Ct. 2301, 2316 n. 18, 442 U.S. 289, 309 n. 18, 60 L.Ed.2d 895;

Romany v. Colegio de Abogados de Puerto Rico, C.A.1st, 1984, 742 F.2d 32, 44–45; Deck House, Inc. v. New Jersey State Bd. of Architects, D.C.N.J.1982, 531 F.Supp. 633, 645–648; Report, note 1 above, at 106; Wells, Preliminary Injunctions and Abstention: Some Problems in Federalism, 1977, 63 Cornell L.Rev. 65.

30. 1943, 63 S.Ct. 1098, 319 U.S. 315, 87 L.Ed. 1424.

The strong feelings the Burford case produced within the Supreme Court are reported in Lash, From the Diaries of Felix Frankfurter, 1975, pp. 226–228.

question. The Supreme Court said: "As adequate state court review of an administrative order based upon predominantly local factors is available to appellee, intervention of a federal court is not necessary for the protection of federal rights." [31]

In Burford-type abstention, where the federal court defers to avoid interference with state activities, dismissal of the action, rather than retention of jurisdiction pending a state determination, is normally appropriate.[32] If the state court to which deference is thus shown prejudices any federal rights of the parties, this can be redressed by review of the state decision in the United States Supreme Court.

Two important cases, decided on the same day in 1959, must now be considered. It may be that they are only further examples of when Burford-type abstention is appropriate, but it is possible that they represent an extension of the third type of abstention, because of unsettled state law, which is yet to be discussed. Both cases grew out of state eminent-domain proceedings. In County of Allegheny v. Frank Mashuda Co.,[33] the landowner brought an independent action of ouster, as the state law permitted, to challenge the validity of the taking, and brought it in federal court on the basis of diversity. Though the state law was regarded, rightly or not, as clearly settled, the district court, believing it should not interfere with the administration of the affairs of a political subdivision acting under color of state law, dismissed the action. In the other case, Louisiana Power & Light Co. v. City of Thibodaux,[34] the condemnee removed the condemnation action itself to federal court on the basis of diversity, and challenged the taking in that action. The state law here was regarded, rightly or not, as confused. The state statute seemed to permit the taking, but it was old and unconstrued by the courts, and an opinion of the state attorney general appeared to deny such a power. The trial judge, on his own motion, ordered the condemnation action stayed until the state court had had an opportunity to construe the statute relied on.

31. Alabama Public Serv. Commn. v. Southern R. Co., 1951, 71 S.Ct. 762, 768, 341 U.S. 341, 349, 95 L.Ed. 1002.

32. 17A Wright, Miller & Cooper, Jurisdiction 2d § 4245.

This is not inconsistent with ordering retention of jurisdiction simply against the possibility that something should prevent a prompt state court determination. Ankenbrandt v. Richards, 1992, 112 S.Ct. 2206, 2216 n. 5, ___ U.S. ___, ___ n. 5, 119 L.Ed.2d 468; Kaiser Steel Corp. v. W.S. Ranch Co., 1968, 88 S.Ct. 1753, 391 U.S. 593, 20 L.Ed.2d 835; ALI Study, § 1371(d). In the Kaiser Steel case, abstention was ordered so that the state courts could decide a novel question of water law of vital concern to a dry state such as New Mexico. This is probably best understood as Bur-

ford-type abstention, and it is so explained in a concurring opinion by three justices. The opinion of the Court is silent on the point. Cf. ALI Study, § 1371(b).

If the case is one that has been removed from state court to federal court, and it is determined that Burford-type abstention is appropriate, there is now authority that the federal court may remand the case to state court rather than dismiss. Melahn v. Pennock Ins. Co., C.A.8th, 1992, 965 F.2d 1497, 1501; Corcoran v. Ardra Ins. Co., C.A.2d, 1988, 842 F.2d 31, 36–37.

33. 1959, 79 S.Ct. 1060, 360 U.S. 185, 3 L.Ed.2d 1163.

34. 1959, 79 S.Ct. 1070, 360 U.S. 25, 3 L.Ed.2d 1058.

The cases are distinguishable in only two respects. In the Allegheny County case, the state law was thought to be clear; in the City of Thibodaux case, it was thought to be unclear. In the Allegheny County case, the trial court ordered the action dismissed, while in the other case it had merely ordered the federal action stayed. The Supreme Court held, 5–4, that it was error for the court in the Allegheny County case to dismiss the action and directed it to decide the case. At the same time the Court, by a vote of 6–3, upheld the stay of the federal action ordered in the City of Thibodaux. Perhaps the results can be reconciled on the basis of the two factual distinctions between the cases, but the opinions cannot be reconciled. The opinion in the City of Thibodaux case, upholding the stay, rested heavily on "the special nature of eminent domain" proceedings. A majority of the Court declared of eminent domain, "it is intimately involved with sovereign prerogative." [35] A majority of the same Court, on the same day, declared in the Allegheny County case that "surely eminent domain is no more mystically involved with 'sovereign prerogative' than" [36] a number of other matters on which abstention has been refused. Nor is difficulty dispelled by the fact that the dissenting opinion in City of Thibodaux is in all respects similar to, and in many passages taken verbatim from, the opinion for the Court in Allegheny County.

The two cases, taken together, do establish that an abstention doctrine can apply in eminent-domain cases. Beyond this two explanations are possible. One is that abstention is proper in eminent-domain cases where the state law is unsettled. If this explanation be sound, then the special nature of eminent-domain proceedings, combined with difficulties of state law, will permit abstention though neither of the circumstances individually would suffice. An alternative explanation is that the grant of a stay in an eminent-domain case is a matter of discretion for the trial court. This explanation has its own difficulties. As noted above, in Burford-type abstention, as contrasted with Pullman-type abstention, dismissal of the federal action, rather than a stay, is normally appropriate. Yet the Allegheny County case holds squarely that dismissal was erroneous while the City of Thibodaux case affirms a stay. Further, though the abstention doctrines have their origin in the discretion of equity judges, in the situations heretofore considered no discretion has been recognized. If the case was an appropriate one for abstention, then the trial judge committed reversible error by failure to abstain. Yet the majority opinion in City of Thibodaux speaks broadly of the district court "exercising a fair and well-considered judicial discretion in staying proceedings" [37] while the dissenters in the Allegheny County case argue that in view of peculiar circumstances of the case the trial judge had not "clearly abused his discretion." [38] That the Court may be willing to confide more to the discretion of the trial court in determining whether to abstain is suggested also by a decision two weeks

---

35. 79 S.Ct. at 1073, 360 U.S. at 28.

36. 79 S.Ct. at 1064–1065, 360 U.S. at 190–192.

37. 79 S.Ct. at 1074, 360 U.S. at 30.

38. 79 S.Ct. at 1070, 360 U.S. at 25.

after the cases just considered in which, in a Pullman-type situation, the Court ruled that reference to the state courts for construction of the state statute should not automatically be made; it remanded for the trial court to exercise its considered discretion.[39]

It may even be that attempts to explain the two decisions are a futile exercise. Seven of the nine members of the Court found the two cases indistinguishable and would have reached the same result in both cases, though differing as to what that result should be. Thus, any nice distinction that might have been drawn between the two cases probably would not have been acceptable to a majority of the Court.[40]

As good a summary of Burford as can be hoped for was given by Justice Scalia, writing for the Court in a 1989 case: "Where timely and adequate state court review is available, a federal court sitting in equity must decline to interfere with the proceedings or orders of state administrative agencies: (1) when there are 'difficult questions of state law bearing on policy problems of substantial public import whose importance transcends the result in the case at bar'; or (2) where the 'exercise of federal review of the question in a case and in similar cases would be disruptive of state efforts to establish a coherent policy with respect to a matter of substantial public concern.' "[41] It would be wrong, however, to suppose that Burford is limited to "the proceedings or orders of state administrative agencies." In the 1976 decision from which the Court quoted in the passage just set out, the first two cases cited as examples of "difficult questions of state law" were cases in which the state proceedings were judicial rather than administrative.[42] And in a 1992 case the Supreme Court has said that there are circumstances in which Burford-type abstention might be appropriate prior to effectuation of a state decree in a domestic-relations matter.[43]

39. National Assn. for the Advancement of Colored People v. Bennett, 1959, 79 S.Ct. 1192, 360 U.S. 471, 3 L.Ed.2d 1375.

In his concurring opinion in England v. Louisiana State Bd. of Medical Examiners, 1964, 84 S.Ct. 461, 473, 375 U.S. 411, 432, 11 L.Ed.2d 440, Justice Douglas argued that Pullman-type abstention should be made "less of a mandatory and more a discretionary procedure." Abstention would always be discretionary under the proposals of the American Law Institute. ALI Study, § 1371(c).

40. See 17A Wright, Miller & Cooper, Jurisdiction 2d § 4241, pp. 13–17; Redish, note 28 above, at pp. 240–243; Comment, Abstention by Federal Courts in Suits Challenging State Administrative Decisions: The Scope of the Burford Doctrine, 1979, 46 U.Chi.L.Rev. 971.

41. New Orleans Public Service, Inc. v. Council of City of New Orleans, 1989, 109 S.Ct. 2506, 2514, 491 U.S. 350, 361, 105 L.Ed.2d 298. The internal quotations are

from Colorado River Water Conservation Dist. v. U.S., 1976, 96 S.Ct. 1236, 1244–1245, 424 U.S. 800, 814, 47 L.Ed.2d 483. The holding of the NOPSI case, as it is known, is that Burford-type abstention is not proper where the claim is that federal law has preempted the authority of the state to act on the matter. 109 S.Ct. at 2514–2515, 491 U.S. at 361–364.

For cases in which the lower courts have thought Burford-type abstention was or was not proper, see 17A Wright, Miller & Cooper, Jurisdiction § 4244. A particularly instructive case is Property & Cas. Ins. Ltd. v. Central Nat. Ins. Co. of Omaha, C.A.7th, 1991, 936 F.2d 319, 323.

42. Colorado River, 96 S.Ct. at 1244–1245, 424 U.S. at 814, citing the City of Thibodaux case, note 34 above, and the Kaiser Steel case, note 32 above.

43. Ankenbrandt v. Richards, 1992, 112 S.Ct. 2206, 2216, ___ U.S. ___, ___, 119 L.Ed.2d 468. See generally Young, Federal Court Abstention and State Administrative

All of the abstention cases prior to 1959 had involved equitable actions. It appeared in City of Thibodaux that the Court was about to demolish any such limitation on abstention when it said that the cases did not apply a technical rule of equity procedure but reflected a deeper policy derived from our federalism. In the same paragraph, however, the Court went on to emphasize that eminent domain is a special and peculiar kind of common-law action and seemingly analogized eminent-domain cases to equitable proceedings.[44] Nevertheless a year later, in Clay v. Sun Insurance Office Ltd.,[45] the Court actually ordered abstention in a common-law action to recover money from an insurance company, in a Pullman-type situation where the meaning of a state statute was deemed unclear and a supposedly difficult federal constitutional question would be raised if the statute applied to the suit before the Court.[46]

An important question, only recently resolved, is whether a third type of abstention is proper. All of the cases thus far considered have involved constitutional and statutory issues of a public nature. Is abstention appropriate in private litigation to avoid having to decide difficult questions of state law? At least until 1959, the rule seemed to be that the mere difficulty of determining state law did not justify abstention.

The leading case was Meredith v. City of Winter Haven.[47] In a diversity action seeking equitable relief, question was raised about a city's power to issue certain bonds without a referendum. The trial court dismissed the action on the merits, but the court of appeals ordered that the dismissal be on abstention grounds. The Supreme Court reversed and ordered the lower court to reinstate the complaint and to decide the case. Chief Justice Stone announced broadly that "the difficulties of ascertaining what the state courts may hereafter determine the state law to be do not in themselves afford a sufficient ground for a federal court to decline to exercise its jurisdiction to decide a case which is properly brought to it for decision." [48]

Law from Burford to Ankenbrandt: Fifty Years of Judicial Federalism Under Burford v. Sun Oil Co. and Kindred Doctrines, 1993, 42 DePaul L.Rev. 859.

44. 79 S.Ct. at 1072, 360 U.S. at 28.

45. 1960, 80 S.Ct. 1222, 363 U.S. 207, 4 L.Ed.2d 1170. See Cardozo, Choosing and Declaring State Law: Deference to State Courts Versus Federal Responsibility, 1960, 55 Nw.U.L.Rev. 419.

46. Although four members of the Court, speaking through Justice Brennan, have recently sought to limit the "principle of comity" to cases "where a federal court is asked to employ its historic powers as a court of equity," and have said somewhat grudgingly that "even assuming 'absten-tion' might have some application in actions at law," Fair Assessment in Real Estate Assn., Inc. v. McNary, 1981, 102 S.Ct. 177, 188 and n. 3, 454 U.S. 100, 119–120 and n. 3, 70 L.Ed.2d 271 (concurring opinion), other cases after Clay have ordered abstention in private damage actions. E.g., Fornaris v. Ridge Tool Co., 1970, 91 S.Ct. 156, 400 U.S. 41, 27 L.Ed.2d 174; United Gas Pipe Line Co. v. Ideal Cement Co., 1962, 82 S.Ct. 676, 369 U.S. 134, 7 L.Ed.2d 623; Lac D'Amiante du Quebec v. American Home Assur. Co., C.A.3d, 1988, 864 F.2d 1033, 1044–1045. See also Shapiro, note 2 above, at 551–552.

47. 1943, 64 S.Ct. 7, 320 U.S. 228, 88 L.Ed. 9.

48. 64 S.Ct. at 11, 320 U.S. at 235.

The Court frequently applied the Meredith principle, and refused to order abstention though a case presented difficult questions of state law.[49]   The 1959 condemnation cases raised doubts.   In City of Thibodaux the Court was at pains to say that the issue before it was "decisively different" from that involved in Meredith,[50] but the difference six Justices detected did not seem a persuasive distinction to everyone.[51]   To the extent that City of Thibodaux and Allegheny County may have turned on the fact that the law was settled in one case and not in the other, they gave support to the notion that a federal court may or should leave to the states the decision of unsettled questions of state law. Yet four years after those cases the Court seemed to be at pains to reaffirm the Meredith principle.[52]   The decisions of the lower courts were not entirely consistent.   The Fifth Circuit, with scattered support elsewhere, thought abstention proper in a routine diversity case simply because the state law was unclear.[53]   Other courts consistently rejected this view.[54]

The Clay case, discussed above, was unique in being the first decision in which the Supreme Court ordered abstention in a common-law action.   It was unique also in that the Court ordered resort to the new device of certification of the state questions involved to the highest state court for decision.   Florida had had on its books for some years a statute permitting a federal court of appeals to certify a question of Florida law to the Florida Supreme Court.   The Florida statute had

49. See 17A Wright, Miller & Cooper, Jurisdiction 2d § 4246 n. 10.

50. 79 S.Ct. at 1072 n. 2, 360 U.S. at 27 n. 2.

51. The distinction was not persuasive to the dissenters in City of Thibodaux. See 79 S.Ct. at 1078 n. 4, 360 U.S. at 38 n. 4 (dissenting opinion).

In private correspondence at that time Justice Frankfurter, the spokesman for the majority in City of Thibodaux, expressed regret that he had joined in the Meredith decision. See 17A Wright, Miller & Cooper, Jurisdiction 2d § 4241 n. 39.

52. In McNeese v. Board of Educ., 1963, 83 S.Ct. 1433, 1436 n. 5, 373 U.S. 668, 673 n. 5, 10 L.Ed.2d 622, the Court said: "Yet where Congress creates a head of federal jurisdiction which entails a responsibility to adjudicate the claim on the basis of state law, viz., diversity of citizenship, as was true in Meredith v. Winter Haven, 320 U.S. 228, we hold that difficulties and perplexities of state law are no reason for referral of the problem to the state court * * *."

Meredith is also cited in Colorado River Water Conservation Dist. v. U.S., 1976, 96 S.Ct. 1236, 1245, 424 U.S. 800, 816, 47 L.Ed.2d 483, for the proposition that "the mere potential for conflict in the results of adjudication, does not, without more, war-

rant staying exercise of federal jurisdiction."

53. The best-known Fifth Circuit case is United Services Life Ins. Co. v. Delaney, C.A.5th, 1964, 328 F.2d 483, certiorari denied 84 S.Ct. 1335, 377 U.S. 935, 12 L.Ed.2d 298.   The case was vigorously criticized.   See Currie, note 14 above, at 313–314; Agata, Delaney, Diversity, and Delay: Abstention or Abdication, 1966, 4 Hous. L.Rev. 422, 447.   One commentator has suggested that the Fifth Circuit abstained in Delaney not because the state law was unclear but "because it did not believe the state law was what the state court had said it was."   Comment, Abstention under Delaney: A Current Appraisal, 1971, 49 Texas L.Rev. 247, 258.   There is a spirited defense of Delaney by Chief Judge John R. Brown of the Fifth Circuit, sitting by designation with the Tenth Circuit, in his separate opinion in W.S. Ranch Co. v. Kaiser Steel Corp., C.A.10th, 1967, 388 F.2d 257, 262, reversed 1968, 88 S.Ct. 1753, 391 U.S. 593, 20 L.Ed.2d 835.

54. See cases cited in 17A Wright, Miller & Cooper, Jurisdiction 2d § 4246 n. 28. Indeed even the Fifth Circuit later referred to Delaney as an "unfortunate decision." Barrett v. Atlantic Richfield Co., C.A.5th, 1971, 444 F.2d 38, 45.

never been implemented by court rules setting up such a procedure, but after certification was ordered by the Supreme Court in the Clay case the Florida Supreme Court adopted such rules and determined the questions certified to it by the Fifth Circuit.[55] The Clay case itself was an example of Pullman-type abstention, since decision of the state issues might—though in the result it did not—obviate deciding a federal constitutional question.

The certification procedure has been regarded with quite an extraordinary enthusiasm by the commentators,[56] and three-fourths of the states now have followed Florida's lead and have made such a procedure available.[57] In some states it is thought that for the state court to answer certified questions would be to give an impermissible advisory opinion,[58] while in other states the rule against advisory opinions limits the circumstances in which the court can answer certified questions.[59]

In the 1974 decision in Lehman Brothers v. Schein,[60] the Supreme Court gave strong endorsement to the use of certification in cases where

55. Sun Ins. Office, Ltd. v. Clay, Fla. 1961, 133 So.2d 735.

The Fifth Circuit adhered to its earlier decision despite the answers to the certified questions provided by the Florida court. Sun Ins. Office, Ltd. v. Clay, C.A.5th, 1963, 319 F.2d 505. The Supreme Court, four years after first hearing the case, reversed the Fifth Circuit and held the Florida statute applicable. Clay v. Sun Ins. Office, Ltd., 1964, 84 S.Ct. 1197, 377 U.S. 179, 12 L.Ed.2d 229.

56. The literature is immense. See Robbins, The Uniform Certification of Questions of Law Act: A Proposal for Reform, 1992, 18 J.Legis. 127; LeBel, Legal Positivism and Federalism: The Certification Experience, 1985, 19 Ga.L.Rev. 999; and commentaries cited 17A Wright, Miller & Cooper, Jurisdiction 2d § 4248 n. 1.

57. The statutes and rules are cited, and their variations in matters of detail noted, in 17A Wright, Miller & Cooper, Jurisdiction 2d § 4248 nn. 30–33. Most, but not all, of them are based on the Uniform Certification of Questions of Law Act, approved in 1967. 12 U.L.A., pp. 49–56. See also ALI Study, § 1371(e).

A federal court cannot certify a question to the court of a state that has no certification procedure. Planned Parenthood Assn. of Kansas City v. Ashcroft, 1983, 103 S.Ct. 2517, 2526 n. 21, 462 U.S. 476, 493 n. 21, 76 L.Ed.2d 733.

58. The Florida court concluded that advisory opinions were permissible under the state constitution. Sun Ins. Office, Ltd. v. Clay, Fla.1961, 133 So.2d 735, 739–743.

The Washington certification statute was upheld by vote of 6–3. The majority

thought that they were not being asked to give an advisory opinion, but held that they had power to give advisory opinions if this were what was involved. In re Elliott, 1968, 446 P.2d 347, 74 Wash.2d 600.

See also note 26 above.

59. The usual rule is that the state court will not answer the certified question unless one of the possible answers it can give will be determinative of the case. Pan American Computer Corp. v. Data General Corp., 1982, 112 D.P.R. 780; White v. Edgar, Me.1974, 320 A.2d 668; In re Richards, Me.1966, 223 A.2d 827.

In Wyoming, however, the state court has taken the much more restrictive view that it will not answer a certified question until there is nothing left for the federal court to do but apply the state court's answer to the question and enter judgment consistent with the answer. Matter of Certified Question, Wyo.1976, 549 P.2d 1310, noted 1977, 12 Land & Water L.Rev. 337. See also the discussion of the Mississippi certification rule in Brewer v. Memphis Pub. Co., Inc., C.A.5th, 1980, 626 F.2d 1238, 1242 n. 5.

State courts have also refused to answer certified questions if they involve state constitutional provisions that mirror provisions of the federal Constitution. Pan American Computer Corp. v. Data General Corp., 1982, 112 D.P.R. 780; WXYZ, Inc. v. Hand, C.A.6th, 1981, 658 F.2d 420, 422 n. 3 (Michigan Supreme Court's action).

60. 1974, 94 S.Ct. 1741, 416 U.S. 386, 40 L.Ed.2d 215.

state law is difficult to ascertain. The case was a private diversity case in New York that turned on an unsettled issue of Florida law. The Court vacated a decision of the case by the Second Circuit so that that court might reconsider whether to certify the question to the Florida Supreme Court. The Court restated the Meredith rule, that mere difficulty in ascertaining local law does not justify "remitting the parties to a state tribunal for the start of another lawsuit." [61] It then spoke warmly of certification. "We do not suggest that where there is doubt as to local law and where the certification procedure is available, resort to it is obligatory. It does of course in the long run save time, energy, and resources and helps build a cooperative judicial federalism. Its use in a given case rests in the sound discretion of the federal court." [62] Lower courts have accepted the invitation of the Lehman Brothers case and have often certified unclear questions of state law to state courts where that procedure was available, though they have not done so indiscriminately.[63]

Although there is still disagreement on the desirability of certification in cases of unclear state law, there is no such disagreement about the value of certification in situations of the Pullman type. The state-law questions that are intertwined with federal constitutional issues in Pullman-type cases can be resolved more expeditiously by certification than by the traditional method of requiring a party to commence a declaratory judgment action in the state trial court and take the decision there to the highest court of the state. Thus, the availability of a certification procedure may tip the scales in favor of having the state court first decide the state-law questions in Pullman-type cases.[64] But "the availability of certification is not in itself sufficient to render abstention appropriate." [65]

The fourth, and presently the most disputed, of the abstention doctrines concerns whether a federal court may stay or dismiss an action on the sole ground that there is a similar action pending in state court in which the controversy between the parties can be resolved. This may be

61. 94 S.Ct. at 1744, 416 U.S. at 386.

62. 94 S.Ct. at 1744, 416 U.S. at 386.

63. See cases cited 17A Wright, Miller & Cooper, Jurisdiction 2d § 4246 nn. 37, 38.

64. "Although we do not mean to intimate that abstention would be improper in this case were certification not possible, the availability of certification greatly simplifies the analysis." Bellotti v. Baird, 1976, 96 S.Ct. 2857, 2868, 428 U.S. 132, 151, 49 L.Ed.2d 844.

Certification has also been imaginatively used in a habeas-corpus case that was analytically similar to a Pullman-type case. Adams v. Murphy, C.A.5th, 1979, 598 F.2d 982. See the same case, C.A.5th, 1981, 653 F.2d 224.

A leading scholar of Pullman-type abstention now concludes that "Pullman abstention is not worth its costs" and that it

should be preserved only where certification procedures are available. Field, note 1 above, at 605–609. The same view is taken in Report, note 1 above, at 506.

Abstention of the traditional type has been refused when the state court has already refused to answer certified questions in the case. WXYZ, Inc. v. Hand, C.A.6th, 1981, 658 F.2d 420.

65. City of Houston v. Hill, 1987, 107 S.Ct. 2502, 2514, 482 U.S. 451, 470–471, 96 L.Ed.2d 398. In that case the majority found the ordinance in question "neither ambiguous nor obviously susceptible of a limiting construction," and said: "A federal court may not properly ask a state court if it would care in effect to rewrite a statute." 107 S.Ct. at 2514–2515, 482 U.S. at 471.

regarded as abstention merely to serve the convenience of the federal courts or, to put a more prepossessing name on it, to avoid duplicative litigation.

Of course the doctrine of forum non conveniens permits dismissal in unusual cases.[66] If a state court has already taken jurisdiction of a res, a federal court must decline jurisdiction.[67] If a state action is already pending in which all issues can be effectively determined, a federal court may refuse to entertain a declaratory-judgment action,[68] but this rests on the special nature of declaratory-judgment procedure and the fact that there is no need for that procedure in the situation outlined.[69] Also it is clear that a federal court can stay an action where the same issues are presented in an action pending in another federal court.[70]

Beyond the situations outlined, it had been thought to be the rule that the mere pendency of an action in personam in state court would not require, nor even permit, a federal court to refuse to hear an action or to stay an action, and that instead both state and federal actions should go forward until one of them resulted in a judgment that might be asserted as res judicata in the other.[71] Two decisions of the Second Circuit, and some cases elsewhere, cast doubt even on that proposition. In one a federal judge ordered a stay of a shareholder's action brought in federal court pending determination of a state suit in which nine similar actions had been consolidated. The Second Circuit upheld the stay, on condition that the defendants consent to discovery of the same scope in the state action as would be available in the federal action.[72] In the second case, a federal judge, relying solely on the fact of a crowded docket in his district, ordered a stay of a trademark-infringement action pending determination of an earlier declaratory-judgment action in state court that raised the same issues. The stay was upheld.[73] Though these decisions had some support from commentators,[74] they seemed to go

66. Piper Aircraft Co. v. Reyno, 1981, 102 S.Ct. 252, 454 U.S. 235, 70 L.Ed.2d 419. The enactment in 1948 of the change-of-venue statute, 28 U.S.C.A. § 1404(a), see § 44 above, has left only vestiges of this doctrine available in federal court.

67. Princess Lida of Thurn and Taxis v. Thompson, 1939, 59 S.Ct. 275, 305 U.S. 456, 83 L.Ed. 285; 14 Wright, Miller & Cooper, Jurisdiction 2d § 3631.

68. Brillhart v. Excess Ins. Co. of America, 1942, 62 S.Ct. 1173, 316 U.S. 491, 86 L.Ed. 1620. See § 100 below.

69. The Fifth Circuit has extended the doctrine of the Brillhart case, note 68 above, to permit a stay in ordinary equity suits in deference to a parallel state action. PPG Indus., Inc. v. Continental Oil Co., C.A.5th, 1973, 478 F.2d 674, noted 1973, 51 Texas L.Rev. 1252.

70. Kerotest Mfg. Co. v. C–O–Two Fire Equipment Co., 1952, 72 S.Ct. 219, 342 U.S. 180, 96 L.Ed. 200; Semmes Motors, Inc. v.

Ford Motor Co., C.A.2d, 1970, 429 F.2d 1197.

71. McClellan v. Carland, 1910, 30 S.Ct. 501, 217 U.S. 268, 54 L.Ed. 762; see Kline v. Burke Constr. Co., 1922, 43 S.Ct. 79, 260 U.S. 226, 67 L.Ed. 226; Vestal, Repetitive Litigation, 1960, 45 Iowa L.Rev. 527; Note, Stays of Federal Proceedings in Deference to Concurrently Pending State Court Suits, 1960, 60 Col.L.Rev. 684.

72. Mottolese v. Kaufman, C.A.2d, 1949, 176 F.2d 301.

73. P. Beiersdorf & Co. v. McGohey, C.A.2d, 1951, 187 F.2d 14.

74. Kurland, Toward a Co-operative Judicial Federalism: The Federal Court Abstention Doctrine, 1960, 24 F.R.D. 481, 490–492; Notes, 1950, 59 Yale L.J. 978, 1952, 37 Minn.L.Rev. 46, 1960, 60 Col. L.Rev. 684.

beyond anything required by the demands of federalism that are at the heart of the abstention doctrine.[75]

The propriety of this type of abstention came to the Supreme Court in 1976 in Colorado River Water Conservation District v. United States.[76] In that case the Court stated the general rule that the pendency of an action in the state court is no bar to proceedings concerning the same matter in the federal court and that none of the abstention doctrines apply merely because there is a pending state action raising the same issue. But it did not make the general rule into an absolute. It concluded by saying "the circumstances permitting the dismissal of a federal suit due to the presence of a concurrent state proceeding for reasons of wise judicial administration are considerably more limited than the circumstances appropriate for abstention. The former circumstances, though exceptional, do nevertheless exist." [77] It found the case before it to be one of those exceptional cases in which a federal action should be dismissed in favor of a pending state action. Nevertheless, the factual situation in that case was so unusual, and the Court's emphasis on "the virtually unflagging obligation of the federal courts to exercise the jurisdiction given them" [78] and that only "exceptional" circumstances permit dismissals of this kind was so strong, that the case argues against, rather than for, the use of this practice in routine cases.

What had seemed the clear teaching of Colorado River, that a federal court cannot dismiss or stay a federal action in deference to a concurrent state proceeding save in "exceptional" circumstances, was muddied by the Court's decision two years later in Will v. Calvert Fire Insurance Co.[79] It was inevitable that Will would raise questions rather than answering them. The order the Supreme Court was reviewing in Will was a grant of a writ of mandamus by the Seventh Circuit to require Judge Will to proceed immediately to consider Calvert's federal antitrust action, which he had stayed in deference to a state-court contract action in which Calvert had raised the federal antitrust issues as a defense. This meant, first, that the case was complicated by questions about when mandamus may be used to review interlocutory orders of district courts.[80] Second, the federal action was one of which the federal courts have exclusive jurisdiction. There are significant questions, still unanswered, about whether any form of abstention is proper in an exclusive-jurisdiction case [81] and also about how the usual

75. Ashman, Alfini & Shapiro, Federal Abstention: New Perspectives on Its Current Vitality, 1975, 46 Miss.L.J. 629, 652; Pell, Abstention—A Primrose Path by Any Other Name, 1972, 21 DePaul L.Rev. 926, 950; Wright, The Abstention Doctrine Reconsidered, 1959, 37 Texas L.Rev. 815, 824; Comment, 1952, 19 U.Chi.L.Rev. 361.

76. 1976, 96 S.Ct. 1236, 424 U.S. 800, 47 L.Ed.2d 438.

77. 96 S.Ct. at 1246, 424 U.S. at 818. Doubt has been expressed on whether or why the Colorado River case was "excep-

tional." See Redish, note 28 above, at 251–252.

78. 96 S.Ct. at 1246, 424 U.S. at 818.

79. 1978, 98 S.Ct. 2552, 437 U.S. 655, 57 L.Ed.2d 504, on remand C.A.7th, 1978, 586 F.2d 12.

80. See § 102 below.

81. See Key v. Wise, C.A.5th, 1980, 629 F.2d 1049, and the dissent by three Justices from the denial of certiorari in that case, 102 S.Ct. 682, 454 U.S. 1103, 70 L.Ed.2d 647. See also Medema v. Medema Builders rules of issue preclusion apply if a state court has decided issues that then arise in a case exclusively for the federal courts.[82]   All of this would have been bad enough, but the case is further complicated by the fragmentation in the Court, so that the plurality opinion states a view that is expressly rejected by five of the Justices.[83]

Some matters that had been made more confusing by the Will case were clarified when the Court returned to this topic again in 1983 in Moses H. Cone Memorial Hospital v. Mercury Construction Corporation.[84]   The Hospital had sued in state court for a declaratory judgment that it owed Mercury nothing under a construction contract and that Mercury had waived its right under the contract to arbitration of the dispute by failure to make a timely demand.   Nineteen days later Mercury brought a diversity action in state court to compel arbitration under § 4 of the United States Arbitration Act.[85]   The district court ordered the federal action stayed pending resolution of the state suit, since the two actions involved the identical issues whether Mercury was entitled to arbitration.   The Fourth Circuit reversed the grant of a stay and held that arbitration should be compelled.

The Supreme Court affirmed the Fourth Circuit.   In an opinion by Justice Brennan it first held that grant of the stay was in fact an appealable order.   On the merits it held that the "exceptional circumstances" test announced in Colorado River was controlling.[86]   The Court found present in Cone none of the four factors mentioned in Colorado River as relevant in deciding whether "exceptional circumstances" are present.   There was no assumption by either court of jurisdiction over any res or property, there was no contention that the federal forum was less convenient to the parties than the state forum, and "the remaining factors—avoidance of piecemeal litigation and the order in which jurisdiction was obtained by the concurrent forums—far from supporting the stay, actually counsel against it.[87]   The Court then examined two factors that had not been discussed in Colorado River.   It noted that federal law, the Arbitration Act, provided the rule of decision on the merits and thought that "the presence of federal-law issues must always be a major

Inc., C.A.7th, 1988, 854 F.2d 210, and cases there cited; Note, Judicial Abstention and Exclusive Federal Jurisdiction: A Reconciliation, 1981, 67 Cornell L.Rev. 219.

82.   See § 100A below; 18 Wright, Miller & Cooper, Jurisdiction § 4470; Note, The Collateral Estoppel Effect of Prior State Court Findings in Cases Within Exclusive Federal Jurisdiction, 1978, 91 Harv. L.Rev. 1281.

83.   The plurality opinion by Justice Rehnquist, holding that mandamus should not have issued, spoke for only three other Justices.   Justice Blackmun joined in the result only because he thought issuance of mandamus was premature.   He believed that Judge Will should be given an opportu

nity to reconsider the stay in the light of Colorado River.   Justice Brennan dissented in an opinion joined by three other Justices.

84.   1983, 103 S.Ct. 927, 460 U.S. 1, 74 L.Ed.2d 765, noted 1985, 46 Ohio St.L.J. 435.   See generally Mullenix, A Branch Too Far: Pruning the Abstention Doctrine, 1986, 75 Geo.L.J. 99.

85.   9 U.S.C.A. § 4.

86.   103 S.Ct. at 938, 460 U.S. at 17. See also Deakins v. Monaghan, 1988, 108 S.Ct. 523, 530, 484 U.S. 193, 203, 98 L.Ed.2d 529.

87.   103 S.Ct. at 939, 460 U.S. at 19.

consideration weighing against surrender." [88] A final reason not to stay the federal action was "the probable inadequacy of the state-court proceeding to protect Mercury's rights." [89]

Finally, the Court rejected the Hospital's argument that Colorado River was not controlling because here the district court had merely stayed the federal action rather than dismissing it outright as had happened in Colorado River. The Supreme Court thought that "a stay is as much a refusal to exercise federal jurisdiction as a dismissal" and said that "the decision to invoke Colorado River necessarily contemplates that the federal court will have nothing further to do in resolving any substantive part of the case, where it stays or dismisses." [90]

Justice Brennan was always quite insistent that what was allowed in Colorado River and discussed in Cone is something other than abstention.[91] Most lower courts, and even some of Justice Brennan's colleagues, use the name "abstention" for the procedure there involved.[92] By whatever name it is called the lower courts must struggle as best they can with the six factors announced in Colorado River and in Cone.[93] After Cone there will be rare cases in which "exceptional circumstances" will exist justifying stay or dismissal because of a concurrent state proceeding, but in most cases neither stay nor dismissal will be proper and the federal court will be obliged to exercise its jurisdiction." [94]

§ 52A. "Our Federalism" [1]

There is no more controversial doctrine in the federal courts today than the doctrine of "Our Federalism," which teaches that federal courts

88. 103 S.Ct. at 942, 460 U.S. at 26.

89. 103 S.Ct. at 942, 460 U.S. at 26. This came about because it is clear that state courts, as much as federal courts, are obliged to grant stays of litigation under § 3 of the Arbitration Act, but it was not clear whether state courts are required to compel arbitration under § 4. This meant that there was substantial room for doubt that Mercury could obtain from the state court an order compelling the Hospital to arbitrate.

90. 103 S.Ct. at 943, 460 U.S. at 28.

91. Colorado River, 96 S.Ct. at 1246, 424 U.S. at 817; Cone, 103 S.Ct. at 936, 460 U.S. at 14–15.

92. See 17A Wright, Miller & Cooper, Jurisdiction 2d § 4247, pp. 150–151.

93. The factors are clearly listed and comprehensively discussed in Mullenix, note 84 above, but she does not find the list of factors helpful. She says it "amounts to little more than a laundry list" and that "[v]irtually no meaning, analysis, or content is given to these factors * * *." 75 Geo.L.J. at 119.

94. Cases both ways are cited in 17A Wright, Miller & Cooper, Jurisdiction 2d § 4247 nn. 81, 82.

§ 52A

1. 17A Wright, Miller & Cooper, Jurisdiction 2d §§ 5251–5255. The literature is immense, and tends to become quickly dated as new cases reshape the doctrine. It is cited in 17A id. § 4251 nn. 16, 39, and § 4252 n. 1. The following general discussions are current and helpful: Marcus, Wanted a Federal Standard for Evaluating the Adequate State Forum, 1991, 50 Md. L.Rev. 131; Baker, "Our Federalism" in Pennzoil Co. v. Texaco, Inc. or How the Younger Doctrine Keeps Getting Older Not Better, 1990, 9 Rev.Lit. 303; Brown, When Federalism and Separation of Powers Collide—Rethinking Younger Abstention, 1990, 59 Geo.Wash.L.Rev. 114; Dennis, The Illegitimate Foundations of the Younger Abstention Doctrine, 1990, 10 Bridgeport L.Rev. 311; Lee & Wilkins, An Analysis of Supplemental Jurisdiction and Abstention with Recommendations for Legislative Action, 1990 B.Y.U.L.Rev. 321; Stravitz, Younger Abstention Reaches a Civil Maturity: Pennzoil Co. v. Texaco, Inc., 1989, 57 must refrain from hearing constitutional challenges to state action under certain circumstances in which federal action is regarded as an improper intrusion on the right of a state to enforce its laws in its own courts. The doctrine is identified with the 1971 decision in Younger v. Harris,[2] though the Supreme Court has spoken a number of times since, and doubtless will have to speak often again, to resolve questions left open by Younger and its companion cases. The doctrine seems to be a special application of the abstention doctrines[3] but it has taken on such a robust life of its own that it is here discussed in a separate section.

The Younger case can only be understood against the background of the 1965 decision in Dombrowski v. Pfister.[4] The holding in Dombrowski was simple enough. Plaintiffs were held entitled to an injunction to prevent state officers from prosecuting them or threatening to prosecute them under a state statute that was so broad and vague that it interfered unconstitutionally with First Amendment rights. The holding seemed surprising, because to obtain this injunction plaintiffs had to overcome three hurdles: the Anti–Injunction Act; the notion that equity will not interfere with enforcement of the criminal law; and the abstention doctrines. But when each of these was examined individually, the holding that it did not bar injunctive relief could be made to fit comfortably within prior learning.

At the time of Dombrowski it was still unsettled whether civil-rights actions came within an exception to the Anti–Injunction Act, 28 U.S.C.A. § 2283, and indeed it was not until 1972 that it was held that they do.[5] But the settled rule has long been that the statute applies only to injunctions against pending proceedings and does not bar an injunction against the initiation of state proceedings in the future. On the facts of Dombrowski this rule was enough to avoid any problems with § 2283.[6]

It was necessary next to consider the practice, stemming from comity and the federal framework, that a federal equity court should not interfere with a state's good-faith administration of its criminal laws.

Fordham L.Rev. 997; Vairo, Making Younger Civil: The Consequences of Federal Court Deference to State Court Proceedings: A Response to Professor Stravitz, 1989, 58 Fordham L.Rev. 173; Edwards, The Changing Notion of "Our Federalism," 33 Wayne L.Rev. 1015 (1987); Zeigler, Federal Court Reform of State Criminal Justice Systems: A Reassessment of the Younger Doctrine from a Modern Perspective, 1985, 19 U.C.Davis L.Rev. 31; Note, Younger Abstention Doctrine: A Morass of Confusion, 1991 B.Y.U.L.Rev. 1445; Note, Slogan or Substance? Understanding "Our Federalism" and Younger Abstention, 1988, 73 Cornell L.Rev. 852.

2. 1971, 91 S.Ct. 746, 401 U.S. 37, 27 L.Ed.2d 669.

3. It has repeatedly been so characterized by the Supreme Court, most recently in Ankenbrandt v. Richards, 1992, 112 S.Ct.

2206, 2215, ___ U.S. ___, ___, 119 L.Ed.2d 468. But see Hart & Wechsler, The Federal Courts and the Federal System, Bator, Mishkin, Shapiro & Wechsler, 2d ed. 1973, p. 1043 n. 1. The question whether it is right to characterize this as abstention is not repeated in the 1988 Third Edition.

4. 1965, 85 S.Ct. 1116, 380 U.S. 479, 14 L.Ed.2d 22. There is a brilliant—and fascinating—discussion of the case and its aftermath in Fiss, Dombrowski, 1977, 86 Yale L.J. 1103.

5. Mitchum v. Foster, 1972, 92 S.Ct. 2151, 407 U.S. 225, 32 L.Ed.2d 705. See § 47 above.

6. 85 S.Ct. at 1119 n. 2, 380 U.S. at 484, n. 2. But see Fiss, note 4 above, at 1109–1111.

This practice has origins also in the traditional requirements for equitable relief. Even if a state statute is unconstitutional, a person charged under it normally has an adequate remedy at law by raising the constitutional defense in the state proceeding. Although this practice had frequently been followed in the federal courts,[7] it had never been stated as an absolute and both the statements of the practice and decisions under it had recognized that it could be departed from if necessary to prevent irreparable injury. In Dombrowski the Court thought that "the chilling effect upon the exercise of First Amendment rights may derive from the fact of the prosecution, unaffected by the prospect of its success or failure,"[8] and it found sufficient irreparable injury to justify equitable relief in the substantial loss or impairment of freedoms of expression that would occur if it were necessary to await disposition of the criminal actions in the state courts.[9]

Finally, the Court held that the lower court had been in error in abstaining to await authoritative interpretation of the state statutes by the state court. It found the abstention doctrine inappropriate for cases where "statutes are justifiably attacked on their face as abridging free expression, or as applied for the purpose of discouraging protected activities."[10] Again it said that "abstention serves no legitimate purpose where a statute regulating speech is properly attacked on its face, and where, as here, the conduct charged in the indictments is not within the reach of an acceptable limiting construction readily to be anticipated as the result of a single criminal prosecution and is not the sort of 'hardcore' conduct that would obviously be prohibited under any construction."[11] The formulations were new but the result was not. It had been well established that abstention is improper if the state statute is unconstitutional regardless of the construction the state court might give it.[12] The Court found this to be true in Dombrowski.

Between Dombrowski, in 1965, and Younger, in 1971, there was not much of significance from the Supreme Court on this subject. Indeed the little the Court did suggested a rather modest view of the Dombrowski holding.[13] Many litigants, however, thought that they discerned in

---

7. The leading case was Douglas v. City of Jeannette, 1943, 63 S.Ct. 877, 319 U.S. 157, 87 L.Ed. 1324.

It has been argued, however, that in Dombrowski the Court overlooked many cases showing that injunctions against threatened prosecutions had issued routinely. Laycock, Federal Interference with State Prosecutions: The Cases Dombrowski Forgot, 1979, 46 U.Chi.L.Rev. 636. See also Dennis, note 1 above.

8. 85 S.Ct. at 1121, 380 U.S. at 487.

9. 85 S.Ct. at 1120–1122, 380 U.S. at 485–489.

10. 85 S.Ct. at 1122, 380 U.S. at 489–490.

11. 85 S.Ct. at 1123–1124, 380 U.S. at 491–492.

12. See § 52 n. 11 above.

13. In Cameron v. Johnson, 1968, 88 S.Ct. 1335, 390 U.S. 611, 20 L.Ed.2d 182, the district court entered a declaratory judgment that a state statute was valid on its face and, finding no bad faith in enforcement of the statute, refused injunctive relief. The Court, with two justices dissenting, affirmed both aspects of the decision below. In four other cases the Court, without opinion, summarily affirmed lower-court decisions that had refused relief under Dombrowski.

In Zwickler v. Koota, 1967, 88 S.Ct. 391, 389 U.S. 241, 19 L.Ed.2d 444, the Court

Dombrowski a major change in federal-state relations. They read Dombrowski as meaning that every person prosecuted under state law for conduct arguably protected by the First Amendment could, by murmuring the words "chilling effect," halt the state prosecution while a federal court, ordinarily of three judges, passed on the validity of the statute and the bona fides of the state law-enforcement officers. Lower-court cases in which litigants attempted to claim the benefit of what they understood to be the Dombrowski doctrine numbered in the hundreds and went in every possible direction.[14]

Those who had read a great deal into Dombrowski had their hopes dashed, and the Dombrowski decision itself was sharply limited, on February 23, 1971, when the Court announced its decisions in Younger v. Harris[15] and five other cases, of which the most significant are Samuels v. Mackell,[16] Perez v. Ledesma,[17] and Boyle v. Landry.[18] Five of the justices, speaking in every instance through Justice Black, announced a major retreat from Dombrowski. Three other justices, speaking through Justice Brennan, agreed in part with Justice Black. Justice Douglas opposed the retreat though he agreed with the result in one of the cases.

The Court in the Younger cases continued to leave open whether 28 U.S.C.A. § 2283 applied to civil-rights actions.[19] Instead it held that relief was barred in all of these cases because of "the fundamental policy against federal intervention with state criminal proceedings"[20] and "the absence of the factors necessary under equitable principles to justify federal intervention."[21] The Court gave the name, "Our Federalism," to the concept of comity that was at the heart of its decisions. "Our Federalism," Justice Black wrote, represents "a system in which there is

---

held that the rule against an injunction interfering with a state's enforcement of its criminal laws did not apply to a request for a declaratory judgment and that it was error for a lower court to abstain in a case challenging the constitutionality of a state statute prohibiting anonymous election literature. On remand the district court entered a declaratory judgment but on a second appeal the Supreme Court vacated this on the ground that there was no longer an actual controversy in the circumstances of the particular case. Golden v. Zwickler, 1969, 89 S.Ct. 956, 394 U.S. 103, 22 L.Ed.2d 113.

14. The state of the decisions at that point is carefully examined in Maraist, Federal Injunctive Relief Against State Court Proceedings: The Significance of Dombrowski, 1970, 48 Texas L.Rev. 535.

15. 1971, 91 S.Ct. 746, 401 U.S. 37, 27 L.Ed.2d 669.

16. 1971, 91 S.Ct. 764, 401 U.S. 66, 27 L.Ed.2d 688.

17. 1971, 91 S.Ct. 674, 401 U.S. 82, 27 L.Ed.2d 701.

The majority opinion in Perez adds little to the other cases decided that day, but Justice Brennan chose a separate opinion in that case as the vehicle for the major expression of his approach to the cases, a view shared by Justices White and Marshall.

18. 1971, 91 S.Ct. 758, 401 U.S. 77, 27 L.Ed.2d 696.

The other two cases of the Younger sextet were Dyson v. Stein, 1971, 91 S.Ct. 769, 401 U.S. 200, 27 L.Ed.2d 781, and Byrne v. Karalexis, 1971, 91 S.Ct. 777, 401 U.S. 216, 27 L.Ed.2d 792.

19. See note 5 above.

20. Younger, 91 S.Ct. at 751, 401 U.S. at 46.

21. Younger, 91 S.Ct. at 755, 401 U.S. at 54.

sensitivity to the legitimate interests of both State and National Governments, and in which the National Government, anxious though it may be to vindicate and protect federal rights and federal interests, always endeavors to do so in ways that will not unduly interfere with the legitimate activities of the States." [22]

The bare holding of the cases is that "a federal court should not enjoin a state criminal prosecution begun prior to the institution of the federal suit except in very unusual situations, where necessary to prevent immediate irreparable injury." [23] There is ordinarily no irreparable injury if the threat to plaintiff's federally protected rights can be eliminated by the defense of a single criminal prosecution, and "even irreparable injury is insufficient unless it is 'both great and immediate.' " [24] In a major change from what had been said in Dombrowski, the Court said that the possibility of a "chilling effect" on First Amendment freedoms does not by itself justify federal intervention. [25] Nor are federal courts to test the constitutionality of a state statute "on its face" and then enjoin all action to enforce the statute until the state can obtain court approval for a modified version. [26] A federal injunction can run against a pending state criminal prosecution only on a "showing of bad faith, harassment, or any other unusual circumstance that would call for equitable relief." [27]

Several other important propositions were announced in that group of decisions. If injunctive relief against a pending state prosecution is barred because there is no showing of irreparable injury, declaratory relief should ordinarily be denied as well and the action should be dismissed without any consideration of the constitutionality of the state statute in question. [28] In addition, the Court tightened the rules on standing to challenge the constitutionality of state statutes. Persons who claim to be inhibited by a statute but who have not been indicted, arrested, or even threatened by the prosecutor lack standing since "persons having no fears of state prosecution except those that are imaginary or speculative, are not to be accepted as appropriate in such

---

22. Younger, 91 S.Ct. at 750–751, 401 U.S. at 44. See also Koury, Section 1983 and Civil Comity: Two for the Federalism Seesaw, 1979, 25 Loy.L.Rev. 659, 709.

23. Samuels, 91 S.Ct. at 766, 401 U.S. at 69.

24. Younger, 91 S.Ct. at 751, 401 U.S. at 46. The internal quotation is from Fenner v. Boykin, 1926, 46 S.Ct. 492, 493, 271 U.S. 240, 243, 70 L.Ed. 927, a precedent on which the Court relied heavily in Younger.

25. Younger, 91 S.Ct. at 753–754, 401 U.S. at 50–52.

26. Younger, 91 S.Ct. at 754–755, 401 U.S. at 52–54.

27. Younger, 91 S.Ct. at 755, 401 U.S. at 54.

In Kugler v. Helfant, 1975, 95 S.Ct. 1524, 1531 n. 4, 421 U.S. 117, 125 n. 4, 44 L.Ed.2d 15, the Court agreed that the scope of the exception for other extraordinary circumstances "has been left largely undefined * * *." It pointed to Gibson v. Berryhill, 1973, 93 S.Ct. 1689, 411 U.S. 564, 36 L.Ed.2d 488, as a case that might be explained on that ground.

28. Samuels, 91 S.Ct. at 768, 401 U.S. at 73–74.

The holding in Samuels is inconsistent with Cameron v. Johnson, 1968, 88 S.Ct. 1335, 390 U.S. 611, 20 L.Ed.2d 182, discussed in note 13 above. Cameron is not mentioned by the Court in Samuels.

cases."[29]   Finally, the Court reiterated the rule that a federal injunction is not to be used to test the validity of an arrest or the admissibility of evidence in a state criminal proceeding.[30]

In Younger the opinion of the Court purported to express no view about the circumstances under which federal courts may act if there is no state prosecution pending when the federal action is begun.[31]   Nevertheless the principal precedent on which the Court relied held that an injunction should not have issued at the instance of one who had been threatened with criminal prosecution but who had not yet been arrested or otherwise formally charged.[32]   The Court also referred approvingly to other cases "involving threatened prosecutions."[33]

The question that this seemed to leave open was largely resolved in 1974 in Steffel v. Thompson.[34]   Justice Brennan, writing for the Court in Steffel, relied heavily on his separate opinion in Perez v. Ledesma for the proposition that declaratory relief is quite different from injunctive relief.   Thus, "regardless of whether injunctive relief may be appropriate, federal declaratory relief is not precluded when no state prosecution is pending and a federal plaintiff demonstrates a genuine threat of enforcement of a disputed state criminal statute, whether an attack is made on the constitutionality of the statute on its face or as applied."[35]

The Court was unanimous in Steffel,[36] and the result seems unavoidable.   A person against whom state criminal charges are pending may vindicate his or her rights, if they exist, through the defense of a single criminal action, but the person against whom no charges are pending would have no remedy, except that provided by Steffel, to vindicate the constitutionality of the conduct in which he or she wishes to engage.   Thus, Steffel stands for "the sensible proposition that both a potential state defendant, threatened with prosecution but not charged, and the State itself, confronted by a possible violation of its criminal laws, may benefit from a procedure which provides for a declaration of rights without activation of the criminal process."[37]

Steffel laid heavy emphasis on the distinction between a declaratory judgment and an injunction, and purported not to decide whether an

---

29.   Younger, 91 S.Ct. at 749, 401 U.S. at 42.   See also Boyle, 91 S.Ct. at 760, 401 U.S. at 80–81.

30.   Perez, 91 S.Ct. at 676–677, 401 U.S. at 83–85.

This was followed in Kugler v. Helfant, 1975, 95 S.Ct. 1524, 1533–1534, 421 U.S. 117, 128–131, 44 L.Ed.2d 15.

31.   Younger, 91 S.Ct. at 749, 401 U.S. at 41.   See also the concurring opinion of Justices Stewart and Harlan, 91 S.Ct. at 757, 401 U.S. at 54–55.

32.   Fenner v. Boykin, 1926, 46 S.Ct. 492, 271 U.S. 240, 70 L.Ed. 927, discussed in Younger, 91 S.Ct. at 751, 401 U.S. at 45–46.

33.   Younger, 91 S.Ct. at 751, 401 U.S. at 45.   But see Laycock, note 7 above.

34.   1974, 94 S.Ct. 1209, 415 U.S. 452, 39 L.Ed.2d 505.

35.   94 S.Ct. at 1223–1224, 415 U.S. at 475.

36.   Concurring opinions by Justice White and by Justice Rehnquist, joined by Chief Justice Burger, do differ on the effect state officials must give to a declaration of unconstitutionality.   94 S.Ct. at 1224, 1225, 415 U.S. at 476, 478.

37.   94 S.Ct. at 1228, 415 U.S. at 484 (Rehnquist, J., concurring).

injunction could issue, without satisfying the Younger tests, if no state action is pending.[38] The following year, however, the Court held that in a case within the Steffel principle, in which no state action is pending, a preliminary injunction can issue, without satisfying the Younger tests, to preserve the status quo while the court considers whether to grant declaratory relief.[39] In a still later case the Court held that a permanent injunction could be given, as well as declaratory relief, if there is no pending prosecution and there is a clear showing that an injunction is necessary to afford adequate protection of constitutional rights.[40]

Thus, whether a state action is pending is critical to the application of Younger. If a state criminal action is pending when the federal action is commenced, the federal court cannot give either injunctive or declaratory relief and must dismiss the action [41] except in the rare case in which the Younger standard of bad faith, harassment, or other extraordinary circumstance is satisfied.[42] But if the state action, though threatened, is not yet pending, the federal court can consider the request for the declaration without regard to the Younger restrictions and can also give at least preliminary injunctive relief if the usual equitable tests for that kind of relief are satisfied.[43]

Although the rules stated in the preceding paragraph continue to be valid, the cosmology of "Our Federalism" seems to require continuous refining,[44] and the application of those rules was significantly altered by

---

38. 94 S.Ct. at 1217–1218, 415 U.S. at 463.

39. Doran v. Salem Inn, Inc., 1975, 95 S.Ct. 2561, 2567–2568, 422 U.S. 922, 930–931, 45 L.Ed.2d 648.

40. Wooley v. Maynard, 1977, 97 S.Ct. 1428, 1434, 430 U.S. 705, 712, 51 L.Ed.2d 752. There is an interesting analysis of the Wooley case from "a post-Newtonian perspective" in Tribe, The Curvature of Constitutional Space: What Lawyers Can Learn from Modern Physics, 1989, 103 Harv.L.Rev. 1, 20–23.

Compare Fiss, note 4 above, at 1143–1148 with Redish, Federal Jurisdiction: Tension in the Allocation of Judicial Power, 1980, pp. 311–314. See cases cited 17A Wright, Miller & Cooper, Jurisdiction 2d § 4253 n. 21.

41. "Younger v. Harris contemplates the outright dismissal of the federal suit, and the presentation of all claims, both state and federal, to the state courts." Gibson v. Berryhill, 1973, 93 S.Ct. 1689, 1697, 411 U.S. 564, 577, 36 L.Ed.2d 488.

42. A rare instance in which the Court has found that the Younger standard was satisfied is Gibson v. Berryhill, 1973, 93 S.Ct. 1689, 1697, 411 U.S. 564, 577, 36 L.Ed.2d 488, where the state tribunal was found incompetent by reason of bias to adjudicate the issues. See note 27 above. See also Wall v. American Optometric Assn., Inc., D.C.Ga.1974, 379 F.Supp. 175, 185, affirmed without opinion 1974, 95 S.Ct. 166, 419 U.S. 888, 42 L.Ed.2d 134.

On the exceptions to Younger generally, which are almost never found applicable, see 17A Wright, Miller & Cooper, Jurisdiction 2d § 4255; Collins, The Right to Avoid Trial: Justifying Federal Court Intervention into Ongoing State Court Proceedings, 1987, 66 N.C.L.Rev. 49.

43. The threat must be a real, rather than a speculative, one or plaintiffs will be held to lack standing, see note 29 above, and there will not be the actual controversy required by the Declaratory Judgment Act. See Steffel, 94 S.Ct. at 1215–1216, 415 U.S. at 458–460. See also City of Houston v. Hill, 1987, 107 S.Ct. 2502, 2508 n. 7, 482 U.S. 451, 459 n. 7, 96 L.Ed.2d 398; and cases cited 17A Wright, Miller & Cooper, Jurisdiction 2d § 4253 n. 24.

44. "[A]s our cases abundantly illustrate, this area of law is in constant litigation, and it is an area through which our decisions have traced a path that may accurately be described as sinuous." Steffel, 94 S.Ct. at 1225, 415 U.S. at 479 (Rehnquist, J., concurring).

two decisions in 1975. In Hicks v. Miranda [45] a theater owner sued in federal court for declaratory and injunctive relief against a state obscenity statute. At the time the federal action was brought, state criminal charges were pending against two of the theater's employees and copies of a film had been seized. The district court denied a temporary restraining order and requested convening of a three-judge court. One day after service of the federal complaint was completed the state criminal charges were amended to include the theater owner as a defendant.

On these facts it was held, over the vigorous dissent of four justices, that the three-judge court erred in granting relief because the Younger tests had not been met and a state criminal proceeding was pending. Even though the theater owner was not a party to the state proceedings at the time the federal action was brought, his interest and that of his employees was intertwined and the relief sought in federal court would have interfered with the pending state prosecution.[46]

But as a second, and more significant, ground for decision the Court held that "where state criminal proceedings are begun against the federal plaintiffs after the federal complaint is filed but before any proceedings of substance on the merits have taken place in the federal court, the principles of Younger v. Harris should apply in full force." [47] Thus, the dividing line between Younger and Steffel continues to turn on the pendency of a state proceeding, but the commencement of the federal action is not the controlling date in determining whether a state action is pending. Instead the federal court is to make that determination when it is ready to commence "proceedings of substance on the merits." [48]

In the other case, Doran v. Salem Inn, Inc.,[49] decided six days after Hicks, three bar owners brought a federal action asking for a preliminary injunction and declaratory relief against a newly enacted ordinance regulating the clothing of their waitresses and entertainers. Two of the bars complied with the ordinance until they were granted a preliminary injunction nearly a month later but the third bar disobeyed the ordinance and criminal proceedings were begun against it by the state one day after the federal action was filed. The Court held that while there may be circumstances in which legally distinct parties are so closely related that they should all be subject to the Younger considerations that govern any one of them, the case before it, where the bars were unrelated in terms of ownership and management, was not such a case.[50]

45. 1975, 95 S.Ct. 2281, 422 U.S. 332, 45 L.Ed.2d 223.

46. See cases cited 17A Wright, Miller & Cooper, Jurisdiction 2d § 4252 n. 22.

47. 95 S.Ct. at 2292, 422 U.S. at 349.

48. The majority did not define the quoted phrase and the dissenters found its meaning "a good deal less than apparent." 95 S.Ct. at 2294 n. 1, 422 U.S. at 353 n. 1.

49. 1975, 95 S.Ct. 2561, 422 U.S. 922, 45 L.Ed.2d 648.

50. See also U.S. v. Composite State Bd. of Medical Examiners, C.A.5th, 1981, 656 F.2d 131; New Jersey–Philadelphia Presbytery v. New Jersey State Bd. of Higher Educ., C.A.3d, 1981, 654 F.2d 868; Bickham v. Lashof, C.A.7th, 1980, 620 F.2d 1238.

Since there were never any criminal proceedings against the bars that had complied with the law, the grant of a preliminary injunction in their favor until final determination of their request for a declaration was upheld. This relief was denied, however, to the bar that had violated the ordinance. The federal litigation was "in an embryonic stage and no contested matter had been decided"[51] when criminal summonses were issued against it, and its case was covered by the Younger rule.

The Court continues to use the Hicks formulation of "proceedings of substance on the merits,"[52] though there is still much uncertainty on what the phrase means.[53] Hicks certainly means that the dividing line between Younger and Steffel is no longer drawn in terms of whether a state action was pending on the day the federal action was begun. It is true, as the dissenters in Hicks feared, that in many cases the state may be able to abort a federal action by commencing state-court proceedings immediately after the federal action is filed. But this will not always be the case. As Doran shows, one who has not yet broken the law may commence a federal action and obtain a preliminary injunction so that he or she will not be subject to prosecution for violating the law while the attack on its constitutionality is being determined.

A related question also came before the Court in 1975 in Huffman v. Pursue, Ltd.[54] The state brought an action in state court under a statute providing that a place that exhibits obscene films is a nuisance and can be ordered closed for a year. Judgment was granted for the state. The theater did not appeal the state judgment but brought a federal action against the state authorities to enjoin enforcement of the state court's judgment insofar as it barred the theater from showing films that had not been adjudged obscene. The theater sought to avoid application of Younger by arguing that there was no pending state proceeding since the action in the state trial court had gone to judgment and no appeal was taken. This argument was rejected by the Court, which found that posttrial federal intervention would be if anything more offensive than intervention at an earlier stage. For this reason it held that Younger standards must be met to justify federal intervention in a state judicial proceeding as to which a losing litigant has not exhausted its state appellate remedies.[55]

This aspect of Huffman was distinguished two years later in Wooley

51. 95 S.Ct. at 2566, 422 U.S. at 927. The Court made no reference to the Hicks case, six days earlier, in which it had spoken of "proceedings of substance on the merits."

52. See Hawaii Housing Authority v. Midkiff, 1984, 104 S.Ct. 2321, 2328, 467 U.S. 229, 238, 81 L.Ed.2d 186, where the Court conflates the tests announced in Hicks and in Doran. In holding that the actions in the federal court in the case before it were "proceedings of substance on the merits," the Court said that the case had "proceeded well beyond the 'embryonic stage'."

53. See 17A Wright, Miller & Cooper, Jurisdiction 2d § 4253, pp. 225–230. In the Hawaii Housing Authority case, note 52 above, grant of a preliminary injunction was held to satisfy the test.

54. 1975, 95 S.Ct. 1200, 420 U.S. 592, 43 L.Ed.2d 482.

55. 95 S.Ct. at 1211, 420 U.S. at 610.

v. Maynard.[56] Maynard had been convicted three times of violating a state statute by covering up the state motto, "Live Free or Die," on the license plate of his car. He did not appeal those convictions, but subsequently brought a federal action to enjoin future prosecutions for violating that statute. The Court found Huffman inapposite, since in Huffman the theater was seeking to prevent enforcement of the state court judgment, while Maynard was not seeking to have the record of his convictions expunged nor to annul any collateral effects those convictions might have, but instead was seeking purely prospective relief to preclude further prosecution under the statute.[57]

In Huffman the Court also spoke to another major question that had been left open in Younger and its companion cases. Those cases had all concerned interference with state criminal proceedings and shed no light on how far, if at all, "Our Federalism" restricts a federal court from interfering with civil actions in state courts in which the state, or its officer or agency, is seeking to enforce state laws. The nuisance action the state had brought against the theater was a civil action. The Court found that it "need make no general pronouncements upon the applicability of Younger to all civil litigation," [58] since the state was a party to the nuisance action, it was brought in aid of and closely related to criminal statutes on obscenity, and thus the Court was dealing with "a state proceeding which in important respects is more akin to a criminal prosecution than are most civil cases." [59] Later cases broadened the rule announced in Huffman so that the Court could say that the Younger rules "are fully applicable to noncriminal judicial proceedings when important state interests are involved." [60]

Two other cases shed additional light on the application of the Younger rules in noncriminal matters. Ohio Civil Rights Commission v.

---

56. 1977, 97 S.Ct. 1428, 430 U.S. 705, 51 L.Ed.2d 752.

57. 97 S.Ct. at 1433, 430 U.S. at 710–711. See Fiss, note 4 above, at 1142, and Laycock, Federal Interference with State Prosecutions: The Need for Prospective Relief, 1977 Sup.Ct.Rev. 193, 213–214.

Wooley was held inapplicable, and Younger and Huffman barred relief, in Schall v. Joyce, C.A.3d, 1989, 885 F.2d 101, 111, and Ballard v. Wilson, C.A.5th, 1988, 856 F.2d 1568, 1570.

If Maynard had raised his constitutional objection unsuccessfully in the state-court proceeding, he would be barred from a later federal action. Allen v. McCurry, 1980, 101 S.Ct. 411, 449 U.S. 90, 66 L.Ed.2d 308. See § 100A. The lower court in the Maynard case held that he was not barred since issue preclusion applies only to an issue actually litigated and at that time the lower court thought that claim preclusion did not apply to civil-rights actions under 42 U.S.C.A. § 1983. Maynard v. Wooley, D.C.N.H.

1976, 406 F.Supp. 1381, 1385 n. 6, affirmed 1977, 97 S.Ct. 1428, 430 U.S. 705, 51 L.Ed.2d 752.

58. 95 S.Ct. at 1209, 420 U.S. at 605.

59. 95 S.Ct. at 1208, 420 U.S. at 603.

60. Middlesex County Ethics Committee v. Garden State Bar Assn., 1982, 102 S.Ct. 2515, 2521, 457 U.S. 423, 432, 73 L.Ed.2d 116 (disciplinary proceeding against an attorney). See also Moore v. Sims, 1979, 99 S.Ct. 2371, 442 U.S. 415, 60 L.Ed.2d 994 (child custody proceeding); Trainor v. Hernandez, 1977, 97 S.Ct. 1911, 431 U.S. 434, 52 L.Ed.2d 486, on remand D.C.Ill., 1978, 471 F.Supp. 516 (civil action by state to recover welfare payments wrongfully received); Juidice v. Vail, 1977, 97 S.Ct. 1211, 430 U.S. 327, 51 L.Ed.2d 376 (contempt proceeding for failure to obey court order in a private civil action).

See generally 17A Wright, Miller & Cooper, Jurisdiction 2d § 4254.

Dayton Christian Schools, Inc.,[61] held that the Younger rules apply "to state administrative proceedings in which important state interests are vindicated, so long as in the course of these proceedings the federal plaintiff would have a full and fair opportunity to litigate the federal constitutional claim." [62] In Pennzoil Co. v. Texaco, Inc.,[63] the Court shed additional light on what state interests are "important" enough to invoke Younger [64] and it held for the first time that there can be a sufficiently important state interest even though the state proceeding is entirely between two private parties.[65]

Although the exceptions to Younger that Justice Black discussed in that case have been found to be largely illusory,[66] there is one exception, probably implicit in Younger but not discussed there in terms, that is now well recognized. Federal intervention is proper if the federal claim is one that cannot be raised in the state action.[67]

Finally the Court has not limited considerations of "Our Federalism" to cases in which an injunction is being sought against the judicial branch of the state government. That concept must also be taken into account when relief is sought against those in charge of an executive branch of an agency of state or local government. Because of these considerations it was held error for a lower court to issue an injunction that sharply limited a police department's latitude in the dispatch of its internal affairs in an effort to provide prophylactic procedures to minimize misconduct by a handful of state employees.[68]

61. 1986, 106 S.Ct. 2718, 477 U.S. 619, 91 L.Ed.2d 512. The case is sharply criticized in Edwards, note 1 above, at 1028–1029.

62. 106 S.Ct. at 2723, 477 U.S. at 627. That case hinted that this is true only if the administrative proceedings are "judicial in nature." This is declared to be the law in New Orleans Public Service, Inc. v. Council of City of New Orleans, 1989, 109 S.Ct. 2506, 2517–2520, 491 U.S. 350, 366–373, 105 L.Ed.2d 298.

63. 1987, 107 S.Ct. 1519, 481 U.S. 1, 95 L.Ed.2d 1. See the articles by Baker, Stravitz, Vairo, and Edwards, all note 1 above. See also Gibson, Private Concurrent Litigation in Light of Younger, Pennzoil, and Colorado River, 1989, 14 Okla.City U.L.Rev. 185; Althouse, The Misguided Search for State Interest in Abstention Cases: Observations on the Occasion of Pennzoil v. Texas, 1988, 63 N.Y.U.L.Rev. 1051.

64. The Court found sufficient "the State's interest in protecting 'the authority of the judicial system, so that its orders and judgments are not rendered nugatory.'" 107 S.Ct. at 1527 n. 12, 481 U.S. at 14 n. 12. The internal quotation is from Juidice v. Vail, note 60 above, 97 S.Ct. at 1217 n. 12, 430 U.S. at 336 n. 12.

65. The winning counsel in the Pennzoil case has said that as a result of that decision Younger "applies to any case where pending state judicial proceedings are structurally capable of resolving the problem." Constitutional Law Conference, 1987, 56 U.S.L.W. 2233, quoting Professor Laurence H. Tribe.

66. See note 42 above.

67. Gerstein v. Pugh, 1975, 95 S.Ct. 854, 420 U.S. 103, 43 L.Ed.2d 54. See also Trainor v. Hernandez, 1977, 97 S.Ct. 1911, 431 U.S. 434, 52 L.Ed.2d 486, on remand D.C.Ill.1978, 471 F.Supp. 516, and its aftermath, Quern v. Hernandez, 1979, 99 S.Ct. 1488, 440 U.S. 951, 59 L.Ed.2d 765, noted 1979, 28 De Paul L.Rev. 901.

This principle is recognized, but found inapplicable, in Pennzoil Co. v. Texaco, Inc., 1987, 107 S.Ct. 1519, 1527–1529, 481 U.S. 1, 14–16, 95 L.Ed.2d 1, Middlesex County Ethics Committee v. Garden State Bar Assn., 1982, 102 S.Ct. 2515, 457 U.S. 423, 73 L.Ed.2d 116, and in Moore v. Sims, 1979, 99 S.Ct. 2371, 442 U.S. 415, 60 L.Ed.2d 994.

68. Rizzo v. Goode, 1976, 96 S.Ct. 598, 423 U.S. 362, 46 L.Ed.2d 561. See also City of Los Angeles v. Lyons, 1983, 103 S.Ct. 1660, 461 U.S. 95, 75 L.Ed.2d 675.

The Younger rules also apply to bar interference in pending military court-martial

In Younger Justice Black wrote that "this slogan, 'Our Federalism,' born in the early struggling days of our Union of States, occupies a highly important place in our Nation's history and its future." [69]   The multitude of decisions in the years since he wrote confirms his prediction about the future but demonstrates also the difficulty in turning a slogan into workable and understandable legal rules.

§ 53. Habeas Corpus [1]

The writ of habeas corpus, by which the legal authority under which a person may be detained can be challenged, is of immemorial antiquity.[2] After a checkered career in which it was involved in the struggles between the common-law courts and the Courts of Chancery and the Star Chamber, as well as in the conflicts between Parliament and the crown, the protection of the writ was firmly written into English law by the Habeas Corpus Act of 1679.[3]   Today it is said to be "perhaps the most important writ known to the constitutional law of England * * *."[4]

Its significance in the United States has been no less great.   Article I, § 9, of the Constitution gives assurance that the privilege of the writ of habeas corpus shall not be suspended, unless when in cases of rebellion or invasion the public safety may require it,[5] and its use by the

---

proceedings. Schlesinger v. Councilman, 1975, 95 S.Ct. 1300, 1313, 420 U.S. 738, 758, 43 L.Ed.2d 591.

69. Younger, 91 S.Ct. at 751, 401 U.S. at 44–45.

§ 53

1. 17A Wright, Miller & Cooper, Jurisdiction 2d §§ 4261–4268.5; Hughes, The Decline of Habeas Corpus, 1990; Duker, A Constitutional History of Habeas Corpus, 1980; Lay, The Writ of Habeas Corpus: A Complex Procedure for a Simple Process, 1993, 77 Minn.L.Rev. 1015; Steiker, Innocence and Federal Habeas, 1993, 41 UCLA L.Rev. 303; Sullivan, A Practical Guide to Recent Developments in Federal Habeas Corpus for Practicing Attorneys, 1993, 25 Ariz.St.L.Rev. 317; Woolhandler, Demodeling Habeas, 1993, 45 Stan.L.Rev. 575; Yackle, The Habeas Hagioscope, 1993, 66 S.Cal.L.Rev. 2331; Patchel, The New Habeas, 1991, 42 Hastings L.J. 939; Hoffman, The Supreme Court's New Vision of Federal Habeas Corpus for State Prisoners, 1989 Sup.Ct.Rev. 165; Wechsler, Habeas Corpus and the Supreme Court: Reconsidering the Reach of the Great Writ, 1988, 59 U.Colo. L.Rev. 167; Friedman, A Tale of Two Habeas, 1988, 73 Minn.L.Rev. 247; Robbins, Whither (or Wither) Habeas Corpus?: Observations on the Supreme Court's 1985 Term, 1986, 111 F.R.D. 265; Yackle, Ex-

plaining Habeas Corpus, 1985, 60 N.Y.U.L.Rev. 991; Wright, Habeas Corpus: Its History and Its Future, 1983, 81 Mich. L.Rev. 802; Allen, Schachtman & Wilson, Federal Habeas Corpus and Its Reform: An Empirical Analysis, 1982, 13 Rutgers L.J. 675; Cover & Aleinikoff, Dialectical Federalism: Habeas Corpus and the Court, 1977, 86 Yale L.J. 1035; Shapiro, Federal Habeas Corpus: A Study in Massachusetts, 1973, 87 Harv.L.Rev. 321; Gibbons, Waiver: The Quest for Functional Limitations on Habeas Corpus Jurisdiction, 1971, 2 Seton Hall L.Rev. 291; Friendly, Is Innocence Irrelevant? Collateral Attack on Criminal Judgments, 1970, 38 U.Chi.L.Rev. 142.

2. Duker, The English Origins of the Writ of Habeas Corpus: A Peculiar Path to Fame, 1978, 53 N.Y.U.L.Rev. 983; Glass, Historical Aspects of Habeas Corpus, 1934, 9 St. John's L.Rev. 55.

3. 31 Car. II, c. 2.

4. Secretary of State for Home Affairs v. O'Brien, [1923] A.C. 603, 609.

5. The implications of the Suspension Clause are considered in all three of the opinions in Swain v. Pressley, 1977, 97 S.Ct. 1224, 430 U.S. 372, 51 L.Ed.2d 411. See also Steiker, Incorporating the Suspension Clause: Is there a Constitutional Right to Federal Habeas Corpus for State Prisoners?, 1994, 92 Mich.L.Rev. 862.

federal courts was authorized in § 14 of the Judiciary Act of 1789. The situations in which the writ might issue were extended in 1833 and 1842 to meet particular exigencies, but the great expansion came in 1867. Congress, anticipating difficulty in enforcing Reconstruction, authorized the federal courts to grant the writ "in all cases where any person may be restrained of his or her liberty in violation of the constitution, or of any treaty or law of the United States." [6] The statutory provisions on habeas corpus appear as sections 2241 to 2255 of the 1948 Judicial Code. The recodification of that year set out important procedural limitations and additional procedural changes were added in 1966, but the scope of the writ, insofar as the statutory language is concerned, has not been altered since 1867.

The "Great Writ," as it has been called by the Supreme Court from John Marshall's day to this,[7] is available by statute in four different situations.[8] A little-used provision permits it to issue where a foreign citizen is in custody for some act done under color of authority from his country and international law is involved.[9] It will issue also where a person is held by a state for some act done pursuant to federal authority,[10] but provisions for removal of such cases [11] diminish the need for habeas corpus in such situations. The writ will issue to test the detention of any person held under custody of the United States.[12] This

---

6. Act of Feb. 5, 1867, c. 28, § 1, 14 Stat. 385. Although the reason stated in the text seems the most likely, the legislative history is unclear and there is dispute about this. Mayers, The Habeas Corpus Act of 1867: The Supreme Court as Legal Historian, 1965, 33 U.Chi.L.Rev. 31.

7. See Ex parte Bollman, 1807, 4 Cranch 75, 95, 2 L.Ed. 554; Engle v. Isaac, 1982, 102 S.Ct. 1558, 1571, 456 U.S. 107, 126, 71 L.Ed.2d 783; Pennsylvania Bureau of Correction v. United States Marshals Service, 1985, 106 S.Ct. 355, 359 n. 5, 474 U.S. 34, 39 n. 5, 88 L.Ed.2d 189. Since 1985, except in quotations from earlier cases, the term has appeared only in dissenting and concurring opinions.

8. The "Great Writ" is the writ of habeas corpus ad subjiciendum. The statute also authorizes issuance of the writ to bring a person into court to testify or for trial, 28 U.S.C.A. § 2241(c)(5), thus providing an analogue to the common-law writs of habeas corpus ad prosequendum, testificandum, etc. Carbo v. U.S., 1961, 81 S.Ct. 338, 364 U.S. 611, 5 L.Ed.2d 329.

9. This provision—now 28 U.S.C.A. § 2241(c)(4)—was first added by Act of Aug. 29, 1842, c. 257, 5 Stat. 539. England had protested that the trial of a Canadian soldier for murder in the New York court, People v. McLeod, N.Y.1841, 25 Wend. 483, 37 Am.Dec. 328, was a violation of

international law. The statute was designed to give jurisdiction of such matters to the federal courts. Horn v. Mitchell, D.C.Mass.1915, 223 F. 549, affirmed C.C.A. 1st, 1916, 232 F. 819, appeal dismissed 1917, 37 S.Ct. 293, 243 U.S. 247, 61 L.Ed. 700.

It is arguable that the 1966 amendment of 28 U.S.C.A. § 2254(a) makes § 2241(c)(4) no longer available to state prisoners. If so, this was certainly inadvertent, but the provision has been used so rarely that its inadvertent repeal, if this happened, is of little practical consequence.

10. This provision—now 28 U.S.C.A. § 2241(c)(2)—was originally § 7 of the Force Act of 1833, 4 Stats. 634, and was the result of state imprisonment of federal marshals seeking to enforce the controversial Tariff Act. The most famous and colorful case involving this authorization for habeas corpus is In re Neagle, 1890, 10 S.Ct. 658, 135 U.S. 1, 34 L.Ed. 55. See Swisher, Stephen J. Field: Craftsman of the Law, 1930, pp. 321–361. The background of the Neagle case is also described in a fascinating book, Kroninger, Sarah and the Senator, 1964.

11. 28 U.S.C.A. §§ 1442, 1442a.

12. 28 U.S.C.A. § 2241(c)(1). This provision stems from § 14 of the Judiciary Act of 1789, 1 Stat. 81.

provision, though still of much importance in noncriminal cases,[13] is not of significance with regard to federal criminal prisoners. The writ will not issue to test the sufficiency of an indictment,[14] and after the prisoners are convicted a statutory motion, covering the same scope as the writ of habeas corpus, is the remedy they must pursue.[15]

The most important part of the statute today is that provision, first adopted in 1867, authorizing issuance of the writ where persons are held in violation of the federal Constitution or laws,[16] which permits a federal court to order discharge of any person held by a state in violation of the supreme law of the land. The constitutionality of vesting this power in the federal courts is entirely settled.[17] The writ need not actually result in the discharge of the prisoner. Indeed in most cases grant of the writ is expressly made conditional in order that the state may retry the prisoner in a fashion meeting constitutional demands.[18]

It was once the law that the writ was not available unless it could potentially lead to discharge from custody under the sentence being attacked. This requirement has been considerably attenuated by the courts. A prisoner serving consecutive sentences is regarded as being "in custody" under any one of them, and may attack the validity of either the one he is serving or the one he is to serve in the future.[19] A prisoner being held as a multiple offender can use habeas corpus to challenge an earlier conviction that is being used to enhance his punishment on his latest conviction.[20] The writ may be used though the prisoner has been released on parole,[21] or is free on his own recognizance pending execution of sentence,[22] and even an unconditional release does not make moot a pending application for habeas corpus.[23] A prisoner in

---

13. For its use to challenge a deportation order, a court-martial conviction, commitment to a mental hospital, denial of parole, and other matters, see 17A Wright, Miller & Cooper, Jurisdiction 2d § 4261 pp. 275–280.

14. Riggins v. U.S., 1905, 26 S.Ct. 147, 199 U.S. 547, 50 L.Ed. 303.

15. 28 U.S.C.A. § 2255; U.S. v. Hayman, 1952, 72 S.Ct. 263, 342 U.S. 205, 96 L.Ed. 232; Hill v. U.S., 1962, 82 S.Ct. 468, 368 U.S. 424, 7 L.Ed.2d 417. For extended discussion of the vast litigation this statute has spawned, see 2 Wright, Criminal 2d §§ 589–602. U.S. v. Frady, 1982, 102 S.Ct. 1584, 456 U.S. 152, 71 L.Ed.2d 816.

16. 28 U.S.C.A. § 2241(c)(3).

17. U.S. ex rel. Elliott v. Hendricks, C.A.3d, 1954, 213 F.2d 922, certiorari denied 75 S.Ct. 77, 348 U.S. 851, 99 L.Ed. 670. See Ex parte Royall, 1886, 6 S.Ct. 734, 739, 117 U.S. 241, 249, 29 L.Ed. 868; Frank v. Mangum, 1915, 35 S.Ct. 582, 588, 237 U.S. 309, 311, 59 L.Ed. 969.

18. E.g., Rogers v. Richmond, 1961, 81 S.Ct. 735, 365 U.S. 534, 5 L.Ed.2d 760;

Irvin v. Dowd, 1961, 81 S.Ct. 1639, 366 U.S. 717, 6 L.Ed.2d 751.

19. Peyton v. Rowe, 1968, 88 S.Ct. 1549, 391 U.S. 54, 20 L.Ed.2d 426, overruling McNally v. Hill, 1934, 55 S.Ct. 24, 293 U.S. 131, 79 L.Ed. 238.

See generally 17A Wright, Miller & Cooper, Jurisdiction 2d § 4262; Smith, Federal Habeas Corpus: State Prisoners and the Concept of Custody, 1969, 4 U.Rich.L.Rev. 1; Note, Beyond Custody: Expanding Collateral Review of State Convictions, 1981, 14 U.Mich.J.L.Ref. 465.

20. Bernard v. Garraghty, C.A.4th, 1991, 934 F.2d 52; Stubblefield v. Beto, C.A.5th, 1968, 399 F.2d 424, certiorari denied 89 S.Ct. 731, 393 U.S. 1072, 21 L.Ed.2d 715.

21. Jones v. Cunningham, 1963, 83 S.Ct. 373, 371 U.S. 236, 9 L.Ed.2d 285.

22. Hensley v. Municipal Court, 1973, 93 S.Ct. 1571, 411 U.S. 345, 36 L.Ed.2d 294.

23. Carafas v. LaVallee, 1968, 88 S.Ct. 1556, 391 U.S. 234, 20 L.Ed.2d 554, overruling Parker v. Ellis, 1960, 80 S.Ct. 909, 362 U.S. 574, 4 L.Ed.2d 963. See also custody in one state against whom another state has a detainer may challenge the sentence or indictment that is the basis for the detainer by habeas corpus in federal court in either state.[24]

The statute permits granting of the writ "within their respective jurisdictions" by the district court, a judge of a court of appeals, and by the Supreme Court or a justice thereof.[25] In practice the application will normally be made to the district court; higher courts, and judges thereof, are authorized to transfer to the district court any application made to them.[26] By statute a state prisoner may seek the writ either in the district in which he is being held or the district in which he was convicted,[27] and the former rigid rule that both the prisoner and the custodian must be within the territorial jurisdiction of the court has been greatly watered down by decisions.[28]

The early concept of habeas corpus was that it guaranteed only that all the proper legal processes had been used, "thus assuring only a formalistic, check-list freedom."[29] The stated doctrine was that the writ would issue only if the court that had committed the prisoner lacked "jurisdiction" to do so.[30] The concept of jurisdictional defects was never entirely rigid, and a great expansion, beginning in 1923, has led to abandonment of the concept as a limit on habeas corpus. In 1923, in

Evitts v. Lucey, 1985, 105 S.Ct. 830, 833 n. 4, 469 U.S. 387, 391 n. 4, 83 L.Ed.2d 821.

This will not be true, however, if the prior conviction has no collateral consequences. Lane v. Williams, 1982, 102 S.Ct. 1322, 455 U.S. 624, 71 L.Ed.2d 508.

24. Nelson v. George, 1970, 90 S.Ct. 1963, 399 U.S. 224, 26 L.Ed.2d 578 (state of custody); Braden v. 30th Judicial Circuit Court, 1973, 93 S.Ct. 1123, 410 U.S. 484, 35 L.Ed.2d 443 (state of detainer). The Braden case suggests that the state of detainer will ordinarily be the more convenient forum, and that if the action is brought in the state of custody it may be transferred to the state of detainer under 28 U.S.C.A. § 1404(a).

25. 28 U.S.C.A. § 2241(a). The writ is in aid of the appellate jurisdiction of the higher courts, and thus the authorization for the Supreme Court to grant it does not violate the constitutional limits on the original jurisdiction of that Court. Ex parte Siebold, 1879, 100 U.S. 371, 25 L.Ed. 717; Oaks, The "Original" Writ of Habeas Corpus in the Supreme Court, 1962 Sup.Ct. Rev. 153. See § 108 below.

26. 28 U.S.C.A. § 2241(b); Ex parte Abernathy, 1943, 64 S.Ct. 13, 320 U.S. 219, 88 L.Ed. 3; In re Tracy, 1919, 39 S.Ct. 374, 249 U.S. 551, 63 L.Ed. 768. Whether an individual justice of the Supreme Court may issue the writ is an open question. Locks v. Commanding General, Sixth Army,

1968, 89 S.Ct. 31, 21 L.Ed.2d 78 (opinion of Circuit Justice Douglas).

27. 28 U.S.C.A. § 2241(d), as amended by Act of Sept. 19, 1966, Pub.L. 89–590, 80 Stat. 811. The court in which the application is filed may transfer it to the other district if this is in the furtherance of justice.

28. Braden v. 30th Judicial Circuit Court, 1973, 93 S.Ct. 1123, 410 U.S. 484, 35 L.Ed.2d 443; compare Strait v. Laird, 1972, 92 S.Ct. 1693, 406 U.S. 341, 32 L.Ed.2d 141, with Schlanger v. Seamans, 1971, 91 S.Ct. 995, 401 U.S. 487, 28 L.Ed.2d 251.

29. Note, 1948, 61 Harv.L.Rev. 657, 660. This view is rejected in Fay v. Noia, 1963, 83 S.Ct. 822, 830–831, 372 U.S. 391, 404–405, 9 L.Ed.2d 837, where it is argued that at common law the writ was not narrowly limited to jurisdictional questions. See Bushell's Case, 1670, Vaughan, 135, 124 Eng.Rep. 1006. But see Justice Powell's concurring opinion in Schneckloth v. Bustamonte, 1973, 93 S.Ct. 2041, 2061, 412 U.S. 218, 254, 36 L.Ed.2d 854, and Justice Thomas's plurality opinion in Wright v. West, 1992, 112 S.Ct. 2482, 2486, ___ U.S. ___, ___, 120 L.Ed.2d 225.

30. Ex parte Siebold, 1879, 100 U.S. 371, 25 L.Ed. 717. In this case it was held, however, that a court lacked jurisdiction if the statute creating the offense for which the prisoner was tried was unconstitutional.

Moore v. Dempsey,[31] it was held that if a court was under the sway of mob rule, the proceedings, though formally entirely proper, would be a mere mask, depriving the court of jurisdiction, and that a prisoner convicted in such circumstances could attack his conviction by habeas corpus. A similar result was reached later where the conviction was allegedly obtained by the knowing use of perjured testimony.[32] In 1938 the Supreme Court held that a federal court that had jurisdiction at the outset of a trial "lost" jurisdiction during the course of the proceedings when it failed to provide the prisoner with counsel as the Sixth Amendment requires.[33] A similar doctrine was applied to state prisoners, and finally, in 1942, the Supreme Court abandoned the overstrained jurisdictional fiction and stated the reality: "the use of the writ in the federal courts to test the constitutional validity of a conviction for crime is not restricted to those cases where the judgment of conviction is void for want of jurisdiction of the trial court to render it. It extends also to those exceptional cases where the conviction has been in disregard of the constitutional rights of the accused, and where the writ is the only effective means of preserving his rights." [34] Despite the language about "exceptional cases" in the passage just quoted, it is now clear that habeas corpus in a federal court is available whenever the state proceeding fails to meet the standards of procedural fairness that the Fourteenth Amendment requires of the states.[35]

There is an important limitation on the broad power of the federal courts to upset criminal convictions thus outlined. The Supreme Court had developed a doctrine that an application for habeas corpus should not be entertained until the prisoner had exhausted his state remedies.[36] This rule of comity was written into the statutes in 1948.[37] The Court

---

31. 1923, 43 S.Ct. 265, 261 U.S. 86, 67 L.Ed. 543. See Waterman & Overton, Federal Habeas Corpus Statutes and Moore v. Dempsey, 1933, 1 U.Chi.L.Rev. 307; Waterman & Overton, The Aftermath of Moore v. Dempsey, 1933, 18 St. Louis L.Rev. 117.

32. Mooney v. Holohan, 1935, 55 S.Ct. 340, 294 U.S. 103, 79 L.Ed. 791.

33. Johnson v. Zerbst, 1938, 58 S.Ct. 1019, 1024, 304 U.S. 458, 468, 82 L.Ed. 1461.

34. Waley v. Johnston, 1942, 62 S.Ct. 964, 966, 316 U.S. 101, 104–105, 86 L.Ed. 1302.

35. See Hensley v. Municipal Court, 1973, 93 S.Ct. 1571, 1574, 411 U.S. 345, 349–350, 36 L.Ed.2d 294; Carafas v. LaVallee, 1968, 88 S.Ct. 1556, 1560, 391 U.S. 234, 238, 20 L.Ed.2d 554.

36. Ex parte Royall, 1886, 6 S.Ct. 734, 117 U.S. 241, 29 L.Ed. 868; Mooney v. Holohan, 1935, 55 S.Ct. 340, 343, 294 U.S. 103, 115, 79 L.Ed. 791; Ex parte Hawk, 1944, 64 S.Ct. 448, 321 U.S. 114, 88 L.Ed. 572; Slayton v. Smith, 1971, 92 S.Ct. 174, 404 U.S. 53, 30 L.Ed.2d 209.

37. 28 U.S.C.A. § 2254(b), (c). See 17A Wright, Miller & Cooper, Jurisdiction 2d § 4264–4264.8.

The exhaustion requirement applies even though it is clear that the prisoner's constitutional rights were violated in the state proceeding. Duckworth v. Serrano, 1981, 102 S.Ct. 18, 454 U.S. 1, 70 L.Ed.2d 1.

The state remedy is not exhausted if the claim presented to the state court is not the same as that presented to the federal court. Picard v. Connor, 1971, 92 S.Ct. 509, 404 U.S. 270, 30 L.Ed.2d 438; Vasquez v. Hillery, 1986, 106 S.Ct.617, 474 U.S. 254, 88 L.Ed.2d 598. See 17A Wright, Miller & Cooper, Jurisdiction 2d § 4264.3.

A federal court must dismiss a "mixed petition," one that contains some claims on which state remedies have been exhausted and others on which they have not been exhausted, and leave the prisoner with the choice of returning to state court to exhaust his claims or of amending or resubmitting the petition to present only the exhausted claims to the federal court. Rose v. Lundy, 1982, 102 S.Ct. 1198, 455 U.S. 509, 71 first construed the statute to mean that the remedies that must be exhausted normally included application to the Supreme Court to review the state proceedings, either by appeal or by certiorari as the case might be.[38] Though the prisoner was thus required to have sought Supreme Court review, denial of review by that Court was not to be given any weight by the district court on a later application for habeas corpus.[39] The wisdom of requiring a resort to the Supreme Court as a part of exhaustion of state remedies was always doubtful, and in 1963 the Court overruled the case that had read this requirement into the statute.[40] But if the Supreme Court has decided the case, its judgment is conclusive in a later habeas corpus proceeding on all issues of fact or law that were actually adjudicated by the Court.[41]

The draftsman of the habeas-corpus provisions incorporated in the 1948 revision of the Judicial Code had anticipated that the state remedies would not be deemed exhausted so long as the prisoner had the right to present his grievance again to the state by some state procedure.[42] The Supreme Court ruled to the contrary, holding squarely that the state remedies are exhausted when the constitutional contention has once been presented to the state courts, with, as then required, review sought, or excused, in the United States Supreme Court.[43] The draftsman had supposed that under this statute "there should be no more cases where proceedings of state courts, affirmed by the highest courts of the state, with denial of certiorari by the Supreme Court of the United

L.Ed.2d 379. See 17A Wright, Miller & Cooper, Jurisdiction 2d § 4264.6.

A state prisoner claiming that he is entitled to immediate or more speedy release from imprisonment cannot avoid the exhaustion requirement by framing his action as a civil-rights action under 42 U.S.C.A. § 1983 but must proceed by habeas corpus. Preiser v. Rodriguez, 1973, 93 S.Ct. 1827, 411 U.S. 475, 36 L.Ed. 439. See 17A Wright, Miller & Cooper, Jurisdiction 2d § 4263, p. 320.

38. Darr v. Burford, 1950, 70 S.Ct. 587, 339 U.S. 200, 94 L.Ed. 761. This may have been the rule prior to the 1948 codification. Ex parte Hawk, 1944, 64 S.Ct. 448, 321 U.S. 114, 88 L.Ed. 572; but cf. Wade v. Mayo, 1948, 68 S.Ct. 1270, 334 U.S. 672, 92 L.Ed. 1647.

39. Brown v. Allen, 1953, 73 S.Ct. 397, 344 U.S. 443, 97 L.Ed. 469, affirmed 73 S.Ct. 437, 344 U.S. 443, 97 L.Ed. 469. This is true even if the prisoner could have appealed as of right to the Supreme Court. County Court of Ulster County v. Allen, 1979, 99 S.Ct. 2213, 2220 n. 7, 442 U.S. 140, 149 n. 7, 60 L.Ed.2d 777.

40. Fay v. Noia, 1963, 83 S.Ct. 822, 847, 372 U.S. 391, 435, 9 L.Ed.2d 837.

41. 28 U.S.C.A. § 2244(c).

An affirmance by an equally divided Court is not an adjudication for this purpose. Neil v. Biggers, 1972, 93 S.Ct. 375, 409 U.S. 188, 34 L.Ed.2d 401. Neither is a denial of certiorari. But dismissal of an appeal for want of a substantial federal question is an adjudication. Howell v. Jones, C.A.5th, 1975, 516 F.2d 53; Connor v. Hutto, C.A.8th, 1975, 516 F.2d 853.

42. Parker, Limiting the Abuse of Habeas Corpus, 1948, 8 F.R.D. 171, 176.

43. Brown v. Allen, 1953, 73 S.Ct. 397, 402–404, 344 U.S. 443, 447–450, 97 L.Ed. 469.

A prisoner who has once exhausted his state remedies need not go back to the state court because an intervening decision by the state court makes it appear that it would now give the relief sought. Francisco v. Gathright, 1974, 95 S.Ct. 257, 419 U.S. 59, 42 L.Ed.2d 226.

Prisoners, who had unsuccessfully sought habeas corpus from the state courts, were not required to exhaust possible alternative state remedies before bringing a federal habeas-corpus action. Wilwording v. Swenson, 1971, 92 S.Ct. 407, 404 U.S. 249, 30 L.Ed.2d 418.

States, will be reviewed by federal circuit or district judges." [44]   The rule that only one state remedy need be exhausted has refuted such a hope. There are a great many such cases every year.

The requirement that state remedies be exhausted leads to the two most difficult problems with regard to federal habeas corpus for state prisoners. Though it appeared that they had been resolved in 1963, that resolution did not prove durable and there has been much subsequent change with regard to them. If the prisoner has been successful when he presented his constitutional contention to the state court, he will have been released, or retried, and has no need to resort to federal court. Applications for habeas corpus come, then, only where the state court has rejected the constitutional contention, or where for one reason or another it has failed to pass upon it. If the state court has held against the prisoner on his federal claim, what weight is to be given that determination in the subsequent federal proceedings? In a concurring opinion in Brown v. Allen,[45] which for 10 years was thought to be authoritative, Justice Frankfurter said that the federal judge could accept the determination of historic facts by the state court, unless there had been a "vital flaw" in the state factfinding process, but that the federal judge had to decide independently mixed questions of law and fact as well as the application of constitutional principles to the facts as found. This formulation, though helpful, did not solve all questions about the effect to be given the state determination.

Suppose a case in which a state defendant is convicted on the basis of a confession obtained after he was arrested but before he was brought before a magistrate. He contends, by analogy to the Mallory–McNabb rule once applicable in federal prosecutions,[46] that the use of such a confession against him is a violation of his rights under the Fourteenth Amendment. The contention is pressed in and rejected by the state courts. He then applies to a federal district court for habeas corpus, raising the same contention.

Despite an occasional aberrational decision to the contrary, the historic rule applies that res judicata does not bar habeas corpus, and the mere fact that the contention has been presented to, and rejected by, the state courts does not prevent the federal court from giving relief.[47]   If

---

44. Parker, note 42 above, at 178.

45. 1953, 73 S.Ct. 397, 446, 344 U.S. 443, 506–507, 97 L.Ed. 469.

46. 1 Wright, Criminal 2d §§ 72–75.

47. Brown v. Allen, 1953, 73 S.Ct. 397, 408, 344 U.S. 443, 456, 97 L.Ed. 469; see Allen v. McCurry, 1980, 101 S.Ct. 411, 417 n. 12, 449 U.S. 90, 98 n. 12, 66 L.Ed.2d 308. See also Kelley, Finality and Habeas Corpus: Is the Rule That Res Judicata May Not Apply to Habeas Corpus or Motion to Vacate Still Viable?, 1975, 78 W.Va.L.Rev. 1.

Whether this was in fact the law prior to Brown v. Allen is a matter of dispute. In an interesting and scholarly article, Professor Paul M. Bator contended that prior to Brown relief would lie for a state prisoner only if the state courts had failed to provide adequate corrective process. Bator, Finality in Criminal Law and Federal Habeas Corpus for State Prisoners, 1963, 76 Harv. L.Rev. 441. This analysis was persuasive to the dissenters in Fay v. Noia, 1963, 83 S.Ct. 822, 858–860, 372 U.S. 391, 457–461, 9 L.Ed.2d 837, but was rejected by the majority as "untenable." 83 S.Ct. at 839 n. 30, 372 U.S. at 421 n. 30. Professor Bator's view of history has been thought unpersuasive by Professor Herbert Wechsler, the state court has held that unreasonable delay in bringing an arrested person before a magistrate is no bar to the admissibility of confessions obtained in the interim, this construction of the Fourteenth Amendment raises a pure question of law that the federal judge is entirely free to decide. Suppose, however, that the prisoner contends that the effect of holding him incommunicado after arrest was to produce coercion upon him, and make his confession involuntary. Such a contention would raise a mixed question of law and fact. The federal judge might accept the state court's finding as to the historical facts but would have to decide independently whether on these facts an inference should be drawn that the confession was involuntary.[48]

The case becomes harder where the dispute goes solely to the historical facts. Perhaps the prisoner has testified that he was held incommunicado for an extended period after arrest, but the police officers have denied this. If there was some "vital flaw" in the state process for finding the historical facts, as if the prisoner had not been given a fair opportunity to produce evidence to support his contention or the state-court finding was contrary to uncontradicted evidence, the state finding could not be accepted by the federal court, which was required to make its own finding. In the absence of such a "vital flaw," however, the federal court, under Brown v. Allen, was free to accept the state findings.[49] It was not, however, required to do so. Even without a "vital flaw," the district court was at liberty if it saw fit to take testimony as to the facts.[50]

The Supreme Court undertook to shed light on these matters in

note 1 above, at 173, and it is challenged by other recent studies of the historical evidence. Peller, In Defense of Federal Habeas Corpus Relitigation, 1982, 16 Harv.C.R.-C.L.L.Rev. 570; Liebman, Apocalypse Next Time?: The Anachronistic Attack on Habeas Corpus/Direct Review Parity, 1992, 92 Col.L.Rev. 1997; Woolhandler, note 1 above. It is regarded more favorably in Oaks, Legal History in the High Court—Habeas Corpus, 1966, 64 Mich.L.Rev. 451, in Friendly, note 1 above, in Justice Powell's concurring opinion (joined by two other justices) in Schneckloth v. Bustamonte, 1973, 93 S.Ct. 2041, 2059, 412 U.S. 218, 250, 36 L.Ed.2d 854, and in Justice Thomas's plurality opinion (joined by two other justices) in Wright v. West, 1992, 112 S.Ct. 2482, 2486–2487, ___ U.S. ___, ___, 120 L.Ed.2d 225. See also Stone v. Powell, 1976, 96 S.Ct. 3037, 3043 n. 9, 428 U.S. 465, 476 n. 9, 49 L.Ed.2d 1067, where the Court merely says: "There has been disagreement among scholars as to whether the result in Brown v. Allen was foreshadowed by the Court's decision in Moore v. Dempsey." See also Steiker, note 1 above,

at 312–320. Writing in 1981, Professor Bator said that his 1963 article, which was published just before Fay v. Noia came down, "had the strange history of being pronounced dead almost as soon as it was written, only to enjoy a mysterious recent resurrection." Bator, The State Courts and Federal Constitutional Litigation, 1981, 22 Wm. & Mary L.Rev. 605, 613. But as Patchel points out, note 1 above, at 953, Bator may have lost the battle at the time of Fay, but his ideas about the appropriate scope of habeas seem in the most recent decisions to have won the war.

48. Cf. Leyra v. Denno, 1954, 74 S.Ct. 716, 347 U.S. 556, 98 L.Ed. 948.

This is still the rule. Miller v. Fenton, 1985, 106 S.Ct. 445, 474 U.S. 104, 88 L.Ed.2d 405.

49. E.g., U.S. ex rel. Salemi v. Denno, C.A.2d, 1956, 235 F.2d 910; Thomas v. Eyman, C.A.9th, 1956, 235 F.2d 775.

50. U.S. ex rel. Rogers v. Richmond, 1958, 78 S.Ct. 1365, 357 U.S. 220, 2 L.Ed.2d 1361.

1963, in Townsend v. Sain.[51] The Court there was unanimous in holding that the federal court has the power to receive evidence and try the facts anew on a habeas corpus petition. The question is not whether the federal court may try the facts, but whether it must. The Court was unanimous also on the following statement as to when independent factfinding by the federal court is mandatory: "Where the facts are in dispute, the federal court on habeas corpus must hold an evidentiary hearing if the habeas applicant did not receive a full and fair evidentiary hearing in a state court, either at the time of the trial or in a collateral proceeding. In other words a federal evidentiary hearing is required unless the state-court trier of fact has after a full hearing reliably found the relevant facts." [52] Finally the Court was unanimous in holding that the district court is not limited to a study of the undisputed portions of the state court record.[53]

The decision in the Townsend case was by a vote of 5–4, because of disagreement as to application of the announced standard on the facts of that case. The dissenters objected, also, to the majority's particularization of the general standard stated as to when independent factfinding is mandatory. The majority, believing that experience teaches that too general a standard, such as the "exceptional circumstances" and "vital flaw" tests of Brown v. Allen, did not give adequate guidance to the district courts, undertook to provide guidelines by listing six circumstances in which a federal evidentiary hearing was mandatory.[54] These were codified in somewhat different form in 1966.[55] The statute now provides that a determination of a fact issue [56] made by a state court

---

51. 1963, 83 S.Ct. 745, 372 U.S. 293, 9 L.Ed.2d 770.

52. 83 S.Ct. at 757, 372 U.S. at 312–313. The Court stated that this test supersedes, to the extent that there is any inconsistency, the tests set out in Brown v. Allen.

See also Smith v. Yeager, 1968, 89 S.Ct. 277, 393 U.S. 122, 21 L.Ed.2d 246.

A new hearing is not required unless the prisoner's version of the events, if true, would entitle him to relief. Procunier v. Atchley, 1971, 91 S.Ct. 485, 400 U.S. 446, 27 L.Ed.2d 524.

53. 83 S.Ct. at 761, 372 U.S. at 320.

54. 83 S.Ct. at 757, 372 U.S. at 313.

55. 28 U.S.C.A. § 2254(d), added by Act of Nov. 2, 1966, Pub.L. 89–711, 80 Stat. 1105.

Though Townsend lists six circumstances and the statute eight, the lists are not entirely overlapping on their face, and Townsend speaks of making a hearing mandatory while the statute is in terms of circumstances dispelling the presumption of correctness, it seems entirely clear that the statute is a determination by Congress that the Townsend guidelines "would be better

understood and applied if they were codified in statutory form," White v. Swenson, D.C.Mo.1966, 261 F.Supp. 42, 61. See also Brewer v. Williams, 1977, 97 S.Ct. 1232, 1238, 430 U.S. 387, 395–396, 51 L.Ed.2d 424.

56. "In the § 2254(d) context, as elsewhere, the appropriate methodology for distinguishing questions of fact from questions of law has been, to say the least, elusive." Miller v. Fenton, 1985, 106 S.Ct. 445, 451, 474 U.S. 104, 113, 88 L.Ed.2d 405. See 17A Wright, Miller & Cooper, Jurisdiction 2d § 4265.1, pp. 416–421.

In Wright v. West, 1992, 112 S.Ct. 2482, ___ U.S. ___, 120 L.Ed.2d 225, the Supreme Court ordered briefing on whether a federal court should afford deference to state-court determinations applying law to the specific facts of a case. Ultimately it held that it need not decide the issue in the case before it, but the issue is extensively discussed in a plurality opinion by Justice Thomas, joined by Chief Justice Rehnquist and Justice Scalia, and in a concurring opinion by Justice O'Connor, joined by Justices Blackmun and Stevens.

after a hearing on the merits and evidenced by reliable and adequate written indicia is presumed to be correct, and the burden is on the petitioner to establish by convincing evidence that the determination is erroneous, unless one of eight specified circumstances exists. These circumstances are: "(1) that the merits of the factual dispute were not resolved in the State court hearing; (2) that the factfinding procedure employed by the State court was not adequate to afford a full and fair hearing; (3) that the material facts were not adequately developed at the State court hearing; [57] (4) that the State court lacked jurisdiction of the subject matter or over the person of the applicant in the State court proceeding; (5) that the applicant was an indigent and the State court, in deprivation of his constitutional right, failed to appoint counsel to represent him in the State court proceeding; (6) that the applicant did not receive a full, fair, and adequate hearing in the State court proceeding; (7) that the applicant was otherwise denied due process of law in the State court proceeding; (8) or unless that part of the record of the State court proceeding in which the determination of such factual issue was made, pertinent to a determination of the sufficiency of the evidence to support such factual determination, is produced as provided for hereinafter, and the Federal court on a consideration of such part of the record as a whole concludes that such factual determination is not fairly supported by the record." Under the statute a state finding cannot be set aside merely on a preponderance of the evidence, and a federal court granting the writ must include in its opinion the reason that it found that one of the first seven factors were present, or the reason that it concluded that the state finding was not fairly supported by the record.[58]

Thus, in the case earlier put, where there was conflicting evidence on whether the prisoner had been held incommunicado after arrest, the test will no longer be whether there was a "vital flaw" in the state process for finding the historical facts. Instead the test will be whether the prisoner received a full and fair evidentiary hearing in the state court, in the light of the principles announced in Townsend and with an eye to the circumstances specified in the statute.

If the state has not decided the federal claim, it will be because the prisoner has not asserted it properly in state court or because there is some adequate state ground that supports the conviction. On the problem of "an abortive state proceeding," the two Supreme Court decisions in point prior to 1963 were inconclusive. In Daniels v. Allen [59] the state defendants had filed their appeal papers in the state supreme

---

57. The Townsend case had held that a habeas petitioner's failure to develop a material fact in the state-court proceeding could be excused unless the petitioner had deliberately bypassed the state courts. That holding of Townsend was overruled in Keeney v. Tamayo–Reyes, 1992, 112 S.Ct. 1715, ___ U.S. ___, 118 L.Ed.2d 318, and it was held that a cause-and-prejudice test must be applied.

58. Sumner v. Mata, 1981, 101 S.Ct. 764, 449 U.S. 539, 66 L.Ed.2d 722. See also Sumner v. Mata, 1982, 102 S.Ct. 1303, 455 U.S. 591, 71 L.Ed.2d 480.

See generally 17A Wright, Miller & Cooper, Jurisdiction 2d § 4265.1.

59. 1953, 73 S.Ct. 397, 420–422, 344 U.S. 443, 482–487, 97 L.Ed. 469 (decided sub nom. Brown v. Allen).

court one day late, and that court had refused to pass on their meritorious claim that they had been denied federal constitutional rights. The United States Supreme Court held that the failure to perfect the appeal in accord with a reasonable state procedural requirement barred subsequent discharge on habeas corpus. In Irvin v. Dowd [60] the state supreme court had held that the trial court had not erred in denying the prisoner's application for a new trial, since he had escaped the day before it was filed, but because the death sentence was involved the state court went on to consider and reject the federal constitutional claim. Four Supreme Court dissenters asserted that an adequate state ground sufficient to bar direct review by the Court was also sufficient to bar habeas corpus. The majority, holding that the application for habeas corpus should be considered on its merits,[61] avoided passing on this assertion directly by reading the state-court opinion as resting decision entirely on the determination that the federal claim was without substance. Since the rule proposed by the dissenters in Irvin was not enunciated in terms in Daniel, nor rejected in terms by the majority in Irvin, the law on the point was not clear. The issue produced a spirited controversy in the law reviews [62] and was temporarily settled by the 1963 decision in Fay v. Noia.[63]

The Noia case was a particularly appealing one. Noia and two others were convicted of murder. Noia did not appeal. The other defendants appealed unsuccessfully. Fourteen years later one of the other defendants was discharged on federal habeas corpus when it was established that his confession had been coerced by "satanic practices." The following year the state court granted reargument of the appeal of Noia's second codefendant, and set his conviction aside on the same ground. Noia, whose conviction had been similarly coerced, then sought relief from the state court, but it was held there that his failure to appeal his conviction barred him from later attacking the conviction. He brought an action in federal court for habeas corpus. The state conceded that his rights under the Fourteenth Amendment had been denied, by use of the coerced confession, but relied on his failure to appeal as an adequate state ground precluding relief, or as showing that he had not exhausted state remedies as required by the statute.

The Supreme Court disagreed. In a sweeping opinion by Justice Brennan, the Court held that federal courts have power to grant relief despite the applicant's failure to have pursued a state remedy not available to him at the time he seeks habeas corpus. The doctrine that a

60. 1959, 79 S.Ct. 825, 359 U.S. 394, 3 L.Ed.2d 900.

61. When the case came back to the Supreme Court on the merits, it was held unanimously that Irvin had been unfairly convicted. Irvin v. Dowd, 1961, 81 S.Ct. 1639, 366 U.S. 717, 6 L.Ed.2d 751.

62. Hart, Foreword: The Time Chart of the Justices, 1959, 73 Harv.L.Rev. 84, 101–125; Arnold, Professor Hart's Theology, 1960, 73 Harv.L.Rev. 1298, 1304–1310; Reitz, Federal Habeas Corpus: Impact of an Abortive State Proceeding, 1961, 74 Harv.L.Rev. 315; Brennan, Federal Habeas Corpus and State Prisoners: An Exercise in Federalism, 1961, 7 Utah L.Rev. 423; R.C., 1962, 76 Harv.L.Rev. 411.

63. 1963, 83 S.Ct. 822, 372 U.S. 391, 9 L.Ed.2d 837.

state procedural default is an adequate and independent state-law ground barring direct review in the Supreme Court does not limit the power of a district court to grant habeas corpus. It held also that the statutory requirement of exhaustion of state remedies applies only to those still open to the applicant at the time he seeks federal habeas corpus; it does not include remedies he might have pursued in the past that are not still open. The Court recognized a discretion to refuse relief because of failure to comply with state procedures, but made it clear that such discretion is very limited. "If a habeas applicant, after consultation with competent counsel or otherwise, understandingly and knowingly forwent the privilege of seeking to vindicate his federal claims in the state courts, whether for strategic, tactical, or any other reasons that can fairly be described as the deliberate bypassing of state procedures, then it is open to the federal court on habeas to deny him all relief if the state courts refused to entertain his federal claims on the merits * * *. At all events we wish it clearly understood that the standard here put forth depends on the considered choice of the petitioner. * * * A choice made by counsel not participated in by the petitioner does not automatically bar relief. Nor does a state court's finding of waiver bar independent determination of the question by the federal courts on habeas, for waiver affecting federal rights is a federal question." [64]

Applying these principles to the case before it, the Court held that Noia's decision not to appeal—though made in consultation with counsel and based on a fear that at a second trial he might receive the death sentence, rather than life imprisonment—was not a deliberate bypassing of the state-court system, and thus did not give the district court discretion to refuse to issue the writ.

To Justice Harlan, and two other dissenters, the Court in Noia had "turned its back on history and struck a heavy blow at the foundations of our federal system." [65] In their view the federal courts are constitutionally without power to order release of a prisoner where the validity of his conviction rests on an adequate and independent state ground.

Fay v. Noia was not to be the last word. The doctrine announced in Fay was decisively changed in 1977 in Wainwright v. Sykes, [66] but other cases between 1963 and 1977 provided the foundation on which the Court built in Wainwright. In Davis v. United States, [67] a 1973 decision involving a federal prisoner, the Court held that the deliberate-bypass standard of Fay did not apply to a postconviction motion challenging the composition of the grand jury. The motion was barred by Criminal Rule 12(b)(2), which provided that challenges of that kind must be made by motion before trial and that only "for cause shown" could a court grant relief from the waiver resulting from failure to make the motion at the

---

64. 83 S.Ct. at 849, 372 U.S. at 439.

65. 83 S.Ct. at 854, 372 U.S. at 449.

Professor Wechsler, note 1 above, at 178, called Fay v. Noia "one of the most dramatic, important and doubtful decisions of the High Court in my lifetime."

66. 1977, 97 S.Ct. 2497, 433 U.S. 72, 53 L.Ed.2d 594.

67. 1973, 93 S.Ct. 1577, 411 U.S. 233, 36 L.Ed.2d 216.

time provided.[68]   A similar attack on the makeup of a grand jury by a state prisoner was rejected in 1976 in Francis v. Henderson.[69]   A state statute required such challenges to be made before trial.   Although the Supreme Court recognized that a district court has power to entertain an application for habeas corpus in a case of that kind, it held that it would not be appropriate to exercise that power.   Without any explanation of how the result could be reconciled with Fay v. Noia, the Court announced that in these circumstances collateral attack on a state conviction required "not only a showing of 'cause' for the defendant's failure to challenge the composition of the grand jury before trial, but also a showing of actual prejudice." [70]

In Wainwright v. Sykes habeas corpus was sought because of the introduction of inculpatory statements Sykes had made when allegedly he had not understood the Miranda warnings given him.   No objection was made at trial to the introduction of the statements.   The Court held that the failure to make a contemporaneous objection, as required by state procedure, could not be regarded as a deliberate bypass, but that it barred Sykes from habeas relief unless he could show cause for his failure to object and actual prejudice from admission of the statements.   "To the extent that the dicta of Fay v. Noia may be thought to have laid down an all-inclusive rule rendering state timely objection rules ineffective to bar review of underlying federal claims in federal habeas proceedings—absent a 'knowing waiver' or a 'deliberate bypass' of the right to so object—its effect was limited by Francis, which applied a different rule and barred a habeas challenge to the makeup of a grand jury." [71]

Wainwright left many questions unanswered.[72]   The "cause" and "prejudice" test it announced surely applies to any failure to comply with a state rule requiring contemporaneous objection to events at the trial or prior to trial.[73]   In Wainwright the Court said it was rejecting "the sweeping language of Fay v. Noia * * *, going far beyond the facts

---

68. What was Rule 12(b)(2) at the time of the Davis case is now divided between Rule 12(b) and Rule 12(f).

69. 1976, 96 S.Ct. 1708, 425 U.S. 536, 48 L.Ed.2d 149.

70. 96 S.Ct. at 1711, 425 U.S. at 542.

On the same day as Francis the Court held in Estelle v. Williams, 1976, 96 S.Ct. 1691, 425 U.S. 501, 48 L.Ed.2d 126, that a prisoner who was required to stand trial in his prison clothes could not obtain habeas corpus, because his failure to object in state court negated the presence of compulsion necessary to establish a constitutional violation.

71. 97 S.Ct. at 2505, 433 U.S. at 85.

72. See 17A Wright, Miller & Cooper, Jurisdiction 2d § 4266; Dooley, Equal Protection and the Procedural Bar Doctrine in Federal Habeas Corpus, 1991, 59 Fordham L.Rev. 737; Hughes, Sandbagging Constitu-

tional Rights: Federal Habeas Corpus and the Procedural Default Principle, 1988, 16 N.Y.U.L.Rev.L. & Soc. Change 321; Goodman, Wainwright v. Sykes, The Lower Federal Courts Respond, 1979, 30 Hastings L.Rev. 1683; Kinnamon, Defenses to the Preclusive Rule of Wainwright v. Sykes, 1979, 28 Drake L.Rev. 571; Hill, The Forfeiture of Constitutional Rights in Criminal Cases, 1978, 78 Col.L.Rev. 1050; Rosenberg, Jettisoning Fay v. Noia: Procedural Defaults by Reasonably Incompetent Counsel, 1978, 62 Minn.L.Rev. 341; Spritzer, Criminal Waiver, Procedural Default and the Burger Court, 1978, 126 U.Pa.L.Rev. 473.

73. Spritzer, note 72 above, at 507–508. See, e.g., Sumner v. Mata, 1981, 101 S.Ct. 764, 769, 449 U.S. 539, 547, 66 L.Ed.2d 722; Lee v. Missouri, 1979, 99 S.Ct. 710, 439 U.S. 461, 58 L.Ed.2d 736.

of the case eliciting it * * *," and expressly refrained from deciding whether failure to comply with state appeal procedures would bar habeas corpus and thus whether the holding of Fay is now overruled.[74] That question was answered in 1991 when any remaining vestiges of Fay v. Noia were rejected and it was expressly held that the "cause" and "prejudice" rule, rather than a "deliberate bypass" standard, applies to all independent and adequate state procedural defaults, including failure to take a direct appeal.[75]

State law must be looked to in deciding if a contemporaneous objection is required,[76] and if a state court considers a defendant's constitutional claim and rejects it on the merits, despite failure to object or some other procedural default that might have made determination of the merits unnecessary, the federal court is free to consider the constitutional claim on habeas corpus.[77] The meaning of "cause" and of "prejudice" remains uncertain, although it has been held that the futility of presenting an objection to the state courts cannot alone constitute cause for a failure to object at trial, nor can the novelty of a constitutional claim if other defense counsel have perceived and litigated that claim.[78] Prejudice must be evaluated in the total context of the events at trial, and the party attacking a conviction must show not merely that the errors at his trial created a possibility of prejudice but that they worked to his actual and substantial disadvantage, infecting his entire trial with error of constitutional dimension.[79]

It had been thought that the use of illegally obtained evidence was not ground for collateral attack, whether on a motion under 28 U.S.C.A.

---

74. 97 S.Ct. at 2507, 433 U.S. at 87–88.

75. Coleman v. Thompson, 1991, 111 S.Ct. 2546, 501 U.S. 722, 115 L.Ed.2d 640.

76. Jenkins v. Anderson, 1980, 100 S.Ct. 2124, 2127 n. 1, 447 U.S. 231, 234 n. 1, 65 L.Ed.2d 86.

77. County Court of Ulster County v. Allen, 1979, 99 S.Ct. 2213, 2223, 442 U.S. 140, 154, 60 L.Ed.2d 777. See also Francis, 96 S.Ct. at 1711 n. 5, 425 U.S. at 542 n. 5.

The "plain statement" rule of Michigan v. Long, 1983, 103 S.Ct. 3469, 463 U.S. 1032, 77 L.Ed.2d 1201—see § 107 below—applies to federal habeas-corpus proceedings so that a procedural default will not bar consideration of a federal claim on habeas review unless the state court rendering judgment in the case has clearly and expressly stated that the judgment rested on a state procedural bar. Harris v. Reed, 1989, 109 S.Ct. 1038, 489 U.S. 255, 103 L.Ed.2d 308, noted 1989, 58 Fordham L.Rev. 493. But this is true only if the decision appears to rest primarily on, or to be interwoven with, federal law. Coleman v. Thompson, 1991, 111 S.Ct. 2546, 501 U.S. 722, 115 L.Ed.2d 640, noted 1991, 23

St. Mary's L.J. 585. And if the last reasoned state-court opinion on a federal claim rests on a finding of procedural default, there is a strong presumption that any subsequent state-court decision on the claim also rested on the default rather than on the merits. Ylst v. Nunnemaker, 1991, 111 S.Ct. 2590, 501 U.S. 722, 115 L.Ed.2d 706.

78. Engle v. Isaac, 1982, 102 S.Ct. 1558, 456 U.S. 107, 71 L.Ed.2d 783. But if the claim was so novel that its legal basis was not reasonably available to counsel, the "cause" test is satisfied. Reed v. Ross, 1984, 104 S.Ct. 2901, 468 U.S. 1, 82 L.Ed.2d 1. The test was also held satisfied in Amadeo v. Zant, 1988, 108 S.Ct. 1771, 486 U.S. 214, 100 L.Ed.2d 249.

An inadvertent failure by counsel to raise a point on appeal is not "cause" within the Wainwright rule. Murray v. Carrier, 1986, 106 S.Ct. 2678, 477 U.S. 478, 91 L.Ed.2d 397.

79. U.S. v. Frady, 1982, 102 S.Ct. 1584, 456 U.S. 152, 71 L.Ed.2d 816. This case holds that the "cause" and "prejudice" test announced in Wainwright applies also to federal prisoners attacking a conviction under 28 U.S.C.A. § 2255.

§ 2255 by a federal prisoner or on a habeas corpus application by a state prisoner.[80] Although the Supreme Court rejected this view in 1969,[81] it substantially returned to it in 1976, when it held, in Stone v. Powell,[82] that if the state "has provided an opportunity for full and fair litigation of a Fourth Amendment claim, a state prisoner may not be granted federal habeas corpus relief on the ground that evidence obtained in an unconstitutional search or seizure was introduced at his trial." [83]

It is possible that the Stone rule will be extended to constitutional violations other than the Fourth Amendment. To date, at least, that has not happened, and in the two cases in which the Court squarely confronted such an argument it refused to apply the Stone rationale to preclude habeas corpus on a claim of racial discrimination in the selection of the grand jury that indicted a state prisoner [84] and it refused to apply it to the use of a statement obtained from a prisoner in violation of the Miranda safeguards.[85]

Not every constitutional violation entitles a prisoner to habeas corpus even where the Stone rule is not a bar. Relief is not to be given if the error was harmless, and the standard for determining whether habeas relief must be granted is whether the constitutional violation had substantial and injurious effect or influence in determining the jury's verdict.[86]

In a major 1989 case, Teague v. Lane,[87] the Supreme Court considered the extent to which prisoners can rely on a "new rule" of constitutional law in a collateral attack on a criminal conviction. It held that a federal court entertaining a state prisoner's habeas petition generally may not reach the merits of the legal claim unless the court determines, as a threshold matter, that a favorable ruling on the claim would flow from the application of legal standards prevailing at the time the prisoner's claim became final. A ruling is "new" for this purpose "if the result was not *dictated* by precedent existing at the time the defendant's conviction became final." [88] There are two exceptions to this general

---

80. Amsterdam, Search, Seizure, and Section 2255: A Comment, 1964, 112 U.Pa. L.Rev. 378; 2 Wright, Criminal, 1969 ed., § 595 n. 57 and cases cited.

81. Kaufman v. U.S., 1969, 89 S.Ct. 1068, 394 U.S. 217, 22 L.Ed.2d 227.

82. 1976, 96 S.Ct. 3037, 428 U.S. 465, 49 L.Ed.2d 1067. See 17A Wright, Miller & Cooper, Jurisdiction 2d § 4263.1; Halpern, Federal Habeas Corpus and the Mapp Exclusionary Rule After Stone v. Powell, 1982, 82 Col.L.Rev. 1; Comment, Development of Federal Habeas Corpus Since Stone v. Powell, 1979 Wis.L.Rev. 1145; Comment, Habeas Corpus After Stone v. Powell: The "Opportunity for Full and Fair Litigation" Standard, 1978, 13 Harv.C.R.C.L.L.Rev. 521.

83. 96 S.Ct. at 3049, 428 U.S. at 489.

84. Rose v. Mitchell, 1979, 99 S.Ct. 2993, 443 U.S. 545, 61 L.Ed.2d 739.

85. Withrow v. Williams, 1993, 113 S.Ct. 1745, ___ U.S. ___, 123 L.Ed.2d 407.

86. Brecht v. Abrahamson, 1993, 113 S.Ct. 1710, ___ U.S. ___, 123 L.Ed.2d 353.

87. 1989, 109 S.Ct. 1060, 489 U.S. 288, 103 L.Ed.2d 334. See Symposium, The Future of Habeas Corpus: Reflections on Teague v. Lane and Beyond, 1993, 66 S.Cal. L.Rev. 2331; Fallon & Meltzer, New Law, Non–Retroactivity, and Constitutional Remedies, 1991, 104 Harv.L.Rev. 1731; Hoffman, Retroactivity and the Great Writ: How Congress Should Respond to Teague v. Lane, 1990 B.Y.U.L.Rev. 183.

88. 109 S.Ct. at 1070, 489 U.S. at 301 (emphasis in original). Although Justice O'Connor's opinion spoke only for a pluralirule, although both exceptions are quite narrow. A new rule can be applied retroactively "if it places 'certain kinds of primary, private individual conduct beyond the power of the criminal law-making authority to proscribe'."[89] It can also be applied retroactively if the new rule establishes "new procedures without which the likelihood of an accurate conviction is seriously diminished."[90] The Teague rule was motivated by a respect for the states' strong interest in the finality of criminal convictions.[91] A prisoner has no such interest in finality, and for that reason the state may rely on a "new" rule to defeat habeas corpus although a prisoner cannot rely on that kind of rule to obtain the writ.[92]

A prisoner is not limited to a single application for federal habeas corpus. A 1963 decision had defined very narrowly the situations in which a federal court could give controlling weight to denial of a prior application.[93] Rule 9(b) of the Habeas Corpus Rules, adopted in 1977, provides, however, that "[a] second or successive petition may be dismissed if the judge finds that it fails to allege new or different grounds for relief and the prior determination was on the merits or, if new and different grounds are alleged, the judge finds that the failure of the petitioner to assert those grounds in a prior petition constituted an abuse of the writ."[94] The Supreme Court has held that unless there is a showing of "cause" and "prejudice", a court may not reach the merits of successive claims that raise grounds identical to grounds heard and decided on the merits in a previous petition,[95] nor can it consider new claims, not previously considered, that constitute an abuse of the writ.[96] There is an exception to these requirements of "cause" and "prejudice",

ty, these principles were endorsed in the opinion of the Court in Penry v. Lynaugh, 1989, 109 S.Ct. 2934, 492 U.S. 302, 106 L.Ed.2d 256. The Court later held that a prisoner's claim asks for a "new rule" if decisions already on the books "inform, or even control or govern" the claim, so long as they do not "compel the rule" that the prisoner seeks. Saffle v. Parks, 1990, 110 S.Ct. 1257, 1261, 494 U.S. 484, 491, 108 L.Ed.2d 415. See also Butler v. McKellar, 1990, 110 S.Ct. 1212, 494 U.S. 407, 108 L.Ed.2d 347; Graham v. Collins, 1993, 113 S.Ct. 892, ___ U.S. ___, 122 L.Ed.2d 260.

89. 109 S.Ct. at 1073, 489 U.S. at 307. The internal quotation is from the separate opinion of Justice Harlan in Mackey v. U.S., 1971, 91 S.Ct. 1160, 1180, 401 U.S. 667, 692, 28 L.Ed.2d 404.

90. 109 S.Ct. at 1076–1077, 489 U.S. at 313.

This exception is limited to new procedures without which the likelihood of an accurate conviction would be seriously diminished. Butler v. McKellar, 1990, 110 S.Ct. 1212, 494 U.S. 407, 108 L.Ed.2d 347.

91. The Teague rule is not jurisdictional and can be waived by the state. Collins v.

Youngblood, 1990, 110 S.Ct. 2715, 2718, 497 U.S. 37, 40–41, 111 L.Ed.2d 30.

92. Lockhart v. Fretwell, 1993, 113 S.Ct. 838, ___ U.S.___, 122 L.Ed.2d 180.

93. Sanders v. U.S., 1963, 83 S.Ct. 1068, 373 U.S. 1, 10 L.Ed.2d 148.

94. The official name of these rules is Rules Governing Section 2254 Cases in the United States District Courts. There is a similar provision applicable to federal prisoners in Rule 9(b) of the Section 2255 Rules, officially known as Rules Governing Section 2255 Proceedings in the United States District Courts.

Rule 9(a) in each of these bodies of rules speaks to the circumstances under which a habeas corpus petition or a § 2255 motion may be dismissed because the government has been prejudiced in its ability to respond to the motion by delay in its filing. See 17A Wright, Miller & Cooper, Federal Practice and Procedure § 4268.2.

95. Kuhlmann v. Wilson, 1986, 106 S.Ct. 2616, 477 U.S. 436, 91 L.Ed.2d 364.

96. McCleskey v. Zant, 1991, 111 S.Ct. 1454, 499 U.S. 467, 113 L.Ed.2d 517.

and to the similar requirement where there has been a procedural default and the rule of Wainwright v. Sykes applies, if the failure to hear the claims would constitute a miscarriage of justice. This is often spoken of as the "actual innocence" exception.[97]

Federal habeas corpus for state prisoners is, and always has been, a controversial and emotion-ridden subject. In the last century there were protests against "the prostitution of the writ of habeas corpus, under which the decisions of the State courts are subjected to the superintendence of the Federal judges * * *."[98] As the scope of the writ has expanded, as the rights found to be protected by the Fourteenth Amendment have increased in number, so has the criticism of this jurisdiction mounted in volume. There is an affront to state sensibilities when a single federal judge can order discharge of a prisoner whose conviction has been affirmed by the highest court of a state. Thus, it is not surprising that the Conference of Chief Justices has called for abolition of such jurisdiction, nor that the attorneys general of 41 states joined in a 1954 attempt to sweep aside nearly a century of history and precedent and have the habeas corpus statute itself, insofar as it applies to state prisoners, declared unconstitutional.[99]

Though there are a great many applications for habeas corpus, it is rare indeed to have the single federal judge set free the prisoner the state has convicted. Comprehensive statistics are lacking, but those that are available indicate that the writ is granted in at most 4% of the cases in which it is sought, and in many of these cases it is possible for the state to retry the petitioner.[100] The number of applications, however, puts a burden on the federal courts, and this burden has increased rapidly as procedural barriers to relief have been removed and Supreme Court decisions have broadened the substantive grounds on which relief is available. In 1953 Justice Jackson complained that "floods of stale, frivolous and repetitious petitions inundate the docket of the lower courts and swell our own." In a footnote at that point he noted that in the preceding year 541 petitions had been filed.[101] The number of petitions reached a peak of 9,063 in 1970 and seemed thereafter to have

97. Sawyer v. Whitley, 1992, 112 S.Ct. 2514, 2518–2519, ___ U.S. ___, ___, 120 L.Ed.2d 269. In a death case, "to show 'actual innocence' one must show by clear and convincing evidence that but for a constitutional error, no reasonable juror would have found the petitioner eligible for the death penalty under the applicable state law." 112 S.Ct. at 2517, ___ U.S. at ___.

"Claims of actual innocence based on newly discovered evidence have never been held to state a ground for federal habeas relief absent an independent constitutional violation occurring in the underlying state criminal proceeding." Herrera v. Collins, 1993, 113 S.Ct. 853, 860, ___ U.S. ___, ___,

122 L.Ed.2d 203. See generally Steiker, note 1 above.

98. Note, Federal Abuses of the Writ of Habeas Corpus, 1898, 25 Am.L.Rev. 149, 153.

99. U.S. ex rel. Elliott v. Hendricks, C.A.3d, 1954, 213 F.2d 922, certiorari denied 75 S.Ct. 77, 348 U.S. 851, 99 L.Ed. 670.

100. See 17A Wright, Miller & Cooper, Jurisdiction 2d §§ 4261 n. 48, 4268.4, pp. 527–530.

101. Brown v. Allen, 1953, 73 S.Ct. 397, 425, 344 U.S. 443, 536, 97 L.Ed. 469 (concurring opinion).

levelled off at about 7,800 per year, but the number has grown again and is now in excess of 12,000 per year.[102]

The great bulk of these applications are utterly unjustified, and it is easy to say, as Justice Jackson did, that "he who must search a haystack for a needle is likely to end up with the attitude that the needle is not worth the search." [103] To that attitude the classic answer has been that of Justice Walter V. Schaefer of the Illinois Supreme Court when he said "it is not a needle we are looking for in these stacks of paper, but the rights of a human being." [104] Nevertheless federal judges, fully sensitive to the importance of human rights, do feel the burden of processing this flood of applications [105] and the Supreme Court, while recognizing the honored position habeas corpus has in our jurisprudence, has gone on to point out that "the Great Writ entails significant costs." [106]

There have been many proposals over the years for legislation restricting habeas corpus, and the interest in such legislation appears to be growing.[107] In addition, the Supreme Court has shown a "historic willingness to overturn or modify its earlier views of the scope of the writ, even where the statutory language authorizing judicial action has remained unchanged." [108] In recent years states that have urged the Court to cut back on the scope of the writ have often found a receptive audience.

---

102. Ann.Rep. of the Director of the Administrative Office of the United States Courts, 1992, Table C–2A. Figures for earlier years can be found in similar tables in earlier reports. See also 17A Wright, Miller & Cooper, Jurisdiction 2d § 4261 n. 51.

103. Brown v. Allen, 1953, 73 S.Ct. 397, 425, 344 U.S. 443, 537, 97 L.Ed. 469 (concurring opinion).

104. Schaefer, Federalism and State Criminal Procedure, 1956, 70 Harv.L.Rev. 1, 25.

105. Although many habeas corpus applications are considered in the first instance by a United States magistrate, 28 U.S.C.A. § 636(b)(1)(B), the magistrate can only make proposed findings of fact and recommendations, and the petition must finally be disposed of by a district judge. See 17A Wright, Miller & Cooper, Jurisdiction 2d § 4268.4, pp. 525–526.

106. Engle v. Isaac, 1982, 102 S.Ct. 1558, 1571, 456 U.S. 107, 126–128, 71 L.Ed.2d 783. The Court itemized the costs: "Collateral review of a conviction extends the ordeal of trial for both society and the accused. * * * Liberal allowance of the writ, moreover, degrades the prominence of the trial itself. * * * [W]rits of habeas corpus frequently cost society the right to punish admitted offenders. * * * Federal intrusions into state criminal trials frustrate both the States' sovereign power to punish offenders and their good faith attempts to honor constitutional rights."

107. E.g., ABA Standards for Criminal Justice, 2d ed. 1980, c. 22; Committee Report, Ad Hoc Committee on Federal Habeas Corpus in Capital Cases, 1989, 45 Crim. L.Rep. (BNA) 3239; Committee Report, Pending Legislation to Amend the Federal Habeas Corpus Statutes, 1980, 35 Record of N.Y.C.B.A. 124; see Hatch, The Importance of Habeas Corpus Reform, 1992, 14 Crim. Just.J. 149; Tabak & Lane, Judicial Activism and Legislative "Reform" of Federal Habeas Corpus: A Critical Analysis of Recent Developments and Current Proposals, 1991, 55 Alb.L.Rev. 1; Remington, Restricting Access to Federal Habeas Corpus: Justice Sacrificed on the Altars of Expediency, Federalism and Deterrence, 1988, 16 Rev.L. & Soc.Change 339; Note, Proposed Modification of Federal Habeas Corpus for State Prisoners—Reform or Revocation?, 1973, 61 Geo.L.J. 1221.

108. Wainwright, 97 S.Ct. at 2497, 433 U.S. at 81.

"Every Justice on the current Court has embraced at least one decision that has sharply restricted the availability of the writ. The issue, then, no longer is *whether* the Court retains power to limit habeas based on equitable considerations, but *when* the Court should do so." Steiker, note 1 above, at 368.

The scope of habeas corpus has never been static in the federal courts and further change seems likely. The Great Writ was long ago hailed as "the best and only sufficient defense of personal freedom" [109] and much more recently was described as "both the symbol and guardian of individual liberty." [110] But in recent years there has been increased support for the view that the writ must be saved from itself.[111]

109. Ex parte Yerger, 1868, 8 Wall. 85, 95, 19 L.Ed. 332 (per Chase, C.J.).

110. Peyton v. Rowe, 1968, 88 S.Ct. 1549, 1551, 391 U.S. 54, 58, 20 L.Ed.2d 426 (per Warren, C.J.).

111. "There has been a halo about the 'Great Writ' that no one would wish to dim. Yet one must wonder whether the stretching of its use far beyond any justifiable purpose will not in the end weaken rather than strengthen the writ's vitality." Schneckloth v. Bustamonte, 1973, 93 S.Ct. 2041, 2072, 412 U.S. 218, 275, 36 L.Ed.2d 854 (Powell, J., concurring).

See also Friendly, note 1 above, at 143.

For a different view, see Wechsler, note 1 above, at 182: "I should myself be quite content to leave future developments to the Supreme Court. Now that its docket has expanded to some 4,000 cases a year seeking review, the logistics of the situation preclude any but a token function on direct review of state court judgments. If federal review is to be available beyond this, something like the present system of collateral attack must be preserved. The alternative, to leave the issues wholly to state courts, is not in my considered judgment an acceptable conception at this time."

Chapter 9

THE LAW APPLIED BY THE FEDERAL COURTS

Analysis

§ 54. The Rules of Decision Act and Swift v. Tyson [1]

Section 34 of the Judiciary Act of 1789 [2]—the famous Rules of Decision Act—provided that "the laws of the several states, except where the constitution, treaties, or statutes of the United States shall otherwise require or provide, shall be regarded as rules of decision in trials at common law in the courts of the United States in cases where they apply." The statute has remained substantially unchanged to this day.[3] No issue in the whole field of federal jurisprudence has been more difficult than determining the meaning of this statute.

The central question has been whether the decisions of state courts are "laws of the several states" within the meaning of the statute, and thus of controlling effect in some situations at least in the federal courts. Despite the claims of some commentators, it seems fair to say that the early decisions of this question were neither consistent nor considered,[4]

---

§ 54

1. Zeigler, The Background of Erie, 1965, 17 S.C.L.Rev. 468; Jackson, The Rise and Fall of Swift v. Tyson, 1938, 24 A.B.A.J. 609; Teton, The Story of Swift v. Tyson, 1941, 35 Ill.L.Rev. 519; Keeffe, In Praise of Joseph Story, Swift v. Tyson and "The" True National Common Law, 1969, 18 Am.U.L.Rev. 316; Note, Swift v. Tyson Exhumed, 1969, 79 Yale L.J. 284.

2. 1 Stat. 92.

3. As revised in 1948, some slight verbal changes were made in the statute that is now 28 U.S.C.A. § 1652, and the phrase "civil actions" was substituted for "trials at common law."

4. The decisions prior to 1842 are reviewed in 2 Crosskey, Politics and the Constitution in the History of the United States, 1953, pp. 816–864. Compare Robinson v. Campbell, 1818, 3 Wheat. 212, 222–223, 4 L.Ed. 372, with Wheaton v. Peters, 1834, 8 Pet. 591, 658, 8 L.Ed. 1055.

and that the first attempt at a definitive answer was in 1842 in the celebrated case of Swift v. Tyson.[5] The precise issue in that case was whether a preexisting debt was good consideration for an endorsement of a bill of exchange so that the endorsee would be a holder in due course. Several decisions of the Supreme Court had regarded this as good consideration, but the New York decisions were unclear. Justice Story, speaking for the Court, assumed that the New York decisions would not regard this as good consideration, but held that an opposite result should be reached by a federal court sitting in a diversity case.

In determining whether the New York decisions were "laws" of that state within the Rules of Decision Act, Justice Story gave no consideration to the legislative history of the act, though, as will be seen, this was to be much argued at a later time. The bases of the decision were, rather, the normal meaning of the word "laws" and considerations of policy deemed of importance by the Court. On the first of these points, he said: "In the ordinary use of language it will hardly be contended that the decisions of courts constitute laws. They are, at most, only evidence of what the laws are, and are not of themselves laws."[6] He was not content to rest decision on this pronouncement as to the nature of law, but went on to distinguish between, on the one hand, matters of a local nature, including state statutes and the construction thereof, and decisions as to real estate and other immovable matters, and, on the other hand, questions of general commercial law, dependent not on "the decisions of the local tribunals, but in the general principles and doctrines of commercial jurisprudence."[7] When Justice Story went on to say that "the law respecting negotiable instruments may be truly declared" in terms of Cicero's remark that law cannot be one thing in Rome and another in Athens, he was being entirely consistent with his earlier views, expressed both on and off the bench, urging uniformity of law.[8]

---

5. 1842, 16 Pet. 1, 10 L.Ed. 865. Ironically the defendant's name, which was a household word to lawyers for a century, was apparently misspelled by the Supreme Court, and was in fact "Tysen." See Teton, The Story of Swift v. Tyson, 1941, 35 Ill.L.Rev. 519, 530 n. 2. This is not the only example of misspelling in Supreme Court cases. The bank cashier in the great case of McCulloch v. Maryland, 1819, 4 Wheat. 316, 4 L.Ed. 579, actually spelled his name McCulloh. Lewis, Without Fear or Favor, 1965, p. 504 n. 163. The defendants in Cohens v. Virginia, 1821, 6 Wheat. 264, 5 L.Ed. 257, were two men with the last name "Cohen". Jackson, The Supreme Court, the Eleventh Amendment, and State Sovereign Immunity, 1988, 98 Yale L.J. 1, 15 n. 65. The defendant in Dred Scott's case was John F.A. Sanford, but the case has gone into the books as Dred Scott v. Sandford, 1857, 19 How. 393, 15 L.Ed. 691. See Latham, The Dred Scott Decision, 1968,

p. 26. The stubborn parents in Minersville Sch. Dist. v. Gobitis, 1940, 60 S.Ct. 1010, 310 U.S. 586, 84 L.Ed. 1375, were really named Gobitas. Harrell & Jones, Equal Justice Under Law, 1965, p. 85.

In Ford Motor Credit Co. v. Milhollin, 1980, 100 S.Ct. 790, 444 U.S. 555, 63 L.Ed.2d 22, the Court, in an introductory footnote *, says that the respondents spell their name "Millhollin", but since it has been misspelled throughout the litigation and since "legal research catalogs and computers are governed by the principle of consistency, not correctness, we feel constrained to adhere to the erroneous spelling."

6. 16 Pet. at 18.

7. 16 Pet. at 19.

8. The quotation is 16 Pet. at 19. Twenty-seven years before Justice Story had made use of the same quotation from

Writing in 1928 of the progeny of Swift v. Tyson, Dean Dobie observed justly that "though the cases here are legion, these rules and their application are notoriously far from clear."[9]   Since the doctrine of Swift v. Tyson is now a museum piece, it would not be worthwhile to develop the distinctions that the courts created in applying the doctrine. The dichotomy between matters of "general" law, which the federal courts were free to find for themselves, and matters of "local" law, on which state decisions were binding, proved particularly elusive.   Though Swift v. Tyson might have been limited to questions of commercial law, it was not so limited, and it was ultimately held that federal courts were to decide for themselves questions of the law of torts.[10]   Usually state law was respected on questions of real property, but even here the federal court was allowed to take its own view if the state decisions were thought to be unsettled.[11]   In general state-court decisions construing a state statute or constitution were followed in the federal courts, but it was held that such decisions need not be followed if they conflicted with an earlier federal construction of the statute or constitution,[12] or if the state decision had come down after the case had been tried in a lower federal court.[13]   Finally, there is the controversial case of Gelpcke v. City of Dubuque.[14]   Municipalities in Iowa had issued bonds to pay for stock in railroads building toward their towns.   The Iowa Supreme Court initially held that such bonds were valid, but subsequently overruled itself and held that the bonds were invalid under the state constitution. Citizens of states other than Iowa sued on the bonds, and invoked the diversity jurisdiction of the federal court.   The Supreme Court followed the earlier decisions and refused to be bound by the later ones holding the bonds invalid.   The Court recognized that ordinarily the federal courts should follow state decisions construing state statutes or constitutions, but said there might be exceptions to the rule, and declared passionately: "We shall never immolate truth, justice, and the law, because a state tribunal has erected the altar and decreed the sacrifice."[15]   On one level Gelpcke v. Dubuque may be thought inconsistent with Swift v. Tyson.   If decisions of a court are not themselves law, as Justice Story had said, then the early Iowa decisions were entitled to no greater respect than the later decisions, and there was no basis for holding, as the Court was to hold, that bonds issued while the early decisions still stood were valid, but that bonds issued after the overrul-

Cicero, only then it was prefaced with the words: "of the great system of maritime law it may be truly said * * *." DeLovio v. Boit, C.C.D.Mass.1815, 7 Fed.Cas. 418, 443, No. 3776.

See also Teton, note 1 above.   There is an engaging discussion of the intellectual underpinnings of Swift in the Yale Note, cited note 1 above.

9. Dobie, Federal Procedure, 1928, p. 558.

10. E.g., Baltimore & O.R. Co. v. Baugh, 1893, 13 S.Ct. 914, 149 U.S. 368, 37 L.Ed. 772.

11. E.g., Kuhn v. Fairmont Coal Co., 1910, 30 S.Ct. 140, 215 U.S. 349, 54 L.Ed. 228.

12. E.g., Rowan v. Runnels, 1847, 5 How. 134, 12 L.Ed. 85.

13. E.g., Burgess v. Seligman, 1883, 2 S.Ct. 10, 107 U.S. 20, 27 L.Ed. 359.

14. 1863, 1 Wall. 175, 17 L.Ed. 520.

15. 1 Wall. at 206–207 (per Swayne, J.).

ing decision were invalid. On another level, however, the Gelpcke case is consistent with the unarticulated assumption of Swift v. Tyson that the federal judiciary has the power, if not indeed the duty, to reach the result that appeals to it as just regardless of what the states may say.

Ultimately the doctrine of Swift v. Tyson was to come under heavy attack. As early as 1893 Justice Field, in a dissent, expressed "an abiding faith that this, like other errors, will, in the end 'die among its worshippers.' "[16] The notion that decisions of a court are not "laws" was ridiculed by a new generation, which was prepared to accept the idea that judges do not merely find the law but in fact make it.[17] Experience was said to show that independent determination by the federal courts of questions of general law had not promoted uniformity in the law.[18] Charles Warren, a distinguished lawyer and historian, uncovered evidence of an earlier draft of the Rules of Decision Act, which had said that "the Statute law of the several States in force for the time being and their unwritten or common law now in use, whether by adoption from the common law of England, the ancient statutes of the same or otherwise," should be rules of decision in federal court. From this Warren deduced that the phrase "laws of the several states," which was substituted by Oliver Ellsworth, in place of the quoted language, before the Act was adopted, was simply a shorthand expression of the same concept, and included decisions of state courts.[19] Other commentators have been less confident that this is the inevitable conclusion from the facts found by Warren.[20]

16. Baltimore & O.R. Co. v. Baugh, 1893, 13 S.Ct. 914, 928, 149 U.S. 368, 403, 37 L.Ed. 772.

17. Gray, The Nature and Sources of the Law, 2d ed. 1927, c. x.; Kuhn v. Fairmont Coal Co., 1910, 30 S.Ct. 140, 147–148, 215 U.S. 349, 370–372, 54 L.Ed. 228 (dissenting opinion of Holmes, J.); Southern Pac. Co. v. Jensen, 1917, 37 S.Ct. 524, 531, 244 U.S. 205, 221, 61 L.Ed. 1086 (dissenting opinion of Holmes, J.). But see Green, The Law as Precedent, Prophecy, and Principle: State Decisions in Federal Courts, 1924, 19 Ill.L.Rev. 217.

Other attacks on Swift from within and without the Court are cited in 19 Wright, Miller & Cooper, Jurisdiction § 4502 n. 22.

18. 2 Warren, The Supreme Court in United States History, Rev. ed. 1935, p. 89; Frankfurter, Distribution of Judicial Power Between Federal and State Courts, 1928, 13 Corn.L.Q. 499, 529 n. 150. But cf. Yntema & Jaffin, Preliminary Analysis of Concurrent Jurisdiction, 1931, 79 U.Pa.L.Rev. 869, 881 n. 23; Keeffe et al., Weary Erie, 1949, 34 Cornell L.Q. 494; 504, 527–531.

19. Warren, New Light on the History of the Federal Judiciary Act of 1789, 1923, 37 Harv.L.Rev. 49, 84–88.

20. See Jackson, note 1 above, at 614; Shulman, The Demise of Swift v. Tyson, 1938, 47 Yale L.J. 1336, 1345; Teton, note 1 above, at 536–551; 2 Crosskey, note 4 above, at p. 867; Friendly, In Praise of Erie—And of the New Federal Common Law, 1964, 39 N.Y.U.L.Rev. 383, 389–391; Field, Sources of Law: The Scope of Federal Common Law, 1986, 99 Harv.L.Rev. 883, 903–904; Comment, 1956, 51 Nw.U.L.Rev. 338, 342 n. 26; Note, note 1 above, at 285 n. 8.

The language in the early draft would have required applying statutes "in force for the time being" but the common law "now in use" and thus would have precluded using state decisions subsequent to 1789.

Mr. Warren's scholarship is criticized, and his thesis sharply attacked, in Ritz, Rewriting the History of the Judiciary Act of 1789, Holt & LaRue eds. 1990, pp. 8–12, 126–148. Ritz argues that: (1) the earlier draft Warren found was not used by the Senate in its work on § 34; (2) "the laws of the several states" was meant to refer to American law, as distinguished from British law; and (3) the purpose of § 34 may have been to allow development of a federal common law of crimes, pending the time when Congress might develop criminal statutes.

The hardest blow to Swift v. Tyson came with the 1928 decision in Black & White Taxicab Co. v. Brown & Yellow Taxicab Co.[21] A Kentucky corporation had contracted with a railroad for the exclusive right to provide taxi service at a particular station. Subsequently it wished to enjoin another Kentucky corporation from operating taxis at the station in violation of its exclusive right. For 35 years, however, the law had been settled in the Kentucky state courts that such exclusive contracts were contrary to public policy and thus unenforceable. The Kentucky corporation was, therefore, dissolved, a new corporation with the same name formed in Tennessee and the contract assigned to it, and suit for an injunction brought against the second taxi company in the federal court on the basis of diversity of citizenship. The Supreme Court upheld grant of the injunction, ruling that this was a question of general law on which Kentucky decisions were not binding, and that the common law permitted such an exclusive contract.

The result could easily have been avoided. The reincorporation in Tennessee in order to create diversity verged on fraud, and it was not necessary to hold that diversity jurisdiction could be so readily abused.[22] Even if jurisdiction were thought present, it would have been easy to classify the question of whether exclusive use may be granted for a particular piece of land as a question of "local" law on which the state could have the final say. The Court did not choose to follow either of these courses, and its decision upholding grant of the injunction provoked a famous dissent from Justice Holmes, in which he was joined by Justices Brandeis and Stone. In this dissent Holmes argued that the rule of Swift v. Tyson was "an unconstitutional assumption of powers by the Courts of the United States," insofar as it permitted the federal courts to declare rules of law in areas beyond the delegated powers of the federal government.[23] Justice Holmes said that Swift v. Tyson should be left undisturbed, but that its doctrine should not be allowed to spread into new fields.

The Black & White Taxicab case was greeted with widespread criticism, and during the next ten years the Supreme Court showed some tendency to retreat from the furthest extensions of the Swift v. Tyson rule. It deferred to state law under circumstances where earlier it would have taken a different view, and it said that as a matter of comity state law should be followed where a question was "balanced with doubt."[24]

See also Borchers, The Origins of Diversity Jurisdiction, the Rise of Legal Positivism, and a Brave New World for Erie and Klaxon, 1993, 72 Texas L.Rev. 79.

21. 1928, 48 S.Ct. 404, 276 U.S. 518, 72 L.Ed. 681.

22. See § 31 above. Under a 1958 amendment to the statute diversity jurisdiction would no longer exist on the facts of this case, since even after reincorporating in Tennessee the company had its principal place of business in Kentucky. See 28 U.S.C.A. § 1332(c), discussed § 27 above.

23. 48 S.Ct. at 408–410, 276 U.S. at 532–536. That the doctrine of Swift v. Tyson was unconstitutional had been argued also by Justice Field in his dissent in Baltimore & O.R. Co. v. Baugh, 1893, 13 S.Ct. 914, 923, 149 U.S. 368, 401, 37 L.Ed. 772.

24. The most important case is Mutual Life Ins. Co. v. Johnson, 1934, 55 S.Ct. 154, 156, 293 U.S. 335, 340, 79 L.Ed. 398. See also Burns Mortg. Co. v. Fried, 1934, 54 S.Ct. 813, 292 U.S. 487, 78 L.Ed. 1380; Trainor v. Aetna Cas. & Sur. Co., 1933, 54 S.Ct. 1, 290 U.S. 47, 78 L.Ed. 162; Note,

Thus, the Swift doctrine was narrowed, but the end did not come until 1938.

Cases in equity presented their own complications. The Judiciary Act of 1789 gave the federal courts equitable jurisdiction, though at that time many of the states did not have courts of equity, the Rules of Decision Act was limited by its express terms to "trials at common law," and the federal courts were required to conform their procedure to that of the state in which they sat in actions at law, but not in proceedings in equity. There was good reason to believe that a system of federal equity jurisprudence independent of the states was intended,[25] and indeed the early decisions seemed to imply as much.[26] Later decisions developed a more subtle doctrine. State statutes defining substantive rights were to be followed by the federal court. The Rules of Decision Act was held applicable to such statutes, though it is limited to "trials at common law," on the theory that the Act was merely declaratory of the rule that would have existed without it.[27] A different result was reached where state statutes affected what came to be known as "equitable remedial rights." The federal court was free to refuse a remedy newly created by state statute,[28] and in equity, unlike law, could give a remedy that state law denied.[29]

§ 55. The Erie Doctrine [1]

In 1938 the Supreme Court of the United States decided what a member of the Court later called "one of the most important cases at

Some Recent Implications of Swift v. Tyson, 1935, 48 Harv.L.Rev. 979.

25. See 2 Crosskey, note 4 above, at pp. 877–902; Morse, The Substantive Equity Historically Applied by the United States Courts, 1949, 54 Dick.L.Rev. 10; Van Moschzisker, Equity Jurisdiction in the Federal Courts, 1927, 75 U.Pa.L.Rev. 287. For a contrary view, see Hill, The Erie Doctrine in Bankruptcy, 1953, 66 Harv.L.Rev. 1013, 1024–1035.

26. Robinson v. Campbell, 1818, 3 Wheat. 212, 4 L.Ed. 372; U.S. v. Howland, 1819, 4 Wheat. 108, 115, 4 L.Ed. 526; Livingston v. Story, 1835, 9 Pet. 632, 9 L.Ed. 255; Neves v. Scott, 1851, 13 How. 268, 14 L.Ed. 140.

27. Mason v. U.S., 1923, 43 S.Ct. 200, 260 U.S. 545, 67 L.Ed. 396.

28. The leading case is Pusey & Jones Co. v. Hanssen, 1923, 43 S.Ct. 454, 261 U.S. 491, 67 L.Ed. 763. See also Whitehead v. Shattuck, 1891, 11 S.Ct. 276, 138 U.S. 146, 34 L.Ed. 873; Scott v. Neely, 1891, 11 S.Ct. 712, 140 U.S. 106, 35 L.Ed. 358.

See generally 19 Wright, Miller & Cooper, Jurisdiction § 4513.

29. This appears very clearly in Guffey v. Smith, 1915, 35 S.Ct. 526, 237 U.S. 101, 59 L.Ed. 856. Under Illinois law holders under a particular kind of lease could not sue in ejectment against a trespasser operating under a subsequent lease, nor could they sue for an injunction, even though the remedy at law was inadequate. The Supreme Court held that a federal court must follow the state law, and refuse to allow ejectment, but that equitable relief, including an injunction, was available.

§ 55

1. See generally 19 Wright, Miller & Cooper, Jurisdiction §§ 4503–4504.

The literature dealing with the subject of the present section, and the remaining sections of this chapter, is voluminous, and much of it is outdated by changes in the doctrine. Thus, the writings of the commentators cited in this and subsequent sections of the chapter are those that the present author has found most helpful and of contemporary relevance.

There was a spirited exchange in the Harvard Law Review. See Ely, The Irrepressible Myth of Erie, 1974, 87 Harv. L.Rev. 693, and the commentaries thereon: Chayes, The Bead Game, 1974, 87 Harv. L.Rev. 741; Ely, The Necklace, 1974, 87 Harv.L.Rev. 753; Mishkin, The Thread, 1974, 87 Harv.L.Rev. 1682.

law in American legal history." [2]   It hardly appeared to be such a case
when it began.   Harry Tompkins was walking along the right of way of
the Erie Railroad at Hughestown, Pa.   A train came by and he was hit
by something that looked like a door projecting from one of the moving
cars.   Under at least one view of Pennsylvania law, the courts of that
state would have regarded Tompkins as a trespasser and held that the
railroad would not be liable except for wanton or willful misconduct.
The "general" law, recognized by the federal courts under Swift v.
Tyson, gave Tompkins the status of a licensee and imposed liability for
ordinary negligence.   Since the railroad was a New York corporation,
and Tompkins was a citizen of Pennsylvania, he brought suit in federal
court in New York City.   He obtained a judgment for $30,000, which was
affirmed by the Second Circuit.   The railroad successfully petitioned for
certiorari.   In its brief in the Supreme Court the railroad said "we do
not question the finality of the holding of this Court in Swift v. Tyson
* * *" and the argument, both in the brief and orally, was that the
Pennsylvania cases on the duty owed those in Tompkins's position
declared a Pennsylvania rule sufficiently "local" in nature to be controlling.

The decision in the case of Erie Railroad Company v. Tompkins [3]
was handed down on April 25, 1938.   "The question for decision,"
Justice Brandeis began his opinion for the Court, "is whether the oft-
challenged doctrine of Swift v. Tyson shall now be disapproved." [4]
Having posed this somewhat surprising question, Justice Brandeis was
quick to answer it in the affirmative.   In the first section of the opinion
he referred to the "more recent research of a competent scholar,"
Charles Warren, whose examination of the original document "established" that the construction given to the Rules of Decision Act in Swift
v. Tyson and thereafter was "erroneous." [5]   Section Two of the opinion
argued that Swift v. Tyson had not produced the hoped-for uniformity
and had introduced grave discrimination by noncitizens against citizens.
These teachings of experience were not enough to justify overruling the
Swift case.   "If only a question of statutory construction were involved
we should not be prepared to abandon a doctrine so widely applied

For another provocative debate, see: Redish & Phillips, Erie and the Rules of Decision Act: In Search of the Appropriate Dilemma, 1977, 91 Harv.L.Rev. 356; Westen
& Lehman, Is There Life for Erie After the
Death of Diversity?, 1980, 78 Mich.L.Rev.
311; Redish, Continuing the Erie Debate:
A Response to Westen and Lehman, 1980,
78 Mich.L.Rev. 959; Westen, After "Life for
Erie"—A Reply, 1980, 78 Mich.L.Rev. 971.

2.   Black, Address, 1942, 13 Mo.B.J. 173,
174.

3.   1938, 58 S.Ct. 817, 304 U.S. 64, 82
L.Ed. 1188.

4.   58 S.Ct. at 818, 304 U.S. at 69.

Though the parties had not raised such a
question, at oral argument Justice Brandeis
had asked counsel's views of Swift v. Tyson.

Hicks, Materials and Methods of Legal Research, 3d ed. 1942, p. 376.   See Friendly,
In Praise of Erie—And of the New Federal
Common Law, 1964, 39 N.Y.U.L.Rev. 383,
399 n. 71.

For a highly entertaining and informative
account of the lawsuit itself, including the
underlying facts, the legal arguments and
litigation strategies, and profiles of some of
the lawyers and judges involved, see Younger, What Happened in Erie, 1978, 56 Texas L.Rev. 1011.

5.   58 S.Ct. at 819, 304 U.S. at 73.   For
discussion of what Mr. Warren found, and
whether it actually "established" anything,
see § 54 above at notes 19 and 20.

throughout nearly a century. But the unconstitutionality of the course pursued has now been made clear, and compels us to do so." [6] This led to the third section of the opinion where the new rule was summarily stated: "Except in matters governed by the Federal Constitution or by acts of Congress, the law to be applied in any case is the law of the state. And whether the law of the state shall be declared by its Legislature in a statute or by its highest court in a decision is not a matter of federal concern. There is no federal general common law. Congress has no power to declare substantive rules of common law applicable in a state whether they be local in their nature or 'general,' be they commercial law or a part of the law of torts. And no clause in the Constitution purports to confer such a power upon the federal courts." [7] These conclusions were supported by extensive quotations from earlier dissents by Justices Field and Holmes. Finally Justice Brandeis said: "In disapproving [the doctrine of Swift v. Tyson] we do not hold unconstitutional section 34 of the Federal Judiciary Act of 1789 or any other act of Congress. We merely declare that in applying the doctrine this Court and the lower courts have invaded rights which in our opinion are reserved by the Constitution to the several states." [8] The case was remanded to the Second Circuit to determine whether Pennsylvania law in fact was as the railroad contended, and on remand Tompkins ended up without his $30,000 judgment.[9]

Since Justice Cardozo was ill and took no part, only eight justices participated in the Erie decision. Four of the other justices joined in the opinion by Justice Brandeis. Justice Reed concurred in part.[10] He agreed with the disapproval of Swift v. Tyson, but said it was sufficient to hold that "the laws" in the Rules of Decision Act referred to state decisions as well as to state statutes. He thought it unnecessary to speak about the constitutionality of the Swift v. Tyson doctrine, and suggested that Article III of the Constitution and the Necessary and Proper Clause of Article I might indeed empower Congress to declare what rules of substantive law should govern the federal courts. Justices Butler and McReynolds dissented from overruling Swift v. Tyson.[11] They pointed out that Justice Field had acquiesced in the doctrine of that case after his one famous protest, and that Justice Holmes, dissenting in the Black & White Taxicab case, had stated specifically that he

---

6. 58 S.Ct. at 822, 304 U.S. at 77–78.

The sentence about statutory construction was put in the opinion at the insistence of Justice Stone. Mason, Harlan Fiske Stone: Pillar of the Law, 1956, pp. 478–481. For his later view, see § 56 n. 4.

In view of this quite explicit sentence in Erie, it is surprising to have Justice Stevens say that Swift was overruled because it rested "upon a discredited interpretation of the relevant historical documents." Florida Dept. of Health & Rehabilitative Services v. Florida Nursing Home Assn., 1981, 101 S.Ct. 1032, 1035, 450 U.S. 147, 153, 67 L.Ed.2d 132 (concurring opinion).

7. 58 S.Ct. at 822, 304 U.S. at 78.

8. 58 S.Ct. at 823, 304 U.S. at 79–80.

9. Tompkins v. Erie R. Co., C.C.A.2d 1938, 98 F.2d 49, certiorari denied 59 S.Ct. 108, 305 U.S. 637, 83 L.Ed. 410.

10. 58 S.Ct. at 828, 304 U.S. at 90–92.

11. 58 S.Ct. at 823–828, 304 U.S. at 80–90. Although their opinion is listed as a dissent in the reports, they would have reversed the decision below on the ground that Tompkins was guilty of contributory negligence as a matter of law.

would not disturb Swift v. Tyson and argued only against extending its doctrine into new fields. They protested the Court's discussion of a constitutional question without having heard counsel on that question, and, with what must have been glee, observed that the Court had failed to follow a 1937 statute, one of the few vestiges of the "court-packing plan" to survive Congress, that required notice to the Attorney General and permission for him to participate whenever the constitutionality of an Act of Congress was questioned in the courts.

It is impossible to overstate the importance of the Erie decision.[12] It announces no technical doctrine of procedure or jurisdiction, but goes to the heart of the relations between the federal government and the states and returns to the states a power that had for nearly a century been exercised by the federal government. Nevertheless the decision attracted no popular attention when it was announced.[13] Lawyers, however, were quick to recognize its significance, and there has hardly been a civil case since Erie was decided that has not felt the effect of that decision.[14] In the process the law has gone far beyond the simple holding of Erie, to the point where one competent scholar refers to "the Erie jurisprudence that has developed a doctrine completely foreign to the decision that is

12. There has been an occasional call for an overruling of Erie and a return to Swift v. Tyson. Corr, Thoughts on the Vitality of Erie, 1992, 41 Am.U.L.Rev. 1087; Keeffe, In Praise of Joseph Story, Swift v. Tyson and "The" True National Common Law, 1969, 18 Am.U.L.Rev. 316; Keeffe et al., Weary Erie, 1949, 34 Cornell L.Q. 494. These are interesting academic exercises that will not turn back the tide of the last half-century.

13. Though other decisions of the Supreme Court on April 25, 1938, received attention in the press the following day, no mention was made of the Erie case. The case was listed by name, along with everything else the Supreme Court had done the preceding day, in the Journal of Proceedings published amid the classified advertisements in N.Y. Times, April 26, 1938, p. 40. It was not referred to, however, in a front-page story about "[t]hree decisions of import to the New Deal" that had come down that day, nor in a sidebar on an inside page about denial of rehearing in a case involving New York utilities. Id. at pp. 1, 7.

On May 2d Justice Stone wrote to Arthur Krock, of the New York Times, prodding him on the matter, Mason, note 6 above, at 477, and Krock then wrote a column entitled "A Momentous Decision of the Supreme Court," Krock, N.Y.Times, May 3, 1938, p. 22. Mr. Krock began his discussion by observing that if the Supreme Court had a publicity agent eight days would not have passed before the importance of the Erie decision became known. He followed

this with another column, entitled "More about the Epochal Tompkins Decision," the next day. N.Y.Times, May 4, 1938, p. 22. See also the Letter to the Editor, by someone who signed himself mysteriously "L.L.B.," defending the constitutional arguments relied on by Justice Brandeis in the Erie decision. N.Y.Times, May 7, 1938, p. 14.

One close observer of the Court did not miss the Erie decision, nor its significance. In a letter of April 27, 1938, to President Roosevelt, Professor Frankfurter said: "I certainly didn't expect to live to see the day when the Court would announce, as they did on Monday, that it itself has usurped power for nearly a hundred years. And think of not a single New York paper—at least none that I saw—having a nose for the significance of such a decision. How fluid it all makes the Constitution!" Freedman, Roosevelt and Frankfurter, 1967, p. 456.

14. "My senior colleague Judge Learned Hand has a way of startling counsel in these 'erieantompkinated' days by saying, as they approach that inevitable citation: 'I don't suppose a civil appeal can now be argued to us without counsel sooner or later quoting large portions of Erie Railroad v. Tompkins.'" Clark, State Law in the Federal Courts: The Brooding Omnipresence of Erie v. Tompkins, 1946, 55 Yale L.J. 267, 269.

For statistics on how often Erie had been referred to up to 1978, see Younger, note 4 above, at 1011–1012.

its putative source." [15]   That doctrine is examined in the succeeding five sections, but three subsequent decisions of the Supreme Court in this area are of such landmark importance as to require special mention here.

The Erie doctrine was substantially redefined in 1945 in the case of Guaranty Trust Co. of New York v. York,[16] to the point where one writer observed that "the governing doctrine might be better described if it took its name from York rather than Erie." [17]   The Guaranty Trust case was a suit in equity brought in federal court because of diversity.   The issue was whether in such a suit a state statute of limitations, which would have barred the suit in state court, operated as a bar also in federal court.   The federal court might be thought free to entertain the action, regardless of the state statute of limitations, if equitable actions are in some way free from the compulsion of Erie, or if a statute of limitation is a mere matter of procedure, not controlling in federal court, within the "substance-procedure" dichotomy that Erie seemed to endorse.   The Court, with Justice Frankfurter speaking for five members,[18] rejected both of these possible escapes from following the state statute.

Though recognizing that in a sense federal equity is a separate legal system, the Court pointed out that the substantive right to be enforced is created by the state, and the federal courts, whether sitting in law or in equity, must respect state law, both statutory and court-made, as to that right.   It was immaterial, the Court thought, that for some purposes statutes of limitation are treated as procedural rather than substantive. "[S]ince a federal court adjudicating a state-created right solely because of the diversity of citizenship of the parties is for that purpose, in effect, only another court of the State, it cannot afford recovery if the right to recover is made unavailable by the State nor can it substantially affect the enforcement of the right as given by the State." [19]   The Erie case, Justice Frankfurter wrote, "was not an endeavor to formulate scientific legal terminology.   It expressed a policy that touches vitally the proper distribution of judicial power between State and federal courts.   In essence, the intent of that decision was to insure that, in all cases where a federal court is exercising jurisdiction solely because of the diversity of citizenship of the parties, the outcome of the litigation in the federal court should be substantially the same, so far as legal rules determine the outcome of a litigation, as it would be if tried in a State court.   The nub of the policy that underlies Erie R. Co. v. Tompkins is that for the same transaction the accident of a suit by a non-resident litigant in a

---

15.   Boner, Erie v. Tompkins: A Study in Judicial Precedent: II, 1962, 40 Texas L.Rev. 619, 625.   Mrs. Boner also observes, at 635, that "its status rose to that of a jurisprudence, which has continued to gain stature until it is practically a religion.   To its critics, the religion may be wearing a little thin, but heresy is still promptly and mercilessly eradicated."

16.   1945, 65 S.Ct. 1464, 326 U.S. 99, 89 L.Ed. 2079.

17.   Kurland, Mr. Justice Frankfurter, The Supreme Court and the Erie Doctrine in Diversity Cases, 1957, 67 Yale L.J. 187–188.

18.   Justices Rutledge and Murphy dissented.   Justices Roberts and Douglas took no part.

19.   65 S.Ct. at 1469–1470, 326 U.S. at 108–109.

federal court instead of in a State court a block away, should not lead to a substantially different result." [20]   It is clear that a state statute that would completely bar recovery in a state court does significantly affect the outcome of the case, and, on the "outcome-determinative" test announced in Guaranty Trust, would be binding in federal court.

For 13 years the lower courts struggled loyally with the rule of Guaranty Trust, but there were inevitable difficulties. Applied literally, very little would remain of the Federal Rules of Civil Procedure in diversity cases, for almost every procedural rule may have a substantial effect on the outcome of a case. If the test was not to be carried to its literal limits, however, there was confusion as to how far it was to go. Professor Henry Hart commented that "the principle having no readily apparent stopping place, the reach of the decisions is unclear." [21]   In the view of Judge Charles E. Clark, the outcome-determinative test carried the very delicate question of federalism "to an absurd extreme." [22]

In 1958 the Supreme Court seemed to retreat from the rigorous view of Guaranty Trust in the case of Byrd v. Blue Ridge Rural Electric Cooperative, Inc. [23]   As a defense to a diversity action for injuries resulting from negligence, defendant asserted that plaintiff was its employee for purposes of the South Carolina Workmen's Compensation Act, and that the act provided plaintiff's exclusive remedy. A state decision had held that this defense is to be passed on by the judge, rather than the jury. The Supreme Court held that, notwithstanding this state rule, in federal actions a jury must pass on this defense.

Justice Brennan, writing for six members of the Court, [24] said first that there was nothing to suggest that the South Carolina rule, leaving this issue for the judge rather than the jury, "was announced as an integral part of the special relationship created by the statute. Thus the requirement appears to be merely a form and mode of enforcing the immunity * * * and not a rule intended to be bound up with the definition of the rights and obligations of the parties." [25]

The Court went on to consider whether such a result was consistent with the rule of the Guaranty Trust case. It conceded that "were 'outcome' the only consideration, a strong case might appear for saying

20. 65 S.Ct. at 1470, 326 U.S. at 109.

21. Hart, The Relations between State and Federal Law, 1954, 54 Col.L.Rev. 489, 512.

See also Judge Friendly's reference to "some overly enthusiastic expressions" in Guaranty Trust. Friendly, note 4 above, at 402.

22. Clark, Federal Procedural Reform and States' Rights; to a More Perfect Union, 1961, 40 Texas L.Rev. 211, 220.

23. 1958, 78 S.Ct. 893, 356 U.S. 525, 2 L.Ed.2d 953. See Smith, Blue Ridge and Beyond: A Byrd's-Eye View of Federalism in Diversity Litigation, 1962, 36 Tul.L.Rev. 443.

24. Justice Whittaker dissented on this point. Justices Harlan and Frankfurter dissented on another issue and did not discuss the Erie features of the case.

25. 78 S.Ct. at 900, 356 U.S. at 536. See also Magenau v. Aetna Freight Lines, Inc., 1959, 79 S.Ct. 1184, 360 U.S. 273, 3 L.Ed.2d 1224.

that the federal court should follow the state practice. But there are affirmative countervailing considerations at work here." [26] Such an affirmative countervailing consideration might have been found in the express command of the Seventh Amendment that actions at law are to be tried to a jury, but the Court was at pains to refrain from deciding whether the Seventh Amendment extends to a factual issue of statutory immunity when asserted as an affirmative defense in a common-law negligence action.[27] Instead it found "a strong federal policy against allowing state rules to disrupt the judge-jury relationship in the federal courts" [28] and held that this policy outweighed the general policy, enunciated in Guaranty Trust, that the outcome of a case should not be different because it is brought in a federal court rather than in the state court a block away. As a final ground for decision, the Court expressed doubt whether the difference between jury and court determination of an issue would in fact lead to a different outcome.

The Court came to grips with the scope of the Erie doctrine again in 1965 in Hanna v. Plumer.[29] The precise holding of that case was that substituted service on an executor by leaving the process at his usual place of abode, as authorized by Rule 4(d)(1), is sufficient even where a state statute requires in hand service on an executor within a specified period. In Hanna Chief Justice Warren, writing for the Court, accepted the teaching of Guaranty Trust that "Erie-type problems were not to be solved by reference to any traditional or common-sense substance-procedure distinction," [30] but he cited the Byrd case for the proposition that the outcome-determinative test "was never intended to serve as a talisman." [31] He read Guaranty Trust as holding only that the choice between federal and state law cannot be made "by application of any automatic, 'litmus paper' criterion, but rather by reference to the policies underlying the Erie rule." [32] These policies he found to be two: "discouragement of forum-shopping and avoidance of inequitable administration of the laws." [33] The Chief Justice went on to say that Erie is not the proper test when the question is governed by one of the Rules of Civil Procedure. If the rule is valid when measured against the standards contained in the Enabling Act and the Constitution,[34] it is to be

26.   78 S.Ct. at 900, 356 U.S. at 537.

27.   78 S.Ct. at 901 n. 10, 356 U.S. at 537 n. 10.

28.   78 S.Ct. at 901, 356 U.S. at 538.

29.   1965, 85 S.Ct. 1136, 380 U.S. 460, 14 L.Ed.2d 8. See Holtzoff, A Landmark in Federal Procedural Reform, 1965, 10 Vill. L.Rev. 701; McCoid, Hanna v. Plumer: The Erie Doctrine Changes Shape, 1965, 51 Va. L.Rev. 884; Stason, Choice of Law Within the Federal System: Erie versus Hanna, 1967, 52 Corn.L.Q. 377; Zabin, The Federal Rules in Diversity Cases: Erie in Retreat, 1967, 53 A.B.A.J. 266; Siegel, The Federal Rules in Diversity Cases: Erie Implemented, Not Retarded, 1968, 54 A.B.A.J. 172.

30.   85 S.Ct. at 1141, 380 U.S. at 465–466.

31.   85 S.Ct. at 1141, 380 U.S. at 466–467.

32.   85 S.Ct. at 1141, 380 U.S. at 467.

33.   85 S.Ct. at 1142, 380 U.S. at 468.

34.   In determining the validity of a rule, a court "need not wholly blind itself to the degree to which the Rule makes the character and result of the federal litigation stray from the course it would follow in state courts * * *." 85 S.Ct. at 1145, 380 U.S. at 473.

applied regardless of contrary state law.[35]

Lawyers commonly refer to "the Erie doctrine," and this practice will be followed in the present work. It is clear, however, that the doctrine today is not what was announced in 1938. All four of the cases here discussed accept the decisions of state courts as forming a part of the "laws" of the state. All four recognize that rights created by state law should be adjudicated in accordance with state law. They differ in their attempts to delineate the issues on which state law is to control and the issues on which the federal courts are free to decide legal points for themselves. This particular problem is examined further in section 59 below.

§ 56. The Erie Doctrine—The Constitutional Basis[1]

"If only a question of statutory construction were involved," Justice Brandeis wrote in Erie, "we should not be prepared to abandon a doctrine so widely applied throughout nearly a century. But the unconstitutionality of the course pursued has now been made clear, and compels us to do so."[2] Perhaps no aspect of the Erie decision so perplexed the commentators for many years as this statement. Justice Brandeis is noted for his insistence that the Court refrain from deciding constitutional issues if any other means of disposing of the case is available.[3] Yet in Erie he seemed to go out of his way to reach the constitutional issue, since it would have been possible—if perhaps not desirable—to resolve the case as a matter of statutory construction, on the basis of what the Court believed Charles Warren's discoveries to have "established." Justice Brandeis put the decision on constitutional

---

35. 85 S.Ct. at 1143–1145, 380 U.S. at 469–474.

Seven members of the Court joined in the opinion of the Chief Justice. Justice Black concurred in result. Justice Harlan wrote a separate concurring opinion. He recognized as "unquestionably true that up to now Erie and the cases following it have not succeeded in articulating a workable doctrine governing choice of law in diversity actions." 85 S.Ct. at 1145, 380 U.S. at 474. He thought, however, that the opinion of the Court erred by oversimplification and by making the rules of procedure inviolate. He thought the inquiry should be whether "the choice of rule would substantially affect those primary decisions respecting human conduct which our constitutional system leaves to state regulation." 85 S.Ct. at 1146, 380 U.S. at 476.

The court of appeals that was reversed in Hanna later concluded that the Supreme Court had misconstrued the state statute it held not controlling in Hanna. Because of this the court of appeals felt justified in giving Hanna a much narrower reading than its words seem to justify and that

most people have given it. Marshall v. Mulrenin, C.A.1st, 1974, 508 F.2d 39, noted 1976, 50 N.Y.U.L.Rev. 952.

§ 56

1. 19 Wright, Miller & Cooper, Jurisdiction § 4505; Westen & Lehman, Is There Life for Erie after the Death of Diversity?, 1980, 78 Mich.L.Rev. 311, 338–344; Ely, The Irrepressible Myth of Erie, 1974, 87 Harv.L.Rev. 693, 700–706; Friendly, In Praise of Erie—And of the New Federal Common Law, 1964, 39 N.Y.U.L.Rev. 383, 394–398; Quigley, Congressional Repair of the Erie Derailment, 1962, 60 Mich.L.Rev. 1031; Hill, The Erie Doctrine and the Constitution, 1958, 53 Nw.U.L.Rev. 427, 541; Comment, the Constitutional Power of Congress to Control Procedure in the Federal Courts, 1961, 56 Nw.U.L.Rev. 560.

2. Erie R. Co. v. Tompkins, 1938, 58 S.Ct. 817, 822, 304 U.S. 64, 77–78, 82 L.Ed. 1188.

3. See his famous concurring opinion in Ashwander v. Tennessee Valley Authority, 1936, 56 S.Ct. 466, 482–484, 297 U.S. 288, 346–348, 80 L.Ed. 688.

grounds though Justice Reed, concurring specially, was unwilling to accept such an argument, and Justice Stone, reluctant to accept all that Brandeis said about the Constitution, three years later referred to it as "unfortunate dicta." [4]

There are other remarkable features of the constitutional discussion in Erie. Though he observed that Congress has no power to declare substantive rules of common law applicable in a state, Justice Brandeis apparently recognized that Congress had not attempted to do so for he stated expressly "we do not hold unconstitutional section 34 of the Federal Judiciary Act of 1789 or any other act of Congress." [5] Instead it was the Court's own conduct that was regarded as unconstitutional. Again the Court does not say which provision of the Constitution was violated by the doctrine of Swift v. Tyson. The courts, we are told, "have invaded rights which in our opinion are reserved by the Constitution to the several states." [6] Presumably the reference is to the Tenth Amendment, but it is unusual to have a constitutional decision that avoids making specific reference to the constitutional provision involved. No authority is cited for the constitutional arguments in the decision except earlier dissents by Justices Field and Holmes, which are themselves quite cryptic as to why Swift v. Tyson is contrary to the Constitution. Finally Justice Brandeis fails to answer the argument of Justice Reed in his concurring opinion that the Judiciary Article of the Constitution and the Necessary and Proper Clause of Article I may indeed give Congress power to enact the substantive rules that are to be applied by the courts.

For 18 years after Erie the Court refrained from referring again to the Constitution in an Erie context. This silence was perhaps most significant in the Guaranty Trust case. In that major redefinition of the Erie doctrine, Justice Frankfurter referred at three separate places to the "policy" of federal jurisdiction embodied in the Erie case. [7] It is odd that what had seemed to Justice Brandeis a constitutional imperative was reduced to a mere "policy," even if an important one, in the eyes of Justice Frankfurter and the Court for which he spoke.

The next reference to the Constitution after Erie itself was in 1956 in Bernhardt v. Polygraphic Co. of America, Inc. [8] Defendant in a diversity breach-of-contract action moved for a stay pending arbitration,

---

4. Mason, Harlan Fiske Stone: Pillar of the Law, 1956, pp. 476–481. The reference to "unfortunate dicta" was in a letter to Justice Roberts in 1941. Id. at 480 n.

5. 58 S.Ct. at 823, 304 U.S. at 79–80.

6. 58 S.Ct. at 823, 304 U.S. at 80.

Earlier in the Erie opinion there is a casual statement that Swift had "rendered impossible equal protection of the law." 58 S.Ct. at 821, 304 U.S. at 75. It was not until many years later, however, that it was first held that the notion of equal protection binds the federal government as well as the states. Bolling v. Sharpe, 1954, 74

S.Ct. 693, 347 U.S. 497, 98 L.Ed. 884. "Needless to say, in speaking of 'equal protection,' Justice Brandeis was not referring to the fourteenth amendment (which, then, applied only to the states) or to any other constitutional limitation." Westen, After "Life for Erie"—A Reply, 1980, 78 Mich. L.Rev. 971, 980 n. 35.

7. Guaranty Trust Co. of New York v. York, 1945, 65 S.Ct. 1464, 1466, 1470, 326 U.S. 99, 101, 109, 89 L.Ed. 2079.

8. 1956, 76 S.Ct. 273, 350 U.S. 198, 100 L.Ed. 199.

since the contract provided that all disputes under it were to be referred to arbitration. Vermont law arguably did not consider arbitration agreements enforceable, but § 3 of the United States Arbitration Act,[9] if applicable, did. Respondent argued that § 3 of the Act was applicable. The Court, through Justice Douglas, said: "If respondent's contention is correct, a constitutional question might be presented. Erie R. Co. v. Tompkins indicated that Congress does not have the constitutional authority to make the law that is applicable to controversies in diversity of citizenship cases. * * * We therefore read § 3 narrowly to avoid that issue." [10] Justice Frankfurter, concurring, said that "in view of the ground that was taken in [the Erie case] for its decision, it would raise a serious question of constitutional law whether Congress could subject to arbitration litigation in the federal courts which is there solely because it is 'between Citizens of different States' ".[11] These vague statements that it "might" or "would raise" a constitutional issue if Congress were to set out the applicable law in diversity cases in themselves cast doubt on how firmly Erie is based on the Constitution.

The only other reference to the Constitution since Erie was in Hanna v. Plumer.[12] The Court there said that "we are reminded by the Erie opinion that neither Congress nor the federal courts can, under the guise of formulating rules of decisions for federal courts, fashion rules which are not supported by a grant of federal authority contained in Article I or some other section of the Constitution; in such areas state law must govern because there can be no other law." [13] This says rather less than it appears to, because it leaves open hard questions about the extent to which the Necessary and Proper Clause of Article I or even Article III itself do support grants of federal authority. Indeed in that same passage the Court in Hanna relied on the "necessary and proper" clause as the source of the power to make rules of procedure and also to regulate matters that are rationally capable of being classified either as substance or procedure.

The earlier commentators had a great deal to say about the constitutional discussion in Erie, most of it critical. The view that the discussion was "a bit of judicial hyperbole which, having served its purpose, should not be permitted to mislead even the most literal-minded reader," [14] had been put forward by many distinguished students of federal

---

9. 9 U.S.C.A. § 3.

10. 76 S.Ct. at 275–276, 350 U.S. at 202.

It was later held that there is no Erie problem in applying the Arbitration Act to a diversity case involving matters over which Congress plainly has power to legislate, such as interstate commerce and admiralty. Prima Paint Corp. v. Flood & Conklin Mfg. Co., 1967, 87 S.Ct. 1801, 1806–1807, 388 U.S. 395, 404–405, 18 L.Ed.2d 1270.

11. 76 S.Ct. at 279, 350 U.S. at 208.

12. 1965, 85 S.Ct. 1136, 380 U.S. 460, 14 L.Ed.2d 8.

13. 85 S.Ct. at 1144, 380 U.S. at 471–472.

14. The phrase was Professor Brainerd Currie's but he later disowned it. Compare Currie, Change of Venue and the Conflict of Laws, 1955, 22 U.Chi.L.Rev. 405, 468–469, with Currie, Change of Venue and the Conflict of Laws: A Retraction, 1960, 27 U.Chi. L.Rev. 341, 351.

jurisdiction,[15] but this view was never unanimous, and as time went past the constitutional framework of the Erie decision attracted more defenders.[16]

On an issue that left the scholarly writers so divided, and about which the Supreme Court has been so cryptic, it would be foolhardy to venture a confident answer. A few observations may help focus the nature of the problem. When Justice Brandeis said that Congress has no power to declare substantive rules of common law applicable in a state, there is a sense in which he is surely right. If Congress were to pass a general statute that persons walking along longitudinal pathways are to be regarded as licensees and entitled to recover for ordinary negligence, such a statute could not be binding in state-court actions because Congress has no power to enact a general code of tort law obligatory upon the states.[17] To say this, however, is to contribute very little to a resolution of the Erie problem, since whatever Erie involved, it surely did not involve any such statute. There are at least three possible arguments for applying "general" law in the Erie situation—none of them at all like the hypothetical statute just described—that Justice Brandeis may have had in mind. It can be argued that Article III, § 2, of the Constitution gives the federal courts judicial power in cases between citizens of different states, and that judicial power itself includes the power to determine the rules of law that are to apply. Alternatively, resort may be had to the provision of Article I, § 8, that empowers Congress to make "all laws which shall be necessary and proper" for carrying into execution any power vested by the Constitution in any department of the government of the United States. Chief Justice Marshall held long ago that this does not confine Congress to those things that are absolutely necessary, but that it permits the use of any means calculated to produce the end and is not confined to those single means without which the end would be entirely unattainable.[18] It can be argued from this that Congress does have power to adopt rules of

15. See Clark, State Law in the Federal Courts: The Brooding Omnipresence of Erie v. Tompkins, 1946, 55 Yale L.J. 267, 273, 278; Crosskey, Politics and the Constitution in the History of the United States, 1953, pp. 563–574, 711–937; Herriott, Has Congress the Power to Modify the Effect of Erie Railroad Co. v. Tompkins?, 1941, 26 Marq.L.Rev. 1; Keeffe, In Praise of Joseph Story, Swift v. Tyson and "The" True National Common Law, 1969, 18 Am.U.L.Rev. 316; Kurland, Mr. Justice Frankfurter, The Supreme Court and the Erie Doctrine in Diversity Cases, 1957, 67 Yale L.J. 187, 188–204; McCormick & Hewins, The Collapse of "General" Law in the Federal Courts, 1938, 33 Ill.L.Rev. 126, 135; and authorities cited 19 Wright, Miller & Cooper, Jurisdiction § 4505 n. 30.

16. See Ely, note 1 above, at 700–706; Friendly, note 1 above, at 384–398; Hart, The Relations Between State and Federal Law, 1954, 54 Col.L.Rev. 489, 509–510;

Hill, note 1 above, at 541; Mishkin, The Thread, 1974, 87 Harv.L.Rev. 1682; Wechsler, Federal Jurisdiction and the Revision of the Judicial Code, 1948, 13 L. & Contemp.Probs. 216, 239 n. 121; Westen & Lehman, note 1 above, at 338–344, 353–356; and authorities cited 19 Wright, Miller & Cooper, Jurisdiction § 4505 n. 31.

17. In the precise situation involved in Erie, that of a railroad involved in interstate commerce, the Commerce Clause is broad enough to authorize legislation as to the tort duties of such carriers. Cf. Friendly, The Gap in Lawmaking—Judges Who Can't and Legislators Who Won't, 1963, 63 Col.L.Rev. 787, 789.

18. McCulloch v. Maryland, 1819, 4 Wheat. 316, 4 L.Ed. 579. See Shepard v. Adams, 1898, 18 S.Ct. 214, 216, 168 U.S. 618, 625, 42 L.Ed. 602.

tort law to be followed by the federal courts in their exercise of the judicial power.[19] Or it can be argued that Congress may tell the federal courts which subjects they may decide for themselves and which must be decided according to state law.

Since Justice Brandeis denounced as unconstitutional the course of conduct of the federal courts, he is surely rejecting the first of these three arguments, and perhaps all three. There has been much learned dispute as to whether his constitutional discussion is holding or dicta, but such discussion seems to miss any mark worth shooting at. The fact is that the Court made a considered statement that it would not overrule Swift v. Tyson if only a question of statutory construction were involved, and that it was overruling that decision only because it was inconsistent with the Constitution of the United States. If the Court believes it is deliberately deciding a constitutional question, it is wise to suppose that the constitutional question has been decided, unless and until some later Court suggests a different answer.[20]

Even if Erie is to be considered, as apparently it must, as deciding that neither Congress nor the Court can create tort rules to be applied in federal court in diversity cases, the constitutional questions raised by Erie are not yet resolved. Surely "judicial power" means something and the Necessary and Proper Clause means something. Suppose that in some state accustomed to moving at a more leisurely pace than are most of its sister states, the local law were to provide that defendants have six months in which to answer the complaint, and that either party may have unlimited continuances as a matter of right. Is the federal judiciary constitutionally compelled to countenance similar delays in diversity cases in that state, or is there rather constitutional power—if not indeed a constitutional duty—for the federal system to enforce its own procedures so that justice will not be delayed to the point where it is denied? There is nothing in the Erie decision that would seem to deny such constitutional power.[21]

Thus, perhaps a proper conclusion is that under the Constitution only Pennsylvania can say what tort duties are to be imposed on Pennsylvania landowners, that under the Constitution only the federal government can say how the federal courts are to administer their proceedings, and that under the Constitution it is a difficult and doubtful question whether New York or the federal government should have the right to determine how promptly a suit must be brought in federal court to vindicate a right created by the state. This is not the only conceivable

---

19. Cf. Panama R. Co. v. Johnson, 1924, 44 S.Ct. 391, 264 U.S. 375, 68 L.Ed. 748; Note, From Judicial Grant to Legislative Power: The Admiralty Clause in the Nineteenth Century, 1954, 67 Harv.L.Rev. 1214.

20. See Friendly, note 1 above, at 386 n. 15.

21. See Wayman v. Southard, 1825, 10 Wheat. 1, 6 L.Ed. 253. In the Hanna case the Court said: "For example, a plaintiff cannot then insist on the right to file subsequent pleadings in accord with the time limits applicable in state courts, even though enforcement of the federal timetable will, if he continues to insist that he must meet only the state time limit, result in determination of the controversy against him." 85 S.Ct. at 1142, 380 U.S. at 468–469.

conclusion. The argument that the Judicial Article and the Necessary and Proper Clause give the federal government power to provide for "juster justice" in federal courts is a compelling one, but the Erie decision, deliberately rested on a constitutional basis, stands in the way. The conclusion here suggested is not a tidy one, but federalism is not a tidy concept.

§ 57. The Erie Doctrine—Which State's Law?[1]

An accident occurs in Pennsylvania. Suit is brought in federal court in New York. Under the Erie doctrine, the federal court is required to apply state law, but is it to apply Pennsylvania law or New York law? To Justice Brandeis the question was simple. The federal court in New York was not "free to disregard the alleged rule of the Pennsylvania Common law."[2] The Court never explained why Pennsylvania law, rather than New York law, was to govern. The opinion could fairly be interpreted as meaning either that the Supreme Court had made its own decision that Pennsylvania law was properly applicable, relying on a federal choice-of-law doctrine,[3] or that it had determined sub silentio that a New York state court in similar circumstance would apply Pennsylvania law. Judge Friendly has said that "a pretty good reason for having 'skimmed over the conflicts problem as if none existed' was that none did exist; counsel were agreed that if state law controlled, Pennsylvania law would govern the rights of a Pennsylvanian injured in Pennsylvania, and no one to this day has ever suggested anything else."[4] Perhaps so, but Professor Hill has shown that while New York would feel bound to apply Pennsylvania law, it would not necessarily feel bound to follow the decisions of the Pennsylvania courts.[5]

---

§ 57

1. 19 Wright, Miller & Cooper, Jurisdiction § 4506; Cavers, Special Memorandum on Change in Choice–of–Law Thinking and Its Bearing on the Klaxon Problem, in A.L.I., Study of the Division of Jurisdiction between State and Federal Courts, Tent.Dr. No. 1, 1963, pp. 154–214; Horowitz, Toward a Federal Common Law of Choice of Law, 1967, 14 U.C.L.A.L.Rev. 1191; Weintraub, The Erie Doctrine and State Conflict of Laws Rules, 1964, 39 Ind.L.J. 228; Baxter, Choice of Law and the Federal System, 1963, 16 Stan.L.Rev. 1; Maltz, Choice of Forum and Choice of Law in the Federal Courts: A Reconsideration of Erie Principles, 1991, 79 Ky.L.J. 231.

2. Erie R. Co. v. Tompkins, 1938, 58 S.Ct. 817, 819, 304 U.S. 64, 71, 82 L.Ed. 1188. There are two other references in the opinion to Pennsylvania law, and no references to New York law.

See also Mutual Benefit, Health & Acc. Assn. v. Bowman, 1938, 58 S.Ct. 1056, 304 U.S. 549, 82 L.Ed. 1521, directing application of New Mexico law in a suit in federal court in Nebraska based on a New Mexico contract.

3. "In Erie itself, Justice Brandeis seemed to assume that a federal court should think for itself on conflicts problems." Hart, The Relations between State and Federal Law, 1954, 54 Col.L.Rev. 489, 514 n. 84.

4. Friendly, In Praise of Erie—And of the New Federal Common Law, 1964, 39 N.Y.U.L.Rev. 383, 401.

5. "It is important to remember that the jurisprudence of Swift v. Tyson had its votaries in the state courts as well as in the federal courts. If the state law concededly applicable to a controversy was the 'general law,' then not only the federal courts but also some of the state courts, among them the courts of New York, took it upon themselves to discover the applicable rules independently and thereby to avoid any 'errors' which might have been committed by the courts of the state whose 'law' was deemed to govern." Hill, The Erie Doctrine and the Constitution: II, 1958, 53 Nw.U.L.Rev. 541, 598.

In a case a week later, the Court expressly left open a similar question. In noting that general conflicts doctrine looks for interpretation of an insurance contract to the law of the place where the policy is delivered, the Court, in a case arising from federal court in Pennsylvania, said: "We do not now determine which principle must be enforced if the Pennsylvania courts follow a different conflict of laws rule." [6]

The courts of appeals, left without guidance by the Supreme Court, divided on whether they were bound by the conflicts rule in the state where the district court was sitting, or whether they were free to make their own choice of law. The best known opinion was that of Judge Magruder of the First Circuit in Sampson v. Channell.[7] In a comprehensive discussion, he concluded that the reasoning of Justice Holmes, adopted by Justice Brandeis in the Erie case, "seems to be applicable to that portion of the Massachusetts common law relating to conflict of laws quite as much as to the common law of contracts or torts. * * * If the federal court in Massachusetts on points of conflict of laws may disregard the law of Massachusetts as formulated by the Supreme Judicial Court and take its own view as a matter of 'general law,' then the ghost of Swift v. Tyson * * * still walks abroad, somewhat shrunken in size, yet capable of much mischief." [8]

It is worth noting that Judge Magruder's conclusion on this point is not an inevitable one. It is not compelled by the Erie decision, nor by the Rules of Decision Act, nor by the Constitution. In the Erie case, as has been seen, the Court directed recourse to Pennsylvania law without any attempt to demonstrate that New York choice-of-law doctrines required such a result. The Rules of Decision Act, from 1789 to the present, has referred to "the laws of the several states * * * in cases where they apply." [9] This leaves the question open of which state's law applies in a particular case. Finally, even if the Erie decision is assumed to be constitutionally compelled,[10] the Constitution does not compel a federal court to follow state conflicts doctrines. The "full faith and credit" clause of Article IV, § 1 is an affirmative grant of power to Congress, and inferentially also to the courts, to create a uniform body of conflicts principles, binding not only on the federal courts but even on the states.[11] Either from this provision, or from the implications of the

---

6. Ruhlin v. New York Life Ins. Co., 1938, 58 S.Ct. 860, 862 n. 2, 304 U.S. 202, 208 n. 2, 82 L.Ed. 1290.

7. Sampson v. Channell, C.C.A.1st, 1940, 110 F.2d 754, certiorari denied 60 S.Ct. 1099, 310 U.S. 650, 84 L.Ed. 1415.

8. 110 F.2d at 761.

9. 28 U.S.C.A. § 1652.

10. See § 56 above.

11. See Baxter, note 1 above, at 22–42; Cheatham, Federal Control of Conflict of Laws, 1953, 6 Vand.L.Rev. 581; Hughes v. Fetter, 1951, 71 S.Ct. 980, 341 U.S. 609, 95 L.Ed. 1212; Sutton v. Leib, 1952, 72 S.Ct.

398, 342 U.S. 402, 96 L.Ed. 448; First Nat. Bank of Chicago v. United Air Lines, 1952, 72 S.Ct. 421, 342 U.S. 396, 96 L.Ed. 441.

See also Jackson, Full Faith and Credit— The Lawyer's Clause of the Constitution, 1945, 45 Col.L.Rev. 1; Cook, The Powers of Congress Under the Full Faith and Credit Clause, 1919, 28 Yale L.J. 421.

Scholars are of various minds on whether Congress should adopt choice-of-law statutes, either for mass-tort cases or for all cases. Compare Gottesman, Draining the Dismal Swamp: The Case for Federal Choice of Law Statutes, 1991, 80 Geo.L.J. 1, and Atwood, The Choice–of–Law Dilemma grant of "judicial power" in Article III, it is possible to find a constitutional basis for independent determination by federal courts of conflicts questions.[12]

A 1941 decision of the Court seemed to point, if without considered discussion, in this direction. The issue was whether Civil Rule 35, authorizing the court to order a physical examination of a party to a lawsuit, was invalid as violating "substantive rights." The suit was brought in federal court in Illinois. That state did not then provide for physical examinations. The accident had occurred in Indiana, which did authorize such examinations. The Court held Rule 35 valid, but in the course of the decision made the interesting observation that "if the right to be exempt from such an order is one of substantive law, the Rules of Decision Act required the District Court, though sitting in Illinois, to apply the law of Indiana, the state where the cause of action arose, and to order the examination."[13] This is interesting because it is beyond belief that an Illinois court would hold that it could order such an examination if an accident had occurred in Indiana when it was the Illinois rule that such examinations could not be compelled in suits arising out of Illinois accidents. Thus, the Court seemed to be saying that if the matter were not governed by a valid federal rule, the federal court should apply the practice of the place of the wrong rather than the practice, and the conflicts doctrine, of the forum state.

Before that term was over the Court had laid any such notions to rest. In two cases, decided the same day, it held clearly that a federal court, in a case governed by the Erie doctrine, is to apply whatever law would be applied by the courts of the state in which the district court is sitting. In Klaxon Co. v. Stentor Electric Manufacturing Co., Inc.,[14] suit on a New York contract had been brought in Delaware federal court, because the defendant corporation was incorporated there. The Third Circuit held that a New York statute providing for interest in contract actions was to be applied. In so holding, it made no examination of Delaware law, but followed what it deemed to be the better view on such an issue. The Supreme Court reversed, in an uninformative opinion. It disposed of this difficult question in a single paragraph, in which it gave, as its sole reason for holding that Delaware's choice-of-law rules must be

in Mass Tort Litigation: Kicking Around Erie, Klaxon, and Van Dusen, 1986, 19 Conn.L.Rev. 9, with Mullenix, Federalizing Choice of Law for Mass–Tort Litigation, 1992, 70 Texas L.Rev. 1624, and Weinberg, Against Comity, 1991, 80 Geo.L.J. 53.

12. See Friendly, note 4 above, at 402; Manderino, Erie v. Tompkins: A Geography Lesson, 1967, 5 Duq.L.Rev. 465.

Professor Borchers thinks that both Erie and Klaxon are bad history. He concludes that it is too late to return to the era of Swift, but that in diversity cases federal

courts should apply an independent choice-of-law approach. Borchers, The Origins of Diversity Jurisdiction, the Rise of Legal Positivism, and a Brave New World for Erie and Klaxon, 1993, 72 Texas L.Rev. 79, 123–133.

13. Sibbach v. Wilson & Co., Inc., 1941, 61 S.Ct. 422, 425, 312 U.S. 1, 10–11, 85 L.Ed. 479. The Court repeated such a statement, 61 S.Ct. at 426 n. 13, 312 U.S. at 13 n. 13.

14. 1941, 61 S.Ct. 1020, 313 U.S. 487, 85 L.Ed. 1477.

applied, that any other ruling would do violence to the principle of uniformity within a state upon which the Tompkins decision is based.[15]

The other case decided the same day, Griffin v. McCoach,[16] is even more extreme. An administrator sued an insurance company in the district court in Texas to collect an insurance policy on the life of his decedent. The company responded with a bill of interpleader, bringing in other claimants to the policy proceeds. The policy had been taken out in New York by members of a syndicate on the life of the insured. Three of the members of the syndicate subsequently had assigned their interest in the policy to individuals not previously interested in the transaction, and these assignees had paid their proportion of the premiums after the assignments. The lower courts, considering the contract to be a New York contract, had applied New York law and awarded the proceeds to the members of the syndicate and their assignees. The Supreme Court reversed. Texas had a unique rule that an assignee of an interest in a life insurance policy who has no insurable interest in the life of the insured cannot collect on the policy, and arguably this was true of the assignees in the Griffin case. The Supreme Court held that if a Texas court would apply this rule to a contract made in another state, so must a federal court in Texas. The case goes beyond Klaxon, because in Griffin the assignees were made parties to a suit in federal court in Texas only by virtue of the nationwide service authorized by the Federal Interpleader Act. They could not have been made parties to an action in a Texas state court against their will, but after the long arm of the federal court had brought them to a Texas forum, they were held bound by whatever law a Texas state court would have applied to them in the unlikely event that they had appeared in a Texas state court.[17]

The Supreme Court has made it clear that the Klaxon rule is not to yield to the more modern thinking of conflicts-of-laws scholars. The premature explosion of an artillery shell in Cambodia injured a soldier from Wisconsin and killed another from Tennessee. Suit was brought for the injury and the death against the manufacturer in federal court in Texas, where the shell was manufactured. The Fifth Circuit reasoned that under Texas conflicts rules the law of Cambodia would certainly apply to the wrongful-death claim and perhaps to the personal-injury claim. It was thought that Cambodian law would require proof of fault by the manufacturer, while Texas, Wisconsin, and Tennessee all apply strict liability to manufacturers. The Fifth Circuit held that Cambodia had no interest in this dispute between American litigants and, on this reasoning, the court felt it could apply the strict-liability rule of all of the

15. On remand the Third Circuit concluded that Delaware would look to New York law on interest. Stentor Elec. Mfg. Co., Inc. v. Klaxon Co., C.C.A.3d, 1942, 125 F.2d 820, certiorari denied 62 S.Ct. 1284, 316 U.S. 865, 86 L.Ed. 1757.

16. 1941, 61 S.Ct. 1023, 313 U.S. 498, 85 L.Ed. 1481.

17. On remand it was held that the Texas rule applied and that the proceeds from those interests in the policy assigned to third parties were payable to the estate of the insured. Griffin v. McCoach, C.C.A.5th, 1941, 123 F.2d 550, certiorari denied 62 S.Ct. 1270, 316 U.S. 683, 86 L.Ed. 1755.

interested jurisdictions.[18]   The Supreme Court summarily reversed without hearing argument.[19]   It said that Klaxon was applicable and controlling.   "A federal court in a diversity case is not free to engraft onto those state rules exceptions or modifications which may commend themselves to the federal court, but which have not commended themselves to the State in which the federal court sits." [20]

The insistence on uniformity with the courts of the state where the district court is sitting would seem to introduce even a further refinement.   In a situation such as Erie, where the accident was in Pennsylvania and suit in New York, Klaxon dictates that New York principles of choice-of-law control.   If New York holds that in such a situation Pennsylvania law is to govern, it would seem that the federal court is then to apply, not Pennsylvania law as the federal court understands it, but the New York conception, if any, of what the Pennsylvania law is.[21]   Indeed the Supreme Court seems to have gone this far in a case where it directed the federal court to decide the relative weights, as authoritative sources for ascertaining the law of the place of the wrong, the forum state would give to direct holdings of an intermediate court of the state of the wrong and a considered dictum of relevant scope of the supreme court of that state.[22]   That this may mean that a federal court in New York "is to determine what the New York courts would think the California courts would think on an issue about which neither has thought" [23] merely highlights the unreality of the process.

The Klaxon case has been criticized on two principal grounds.[24]   By demanding uniformity between the federal and state courts in a particu-

---

18. Challoner v. Day & Zimmerman, Inc., C.A.5th, 1975, 512 F.2d 77.

The Fifth Circuit had taken a similar approach in Lester v. Aetna Life Ins. Co., C.A.5th, 1970, 433 F.2d 884, certiorari denied 91 S.Ct. 1382, 402 U.S. 909, 28 L.Ed.2d 650, criticized 1971, 40 U.Cin. L.Rev. 356, where it held that a federal court in Louisiana correctly applied Louisiana law, since Louisiana was the only state interested in the contract, even though Louisiana law would have looked to the law of Wisconsin, where the contract in question was made.

19. Day & Zimmerman, Inc. v. Challoner, 1975, 96 S.Ct. 167, 423 U.S. 3, 46 L.Ed.2d 3.

20. 96 S.Ct. at 168, 423 U.S. at 4.

On remand it was held that the Supreme Court of Texas would have applied the law of Cambodia. Challoner v. Day & Zimmerman, C.A.5th, 1977, 546 F.2d 26.

21. See Johnson v. Eastern Air Lines, C.A.2d, 1949, 177 F.2d 713, 714.

22. Nolan v. Transocean Air Lines, 1961, 81 S.Ct. 555, 365 U.S. 293, 5 L.Ed.2d 571.

23. See Nolan v. Transocean Air Lines, C.A.2d, 1960, 276 F.2d 280, 281.

The state with the best developed conflicts law is New York, but even in that state in 1941 there were no local authorities either way on 20.1% of the propositions stated in the Restatement of Conflict of Laws.   In Tennessee there was no local authority on 73% of those propositions. Goodrich, Mr. Tompkins Restates the Law, 1941, 27 A.B.A.J. 547, 548.   Thus, there will be difficulty in determining the state's conflicts doctrine generally, much less in determining its conception of the law of some particular state.

For a striking example of the difficulties the Klaxon approach causes for lower courts, see Melville v. American Home Assur. Co., D.C.Pa.1977, 443 F.Supp. 1064, reversed C.A.3d, 1978, 584 F.2d 1306.

24. See Trautman, The Relation between American Choice of Law and Federal Common Law, 1977, 41 L. & Contemp.Probs. (No. 2) 105; Horowitz, note 1 above; Cook, The Federal Courts and the Conflict of Laws, 1942, 36 Ill.L.Rev. 493; Hart, The Relations between State and Federal Law, 1954, 54 Col.L.Rev. 489, 513–515.

lar state, it eliminates the possibility of forum-shopping among the courts sitting in that state, but at the same time opens wide the door to forum-shopping among different states. Before Erie, the substantive law that would govern the parties could not be determined until it was seen whether suit was ultimately brought in state or federal court. After Klaxon, the substantive law that will govern the parties cannot be determined until it is seen in which state suit is brought. Second, the federal courts are likely to be disinterested in questions of conflicts of laws, and are in a uniquely favorable position to develop a rational body of doctrine for that branch of law.[25] Klaxon deprives them of this power.

Even if the Klaxon doctrine is accepted, there is ground to argue that Griffin v. McCoach goes too far, and that in those situations, so far quite limited, where Congress or the federal rules have made it possible to bring a litigant into a federal court located in a state where defendant could not have been sued in state court, the federal court should apply its own doctrine of conflicts and determine for itself which state's law to apply.[26]

§ 58. The Erie Doctrine—The Determination of State Law [1]

Once it is agreed that on a particular issue in a particular case the federal court is to apply state law, the problem arises of determining what the state law is that is to be applied. In Erie Justice Brandeis said that the federal court was to apply state law whether "declared by its Legislature in a statute or by its highest court."[2] The Erie doctrine has advanced—or retrogressed—far beyond this comparatively simple test.

A series of decisions in 1940 held that the federal court must follow the decision of an intermediate state appellate court in the absence of persuasive data that the highest court of the state would decide otherwise.[3] The most notorious of the cases then decided, however, did not

---

25. But see Cavers, note 1 above.

Weintraub, note 1 above, accepts the Klaxon principle generally but says that there must be "separate scrutiny of various diversity jurisdiction cases to determine in which circumstances the policy against intrastate forum-shopping is overcome by countervailing considerations." Id. at 248. Maltz, note 1 above, would modify Klaxon to provide that on issues that the federal courts should apply the law that would have been adopted by the forum state if the party choosing the federal forum had been a resident of that state. Id. at 255.

26. ALI Study, §§ 2361(c), 2374(c); Weintraub, note 1 above, at 253–256; Boner, Erie v. Tompkins: A Study in Judicial Precedent, 1962, 40 Texas L.Rev. 509, 522; Freund, Chief Justice Stone and the Conflict of Laws, 1946, 59 Harv.L.Rev. 1210, 1236 n. 62.

But see Currie, Change of Venue and the Conflicts of Laws: A Retraction, 1960, 27 U.Chi.L.Rev. 341.

§ 58

1. 19 Wright, Miller & Cooper, Jurisdiction § 4507; Yonover, Ascertaining State Law: ; The Continuing Erie Dilemma, 1989, 38 DePaul L.Rev. 1; Thomas, The Erosion of Erie in the Federal Courts: Is State Law Losing Ground?, 1977 B.Y.U.L.Rev. 1; Gibbs, How Does the Federal Judge Determine What is the Law of the State?, 1965, 17 S.C.L.Rev. 487.

2. Erie R. Co. v. Tompkins, 1938, 58 S.Ct. 817, 822, 304 U.S. 64, 78, 82 L.Ed. 1188.

3. West v. American Tel. & Tel. Co., 1940, 61 S.Ct. 179, 311 U.S. 223, 85 L.Ed. 139; Six Companies of California v. Joint Highway Dist. No. 13, 1940, 61 S.Ct. 186, 311 U.S. 180, 85 L.Ed. 114; Stoner v. New involve an intermediate state court at all, but rather a decision at nisi prius. The case is Fidelity Union Trust Co. v. Field.[4] Prior to 1932 New Jersey law had not permitted the so-called "Totten trust," by which a person can make a deposit in a savings bank for himself or herself as trustee for another, and create a tentative trust, revocable at any time before death. In 1932 the New Jersey legislature passed four statutes that seemed, in clearest terms, to change the prior law and permit the Totten trust. In 1935 Miss Peck made such a deposit in trust for her friend, Miss Field. She died shortly thereafter and Miss Field sued the bank, which had denied the validity of the trust, to collect the funds. In the meantime the 1932 legislation came before the Court of Chancery in 1936 in two cases involving other parties and "two vice-chancellors had more respect for the law than to believe it could be made imperfect by a mere legislature, and so they had construed the statute away by decision." [5] The New Jersey Court of Chancery was a court of original jurisdiction, though it had statewide jurisdiction and a standing on the equity side comparable to that of the intermediate appellate courts on the law side. The Third Circuit, in Miss Field's case, recognized that the case before it was indistinguishable from those decided by the two vice-chancellors, and it recognized that it was obliged to apply New Jersey law, but it found the 1932 legislation clearly constitutional and unambiguous and applied the statute, awarding the funds to Miss Field, rather than following the contrary decisions of the vice-chancellors. For doing so it was reversed by the Supreme Court. The decisions of the vice-chancellors would not have been binding on the New Jersey Court of Errors and Appeals, nor on any other vice-chancellor, nor even on the vice-chancellors who had made the decisions if they could be persuaded in a later case to change their mind. Nevertheless they were binding on the federal courts. Miss Field lost the money that Miss Peck wanted to leave to her because the decisions of two inferior judges, in cases to which she was not a party and in which she was not represented by counsel, were held to have, in federal court, an effect not unlike that of res judicata. It is somewhat ironical—though it did not help Miss Field—that a later New Jersey case followed the decision of the Third Circuit as to the 1932 statutes, which, it noted, had been "reversed on other grounds" by the Supreme Court,[6] and that New Jersey law now is what the Third Circuit thought it was, rather than what two vice-chancellors declared it to be in 1936. It is no wonder that Judge Jerome N. Frank said that federal judges were now "to play the role of

York Life Ins. Co., 1940, 61 S.Ct. 336, 311 U.S. 464, 85 L.Ed. 284.

Judge Friendly refers to these decisions as "the excesses of 311 U.S. as to the respect that federal judges must pay to decisions of lower state courts * * *." Friendly, In Praise of Erie—And of the New Federal Common Law, 1964, 39 N.Y.U.L.Rev. 383, 400.

4. 1940, 61 S.Ct. 176, 311 U.S. 169, 85 L.Ed. 109.

5. Clark, State Law in the Federal Courts: The Brooding Omnipresence of Erie v. Tompkins, 1946, 55 Yale L.J. 267, 292.

6. Hickey v. Kahl, 1941, 19 A.2d 33, 129 N.J.Eq. 233.

Miss Field petitioned for rehearing on the basis of the Hickey decision, but the petition was denied. 1941, 62 S.Ct. 118, 314 U.S. 709, 86 L.Ed. 565.

ventriloquist's dummy to the courts of some particular state," [7] nor that Judge Charles E. Clark denounced the Field case as "the most troublesome, the most unsatisfying in its consequence, of all the rules based upon the Tompkins case." [8] Perhaps the highpoint of the Field doctrine came in a case where the Sixth Circuit felt obliged to follow an unreported decision of an intermediate Ohio court in the face of an Ohio statute providing that "only such cases as are hereafter reported in accordance with the provisions of this section shall be recognized by and receive the official sanction of any court within the state." [9]

The first retreat from the rigidity of the Field decision came in 1948, when it was held that an unreported decision of a South Carolina Court of Common Pleas, which would not have even precedential value in any other case in that state and which could be located only with great difficulty, was entitled to "some weight" but was "not controlling" on the federal court.[10]

Unlike the situation under Swift v. Tyson, where the federal court was free to disregard even state decisions construing state statutes if the decision came down after a lower federal court had decided the case,[11] under the Erie rule it is never too late to change in conformity to some new pronouncement of state law, and a court of appeals must rely on the latest state decisions even though they come after the federal court decision that the appellate court is reviewing.[12] This raises the question

---

7. Richardson v. C.I.R., C.C.A.2d, 1942, 126 F.2d 562, 567.

8. Clark, note 5 above, at 290. See also Gibbs, note 1 above, at 487, saying that in the Fidelity Union case "the Erie Railroad ran off the track".

9. Gustin v. Sun Life Assur. Co., C.C.A.6th, 1946, 154 F.2d 961, certiorari denied 66 S.Ct. 1374, 328 U.S. 866, 90 L.Ed. 1636. There are similar decisions in: Craig v. Lake Asbestos of Quebec, Ltd., C.A.3d, 1988, 843 F.2d 145, 152 n. 6; Aviles v. Burgos, C.A.1st, 1986, 783 F.2d 270, 283 n. 4; and in In re Schmelzer, C.A.6th, 1973, 480 F.2d 1074, 1074 n. 1.

But in Southern Ry. Co. v. Foote Mineral Co., C.A.6th, 1967, 384 F.2d 224, 228, the Sixth Circuit said it was not bound by an unpublished opinion of the Tennessee Supreme Court since under Tennessee practice unpublished opinions are binding only on the parties to the particular litigation.

10. King v. Order of United Commercial Travelers of America, 1948, 68 S.Ct. 488, 333 U.S. 153, 92 L.Ed. 608.

For applications of this principle, see e.g., MGM Grand Hotel, Inc. v. Imperial Glass Co., C.A.9th, 1976, 533 F.2d 486, 489 n. 5, certiorari denied 97 S.Ct. 239, 429 U.S. 887, 50 L.Ed.2d 168; U.S. v. Wyoming Nat. Bank of Casper, C.A.10th, 1974, 505 F.2d 1064.

11. Burgess v. Seligman, 1883, 2 S.Ct. 10, 107 U.S. 20, 27 L.Ed. 359. See § 54 above.

12. Vandenbark v. Owens–Illinois Glass Co., 1941, 61 S.Ct. 347, 311 U.S. 538, 85 L.Ed. 327; Huddleston v. Dwyer, 1944, 64 S.Ct. 1015, 322 U.S. 232, 88 L.Ed. 1246; Nolan v. Transocean Air Lines, 1961, 81 S.Ct. 555, 365 U.S. 293, 5 L.Ed.2d 571.

This principle is extended in Maryland Cas. Co. v. Hallatt, C.A.5th, 1964, 326 F.2d 275, and carried to—or perhaps beyond—its limit in Pierce v. Cook & Co., C.A.10th, 1975, 518 F.2d 720, noted 1975, 7 St. Mary's L.J. 594; 1976, 29 Rutgers L.Rev. 921, 62 Va.L.Rev. 414.

But see Boston & M. Corp. v. Town of Hampton, C.A.1st, 1993, 7 F.3d 281, in which the court refused to recall its mandate and consider an otherwise untimely petition for rehearing based on a decision by the state court explicitly declaring that parts of the First Circuit's decision in the case were erroneous assessments of state law. The First Circuit expressed grave doubt about the power to grant the relief that was sought, but held that even if it had power to do so it would not exercise that power since its earlier judgment, as distinguished from its reasoning, was not demonstrably wrong. See also note 39 below.

whether a federal court can anticipate a change in state law that has not yet been authoritatively announced by the state court. Some courts thought that they had this power. They held that they could disregard a decision of the state court that the state court itself had ignored in later decisions, even though the earlier decision had never been expressly overruled,[13] or that they might follow a recent dictum discrediting outdated holdings,[14] or that if the state legislature had spoken since the state court's decision in an apparent effort to change the law as declared in that decision, the legislative enactment, rather than the decision, should take precedence.[15] On all of this there was no unanimity of view. Judge Frank, of the Second Circuit, thought that the test for the federal judge was: "What would be the decision of reasonable intelligent lawyers, sitting as judges of the highest New York court, and fully conversant with New York 'jurisprudence'?"[16] But Judge Warren L. Jones, for the Fifth Circuit, thought that to follow such a process "would be attempting to psychoanalyze state court judges rather than to rationalize state court decisions."[17]

It now seems clear that Judge Frank was right. The Court first hinted at the answer in Bernhardt v. Polygraphic Co. of America.[18] One of the issues there was whether a 1910 Vermont decision, holding arbitration agreements unenforceable, was binding on a federal court in 1956. The Court held that the 1910 decision was controlling, but in doing so pointed out that "there appears to be no confusion in the Vermont decisions, no developing line of authorities that casts a shadow over the established ones, no dicta, doubts or ambiguities in the opinions of Vermont judges on the question, no legislative development that promises to undermine the judicial rule."[19]

The Court was even more explicit in 1967 in Commissioner v. Estate of Bosch.[20] Although the issue there was a different one, the Court drew on what it understood to be the practice where Erie is controlling as providing a useful analogy. Speaking directly to the Erie cases, the Court said that "under some conditions, federal authority may not be bound even by an intermediate state appellate court ruling. * * * [T]he underlying substantive rule involved is based on state law and the

---

13. City of Newark v. U.S., D.C.N.J. 1957, 149 F.Supp. 917, 922, affirmed C.A.3d, 1958, 254 F.2d 93; City of Stockton v. Miles & Sons, Inc., D.C.Cal.1958, 165 F.Supp. 554, 563.

14. Mason v. American Emery Wheel Works, C.A.1st, 1957, 241 F.2d 906, 908. But cf. Nolan v. Transocean Air Lines, C.A.2d, 1961, 290 F.2d 904, certiorari denied 81 S.Ct. 555, 365 U.S. 293, 5 L.Ed.2d 571.

15. U.S. v. Covington Independent Tobacco Warehouse Co., D.C.Ky.1957, 152 F.Supp. 612, 615–616.

16. Cooper v. American Airlines, Inc., C.C.A.2d, 1945, 149 F.2d 355, 359.

17. Polk County v. Lincoln Nat. Life Ins. Co., C.A.5th, 1959, 262 F.2d 486, 489.

18. 1956, 76 S.Ct. 273, 350 U.S. 198, 100 L.Ed. 199.

19. 76 S.Ct. at 277, 350 U.S. at 205. In an interesting concurring opinion, Justice Frankfurter argued that the 1910 Vermont decision was a product of the hostility to arbitration at that time, and that the court of appeals might reasonably "estimate" that Vermont would no longer adhere to it if the question were to be raised now when arbitration is well accepted. 76 S.Ct. at 279–281, 350 U.S. at 208–212.

20. 1967, 87 S.Ct. 1776, 387 U.S. 456, 18 L.Ed.2d 886.

State's highest court is the best authority on its own law. If there be no decision by that court then federal authorities must apply what they find to be the state law after giving 'proper regard' to relevant rulings of other courts of the State. In this respect, it may be said to be, in effect, sitting as a state court." [21] Two dissenters in the Bosch case stated their understanding of "the formula now ordinarily employed to determine state law in diversity cases" to be that "absent a recent judgment of the State's highest court, state cases are only data from which the law must be derived * * *." [22]

Thus, the federal judge need no longer be a ventriloquist's dummy. Instead he or she is free, just as state judges are, to consider all the data the highest court of the state would use in an effort to determine how the highest court of the state would decide.[23] This is as it should be. Unless this much freedom is allowed the federal judge, the Erie doctrine would simply have substituted one kind of forum-shopping for another. The lawyer whose case was dependent on an old or shaky state-court decision that might no longer be followed within the state would have a strong incentive to maneuver the case into federal court, where, on the mechanical jurisprudence that the Erie doctrine was once thought to require, the state decision could not have been impeached.

If there are no holdings from state courts, high or low, on the matter that the federal court is to decide, that court must look for other

21. 87 S.Ct. at 1782–1783, 387 U.S. at 465.

22. 87 S.Ct. at 1788, 387 U.S. at 477.

23. Roginsky v. Richardson–Merrell, Inc., C.A.2d, 1967, 378 F.2d 832, 851. This is the view long urged by the commentators. In addition to the articles cited in note 1 above, see Hart, The Relations between State and Federal Law, 1954, 54 Col. L.Rev. 489, 510; Clark, note 5 above, at 290–295; Corbin, The Laws of the Several States, 1941, 50 Yale L.J. 762; Note, Federal Interpretation of State Law: An Argument for Expanded Scope of Inquiry, 1976, 53 Minn.L.Rev. 806.

There is an excellent statement of the process a federal judge is now to follow in determining state law in McKenna v. Ortho Pharmaceutical Corp., C.A.3d, 1980, 622 F.2d 657, 662–663, certiorari denied 101 S.Ct. 387, 449 U.S. 976, 66 L.Ed.2d 237. Even so, there is force to the argument of the dissenting judge that the majority in that case "disregards Ohio's current (though archaic) doctrine and announces a rule of law that Ohio should adopt." 622 F.2d at 669.

See Vargus v. Pitman Mfg. Co., C.A.3d, 1982, 675 F.2d 73, where the court refused to follow an recent decision of the state supreme court that appeared to abolish the defense of assumption of risk, since only three of the seven judges of the state court joined in the opinion to that effect while a fourth judge merely concurred in the result.

An extraordinary debate has been going on between two judges of the Northern District of Illinois. If the intermediate appellate courts in that state are divided on an issue on which the Illinois Supreme Court has not spoken, should a federal district court in Illinois hearing a diversity case try to predict what result the Illinois Supreme Court would reach if the issue should come before it? Judge Marshall held that it should in Roberts v. Western–Southern Life Ins. Co., D.C.Ill.1983, 568 F.Supp. 536, 539–545. Or is it absolutely bound to follow the rule in the appellate district in which the case would be if it had been filed in state court rather than federal court, as Judge Shadur held in Abbott Laboratories v. Granite State Ins. Co., D.C.Ill. 1983, 573 F.Supp. 193, 196–200, and in Rizzo v. Means Services, Inc., D.C.Ill.1986, 632 F.Supp. 1115, 1131–1133. The issue is carefully examined in Yonover, note 1 above, and the conclusion reached that Judge Shadur's approach is "flawed", while Judge Marshall's approach, "while at times susceptible to error, remains the best method to effectuate Erie's policy of achieving parity between state and federal courts". Id. at 42.

indications of the state law. Though there are various remarks from federal courts about the effect of state-court dicta,[24] such remarks should not be read out of context. Much depends on the character of the dictum. Mere obiter may be entitled to little weight, while a carefully considered statement by the state court, though technically dictum, must carry great weight,[25] and may even, in the absence of any conflicting indication of the law of the state, be regarded as conclusive.[26]

The opinions of a state attorney general are not part of "the laws" of the state within the meaning of the Rules of Decision Act, though they are entitled to weight in determining the legislative intent in enacting a statute.[27] Similarly the long-continued construction of a state statute by the state agency charged with administering it may be accepted by the federal court as representing the state law, even where the language of the statute, to an outsider, might appear to require a different construction.[28]

Inevitably situations will arise where there is no state law of any kind on the particular point involved. It is probably still true, as clearly held in 1943, that a federal court cannot decline jurisdiction of a case simply because it is difficult to ascertain what the state courts may thereafter determine the state law to be.[29] "In the absence of a state court ruling, our duty is tolerably clear. It is to decide, not avoid, the question."[30] In vicariously creating law for a state, the federal court may look to such sources as the Restatements of Law, treatises and law

---

24. Compare Hardy Salt Co. v. Southern Pac. Transp. Co., C.A.10th, 1974, 501 F.2d 1156, 1163, and Rocky Mountain Fire & Cas. Co. v. Dairyland Ins. Co., C.A.9th, 1971, 452 F.2d 603 (state dicta binding), with Nolan v. Transocean Air Lines, C.A.2d, 1961, 290 F.2d 904, certiorari denied 82 S.Ct. 177, 368 U.S. 901, 7 L.Ed.2d 96, and Walker v. Felmont Oil Corp., C.A.6th, 1957, 240 F.2d 912 (state dicta not binding).

25. Thomas v. Hoffman–LaRoche, Inc., C.A.5th, 1992, 949 F.2d 806, 812; Towne Realty, Inc. v. Safeco Ins. Co. of America, C.A.11th, 1988, 854 F.2d 1264, 1269 n. 5; Gee v. Tenneco, Inc., C.A.9th, 1980, 615 F.2d 857, 861; Hartford Acc. & Indem. Co. v. First Nat. Bank & Trust Co. of Tulsa, C.A.10th, 1961, 287 F.2d 69, 73.

26. One commentator, however, argues that if the federal court gives weight to state dicta it has substituted "stare dictis" for "stare decisis," and that the courts doing so "have departed not only from the Erie decision, but also from the very policy that they profess to serve." Boner, Erie v. Tompkins: A Study in Judicial Precedent, II, 1962, 40 Texas L.Rev. 619, 623. See also Harnett & Thornton, Precedent in the Eerie–Tompkins Manner, 1949, 24 N.Y.U.L.Q. 770, 784–786.

27. FDIC v. Municipality of Ponce, C.A.1st, 1990, 904 F.2d 740, 746; Bostick v. Smoot Sand & Gravel Corp., C.A.4th, 1958, 260 F.2d 534, 541.

28. Estate of Dancy v. C.I.R., C.A.4th, 1989, 872 F.2d 84, 85; Dickinson v. First Nat. Bank in Plant City, C.A.5th, 1968, 400 F.2d 548, 558, affirmed 1969, 90 S.Ct. 337, 396 U.S. 122, 24 L.Ed.2d 312; Rosenfield, Administrative Determinations as State Law under Erie v. Tompkins, 1949, 24 N.Y.U.L.Q.Rev. 319.

But see Mogis v. Lyman–Richey Sand & Gravel Corp., C.A.8th, 1951, 189 F.2d 130, certiorari denied 72 S.Ct. 168, 342 U.S. 877, 96 L.Ed. 659, criticized 1951, 36 Minn. L.Rev. 100, where the rule stated in the text was recognized but the court in fact did not follow the administrative construction.

29. Meredith v. City of Winter Haven, 1943, 64 S.Ct. 7, 320 U.S. 228, 88 L.Ed. 9. The recent burgeoning of the abstention doctrines casts some doubt on whether the Meredith case still represents an absolute rule. See § 52 above.

30. Daily v. Parker, C.C.A.7th, 1945, 152 F.2d 174, 177. See Fitzgerald, The Celebrated Case of Daily v. Parker, 1947, 15 U.Kan.City L.Rev. 120. See also Konradi v. U.S., C.A.7th, 1990, 919 F.2d 1207, 1213.

review commentary, and "the majority rule." [31] The federal court must keep in mind, however, that its function is not to choose the rule that it would adopt for itself, if free to do so, but to choose the rule that it believes the state court, from all that is known about its methods of reaching decisions, is likely in the future to adopt.[32]

As a general proposition, a federal-court judge who sits in a particular state and has practiced before its courts may be better able to resolve complex questions about the law of that state than is some other federal judge who has no such personal acquaintance with the law of the state. For this reason federal appellate courts have frequently voiced reluctance to substitute their own view of the state law for that of the district judge who is a member of the state's bar.[33] As a matter of judicial administration, this seems defensible. But there had been some tendency to go beyond that, and to say that if the trial court had reached a permissible conclusion under state law, the appellate court could not reverse even if it thought the state law otherwise, thus treating the question of state law much as if it were a question of fact.[34] It would seem that a party is entitled to review of the trial court's determination of state law just as he is of any other legal question in the case, and that the decision of the local trial judge cannot reasonably be regarded as conclusive.

---

31. Armijo v. Ex Cam, Inc., C.A.10th, 1988, 843 F.2d 406, 407; Seafirst Commercial Corp. v. U.S. Fid. & Guar. Co., C.A.5th, 1986, 780 F.2d 1290, 1295; and cases cited 19 Wright, Miller & Cooper, Jurisdiction § 4507 nn. 49–54.

32. Adams v. Madison Realty & Dev., Inc., C.A.3d, 1988, 853 F.2d 163, 168; Nichols v. Anderson, C.A.5th, 1988, 837 F.2d 1372, 1375; Tucker v. Paxson Machine Co., C.A.8th, 1981, 645 F.2d 620, 624–625; and cases cited 19 Wright, Miller & Cooper, Jurisdiction § 4507 n. 55.

Two cases illustrate this process in interesting fashion. In Yost v. Morrow, C.A.9th, 1959, 262 F.2d 826, 828 n. 3, it was assumed that the Idaho court would follow decisions of its sister state Oregon. In Pomerantz v. Clark, D.C.Mass.1951, 101 F.Supp. 341, 346, Judge Wyzanski based his estimate of what the Massachusetts court would do on his judgment that "subtle variations and blurred lines are not characteristic of that court. Principles are announced and adhered to in broad magisterial terms. The emphasis is on precedent and adherence to the older ways, not on creating new causes of action or encouraging the use of novel judicial remedies that have sprung up in less conservative communities."

A study has shown that federal courts in diversity cases are likely to cite federal cases, rather than state cases, on issues of state law. The authors hypothesize that despite Erie "the federal courts continue to entertain a preference for federal interpretations of common law principles: the federal common law survives despite its formal interment in the Erie decision." Landes & Posner, Legal Change, Judicial Behavior, and the Diversity Jurisdiction, 1980, 9 J.Leg.Studies 367, 375. An earlier study of over 1,400 diversity cases decided in federal courts of appeals between 1938 and 1973 found that 22% of the cases were "decided by applying law other than that of the forum state as the rule of decision, in apparent contravention of Erie." Thomas, note 1 above, at 12.

33. E.g., Gooding v. Wilson, 1972, 92 S.Ct. 1103, 1107, 405 U.S. 518, 524, 31 L.Ed.2d 408; Bernhardt v. Polygraphic Co. of America, 1956, 76 S.Ct. 273, 277, 350 U.S. 198, 204, 100 L.Ed. 199; Huddleston v. Dwyer, 1944, 64 S.Ct. 1015, 1018, 322 U.S. 232, 237, 88 L.Ed. 1246; MacGregor v. State Mut. Life Assur. Co. of Worcester, Mass., 1942, 62 S.Ct. 607, 315 U.S. 280, 281, 86 L.Ed. 846.

34. Cases are collected in Coenen, To Defer or Not to Defer: A Study of Federal Circuit Court Deference to District Rulings on State Law, 1989, 73 Minn.L.Rev. 899. Professor Coenen was critical of the decisions that deferred to the district court's determination of state law.

The latter view was endorsed by the Supreme Court in 1991 in Salve Regina College v. Russell.[35] The Court held that the essence of the Erie doctrine is that the bases of state law are presumed to be communicable to a federal judge no less than to a state judge, and to this it added that "the bases of state law are as equally communicable to the appellate judges as they are to the district judge." [36] Accordingly the courts of appeals are required to review de novo the state-law determinations of district courts.

An interesting variation on the problem just discussed was before the Second Circuit in Factors Etc., Inc. v. Pro Arts, Inc.[37] In a diversity case in federal court in New York, the issue was whether Elvis Presley's right of publicity had survived his death. All of the Second Circuit judges agreed that New York's conflicts rules would turn to Tennessee law for the answer to that question. No Tennessee statute or decision gave any hint of an answer, but the Sixth Circuit, in another case, had held on policy and practical grounds that Presley's right had not survived. The majority in the Second Circuit held that when the court of appeals for the circuit that includes the state has made a prediction of state law on a question of first impression within the state, the other circuits must defer to that holding "at least in all situations except the rare instance when it can be said with conviction that the pertinent court of appeals has disregarded clear signals emanating from the state's highest court pointing toward a different rule." [38] It is hard to see why the decision of one court of appeals should have more than persuasive effect on a coordinate court on an issue about which neither of them can speak with authority.[39] Indeed it is even arguable that the proper question is one not addressed either in the majority opinion or the vigorous dissent in Factors Etc.: what weight would New York's highest

35. 1991, 111 S.Ct. 1217, 499 U.S. 225, 113 L.Ed.2d 190. Justice Blackmun wrote for the Court. Chief Justice Rehnquist dissented, in an opinion joined by Justices White and Stevens.

36. 111 S.Ct. at 1225, 499 U.S. at 239.

37. C.A.2d, 1981, 652 F.2d 278, certiorari denied 102 S.Ct. 1973, 456 U.S. 927, 72 L.Ed.2d 442, noted 1981 B.Y.U.L.Rev. 974; 1982, 67 Cornell L.Rev. 415, 1982 Duke L.J. 704, 10 Hofstra L.Rev. 927, 15 J. Marshall L.Rev. 499, 16 Suffolk U.L.Rev. 787, 27 Vill.L.Rev. 393.

The Factors Etc. case is followed in Abex Corp. v. Maryland Cas. Co., C.A.D.C.1986, 790 F.2d 119, 125–126. But in Independent Petrochemical Corp. v. Aetna Cas. & Sur. Co., C.A.D.C.1991, 944 F.2d 940, 944–945, the District of Columbia Circuit declared that "[d]eference is one thing; blind adherence quite another." It refused to accept an Eighth Circuit determination of Missouri law.

38. 652 F.2d at 283.

39. Indeed only three months after the Second Circuit's decision, a Tennessee court decided the issue, holding that the Sixth and Second Circuits were wrong and that the right did survive. Commerce Union Bank v. Coors, Tenn.Ch.Ct.1981, 7 Media L.Rep. 2204. The federal district court then stayed entry of judgment so that plaintiffs might petition the Second Circuit to recall its mandate and rehear the case in the light of the intervening Tennessee decision. Factors Etc., Inc. v. Pro Arts, Inc., D.C.N.Y.1982, 541 F.Supp. 231. The Second Circuit granted leave to file a petition for rehearing, but at that point a second Tennessee judge held that the right did not survive. Lancaster v. Factors Etc., Inc., Tenn.Ch.Ct.1982, 9 Media L.Rep. 1109. The Second Circuit then held that the appearance of two conflicting decisions of the state courts was no basis for considering that the law of Tennessee had been authoritatively changed since 1981 and denied the motion to recall the mandate and the petition for rehearing. Factors Etc., Inc. v. Pro Arts, Inc., C.A.2d, 1983, 701 F.2d 11.

court have given to the Sixth Circuit's construction of Tennessee common law?[40]

§ 59. The Erie Doctrine—Issues on Which State Law Is Controlling[1]

A central and recurring question in the application of the Erie doctrine has been how to distinguish between those issues on which state law is controlling and those on which a federal court is not bound by state law. The Supreme Court has given different answers to this question at different times over the years. Although in 1965 it gave what appeared to be a durable and reasonably clear answer, both the lower courts and the commentators have found that the answer is not as simple as the 1965 decision seemed to make it.

In the Erie case Justice Brandeis asserted that Congress is powerless to declare "substantive rules of common law applicable in a state."[2] Justice Reed, in his concurring opinion, completed the dichotomy by observing that "no one doubts federal power over procedure."[3] For seven years it was supposed that Erie drew a line between "substance" and "procedure," with the first governed by state law in diversity cases while the second was subject to a federal rule.[4] Commentators were critical of such a distinction, but it gave no undue difficulty in the early years of the Erie era, when the most notable Supreme Court decisions were those holding that the federal court must apply state rules as to burden of proof.[5] To this day the terms "substance" and "procedure"

---

40. That possibility is suggested in Independent Petrochemical Corp. v. Aetna Cas. & Sur. Co., C.A.D.C.1991, 944 F.2d 940, 945 n. 6, but the court there found no indication that the local courts of the District of Columbia would treat the matter of deference any differently from the rule the District of Columbia had announced in the Abex case, note 37 above.

§ 59

1. 19 Wright, Miller & Cooper, Jurisdiction §§ 4508–4513. In addition to the commentaries cited § 55 n. 1, see: Crump, The Twilight Zone of the Erie Doctrine: Is There Really a Different Choice of Equitable Remedies in the "Court a Block Away"?, 1991 Wis.L.Rev. 1233; Brannan & Neumann, The Still Unrepressed Myth of Erie, 1989, 19 U.Balt.L.Rev. 403; Freer, Erie's Mid–Life Crisis, 1989, 63 Tul.L.Rev. 1087; Gelfand & Abrams, Putting Erie on the Right Track, 1988, 49 U.Pitt.L.Rev. 937; Kane, The Golden Wedding Year: Erie Railroad Company v. Tompkins and the Federal Rules, 1988, 63 Notre Dame L.Rev. 671; Weinstein, The Ghost of Process Past: ; The Fiftieth Anniversary of the Federal Rules of Civil Procedure and Erie, 1988, 54 Brooklyn L.Rev. 1.

2. Erie R. Co. v. Tompkins, 1938, 58 S.Ct. 817, 822, 304 U.S. 64, 78, 82 L.Ed. 1188.

3. 58 S.Ct. at 828, 304 U.S. at 92.

4. This line seemed to be accepted by the Supreme Court in Sibbach v. Wilson, 1941, 61 S.Ct. 422, 425, 312 U.S. 1, 10–11, 85 L.Ed. 479. See the discussion of Sibbach in Ely, The Irrepressible Myth of Erie, 1974, 87 Harv.L.Rev. 693, 733–737.

The first case expressly to employ the "substance"-"procedure" dichotomy was Guaranty Trust Co. of New York v. York, 1945, 65 S.Ct. 1464, 1467–1471, 326 U.S. 99, 105–112, 89 L.Ed. 2079. See Gelfand & Abrams, note 1 above, at 961.

5. Cities Serv. Oil Co. v. Dunlap, 1939, 60 S.Ct. 201, 308 U.S. 208, 84 L.Ed. 196; Palmer v. Hoffman, 1943, 63 S.Ct. 477, 318 U.S. 109, 87 L.Ed. 645.

For scholarly criticism of the line, see Cook, Logical and Legal Bases of the Conflict of Laws, 1942, pp. 163–165; Tunks, Categorization and Federalism: "Substance" and "Procedure" After Erie Railroad v. Tompkins, 1939, 34 Ill.L.Rev. 271.

are widely used, not only by lawyers but also by courts. As has already been seen in section 55, the Erie doctrine has been substantially redefined by the Supreme Court, and it is now clear that no simple dichotomy between substance and procedure will determine the issues on which state law is to control. The trouble with such a dichotomy, as Justice Frankfurter pointed out in the Guaranty Trust case, is that " 'substance' and 'procedure' are the same keywords to very different problems. Neither 'substance' nor 'procedure' represents the same invariants. Each implies different variables depending upon the particular problem for which it is used." [6] A particular issue may be classified as substantive or procedural in determining whether it is within the scope of a court's rulemaking power, or in resolving questions of conflict of laws, or in determining whether to apply state law or federal law. These are three very different kinds of problems. Factors that are of decisive importance in making the classification for one purpose may be irrelevant for another. To use the same name for all three purposes is an invitation to a barren and misleading conceptualism by which a decision holding that a particular issue is substantive for one of these purposes would be thought controlling authority when classification for a different purpose is involved.[7]

In the Guaranty Trust case itself the issue was whether a state statute of limitations was controlling on the equity side of federal court. Much of the opinion was devoted to refuting "talk in the cases that federal equity is a separate legal system." One week after Erie it had been held that the Erie principle applied to proceedings in equity,[8] even though the Rules of Decision Act then was limited to "trials at common law." [9] This portion of the Guaranty opinion is not as clear as might be desired. In particular, there is language in the opinion that seems to suggest that the doctrine of "equitable remedial rights" persists, and that a federal court sitting in equity is free to grant or withhold remedies without regard to what a state court would do in a similar case.[10] Probably this is true where an Act of Congress has taken away jurisdic-

---

6. Guaranty Trust Co. of New York v. York, 1945, 65 S.Ct. 1464, 1469, 326 U.S. 99, 108, 89 L.Ed. 2079.

"The line between 'substance' and 'procedure' shifts as the legal context changes." Hanna v. Plumer, 1965, 85 S.Ct. 1136, 1144, 380 U.S. 460, 471, 14 L.Ed.2d 8.

7. Jarvis v. Johnson, C.A.3d, 1982, 668 F.2d 740, 747. The holding here was that although Pa.R.C.P. 238, requiring prejudgment interest in certain cases, had been upheld by the Pennsylvania Supreme Court as a valid exercise of its power to make rules of "procedure," Rule 238 nevertheless must be applied by a federal court in a diversity case.

8. Ruhlin v. New York Life Ins. Co., 1938, 58 S.Ct. 860, 304 U.S. 202, 82 L.Ed.

1290. This had been the rule even under Swift v. Tyson—see Mason v. U.S., 1923, 43 S.Ct. 200, 260 U.S. 545, 67 L.Ed. 396—except insofar as state law sought to define "equitable remedial rights." See § 54 above.

9. In the 1948 revision of the Judicial Code the Rules of Decision Act was altered, and now speaks of "civil actions." 28 U.S.C.A. § 1652.

10. "State law cannot define the remedies which a federal court must give simply because a federal court in diversity jurisdiction is available as an alternative tribunal to the State's courts. Contrariwise, a federal court may afford an equitable remedy for a substantive right recognized by a State even though a State court cannot give it." 65 S.Ct. at 1468–1469, 326 U.S. at 106.

tion to grant an injunction in particular cases [11] or where the constitutional right to trial by jury might be abridged.[12] It seems equally true that federal courts are free to use procedural devices made available by statutes or the Federal Rules despite the absence of similar procedures in the states.[13] Beyond such situations it is difficult to believe that the federal court is free to fashion an independent law of remedies in equitable actions.[14]

The most important, and better-known, aspect of the Guaranty Trust case is its holding that a state statute of limitations must be applied by a federal court in a diversity case, even though statutes of limitations may be regarded as "procedural" for some other purposes, in order to ensure that "the outcome of the litigation in the federal court should be substantially the same, so far as legal rules determine the outcome of a litigation, as it would be if tried in a State court." [15]

It has already been pointed out that to such a principle there is no apparent stopping place.[16] It is difficult to conceive of any rule of procedure that cannot have a significant effect on the outcome of a case. Yet for some years the Supreme Court seemed committed to applying this "outcome-determinative" test to its farthest reach. Three decisions handed down on the same day in 1949 showed the deference to state law that was to be required in matters that, for other purposes, are clearly procedural. One of the decisions held that a federal court, hearing a stockholder's derivative suit based on diversity, must apply a New Jersey statute making unsuccessful plaintiffs in such litigation liable for all expenses, including attorney's fees, of the defense, and requiring security for the payment of such expenses as a condition of prosecuting the action.[17] Clearly it would significantly affect the outcome if the suit would be barred in state court because of the plaintiff's inability to post such security, and on this reasoning the majority held that the policy of Guaranty Trust must apply. Three dissenters, including, interestingly, the author of the Guaranty Trust opinion, took the view that the New

---

11. As with the Norris–La Guardia Act, 29 U.S.C.A. § 101 et seq.

12. In Guaranty Trust the Court cites approvingly, as illustrating this point, Whitehead v. Shattuck, 1891, 11 S.Ct. 276, 138 U.S. 146, 34 L.Ed. 873.

13. E.g., class actions, Oskoian v. Canuel, C.A.1st, 1959, 269 F.2d 311; preliminary injunctions and temporary restraining orders, Southern Milk Sales, Inc. v. Martin, C.A.6th, 1991, 924 F.2d 98, 101–102; declaratory judgments, Cincinnati Ins. Co. v. Holbrook, C.A.11th, 1989, 867 F.2d 1330.

14. 19 Wright, Miller & Cooper, Jurisdiction § 4513; Crump, note 1 above, at 1273. Thus, state law has been held to govern the availability of such equitable remedies as: permanent injunction, System Operations, Inc. v. Scientific Games Development Corp., C.A.3d, 1977, 555 F.2d 1131, 1143; specific performance, Weathersby v.

Gore, C.A.5th, 1977, 556 F.2d 1247, 1257–1259; rescission, Lipsky v. Commonwealth United Corp., C.A.2d, 1976, 551 F.2d 887, 894–898; and accounting, McLeod v. Stevens, C.A.4th, 1980, 617 F.2d 1038, 1041.

But see Perfect Fit Indus., Inc. v. Acme Quilting Co., Inc., C.A.2d, 1981, 646 F.2d 800, 806.

The Supreme Court treated this as still an open question in Stern v. South Chester Tube Co., 1968, 88 S.Ct. 1332, 1334, 390 U.S. 606, 609–610, 20 L.Ed.2d 177.

15. 65 S.Ct. at 1470, 326 U.S. at 109.

16. See § 55 nn. 21, 22 above.

17. Cohen v. Beneficial Indus. Loan Corp., 1949, 69 S.Ct. 1221, 337 U.S. 541, 93 L.Ed. 1528.

Justices Douglas, Frankfurter, and Rutledge dissented.

Jersey statute neither added to nor subtracted from the cause of action, but merely prescribed the method by which the cause of action was to be enforced, and on this reasoning said state law need not be followed.

In a second case, it was held, with three justices dissenting, that a state statute barring foreign corporations that had not qualified to do business in the state from suing in the courts of the state was effective also to bar such a corporation from bringing a diversity action in the federal court sitting in that state.[18]

Finally, in the controversial case of Ragan v. Merchants Transfer & Warehouse Co.,[19] a suit had been filed within the period of a state statute of limitations, but service was not made until after the statutory period had run, and the state law made service within the statutory period an integral part of the state's statute of limitations. It was held, with only one dissent, that the action must be dismissed in federal court, despite Rule 3 of the Federal Rules of Civil Procedure, which provides that an action is commenced by filing a complaint with the court.

It is interesting to note that, though in each of these cases state law was held controlling, only four members of the Court were applying a principle broad enough to encompass all three cases. Five of the justices dissented in one or another of the three cases. This failure to enunciate an understandable principle made application of the teaching of these cases more difficult. Many observers believed, however, that there was no longer much, if any, room for independent federal regulation of procedure.

Prior to 1938 the pattern in federal courts had been conformity to state law on matters of procedure, under the Conformity Act,[20] but substantial uniformity among the federal courts on substantive law, under the aegis of Swift v. Tyson.[21] This arrangement was reversed in 1938. The Federal Rules of Civil Procedure, providing a uniform system of procedure for the federal courts, were adopted by the Court on December 20, 1937, and became effective September 1, 1938.[22] The Erie case, requiring conformity to state decisional law, was decided April 25, 1938.[23]

After the three 1949 decisions the draftsman of the rules said that "hardly a one of the heralded Federal Rules can be considered safe from attack."[24] Several distinguished commentators urged repeal of the rules

---

18. Woods v. Interstate Realty Co., 1949, 69 S.Ct. 1235, 337 U.S. 535, 93 L.Ed. 1524.

Justices Jackson, Rutledge, and Burton dissented.

The result in this case was foreshadowed by Angel v. Bullington, 1947, 67 S.Ct. 657, 330 U.S. 183, 91 L.Ed. 832. See § 46 above.

19. 1949, 69 S.Ct. 1233, 337 U.S. 530, 93 L.Ed. 1520.

Justice Rutledge dissented.

20. See § 61 below.

21. See § 54 above.

22. See § 62 below.

23. The author of the Erie opinion, Justice Brandeis, had dissented from adoption of the Rules of Civil Procedure. Order of Dec. 20, 1937, 302 U.S. 783.

24. Clark, Book Review, 1950, 36 Cornell L.Q. 181, 183.

in diversity cases.[25]   Other writers were more sanguine, and recognized the practical necessity of arriving at a workable policy that would permit the coexistence of the Erie doctrine and the rules.[26]

For the next nine years the lower courts were left to resolve such questions with a minimum of guidance from the Supreme Court.   The only decision in that period from the Court bearing on the question held that a change in forum from a court trial to arbitration might make a radical difference in ultimate result, and thus that antiquated state court decisions, holding unenforceable contract provisions for arbitration, must be applied by the federal court.[27]   Then in 1958 the well-known case of Byrd v. Blue Ridge Rural Electric Cooperative, Inc.,[28] provided a formula by which the rules might indeed coexist with the Erie doctrine. "Outcome" was no longer to be the only test.   Instead it was recognized that the federal judicial system is an independent system for administering justice to litigants who properly invoke its jurisdiction.   Federal policies on how the federal courts should be run—in that case the federal policy favoring jury decisions of disputed fact questions—must be balanced against the policy of providing the same outcome in federal court as in state court.

Though Byrd was a welcome retreat from the more extreme position of Guaranty Trust, and it provided a means for continuing to apply the Civil Rules in many areas, there was considerable difficulty in applying the Byrd test.   Indeed in many respects Byrd is the most Delphic of the Supreme Court's major Erie-doctrine decisions.[29]   Able courts—and judges within a single court—were divided in situations that were distinguishable but perhaps not really different.   The interest of the federal system in having a uniform procedure in its courts was given heavy weight by the Fifth Circuit but only "slight" weight by the Seventh Circuit.[30]   The presence or absence of a specific federal statute or rule was thought decisive by Judge Friendly and a majority of the Second Circuit but Judge Clark of that court gave it little weight as also

25.   Merrigan, Erie to York to Ragan—A Triple Play on the Federal Rules, 1950, 3 Vand.L.Rev. 711; Gavit, States' Rights and Federal Procedure, 1949, 25 Ind.L.Rev. 1, 26.   A later writer proposed "thorough amendment" of the rules to avoid conflicts with state law. Hill, The Erie Doctrine and the Constitution, 1958, 53 Nw.U.L.Rev. 549, 581–584.

26.   Symposium, Federal Trials and the Erie Doctrine, 1956, 51 Nw.U.L.Rev. 338; Note, The Erie Case and the Federal Rules—A Prediction, 1951, 39 Geo.L.J. 600, 612.

27.   Bernhardt v. Polygraphic Co. of America, 1956, 76 S.Ct. 273, 350 U.S. 198, 100 L.Ed. 199.

28.   1958, 78 S.Ct. 893, 356 U.S. 525, 2 L.Ed.2d 953.

29.   See 19 Wright, Miller & Cooper, Jurisdiction § 4504, pp. 31–35.

30.   Compare Monarch Ins. Co. of Ohio v. Spach, C.A.5th, 1960, 281 F.2d 401, 408, with Allstate Ins. Co. v. Charneski, C.A.7th, 1960, 286 F.2d 238, 244.

Professor Freer has said that to rely on a supposed need for uniformity in federal courts is to beg the question.   "Federal uniformity is proper only if the matter is not one entrusted by Erie to state law.   The very point of Erie is that uniformity among federal courts must give way to promote vertical uniformity for citizens of the various states, at least with regard to substantive issues."   Freer, note 1 above, at 1140 n. 241.

did the Seventh Circuit.[31]

The difficulty in applying the Byrd test probably stemmed from the fact that there is no scale in which the balancing process called for by that case can take place. There is no way to say with assurance in a particular case that the federal interest asserted is more or less important than the interest in preserving uniformity of result with the state court. Even if there were such a scale, the weights to be put in it must be whatever the judges say they are. Uniformity of procedure among the federal courts is thought "important" by one court but of only "slight" weight by another. There is no objective standard by which it can be said that one of those evaluations is "wrong" and the other "right."

Perhaps because of these difficulties, the Court again turned its attention to this problem in 1965 in Hanna v. Plumer.[32] All of the fears that the Civil Rules might be limited or made ineffective by Erie were laid to rest, as the Court denounced "the incorrect assumption that the rule of Erie R. Co. v. Tompkins constitutes the appropriate test of the validity and therefore the applicability of a Federal Rule of Civil Procedure."[33] Cases that had seemed to put the rules in jeopardy were explained on the ground that "the holding of each such case was not that Erie commanded displacement of a Federal Rule by an inconsistent state rule, but rather that the scope of the Federal Rule was not as broad as the losing party urged, and therefore, there being no Federal Rule which covered the point in dispute, Erie commanded the enforcement of state law."[34]

Thus, Hanna announces a bifurcated test. If one of the Civil Rules (or a statute) is valid and if, properly construed, it speaks to the question, it is controlling and no regard need be paid to contrary state provisions. "[T]he court has been instructed to apply the Federal Rule, and can refuse to do so only if the Advisory Committee, this Court, and Congress erred in their prima facie judgment that the Rule in question transgressed neither the terms of the Enabling Act nor constitutional restrictions."[35]

The matter is very different if there is no rule directly in point and the court must make "the typical, relatively unguided Erie choice."[36] Such questions cannot be resolved by a talismanic analysis of whether the outcome would be affected. Instead the problem must be viewed in

---

31. Compare Arrowsmith v. United Press Intl., C.A.2d, 1963, 320 F.2d 219, 226, and Iovino v. Waterson, C.A.2d, 1959, 274 F.2d 41, 48, certiorari denied 80 S.Ct. 860, 362 U.S. 949, 4 L.Ed.2d 867, with Jaftex Corp. v. Randolph Mills, Inc., C.A.2d, 1960, 282 F.2d 508, 515–516, and Allstate Ins. Co. v. Charneski, C.A.7th, 1960, 286 F.2d 238, 244.

32. 1965, 85 S.Ct. 1136, 380 U.S. 460, 14 L.Ed.2d 8.

33. 85 S.Ct. at 1143, 380 U.S. at 469–470.

34. 85 S.Ct. at 1143, 380 U.S. at 470.

35. 85 S.Ct. at 1144, 380 U.S. at 471.

See 19 Wright, Miller & Cooper, Jurisdiction § 4508.

36. 85 S.Ct. at 1144, 380 U.S. at 471.

the light of "the twin aims of the Erie rule; discouragement of forum-shopping and avoidance of inequitable administration of the laws." [37]

Each half of the test announced in Hanna leaves significant questions unanswered.[38] The first half of the test, that a valid Civil Rule is to be applied without more, frees the federal courts from Erie concerns in many cases and, in addition, provides the Civil Rules with a presumptive validity if not quite an automatic seal of approval. At the same time this portion of Hanna creates an added burden on the Court and those who advise it in the rulemaking process. In formulating a rule the rulemakers must now consider the extent to which application of a proposed rule, in cases where state law is different, is consistent with the proper ordering of the federal system.[39] As Professor Ronan E. Degnan has put it, the implication of Hanna is not that the federal rules are valid because wise men made them, but because wise men thought carefully before making them.[40]

Under this part of Hanna, a rule is to be applied only if it is valid. Hanna seems to state an easy test: anything that is arguably procedural, in that it falls "within the uncertain area between substance and procedure," is a valid rule.[41] There is reason, however, to think that this states only the constitutional limits on the power of Congress—or the Court as its rulemaking delegate—to make rules of procedure, and that the proviso in the Rules Enabling Act that rules "shall not abridge, enlarge or modify any substantive right" [42] imposes a further, more stringent limitation.[43]

37. 85 S.Ct. at 1142, 380 U.S. at 468.

38. Freer, note 1 above, at 1089–1090, calls the first part of this test "the Hanna prong" and the second part "the Rules of Decision Act or Erie prong."

39. "[A] court, in measuring a Federal Rule against the standards contained in the Enabling Act and the Constitution, need not wholly blind itself to the degree to which the Rule makes the character and result of the federal litigation stray from the course it would follow in state courts * * *." 85 S.Ct. at 1145, 380 U.S. at 473.

Wright, Procedural Reform: Its Limitations and Its Future, 1967, 1 Ga.L.Rev. 563, 571–574.

40. Quoted in Wright, note 39 above, at 574.

See also Ely, note 4 above, arguing that the Court has failed to give sufficient meaning to the second sentence of the Rules Enabling Act, 28 U.S.C.A. § 2072, providing that the rules "shall not abridge, enlarge or modify any substantive right * * *."

41. 85 S.Ct. at 1144, 380 U.S. at 472.

In Burlington Northern R. Co. v. Woods, 1987, 107 S.Ct. 967, 970, 480 U.S. 1, 5, 94 L.Ed.2d 1, the Court says that the process by which the various sets of rules are made gives them "presumptive validity under both the constitutional and statutory restraints."

42. 28 U.S.C.A. § 2072.

43. 19 Wright, Miller & Cooper, Jurisdiction § 4509; Westen & Lehman, Is There Life for Erie after the Death of Diversity?, 1980, 78 Mich.L.Rev. 311, 360–364; Mishkin, The Thread, 1974, 87 Harv. L.Rev. 1682; Ely, note 4 above, at 718–720; McCoid, note 1 above, at 901–903.

In a thoughtful opinion it is held that for purposes of the Enabling Act, a state rule is "substantive" only if it is one "which, if all the facts were stipulated, would be meaningful in analyzing the rights and liabilities of parties to a dispute if they were to settle it on the day of filing suit, taking into account the necessity of filing suit, but without actually filing it." Boggs v. Blue Diamond Coal Co., D.C.Ky.1980, 497 F.Supp. 1105, 1120, noted 1981, 11 Mem.St. U.L.Rev. 413. On this analysis it was held that the time allowed in Rule 25(a) for substitution after death is a valid procedural rule, "because immediately prior to filing the suit the parties would not consider this rule in evaluating their rights and liabilities." 497 F.Supp. at 1121.

A testing case—and one that had given the courts much difficulty—is Rule 15(c), which provides that if the conditions stated in it are satisfied a defendant can be added to an action by amendment even if the applicable statute of limitations has run in the interim between the filing of the original complaint and the filing of the amendment. Application of Rule 15(c) will mean in some instances that the action can go forward against the new defendant even though in state court that party would have a good defense of limitations. In this situation the courts have uniformly held, and properly so, that Rule 15(c) can be applied and that to do so does not violate the "substantive rights" proviso of the Enabling Act.[44]

It is the other application of Rule 15(c) that in the past had caused more difficulty. One of the conditions of that rule is that the party to be added must have received such notice of the institution of the original action within the limitations period that he will not be prejudiced in maintaining a defense and that he must have known or had reason to know that, except for a mistake concerning the identity of the proper party, the action would have been brought against him. Some states have more liberal views on amendments to add parties and would find the statute of limitations not to be a bar even though that condition has not been met. Here the better view had been thought to be that the amendment should be allowed, as permitted by state law, even though Rule 15(c) seemingly did not authorize it.[45] If a state should provide that the filing of a complaint against the wrong defendant tolls the running of the statute of limitations against the correct defendant, a federal court would apply the state's tolling provision.[46] It would honor the state's policy decision that a potential defendant's sense of repose is not so important as to prevent resolution on the merits of state causes of action simply because of an excusable mistake in the denomination of the defendant. The result should not be different because the state has chosen to cast the same policy decision in terms of relation back of

But see McCollum Aviation, Inc. v. CIM Associates, Inc., D.C.Fla.1977, 438 F.Supp. 245. A Florida statute providing that a corporation transacting business in the state cannot sue in Florida courts unless it has obtained authority to transact business in the state must be applied in federal court since it is highly influential in the choice of forum and has the substantive purpose of encouraging corporation qualification for the benefit of the people of the state. Thus, it controls over Rule 17(b).

44. E.g., Freund v. Fleetwood Enterprises, Inc., C.A.1st, 1992, 956 F.2d 354; Welch v. Louisiana Power & Light Co., C.A.5th, 1972, 466 F.2d 1344. See 19 Wright, Miller & Cooper, Jurisdiction § 4509, pp. 148–151.

For a highly debatable application of Rule 15(c) to allow relation back to cure lack of capacity of a plaintiff when state law would not do so, see Davis v. Piper Aircraft Corp.,

C.A.4th, 1980, 615 F.2d 606, certiorari dismissed 101 S.Ct. 25, 448 U.S. 911, 65 L.Ed.2d 1141.

45. Marshall v. Mulrenin, C.A.1st, 1974, 508 F.2d 39; Covel v. Safetech, Inc., D.C.Mass.1981, 90 F.R.D. 427; Carmouche v. Bethlehem Steel Corp., D.C.Nev.1978, 450 F.Supp. 1361; cf. Ingram v. Kumar, C.A.2d, 1978, 585 F.2d 566, certiorari denied 99 S.Ct. 1289, 440 U.S. 940, 59 L.Ed.2d 499.

Contra: Britt v. Arvanitis, C.A.3d, 1978, 590 F.2d 57; Williams v. Avis Transport of Canada, Ltd., D.C.Nev.1972, 57 F.R.D. 53.

46. Lindley v. General Elec. Co., C.A.9th, 1986, 780 F.2d 797, certiorari denied 106 S.Ct. 2926, 476 U.S. 1186, 91 L.Ed.2d 554; Williams v. U.S., D.C.La.1973, 353 F.Supp. 1226.

amendments rather than of tolling of the statute of limitations.[47] Nevertheless the Supreme Court decided the other way. It held that an amendment changing parties related back only if the party to be named had notice of the pendency of the suit before the statute of limitations had run and that notice within a reasonable additional time for serving process was not sufficient. The Court reached this result wholly as a construction of Rule 15(c) and did not discuss, though the case was a diversity case, what a state court might have done.[48] Fortunately Rule 15(c) was amended in 1991, so that an amendment always relates back if relation back is permitted by the law that provides the statute of limitations applicable to the action.[49]

Even if the Civil Rule in question is clearly valid, both in terms of the Constitution and, in the circumstances of the particular case, in terms of the Enabling Act, it still must be decided whether it speaks to the precise issue before the court. A good illustration is the controversy about the continuing vitality of the Ragan case. The holding in Ragan, it will be recalled, was that the mere filing of a complaint with the court is not enough to satisfy a state statute of limitations if the state law makes service within the statutory period essential. This holding was reached despite Rule 3, which provides that an action is commenced by filing a complaint with the court.

In Hanna the Court was at pains to distinguish Ragan as a case in which "the scope of the Federal Rule was not as broad as the losing party urged."[50] Even so, some lower courts thought that Hanna had silently overruled Ragan.[51] In 1980, in Walker v. Armco Steel Corporation,[52] the Court was confronted with facts indistinguishable from those in Ragan, and it unanimously reaffirmed Ragan. Rule 3, it reasoned, does not speak to state statutes of limitations. "There is no indication that the Rule was intended to toll a state statute of limitations, much less that it purported to displace state tolling rules for purposes of state statutes of limitations. In our view, in diversity actions Rule 3 governs the date from which various timing requirements of the federal rules

---

47. 19 Wright, Miller & Cooper, Jurisdiction § 4509, pp. 152–160.

48. Schiavone v. Fortune, 1986, 106 S.Ct. 2379, 477 U.S. 21, 91 L.Ed.2d 18. See Brussack, Outrageous Fortune: The Case for Amending Rule 15(c) Again, 1988, 61 S.Cal.L.Rev. 671; Lewis, The Excessive History of Federal Rule 15(c) and Its Lessons for Civil Rule Revision, 1987, 85 Mich. L.Rev. 1507; Note, 1988, 63 N.Y.U.L.Rev. 131.

49. Rule 15(c)(1). At the same time it was provided in Rule 15(c)(3) that a defect in the pleading with respect to the defendant's name does not defeat relation back. In this way the specific holding of Schiavone was overcome.

50. 85 S.Ct. at 1143, 380 U.S. at 469–470.

The Court, in drawing this distinction, relied primarily on Palmer v. Hoffman, 1943, 63 S.Ct. 477, 482, 318 U.S. 109, 117, 87 L.Ed. 645, where it had held that Rule 8(c) governs the manner of pleading affirmative defenses, but that it is silent on burden of proof and that state law controls on that issue.

51. Sylvestri v. Warner & Swasey Co., C.A.2d, 1968, 398 F.2d 598; and cases cited 19 Wright, Miller & Cooper, Jurisdiction § 4510 n. 10.

52. 1980, 100 S.Ct. 1978, 446 U.S. 740, 64 L.Ed.2d 659. See Diffurth, Rule 3, The Enabling Act, and Statutes of Limitations, 1981 S.Ill.U.L.J. 329.

begin to run, but does not affect state statutes of limitations." [53] By a similar analysis Rule 23.1 (formerly Rule 23(b)) on derivative actions does not speak to whether plaintiffs can be required to give security for expenses [54], and Rule 4, though prescribing how to serve process on a foreign corporation, is silent on when a foreign corporation is amenable to suit. [55] In each of these instances the courts, finding the Civil Rule not to be in point, [56] have in effect gone to the second half of the Hanna test and have held that state law applies.

In two other cases the Court has given surprisingly broad readings to a federal statute and a federal rule and, concluding that the statute or rule spoke to the point in issue, held that, under the first prong of the test announced in Hanna, the federal law should apply regardless of the state rule on the matter. The first of these cases, Burlington Northern Railroad Co. v. Woods, [57] was an Alabama diversity case. An Alabama statute requires an appellate court, upon affirming a money judgment, to impose a 10% penalty on any appellant who had obtained a stay of the judgment by executing a bond. A unanimous Court held that the Alabama statute is not to be applied in federal court. Rule 38 of the Federal Rules of Appellate Procedure affords federal courts of appeals plenary discretion to award damages to an appellee upon determining that the appeal is frivolous, and the purposes of Rule 38 were sufficiently coextensive with the statute's purposes to indicate that the rule occupied the statute's field of operation.

The second case, Stewart Organization, Inc. v. Ricoh Corp, [58] arose out of a contract that contained a clause providing that any disputes could be brought only in a court in New York. A diversity action was brought in federal court in Alabama. Alabama was a proper venue, but defendant, relying on the forum-selection clause, moved to transfer the suit to the Southern District of New York. The Eleventh Circuit, sitting

---

53. 100 S.Ct. at 1985, 446 U.S. at 750–751.

This has been thought to be a "painfully narrow" reading of Rule 3. Freer, note 1 above, at 1122. See also James, Hazard & Leubsdorf, Civil Procedure, 4th ed. 1992, p. 130. In a later case the Court held that Rule 3 does determine when an action is commenced for purposes of a statute of limitations when the underlying cause of action is based on federal law. West v. Conrail, 1987, 107 S.Ct. 1538, 1541, 481 U.S. 35, 39, 95 L.Ed.2d 32.

54. Cohen v. Beneficial Indus. Loan Corp., 1949, 69 S.Ct. 1221, 337 U.S. 541, 93 L.Ed. 1528. See § 73 below.

See also Kamen v. Kemper Financial Services, Inc., 1991, 111 S.Ct. 1711, 500 U.S. 90, 114 L.Ed.2d 152. The Court there held that Civil Rule 23.1, requiring the complaint to allege the plaintiff's efforts to obtain the desired action from the board of directors relates only to the adequacy of

pleadings. The rule does not create a demand requirement of any particular dimension and the applicable substantive law must be looked to.

55. Arrowsmith v. United Press Intl., C.A.2d, 1963, 320 F.2d 219. See § 64 below.

56. See 19 Wright, Miller & Cooper, Jurisdiction § 4510.

57. 1987, 107 S.Ct. 967, 480 U.S. 1, 94 L.Ed.2d 1.

See Whitten, Erie and the Federal Rules: A Review and Reappraisal After Burlington Northern Railroad v. Woods, 1988, 21 Creighton L.Rev. 1.

58. 1988, 108 S.Ct. 2239, 487 U.S. 22, 101 L.Ed.2d 22. Although the article by Freer, note 1 above, speaks generally to the Erie doctrine, it focuses on the Stewart case as an example to make its points and it is very critical of that decision.

en banc, divided sharply on whether in a diversity case a federal court should look to Alabama law, which regards forum-selection clauses as unenforceable, or to federal law, which enforces such clauses if they are not unreasonable. The Supreme Court thought that this was not the right question. It held that 28 U.S.C.A. § 1404(a) governs whether to transfer a case,[59] so that state law is not controlling, and that the forum-selection clause is only one of the factors the federal court should take into account in exercising its discretion under the statute. Although the Hanna and Walker cases had said that the first prong of the Hanna test applies only if there is a "direct collision" between state and federal law, Justice Marshall, writing for the Court in Stewart, said that that phrase "is not meant to mandate that federal law and state law be perfectly coextensive and equally applicable to the issue at hand; rather, the 'direct collision' language, at least where the applicability of a federal statute is at issue, expresses the requirement that the federal statute be sufficiently broad to cover the point in dispute." [60]

If a case is found to be like Walker, rather than like Burlington Northern or Stewart, and there is no valid federal statute or rule addressing the point, the second half of Hanna requires courts to consider the problem in the light of "the twin aims of the Erie rule: discouragement of forum-shopping and avoidance of inequitable administration of the laws." [61] Although many courts have simply applied the Hanna formulae without further discussion, other courts have felt that these issues require some further refinement of analysis, and that it is necessary to balance the strength of the competing federal and state interests.[62] Byrd v. Blue Ridge has not been overruled, nor its interest-balancing technique repudiated, and, when faced with the typical, relatively unguided Erie choice, its approach has been found useful.[63]

---

59. See § 44 above.

60. 108 S.Ct. at 2242 n. 4, 487 U.S. at 26 n. 4.

61. 85 S.Ct. at 1144, 380 U.S. at 471.

62. 19 Wright, Miller & Cooper, Jurisdiction § 4511. See also Crump, note 1 above; Redish & Phillips, Erie and the Rules of Decision Act: In Search of the Appropriate Dilemma, 1977, 91 Harv.L.Rev. 356.

"[W]e must approach a problem such as is presented by the instant case by considering how the constitutional and policy concerns that motivated the Court in Erie and its progeny are implicated by the application or nonapplication of the particular state rule at issue. * * * [T]hese concerns include (1) the effect of application of the state or federal rule on the outcome of the litigation; (2) the likelihood that divergent state and federal rules will result in forum shopping; and (3) the existence of any overriding federal interest in the application of the federal rule." Jarvis v. Johnson, C.A.3d, 1982, 668 F.2d 740, 743–744.

63. A great many cases purporting to apply the second half of the Hanna test on a great variety of issues are collected in 19 Wright, Miller & Cooper, Jurisdiction § 4511 n. 67. The following are a few well-known cases that seem to use some form of the approach described in the text:

Chambers v. NASCO, Inc., 1991, 111 S.Ct. 2123, 2136–2138, 501 U.S. 32, ___-___, 115 L.Ed.2d 27. The twin aims of Erie are not implicated by the assessment of attorney's fees as a sanction for bad-faith conduct that involved disobedience of the court's orders and the attempt to defraud the court itself.

Szantay v. Beech Aircraft Corp., C.A.4th, 1965, 349 F.2d 60, noted 1965, 17 S.C.L.Rev. 631, 1966, 51 Cornell L.Q. 560. The court refused to apply a state's "door-closing statute" where to do so would not further any important state policy but would frustrate the federal interest in encouraging efficient joinder in multi-party actions and the interest in providing a convenient forum for plaintiff's action. Szan-

In his concurring opinion in Hanna Justice Harlan said: "It is unquestionably true that up to now Erie and the cases following it have not succeeded in articulating a workable doctrine governing choice of law in diversity actions." [64] This is still true even after Hanna. Quite possibly this is inevitable in the nature of the Erie problem. Erie and its progeny recognize that the choice of law to be applied in the federal courts in diversity cases is an important question of federalism, and that the constitutional power of the states to regulate the relations among their people does overlap the constitutional power of the federal government to determine how its courts are to be operated. [65] Where these interests come into conflict, there can be no wholly satisfactory answer. [66]

tay has been distinguished in two later Fourth Circuit decisions: Bumgarder v. Keene Corp., C.A.4th, 1979, 593 F.2d 572; Proctor & Schwartz, Inc. v. Rollins, C.A.4th, 1980, 634 F.2d 738. It was followed in rather exotic circumstances in Miller v. Davis, C.A.6th, 1974, 507 F.2d 308. See Leathers, Miller v. Davis: The Sixth Circuit Applies Interest Analysis to an Erie Problem, 1975, 63 Ky.L.J. 923.

Atkins v. Schmutz Mfg. Co., C.A.4th, 1970, 435 F.2d 527, certiorari denied 91 S.Ct. 1526, 402 U.S. 932, 28 L.Ed.2d 867, noted 1971, 50 Texas L.Rev. 162, 1971 Duke L.J. 785. It was held that the pendency of suit in another federal court tolled the state statute of limitations though it would not have done so in state court. See the lucid analysis of Atkins by Professor Ward in Tribute to The Honorable Clement F. Haynsworth, Jr., 1981, 665 F.2d lxxiii, lxxxviii-xc.

Goodman v. Mead Johnson & Co., C.A.3d, 1976, 534 F.2d 566, certiorari denied 97 S.Ct. 732, 429 U.S. 1038, 50 L.Ed.2d 748. A federal jury should decide when plaintiff knew or should have known that she had an actionable claim, although the state had held that application of the "discovery" exception to the statute of limitations is for the court and not the jury. Compare Justice v. Pennzoil Co., C.A.4th, 1979, 598 F.2d 1339, certiorari denied 100 S.Ct. 457, 444 U.S. 967, 62 L.Ed.2d 380, holding that state rules governed the allocation of judge and jury functions to a question of what constitutes unreasonable use of land by a mineral owner.

Hargrave v. OKI Nursery, Inc., C.A.2d, 1980, 646 F.2d 716. A defendant brought in under a state long-arm statute on a claim of fraud must defend also other claims dealing with breach of contract and warranty, although in state court jurisdiction would extend to the fraud claim only.

Feinstein v. Massachusetts Gen. Hosp., C.A.1st, 1981, 643 F.2d 880. A federal plaintiff must comply with a state statutory procedure referring malpractice claims to a special tribunal before a claimant is permitted to pursue a judicial remedy. But see Hibbs v. Yashar, D.C.R.I.1981, 522 F.Supp. 247.

In re Air Crash Disaster Near New Orleans, C.A.5th, 1987, 821 F.2d 1147, 1154–1159, noted 1988, 62 Tul.L.Rev. 813. A federal court is to apply federal notions of whether to dismiss on the ground of forum non conveniens and is not to look to state law on the point. But see Stein, Erie and Court Access, 1991, 100 Yale L.J. 1935.

64. 85 S.Ct. at 1145, 380 U.S. at 474. The test Justice Harlan proposed would be to inquire "if the choice of rule would substantially effect those primary decisions respecting human conduct which our constitutional system leaves to state regulation." 85 S.Ct. at 1146, 380 U.S. at 475. With respect, that too would be a difficult and imprecise test to apply.

65. See § 56 above.

66. "It is, of course, neither possible nor necessary for federal courts to be totally neutral in the adjudication of state-created rights. It is not possible simply because federal courts are not protean and are unable to transform themselves into exact replicas of their state counterparts. That state and federal judicial systems are not identical will inevitably mean that the choice of forum will have some effect upon the course of litigation. Some adoption of state court procedures by federal courts sitting in diversity may be feasible, but it may also be in conflict with fundamental interests of the federal courts in the conduct of their own business and the maintenance of the integrity of their own procedures, the legitimate interests of a federal forum *qua* forum." Atkins v. Schmutz Mfg. Co., C.A.4th, 1970, 435 F.2d 527, 536, certiorari denied 91 S.Ct. 1526, 402 U.S. 932, 28 L.Ed.2d 867.

This is hardly a problem unique to questions of jurisdiction, as anyone who has read, for example, the long line of virtually irreconcilable cases on the power of the states to tax businesses engaged in interstate commerce will attest. There may be no alternative but to leave questions such as these for the ad hoc determination of judges keenly aware of their responsibilities to two sovereigns.[67]

§ 60.   The Erie Doctrine—Federal Common Law [1]

In the Erie case, Justice Brandeis wrote: "Except in matters governed by the Federal Constitution or by acts of Congress, the law to be applied in any case is the law of the state. * * * There is no federal general common law." [2] On that same day, in another case, Justice Brandeis, again speaking for the Court, wrote that "whether the water of an interstate stream must be apportioned between the two States is a question of 'federal common law' upon which neither the statutes nor the decisions of either State can be conclusive." [3]

It is clear, therefore, that there is a "federal common law" even if not a "federal general common law." It is not accurate to say, however, that the law of the state is to be applied in all cases except on matters governed by the Constitution or by Act of Congress. Neither the Constitution nor any statute provides the answer to controversies between states about interstate streams, or similar interstate conflicts, nor do these sources indicate where the governing law is to be found. Yet the Court, of necessity, has developed its own body of law to govern such questions, because of the obvious unsuitability of looking to the law of a particular state when two states are in dispute.[4]

---

67. The view put forward in the text has been rejected as a "free-wheeling approach" that is "too ad hoc to allow the development of meaningful legal categories by which men may judge their everyday affairs * * *." Note, The Operation of Federalism in Diversity Jurisdiction: Erie's Constitutional Basis, 1965, 40 Ind.L.J. 512, 538–539.

But see Freer, note 1 above, at 1090: "To a degree, confusion is to be expected, because the vertical choice of law cases reflect the ongoing, delicate process by which we allocate power between federal and state courts. This process will never, and should never, yield clear, litmus-test answers in all cases."

§ 60

1. 19 Wright, Miller & Cooper, Jurisdiction § 4514; Field, Sources of Law: The Scope of Federal Common Law, 1986, 99 Harv.L.Rev. 881; Merrill, The Common Law Powers of Federal Courts, 1985, 52 U.Chi.L.Rev. 1; Hill, The Law–Making Power of the Federal Courts: Constitutional Preemption, 1967, 67 Col.L.Rev. 1024; Mishkin, The Variousness of "Federal Law": Competence and Discretion in the Choice of National and State Rules for Decision, 1957, 105 U.Pa.L.Rev. 797; Friendly, In Praise of Erie—And of the New Federal Common Law, 1964, 39 N.Y.U.L.Rev. 383.

2. Erie R. Co. v. Tompkins, 1938, 58 S.Ct. 817, 822, 304 U.S. 64, 78, 82 L.Ed. 1188.

3. Hinderlider v. La Plata River & Cherry Creek Ditch Co., 1938, 58 S.Ct. 803, 811, 304 U.S. 92, 110, 82 L.Ed. 1202.

4. Kansas v. Colorado, 1902, 22 S.Ct. 552, 185 U.S. 125, 46 L.Ed. 838; Kansas v. Colorado, 1907, 27 S.Ct. 655, 206 U.S. 46, 51 L.Ed. 956; Kentucky v. Indiana, 1930, 50 S.Ct. 275, 281 U.S. 163, 74 L.Ed. 784; Connecticut v. Massachusetts, 1931, 51 S.Ct. 286, 289–290, 282 U.S. 660, 670–671, 75 L.Ed. 602; West Virginia ex rel. Dyer v. Sims, 1951, 71 S.Ct. 557, 341 U.S. 22, 95 L.Ed. 713; Texas v. New Jersey, 1965, 85 S.Ct. 626, 379 U.S. 674, 13 L.Ed.2d 596; Illinois v. City of Milwaukee, 1972, 92 S.Ct. 1385, 406 U.S. 91, 31 L.Ed.2d 712; Note, What Rule of Decision Should Control in Interstate Controversies, 1907, 21 Harv. L.Rev. 132. See § 109 below.

There has been in recent years a considerable scholarly debate about the legitimacy of federal common law and a variety of views have been put forth.[5] "These range from the prohibitive view, founded on the Rules of Decision Act, through a broad middle ground, emphasizing the need for authorization, that permits a range of federal common law, to an inclusive view under which the federal courts enjoy, presumptively, the same lawmaking powers as Congress."[6] The issue raises important considerations of both separation of powers and federalism, but to date it has interested the scholars far more than it has the Supreme Court. The Court has largely ignored the issue.[7]

It is clear that where the Constitution, or a valid Act of Congress, provides a rule of decision, it must be applied by a federal court—and by a state court—in cases where there is concurrent jurisdiction.[8] Beyond that very little is clear. Whether state law or federal law controls on matters not covered by the Constitution or an Act of Congress is a very complicated question, which yields to no simple answer in terms of the parties to the suit, the basis of jurisdiction, or the source of the right that is to be enforced.[9] Whenever the federal court is free to decide for itself the rule to be applied, and there are many such situations, it is applying, or making, "federal common law."

In a much-admired concurring opinion in D'Oench, Duhme & Co. v.

See, however, the suggestion of Judge Friendly that it is indeed the Constitution that requires the federal courts to fashion law when the interstate nature of a controversy makes it inappropriate that the law of either state should govern. Friendly, note 1 above, at 408 n. 119.

5. There is a fascinating exchange between Professors Martin Redish and Louise Weinberg in 1989, 83 Nw.U.L.Rev. 761; Redish, Federal Common Law, Political Legitimacy, and the Interpretative Process: An Institutional Perspective, 1989, 83 Nw. U.L.Rev. 761; Weinberg, Federal Common Law, 1989, 83 Nw.U.L.Rev. 805; Redish, Federal Common Law and American Political Theory: A Response to Professor Weinberg, 1989, 83 Nw.U.L.Rev. 853; Weinberg, The Curious Notion That the Rules of Decision Act Blocks Supreme Court Federal Common Law, 1989, 83 Nw.U.L.Rev. 860.

There is also a useful Symposium, 1992, 12 Pace L.Rev. 227. It includes: Doernberg, Introduction, 1992, 12 Pace L.Rev. 227; Brown, Federal Common Law and The Role of the Federal Courts in Private Law Adjudication—A (New) Erie Problem?, 1992, 12 Pace L.Rev. 229; Kramer, The Lawmaking Power of the Federal Courts, 1992, 12 Pace L.Rev. 263; Field, The Legitimacy of Federal Common Law, 1992, 12 Pace L.Rev. 303; Merrill, The Judicial Prerogative, 1992, 12 Pace L.Rev. 327.

6. Brown, note 5 above, at 260.

7. Brown, Bright Lines, 1991 Wis.L.Rev. 293, 298.

In a recent leading case, Boyle v. United Technologies Corp., 1988, 108 S.Ct. 2510, 487 U.S. 500, 101 L.Ed.2d 442, the Court divided 5–4 in deciding that state law that holds government contracts liable for design defects in military equipment in some circumstances presents a significant conflict with federal policy and must be displaced by federal common law. The dispute, however, was on whether this was an appropriate situation in which to displace state law. To Justice Scalia, for the majority, "a few areas, involving 'uniquely federal interests,' * * * are so committed by the Constitution and laws of the United States to federal control that state law is preempted and replaced, where necessary, by federal law of a content prescribed (absent explicit statutory directive) by the courts—so-called 'federal common law.'" 108 S.Ct. at 2514, 487 U.S. at 504. To the three dissenters who joined in Justice Brennan's opinion, "federal common law can displace state law in 'few and restricted' instances." 108 S.Ct. at 2521, 487 U.S. at 518.

8. See § 45 above.

9. See 19 Wright, Miller & Cooper, Jurisdiction § 4514 at notes 18–20.

Federal Deposit Insurance Corporation,[10] Justice Jackson said: "A federal court sitting in a non-diversity case such as this does not sit as a local tribunal. In some cases it may see fit for special reasons to give the law of a particular state highly persuasive or even controlling effect, but in the last analysis its decision turns upon the law of the United States, not that of any state. Federal law is no juridical chameleon changing complexion to match that of each state wherein lawsuits happen to be commenced because of the accidents of service of process and of the application of the venue statutes. It is found in the federal Constitution, statutes, or common law. Federal common law implements the federal Constitution and statutes, and is conditioned by them. Within these limits, federal courts are free to apply the traditional common-law technique of decision and to draw upon sources of the common law in cases such as the present." In the D'Oench, Duhme case the issue was whether the accommodation maker of a note could assert a defense of no consideration in a suit by a federal agency to which the note had been assigned. The Court was unanimous in holding that the maker could not, apparently as a matter of independent decision of what the federal rule should be, although the other opinions are less lucid as to the source of the governing rule than is Justice Jackson's.

A somewhat similar case, and perhaps the best-known case in this area, is Clearfield Trust Co. v. United States.[11] A check issued by the United States had been stolen, and it was cashed on the basis of a forged endorsement. The United States sued a bank that had presented the check for payment and had guaranteed prior endorsements. Under the law of Pennsylvania, where the transaction took place, the delay of the United States in notifying the bank that the endorsement was a forgery would bar recovery from the bank, but a unanimous Court held that the rights and duties of the United States on commercial paper that it issues are governed by federal rather than local law. This does not mean that in choosing the applicable federal rule the courts may not occasionally select state law.[12] But it was thought that such a course would be singularly inappropriate in the Clearfield case. "The issuance of commercial paper by the United States is on a vast scale and transactions in that paper from issuance to payment will commonly occur in several states. The application of state law, even without the conflict of laws rules of the forum, would subject the rights and duties of the United States to exceptional uncertainty. It would lead to great diversity in results by making identical transactions subject to the vagaries of the laws of the several states. The desirability of a uniform rule is plain." [13]

---

10. 1942, 62 S.Ct. 676, 686, 315 U.S. 447, 471–472, 86 L.Ed. 956.

11. 1943, 63 S.Ct. 573, 318 U.S. 363, 87 L.Ed. 838.

12. See Board of County Commrs. v. U.S., 1939, 60 S.Ct. 285, 288–289, 308 U.S. 343, 351–352, 84 L.Ed. 313. It was held there that state law does not control on the right to interest in an action by the United

States for taxes improperly collected from an Indian, but that as a matter of choice the state rule would be absorbed and applied as the federal law.

13. 63 S.Ct. at 575, 318 U.S. at 367.

For criticism of this passage, see Friendly, note 1 above, at 410; Mishkin, note 1 above, at 829–832; Note, 1969, 82 Harv. L.Rev. 1512, 1526–1531.

To find such a uniform rule the Court looked to the federal law merchant, and found from this that mere delay in giving notice of a forged endorsement does not bar recovery unless there is a clear showing that the delay in giving notice caused damage to the other party. Federal courts have made similar decisions for themselves as to what the controlling rule is to be in other cases where the United States is a party and the suit involves commercial paper issued by the United States,[14] government contracts,[15] or the effect of a federal lien.[16]

A similar principle has been applied in tort cases, with federal law held to determine whether a tortfeasor who injured a soldier is liable to the United States for hospitalization of the soldier and loss of his services.[17] The Court said in that case that the Erie decision was not intended for "broadening state power over matters essentially of federal character or for determining whether issues are of that nature."[18] Federal common law also controls the validity of a defense by a federal officer sued for having committed a tort in the course of his official duties.[19] And this principle has been extended to some suits by private parties against an independent contractor performing its duty under a government contract.[20]

The Court has held that "an issue concerned with a basic choice regarding the competence and function of the Judiciary and the National Executive in ordering our relationships with other members of the international community must be treated exclusively as an aspect of federal law."[21] It has consistently interpreted the grant of general

14. National Metropolitan Bank v. U.S., 1945, 65 S.Ct. 354, 323 U.S. 454, 89 L.Ed. 383; Comment, Federal Law of Negotiable Instruments, 1961, 6 Vill.L.Rev. 388.

It has been said that the Uniform Commercial Code should generally be considered as the federal law of commerce. Sierra Pacific Indus. v. Lyng, C.A.9th, 1989, 866 F.2d 1099, 1110 n. 16; In re King–Porter Co., C.A.5th, 1971, 446 F.2d 722, 732; U.S. v. Wegematic Corp., C.A.2d, 1966, 360 F.2d 674, 676, noted 1966, 20 Sw.L.J. 688; In re Quantum Development Corp., D.C.V.I.1975, 397 F.Supp. 329, 336. But courts have continued to apply the particular rule of commercial paper announced in the National Metropolitan Bank case, above, although the Uniform Commercial Code, now adopted in 49 states, lays down a different rule. U.S. v. City Nat. Bank & Trust Co., C.A.8th, 1974, 491 F.2d 851, 854; U.S. v. Bank of America Nat. Trust & Sav. Assn., C.A.9th, 1971, 438 F.2d 1213, 1214, certiorari denied 92 S.Ct. 54, 404 U.S. 864, 30 L.Ed.2d 108.

15. West Virginia v. U.S., 1987, 107 S.Ct. 702, 479 U.S. 305, 93 L.Ed.2d 639; U.S. v. Seckinger, 1970, 90 S.Ct. 880, 397 U.S. 203, 25 L.Ed.2d 224; Wissner v. Wissner, 1950, 70 S.Ct. 398, 338 U.S. 655, 94 L.Ed. 424; U.S. v. Standard Rice Co., 1944, 65 S.Ct. 145, 147, 323 U.S. 106, 111, 89 L.Ed. 104.

16. U.S. v. Kimbell Foods, Inc., 1979, 99 S.Ct. 1448, 440 U.S. 715, 59 L.Ed.2d 711; U.S. v. Brosnan, 1960, 80 S.Ct. 1108, 363 U.S. 237, 4 L.Ed.2d 1192; U.S. v. Acri, 1955, 75 S.Ct. 239, 348 U.S. 211, 99 L.Ed. 264.

17. U.S. v. Standard Oil Co., 1947, 67 S.Ct. 1604, 332 U.S. 301, 91 L.Ed. 2067.

18. 67 S.Ct. at 1608, 332 U.S. at 307.

19. Howard v. Lyons, 1959, 79 S.Ct. 1331, 1333, 360 U.S. 593, 597, 3 L.Ed.2d 1454.

20. Boyle v. United Technologies Corp., note 7 above. See Cass & Gillette, The Government Contractor Defense: Contractual Allocation of Public Risk, 1991, 77 Va. L.Rev. 257; Green & Matasar, The Supreme Court and the Products Liability Crisis: Lessons from Boyle's Government Contractor Defense, 1990, 63 S.Cal.L.Rev. 637.

21. Banco Nacional de Cuba v. Sabbatino, 1964, 84 S.Ct. 923, 939, 376 U.S. 398, 425, 11 L.Ed.2d 804. See Chow, Limiting Erie in a New Age of International Law:

admiralty jurisdiction to the federal courts as a proper basis for the development of judge-made rules of maritime law.[22] And in Illinois v. City of Milwaukee,[23] the Court rejected its own dictum of barely a year before [24] and held that federal common law controls in an action to abate pollution of interstate or navigable waters. The significance of that decision proved to be short-lived. In a later phase of the same litigation the Court held that in legislation six months after the decision Congress implicitly extinguished the common-law remedy there recognized.[25]

"Federal common law also may come into play when Congress has vested jurisdiction in the federal courts and empowered them to create governing rules of law." [26] In the best-known example of this the Court read a statute that on its face only grants jurisdiction to federal courts of suits for violation of contracts between an employer and a labor union [27] as meaning that the substantive law to apply in these suits is federal law, which the courts through judicial inventiveness are to fashion from the policy of the national labor laws.[28]

If an issue is controlled by federal common law, this is binding on both state and federal courts.[29] A case "arising under" federal common law is a federal-question case, and is within the original jurisdiction of the federal courts as such.[30]

Toward a Federal Common Law of International Choice of Law, 1988, 74 Iowa L.Rev. 165; Hill, note 1 above, at 1042–1068; Edwards, The Erie Doctrine in Foreign Affairs Cases, 1967, 42 N.Y.U.L.Rev. 42; Moore, Federalism and Foreign Relations, 1965 Duke L.J. 248. But see Henkin, The Foreign Affairs Power of the Federal Courts: Sabbatino, 1964, 64 Col.L.Rev. 805.

22. Edmonds v. Compagnie Generale Transatlantique, 1979, 99 S.Ct. 2753, 443 U.S. 256, 61 L.Ed.2d 521; Cooper Stevedoring Co. v. Fritz Kopke, Inc., 1974, 94 S.Ct. 2174, 417 U.S. 106, 40 L.Ed.2d 694; Fitzgerald v. United States Lines Co., 1963, 83 S.Ct. 1646, 374 U.S. 16, 10 L.Ed.2d 720; Southern Pac. Co. v. Jensen, 1917, 37 S.Ct. 524, 244 U.S. 205, 61 L.Ed. 1086. See Robertson, Admiralty and Federalism, 1970.

23. 1972, 92 S.Ct. 1385, 406 U.S. 91, 31 L.Ed.2d 712. See Comment, The Expansion of Federal Common Law and Federal Question Jurisdiction to Interstate Pollution, 1972, 10 Hous.L.Rev. 121; Note, Federal Common Law and Interstate Pollution, 1972, 85 Harv.L.Rev. 1439.

24. Ohio v. Wyandotte Chemicals Corp., 1971, 91 S.Ct. 1005, 1009 n. 3, 401 U.S. 493, 498 n. 3, 28 L.Ed.2d 256.

25. City of Milwaukee v. Illinois, 1981, 101 S.Ct. 1784, 451 U.S. 304, 68 L.Ed.2d 114. See 19 Wright, Miller & Cooper, Jurisdiction § 4514, pp. 251–256.

26. Texas Indus., Inc. v. Radcliff Materials, Inc., 1981, 101 S.Ct. 2061, 2068, 451 U.S. 630, 642, 68 L.Ed.2d 500.

27. 29 U.S.C.A. § 185(a).

28. Textile Workers Union of America v. Lincoln Mills of Alabama, 1957, 77 S.Ct. 912, 353 U.S. 448, 1 L.Ed.2d 972. See Bickel & Wellington, Legislative Purpose and the Judicial Process: The Lincoln Mills Case, 1957, 71 Harv.L.Rev. 1. The decision is defended in Note, 1969, 82 Harv.L.Rev. 1512, 1531–1535.

29. Free v. Bland, 1962, 82 S.Ct. 1089, 369 U.S. 663, 8 L.Ed.2d 180; Yiatchos v. Yiatchos, 1964, 84 S.Ct. 742, 376 U.S. 306, 11 L.Ed.2d 724, noted 1965, 38 So.Cal. L.Rev. 335; Local 174, Teamsters, Chauffeurs, Warehousemen & Helpers of America v. Lucas Flour Co., 1962, 82 S.Ct. 571, 369 U.S. 95, 7 L.Ed.2d 593; Banco Nacional de Cuba v. Sabbatino, 1964, 84 S.Ct. 923, 939, 376 U.S. 398, 426, 11 L.Ed.2d 804. See Comment, The State Courts and the Federal Common Law, 1963, 27 Alb. L.Rev. 73.

30. Illinois v. City of Milwaukee, 1972, 92 S.Ct. 1385, 406 U.S. 91, 31 L.Ed.2d 712. This view had been anticipated in Ivy Broadcasting Co. v. American Tel. & Tel. Co., C.A.2d, 1968, 391 F.2d 486, 492–493. See also Comment, Federal Common Law and Article III: A Jurisdictional Approach to Erie, 1964, 74 Yale L.J. 325.

The burgeoning of a federal common law binding on federal and state courts alike occurred at the same time as the development of the Erie doctrine, and these two simultaneous developments are probably more than coincidental. Although one distinguished commentator waxed rhapsodic in his praise of the two taken together,[31] others were less enthusiastic and fears were expressed that the doctrine of federal common law meant that "further inroads may be made upon the clear provisions of the Rules of Decision Act on vague grounds of federal interest."[32] A few extreme decisions from courts of appeals gave substance to such fears. In one it was held that the federal interest in telephone companies is so strong and the legislation regulating such companies is so comprehensive that federal common law gives a remedy for tort or breach of contract against these carriers though the statutes provide no such remedy, either expressly or implicitly.[33] Another very questionable decision from a court of appeals held that the predominant interest of the federal government in regulating the nation's airways justifies application, as a matter of federal common law, of a rule that there is a right to contribution and indemnity, on a comparative negligence basis, among joint tortfeasors in aviation collision cases.[34]

31. "The complementary concepts—that federal courts must follow state decisions on matters of substantive law appropriately cognizable by the states whereas state courts must follow federal decisions on subjects within national legislative power where Congress has so directed—seems so beautifully simple, and so simply beautiful, that we must wonder why a century and a half were needed to discover them, and must wonder even more why anyone should want to shy away once the discovery was made. We may not yet have achieved the best of all possible worlds with respect to the relationship between state and federal law. But the combination of Erie with Clearfield and Lincoln Mills has brought us to a far, far better one than we have ever known before." Friendly, note 1 above, at 422.

32. Currie, Federal Jurisdiction in a Nutshell, 4th ed. 1990, p. 228. See also Comment, The Invalid Growth of the New Federal Common Law Dictates the Need for a Second Erie, 1971, 9 Hous.L.Rev. 329.

33. Ivy Broadcasting Co. v. American Tel. & Tel. Co., C.A.2d, 1968, 391 F.2d 486, noted 1968, 37 Geo.Wash.L.Rev. 425, 82 Harv.L.Rev. 479, 43 Tul.L.Rev. 168, 1969, 47 N.C.L.Rev. 447. The commentators were generally critical, and one went so far as to call the decision "a pernicious sub rosa attack on state substantive law." 35 Geo.Wash.L.Rev. at 431.

The Second Circuit continues to apply Ivy, Nordlicht v. New York Telephone Co., C.A.2d, 1986, 799 F.2d 859, and the Eighth Circuit has recently followed it. MCI Telecommunications Corp. v. Garden State Investment Corp., C.A.8th, 1992, 981 F.2d 385. The Fifth Circuit, however, has said it is not persuaded by Ivy and has refused to follow it. MCI Telecommunications Corp. v. Credit Builders of America, Inc., C.A.5th, 1993, 980 F.2d 1021, opinion reinstated C.A.5th, 1993, 2 F.3d 103, certiorari denied 114 S.Ct. 472, ___ U.S. ___, 126 L.Ed.2d 424.

34. Kohr v. Allegheny Airlines, Inc., C.A.7th, 1974, 504 F.2d 400, certiorari denied 95 S.Ct. 1980, 421 U.S. 978, 44 L.Ed.2d 470, noted 1975, 41 J.Air L. & Com. 347, 6 Sw.U.L.Rev. 661, 28 Vand. L.Rev. 621.

Professor Currie's comment on the Kohr decision is: "Much of the same could have been said, of course, as to interstate railroads in Erie itself." Currie, Federal Jurisdiction in a Nutshell, 4th ed. 1990, p. 244. See also Redish, Federal Jurisdiction: Tensions in the Allocation of Judicial Power, 1980, pp. 93–94.

It seems inconceivable that Kohr can have survived Miree v. DeKalb County, 1977, 97 S.Ct. 2490, 433 U.S. 25, 53 L.Ed.2d 557. A unanimous Court there held that state law, rather than federal common law, governed whether victims of an air crash could sue as third-party beneficiaries of a contract between the county, which owned the airport where the crash occurred, and the Federal Aviation Administration. The Court found the substantial interest of the

The Court, however, more recently has taken a cautious course toward the recognition of federal common law. It has emphasized that federal common law is appropriate in only a "few and restricted" instances.[35] "[A]bsent some congressional authorization to formulate substantive rules of decision, federal common law exists only in such narrow areas as those concerned with the rights and obligations of the United States, interstate and international disputes implicating the conflicting rights of States or our relations with foreign nations, and admiralty cases. In these instances, our federal system does not permit the controversy to be resolved under state law, either because the authority and duties of the United States as sovereign are intimately involved or because the interstate or international nature of the controversy makes it inappropriate for state law to control."[36]

An issue that seems quite similar to that of federal common law is determining when it is appropriate to find an implied federal right of action for damages from an Act of Congress, although the Court treats these as being "two quite different theories."[37] The cases are not all one way, but the more recent decisions have shown a reluctance to infer

---

United States in regulating aircraft travel and promoting air safety insufficient to make federal common law appropriate, and said "the issue of whether to displace state law on an issue such as this is primarily a decision for Congress. Congress has chosen not to do so in this case." 97 S.Ct. at 2495, 433 U.S. at 32. Nevertheless, Kohr is cited in Northwest Airlines, Inc. v. Transport Workers Union of America, 1981, 101 S.Ct. 1571, 1580, 451 U.S. 77, 90–91, 67 L.Ed.2d 750.

35. City of Milwaukee v. Illinois, 1981, 101 S.Ct. 1784, 1790, 451 U.S. 304, 313, 68 L.Ed.2d 114, quoting Wheeldin v. Wheeler, 1963, 83 S.Ct. 1441, 1445, 373 U.S. 647, 651, 10 L.Ed.2d 605. In the Boyle case, note 7 above, the majority speak of "a few areas" as appropriate for federal common law, 108 S.Ct. at 2514, 487 U.S. at 504, while Justice Brennan's dissent quotes the language from Wheeldin about "few and restricted." 108 S.Ct. at 2521, 487 U.S. at 518.

An instructive earlier case is Bank of America Nat. Trust & Sav. Assn. v. Parnell, 1956, 77 S.Ct. 119, 352 U.S. 29, 1 L.Ed.2d 93. This was a diversity action between private parties but involving United States bonds. The bank was suing Parnell to recover money he had obtained by cashing bonds that had been stolen from the bank. One issue was whether the bonds, which were not yet to mature but which had been called by the government, were "overdue." The other issue was whether Parnell had

acted in good faith in redeeming the bonds, and whether he had the burden of proving good faith or the bank had the burden of proving lack of it. It was held that whether the bonds were "overdue" concerned the interpretation of the nature of the rights and obligations created by the government bonds themselves, and was controlled by federal law, but that the burden of proof of good faith represented essentially a private transaction to be dealt with by the local law of the state where the transactions took place.

See also Wallis v. Pan American Petroleum Corp., 1966, 86 S.Ct. 1301, 384 U.S. 63, 16 L.Ed.2d 369, holding that conflicting private claims to federal lands leased under the Mineral Leasing Act of 1920 were governed by state law rather than federal law. The Court could discern "no significant threat to any identifiable federal policy or interest." 86 S.Ct. at 1304, 384 U.S. at 68.

36. Texas Indus., Inc. v. Radcliff Materials, Inc., 1981, 101 S.Ct. 2061, 2067, 451 U.S. 630, 641, 68 L.Ed.2d 500.

37. Northwest Airlines, Inc. v. Transport Workers Union of America, 1981, 101 S.Ct. 1571, 1578, 451 U.S. 77, 86, 67 L.Ed.2d 750. See also Texas Indus., Inc. v. Radcliff Materials, Inc., 1981, 101 S.Ct. 2061, 2066, 451 U.S. 630, 638, 68 L.Ed.2d 500; Middlesex County Sewage Auth. v. National Sea Clammers Assn., 1981, 101 S.Ct. 2615, 2627, 453 U.S. 1, 21, 69 L.Ed.2d 435.

remedies that Congress has not given.[38]

In federal-question cases, it may be that the federal statute or constitutional provision in question sets out the applicable rule. In such a case, this rule must, of course, be applied regardless of state law. Sometimes the federal statute will direct that state law be applied, as is the case with the Federal Tort Claims Act,[39] and in such a case the state rule will control regardless of the federal interest in the matter. "The variousness of federal law," to use Professor Mishkin's apt phrase,[40] is present when the federal statute is silent on a particular issue. Here the federal court must choose whether to incorporate state law to resolve that issue or to fashion an independent federal doctrine for it. Quite commonly, for example, federal statutes will create a right of action without stating the time within which such action must be brought. The usual rule in such situations is to apply whatever statute of limitations the state has for analogous types of suits.[41] If the case were

38. E.g., Karahalios v. National Federation of Federal Employees, 1989, 109 S.Ct. 1282, 489 U.S. 527, 103 L.Ed.2d 539, refusing to find an implied right of action for breach of a duty of fair representations in Title VII of the Civil Service Reform Act of 1978, 5 U.S.C.A. § 7101 et seq., and Thompson v. Thompson, 1988, 108 S.Ct. 513, 484 U.S. 174, 98 L.Ed.2d 512, noted 1989, 16 Pepperdine L.Rev. 409, 11 U.Ark. Little Rock L.J. 97, holding that there is no implied right of action in federal court under the Parental Kidnapping Prevention Act of 1980, 28 U.S.C.A. § 1738A, to determine which of two conflicting state custody decisions is valid.

The Court had been more willing to infer a right of action from the Constitution than from an Act of Congress. Davis v. Passman, 1979, 99 S.Ct. 2264, 2274–2276, 442 U.S. 228, 239–243, 60 L.Ed.2d 846. But even there the more recent decisions have been reluctant to find a remedy. E.g., Schweiker v. Chilicky, 1988, 108 S.Ct. 2460, 487 U.S. 412, 101 L.Ed.2d 370; Bush v. Lucas, 1983, 103 S.Ct. 2404, 462 U.S. 367, 76 L.Ed.2d 648. See Fallon & Meltzer, New Law, Non–Retroactivity, and Constitutional Remedies, 1991, 104 Harv.L.Rev. 1731; Brown, Letting Statutory Tails Wag Constitutional Dogs—Have the Bivens Dissenters Prevailed, 1989, 64 Ind.L.J. 263.

In Cannon v. University of Chicago, 1979, 99 S.Ct. 1946, 441 U.S. 677, 60 L.Ed.2d 560, the Court had held that there is an implied right of action under Title IX, which precludes discrimination on the basis of sex. In Franklin v. Gwinnett County Public Schools, 1992, 112 S.Ct. 1028, ___ U.S. ___, 117 L.Ed.2d 208, it was held that this allows a suit for damages by a high-school student claiming sexual harassment. The

general rule, absent any clear direction to the contrary from Congress, is that "the federal courts have the power to award any appropriate relief in a cognizable cause of action brought pursuant to a federal statute." 112 S.Ct. at 1035, ___ U.S. at ___.

See generally 19 Wright, Miller & Cooper, Jurisdiction § 4514, pp. 238–245; Ziegler, Rights Require Remedies: A New Approach to the Enforcement of Rights in the Federal Courts, 1987, 38 Hastings L.J. 665; Ashford, Implied Causes of Action under Federal Law: Calling the Court Back to Borak, 1984, 79 Nw.U.L.Rev. 227.

39. 28 U.S.C.A. §§ 1346(b), 2674. As the latter section shows, Congress has rejected local law, and set out a measure of damages of its own, in any state in which punitive damages are the only damages recoverable for wrongful death. Massachusetts Bonding & Ins. Co. v. U.S., 1956, 77 S.Ct. 186, 352 U.S. 128, 1 L.Ed.2d 189.

40. Mishkin, note 1 above.

41. Campbell v. City of Haverhill, 1895, 15 S.Ct. 217, 155 U.S. 610, 39 L.Ed. 280; Cope v. Anderson, 1947, 67 S.Ct. 1340, 331 U.S. 461, 91 L.Ed. 1602; Johnson v. Railway Exp. Agency, Inc., 1975, 95 S.Ct. 1716, 1721–1723, 421 U.S. 454, 462–466, 44 L.Ed.2d 295; Blume & George, Limitations and the Federal Courts, 1951, 49 Mich. L.Rev. 937; Note, Federal Statutes Without Limitations Provisions, 1953, 53 Col.L.Rev. 68.

The same result may be reached where the claim is one controlled by federal common law. International Union, United Automobile, Aerospace & Agric. Implement Workers v. Hoosier Cardinal Corp., 1966, 86 S.Ct. 1107, 383 U.S. 696, 16 L.Ed.2d 192.

subject to the Erie doctrine, then the state limitations doctrine would have to be applied in its full force.[42] The Erie doctrine does not apply, and the federal court has much more freedom, where the state rule has merely been absorbed as the relevant federal rule. This is illustrated by Holmberg v. Armbrecht.[43] That was a suit between private parties to enforce the liability imposed upon bank stockholders by the Federal Farm Loan Act. The suit would have been barred by the statute of limitations of New York, where it was brought, but the delay in bringing the suit had been caused by fraud on the part of the defendants. The Court held that the federal equitable rule that a statute of limitations does not begin to run until the fraud has been discovered, which would be read into even an explicit federal statutory limitation, must also be read into the state limitations statute if suit is on a federal claim.[44]

On some issues in private federal-question cases, there may be compelling reasons for ignoring state law and following an independent federal rule, as where Congress has clearly indicated a substantive policy it wishes to have followed, or there are indications of a leaning toward uniformity and there is no significant state interest to be served by absorption of the state law as the rule of decision.[45] In other cases application of the state law may seem the wiser choice.[46] De Sylva v.

For the application of this rule to civil-rights actions under 42 U.S.C.A. § 1983, see § 22A n. 32 above.

In 1990, in response to a recommendation of the Federal Courts Study Committee, Congress adopted a general four-year statute of limitations for civil actions "arising under an Act of Congress enacted after the date of enactment of this section." 28 U.S.C.A. § 1658. By its terms § 1658 does not apply to actions brought under pre–1990 statutes or to later statutes that contain their own limitations period. See Norwood, 28 U.S.C.A. § 1658: A Limitation Period with Real Limitations, 1994, 69 Ind. L.J. 477; McDowell, Limitation Periods for Federal Causes of Action After the Judicial Improvements Act of 1990, 1991, 44 Vand. L.Rev. 1355.

42. Guaranty Trust Co. of New York v. York, 1945, 65 S.Ct. 1464, 326 U.S. 99, 89 L.Ed. 2079.

43. 1946, 66 S.Ct. 582, 327 U.S. 392, 90 L.Ed. 743.

44. See also Bomar v. Keyes, C.C.A.2d, 1947, 162 F.2d 136, holding that regardless of state law, filing of the complaint tolls the state statute of limitations where suit is on a federal claim. The later decision by the Supreme Court, reaching a different result in a diversity action on a state-created right, Ragan v. Merchants Transfer & Warehouse Co., 1949, 69 S.Ct. 1233, 1235, 337 U.S. 530, 533, 93 L.Ed. 1520, cited and distinguished the Bomar case on the ground

that it was a suit to enforce a federal claim. But in Johnson v. Railway Exp. Agency, Inc., 1975, 95 S.Ct. 1716, 421 U.S. 454, 44 L.Ed.2d 295, the timely filing of a complaint of racial discrimination with the Equal Employment Opportunity Commission was held not to toll the state statute of limitations applicable to an action under the Civil Rights Act of 1866, 42 U.S.C.A. § 1981.

45. E.g., Deitrick v. Greaney, 1940, 60 S.Ct. 480, 309 U.S. 190, 84 L.Ed. 694; Dyke v. Dyke, C.A.6th, 1955, 227 F.2d 461. See discussion of these cases by Mishkin, note 1 above, at 814–820.

See also 19 Wright, Miller & Cooper, Jurisdiction § 4514, pp. 263–274; Comment, Adopting State Law as the Federal Rule of Decision: A Proposed Test, 1976, 43 U.Chi. L.Rev. 823.

46. In the following cases it is held that federal law governs an issue but that a uniform national rule is not necessary, and state law is to be looked to so long as it is not discriminatory or in conflict with federal statutes: Kamen v. Kemper Financial Services, Inc., 1991, 111 S.Ct. 1711, 500 U.S. 90, 114 L.Ed.2d 152 (whether a stockholder's failure to demand action by the board of directors before bringing suit under the Investment Company Act was excused by futility): U.S. v. Kimbell Foods, Inc., 1979, 99 S.Ct. 1448, 440 U.S. 715, 59 L.Ed.2d 711 (priority of liens under two federal loan programs); Burks v. Lasker, 1979, 99 S.Ct. 1831, 441 U.S. 471, 60

Ballentine [47] was such a case. The issue there was whether the illegitimate son of a copyright owner is one of the "children" of the owner within the meaning of the copyright statute. The Court recognized that the meaning of the word in the statute is a federal question, but since there is no federal law of domestic relations, and this is primarily a matter of state concern, the Court thought it best to draw on "the ready-made body of state law" to define what Congress meant by "children." The case shows, however, the greater flexibility that a court has when state law is absorbed, as compared to the Erie-type situations where it is controlling of its own force. The Court said that a state would not be entitled to use the word "children" in a way entirely strange to its ordinary usage, and that only to the extent that there are permissible variations in the ordinary concept of "children" would the state definition be adopted. It also indicated that the federal court is free to decide for itself which state's law is applicable—as it would not be if the Erie doctrine applied [48]—although only one state was involved in the De Sylva case and there was no need to make a conflict-of-laws decision.

It is frequently said that the Erie doctrine applies only in cases in which jurisdiction is based on diversity of citizenship. Indeed in an action for wrongful-death caused by a maritime tort committed on navigable waters, the Court curtly dismissed Erie as "irrelevant," since the district court was exercising its admiralty jurisdiction, even though it was enforcing a state-created right.[49] The Erie doctrine itself may be irrelevant, but, as has just been seen, state law is frequently quite relevant though the basis of the jurisdiction is something other than diversity.[50]

At the same time Erie is not always controlling even on clearly "substantive" issues in diversity cases. There is a limited scope for "federal common law" even within the diversity jurisdiction. This is illustrated most clearly by Francis v. Southern Pacific Co.,[51] a wrongful

---

L.Ed.2d 404 (whether disinterested directors can terminate a stockholders' suit under federal statutes); Wilson v. Omaha Indian Tribe, 1979, 99 S.Ct. 2529, 442 U.S. 653, 61 L.Ed.2d 153 (effect of the change of course of a stream on Indian title to adjoining land).

See also 42 U.S.C.A. § 1988, providing that state law is to be looked to in federal civil-rights actions on issues on which the federal statutes are "deficient in the provisions necessary to furnish suitable remedies," so far as state law is not inconsistent with the federal Constitution and laws. See Robertson v. Wegmann, 1978, 98 S.Ct. 1991, 436 U.S. 584, 56 L.Ed.2d 554.

47. 1956, 76 S.Ct. 974, 351 U.S. 570, 100 L.Ed. 1415.

48. See § 57 above.

49. Levinson v. Deupree, 1953, 73 S.Ct. 914, 916, 345 U.S. 648, 651, 97 L.Ed. 1319. The specific holding of Levinson is no long-

er of any force. That case comes from the era in which it was thought that maritime law did not allow recovery for wrongful death. That era was ended by Moragne v. States Marine Lines, Inc., 1970, 90 S.Ct. 1772, 398 U.S. 375, 26 L.Ed.2d 339.

50. "[D]espite repeated statements implying the contrary, it is the *source* of the right sued upon, and not the ground on which federal jurisdiction is founded, which determines the governing law." Maternally Yours, Inc. v. Your Maternity Shop, Inc., C.A.2d, 1956, 234 F.2d 538, 540 n. 1. See also Westen & Lehman, Is There Life for Erie After the Death of Diversity?, 1980, 78 Mich.L.Rev. 311; 19 Wright, Miller & Cooper, Jurisdiction § 4515.

51. 1948, 68 S.Ct. 611, 333 U.S. 445, 92 L.Ed. 798.

See also Banco Nacional de Cuba v. Sabbatino, 1964, 84 S.Ct. 923, 376 U.S. 398, 11 L.Ed.2d 804.

death action for the death of a railroad employee who was riding on a free pass when he was killed. The basis of jurisdiction was diversity. The right of action was created by Utah law, and under that law a railroad is liable for ordinary negligence even to those riding on free passes. Old federal decisions, in the era of Swift v. Tyson, had reached a different result and had said that if no fare is paid, the railroad is liable only for gross negligence. Since the earliest of those federal decisions, federal statutes had provided extensive regulation of the giving of free passes by railroads, although these statutes are silent as to the tort duties of a railroad to the recipient of such a pass. In these circumstances a majority of the Court held that federal law controlled and that the federal law was that defined in the old cases. Although at first it appears that here the federal court is not acting as "another court of the state," in fact the conflict is illusory. Utah law purported to create liability for ordinary negligence, but on this point the state law had been superseded by the federal common law to the contrary.

The Francis case does not stand alone in requiring application of federal law in diversity cases. Where a patent owner sues its licensee for unpaid royalties, federal rather than state law governs whether the licensee is estopped from raising the defenses that the patents are invalid or that the license agreement violated the federal antitrust laws.[52] Again in an extension of the doctrine that federal law is controlling in suits involving the United States on government contracts,[53] it has been held that federal common law governs in a diversity action by a subcontractor against a government prime contractor.[54] Finally where federal law creates a right of action, but does not grant jurisdiction, and suit is brought in the federal court only on the basis of diversity, the Erie doctrine does not apply and federal law controls.[55]

It may be, as Justice Brandeis said, that there is no federal *general* common law, but there remains a substantial area for the application of federal common law.

52. Sola Elec. Co. v. Jefferson Elec. Co., 1942, 63 S.Ct. 172, 317 U.S. 173, 87 L.Ed. 165; Kelly v. Kosuga, 1959, 79 S.Ct. 429, 358 U.S. 516, 3 L.Ed.2d 475.

The same result has been reached on the assignability of a patent license agreement. Unarco Indus., Inc. v. Kelley Co., C.A.7th, 1972, 465 F.2d 1303, certiorari denied 93 S.Ct. 1365, 410 U.S. 929, 35 L.Ed.2d 590.

53. See note 15 above.

54. American Pipe & Steel Corp. v. Firestone Tire & Rubber Co., C.A.9th, 1961,

292 F.2d 640, 643–644, noted 1961, 61 Col. L.Rev. 1519, 1962, 75 Harv.L.Rev. 1656; U.S. v. Taylor, C.A.5th, 1964, 333 F.2d 633, adhered to C.A.5th, 1964, 336 F.2d 149, noted 1964, 39 Tul.L.Rev. 137.

55. Huber Baking Co. v. Stroehmann Bros. Co., C.A.2d, 1958, 252 F.2d 945, certiorari denied 79 S.Ct. 50, 358 U.S. 829, 3 L.Ed.2d 69.

Chapter 10

PROCEDURE IN THE DISTRICT COURTS

Analysis

A. INTRODUCTION

Sec.
61. The Conformity Act and the Equity Rules.
62. The Federal Rules of Civil Procedure.
63. Rules of Procedure in Non-Civil Cases.
63A. The Civil Justice Reform Act of 1990.

B. PROCESS

64. Service of Summons and Complaint.
65. Service According to State Law.

C. PLEADINGS

66. Pleadings In General.
67. One Form of Action.
68. The Theory of Modern Pleading.
69. Pleading Jurisdiction.
69A. Sanctions.

D. JOINDER OF CLAIMS AND PARTIES

70. Parties Classified.
71. Joinder of Parties.
72. Class Actions.
73. Stockholders' Derivative Actions.
74. Interpleader.
75. Intervention.
76. Impleader.
77. Substitution of Parties.
78. Joinder of Claims.

A. INTRODUCTION

Analysis

---

§ 61. The Conformity Act and the Equity Rules [1]

Although the Judiciary Act of 1789 gave the federal courts power to

§ 61

1. 4 Wright & Miller, Civil 2d § 1002; Clark & Moore, A New Federal Civil Procedure: I. The Background, 1935, 44 Yale L.J. 387; Lane, Twenty Years Under the Federal Equity Rules, 1933, 46 Harv.L.Rev. 638; Comment, Ineffectiveness of the Conformity Act, 1927, 36 Yale L.J. 853.

make necessary rules for the orderly conduct of business in those courts,[2] another statute, enacted five days later, provided that in actions at law procedures in federal court should be the same in each state "as are now used or allowed in the supreme courts of the same."[3] Conformity to state procedure in actions at law, with independent federal regulation of procedure in admiralty and equity proceedings, was reaffirmed in a permanent statute adopted in 1792.[4] The conformity thus called for in actions at law was a static conformity. The state practice as of September 29, 1789, was to be followed, regardless of changes that the states might thereafter have made. Further the conformity statute made no provision for states subsequently admitted to the union; in those states the federal court could follow whatever procedure it chose. The rule-making power, though utilized in admiralty and equity, was not employed in actions at law, where the Court considered it its duty "to yield rather than encroach" upon state practice.[5]

The static conformity required by the statute was of considerable practical importance, because it made unavailable in federal court laws enacted subsequent to 1789 by the states for the relief of debtors. The matter came to a head in 1825 in the leading case of Wayman v. Southard,[6] where the Court, through Chief Justice Marshall, held that a federal court sitting in Kentucky could not apply a Kentucky statute altering the rules as to execution on a judgment in a manner favorable to debtors. The opinion in that case contained some intimation that a dynamic conformity, by which federal courts would follow the state procedure in effect as of the time they heard a case, would be an intolerable delegation of rulemaking power to the state legislatures. The holding in Wayman v. Southard was politically unpalatable, but the congressional solution to the problem posed its own difficulties. Under an 1828 statute procedure in the federal courts sitting in the original states was still to conform to the 1789 state procedure, while procedure in states subsequently admitted was to conform to the 1828 state procedure. It was provided, however, that all federal courts were to follow the 1828 state procedure with regard to writs of execution and other final process issued on judgments, and that the courts might, in their discretion, alter the procedure on executions to conform to any subsequent legislative changes by the state in which they were sitting.[7] This pattern continued in effect until 1872.[8]

---

2. Act of Sept. 24, 1789, c. 20, § 17, 1 Stat. 73, 83.

3. Act of Sept. 29, 1789, c. 21, § 2, 1 Stat. 93.

4. Act of May 8, 1792, c. 36, § 2, 1 Stat. 275, 276.

5. Fullerton v. Bank of United States, 1828, 1 Pet. 604, 614, 7 L.Ed. 280.

6. 1825, 10 Wheat. 1, 6 L.Ed. 253.

7. Act of May 19, 1828, c. 68, 4 Stat. 278.

8. In 1842 a similar statute was adopted to cover states admitted between 1828 and 1842. Act of Aug. 1, 1842, c. 109, 5 Stat. 499. For states admitted after 1842, a similar result was reached by judicial construction of language in the acts admitting them to the union. U.S. v. City Council of Keokuk, 1868, 6 Wall. 514, 516–517, 18 L.Ed. 933; Smith v. Cockrill, 1868, 6 Wall. 756, 18 L.Ed. 973.

Static conformity was unsatisfactory. During this period many states were following the lead of the New York Code of 1848 by merging law and equity and substituting a simplified form of code pleading for the common-law pleading formerly required. Under the statutes then in force, these new state procedures were not available in federal actions, which were required to proceed according to the earlier, discarded procedure of a state.

The situation was changed by the famous Conformity Act of 1872.[9] Among other things, that statute repealed the unused rulemaking power of the Supreme Court in common-law actions. Its more important accomplishment was to provide that "the practice, pleadings, and forms and modes of proceeding in civil causes, other than equity and admiralty causes, in the district courts, shall conform, as near as may be, to the practice, pleadings, and forms and modes of proceeding existing at the time in like causes in the courts of record of the State within which such district courts are held."

Thus a continuing or dynamic conformity was substituted for the static conformity earlier required. In theory the lawyer would now need to know but one system of procedure, since the federal courts would follow the same procedure as that currently used in the state court. The theory was largely illusory. The state practice was required to give way to any federal statute in point.[10] The state practice did not control on questions of jurisdiction or validity of service of process.[11] The state practice did not control the conduct of the federal judge in administration of the trial, which carried with it an independent federal rule on such important matters as the right of the judge to comment on the evidence,[12] the division of function between judge and jury,[13] whether instructions must be in writing,[14] and investigation of jury misconduct.[15] The state practice did not control appellate procedure.[16] Finally, even where there was conformity, it was to be "as near as may be," and this was understood by the Court to make the Conformity Act "to some extent only directory and advisory" and to permit the federal judge to disregard a state practice that would, in his view, "unwisely encumber the administration of the law, or tend to defeat the ends of justice." [17] With all these exceptions to conformity, and with the judge left some-

---

9. Act of June 1, 1872, c. 255, 17 Stat. 197; Rev.Stat. § 914.

10. Amy v. City of Watertown, 1889, 9 S.Ct. 530, 531, 130 U.S. 301, 304, 32 L.Ed. 946; Henkel v. Chicago, St. P., M. & O. Ry., 1932, 52 S.Ct. 223, 284 U.S. 444, 76 L.Ed. 386.

11. Davenport v. City of Dodge, 1881, 105 U.S. 237, 26 L.Ed. 1018; Southern Pac. Co. v. Denton, 1892, 13 S.Ct. 44, 146 U.S. 202, 36 L.Ed. 942; Munter v. Weil Corset Co., 1922, 43 S.Ct. 347, 261 U.S. 276, 67 L.Ed. 652.

12. Nudd v. Burrows, 1875, 91 U.S. 426, 23 L.Ed. 286; Vicksburg & M.R. Co. v.

Putnam, 1886, 7 S.Ct. 1, 118 U.S. 545, 30 L.Ed. 257.

13. Herron v. Southern Pac. Co., 1931, 51 S.Ct. 383, 283 U.S. 91, 75 L.Ed. 857.

14. City of Lincoln v. Power, 1894, 14 S.Ct. 387, 151 U.S. 436, 38 L.Ed. 224.

15. McDonald v. Pless, 1915, 35 S.Ct. 783, 238 U.S. 264, 59 L.Ed. 1300.

16. St. Clair v. U.S., 1894, 14 S.Ct. 1002, 1009, 154 U.S. 134, 153, 38 L.Ed. 936.

17. Indianapolis & St. L. Ry. Co. v. Horst, 1876, 93 U.S. 291, 300–301, 23 L.Ed. 898 (per Swayne, J.).

what at large to decide when he would conform, it is hardly surprising that the result was, in the view of a distinguished commentator, "a mixture of conflicting decisions, which have served to cloud the whole subject in hideous confusion and shifting uncertainty."[18]

The situation in equity was better than at law, though far from perfect, as indeed no system that continued the separation of law and equity could be. The Act of 1792 had provided that procedure in equity was to be "according to the principles, rules and usages which belong to courts of equity," with power in the Supreme Court to make such alterations by rule as it thought proper.[19] Rules of equity were adopted by the Supreme Court in 1822 and again in 1842. The 1842 rules continued in effect long after events had made them obsolete, so that, in the words of Judge Learned Hand, "the rules of Equity pleading fit the pleadings no better than small clothes would suit as professional costumes for the counsel."[20] The Equity Rules of 1912 were a considerable improvement,[21] and Congress helped with a 1915 statute which took a long step toward the consolidation of law and equity by permitting transfer of actions brought on the "wrong" side of the court to the "right" side, and also authorizing equitable defenses in actions at law.[22]

§ 62. The Federal Rules of Civil Procedure [1]

In the preceding section the difficulties with procedure in federal courts prior to 1938 were described. An erratic conformity to state procedure, an anachronistic survival of the separation between law and equity, and a failure to take advantage of the possibilities of judicial rulemaking were hallmarks of the system. The last of these points, that procedure is better regulated by the courts than by legislative bodies, was seen to be the key to the problem. It is doubtful whether, as some have contended, the legislature lacks constitutional power to regulate

---

18. Dobie, Federal Procedure, 1928, p. 585. See also Clark & Moore, note 1 above, at 401–411.

19. Act of May 8, 1792, c. 36, § 2, 1 Stat. 275, 276.

20. Monarch Vacuum Cleaner Co. v. Vacuum Cleaner Co., D.C.N.Y.1912, 194 F. 172, 174.

21. Talley, The New and the Old Federal Equity Rules Compared, 1913, 18 Va. L.Rev. 663.

22. Act of March 3, 1915, c. 90, 38 Stat. 956. See Liberty Oil Co. v. Condon Nat. Bank, 1922, 43 S.Ct. 118, 260 U.S. 235, 67 L.Ed. 232.

§ 62

1. 4 Wright & Miller, Civil 2d §§ 1003–1008; Tolman, Historical Beginnings of Procedural Reform, 1936, 22 A.B.A.J. 783; Sunderland, The Grant of Rule–Making Power to the Supreme Court of the United States, 1934, 32 Mich.L.Rev. 1116; Holt-

zoff, Origin and Sources of the Federal Rules of Civil Procedure, 1955, 30 N.Y.U.L.Rev. 1057; Clark, Two Decades of the Federal Civil Rules, 1958, 58 Col.L.Rev. 435; Chandler, Some Major Advances in the Federal Judicial System, 1922–1947, 1963, 31 F.R.D. 307, 477–516; Clark, The Role of the Supreme Court in Federal Rule–Making, 1963, 46 J.Am.Jud.Soc. 250; Goodman, On the Fiftieth Anniversary of the Federal Rules of Civil Procedure: What Did the Drafters Intend?, 1987, 21 Suffolk U.L.Rev. 351; Subrin, How Equity Conquered Common Law: The Federal Rules of Civil Procedure in Historical Perspective, 1987, 135 U.Pa.L.Rev. 909; Weinstein, The Ghost of Process Past: The Fiftieth Anniversary of the Federal Rules of Civil Procedure and Erie, 1988, 54 Brooklyn L.Rev. 1; Burbank, The Transformation of American Civil Procedure: The Example of Rule 11, 1989, 137 U.Pa.L.Rev. 1925; Toran, 'Tis A Gift To Be Simple: Aesthetics and Procedural Reform, 1990, 89 Mich.L.Rev. 352.

procedure,[2] but it is certainly clear that this power can be delegated by the legislature to the courts.[3] It cannot be doubted that legislative regulation is less satisfactory than regulation by court-made rules.[4]

The fight for court-made rules of civil procedure for the federal courts began in 1911 when the American Bar Association, at the instigation of Thomas Shelton, adopted a resolution favoring such a system. For almost 20 years a bill to give the Supreme Court power to make such rules was introduced in every Congress, but never was passed, despite the gallant efforts of Mr. Shelton. In later years, in response to a suggestion by Chief Justice Taft,[5] the bill included a provision authorizing the Court to unify law and equity. Opposition to the bill was led by Senator Walsh of Montana, and was based in large measure on the fear that grant of the rulemaking power would result in the rather simplified code practice of the western states being superseded by the involved practice that had developed in New York.[6] In 1930 Mr. Shelton died, and the American Bar Association lost interest, even to the point of abolishing its committee that had been pressing for this reform.

Senator Walsh was to have been appointed Attorney General in 1933, which would surely have ended, for the time at least, any hope of obtaining rulemaking power for the Supreme Court. He died, however, on the eve of his appointment, and the new Attorney General, Homer Cummings, assumed sponsorship of the bill authorizing the court to make procedural rules and to unite law and equity. So effective was his leadership that the bill was adopted unanimously by Congress in 1934 with very little discussion.[7]

It is a long step from a grant of rulemaking power to the adoption of effective rules. Indeed one familiar argument against rulemaking power

2. Compare Wigmore, Legislative Rules for Judicial Procedure are Void Constitutionally, 1928, 23 Ill.L.Rev. 276, with Kaplan & Greene, The Legislature's Relation to Judicial Rule–Making: An Appraisal of Winberry v. Salisbury, 1951, 65 Harv.L.Rev. 234.

Indeed Professor Whitten argues that separation-of-powers principles restrict the authority of the Court to make even "purely procedural" rules under a general delegation of rulemaking power if Congress has occupied the procedural field in question. Whitten, Separation of Powers Restrictions on Judicial Rulemaking: A Case Study of Federal Rule 4, 1988, 40 Me.L.Rev. 41.

3. See Mistretta v. U.S., 1989, 109 S.Ct. 647, 662–664, 488 U.S. 361, 386–390, 102 L.Ed.2d 714, and cases there cited. The principle was recognized as early as Wayman v. Southard, 1825, 10 Wheat. 1, 43, 6 L.Ed. 253.

4. 4 Wright & Miller, Civil 2d § 1001; Clark & Wright, The Judicial Council and the Rule–Making Power: A Dissent and a Protest, 1950, 1 Syracuse L.Rev. 346; Join-

er & Miller, Rules of Practice and Procedure: A Study of Judicial Rule–Making, 1957, 55 Mich.L.Rev. 623; Levin & Amsterdam, Legislative Control over Judicial Rule–Making: A Problem in Constitutional Revision, 1958, 107 U.Pa.L.Rev. 1.

5. Taft, Three Needed Steps of Progress, 1922, 8 A.B.A.J. 34, 35; Taft, Possible and Needed Reforms in the Administration of Justice in Federal Courts, 1922, 8 A.B.A.J. 601, 604, 607.

6. Walsh, Rule–Making Power on Law Side of Federal Practice, 1927, 13 A.B.A.J. 84. See Clark, Code Pleading, 2d ed. 1947, p. 35.

7. Act of June 19, 1934, c. 651, 48 Stat. 1064; 4 Wright & Miller, Civil 2d § 1003, p. 20; Burbank, The Rules Enabling Act of 1934, 1982, 130 U.Pa.L.Rev. 1015. See Cummings, Immediate Problems of the Bar, 1934, 20 A.B.A.J. 212. The Enabling Act, as subsequently revised, is now 28 U.S.C.A. §§ 2072–2074.

is that it will not be exercised. For almost a year after the Enabling Act was passed the Supreme Court took no action with regard to it. The Department of Justice and the Conference of Senior Circuit Judges apparently contemplated that no more would be required than the drafting of uniform rules for actions at law to supplement the existing Equity Rules of 1912.[8]

That the reform was not so limited, that law and equity were merged under a single set of simple and effective rules, was due primarily to the efforts of William D. Mitchell, a former Attorney General of the United States, and Charles E. Clark, then Dean of the Yale Law School and later Chief Judge of the Court of Appeals for the Second Circuit. In January 1935, Dean Clark, in collaboration with James Wm. Moore, published a major article summarizing the history of federal procedure and predicting that reform would be a failure unless it included a merger of law and equity.[9] Aroused by this article, General Mitchell wrote Chief Justice Hughes, on February 9, 1935, setting forth powerfully and persuasively the need for the full reform.[10] Three months later the Chief Justice, addressing the American Law Institute, made the dramatic announcement that the rules would not be limited to common-law cases, but would unify the procedure for cases in equity and actions at law "so as to secure one form of civil action and procedure for both."[11] A few weeks later the Court appointed an Advisory Committee of the most distinguished lawyers and law professors in the country to prepare and submit a draft of unified rules. General Mitchell was named by the Court as chairman, a post he filled with distinction until his death in 1955, and Dean Clark was designated as Reporter for the Committee.[12]

The Committee circulated three printed drafts for comment and criticism by the profession. The third draft, which was the Final Report of the Committee, was submitted to the Supreme Court in November 1937, and on December 20, 1937, the Court adopted the rules proposed by the Committee with some changes of its own.[13] The rules were submitted to Congress, as the Enabling Act required, and when Congress adjourned without any adverse legislation,[14] the rules became effective September 16, 1938.

8. Subrin, Charles E. Clark and His Procedural Outlook: The Disciplined Champion of Undisciplined Rules, in Judge Charles E. Clark, Petruck ed. 1991, p. 115.

9. Clark & Moore, A New Federal Civil Procedure: I. The Background, 1935, 44 Yale L.J. 387.

10. Subrin, note 8 above, at pp. 128–131. The letter appears in full in Mitchell, The Federal Rules of Civil Procedure, in David Dudley Field Centenary Essays, 1949, pp. 73, 76–78.

11. Address of Chief Justice Hughes, 1935, 55 S.Ct. xxxv, xxxvii, 21 A.B.A.J. 340, 12 A.L.I.Proc. 54.

12. Order of June 3, 1935, 295 U.S. 774. For a full list of members of the committee,

see 4 Wright & Miller, Civil 2d § 1003, pp. 21–24.

The contributions of Dean—later Judge—Clark are described in Smith, Judge Charles E. Clark and The Federal Rules of Civil Procedure, 1976, 85 Yale L.J. 914. See also Subrin, note 8 above.

13. Order of Dec. 20, 1937, 302 U.S. 783. Justice Brandeis dissented from adoption of the rules.

14. There was opposition to the rules in the Senate, but that body took no action, since the House of Representatives favored the rules, and concurrent action of both houses would have been required to delay or defeat adoption of the rules. See Chan-

Even the best system of court rules cannot remain static. Experience under the rules, and continued scholarly thinking about problems of procedure, will disclose places in which improvement is possible. Amendment will be necessary in other instances to remove unsound judicial glosses on the rules, or to codify desirable lines of decision. It is essential, therefore, that there be a continuing body charged with the responsibility of examining the rules in action and recommending change to the Court when this seems desirable.[15] The Advisory Committee that drafted the federal rules was reconstituted in 1942 to serve this function, and did so until its discharge in 1956. Various amendments were made by the Court, on the recommendation of that Committee, but the most significant was the set of amendments adopted in 1946, effective March 19, 1948, which reflected the results of a general study of the rules in operation.

The old Advisory Committee was discharged in 1956. In 1958 Congress amended the act creating the Judicial Conference to include among the duties of that body advising the Supreme Court with regard to necessary changes in the various rules the Court has power to make or amend.[16] An elaborate structure was created to assist the Judicial Conference, and ultimately the Court, in this task. There have been, as needed, advisory committees of practitioners, judges, and scholars for civil procedure, criminal procedure, appellate procedure, admiralty, bankruptcy, and evidence. These report to a standing Committee on Rules of Practice and Procedure and it in turn reports to the Judicial Conference.[17] The Judicial Conference transmits such of the recommendations as it approves to the Supreme Court, for under this new plan, as under that in effect from 1934 to 1956, the Court retains ultimate responsibility for the adoption of amendments to the rules.

This new machinery led to significant amendments to the Civil Rules in 1961, 1963, 1966, 1970, 1980, and 1983. More recently there have been amendments almost every other year.

The success of the Federal Rules of Civil Procedure has been quite phenomenal. They provide for the federal courts a uniform procedure in civil actions. This in itself would be a fine accomplishment, but the rules go beyond this to create a uniform procedure that is flexible, simple, clear, and efficient. It may smack of hyperbole to say, as one commentator has, that the rules are "one of the greatest contributions

dler, Some Major Advances in the Federal Judicial System, 1922–1947, 1963, 31 F.R.D. 307, 505–512.

15. Clark, "Clarifying" Amendments to the Federal Rules, 1953, 14 Ohio St.L.J. 241; Wright, Amendments to the Federal Rules: The Function of a Continuing Rules Committee, 1954, 7 Vand.L.Rev. 521; Wright, Rule 56(e): A Case Study on the Need for Amending the Federal Rules, 1956, 69 Harv.L.Rev. 839.

16. 28 U.S.C.A. § 331, as amended by Act of July 11, 1958, 72 Stat. 356. For

discussion of this amendment prior to its adoption, see Symposium, 1957, 21 F.R.D. 117.

17. The work of the new committees is described by the chairman of the Judicial Conference's Standing Committee on Rules of Practice and Procedure in Maris, Federal Procedural Rule–Making: The Program of the Judicial Conference, 1961, 37 A.B.A.J. 772. Their members are listed in 4 Wright & Miller, Civil 2d § 1007.

to the free and unhampered administration of law and justice ever struck off by any group of men since the dawn of civilized law." [18] It is nevertheless true that the chorus of approval of the rules by judges, lawyers, and commentators had been, until very recently, unanimous, unstinted, and spontaneous. [19] In the last few years, however, there has been questioning and reexamination of the assumptions about the proper goals of procedure that are at the heart of the Civil Rules. [20] This questioning has been sparked particularly by what some think is abuse of the discovery procedures made available by the rules. [21]

The impact of the rules has not been limited to the federal courts. The excellence of the rules is such that in more than half the states the rules have been adapted for state use virtually unchanged, and there is not a jurisdiction that has not revised its procedure in some way that reflects the influence of the federal rules. [22]

The Enabling Act declares that the rules are to regulate only "practice and procedure" and are not to "abridge, enlarge or modify any substantive rights." [23] Particular rules have been attacked as affecting matters of substance, but the Supreme Court, in a notable series of decisions, has upheld all such rules challenged before it. [24]

The success of the Civil Rules caused many to think that formulation of Federal Rules of Evidence would be desirable. An Advisory Committee on Rules of Evidence was created in 1965 and followed the methods of the committee that had drafted the Civil Rules in its work. Ultimately Federal Rules of Evidence became effective July 1, 1975, but their gestation period was as troubled as it was lengthy. As is recounted

---

18. Carey, In Favor of Uniformity, 1943, 3 F.R.D. 507, 18 Temp.L.Q. 145.

19. See 4 Wright & Miller, Civil § 1008, and particularly n. 6.

20. Subrin, The New Era in American Civil Procedure, 1981, 67 A.B.A.J. 1648.

21. See §§ 81, 83 below.

22. A commentator has pointed out, however, that certain provisions in the Civil Rules respond to special problems of a federal system and of courts of constitutionally limited jurisdiction, and that those provisions ought not be blindly adopted by the states. Rowe, A Comment on the Federalism of the Federal Rules, 1979 Duke L.J. 843.

23. 28 U.S.C.A. § 2072(b). See Carrington, "Substance" and "Procedure" in the Rules Enabling Act, 1989 Duke L.J. 281.

24. Sibbach v. Wilson & Co., 1941, 61 S.Ct. 422, 312 U.S. 1, 85 L.Ed. 479 (Rule 35(a)); Mississippi Pub. Co. v. Murphree, 1946, 66 S.Ct. 242, 326 U.S. 438, 90 L.Ed. 185 (Rule 4(f)); Cold Metal Process Co. v. United Engineering & Foundry Co., 1956,

76 S.Ct. 904, 351 U.S. 445, 100 L.Ed. 1311 (amended Rule 54(b)); Hanna v. Plumer, 1965, 85 S.Ct. 1136, 380 U.S. 460, 14 L.Ed.2d 8 (Rule 4(d)(1)).

It has been argued, however, that the Court has been too permissive in upholding rules that do affect substantive rights, contrary to the Enabling Act. Ely, The Irrepressible Myth of Erie, 1974, 87 Harv. L.Rev. 693. Professor Ely's view is rejected, in the course of a thoughtful decision holding that Rule 25(a) is valid, in Boggs v. Blue Diamond Coal Co., D.C.Ky.1980, 497 F.Supp. 1105, 1118–1121, noted 1981, 11 Mem.St.U.L.Rev. 413.

It has also been argued that the Supreme Court has become increasingly fond of using the plain-meaning doctrine to interpret the Federal Rules. Moore, The Supreme Court's Role in Interpreting the Federal Rules of Civil Procedure, 1993, 44 Hastings L.J. 1039. The author argues that because of the Court's dual roles as rulemaker and rule interpreter, the determination of the proper interpretation and application of a rule should be informed by many considerations beyond the simple literal language of the rule.

in more detail in a later section,[25] a draft of Evidence Rules was promulgated by the Supreme Court in 1972, but they caused so much controversy that Congress passed a statute providing that they could not take effect until they were expressly approved by Act of Congress. Congress then made very substantial revisions in the rules as they had been promulgated by the Supreme Court before permitting them to become effective in 1975.

The controversy over the Evidence Rules, and a similar furor over amendments to the Criminal Rules that the Supreme Court had approved in 1974,[26] has led to some reappraisal of the rulemaking process.[27] The critics have not been directing themselves particularly to the Civil Rules, but insofar as the criticism goes to the methods that the rulemaking committees have used over the years, they must inevitably have an impact on future amendments of the Civil Rules. Legislation in 1988 amended the Enabling Act to respond to some of the arguments of the critics,[28] but the more important changes go to rules made by district courts and courts of appeals. Rulemaking by the Supreme Court for the federal courts generally is now subjected to closer public and congressional scrutiny, but is not changed in substance.[29]

Another threat to the integrity of the Civil Rules has come from the proliferation of local rules for particular districts. Although Rule 83 authorizes local rules, it had been expected that these would be few in number and confined to purely housekeeping matters. Instead the use of local rules has been extensive and they cover a great variety of important matters.[30] This in itself is a threat to uniformity of procedure throughout the country, the local rules often provide "a series of traps"[31] for lawyers from other districts, and the casual manner in

---

25. See § 93 below.

26. See § 63 below.

27. Weinstein, Reform of Court Rule–Making Procedures, 1977 (shorter versions of this book appeared in 1977, 63 A.B.A.J. 47, and 1976, 76 Col.L.Rev. 905). See also Wright, Book Review, 1978, 9 St. Mary's L.J. 652; Clinton, Rule 9 of the Federal Habeas Corpus Rules: A Case Study on the Need for Reform of the Rules Enabling Acts, 1977, 63 Iowa L.Rev. 15; Friedenthal, The Rulemaking Power of the Supreme Court: A Contemporary Crisis, 1975, 27 Stan.L.Rev. 673; Lesnick, The Federal Rule–Making Process: Time for Re-examination, 1975, 61 A.B.A.J. 579.

28. Act of Nov. 19, 1988, Pub.L. 100–702, Title IV, 102 Stat. 4648.

29. Carrington, The New Order in Judicial Rulemaking, 1991, 75 Judicature 161; Mullenix, Hope Over Experience: Mandatory Informal Discovery and the Politics of Rulemaking, 1991, 69 N.C.L.Rev. 795.

It has been argued, however, that recent controversies suggest that rulemaking should be reformed and follow what is done in modern administrative law. Walker, A Comprehensive Reform for Federal Civil Rulemaking, 1993, 61 Geo.Wash.L.Rev. 455.

30. 12 Wright & Miller, Civil § 3154. See also Coquilette, Squiers & Subrin, The Role of Local Rules, A.B.A.J., Jan. 1989, p. 62; Subrin, Federal Rules, Local Rules, and State Rules: Uniformity, Divergence, and Emerging Procedural Patterns, 1989, 137 U.Pa.L.Rev. 1999.

31. Woodham v. American Cystoscope Co. of Pelham, C.A.5th, 1964, 335 F.2d 551, 552.

The difficulty in finding out what local rules are in effect is illustrated by Doran v. U.S., C.A.1st, 1973, 475 F.2d 742, where the United States attorney had no knowledge of a local rule in effect for 20 years. See also U.S. v. Ferretti, C.A.3d, 1980, 635 F.2d 1089, in which the judges in the district were uncertain about the continued existence of a local rule.

which until recently the judges in a district have decided to adopt a rule or set of rules is in striking contrast to the care with which the Civil Rules themselves are made and amended. Almost every study of experience with local rules has demonstrated how unsatisfactory it has been.[32]

The Supreme Court sought to provide a check when it ruled in 1960 that the power to make local rules is not to be used to introduce "basic procedural innovations," [33] but it seemed to retreat from this when it later held that local rules reducing the size of civil juries from 12 to six did not fall afoul of that restriction.[34] Many local rules have been held invalid for this reason, or because they are inconsistent with the Civil Rules, an Act of Congress, or the Constitution,[35] but patently there are many other invalid local rules on the books that have escaped scrutiny in a contested case.[36]

Rule 83 was amended in 1985 to provide that local rules can be made only after appropriate public notice and an opportunity to comment, and to give the judicial council of the circuit power to abrogate any local rule of a district. These provisions were made statutory in 1988. The statutes also require each district court and court of appeals to appoint an advisory committee to study and make recommendations about the rules of the court [37] and they give the Judicial Conference of the United States power to modify or abrogate a rule adopted by any court other than a district court or the Supreme Court.[38] These changes, if they stood alone, could improve the local rulemaking process. But the Civil Justice Reform Act of 1990 [39] has led to the adoption in many districts of procedures that vary among themselves and that are often inconsistent with the Federal Rules of Civil Procedure. That Act and its progeny are discussed elsewhere.[40]

---

32. 12 Wright & Miller, Civil § 3152; Weinstein, note 27 above, at pp. 117–137; Tobias, Civil Justice Reform and the Balkanization of Federal Civil Procedure, 1992, 24 Ariz.St.L.J. 1393, 1397–1401; Roberts, The Myth of Uniformity in Federal Civil Procedure: Federal Civil Rule 83 and District Court Local Rulemaking Powers, 1985, 8 U.Puget Sound L.Rev. 537; Note, Rule 83 and the Local Federal Rules, 1967, 67 Col. L.Rev. 1251; Note, The Local Rules of Civil Procedure in the Federal District Courts— A Survey, 1966 Duke L.J. 1011.

But see Flanders, Local Rules in Federal District Courts: Usurpation, Legislation, or Information?, 1981, 14 Loy.L.A.L.Rev. 213; Flanders, In Praise of Local Rules, 1978, 62 Judicature 28.

33. Miner v. Atlass, 1960, 80 S.Ct. 1300, 1306, 363 U.S. 641, 650, 4 L.Ed.2d 1462.

34. Colgrove v. Battin, 1973, 93 S.Ct. 2448, 2456 n. 23, 413 U.S. 149, 163 n. 23, 37 L.Ed.2d 522.

35. See Frazier v. Heebe, 1987, 107 S.Ct. 2607, 482 U.S. 641, 96 L.Ed.2d 557; Carver v. Bunch, C.A.6th, 1991, 946 F.2d 451; Bailey v. Systems Innovation, Inc., C.A.3d, 1988, 852 F.2d 93; Carter v. Clark, C.A.5th, 1980, 616 F.2d 228; and cases cited 12 Wright & Miller, Civil § 3153 nn. 53–55.

36. "[A]nother failure of rule 83 flows from the fact that occasions for judicially testing local rules have been and will continue to be infrequent. Given practical realities and economic constraints, few litigants will venture into battle over issues that seem so arcane." Roberts, note 32 above, at 546–547.

37. 28 U.S.C.A. §§ 2071, 2077(b). See also 28 U.S.C.A. § 332(d)(4).

38. 28 U.S.C.A. § 2071(c)(2).

39. 28 U.S.C.A. §§ 471–482, added by Act of Dec. 1, 1990, Pub.L. No. 101–650, 104 Stat. 5089.

40. See § 63A below.

§ 63.   Rules of Procedure in Non–Civil Cases [1]

In the title of this section, "Non–Civil" is used in somewhat arbitrary fashion to refer to all federal actions governed by systems of procedure other than the Federal Rules of Civil Procedure. It is beyond the scope of this book to make a detailed examination of such other systems of procedure, and the purpose of the section is simply to note their existence.

Prior to 1966 procedure in admiralty cases was different than in "civil actions." Conformity to state procedure was never required in admiralty, where the federal courts from the first were free to apply the procedure historically associated with the courts of admiralty. Although the Supreme Court had rulemaking power in admiralty matters since 1792, the first set of admiralty rules was not promulgated until 1844. This was superseded by the Admiralty Rules of 1920, which, as amended, remained in effect until 1966. In that year admiralty cases were brought within Civil Rules, and treated as civil actions, with certain minor variations for admiralty and maritime claims identified as such.[2]

Procedure in bankruptcy initially was to follow the Civil Rules "as nearly as may be" except insofar as those rules were inconsistent with the Bankruptcy Act [3] or with the General Orders in Bankruptcy, first adopted by the Supreme Court in 1898 and frequently since amended.[4] This came to an end in 1973 when a complete set of Bankruptcy Rules was adopted.[5] These were replaced by the 1983 Bankruptcy Rules and those in turn had to be significantly amended to take account of the changes in the Bankruptcy Act of 1978 that were made by Congress in 1984.[6]

The Civil Rules themselves provide that they do not apply to copyright proceedings "except in so far as they may be made applicable thereto by rules promulgated by the Supreme Court of the United States." [7] That Court, since 1909, has made special rules of practice for

---

§ 63

1. Admiralty: 4 Wright & Miller, Civil 2d § 1014. Bankruptcy: 4 id. § 1016. Copyright: 4 id. § 1018. Criminal prosecutions: 1 Wright, Criminal 2d, §§ 1–4. Habeas corpus, 17A Wright, Miller & Cooper, Jurisdiction 2d § 4268. Section 2255 motions: 3 Wright, Criminal 2d §§ 597–600.

2. Civil Rule 9(h). The variations relate to third-party practice (Rule 14(c)), deposition procedure (Rule 26(a)), jury trial (Rule 38(e)), and venue (Rule 82). There are also six "Supplemental Rules for Certain Admiralty and Maritime Claims." See 12 Wright & Miller, Civil §§ 3201–3256.

See generally 4 Wright & Miller, Civil 2d § 1014; Robertson, Admiralty Procedure and Jurisdiction After the 1966 Unification, 1976, 74 Mich.L.Rev. 1627; Landers, By Sleight of Rule: Admiralty Unification and Ancillary and Pendent Jurisdiction, 1972,

51 Texas L.Rev. 50; Bradley, Admiralty Aspects of the Civil Rules, 1967, 41 F.R.D. 257; Colby, Admiralty Unification, 1966, 54 Geo.L.J. 1258; Currie, Unification of the Civil and Admiralty Rules: Why and How, 1965, 17 Me. L.Rev. 1; Note, Admiralty Practice After Unification: Barnacles on the Procedural Hull, 1972, 81 Yale L.J. 1154.

3. Title 11, U.S.C.A.

4. 11 U.S.C.A. following § 53.

5. These rules were promulgated under the authority granted by 28 U.S.C.A. § 2075.

6. King, Jurisdiction and Procedure under the Bankruptcy Amendments of 1984, 38 Vand.L.Rev. 675.

7. Civil Rule 81(a)(1).

infringement actions,[8] acting under a statute that has since been repealed as covered by the general rulemaking statute. In 1939 the Court amended Rule 1 of the Copyright Rules to provide that infringement proceedings should be governed by the Civil Rules insofar as they are not inconsistent with the Copyright Rules. Thus the Court made proper the application of the Civil Rules in infringement proceedings, which many of the courts were already doing even without the change in the Copyright Rules. This arrangement has given no difficulty. The Copyright Rules prescribe certain special procedures that at most supplement, rather than contradict, the Civil Rules, and indeed there is probably no necessity for the continued existence of separate Copyright Rules.[9]

There are a number of other kinds of cases where the Civil Rules are applicable only to the extent that they do not contradict procedures required by statute or otherwise. These are listed in Civil Rule 81(a).[10]

The most interesting of the federal procedures not regulated by the Civil Rules is that for criminal actions. The federal courts never conformed to state procedure, as such, in criminal actions. From 1789 to 1946 the uncoded federal criminal procedure was the criminal procedure followed at common law, save as modified by constitutional limitations and by fragmentary statutory changes. State procedure was occasionally looked to—as it still is—where a statute so required or where it was necessary to fill the interstices of federal procedure.

Two of the men most responsible for reform of federal civil procedure are entitled to similar credit for the reform of criminal procedure. Attorney General William D. Mitchell was instrumental in the passage of 1933 legislation that gave the Supreme Court rulemaking power with respect to criminal proceedings after verdict.[11] This power was exercised by the Court in 1934. His successor as attorney general, Homer Cummings, recommended in 1938 that the Court be given similar authority to make rules in criminal cases prior to verdict. This legislation was adopted in 1940.[12] The Supreme Court determined to adopt a single set of rules that would govern proceedings both before and after verdict. The same careful methods that had proven so successful in the formulation of the Civil Rules were employed. A distinguished Advisory Committee was appointed, with Arthur T. Vanderbilt, later Chief Justice of New Jersey, as chairman, and Professor James J. Robinson, of the Indiana Law School, as Reporter.[13] The committee circulated to the profession two printed drafts of rules. Its final draft was, with some changes, approved by the Supreme Court in 1944,[14] and the Federal

---

8. 17 U.S.C.A. following § 101.

9. 4 Wright & Miller, Civil 2d § 1018; Kaplan, Continuing Work of the Civil Committee: 1966 Amendments of the Federal Rules of Civil Procedure (II), 1968, 81 Harv. L.Rev. 591, 617–620.

10. For discussion of these, see 4 Wright & Miller, Civil 2d §§ 1013 (review of administrative proceedings), 1015 (arbitration), 1020 (forfeiture and penalty actions), 1021 (habeas corpus, quo warranto, citizen-

ship, and naturalization), and 1028 (miscellaneous actions and proceedings).

11. Act of Feb. 24, 1933, c. 119, 47 Stat. 904, now codified as 18 U.S.C.A. § 3772.

12. Act of June 29, 1940, 54 Stat. 688, now codified as 18 U.S.C.A. § 3771.

13. For the other members of the committee, see 1 Wright, Criminal 2d § 2 n. 2.

14. Order of December 26, 1944, 323 U.S. 821. Justices Black and Frankfurter

Rules of Criminal Procedure became effective on March 21, 1946. The great achievement of these rules was the codification and simplification of the prior practice, although important reforms were also made.

The Criminal Rules have worked well. They have not been adopted by the states, however, as widely as have the Civil Rules. They remained unchanged for twenty years after they became effective, but since 1966, when the first amendments were made, they have been amended so frequently that even scholars in the field find it difficult to follow the constant changes or to be certain what a particular rule provided at a particular time.[15] In addition, it has become commonplace in the last decade for Congress to postpone the effectiveness of part or all of a set of amendments to the Criminal Rules approved by the Supreme Court, so that Congress may decide for itself whether it will allow the amendments to become effective and, if so, in what form. On occasion this has led courts to act on the basis of amendments approved by the Supreme Court, not knowing that those amendments have been disapproved by Congress.[16]

There had been a special set of rules governing the trial of misdemeanors before United States magistrates. These were abrogated in 1990 and Criminal Rule 58 has been extensively rewritten to govern the procedure and practice for the conduct of proceedings involving misdemeanors and other petty offenses and for appeals to judges of the district courts in such cases tried by magistrate judges.[17] There are also special sets of rules for collateral attacks on criminal convictions, whether by habeas corpus for a state prisoner or by a motion under 28 U.S.C.A. § 2255 by a federal prisoner.[18]

§ 63A. The Civil Justice Reform Act of 1990 [1]

In an earlier section [2] it was seen that the integrity of the Federal Rules of Civil Procedure has been threatened by controversy that, since

did not join in adoption of the rules. Rules 32 to 39 regulated proceedings after verdict, and were adopted in the exercise of the Court's power under 18 U.S.C.A. § 3772, which, unlike 18 U.S.C.A. § 3771, does not require that rules be submitted to Congress and subject to its disapproval. Thus, these rules were separately adopted by the Court by Order of Feb. 8, 1946, 327 U.S. 825, to be effective on the same day as the other rules.

15. For details, see 1 Wright, Criminal 2d § 4. See generally Remington, A Quarter Century of Rulemaking with Particular Attention to the Federal Rules of Criminal Procedure, 1984, 36 Me.L.Rev. 219.

16. E.g., U.S. v. Gonzalez Vargas, C.A.1st, 1978, 585 F.2d 546; Government of Virgin Islands v. Bradshaw, C.A.3d, 1978, 569 F.2d 777, certiorari denied 98 S.Ct. 3070, 436 U.S. 956, 57 L.Ed.2d 1121.

17. See 3A Wright, Criminal 2d § 912.

18. These rules became effective in 1976, and have been amended since. The Habeas Corpus Rules appear in 28 U.S.C.A. following § 2254. The Section 2255 Rules appear in 28 U.S.C.A. following § 2255.

See Clinton, Rule 9 of the Federal Habeas Corpus Rules: A Case Study on the Need for Reform of the Rules Enabling Acts, 1977, 63 Iowa L.Rev. 15.

§ 63A

1. Symposium on Implementing Civil Justice Reform, 1992, 11 Rev.Litig. 165; Johnston, Civil Justice Reform: Juggling Between Politics and Perfection, 1994, 62 Fordham L.Rev. 833; Dessem, Judicial Reporting under the Civil Justice Reform Act: Look, Mom, No Cases!, 1993, 54 U.Pitt. L.Rev. 685; Mullenix, The Counter–Reformation in Procedural Justice, 1992, 77 Minn.L.Rev. 375; Tobias, Civil Justice Reform and the Balkanization of Federal Civil

2. See note 2 on page 436.

1970, has surrounded the rulemaking process itself and by the proliferation of local rules. A threat far greater than either of these has come with adoption of the Civil Justice Reform Act of 1990.[3]

The enactment of that statute followed a decade of pronounced concern about the increased cost and delay of civil litigation.[4] Even though during that decade the Supreme Court amended the rules twice in order to combat the problems of expense and delay,[5] dissatisfaction still remained.[6] This dissatisfaction culminated in 1990 when two separate reports were issued regarding the delivery of civil justice in the federal courts.[7] The report of a Brookings Institution Task Force was particularly influential [8] and led to swift enactment by Congress of the Civil Justice Reform Act of 1990.[9] The Act was adopted despite opposition from the Judicial Conference of the United States, the American Bar Association, and the Department of Justice.[10]

The Act required each of the 94 federal district courts to create and implement within three years an expense- and delay-reduction plan based on the recommendations of a local advisory group.[11] The purpose of these plans is "to facilitate deliberate adjudication of civil cases on the merits, monitor discovery, improve litigation management, and ensure

---

Procedure, 1992, 24 Ariz.St.L.J. 1393; Peck, "Users United"; The Civil Justice Reform Act of 1990, 1991, 54 Law & Contemp.Probs. 105.

The author is indebted to Pamela B. Roe for her valuable assistance in preparing this section.

2. See § 62 above.

3. 28 U.S.C.A. §§ 471–482, added by Act of Dec. 1, 1990, Pub.L. No. 101–416, Title I, 104 Stat. 5089.

4. See, e.g., McManamon, Is the Recent Frenzy of Civil Justice Reform a Cure-all or a Placebo? An Examination of the Plans of Two Pilot Districts, 1991, 11 Rev. Litig. 329.

5. Id. at 331.

6. Justice Powell, joined by Justices Stewart and Rehnquist, dissented from the Supreme Court's promulgation of the 1980 Amendments and warned that without substantial change, the rules will "continue to deny justice to those least able to bear the burdens of delay, escalating legal fees and rising court costs". Order, 1980, 446 U.S. 997, 1000–1001, 85 F.R.D. 521, 523. See also Blue Chip Stamps v. Manor Drug Stores, 95 S.Ct. 1917, 1928, 421 U.S. 723, 741, 44 L.Ed.2d 539.

7. See Mullenix, Civil Justice Reform Comes to the Southern District of Texas: Creating and Implementing a Cost and Re-

duction Plan Under the Civil Justice Reform Act of 1990, 1991, 11 Rev. Litig. 165, 171 (1991).

8. "The genesis for many of the ideas embraced within Title I is the report of a Brookings Institution Task Force entitled 'Justice For All: Reducing Costs and Delays in Civil Litigation.' " S. Rep. No. 101–416, 101st Cong., 2d Sess. 13 (1990), reprinted in 1990 U.S.Code Cong. & Adm. News 6802, 6816. For skepticism concerning the report, see Mullenix, note 1 above, at 397.

9. "Less than twelve months passed between the introduction of the Act and its enactment—a rather remarkable feat, even the critics of the Act must concede, in an area of the law in which reform has been both incremental in scope and languid in pace." Peck, note 1 above, at 106.

10. Mullenix, note 1 above, at 411–424.

11. 28 U.S.C.A. § 471. The time limit is not codified and can be found in Act of Dec. 1, 1990, Pub.L. 101–650, Title I, § 103(b), 104 Stat. 5090. The Act also makes provision for Early Implementation District Courts, popularly known as EIDCs, id. § 103(c), for a demonstration program, id. § 104, and for a pilot program, id. § 105. See Tobias, Judicial Oversight of Civil Justice Reform, 1992, 140 F.R.D. 49.

just, speedy, and inexpensive resolutions of civil disputes." [12] The congressionally mandated guidelines and techniques that form the basis of the plans emphasize increased judicial management. [13] The guidelines set forth in 28 U.S.C.A. § 473(a) are aimed at limiting pretrial activities, controlling pretrial discovery, arriving at a settlement as early as possible, and ensuring well-focused trials. [14] Section 473(b) then provides six specific techniques that each district court, in consultation with its advisory group, is to consider in formulating its particular plan. [15]

The beneficial effects of this emphasis on aggressive judicial management, however, are questionable. There exists concern that the increase in management constraints will lessen the freedom of the district judge to manage his or her docket. [16] The possibility exists that tighter managerial control of the judicial officer will infringe upon the litigant's autonomy and control over the litigation process. [17] In addition, local rules will become increasingly more complex and specific, which could further complicate the practitioner's life. [18]

Although Congress provided guidance for developing the plans, the main thrust of the Act is directed toward the principle that reform must come from the bottom up. [19] Thus, Congress leaves the creation and implementation of the expense- and delay-reduction plans to local advisory groups appointed by the chief judge of each court. Once the plan is developed, the chief judge reviews and makes any necessary modifications for reducing cost and delay. After implementation of the plan, the chief judge in consultation with the advisory group annually assesses the condition of the docket in regard to cost and delay of litigation.

In stressing the need for local input, Congress intends the composition of the advisory groups to include not only plaintiffs' and defense lawyers, but also corporate and public-interest lawyers representing different philosophic positions. [20] Although the purpose of this broad composition is to ensure that the entire litigating community share in the development of the plan and that the plan addresses the needs and demands of local conditions, [21] the possible result of this broad composi-

---

12. 28 U.S.C.A. § 471.

13. Peck, note 1 above, at 110–111; Mullenix, note 7 above, at 174.

14. S. Rep. No. 416, note 8 above, at p. 57.

15. 28 U.S.C.A. § 473(b).

16. Lay, Rethinking the Guidelines: A Call for Cooperation, 1992, 101 Yale L.J. 1755, 1757.

17. Mullenix, note 7 above, at 169.

18. "Increased complexity is evidenced by the growing number of procedures, many of which have become more complicated, impose onerous obligations, or are obscure or otherwise difficult to find. This complexity has deleterious ramifications for all judges, lawyers, and litigants, but especially for counsel and parties with limited resources." Tobias, note 1 above, at 1422.

19. S. Rep. No. 416, note 8 above, at p. 14 (1990). See also Peck, note 1 above, at 105: "The linchpin of the Act is user involvement in the establishment and promulgation of policies for the management of litigation in the federal courts." See also id. at 109–110.

20. S. Rep. No. 416, note 1 above, at p. 62 (1990). See also Mullenix, note 7 above, at 173.

21. S. Rep. No. 416, note 8 above, at p. 15.

tion is to allow amateur and ill-equipped advisory groups with individual political objectives to control federal rulemaking.[22]

As early as December 31, 1991, the advisory groups of 34 district courts had developed their plans and became Early Implementation Districts. Although each plan is unique to its district, several similar themes appear in the plans. The most pronounced theme is the belief that Congress must accept some blame for civil-justice expense and delay in the form of inadequate resources and increased criminal statutes.[23] Many district courts provided for various forms of mandatory disclosure[24] and many required the use of alternative dispute resolution.[25] There is dispute on how effectively these plans address issues of expense. One commentator thinks that the "ubiquitous flaw" of the early plans is that they focus on reducing delay but address only lightly, if at all, the problems of cost,[26] while another is more sanguine on these aspects of the plans.[27]

Many of the provisions of the Early Implementation District Courts' plans also establish new local rules of procedure that are potentially inconsistent with the Federal Rules of Civil Procedure[28]. In fact, the Eastern District of Texas flatly proclaims that "to the extent that the Federal Rules of Civil Procedure are inconsistent with this Plan, the Plan has precedence and is controlling."[29]

The question arises whether these new local rules issued under the authority of the Civil Justice Reform Act infringe on the Supreme Court's authority to enact rules of procedure as delegated by the Rules Enabling Act.[30] Congress felt obliged to answer this question and concluded that it may pass procedural rules that advance substantive policy goals, since its power is limited only by the Constitution, and not

22. "[L]ocal amateur rulemaking groups, however intelligent, diligent, and well-intentioned, are ill-equipped to perform the basic tasks the Act requires, such as conducting docket assessments and evaluating the reasons for cost and delay in the district." Mullenix, note 1 above, at 380. See also id. at 400, 439.

23. See McManamon, note 4 above, at 359. See also Mullenix, note 1 above, at 401 for a discussion of the impact of this oversight.

24. See Bell, Varner & Gottschalk, Automatic Disclosure in Discovery—The Rush to Reform, 1992, 27 Ga.L.Rev. 1, 18–20, 53–58. Professor Tobias calls these mandatory disclosure provisions "the most troubling example" of procedures that seem inconsistent with the Civil Rules or with statutes. Tobias, Recalibrating the Civil Justice Reform Act, 1993, 30 Harv.J.Legis. 115, 125.

On mandatory disclosure generally, see § 83A below.

25. See Mullenix, note 1 above, at 378.

26. Slate, Early Implementation Districts: Pioneers and a Plethora of New Local Rules, 1991, 11 Rev.Litig. 367, 383.

27. "[T]he courts adopted numerous procedures that will help achieve the statute's goals of reducing expense and delay, while the EIDCs thus far seem to be relatively efficacious laboratories of experimentation." Tobias, note 24 above, at 123.

28. See the quotation from Tobias in note 24 above. See also Slate, note 26 above, at 372; Tobias, note 1 above, at 1416–1422.

29. See Tobias, note 11 above, at 51.

30. See Mullenix, Unconstitutional Rulemaking: The Civil Justice Reform Act and Separation of Powers, 1993, 77 Minn. L.Rev. 1283.

the Rules Enabling Act.[31]   The logic of this analysis and other Congressional justifications for the authority to enact the Civil Justice Reform Act has been questioned.[32]   But Congress concluded that the Act is within its exclusive rulemaking authority, and indeed that the Supreme Court would be barred from proposing this legislation.[33]

The verdict is not yet in on the Civil Justice Reform Act.   One commentator, who thinks that what has been done so far under the Act "has had considerable promise," [34] is concerned nevertheless that Congress attempted "to accomplish more than could be efficaciously achieved at one time by employing too many instrumentalities and procedures.   Congress may have so drafted the legislation that its implementation could undermine the Act's expressly stated purpose to reduce cost and delay." [35]   A federal judge has written that the Act "is premised on a number of invalid assumptions, or assumptions for which proof is lacking," and that the "good aspects of the bill could easily be implemented by the Judicial Conference as the managing head of the federal court system." [36]

Another commentator is even gloomier.   "[T]he Act ought to be repudiated as a noble but ill-conceived piece of legislation that will produce more harm than good for civil justice in this country.   Civil procedural rulemaking ought not to be in the hands of ninety-four local amateur rulemaking groups who are destined to wreak mischief, if not havoc, on the federal court system.   Procedural rulemaking should be restored to the federal judiciary, to be accomplished in slow and deliberative fashion by procedural experts through the existing Advisory Committee system." [37]

B.   PROCESS

Analysis

Sec.
64.   Service of Summons and Complaint.
65.   Service According to State Law.

---

31. S. Rep. No. 416, note 8 above, at p. 10 (1990).

32. See Mullenix, note 1 above, at 424–438.   See also Mullenix, note 30 above.

33. S. Rep. No. 416, at p. 11.   See also Peck, note 1 above, at 114–117.

34. Tobias, note 24 above, at 133.

35. Id. at 128.   In another article Professor Tobias said: "The consummate irony of civil justice reform is that the increased balkanization manifested in CJRA's implementation probably will have effects very different from those that Congress intended; it may well lead to greater delay and expense in civil litigation, decreased federal court access, fewer fair resolutions and fewer merit-based dispositions." Tobias, note 1 above, at 1426.

36. Cohn, A Judge's View of Congressional Action Affecting the Courts, 1991, 54 Law & Contemp.Probs. 99, 100–101.

37. Mullenix, note 1 above, at 385.

§ 64. Service of Summons and Complaint

Service of process in federal actions was changed drastically in 1983 and again in 1993. In 1982 the Supreme Court had proposed amendments to Rule 4 for this purpose. Congress first postponed the effectiveness of the Court's amendments and then rewrote those amendments before adopting them by statute to be effective February 26, 1983.[1] That version of Rule 4 was unsatisfactory in many ways.[2] A completely rewritten version of Rule 4 was approved by the Supreme Court and became effective December 1, 1993.[3]

In some states an action is commenced by the service of process on the defendant. This "hip-pocket" method of commencing an action, as it is known, was at one time favored by a majority of the Advisory Committee, but the committee finally took a contrary view and provided that a civil action is commenced by filing a complaint with the court.[4] This recognizes that a law suit is a matter of public record and that there is a need for certainty with regard to the time of institution of the suit and its consequent effect upon limitations and priorities.

From 1938 to 1993 the rule had provided that after the action had been commenced by filing the complaint with the clerk, the clerk must "forthwith" issue a summons and deliver it to the plaintiff or the plaintiff's attorney, who was responsible for prompt service of the summons and a copy of the complaint.[5] This mandate was not always followed, and even where it was, the passage of time between the filing of the complaint and the service of process raised some difficult questions. Of these undoubtedly the effect of the filing alone as satisfying a controlling statute of limitations is the most important.

If suit is on a right created by federal law, filing of the complaint, as called for by Rule 3, is sufficient, without more, to satisfy the statute of limitations.[6] Despite Rule 3, however, in a suit on a state-created right plaintiff must do, before the statute of limitations has run, whatever he would be required to do in a similar suit in state court. This is the rule

---

§ 64

1. See generally 4 Wright & Miller, Civil 2d §§ 1036–1051.

Those amendments were adopted by Act of January 12, 1983, Pub.L. 97–462, 96 Stat. 2527. Their text appears at 96 F.R.D. 75. Much of their legislative history appears as appendices to Siegel, Practice Commentary on Amendment of Federal Rule 4 (Eff. Feb. 26, 1983) with Special Statute of Limitations Precautions, 1983, 96 F.R.D. 88. The text and Committee Note to the amendments the Supreme Court had approved appear at 93 F.R.D. 255.

2. See Sinclair, Service of Process: Rethinking the Theory and Procedure of Serving Process Under Federal Rule 4(c), 1987, 73 Va.L.Rev. 1183.

3. The Reporter for the Civil Rules Committee discussed many of the issues

involved in rewriting the rule in Carrington, Continuing Work on the Civil Rules: The Summons, 1988, 63 Notre Dame L.Rev. 733.

4. Rule 3.

5. 4A Wright & Miller, Civil 2d §§ 1084–1086.

As amended in 1983, Rule 4(b) provides that upon or after filing the complaint the plaintiff may present a summons to the clerk for signature and seal. If the summons is in proper form, the clerk is to sign, seal, and issue it to the plaintiff for service on defendant.

6. West v. Conrail, 1987, 107 S.Ct. 1538, 481 U.S. 35, 95 L.Ed.2d 32; and cases cited 4 Wright & Miller, Civil 2d § 1056 n. 3.

of Ragan v. Merchants Transfer & Warehouse Co.[7] The holding there, it will be recalled, is that a federal court sitting in diversity cannot give an action longer life than it would have had in the state court, and that if state law requires something more than filing the complaint, such as service on the defendant, within the limitations period, the same formalities must be completed for the action in federal court to be timely. Although there had been some question about the continuing vitality of the Ragan case, its holding was expressly reaffirmed in 1980 in Walker v. Armco Steel Corporation.[8]

Even where the action is commenced for purposes of the statute of limitations merely by filing the complaint, whether because the suit is governed by federal law or because the relevant state law so provides, there had been an implied qualification, of equitable origin,[9] that to avoid the bar of the statute of limitations there must have been a bona fide intent to prosecute the suit diligently and no unreasonable delay in the issuance or service of the summons. The decisions turned heavily on their particular facts.[10] Since 1983, however, the rules have spoken to this question. There is a presumption that service within 120 days of filing the complaint equals due diligence, with the courts given discretion to decide what constitutes "good cause" for extending that time period.[11]

Many time periods in the rules are dated from the commencement of the action. Undoubtedly this can be abused, and plaintiff can secure an advantage that the rules do not intend if service is delayed for whatever cause. The alternative of measuring time periods from the date of service would cause administrative difficulties, especially where there are several defendants and service is made on different days. By contrast, the date of filing the complaint with the clerk, which is the commencement of the action, is a readily discernible and easily administered point in time.[12] The courts have ample power to protect defendant in a case where plaintiff has sought to gain an advantage from the delay in making service.[13]

In the past the summons and complaint [14] had normally been served by the marshal.[15] The principal purpose of the amendments adopted in

7. 1949, 69 S.Ct. 1233, 337 U.S. 530, 93 L.Ed. 1520. See 4 Wright & Miller, Civil 2d § 1057.

8. 1980, 100 S.Ct. 1978, 446 U.S. 740, 64 L.Ed.2d 659.

9. See Linn & Lane Timber Co. v. U.S., 1915, 35 S.Ct. 440, 236 U.S. 574, 59 L.Ed. 725.

10. See cases cited 4 Wright & Miller, Civil 2d § 1056 nn. 8–14.

11. Under the 1983 version of Rule 4 this was in Rule 4(j). It is now Rule 4(m).

12. Edwin H. Morris & Co. v. Warner Bros. Pictures, D.C.N.Y.1950, 10 F.R.D. 236, 238.

13. See, e.g., Caribbean Constr. Corp. v. Kennedy Van Saun Mfg. & Engineering Corp., D.C.N.Y.1952, 13 F.R.D. 124; 4 Wright & Miller, Civil 2d § 1053.

14. Much less formal methods of service have always been provided for papers subsequent to the original complaint. Subpoenas may be served by any person 18 years of age or over who is not a party to the lawsuit. Rule 45(c); 9 Wright & Miller, Civil § 2461. Service of other papers may be made on the party's attorney either by delivering a copy to him or mailing a copy to his last known address. Rule 5(b); 4A Wright & Miller, Civil 2d §§ 1145–1147.

15. There had been a little used provision allowing the court to appoint a special person to make service where substantial savings in travel fees would result. In addi-

1983 was to end this. Because of the reduction in appropriations available to the Marshal's Service, it was thought desirable to relieve the marshals of the duty of serving summonses and complaints in private civil litigation.[16] As things have stood since 1983, a marshal will not ordinarily [17] make service and service can be by any person who is not a party and is not less than 18 years old.[18]

The methods of making service on various kinds of defendants are set out in the several subdivisions of Rule 4(d). The procedures set out for service on infants and incompetent persons, and on the United States or officers or agencies thereof, and on states and subdivisions of states, are largely self-explanatory, and have given little difficulty.[19] This cannot be said of service on individuals or corporations.

It should be noted immediately that the procedures of Rules 4(e) and (h) [20] with regard to service on individuals or corporations and other associations are merely one way by which such service can be made. There has always been the alternative in such cases, discussed below in section 65, of service on defendants of this character in the manner prescribed by the law of the state in which the district court is held. This was broadened in 1993 to authorize also use of the law of the state in which service is effected.[21]

The 1983 amendments, however, also allowed service by mailing a copy of the summons and complaint by first-class mail, postage prepaid, as an alternative to the procedures of subdivisions (1) and (3). The idea

---

tion, the rule had been amended in 1980 to allow service to be made by any person authorized to serve process in the courts of the state in which the federal court was held.

16. See Sinclair, note 2 above, at 1197–1212. Although the appropriations for the Marshal's Service were the principal impetus for the 1983 changes, Professor Carrington speculates that it is "possible that other facts are at play, such as the professional status of marshals who find service of a summons to be demeaningly easy, or a slight tension between the Justice Department and the federal judiciary over control of these officers." Carrington, note 3 above, at 750.

17. Under the 1993 amendments, which limit the use of marshals even more than did the 1983 amendments, the court may on request of plaintiff order that service be made by a marshal or a special appointee and such an appointment must be made in cases of paupers and seamen. Rule 4(c)(2). The marshal or a special appointee will continue to serve forms of process other than a summons or a subpoena. Rule 4.1(a).

18. Rule 4(c)(2).

19. Rule 4(g), (i), (j)(2) 4A Wright & Miller, Civil 2d §§ 1099, 1106–1110.

The rules did not deal satisfactorily with service on foreign governments or agencies thereof, and judicial inventiveness had been required to fill that gap, but the matter is now covered by the provisions of the Foreign Sovereign Immunities Act of 1976. See 28 U.S.C.A. § 1608; Rule 4(j)(1); 4A Wright & Miller, Civil 2d § 1111; Kane, Suing Foreign Sovereigns: A Procedural Compass, 1981, 34 Stan.L.Rev. 385.

There is a sensible and liberal provision for service on federal officers or agencies in 28 U.S.C.A. § 1391(e). 4A Wright & Miller, Civil 2d § 1107. It does not apply to a suit against a former government official or to an action for money damages brought against a federal official in his individual capacity. Stafford v. Briggs, 1980, 100 S.Ct. 774, 444 U.S. 527, 63 L.Ed.2d 1, noted 1980, 49 U.Cin.L.Rev. 675.

20. From 1938 to 1993 the corresponding provisions were Rule 4(d)(1), (3).

21. Rule 4(e)(1), 4(h)(2). This had originally been in Rule 4(d)(7) and in the 1983 revision appeared in Rule 4(c)(1).

was innovative but the provisions, which came from Congress rather than from the Advisory Committee, were poorly drafted and the implementation of the procedure was deeply flawed.[22]   Perhaps the most basic flaw was referring to this as service-by-mail.[23]

Rule 4(d), in the 1993 version, builds on this earlier idea of using the mail, but it is much better drafted than its predecessor and it now calls the device what it is: waiver of service.   In a suit against an individual, a corporation, or an association, plaintiff may notify the defendant by first-class mail or other reliable means of the commencement of the action and request that the defendant waive service of a summons.[24] The rule is explicit that a defendant who waives service of a summons does not thereby waive any objection to venue or to personal jurisdiction of the court over him.[25]   As an inducement to waiver, the rule provides that a defendant who waives formal service does not need to respond to the complaint until 60 days from the date the notice was sent,[26] rather than 20 days from the date of service as Rule 12 would otherwise specify.

A key provision in the 1993 rule is Rule 4(d)(4).   It provides that if defendant waives service and plaintiff files that waiver with the court, the action proceeds as if a summons and complaint had been served at the time of filing the waiver.   This makes it clear that if the applicable law requires service of process to toll the statute of limitations, it is the filing of the waiver, not the mere receipt by defendant of a request for waiver, that is effective for this purpose.[27]   In the light of this, the device of requested waiver of service is not suitable if a limitations period that is about to expire is not tolled by mere filing of the complaint.   Unless there is ample time, the plaintiff should proceed directly to the formal methods for service identified in subdivision (e), (f), or (h).

If defendant does not waive service, under the procedure set out in Rule 4(d), then plaintiff must serve the defendant in the traditional way. But Rule 4(d)(2) states that a defendant who receives a notice and request for waiver has a duty to avoid unnecessary costs of serving the summons.   If the defendant fails to comply with the request for waiver, the court is to impose the costs subsequently incurred in effecting service

---

22.   Sinclair, note 2 above, at 1186.   See 4A Wright & Miller, Civil 2d § 1092.1.

23.   The Advisory Committee Note to the 1993 amendment of Rule 4(d) says in part that calling this service-by-mail "misled some plaintiffs into thinking that service could be effected by mail without the affirmative cooperation of the defendant. E.g., Gulley v. Mayo Foundation, 886 F.2d 161 (8th Cir.1989).   It is more accurate to describe the communication sent to the defendant as a request for a waiver of formal service."   146 F.R.D. at 561.

24.   Rule 4(d)(2).   The rule spells out in detail the contents of the notice and re-

quest.   It is supplemented by Official Forms 1A and 1B.

25.   Rule 4(d)(1).

26.   Rule 4(d)(3).   If the notice was sent to a foreign country, 90 days are allowed.

27.   Under the 1983 provisions one court had held that mere receipt by the defendant was enough.   Morse v. Elmira Country Club, C.A.2d, 1984, 752 F.2d 35.   This "fanciful interpretation of the rule"—Sinclair, note 2 above, at 1266—was rejected by all the other circuits that spoke to the point.   Media Duplication Services, Ltd., v. HDG Software, Inc., C.A.1st, 1991, 928 F.2d 1228, 1233–1234.   The new Rule 4(d)(4) explicitly rejects the view taken in Morse.

on the defendant unless good cause for the failure is shown.[28]

If there has been no waiver of service, Rule 4(e)(2) offers three possible methods of service on an individual in the United States.[29] Probably the most common, and surely the most desirable, method is to deliver the summons and complaint to the individual personally. Where this method is followed there can be no question whether defendant had notice of the suit. Personal service may also be made by leaving copies of the summons and complaint at defendant's dwelling house or usual place of abode with some person of suitable age and discretion then residing therein. Service that meets these tests is good even though defendant never personally receives the papers.[30] Unlike some state statutes, this rule does not require an order of court or a showing of inability to find the defendant before making service in this manner. There have been elaborate attempts to define "usual place of abode," but whether defendant actually received notice is likely to have more influence on the result than any conceptual notions of whether the place where the summons and complaint were left is the "usual place of abode." [31] A third method of service on an individual is by delivery to an agent authorized by appointment or by law to receive process. A person who is an agent of an individual for other purposes is not necessarily authorized to receive service of process, and thus this method of service must be used with care.[32]

An individual who is personally within the state or one who is domiciled within the state although absent from it is subject to the jurisdiction of the state, and may be served in federal court if the procedure for service satisfies due-process requirements by providing a means reasonably calculated to give him notice of the proceeding and an

---

28. Rule 4(d)(2). This sanction applies only if both the defendant and plaintiff are located within the United States. There is no cost sanction if the request-for-waiver procedure is attempted, but not complied with, on a foreign defendant.

29. 4A Wright & Miller, Civil 2d §§ 1094–1098. These are in addition to service pursuant to state law. Rule 4(e)(1). See § 65 below.

Rule 4(f) provides a variety of methods for service on an individual in a foreign country. See 4A Wright & Miller, Civil 2d §§ 1133–1136; Carrington, note 3 above, at 747–750; Born & Vollmer, The Effect of the Revised Federal Rules of Civil Procedure on Personal Jurisdiction, Service and Discovery in International Cases, 1993, 150 F.R.D. 221; Degnan & Kane, The Exercise of Jurisdiction Over and Enforcement of Judgments Against Alien Defendants, 1988, 37 Hastings L.J. 799.

30. Smith v. Kincaid, C.A.6th, 1957, 249 F.2d 243; Adams v. School Bd. of Wyoming Val. West Sch. Dist., D.C.Pa.1971, 53 F.R.D. 267.

31. Karlsson v. Rabinowitz, C.A.4th, 1963, 318 F.2d 666, 668, noted 1964, 24 Md.L.Rev. 356, 9 Utah L.Rev. 192; Williams v. Capital Transit Co., C.A.D.C. 1954, 215 F.2d 487; Minnesota Mining & Mfg. Co. v. Kirkevold, D.C.Minn.1980, 87 F.R.D. 317; 4A Wright & Miller, Civil 2d § 1096.

32. 4A Wright & Miller, Civil 2d §§ 1097–1098.

Hohensee v. News Syndicate, Inc., C.A.3d, 1961, 286 F.2d 527, vacated on other grounds 1962, 82 S.Ct. 1035, 369 U.S. 659, 8 L.Ed.2d 273; Nelson v. Swift, C.A.D.C.1959, 271 F.2d 504; Impoco v. Lauro, D.C.Mass.1955, 16 F.R.D. 522.

A contractual provision designating an agent for receipt of process is valid, even if the contract does not expressly require the agent to notify the defendant when service is made. National Equipment Rental, Ltd. v. Szukhent, 1964, 84 S.Ct. 411, 375 U.S. 311, 11 L.Ed.2d 354.

opportunity to be heard.[33]   There are circumstances, however, where a person within the state may be immune from service there, and this is a question that the federal courts resolve for themselves and on which they are not controlled by state law.   In general the federal courts recognize the principles that parties, witnesses, and attorneys coming from another state, in order to attend court under subpoena or other process, or to represent a party, in connection with one suit are immune from service of process in another and that service on a party induced to come into the jurisdiction for the purpose by the fraud or deceit of the plaintiff is invalid.[34]   The immunity is granted not for the convenience of the person seeking to invoke it but for the convenience of the court. The underlying idea of immunity is to encourage voluntary appearance to secure the better administration of justice.   If a defendant is willing to enter the jurisdiction and submit to it, the court will encourage him to do so by assuring him that he will not be served with process in any other suit.   Thus, where the subsequent suit, in which immunity is sought, is part of, or a continuation of, the suit in which the party appeared, the courts have refused to invoke the immunity.[35]   The lower courts are not in agreement, and the Supreme Court has not yet spoken, on whether a person who comes into the state to answer a criminal indictment is immune from the service of civil process.   It would seem that the purpose of granting immunity is not present here, where there is nothing voluntary about the person's appearance, and thus that the better view is that denying immunity under these circumstances.[36]

Service within the United States on a corporation or other association that is subject to suit under a common name is made by delivery of the summons and complaint to an officer, a managing or general agent, or to any other agent authorized by appointment or by law to receive service of process.[37]   As with an individual, other methods of service are proper where authorized by the law of the state in which the district

---

33. See Milliken v. Meyer, 1940, 61 S.Ct. 339, 311 U.S. 457, 85 L.Ed. 278.   This principle is recognized in Rule 4(d)(1) by the authorization for leaving the summons and complaint at the defendant's usual place of abode.

34.   Lamb v. Schmitt, 1932, 52 S.Ct. 317, 285 U.S. 222, 76 L.Ed. 720; Stewart v. Ramsay, 1916, 37 S.Ct. 44, 242 U.S. 128, 61 L.Ed. 192; Jacobs/Kahan & Co. v. Marsh, C.A.7th, 1984, 740 F.2d 587; and 4 Wright & Miller, Civil 2d §§ 1076–1081.

Immunity is unnecessary if the person could be served in his home jurisdiction under the forum's long-arm statute.   4 Wright & Miller, Civil 2d § 1076, pp. 505–506; Note, Long Arm Statutes and the Denial of the Immunity Privilege, 1974, 9 New Eng.L.Rev. 589.

35.   Page Co. v. Macdonald, 1923, 43 S.Ct. 416, 261 U.S. 446, 67 L.Ed. 737; McDonnell v. American Leduc Petroleums, Ltd., C.A.2d, 1972, 456 F.2d 1170; Pointer

v. Ghavam, D.C.Ark.1985, 107 F.R.D. 262. It has been thought not enough, however, that there is some similarity between the two suits and that denial of immunity would be desirable as a matter of judicial administration.   Matter of Equitable Plan Co., C.A.2d, 1960, 277 F.2d 319, criticized 1961, 61 Col.L.Rev. 278; Atkinson v. Jory, C.A.10th, 1961, 292 F.2d 169.   But see 4 Wright & Miller, Civil 2d § 1080.

36.   Greene v. Weatherington, C.A.D.C. 1962, 301 F.2d 565, noted 1962, 48 Va. L.Rev. 1163, 1963, 12 Am.U.L.Rev. 101, 20 Wash. & Lee L.Rev. 375; Employers Mut. Liab. Ins. Co. of Wisconsin v. Hitchcock, D.C.Mo.1958, 158 F.Supp. 783.   Contra: Alla v. Kornfeld, D.C.Ill.1949, 84 F.Supp. 823.   See 4 Wright & Miller, Civil 2d § 1081.

37.   Rule 4(h)(1); 4A Wright & Miller, Civil 2d §§ 1100–1105.

court is located or in which service is made and there are other provisions if service must be made in a foreign country [38].

If the person served is an officer, or a managing agent, or a general agent of the corporation, service on him is proper even though he is not specifically authorized by the corporation to accept service of process.[39] Whether a person is a managing or general agent within the rule depends upon the nature of his duties and authority and not upon the name of his office. There are a great many decisions as to whether particular persons were proper agents to receive service for corporations,[40] but the underlying principle is that service must be made on a representative so integrated with the corporation sued as to make it likely that he will realize his responsibilities and know what he should do with any legal papers served on him.[41] The required agency must exist at the time service is made, and it is important that the person served on behalf of the corporation is at the time of service acting in the capacity that permits him to accept service.[42] An officer or agent may be disqualified to receive service of process on the corporation if his interests are adverse to those of the corporation.[43]

Even if service is made on an appropriate corporate agent, it is ineffective unless the corporation is subject to suit in the state where service is made. This is an issue with a long history and considerable change of view. Concepts of jurisdiction have altered through the years and the older precedents can be regarded as authoritative only to the extent that they are consistent with what one justice has called "the enlightened rationale of our more recent cases."[44] The Court has declared unanimously that "a trend is clearly discernible toward expanding the permissible scope of state jurisdiction over foreign corporations and other nonresidents. In part this is attributable to the fundamental transformation of our national economy over the years. Today many commercial transactions touch two or more States and may involve parties separated by the full continent. With this increasing nationalization of commerce has come a great increase in the amount of business conducted by mail cross state lines. At the same time modern transpor-

---

38. Rule 4(h)(2), incorporating most of the methods for service of an individual in a foreign country authorized by Rule 4(f).

39. Bergold v. Commercial Nat. Underwriters, D.C.Kan.1945, 61 F.Supp. 639; U.S. v. Central States Theatre Corp., D.C.Neb.1960, 187 F.Supp. 114.

40. See 4A Wright & Miller, Civil 2d § 1103.

41. Goetz v. Interlake S.S. Co., D.C.N.Y. 1931, 47 F.2d 753, 757. The test has been similarly stated in more recent cases. Montclair Electronics, Inc. v. Electra/Midland Corp., D.C.N.Y.1971, 326 F.Supp. 839, 842; Van Hoven Co. v. Stans, D.C.Minn. 1970, 319 F.Supp. 180, 182.

42. Westcott–Alexander, Inc. v. Dailey, C.A.4th, 1959, 264 F.2d 853; Granite Chem. Corp. v. Northeast Coal & Dock Corp., D.C.Me.1966, 249 F.Supp. 597; Pacific Employers Ins. Co. v. The Paul David Jones, D.C.Tex.1950, 98 F.Supp. 668, affirmed C.A.5th, 1952, 195 F.2d 372; and cases cited 4A Wright & Miller, Civil 2d § 1101 nn. 15, 16.

43. Hartsock v. Commodity Credit Corp., D.C.Iowa 1950, 10 F.R.D. 181; Bishop v. Everson Mfg. Co., D.C.N.Y.1943, 50 F.Supp. 792.

44. Burton, J., concurring in part in Polizzi v. Cowles Magazines, Inc., 1953, 73 S.Ct. 900, 905, 345 U.S. 663, 672, 97 L.Ed. 1331.

tation and communication have made it much less burdensome for a party sued to defend himself in a State where he engages in economic activity." [45]

There are conceptual difficulties in deciding whether a corporation is "in" a state other than that of its incorporation so as to be subject to process. The early cases developed fictional doctrines that the corporation had given "consent" to be sued in a state other than that of its incorporation as a condition to doing business there,[46] or that simply by doing business it was "present" there and subject to the jurisdiction of the courts of that state.[47] Such metaphysical questions naturally led to confusion in the decisions. Judge Learned Hand observed that "it is quite impossible to establish any rule from the decided cases; we must step from tuft to tuft across the morass." [48]

The first, and the most important, of the "more enlightened" recent decisions on jurisdiction over foreign corporations is International Shoe Co. v. Washington,[49] in which Chief Justice Stone reviewed comprehensively the entire problem. He adopted Judge Hand's view that talk of "presence" or "consent" is a mere fiction, used to symbolize those activities of corporate agents within a state that the courts will deem sufficient to satisfy due process, and that the corporation should be subject to suit in any state where it had certain minimum contacts such that the maintenance of the suit would not offend "traditional notions of fair play and effective justice." He went on to say: "It is evident that the criteria by which we mark the boundary line between those activities which subject the corporation to suit, and those which do not, cannot be simply mechanical or quantitative. The test is not merely, as has sometimes been suggested, whether the activity, which the corporation has seen fit to procure through its agents in another state, is a little more or a little less. * * * Whether due process is satisfied must depend rather upon the quality and nature of the activity in relation to the fair and orderly administration of the laws which it was the purpose of the due process clause to insure. * * * [T]o the extent that a corporation exercises the privilege of conducting activities within a state, it enjoys the benefits and protection of the laws of that state. The exercise of that privilege may give rise to obligations; and, so far as those obligations arise out of or are connected with activities within the state, a procedure which requires the corporation to respond to a suit brought to

45. McGee v. International Life Ins. Co., 1957, 78 S.Ct. 199, 201, 355 U.S. 220, 222–223, 2 L.Ed.2d 223.

This development is described in 4 Wright & Miller, Civil 2d §§ 1064–1072.

In World–Wide Volkswagen Corp. v. Woodson, 1980, 100 S.Ct. 559, 565, 444 U.S. 286, 293, 62 L.Ed.2d 490, the Court quoted this passage from McGee, and added: "The historical developments noted in McGee, of course, have only accelerated in the generation since that case was decided."

46. Lafayette Ins. Co. v. French, 1855, 18 How. 404, 15 L.Ed. 451.

47. Philadelphia & R. Co. v. McKibbin, 1916, 37 S.Ct. 280, 243 U.S. 264, 61 L.Ed. 710.

48. Hutchinson v. Chase & Gilbert, C.C.A.2d 1930, 45 F.2d 139, 142.

49. 1945, 66 S.Ct. 154, 326 U.S. 310, 90 L.Ed. 95.

enforce them can, in most instances, hardly be said to be undue."[50]

In the wake of International Shoe there has been a flood of decisions, including several from the Supreme Court, undertaking to say whether the contacts of a corporation with a particular state were substantial enough to make the corporation amenable to process in that state.[51] Of these the best known, and the most important, are McGee v. International Life Insurance Company,[52] Hanson v. Denckla,[53] World-Wide Volkswagen Corporation v. Woodson,[54] Helicopteros Nacionales de Colombia, S.A. v. Hall,[55] and Burger King Corporation v. Rudzewicz.[56] The McGee case held that a Texas insurance company was subject to process in a California state court in a suit on an insurance policy on the life of a California resident, though the company never had an office or agent in California, and never solicited or did any insurance business in that state other than the policy in question. The facts that the contract was delivered in California, that the premiums were mailed from there, and that the insured resided there when he died were held to give California sufficient interest in the transaction to require the insurer to defend there. The facts of Hanson v. Denckla defy brief summarization and both the majority and dissenting opinions have a somewhat Delphic quality. The case is significant as demonstrating that the McGee case did not remove all bars against service on a foreign corporation, and that the corporation must have done some act by which it purposefully availed itself of the privilege of conducting activities within the forum state to be subject to suit there.

World-Wide Volkswagen was a suit by the owners of a car against the dealer from whom they had bought the car in New York and its wholesaler. The suit arose out of an accident in Oklahoma. The defendants were New York corporations that did no business in Oklahoma. A divided Court held that the Oklahoma courts could not exercise jurisdiction over defendants. The requirement of minimum contacts, Justice White wrote, performs "two related, but distinguishable, functions. It protects the defendant against the burdens of litigating in a distant or inconvenient forum. And it acts to ensure that the States through their courts, do not reach out beyond the limits imposed on them by their status as coequal sovereigns in a federal system."[57]

50. 66 S.Ct. at 159–160, 326 U.S. at 319–320.

51. See 4 Wright & Miller, Civil 2d § 1069.

52. 1957, 78 S.Ct. 199, 355 U.S. 220, 2 L.Ed.2d 223.

53. 1958, 78 S.Ct. 1228, 357 U.S. 235, 2 L.Ed.2d 1283.

54. 1980, 100 S.Ct. 559, 444 U.S. 286, 62 L.Ed.2d 490. See Louis, The Grasp of Long Arm Jurisdiction Finally Exceeds Its Reach: A Comment on World-Wide Volkswagen Corp. v. Woodson and Rush v. Savchuk, 1980, 58 N.C.L.Rev. 407; Note, Fed-

eralism, Due Process, and Minimum Contacts, 1980, 80 Col.L.Rev. 1341.

55. 1984, 104 S.Ct. 1868, 466 U.S. 408, 80 L.Ed.2d 404.

56. 1985, 105 S.Ct. 2174, 471 U.S. 462, 85 L.Ed.2d 528.

57. 100 S.Ct. at 564, 444 U.S. at 291–292.

In Insurance Corp. of Ireland, Ltd. v. Compagnie des Bauxites de Guinee, 1982, 102 S.Ct. 2099, 2104, 456 U.S. 694, 702, 72 L.Ed.2d 492, however, with Justice White again writing for the Court, it was said that the personal-jurisdiction requirement of the Due Process Clause "recognizes and pro-

The Court put great emphasis on the notion of sovereignty as a limitation on jurisdiction, and it rejected the argument that jurisdiction could rest on the fact that it was foreseeable that an automobile sold in New York might travel through Oklahoma and become involved in an accident there.[58] The Court agreed that foreseeability is not wholly irrelevant, but thought that the foreseeability that is critical is not the mere likelihood that a product will find its way into the forum state, but that the defendant's conduct and connection with the forum state must be such that he should reasonably anticipate being haled into court there.[59]

In the Helicopteros case the Supreme Court recognized a distinction that had been suggested by commentators and drawn by some lower courts between "general jurisdiction" and "special jurisdiction." [60] When the claim sued on does not arise from the defendant's contacts with the forum state, general jurisdiction must be predicated on contacts sufficiently continuous and systematic to justify haling the defendant into court. Special jurisdiction is asserted when the defendant's forum contacts are sporadic, but the claim arises out of those contacts.[61] The distinction is significant because in order to assert general jurisdiction there must be substantial forum-related activity on the part of the defendant. Thus, the threshold for satisfying minimum contacts before considering convenience or more general fairness concerns is higher than in special-jurisdiction cases.

In the Burger King case two Michigan residents had entered into a long-term franchise agreement to operate a Burger King restaurant in

tects an individual liberty interest. It represents a restriction on judicial power not as a matter of sovereignty, but as a matter of individual liberty." This led Justice Powell, in a concurring opinion, to express concern that the Court was abandoning the rationale of World–Wide Volkswagen and of Hanson v. Denckla, and that it was abandoning "reliance on the concept of minimum contacts as a 'sovereign' limitation on the power of States" in favor of "abstract notions of fair play." 102 S.Ct. at 2110, 456 U.S. at 714. Distinguished commentators have said that Justice White's view of the basis of the personal-jurisdiction requirement is "historically, analytically, and functionally incorrect." James, Hazard & Leubsdorf, Civil Procedure, 4th ed. 1992, p. 60.

58. 100 S.Ct. at 566–567, 444 U.S. at 295–296. For the proposition that foreseeability by itself is not enough, the Court cited Hanson v. Denckla, and it also read Kulko v. California Superior Court, 1978, 98 S.Ct. 1690, 436 U.S. 84, 56 L.Ed.2d 132, as supporting that result. In Kulko it had held that California could not exercise jurisdiction in a child-support action over a former husband who had remained in New York, and in World–Wide Volkswagen the

Court said that it was foreseeable that the divorced wife in Kulko would move to California from New York and that the minor child would move there with her. The Court also noted in World–Wide Volkswagen that in Shaffer v. Heitner, 1977, 97 S.Ct. 2569, 433 U.S. 186, 53 L.Ed.2d 683, it had repudiated the former rule that a creditor is subject to suit quasi-in-rem in any state having transitory jurisdiction over his or her debtor.

59. 100 S.Ct. at 567, 444 U.S. at 297.

The various opinions in Asahi Metal Industry Co. v. Superior Court, 1987, 107 S.Ct. 1026, 480 U.S. 102, 94 L.Ed.2d 92, express differing views on whether the mere placement of a product into the stream of commerce is enough for jurisdiction.

60. Von Mehren & Trautman, Jurisdiction to Adjudicate: A Suggested Analysis, 1966, 79 Harv.L.Rev. 1121, 1136–1164; Brilmayer, How Contacts Count: Due Process Limitations on State Court Jurisdiction, 1980 S.Ct.Rev. 77, 80–81.

61. 104 S.Ct. at 1872 nn. 8, 9, 466 U.S. at 414 nn. 8, 9. See Weinberg, The Helicopter Case and the Jurisprudence of Jurisdiction, 1985, 58 S.Cal.L.Rev. 913.

Michigan. Burger King was a Florida corporation and the contract provided that the franchise relationship was established in Miami and governed by Florida law and called for payment of all required fees to Burger King's Miami headquarters. When the franchisees fell behind in their payments, Burger King brought a diversity action against them in federal court in Florida. The Supreme Court held that once minimum contacts have been established through application of the "purposeful availment" standard, courts may consider those contacts "in light of other factors to determine whether the assertion of personal jurisdiction would comport with 'fair play and substantial justice'." [62] The Court found no lack of fairness in upholding jurisdiction in Florida over Rudzewicz and his partner. They were experienced and sophisticated businessmen who had deliberately entered into a long-term arrangement contemplating ongoing interactions with Burger King's Florida headquarters.

The due-process limitations on the amenability of a foreign corporation [63] to suit within a state are not peculiarly, nor even particularly, a problem for the federal courts. Thus, it is not necessary, were it possible, to spell out here what those limits are now thought by the courts to be. A substantial literature is available on this subject. [64]

There is an aspect of the problem, however, that is peculiar to the federal courts. The principles discussed so far represent federal constitutional limitations. If suit in federal court is on a federally created right, these federal general-law concepts are the sole guide on whether a foreign corporation is amenable to process. [65] The matter is not so simple, however, where the right sued on is state-created and jurisdiction rests on diversity. The landmark jurisdictional decisions of the Supreme Court show the extent to which the states may go, consistent with due process, in making foreign corporations suable in their courts,

---

62. 105 S.Ct. at 2184, 471 U.S. at 476.

63. These due-process concerns occasionally arise in suits against individuals. Indeed the famous early case of Pennoyer v. Neff, 1877, 95 U.S. 714, 24 L.Ed. 565, was such a case. In Phillips Petroleum Co. v. Shutts, 1985, 105 S.Ct. 2965, 472 U.S. 797, 86 L.Ed.2d 628, the Court held that a state court can decide a damages class action with binding effect on absent members of the class of plaintiffs, provided that those class members outside the state received notice of the action and an opportunity to opt out. And in Burnham v. Superior Court, 1990, 110 S.Ct. 2105, 495 U.S. 604, 109 L.Ed.2d 631, the Court held that a state can obtain personal jurisdiction over an individual by service on him or her within the state when defendant was there temporarily for activities unrelated to the suit. See also the Kulko case, discussed note 58 above.

64. See, e.g., Transgrud, The Federal Common Law of Personal Jurisdiction, 1989, 57 Geo.Wash.L.Rev. 849; Murphy,

Personal Jurisdiction and the Stream of Commerce Theory: A Reappraisal and a Revised Approach, 1989, 77 Ky.L.J. 243; Stravitz, Sayonara to Minimum Contacts: Asahi Metal Indus. Co. v. Superior Court, 1988, 31 S.C.L.Rev. 1; Dessem, Personal Jurisdiction After Asahi: The Other (International) Shoe Drops, 1987, 55 Tenn.L.Rev. 41; Knudson, Keeton, Calder, Helicopteros and Burger King—International Shoe's Most Recent Progeny, 1985, 39 U.Miami L.Rev. 809. See also Restatement Second of Judgments, 1982, §§ 4–9, and the Reporter's Notes thereto.

65. Terry v. Raymond Intl., Inc., C.A.5th, 1981, 658 F.2d 398, certiorari denied 102 S.Ct. 1975, 456 U.S. 928, 72 L.Ed.2d 443; Fraley v. Chesapeake & O. Ry., C.A.3d, 1968, 397 F.2d 1; and cases cited 4 Wright & Miller, Civil 2d § 1075 n. 3. But cf. Gkiafis v. S.S. Yiosonas, C.A.4th, 1965, 342 F.2d 546, 548–549.

but due process does not compel the states to go this far if they do not choose to do so.[66] If a corporation cannot be sued in state court, because the state has not gone as far as the Constitution permits, is it consistent with the Erie doctrine for a federal court to entertain a diversity action against the corporation in that state? This question led to an extraordinary debate within the Second Circuit. In Jaftex Corp. v. Randolph Mills, Inc.,[67] the majority, speaking through the draftsman of the rules, Chief Judge Charles E. Clark, said that amenability to federal process in a diversity case where service is made under what was then Rule 4(d)(3) is governed only by a federal test. Judge Henry J. Friendly disagreed, and argued that a corporation is not suable in federal court unless it could also be sued in the courts of the state. Three years later the court, this time sitting en banc, considered the issue again, in Arrowsmith v. United Press International.[68] In that case Judge Friendly spoke for the court in holding that the state test of amenability must be satisfied, while Judge Clark was alone in dissent. The commentators thought Judge Clark had the better of the argument,[69] but the courts have accepted Judge Friendly's position. Accordingly they hold that in diversity cases state law determines whether a corporation is subject to suit in the state, and the federal decisions are important only in ascertaining whether the state law is within constitutional bounds.[70]

As has been implicit in all that has been said thus far, federal process can ordinarily be served only within the territorial limits of the state in which the court is sitting.[71] This is not a necessary limitation. Congress has power to provide for the service of process anywhere within the United States[72]—or in some circumstances in foreign countries[73]— and there are not a few instances in which it has done so.[74] These are expressly recognized as exceptions to the usual limits.[75] This has never been true of process in an ordinary civil action. Indeed prior to adoption

---

66. Perkins v. Benguet Consol. Mining Co., 1952, 72 S.Ct. 413, 342 U.S. 437, 96 L.Ed. 485.

67. C.A.2d, 1960, 282 F.2d 508.

68. C.A.2d, 1963, 320 F.2d 219.

69. Transgrud, note 64 above; Comment, 1964, 64 Col.L.Rev. 685; Comment, 1964, 31 U.Chi.L.Rev. 752; Note, 1964, 49 Iowa L.Rev. 1224; Note, 1964, 48 Minn. L.Rev. 1131. Contra: ALI Study, pp. 133–134.

70. See the many cases cited 4 Wright & Miller, Civil 2d § 1075 n. 32.

71. 4A Wright & Miller, Civil 2d § 1124. From 1938 to 1993 this limit appeared in Rule 4(f). It is now set out in Rule 4(k)(1)(A) and is couched in terms of service—or waiver of service—being effective to establish jurisdiction over the person of a defendant who could be subjected to the jurisdiction of a court of general jurisdiction in the state in which the district court is located.

72. Mississippi Pub. Corp. v. Murphree, 1946, 66 S.Ct. 242, 245, 326 U.S. 438, 442, 90 L.Ed. 185. See also Robertson v. Railroad Labor Bd., 1925, 45 S.Ct. 621, 623, 268 U.S. 619, 622, 69 L.Ed. 1119; U.S. v. Union Pac. R. Co., 1878, 98 U.S. 569, 604, 25 L.Ed. 143; Toland v. Sprague, 1838, 12 Pet. 300, 328, 9 L.Ed. 1093.

To the same effect, see Restatement Second of Judgments, 1982, § 4(2), and comm. f; ALI Study, pp. 437–441. But see Seeburger, The Federal Long–Arm: The Uses of Diversity, or "Tain't So, McGee," 1977, 10 Ind.L.Rev. 480; Abraham, Constitutional Limitations Upon the Territorial Reach of Federal Process, 1963, 8 Vill.L.Rev. 520.

73. Rule 4(f), (h)(2); 4A Wright & Miller, Civil 2d §§ 1133–1136.

74. See 4A Wright & Miller, Civil 2d §§ 1118, 1125.

75. Rule 4(k)(1)(C), (D).

of the rules process normally ran only throughout the district, and the extension of the territorial limits to the borders of the state was challenged as going beyond the rulemaking power, but this challenge was rebuffed by a unanimous Court.[76]

Though the enlargement of the territorial limits of process effected in 1938 was a desirable change, the need was clear for further expansion of those limits. The problem was particularly pressing in great metropolitan areas that stretch across state lines. Under the rules prior to 1963, a person who had failed to pay alimony called for by a divorce in the District of Columbia was beyond the power of the court to compel such payment so long as he remained across the Potomac River in Virginia, since an order of commitment for civil contempt could not validly be served outside the district.[77] Third-party practice was seriously limited by the inability to implead a third party who lived in a state other than that in which the original action was brought.[78] Suit was not possible in any federal court, even though venue problems were not present or were waived, if one of two "indispensable" parties defendant lived across the state line from the other.[79]

To meet these particular problems, a 1963 amendment made a modest liberalization of what was then Rule 4(f) to meet the most-pressing needs. This amendment permits service outside the state, but within 100 miles of the place where the action is commenced or is to be tried, if this is necessary to add a third-party defendant under Rule 14, or to join an indispensable party without whose joinder the existing action or a counterclaim therein must be dismissed, or to require a person to respond to an order of commitment for civil contempt.[80] This provision was carried forward, with one slight expansion, in the 1993 amendments of the rules.[81] Though the amended rule takes care of the

---

76. Mississippi Pub. Corp. v. Murphree, 1946, 66 S.Ct. 242, 326 U.S. 438, 90 L.Ed. 185.

The power of the Supreme Court to extend the reach of process through the rule-making power is questioned in Whitten, Separation of Powers Restrictions on Judicial Rulemaking: A Case Study of Federal Rule 4, 1988, 40 Me.L.Rev. 41. In Wright, Procedural Reform: Its Limitations and Its Future, 1967, 1 Ga.L.Rev. 563, 571, the Supreme Court's power even to allow nationwide service by rule is fully accepted, but it is argued that this is "so basic an alteration in the way of doing things that the change should be made by Congress rather than the Court."

77. Graber v. Graber, D.C.D.C.1950, 93 F.Supp. 281.

78. See § 76 below.

79. See § 70 below.

80. 4A Wright & Miller, Civil 2d §§ 1127–1129. Although it has been held that in a diversity case in which service is

made in the 100–mile "bulge," the law of the state in which the service is made determines the defendant's amenability to suit, Coleman v. American Export Isbrandtsen Lines, Inc., C.A.2d, 1968, 405 F.2d 250, the better view is that state tests are of no significance and that it is enough that the person to be served has minimum contacts with either the forum state or the "bulge" area. Sprow v. Hartford Ins. Co., C.A.5th, 1979, 594 F.2d 412; Gamble v. Lyons Precast Erectors, Inc., D.C.Pa.1993, 825 F.Supp. 92. See also 4 Wright & Miller, Civil 2d § 1075, pp. 496–498, 4A id. § 1127, pp. 335–337; Kaplan, Amendments to the Federal Rules of Civil Procedure, 1961–1963, 1964, 77 Harv.L.Rev. 601, 633. But cf. Note, The Limits of Federal Diversity Jurisdiction Under Rule 4(f) of the Federal Rules of Civil Procedure, 1980, 68 Geo. Wash.L.Rev. 269.

81. Rule 4(k)(1)(B) has the 100–mile bulge provision for third-party defendants and "indispensable" parties. The provision for civil-contempt cases is now in Rule problems that exist in metropolitan areas, the ultimate solution seems likely to be that of permitting nationwide service of process in all cases, with inconvenience to parties avoided by adjustment of the venue requirements and provision for transfer to the most convenient forum.[82]

§ 65. Service According to State Law [1]

From the earliest days of the nation, service of process in federal actions was required to conform to state law. This tradition was broken in 1938 when the Federal Rules of Civil Procedure made their own provisions for modes of service.[2] As was noted in section 64, the rules provide methods of service on various classes of defendants, but they also provide that service on an individual or corporation is sufficient if the summons and complaint are served in the manner prescribed by state law for the service of summons or other like process upon any such defendant in an action brought in the courts of general jurisdiction of that state.

The key provision, under the 1993 revision, is Rule 4(e)(1).[3] Although it applies of its own force only to service upon individuals within the United States, it is incorporated by reference in Rule 4(h)(1) as a method of service upon corporations and associations. These provisions go beyond the previous law in that they not only allow service pursuant to the law of the state in which the district court is located, as the former rules had done, but also allow service pursuant to the law of the state in which service is effected. Two other provisions for service in accordance with state law carry forth language that had already appeared in the rules. Service in the manner prescribed by state law is authorized upon infants and incompetents, but in those cases it must be the law of the state in which the service is made.[4] Service upon a state,

---

4.1(b); it continues the 100–mile bulge for most civil-contempt proceedings, but allows nationwide service if a person is held in contempt of a decree or injunction issues to enforce the laws of the United States.

82. See 4A Wright & Miller, Civil 2d § 1127, pp. 332–334; Barrett, Venue and Service of Process in the Federal Courts—Suggestions for Reform, 1954, 7 Vand. L.Rev. 608.

§ 65

1. 4A Wright & Miller, Civil 2d §§ 1112–1116, 1119–1123; Foster, Long-arm Jurisdiction in Federal Courts, 1969 Wis.L.Rev. 9.

2. Carrington, Continuing Work on the Civil Rules: The Summons, 1988, 63 Notre Dame L.Rev. 733, 738–739.

3. In the original Civil Rules the relevant provision was Rule 4(d)(7). In 1983 it became Rule 4(c)(2)(C)(i).

In addition, prior to 1993 Rule 4(e) had provided that whenever a statute or rule of court of the state in which the district court is held allowed service on a person not an inhabitant of or found within the state, service might be made under the circumstances and in the manner prescribed by the state statute or rule. Although it was possible to draw nice distinctions about the scope and interrelation of this provision with what was first Rule 4(d)(7) and later Rule 4(c)(2)(C)(i), it was generally recognized that there was considerable overlap between them and that no useful purpose would be served by trying to bifurcate them in a mechanical fashion. 4A Wright & Miller, Civil 2d § 1114.

4. Rule 4(g). Prior to 1993 this had been Rule 4(d)(2). See 4A Wright & Miller, Civil 2d § 1099.

municipal corporation, or other governmental organization may be made in the manner prescribed by the law of "that state".[5]

The alternative of service as authorized by state law has been frequently used, ordinarily in conjunction with a state long-arm statute.[6] There had been uncertainty whether Rule 4(c) or state law controlled on who should make service when the state procedures are used.[7] This problem was cured by amendments of Rule 4(c) effective in 1983, which allowed service by any person who is 18 or over and who is not a party to the lawsuit, and this has been carried forward in the 1993 revision.[8]

Frequently state law conditions use of a particular means of service, as under the nonresident motorist statutes, on the action being brought in the county in which the transaction occurred. Such restrictions on venue are not binding in federal court; instead it is enough that suit is brought in the federal district that includes the county in question.[9] It may be that there are other details relating to the manner of service as prescribed by state law that cannot be literally followed in federal court. In such cases conformity as nearly as may be with the state practice should be sufficient compliance with the federal authorization of state methods of service.

The state method of service is not limited to diversity cases or to cases in which state law governs amenability to process. As has always been true, the provisions of Rule 4 allowing this alternative means of service are available for use in any case, whatever its jurisdictional basis.[10]

Prior to 1963 there were questions about the use of state statutes authorizing so-called "quasi-in-rem" actions. These were commenced by attachment or garnishment of property within the state, with notice to the person outside the state against whom the claims were asserted. Actions commenced in this fashion could be removed to federal court if ordinary conditions for removal were satisfied,[11] but, as a result of a historical anomaly,[12] it was repeatedly held that an original action could not be commenced in federal court in this manner.[13] Rule 4 was amended in 1963 to permit actions to be commenced in this fashion if state law so provided.[14]

5. Rule 4(j)(2). Prior to 1993 this had been Rule 4(d)(6). This apparently refers to the law of the state in which the governmental entity is located rather than the state in which the district court is sitting. 4A Wright & Miller, Civil 2d § 1009.

6. 4A Wright & Miller, Civil 2d § 1115.

7. 4A Wright & Miller, Civil 2d § 1092.

8. See § 64 above at notes 15–18.

9. FDIC v. Greenberg, C.A.3d, 1973, 487 F.2d 9, 12–13; and cases cited 4A Wright & Miller, Civil 2d § 1112 nn. 21–23.

10. U.S. v. First Nat. City Bank, 1965, 85 S.Ct. 528, 379 U.S. 378, 13 L.Ed.2d 365; and cases cited 4A Wright & Miller, Civil 2d § 1115 n. 3.

11. Rorick v. Devon Syndicate, Ltd., 1939, 59 S.Ct. 877, 307 U.S. 299, 83 L.Ed. 1303; Clark v. Wells, 1906, 27 S.Ct. 43, 203 U.S. 164, 51 L.Ed. 138; see 28 U.S.C.A. § 1450.

12. Currie, Attachment and Garnishment in the Federal Courts, 1961, 59 Mich. L.Rev. 337; 4A Wright & Miller, Civil 2d § 1119.

13. Big Vein Coal Co. v. Read, 1913, 33 S.Ct. 694, 229 U.S. 31, 57 L.Ed. 1053; Davis v. Ensign–Bickford Co., C.C.A.8th, 1944, 139 F.2d 624.

14. This language appeared in Rule 4(e)(2) from 1963 to 1993. Practice under the amendment is described in 4A Wright & Miller, Civil 2d §§ 1421–1423. This 1963

The 1963 amendment permitting "quasi-in-rem" actions was little used,[15] and its possible utility was further diminished by Supreme Court decisions holding that the mere presence of property in a state does not establish a sufficient relationship between the owner of the property and the state to support the exercise of jurisdiction over an unrelated cause of action.[16] Thus, unless there are other ties sufficient to satisfy the minimum contacts standard, there cannot be a valid exercise of jurisdiction quasi-in-rem.[17]

For these reasons, when Rule 4 was rewritten in 1993 the authorization for quasi-in-rem actions was sharply narrowed. It now appears in Rule 4(n)(2) and applies only upon a showing that personal jurisdiction over a defendant in the district where the action is brought cannot be obtained with reasonable efforts by service of process in any manner authorized by Rule 4. The Advisory Committee Note to the 1993 amendment says that "occasions for the use of this provision should be rare, as where the defendant is a fugitive or asserts are in imminent danger of disappearing."[18]

C. PLEADINGS

Analysis

---

amendment was sharply criticized by Carrington, The Modern Utility of Quasi in Rem Jurisdiction, 1962, 76 Harv.L.Rev. 303, partly because of the limited utility it would have. Doubt whether the amendment was a valid "procedural" provision was raised by Elliott & Green, Quasi in Rem Jurisdiction in Federal Courts: The Proposed Amendments to Rule 4, 1963, 48 Iowa L.Rev. 300. But cf. 4A Wright & Miller, Civil 2d §§ 1119, 1120. Recent Supreme Court decisions imposing due process requirements on garnishment and attachment also had to be taken into account. See 4 Wright & Miller, Civil 2d § 1074.

15. The state attachment procedure may be used in federal court though the property is in a different county of the district than that in which the federal court sits. FDIC v. Greenberg, C.A.3d, 1973, 487 F.2d 9. See 4A Wright & Miller, Civil 2d § 1121.

16. The leading case is Shaffer v. Heitner, 1977, 97 S.Ct. 2569, 433 U.S. 186, 53 L.Ed.2d 683. See also Rush v. Savchuk, 1980, 100 S.Ct. 571, 444 U.S. 320, 62 L.Ed.2d 516.

See 4 Wright & Miller, Civil § 2d 1070. Some of the vast literature provoked by these cases is cited, id. at n. 14.

17. Restatement Second of Judgments, 1982, § 8.

18. 146 F.R.D. at 573–574. The Note also says that "[g]iven the liberal availability of long-arm jurisdiction, the exercise of power quasi-in-rem has become almost an anachronism." The Reporter for the Civil Rules Committee at the time the 1993 amendments were prepared, and therefore the draftsman of the Note, was Professor Paul D. Carrington, whose article critical of the 1963 amendment allowing use of quasi-in-rem actions is cited note 14 above.

§ 66. Pleadings in General[1]

The draftsmen of the Civil Rules proceeded on the conviction, based on experience at common law and under the codes, that pleadings are not of great importance in a lawsuit. This is evident from the basic rule, discussed later,[2] on what a pleading must contain in order to state a claim that will be heard, but it is evident also from the flexible rules on the form of pleadings and the limitation on the number of pleadings.

At common law the pleadings could continue indefinitely, until they had produced a single issue of law or fact that would then be decided. The Field Code, adopted in New York in 1848 and widely imitated, limited the pleadings to three, a complaint, an answer, and a reply. In the federal system, under Rule 7(a), normally there will be only two pleadings, a complaint and an answer, though in some cases a reply is permissible.[3] The theory is that by the complaint and the answer each of the parties will have indicated the general position he is taking in the litigation, and that further pleading is not worth the trouble.

In the complaint the plaintiff is required to set forth a short and plain statement of the claim showing that he is entitled to relief, and to demand the relief to which he deems himself entitled.[4] In the answer the defendant must admit or deny each of the allegations of the complaint, or state that he is without knowledge or information sufficient to form a belief as to the truth of the allegation, which has the effect of a denial. He must also set forth anything that constitutes an avoidance or affirmative defense.[5]

A reply is allowed in only two situations. A reply must be made if the answer contains "a counterclaim denominated as such."[6] This phrase contains two elements: the answer must in fact contain a counterclaim and it must be so denominated. If the answer contains a counterclaim not so labeled, a reply is not required and is theoretically not permitted, though under Rule 8(c) the court, on terms, may treat the pleading as if it had been properly labeled and allow a reply. Similarly, if a party labels as a counterclaim what is actually a defense, a reply is again improper, though the cautious lawyer will plead the reply rather than get involved in the maze of niceties as to what is a "counterclaim"

§ 66

1. See 5 Wright & Miller, Civil 2d §§ 1181–1196 (pleadings allowed; form of motions), 1261–1278 (denials and defenses), 1321–1327 (form of pleadings), 5A id. §§ 1331–1335 (signing of pleadings), 1390–1397 (waiver of defenses or objections), and 6 Wright, Miller & Kane, Civil 2d §§ 1471–1490, 6A id. §§ 1491–1510 (amended and supplemental pleadings).

2. See § 68 below.

3. The rule also permits an answer to a cross-claim, where such a claim has been asserted by one defendant against another, see § 80 below, and a third-party complaint and a third-party answer, if a third party is impleaded, see § 76 below.

4. Rule 8(a). See § 68 below.

5. As to denials, see Rule 8(b); 5 Wright & Miller, Civil 2d §§ 1261–1269. That rule seriously restricted use of the time-honored general denial, and under Rule 11(b)(4), as amended in 1993, such a pleading could lead to the imposition of sanctions. Failure to deny an allegation in the complaint amounts to an admission of that allegation. Rule 8(d).

As to affirmative defenses, see Rule 8(c); 5 Wright & Miller, Civil 2d §§ 1270–1278.

6. Rule 7(a).

and what is a "defense." Where the answer does contain a counterclaim denominated as such, the reply, which is then mandatory, is only to the counterclaim. It should not traverse allegations of the answer that are not part of the counterclaim, but should respond to the counterclaim in the same fashion that an answer responds to a complaint.

Rule 7(a) also allows the court to order a reply, either on its own motion or that of a party, but occasions when this power should be or has been exercised are extremely rare.[7] Where no reply is required, allegations of the answer are deemed denied or avoided, and the plaintiff can meet such allegations at the trial in any fashion that would have been open to him had a reply been proper.[8] Thus, while occasionally a reply is ordered by the court,[9] the mere fact that the answer raises affirmative defenses is not enough reason to call for a reply.

Rule 10 makes very flexible requirements for the form of pleadings. In addition to a caption,[10] the pleading must set out the averments in numbered paragraphs, each of which is limited so far as is practicable to the statement of a single set of circumstances.[11] Claims that are founded upon separate transactions or occurrences, and defenses other than denials, are to be stated in separate counts or defenses if such a separation will facilitate the clear presentation of the matters set forth.[12] Statements in one part of a pleading may be adopted by reference in other parts.[13] It is worthy of note that the requirement of numbered paragraphs limited to a single set of circumstances applies only "as far as practicable," while claims arising out of separate transactions or occurrences need be set forth in separate counts only when such a separation will facilitate the clear presentation of the matters set forth. The emphasis is on clarity and on practicality, rather than on any mechanical rule as to form. The Supreme Court has observed: "We no longer insist upon technical rules of pleading, but it will ever be difficult in a jury trial to segregate issues which counsel do not separate in their pleading, preparation or thinking."[14] Thus, the rule commands only what a lawyer who has analyzed his case clearly would do in any event.

The requirement that pleadings be verified is abolished by Rule 11, except insofar as other rules or statutes call for verification. Instead every pleading must be signed by at least one attorney of record in his

7. 5 Wright & Miller, Civil 2d § 1185.

8. Rule 8(d); Neeff v. Emery Transp. Co., C.A.2d, 1960, 284 F.2d 432; Cowling v. Deep Vein Coal Co., C.A.7th, 1950, 183 F.2d 652; First Presbyterian Church of Santa Barbara, California v. Rabbitt, C.C.A.9th, 1940, 118 F.2d 732; 5 Wright & Miller, Civil 2d § 1186.

9. Reynolds v. Needle, C.C.A.D.C.1942, 132 F.2d 161; Beckstrom v. Coastwise Line, D.C.Alaska 1953, 13 F.R.D. 480; Columbia Pictures Corp. v. Rogers, D.C.W.Va.1949, 81 F.Supp. 580; U.S. v. Hole, D.C.Mont.1941, 38 F.Supp. 600.

10. Rule 10(a); 5 Wright & Miller, Civil 2d § 1321.

11. Rule 10(b); 5 Wright & Miller, Civil 2d §§ 1322–1323; Browne, Civil Rule 10(b) and the Three Basic Rules of Form Applicable to the Drafting of Documents Used in Civil Litigation, 1978, 6 Cap.U.L.Rev. 199.

12. Rule 10(b); 5 Wright & Miller, Civil 2d §§ 1324–1325.

13. Rule 10(c); 5 Wright & Miller, Civil 2d § 1326.

14. O'Donnell v. Elgin, J. & E. Ry. Co., 1949, 70 S.Ct. 200, 205, 338 U.S. 384, 392, 94 L.Ed. 187.

individual name, or by the party if he is not represented by counsel.[15] The signature of the attorney has always constituted a certificate by the signed that the document merits the attention of the court, but Rule 11, as it stood from 1938 to 1983, was ineffective in this regard and its sanction provisions were useless as a practical matter. The rule was dramatically changed in 1983 and revised again in 1993.[16] Rule 11 in its present form is discussed elsewhere.[17]

Great freedom is allowed in amending pleadings in order to assert matters that occurred before the filing of the original pleading but were overlooked by the pleader or were unknown to it at the time.[18] A party may amend its pleading once as a matter of course at any time before a responsive pleading has been served, or within 20 days after service of his pleading, if no responsive pleading is required. A motion is not a "responsive pleading," within the meaning of rule 15(a), and thus the right to amend as of course is not defeated because the other party has filed a motion attacking the pleading.[19] Indeed even where the motion is granted, as where a complaint is dismissed for failure to state a claim on which relief can be granted, the party has the right to file an amended pleading as of course, though this right must be exercised in a reasonable time, and the party may amend with leave of court if it has not acted promptly.[20]

The provisions of Rule 15(a) allowing amendment as of right should control over other, more guarded, provisions of the rules. Thus, while the cases are divided, the better view is that so long as amendment as of right is possible, a party may amend to add an omitted counterclaim without satisfying the test of Rule 13(f)[21] and may add or drop parties without obtaining a court order under Rule 21.[22]

After a responsive pleading has been filed, or the time for amending as of course has otherwise expired, amendment may be made only by leave of court or with the written consent of the adverse party. The rule

15. 5A Wright & Miller, Civil 2d §§ 1333–1334; Browne, Civil Rule 11: The Signature and Signature Block, 1979, 9 Cap.U.L.Rev. 291.

A 1976 statute, 28 U.S.C.A. § 1746, abolished verification and the use of affidavits generally in the federal system.

16. See 5A Wright & Miller, Civil 2d § 1331.

17. See § 69A below.

18. Rule 15(a); 6 Wright, Miller & Kane, Civil 2d §§ 1473–1503.

19. Allen v. Veterans Administration, C.A.9th, 1984, 749 F.2d 1386, 1388; Smith v. Blackledge, C.A.4th, 1971, 451 F.2d 1201; Keene Lumber Co. v. Leventhal, C.C.A.1st, 1948, 165 F.2d 815; and cases cited 6 Wright, Miller & Kane, Civil 2d § 1483 n. 9.

20. Graue Mill Devel. Corp. v. Colonial Bank & Trust Co. of Chicago, C.A.7th, 1991, 927 F.2d 988, 992; Exxon Corp. v.

Maryland Cas. Co., C.A.5th, 1979, 599 F.2d 659, 662 n. 10; and cases cited 6 Wright, Miller & Kane, Civil 2d § 1483, pp. 587–591.

One circuit attaches great importance to a distinction between dismissal of the complaint and dismissal of the action. E.g., Firchau v. Diamond Nat. Corp., C.A.9th, 1965, 345 F.2d 269.

21. See A.J. Indus., Inc. v. United States Dist. Court, C.A.9th, 1974, 503 F.2d 384, 388; 6 Wright, Miller & Kane, Civil 2d § 1479, pp. 573–574. Contra: Stoner v. Terranella, C.A.6th, 1967, 372 F.2d 89.

22. McLellan v. Mississippi Power & Light Co., C.A.5th, 1976, 526 F.2d 870, citing the divided cases from the district courts. See also 6 Wright, Miller & Kane, Civil 2d § 1479, pp. 569–573.

provides, however, that "leave shall be freely given when justice so requires," and refusal to permit amendment is an abuse of discretion in the absence of some justification for the refusal.[23] Leave to amend may be accompanied with conditions that the pleader must satisfy if there is some reason that such conditions are necessary.[24] The test whether amendment is proper is functional rather than conceptual. It is entirely irrelevant that a proposed amendment changes the cause of action or the theory of the case, or that it states a claim arising out of a transaction different from that originally sued on, or that it causes a change in parties.[25] Normally leave to amend should be denied only if it would cause actual prejudice to an adverse party, but a busy court does not abuse its discretion if it protects itself from being imposed on by the presentation of theories seriatim, and may deny a belated application to amend that makes a drastic change in the case in the absence of some good reason why the amendment is offered at a late stage.[26]

Rule 15(c) provides that whenever "the claim or defense asserted in the amended pleading arose out of the conduct, transaction, or occurrence set forth or attempted to be set forth in the original pleading the amendment relates back to the date of the original pleading." This fiction of "relation back" is of great importance in avoiding the bar of the statute of limitations. Thus, where plaintiff sued for wrongful death, alleging various negligent acts that would constitute a violation of the Federal Employers' Liability Act, plaintiff was permitted to amend, after the statute of limitations would otherwise have run, to add a claim under the Federal Boiler Inspection Act for failure to have a locomotive properly lighted. Since the amendment related to the same general conduct, transaction, and occurrence as did the original complaint, the amendment related back even though it was based on a different legal theory than was the original complaint, and it rested on facts not asserted originally.[27] In a diversity action, a federal court may apply the

---

23. Foman v. Davis, 1962, 83 S.Ct. 227, 230, 371 U.S. 178, 182, 9 L.Ed.2d 222; Bank v. Pitt, C.A.11th, 1991, 928 F.2d 1108; 6 Wright, Miller & Kane, Civil 2d §§ 1484, 1487.

24. E.g., Phoenix Hardware Co. v. Paragon Paint & Hardware Corp., D.C.N.Y. 1940, 1 F.R.D. 116 (limiting time of service of amended pleading); Bercovici v. Chaplin, D.C.N.Y.1944, 56 F.Supp. 417 (trial without a jury); Affron Fuel Oil v. Firemen's Ins. Co., D.C.N.Y.1955, 143 F.Supp. 38 (granting jury trial on new issues to opposing party); Shelley v. The Maccabees, D.C.N.Y. 1960, 26 F.R.D. 10 (restoration of status quo); Prandini v. National Tea Co., D.C.Pa. 1974, 62 F.R.D. 503 (waive relation back of added claim); Leased Optical Departments–Montgomery Ward v. Opti–Center, Inc., D.C.N.J.1988, 120 F.R.D. 476 (payment of costs).

25. Samaha v. Presbyterian Hospital, C.A.2d,1985, 757 F.2d 529; Goodman v.

Mead Johnson & Co., C.A.3d, 1976, 534 F.2d 566, certiorari denied 97 S.Ct. 732, 429 U.S. 1038, 50 L.Ed.2d 748; Sherman v. Hallbauer, C.A.5th, 1972, 455 F.2d 1236; and cases cited 6 Wright, Miller & Kane, Civil 2d § 1474 nn. 10–21.

26. Freeman v. Continental Gin Co., C.A.5th, 1967, 381 F.2d 459, 469. See also Federal Ins. Co. v. Gates Learjet Corp., C.A.10th, 1987, 823 F.2d 383, 387.

27. Tiller v. Atlantic Coast Line R. Co., 1945, 65 S.Ct. 421, 323 U.S. 574, 89 L.Ed. 465. For cases on application of relation back, see 6A Wright, Miller & Kane, Civil 2d § 1497. A discriminating opinion, rejecting mechanical tests for relation back and looking instead to the interests of justice, is Green v. Walsh, D.C.Wis.1957, 21 F.R.D. 15, noted 1958, 4 How.L.J. 117. See also Smyser, Rule 15(c) Relation Back of Amendments: A Workable Test, 1978, 23 S.D.L.Rev. 55.

federal rule to allow relation back and is not bound by a more restrictive state rule on the subject. The cases were once in conflict on this point, but the decision in Hanna v. Plumer [28] should have removed any doubt about this.[29] The matter is more complicated if state law would not regard the statute of limitations as a bar to an amendment even though the conditions stated for relation back in Rule 15(c) have not been satisfied. Here the better view had been thought to be that the amendment should be allowed, even though Rule 15(c) seemingly did not allow it, and Rule 15(c)(1) was added by amendment in 1991 to provide specifically for this result and to avoid implications to the contrary in a 1986 decision of the Supreme Court.[30]

Rule 15(d) gives the court discretionary power to permit supplementary pleadings. A supplemental pleading deals with events that have occurred since the original pleading was filed. Thus, it differs from an amended pleading, which covers matters occurring before the filing of the original pleading but overlooked at that time.[31]

There was a very strange distinction, supported by some cases, by which it was held that a supplemental complaint was improper if the original complaint was insufficient, even though it has always been quite clear that an amendment is proper to cure a defective complaint. On this view, if parties were before the court on a defective complaint it was held necessary to dismiss their action and make them start again, even though events occurring after commencement of the action had made clear their right to judicial relief. Such a distinction had no support in the language of Rule 15(d) and was the kind of arbitrary and mechanical procedural barrier that the rules generally do not countenance. There was case law to the contrary, holding that a supplemental complaint was to be tested on its own merits and entertained if it stated a claim on which relief could be granted even though the complaint which it purported to supplement was defective in its statement of such a claim. In 1963 Rule 15(d) was amended to codify this latter line of cases.[32]

The case law is not clearly developed on the extent to which a supplemental complaint will be held to relate back for purposes of the

28. 1965, 85 S.Ct. 1136, 380 U.S. 460, 14 L.Ed.2d 8. See § 59 above.

29. Johansen v. E.I. Du Pont de Nemours & Co., C.A.5th, 1987, 810 F.2d 1377, 1380, certiorari denied 108 S.Ct. 148, 484 U.S. 849, 98 L.Ed.2d 104; and cases cited 6A Wright, Miller & Kane, Civil 2d § 1503 nn. 13, 16.

The holding in Stoner v. Terranella, C.A.6th, 1967, 372 F.2d 89, that Rule 15(c) does not apply to an amendment to set up an omitted counterclaim and that state law therefore controls on relation back of such a counterclaim, seems very dubious. See 6A Wright, Miller & Kane, Civil 2d § 1496, pp. 67–70. In Butler v. Poffinberger,

D.C.W.Va.1970, 49 F.R.D. 8, the court refused to follow the Stoner case.

30. See § 59 above at notes 45–49.

31. Slavenburg Corp. v. Boston Ins. Co., D.C.N.Y.1962, 30 F.R.D. 123; Berssenbrugge v. Luce Mfg. Co., D.C.Mo.1939, 30 F.Supp. 101.

On supplemental pleadings generally, see 6A Wright, Miller & Kane, Civil 2d §§ 1504–1510.

32. Ridgeway v. International Broth. of Elec. Workers, D.C.Ill.1979, 466 F.Supp. 595; Lynam v. Livingston, D.C.Del.1966, 257 F.Supp. 520; 6A Wright, Miller & Kane, Civil 2d § 1505.

statute of limitations. The problem is not likely to arise often, since a supplemental complaint is limited to events that have occurred since the filing of the original complaint and usually the claim based on these recent events will not be barred by limitations. But with delays in litigation, and a short statute of limitations, such a case can arise. Where it does arise, the supplemental complaint should be treated as an amended complaint would be. If it relies on a different transaction from that originally sued on, there should be no relation back,[33] but where, as is usual, the supplemental complaint is designed to obtain relief along the same lines, pertaining to the same cause, and based on the same subject matter or claim for relief, as set out in the original complaint, it should be held to relate back, as an amended complaint would. The defendant will have had notice from the beginning that a claim was being asserted against it arising out of this subject matter, and this is usually thought enough to satisfy the statute of limitations.[34]

In addition to the pleadings, Rule 12 authorizes a variety of motions attacking pleadings. A party may move to strike any insufficient defense or any redundant, immaterial, impertinent, or scandalous matter.[35] Such motions are not favored; the motion should be denied unless the allegations attacked have no possible relation to the controversy and may prejudice the other party.[36]

Another disfavored motion is the motion for a more definite statement. By a 1948 amendment to the rules, the old bill of particulars was abolished. The motion for more definite statement, which serves much the same function, is to be granted only where a pleading to which a responsive pleading is permitted is so vague or ambiguous that the party cannot reasonably be required to frame a responsive pleading.[37] If the pleading is sufficiently definite that the opponent can reply to it, the motion for more definite statement should be denied and any particulars that the opponent needs to prepare for trial obtained by depositions, interrogatories, and similar discovery procedures.[38] The motion is never proper where no responsive pleading is permitted,[39] nor should it be used to force the plaintiff to include additional particulars that may make the

33. U.S. for Use & Benefit of Wulff v. CMA, Inc., C.A.9th, 1989, 890 F.2d 1070, 1072–1074.

34. New York Central & H.R.R. Co. v. Kinney, 1922, 43 S.Ct. 122, 123, 260 U.S. 340, 346, 67 L.Ed. 294.

A supplemental complaint is treated as an amendment, and Rule 15(c) applied, in Davis v. Piper Aircraft Corp., C.A.4th, 1980, 615 F.2d 606, 609 n. 3, certiorari dismissed 101 S.Ct. 25, 448 U.S. 911, 65 L.Ed.2d 1141. See 6A Wright, Miller & Kane, Civil 2d § 1508.

35. Rule 12(f); 5A Wright & Miller, Civil 2d §§ 1380–1383.

36. E.g., Beiswenger Enterprises Corp. v. Carletta, D.C.Fla.1991, 779 F.Supp. 160, 161; U.S. v. Kramer, D.C.N.J.1991, 757 F.Supp. 397, 409–410; and cases cited 5A Wright & Miller, Civil 2d § 1380 n. 11.

37. Rule 12(e); Kirby v. Turner–Day & Woolworth Handle Co., D.C.Tenn.1943, 50 F.Supp. 469; 5A Wright & Miller, Civil 2d §§ 1374–1379; Comment, 1963, 61 Mich. L.Rev. 1126.

38. E.g., CMAX Inc. v. Hall, C.A.9th, 1961, 290 F.2d 736; Prudhomme v. Procter & Gamble Co., D.C.La.1992, 800 F.Supp. 390, 396.

39. Armstrong v. Snyder, D.C.Wis.1984, 103 F.R.D. 96.

complaint vulnerable to a motion to dismiss.[40]

The most familiar motion is a motion to dismiss under Rule 12(b). This rule lists seven defenses that could be set out in the answer but that may, at the option of the pleader, be made by preliminary motion.[41] By such a motion the defendant can raise the defense that the complaint fails to state a claim upon which relief can be granted, although the liberal rules as to sufficiency of a complaint make it a rare case in which a motion on this ground should properly be granted.[42] By such a motion the defendant can also challenge whether the court has jurisdiction over the subject matter, raise the failure to join an indispensable party, and assert the dilatory defenses of lack of jurisdiction over the person, improper venue, insufficiency of process, and insufficiency of service of process.

Though these motions under Rule 12(b) are much discussed, they are of limited efficacy. A sampling made in 1962 for the information of the Advisory Committee on Civil Rules suggested that such motions were made in only about 5% of all cases, and that in fewer than 2% of all cases did such motions lead to a final termination of the action.

All motions, except those made during a hearing or trial, must be made in writing, and are to state with particularity the grounds therefor, and set forth the relief or order sought.[43] In practice the requirement that the grounds be stated with particularity is frequently ignored. Motions to dismiss for failure to state a claim on which relief can be granted rarely, if ever, set forth the detailed grounds on which the party relies, and such motions have the support of Official Form 19, which is equally unspecific and which, by virtue of Rule 84, is expressly made sufficient. Thus, there can be no doubt that such a general motion is proper, despite the language of Rule 7(b)(1).[44] Many of the district courts have met this situation by adoption of a local rule requiring the moving party to submit a brief or memorandum in support of his motion at the time the motion is made.[45]

It is now quite clear that any common-law rule against "speaking motions" is ended. The court is not confined to the pleadings and motion in ruling, but may consider evidentiary matter presented by affidavit or otherwise. It has always been the rule that such other

---

40. E.g., Lodge 743, Intl. Assn. of Machinists, AFL–CIO v. United Aircraft Corp., D.C.Conn.1962, 30 F.R.D. 142.

41. 5A Wright & Miller, Civil 2d §§ 1347–1366.

42. See § 68 below. For similar reasons a motion for judgment on the pleadings, made after the close of all the pleadings, though authorized by Rule 12(c), can rarely be granted. See 5A Wright & Miller, Civil 2d §§ 1367–1372.

43. Rule 7(b)(1); 5 Wright & Miller, Civil 2d §§ 1191–1193.

44. Sheppard v. Moore, D.C.N.C.1981, 514 F.Supp. 1372, 1374 n. 2; Sapero v. Shackelford, D.C.Va.1944, 109 F.Supp. 321. But cf. Smeed v. Carpenter, C.A.9th, 1960, 274 F.2d 414.

45. See 12 Wright & Miller, Civil § 3154 nn. 75, 76; Mitchell v. Public Serv. Coordinated Transp., D.C.N.J.1952, 13 F.R.D. 96.

These local rules cannot be applied as a trap for the unwary and cause a litigant to be deprived of a day in court. Woodham v. American Cystoscope Co., C.A.5th, 1964, 335 F.2d 551.

matter is proper where jurisdiction is challenged or a dilatory defense is being raised.[46] Amendments to the rules in 1948 provide that where a party moves to dismiss for failure to state a claim on which relief can be granted, or moves for judgment on the pleadings, and matters outside the pleadings are presented to and not excluded by the court, the motion is to be treated as if it were a motion for summary judgment under Rule 56.[47] This convenient practice has been followed in innumerable cases.[48] Where it is used, the parties are able to present to the court the merits of the case, to see if there is any genuine issue which requires trial, and they are not limited to an attack on the paper allegations.

Ordinarily a motion to dismiss or a motion for judgment on the pleadings will be heard in advance of trial, although the court has discretion to order that the hearing and determination thereof be deferred until the trial. If the defenses listed in Rule 12(b) are included in the answer, rather than raised by motion to dismiss, they will still be heard before trial, on application of any party, unless the court chooses to defer them.[49]

The time-honored ritual of a "special appearance" has no place under the rules. At an earlier time an answer on the merits was thought to be a general appearance, submitting the party to the jurisdiction of the court for all purposes. The party who wished to challenge jurisdiction without so submitting was required to come in and make a special appearance. This is no longer the law. Rule 12(b) provides that no defense or objection is waived by being joined with one or more other defenses or objections in a responsive pleading or motion.[50] There is a possible qualification of this general principle. There have been cases continuing to apply the former practice that a defendant waives objection to venue or jurisdiction over his person by the assertion of a counterclaim,[51] while other cases have been to the contrary.[52] A finding of waiver is wholly impermissible if the counterclaim is compulsory,[53]

46. Williams v. Minnesota Mining & Mfg. Co., D.C.Cal.1953, 14 F.R.D. 1; Central Mexico Light & Power Co. v. Munch, C.C.A.2d, 1940, 116 F.2d 85.

47. As to summary judgment, see § 99 below.

48. See 5A Wright & Miller, Civil 2d § 1366.

49. Rule 12(d); 5A Wright & Miller, Civil 2d § 1373.

50. Orange Theatre Corp. v. Rayherstz Amusement Corp., C.C.A.3d, 1944, 139 F.2d 871, certiorari denied 64 S.Ct. 1057, 322 U.S. 740, 88 L.Ed. 1573; Product Promotions, Inc. v. Cousteau, C.A.5th, 1974, 495 F.2d 483, 490; 5A Wright & Miller, Civil 2d § 1344. A defense or objection overruled by the trial court may be asserted on appeal, even though the party has gone on to defend on the merits after his objection was denied. Speir v. Robert C. Herd &

Co., D.C.Md.1960, 189 F.Supp. 436; Lisle Mills v. Arkay Infants Wear, D.C.N.Y.1950, 90 F.Supp. 676.

51. North Branch Products, Inc. v. Fisher, C.A.D.C.1960, 284 F.2d 611, certiorari denied 81 S.Ct. 713, 365 U.S. 827, 5 L.Ed.2d 705; Beaunit Mills, Inc. v. Industrias Reunidas F. Matarazzo, S.A., D.C.N.Y. 1959, 23 F.R.D. 654; Hook & Ackerman v. Hirsh, D.C.D.C.1951, 98 F.Supp. 477. This was clearly the old rule. Merchants' Heat & Light Co. v. James B. Clow & Sons, 1907, 27 S.Ct. 285, 204 U.S. 286, 51 L.Ed. 488.

52. Knapp–Monarch Co. v. Dominion Elec. Corp., C.A.7th, 1966, 365 F.2d 175; Keil Lock Co., Inc. v. Earle Hardware Mfg. Co., D.C.N.Y.1954, 16 F.R.D. 388; Sadler v. Pennsylvania Ref. Co., D.C.S.C.1940, 33 F.Supp. 414.

53. Dragor Shipping Corp. v. Union Tank Car Co., C.A.9th, 1967, 378 F.2d 241, 244; Hasse v. American Photograph Corp., and the better-reasoned, and increasingly the prevailing, view is that there can be no finding of waiver even if the counterclaim was permissive only.[54]

If a defendant chooses to assert its defenses and objections by answer, rather than raising some of them, as it may, in a Rule 12(b) motion, it waives any defenses or objections not included in the answer, with certain exceptions noted below.[55]   And if a defendant moves for summary judgment prior to filing a motion to dismiss for improper venue, it waives that defense.[56]   If the defendant chooses to make a motion to dismiss under Rule 12(b), it must include all defenses and objections then available to it that Rule 12 permits to be raised by motion, and cannot make a second motion raising other such defenses or objections.[57]   The rule was amended in 1966 to resolve a conflict in the cases and make it clear that a defendant who makes a motion under Rule 12(b), asserting, for example, that the complaint should be dismissed for failure to state a claim on which relief can be granted, cannot thereafter raise, either by further motion or in its answer, such dilatory defenses as lack of personal jurisdiction, improper venue, or insufficiency of process or service of process.[58]

There are four exceptions to the rule that a defense or objection is waived if not made by answer or by motion, as the case may be.   Lack of jurisdiction of the subject matter is never waived, and if such lack of jurisdiction appears at any time in the case, the court must dismiss the action.[59]   The defense of failure to state a claim upon which relief can be granted, the defense of failure to join an indispensable party, and the objection of failure to state a legal defense to a claim, need not be asserted at the earliest opportunity.   They may be made by a later

C.A.10th, 1962, 299 F.2d 666, 668–669; Medicenters of America, Inc. v. T & V Realty & Equip. Corp., D.C.Va.1974, 371 F.Supp. 1180; Ryan v. Glenn, D.C.Miss. 1971, 336 F.Supp. 555.

54. Chase v. Pan–Pacific Broadcasting, Inc., C.A.D.C.1984, 750 F.2d 131.   See also Bayou Steel Corp. v. M/V Amstelvoorn, C.A.5th, 1987, 809 F.2d 1147, 1148–1149; Neifeld v. Steinberg, C.A.3d, 1971, 438 F.2d 423, 429 n. 13, noted 1972, 32 Md.L.Rev. 156; 5A Wright & Miller, Civil 2d § 1397.

55. Chatman–Bey v. Thornburgh, C.A.D.C.1988, 864 F.2d 804, 813; Pila v. G.R. Leasing & Rental Corp., C.A.1st, 1977, 551 F.2d 941, 943; and cases cited 5A Wright & Miller, Civil 2d § 1391 n. 19.

The answer, like any pleading, may be amended to incorporate affirmative defenses inadvertently omitted, and this may be done either by express amendment, e.g., U.S. v. Continental Illinois Nat. Bank & Trust Co. of Chicago, C.A.2d, 1989, 889 F.2d 1248, 1253–1255, or by amendment to conform to the evidence, e.g., Mazer v. Lipshutz, C.A.3d, 1966, 360 F.2d 275, certiorari

denied 87 S.Ct. 72, 385 U.S. 833, 17 L.Ed.2d 68.   But amendment to assert the objections of lack of jurisdiction over the person, improper venue, insufficiency of process, or insufficiency of service of process may only be made if Rule 15(a) allows amendment as a matter of course.   Rule 12(h)(1).

56. Misch v. Zee Enterprises, Inc., C.A.9th, 1989, 879 F.2d 628, 631; Reliable Tire Distribs., Inc. v. Kelly Springfield Tire Co., D.C.Pa.1985, 623 F.Supp. 153, 156.

57. Rule 12(g); 5A Wright & Miller, Civil 2d §§ 1384–1389.

58. The amendment accepts the view previously taken in Keefe v. Derounian, D.C.Ill.1946, 6 F.R.D. 11, and rejects the view taken in Phillips v. Baker, C.C.A.9th, 1941, 121 F.2d 752, certiorari denied 62 S.Ct. 301, 314 U.S. 688, 86 L.Ed. 551.   See Rowley v. McMillan, C.A.4th, 1974, 502 F.2d 1326, 1332–1333; 5A Wright & Miller, Civil 2d § 1391.

59. Rule 12(h)(3); 5A Wright & Miller, Civil 2d § 1393.

pleading, if one is permitted, or by motion for judgment on the pleadings, or at the trial.[60] It is too late, however, to raise these last three defenses and objections after trial.[61]

The Erie doctrine has very little application to pleading in federal court. A complaint is sufficient if it meets the test of Rule 8(a), though it would be subject to demurrer in state court for failure to set forth the detailed facts cherished in the state system.[62] An affirmative defense listed in Rule 8(c) must be pleaded in the answer, regardless of state law, though the state law will control the burden of proof on that defense.[63] The state law also continues to control the substantive elements of the claim, and the pleading may be required to set forth these elements,[64] though the form of stating them is governed by a federal standard.[65]

§ 67. One Form of Action [1]

Ever since the Field Code was adopted in New York in 1848, it has been recognized that the two most prominent features of that code, the abolition of the common-law forms of action and the union of law and equity, are essential to any significant procedural reform.[2] Chief Justice Taft gave impetus to such a change in the federal system,[3] and when the Supreme Court determined to exercise its rulemaking power under the

---

60. Rule 12(h)(2); Coyne v. City of Somerville, C.A.1st, 1992, 972 F.2d 440, 445–446; Wright Farms Constr., Inc. v. Kreps, D.C.Vt.1977, 444 F.Supp. 1023; 5A Wright & Miller, Civil 2d § 1392.

61. Brown v. Trustees of Brown Univ., C.A.1st, 1989, 891 F.2d 337, 355–357.

62. Bank of St. Louis v. Morrissey, C.A.8th, 1979, 597 F.2d 1131; and cases cited 5 Wright & Miller, Civil § 2d 1204 n. 4.

63. Palmer v. Hoffman, 1943, 63 S.Ct. 477, 482, 318 U.S. 109, 117, 87 L.Ed. 645; A.D.E., Inc. v. Louis Joliet Bank & Trust Co., C.A.7th, 1984, 742 F.2d 395, 397; Sampson v. Channell, C.C.A.1st, 1940, 110 F.2d 754, 757, certiorari denied 60 S.Ct. 1099, 310 U.S. 650, 84 L.Ed. 1415; 5 Wright & Miller, Civil 2d § 1272.

However, if Rule 8(c) is silent about a particular defense, state law, though not controlling, is frequently looked to in deciding whether it is an affirmative defense. E.g., Charpentier v. Godsil, C.A.3d, 1991, 937 F.2d 859, 863; 5 Wright & Miller, Civil 2d § 1271.

64. Mitchell v. White Consol., C.A.7th, 1949, 177 F.2d 500, certiorari denied 70 S.Ct. 574, 339 U.S. 913, 94 L.Ed. 1339; Whitehall Constr. Co. v. Washington Suburban Sanitary Commn., D.C.Md.1958, 165 F.Supp. 730.

65. In the Matter of Johns Manville/Asbestosis Cases, D.C.Ill.1981, 511 F.Supp.

1229; Korry v. International Tel. & Tel. Corp., D.C.N.Y.1978, 444 F.Supp. 193.

§ 67

1. 4 Wright & Miller, Civil 2d §§ 1041–1045; Hazard, Forms of Actions under the Federal Rules of Civil Procedure, 1988, 63 Notre Dame L.Rev. 628.

2. See Joiner & Geddes, The Union of Law and Equity: A Prerequisite to Procedural Revision, 1957, 55 Mich.L.Rev. 1059.

"Law and equity are two things which God has joined together but New South Wales has kept asunder. In a land where natural curiosities abound, and such anachronisms as the platypus still survive, perhaps nothing is surprising; but the continued refusal of this State to adopt the judicature system is anomalous enough to excite interest." Adam, 1951, 25 Aust.L.J. 354. Though the platypus presumably still survives in New South Wales, the separation of law and equity does not. See Law Reform (Law and Equity) Act, 1972 Stat. N.S.W. 424.

3. Taft, Three Needed Steps of Progress, 1922, 8 A.B.A.J. 34, 35; Taft, Possible and Needed Reforms in Administration of Justice in Federal Courts, 1922, 8 A.B.A.J. 601, 604, 607. See also his famous opinion in Liberty Oil Co. v. Condon Nat. Bank, 1922, 43 S.Ct. 118, 260 U.S. 235, 67 L.Ed. 232.

Enabling Act of 1934, it decided at the outset to incorporate this change in the rules it promulgated.[4] Thus, Rule 2 declares: "There shall be one form of action to be known as 'civil action.'"

The creation of a single form of action for the federal courts has been uniquely successful. The courts construed the change in a sympathetic fashion, with a clear understanding of the purposes it was intended to achieve. This was in striking contrast to "the cold, not to say inhuman, treatment"[5] that judges in many states had given to the initial Field Code nearly a century before. As a result, the single form of action has worked without difficulty, and virtually without comment, in federal court. There has been an occasional nostalgic look to the past,[6] but much more common is a glad acceptance of the fact that the old distinctions are now almost without procedural significance.[7]

The forms of action are abolished. No longer is a judgment to be reversed because the pleader chose the wrong form.[8] Law and equity are merged. There is no longer, in federal practice, such a thing as a "suit in equity."[9]

Rule 2 does not affect the various remedies that have heretofore been available. Instead the merger of law and equity and the abolition of the forms of action supply one uniform procedure by which a litigant may present his claim in an orderly manner to a court empowered to give him whatever relief is appropriate and just. The substantive principles that applied previously are not changed,[10] and it remains for the court to decide, in accordance with those principles, what form of relief is proper on the particular facts proven. Because courts can now give specific relief without interference with another independent system of courts, there is a natural tendency to grant specific relief more frequently than was true in olden days. Eventually it may well be that courts will feel free to ask only "What remedy is best adapted to making the plaintiff whole?" and will ignore the historic origins of the various remedies.[11] The rules neither hasten nor retard such a development.

4. It was by no means a foregone conclusion that the Supreme Court would do this. See § 62 above.

5. Winslow, C.J., in McArthur v. Moffett, 1910, 128 N.W. 445, 446, 143 Wis. 564, 567.

6. See, e.g., Frank, J., in Bereslavsky v. Caffey, C.C.A.2d, 1947, 161 F.2d 499, 500, certiorari denied 68 S.Ct. 82, 332 U.S. 770, 92 L.Ed. 355.

7. See, e.g., Arnold, J., in Groome v. Steward, C.C.A.D.C.1944, 142 F.2d 756.

"Under the rules, law and equity are procedurally combined; nothing turns now upon the form of the action or the procedural devices by which the parties happen to come before the court." Ross v. Bernhard, 1970, 90 S.Ct. 733, 739, 396 U.S. 531, 540, 24 L.Ed.2d 729.

8. C & H Air Conditioning Fan Co. v. Haffner, C.A.5th, 1954, 216 F.2d 256; 4 Wright & Miller, Civil 2d § 1042.

9. Union Mut. Life Ins. Co. v. Friedman, C.C.A.2d, 1944, 139 F.2d 542; Rodgers v. U.S., D.C.Cal.1958, 158 F.Supp. 670; U.S. v. Rosenbluth, D.C.Ohio 1952, 102 F.Supp. 996.

10. Stainback v. Mo Hock Ke Lok Po, 1949, 69 S.Ct. 606, 614 n. 26, 336 U.S. 368, 382 n. 26, 93 L.Ed. 741; Hanson v. Aetna Life & Cas., C.A.5th, 1980, 625 F.2d 573; 4 Wright & Miller, Civil 2d § 1043.

11. See Beacon Theatres, Inc. v. Westover, 1959, 79 S.Ct. 948, 955, 359 U.S. 500, 501, 3 L.Ed.2d 988; Laycock, The Death of the Irreparable Injury Rule, 1991; Wright, The Law of Remedies as a Social Institution, 1955, 18 U.Det.L.J. 376; Sedler, Equi-

Their function is limited to that of supplying a procedure by which a party may present his claim in an orderly manner.

Because the creation of a single form of action is a procedural reform only, the court may still find it necessary to consider the nature of the action to determine what statute of limitations is applicable, where such statutes are couched in terms of the old distinctions.[12] The right to jury trial turns—though decreasingly so in the light of recent decisions—on the historical characterization of the action.[13] But such instances in which the old distinctions continue to rule from their graves are quite rare.[14]

The one civil action under the rules is used to vindicate any civil power the district court has. The demand for judgment forms no part of the claim for relief, and does not restrict the relief to be granted against those appearing and defendant: as against such parties the final judgment must grant all the relief to which a plaintiff is entitled, whether or not demanded in the pleadings.[15] Rule 8(e)(2) authorizes a party to state as many separate claims or defenses as it has, regardless of whether they are based on legal or equitable or maritime grounds,[16] and this mandate is reinforced by Rule 18(a), which permits, either as a claim or a counterclaim, as many claims, either legal or equitable or maritime, as the party may have against an opposing party.[17]

§ 68. The Theory of Modern Pleading [1]

The keystone of the system of procedure embodied in the rules is Rule 8, and specifically subsections 8(a)(2), 8(e)(1), and 8(f). These provisions state that technical forms of pleading are not required, that pleadings are to be construed liberally so as to do substantial justice, and, most important of all, they substitute the requirement of "a short and plain statement of the claim showing that the pleader is entitled to relief" for the familiar "facts constituting a cause of action" of the codes. The other procedural devices of the rules—broad joinder, discovery, free

---

table Relief, But Not Equity, 1963, 15 J.Legal Ed. 293; Frank, Bringing Equity Up to Date, 1975, 61 A.B.A.J. 91.

12. Williamson v. Columbia Gas & Elec. Corp., C.C.A.3d, 1940, 110 F.2d 15, certiorari denied 60 S.Ct. 1087, 310 U.S. 639, 84 L.Ed. 1407.

13. See § 92 below.

14. See 4 Wright & Miller, Civil 2d §§ 1044, 1045.

But see Hazard, note 1 above, at 645: "[T]hese substantively transparent rules have been modified into substantively particularized variations. Maitland observed nearly a century ago that 'the forms of action we have buried, but they still rule us from their graves.' Forms of action *redux*."

15. Rule 54(c); Zunamon v. Brown, C.A.8th, 1969, 418 F.2d 883, 888–889; Fanchon & Marco v. Paramount Pictures,

C.A.2d, 1953, 202 F.2d 731; 4 Wright & Miller, Civil 2d §§ 1255–1257. See also § 98 below.

16. 4 Wright & Miller, Civil 2d §§ 1282–1285.

17. DePinto v. Provident Sec. Life Ins. Co., C.A.9th, 1963, 323 F.2d 826, certiorari denied 84 S.Ct. 968, 376 U.S. 950, 11 L.Ed.2d 970. See also § 78 below.

§ 68

1. 5 Wright & Miller, Civil 2d §§ 1202, 1215–1226; Marcus, The Revival of Fact Pleading Under the Federal Rules of Civil Procedure, 1986, 86 Col.L.Rev. 433; James, The Objective and Function of the Complaint—Common Law—Codes—Federal Rules, 1961, 14 Vand.L.Rev. 899; Clark, Simplified Pleading, 1942, 2 F.R.D. 456.

amendment, and summary judgment—rest on these provisions about pleadings.

Historically pleadings have had four functions: (1) giving notice of the nature of a claim or defense; (2) stating the facts each party believes to exist; (3) narrowing the issues; and (4) providing a means for speedy disposition of sham claims and unsubstantial defenses. The emphasis as among these four functions varied greatly with the passage of years and from jurisdiction to jurisdiction, but both at common law and under the codes all four were expected to be performed by the pleadings. The complaint not only gave notice of the nature of the case but also was required to state the facts constituting the cause of action. Subsequent pleadings were expected to narrow the issues until the case was ready for trial. Failure to incorporate an essential allegation might lead to a speedy end of the litigation. Since the pleadings were expected to do so much, it was natural that strict rules should develop about them, and this in turn meant that many cases were disposed of on pleading defects without regard to the merits of the controversy.

The rules provide techniques more efficient than pleadings for performing the last three functions.[2] The facts may be determined by discovery. The issues may likewise be narrowed by discovery or at a pretrial conference, or by "partial summary judgment" under Rule 56(d). Cases where there is no real controversy may be disposed of speedily and finally, on the merits, by summary judgment. This is not to say that the pleadings will not, in some cases, still assist in performing those functions, but rather that the pleadings no longer carry exclusive responsibility for them. The only function left to be performed by the pleadings alone is that of notice. For these reasons, pleadings under the rule may properly be a generalized summary of the party's position, sufficient to advise the party what the incident is for which it is being sued, sufficient to show what was decided for purposes of res judicata, and sufficient to indicate whether the case should be tried to the court or to a jury. No more is demanded of pleadings than this; history shows that no more can be successfully performed by pleadings.

At common law there was a great belief in the efficacy of pleadings. The whole grand scheme was, by rigid stages of denial, avoidance, or demurrer, eventually to reach a single issue of law or fact that would dispose of the case. This system was wonderfully scientific. It was also wonderfully slow, expensive, and unworkable. The system was better calculated to vindicate scientific rules of pleading than it was to dispense justice. The great Baron Parke is said to have boasted to Sir William Erle that he had aided in building up sixteen volumes of Meeson & Welsby, reports of the Court of Exchequer that usually went off on procedural points. "It's a lucky thing," Sir William replied, "that there was not a seventeenth volume, because if there had been, the common

2. Hickman v. Taylor, 1947, 67 S.Ct. 385, 388, 329 U.S. 495, 500, 91 L.Ed. 451; Conley v. Gibson, 1957, 78 S.Ct. 99, 103, 355 U.S. 41, 47–48, 2 L.Ed.2d 80.

law itself would have disappeared altogether amidst the jeers and hisses of mankind."[3]

Under the codes the important emphasis was on developing the facts by pleadings. The pleader was asked to give the "dry, naked, actual facts,"[4] avoiding the pitfalls of stating conclusions on the one hand and pleading evidence on the other. This requirement was based on a failure to perceive that the distinction between facts and conclusions is one of degree only, not of kind.[5] But it had a further weakness. The pleader who set forth too little could be attacked by demurrer. The pleader who set forth exactly the right amount in his pleading found himself committed unreservedly to a course of action and a factual statement from which he could not deviate at the trial. Many pleaders discovered that an obvious solution was to plead too much, to include every possible allegation regardless of the unlikelihood that the evidence would support it. The result of such overpleading was "frightful expense, endless delay and an enormous loss of motion."[6]

Thus, the rules do not ask more of the pleadings than can reasonably be expected. The short and plain statement of the claim showing that the pleader is entitled to relief is enough to give the opposing party fair notice of the occurrences being sued on, and other devices are provided for the other functions previously entrusted to the pleadings. A series of Official Forms appended to the rules, and expressly made sufficient by virtue of Rule 84, indicate the brevity and the simplicity that Rule 8(a) contemplates. The common law emphasized scientific symmetry and issue formulation in the pleadings. The codes emphasized statement of facts. The rules emphasize fair notice and the doing of justice. "Cases are generally to be tried on the proofs rather than the pleadings."[7]

The leading case on the pleading requirements of the rules is the decision of the Supreme Court in Conley v. Gibson.[8] This was a class suit brought by certain black members of a labor union claiming that the union had breached its statutory duty to represent fairly and without hostile discrimination all of the employees in the union. The union contended, among other things, that the complaint failed adequately to set forth a claim upon which relief could be granted. A unanimous

---

3. Coleridge, The Law in 1847 and The Law in 1889, 1890, 57 Contemp.Rev. 797, 799.

Perhaps the most amusing piece ever to appear in the solemn pages of the Harvard Law Review is Note, Common Law Pleading, 1896, 10 Harv.L.Rev. 238, in which the editors quote and endorse the spirited defense of the old ways by Sir Montague Crackenthorpe, Q.C. The Note is reprinted in 5 Wright & Miller, Civil 2d § 1202 n. 6.

4. Pomeroy, Code Remedies, 5th ed. 1929, p. 640.

5. Cook, Statements of Fact in Pleading Under the Codes, 1921, 21 Col.L.Rev. 416;

Cook, "Facts" and "Statements of Fact," 1937, 4 U.Chi.L.Rev. 233; Gavit, Legal Conclusions, 1932, 16 Minn.L.Rev. 378; Clark, Code Pleading, 2d ed. 1947, § 38.

6. Skinner, Pre–Trial and Discovery under the Alabama Rules of Civil Procedure, 1957, 9 Ala.L.Rev. 202, 204, quoted in 5 Wright & Miller, Civil 2d § 1202, pp. 71–72.

7. De Loach v. Crowley's, Inc., C.C.A.5th, 1942, 128 F.2d 378, 380.

8. 1957, 78 S.Ct. 99, 355 U.S. 41, 2 L.Ed.2d 80.

Court, speaking through Justice Black, said: "In appraising the sufficiency of the complaint we follow, of course, the accepted rule that a complaint should not be dismissed for failure to state a claim unless it appears beyond doubt that the plaintiff can prove no set of facts in support of his claim which would entitle him to relief." [9] The complaint in question alleged that petitioners were discharged wrongfully by the railroad and that the union, acting according to plan, refused to protect their jobs as it did those of white employees or to help blacks with their grievances, all because of their race. The Court asserted that if these allegations were proven they would show a manifest breach of the union's statutory duty to represent fairly and without hostile discrimination all of the employees in the bargaining unit.

The union also contended that the complaint failed to set forth specific facts to support its general allegations of discrimination. The Court said of this contention: "The decisive answer to this is that the Federal Rules of Civil Procedure do not require a claimant to set out in detail the facts upon which he bases his claim. To the contrary, all the Rules require is 'a short and plain statement of the claim' that will give the defendant fair notice of what the plaintiff's claim is and the grounds upon which it rests. The illustrative forms appended to the Rules plainly demonstrate this. Such simplified 'notice pleading' is made possible by the liberal opportunity for discovery and the other pretrial procedures established by the Rules to disclose more precisely the basis of both claim and defense and to define more narrowly the disputed facts and issues. Following the simple guide of Rule 8(f) that 'all pleadings shall be so construed as to do substantial justice', we have no doubt that petitioner's complaint adequately set forth a claim and gave the respondents fair notice of its basis. The Federal Rules reject the approach that pleading is a game of skill in which one misstep by counsel may be decisive to the outcome and accept the principle that the purpose of pleading is to facilitate a proper decision on the merits." [10]

In line with the general philosophy of pleading that the rules embody, six specific principles are authoritatively accepted.

(1) No distinction is to be drawn between "evidence," "ultimate facts," and "conclusions." [11] The rules permit the claim to be stated in general terms, and are intended to discourage battles over mere form of statement.[12] The former distinctions, as has already been pointed out, were quite unworkable.

9. 78 S.Ct. at 9, 35 U.S. at 45, citing, in support of "the accepted rule," such well-known cases as Leimer v. State Mut. Life Assur. Co., C.C.A.8th, 1940, 108 F.2d 302; Dioguardi v. Durning, C.C.A.2d, 1944, 139 F.2d 774, and Continental Collieries, Inc. v. Shober, C.C.A.3d, 1942, 130 F.2d 631.

10. 78 S.Ct. at 103, 355 U.S. at 48.

11. U.S. v. Employing Plasterers' Assn., 1954, 74 S.Ct. 452, 454, 347 U.S. 186, 188, 98 L.Ed. 618; Garcia v. Bernabe, C.A.1st, 1961, 289 F.2d 690; Oil, Chem. and Atomic Workers Intl. Union, AFL–CIO v. Delta Ref. Co., C.A.6th, 1960, 277 F.2d 694, 697; and 5 Wright & Miller, Civil 2d § 1218.

12. Note to Rule 8(a), Advisory Committee Report of October, 1955, reprinted at 5 Wright & Miller, Civil 2d § 1201 n. 11.

(2) There is no requirement of any particular "theory of the pleadings." Contrary to the rule in some code states, the complaint is not to be dismissed because the plaintiff's lawyer has misconceived the proper legal theory of the claim, if he is entitled to any relief on any theory.[13] "A simple statement in sequence of the events which have transpired, coupled with a direct claim by way of demand for judgment of what the plaintiff expects and hopes to recover, is a measure of clarity and safety; and even the demand for judgment loses its restrictive nature when the parties are at issue, for particular legal theories of counsel yield to the court's duty to grant the relief to which the prevailing party is entitled, whether demanded or not." [14]

(3) Pleadings are to be so construed as to do substantial justice.[15] The old rule that a pleading must be construed most strongly against the pleader is no longer followed. Instead the court will not require technical exactness or make refined inferences against the pleader but will construe the pleading in the pleader's favor if justice so requires.

(4) A complaint is not subject to dismissal unless it appears to a certainty that no relief can be granted under any set of facts that can be proved in support of its allegations.[16] This rule, which has been stated literally hundreds of times, precludes final dismissal for insufficiency of the complaint except in the extraordinary case where the pleader makes allegations that show on the face of the complaint some insuperable bar to relief.[17]

(5) The pleader may allege matters alternatively or hypothetically, and except for the good-faith requirements of Rule 11, the allegations may even be inconsistent.[18] The pleader cannot be required to elect among his allegations, but is entitled to have all his claims and defenses considered by the trier of facts.[19] Similarly there is no requirement of

---

13. "A drafter who lacks a legal theory is likely to bungle the complaint (and the trial); you need a theory to decide which facts to allege and prove. But the complaint need not identify a legal theory, and specifying an incorrect theory is not fatal." See also 5 Wright & Miller, Civil 2d § 1219.

14. Gins v. Mauser Plumbing Supply Co., C.C.A.2d, 1945, 148 F.2d 974, 976.

15. Rule 8(f); 5 Wright & Miller, Civil 2d § 1286.

16. Conley v. Gibson, 1957, 78 S.Ct. 99, 102, 355 U.S. 41, 45, 2 L.Ed.2d 80; Hospital Bldg. Co. v. Trustees of Rex Hosp., 1976, 96 S.Ct. 1848, 1853, 425 U.S. 738, 746, 48 L.Ed.2d 338; 5 Wright & Miller, Civil 2d §§ 1215, 1216.

Professor James has pointed out that the many statements to this effect are intended to evoke a frame of mind about pleading rather than state a precise test. James, Civil Procedure, 1965, pp. 86–88. See also James, Hazard, & Leubsdorf, Civil Procedure, 4th ed. 1988, pp. 147–148; Hoshman

v. Esso Standard Oil Co., C.A.5th, 1959, 263 F.2d 499, 501, certiorari denied 80 S.Ct. 60, 361 U.S. 818, 4 L.Ed.2d 64; 5 Wright & Miller, Civil 2d § 1216.

17. E.g., Leggett v. Montgomery Ward & Co., C.A.10th, 1949, 178 F.2d 436; Nazarenus v. J. F. Daly Intl., Ltd., D.C.Ill. 1989, 714 F.Supp. 361; Bach v. Quigan, D.C.N.Y.1945, 5 F.R.D. 34. See Trevino v. Union Pac. R. Co., C.A.7th, 1990, 916 F.2d 1230, 1234; 5 Wright & Miller, Civil 2d § 1226.

18. Rule 8(e)(2); 5 Wright & Miller, Civil 2d §§ 1282–1285.

19. United Roasters, Inc. v. Colgate–Palmolive Co., C.A.4th, 1981, 649 F.2d 985, certiorari denied 102 S.Ct. 599, 454 U.S. 1054, 70 L.Ed.2d 590. Fidelity & Deposit Co. of Maryland v. Krout, C.C.A.2d 1945, 146 F.2d 531; McAndrews v. Goody Co., D.C.Neb.1978, 460 F.Supp. 104; 5 Wright & Miller, Civil 2d § 1283.

election of remedies.[20]

(6) Once the case is tried, the pleadings lose such little significance as they had before, and judgment is to be in accordance with the evidence. This is provided by Rule 15(b). It authorizes two different procedures, both intended "to avoid the tyranny of formalism" [21] and both usually referred to as "amendments to conform to the evidence." [22] Under this rule the pleadings shall be deemed amended to conform to the proof on any issues that were tried by express or implied consent of the parties, though not raised by the pleadings. "[A] litigant cannot, for tactical purposes, stand by silently while evidence is being admitted and then claim later that no relief can be given because the matter was not plead." [23] If the litigant does raise his voice, and timely objection is made that evidence is outside the pleadings, the court may permit the pleadings to be amended and shall do so freely when presentation of the merits of the case will be thus served and the opposing party will not be prejudiced by the amendment. The first of these procedures effectively abolishes the old doctrine of "variance." The second, liberally applied as it must be,[24] ensures that the pleadings will not restrict proof of the actual facts of the case.

The simplified pleading required by the rules is not infrequently referred to as "notice pleading." This term, which was rejected by the rulemakers and never employed by them, is prejudicial to a proper operation of federal procedure, because it is a pure abstraction, without content except as injected by the immediate user, and because it suggests the absence of all pleadings.[25] The rules require the pleader to disclose adequate information about the basis of his claim for relief as distinguished from a bare averment that he wants relief and is entitled to it. It is true that in Conley v. Gibson the Supreme Court referred to "simplified 'notice pleading,'" [26] but in context it is plain that the

---

20. Guy James Constr. Co. v. Trinity Indus., Inc., C.A.5th, 1981, 644 F.2d 525; Gins v. Mauser Plumbing Supply Co., C.C.A.2d, 1945, 148 F.2d 974; Bauman, Multiple Liability, Multiple Remedies, and the Federal Rules of Civil Procedure, 1962, 46 Minn.L.Rev. 729.

It is most unlikely that, as one case has sometimes been thought to have held, the Erie doctrine requires application of state law as to election of remedies. Berger v. State Farm Mut. Auto. Ins. Co., C.A.10th, 1961, 291 F.2d 666, criticized 1962, 15 Okla.L.Rev. 186.

21. In re Santa Fe Downs, Inc., C.A.10th, 1980, 611 F.2d 815, 817.

22. 6A Wright, Miller & Kane, Civil 2d §§ 1491–1495.

23. Niedland v. U.S., C.A.3d, 1964, 338 F.2d 254, 259. See also 6A Wright, Miller & Kane, Civil 2d § 1493; Note, Amendment of Pleadings to Conform to the Evidence, 1973, 9 Wake Forest L.Rev. 247.

But implied consent to try new issues cannot be derived from a failure to object to evidence that is relevant to existing issues. U.S. v. Texas, C.A.5th, 1982, 680 F.2d 356, 361.

24. See, e.g., Robbins v. Jordan, C.A.D.C.1950, 181 F.2d 793, where it is held that the proper remedy for surprise from a change of theory is a continuance, and that it is an abuse of judicial discretion to refuse to allow the amendment. Accord: Green v. Baltimore & O.R. Co., C.A.6th, 1962, 299 F.2d 837. But cf. Thermo King Corp. v. White's Trucking Serv., Inc., C.A.5th, 1961, 292 F.2d 668; Hargrave v. Wellman, C.A.9th, 1960, 276 F.2d 948.

25. Padovani v. Bruchhausen, C.A.2d, 1961, 293 F.2d 546, 550–551; Clark, Two Decades of the Federal Civil Rules, 1958, 58 Col.L.Rev. 435, 450–451.

26. 78 S.Ct. at 103, 355 U.S. at 48.

Court's statement was one of aim rather than definition. Only two sentences before the phrase in question the Court had emphasized that the rules require the complaint to give the defendant "fair notice of what the plaintiff's claim is and the grounds upon which it rests." [27] Thus the Court recognized that the rule does contemplate the statement of circumstances, occurrences, and events in support of the claim presented, even though it permits these circumstances to be stated with great generality. [28]

The modern philosophy of pleading has been received with general approval and applied with success. Reviewing its operation, after 17 years' experience, the Advisory Committee on Civil Rules said: "While there has been some minority criticism, the consensus favors the rule and the reported cases indicate that it has worked satisfactorily and has advanced the administration of justice in the district courts." [29]

Minority criticism there has been, [30] though some of it may be nostalgia by those who were expert in the old ways. The principal target for the criticism has been the decision in Dioguardi v. Durning. [31] The case itself seems but a routine application of principles that are universally accepted, but it has attracted unusual attention, perhaps because of its rather colorful facts and because the opinion is by Judge Charles E. Clark, the draftsman of the federal rules.

Dioguardi was the consignee of a shipment of "tonics," which was tied up in customs for failure of the consignee to pay some charges he claimed should have been paid by the consignor. The Collector of Customs, after holding the goods for a year, sold them at auction. Dioguardi, who had but limited ability to write and speak English, scorned the help of a lawyer and brought suit against the Collector with his own "obviously home drawn" complaint. In that complaint he alleged that on the auction day defendant "sold my merchandise to another bidder with my price of $110, and not of his price of $120." He also alleged that "three weeks before the sale, two cases, of 19 bottles each case disappeared." The United States Attorney moved to dismiss the complaint on the ground that it "fails to state facts sufficient to constitute a cause of action." The trial court granted the motion with leave to amend. Plaintiff reiterated his claims, "with an obviously heightened conviction that he was being unjustly treated", in an amend-

---

27. Ibid.

28. Toberman v. Copas, D.C.Pa.1992, 800 F.Supp. 1239, 1243; City of Gainesville v. Florida Power & Light Co., D.C.Fla.1980, 488 F.Supp. 1258, 1263; Frank v. Mracek, D.C.Ala.1973, 58 F.R.D. 365, 369.

29. Note to Rule 8(a), Advisory Committee Report of October, 1955, reprinted in 5 Wright & Miller, Civil § 1201 n. 11.

30. McCaskill, Easy Pleading, 1941, 35 Ill.L.Rev. 28; Fee, The Lost Horizon in Pleading under the Federal Rules of Civil Procedure, 1948, 48 Col.L.Rev. 491; Claim or Cause of Action, 1951, 13 F.R.D. 253; McCaskill, Modern Philosophy of Pleading: A Dialogue Outside the Shades, 1952, 38 A.B.A.J. 123; Dawson, The Place of the Pleading in a Proper Definition of the Issues in the "Big Case," 1958, 23 F.R.D. 430; Rosen v. Texas Co., D.C.N.Y.1958, 161 F.Supp. 55 (per Dimock, J.).

31. C.C.A.2d, 1944, 139 F.2d 774, see 5 Wright & Miller, Civil 2d § 1220.

ed complaint, but this too was dismissed and final judgment entered for the defendant.

The Second Circuit, speaking through Judge Clark, reversed. It said that Dioguardi had "stated enough to withstand a mere formal motion, directed only to the face of the complaint, and that here is another instance of judicial haste which in the long run makes waste. * * * We think that, however inartistically they may be stated, the plaintiff has disclosed his claims that the collector has converted or otherwise done away with two of his cases of medicinal tonics and has sold the rest in a manner incompatible with the public auction he had announced—and indeed required * * *." [32]

It is difficult to see what the Second Circuit could have done other than reverse in the Dioguardi case. Had it affirmed the judgment below, Dioguardi would have been out of court without ever having any hearing on the merits of his claims. These claims had merit if the facts were as Dioguardi believed them to be. The Collector of Customs would have been liable had he done away with part of the merchandise, or conducted the auction other than in accordance with regulations. The trial court had no means of knowing whether the facts were as Dioguardi claimed them to be or not, for the government made a purely formal motion, rather than going to the merits by a motion for summary judgment with supporting affidavits.

The critics have made much of the fact that, after the decision here noted, the case went to trial, Dioguardi failed to prove his claims, and a judgment was entered against him and affirmed by the Second Circuit. [33] The fact, however, that a litigant ultimately loses on the merits hardly shows that he should be thrown out of court without any opportunity to prove the merits of his case.

Those who criticize the result in the Dioguardi case necessarily must believe that "good pleading" is a sufficiently important goal that even possibly meritorious claims should be dismissed if they are not properly pleaded. Indeed one of the critics says virtually this much, when he attacks the federal rules, as they have been interpreted, on the ground that they lower "the standards of pleading to fit the incompetent or lazy lawyer, instead of keeping the standards where pleadings will be of some use to the courts, and making those who wish to practice in the courts meet those standards." [34] This is an arguable position, but it is contrary to the fundamental notion of all modern procedural reform, that the object of procedure should be to secure a determination on the merits rather than to penalize litigants because of procedural blunders.

Some of the critics have read the Dioguardi case as meaning that a pleader need no longer set forth facts from which it can be seen that he

32. 139 F.2d at 775.

33. Dioguardi v. Durning, C.C.A.2d, 1945, 151 F.2d 501.

34. McCaskill, The Modern Philosophy of Pleading: A Dialogue Outside the Shades, 1952, 38 A.B.A.J. 123, 125. This expression by Professor McCaskill is strikingly reminiscent of the views of Sir Montague Crackenthorpe, Q.C., cited note 3 above.

has a right to relief. As the Advisory Committee has correctly pointed out, Dioguardi was not based on any such holding. "The complaint in that case stated a plethora of facts and the court so construed them as to sustain the validity of the pleading."[35] The statement by the court in Dioguardi that "under the new rules of civil procedure, there is no pleading requirement of stating 'facts sufficient to constitute a cause of action', but only that there be 'a short and plain statement of the claim showing that the pleader is entitled to relief,' "[36] seems but an obvious truth, which many decisions have announced, pointing up the fact that a different standard now applies than did formerly, and that the language of the United States Attorney's motion in the trial court in Dioguardi was unfortunate.[37]

Even some of those who agree that Judge Clark was basically right in the Dioguardi case and his critics basically wrong have voiced the view that he was ill-advised to choose the Dioguardi case as a vehicle to set forth his pleading theories. It is hard to understand what is meant by this criticism. The Dioguardi opinion is not a treatise on pleading, nor does it purport to be. Indeed it confines itself very closely to the problem presented by the particular case and discusses pleading theory only to the extent needed to dispose of that case. It does not enter into a discussion of pleading philosophy at all comparable to that, say, of the Supreme Court in Conley v. Gibson. Perhaps Conley v. Gibson will bring to a close the unnecessary controversy that some have raised about the Dioguardi case, both because Dioguardi is cited with approval by the Supreme Court in Conley[38] and because the Court in Conley lends ringing endorsement to the principles for which the Dioguardi decision stands.

Despite the general acceptance of modern pleading, there is always a tendency to imagine that strict pleading rules will save judicial work. This has been seen in recent years with regard to antitrust litigation, stockholders' derivative actions, and similar protracted lawsuits, now popularly referred to as "the big case." These cases do impose a heavy burden on the courts, and a number of district judges have sought to discourage them at the outset by applying strict rules as to the contents of the complaint. In fact such efforts usually resulted only in waste of time and much longer pleadings, without any corresponding gain. The sad truth is that, tedious and laborious as these cases are likely to prove, there is no real substitute for trial. Recognizing this, several courts of appeals have written strong opinions pointing out that the same liberal

---

35. Note to Rule 8(a), Advisory Committee Report of October, 1955, reprinted 5 Wright & Miller, Civil 2d § 1201 n. 11.

36. 139 F.2d at 775.

37. 5 Wright & Miller, Civil 2d § 1216.

38. 78 S.Ct. at 102 n. 5, 355 U.S. at 41 n. 5.

The Dioguardi case is also cited with approval in Haines v. Kerner, 1972, 92 S.Ct. 594, 596, 404 U.S. 519, 521, 30 L.Ed.2d 652, and in Kosak v. U.S, 1984, 104 S.Ct. 1519, 1526 n. 20, 465 U.S. 848, 860 n. 20, 79 L.Ed.2d 860. See also Estelle v. Gamble, 1976, 97 S.Ct. 285, 295, 429 U.S. 97, 113, 50 L.Ed.2d 251 (Stevens, J., dissenting).

pleading rules that apply in ordinary litigation are applicable to the "big case." [39]

Similarly, it is tempting to think that the flood of civil-rights cases, and especially of petitions and complaints filed by prisoners, most of them wholly without merit, could be quickly disposed of by strict pleading rules. The Civil Rules, after all, are based "on the working assumption that powerful extra-judicial constraints would operate to screen out most claims completely lacking factual or legal merit before the judicial process was invoked." [40] These constraints are ordinarily of no effect on those in prison. [41] Even so, the Supreme Court has insisted that pro se complaints must be tested by "less stringent standards than formal pleadings drafted by lawyers." [42] Procedures have been devised that ease the task of identifying those habeas corpus and § 2255 cases that deserve an evidentiary hearing. [43] For other cases brought by prisoners, the courts have broad discretion to dismiss suits brought in forma pauperis if "the action is frivolous or malicious," [44] and there are other promising remedies for prisoners' suits that are worth exploring. [45]

The Supreme Court should have put an end to any thought that there are special pleading requirements for civil-rights cases by its 1993 decision in Leatherman v. Tarrant County Narcotics Intelligence and Coordination Unit. [46] Some courts of appeals had held that a "heightened pleading standard", more stringent than the usual pleading requirements of Rule 8(a), applied in civil-rights cases alleging municipal liability under 42 U.S.C.A. § 1983. Chief Justice Rehnquist, writing for

---

39. Nagler v. Admiral Corp., C.A.2d, 1957, 248 F.2d 319; New Home Appliance Center, Inc. v. Thompson, C.A.10th, 1957, 250 F.2d 881; Austin v. House of Vision, Inc., C.A.7th, 1967, 385 F.2d 171; Control Data Corp. v. International Business Machines Corp., C.A.8th, 1970, 421 F.2d 323; General Acquisition, Inc. v. GenCorp Inc., D.C.Ohio 1990, 766 F.Supp. 1460, 1464–1465. See 5 Wright & Miller, Civil 2d § 1221; Clark, Special Pleading in the "Big Case", 1957, 21 F.R.D. 45; Dawson, The Place of the Pleading in a Proper Definition of the Issues in the "Big Case," 1958, 23 F.R.D. 430; Clark, Comment on Judge Dawson's Paper, 1958, 23 F.R.D. 435; Freund, The Pleading and Pre-Trial of an Anti-Trust Claim, 1961, 46 Corn.L.Q. 555.

The problems of "the big case" may require the court to make special provisions concerning discovery and otherwise to control the case more closely than in ordinary litigation. See Manual for Complex Litigation, Second, 1985, 15 Wright, Miller & Cooper, Jurisdiction 2d §§ 3861, 3868.

40. Phillips, Foreword, 1982, 39 Wash. & Lee L.Rev. 425, 427–428.

41. Marcus, note 1 above, at 477; Phillips, note 40 above, at 428.

42. Haines v. Kerner, 1972, 92 S.Ct. 594, 596, 404 U.S. 519, 520, 30 L.Ed.2d 652. See also Boag v. MacDougall, 1982, 102 S.Ct. 700, 701, 454 U.S. 364, 365, 70 L.Ed.2d 551. See cases cited 5 Wright & Miller, Civil 2d § 1230 n. 7.

43. The petition or motion can be on a model form, which is readily available to prisoners. It is appended to the Habeas Corpus Rules and the Section 2255 Rules. Those sets of rules make provision for summary judgment and for "a variety of measures in an effort to avoid the need for an evidentiary hearing." Blackledge v. Allison, 1977, 97 S.Ct. 1621, 1633, 431 U.S. 63, 81, 52 L.Ed.2d 136. See 3 Wright, Federal Practice and Procedure: Criminal 2d, §§ 598, 599; 17A Wright, Miller & Cooper, Jurisdiction 2d §§ 4268.3–4268.4.

44. 28 U.S.C.A. § 1915(d). See Boag v. MacDougall, 1982, 102 S.Ct. 700, 701, n. *, 454 U.S. 364, 365 n. *, 70 L.Ed.2d 551.

45. See Phillips, note 39 above, at 429; Report of the Study Group on the Caseload of the Supreme Court, 1972, 57 F.R.D. 573, 586–588.

46. 1993, 113 S.Ct. 1160, ___ U.S. ___, 122 L.Ed.2d 517.

a unanimous Court, rejected this notion. It "is impossible," he said, "to square the 'heightened pleading standard' * * * with the liberal system of 'notice pleading' set up by the Federal Rules."[47] He quoted from Conley v. Gibson for the proposition that Rule 8(a)(2) means what it says and that it does not require a claimant to set out in detail the facts upon which he bases his claim. The Chief Justice recognized that suits against municipal corporations based on claimed constitutional violations for their employees could not have been brought before 1978.[48] "Perhaps if Rules 8 and 9 were rewritten today, claims against municipalities under 1983 might be subjected to the added specificity requirement of Rule 9(b). But that is a result which must be obtained by the process of amending the Federal Rules, and not by judicial interpretation."[49]

Rule 9 contains special provisions, which are largely self-explanatory, as to pleading such matters as capacity, fraud or other condition of mind, conditions precedent, official document or act, judgment, time and place, and special damage.[50] Of these provisions, the only one that has given any difficulty is Rule 9(b), which says that in all averments of fraud or mistake, the circumstances constituting fraud or mistake shall be stated with particularity. Occasional cases have read this as if it were in a vacuum, and have given it a strict application that fails to take into account the general simplicity of pleadings contemplated by the rules.[51] Rule 9(b) must be read in the light of Rule 8(a). While fraud must be particularized, the allegations must still be as short, plain, simple, concise, and direct as is reasonable under the circumstances.[52] If the allegations of fraud are not sufficiently particularized, the remedy is not to dismiss the complaint, but to require a more definite statement or to permit defendant to ascertain the facts by discovery.[53] In these special matters, as generally, the aim of the rules to deemphasize the pleadings and to try the case on the proofs must be kept in mind.

§ 69. Pleading Jurisdiction[1]

The general requirements for pleading have been stated in the three preceding sections. In the federal system, however, there is an additional requirement not commonly found in the states. Rule 8(a)(1) requires that a pleading setting forth a claim for relief contain a short and plain statement of the grounds upon which the court's jurisdiction depends, unless the court already has jurisdiction and the claim needs no new grounds of jurisdiction to support it. The reason for the rule is clear.

---

47. 113 S.Ct. at 1163, ___ U.S. at ___.

48. See § 22A above.

49. 113 S.Ct. at 1163, ___ U.S. at ___.

50. 5 Wright & Miller, Civil 2d §§ 1291–1315.

51. Cases holding particular allegations sufficient or insufficient are set out in 5 Wright & Miller, Civil 2d §§ 1297–1298.

52. Seattle–First Nat. Bank v. Carlstedt, C.A.10th, 1986, 800 F.2d 1008, 1011;

McGinty v. Beranger Volkswagen, Inc., C.A.1st, 1980, 633 F.2d 226, 228–229.

53. Glus v. Brooklyn Eastern Dist. Terminal, 1959, 79 S.Ct. 760, 763, 359 U.S. 231, 235, 3 L.Ed.2d 770. See 5 Wright & Miller, Civil 2d § 1300.

§ 69

1. 5 Wright & Miller, Civil 2d §§ 1206–1214.

The federal courts are courts of limited jurisdiction.[2] There is no presumption in favor of jurisdiction, and the basis for jurisdiction must be affirmatively shown.[3] In the past, some decisions have taken a quite technical view as to the sufficiency of jurisdictional allegations. One extreme case held that an allegation that a party was "a citizen of London, England" was not a sufficient allegation that the party was an alien.[4] Since such decisions are on the books, care is indicated in jurisdictional allegations, though Rule 8(f), requiring pleadings to be construed so as to do substantial justice, applies as well to jurisdictional allegations as to other portions of the complaint.[5]

Official Form 2, appended to the rules, gives illustrative forms for the pleading of jurisdiction. Where jurisdiction is based on diversity, the complaint should allege the citizenship of each of the parties. An allegation of residence is insufficient.[6] Nor is it enough to allege that plaintiff is a citizen of state X and that defendant is not a citizen of state X, since this leaves open the possibility that defendant may be a citizen of the United States but not of any state, or that he or she may have no citizenship.[7]

A corporation is not a citizen of any state, though it is treated for jurisdictional purposes as if it were.[8] Thus, an allegation that a corporate party is a citizen of state X will not do.[9] Instead it must be alleged that the party is a corporation incorporated under the laws of state X and having its principal place of business in state Y. Though this is always the preferable method of allegation where there is a corporate party, it may be that plaintiff will not know the principal place of business of a corporate defendant. In this case, Official Form 2 permits the following form of allegation: "Plaintiff is a citizen of the state of Connecticut and defendant is a corporation incorporated under the laws of the state of New York having its principal place of business in a state other than the state of Connecticut."[10]

---

2. See § 7 above.

3. Hanford v. Davies, 1896, 16 S.Ct. 1051, 163 U.S. 273, 41 L.Ed. 157; Smith v. McCullough, 1926, 46 S.Ct. 338, 270 U.S. 456, 70 L.Ed. 682; Bowman v. White, C.A.4th, 1968, 388 F.2d 756; Le Mieux Bros. v. Tremont Lumber Co., C.C.A.5th, 1944, 140 F.2d 387.

4. Stuart v. City of Easton, 1895, 15 S.Ct. 268, 156 U.S. 46, 39 L.Ed. 341.

5. Neagle v. Johnson, C.A.8th, 1967, 381 F.2d 9; Bartle v. Markson, C.A.2d, 1966, 357 F.2d 517; Holy Eagle v. Towle, D.C.S.D.1963, 32 F.R.D. 591; 5 Wright & Miller, Civil 2d § 1206.

6. Robertson v. Cease, 1878, 97 U.S. 646, 648, 24 L.Ed. 1057; Southern Pac. Co. v. Denton, 1892, 13 S.Ct. 44, 146 U.S. 202, 36 L.Ed. 942; Nadler v. American Motors Sales Corp., C.A.5th, 1985, 764 F.2d 409. This defect, however, is often disregarded if it is clear that citizenship was intended.

E.g., National Farmers Union Property & Cas. Co. v. Fisher, C.A.8th, 1960, 284 F.2d 421; Holm v. Shilensky, D.C.N.Y.1967, 269 F.Supp. 359, affirmed C.A.2d, 1968, 388 F.2d 54.

7. Cameron v. Hodges, 1888, 8 S.Ct. 1154, 127 U.S. 322, 32 L.Ed. 132; Bryant v. Harrelson, D.C.Tex.1960, 187 F.Supp. 738. See § 24 above.

8. 28 U.S.C.A. § 1332(c). See § 27 above.

9. Thomas v. Board of Trustees of Ohio State Univ., 1904, 25 S.Ct. 24, 195 U.S. 207, 49 L.Ed. 160; Fifty Associates v. Prudential Ins. Co., C.A.9th, 1970, 446 F.2d 1187. But cf. 5 Wright & Miller, Civil 2d § 1208, p. 107.

10. McAndrews v. Goody Co., D.C.Neb. 1978, 460 F.Supp. 104; Kurtz v. Draur, D.C.Pa.1977, 434 F.Supp. 958; Gorman v. King, D.C.Wis.1970, 50 F.R.D. 195.

Where jurisdiction is based on the existence of a federal question, the jurisdictional allegation should state that the action arises under a particular statute or provision of the Constitution "as hereinafter more fully appears", and the body of the complaint must state facts showing that the case does in fact arise under federal law. Failure to cite the federal law involved is not fatal, if the balance of the complaint shows that a federal question is involved,[11] and correspondingly a general allegation of a federal question will not suffice if it is not supported by the matters constituting the claim for relief as set forth in the complaint.[12]

With respect to jurisdictional amount, where this is required,[13] an allegation that the matter in controversy exceeds, exclusive of interest and costs, the sum of $50,000 (or whatever other sum a particular statute may require) is sufficient unless the other allegations of the complaint show that less than that amount is involved.[14]

All of these rules as to pleading jurisdiction must be read in the light of the principle that the whole record may be looked to, for the purpose of curing a defective jurisdictional allegation, and that where diversity is the basis of jurisdiction it is sufficient if the requisite citizenship is anywhere expressly averred in the record, or facts are there stated that in legal intendment constitute such allegation.[15]

Defective allegations of jurisdiction may be amended. Indeed a statute permits such amendment, on terms, in the trial or appellate court.[16] If the plaintiff, fearful that it is losing on the merits and preferring a dismissal without prejudice for want of jurisdiction, refuses to make such an amendment, the defendant may present the needed

---

But an allegation that plaintiff was a citizen of South Dakota and that defendants were corporations that were incorporated and had their principal places of business in states other than South Dakota was held insufficient. McGovern v. American Airlines, Inc., C.A.5th, 1975, 511 F.2d 653.

11. Schlesinger v. Councilman, 1975, 95 S.Ct. 1300, 1306 n. 9, 420 U.S. 738, 744 n. 9, 43 L.Ed.2d 591; Boarhead Corp. v. Erickson, C.A.3d, 1991, 923 F.2d 1011, 1018; and cases cited 5 Wright & Miller, Civil 2d § 1209 n. 7.

12. See note 2 to Official Form 2; Mantin v. Broadcast Music, Inc., C.A.9th, 1957, 244 F.2d 204; Fountain v. New Orleans Public Serv., Inc., D.C.La.1967, 265 F.Supp. 630; North Allegheny Joint Sch. System v. Secretary of Health, Educ. and Welfare, D.C.Pa.1961, 196 F.Supp. 144.

13. See § 32 above.

14. KVOS, Inc. v. Associated Press, 1936, 57 S.Ct. 197, 299 U.S. 269, 81 L.Ed. 183; Beneficial Indus. Loan Corp. v. Kline, C.C.A.8th, 1942, 132 F.2d 520; Maryland Cas. Co. v. Baker, D.C.Ky.1961, 196 F.Supp.

234. See 5 Wright & Miller, Civil 2d § 1213; Note, Good Faith Pleading of Jurisdictional Amount, 1963, 48 Iowa L.Rev. 426.

15. Pittsburgh, C. & St. L. R. Co. v. Ramsey, 1874, 22 Wall. 322, 326, 22 L.Ed. 823; Sun Printing & Pub. Assn. v. Edwards, 1904, 24 S.Ct. 696, 194 U.S. 377, 48 L.Ed. 1027.

The complaint alone must be looked to in determining the existence of a federal question. See § 18 above.

16. 28 U.S.C.A. § 1653; Miller v. Stanmore, C.A.5th, 1981, 636 F.2d 986, 990; Miller v. Davis, C.A.6th, 1974, 507 F.2d 308; and cases cited 6 Wright, Miller & Kane, Civil 2d § 1474 n. 1.

The statute allows appellate courts to remedy inadequate jurisdictional allegations, but not defective jurisdictional facts. Newman–Green, Inc. v. Alfonzo–Larrain, 1989, 109 S.Ct. 2218, 490 U.S. 826, 104 L.Ed.2d 893.

amendment to show the existence of jurisdiction.[17] The statute permitting amendment of jurisdictional allegations has been of particular importance since the adoption of the 1958 statute making diversity, with regard to a corporate party, dependent on its principal place of business as well as on the state of its incorporation. Many pleaders have failed to allege the principal place of business of a corporate party, and amendment has frequently been allowed, even on appeal, to cure such an allegation.[18] Some cases have refused to allow an amendment to show the principal place of business in a removed case after the time for removal has run,[19] but the statute permitting amendment of jurisdictional allegations is broad enough to permit this, and other cases allow the amendment, even on appeal.[20]

It is never too late for a party, or the court on its own motion, to assert lack of jurisdiction over the subject matter.[21] If the defect is curable, as where diversity is destroyed by the presence of a party who is not indispensable, it is possible to cure the defect by dropping the nondiverse party. The Supreme Court has now resolved what had been a conflict of circuits about the proper procedure where the defect comes to light on appeal after judgment for the plaintiff. The court of appeals may grant a motion to dismiss a dispensable party whose presence spoils statutory diversity jurisdiction.[22] This authority is to be exercised sparingly. The appellate court must always consider whether the dismissal will prejudice any party in the litigation, and if factual disputes arise, it may be appropriate to remand the case to the district court to make the prejudice determination.[23]

If the jurisdictional allegations are challenged, they must be proved,[24] and the party invoking federal jurisdiction has the burden of proof.[25] Where there is such a challenge, the court has discretion either to decide the question itself or to submit it to a jury,[26] though ordinarily the court will determine the jurisdictional facts itself.

17. Keene Lumber Co. v. Leventhal, C.A.1st, 1948, 165 F.2d 815; Maryland Cas. Co. v. Baker, D.C.Ky.1961, 196 F.Supp. 234.

18. McCurdy v. Greyhound Corp., C.A.3d, 1965, 346 F.2d 224; Burkhardt v. Bates, C.A.8th, 1961, 296 F.2d 315; Niagara Fire Ins. Co. v. Dyess Furniture Co., C.A.5th, 1961, 292 F.2d 232; cf. Wymard v. McCloskey & Co., C.A.3d, 1965, 342 F.2d 495, certiorari denied 86 S.Ct. 52, 382 U.S. 823, 15 L.Ed.2d 68.

19. See Richmond, F. & P. R. Co. v. Intermodal Services, Inc., D.C.Va.1981, 508 F.Supp. 804; and cases cited 14A Wright, Miller & Cooper, Jurisdiction 2d § 3733 n. 14.

20. E.g., Stanley Elec. Contractors, Inc. v. Darin & Armstrong Co., D.C.Ky.1980, 486 F.Supp. 769; Board of Educ. of Charles County v. Travelers Indem. Co., D.C.Md. 1980, 486 F.Supp. 129; and cases cited 14A

Wright, Miller & Cooper, Jurisdiction 2d § 3733 n. 15.

21. See § 7 above at notes 16 to 22.

22. Newman–Green, Inc. v. Alfonzo–Larrain, 1989, 109 S.Ct. 2218, 490 U.S. 826, 104 L.Ed.2d 893.

23. 109 S.Ct. at 2225, 490 U.S. at 838.

24. Roberts v. Lewis, 1892, 12 S.Ct. 781, 144 U.S. 653, 36 L.Ed. 579.

25. McNutt v. General Motors Acceptance Corp., 1936, 56 S.Ct. 780, 298 U.S. 178, 80 L.Ed. 1135; Dept. of Recreation & Sports of Puerto Rico v. World Boxing Association, C.A.1st, 1991, 942 F.2d 84, 88; Georgiades v. Martin–Trigona, C.A.D.C. 1984, 729 F.2d 831, 834 n. 4.

26. Gilbert v. David, 1915, 35 S.Ct. 164, 235 U.S. 561, 59 L.Ed. 360; Katz v. Goodyear Tire & Rubber Co., C.A.2d, 1984, 737 F.2d 238, 242 n. 2; Williamson v. Tucker,

§ 69A.   Sanctions [1]

The law of sanctions today is as volatile as it once was dormant. In the years since 1983, when the Federal Rules were amended to encourage courts to make greater use of their sanctioning powers, hundreds of opinions have appeared in the reporters dealing with the issues involved in whether, when, and why a court might sanction an attorney. The law reviews and journals also bear the mark of the change in the form of numerous articles and there are even books on the subject. Faced with a vast increase in the volume of litigation, rulemakers and courts alike have turned to sanctions as a deterrent.

The law of sanctions, like much of the law of federal courts, begins with a grant of power. In the particular case of the power to sanction, the courts have multiple sources of power, each with its own limits and requirements. First, the courts have an "inherent power" to control their dockets and the people appearing before them. This power is traced from Article III itself. Second, by enacting 28 U.S.C.A. § 1927, Congress has granted to the courts a power to sanction attorneys. Finally, several of the Federal Rules of Civil Procedure permit a district court to impose sanctions on parties or on their attorneys when the mandates of the rules are violated.

The Supreme Court discussed the "inherent power" of the district courts in Chambers v. NASCO, Inc.[2] The case began as an action to compel specific performance of a contract to convey a television station and broadcast license. Although the trial court warned the defendant on several occasions and even assessed a $25,000 fine for civil contempt during the pretrial proceedings, the defendant repeatedly attempted to moot the issue before the court by conveying the television station to others. As the trial court put it, the defendant "(1) attempted to deprive [the trial] Court of jurisdiction by acts of fraud, nearly all of which were performed outside the confines of [the] Court, (2) filed false and frivolous pleadings, and (3) attempted, by other tactics of delay, oppression, harassment and massive expense to reduce plaintiff to exhausted compliance."[3] The trial court considered imposing Rule 11 sanctions, but

C.A.5th, 1981, 645 F.2d 404, 412–415; Seideman v. Hamilton, C.A.3d, 1960, 275 F.2d 224, certiorari denied 80 S.Ct. 1258, 363 U.S. 820, 4 L.Ed.2d 1517.

See also Shaffer v. Coty, Inc., D.C.Cal. 1960, 183 F.Supp. 662. See Note, Trial by Jury of Preliminary Jurisdictional Facts in Federal Cases, 1963, 48 Iowa L.Rev. 471.

§ 69A

1. 5A Wright & Miller, Civil 2d §§ 1331–1338 (Rule 11); 8 Wright, Miller & Marcus: Civil 2d §§ 2281–2293 (Rule 37); 10 Wright, Miller & Kane, Civil 2d § 2670 (28 U.S.C.A. § 1927); 15B Wright, Miller & Cooper, Jurisdiction 2d § 3914.30 (appellate review of sanctions); 16 Wright, Miller & Cooper, Jurisdiction § 3984 (Appellate

Rule 38 and 28 U.S.C.A. § 1912). See also Vairo, Rule 11 Sanctions: Case Perspectives and Preventive Measures, 2d ed. 1992; Solovy, The Federal Law of Sanctions, 1991; Joseph, Sanctions: The Federal Law of Litigation Abuse, 1989; Tobias, Reconsidering Rule 11, 1992, 46 U.Miami L.Rev. 855.

The author is indebted to John Mollenkamp, of the Missouri bar, for his valuable assistance in the preparation of this section.

2. 1991, 111 S.Ct. 2123, 501 U.S. 32, 115 L.Ed.2d 27. Justice White wrote for the Court. There were dissents by Justice Kennedy, joined by Chief Justice Rehnquist and Justice Souter, and by Justice Scalia.

3. 111 S.Ct. at 2131, 501 U.S. at ___.

found them lacking, in part because they could not reach out-of-court behavior. Instead, the court imposed sanctions based on its inherent power to control litigants.

The Supreme Court found that courts necessarily have some inherent powers that cannot be dispensed with because they are necessary to the execution of all other powers of the court.[4] A few examples of these powers are the powers to discipline attorneys,[5] to impose silence and decorum in their presence,[6] to punish contempt,[7] and to dismiss a suit for failure to prosecute.[8] In the past each of these powers has been discussed separately, as a part of discussions of when the courts might properly exercise that particular power. In Chambers the Court mentioned them in sequence, all as flowing from a common source of power.

The Court then moved on to the specific exercise of power at issue in the case, the order to pay attorneys' fees. The Court discussed the "American Rule," which mandates that courts not charge the losing party with the attorneys' fees of the victorious side, and the recognized exceptions to the rule. One recognized exception to the "American Rule" is where a party has acted in bad faith and the Court found that this case fell within that exception. The Court rejected the argument, presented by Chambers, that the enactment of 28 U.S.C.A. § 1927 and the adoption of rules of procedure, including Rule 11, which provide for the imposition of sanctions replaced the inherent power. Justice White noted that the inherent power is both broader and narrower than the other grants of power to sanction. While the inherent power may be used to punish conduct not taking place within the courtroom or as a formal part of the litigation, it may only be imposed for "bad faith" conduct.[9]

The courts also draw authority to sanction attorneys from an explicit grant of authority by Congress. As amended in 1980, 28 U.S.C.A. § 1927 provides: "Any attorney or other person admitted to conduct cases in any court of the United States or any Territory thereof who so multiplies the proceedings in any case unreasonably and vexatiously may be required by the court to satisfy personally the excess costs, expenses, and attorneys' fees reasonably incurred because of such conduct."[10] The statute, by its terms, applies only to conduct that is both unreasonable and vexatious and in this way effectively requires a showing of bad faith.[11] Section 1927 has not been used much by the

---

4. 111 S.Ct. at 2132, 501 U.S. at ___.

5. Citing Ex parte Burr, 1824, 9 Wheat. 529, 531, 6 L.Ed. 152.

6. Citing Anderson v. Dunn, 1821, 6 Wheat. 204, 227, 5 L.Ed. 242.

7. Citing Ex parte Robinson, 1874, 19 Wall. 505, 510, 22 L.Ed. 205.

8. Citing Link v. Wabash R. Co., 1962, 82 S.Ct. 1386, 1388–1389, 370 U.S. 626, 630–631, 8 L.Ed.2d 734.

9. Resolution Trust Corp. v. Bright, C.A.5th, 1993, 6 F.3d 336.

10. See 10 Wright, Miller & Kane, Civil 2d § 2670, pp. 225–226; Note, 1990, 31 B.C.L.Rev. 477. Prior to its amendment in 1980 § 1927 did not authorize requiring payment of attorneys' fees. Roadway Express, Inc. v. Piper, 1980, 100 S.Ct. 2455, 447 U.S. 752, 65 L.Ed.2d 488.

11. In the debate on the 1980 amendment of § 1927 Congress made it clear that it did not want to allow fee-shifting in the absence of bad faith. 5A Wright & Miller, Civil 2d, § 1332, p. 39.

courts, whether because they are unfamiliar with it and its contours or because sanctions are more frequently requested under the Federal Rules of Civil Procedure.

Civil Rule 37 has long provided sweeping authority to sanction litigants, and on occasion their attorneys, for violations of the discovery rules.[12] The Supreme Court's 1976 decision in National Hockey League v. Metropolitan Hockey Club, Inc.[13] encouraged broader use of that authority by emphasizing that severe sanctions may be needed "not merely to penalize those whose conduct may be deemed to warrant such a sanction, but to deter those who might be tempted to such conduct in the absence of such a deterrent."[14]

These other sources of power to impose sanctions are not insignificant. Nevertheless since 1983 most of the cases and nearly all of the controversy have centered around Rule 11. From the enactment of the Federal Rules in 1938 until 1983, Rule 11 required that pleadings be signed by an attorney, or by the party if the party was not represented by an attorney. The signature of the party meant little, perhaps no more than that the party was aware of the action and it had not been filed by someone else without the party's permission. The signature of an attorney, however, "constitute[d] a certificate by him that he has read the pleading; that to the best of his knowledge, information, and belief there is good ground to support it; and that it is not interposed for delay." The rule also provided that pleadings not signed or "signed with intent to defeat the purpose of the rule" might be stricken. Willful violations of the rule might be enough to subject the attorney to "appropriate disciplinary action." The rule also provided for similar action upon the insertion of "scandalous or indecent matter" in the pleadings. Under no circumstances were the sanctions mandatory and only upon a finding of "bad faith" were they ever imposed. Sanctions under this version of the rule were few.[15]

While Rule 11 lay unused and ineffective, litigation in federal courts was increasing dramatically. The Advisory Committee on Civil Rules traced the increase in litigation to four factors.[16] First, our judicial

---

12. See § 90 below. Rule 26(g) states, in terms reminiscent of Rule 11, the effect of signing a discovery request, response, or objection, and provides for sanctions if that rule is violated. Rule 16(f) makes similar provisions for pretrial conferences.

13. 1976, 96 S.Ct. 2778, 427 U.S. 639, 49 L.Ed.2d 747.

14. 96 S.Ct. at 2781, 427 U.S. at 643.

15. Risinger, Honesty in Pleading and Its Enforcement: Some "Striking" Problems with Fed.R.Civ.P. 11, 1976, 61 Minn. L.Rev. 1. Stempel, Sanctions, Symmetry, and Safe Harbors: Limiting Misapplication of Rule 11 by Harmonizing it with Pre–Verdict Dismissal Devices, 1991, 60 Fordham L.Rev. 257.

"First, the Rule engendered confusion regarding when a pleading should be struck, what standard of conduct would make an attorney liable to sanctions, and what sanctions were available. Second, courts were reluctant to impose disciplinary measures on attorneys * * * and attorneys were slow to invoke the rule." Cooter & Gell v. Hartmarx Corp., 1990, 110 S.Ct. 2447, 2454, 496 U.S. 384, 393, 110 L.Ed.2d 359.

16. 5A Wright & Miller, Civil 2d § 1331; Miller, The August 1983 Amendments to the Federal Rules of Civil Procedure: Promoting Effective Case Management and Lawyer Responsibility 1984, pp. 2–9.

system has economic incentives to litigate. The existence and growing number of fee-shifting statutes encourage litigation insofar as they increase the potential economic benefit to winning plaintiffs. The "American rule," on the other hand, limits the possible losses by prohibiting, with some exceptions, the charging of the winning-side's attorneys' fees to the losing party, whether plaintiff or defendant. Where statutes provide that plaintiffs may recover their attorneys' fees if they win, and a common-law rule provides that plaintiffs will not have to pay the defendants' attorneys' fees if they lose, it is not unreasonable to assume that some suits might be brought that would not be brought if it were not for the lopsided fee-shifting rules. Further the availability of contingent-fee representation makes lawsuits less costly to file.

Second, the committee perceived the growing number of substantive federal rights as an obvious cause of the increased number of cases in federal courts. As Congress created new rights by statute, courts in recent years had been willing to find implied causes of action in other statutes. Together these activities added considerably to the number of rights people had, and consequently added to the number of cases filed to protect or recover for the violation of these new rights.

Third, the increase in the number of attorneys practicing in America was seen as adding to the problem. Just as more rights lead to more cases, so do more advocates. Further, the increased freedom to advertise legal services has led to greater contact with and representation of clients. This in turn leads to more litigation.

Fourth, the committee saw the open access to the courts inherent in the system of the Federal Rules as doing little to stem the tide of litigation. With its emphasis on notice pleading and resolution of cases on the merits as opposed to the technicalities of fact pleading, the federal court system was open to all.

These causes of more litigation were not seen as wrong or as flaws, simply as explanations. Few would suggest the repeal of substantive rights or limits on the number of attorneys as rational solutions to overcrowded federal trial dockets. But this perception of the problem and these ideas as to the underlying causes formed the backdrop for the 1983 amendments to the rules, including Rule 11. In particular, the view that pretrial was the time and place to reduce the logjam affected the amendments greatly.[17] The committee sought to alleviate the problem by proposing a package of amendments to the rules. Amendments to Rules 7, 11, 16, and 26 were interrelated as parts of a single solution to the single problem of overcrowded courts.[18]

For reasons that will be discussed later, the 1983 version of Rule 11 proved quite controversial. In 1993 the rule was rewritten in the light of the experience of the preceding ten years and of the criticism it had aroused. In some respects the sweep of the rule was broadened, while in

17. Miller, note 16 above, at p. 9.   **18.** Id. at 2.

others the rule was made less Draconian [19]. The discussion here is of the 1993 version of the rule, but with reference made where necessary to the 1983 version and to the changes that were made in 1993.

Rule 11 is no longer limited to pleadings. It now applies to "[e]very pleading, written motion, and other paper." [20] The rule now requires the striking of an unsigned paper if the defect is not corrected.[21] The 1983 version of the rule now made sanctions mandatory upon violation of the rule, but in the 1993 revision the imposition of sanctions is once again discretionary with the court.[22] The 1983 rule expanded the range of sanctions available to encompass nonmonetary and monetary sanctions, including attorneys' fees. This continues to be true under the 1993 revision, but limits have been placed on monetary sanctions.[23] As the Advisory Committee Note to the 1993 amendments says, "if a monetary sanction is imposed, it should ordinarily be paid into court as a penalty."[24] It is still permissible to order payment to the other party, as had been commonly done under the 1983 version of Rule 11, but payment to the other party is only to be ordered where "warranted for effective deterrence" and is limited to the fees and expenses "incurred as a direct result of the violation."[25] Sanctions for violation of Rule 11 can be imposed upon "the attorneys, law firms, or parties" that have violated the rule or are responsible for the violation.[26]

Undoubtedly the most important change made in 1983, and strengthened in 1993, was the certification that the signer of a document makes. As Justice O'Connor put it, the "heart of Rule 11" as it was amended in 1983 was the sentence that "explains in detail the message conveyed by the signing of a document. A signature certifies to the court that the signer has read the document, has conducted a reasonable inquiry into the facts and the law and is satisfied that the document is well-grounded in both, and is acting without any improper motive." [27] In the 1993 revision this is still a sentence, but it is now a sentence 22

19. Comment, Proposed Amendments to Federal Rule of Civil Procedure 11: New, But Not Necessarily Improved, 1993, 21 Fla.St.U.L.Rev. 111.

20. Rule 11(a). See 5A Wright & Miller, Civil 2d § 1331.

21. Rule 11(a).

22. See 5A Wright & Miller, Civil 2d § 1336.

23. Rule 11(c)(2). See 5A Wright & Miller, Civil 2d § 1336.

24. 146 F.R.D. at 587–588. See also Parness, Fines Under New Federal Civil Rule 11: The New Monetary Sanctions for the "Stop–and–Think–Again" Rule, 1993 B.Y.U.L.Rev. 879.

25. Rule 11(c)(2). A party that is represented by an attorney cannot itself be ordered to pay a monetary sanction for making a frivolous legal contention. Rule 11(c)(2)(A). And the court may not order payment of monetary sanctions on its own initiative unless it has issued an order to show cause before voluntary dismissal or settlement of the case. Rule 11(c)(2)(B).

26. The imposition of sanctions on parties, even those represented by counsel, had been allowed under the 1983 version of the rule in Business Guides, Inc. v. Chromatic Communications Enterprises, Inc., 1991, 111 S.Ct. 922, 498 U.S. 533, 112 L.Ed.2d 1140. The authorization of sanctions against a law firm changes the construction put on the 1983 version in Pavelic & Le-Flore v. Marvel Entertainment Group, 1989, 110 S.Ct. 456, 493 U.S. 120, 107 L.Ed.2d 438.

27. Business Guides, Inc. v. Chromatic Communications Enterprises, Inc., 1991, 111 S.Ct. 922, 929, 498 U.S. 533, 542, 112 L.Ed.2d 1140. See 5A Wright & Miller, Civil 2d § 1335.

lines long and with four numbered subdivisions. The certification that the document be well grounded in law is now that the legal contentions "are warranted by existing law or by a nonfrivolous argument for the extension, modification, or reversal of existing law or the establishment of new law." [28] The certification as to factual contentions is now that they "have evidentiary support or, if specifically so identified, are likely to have evidentiary support after a reasonable opportunity for further investigation or discovery." [29]

The 1993 revision speaks to one point on which the cases had been divided under the 1983 version. The certification is made by "presenting to the court (whether by signing, filing, submitting, or later advocating) a pleading, written motion, or other paper." [30] This makes it clear that there is a continuing duty. Rule 11 is violated if a litigant reaffirms to the court and advocates a position contained in an earlier pleading or motion after it has been learned that there is no merit to that position. But the 1993 revision also contains what is known as a "safe harbor" provision. A request for sanctions must be made as a separate motion and this motion is not to be filed until at least 21 days after it has been served. If during those 21 days "the alleged violation is corrected, as by withdrawing (whether formally or informally) some allegation or contention, the motion should not be filed with the court." [31]

The standard by which a certification is to be measured was one of the issues resolved by the Supreme Court in a 1991 decision, Business Guides, Inc. v. Chromatic Communications Enterprises, Inc.[32] It held that Rule 11 imposed an objective standard of reasonable inquiry.[33] "Giving the text its plain meaning, we hold that it imposes on any party who signs a pleading, motion, or other paper—whether the party's signature is required by the Rule or is provided voluntarily—an affirmative duty to conduct a reasonable inquiry into the facts and the law before filing, and that the applicable standard is one of reasonableness under the circumstances." [34] It seems clear that this will still be the applicable standard under the 1993 revision.

In the Business Guides case the Court dealt briefly with the argument that the 1983 version of Rule 11 was not authorized by the Rules

28. Rule 11(b)(2).

29. Rule 11(b)(3).

In order to equalize the burden of the rule upon plaintiffs and defendants, Rule 11(b)(4) now makes signature of a document a certification that denials of factual contentions are warranted on the evidence or, if specifically so identified, are reasonably based on a lack of information or belief.

30. Rule 11(b). For discussion of the prior case law on this point, see 5A Wright & Miller, Civil 2d § 1333, pp. 51–53.

31. Rule 11(c)(1)(A). The quotation is from the Advisory Committee Note to that

portion of the 1993 amendments, 146 F.R.D. at 591.

The continuing-duty requirement, even with the "safe harbor" provisions, is criticized as too ambiguous and too onerous in Comment, note 19 above.

32. 1991, 111 S.Ct. 922, 498 U.S. 533, 112 L.Ed.2d 1140. Justice O'Connor wrote for the Court. Justice Kennedy dissented, in an opinion joined by Justices Marshall and Stevens and in part by Justice Scalia.

33. 111 S.Ct. at 934, 498 U.S. at 554.

34. 111 S.Ct. at 933, 498 U.S. at 551.

Enabling Act. The Court stated that "[t]here is little doubt that Rule 11 is reasonably necessary to maintain the integrity of the system of federal practice and procedure, and that any effect on substantive rights is incidental. We held as much only last Term in Cooter & Gell: 'It is now clear that the central purpose of Rule 11 is to deter baseless filings in District Court and thus, consistent with the Rule Enabling Act's grant of authority, streamline the administration and procedure of the federal courts.' " [35]

The Cooter & Gell case, quoted by the Court in Business Guides, dealt primarily with three other issues about the application of Rule 11.[36] Before treating any of the issues involved, the Court first discussed the history of Rule 11 and its underlying purpose and concluded that "[a]lthough the rule must be read in light of concerns that it will spawn satellite litigation and chill vigorous advocacy, any interpretation must give effect to the rule's central goal of deterrence." [37]

First, the Court considered whether the district court might still impose Rule 11 sanctions after the plaintiff had voluntarily dismissed the action under Rule 41(a)(1)(i) of the Federal Rules. The Court found that the filing of the complaint invoked the jurisdiction of the district court to determine the merits of the action and the motion for Rule 11 sanctions arising from the complaint, and that voluntary dismissal did not undo the wrong of the Rule 11 violation. The Court likened the Rule 11 inquiry and imposition of sanctions to the imposition of costs, attorney's fees, and contempt sanctions. All of these collateral issues, including Rule 11 sanctions, may be considered by a court after the termination of the proceeding.[38] The second issue decided by the Court in Cooter & Gell was the appropriate standard of review to be applied by appellate courts reviewing Rule 11 sanctions. The Court discussed the various standards applied by the Courts of Appeals for the various circuits and determined that "an appellate court should apply an abuse-of-discretion standard in reviewing all aspects of a district court's Rule 11 determination. A district court would necessarily abuse its discretion if it based its ruling on an erroneous view of the law or on a clearly erroneous assessment of the evidence." [39] Finally, the Court determined that Rule 11 did not, by its terms or otherwise, authorize the award of attorney's fees incurred defending the original award on appeal.[40]

The 1983 version of Rule 11 had its enthusiastic advocates, but it

35. 111 S.Ct. at 934, 498 U.S. at 552.

36. Cooter & Gell v. Hartmarx Corp., 1990, 110 S.Ct. 2447, 496 U.S. 384, 110 L.Ed.2d 359. Justice O'Connor wrote for the Court. Justice Stevens dissented in part.

37. 110 S.Ct. at 2454, 496 U.S. at 393.

38. 110 S.Ct. at 2454–2457, 496 U.S. at 393–398.

See also Willy v. Coastal Corporation, 1992, 112 S.Ct. 1076, ___ U.S. ___, 117 L.Ed.2d 280, noted 1993, 13 Rev.Litig. 105, holding that the imposition of sanctions may be proper even though it is later held that the district court lacked subject-matter jurisdiction of the action.

39. 110 S.Ct. at 2461, 496 U.S. at 405.

40. 110 S.Ct. at 2461–2462, 496 U.S. at 405–409.

also had been harshly criticized.[41] Some of the supposed defects in the rule were corrected by the recent decisions of the Supreme Court. Others have been addressed by the 1993 revision of the rule. Two of the grounds of criticism are of such importance that they require continued study under the rule as it now stands.

Critics argue, and with some statistical support, that plaintiffs in general and civil-rights plaintiffs in particular have suffered a disproportionate amount under the rule. This "pro-defendant" bias in the application of the rule is said to have been demonstrated by the higher number of sanctions against plaintiffs and the higher rate of sanctions per motion for sanctions.[42] With the passage of time has come the opportunity to conduct more thorough studies of the application of the rule. The Federal Judicial Center, at the request of the Advisory Committee, conducted an extensive study of five circuits, in part to determine if this was an accurate assessment of the application of Rule 11. The conclusions of the authors of the study were that civil-rights plaintiffs, though more frequently the target of Rule 11 motions, were not being unfairly sanctioned.[43] This was based upon an analysis of the actual pleadings that gave rise to the sanctions, as well as a study of the statistical rates of sanctioning. This conclusion highlights the difference between a greater number of sanctions than the average and the imposition of sanctions on nonfrivolous claims. While a higher rate of sanctions could be evidence of the use of the rule by "pro-defendant" judges to keep civil-rights plaintiffs from recovering, it could also be evidence of a higher rate of frivolous claims in the civil-rights area.

Further, if the claim is before the court (as it must for sanctions to be imposed), then the harm of a discriminatory sanction is less drastic than if the claim is not brought. If the claim is meritorious, and a court of appeals or the Supreme Court so finds, then the sanction will be reversed and the law will still advance. However, if the plaintiffs are deterred from offering their claim at all, then the problem is worse. A study commissioned by the American Judicature Society examined, among other effects of the rule, whether and how often attorneys did not bring claims that they thought were meritorious for fear of Rule 11 sanctions.[44] The study found that because of the rule 20.5% of the plaintiffs' attorneys and 17.5% of the defense attorneys responding to the survey had decided not to assert a claim or defense that they felt had potential merit.[45] This figure is potentially quite disturbing. If all of these claims are actually meritorious, then effective advocacy is being deterred by the rule and the "chilling effect" feared by some critics has become a reality. But standing by itself this number alone evidences

41. There is a full discussion of the criticisms, and of possible answers to the critics, in 5A Wright & Miller, Civil 2d § 1332.

42. Vairo, note 1 above, § 2.02(b)(3); Marino, Rule 11 and Public Interest Litigation: The Trend Toward Limiting Access to the Federal Courts, 1992, 44 Rutgers L.Rev. 923.

43. Wiggins, Willging & Stienstra, The Federal Judicial Center's Study of Rule 11, 1991, 2 FJC Directions 19–26.

44. Kritzer, Marshall & Zemans, Rule 11: Moving Beyond the Cosmic Anecdote, 1992, 75 Judicature 269.

45. Id. at 271.

either the chilling effect of a discriminatory rule or the proper effect of a well-written rule. When the Committee removed the requirement of "bad faith" from the rule, it was to deter attorneys from bringing claims that were frivolous, but which the attorneys believed in, whether because they had not investigated properly or were incompetent. If there are some incompetent or unreasonably lax attorneys practicing (who are aware of Rule 11 and its import), they will probably refrain from filing some claims that they subjectively believe are meritorious, but that are objectively frivolous. If any of these attorneys responded to the poll, then they would answer that they had been deterred. Their affirmative response, however, is not evidence of the chilling of creativity or good advocacy, but rather is evidence that the rule is working as it was intended and is deterring baseless litigation in federal courts.

The 1993 amendments will quiet some of the controversy that Rule 11 has aroused. There are still legitimate concerns about the amended rule and its application [46] and more studies and more experience are needed before any truly conclusive determinations about the effectiveness of the rule can be made.

D. JOINDER OF CLAIMS AND PARTIES

Analysis

§ 70. Parties Classified [1]

Three different, but easily confused, concepts must be kept in mind in considering joinder of parties in federal court. Only the real party in interest can be a party. This is governed by Rule 17(a). A person must have capacity to sue or be sued. This is governed by Rule 17(b) and (c).

---

46. See, e.g., Lazaroff, Rule 11 and Federal Antitrust Litigation, 1993, 67 Tul. L.Rev. 1034.

§ 70

1. 6A Wright, Miller & Kane, Civil 2d §§ 1543–1558 (real party in interest), 1559– 1569 (capacity to sue or be sued); 7 Wright, Miller & Kane, Civil 2d §§ 1604–1608 (parties classified).

If these tests are met, the relation of a particular person to the suit must be examined in order to determine whether his or her joinder ought to be compelled by Rule 19 or is permitted by Rule 20.

Rule 17(a), stating that every action shall be brought in the name of the real party in interest, follows the usual code formula. It was intended to change the common-law rule, which permitted suit to be brought only in the name of the person having the legal title to the right of action, and thus precluded suit by persons who had only equitable or beneficial interests. Under the rule the "real party in interest" is the party who, by the substantive law, possesses the right sought to be enforced,[2] and not necessarily the person who will ultimately benefit from the recovery.[3] This is illustrated by the further language stating that executors, administrators, and other named representatives may sue in their own name without joining with them the party for whose benefit the action is brought. This further language is not an exception to the real-party-in-interest provision, but was inserted as a precautionary measure in order that the "real party in interest" would not be confined to the person beneficially interested.[4] Indeed of late the existence of such a rule has come in for severe criticism. The critics argue that if the effect of the rule is merely to provide that the person who has the substantive right shall sue, the rule itself is unnecessary and the same results can be reached simply by application of the substantive law.[5] About the best that can be said for the rule is that "it conveys a certain amount of correct information about naming plaintiffs, but to the average reader innocent of history it probably suggests as much or more that is quite incorrect. It does stand as a warning, which is perhaps unnecessary, that the defendant can insist upon a plaintiff

2. E.g., Lubbock Feed Lots, Inc. v. Iowa Beef Processors, Inc., C.A.5th, 1980, 630 F.2d 250, 256–258; Bass v. Campagnone, D.C.R.I.1987, 655 F.Supp. 1390; and cases cited 6A Wright, Miller & Kane, Civil 2d § 1543 n. 1.

The concept of real party in interest should not be confused with the concept of standing. The standing question arises in the realm of public law, when governmental action is attacked on the ground that it violates private rights or some constitutional principle. See § 13 above. " 'Real party in interest' is very different from standing." Kent v. Northern California Regional Office of American Friends Serv. Committee, C.A.9th, 1974, 497 F.2d 1325, 1329. See also K–B Trucking Co. v. Riss Intl. Corp., C.A.10th, 1985, 763 F.2d 1148, 1154 n. 7. Unfortunately, as shown by the cases cited in 13 Wright, Miller & Cooper, Jurisdiction 2d § 3531 n. 2, confusion between standing on the one hand and real party in interest or capacity on the other has been increasing.

3. Proctor v. Gissendaner, C.A.5th, 1978, 579 F.2d 876, 880; Armour Pharmaceutical Co. v. Home Ins. Co., D.C.Ill.1973, 60 F.R.D. 592; Allen v. Baker, D.C.Miss. 1968, 327 F.Supp. 706; Clark & Moore, A New Federal Civil Procedure, 1935, 44 Yale L.J. 1291, 1310–1312.

4. Horwich v. Price, D.C.Mich.1960, 25 F.R.D. 500; Clark, Code Pleading, 2d ed. 1947, p. 190.

5. Entman, More Reasons for Abolishing Federal Rule of Civil Procedure 17(a): The Problem of the Proper Plaintiff and Insurance Subrogation, 1990, 68 N.C.L.Rev. 893, 951 ("a computer virus in the systems of federal procedure and jurisdiction"); Kennedy, Federal Rule 17(a): Will the Real Party in Interest Please Stand?, 1967, 51 Minn.L.Rev. 675, 724 ("barnacle on the federal practice ship"); Atkinson, The Real Party in Interest Rule: A Plea for its Abolition, 1957, 32 N.Y.U.L.Rev. 926. See also Jefferson v. Ametek, Inc., D.C.Md.1980, 86 F.R.D. 425, 427.

who will afford him a setup providing good res judicata protection if the struggle is carried through on the merits to the end." [6]

Since the rule does direct attention to the person with the substantive right sought to be enforced, state law must be looked to in diversity cases to see who this person is, although the federal rule then governs the procedural question of joinder.[7] Despite the criticisms directed at the text of the rule itself, whether a person with a particular relation to a case is "the real party in interest" has been worked out in many specific contexts,[8] and generally quite satisfactorily.

The most important application of the rule is with regard to assignment and subrogation. One of the main purposes of the provision is to allow the assignee of a chose in action to sue upon it in his or her own name instead of in the name of the assignor. It is now quite settled that the assignee is a real party in interest,[9] and that an assignor that has assigned its entire claim is not a real party in interest.[10] Where there has been a partial assignment, both assignor and assignee are real parties in interest; in order to avoid a split judgment, the defendant, on motion, may be able to compel both to be joined as parties plaintiff.[11]

Except as relevant state law may require a different treatment, the same results are reached in cases of subrogation as in cases of assignment. The most common situation is that of the insurer that has paid its insured and thus is subrogated to the insured's right against some third party. If the insurer has paid the entire loss, it is the real party in

---

6. Kaplan, Continuing Work of the Civil Committee: 1966 Amendments of the Federal Rules of Civil Procedure, 1967, 81 Harv.L.Rev. 356, 412.

This understanding that the modern function of the rule is the negative one of protecting the defendant against a subsequent action by the party actually entitled to recover and insuring that the judgment will have its proper effect as res judicata was first enunciated by Judge Hutcheson in Celanese Corp. v. John Clark Indus., Inc., C.A.5th, 1954, 214 F.2d 551, 556, and has had wide acceptance. E.g., Gogolin & Steiter v. Kern's Auto Imports, Inc., C.A.5th, 1989, 886 F.2d 100, 102, certiorari denied 110 S.Ct. 1480, 494 U.S. 1031, 108 L.Ed.2d 617; and cases cited 6A Wright, Miller & Kane, Civil 2d § 1541 n. 9.

7. Brocklesby Transport v. Eastern States Escort Servs., C.A.2d, 1990, 904 F.2d 131, 133; McNeil Constr. Co. v. Livingston State Bank, C.A.9th, 1962, 300 F.2d 88; American Fidelity & Cas. Co. v. All American Bus Lines, C.A.10th, 1949, 179 F.2d 7; 6A Wright, Miller & Kane, Civil 2d § 1544.

8. 6A Wright, Miller & Kane, 2d Civil §§ 1545–1553.

9. Fox–Greenwald Sheet Metal Co. v. Markowitz Bros., Inc., C.A.D.C.1971, 452 F.2d 1346; Amico v. New Castle County, D.C.Del.1983, 571 F.Supp. 160; and cases cited 6A Wright, Miller & Kane, Civil 2d § 1545 n. 2.

This result is not changed by the fact that the assignment was for collection only. Titus v. Wallick, 1939, 59 S.Ct. 557, 561, 306 U.S. 282, 288–289, 83 L.Ed. 653; Staggers v. Otto Gerdau Co., C.A.2d, 1966, 359 F.2d 292.

10. Rodriguez v. Compass Shipping Co., C.A.2d, 1980, 617 F.2d 955, affirmed 1981, 101 S.Ct. 1945, 451 U.S. 596, 68 L.Ed.2d 472; Horwich v. Price, D.C.Mich.1960, 25 F.R.D. 500.

11. Hoeppner Constr. Co. v. U.S. for Use of Mangum, C.A.10th, 1960, 287 F.2d 108; Verdi v. City of Philadelphia, D.C.Pa. 1982, 553 F.Supp. 334; Texas San Juan Oil Corp. v. An–Son Offshore Drilling Co., D.C.N.Y.1961, 194 F.Supp. 396. See 6A Wright, Miller & Kane, Civil § 1545, pp. 353–354.

interest and must sue in its own name.[12]   The insured, who no longer
has any interest in the recovery, cannot sue.[13]   If the insurer has paid
only part of the loss, either the insured or the insurer may sue, but the
defendant may be able to compel joinder of the other in order to avoid
being subjected to a multiplicity of suits.[14]   If instead of paying the loss
the insurer makes a loan to the insured under an agreement whereby
the loan is to be repaid only out of any recovery which may be obtained
from the third person, the insured rather than the insurer is usually, but
not always, considered to be the real party in interest.[15]

   Though the two concepts are sometimes confused, there is a clear
distinction between "real party in interest," governed by Rule 17(a), and
"capacity," governed by Rule 17(b) and (c).[16]   A litigant could be the real
party in interest and yet lack capacity to sue, as for example a person
who has become mentally incompetent.   A person could have capacity to
sue and yet not be the real party in interest, as for example a plaintiff
who has assigned away all his interest in the claim before suit is
brought.   The distinction has procedural significance since the burden is

12.   U.S. v. Aetna Cas. & Sur. Co., 1949,
70 S.Ct. 207, 215, 338 U.S. 366, 380, 94
L.Ed. 171; Hilbrands v. Far East Trading
Co., C.A.9th, 1975, 509 F.2d 1321; and
cases cited 6A Wright, Miller & Kane, Civil
2d § 1546 n. 1.   The Aetna Casualty case
has been criticized as "an unfortunate landmark" and its treatment of Rule 17(a)
called "dreadfully superficial and misleading".   Entman, note 5 above, at 914.

13.   American Fidelity & Cas. Co. v. All
American Bus Lines, C.A.10th, 1949, 179
F.2d 7; McCoy v. Wean United, Inc.,
D.C.Tenn.1973, 67 F.R.D. 491.

14.   U.S. v. Aetna Cas. & Sur. Co., 1949,
70 S.Ct. 207, 338 U.S. 366, 94 L.Ed. 171;
Public Serv. Co. of Oklahoma v. Black &
Veatch, C.A.10th, 1972, 467 F.2d 1143; 6A
Wright, Miller & Kane, Civil § 1546, pp.
360–363.   The position taken in the text
and in these cases is rejected, however, in
Glacier General Assurance Co. v. G. Gordon
Symons Co., C.A.9th, 1980, 631 F.2d 131,
134, and in Dudley v. Smith, C.A.5th, 1974,
504 F.2d 979, 983.

Joinder of the insurer will not be compelled if this would destroy diversity and
the insurer will be bound by the judgment.
Virginia Elec. & Power Co. v. Westinghouse
Elec. Corp., C.A.4th, 1973, 485 F.2d 78, 84–
85, certiorari denied 94 S.Ct. 1450, 415 U.S.
935, 39 L.Ed.2d 493.   The case is sharply
criticized in Entman, note 5 above, at 947–
949.

The deference to state law precluding in-
voluntary joinder of the insurer in Race v.
Hay, D.C.Ind.1961, 28 F.R.D. 354, seems to
be unsound.   See, e.g., Gas Service Co. v.
Hunt, C.A.10th, 1950, 183 F.2d 417; White
Hall Bldg. Corp. v. Profexray Div. of Litton

Indus., Inc., D.C.Pa.1974, 387 F.Supp. 1202;
Hughey v. Aetna Cas. & Sur. Co., D.C.Del.
1963, 32 F.R.D. 340.

15.   E.g., R.J. Enstrom Corp. v. Intercep-
tor Corp., C.A.10th, 1975, 520 F.2d 1217;
Ketona Chemical Corp. v. Globe Indem. Co.,
C.A.5th, 1968, 404 F.2d 181; Export Leaf
Tobacco Co. v. American Ins. Co., C.A.4th,
1958, 260 F.2d 839; Industrial Dev. Bd. of
City of Prattville v. Brown & Root, Inc.,
D.C.Ala.1983, 99 F.R.D. 58; and cases cited
6A Wright, Miller & Kane, Civil 2d § 1546
n. 9.

Contra: Executive Jet Aviation, Inc. v.
U.S., C.A.6th, 1974, 507 F.2d 508; City
Stores Co. v. Lerner Shops, Inc., C.A.D.C.
1969, 410 F.2d 1010; McNeil Constr. Co. v.
Livingston State Bank, C.A.9th, 1962, 300
F.2d 88; F.L. Crane Co. v. Cessna Aircraft
Co., D.C.Miss.1977, 74 F.R.D. 414; Ent-
man, note 5 above, at 925–931; Boynton,
The Myth of the "Loan Receipt" Revisited
Under Rule 17(a), 1966, 18 S.C.L.Rev. 624;
Note, 1990, 74 Minn.L.Rev. 1107.

16.   The concepts are discriminatingly
distinguished, under rules based on the federal rules, in Catalfano v. Higgins, 1962,
182 A.2d 637, 4 Storey 548, vacated on
other grounds Del.1962, 188 A.2d 357, 5
Storey 470.   The concepts were confused in,
e.g., E. Brooke Matlack, Inc. v. Walrath,
D.C.Md.1959, 24 F.R.D. 263.

See generally Kennedy, Federal Civil
Rule 17(b) and (c): Qualifying to Litigate in
Federal Court, 1968, 43 Notre Dame Law.
273; 6A Wright, Miller & Kane, Civil 2d
§ 1542.

on plaintiff to show that he has a substantive right to recover and thus that he is the real party in interest, while Rule 9(a) requires a specific negative averment if defendant wishes to object that plaintiff lacks capacity to sue.

The capacity of an individual, other than one acting in a representative capacity, to sue or be sued is determined according to the law of the individual's domicile.[17] The capacity of a corporation is determined by the law under which it was organized.[18] The capacity of a representative is determined by the law of the state where the district court is held.[19] This is usually the test, also, for determining the capacity of partnerships and unincorporated associations,[20] but such an association may sue or be sued in its common name, even though it lacks capacity under state law, where the suit is to enforce a substantive right existing under the Constitution or laws of the United States.[21]

Rule 17(c)[22] provides that if an infant or incompetent person has a representative, such as a general guardian, the representative may sue or defend in behalf of his ward. If there is no such representative, suit may be brought by the next friend or a guardian ad litem. The court is authorized to appoint a guardian ad litem or otherwise take steps to protect an infant or incompetent not represented in an action.[23] There is some lack of clarity with regard to the relation between 17(b) and 17(c). One line of cases holds that the language of the first sentence of Rule 17(c), authorizing a guardian or other representative to sue on behalf of an infant or incompetent, is subject to Rule 17(b), which makes the capacity of a representative dependent on the law of the state where the district court is held.[24] Another line of cases permits appointment of a guardian ad litem even though the state law does not recognize such a representative.[25] It is possible to reconcile these two lines of authority by holding that state law controls where the ward already has a repre-

17. Rule 17(b); Donnelly v. Parker, C.A.D.C.1973, 486 F.2d 402; 6A Wright, Miller & Kane, Civil 2d § 1560.

18. Rule 17(b); 6A Wright, Miller & Kane, Civil 2d §§ 1561–1563.

But see Woods v. Interstate Realty Co., 1949, 69 S.Ct. 1235, 337 U.S. 535, 93 L.Ed. 1524; McCollum Aviation, Inc. v. Cim Associates, Inc., D.C.Fla.1977, 438 F.Supp. 245. The cases just cited are criticized in Little, Out of Woods and into the Rules: The Relationship Between State Foreign Corporation Door–Closing Statutes and Federal Rule of Civil Procedure 17(b), 1986, 72 Va. L.Rev. 676.

19. Rule 17(b); 6A Wright, Miller & Kane, Civil 2d § 1565.

20. Rule 17(b); In re Vento Development Corp., C.A.1st, 1977, 560 F.2d 2; 6A Wright, Miller & Kane, Civil 2d § 1564.

21. Rule 17(b)(1). This is a generalization of the doctrine first announced in United Mine Workers of America v. Coronado

Coal Co., 1922, 42 S.Ct. 570, 259 U.S. 344, 66 L.Ed. 975, 27 A.L.R. 762.

22. 6A Wright, Miller & Kane, Civil 2d §§ 1570–1572.

23. See Chrissy F. v. Mississippi Dept. of Public Welfare, C.A.5th, 1989, 883 F.2d 25; Noe v. True, C.A.6th, 1974, 507 F.2d 9.

24. Chrissy F. v. Mississippi Dept.of Public Welfare, C.A.5th, 1989, 883 F.2d 25; Brimhall v. Simmons, C.A.6th, 1964, 338 F.2d 702, noted 1965, 67 W.Va.L.Rev. 249; Vroon v. Templin, C.A.4th, 1960, 278 F.2d 345; Greenstreet v. Simmons, D.C.Ill.1972, 54 F.R.D. 554; Southern Ohio Sav. Bank & Trust Co. v. Guaranty Trust Co. of New York, D.C.N.Y.1939, 27 F.Supp. 485.

25. Montgomery Ward & Co. v. Callahan, C.C.A.10th, 1942, 127 F.2d 32; Constantine v. Southwestern Louisiana Institute, D.C.La.1954, 120 F.Supp. 417.

sentative appointed and qualified by a state court, but that if the ward has no such representative, the federal court may appoint one for him regardless of state law.[26]

This is not the only respect in which the effect of state law on Rule 17(b) and (c) is unclear. The rule itself looks to state law, but looks variously, in Rule 17(b), to the domicile, the state in which a corporation was organized, and the forum. To what extent are the various provisions stated in the rule qualified if the law of the forum would require a contrary result than the rule provides? Here there is a conflict of view,[27] and in light of Hanna v. Plumer[28] it would seem to turn on whether "capacity" in Rule 17(b) refers "only to the range of rules concerned with the administration of the judicial process or whether all limitations of the right to bring suit were covered."[29]

Once the requirements of Rule 17 have been complied with, and it has been decided that a particular individual or entity is a party in interest with capacity to sue or be sued, it is necessary to go one more step and decide whether the person has such a strong interest in the litigation that his or her joinder ought to be compelled. Compulsory joinder of parties is an exception to the usual practice that leaves a plaintiff free to decide who shall be parties to its lawsuit. Plaintiff cannot be permitted an unfettered choice in this respect, because there may be others, not named by plaintiff, so closely connected with the controversy that it would be desirable to have them as parties. "There are three classes of interests which may be served by requiring the presence of additional parties in an action: (1) the interests of the present defendant; (2) the interests of potential but absent plaintiffs and defendants; (3) the social interest in the orderly, expeditious administration of justice."[30] In some cases the connection of the absentees with

---

26. Bengtson v. Travelers Indem. Co., D.C.La.1955, 132 F.Supp. 512, affirmed C.A.5th, 1956, 231 F.2d 263. See also M.S. v. Wermers, C.A.8th, 1977, 557 F.2d 170, 174 n. 4; Donnelly v. Parker, C.A.D.C.1973, 486 F.2d 402, 406; 6A Wright, Miller & Kane, Civil 2d § 1571.

27. Compare Urbano v. News Syndicate Co., C.A.2d, 1966, 358 F.2d 145, certiorari denied 87 S.Ct. 68, 385 U.S. 831, 17 L.Ed.2d 66, with McCollum Aviation, Inc. v. Cim Associates, Inc., D.C.Fla.1977, 438 F.Supp. 245.

See generally the article by Professor Kennedy cited note 16 above.

28. 1965, 85 S.Ct. 1136, 380 U.S. 460, 14 L.Ed.2d 8. See § 59 above.

29. R.C., 1969, 82 Harv.L.Rev. 708, 710–711. The notewriter thinks that "capacity" should be read in the narrower of these two senses, and thus that Rule 17(b) does not bar application of state "door-closing" statutes.

A similar thought about "door-closing" statutes is expressed in 6A Wright, Miller & Kane, Civil 2d § 1569, but with the caveat that the state rule may still yield to the federal if the state interest is significantly outweighed by the federal interest, as in: Szantay v. Beech Aircraft Corp., C.A.4th, 1965, 349 F.2d 60, noted 1965, 17 S.C.L.Rev. 631, 1966, 51 Cornell L.Q. 560; Tolson v. Hodge, C.A.4th, 1969, 411 F.2d 123; and Avondale Shipyards, Inc. v. Propulsion Systems, Inc., D.C.La.1971, 53 F.R.D. 341, noted 1972, 18 Wayne L.Rev. 1619.

30. Reed, Compulsory Joinder of Parties in Civil Actions, 1957, 55 Mich.L.Rev. 327, 330.

See also McCoid, A Single Package for Multiparty Disputes, 1976, 28 Stan.L.Rev. 707, arguing that broadened mandatory joinder is superior to expanded collateral estoppel and to compulsory intervention as a means of dealing with the problem of multiple disputes.

the controversy will be so compelling that the three interests listed will dictate that the suit should not proceed without the absentees. In other cases the connection will be less close, and though it would be desirable to have them as parties, the action should proceed without them if it is impossible to obtain jurisdiction over them or if their joinder would destroy diversity and thus deprive the court of subject matter jurisdiction. The label "indispensable" is used if the connection is so close that the action should be dismissed unless the party is joined. The label "necessary" is used if the party is one who ought to be joined if this is possible. The label "proper" is used if the party is one who can be joined or not at plaintiff's option. That there should be such a tripartite classification of parties makes sense. Judicial attempts to define when one label or another is appropriate do not.

The leading case is Shields v. Barrow,[31] cited hundred of times and vastly influential in the states as well as in federal courts. Barrow, a citizen of Louisiana, sold a plantation to Shields, also a citizen of Louisiana, and was given notes for the purchase price. The notes were endorsed by six persons, four from Louisiana and two from Mississippi. After about half the price had been paid, Shields defaulted. Later a compromise was worked out between Barrow on the one hand and Shields and the endorsers on the other. The plantation was returned to Barrow, who was allowed to keep the amount already paid, and the endorsers gave new notes for a fraction of the unpaid balance. Shortly thereafter Barrow became dissatisfied with the agreement and brought suit in federal court in Louisiana against the two Mississippi parties to rescind it. The Supreme Court held that the rights of the parties to the compromise agreement were "inseparable," and that the action could not proceed without joinder of all the parties to the agreement. Since the joinder of the Louisiana parties would defeat diversity, the result was to prevent suit in federal court, and it is quite possible that Barrow's attempt to rescind was defeated altogether, since it might have been difficult for any state court to obtain jurisdiction of all the parties.

Both the reasoning and the result in Shields v. Barrow have been criticized. Whether the result there was right or wrong is of little importance. The facts in Shields v. Barrow have been virtually forgotten. What has been remembered, and much quoted, is the language of the Court defining the classes of parties. "Indispensable" parties were defined as "persons who not only have an interest in the controversy, but an interest of such a nature that a final decree cannot be made without either affecting that interest, or leaving the controversy in such a condition that its final termination may be wholly inconsistent with equity and good conscience," while "necessary" parties were "persons having an interest in the controversy, and who ought to be made parties, in order that the court may act on that rule which requires it to decide on, and finally determine the entire controversy, and do complete justice,

31. 1854, 17 How. 130, 15 L.Ed. 158.

by adjusting all the rights involved in it * * * [but whose] interests are separable from those of the parties before the court, so that the court can proceed to a decree, and do complete and final justice, without affecting other persons not before the court." [32]

The sonorous generalities of Shields v. Barrow led, perhaps inevitably, to a jurisprudence of labels. Labels are not bad things in the law if they are understood for what they are, a shorthand way of expressing the result of a more complicated reasoning process. Labels become treacherous and misleading if they are applied as a substitute for reasoning. It is perfectly appropriate to say that "this absentee has such a strong interest in this case that it would be unjust to let it go to decision in his absence. Therefore we will refer to him as 'indispensable.' " It is not appropriate to say, as many courts seemed to do, that "this person is 'indispensable.' Therefore we will not let the case go to decision in his absence." The latter reasoning—or nonreasoning— suggests that absent parties wear labels indicating their relation to a controversy [33] and obscures the pragmatic examination of all the circumstances that is required in the light of the very particular facts of a particular case. This jurisprudence of labels reached its high point in a decision suggesting that the category of "indispensable" parties formed such a rigid class that it had become a matter of "substantive" law and could not be altered through the process of judicial rulemaking.[34]

Rule 19, as it stood from 1938 to 1966, did little to improve this situation. "Persons having a joint interest" were required to be joined, but the action could proceed in their absence if they were "not indispensable." Thus, the conceptual test of a "joint interest" was made the dividing line between permissive joinder and compulsory joinder, while once that line had been crossed, and it had been found that the party must be joined if possible, the rule offered no guidance on whether a particular party with a "joint interest" was "indispensable" or merely "necessary." In both respects the rule was unsatisfactory, not because it necessarily led to bad results but because it did not point to the factors properly relevant to decision.[35]

The "joint interest" test was not a workable division between compulsory joinder and permissive joinder. One would hardly expect that, under such a test, it would uniformly be held that joint tortfeasors

---

32. 17 How. at 139.

33. See Wright, Recent Changes in the Federal Rules of Procedure, 1966, 42 F.R.D. 552, 561.

34. Provident Tradesmens Bank and Trust Co. v. Lumbermens Mut. Cas. Co., C.A.3d, 1966, 365 F.2d 802. The decision was heavily criticized. Kaplan, Continuing Work of the Civil Committee: 1966 Amendments of the Federal Rules of Civil Procedure, 1967, 81 Harv.L.Rev. 356, 371–375; Comment, The Mechanics of New Rule 19

and the Challenges to Its Validity, 1967, 12 St. Louis U.L.J. 119; Note, Rule 19 and Indispensable Parties, 1967, 65 Mich.L.Rev. 968. As will be seen, the Supreme Court reversed this decision.

35. Provident Tradesmens Bank & Trust Co. v. Patterson, 1968, 88 S.Ct. 733, 741 n. 12, 390 U.S. 102, 116 n. 12, 19 L.Ed.2d 936; Kaplan, Continuing Work of the Civil Committee: 1966 Amendments of the Federal Rules of Civil Procedure, 1967, 81 Harv.L.Rev. 356, 366–367.

were merely "proper" parties and their joinder was entirely optional,[36] or that joint obligees would be thought to be "indispensable"[37] while joint obligors were quite possibly only "proper" parties.[38] The ancient concept of "joint interest" simply made no sense when applied to questions such as whether a majority of a board of directors must be parties to a suit to compel declaration of a dividend,[39] or whether, in an action against a local federal officer, a superior in Washington must be joined.[40]

The rule was also no help at all in deciding whether an absentee, who ought to be joined if possible, had such a relation to the controversy that he should be regarded as "indispensable" and the action dismissed if he could not be joined. Behind the lofty language of Shields v. Barrow, and the attempts to reformulate the test there announced in terms of seeming precision,[41] what was really involved was the desire of the courts, on the one hand, to avoid a multiplicity of suits and to give

---

36. Ward v. Deavers, C.A.D.C.1953, 203 F.2d 72, 76; Union Paving Co. v. Downer Corp., C.A.9th, 1960, 276 F.2d 468; 7 Wright, Miller & Kane, Civil 2d § 1623.

The same result is reached under the amended rule. Temple v. Synthes Corp., 1990, 111 S.Ct. 315, 498 U.S. 5, 112 L.Ed.2d 263.

37. Jenkins v. Reneau, C.A.6th, 1983, 697 F.2d 160; and cases cited 7 Wright, Miller & Kane, Civil 2d § 1613 n. 12. But see Reed, Compulsory Joinder of Parties in Civil Actions, 1957, 55 Mich.L.Rev. 327, 367–374; James, Necessary and Indispensable Parties, 1963, 18 U.Miami L.Rev. 68, 83–85.

See note 38 below.

38. Park v. Didden, C.A.D.C.1982, 695 F.2d 626; Greenleaf v. Safeway Trails, C.C.A.2d, 1944, 140 F.2d 889, 892 (concurring opinion). That they were not "indispensable" was held in Camp v. Gress, 1919, 39 S.Ct. 478, 250 U.S. 308, 63 L.Ed. 997.

Under the 1966 amendment the result, with regard both to joint obligors and joint obligees, depends on a practical appraisal of the substantiality of the interest of the absentee and on other pragmatic factors rather than on the conceptual nature of the interest. See 7 Wright, Miller & Kane, Civil 2d § 1613; Bank of America Nat. Trust & Savings Assn. v. Hotel Rittenhouse Associates, C.A.3d, 1988, 844 F.2d 1050, 1053–1055; Harrell & Sumner Contracting Co. v. Peabody Petersen Co., D.C.Fla.1976, 415 F.Supp. 573, 575, affirmed C.A.5th, 1977, 546 F.2d 1227.

39. Compare Kroese v. General Steel Castings Corp., C.A.3d, 1950, 179 F.2d 760, certiorari denied 70 S.Ct. 1026, 339 U.S. 983, 94 L.Ed. 1386, and Doherty v. Mutual Warehouse Co., C.A.5th, 1957, 245 F.2d

609, with Schuckman v. Rubenstein, C.A.6th, 1947, 164 F.2d 952. See 7 Wright, Miller & Kane, Civil 2d § 1615, pp. 235–236.

Joinder of directors not amendable to process was held not required, under the 1966 amendment, in Levin v. Mississippi River Corp., D.C.N.Y.1968, 289 F.Supp. 353, 360–362.

40. See Williams v. Fanning, 1947, 68 S.Ct. 188, 332 U.S. 490, 92 L.Ed. 95. Whether the superior must be joined produced a multitude of irreconcilable decisions. See Byse, Proposed Reforms in Federal "Nonstatutory" Judicial Review: Sovereign Immunity, Indispensable Parties, Mandamus, 1962, 75 Harv.L.Rev. 1479, 1493–1499. A 1962 statute allowing a broad choice of venue and extraterritorial service of process has diminished the importance of the problem. 28 U.S.C.A. § 1391(e), added by Act of Oct. 5, 1962, Pub.L. 87–748. So too has the Act of Oct. 21, 1976, Pub.L. 94–574, amending 5 U.S.C.A. §§ 702, 703, providing a right of review of federal official action in suits seeking relief other than money damages, and further providing that those suits cannot be dismissed on the ground that the United States is an indispensable party and immune from suit.

To the extent that the problem is still of significance after passage of the 1962 statute, it must now be resolved by the balancing process called for by amended Rule 19. Compare, e.g., Washington v. Cameron, C.A.D.C.1969, 411 F.2d 705, with Chicago Teachers Union v. Johnson, C.A.7th, 1980, 639 F.2d 353. See generally 7 Wright, Miller & Kane, Civil 2d § 1622.

41. See, e.g., Washington v. U.S., C.C.A.9th, 1936, 87 F.2d 421, 427–428; Montfort v. Korte, C.C.A.7th, 1939, 100 F.2d 615, 617.

parties their day in court before making decisions that would affect their interests, and, on the other hand, the desire to make some judgment, if at all possible, rather than leaving the parties without a remedy because, if the absentees could be ordered in, a better decision might be reached.[42]

Because of the need to reconcile these conflicting interests, the courts, though they rarely articulated it, commonly strained hard to classify a missing party was not "indispensable" if the alternative was to dismiss the action and perhaps preclude the present parties from any effective relief.[43]   Only an occasional statement in the cases revealed the true nature of the problem.   The Supreme Court said, for example, that "there is no prescribed formula for determining in every case whether a person is an indispensable party," [44] and again that "indispensability of parties is determined on practical considerations." [45]   Other courts reached sound results by anomalous reasoning, as where a party was expressly characterized as "indispensable" but the court nevertheless proceeded to judgment in his absence because justice so required.[46]

Modern scholarship exposed the inadequacies of Rule 19, and of the traditional approach to compulsory joinder of parties,[47] and the rule was extensively amended in 1966 to reflect this thinking.   The amended rule was held valid, and given a discriminating and sympathetic reading, in Provident Tradesmens Bank & Trust Co. v. Patterson.[48]   The amended rule, as the Supreme Court said, "was not intended as a change in principles." [49]   Instead it sought to "eliminate the confusion which has long surrounded the old Rule 19 by eliminating the categories and the ritual inherited from Shields v. Barrow" [50] and substituting instead

---

42.   Comment, The Litigant and the Absentee in Federal Multiparty Practice, 1968, 116 U.Pa.L.Rev. 531, 532.

43.   An excellent example is Kroese v. General Steel Castings Corp., C.A.3d, 1950, 179 F.2d 760, certiorari denied 70 S.Ct. 1026, 339 U.S. 983, 94 L.Ed. 1386, where a holding that a majority of the directors were indispensable in an action to compel declaration of a dividend would have barred any relief in any forum.   See also Standard Oil Co. of Texas v. Marshall, C.A.5th, 1959, 265 F.2d 46, 56, certiorari denied 80 S.Ct. 259, 361 U.S. 915, 4 L.Ed.2d 185; New England Mut. Life Ins. Co. v. Brandenburg, D.C.N.Y.1948, 8 F.R.D. 151.

44.   Niles–Bement–Pond Co. v. Iron Moulders' Union Local No. 68, 1920, 41 S.Ct. 39, 41, 254 U.S. 77, 80, 65 L.Ed. 145.

45.   Shaugnessy v. Pedreiro, 1955, 75 S.Ct. 591, 595, 349 U.S. 48, 54, 99 L.Ed. 868.

See also Roos v. Texas Co., C.C.A.2d, 1927, 23 F.2d 171, 172, certiorari denied 48 S.Ct. 434, 277 U.S. 587, 72 L.Ed. 1001.

46.   Parker Rust–Proof Co. v. Western Union Tel. Co., C.C.A.2d, 1939, 105 F.2d 976, certiorari denied 60 S.Ct. 128, 308 U.S.

597, 84 L.Ed. 500; Benger Laboratories, Ltd. v. R.K. Laros Co., Inc., D.C.Pa.1959, 24 F.R.D. 450.

47.   Reed, Compulsory Joinder of Parties in Civil Actions, 1957, 55 Mich.L.Rev. 327, 483; Hazard, Indispensable Party: The Historical Origin of a Procedural Phantom, 1961, 61 Col.L.Rev. 1254.   See also Developments in the Law—Multiparty Litigation in the Federal Courts, 1958, 71 Harv.L.Rev. 874, 879–889; Note, Indispensable Parties in the Federal Courts, 1952, 65 Harv.L.Rev. 1050.

48.   1968, 88 S.Ct. 733, 390 U.S. 102, 19 L.Ed.2d 936.   See also the decision on remand C.A.3d, 1969, 411 F.2d 88.

49.   88 S.Ct. at 741 n. 12, 390 U.S. at 116 n. 12.

50.   Rippey v. Denver U.S. Nat. Bank, D.C.Colo.1966, 260 F.Supp. 704, 708.   See also Haas v. Jefferson Nat. Bank of Miami Beach, C.A.5th, 1971, 442 F.2d 394, 396–397.

"stated pragmatic considerations." [51]

Rule 19(a) defines the class of persons who are needed for just adjudication. A person falls into this class if in his absence complete relief cannot be accorded to the existing parties, or if he has some interest in the controversy and is so situated that disposition of the action in his absence might as a practical matter impair his ability to protect that interest, or if judgment in his absence would expose any of the existing parties to a substantial risk of double obligation by reason of his claimed interest. If an absentee meets this test, and if he is subject to process and his joinder will not destroy diversity, the court must require that he be joined. This class of persons needed for a just adjudication is roughly equivalent to those who would in the past have been classified as either "indispensable" or "necessary," but the old labels are not used, and old decisions applying the labels are not controlling.[52]

If the absentee is needed for just adjudication and is not subject to process or his joinder would destroy diversity, Rule 19(b) states the factors to be considered in deciding whether to proceed in his absence or to dismiss the action. The ultimate question is whether "equity and good conscience" permit the action to proceed, but in deciding this the court is required to weigh whether judgment in the absence of the person would prejudice him or those already parties, whether protective provisions in the decree might lessen or void this prejudice, whether a judgment rendered in the person's absence will be adequate, and whether the plaintiff will have a satisfactory remedy if the action is dismissed.

The decision by the Supreme Court in the Provident Tradesmens case not only upheld the validity of the amended rule, against a claim that it exceeded the rulemaking power by altering the "substantive" rights of "indispensable" parties, but also indicated how the new rule is to work. A collision between a truck and a borrowed car led to several deaths and serious injuries. The estate of one of the persons killed obtained a $50,000 judgment against the estate of the driver of the car, but the driver's estate was penniless and the judgment had not been paid. The owner of the car had $100,000 liability insurance. The estate of the person killed then brought an action for a declaratory judgment that the driver's use of the car had been with permission of the owner, and thus that the owner's insurance covered the $50,000 judgment. The defendants in the declaratory-judgment action were the insurance company and the estate of the driver. The owner was not a party and his presence would have defeated diversity if he had been a party. A jury found that the use of the car had been with the owner's permission and a declaratory judgment was entered that the policy coverage extended to the $50,000 judgment.

---

51. 88 S.Ct. at 736, 390 U.S. at 107. See also Smith v. State Farm Fire & Cas. Co., C.A.5th, 1980, 633 F.2d 401, 405; Lewis, Mandatory Joinder of Parties in Civil Proceedings: The Case for Analytical Pragmatism, 1974, 26 U.Fla.L.Rev. 381.

52. See generally 7 Wright, Miller & Kane, Civil 2d § 1604.

Though the issue had not been raised by the parties in the trial court or by the appellant on appeal, the court of appeals held that the owner was an "indispensable" party and that the action must be dismissed because he had not been joined.[53] The Supreme Court reversed. It had no trouble agreeing that the owner was a person needed for a just adjudication who should be "joined if feasible," since at the time the case went to trial there was at least a possibility that a judgment might impede his ability to protect his interest or lead to later relitigation by him. But from an appellate perspective, after a judgment following extensive litigation in which the owner's absence was not raised, it thought that the criteria of Rule 19(b) clearly required that the owner's absence be held not fatal to that judgment.

Although the Court indicated that the matter might have been different if the nonjoinder of the owner had been raised at the outset, it concluded that the only one of the factors mentioned in Rule 19(b) that might argue in favor of requiring dismissal at the appellate level because of the nonjoinder was the possibility of prejudice to the owner. The argument was that a judgment that the policy coverage protected the estate of the driver would deplete the policy proceeds available if, in later litigation by others killed or injured in the accident, the owner of the car should have a judgment entered against him on a theory of vicarious liability. The Court thought that "supposed threat neither large nor unavoidable."[54] The chance that the owner might be found vicariously liable was apparently slim, he would still be free to relitigate the issue whether the driver had had his permission and thus whether the insurance proceeds should not be credited against his personal liability, and in any event the judgment could be shaped to give him full protection. Thus, "there was no reason then to throw away a valid judgment just because it did not theoretically settle the whole controversy."[55]

As then-Judge Clarence Thomas put it: "When a party moves to join a nonparty resisting joinder, the district court must answer three questions: Should the absentee be joined? If the absentee should be joined, can the absentee be joined? If the absentee cannot be joined, should the lawsuit proceed without her nonetheless?"[56]

Other cases asked those questions and have made a practical analysis similar to that in the Provident Tradesmens case in allowing suit to proceed despite the absence of a party needed for a just adjudication.[57]

---

53. See note 34 above. See 7 Wright, Miller & Kane, Civil 2d § 1609.

54. 88 S.Ct. at 740, 390 U.S. at 115.

55. 88 S.Ct. at 741, 390 U.S. at 116. On remand the judgment was shaped to protect the owner. C.A.3d, 1969, 411 F.2d 88, 98–99.

56. Western Md. Ry. Co. v. Harbor Ins. Co., C.A.D.C.1990, 910 F.2d 960, 961.

57. E.g., Jaser v. New York Property Ins. Underwriting Assn., C.A.2d, 1987, 815 F.2d 240; Pasco Intl. (London) Ltd. v. Stenograph Corp., C.A.7th, 1980, 637 F.2d 496; U.S. v. Allegheny–Ludlum Indus., Inc., C.A.5th, 1975, 517 F.2d 826; Virginia Elec. & Power Co. v. Westinghouse Elec. Corp., C.A.4th, 1973, 485 F.2d 78, certiorari denied 94 S.Ct. 1450, 415 U.S. 935, 39 L.Ed.2d 493; Bethell v. Peace, C.A.5th, 1971, 441 F.2d 495; Staten Island Rapid Transit Ry. Co. v. S.T.G. Constr. Co., C.A.2d, 1970, 421 F.2d 53, certiorari denied

There are, of course, cases in which a contrary result has been reached, particularly where there is a state forum in which joinder of all parties is possible,[58] but these cases too show the kind of pragmatic approach Rule 19 was intended to produce. If the action is dismissed for want of the absentee, he may then be referred to as "indispensable," but it is clear that the old label is now being used in a wholly conclusory sense.[59]

The Provident Tradesmens case also laid to rest one other matter that had been subject to dispute. It said that "in a diversity case the question of joinder is one of federal law. * * * To be sure, state-law questions may arise in determining what interest the outsider actually has, * * * but the ultimate question whether, given those state-defined interests, a federal court may proceed without the outsider is a federal matter."[60] This is in accord with the better earlier decisions, and is a sound resolution of the question. It seems not inconsistent with that rule to say that if, as a matter of substantive law, a state does not recognize that a plaintiff has a particular right of action unless he joins with him certain others, then the federal court in a diversity action is precluded from giving a plaintiff who fails to join those others an opportunity to proceed as though alone he had the substantive right.[61]

§ 71. Joinder of Parties [1]

The general principles about compulsory joinder of parties have been sufficiently discussed in the preceding section. As there suggested, if an absent party is found to be needed for a just adjudication, the court will order his joinder if feasible. If his joinder is not feasible, there are some circumstances in which the action cannot proceed in his absence, and the absentee is regarded as "indispensable."

If the absentee needed for just adjudication is a defendant, the plaintiff may join him as plaintiff would any other defendant. If a person who is required to join as a party plaintiff refuses to do so, the

---

90 S.Ct. 1871, 398 U.S. 951, 26 L.Ed.2d 291; Bennie v. Pastor, C.A.10th, 1968, 393 F.2d 1.

58. E.g., Pulitzer–Polster v. Pulitzer, C.A.5th, 1986, 784 F.2d 1305; Takeda v. Northwestern Nat. Life Ins. Co., C.A.9th, 1985, 765 F.2d 815; Kamhi v. Cohen, C.A.2d, 1975, 512 F.2d 1051; Glenny v. American Metal Climax, Inc., C.A.10th, 1974, 494 F.2d 651; Haas v. Jefferson Nat. Bank of Miami Beach, C.A.5th, 1971, 442 F.2d 394; Evergreen Park Nursing Home, Inc. v. American Equitable Assur. Co., C.A.7th, 1969, 417 F.2d 1113.

The application of the four factors of Rule 19(b) is discussed in 7 Wright, Miller & Kane, Civil 2d § 1608.

On the scope of appellate review of dismissals under Rule 19(b), see Walsh v. Centeio, C.A.9th, 1982, 692 F.2d 1239.

59. 88 S.Ct. at 742 n. 15, 390 U.S. at 118 n. 15.

60. 88 S.Ct. at 746 n. 22, 390 U.S. at 125 n. 22. There is a particularly careful discussion of this problem by Judge John Minor Wisdom in Kuchenig v. California Co., C.A.5th, 1965, 350 F.2d 551, certiorari denied 86 S.Ct. 561, 382 U.S. 985, 15 L.Ed.2d 473. See 7 Wright, Miller & Kane, Civil 2d § 1603.

61. Stevens v. Loomis, D.C.Mass.1963, 223 F.Supp. 534, 536, affirmed C.A.1st, 1964, 334 F.2d 775. But see Note, Rule 19 and Indispensable Parties, 1967, 65 Mich. L.Rev. 968, 980.

See generally Yonofsky v. Wernick, D.C.N.Y.1973, 362 F.Supp. 1005, 1021.

§ 71

1. 7 Wright, Miller & Kane, Civil 2d §§ 1651–1660.

situation is more difficult. In one particular circumstance, where the exclusive licensee of a patent or copyright wishes to sue for infringement but the patent or copyright owner refuses to join as a plaintiff, the licensee may name the owner as an "involuntary plaintiff." [2] Though this procedure is recognized in general terms in Rule 19(a), the courts have shown no tendency to permit broader use of the involuntary-plaintiff device beyond the exclusive-licensee situation in which it was developed. Thus, it is held that the involuntary-plaintiff procedure may be invoked only when the party sought to be joined has a duty to allow plaintiff to use his name in the action. [3] In other situations where one who should be a plaintiff refuses to join as such, the remedy, also recognized by Rule 19(a), is for plaintiff to name the person as a defendant and serve process upon the person. [4] Presumably such a party will then be realigned as a plaintiff in determining whether diversity exists. [5]

The cases sometimes speak, and even act, as if the failure to join a party who may be regarded as "indispensable" is a "jurisdictional" defect. [6] This heresy has been rejected over and over again by authoritative cases. [7] The court has no jurisdiction of the absentee, and it cannot enter a judgment that will be legally binding on him, but it does have jurisdiction of the existing parties and has the power to make a judgment affecting their interests. It is for discretionary reasons, not for any want of jurisdiction, that the court may decline to proceed without the absentee. [8]

Rule 20 deals with permissive joinder of parties. If a party has some relation to the action, but it is not so close as to make him a person needed for just adjudication within Rule 19(a), he is a "proper" party, and the plaintiff has an option whether to join him if the tests of Rule 20

---

2. Independent Wireless Tel. Co. v. Radio Corp. of America, 1926, 46 S.Ct. 166, 269 U.S. 459, 70 L.Ed. 357; Ferrara v. Rodale Press, Inc., D.C.Pa.1972, 54 F.R.D. 3.

The requirements for joining an involuntary plaintiff were held not to have been met in Followay Productions, Inc. v. Maurer, C.A.9th, 1979, 603 F.2d 72.

3. Caprio v. Wilson, C.A.9th, 1975, 513 F.2d 837; Eikel v. States Marine Lines, Inc., C.A.5th, 1973, 473 F.2d 959.

See generally 7 Wright, Miller & Kane, Civil 2d § 1606.

4. International Rediscount Corp. v. Hartford Acc. & Indem. Co., D.C.Del.1977, 425 F.Supp. 669, 674; Dental Precision Shoulder v. L.D. Caulk Co., D.C.N.Y.1947, 7 F.R.D. 203; Hoffman v. Santly–Joy, Inc., D.C.N.Y.1943, 51 F.Supp. 778.

5. Eikel v. States Marine Lines, Inc., C.A.5th, 1973, 473 F.2d 959. See 7 Wright, Miller & Kane, Civil 2d § 1605, and § 30 above.

6. See, e.g., Agrashell, Inc. v. Hammons Products Co., C.A.8th, 1965, 352 F.2d 443, 447; Samuel Goldwyn, Inc. v. United Artists Corp., C.C.A.3d, 1940, 113 F.2d 703, 707; Coughlin v. Ryder, D.C.Pa.1966, 260 F.Supp. 256, 257–258.

7. Elmendorf v. Taylor, 1825, 10 Wheat. 152, 166–168, 6 L.Ed. 289; Mallow v. Hinde, 1827, 12 Wheat. 193, 198, 6 L.Ed. 599; Provident Tradesmens Bank & Trust Co. v. Patterson, 1968, 88 S.Ct. 733, 744, 390 U.S. 102, 122, 19 L.Ed.2d 936.

8. Reed, Compulsory Joinder of Parties in Civil Actions, 1957, 55 Mich.L.Rev. 327, 332–334; Kaplan, Continuing Work of the Civil Committee: 1966 Amendments of the Federal Rules of Civil Procedure, 1967, 81 Harv.L.Rev. 356, 364; Lewis, Mandatory Joinder of Parties in Civil Proceedings: The Case for Analytical Pragmatism, 1974, 26 U.Fla.L.Rev. 381, 386; 7 Wright, Miller & Kane, Civil 2d § 1611.

are met. The rule well exemplifies the modern philosophy of joinder. The provisions for joinder are very broad, but the court is then given discretion to order separate trials or to make such other orders as will prevent delay or prejudice.[9] In this way the scope of a civil action is made a question for the discretion of the judge, to be decided on practical considerations in a particular case, rather than a question governed by conceptual tests, as was true under some of the codes and at common law.

Rule 20(a) applies in similar terms to joinder of plaintiffs and joinder of defendants. It creates two tests for joinder. (1) There must be some question of law or fact common to all parties which will arise in the action. (2) There must be some right to relief asserted on behalf of each of the plaintiffs, and against each of the defendants, relating to, or arising out of, a single transaction or occurrence or series of transactions or occurrences. These tests are cumulative and both of them must be satisfied to permit joinder.[10]

It has been said that the phrase "questions of law" has reference to those arising upon the facts of the particular case, and not general principles of law.[11] The argument for such an interpretation is that otherwise a creditor, such as a bank, could bring a single action against all debtors whose obligations arose out of promissory notes, upon the theory that a common question of law was involved. This argument overlooks the fact that such joinder would not be permitted, even though it were said that a common question of law was presented, unless the notes involved a single transaction or series of transactions. Of course it will not be enough to permit joinder that there is some inconsequential or theoretical issue common to all the plaintiffs. As said by the New York Court of Appeals, construing a statute on which Rule 20 was based, "such common questions must be of substantial importance as compared with all of the issues, and * * * the question of the comparative weight and importance of common and separate issues involved in each cause of action is quite largely a matter of judgment." [12] In that case 193 persons who had been individually induced, by means of a fraudulent prospectus, to invest their money in a sham corporation were permitted to join in one action for fraud against the promoters. The common question whether the prospectus was fraudulent was enough to justify joinder,

9. Rules 20(b), 42(b). See United Mine Workers of America v. Gibbs, 1966, 86 S.Ct. 1130, 1138, 383 U.S. 715, 724, 16 L.Ed.2d 218; 7 Wright, Miller & Kane, Civil 2d § 1660; 9 Wright & Miller, Civil §§ 2387–2392.

10. Magnavox Co. v. APF Electronics, Inc., D.C.Ill.1980, 496 F.Supp. 29, 34; King v. Pepsi Cola Metropolitan Bottling Co., D.C.Pa.1979, 86 F.R.D. 4, 5. But see Note, Is Federal Rule 20(a) Too Restrictive?, 1965, 18 Okla.L.Rev. 195.

Note, however, that if there is a common question of law or fact, the cases may be consolidated for trial, under Rule 42(a), even though the "same transaction or occurrence" test is not met. Hanes Dye & Finishing Co. v. Caisson Corp., D.C.N.C. 1970, 309 F.Supp. 237; 9 Wright & Miller, Civil § 2382.

11. Federal Housing Admr. v. Christianson, D.C.Conn.1939, 26 F.Supp. 419; Smith v. North American Rockwell Corp.—Tulsa Div., D.C.Okl.1970, 50 F.R.D. 515, 524.

12. Akely v. Kinnicutt, 1924, 144 N.E. 682, 684, 238 N.Y. 466, 473. See also Music Merchants, Inc. v. Capitol Records, Inc., D.C.N.Y.1957, 20 F.R.D. 462.

even though there were separate issues of whether each plaintiff saw the prospectus and relied on it to plaintiff's detriment. By the same token permissive joinder of plaintiffs is quite common in automobile-collision cases, where there is a common question of fact and law about defendant's negligence, even though there are also separate questions about damages and contributory negligence.[13] And in a suit against an employer for discrimination, the discriminatory character of defendant's conduct is common to all of the plaintiffs, even though particular plaintiffs may have suffered different effects from it.[14]

There is very little discussion in the cases about what constitutes the same transaction or occurrence or series of transactions or occurrences. One court has suggested that there can be no hard and fast rule and that the approach must be generally whether there are enough factual concurrences that it would be fair to the parties to litigate the matters at one time, having in mind also the convenience of the court.[15] This seems a sensible approach, particularly in so far as it is reminiscent of the "logical relationship" test that the case law has developed as the meaning of "transaction or occurrence" in the compulsory-counterclaim rule.[16] It is worth observing, however, that the convenience of the parties and the court can be fully protected, though joinder is allowed, by separate trials, pursuant to Rules 20(b) and 42(b), and thus it seems practically desirable to give the broadest possible reading to the permissive language of Rule 20(a).[17]

A state court, construing a statute identical to Rule 20(a), has tried to differentiate between a "transaction" and an "occurrence." Certain property was allegedly destroyed by an explosion. Plaintiffs sought to join a claim against the persons who set off the dynamite causing the explosion with a claim against insurance companies that had issued explosion policies covering the property. There was a question of fact, admittedly common to all defendants, on whether the damage had been done by an explosion or by some other cause. The court held nevertheless that joinder was not proper. It reasoned that the dynamiting was an "occurrence," the insurance was a "transaction," and thus that the

---

13. E.g., Franklin v. Shelton, C.A.10th, 1957, 250 F.2d 92, certiorari denied 78 S.Ct. 544, 355 U.S. 959, 2 L.Ed.2d 533; 7 Wright, Miller & Kane, Civil 2d § 1656; James, Hazard & Leubsdorf, Civil Procedure, 4th ed. 1992, § 9.7.

14. Mosley v. General Motors Corp., C.A.8th, 1974, 497 F.2d 1330; Mack v. J.C. Penney Co., D.C.Ga.1985, 108 F.R.D. 30.

15. Eastern Fireproofing Co. v. U.S. Gypsum Co., D.C.Mass.1958, 160 F.Supp. 580, 581. See also Mosley v. General Motors Corp., C.A.8th, 1974, 497 F.2d 1330, 1333; McLernon v. Source Intl., Inc., D.C.Wis.1988, 701 F.Supp. 1422, 1425.. Under a state statute similar to Rule 20(a), two rear-end collisions five months apart were held to be a "series of occurrences."

Ryan v. Mackolin, 1968, 237 N.E.2d 377, 14 Ohio St.2d 213, noted 1968, 20 Syracuse L.Rev. 67, 37 U.Cin.L.Rev. 826, 1969, 1 U.Tol.L.Rev. 287.

The Supreme Court has held that a common practice among voter registrars to deny black persons their right to vote constituted a series of transactions and allowed joinder. U.S. v. Mississippi, 1965, 85 S.Ct. 808, 815–816, 380 U.S. 128, 142–143, 13 L.Ed.2d 717.

16. See § 79 below.

17. Wheat v. Safeway Stores, Inc., 1965, 404 P.2d 317, 321, 146 Mont. 105, 113. See also Friedenthal, Kane & Miller, Civil Procedure, 2d ed. 1993, pp. 334–335.

claims did not arise from a single transaction nor from a single occurrence.[18] This is an undesirable overrefinement. The word "transaction" is normally defined in terms of "occurrences," [19] and the history of the drafting of Rule 20(a) [20] suggests clearly that "occurrence" was added merely to guard against any over-restrictive definition of "transaction" and was not intended to add a new and independent concept. Such, it is believed, is the construction most courts have put upon the rule.[21]

A significant innovation made by Rule 20(a) is the provision allowing joinder even though liability is asserted severally or in the alternative, provided the "same transaction" and "common question" tests are met. This is a departure from the common law and older code rules, which restricted joinder to persons having a joint interest or liability. The classic case illustrating the need for joinder in the alternative is an English case decided under a rule that was the forerunner of Rule 20(a). An office-supply company had contracted to sell to a particular customer time cards meeting certain specifications. It then contracted with a manufacturer to purchase such time cards from it. When the cards were shipped, the customer refused to pay for them, claiming that they failed to meet the required specifications. The supply company then sued the customer and the manufacturer, demanding the price from the customer, or, in the alternative, damages for breach of contract in not meeting the specifications from the manufacturer. The case presented one common question: "Did the goods furnished by the manufacturer conform to the specifications?" If they did, then the customer was obliged to pay the price. If they did not, then the manufacturer had breached its contract. No matter how many other questions might appear in the case, this common question was fundamental. Every instinct for procedural economy and simplicity suggests that this controversy be resolved in one suit, and the court properly permitted the joinder.[22] Similar joinder in the alternative is allowed under Rule 20(a).[23]

The only real difficulty in joinder of parties has come in cases involving both multiple parties and multiple claims. Here, as is discussed in a later section, there was, prior to a 1966 amendment, an

---

18.   State ex rel. Campbell v. James, Mo. 1953, 263 S.W.2d 402, 407.

19.   " 'Transaction' is a word of flexible meaning. It may comprehend a series of many occurrences * * *." Moore v. New York Cotton Exchange, 1926, 46 S.Ct. 367, 371, 270 U.S. 593, 610, 70 L.Ed. 750; Wheaton, A Study of the Statutes Which Contain the Term "Subject of the Action" and Which Relate to Joinder of Actions and Plaintiffs and to Counterclaims, 1933, 18 Corn.L.Q. 232, 242.

20.   The history is set out in Wright, Estoppel by Rule: The Compulsory Counterclaim Under Modern Pleading, 1954, 38 Minn.L.Rev. 423, 448–450.

21.   Decisions passing on the propriety of joinder in particular circumstances are collected in 7 Wright, Miller & Kane, Civil 2d §§ 1656, 1657.

22.   Payne v. British Time Recorder Co., [1921] 2 K.B. 1 (C.A.).

23.   E.g., Texas Employers Ins. Assn. v. Felt, C.C.A.5th, 1945, 150 F.2d 227 (three insurance companies joined as defendants where there was doubt about which was liable for workmen's compensation); Amalgamated Packaging Indus., Ltd. v. National Container Corp., D.C.N.Y.1953, 14 F.R.D. 194 (alternative joinder as plaintiffs of purchaser and its subsequent vendee in breach of warranty action). See 7 Wright, Miller & Kane, Civil 2d § 1654.

unfortunate tendency in some cases to read Rule 20(a), on joinder of parties, as limiting Rule 18 on joinder of claims.[24]

State restrictions on joinder do not limit the application of Rule 20(a) in federal court,[25] but the federal court may honor some strong state policy, such as that prohibiting joinder of an insurance company in a suit against its insured.[26] The rule, of course, does not alter usual requirements of federal jurisdiction, and with regard to this rule, unlike some of the special joinder devices to be considered later, the concept of "ancillary jurisdiction," or "supplemental jurisdiction" as it is now called,[27] had until recently not been applied.[28] Thus, complete diversity is required between all the plaintiffs and all the defendants.[29] The requirements of the venue statutes, which usually speak in terms of all the parties on one side, must be met.[30] Normally the jurisdictional-amount test must be satisfied with regard to each of the parties. Aggregation is permitted if there are several parties on one side with a common undivided interest,[31] but not if the demands for and against them are separate and distinct.[32] Nor, on the orthodox view, may a party with a claim for less than the jurisdictional amount be joined with one who has a sufficient claim.[33] There had been considerable uncertainty on when or whether the concept of "pendent parties" could properly be used to allow joinder of one defendant in a nondiversity case against whom there is a jurisdictional basis with a second defendant for whom there is no independent basis of jurisdiction. That uncertainty was ended by the adoption in 1990 of 28 U.S.C.A. § 1367, which gives the courts jurisdiction in the situation described.[34]

Under Rule 21 the remedy for misjoinder or nonjoinder of parties is corrective action, rather than a punitive dismissal. If a party has been

---

24. See § 78 below.

25. Siebrand v. Gossnell, C.A.9th, 1956, 234 F.2d 81; Doyle v. Stanolind Oil & Gas Co., C.C.A.5th, 1941, 123 F.2d 900; Sypherd v. Haeckl's Exp., Inc., D.C.Ohio 1962, 31 F.R.D. 255; Campbell v. Pacific Fruit Exp. Co., D.C.Idaho 1957, 148 F.Supp. 209; Stanford v. Tennessee Val. Auth., D.C.Tenn.1955, 18 F.R.D. 152.

26. American Fidelity Fire Ins. Co. v. Hood, D.C.S.C.1965, 37 F.R.D. 17; Globe Indem. Co. v. Teixeira, D.C.Hawaii 1963, 230 F.Supp. 444; Hoosier Cas. Co. of Indianapolis, Ind. v. Fox, D.C.Iowa 1952, 102 F.Supp. 214; Pennsylvania R. Co. v. Lattavo Bros., Inc., D.C.Ohio 1949, 9 F.R.D. 205. But cf. Plains Ins. Co. v. Sandoval, D.C.Colo.1964, 35 F.R.D. 293. Joinder of the insurer will be allowed in federal court in states such as Louisiana and Wisconsin that permit such joinder. Cf. Lumbermen's Mut. Cas. Co. v. Elbert, 1954, 75 S.Ct. 151, 348 U.S. 48, 99 L.Ed. 59.

27. See § 9 above.

28. Olivieri v. Adams, D.C.Pa.1968, 280 F.Supp. 428.

29. See § 24 above at notes 41 to 45.

30. See § 42 above; 15 Wright, Miller & Cooper, Jurisdiction 2d § 3807.

31. E.g., Troy Bank of Troy, Ind. v. G.A. Whitehead & Co., 1911, 32 S.Ct. 9, 222 U.S. 39, 56 L.Ed. 81. See § 36 above.

32. E.g., Pinel v. Pinel, 1916, 36 S.Ct. 416, 240 U.S. 594, 60 L.Ed. 817. See § 36 above.

33. A number of courts of appeals had sensibly moved to a different rule on this point, but that movement seems to be clearly wrong in the light of what the Supreme Court said in Zahn v. International Paper Co., 1973, 94 S.Ct. 505, 509, 414 U.S. 291, 295, 38 L.Ed.2d 511. See § 36 above.

34. See § 19 above. But § 1367(b) makes it clear that supplemental jurisdiction cannot be used in a diversity case to permit joinder under Rule 20 of a party whose citizenship would defeat complete diversity.

omitted who ought to be joined under Rule 19, the remedy is to join him, and dismissal is called for only if he cannot be served or his presence would destroy diversity.[35] If a party has been joined whose joinder is not proper under Rule 20, that party may be dropped by order of the court on motion of any party or on its own initiative at any stage of the action and on such terms as are just.[36] As was developed in an earlier section, this can be done even after verdict to eliminate from the case a party of nondiverse citizenship.[37]

§ 72. Class Actions [1]

"One of the most controversial recent developments in the law of federal procedure is the growth of the class action. The crucial event was the amendment in 1966 of Rule 23 of the Federal Rules of Civil Procedure."[2] The controversy has indeed been a hot one. The class action, as it was reformed in 1966, has been described as everything from "one of the most socially useful remedies in history"[3] to "legalized blackmail."[4] In less than three decades under the amended rule both the case law and the literature have become vast. Indeed it would be possible to write a book much larger than the present work on class actions alone,[5] and in this section it will be possible only to touch on the more important features.

"The class action was an invention of equity * * * mothered by the practical necessity of providing a procedural device so that mere numbers would not disable large groups of individuals, united in interest, from enforcing their equitable rights nor grant them immunity from their equitable wrongs. * * * By Rule 23 the Supreme Court has extended the use of the class action device to the entire field of federal civil litigation by making it applicable to all civil actions."[6] It provides a means by which, where a large group of persons are interested in a matter, one or more may sue or be sued as representatives of the class without needing to join every member of the class. This procedure is

---

35. 7 Wright, Miller & Kane, Civil 2d § 1684.

36. 7 Wright, Miller & Kane, Civil 2d § 1684.

37. Finn v. American Fire & Cas. Co., C.A.5th, 1953, 207 F.2d 113, certiorari denied 74 S.Ct. 476, 347 U.S. 912, 98 L.Ed. 1069; Dollar S.S. Lines v. Merz, C.C.A.9th, 1934, 68 F.2d 594. See § 69 above.

§ 72

1. 7A Wright, Miller & Kane, Civil 2d §§ 1751–1780; 7B id., §§ 1781–1805; Garth, Nagel & Plager, The Institution of the Private Attorney General: Perspectives from an Empirical Study of Class Action Litigation, 1988, 61 S.Cal.L.Rev. 353; Miller, Of Frankenstein Monsters and Shining Knights: Myth, Reality, and the "Class Action Problem," 1979, 92 Harv.L.Rev. 664; Dam, Class Actions: Efficiency, Compensa-

tion, Deterrence, and Conflict of Interest, 1975, 4 J.Legal Stud. 47.

2. Dam, note 1 above, at 47.

3. Pomerantz, New Developments in Class Actions—Has Their Death Knell Been Sounded?, 1970, 25 Bus.Law. 1259.

4. Handler, The Shift from Substantive to Procedural Innovations in Antitrust Suits, 1971, 71 Col.L.Rev. 1, 9.

5. The discussion of Rule 23 in 7A and 7B Wright, Miller & Kane, Civil 2d, including the 1993 pocket parts, occupies 1,240 pages.

6. Montgomery Ward & Co. v. Langer, C.C.A.8th, 1948, 168 F.2d 182, 187.

See generally Yeazell, From Medieval Group Litigation to the Modern Class Action, 1987.

available in federal court, even in diversity actions in states that do not recognize the class suit, though the state law will define the substantive interest of the members of the class and the capacity to sue or be sued of the named representatives.[7]

As originally adopted in 1938, Rule 23 made a bold and well-intentioned attempt to encourage more frequent use of class actions. The rule made this procedure available in actions for legal relief as well as in those that were historically equitable, and it sought to give guidance on the kind of cases for which class treatment was appropriate. But, as was often pointed out,[8] and as will be referred to more specifically later in this section, a quarter-century of experience demonstrated very serious defects in the original rule. Accordingly in 1966 the rule was extensively amended. The amended rule, like the companion amendments that year to Rules 19 and 24, sought to substitute functional tests for the conceptualisms of the old rule. In addition, it sought to provide better guidance on the measures that may be taken by the court in managing the class action. Unfortunately the new rule, though generously described as "complicated,"[9] still "tends to ask more questions than it answers."[10] The Supreme Court, in a series of decisions construing the amended rule, has answered some of the questions the rule poses, but the effect of its decisions has been to limit the rule's use. Finally, the amended rule is in jeopardy from those who embrace it too enthusiastically just as it is from those who approach it with distaste. Admonitions that "if there is to be an error made, let it be in favor and not against the maintenance of the class action"[11] conveyed a receptive spirit. But to the extent that they encouraged plaintiffs to bring, and the courts to allow, maintenance of class actions in controversies that

7. Minnesota v. U.S. Steel Corp., D.C.Minn.1968, 44 F.R.D. 559, 568; cf. Hanna v. Plumer, 1965, 85 S.Ct. 1136, 380 U.S. 460, 14 L.Ed.2d 8, discussed § 59 above. Compare Oskoian v. Canuel, C.A.1st, 1959, 269 F.2d 311, with Underwood v. Maloney, C.A.3d, 1958, 256 F.2d 334, certiorari denied 79 S.Ct. 93, 358 U.S. 864, 3 L.Ed.2d 97. The last two cases are discussed, and distinguished in 7A Wright, Miller & Kane, Civil 2d § 1758.

8. 7A Wright, Miller & Kane, Civil 2d § 1752; Chafee, Some Problems of Equity, 1950, pp. 199–295; Advisory Committee Note to 1966 Amendment, 1966, 39 F.R.D. 98–99; Kalven & Rosenfield, The Contemporary Function of the Class Suit, 1941, 8 U.Chi.L.Rev. 684; Keeffe, Levy & Donovan, Lee Defeats Ben Hur, 1948, 33 Cornell L.Q. 327; Weinstein, Revision of Procedure: Some Problems in Class Actions, 1960, 9 Buffalo L.Rev. 433; Simeone, Procedure Problems of Class Suits, 1962, 60 Mich. L.Rev. 905.

9. Note, Revised Federal Rule 23, Class Actions: Surviving Difficulties and New Problems Require Further Amendment,

1967, 52 Minn.L.Rev. 509. The present author, less generously, has referred to the amended rule as "extremely complicated." Wright, Recent Changes in the Federal Rules of Procedure, 1966, 42 F.R.D. 552, 563.

10. Frankel, Some Preliminary Observations Concerning Civil Rule 23, 1967, 43 F.R.D. 39.

In a letter to the present author, the draftsman of the rule, Professor Benjamin Kaplan, has suggested that "a rule that came out looking smoother would simply have remitted a series of problems to the courts with fewer guides; and that the purpose of procedural rules of this order of difficulty must be precisely that of asking questions—I mean the right ones."

11. Esplin v. Hirschi, C.A.10th, 1968, 402 F.2d 94, 99; Green v. Wolf Corp., C.A.2d, 1968, 406 F.2d 291, 298, certiorari denied 89 S.Ct. 2131, 395 U.S. 977, 23 L.Ed.2d 766. See also Eisen v. Carlisle & Jacquelin, C.A.2d, 1968, 391 F.2d 555, 563.

are unmanageable by this device, they brought the rule into disrepute even for the cases to which it is well suited. Thus, the same court that made the remark just quoted was to speak five years later of the need "to employ realism and good sense in denying class action status" and warned that Rule 23 "bears the seeds of its own destruction through unrealistic applications within its theoretical span." [12] It may well be that "it will take a generation or so before we can fully appreciate the scope, the virtues, and the vices of the new Rule 23." [13] It was with that thought in mind that the Advisory Committee on Civil Rules declared a general moratorium on possible amendments to Rule 23 to await further case-law development. In 1993 it began work on a complete revision of the rule,[14] but amendment of the rules—and particularly a rule as controversial as Rule 23—is a slow process. Any rewriting of the rule is several years in the future and it is impossible to say what form it will ultimately take.

There are two general requirements for the maintenance of any class suit.[15] These are that the persons constituting the class must be so

12. Wilcox v. Commerce Bank of Kansas City, C.A.10th, 1973, 474 F.2d 336, 347.

13. Frankel, Some Preliminary Observations Concerning Civil Rule 23, 1967, 43 F.R.D. 39, 52, quoting Professor Benjamin Kaplan.

For a pessimistic view, see Friendly, Federal Jurisdiction: A General View, 1973, p. 120: "Something seems to have gone radically wrong with a well-intentioned effort." See also Dam, Class Action Notice: Who Needs It?, 1974 Sup.Ct.Rev. 97, 119: "In the light of Eisen the 1966 amendment becomes a clever bit of legal architecture that has collapsed." The discussion in James, Hazard & Leubsdorf, Civil Procedure, 4th ed. 1992, §§ 10.20–10.23, is less than enthusiastic.

For a more optimistic view, though written before the Supreme Court's decision in the Eisen case, see Miller, Problems of Giving Notice in Class Actions, 1973, 58 F.R.D. 313, 334: "With the passage of time and the accumulation of experience under the rule, which, after all, is only six years old at this point, I believe Rule 23 will prove to be a very valuable keystone in making federal procedure responsive to the exigencies of the Twentieth Century and particularly the needs of contemporary litigation."

Professor Miller has suggested more recently that the period from 1964 to 1969 was one of overenthusiasm and euphoria about amended Rule 23, that a reaction set in and from 1969 to 1973 or 1974 antipathy to the class action was palpable, and that the pendulum swung again about 1974 beginning a phase, which may last until the end of the generation-long period Professor

Kaplan envisioned, of increasing sophistication, restraint, and stabilization in class-action practice. Miller, note 1 above, at 679–680.

In 1978 the Department of Justice proposed legislation that would have made drastic changes in class actions. See Miller, note 1 above, at 684–693; Wells, Reforming Federal Class Action Procedure: An Analysis of the Justice Department Proposal, 1979, 16 Harv.J.Legis. 543. That proposal got nowhere.

14. The initial draft being considered by the Advisory Committee builds on ABA Section on Litigation, Report and Recommendations of the Special Committee on Class Action Improvements, 1986, 110 F.R.D. 195. This in turn adopted an approach taken by the National Conference of Commissioners on Uniform State Laws. That group approved a Uniform Class Actions Act in 1976 and changed it to a Model Class Actions Act in 1987.

15. The requirement in Rule 23(a)(2) that there must be questions of law or fact common to the class will always be met when the further tests of Rule 23(b) are satisfied. Smith v. MCI Telecommunications Corp., D.C.Kan.1989, 124 F.R.D. 665, 6755 n. 7; 7A Wright, Miller & Kane, Civil 2d § 1763, pp. 227–228. The requirement in Rule 23(a)(3) that the claims or defenses of the representatives must be typical of those of the class may have some independent significance, e.g., Koos v. First Nat. Bank of Peoria, C.A.7th, 1974, 496 F.2d 1162, 1164, but in general seems only a further particularization of the requirement numerous that it is impracticable to bring them all before the court, and the named representatives must be such as will fairly insure the adequate representation of them all.

For the class to be large enough to permit a class suit, impossibility of joinder is not required. Extreme difficulty or impracticability of joinder is sufficient.[16] One court has referred to "the numbers game aspect of Rule 23,"[17] but it is clear that no numerical test is possible. Groups of as many as 350 have been held too small for a class action,[18] while groups of 25 or more have been held sufficient.[19] The requirement of a numerous class is intended to protect members of a small class from being deprived of their rights without a day in court,[20] and in a particular case this object should be weighed in the light of the situation that exists.[21]

Adequacy of representation is essential. The representative must not hold interests that conflict with those of the class he or she seeks to represent.[22] The adequacy of representation should be scrutinized with particular care where suit is brought, as the rule has always permitted,[23]

that the named representatives will adequately represent the entire class. See General Telephone Co. of the Southwest v. Falcon, 1982, 102 S.Ct. 2364, 457 U.S. 147, 72 L.Ed.2d 740. "[T]he adversary system is confident that it works well only when the litigant who does his best for himself also inescapably benefits his fellow class members." Degnan, Adequacy of Representation in Class Actions, 1972, 60 Calif.L.Rev. 705, 716.

16. Harris v. Palm Springs Alpine Estates, Inc., C.A.9th, 1964, 329 F.2d 909, 913–914; Hoffman Elec., Inc. v. Emerson Elec. Co., D.C.Pa.1991, 754 F.Supp. 1070, 1075.

17. Phillips v. Sherman, D.C.N.Y.1961, 197 F.Supp. 866, 869.

18. Utah v. American Pipe & Constr. Co., D.C.Cal.1969, 49 F.R.D. 17. See also Minersville Coal Co. v. Anthracite Export Assn., D.C.Pa.1971, 55 F.R.D. 426 (330 members).

19. Philadelphia Elec. Co. v. Anaconda American Brass Co., D.C.Pa.1968, 43 F.R.D. 452, 463. For other cases ruling whether a particular class was large enough, see 7A Wright, Miller & Kane, Civil 2d § 1762 nn. 17–53.

20. Matthies v. Seymour Mfg. Co., C.A.2d, 1959, 270 F.2d 365, 372, certiorari denied 80 S.Ct. 591, 361 U.S. 962, 4 L.Ed.2d 544, noted 1960, 69 Yale L.J. 816; Rippey v. Denver U.S. Nat. Bank, D.C.Colo. 1966, 260 F.Supp. 704, 712.

21. Demarco v. Edens, C.A.2d, 1968, 390 F.2d 836, 845; Barnes v. Board of

Trustees, Michigan Veterans Trust Fund, D.C.Mich.1973, 369 F.Supp. 1327, 1332–1333.

22. Albertson's, Inc. v. Amalgamated Sugar Co., C.A.10th, 1974, 503 F.2d 459; Schy v. Susquehanna Corp., C.A.7th, 1970, 419 F.2d 1112, certiorari denied 91 S.Ct. 51, 400 U.S. 826, 27 L.Ed.2d 55; Degnan, note 15 above; Comment, Representation in Class Actions: Is Personal Interest Replacing Personal Stake?, 1981 Ariz.St.L.J. 1007; 7A Wright, Miller & Kane, Civil 2d § 1768.

The class representative must be part of the class and possess the same interest and suffer the same injury as the class members. East Texas Motor Freight System Inc. v. Rodriguez, 1977, 97 S.Ct. 1891, 431 U.S. 395, 52 L.Ed.2d 453. However, the fact that the representative's claim becomes moot after the class has been certified but before the action terminates does not necessarily require dismissal of the action. Compare Sosna v. Iowa, 1975, 95 S.Ct. 553, 419 U.S. 393, 42 L.Ed.2d 532, and Zablocki v. Redhail, 1978, 98 S.Ct. 673, 434 U.S. 374, 54 L.Ed.2d 618, with Kremens v. Bartley, 1977, 97 S.Ct. 1709, 431 U.S. 119, 52 L.Ed.2d 184. See 7B Wright, Miller & Kane, Civil 2d § 1785.1, pp. 150–173; Kane, Standing, Mootness, and Federal Rule 23—Balancing Perspectives, 1976, 26 Buff. L.Rev. 83.

23. 7A Wright, Miller, & Kane, Civil 2d § 1770; Taylor, Defendant Class Actions Under Rule 23(b)(2): Resolving the Language Dilemma, 1991, 40 U.Kan.L.Rev. 77; Note, Defendant Class Actions, 1978, 91 Harv.L.Rev. 630.

against a class of defendants. Plaintiffs must not be allowed to succumb to the temptation to name as representatives of the defendant class persons whose defense will be less than zealous.[24] It seems fairly obvious that the members of a class cannot be adequately represented if their interests are in conflict, but the application of this principle leads to considerable difficulty. In the leading case of Hansberry v. Lee,[25] involving the validity of a class action testing whether a restrictive agreement had been adopted by a group of landowners, it was held that landowners who sought to secure the benefits of the agreement could not be regarded as members of the same class as those who wished to challenge the agreement. In the course of the opinion Chief Justice Stone wrote, for the Court: "It is one thing to say that some members of a class may represent other members in a litigation where the sole and common interest of the class in the litigation, is either to assert a common right or to challenge an asserted obligation. * * * It is quite another to hold that all those who are free alternatively either to assert rights or to challenge them are of a single class, so that any group merely because it is of the class so constituted, may be deemed adequately to represent others of the class in litigating their interests in either alternative."[26]

There were excellent reasons for deciding Hansberry v. Lee as the Court did. The action that was claimed to bind all members of the class was a collusive action in which the crucial fact was established by a false stipulation.[27] The language of the Court, however, seems unduly broad. In any conceivable case, some of the members of the class will wish to assert their rights while others will not wish to do so.[28] Thus, the familiar case of the stockholders' derivative suit is almost invariably brought by minority stockholders to challenge action that a majority of the stockholders approve. Yet it is routinely regarded as an appropriate

---

24. The danger is illustrated by a well-known state case, where the whole class was held bound by a suit against carefully picked members of the class with a very small financial interest who made only a token defense. Richardson v. Kelly, 1945, 191 S.W.2d 857, 144 Tex. 497, certiorari denied 67 S.Ct. 487, 329 U.S. 798, 91 L.Ed. 683, criticized in Notes, 1946, 55 Yale L.J. 831, 25 Texas L.Rev. 64, and by Chafee, Some Problems of Equity, 1950, pp. 239–242.

25. 1940, 61 S.Ct. 115, 311 U.S. 32, 85 L.Ed. 22.

26. 61 S.Ct. at 119, 311 U.S. at 44–45.

27. In the earlier case it had been stipulated that more than 95% of the owners had signed the restrictive agreement, as was required by its terms before it could take effect. In fact only 54% had signed. See Weinstein, Revision of Procedure: Some Problems in Class Actions, 1960, 9 Buff. L.Rev. 433, 460; Keeffe, Levy & Donovan,

Lee Defeats Ben Hur, 1948, 33 Cornell L.Q. 327, 337–339.

28. A class action seeking more aggressive management of an investment fund was allowed to proceed in Dierks v. Thompson, C.A.1st, 1969, 414 F.2d 453, since the interests of the participants in the plan who preferred investments with little or no risk was adequately represented by the defendants.

The amended rule is helpful on this point, by providing that a class may be divided into subclasses. Rule 23(c)(4)(B). See In re Joint Eastern & Southern Dist. Asbestos Litigation, C.A.2d, 1992, 982 F.2d 721, modified on rehearing C.A.2d, 1993, 993 F.2d 7; Carr v. Conoco Plastics, Inc., C.A.5th, 1970, 423 F.2d 57, 58, certiorari denied 91 S.Ct. 241, 400 U.S. 951, 28 L.Ed.2d 257; 7B Wright, Miller, & Kane, Civil 2d § 1790.

class suit.[29]   Another familiar class suit is that in which one or more taxpayers of a community, suing on behalf of all, challenge the validity of a proposed public expenditure.   It is difficult to believe that there has ever been such a case in which a good many of the taxpayers would not have preferred that their rights not be enforced, because of their interest in having the expenditure made.   Yet no one has ever doubted the propriety of bringing such a suit as a class action.[30]

It has sometimes been said that a sufficient number of members of the class must appear as parties to insure a fair representation of the class,[31] but it has increasingly come to be recognized that the quality of the representation is more important than numbers, and that even a single representative of the class may be enough.[32]   One factor that the court will consider in determining the adequacy of the representation is the quality and experience of the attorneys for the class.[33]   There are problems here, however, that should not be overlooked.   Conflicts of interest between the members of the class and the attorneys are not uncommon in class actions.[34]

---

29. See § 73 below. The suggestion that derivative suits are not actually class actions at all—see Note, Shareholder Derivative Suits: Are They Class Actions?, 1957, 42 Iowa L.Rev. 568—is heretical and unhistorical. See Louisell & Hazard, Cases on Pleading and Procedure, 1962, p. 721. See also Ross v. Bernhard, 1970, 90 S.Ct. 733, 739–740, 396 U.S. 531, 541, 24 L.Ed.2d 729.

30. E.g., Booth v. General Dynamics Corp., D.C.Ill.1967, 264 F.Supp. 465.

Thus, it has been held that a class action could be brought although: many parents and children supported the use of dogs to sniff school lockers, the constitutionality of which was being challenged, Horton v. Goose Creek Ind. Sch. Dist., C.A.5th, 1982, 690 F.2d 470, certiorari denied 103 S.Ct. 3536, 463 U.S. 1207, 77 L.Ed.2d 1387; some children might be happy with the childcare system in New York, despite its discriminatory character, Wilder v. Bernstein, D.C.N.Y.1980, 499 F.Supp. 980; many cancer patients have no interest in the use of laetrile, Rutherford v. U.S., D.C.Okl.1977, 429 F.Supp. 506.

But compare Bailey v. Patterson, D.C.Miss.1962, 206 F.Supp. 67, an action to enjoin segregation on common carriers, in which the court found that the interest of the black plaintiffs was "antagonistic to and not wholly compatible with the interests of those whom they purport to represent," and held that the suit was not a proper class action. The decree thus provided that only the named plaintiffs were entitled to unsegregated transportation. This strange decision was properly reversed. Bailey v. Patterson, C.A.5th, 1963,

323 F.2d 201, certiorari denied 84 S.Ct. 666, 376 U.S. 910, 11 L.Ed.2d 609.

31. Knowles v. War Damage Corp., C.A.D.C.1948, 171 F.2d 15, certiorari denied 69 S.Ct. 604, 336 U.S. 914, 93 L.Ed. 1077; Pelelas v. Caterpillar Tractor Co., C.C.A.7th, 1940, 113 F.2d 629, certiorari denied 61 S.Ct. 138, 311 U.S. 700, 85 L.Ed. 454.

32. Hohmann v. Packard Instrument Co., C.A.7th, 1968, 399 F.2d 711; Eisen v. Carlisle & Jacquelin, C.A.2d, 1968, 391 F.2d 555, 562–563, noted 1968, 18 Am.U.L.Rev. 225, 44 Notre Dame Law. 151, 43 Tul. L.Rev. 369, 21 Vand.L.Rev. 1124, 1969, 47 N.C.L.Rev. 393; Lerwill v. Inflight Services, Inc., D.C.Cal.1974, 379 F.Supp. 690; Green v. Cauthen, D.C.S.C.1974, 379 F.Supp. 361; 7A Wright, Miller, & Kane, Civil 2d § 1766.

33. Eisen v. Carlisle & Jacquelin, C.A.2d, 1968, 391 F.2d 555, 562; Weinberger v. Jackson, D.C.Cal.1984, 102 F.R.D. 839, 845.

34. Indeed distinguished scholars have said that conflict between the attorney and the class members "is almost inevitable." James, Hazard & Leubsdorf, Civil Procedure, 4th ed.1992, p. 572. See generally 7A Wright, Miller & Kane, Civil 2d § 1769.1, pp. 383–395; Macey & Miller, The Plaintiffs' Attorney's Role in Class Action and Derivative Litigation: Economic Analysis and Recommendations for Reform, 1991, 58 U.Chi.L.Rev. 1; Underwood, Legal Ethics and Class Actions: Problems, Tactics and Judicial Responses, 1983, 71 Ky.L.J. 787; Garth, Conflict and Dissent in Class Actions: A Suggested Perspective, 1982, 77

If the requirements of a sufficiently large class and adequate representation are met, it is still necessary to decide whether the action falls into one of the categories for which a class suit is permissible. The original rule permitted three kinds of class suits, popularly known as "true," "hybrid," and "spurious." The rule was cast in terms of jural relations, with a particular suit falling in one class or another according to the character of the right sought to be enforced for or against the class.[35] Thus, a "true" class action was permitted if the right involved was "joint, or common or secondary in the sense that the owner of a primary right refuses to enforce that right and a member of the class thereby becomes entitled to enforce it." Where the right involved was "several" but the object of the action was adjudication of claims that did or might affect specific property involved in the action, the label "hybrid" was applied. Finally an action to enforce "several" rights, where there was a common question of law or fact affecting such rights and "common relief" was sought was a "spurious" class action.[36]

The "spurious" class action was a particularly puzzling creation. In any case in which such an action could have been brought under the former rule, it would have been possible to join all the parties under Rule 20(a). Thus, it was said that the "spurious" action was only a permissive-joinder device,[37] though if this were true it duplicated Rule 20(a).[38] It was thought not to have any binding effect on those who were not named as parties,[39] even though a nonbinding class suit seems to involve a contradiction in terms. If the judgment were effective only with regard to the named parties, it was mere surplusage to say in the pleadings that others similarly situated were involved.

Under the old rule the limited effect given the judgment in the "spurious" action was in contrast to a "true" class suit, in which all the members of the class were bound, and the "hybrid" class suit, where the members of the class were bound only about their rights, if any, in the property involved. But this was not the only respect in which important consequences turned on the label applied to the class suit. Such matters as jurisdiction, venue, intervention, and tolling of the statute of limita-

---

Nw.U.L.Rev. 492; Rhode, Class Conflicts in Class Actions, 1982, 34 Stan.L.Rev. 1183.

35. "This tribute to the memory of Wesley Hohfeld would be more suitable in a law review article than in an enactment which is to guide the actions of practical men day in and day out." Chafee, Some Problems of Equity, 1950, p. 246.

A lonely minority view, finding meaning and value in the tripartite classification, was that of VanDercreek, The "Is" and "Ought" of Class Actions Under Federal Rule 23, 1963, 48 Iowa L.Rev. 273, 280–283.

36. The tripartite classification under the former rule is discussed in 7A Wright, Miller, & Kane, Civil 2d § 1752.

37. See cases cited 7A Wright, Miller, & Kane, Civil 2d § 1752 n. 51.

38. Union Carbide & Carbon Corp. v. Nisley, C.A.10th, 1961, 300 F.2d 561, 589, certiorari dismissed 1962, 83 S.Ct. 13, 371 U.S. 801, 9 L.Ed.2d 46.

39. All American Airways v. Elderd, C.A.2d, 1954, 209 F.2d 247, 248; and cases cited 7B Wright, Miller, & Kane, Civil 2d § 1789 n. 6. This was in accord with the view of Professor Moore, a view that was properly given great influence because of his important role in drafting original Rule 23. Moore, Federal Rules of Civil Procedure: Some Problems Raised by the Preliminary Draft, 1937, 25 Geo.L.J. 511; Moore & Cohn, Federal Class Actions, Jurisdiction and Effect of Judgment, 1938, 22 Ill.L.Rev. 555.

tions were all thought to vary depending on which kind of class suit was involved.

This was the most serious defect in the old rule, and was of much more consequence than the anomaly of a class suit that did not bind the class. If matters of importance turn on the classification given a particular suit, then it is vital that it be clearly understood which classification applies. The fact was that the task of determining which label was appropriate for a particular suit "baffled both courts and commentators." [40] The terms "joint," "common," and "several" had "little or no clear and ascertainable meaning in or out of the context of class actions," [41] and most persons who had to work with them shared the frustration of Professor Chafee, who confessed that he was having as much trouble telling a "common" right from a "several" one as in deciding whether some ties were green or blue.[42] Cases challenging racial discrimination provided a particularly striking example. Some courts thought this a "true" class action, others called it "spurious," while most simply said that it was a permissible class action and avoided the unrewarding task of further identification.[43]

The principal reason for rewriting Rule 23 in 1966 was to get away from the conceptually defined categories of the old rule. The amended rule does describe categories of cases that may be appropriate for class treatment, and procedural consequences may depend on which category is involved, but the new categories are described functionally rather than conceptually. Inevitably there is some overlap among the categories.[44] Because there are three categories in the new rule, just as there were in the old, there was at first some tendency to suppose that the old names, "true," "hybrid," and "spurious," could still be used, though with their definitions in the rule altered.[45] This is not only wrong but dangerously wrong. Nothing in the amended rule corresponds to the former "spurious" class action, since it is expected that the judgment in a class action under the amended rule will bind all members of the class, except those

---

40. Note, Federal Class Actions: A Suggested Revision of Rule 23, 1946, 46 Col. L.Rev. 818, 822. One well-known case was variously characterized as "a class bill," Deckert v. Independence Shares Corp., D.C.Pa.1939, 27 F.Supp. 763, 769, as "spurious," C.C.A.3d, 108 F.2d 51, 55, and as "hybrid," D.C.Pa.1941, 39 F.Supp. 592, 595. Finally the court of appeals said "names are not important." Pennsylvania Co. for Insurances v. Deckert, C.C.A.3d, 1941, 123 F.2d 979, 983.

41. Kaplan, Continuing Work of the Civil Committee: 1966 Amendments of the Federal Rules of Civil Procedure, 1967, 81 Harv.L.Rev. 356, 380. See also the authorities cited note 8 above.

42. Chafee, Some Problems of Equity, 1950, p. 257.

43. See cases cited at 7A Wright, Miller, & Kane, Civil 2d § 1752 nn. 31–42.

44. Kaplan, note 41 above, at 390 n. 130. Problems that this overlap may cause are discussed in Note, Revised Federal Rules 23, Class Actions: Surviving Difficulties and New Problems Require Further Amendment, 1967, 52 Minn.L.Rev. 483, 515–527.

45. E.g., La Mar v. H & B Novelty & Loan Co., C.A.9th, 1973, 489 F.2d 461, 467; Eisen v. Carlisle & Jacquelin, C.A.2d, 1968, 391 F.2d 555, 565; Hartman v. Secretary of Dept. of Housing and Urban Development, D.C.Mass.1968, 294 F.Supp. 794, 796; see Frankel, Some Preliminary Observations Concerning Civil Rule 23, 1967, 43 F.R.D. 39, 43.

who have been expressly excluded. Nor do any of the clauses of amended Rule 23(b) correspond with the old "true" or "hybrid" class actions. The amended rule must be approached on its own pragmatic terms, rather than with preconceptions derived from the old conceptual categories.[46]

Rule 23(b)(1) permits a class action where this is necessary to avoid possible adverse effects on the opponents of the class or on absent members of the class. The party opposing the class would be prejudiced if inconsistent results in individual adjudications establish incompatible standards of conduct to which it must adhere, as in a suit by taxpayers to invalidate municipal action or in a suit involving the rights and duties of riparian owners.[47] Individual members of the class would be prejudiced if individual actions "as a practical matter" would impair their ability to protect their interests, as in a suit to compel reorganization of a fraternal association or a suit by stockholders to compel declaration of a dividend.[48]

Rule 23(b)(2) permits a class action where the party opposing the class has acted or refused to act on grounds generally applicable to the class. It is intended primarily for civil-rights cases though there are other kinds of cases that fall within it.[49] It is expressly limited to cases in which "final injunctive relief or corresponding declaratory relief with respect to the class as a whole" will be appropriate, and thus deliberately excludes actions for damages,[50] in which it might otherwise be asserted that a party's denial of fault, and refusal to pay claims against it, was a refusal to act on a ground generally applicable to a class. On the better view, Rule 23(b)(2) does not apply to defendant class actions.[51]

The most complicated and controversial portion of the 1966 revision is Rule 23(b)(3). This authorizes a class action where the only justifica-

46. See Van Gemert v. Boeing Co., D.C.N.Y.1966, 259 F.Supp. 125, 129; Booth v. General Dynamics Corp., D.C.Ill.1967, 264 F.Supp. 465, 470–471.

47. Rule 23(b)(1)(A). See Advisory Committee Note, 39 F.R.D. 98, 100; U.S. v. Truckee–Carson Irrigation Dist., D.C.Nev. 1975, 71 F.R.D. 10; Guadamuz v. Ash, D.C.D.C.1973, 368 F.Supp. 1233; Booth v. General Dynamics Corp., D.C.Ill.1967, 264 F.Supp. 465; 7A Wright, Miller, & Kane, Civil 2d § 1773.

48. Rule 23(b)(1)(B). See, e.g., Robertson v. National Basketball Assn., C.A.2d, 1977, 556 F.2d 682; Lynch Corp. v. MII Liquidating Co., D.C.S.D.1979, 82 F.R.D. 478; 7A Wright, Miller, & Kane, Civil 2d § 1774.

49. See 7A Wright, Miller & Kane, Civil 2d §§ 1775, 1776. On the use generally of class actions in civil-rights and constitutional cases, see 7A id. § 1771.

50. In re School Asbestos Litigation, C.A.3d, 1986, 789 F.2d 996, 1007–1008, certiorari denied 107 S.Ct. 182, 479 U.S. 852, 93 L.Ed.2d 117; Lukenas v. Bryce's Mountain Resort, Inc., C.A.4th, 1976, 538 F.2d 594, 595–596. But if the predominant purpose of the suit is for injunctive relief, an incidental award of damages or back pay is permissible. Probe v. State Teachers' Retirement Sys., C.A.9th, 1986, 780 F.2d 776, 780, certiorari denied 106 S.Ct. 2891, 476 U.S. 1170, 90 L.Ed.2d 978. See generally 7A Wright, Miller & Kane, Civil 2d § 1775 at notes 13 to 27.

51. Henson v. East Lincoln Township, C.A.7th, 1987, 814 F.2d 410, 417, certiorari dismissed 113 S.Ct. 1035, ___ U.S. ___, 122 L.Ed.2d 111; 7A Wright, Miller & Kane, Civil 2d § 1775, pp. 461–462; Comment, Defendant Class Actions and Federal Civil Rights Litigation, 1985, 38 UCLA L.Rev. 283, 311–317.

tion for such a procedure is the presence of common questions of law or fact. Though this bears a superficial resemblance to the old "spurious" action, the "spurious" action was not really a class action at all while a suit under (b)(3) is a class action in all respects. The court has discretion whether to allow a (b)(3) action. Before permitting it to be maintained the court must find that the questions of law or fact common to the members of the class predominate over any questions affecting only individual members,[52] and that a class action is superior to other available methods for the fair and efficient adjudication of the controversy.[53] The rule itself lists four factors that the court is to consider, among others, in determining whether a class action is superior to other methods.[54]

As soon as practicable after the commencement of an action brought as a class action, the court must determine by order whether it will be allowed to proceed as a class action.[55] Discovery may be proper to obtain information relevant to whether the action ought to be certified as a class action,[56] but it is not proper to have a preliminary hearing on plaintiff's probability of success before making the determination about class-action status.[57] That determination is always subject to change at a later time.[58]

Predictions that not "very many actions" would be allowed to

---

52. E.g., Cameron v. E.M. Adams & Co., C.A.9th, 1976, 547 F.2d 473; Payton v. Abbott Labs, D.C.Mass.1979, 83 F.R.D. 382, vacated on other grounds D.C.Mass.1983, 100 F.R.D. 336; and cases cited 7A Wright, Miller & Kane, Civil 2d § 1778 n. 1.

Individual issues were found to dominate in, e.g., Marcial v. Coronet Ins. Co., C.A.7th, 1989, 880 F.2d 954; Zimmerman v. Bell, C.A.4th, 1986, 800 F.2d 386, 390; and cases cited 7A Wright, Miller & Kane, Civil 2d § 1778 n. 22.

53. See 7A Wright, Miller & Kane, Civil 2d § 1779. With the expansion of issue preclusion and the demise of the requirement of mutuality, the possible binding effect of a test case must be considered in determining whether a class action is superior. Katz v. Carte Blanche Corp., C.A.3d, 1974, 496 F.2d 747, certiorari denied 95 S.Ct. 152, 419 U.S. 885, 42 L.Ed.2d 125, noted 1975, 88 Harv.L.Rev. 825, 21 Wayne L.Rev. 1195.

Although there is a decision to the contrary, Amalgamated Workers Union v. Hess Oil Virgin Islands Corp., C.A.3d, 1973, 478 F.2d 540, it would seem that the court should consider whether administrative remedies would be superior to a class action. Pattillo v. Schlesinger, C.A.9th, 1980, 625 F.2d 262.

54. As listed in Rule 23(b)(3), these are: "(A) the interest of members of the class in

individually controlling the prosecution or defense of separate actions; (B) the extent and nature of any litigation concerning the controversy already commenced by or against members of the class; (C) the desirability or undesirability of concentrating the litigation of the claims in the particular forum; (D) the difficulties likely to be encountered in the management of a class action."

The listing of factors to be considered in Rule 23(b)(3) is not exhaustive and other factors may be considered. Wilcox v. Commerce Bank of Kansas City, C.A.10th, 1973, 474 F.2d 336. See generally 7A Wright, Miller & Kane, Civil 2d § 1780.

55. Rule 23(c)(1); 7B Wright, Miller & Kane, Civil 2d § 1785. The appealability of this determination is discussed in § 101 below and in 15A Wright, Miller & Cooper, Jurisdiction 2d § 3912.

56. Oppenheimer Fund, Inc. v. Sanders, 1978, 98 S.Ct. 2380, 2389 n. 13, 437 U.S. 340, 351 n. 13, 57 L.Ed.2d 253.

57. Eisen v. Carlisle & Jacquelin, 1974, 94 S.Ct. 2140, 2152, 417 U.S. 156, 177–178, 40 L.Ed.2d 732.

58. Kuehner v. Heckler, C.A.3d, 1985, 778 F.2d 152, 163; Gerstle v. Continental Airlines, Inc., C.A.10th, 1972, 466 F.2d 1374; and cases cited 7B Wright, Miller & Kane, Civil 2d § 1785 nn. 68–70.

proceed under (b)(3) [59] have proved quite ill-founded. The great bulk of reported cases in which class actions have been allowed under the revised rule have been (b)(3) actions. This device has been especially popular in antitrust and securities fraud cases, where individual persons allegedly injured are in a poor position to seek redress, either because they do not know enough or because the cost of suit is disproportionate to each individual claim.[60] The use of class actions for the protection of consumers or for environmental litigation was uncommon in the early days of the amended rule, but now occurs regularly.[61]

In drafting the amended rule the Advisory Committee observed that a class action is "ordinarily not appropriate" in cases of mass tort, because of the likelihood that significant questions of damages, liability, and defenses to liability would affect the individuals in different ways.[62] This view has often been followed by the courts,[63] but the need for more efficient methods of disposing of large numbers of cases arising out of a single disaster or a single course of conduct has an increasingly insistent priority in improving judicial administration,[64] and in a number of mass-tort cases class actions have been allowed.[65]

59. Wright, Recent Changes in the Federal Rules of Procedure, 1966, 42 F.R.D. 552, 567.

60. 7B Wright, Miller & Kane, Civil 2d § 1781.

61. 7B Wright, Miller & Kane, Civil 2d § 1782; Miller, note 1 above, at 674–675; Schuck & Cohen, The Consumer Class Action: An Endangered Species, 1974, 12 San Diego L.Rev. 39; Comment, The Use of Federal Class Actions in Mass Toxic Pollution Torts, 1988, 56 Tenn.L.Rev. 243; Note, The Products Liability Class Suit: Preventive Relief for the Consumer, 1975, 27 S.C.L.Rev. 229; Note, Consumer Class Actions Under Federal Rule 23, 1973, 25 S.C.L.Rev. 239; Comment, The Federal Class Action in Environmental Litigation: Problems and Possibilities, 1973, 51 N.C.L.Rev. 1385.

Congress has amended the Truth in Lending Act to provide for class relief, but it has limited recoveries in class actions under the Act to the lesser of $500,000 or 1% of the creditor's net worth. 15 U.S.C.A. § 1640(a)(2)(B). See 7B Wright, Miller & Kane, Civil 2d § 1804.

62. See Advisory Committee Note, 39 F.R.D. 98, 103. See generally 7B Wright, Miller & Kane, Civil 2d § 1783.

63. In re Northern District of California Dalkon Shield IUD Products Liab. Litigation, C.A.9th, 1982, 693 F.2d 847; McDonnell Douglas Corp. v. United States Dist. Court, C.A.9th, 1975, 523 F.2d 1083, certiorari denied 96 S.Ct. 1506, 425 U.S. 911, 47 L.Ed.2d 761; In re Tetracycline Cases, D.C.Mo.1985, 107 F.R.D. 719; Mertens v.

Abbott Labs., D.C.N.H.1983, 99 F.R.D. 38; In re Three Mile Island Litigation, D.C.Pa. 1980, 87 F.R.D. 433; Causey v. Pan American World Airways, Inc., D.C.Va.1975, 66 F.R.D. 392; Yandle v. PPG Indus., Inc., D.C.Tex.1974, 65 F.R.D. 566.

64. 7B Wright, Miller & Kane, Civil 2d § 1783; and for the special problems of products-liability litigation, see 7B id. § 1805. See also A.L.I., Complex Litigation Project, Proposed Final Draft 1993; Nielson, Was the 1966 Advisory Committee Right?: Suggested Revisions of Rule 23 to Allow More Frequent Use of Class Actions in Mass Tort Litigation, 1988, 25 Harv.J. on Legis. 461; Rosenberg, Class Actions for Mass Torts: Doing Individual Justice by Collective Means, 1987, 62 Ind.L.J. 561; Williams, Mass Tort Class Actions: Going, Going, Gone?, 1983, 98 F.R.D. 323; Comment, The Propriety of Class Actions in Mass Aviation Disaster Litigation, 1990, 56 J.Air L. & Com. 559. But see Mullenix, Class Resolution of the Mass–Tort Cases: A Proposed Federal Procedure Act, 1986, 64 Texas L.Rev. 1039 (arguing that reluctance to use Rule 23 is justified and that a statutory solution is needed).

65. Sterling v. Velsicol Chem. Corp., C.A.6th, 1988, 855 F.2d 1188; Jenkins v. Raymark Indus., Inc., C.A.5th, 1986, 782 F.2d 468; Sala v. National R.R. Passenger Corp., D.C.Pa.1988, 120 F.R.D. 494; Wehner v. Syntex Corp., D.C.Cal.1987, 117 F.R.D. 641; Coburn v. 4–R Corp., D.C.Ky. 1977, 77 F.R.D. 43, mandamus denied C.A.6th, 1978, 588 F.2d 543; Bentkowski v. Marfuerza Compania Maritima, S.A.,

If the court permits a (b)(3) class action to be maintained, it must direct to the members of the class the best notice practicable under the circumstances, including individual notice to all members who can be identified through reasonable effort.[66] This notice is crucial to the whole scheme of (b)(3). Arguably notice is not constitutionally compelled as a condition to binding absentees. In the leading case of Hansberry v. Lee, the Supreme Court said that a judgment in a class action will bind absentees whenever the procedure adopted "fairly insures the protection of the absent parties who are to be bound by it,"[67] and that even where the only circumstance defining the class is a common issue of fact or law, as in the (b)(3) action, the judgment might be made binding on all members of the class "provided that the procedure were so devised and applied as to insure that those present are of the same class as those absent and that the litigation is so conducted as to insure the full and fair consideration of the common issue."[68] Nevertheless it is clear that effective notice greatly strengthens the argument that the absentee is bound.[69]

In Eisen v. Carlisle & Jacquelin[70] the Supreme Court held that in a (b)(3) class action it is mandatory that individual notice be provided to those members of the class who are identifiable through reasonable effort. Notice by publication is not permissible even where the cost of individual notice is prohibitively high.[71] Nor may the cost of notice be imposed on the defendant. Instead the plaintiff must pay for the cost of notice as a part of the ordinary burden of financing his or her own suit,

D.C.Pa.1976, 70 F.R.D. 401; Hernandez v. Motor Vessel Skyward, D.C.Fla.1973, 61 F.R.D. 558, affirmed C.A.5th, 1975, 507 F.2d 1279.

66. Rule 23(c)(2); 7B Wright, Miller & Kane, Civil 2d §§ 1786–1788; Dam, note 13 above; Ward & Elliott, The Contents and Mechanics of Rule 23 Notice, 1969, 10 B.C.Ind. & Com.L.Rev. 557.

The Supreme Court has severely restricted "gag orders" barring communications between parties or their counsel and actual or potential class members. Gulf Oil Co. v. Bernard, 1981, 101 S.Ct. 2193, 452 U.S. 89, 68 L.Ed.2d 693. But the potential for misuse in communications from counsel can be countered by court-authorized notice. Hoffman–La Roche Inc. v. Sperling, 1989, 110 S.Ct. 482, 493 U.S. 165, 107 L.Ed.2d 480.

67. 61 S.Ct. at 118, 311 U.S. at 42. See also Sam Fox Pub. Co. v. U.S., 1961, 81 S.Ct. 1309, 1314, 366 U.S. 683, 691, 6 L.Ed.2d 604.

68. 61 S.Ct. at 119, 311 U.S. at 43.

69. It is not clear that what the Supreme Court said in Phillips Petroleum Co. v. Shutts, 1985, 105 S.Ct. 2965, 472 U.S. 797, 86 L.Ed.2d 628, necessarily applies to a class action in federal court. The Court in that case was concerned with whether or when a state court can include absent members of a plaintiff class who lack even minimum contacts with the forum. The Court held that a state court could do so if it provides "minimal procedural due process protection. The plaintiff must receive notice plus an opportunity to be heard and participate in the litigation, whether in person or through counsel. * * * The notice should describe the action and the plaintiff's rights in it. Additionally, we hold that due process requires at a minimum that an absent plaintiff be provided with an opportunity to remove himself from the class by executing and returning an 'opt out' or 'request for exclusion' form to the court." 105 S.Ct. at 2974, 472 U.S. at 811–812. See Miller & Crump, Jurisdiction and Choice of Law in Multistate Class Actions after Phillips Petroleum Co. v. Shutts, 1986, 96 Yale L.J. 8.

70. 1974, 94 S.Ct. 2140, 417 U.S. 156, 40 L.Ed.2d 732. See Benett, Eisen v. Carlisle & Jacquelin: Supreme Court Calls for Revamping of Class Action Strategy, 1974 Wis.L.Rev. 801.

71. 94 S.Ct. at 2150–2152, 417 U.S. at 173–177.

and if plaintiff will not bear the cost of notice the action cannot proceed as a class action.[72]

The Court in Eisen was at pains to base its decision on the language of Rule 23(c)(2) and to point out that that subdivision applies only to (b)(3) class actions.[73] Rule 23(d)(2) permits, but does not require, notice to members of the class in class actions that proceed under sections of Rule 23 other than (b)(3)[74] and the better view is that there is no constitutional requirement of notice to members of the class in (b)(1) or (b)(2) actions.[75]

Notice is particularly critical in (b)(3) class actions, and is made mandatory by the rules, in part because the class members are only loosely associated by common questions of law or fact, rather than by any preexisting or continuing legal relationship, and thus it is less certain that they will be fully protected by the named representatives. The other reason for making notice mandatory in these cases is because of the unusual procedural provisions that apply. The notice to the absentee in a (b)(3) action advises him of his rights in the action, that he may appear through his counsel if he wishes, that he will be excluded from the class if he so requests by a date and procedure specified in the notice, and that the judgment will include him if he has not requested exclusion.[76] It is only in actions that are brought under (b)(3) that absent members of the class have the unique privilege to "opt out."[77]

72. 94 S.Ct. at 2152–2153, 417 U.S. at 177–179.

The Court has also held that the defendant cannot be required to bear the cost of compiling a list of members of the class, so that notice can be sent them, unless the expense is so insubstantial as not to warrant the effort required to calculate it and shift it to the plaintiff. A cost of $16,000 was held not to be insubstantial. Oppenheimer Fund, Inc. v. Sanders, 1978, 98 S.Ct. 2380, 437 U.S. 340, 57 L.Ed.2d 253. But discovery of the names and addresses of all similarly situated employees was held proper in an action under the Age Discrimination in Employment Act. Hoffman–La Roche Inc. v. Sperling, 1989, 110 S.Ct. 482, 493 U.S. 165, 107 L.Ed.2d 480.

73. 94 S.Ct. at 2152 n. 14, 417 U.S. at 177 n. 14.

"[I]t seems conceded that a Rule 23(b)(1) or 23(b)(2) class suit can bind the class membership without their having been given notice, thus finally determining such important matters as the life insurance benefits of a class of insured persons or the right of a group of children to go to a desegregated school. Why should more elaborate notice be required to persons having small tort claims, as was the situation in Eisen? As for procedural policy, why should the damages class suit be so strongly disfa-

vored?" James, Hazard & Leubsdorf, Civil Procedure, 4th ed. 1992, p. 566.

74. 7B Wright, Miller & Kane, Civil 2d § 1793.

75. Stoetzner v. U.S. Steel Corp., C.A.3d, 1990, 897 F.2d 115, 119; Society for Individual Rights, Inc. v. Hampton, C.A.9th, 1975, 528 F.2d 905, 906; and cases cited 7B Wright, Miller & Kane, Civil 2d § 1786 n. 9.

The contrary view announced in Schrader v. Selective Serv. System Local Bd. No. 76, C.A.7th, 1972, 470 F.2d 73, 75, certiorari denied 93 S.Ct. 689, 409 U.S. 1085, 34 L.Ed.2d 672, was based on a dictum from the Second Circuit that since has been repudiated by its home court. Nevertheless it has had some scholarly support. Reno, Notice and Due Process in Federal Class Actions: A Requiem for Revised Rule 23?, 1975, 2 Hast.Const.L.Q. 479; Maraist & Sharp, Federal Procedure's Troubled Marriage: Due Process and the Class Action, 1970, 49 Texas L.Rev. 1. But see Miller, Problems of Giving Notice in Class Actions, 1973, 58 F.R.D. 313, 313–317.

76. 7B Wright, Miller & Kane, Civil 2d § 1787.

77. Cox v. American Cast Iron Pipe Co., C.A.11th, 1986, 784 F.2d 1546, 1553–1555; Dosier v. Miami Val. Broadcasting Corp.,

Critical to the entire operation of the revised rule is the effect of the judgment. It is clearly contemplated that every judgment in every class action will bind all of the members of the class, except for those who have asked to be excluded in a (b)(3) action.[78] The rule does not say this. It says only that the judgment "shall include and describe those whom the court finds to be members of the class," and who have not asked to be excluded from a (b)(3) action.[79] This recognizes that a court conducting an action cannot predetermine its res judicata effect, and that this can be tested only in a subsequent action.[80] It recognizes, too, that even a party named in the judgment will not be bound if he or she has been denied due process of law.[81] But the rule is intended to provide due process to absentees and it plainly contemplates that they will be bound.

The absentee has an absolute right to be excluded from a (b)(3) action. If he does "opt out," and the judgment ultimately is favorable to the class, he should not be entitled to rely on it as collateral estoppel—or issue preclusion, as it is now known—in those jurisdictions that have departed from the requirement of mutuality for estoppel. To permit him to do this would make a mockery of the (b)(3) procedure, and would restore in a different form the "one way" intervention that the amended rule was expressly intended to preclude.[82] Notions of issue preclusion are not so inexorable that a party who has affirmatively obtained exclusion from a judgment need be allowed later to claim the benefits of the judgment.[83]

C.A.9th, 1981, 656 F.2d 1295, 1299. If a class action meets the requirement of (b)(3) but also qualifies as a class action under (b)(1) or (b)(2), it has not been treated as a (b)(3) action for purposes of the notice requirements and the "opt out" provision. In re A.H. Robins Co., C.A.4th, 1989, 880 F.2d 709, 728, certiorari denied 110 S.Ct. 377, 493 U.S. 959, 107 L.Ed.2d 362; and cases cited 7A Wright, Miller & Kane, Civil 2d § 1772 n. 13. But the Supreme Court has now treated this as an open and difficult question. Ticor Title Ins. Co. v. Brown, 1994, 114 S.Ct. 1359, ___ U.S. ___, 128 L.Ed.2d 33.

Flexibility has been used in determining what a class member must do in order to "opt out." See In re Four Seasons Securities Laws Litigation, C.A.10th, 1974, 493 F.2d 1288, 1291, certiorari denied 95 S.Ct. 516, 419 U.S. 1034, 42 L.Ed.2d 309.

78. "The 1966 amendments were designed in part, * * * to assure that members of the class would be identified before trial on the merits and would be bound by all subsequent orders and judgments." American Pipe & Constr. Co. v. Utah, 1974, 94 S.Ct. 756, 763, 414 U.S. 538, 547, 38 L.Ed.2d 713. See 7B Wright, Miller & Kane, Civil 2d § 1789; 18 Wright, Miller & Cooper, Jurisdiction § 4455.

79. Rule 23(c)(3).

"This is a statement of how the judgment shall read, not an attempted prescription of its subsequent res judicata effect, although looking ahead with hope to that effect." Kaplan, note 41 above, at 393.

80. Taunton Gardens Co. v. Hills, C.A.1st, 1977, 557 F.2d 877, 878; Restatement Second of Judgments, 1982, § 42; Note, Binding Effect of Class Actions, 1954, 67 Harv.L.Rev. 1059, 1060. But see Note, 1965, 51 Va.L.Rev. 629, 655–660.

81. Gonzales v. Cassidy, C.A.5th, 1973, 474 F.2d 67, 74; Note, Collateral Attack on the Binding Effect of Class Action Judgments, 1974, 87 Harv.L.Rev. 589.

82. Advisory Committee Note, 39 F.R.D. 98, 105–106. See American Pipe & Constr. Co. v. Utah, 1974, 94 S.Ct. 756, 762–764, 414 U.S. 538, 545–549, 38 L.Ed.2d 713.

83. Restatement Second of Judgments, 1982, § 42 Ill. 6; Premier Elec. Constr. Co. v. National Elec. Contractors Assn., C.A.7th, 1987, 814 F.2d 358, 364; Polk v. Montgomery County, C.A.4th, 1986, 782 F.2d 1196, 1202; Sarasota Oil Co. v. Greyhound Leasing & Financial Corp., C.A.10th, 1973, 483 F.2d 450, 452. See generally George, Sweet Use of Adversity: Parklane

Despite the fact that Rule 23(c)(2)(B) specifically states that the judgment in a (b)(3) action "will include all members who do not request exclusion," a few courts in actions involving extremely large classes of plaintiffs seeking a damage recovery have held that the court may require members of the class to take some affirmative action to remain in the class.[84] This is directly contrary to the language and the philosophy of the rule.[85] It is perfectly proper, however, after defendant's liability has been established, to send a second notice to the class members requiring them to file statements of their individual claims by a stated date.[86]

It has long been the rule that in a class action only the citizenship of the named representatives is to be considered, and that it is no objection to jurisdiction that other members of the class, not named as parties, are of such citizenship as would defeat diversity.[87] This continues to be held under the amended rule. It is true that (b)(3) now permits persons to be bound by a judgment though they are linked only by common questions of law and fact. Nevertheless (b)(3), and perhaps the whole rule, would be totally unworkable in a diversity case if the citizenship of all members of the class, many of them unknown, had to be considered.[88] Similarly for purposes of venue only the residence of the named parties should be considered.[89]

Amount in controversy is a different matter.[90] The decisions in

Hosiery and the Collateral Class Action, 1980, 32 Stan.L.Rev. 655; Note, Offensive Assertion of Collateral Estoppel by Persons Opting Out of a Class Action, 1980, 31 Hastings L.J. 1189.

84. Kyriazi v. Western Elec. Co., C.A.3d, 1981, 647 F.2d 388; In re Antibiotic Antitrust Actions, D.C.N.Y.1971, 333 F.Supp. 267; Iowa v. Union Asphalt & Roadoils, Inc., D.C.Iowa 1968, 281 F.Supp. 391, 403, affirmed C.A.8th, 1969, 409 F.2d 1239; Minnesota v. United States Steel Corp., D.C.Minn.1968, 44 F.R.D. 559, 577; Philadelphia Elec. Co. v. Anaconda American Brass Co., D.C.Pa.1968, 43 F.R.D. 452, 459; Ward & Elliott, The Contents and Mechanics of Rule 23 Notice, 1969, 10 B.C.Ind. & Com.L.Rev. 557, 568.

85. Clark v. Universal Builders, Inc., C.A.7th, 1974, 501 F.2d 324, 340, certiorari denied 95 S.Ct. 657, 419 U.S. 1070, 42 L.Ed.2d 666; In re Crazy Eddie Secs. Litigation, D.C.N.Y.1991, 135 F.R.D. 39, 42; and cases cited 7B Wright, Miller & Kane, Civil 2d § 1787 n. 24. See also Manual for Complex Litigation, Second, § 30.14.

86. B & B Inv. Club v. Kleinert's Inc., D.C.Pa.1974, 62 F.R.D. 140, 149 n. 6; Forbes v. Greater Minneapolis Area Bd. of Realtors, D.C.Minn.1973, 61 F.R.D. 416;

Harris v. Jones, D.C.Utah 1966, 41 F.R.D. 70.

It has also been held that a proof of claim can be required in a (b)(2) class action in which back pay is awarded as incidental to injunctive or declaratory relief. Kyriazi v. Western Elec. Co., C.A.3d, 1981, 647 F.2d 388.

87. Supreme Tribe of Ben Hur v. Cauble, 1921, 41 S.Ct. 338, 255 U.S. 356, 65 L.Ed. 673.

88. 7A Wright, Miller & Kane, Civil 2d § 1755. That this is still the rule was affirmed, against strenuous attack, in In re School Asbestos Litigation, C.A.3d, 1990, 921 F.2d 1310, 1317–1318, certiorari denied 111 S.Ct. 1623, 499 U.S. 976, 113 L.Ed.2d 720.

89. Appleton Elec. Co. v. Advance–United Expressways, C.A.7th, 1974, 494 F.2d 126; Research Corp. v. Pfister Associated Growers, Inc., D.C.Ill.1969, 301 F.Supp. 497, appeal dismissed C.A.7th, 1970, 425 F.2d 1059; 7A Wright, Miller & Kane, Civil 2d § 1757.

90. See 7A Wright, Miller & Kane, Civil 2d § 1756; 14A Wright, Miller & Cooper, Jurisdiction 2d § 3705.

Snyder v. Harris [91] and in Zahn v. International Paper Co.[92] have, in effect, made class actions unavailable in those diversity cases in which more than $50,000 must be in controversy.[93]

The Snyder case held that traditional rules on aggregation of claims for purposes of jurisdictional amount [94] apply to class actions. Thus, if a large class of plaintiffs each have small claims, they cannot aggregate their claims to satisfy the amount requirement if their claims are "separate and distinct." This is true even though the entire class is now bound by the judgment, the result cannot vary from one member of the class to another, and realistically the amount in controversy is the amount sought on behalf of the entire class. It is only if the claims can be regarded as "joint" or "common" that aggregation is permitted.[95] Zahn closed the door even farther. Although the named representatives have claims for more than the required amount, the action cannot go forward as a class action on behalf of absentees whose claims are for less than that amount. "Each plaintiff in a Rule 23(b)(3) class action must satisfy the jurisdictional amount, and any plaintiff who does not must be dismissed from the case— 'one plaintiff may not ride in on another's coattails.' " [96] Perhaps the most surprising feature of Zahn is its failure even to discuss the argument of the dissent that the concept of ancillary jurisdiction could permit hearing the smaller claims as ancillary to those for more than the $10,000 then required.[97] That argument was surely rejected by Zahn, and there may well be good reasons for rejecting it, but the Court did not articulate them.

Although, in the passage just quoted, the Zahn Court spoke of (b)(3) class actions, there is nothing in its reasoning that would suggest that

91. 1969, 89 S.Ct. 1053, 394 U.S. 332, 22 L.Ed.2d 319.

92. 1974, 94 S.Ct. 505, 414 U.S. 291, 38 L.Ed.2d 511. Zahn has produced extensive commentary, mostly critical in nature. See 7A Wright, Miller & Kane, Civil 2d § 1756 nn. 31, 32.

93. See § 32 above.

In fiscal 1977, the most recent year for which these figures have been given, 3,153 class actions were commenced in federal courts. Only 107 of these were based on diversity. Ann.Rep. of the Director of the Administrative Office of the U.S. Courts, 1977, p. 238. The required amount for diversity cases was raised from $10,000 to $50,000 in 1988. It seems unlikely that there will be many cases in which persons, numerous enough to require class-action treatment, each have claims in excess of $50,000.

94. See § 36 above.

95. Gallagher v. Continental Ins. Co., C.A.10th, 1974, 502 F.2d 827; New Jersey Welfare Rights Organization v. Cahill, C.A.3d, 1973, 483 F.2d 723, 725 n. 3;

Dierks v. Thompson, C.A.1st, 1969, 414 F.2d 453; Berman v. Narragansett Racing Assn., C.A.1st, 1969, 414 F.2d 311, certiorari denied 90 S.Ct. 682, 396 U.S. 1037, 24 L.Ed.2d 681; Meyer v. Citizens & So. Nat. Bank, D.C.Ga.1985, 106 F.R.D. 356. For other cases in which claims have been found "joint" or "common" and aggregation permitted, and for the more numerous cases in which the claims were thought "separate and distinct" and aggregation not allowed, see 7A Wright, Miller & Kane, Civil 2d § 1756, pp. 76–85.

96. 94 S.Ct. at 512, 414 U.S. at 301.

This does not require these persons to be dismissed at the outset of the action. The district court has discretionary authority to delay until trial the dismissal of those class members that cannot meet the amount in controversy. In re School Asbestos Litigation, C.A.3d, 1990, 921 F.2d 1310, 1315–1316, certiorari denied 111 S.Ct. 1623, 499 U.S. 976, 113 L.Ed.2d 720; Sterling v. Velsicol Chem. Corp., C.A.6th, 1988, 855 F.2d 1188.

97. 94 S.Ct. at 512, 414 U.S. at 301–302 (Brennan, J., dissenting).

any other rule will govern other kinds of class actions. Even so, Snyder and Zahn should pose no problems in (b)(2) class actions, at least so long as those actions are to redress racial discrimination, since that kind of action can be brought without regard to amount in controversy.[98] In most (b)(1) actions aggregation is apparently permissible, but the (b)(1) action is not coextensive with the former "true" class action, and it cannot automatically be assumed that aggregation is always permissible. It will be necessary in those cases to determine whether the right involved is "joint" or "common" on the one hand, or "several" on the other, no matter how meaningless and arbitrary such a distinction may seem.[99] In a (b)(3) action it appears that the right being enforced must always be labelled "several," and thus Snyder and Zahn preclude aggregation.[100] This will not affect federal-question cases, in which no amount in controversy is required.

It is possible that the 1990 enactment of a supplemental-jurisdiction statute has had the effect of overruling Zahn.[101] The legislative history says that the statute was "not intended to affect the jurisdictional requirements of 28 U.S.C. § 1332 in diversity-only class actions, as those requirements were interpreted prior to Finley."[102] But § 1367(a) is a broad grant of supplemental jurisdiction and Rule 23 is not among the rules listed in § 1367(b) as exceptions to that broad grant.[103] Though the early cases are divided, most of the courts that have passed on the question to date have relied on the legislative history, rather than the words of the statute, and have held that Zahn is still authoritative.[104]

---

98. See § 32 above. Even where amount in controversy is required, it may be found that the plaintiffs in a (b)(2) action have a common, undivided interest so that aggregation will be allowed. Brandt v. Owens–Illinois, Inc., D.C.N.Y.1973, 62 F.R.D. 160. But see U.S. v. Southern Pac. Transp. Co., C.A.9th, 1976, 543 F.2d 676, 682–684.

99. Amen v. City of Dearborn, C.A.6th, 1976, 532 F.2d 554, 559.

100. Snow v. Ford Motor Co., C.A.9th, 1977, 561 F.2d 787.

101. 28 U.S.C.A. § 1367. The statute is discussed in § 9 above.

102. H.R.Rep. No. 101–734, 91st Cong., 2d Sess., 1991, at 29, reprinted in 1991 U.S. Code Cong. & Adm. News 6860, 6875.

103. This point is made by Steinman, Section 1367—Another Party Heard From, 1992, 41 Emory L.J. 85, 102; Arthur & Freer, Grasping At Burnt Straws: The Disaster of the Supplemental Jurisdiction Statute, 1991, 40 Emory L.J. 963, 981. The problem is recognized, but it is thought that the legislative history corrects the problem, in Rowe, Burbank & Mengler, Compounding or Creating Confusion About Supplemental Jurisdiction? A Reply to Professor

Freer, 1991, 40 Emory L.J. 943, 960 n. 90. This is the view taken also in McLaughlin, The Federal Supplemental Jurisdiction Statute—A Constitutional and Statutory Analysis, 1992, 24 Ariz.St.L.J. 849, 972–974, though recognizing "the inherent difficulty in judicial interpretation of a statute contrary to its plain wording." Id. at 973.

104. The following cases hold that Zahn still controls: Benfield v. Mocatta Metals Corp., D.C.N.Y.1993, 1993 WL 148978; Hairston v. Home Loan & Inv. Bank, D.C.Mass.1993, 814 F.Supp. 180, 181; Mayo v. Key Fin. Servs., Inc., D.C.Mass. 1993, 812 F.Supp. 277, 278; Averdick v. Republic Fin. Servs., Inc., D.C.Ky.1992, 803 F.Supp. 37, 45–46; Bradbury v. Robertson–Ceco Corp., D.C.Ill. 1992, 1992 WL 178648; Griffin v. Dana Point Condominium Assn., D.C.Ill.1991, 768 F.Supp. 1299, 1301–1302.

The following cases are to the contrary and hold that § 1367 has overruled Zahn: Patterson Enterprises, Inc. v. Bridgestone/Firestone, Inc., D.C.Kan.1993, 812 F.Supp. 1152, 1154–1155, and in Garza v. National American Ins. Co., D.C.La.1992, 807 F.Supp. 1256, 1258 n. 6.

The question is discussed, but not decided, in Packard v. Provident Nat. Bank, C.A.3d, 1993, 994 F.2d 1039, 1045 n. 9,

There is no problem with regard to the statute of limitations under the amended rule. Since the judgment is now binding in all class actions, commencement of the action tolls the statute of limitations for all members of the class.[105] This result is reached even if the court, for reasons of judicial housekeeping, ultimately holds that it will not allow the suit to proceed as a class action, since otherwise members of the class would have to file a protective individual suit pending that determination.[106]

Because of the representative nature of a class action, the court has more control over it than over ordinary actions, and must assume "a more active role than it normally does."[107] Rule 23(d), added in 1966, spells out in some detail the flexible powers the court has over the conduct of the action.[108] The action may not be dismissed or compromised without the approval of the court, and notice of the proposed dismissal or compromise must be given to all members of the class in such manner as the court directs.[109] If the suit results in a recovery beneficial to the class, the court may award an attorneys' fee to the attorneys for the representatives out of the sum recovered,[110] though recent cases are taking a restrictive approach to the size of the fee that can be awarded.[111]

certiorari denied 114 S.Ct. 440, ___ U.S. ___, 126 L.Ed.2d 373.

105. Esplin v. Hirschi, C.A.10th, 1968, 402 F.2d 94, certiorari denied 89 S.Ct. 1194, 394 U.S. 928, 22 L.Ed.2d 459; Comment, 1968, 13 Vill.L.Rev. 370; 7B Wright, Miller & Kane, Civil 2d § 1800.

106. American Pipe & Constr. Co. v. Utah, 1974, 94 S.Ct. 756, 414 U.S. 538, 38 L.Ed.2d 713; Wheeler, Predismissal Notice and Statute of Limitations in Federal Class Actions After American Pipe and Construction Co. v. Utah, 1975, 48 S.Cal.L.Rev. 771; Note, 1982, 67 Iowa L.Rev. 743; Comment, 1974, 12 San Diego L.Rev. 169.

See also Crown, Cork & Seal Co. v. Parker, 1983, 103 S.Ct. 2392, 462 U.S. 345, 76 L.Ed.2d 628; 7B Wright, Miller & Kane, Civil 2d § 1795, pp. 324–331.

107. Dolgow v. Anderson, D.C.N.Y.1968, 43 F.R.D. 472, 481.

108. Newberg, Orders in the Conduct of Class Actions: A Consideration of Subdivision (d), 1969, 10 B.C.Ind. & Com.L.Rev. 577; 7B Wright, Miller & Kane, Civil 2d §§ 1791–1796.

There has been uncertainty about obtaining discovery from absent class members. The rule that has evolved is that discovery against the absentees is not a matter of right. The court must balance on a case-by-case basis defendant's need for detailed information against the burden on the absent class members. Brennan v. Midwestern United Life Ins. Co., C.A.7th, 1971, 450

F.2d 999; 7B Wright, Miller & Kane, Civil 2d § 1796.1.

109. Rule 23(e); 7B Wright, Miller & Kane, Civil 2d § 1797; McGough & Lerach, Termination of Class Actions: The Judicial Role, 1972, 33 U.Pitt.L.Rev. 445. For the kinds of factors the court considers in passing on a settlement, see 7B Wright, Miller & Kane, Civil 2d § 1797.1.

If an action is brought as a class action, Rule 23(e) applies to its dismissal or compromise even though it has not yet been certified as a class action. Philadelphia Elec. Co. v. Anaconda American Brass Co., D.C.Pa.1967, 42 F.R.D. 324; and cases cited 7B Wright, Miller & Kane, Civil 2d § 1797 nn. 18, 19.

If an action is dismissed by the court as a sanction for noncompliance with the discovery rules, and the absent members of the class are not given notice before the dismissal, the dismissal is not binding on them and they may bring a second suit. Papilsky v. Berndt, C.A.2d, 1972, 466 F.2d 251, certiorari denied 93 S.Ct. 689, 409 U.S. 1077, 34 L.Ed.2d 665. See Comment, Involuntary Dismissals of Class Actions, 1973, 40 U.Chi.L.Rev. 783.

110. Boeing Co. v. Van Gemert, 1980, 100 S.Ct. 745, 444 U.S. 472, 62 L.Ed.2d 676. See 7B Wright, Miller & Kane, Civil 2d § 1803.

111. See 7B Wright, Miller & Kane, Civil 2d § 1803; Miller, Attorneys' Fees in

Until 1966 actions involving unincorporated associations were often brought under the general rule applicable to all class actions, in situations in which the association could not be treated as an entity under Rule 17(b).[112] In 1966 a new Rule 23.2 was adopted, permitting suit by or against the members of an unincorporated association as a class only if it appears that the members named as representatives will fairly and adequately protect the interests of the association and its members. Rule 23(d), listing orders the court may make in the conduct of a class action, is specifically incorporated by reference for unincorporated association actions, as is Rule 23(e), requiring approval of the court, after notice, for the dismissal or compromise of any class action. The explicit incorporation by reference of two subdivisions of Rule 23 suggests that the other parts of Rule 23, including notably the limitations in subdivisions (a) and (b) on when a class action may be maintained, do not apply to actions relating to unincorporated associations, but the committee note is wholly silent on this question.[113]

§ 73. Stockholders' Derivative Actions [1]

A derivative action "in essence is nothing more than a suit by a beneficiary of a fiduciary to enforce a right running to the fiduciary as such."[2] Easily the most common example of such an action is a suit by minority stockholders in a corporation who claim that the corporation has been wronged but that the majority will not seek redress on behalf of the corporation. Special requirements for this kind of suit appear in Rule 23.1.[3] This is not the only derivative action that is possible. Trust beneficiaries may bring claims derivatively on behalf of the trust if the trustee refuses to bring them, and the same general principles will apply as in stockholders' suits,[4] but the specific provisions of Rule 23.1 are not controlling.

Class Actions, Federal Judicial Center 1980; Manual for Complex Litigation, Second, 1985, §§ 24.11, 24.12; Silver, A Restitutionary Theory of Attorneys' Fees in Class Actions, 1991, 76 Cornell L.Rev. 656. Among the leading cases are Lindy Bros. Builders, Inc. v. American Radiator & Standard Sanitary Corp., C.A.3d, 1976, 540 F.2d 102, and Detroit v. Grinnell Corp., C.A.2d, 1974, 495 F.2d 448.

112. See generally 7C Wright, Miller & Kane, Civil 2d § 1861.

113. Advisory Committee Note, 39 F.R.D. 108. Compare Management Television Systems, Inc. v. National Football League, D.C.Pa.1971, 52 F.R.D. 162, with Sembach v. McMahon College, Inc., D.C.Tex.1980, 86 F.R.D. 188.

§ 73

1. 7C Wright, Miller & Kane, Civil 2d §§ 1821–1841; Kessler, Shareholder Deriv-

ative Actions: A Modest Proposal to Revise Federal Rule 23.1, 1973, 7 U.Mich.J.L.Reform 90; Dykstra, The Revival of the Derivative Suit, 1967, 116 U.Pa.L.Rev. 74; Sullivan, The Federal Courts as an Effective Forum in Shareholders' Derivative Actions, 1962, 22 La.L.Rev. 580.

2. Goldstein v. Groesbeck, C.C.A.2d, 1944, 142 F.2d 422, 425, certiorari denied 65 S.Ct. 36, 323 U.S. 737, 89 L.Ed. 590. As the cited case indicates, there may also be "double derivative" actions "in which the beneficiary is in his turn a fiduciary, and as such refuses to enforce the right which is his as beneficiary of the first fiduciary."

3. A similar rule, Rule 23.2, applies to suits by minority members of an unincorporated association. See 7C Wright, Miller & Kane, Civil 2d § 1861.

4. Helm v. Zarecor, 1911, 32 S.Ct. 10, 12, 222 U.S. 32, 36, 56 L.Ed. 77; Reed v. Robilio, C.A.6th, 1967, 376 F.2d 392, 395–

It is possible to have a stockholders' derivative suit that is not also a class action, as where the minority stock is held by one person or a few persons,[5] but in almost all derivative actions the stockholder is suing on behalf of a large class of other minority stockholders similarly situated. Because of this, in the original rules these actions were treated in Rule 23(b), as a part of class actions generally. In the 1966 revision it was decided to deal independently with derivative actions by stockholders in a separate Rule 23.1. Thus, the general class action rule, Rule 23, no longer applies to stockholders' derivative suits.[6] By the same token, suits by stockholders that are not derivative, in which they are asserting their individual claims against a corporation, such as suits to compel declaration of a dividend, or to restrain a merger, are not subject to Rule 23.1. If they are brought, as they usually will be, as class actions, they must meet the tests of Rule 23, and generally will come under Rule 23(b)(1).[7]

Rule 23.1 makes no change of substance in the previous rules applicable to stockholders' derivative suits. Indeed it was deliberately determined not to "disturb the procedural balance previously established in this kind of litigation."[8] Thus, pre–1966 decisions remain completely authoritative.

In a stockholders' derivative suit the stockholder is suing to enforce a claim that belongs to the corporation. Accordingly the corporation must be joined as a party, and the relief granted is a judgment against third persons, also named as defendants, in favor of the corporation.[9]

Rule 23.1 requires the complaint in a derivative action to allege that a demand for action has been made on the directors and, if necessary, the stockholders, or that such a demand was excused. This is a requirement of long standing in federal practice,[10] and would lead to little difficulty except for the now-vexing question of the extent to which state law is to be controlling. Since the states universally require demand on the directors, that phase of the requirement has caused no controversy, but the states are divided on whether demand must be made also on the stockholders and on the circumstances that will excuse such a demand. That state law on this issue must be followed in a diversity case seems clearly required by the Erie doctrine.[11] While state

396; Hellenthal v. John Hancock Mut. Life Ins. Co., D.C.Wash.1929, 31 F.2d 997, 998.

5. Galdi v. Jones, C.C.A.2d, 1944, 141 F.2d 984, 992.

6. Kauffman v. Dreyfus Fund, Inc., C.A.3d, 1970, 434 F.2d 727, 734–736.

7. Advisory Committee Note, 39 F.R.D. 98, 101; Simcox v. San Juan Shipyard, Inc., C.A.1st, 1985, 754 F.2d 430, 438; King v. Kansas City Southern Indus., Inc., C.A.7th, 1975, 519 F.2d 20; Tankersley v. Albright, D.C.Ill.1978, 80 F.R.D. 441.

8. Kaplan, Continuing Work of the Civil Committee: 1966 Amendments of the Fed-

eral Rules of Civil Procedure, 1967 81 Harv. L.Rev. 356, 387 n. 118. See also Papilsky v. Berndt, C.A.2d, 1972, 466 F.2d 251, 257 n. 7, certiorari denied 93 S.Ct. 689, 409 U.S. 1077, 34 L.Ed.2d 665.

9. Ross v. Bernhard, 1970, 90 S.Ct. 733, 738, 396 U.S. 531, 538, 24 L.Ed.2d 729; 7C Wright, Miller & Kane, Civil 2d § 1821.

10. Hawes v. City of Oakland, 1882, 104 U.S. 450, 26 L.Ed. 827.

11. Wolgin v. Simon, C.A.8th, 1983, 722 F.2d 389; Jacobs v. Adams, C.A.5th, 1979, 601 F.2d 176; Brody v. Chemical Bank, C.A.2d, 1973, 482 F.2d 1111, certiorari de-law is looked to for the requirement of a demand, the federal court is free to decide for itself whether the demand, or the reasons that excuse the failure to make a demand, have been pleaded with the particularity required by Rule 23.1.[12]

The Supreme Court's 1991 decision in Kamen v. Kemper Financial Services, Inc.,[13] emphasizes the points just made. A unanimous Court there held that Rule 23.1 speaks only to the adequacy of the pleadings and does not create a demand requirement. Indeed since "the function of the demand doctrine in delimiting the respective powers of the individual shareholder and of the directors to control corporate litigation clearly is a matter of 'substance,' not 'procedure'," it would be inconsistent with the Rules Enabling Act[14] to interpret Rule 23.1 in any other way.[15] Although the Kamen case was a suit under a federal statute, and the contours of the demand requirement therefore were governed by federal law, the Court held that particularly in the corporate-law area there is a strong presumption to incorporate state law into federal common law and that this presumption applied in the case before it, since the use of a state-law futility exception to the demand requirement would not impede the purposes of the federal statute.[16]

Rule 23.1 also requires the plaintiff to aver that he or she "was a shareholder or member at the time of the transaction of which the plaintiff complains or that the plaintiff's share or membership thereafter devolved on the plaintiff by operation of law."[17] This requirement is based on "a sound and wholesome principle of equity,"[18] in that it prevents a person from buying a lawsuit. It serves the further purpose in federal court of preventing collusive attempts to invoke federal jurisdiction,[19] and is related to the additional requirement of the rule that plaintiff allege that the action is not a collusive one to confer on a

nied 94 S.Ct. 737, 414 U.S. 1104, 38 L.Ed.2d 559; Zimmerman v. Bell, D.C.Md. 1984, 585 F.Supp. 512, 515.

In Burks v. Lasker, 1979, 99 S.Ct. 1831, 441 U.S. 471, 60 L.Ed.2d 404, it is held that whether the disinterested directors of a corporation have power to terminate a derivative action based on the Investment Company Act and the Investment Advisers Act is a question of federal law, but that, as a matter of federal law, state law on the issue will be applied to the extent that it is consistent with the policies of the federal statutes in question. This holding would seem clearly to apply to the closely related question whether a demand on the directors must be made before commencing the action.

12. Sax v. World Wide Press, Inc., C.A.9th, 1987, 809 F.2d 610, 613. See 7C Wright, Miller & Kane, Civil 2d §§ 1831–1832, for decisions about the sufficiency of the pleading, the sufficiency of the demand, and the circumstances which excuse de-

mand. See also Note, The Demand and Standing Requirements in Stockholder Derivative Actions, 1976, 44 U.Chi.L.Rev. 168.

13. 1991, 111 S.Ct. 1711, 500 U.S. 90, 114 L.Ed.2d 152.

14. 28 U.S.C.A. § 2072(b).

15. 111 S.Ct. at 1716, 500 U.S. at ___.

16. 111 S.Ct. at 1717–1723, 500 U.S. at ___–___. With regard generally to federal common law, see § 60 above.

17. 7C Wright, Miller & Kane, Civil 2d § 1828; Harbrecht, The Contemporaneous Ownership Rule in Shareholders' Derivative Suits, 1978, 25 U.C.L.A.L.Rev. 1041.

18. Home Fire Ins. Co. v. Barber, 1903, 93 N.W. 1024, 1029, 67 Neb. 644 (per Pound, C.). See also Bangor Punta Operations, Inc. v. Bangor & A.R. Co., 1974, 94 S.Ct. 2578, 417 U.S. 703, 41 L.Ed.2d 418.

19. Hawes v. City of Oakland, 1882, 104 U.S. 450, 26 L.Ed. 827.

court of the United States jurisdiction of any action of which it would not otherwise have jurisdiction.[20]

The requirement that the plaintiff allege that he or she was a shareholder at the time of the transaction complained of is applicable in federal question cases,[21] except where a specific provision in a federal statute makes an exception to it.[22] It has led to difficulty in diversity cases, since such a requirement is not yet universal in the states, and poses questions under the Erie doctrine. A few courts and commentators take the view that an allegation of this kind is unnecessary, and that plaintiff need not have been a shareholder at the time of the transaction, if the law of the state in which suit is brought or the state of incorporation would permit him to sue without meeting this requirement.[23] Other courts and writers have thought, however, that the rule must be met regardless of state law.[24] The decisions both ways are old—perhaps because most states now have a contemporaneous-ownership requirement—and if the issue were to arise now, a court passing on it would have to take into account the strong emphasis the Supreme Court put in the Kamen case on the importance of allowing state law to control on these issues of corporate governance.

There is a related question, not always clearly distinguished from the one just discussed, about whether state or federal law determines if a person was a stockholder within the meaning of Rule 23.1. The older federal doctrine, and that of a majority of states, is that an equitable owner of shares at the time of the transactions complained of is entitled to maintain a derivative action, and a number of decisions continue to apply such a rule in federal court.[25] Other cases hold, however, that the equitable owner may maintain such an action in a diversity case only if the applicable state law—which ordinarily will be the law of the state of

20. Collusion was found in Amar v. Garnier Enterprises, Inc., D.C.Cal.1966, 41 F.R.D. 211. See 7C Wright, Miller & Kane, Civil 2d § 1830; Rowe, A Comment on the Federalism of the Federal Rules, 1979 Duke L.J. 843.

21. Surowitz v. Hilton Hotels Corp., 1966, 86 S.Ct. 845, 383 U.S. 363, 15 L.Ed.2d 807.

22. E.g., 15 U.S.C.A. § 78p(b), Pellegrino v. Nesbit, C.A.9th, 1953, 203 F.2d 463, 466; 15 U.S.C.A. § 80a–17(e), Entel v. Guilden, D.C.N.Y.1963, 223 F.Supp. 129.

23. Milvy v. Adams, D.C.N.Y.1954, 16 F.R.D. 105, remanded C.A.2d, 1954, 217 F.2d 647; Fuller v. American Machine & Foundry Co., D.C.N.Y.1951, 95 F.Supp. 764; Notes, 1952, 40 Calif.L.Rev. 433, 1949, 62 Harv.L.Rev. 1030, 1040.

24. Elkins v. Bricker, D.C.N.Y.1956, 147 F.Supp. 609; Kaufman v. Wolfson, D.C.N.Y. 1955, 136 F.Supp. 939; Perrott v. United States Banking Corp., D.C.Del.1944, 53 F.Supp. 953; Developments in the Law—Multiparty Litigation in the Federal Courts,

1958, 71 Harv.L.Rev. 874, 964–966. See 7C Wright, Miller & Kane, Civil 2d § 1829; 19 Wright, Miller & Cooper, Jurisdiction § 4509, pp. 160–162.

"Although most cases treat the requirement as one of procedure, this Court has never resolved the issue." Bangor Punta Operations, Inc. v. Bangor & A.R. Co., 1974, 94 S.Ct. 2578, 2582 n. 4, 417 U.S. 703, 708 n. 4, 41 L.Ed.2d 418.

25. deHaas v. Empire Petroleum Co., C.A.10th, 1970, 435 F.2d 1223; H.F.G. Co. v. Pioneer Pub. Co., C.C.A.7th, 1947, 162 F.2d 536; Hurt v. Cotton States Fertilizer Co., C.C.A.5th, 1944, 145 F.2d 293, certiorari denied 65 S.Ct. 679, 324 U.S. 844, 89 L.Ed. 1406; Schupack v. Covelli, D.C.Pa. 1980, 498 F.Supp. 704.

This seems clearly the law if the suit is based on a federal right of action. In re Pittsburgh & L.E.R. Co. Securities & Antitrust Litigation, C.A.3d, 1976, 543 F.2d 1058.

incorporation—permits it.[26] The latter view seems clearly sound. Even if Rule 23.1 may validly be applied regardless of state law to close the doors of federal court to suits by persons who became stockholders after the events complained of, and this in itself is doubtful, the determination of who is a stockholder is not a mere procedural regulation and should be left to state law.

The corporation must be made a party in a derivative action, and is always named as a defendant, along with the third persons against whom the corporation has a claim. Since the ultimate interest of the corporation is similar to that of the stockholders bringing suit, it is frequently claimed that it should be realigned as a plaintiff, thus, in many cases, destroying diversity. It has been settled that if the corporation is under a control antagonistic to the plaintiffs, and made to act in a way detrimental to their rights, it should not be realigned, regardless of its ultimate interest.[27] A sharply divided Court has held that if the pleadings allege that the corporate management refuses to take action to undo a business transaction, or so solidly approves the transaction that any demand to rescind would be futile, this is sufficient to show that the corporation is properly aligned as a defendant, and the court is not to hear evidence to determine whether the corporation is actually under antagonistic control.[28]

In a derivative action, plaintiff recovers nothing and judgment runs in favor of the corporation. For the purpose of jurisdictional amount, therefore, the test is the damage asserted to have been sustained by the defendant corporation.[29] It had been the rule that other stockholders could intervene regardless of the amount of their claim or their citizenship,[30] but the 1990 supplemental-jurisdiction statute may well have ended that and required an independent basis of jurisdiction for intervenors.[31]

Historically the derivative action was available only in equity, where there was no right to jury trial. But the issues a derivative action poses on behalf of the corporation against those who are alleged to have wronged it may well be legal in nature and of a sort that would be triable to a jury on demand of either party if the corporation had brought its own action. In a merged system it makes no sense to deny a jury right

---

26. Drachman v. Harvey, C.A.2d, 1971, 453 F.2d 722, 727; Gallup v. Caldwell, C.C.A.3d, 1941, 120 F.2d 90, 93; Kreuzfeld A.G. v. Carnehammar, D.C.Fla.1991, 138 F.R.D. 594, 605; and cases cited 7C Wright, Miller & Kane, Civil 2d § 1826 n. 10.

27. Doctor v. Harrington, 1905, 25 S.Ct. 355, 196 U.S. 579, 49 L.Ed. 606; Koster v. (American) Lumbermens Mut. Cas. Co., 1947, 67 S.Ct. 828, 330 U.S. 518, 91 L.Ed. 1067.

28. Smith v. Sperling, 1957, 77 S.Ct. 1112, 354 U.S. 91, 1 L.Ed.2d 1205. See 7C Wright, Miller & Kane, Civil 2d § 1822.

Realignment of the corporation as a plaintiff was ordered, in quite unusual circumstances, in Taylor v. Swirnow, D.C.Md. 1978, 80 F.R.D. 79. See also Gibson v. BoPar Dock Co., D.C.Va.1991, 780 F.Supp. 371.

29. Koster v. (American) Lumbermens Mut. Cas. Co., 1947, 67 S.Ct. 828, 330 U.S. 518, 91 L.Ed. 1067; Bernstein v. Levenson, C.A.4th, 1971, 437 F.2d 756.

30. Weinstock v. Kallet, D.C.N.Y.1951, 11 F.R.D. 270.

31. 28 U.S.C.A. § 1367(b). See § 75 below.

that would otherwise exist merely because the action is brought by virtue of a procedural device that was borrowed from the practice in equity.[32] In Ross v. Bernhard[33] the Supreme Court accepted this reasoning and held that there is a right to jury trial in a derivative action if the claim is one that would have been triable to a jury in a suit by the corporation.

A special statute provides that a derivative action by a stockholder on behalf of his corporation may be prosecuted in any district where the corporation might have sued the same defendants.[34] There have been surprising difficulties in construing this seemingly simple statute,[35] but fortunately those problems should no longer be of importance. The liberalization of the general venue statutes in 1988[36] should now allow every derivative action to be brought in a convenient forum without regard to the special venue statute.

Another special statute provides that in a derivative suit process may be served upon the corporation outside the district in which suit is brought.[37] This applies only where suit is brought in a district where the corporation might have sued the wrongdoers, under the other special statute just discussed.[38]

A derivative action cannot be maintained if it appears that the plaintiff does not fairly and adequately represent the interests of other shareholders similarly situated. The rule does not spell out the power of the court over conduct of the action, and relies instead on the inherent power of the court to determine the course of the proceedings and to require notice to other shareholders.[39] State provisions with regard to security for expenses must be followed in a diversity case.[40] Compromise or voluntary dismissal of the action must be with the approval of the court, and notice must be given of the proposed dismissal or compromise to all stockholders in such manner as the court may direct.[41] By its

32. See 9 Wright & Miller, Civil § 2306.

33. 1970, 90 S.Ct. 733, 396 U.S. 531, 24 L.Ed.2d 729. See 7C Wright, Miller & Kane, Civil 2d § 1837.

34. 28 U.S.C.A. § 1401.

35. See 7C Wright, Miller & Kane, Civil 2d § 1825, pp. 29–32.

36. 28 U.S.C.A. § 1391(a), (b). See § 42 above.

37. 28 U.S.C.A. § 1695.

38. Koster v. (American) Lumbermens Mut. Cas. Co., 1947, 67 S.Ct. 828, 831 n. 2, 330 U.S. 518, 522 n. 2, 91 L.Ed. 1067; and cases cited 7C Wright, Miller & Kane, Civil 2d § 1825 nn. 18, 19.

39. G.A. Enterprises, Inc. v. Leisure Living Communities, Inc., C.A.1st, 1975, 517 F.2d 24; Kauffman v. Dreyfus Fund, Inc., C.A.3d, 1970, 434 F.2d 727, certiorari denied 91 S.Ct. 1190, 401 U.S. 974, 28 L.Ed.2d 323; Note, Res Judicata in the Derivative Action: Adequacy of Representa-tion and the Inadequate Plaintiff, 1973, 71 Mich.L.Rev. 1042; 7C Wright, Miller, & Kane, Civil 2d § 1833.

40. Cohen v. Beneficial Indus. Loan Corp., 1949, 69 S.Ct. 1221, 337 U.S. 541, 93 L.Ed. 1528; 7C Wright, Miller & Kane, Civil 2d § 1835.

41. Rule 23.1: 7C Wright, Miller & Kane, Civil 2d § 1839; Haudek, The Settlement and Dismissal of Stockholders' Actions, 1968, 22 Sw.L.J. 767.

This provision of Rule 23.1 does not apply if the derivative action is involuntarily dismissed by a court. Burks v. Lasker, 1979, 99 S.Ct. 1831, 1841 n. 16, 441 U.S. 471, 485 n. 16, 60 L.Ed.2d 404. See also Papilsky v. Berndt, C.A.2d, 1972, 466 F.2d 251, certiorari denied 93 S.Ct. 689, 409 U.S. 1077, 34 L.Ed.2d 665.

power to approve or disapprove any compromise of the suit, the court retains substantial control over the fee which may be paid to the attorneys for the plaintiff.[42]

§ 74. Interpleader [1]

Interpleader is a form of joinder open to one who does not know to which of several claimants he or she is liable, if liable at all. It permits him or her to bring the claimants into a single action, and to require them to litigate among themselves to determine which, if any, has a valid claim. Although the earliest records of a procedure similar to interpleader were at common law, it soon became an equitable rather than a legal procedure.[2] The contemporary importance of interpleader is in large measure due to the efforts of Professor Zechariah Chafee, Jr., who, in a notable group of articles,[3] paved the way for the series of reforms by which federal interpleader was modernized and made available in situations where no state court could provide an adequate remedy. There are two kinds of interpleader available in federal court. A statute, 28 U.S.C.A. § 1335, authorizes interpleader and makes very liberal provisions for jurisdiction, venue, and service of process. Nonstatutory interpleader is available under Rule 22, but the jurisdictional and procedural requirements there are the same as in an ordinary civil action.

Before enactment of the federal interpleader statute, there was no effective procedure by which rival claimants of diverse citizenship and residence could be sued in any district in federal court, and territorial limitations on service of process barred state courts from giving relief. This situation is cured by the statute, and the rule supplements the statute.

Rule 22 permits interpleader whenever there are multiple claimants whose claims are such that the plaintiff is or may be exposed to double or multiple liability. The statute requires that there be two or more adverse claimants who are claiming or may claim the same money or property. Under both the statute and the rule, the purpose is to protect against double vexation in respect to a single liability,[4] rather than to a double liability as such, and interpleader will be allowed even though one

---

42. 7C Wright, Miller & Kane, Civil 2d § 1841.

§ 74

1. 7 Wright, Miller & Kane, Civil 2d §§ 1701–1721; Hazard & Moskovitz, An Historical and Critical Analysis of Interpleader, 1964, 52 Calif.L.Rev. 706; Ilsen & Sardell, Interpleader in the Federal Courts, 1960, 35 St. John's L.Rev. 1; Comment, Deference to State Courts in Federal Interpleader Actions, 1980, 47 U.Chi.L.Rev. 824.

2. The earliest reported instance of relief similar to interpleader at law is in 1313, while the first reported bill of interpleader in equity is in 1484. See Rogers, Historical

Origins of Interpleader, 1942, 51 Yale L.J. 924.

3. The following articles are all by Professor Chafee: Modernizing Interpleader, 1921, 30 Yale L.J. 814; Interstate Interpleader, 1924, 33 Yale L.J. 685; Interpleader in the United States Courts, 1932, 41 Yale L.J. 1134, 42 Yale L.J. 41; The Federal Interpleader Act of 1936, 1936, 45 Yale L.J. 963, 1161; Federal Interpleader Since the Act of 1936, 1940, 49 Yale L.J. 377; Broadening the Second Stage of Interpleader, 1943, 56 Harv.L.Rev. 541, 929.

4. State Farm Fire & Cas. Co. v. Tashire, 1967, 87 S.Ct. 1199, 1205, 386 U.S. 523, 534, 18 L.Ed.2d 270.

of the claims is not meritorious, so long as it is not so utterly baseless that the possibility of conflicting claims falls below a minimal threshold level of substantiality.[5]

Pomeroy's list of four restrictions on interpleader may well have been, as has recently been suggested, "the product of uncritical reading and uncritical thinking," [6] but it was widely accepted by the courts. The four restrictions Pomeroy described were: (1) The same thing, debt, or duty must have been claimed by both or all the parties against whom the relief was demanded. (2) All their adverse titles or claims must have been dependent on or be derived from a common source. (3) The person seeking relief—the plaintiff—must not have had or claimed any interest in the subject matter. (4) The plaintiff must have incurred no independent liability to either of the claimants.[7] This was the strict bill of interpleader. A bill in the nature of a bill of interpleader was available, where the plaintiff was not disinterested and had some special ground for equitable relief beyond the assertion of multiple claims against him.

The first of the four conditions, that the claims be identical, and the second, that they be of common origin, are abolished in express terms both by the rule and by the statute.[8] The third requirement, that the plaintiff be disinterested, is abolished in express terms by the rule and by fair implication in the statute. Thus, one who is not disinterested can bring an action of interpleader, even without any special basis for equitable relief other than the danger of multiple vexation.[9] Indeed, interpleader will lie even where the claims are unliquidated tort claims, if the remedy is sought by an insurer with limited liability so that the claims are adverse.[10]

The situation is less clear on whether the fourth condition on equitable interpleader, that the plaintiff must have incurred no independent liability to either of the claimants, survives in modern practice. The situation arises where one of the claimants asserts that the basis of his or her claim is such that he or she is entitled to recover even though the stakeholder may also be liable on some other basis to some other claimant or claimants. Prior to the Act of 1936 it was held that such an

---

5. E.g., Equitable Life Assur. Soc. v. Porter–Englehart, C.A.1st, 1989, 867 F.2d 79, 84. The rule stated in the text was recognized, but the possibility of conflicting claims found too remote to support interpleader, in Indianapolis Colts v. Mayor & City Council of Baltimore, C.A.7th, 1984, 741 F.2d 954, 958, certiorari denied 105 S.Ct. 1753, 470 U.S. 1052, 84 L.Ed.2d 817, and in Dunbar v. U.S., C.A.5th, 1974, 502 F.2d 506.

6. Hazard & Moskovitz, note 1 above, at 708.

7. 4 Pomeroy, Equity Jurisprudence, 5th ed. 1941, § 1322.

8. Standard Sur. & Cas. Co. of New York v. Baker, C.C.A.8th, 1939, 105 F.2d 578, 581.

9. Holcomb v. Aetna Life Ins. Co., C.A.10th, 1955, 228 F.2d 75, certiorari denied 76 S.Ct. 473, 350 U.S. 986, 100 L.Ed. 853; Maryland Cas. Co. v. Glassell–Taylor & Robinson, C.C.A.5th, 1946, 156 F.2d 519; Standard Sur. & Cas. Co. of New York v. Baker, C.C.A.8th, 1939, 105 F.2d 578; John Hancock Mut. Life Ins. Co. v. Kegan, D.C.Md.1938, 22 F.Supp. 326.

10. State Farm Fire & Cas. Co. v. Tashire, 1967, 87 S.Ct. 1199, 386 U.S. 523, 18 L.Ed.2d 270. See 7 Wright, Miller & Kane, Civil 2d § 1707.

independent liability would bar interpleader.[11] The 1936 statute, now 28 U.S.C.A. § 1335, does not do away with the independent-liability restriction in express terms, though it probably was the thought of Professor Chafee, who drafted it, that this restriction was merely a special application of the equitable requirement that the claims must be of common origin, which the statute does expressly end.[12] In England similar language abolishing the common-origin restriction had been held to end the independent-liability restriction,[13] but there have been some federal decisions holding that the restriction is still applicable.[14] In the courts that take this view the practice is for the court to try the facts about independent liability. If no independent liability is found, interpleader is ordered; if such liability exists, the request for interpleader is denied.[15] Increasingly, however, a different view has been taken, and it has been thought that the independent-liability restriction is no longer a bar to interpleader under either the statute or the rule.[16] This is as it should be. Contemporary procedure, with its flexible provisions for wide joinder of parties and claims, for separate trial of separate issues where necessary, and for shaping the judgment to the necessities of the case, is well adapted to disposing of interpleader cases where independent liability is asserted, and there is no reason today, under either the statute or the rule, for continuing to impose a restriction that has no claim to validity save that it is old.

It seems clear, though there is no case authority, that interpleader is available in federal court, under either the rule or the statute, even though the state in which the court is sitting preserves the old equitable restrictions on interpleader and would not allow it under similar circumstances.[17] But to determine the law to be applied in passing on the merits of the case, the federal court must look to the state law, including the conflicts rules of the state, despite the fact that the case is one where the state could not have obtained jurisdiction over all the parties, and

---

11. Dee v. Kansas City Life Ins. Co., C.C.A.7th, 1936, 86 F.2d 813.

12. Chafee, Federal Interpleader Since the Act of 1936, 1940, 49 Yale L.J. 377, 412; Note, the Independent Liability Rule as a Bar to Interpleader in the Federal Courts, 1956, 65 Yale L.J. 714, 719.

13. Ex parte Mersey Docks and Harbour Bd., [1899] 1 Q.B. 546.

14. Nevada Eighty–Eight, Inc. v. Title Ins. Co. of Minnesota, D.C.Nev.1990, 753 F.Supp. 1516, 1527–1528; Equitable Life Ins. Co. of Iowa v. Gilman, D.C.Mo.1953, 14 F.R.D. 243; First State Bank of Chariton, Iowa v. Citizens State Bank of Thedford, D.C.Neb.1950, 10 F.R.D. 424; Boice v. Boice, D.C.N.J.1943, 48 F.Supp. 183, affirmed C.C.A.3d, 135 F.2d 919. See also cases cited note 15 below.

15. Poland v. Atlantis Credit Corp., D.C.N.Y.1960, 179 F.Supp. 863; American–

Hawaiian S.S. Co. (Del.) v. Bowring & Co., D.C.N.Y.1957, 150 F.Supp. 449. But see Hurlbut v. Shell Oil Co., D.C.La.1955, 131 F.Supp. 466, 468.

16. Dakota Livestock Co. v. Keim, C.A.8th, 1977, 552 F.2d 1302, 1306; Knoll v. Socony Mobil Oil Co., C.A.10th, 1966, 369 F.2d 425, 428–429, certiorari denied 87 S.Ct. 1173, 386 U.S. 977, 18 L.Ed.2d 138; Builders & Developers Corp. v. Manassas Iron & Steel Co., D.C.Md.1962, 208 F.Supp. 485, 490; and cases cited 7 Wright, Miller & Kane, Civil 2d § 1706 nn. 10–14.

17. Wright, Miller & Kane, Civil 2d § 1713, pp. 577–578; Developments in the Law—Multiparty Litigation in the Federal Courts, 1958, 71 Harv.L.Rev. 874, 926. See Perkins State Bank v. Connolly, C.A.5th, 1980, 632 F.2d 1306, 1310–1311.

that, therefore, no state court could have heard.[18] And since the basis of jurisdiction is diversity, whether suit is under the rule or the statute, there is some authority that state law is controlling on such matters as the award of an attorney's fee to the plaintiff, although on this point the better view is to the contrary.[19]

The principal difference between statutory interpleader and interpleader under the rule is in the matter of jurisdiction.[20] Statutory interpleader is available if the amount involved exceeds $500 and there are "two or more adverse claimants, of diverse citizenship." [21] Where each of the claimants is a citizen of a different state, and the stakeholder is disinterested, its citizenship is immaterial, since the actual controversy is between the claimants.[22] The courts have gone far beyond this, however, and have entertained statutory interpleader on the basis of what is called "minimal diversity": so long as there are at least two opposing claimants of diverse citizenship,[23] they have held that jurisdiction exists, even though there may be other claimants,[24] or a stakeholder who is not disinterested,[25] of the same citizenship. This departure from the usual rule of complete diversity [26] is a healthy one. Whatever the merits may be in the continuing argument about the desirability of diversity jurisdiction in general,[27] the jurisdiction serves an important

18. Griffin v. McCoach, 1941, 61 S.Ct. 1023, 313 U.S. 498, 85 L.Ed. 1481. See § 57 above.

19. 7 Wright, Miller & Kane, Civil 2d § 1719, pp. 647–651; Bank of China v. Wells Fargo Bank & Union Trust Co., C.A.9th, 1953, 209 F.2d 467; Brose v. International Fidelity Ins. Co., D.C.Pa.1982, 547 F.Supp. 149; Lincoln Income Life Ins. Co. v. Harrison, D.C.Okl.1976, 71 F.R.D. 27; Minnesota Mut. Life Ins. Co. v. Gustafson, D.C.Ill.1976, 415 F.Supp. 615. Contra: Ohio Cas. Ins. Co. v. Berger, D.C.Ky.1970, 311 F.Supp. 840; Aetna Life Ins. Co. v. Johnson, D.C.Ill.1962, 206 F.Supp. 63.

In Perkins State Bank v. Connolly, C.A.5th, 1980, 632 F.2d 1306, 1310–1311, it is held that state law does not control an award of an attorney's fee to a disinterested stakeholder but that it does control award of a fee to one of the claimants.

20. See 7 Wright, Miller & Kane, Civil 2d § 1710: 14 Wright, Miller, & Cooper, Jurisdiction 2d § 3636.

21. Statutory interpleader is not possible on the basis of a federal question if there is no diversity. Sun Shipbuilding & Dry–Dock Co. v. Industrial Union of Marine & Shipbuilding Workers of America, D.C.Pa.1951, 95 F.Supp. 50.

22. Treinies v. Sunshine Mining Co., 1939, 60 S.Ct. 44, 308 U.S. 66, 84 L.Ed. 85.

23. There is no jurisdiction under the statute if all the claimants are citizens of a single state, even though the plaintiff stakeholder is a citizen of a different state. Travelers Ins. Co. v. Harville, D.C.Ala.1985, 622 F.Supp. 68. This result is reached even if the stakeholder is interested. American Family Mut. Ins. Co. v. Roche, D.C.Wis. 1993, 830 F.Supp. 1241. Nor is there jurisdiction if all the claimants are aliens. Geler v. National Westminster Bank USA, D.C.N.Y.1991, 763 F.Supp. 722.

Only claimants who have been served may be counted. Cripps v. Life Ins. Co. of North America, C.A.9th, 1992, 980 F.2d 1261, 1265–1266.

24. State Farm Fire & Cas. Co. v. Tashire, 1967, 87 S.Ct. 1199, 1203–1204, 386 U.S. 523, 530–531, 18 L.Ed.2d 270. An important earlier decision anticipating this result was Haynes v. Felder, C.A.5th, 1957, 239 F.2d 868.

25. Builders and Developers Corp. v. Manassas Iron & Steel Co., D.C.Md.1962, 208 F.Supp. 485; Georgia Sav. Bank & Trust Co. v. Sims, D.C.Ga.1971, 321 F.Supp. 307; Girard Trust Co. v. Vance, D.C.Pa.1946, 5 F.R.D. 109; cf. U.S. v. Sentinel Fire Ins. Co., C.A.5th, 1949, 178 F.2d 217.

Contra: Boice v. Boice, C.C.A.3d, 1943, 135 F.2d 919.

26. Strawbridge v. Curtiss, 1806, 3 Cranch 267, 2 L.Ed. 435. See § 24 above.

27. See § 23 above.

function, as here, in providing a federal forum for cases that would be beyond the jurisdiction of any state court. This function would be severely limited were complete diversity required, and it is good that the courts have recognized the power of Congress to provide by statute for less than complete diversity.

Unlike the statute, Rule 22 does not have, nor purport to have, any effect on jurisdictional requirements. Thus, there must be either complete diversity of citizenship between the stakeholder on the one hand and all of the claimants on the other, with more than $50,000 in controversy,[28] or else there must be a federal question.[29] If, as the Supreme Court has held in a case of statutory interpleader,[30] a disinterested stakeholder is merely a nominal party whose citizenship can be disregarded in determining diversity, it might be argued that there is no diversity jurisdiction in an action under the rule where the plaintiff, a disinterested stakeholder, is a citizen of one state, and all the claimants, among whom the real controversy will lie, are citizens of another state. The courts have not reached this result, perhaps reasoning that the stakeholder is not merely a nominal party since it has a substantial interest in obtaining interpleader and thus avoiding the dangers of multiple liability.[31]

The jurisdictional amount, whether $500 for statutory interpleader or $50,000 for interpleader under the rule, is determined as in other cases.[32] The total amount to be distributed is the amount in controversy, and supports jurisdiction though individual claims may be for less than this amount.[33]

For statutory interpleader, venue will lie in any district in which any claimant resides,[34] and process may be served anywhere in the United

---

28. Underwriters at Lloyd's v. Nichols, C.A.8th, 1966, 363 F.2d 357; John Hancock Mut. Life Ins. Co. v. Kraft, C.A.2d, 1953, 200 F.2d 952; Lincoln Income Life Ins. Co. v. Harrison, D.C.Okl.1976, 71 F.R.D. 27.

29. Interpleader based on a federal question is largely a theoretical matter because of the requirement that a federal question appear in the well-pleaded complaint. The courts look to see if the coercive actions anticipated by the interpleader claim would be federal claims and generally have found that they would not. Morongo Band of Indians v. Cal. St. Bd. of Equal., C.A.9th, 1988, 858 F.2d 1376, 1383–1386, certiorari denied 109 S.Ct. 787, 488 U.S. 1006, 102 L.Ed.2d 779; Bell & Beckwith v. U.S., C.A.6th, 1985, 766 F.2d 910, 912–916. But jurisdiction has been found to exist. Gelfgren v. Republic Nat. Life Ins. Co., C.A.9th, 1982, 680 F.2d 79; St. Louis Union Trust Co. v. Stone, C.A.8th, 1978, 570 F.2d 833. See Banco de Ponce v. Hinsdale Supermarket Corp., D.C.N.Y.1987, 663 F.Supp. 813.

30. Treinies v. Sunshine Mining Co., 1939, 60 S.Ct. 44, 308 U.S. 66, 84 L.Ed. 85.

31. Aetna Life & Cas. Co. v. Spain, C.A.5th, 1977, 556 F.2d 747; Stewart Oil Co. v. Sohio Petroleum Co., C.A.7th, 1963, 315 F.2d 759, 762, certiorari denied 84 S.Ct. 71, 375 U.S. 828, 11 L.Ed.2d 60; Developments in the Law—Multiparty Litigation in the Federal Courts, 1958, 71 Harv.L.Rev. 874, 922–923; 7 Wright, Miller & Kane, Civil 2d § 1710, pp. 547–549.

32. See §§ 33–35 above.

33. Pan American Fire & Cas. Co. v. Revere, D.C.La.1960, 188 F.Supp. 474; Massachusetts Bonding & Ins. Co. v. City of St. Louis, D.C.Mo.1952, 109 F.Supp. 137; see United Benefit Life Ins. Co. v. Leech, D.C.Pa.1971, 326 F.Supp. 598, 600.

34. 28 U.S.C.A. § 1397; Watson v. Manhattan & Bronx Surface Transit Operating Auth., D.C.N.J.1980, 487 F.Supp. 1273; 7 Wright, Miller & Kane, Civil 2d § 1712.

As amended in 1988, 28 U.S.C.A. § 1391(c) provides that a corporation is

States.[35] Interpleader under the rule must be brought in a district in which any defendant resides if all defendants reside in the same state, or in the district in which the claim arose, or, if there is no district in which the action may otherwise be brought, in a district in which the defendants may be served.[36] And as in ordinary civil actions, process must be served in accordance with Rule 4, which normally limits service to the borders of the state in which the court is sitting.[37] Since interpleader under the rule will be used only where all the claimants are citizens of the same state, these restrictions on venue and service should not ordinarily cause any problem.[38]

The present interpleader statute continues a provision, first adopted in 1926, authorizing a federal court that has taken jurisdiction of an interpleader action to enjoin other proceedings in state or federal court affecting the property, instrument, or obligation involved in the interpleader action.[39] Under the 1948 revision of the anti-injunction statute,[40] a similar injunction can now be issued in interpleader under the rule, since a preliminary injunction to stay state-court action while the federal court determines the case is "necessary in aid of its jurisdiction," and a permanent injunction at the conclusion of the federal action is needed "to protect or effectuate its judgments." [41]

It is a condition to jurisdiction under the interpleader statute that the stakeholder deposit with the court the money or property demanded by the claimants, or that it give bond in sufficient amount that it will comply with the future order or judgment of the court.[42] Since it is no longer necessary that the stakeholder be disinterested, it can do this

"deemed to reside in any judicial district in which it is subject to personal jurisdiction at the time the action is commenced." Since there is nationwide service of process in statutory-interpleader actions, this seems to mean that venue is now proper anywhere in the United States if one of the claimants is a corporation. Welkowitz, Some Thoughts on Corporate Venue and Other Foibles, 1989, 10 Whittier L.Rev. 721, 722–723.

35. 28 U.S.C.A. § 2361; 7 Wright, Miller & Kane, Civil 2d § 1711.

36. 28 U.S.C.A. § 1391(a), (b). See § 42 above.

There is considerable room for speculation—and no case law—on where the claim arises in an action for interpleader. See 7 Wright, Miller & Kane, Civil 2d § 1712, pp. 568–569.

37. Metropolitan Life Ins. Co. v. Chase, C.A.3d, 1961, 294 F.2d 500. See § 64 above.

38. Pan American Fire & Cas. Co. v. Revere, D.C.La.1960, 188 F.Supp. 474.

But see Cordner v. Metropolitan Life Ins. Co., D.C.N.Y.1964, 234 F.Supp. 765, where the combined effect of the venue limitation

on statutory interpleader and the service-of-process limitation on interpleader under Rule 22 was to prevent defendant from being able to counterclaim for interpleader.

39. 28 U.S.C.A. § 2361; 7 Wright, Miller & Kane, Civil 2d § 1717.

40. 28 U.S.C.A. § 2283. See § 47 above.

41. General Ry. Signal Co. v. Corcoran, C.A.7th, 1991, 921 F.2d 700; U.S. v. Major Oil Corp., C.A.10th, 1978, 583 F.2d 1152, 1158; Pan American Fire & Cas. Co. v. Revere, D.C.La.1960, 188 F.Supp. 474, 483–485; Ilsen & Sardell, note 1 above, at 55–56. This principle is recognized in Geler v. National Westminster Bank USA, D.C.N.Y. 1991, 763 F.Supp. 722, 727–729, but it is held there that as a matter of comity the stakeholder should first ask the state court to stay its action.

42. 28 U.S.C.A. § 1335(a)(2); Miller & Miller Auctioneers, Inc. v. G.W. Murphy Indus., Inc., C.A.10th, 1973, 472 F.2d 893. On the amount of the deposit, see 7 Wright, Miller & Kane, Civil 2d § 1716.

without waiving its contention that it is not liable to any of the claimants, or that it is not liable for the full sum demanded and paid into court.[43] If it is in fact disinterested, the court can then dismiss it from the action.[44] A deposit is not required in interpleader under the rule, but general equitable powers of the court permit it to receive a deposit and to discharge the stakeholder if it is indifferent.[45]

If interpleader is sought by an insurance company against persons with unliquidated tort claims against its insured, such persons may be enjoined from claiming the proceeds of the insurance policy except in the interpleader proceeding, but they cannot be enjoined from establishing their claims against the insured in a forum of their own choosing.[46] In this way the difficulties that a race to judgment may pose for the insurer, and the resulting unfairness to some claimants, may be avoided without converting interpleader into "an all-purpose 'bill of peace' "[47] for mass torts.

Interpleader under the rule is not limited to an action by a plaintiff. Rule 22(1) makes it clear that a defendant exposed to a multiple liability may obtain interpleader by way of cross-claim or counterclaim.[48] The same result should be reached under the statute, though the statute is not explicit.[49] The interpleader must have some nexus with a party who is already in the case. Defendant will not be allowed to counterclaim or cross-claim for interpleader when he or she is not seeking relief against

---

43. Federal Sav. & Loan Ins. Co. v. Bass, D.C.Ill.1983, 576 F.Supp. 848; United Benefit Life Ins. Co. v. Leech, D.C.Pa.1971, 326 F.Supp. 598; Moseley v. Sunshine Biscuits, Inc., D.C.Mo.1952, 110 F.Supp. 157; John Hancock Mut. Life Ins. Co. v. Yarrow, D.C.Pa.1951, 95 F.Supp. 185. But cf. Doering v. Buechler, C.C.A.8th, 1945, 146 F.2d 784.

44. 28 U.S.C.A. § 2361; Rosenberger v. Northwestern Mut. Life Ins. Co., D.C.Kan. 1959, 176 F.Supp. 379; Savannah Bank & Trust Co. of Savannah v. Block, D.C.Ga. 1959, 175 F.Supp. 798.

45. Bank of China v. Wells Fargo Bank & Union Trust Co., C.A.9th, 1953, 209 F.2d 467, 473; U.S. v. Henry's Bay View Inn, Inc., D.C.N.Y.1960, 191 F.Supp. 632. Deposit in court is authorized by Rule 67. See 12 Wright & Miller, Civil § 2991.

46. State Farm Fire & Cas. Co. v. Tashire, 1967, 87 S.Ct. 1199, 386 U.S. 523, 18 L.Ed.2d 270; General Acc. Group v. Gagliardi, D.C.Conn.1984, 593 F.Supp. 1080; 7 Wright, Miller & Kane, Civil 2d § 1707.

47. State Farm Fire & Cas. Co. v. Tashire, 1967, 87 S.Ct. 1199, 1206, 386 U.S. 523, 535, 18 L.Ed.2d 270.

But see Comment, Promoting Judicial Economy Through the Extension of Inter-

pleader to the Tortfeasor in the Mass Tort Area, 1971, 17 Wayne L.Rev. 1241.

Reasoning similar to that in Tashire was relied on to hold that interpleader was not available to a uranium dealer caught between claims from utilities that it must deliver uranium to them at the contract price and the position of its supplier that it would not supply uranium to the dealer except at the current market price. General Atomic Co. v. Duke Power Co., C.A.10th, 1977, 553 F.2d 53. The court thought that the dealer was not a stakeholder and that the supplier and the utilities were not conflicting claimants. Although the court recognized the "serious problem" the dealer confronted, it held it could not "redesign the interpleader statute in order for it to accommodate this unusual lawsuit." 553 F.2d at 58.

48. U.S. v. Major Oil Corp., C.A.10th, 1978, 583 F.2d 1152; Powers v. Metropolitan Life Ins. Co., C.A.D.C.1971, 439 F.2d 605; and cases cited 7 Wright, Miller & Kane, Civil 2d § 1708 n. 1.

49. Humble Oil & Ref. Co. v. Copeland, C.A.4th, 1968, 398 F.2d 364; and cases cited 7 Wright, Miller & Kane, Civil 2d § 1708 n. 7.

any of the other parties to the action.[50]

Interpleader will not lie against the United States if it has not waived its sovereign immunity,[51] nor may a state be required to interplead contrary to the Eleventh Amendment.[52] The same principles apply here as in an ordinary civil action, and indeed the procedure in an interpleader action follows generally that of the ordinary action,[53] although there has been some confusion about the availability of counterclaims[54] and, in cases where a nonresident claimant has been brought in by extraterritorial service under statutory interpleader, cross-claims.[55] In considering issues of this kind, it will now be necessary to consider the broad grant of supplemental jurisdiction in a 1990 statute.[56]

The historic origin of interpleader in the courts of equity, coupled with a famous dictum from Chief Justice Taft,[57] had caused some courts to suppose that there was no right to jury trial in an interpleader action.[58] But interpleader today is simply a joinder device, not confined to equitable actions and not restricted by the conditions that limited its use in equity. It would raise doubts of constitutional dimension to say that the statute or rule, by making available a flexible and useful procedural tool, can deprive a party of a right to jury trial on a claim that heretofore would have been heard to a jury. Of course the "first stage of interpleader," the decision whether to require the claimants to

50. Grubbs v. General Elec. Credit Corp., 1972, 92 S.Ct. 1344, 405 U.S. 699, 31 L.Ed.2d 612. See also Metropolitan Life Ins. Co. v. O'Ferrall Ochart, D.C.Puerto Rico 1986, 635 F.Supp. 119.

51. U.S. v. Dry Dock Sav. Institution, C.C.A.2d, 1945, 149 F.2d 917; U.S. v. Commercial Bank of North America, D.C.N.Y. 1962, 31 F.R.D. 133; Cowan v. U.S., D.C.N.Y.1959, 172 F.Supp. 291; 7 Wright, Miller & Kane, Civil 2d § 1721. See § 22 above.

52. Cory v. White, 1982, 102 S.Ct. 2325, 457 U.S. 85, 72 L.Ed.2d 694. States can be required to interplead in actions within the original jurisdiction of the Supreme Court, where the Eleventh Amendment is no bar. Texas v. New Jersey,1965, 85 S.Ct. 626, 379 U.S. 674, 13 L.Ed.2d 596; Texas v. Florida, 1939, 59 S.Ct. 563, 306 U.S. 398, 83 L.Ed. 817.

53. 7 Wright, Miller & Kane, Civil 2d §§ 1714, 1715.

54. In Liberty Nat. Bank & Trust Co. of Oklahoma City v. Acme Tool Div. of Rucker Co., C.A.10th, 1976, 540 F.2d 1375, 1379–1381, the Tenth Circuit overruled earlier decisions in which it had held that a disinterested stakeholder was not an "opposing party" against whom a counterclaim would lie. The earlier decisions had been criticized in 7 Wright, Miller & Kane, Civil 2d § 1715, pp. 592–593, and were not followed

in Bell v. Nutmeg Airways Corp., D.C.Conn. 1975, 66 F.R.D. 1.

55. Compare Marine Bank & Trust Co. v. Hamilton Bros., Inc., D.C.Fla.1972, 55 F.R.D. 505, with Dean Witter Reynolds Inc. v. Fernandez, D.C.Fla.1979, 489 F.Supp. 434. See also Allstate Ins. Co. v. McNeill, C.A.4th, 1967, 382 F.2d 84, certiorari denied 88 S.Ct. 2290, 392 U.S. 931, 20 L.Ed.2d 1390. This problem is discussed in 7 Wright, Miller & Kane, Civil 2d § 1715, pp. 593–600.

56. 28 U.S.C.A. § 1367. See § 9 above. Although § 1367(b) limits supplemental jurisdiction in diversity cases with regard to many procedural devices, it makes no limitation with regard to either statutory or rule interpleader.

57. Liberty Oil Co. v. Condon Nat. Bank, 1922, 43 S.Ct. 118, 121, 260 U.S. 235, 244, 67 L.Ed. 232.

58. Bynum v. Prudential Life Ins. Co. of America, D.C.S.C.1947, 7 F.R.D. 585; Liberty Nat. Life Ins. Co. v. Brown, D.C.Ala. 1954, 119 F.Supp. 920; Pennsylvania Fire Ins. Co. v. American Airlines, Inc., D.C.N.Y. 1960, 180 F.Supp. 239; Plaza Exp. Co. v. Galloway, 1955, 280 S.W.2d 17, 365 Mo. 166, noted 1956, 54 Mich.L.Rev. 1171, 1956 Wash.U.L.Rev. 264.

interplead, is for the court alone.[59] But unless the issues are such that there would be no right of jury trial if they arose in an independent action,[60] issues among the claimants [61] and issues between the stakeholder and the claimants [62] are triable as of right to a jury.[63]

§ 75. Intervention [1]

Rule 24, permitting persons not named as parties to a lawsuit to intervene in it, provides a procedure by which one not made a party can protect itself from being excluded from an action that might be detrimental to it, or from an action where it might be able inexpensively to litigate its claim. Rule 24(a) describes situations in which intervention is "of right" while Rule 24(b) authorizes "permissive intervention" in the discretion of the court. Intervention in federal actions is governed by this rule and not by state law.[2]

Both before and after its amendment in 1966, Rule 24(a) has allowed intervention of right if a statute grants an absolute right of intervention. The most important such statute is that authorizing the United States or a state to intervene in cases in which the constitutionality of an Act of Congress or a state statute is in question.[3]

Prior to the 1966 amendment Rule 24(a) had recognized two other situations in which intervention might be had of right. One was where the representation of the applicant by existing parties was inadequate and it "is or may be bound by a judgment in the action." [4] The other was where the applicant was so situated that it would be adversely affected by a distribution or other disposition of property under the control of the court.[5]

59. Savannah Bank & Trust Co. of Savannah v. Block, D.C.Ga.1959, 175 F.Supp. 798; American–Hawaiian S.S. Co. (Del.) v. Bowring & Co., D.C.N.Y.1957, 150 F.Supp. 449.

60. Hyde Properties v. McCoy, C.A.6th, 1974, 507 F.2d 301; Edward B. Marks Music Corp. v. Wonnell, D.C.N.Y.1944, 4 F.R.D. 146.

61. Jefferson Standard Ins. Co. v. Craven, D.C.Pa.1973, 365 F.Supp. 861; Pan American Fire & Cas. Co. v. Revere, D.C.La.1960, 188 F.Supp. 474, 483; Savannah Bank & Trust Co. v. Block, D.C.Ga. 1959, 175 F.Supp. 798, 801.

62. John Hancock Mut. Life Ins. Co. v. Yarrow, D.C.Pa.1951, 95 F.Supp. 185, 188.

63. See Ross v. Bernhard, 1970, 90 S.Ct. 733, 740 n. 15, 396 U.S. 531, 541 n. 15, 24 L.Ed.2d 729; 7 Wright, Miller & Kane, Civil 2d § 1718.

§ 75

1. 7A Wright, Miller & Kane, Civil 2d §§ 1901–1923; Tobias, Standing to Intervene, 1991 Wis.L.Rev. 415; Shreve, Questioning Intervention of Right—Toward a New Methodology of Decisionmaking, 1980, 74 Nw.U.L.Rev. 894; Brunet, A Study in the Allocation of Scarce Judicial Resources: The Efficiency of Federal Intervention Criteria, 1978, 12 Ga.L.Rev. 701; Kennedy, Let's All Join In: Intervention under Federal Rule 24, 1969, 57 Ky.L.J. 329; Shapiro, Some Thoughts on Intervention Before Courts, Agencies, and Arbitrators, 1968, 81 Harv.L.Rev. 721.

2. Venegas v. Skaggs, C.A.9th, 1989, 867 F.2d 527, 530 n. 2, affirmed on other grounds 1990, 110 S.Ct. 1679, 495 U.S. 82, 109 L.Ed.2d 74; 7C Wright, Miller & Kane, Civil 2d § 1905.

3. 28 U.S.C.A. § 2403, as amended by act of Aug. 12, 1976, Pub.L. 94–381, § 5, 90 Stat. 1119. See 7C Wright, Miller & Kane, Civil 2d § 1906.

4. 7C Wright, Miller & Kane, Civil 2d § 1907.

5. 7C Wright, Miller & Kane, Civil 2d § 1907.

The courts had given a very loose reading to the requirement of property in the last of these categories.[6] Although this was a desirable result, it distorted the language of the rule. On the other hand the category dealing with one who might be bound by the judgment was read too narrowly. The Supreme Court had equated the language of the rule with res judicata, and said that it applied only if the would-be intervenor was "legally bound."[7] This created a dilemma, since intervention under that branch of the rule also required a showing of inadequacy of representation. An absent party cannot be legally bound by a judgment in an action in which it was inadequately represented.[8] Thus, no absentee could satisfy this reading of the rule, since no one could show both that it was inadequately represented and that it would be legally bound.[9]

The rule was amended in 1966 to avoid these defects in the former rule. The amendment was intended to substitute a practical rather than a conceptual emphasis in questions of intervention and to tie the intervention rule more closely to Rule 19, on compulsory joinder of parties,[10] and Rule 23, on class actions.[11] The amended rule substitutes a single category, Rule 24(a)(2), for the two categories just discussed in the old rule. It permits intervention of right "when the applicant claims an interest relating to the property or transaction which is the subject of the action and the applicant is so situated that the disposition of the action may as a practical matter impair or impede the applicant's ability to protect that interest, unless the applicant's interest is adequately represented by existing parties."

Thus, the amended rule requires the applicant to show three things: (1) that it has an interest relating to the property or transaction involved in the action; (2) that disposition of the action may impair the applicant's ability to protect its interest "as a practical matter"; and (3) that its interest is not adequately represented by the present parties.

There is as yet no consensus about the kind of "interest" that the would-be intervenor must have. Although the Supreme Court has added the gloss that Rule 24(a)(2) is referring to "a significantly protectable

---

6. E.g., Formulabs, Inc. v. Hartley Pen Co., C.A.9th, 1960, 275 F.2d 52; International Mortg. & Inv. Corp. v. Von Clemm, C.A.2d, 1962, 301 F.2d 857.

7. Sam Fox Pub. Co. v. U.S., 1961, 81 S.Ct. 1309, 1315, 366 U.S. 683, 694, 6 L.Ed.2d 604; Sutphen Estates, Inc. v. U.S., 1951, 72 S.Ct. 14, 16, 342 U.S. 19, 21, 96 L.Ed. 19.

8. Hansberry v. Lee, 1940, 61 S.Ct. 115, 311 U.S. 32, 85 L.Ed. 22.

9. Note, Intervention of Right in Class Actions: The Dilemma of Federal Rule of Civil Procedure 24(a)(2), 1962, 50 Calif.L.Rev. 89.

10. See § 70 above.

11. See § 72 above. On the interrelation of Rules 19, 23, and 24, see Atlantis Development Corp. v. U.S., C.A.5th, 1967, 379 F.2d 818, 824–825.

The amended rule has been criticized, however, as not being "totally faithful to the revision theory of new Rules 19 and 23. That theory is that the rules should express factors for decision rather than definitional categories." Kennedy, note 1 above, at 374.

interest," [12] this has not been a term of art in the law of intervention and provides little more guidance than does the bare term used in the rule itself. Some courts look to the pre–1966 decisions for guidance and continue to call for "a direct substantial, legally protectable interest" [13] while others have permitted intervention on the basis of interests that hardly seem to satisfy the adjectives just quoted.[14]

The second requirement, that the would-be intervenor must be so situated that the disposition of the action "may as a practical matter impair or impede" its ability to protect its interest has been sympathetically applied. It has been clear to all courts that the principal purpose of the amendment was to eliminate the old reading that a would-be intervenor must be legally bound, and that instead the court is to view the effect on his interest with a practical eye. Indeed it is significant that, as finally adopted, the amendment did not require, as an earlier draft would have, that the judgment must "substantially" impair or impede the applicant's ability to protect his interest. Thus, contrary to decisions under the pre–1966 rule, even the stare decisis effect of the judgment in the existing action may, in proper circumstances, create sufficient practical disadvantage to warrant intervention as of right.[15]

12. Donaldson v. U.S., 1971, 91 S.Ct. 534, 542, 400 U.S. 517, 531, 27 L.Ed.2d 580. The Court had seemed to take a very permissive view of the kind of interest that would justify intervention in Cascade Natural Gas Corp. v. El Paso Natural Gas Co., 1967, 87 S.Ct. 932, 386 U.S. 129, 17 L.Ed.2d 814. Both cases are heavily colored by their unusual facts and are less than conclusive on when intervention should be allowed in routine litigation. See 7C Wright, Miller & Kane, Civil 2d § 1908, pp. 264–270; Shreve, note 1 above, at 923–924.

13. Hobson v. Hansen, D.C.D.C.1968, 44 F.R.D. 18, 24. See also Keith v. Daley, C.A.7th, 1985, 764 F.2d 1265, certiorari denied 106 S.Ct. 383, 474 U.S.980, 88 L.Ed.2d 336; Smoot v. Mobil Oil Corp., D.C.Mass. 1989, 722 F.Supp. 849, 860; In re Penn Central Commercial Paper Litigation, D.C.N.Y.1974, 62 F.R.D. 341, 346, affirmed C.A.2d, 1975, 515 F.2d 505; and cases cited 7C Wright, Miller & Kane, Civil 2d § 1908 nn. 25, 44.

Some lower courts have demanded that would-be intervenors possess an interest equivalent to standing. E.g., Panola Land Buying Assn. v. Clark, C.A.11th, 1988, 844 F.2d 1506, 1509; Southern Christian Leadership Conference v. Kelley, C.A.D.C.1984, 747 F.2d 777, 779. These cases are criticized in Tobias, note 1 above. The Supreme Court refrained from deciding this question in Diamond v. Charles, 1986, 106

S.Ct. 1697, 1707, 476 U.S. 54, 68–69, 90 L.Ed.2d 48.

14. E.g., Portland Audubon Soc. v. Hodel, C.A.9th, 1989, 866 F.2d 302, 308; Feller v. Brock, C.A.4th, 1986, 802 F.2d 722, 729; Smuck v. Hobson, C.A.D.C.1969, 408 F.2d 175; Brotherhood of Locomotive Firemen & Enginemen v. Louisville & N.R. Co., C.A.6th, 1968, 400 F.2d 572, certiorari denied 89 S.Ct. 689, 393 U.S. 1050, 21 L.Ed.2d 692; Nuesse v. Camp, C.A.D.C. 1967, 385 F.2d 694, 700. See 7C Wright, Miller & Kane, Civil 2d § 1908, pp. 272–288.

15. Chiles v. Thornburgh, C.A.11th, 1989, 865 F.2d 1197; U.S. v. Oregon, C.A.9th, 1988, 839 F.2d 635; Oneida Indian Nation of Wisconsin v. New York, C.A.2d, 1984, 732 F.2d 261; Corby Recreation, Inc. v. General Elec. Co., C.A.8th, 1978, 581 F.2d 175; Nuesse v. Camp, C.A.D.C.1967, 385 F.2d 694, 701–702, noted 1968, 18 Am. U.L.Rev. 202; Atlantis Development Corp. v. U.S., C.A.5th, 1967, 379 F.2d 818, 828–829, noted, 1967 Duke L.J. 1251, 1968, 33 Mo.L.Rev. 655. A more guarded view is taken on this point in International Paper Co. v. Inhabitants of the Town of Jay, C.A.1st, 1989, 887 F.2d 338, and in Bethune Plaza, Inc. v. Lumpkin, C.A.7th, 1988, 863 F.2d 525.

For other illustrations of the reading the courts have given to this requirement of the rule, see 7C Wright, Miller & Kane, Civil 2d § 1908 nn. 68–71.

The Supreme Court has said that the third requirement, that the applicant not be adequately represented by the existing parties, "is satisfied if the applicant shows that representation of his interest 'may be' inadequate; and the burden of making that showing should be treated as minimal."[16] If the absentee's interest will be affected, and the applicant is not represented at all, or the existing parties are adverse to it, the applicant he must be allowed to intervene.[17] At the other extreme are cases in which the interest of the absentee is identical with that of one of the existing parties or there is a party charged by law with representing the interests of the absentee. In these situations representation will be presumed adequate unless special circumstances are shown.[18] The final situation is that in which the interests of the absentee and of the party thought to represent it are different, though perhaps similar. If there is a serious possibility that the applicant is not adequately represented in these situations, it should be allowed to intervene, rather than being obliged to test the validity of the judgment as applied to its interest by a later collateral attack.[19]

Permissive intervention may be allowed where a governmental officer or agency wishes to come into a case involving a statute or regulation.[20] The more common ground for permissive intervention is that the would-be intervenor's claim or defense and the existing action have a question of law or fact in common.[21] The intervenor need not have a direct personal or pecuniary interest in the subject of the litigation.[22] Indeed it would seem that the intervenor need not be a person who would have been a proper party at the beginning of the suit, since of the two tests for permissive joinder of parties, a common question of law or fact and some right to relief arising from the same transaction, only the former is stated as a limitation on intervention.[23]

16. Trbovich v. United Mine Workers of America, 1972, 92 S.Ct. 630, 636 n. 10, 404 U.S. 528, 538 n. 10, 30 L.Ed.2d 686. See Brunet, note 1 above, at 733–738.

"The number of recent cases denying intervention on the basis of adequate representation, however, suggests the requirement is still formidable." Shreve, note 1 above, at 919 n. 106.

17. Purnell v. City of Akron, C.A.6th, 1991, 925 F.2d 941, 950; Natural Resources Defense Council, Inc. v. U.S. Nuclear Regulatory Comm., C.A.10th, 1978, 578 F.2d 1341, 1346; and cases cited 7C Wright, Miller & Kane, Civil 2d § 1909 nn. 17, 18.

18. Bush v. Viterna, C.A.5th, 1984, 740 F.2d 350, 358; McClune v. Shamah, C.A.3d, 1979, 593 F.2d 482; and cases cited 7C Wright, Miller & Kane, Civil 2d § 1909 nn. 19–38.

19. Chiles v. Thornburgh, C.A.11th, 1989, 865 F.2d 1197, 1214; Johnson v. San Francisco Unified Sch. Dist., C.A.9th, 1974, 500 F.2d 349, 353; Nuesse v. Camp, C.A.D.C.1967, 385 F.2d 694, 702–704; and

cases cited 7C Wright, Miller & Kane, Civil 2d § 1909 nn. 39–46.

20. Rule 24(b)(2); Securities and Exchange Comm. v. U.S. Realty & Improvement Co., 1940, 60 S.Ct. 1044, 310 U.S. 434, 84 L.Ed. 1293; Miami Health Studios, Inc. v. City of Miami Beach, C.A.5th, 1974, 491 F.2d 98; Nuesse v. Camp, C.A.D.C.1967, 385 F.2d 694, 704–706. But cf. Philadelphia Elec. Co. v. Westinghouse Elec. Corp., C.A.3d, 1962, 308 F.2d 856, certiorari denied 83 S.Ct. 883, 372 U.S. 936, 9 L.Ed.2d 767. See 7C Wright, Miller & Kane, Civil 2d § 1912.

21. Rule 24(b)(2); 7C Wright, Miller & Kane, Civil 2d § 1911.

22. Securities and Exchange Comm. v. U.S. Realty & Improvement Co., 1940, 60 S.Ct. 1044, 1055, 310 U.S. 434, 459, 84 L.Ed. 1293.

23. Usery v. Brandel, D.C.Mich.1980, 87 F.R.D. 670, 677.

Even under the pre–1966 rule, permissive intervention was often allowed where the intervenor had an economic interest in the outcome of the suit, although not a direct or a legal interest. It was on this basis that neighbors were allowed to come into an action to set aside a zoning order,[24] and that in an action in which the Brotherhood of Locomotive Engineers sought a declaratory judgment that its agreement with the railroad allowed its members to work more miles and days than they were working, the firemen's union, arguing that the more days engineers work the fewer days firemen work, was allowed to intervene.[25] Indeed, permissive intervention had even been allowed when the intervenor had little more interest than the avoiding of a precedent that might someday come back to haunt him,[26] although here the courts were more doubtful and on occasion said that the applicant could protect itself sufficiently by appearing as amicus curiae.[27] The broadened scope of intervention of right may now encompass some of these situations formerly thought appropriate for permissive intervention if the applicant's interest is not adequately represented.

All applications to intervene, whether as of right or permissively, are required to be "timely."[28] To this extent the court has discretion in all cases of intervention, because it must determine the timeliness of the application, but since in intervention-of-right situations the applicant may be seriously harmed if it is not permitted to intervene, courts should be especially reluctant to dismiss such applications as untimely.[29] In considering whether an application is timely, the court will look to the time element itself but will evaluate it in the light of all the circumstances of the case, and will weigh particularly whether the delay in moving for intervention has prejudiced the existing parties to the case.[30] Intervention may be disallowed where trial of the case is about to begin,[31] but it may not be too late to intervene even after final judgment

24. Wolpe v. Poretsky, C.C.A.D.C.1944, 144 F.2d 505, certiorari denied 65 S.Ct. 190, 323 U.S. 777, 89 L.Ed. 621.

25. Brotherhood of Locomotive Engineers v. Chicago, M., St.P. & P.R. Co., D.C.Wis.1940, 34 F.Supp. 594. See also Ruby v. Pan American World Airways, Inc., D.C.N.Y.1966, 252 F.Supp. 393, appeal dismissed C.A.2d, 1966, 360 F.2d 691.

26. Cf. Fishgold v. Sullivan Drydock & Repair Corp., 1946, 66 S.Ct. 1105, 328 U.S. 275, 90 L.Ed. 1230.

27. Peterson v. U.S., D.C.Minn.1966, 41 F.R.D. 131; Jewell Ridge Coal Corp. v. Local No. 6167, United Mine Workers of America, D.C.Va.1943, 3 F.R.D. 251.

28. 7C Wright, Miller & Kane, Civil 2d § 1916.

29. Alaniz v. Tillie Lewis Foods, C.A.9th, 1978, 572 F.2d 657, 659, certiorari denied 99 S.Ct. 123, 439 U.S. 837, 58 L.Ed.2d 134; and cases cited 7C Wright, Miller & Kane, Civil 2d § 1916 n. 5. See

Note, The Timeliness Threat to Intervention of Right, 1980, 89 Yale L.J. 586.

30. The factors to be considered are: the length of time the intervenor knew or reasonably should have known of its interest before it moved to intervene; prejudice to the existing parties due to failure to move promptly; the prejudice the intervenor would suffer if not allowed to intervene; and the existence of unusual circumstances mitigating either for or against intervention. Culbreath v. Dukakis, C.A.1st, 1980, 630 F.2d 15, 20; Stallworth v. Monsanto Co., C.A.5th, 1977, 558 F.2d 257, 264–266.

See cases cited 7C Wright, Miller & Kane, Civil 2d § 1916 nn. 9–15.

31. National Assn. for the Advancement of Colored People v. New York, 1973, 93 S.Ct. 2591, 2603, 413 U.S. 345, 366–369, 37 L.Ed.2d 648; Equal Employment Opportunity Comm. v. United Airlines, Inc., C.A.7th, 1975, 515 F.2d 946; Janousek v. Wells, C.A.8th, 1962, 303 F.2d 118.

if it is necessary to preserve some right that cannot otherwise be protected.[32]

If the application comes under Rule 24(b) and is permissive, the court has a broader discretion with regard to it.[33] It is required by the rule to consider "whether the intervention will unduly delay or prejudice the adjudication of the rights of the original parties."[34] There is no such provision in subdivision (a). The rulemakers have made a judgment that in the situations described in subdivision (a) justice demands that the interest of the absentee should predominate over the interests of the original parties and of trial convenience. Thus, in determining whether an application for intervention of right is timely, the court may consider whether delay in moving has prejudiced the existing parties, but except for that cannot consider prejudice under subdivision (a).[35] On an application for permissive intervention, however, the court is not so bound and may exercise its discretion in weighing the fact that additional parties always take additional time against the advantages of disposition of all the claims or defenses in one litigation.[36]

The cases on jurisdiction were not easily reconciled prior to the 1966 amendment, and the courts never fully considered what effect, if any, that amendment had on jurisdictional issues. The whole matter is now made vastly more complicated by the poorly drafted 1990 statute on supplemental jurisdiction.[37] The principle, prior to the 1990 statute, was clear enough: if the claim of the intervenor was so closely related to the main action that the claim could be regarded as ancillary, no independent grounds of jurisdiction needed to exist.[38] The difficulty came in

---

32. United Airlines, Inc. v. McDonald, 1977, 97 S.Ct. 2464, 432 U.S. 385, 53 L.Ed.2d 423; Securities & Exchange Comm. v. U.S. Realty & Improvement Co., 1940, 60 S.Ct. 1044, 310 U.S. 434, 84 L.Ed. 1293; Fleming v. Citizens For Albemarle, Inc., C.A.4th, 1978, 577 F.2d 236, certiorari denied 99 S.Ct. 842, 439 U.S. 1071, 59 L.Ed.2d 37. A strong showing is required to intervene at this late stage. Meredith v. Schreiner Transport, Inc., D.C.Kan.1993, 814 F.Supp. 1001, 1003. See 7C Wright, Miller & Kane, Civil 2d § 1916 nn. 16–21.

Although, as held in the United Airlines case, cited above, intervention can be allowed after judgment to allow the intervenor to take an appeal that the existing parties have decided not to take, "an intervenor's right to continue a suit in the absence of the party on whose side intervention was permitted is contingent upon a showing by the intervenor that he fulfills the requirements of Art. III." Diamond v. Charles, 1986, 106 S.Ct. 1697, 1706, 476 U.S. 54, 68, 90 L.Ed.2d 48.

33. 7C Wright, Miller & Kane, Civil 2d § 1913.

34. U.S. Postal Serv. v. Brennan, C.A.2d, 1978, 579 F.2d 188; Gerstle v. Continental Airlines, Inc., C.A.10th, 1972, 466 F.2d 1374; and cases cited 7C Wright, Miller & Kane, Civil 2d § 1913 nn. 13, 14.

35. Stallworth v. Monsanto Co., C.A.5th, 1977, 558 F.2d 257, 265.

Professor Shreve has made an interesting argument that the distinction between intervention of right and permissive intervention should be ended and the courts given broad discretion, with only minimal appellate involvement, on all requests to intervene. Shreve, note 1 above. A similar view is taken by Tobias, note 1 above, at 445–463.

36. Spangler v. Pasadena City Bd. of Educ., C.A.9th, 1977, 552 F.2d 1326, 1329; Pace v. First Nat. Bank of Osawatomie, D.C.Kan.1965, 277 F.Supp. 19, 20.

37. 28 U.S.C.A. § 1367. See § 9 above.

38. Phelps v. Oaks, 1886, 6 S.Ct. 714, 117 U.S. 236, 29 L.Ed. 888; Wichita R. & Light Co. v. Public Util. Comm. of Kansas, 1922, 43 S.Ct. 51, 260 U.S. 48, 67 L.Ed. 124; 7C Wright, Miller & Kane, Civil 2d § 1917.

seeking to determine how close the relationship had to be to justify use of the concept of ancillary jurisdiction. The usual rule was that independent jurisdictional grounds were required for permissive intervention under Rule 24(b), but not for intervention of right.[39]

The 1990 supplemental-jurisdiction statute, 28 U.S.C.A. § 1367, has changed and confused the situation. Section 1367(a) provides that if a district court has original jurisdiction of a case it also has supplemental jurisdiction—the new name for what used to be called "ancillary" and "pendent" jurisdiction—"over all other claims that are so related to claims in the action with such original jurisdiction that they form part of the same case or controversy under Article III of the United States Constitution." The second sentence of (a) says that this includes claims that involve "the joinder or intervention of additional parties." It is clear that this was intended to, and does, bring into play the constitutional test announced in United Mine Workers v. Gibbs [40] and that supplemental jurisdiction will extend to claims arising out of a common nucleus of operative fact.[41] It no longer will make any difference for purposes of jurisdiction whether intervention is under Rule 24(a) or Rule 24(b).

But this grant of supplemental jurisdiction is greatly limited for diversity cases by § 1367(b). In cases in which jurisdiction is founded solely on 28 U.S.C.A. § 1332, the general diversity statute, "the district courts shall not have supplemental jurisdiction under subsection (a) over claims by plaintiffs against persons made parties under Rule * * * 24 of the Federal Rules of Civil Procedure, or over claims by persons * * * seeking to intervene as plaintiffs under Rule 24 of such rules, when exercising supplemental jurisdiction over such claims would be inconsistent with the jurisdictional requirements of section 1332." [42] This means that plaintiff cannot assert a claim against an intervenor nor can a person intervene as a plaintiff if this would be inconsistent with the requirement of complete diversity that has been read into § 1332.[43] It

---

39. See 7C Wright, Miller & Kane, Civil 2d § 1917, pp. 464–475.

40. 1966, 86 S.Ct. 1130, 383 U.S. 715, 16 L.Ed.2d 218. See § 19 above.

41. 88 S.Ct. at 1138, 383 U.S. at 725. The Gibbs Court included a second element in the test of constitutional power: the claims must be such that a plaintiff "would ordinarily be expected to try them all in one judicial proceeding." It is unclear how, if at all, this element of the test can be applied to intervenors, since separate parties are not ordinarily expected to join their claims in one judicial proceeding.

42. See generally Teply & Whitten, Civil Procedure, 1991, pp. 508–514; Ireland, Supplemental Jurisdiction Over Claims in Intervention, 1993, 23 N.M.L.Rev. 57; McLaughlin, The Federal Supplemental Jurisdiction Statute—A Constitutional and

Statutory Analysis, 1992, 24 Ariz.St.L.J. 849, 952–971. Not surprisingly, given the language of § 1367(b) and the sparse legislative history on it, these commentators differ in how they think it will apply to claims by and against intervenors.

43. On the requirement of complete diversity, see § 24 above. The principal purpose of § 1367(b) was to preserve that requirement. But § 1367(b) was also intended to cure what the drafters of the statute regarded as the "anomaly" that a person might intervene of right under Rule 24(a)(2) even though that person, because only a "necessary" party, could not be joined under Rule 19. Whether there really was such an anomaly, and, if so, whether the 1990 statute solves it correctly, has been hotly debated by the commentators. See Freer, Compounding Confusion and Hampering Diversity: Life After Finley and also means that claims against an intervenor or by an intervening plaintiff must be in excess of $50,000.[44]

The procedure for intervention is set out in Rule 24(c).[45] The party desiring to intervene must serve a motion for leave to intervene upon all parties, stating the grounds for intervention and accompanied by a pleading setting forth the claim or defense for which intervention is sought.[46] Since the opposing parties are already subject to the jurisdiction of the court, personal service under Rule 4 is not required and the motion may be served as provided in Rule 5. The requirement of the former Equity Rule that intervention "shall be in subordination to and in recognition of the propriety of the main proceeding" was deliberately omitted from Rule 24 and should not be read back in by the courts.[47] The intervenor may assert a counterclaim—and must do so if the compulsory-counterclaim rule is applicable.[48] Where intervention is permissive, however, the court may refuse intervention if a counterclaim will delay or prejudice the existing parties.[49]

the Supplemental Jurisdiction Statute, 1991, 40 Emory L.J. 445, 476–478; Rowe, Burbank & Mengler, Compounding of Creating Confusion About Supplemental Jurisdiction: A Reply to Professor Freer, 1991, 40 Emory L.J. 943, 955–957; Arthur & Freer, Grasping at Burnt Straws: The Disaster of the Supplemental Jurisdiction Statute, 1991, 40 Emory L.J. 963, 973–974. Professor Oakley thinks that the "vague phrasing" of § 1367(b) need not be construed as changing the law on this particular point. Oakley, Recent Statutory Changes in the Law of Federal Jurisdiction and Venue, The Judicial Improvements Acts of 1988 and 1990, 1991, 24 U.C.Davis L.Rev. 735, 765–766. But as pointed out in McLaughlin, note 42 above, at 960: "Of all the changes effectuated by § 1367(b), this is the only one that is actually identified in the legislative history."

44. Meredith v. Schreiner Transport, Inc., D.C.Kan.1993, 814 F.Supp. 1001.

There is nothing in the legislative history to suggest that the drafters of § 1367 were concerned about amount in controversy, but that is an express jurisdictional requirement of § 1332, while the requirement of complete diversity is only a court-made gloss on the statute. See McLaughlin, note 42 above, at 970–971.

45. 7C Wright, Miller & Kane, Civil 2d § 1914.

46. Courts should be liberal, however, in disregarding procedural errors by the would-be intervenor. Beckman Industries, Inc. v. International Ins. Co., C.A.9th, 1992, 966 F.2d 470, 474, certiorari denied 113 S.Ct. 197, ___ U.S. ___, 121 L.Ed.2d 140;

Spring Constr. Co. v. Harris, C.A.4th, 1980, 614 F.2d 374; 7C Wright, Miller & Kane, Civil 2d § 1914, pp. 410–416. But cf. Shevlin v. Schewe, C.A.7th, 1987, 809 F.2d 447; Spangler v. Pasadena City Bd. of Educ., C.A.9th, 1977, 552 F.2d 1326.

47. 7C Wright, Miller & Kane, Civil 2d § 1920; Spangler v. U.S., C.A.9th, 1969, 415 F.2d 1242; Park & Tilford, Inc. v. Schulte, C.C.A.2d, 1947, 160 F.2d 984, 989 n. 1, certiorari denied 68 S.Ct. 64, 332 U.S. 761, 92 L.Ed. 347; Hartley Pen Co. v. Lindy Pen Co., Inc., D.C.Cal.1954, 16 F.R.D. 141. But cf. Keystone Freight Lines v. Pratt Thomas Truck Line, D.C.Okl.1941, 37 F.Supp. 635; Dolcater v. Manufacturers & Traders Trust Co., D.C.N.Y.1938, 25 F.Supp. 637.

48. U.S. v. Martin, C.A.10th, 1959, 267 F.2d 764; Lenz v. Wagner, C.A.5th, 1957, 240 F.2d 666; Switzer Bros. v. Locklin, C.A.7th, 1953, 207 F.2d 483, noted 1954, 67 Harv.L.Rev. 1265; cf. Stewart–Warner Corp. v. Westinghouse Elec. Corp., C.A.2d, 1963, 325 F.2d 822, certiorari denied 84 S.Ct. 800, 376 U.S. 944, 11 L.Ed.2d 767. Contra: Kauffman v. Kebert, D.C.Pa.1954, 16 F.R.D. 225, appeal dismissed C.A.3d, 1955, 219 F.2d 113; E.G. Staude Mfg. Co. v. Berles Carton Co., Inc., D.C.N.Y.1939, 31 F.Supp. 178. See 7C Wright, Miller & Kane, Civil 2d § 1921.

49. McKersie v. IU Intl., D.C.Ill.1988, 120 F.R.D. 60; Northwest Airlines, Inc. v. Intl. Assn. of Machinists & Aerospace Workers, AFL–CIO, D.C.Minn.1970, 323 F.Supp. 107; Finck v. Gilman Bros. Co., D.C.Conn.1951, 11 F.R.D. 198; cf. Brown v. Lee, C.A.4th, 1964, 331 F.2d 142.

An order granting leave to intervene is not final and is not appealable as of right.[50] The situation is more complicated if intervention is denied. Here the traditional doctrine is that if the applicant has contended it may intervene as of right, denial of leave to intervene is appealable. The appellate court will consider the merits of the claim and will reverse if it determines that intervention was in fact a matter of right.[51] If, however, the appellate court concludes that there was no right to intervene, the common practice has been to dismiss the appeal for want of jurisdiction, on the ground that the order was not final.[52] The practical consequences to the appellant are the same as if the denial of intervention were affirmed on the merits, and there is now a strong trend toward considering all such orders appealable since the appellate court does in fact look into the merits of the claim.[53]

It is commonly said that a denial of permissive intervention may be reversed for abuse of discretion. This is an illusory doctrine. There seems to be only one case in which a district court has been reversed solely because of an abuse of discretion in denying permissive intervention.[54] It makes little sense to maintain a stated doctrine that invites litigants to raise an issue on appeal when there is so little prospect that it will win them a reversal.[55]

§ 76. Impleader[1]

Rule 14 introduced into federal civil practice the procedure of impleader, long familiar in England and in admiralty, by which a defendant[2] can bring in as a third-party defendant one claimed by the defendant to be liable to it for all or part of the plaintiff's claim against the defendant. This procedure is intended to avoid circuity of action and to dispose of the entire subject matter arising from one set of facts in one action, thus administering complete and evenhanded justice, expeditiously and economically.[3] The rule is not mandatory; defendant may refrain

---

50. Shore v. Parklane Hosiery Co., C.A.2d, 1979, 606 F.2d 354; and cases cited 7C Wright, Miller & Kane, Civil 2d § 1923 n. 1.

51. Cascade Natural Gas Corp. v. El Paso Natural Gas Co., 1967, 87 S.Ct. 932, 386 U.S. 129, 17 L.Ed.2d 814; Brotherhood of R. Trainmen v. Baltimore & O.R. Co., 1947, 67 S.Ct. 1387, 1390, 331 U.S. 519, 524–525, 91 L.Ed. 1646.

52. Sam Fox Pub. Co. v. U.S., 1961, 81 S.Ct. 1309, 366 U.S. 683, 6 L.Ed.2d 604; Sutphen Estates v. U.S., 1951, 72 S.Ct. 14, 342 U.S. 19, 96 L.Ed. 19; Equal Employment Opportunity Commn. v. Eastern Airlines, Inc., C.A.11th, 1984, 736 F.2d 635.

53. Blake v. Pallan, C.A.9th, 1977, 554 F.2d 947, 951 n. 5; Pennsylvania v. Rizzo, C.A.3d, 1976, 530 F.2d 501, 504, certiorari denied 96 S.Ct. 2628, 426 U.S. 921, 49 L.Ed.2d 375; Reedsburg Bank v. Apollo, C.A.7th, 1975, 508 F.2d 995, 997; Ionian

Shipping Co. v. British Law Ins. Co., C.A.2d, 1970, 426 F.2d 186, 188–189. See Stallworth v. Monsanto Co., C.A.5th, 1977, 558 F.2d 257, 263 n. 7; 7C Wright, Miller & Kane, Civil 2d § 1923.

54. Crumble v. Blumthal, C.A.7th, 1977, 549 F.2d 462.

55. 7C Wright, Miller & Kane, Civil 2d § 1923, pp. 512–516. See Shreve, note 1 above, at 921–924.

§ 76

1. 6 Wright, Miller & Kane, Civil 2d §§ 1441–1465; Brill, Federal Rule of Civil Procedure 14 and Ancillary Jurisdiction, 1980, 59 Neb.L.Rev. 631.

2. Or a plaintiff against whom a counterclaim has been asserted. Rule 14(b).

3. 6 Wright, Miller & Kane, Civil 2d § 1442.

from impleader and assert its claim instead in an independent action if it prefers.[4]

Defendant may invoke this procedure by service of a summons and third-party complaint on the third party if it acts expeditiously. Otherwise it must obtain leave of court to bring in the third party. In either event the court has discretion whether to allow impleader. Where impleader is had promptly, and leave of court is not required, this discretion can be invoked by a motion of any party to strike the third-party claim, or for its severance or separate trial. A court, called upon to exercise its discretion about impleader, must balance the desire to avoid circuity of actions and to obtain consistent results against any prejudice that the plaintiff might suffer from complication of the case.[5] There should be little occasion, however, to deny impleader. The power to order separate trial of separate issues, under Rule 42(b), is sufficient to prevent any harm from impleader.[6]

There have been cases in which impleader to assert a claim for indemnity, as against an employee of the original defendant, has been refused.[7] If the proposed third-party defendant lacks the financial ability to indemnify the original defendant, the courts have thought that the third party would be a straw man, and that the only purpose of impleading the employee would be to induce the jury to proceed on the false supposition that the employee might have to pay the judgment. The feeling that using impleader for this purpose is improper is realistic and persuasive, though in most cases sufficient protection can be given by ordering a separate trial of the third-party claim.[8]

A third-party complaint may be served only against one not already a party to the action. Counterclaims and cross-claims under Rule 13 are the appropriate procedure for asserting a claim against one already a party.[9] Under the rule as it was amended in 1948, the claim must be that the third party is liable over to defendant for all or part of plaintiff's claim against defendant. Except where the original claim is maritime in nature, and the special provisions of Rule 14(c) apply, it is no longer

---

4. Union Paving Co. v. Thomas, D.C.Pa. 1949, 9 F.R.D. 612.

5. Somportex Ltd. v. Philadelphia Chewing Gum Corp., C.A.3d, 1971, 453 F.2d 435; Local 144, Hotel, Hosp., Nursing Home & Allied Servs. Union v. C.N.H. Management Assocs., D.C.N.Y.1990, 741 F.Supp. 415, 419; Johns Hopkins Univ. v. Hutton, D.C.Md.1966, 40 F.R.D. 338, 346–348; 6 Wright, Miller & Kane, Civil 2d § 1443.

6. Schwab v. Erie Lackawanna R. Co., C.A.3d, 1971, 438 F.2d 62, 71–72; Caplen v. Sturge, D.C.Pa.1964, 35 F.R.D. 176. See also cases cited note 8 below.

7. Goodhart v. U.S. Lines Co., D.C.N.Y. 1960, 26 F.R.D. 163; Sox v. Hertz Corp., D.C.S.C.1967, 262 F.Supp. 531.

Impleader has also been refused where the same insurance company would have to pay the judgment whether it were against the defendant employer or the third-party defendant employee. List v. Roto–Broil Corp. of America, D.C.Pa.1966, 40 F.R.D. 31; Buchholz v. Michigan Motor Freight Lines, Inc., D.C.Mich.1956, 19 F.R.D. 407.

8. Lankford v. Ryder Truck Systems, Inc., D.C.S.C.1967, 41 F.R.D. 430; Smith v. Moore–McCormack Lines, Inc., D.C.N.Y. 1962, 31 F.R.D. 239.

9. Horton v. Continental Can Co., D.C.Neb.1956, 19 F.R.D. 429; cf. Field v. Volkswagenwerk AG, C.A.3d, 1980, 626 F.2d 293, 298 n. 9; 6 Wright, Miller & Kane, Civil 2d § 1446, pp. 374–376.

possible, as it was theoretically prior to 1948, to implead a third party claimed to be solely liable to the plaintiff.[10]   Third-party practice is typically used to assert claims for indemnity, subrogation, contribution, and for breach of warranty.[11]   The third-party claim need not be based on the same theory as the main claim; one sued for negligence, for example, may implead a third party against whom he or she has a contractual right of indemnity.[12]

Prior to amendments of the rules in 1966, there was uncertainty about the extent to which a defendant could join other claims it might have against a third-party defendant with the claim for liability over that formed the basis of impleader, and whether it might demand damages in excess of those plaintiff was seeking from it.[13]   Rule 18(a), as amended in 1966, now states explicitly that "a party asserting a claim to relief as * * * [a] third-party claim, may join, either as independent or as alternate claims, as many claims * * * as he has against an opposing party."   Thus, it is now clear that, as a matter of pleading, once a defendant has asserted a claim suitable for impleader under Rule 14(a), it may join with it all of its other claims against the third-party defendant.[14]   But questions of federal jurisdiction may still limit this kind of joinder.   There must be an independent basis for federal jurisdiction of the additional claims unless they arise out of the same transaction or occurrence as a claim of which the federal court has original jurisdiction, and thus can be considered to be within the ancillary—or, as it is now called, supplemental—jurisdiction of the court.[15]

10. McCain v. Clearview Dodge Sales, Inc., C.A.5th, 1978, 574 F.2d 848; Parr v. Great Lakes Exp. Co., C.A.7th, 1973, 484 F.2d 767; Toberman v. Copas, D.C.Pa.1992, 800 F.Supp. 1239, 1241–1242.

See Ciolino & Roberts, The Missing Direct–Tender Option in Federal Third–Party Practice, 1990, 68 N.C.L.Rev. 423; Comment, Impleader of Nonmaritime Claims Under Rule 14(c), 1968, 47 Texas L.Rev. 120.

11. 6 Wright, Miller & Kane, Civil 2d § 1446 nn. 5–9; § 1448.

12. E.g., U.S. for Use of Payne v. United Pac. Ins. Co., C.A.9th, 1973, 472 F.2d 792, certiorari denied 93 S.Ct. 2273, 411 U.S. 982, 36 L.Ed.2d 958; Southern R. Co. v. Fox, C.A.5th, 1964, 339 F.2d 560; Judd v. General Motors Corp., D.C.Pa.1974, 65 F.R.D. 612.

13. Compare Noland Co. v. Graver Tank & Mfg. Co., C.A.4th, 1962, 301 F.2d 43, and Ruckman & Hansen, Inc. v. Contracting & Material Co., C.A.7th, 1964, 328 F.2d 744, with U.S. v. Scott, D.C.N.Y.1955, 18 F.R.D. 324, C.W. Humphrey Co. v. Security Aluminum Co., D.C.Mich.1962, 31 F.R.D. 41, and Gebhardt v. Edgar, D.C.Pa. 1966, 251 F.Supp. 678.

14. Crompton–Richmond Co., Inc., Factors v. U.S., D.C.N.Y.1967, 273 F.Supp. 219. See also 6 Wright, Miller & Kane, Civil 2d § 1452.

15. King Fisher Marine Serv., Inc. v. 21st Phoenix Corp., C.A.10th, 1990, 893 F.2d 1155, certiorari denied 110 S.Ct. 2603, 496 U.S. 912, 110 L.Ed.2d 283; Nishimatsu Constr. Co., Ltd. v. Houston Nat. Bank, C.A.5th, 1975, 515 F.2d 1200; Schwab v. Erie Lackawanna R. Co., C.A.3d, 1971, 438 F.2d 62.   There is language in these three cases that it is enough that the additional claim arises out of the same transaction or occurrence as the claim for liability over. This is rejected in U.S. for Use of Payne v. United Pac. Ins. Co., C.A.9th, 1973, 472 F.2d 792, certiorari denied 93 S.Ct. 2273, 411 U.S. 982, 36 L.Ed.2d 958 and in Note, 1971, 46 N.Y.U.L.Rev. 634 where it is argued that the additional claim must be ancillary to the original claim of the plaintiff and not to the defendant's claim of liability over.   On this point the new supplemental-jurisdiction statute, see § 9 above, though cryptic, seems to support the view of the three cases first cited.   28 U.S.C.A. § 1367(a) allows supplemental jurisdiction to everything that is part of the same case or controversy under Article III.   Section

Impleader is proper only where there is a substantive right to the relief sought. In diversity actions the law of the state governs on the existence of such substantive rights, and if, for example, the state recognizes no substantive right to contribution in particular circumstances, impleader for contribution cannot be allowed in federal court.[16] Impleader itself, however, is not governed by state law, and is available in federal court, if there is a substantive right to the relief sought, though in state court an independent action would be required to vindicate that substantive right.[17]

One of the most important features of Rule 14 is that it permits impleader of one "who is or may be liable" to the defendant. The express use of the words "may be" indicates, as has been repeatedly held, that the rule permits impleader where liability is only contingent, and thus can accelerate the determination of liability.[18] The court may issue a conditional judgment, where impleader is on a contingent liability.[19] Thus, if state law gives a substantive right to contribution or indemnity, this may be asserted by impleader even though the state has no procedure for determination of such liability until it has been fixed by judgment, with the form of the judgment shaped to reflect the state law.[20] A particularly important application of this principle is that when an insurance company denies liability on the policy and refuses to defend a tort action against its insured, he or she may implead the insurer in the tort action and have the issue of policy coverage decided in the same case as is the issue of tort liability.[21] The usual "no action" clause of insurance policies, which bars suit against the insurer until the liability of the insured has been determined by a judgment, does not bar impleader, because Rule 14 is intended to accelerate the determination of liability.[22] Separate trial of the third-party claim may be ordered, if this is in the interest of sound judicial administration, but the courts have viewed skeptically contentions that separate trials should be ordered as a matter of course on the fear that the presence of the insurer as a party

1367(b) limits claims by plaintiffs in diversity cases against persons brought in under Rule 14, but it is silent about claims by defendants against third-party defendants.

16. The leading cases are Brown v. Cranston, C.C.A.2d, 1942, 132 F.2d 631, certiorari denied 63 S.Ct. 1028, 319 U.S. 741, 87 L.Ed. 1698, and Goldlawr, Inc. v. Shubert, C.A.3d, 1960, 276 F.2d 614. See also Kim v. Fujikawa, C.A.9th, 1989, 871 F.2d 1427; and cases cited 6 Wright, Miller & Kane, Civil 2d § 1446 nn. 10, 15.

17. D'Onofrio Constr. Co. v. Recon Co., C.A.1st, 1958, 255 F.2d 904. The D'Onofrio case is cited with approval in Hanna v. Plumer, 1965, 85 S.Ct. 1136, 1145 n. 16, 380 U.S. 460, 473 n. 16, 14 L.Ed.2d 8.

18. Jeub v. B/G Foods, Inc., D.C.Minn. 1942, 2 F.R.D. 238; 6 Wright, Miller &

Kane, Civil 2d § 1451. Liability is contingent where the third party will be liable to the defendant only if defendant is found liable to plaintiff.

19. Williams v. Ford Motor Credit Co., C.A.8th, 1980, 627 F.2d 158, 160; Travelers Ins. Co. v. Busy Elec. Co., C.A.5th, 1961, 294 F.2d 139, 145.

20. Glens Falls Indem. Co. v. Atlantic Bldg. Corp., C.A.4th, 1952, 199 F.2d 60; Rambone v. Critzer, D.C.Va.1982, 548 F.Supp. 660, 662.

21. 6 Wright, Miller & Kane, Civil 2d § 1449.

22. Colton v. Swain, C.A.7th, 1975, 527 F.2d 296; Jordan v. Stephens, D.C.Mo. 1945, 7 F.R.D. 140.

will prejudice the jury.[23]

There is confusion whether a defendant may implead a third party liable over to it for plaintiff's claim when the plaintiff is under a disability that would bar plaintiff from suing the third party directly.[24] It has been held that defendant may implead plaintiff's employer, even though the state compensation act would bar the plaintiff from suing the employer.[25] There is some authority that the third party may be impleaded although the statute of limitations would bar a suit against it directly by plaintiff.[26] Many decisions refuse to permit impleader of plaintiff's spouse for contribution, where the plaintiff could not sue the spouse directly, though the cases on this point are quite divided.[27] And the United States may implead a state even though the Eleventh Amendment would bar the plaintiff from suing the state.[28]

Even though it is no longer possible, except in maritime cases falling within Rule 14(c), for defendant to implead a third party as solely liable to plaintiff,[29] where a third party has been properly brought in, plaintiff may, if it chooses, assert directly against the third-party defendant either by amendment or by new pleading any claim it may have against the third party arising out of the transaction or occurrence that is the subject matter of the plaintiff's claim against the original defendant.[30] Even if no formal amendment is made, Rule 15(b), on amendments to conform to the evidence, is relevant, and the plaintiff will be considered to have asserted such a claim where the parties have treated themselves as adverse.[31]

The third-party defendant may always assert any defenses it has to the original defendant's claim over against it, and it may also assert any

23. Baker v. Moors, D.C.Ky.1971, 51 F.R.D. 507, 510; Schevling v. Johnson, D.C.Conn.1953, 122 F.Supp. 87, 89–90, affirmed on the opinion below C.A.2d, 1954, 213 F.2d 959; and cases cited 6 Wright, Miller & Kane, Civil 2d § 1449 n. 15.

24. 6 Wright, Miller & Kane, Civil 2d § 1447.

25. Atella v. General Elec. Co., D.C.R.I. 1957, 21 F.R.D. 372; Whitmarsh v. Durastone Co., D.C.R.I.1954, 122 F.Supp. 806; Corrao v. Waterman S.S. Corp., D.C.N.Y. 1948, 75 F.Supp. 482; Severn v. U.S., D.C.N.Y.1946, 69 F.Supp. 21, Contra: Cox v. E.I. Du Pont de Nemours & Co., D.C.S.C. 1965, 39 F.R.D. 47.

26. Keleket X–Ray Corp. v. U.S., C.A.D.C.1960, 275 F.2d 167; TSZ Ki Yim v. Home Indem. Co., D.C.D.C.1982, 95 F.R.D. 349. But see Rambone v. Critzer, D.C.Va. 1982, 548 F.Supp. 660, 663–664.

27. Yellow Cab Co. of D.C. v. Dreslin, C.A.D.C.1950, 181 F.2d 626, 19 A.L.R.2d 1001; Koenigs v. Travis, 1956, 75 N.W.2d 478, 246 Minn. 466; Guerriero v. U–Drive–It Co. of N.J., 1952, 92 A.2d 140, 22 N.J.Super. 588; Norfolk Southern R. Co. v. Gre-

takis, 1934, 174 S.E. 841, 162 Va. 597. Contra: Gray v. Hartford Acc. & Indem. Co., D.C.La.1940, 31 F.Supp. 299; Slavics v. Wood, D.C.Pa.1964, 36 F.R.D. 47; Smith v. Southern Farm Bureau Cas. Ins. Co., 1965, 174 So.2d 122, 247 La. 695; Bedell v. Reagan, 1963, 192 A.2d 24, 159 Me. 292; Fisher v. Diehl, 1945, 40 A.2d 912, 156 Pa.Super. 476. Other cases seemingly in point are distinguishable because of different state rules on contribution or on interspousal immunity.

28. U.S. v. Illinois, C.A.7th, 1971, 454 F.2d 297, 301, certiorari denied 92 S.Ct. 1767, 406 U.S. 918, 32 L.Ed.2d 117.

29. See note 10 above.

30. 6 Wright, Miller & Kane, Civil 2d § 1459.

31. Falls Indus. Inc. v. Consolidated Chem. Indus., Inc., C.A.5th, 1958, 258 F.2d 277; see Patton v. Baltimore & O.R. Co., C.A.3d, 1952, 197 F.2d 732, 743; Feldman, A Puzzle under the Federal Impleader Rule, 1959, 34 Tul.L.Rev. 77.

defenses that the original defendant has to plaintiff's claim. This protects the third-party defendant if the original defendant fails or neglects to assert a proper defense to the plaintiff's claim on which the third party may be liable over.[32] The third-party defendant also has the right to assert directly against the plaintiff any claim arising out of the transaction or occurrence that is the subject matter of the plaintiff's claim against the original defendant.[33]

Joinder of claims and of parties in federal court always raises two questions that seem similar but are completely independent. Is the particular joinder procedurally proper? Is it jurisdictionally proper? If Hart of Massachusetts and Wechsler of New York are injured when the car in which they are riding is hit by a car driven by Shapiro of Massachusetts, they could join as plaintiffs in a suit against Shapiro. The joinder would be procedurally proper under Rule 20.[34] It would fail jurisdictionally, however, because of the requirement of complete diversity.[35]

This distinction between what is procedurally proper and what is jurisdictionally proper is particularly important with regard to impleader. As has just been seen, Rule 14 makes very generous provision for impleading third parties and for assertion of claims on all three sides of the resulting lawsuit. While a great deal is thus procedurally proper, the limitations on jurisdiction and venue in the federal courts would make impleader of little utility there if the courts had not given a commodious scope to the concept of ancillary jurisdiction—or supplemental jurisdiction as it is called in a 1990 statute [36]—when applied to Rule 14. Indeed the Supreme Court's first full-dress examination of the ancillary-jurisdiction concept came in a Rule 14 context.

The case is Owen Equipment and Erection Co. v. Kroger.[37] Kroger was electrocuted when the boom of a steel crane next to which he was walking came too close to a high-tension power line. His widow, a citizen of Iowa, sued the Omaha Public Power District (OPPD), a Nebraska corporation, claiming that it had negligently operated the power line. The utility then impleaded Owen Equipment, a Nebraska corporation that owned the crane. OPPD claimed a right of contribution against Owen Equipment for negligence. Mrs. Kroger then amended her complaint, as Rule 14 allows, to state a claim directly against Owen Equipment for negligence.

---

32. Glick v. White Motor Co., C.A.3d, 1972, 458 F.2d 1287; F & D Property Co. v. Alkire, C.A.10th, 1967, 385 F.2d 97; 6 Wright, Miller & Kane, Civil 2d § 1457. The third-party defendant can also raise on appeal claims of error in the main action as well as those relating to the third-party action. U.S. v. Lumbermens Mut. Cas. Co., C.A.1st, 1990, 917 F.2d 654, 658 n. 5.

33. Stahl v. Ohio River Co., C.A.3d, 1970, 424 F.2d 52; Grace v. United Found-

ers Life Ins. Co., D.C.Okl.1971, 53 F.R.D. 8; 6 Wright, Miller & Kane, Civil 2d § 1458.

34. See § 71 above.

35. See § 24 above.

36. 28 U.S.C.A. § 1367. See § 9 above.

37. 1978, 98 S.Ct. 2396, 437 U.S. 365, 57 L.Ed.2d 274. See Brill, note 1 above, and Comment, Ancillary Jurisdiction: The Kroger Approach and the Federal Rules, 1979, 28 Emory L.Rev. 463.

Thereafter summary judgment was granted to OPPD on Mrs. Kroger's claim against it. It did not own the power line and under the applicable Iowa law had no duty to maintain it. The case then went to trial on Mrs. Kroger's claim against the third-party defendant, Owen Erection. During the third day of trial it was disclosed that Owen Erection's principal place of business was Iowa, not Nebraska, and that Mrs. Kroger and Owen Equipment were, therefore, both citizens of Iowa. The trial court refused to dismiss the action, and the jury returned a substantial verdict for Mrs. Kroger, but the Supreme Court held that there was no jurisdiction of this claim by one citizen of Iowa against another and set the judgment aside.

In his opinion for the Court, Justice Stewart recognized that "the exercise of ancillary jurisdiction over nonfederal claims has often been upheld in situations involving impleader, cross-claims or counter-claims." [38] He thought, however, that it is one thing to extend ancillary jurisdiction to the original defendant's claim against a third party and something quite different to apply it, as was sought in the case before the Court, to the original plaintiff's claim against a third-party defendant. "First, the nonfederal claim in this case was simply not ancillary to the federal one in the same sense that, for example, the impleader by a defendant of a third-party defendant always is. A third-party complaint depends at least in part upon the resolution of the primary lawsuit. * * * Its relation to the original complaint is thus not mere factual similarity but logical dependence. * * * [Mrs. Kroger's] claim against [Owen Equipment], however, was entirely separate from her original claim against OPPD, since [Owen Equipment's] liability to her depended not at all upon whether or not OPPD was also liable. Far from being an ancillary and dependent claim, it was a new and independent one.

"Second, the nonfederal claim here was asserted by the plaintiff, who voluntarily chose to bring suit upon a state-law claim in a federal court. By contrast, ancillary jurisdiction typically involves claims by defending party haled into court against his will, or by another person whose rights might be irretrievably lost unless he could assert them in an ongoing action in a federal court. A plaintiff cannot complain if ancillary jurisdiction does not encompass all of his possible claims in a case such as this one, since it is he who has chosen the federal rather than the state forum and must thus accept its limitations." [39]

It had been well settled before Owen Equipment that there is ancillary jurisdiction over the claim by the original defendant against the third-party defendant, and that there need be no independent jurisdictional grounds for such a claim if there was diversity between the original parties or if plaintiff's claim against the original defendant

---

38. 98 S.Ct. at 2403, 437 U.S. at 375. In footnote 18, at this point, the Court cited with apparent approval cases that had ap-plied ancillary jurisdiction to compulsory counterclaims, impleader, cross-claims, and intervention of right.

39. 98 S.Ct. at 2404, 437 U.S. at 376.

raised a federal question.[40] This was not changed by Owen Equipment.[41] Such a claim, the Court said, "always is" ancillary.[42] Dismissal or settlement of the main action does not require dismissal of the third-party complaint, even though there are no independent grounds of jurisdiction for the third-party claim,[43] but if considerations of convenience will be equally well served, the court has discretion in such a situation to dismiss the third-party proceeding and leave these ancillary matters to be determined in the state courts.[44]

A few cases refused to extend the ancillary concept to questions of venue, and refused to allow impleader unless venue was proper for the third-party defendant.[45] It would be quite extraordinary to hold that the third-party claim is sufficiently ancillary to avoid the constitutional limits on jurisdiction, but that the statutory venue privilege must still be respected, and there is now much authority to the contrary.[46] If there is really a showing of great inconvenience to the third party, the court can consider this in its discretion in deciding whether to allow impleader.[47]

Before Owen Equipment was decided, the cases were divided on whether independent jurisdictional grounds were required if plaintiff exercised his or her right to assert a claim against the third-party defendant. In that case the Supreme Court endorsed what had been the more usual view of the lower courts and held that ancillary jurisdiction

40. 6 Wright, Miller & Kane, Civil 2d § 1444 at notes 20 to 31.

41. Field v. Volkswagenwerk AG, C.A.3d, 1980, 626 F.2d 293, 298–299; Curtis v. Radiation Dynamics, Inc., D.C.Md. 1981, 515 F.Supp. 1176.

42. 98 S.Ct. at 2404, 437 U.S. at 376.

This is also clearly the law under the 1990 statute. 28 U.S.C.A. § 1367(a) grants supplemental jurisdiction to the constitutional limits, and though § 1367(b) limits that grant of jurisdiction in some respects in diversity cases, it does not limit the assertion of claims by defendants against third-party defendants.

43. Washington Hospital Center National Rehabilitation Hospital v. Collier, C.A.D.C.1991, 947 F.2d 1498, 1501; Nishimatsu Constr. Co., Ltd. v. Houston Nat. Bank, C.A.5th, 1975, 515 F.2d 1200, 1204 n. 2; and cases cited 6 Wright, Miller & Kane, Civil 2d § 1444 n. 63.

44. Propps v. Weihe, Black & Jeffries, C.A.4th, 1978, 582 F.2d 1354; Duke v. RFC, C.A.4th, 1954, 209 F.2d 204, certiorari denied 74 S.Ct. 777, 347 U.S. 966, 98 L.Ed. 1108; Point of Americas Condominium Apartments, Inc.—Phase II v. General Builders Corp., D.C.Fla.1976, 424 F.Supp. 1322; Maryland for Use and Benefit of Wood v. Robinson, D.C.Md.1947, 74 F.Supp.

279, 281–282. See generally 6 Wright, Miller & Kane, Civil 2d § 1444, pp. 340–344.

The principles stated in the text should remain true under the 1990 statute. Under 28 U.S.C.A. § 1367(c)(3) the court "may decline to exercise supplemental jurisdiction" if it "has dismissed all claims over which it has original jurisdiction."

45. Lewis v. United Air Lines Transport Corp., D.C.Conn.1939, 29 F.Supp. 112; King v. Shepherd, D.C.Ark.1938, 26 F.Supp. 357. This view is supported by Developments in the Law—Multiparty Litigation in the Federal Courts, 1958, 71 Harv.L.Rev. 874, 912.

46. Lesnik v. Public Indus. Corp., C.C.A.2d, 1944, 144 F.2d 968; Carcella v. L & L Coach Lines, Inc., D.C.Md.1984, 591 F.Supp. 1272, 1278; Moncrief v. Pennsylvania R. Co., D.C.Pa.1947, 73 F.Supp. 815; and cases cited 6 Wright, Miller & Kane, Civil 2d § 1445 n. 9.

47. U.S. v. Acord, C.A.10th, 1954, 209 F.2d 709, certiorari denied 74 S.Ct. 786, 347 U.S. 975, 98 L.Ed. 1115; Manley v. Standard Oil Co. of Tex., D.C.Tex.1948, 8 F.R.D. 354. Great inconvenience must be shown. Brown v. U.S., C.A.9th, 1959, 270 F.2d 80; Globig v. Greene & Gust Co., D.C.Wis.1960, 184 F.Supp. 530; Gore v. U.S., D.C.Mass. 1959, 171 F.Supp. 136.

does not extend to this situation.[48] This view was deliberately codified in the 1990 supplemental-jurisdiction statute. In a diversity case the district courts do not have supplemental jurisdiction "over claims by plaintiffs against persons made parties under Rule 14 * * * when exercising supplemental jurisdiction over such claims would be inconsistent with the jurisdictional requirements of section 1332." [49]

Though the cases were divided, the better view had been that no independent jurisdictional ground was required if the third-party defendant exercised its right under Rule 14 to assert a claim against the plaintiff arising out of the transaction sued on by the plaintiff.[50] Although the matter is not free of doubt, this should still be the result reached after Owen Equipment and under the 1990 statute.[51] Though there are no cases in point, the claim by the third party against the plaintiff should also be treated as ancillary for purposes of venue.

Although subject-matter jurisdiction, and the extent of ancillary jurisdiction, have attracted most attention under Rule 14, personal jurisdiction must also be obtained over the third-party defendant. The third-party summons and complaint ordinarily cannot be served outside the territorial limits of the state in which the main action is brought,[52] except where there is statutory authority for wider service,[53] and on occasion this has been an effective limitation on the use of Rule 14. The 1963 amendment of Rule 4(f) eased this problem somewhat by permitting service of the third-party complaint outside the state within 100 miles of the place where the action is to be tried.[54]

---

48. See 6 Wright, Miller & Kane, Civil 2d § 1444, pp. 330–340.

49. 28 U.S.C.A. § 1367(b). See McLaughlin, The Federal Supplemental Jurisdiction Statute—A Constitutional and Statutory Analysis, 1992, 24 Ariz.St.L.J. 849, 935–940.

The literal language of § 1367(b) means that the court cannot exercise supplemental jurisdiction over a third party impleaded by plaintiff on a counterclaim against the plaintiff, although exercise of jurisdiction in a case such as that would have been permissible under Owen Equipment. Guaranteed Systems, Inc. v. American Nat. Can Co., D.C.N.C.1994, 842 F.Supp. 855.

50. Mayer Paving & Asphalt Co. v. General Dynamics Corp., C.A.7th, 1973, 486 F.2d 763, certiorari denied 94 S.Ct. 899, 414 U.S. 1146, 39 L.Ed.2d 102; Revere Copper & Brass Inc. v. Aetna Cas. & Sur. Co., C.A.5th, 1970, 426 F.2d 709, noted 1971, 59 Ky.L.J. 506, 49 N.C.L.Rev. 503; and cases cited 6 Wright, Miller & Kane, Civil 2d § 1444 n. 56.

But see James King & Son, Inc. v. Indemnity Ins. Co. of North America, D.C.N.Y.

1959, 178 F.Supp. 146, and Shverha v. Maryland Cas. Co., D.C.Pa.1953, 110 F.Supp. 173. The result in these cases is criticized in Note, 1971, 57 Va.L.Rev. 265, 275–282.

51. See Brill, note 1 above, at 661–669; Berch, The Erection of a Barrier Against Assertion of Ancillary Claims: An Examination of Owen Equipment and Erection Company v. Kroger, 1979 Ariz.St.L.J. 253, 260–261. The 1990 statute extends supplemental jurisdiction to the constitutional limits. 28 U.S.C.A. § 1367(a). The exceptions to this broad grant for diversity cases, stated in § 1367(b), apply to claims by plaintiffs and do not limit claims against plaintiffs.

52. James Talcott, Inc. v. Allahabad Bank, Ltd., C.A.5th, 1971, 444 F.2d 451, certiorari denied 92 S.Ct. 280, 404 U.S. 940, 30 L.Ed.2d 253; and cases cited 6 Wright, Miller & Kane, Civil 2d § 1445 nn. 2, 3.

53. Moreno v. U.S., C.C.A.1st, 1941, 120 F.2d 128; Brandt v. Olson, D.C.Iowa 1959, 179 F.Supp. 363.

54. See § 64 above; Sprow v. Hartford Ins. Co., C.A.5th, 1979, 594 F.2d 412; Lee v. Ohio Cas. Ins. Co., D.C.Del.1978, 445 F.Supp. 189.

§ 77. Substitution of Parties [1]

Rule 25 provides, in four subsections, for substitution of parties where a party has died, become incompetent, transferred his or her interest, or where a public officer has been succeeded by someone else. Where a change of parties is desired for some other reason, Rule 15, on amendment, Rule 21, on adding or dropping parties, and Rule 24, on intervention, must be looked to rather than Rule 25.

Rule 25, as it stood prior to 1961, was not satisfactory. The time limits it provided for substitution, enforced rigorously as they were, often proved to be traps for the unwary, and led to harsh results contrary to the beneficial purposes stated in Rule 1. The requirement of substitution of public officers was at best a time-consuming formality and at worst a cause of positive injustice. Rule 25(d), as it stood before the 1961 amendment, enjoyed what is probably the unique distinction of having been criticized editorially by a lay newspaper. Thus, it is not surprising that there were persistent attempts to amend the rule. In 1961 Rule 25(d), on substitution of public officers, was amended, and in 1963 amendment was made to Rule 25(a), on substitution after death of a party. These amendments have removed most, if not all, of the earlier difficulties.

Whether an action abates on the death of a party or survives to the personal representative is not governed by the rules. State law must be looked to in a diversity action [2] and federal law and federal decisions in a federal-question case.[3] Rule 25(a) provides the mechanics of substitution if the action survives, and is controlling regardless of what the state law about such mechanics may be.[4]

The original Rule 25 provided that substitution could only be made within two years after the death of a party, and that the action must be dismissed if substitution was not so made. Such a rigid bar led to harsh results. Thus, in one case the Supreme Court noted that it was through no lack of diligence that the plaintiff, who was seeking to enforce assessments against more than 5,000 stockholders, failed to learn of the

---

§ 77

1. 7C Wright, Miller & Kane, Civil 2d §§ 1951–1962; Comment, Federal Civil Procedure: Substitution Under Amended Rule 25(a)(1), 1963 Duke L.J. 733.

2. E.g., McManus v. Lykes Bros. S.S. Co., D.C.La.1967, 275 F.Supp. 361; 7C Wright, Miller & Kane, Civil 2d §§ 1952, 1954.

3. Smith v. Department of Human Services, C.A.10th, 1989, 876 F.2d 832, 834.

On occasion federal law adopts the law of the state on whether an action survives. E.g., Robertson v. Wegmann, 1978, 98 S.Ct. 1991, 436 U.S. 584, 56 L.Ed.2d 554.

4. U.S. for Use of Acme Granite & Tile Co. v. F. D. Rich Co., C.A.9th, 1971, 441 F.2d 1143, certiorari denied 92 S.Ct. 48, 404

U.S. 823, 30 L.Ed.2d 51; Iovino v. Waterson, C.A.2d, 1959, 274 F.2d 41, certiorari denied 80 S.Ct. 860, 362 U.S. 949, 4 L.Ed.2d 867, approved 1960, 60 Col.L.Rev. 738, 73 Harv.L.Rev. 1618; Hofheimer v. McIntee, C.A.7th, 1950, 179 F.2d 789; Boggs v. Blue Diamond Coal Co., D.C.Ky. 1980, 497 F.Supp. 1105, noted 1981, 11 Mem.St.U.L.Rev. 413; Millich v. Schlesinger, D.C.Ind.1957, 156 F.Supp. 658; Commercial Solvents Corp. v. Jasspon, D.C.N.Y. 1950, 92 F.Supp. 20.

See, however, the more complicated analysis made in Ransom v. Brennan, C.A.5th, 1971, 437 F.2d 513, certiorari denied 91 S.Ct. 2205, 403 U.S. 904, 29 L.Ed.2d 680, discussed in 7C Wright, Miller & Kane, Civil 2d § 1952, pp. 529–530.

deaths of a few of these stockholders until more than two years after the event. Nevertheless plaintiff's failure to move for substitution within two years of the deaths was held to bar further action against the estates of the dead stockholders.[5]

An amendment to Rule 25(a), adopted in 1963, cures such injustice. The amendment eliminates the two-year time limit. A party, or the successors or representatives of the deceased party, may now move for substitution at any time, subject to two limitations. First, either a party, or the successors or representatives of a deceased party, may suggest on the record the fact of death. Where such a suggestion is made on the record, the action will be dismissed unless a motion to substitute is made within 90 days after service of the suggestion of death, or such extended time as the court may allow under Rule 6(b).[6] Second, substitution may be denied, even though the time limit has not run, if circumstances have arisen rendering it unfair to allow substitution, as where settlement and distribution of the estate of a deceased defendant is far advanced by the time the motion for substitution is made.[7] Thus, it is still the safe course to move for substitution as soon as the fact of death becomes known, rather than waiting indefinitely for the suggestion of death upon the record.

The former Rule 25(d), on substitution of public officers, produced incredible results. It required substitution within six months of the time a public officer replaced another person who, as such officer, had been a party to a lawsuit.[8] Where the public officer was plaintiff, this led to much needless formality, as in the making of formal orders of substitution in thousands of pending cases whenever there was a change in the person who was charged with enforcing price controls. The consequences where the public officer was defendant were even worse. The remarkable decision of Snyder v. Buck[9] illustrates the problem. Mrs. Snyder sued Admiral Buck, then Paymaster General of the Navy, to collect an allowance she claimed was due her as the widow of a member of the naval service. On January 30, 1948, the district court entered judgment in her favor for $1365. The suit, as all members of the Supreme Court explicitly recognized, was in form against Buck but in substance against the United States. Government attorneys defended

---

5. Anderson v. Yungkau, 1947, 67 S.Ct. 428, 329 U.S. 482, 91 L.Ed. 436.

6. Compare Staggers v. Otto Gerdau Co., C.A.2d, 1966, 359 F.2d 292 (belated substitution should have been permitted), with Zeidman v. General Accident Ins. Co., D.C.N.Y.1988, 122 F.R.D. 160, refusing enlargement of time. See 7C Wright, Miller & Kane, Civil 2d § 1955.

See also Anderson v. Republic Motor Inns, Inc., C.A.3d, 1971, 444 F.2d 87, where no motion to substitute had been filed but a pretrial memorandum filed within the 90-day period that set forth the intention to substitute was held adequate to comply with Rule 25(a).

A motion to substitute made on the 89th day was denied in Ashley v. Illinois Cent. Gulf R.R. Co., D.C.Miss.1983, 98 F.R.D. 722. But in Saylor v. Bastedo, C.A.2d, 1980, 623 F.2d 230, denial of a motion to substitute, made within the time limits of amended Rule 25(a), was reversed.

7. See Anderson v. Yungkau, 1947, 67 S.Ct. 428, 430–431, 329 U.S. 482, 485–486, 91 L.Ed. 436.

8. 7C Wright, Miller & Kane, Civil 2d § 1959.

9. 1950, 71 S.Ct. 93, 340 U.S. 15, 95 L.Ed. 15.

the suit; government funds would have been used to satisfy the judgment. On March 18th notice of appeal was filed in the name of Rear Admiral W.A. Buck, Paymaster General of the Navy. Unfortunately Admiral Buck had retired on March 1st and had been succeeded as Paymaster General by Admiral Foster. A bare majority of the Supreme Court held that the action abated when Buck retired and no substitution was made within six months. "Petitioner loses her judgment and must start over," the Court said.[10] As a distinguished commentator put it, "the principle of justice seems to be that when one party's attorneys (or their stenographer) are at fault in failing to substitute the name of the successor officer, the court should penalize the opposing party."[11]

The lower courts were not happy with such a doctrine. One court called it "a trap for unsuspecting litigants which seems unworthy of a great government."[12] Another commented that "it all seems so foolish."[13] But in later cases the Supreme Court adhered to the doctrine, if indeed it did not expand it.[14] Finally in 1961 Rule 25(d) was amended to put substitution of public officers on a more sensible basis.

The amended rule does two things. It provides for automatic substitution of public officers, and it also permits suit by the official title of the officer rather than by name.[15] The rule should operate without difficulty where the public officer is the plaintiff; it will eliminate the needless formality of numerous orders of substitution where a public officer, who has instituted many actions, dies or resigns. The matter is more complex where the officer is defending the action. Here the substitution of public officers becomes entangled with notions of sovereign immunity and with fictional devices the courts have developed to avoid those barriers to suit.

The new rule applies in any case in which "a public officer is a party to an action in his official capacity." The old law made a distinction, so confused that it was quite unworkable, between suits nominally against officers personally but in reality against the government, and suits nominally against officers in their official capacity but in reality against the government.[16] Rule 25(d) will be ineffective if this distinction governs its applicability; it should be read, as the Civil Rules Committee

---

10. 71 S.Ct. at 97, 340 U.S. at 22.

11. Davis, Government Officers as Defendants: Two Troublesome Problems, 1955, 104 U.Pa.L.Rev. 69, 83.

12. Vibra Brush Corp. v. Schaffer, C.A.2d, 1958, 256 F.2d 681, 684.

13. Rossello v. Marshall, D.C.N.Y.1952, 12 F.R.D. 352, 355.

14. E.g., Blackmar v. Guerre, 1952, 72 S.Ct. 410, 342 U.S. 512, 96 L.Ed. 534; McGrath v. National Assn. of Mfrs., 1952, 73 S.Ct. 31, 344 U.S. 804, 97 L.Ed. 627; Klaw v. Schaffer, 1958, 78 S.Ct. 1369, 357 U.S. 346, 2 L.Ed.2d 1368. The cases are described in 7C Wright, Miller & Kane, Civil 2d § 1959 at nn. 17–21.

15. 7C Wright, Miller & Kane, Civil 2d §§ 1960, 1961.

16. Davis, Government Officers as Defendants: Two Troublesome Problems, 1955, 104 U.Pa.L.Rev. 69, 87.

The distinction still exists in deciding whether a state officer is a "person" within the meaning of 42 U.S.C.A. § 1983. Will v. Michigan Dept. of State Police, 1989, 109 S.Ct. 2304, 491 U.S. 58, 105 L.Ed.2d 45. But state officers can be held personally liable for damages under § 1983 for actions taken in their official capacities. Hafer v. Melo, 1991, 112 S.Ct. 358, ___ U.S. ___, 116 L.Ed.2d 301.

clearly intended, to apply to all suits that are against the government in reality, regardless of this old distinction.[17] Of course a public officer may commit torts, make or break contracts, or otherwise get involved in litigation that has nothing to do with the officer's official duties, and in which any judgment must be satisfied from his or her personal assets. Rule 25(d) has no application to such cases.[18]

The new rule makes substitution automatic. Though an order of substitution can be made at any time, misnomers are to be disregarded and the litigation will be valid, unless the substantial rights of the parties are affected even though no substitution is ever made.[19] Such a result as in Snyder v. Buck is not possible under the amended rule.

Since substitution is now automatic, the new rule does not contain the requirement of the old rule that a showing be made of a substantial need for continuing and maintaining the action against the successor officer. It thus purports to end a requirement that, in the case of state officers at least, may well be of constitutional origin. In Ex parte La Prade[20] the Supreme Court said that "it is to be borne in mind that Congress had authority to direct the conduct of federal officers in proceedings brought by or against them as such and may ordain that they may sue or be sued as representatives of the United States and stand in judgment on its behalf * * * but that Congress is not so empowered as to state officers." That case was a suit against a state attorney general to restrain enforcement of an allegedly unconstitutional statute. Though substitution was clearly authorized by the then-applicable statute, the Court held substitution improper since the successor officer was not liable on account of anything done or threatened by his predecessor "individually." The Court was here loyal to the fiction permitting suits against state officers despite the Eleventh Amendment, which pretends that the officer is stripped of his or her official character and may be proceeded against individually if he or she threatens to act unconstitutionally.[21] A later case held that the successor state officer might be substituted if the successor adopted the attitude of the former officer and was proceeding or threatening to proceed to enforce an unconstitutional statute.[22]

Accordingly, original Rule 25(d) required a showing of substantial need for continuing the action, and made this requirement applicable to

17. 7C Wright, Miller & Kane, Civil 2d § 1960 at nn. 8–14.

18. Moran v. Commanding Gen. of the United States Army Fin. Center, C.A.7th, 1966, 360 F.2d 920. This will be true also in suits under the doctrine of Hafer v. Melo, described note 16 above.

19. Gonzalez Torres v. Toledo, C.A.1st, 1978, 586 F.2d 858; Lucas v. Gardner, C.A.4th, 1972, 453 F.2d 1255, 1256 n. 1; Barnett v. Rodgers, C.A.D.C.1969, 410 F.2d 995, 997 n. 2; Lankford v. Gelston, C.A.4th, 1966, 364 F.2d 197, 205 n. 9.

20. 1933, 53 S.Ct. 682, 686, 289 U.S. 444, 458, 77 L.Ed. 1311.

21. Ex parte Young, 1908, 28 S.Ct. 441, 209 U.S. 123, 52 L.Ed. 714. See § 48 above.

22. Allen v. Regents of Univ. System of Georgia, 1938, 58 S.Ct. 980, 304 U.S. 439, 82 L.Ed. 1448.

all suits against public officers, whether state or federal, though in the light of Ex parte La Prade it could have been limited to state officers. The amended rule does not require such a showing in any case. With federal officers the situation would seem now to be the same as it was when Ex parte La Prade was decided. The rule has as much force as an Act of Congress and authorizes automatic substitution of a successor federal officer in all cases. If the successor does in fact disavow the policy of the predecessor, he or she can make such a showing, and if this does make the suit moot by usual standards, it should be dismissed as such. The burden will be on the officer to show that the suit is moot.

Where the suit is against a state officer, however, the mere fact that the rule purports to authorize substitution cannot make such substitution proper, any more than did the statute in force when Ex parte La Prade was decided. Substitution will still be within the letter of the rule, and will avoid much waste motion in the judicial process, but here the action must be dismissed as moot unless the plaintiff makes the needed showing that the officer threatens to continue the policy of the predecessor.[23]

Rule 25(d)(2) provides that when a public officer sues or is sued in his official capacity, he or she may be described as a party by his or her official title rather than by name.[24] Encouragement of this practice will minimize formal proceedings to change the name on the pleadings. Wherever automatic substitution is possible under Rule 25(d)(1) there will be no difficulty. The successor will be deemed to have been substituted and the action will continue under the official title just as it began under the predecessor's official title. But where Rule 25(d)(1) is ineffective without more to work a substitution, the action cannot be continued simply because the title of the officer, rather than a name, is contained on the pleadings. Thus, it has been seen that if La Prade succeeds Peterson as Attorney General of Arizona, the suit, for constitutional reasons, cannot be continued against La Prade in the absence of a showing that he intends to continue Peterson's policy of enforcement of the challenged statute. The same result would have to be reached even if the litigation had originally been entitled "Atchison, T. & S.F.R. Co. v. Attorney General of Arizona," rather than naming Peterson as defendant. Indeed to caption the suit as against the Attorney General, rather than against Peterson, would expose so conspicuously the fiction on which suits against state officers rest that it may well be doubted whether use of the title, rather than the name, is ever proper in such a suit.

---

23. Spomer v. Littleton, 1974, 94 S.Ct. 685, 414 U.S. 514, 38 L.Ed.2d 694; Four Star Publications, Inc. v. Erbe, C.A.8th, 1962, 304 F.2d 872; Hirsch v. Green, D.C.Md.1974, 382 F.Supp. 187. Comment, Substitution Under Federal Rule of Civil Procedure 25(d): Mootness and Related Problems, 1975, 43 U.Chi.L.Rev. 151, takes the position that it is for the successor to show that the case is moot rather than for plaintiff to show that it is not. This seems unsound in principle and inconsistent with the cases.

24. 7C Wright, Miller & Kane, Civil 2d § 1961.

§ 78. Joinder of Claims [1]

At common law the joinder of claims was limited by the system of the forms of action. With certain limited exceptions only those claims that fell under the same form might be joined. Joinder was much freer in equity, with the discretion of the court in permitting joinder limited only by a vague doctrine of avoiding "multifariousness," although there were statements from the chancellors that the claims joined should arise out of the same transaction or transactions connected with the same subject matter. Because of the separate systems of law and equity, it was not possible in either court to join a legal claim with an equitable claim. The Field Code attempted to combine the legal and equitable rules on joinder. It listed a number of classes of claims that might be joined. These permitted joinder of claims based on legal similarities, and resembled, though they did not follow, the joinder permitted at law under the forms of action. In addition a final class permitted joinder of all claims that arose out of the same transaction or transactions connected with the same subject of action, and thus incorporated what was thought to be the equitable rule. These provisions were not satisfactory. The specified classes were entirely arbitrary and little used, while the "same transaction" clause suffered from its own vice of being so vague as to defy definition.

The rules, in accord with later developments under more modern codes, proceed on an entirely different basis. All the restrictions on joinder of claims are abrogated. Rule 18 must be read, however, in connection with Rule 42(b), which permits the court to order separate trial of any claim or any issue. Thus joinder of claims is no longer a matter rigidly restricted at the pleading stage, but instead is made a matter of the court's discretion in shaping the trial.

Under Rule 18(a) it is true that "where the claims are against the same defendants, certainly there can be no misjoinder of claims in a civil action." [2] It is equally true that there can be no misjoinder of claims on behalf of the same plaintiffs. The rule permits joinder of legal claims with equitable claims, of claims resting on different legal theories, and even of inconsistent claims. [3]

Rule 18(b) expressly authorizes joinder of two claims though in the past one of them would have been cognizable only after the other claim had been prosecuted to a conclusion. This is particularly intended to permit joinder of a claim for a sum of money and a claim to set aside a fraudulent conveyance of property that would be subject to the money

§ 78

1. 6A Wright, Miller & Kane, Civil 2d §§ 1581–1594; James, Hazard, & Leubsdorf, Civil Procedure, 4th ed. 1993, §§ 9.1–9.4, 9.8. Bauman, Multiple Liability, Multiple Remedies, and the Federal Rules of Civil Procedure, 1962, 46 Minn.L.Rev. 729;

Note, Joinder of Actions, 1952, 40 Ky. L.Rev. 105.

2. Atlantic Lumber Corp. v. Southern Pac. Co., D.C.Or.1941, 2 F.R.D. 313, 314.

3. 6A Wright, Miller & Kane, Civil 2d § 1582.

judgment except for the conveyance.[4] On its face it would seem to permit joinder of a claim against a tortfeasor with a claim against his or her liability insurer but the cases—all of which are rather old—have been divided on whether to permit such joinder under the rule.[5]

Rule 18 permits joinder. It does not compel it. Some commentators have suggested that for efficient dispatch of litigation there should be compulsory joinder of all claims one litigant has against another.[6] The rules do not go so far,[7] but the doctrine of res judicata—or "claim preclusion," as it is now known—prevents "splitting" and requires all grounds upon which a single claim is based to be asserted and concluded in one action, on pain of being barred from separate suit.[8]

Whether joinder is permitted is governed by Rule 18 regardless of what state law may be.[9] Federal jurisdictional requirements must of course be observed in joining claims, but these will not usually be restrictive.[10] If there is diversity between the parties permitting suit on one claim, the same diversity will exist for all other claims that may be joined. In a suit between a single plaintiff and a single defendant, the claims may be aggregated in determining the amount in controversy.[11]

4. Nowell v. Dick, C.A.5th, 1969, 413 F.2d 1204; Graff v. Nieberg, C.A.7th, 1956, 233 F.2d 860; Super Value Stores, Inc. v. Parker's Food Town, Inc., D.C.Ga.1981, 525 F.Supp. 730; 6A Wright, Miller & Kane, Civil 2d §§ 1590–1593.

5. Joinder is denied in the following cases: Headrick v. Smoky Mountain Stages, Inc., D.C.Tenn.1950, 11 F.R.D. 205; Pennsylvania R. Co. v. Lattavo Bros., Inc., D.C.Ohio 1949, 9 F.R.D. 205; Pitcairn v. Rumsey, D.C.Mich.1940, 32 F.Supp. 146. It is allowed in the following cases: U.S. v. Cisco Aircraft, Inc., D.C.Mont.1972, 54 F.R.D. 181; cf. Millers' Nat. Ins. Co., Chicago, Ill. v. Wichita Flour Mills Co., C.A.10th, 1958, 257 F.2d 93, 104. See 6A Wright, Miller & Kane, Civil 2d § 1594.

6. Blume, Required Joinder of Claims, 1947, 45 Mich.L.Rev. 797, 812; Clark, Cases on Modern Pleading, 1952, p. 730; Schopflocher, What Is A Single Cause of Action for the Purpose of the Doctrine of Res Judicata?, 1942, 21 Or.L.Rev. 319; Hyde, J., in Chamberlain v. Mo.–Ark. Coach Lines, Inc., 1945, 189 S.W.2d 538, 540, 354 Mo. 461, 467.

Mich.Ct.R. 2.203(A) requires the joinder of all claims arising out of the subject of the action that do not require for their adjudication the presence of third parties over whom the court cannot acquire jurisdiction.

7. Dore v. Kleppe, C.A.5th, 1975, 522 F.2d 1369; Leimer v. Woods, C.A.8th, 1952, 196 F.2d 828. But see Shelley v. The Maccabees, D.C.N.Y.1961, 191 F.Supp. 742, 745.

8. Restatement Second of Judgments, 1982, §§ 24–26. Section 24(1) defines the

"claim" as including "all rights of the plaintiff to remedies against the defendant with respect to all or any part of the transaction, or series of connected transactions, out of which the action arose." Section 24(2) goes on to say that whether factual groupings constitute a "transaction" or a "series" is to be "determined pragmatically, giving weight to such considerations as to whether the facts are related in time, space, origin, or motivation, whether they form a convenient trial unit, and whether their treatment as a unit conforms to the parties' expectations or business understanding or usage." See 18 Wright, Miller & Cooper, Jurisdiction §§ 4407, 4408.

9. Har–Pen Truck Lines, Inc. v. Mills, C.A.5th, 1967, 378 F.2d 705, 708–709; Huntress v. Huntress' Estate, C.A.7th, 1956, 235 F.2d 205; cf. Provident Tradesmens Bank & Trust Co. v. Patterson, 1968, 88 S.Ct. 733, 746 n. 22, 390 U.S. 102, 125 n. 22, 19 L.Ed.2d 936.

10. 6A Wright, Miller & Kane, Civil 2d § 1588.

11. Griffin v. Red Run Lodge, Inc., C.A.4th, 1979, 610 F.2d 1198, 1204; Hales v. Winn–Dixie Stores, Inc., C.A.4th, 1974, 500 F.2d 836, 846; Jones Motor Co. v. Teledyne, Inc., D.C.Del.1988, 690 F.Supp. 310. See § 36 above.

This result has been reached even when plaintiff holds the claims in different capacities, DeLorenzo v. Federal Deposit Ins. Corp., D.C.N.Y.1966, 259 F.Supp. 193, 197, or is the assignee of some of the claims, National Recovery Systems v. Ornstein, D.C.Pa.1982, 541 F.Supp. 1131.

Where the basis of jurisdiction is a federal claim, however, plaintiff may not join with it a separate and distinct nonfederal claim, unless diversity exists.[12] If, however, the two claims are closely enough related on their facts, the court has power to exercise what used to be called "pendent jurisdiction," and is now called "supplemental jurisdiction," over the nonfederal claim if it chooses to do so.[13]

The only difficult problem the courts discovered was where there were both multiple claims and multiple parties. This problem was resolved by amendments of Rules 18 and 20 in 1966. The problem is clearly presented by the case of Federal Housing Administrator v. Christianson,[14] decided soon after the rules went into effect. Plaintiff held two promissory notes, each of which had been made and endorsed to it the same day. Three persons, whom it joined as defendants, were liable to plaintiff on one of the notes, while two of the same three persons were liable on the other note. The court held that there was no question of law or fact common to both notes and that the joinder was improper. Accordingly it ordered the claims severed under Rule 21. The case was probably too restrictive in its understanding of what is a common question,[15] but for present purposes the significant feature of the case was its assumption that the question of law or fact must be common to the claims joined, rather than to the parties. This was similar to the assumption of some courts and writers that multiple claims could be joined in a multiple-party case only if the claims arose out of the same transaction, occurrence, or series of transactions or occurrences.

This kind of problem arose in many cases. Probably a majority of them took the same approach as in Christianson, and applied the limitations of Rule 20 to the claims sought to be joined rather than the parties. There is good reason to think that this was an incorrect construction of the former rules as they stood.[16] However that may be, it surely was an undesirable result since it put a limitation on joinder at the pleading stage and thus provided "a ready-made issue to be wrangled over upon the pleadings." [17] It makes much more sense to allow joinder in a case like Christianson and then allow the court to decide whether to order separate trials under Rule 42(b). Indeed in Christianson itself the court, after ordering severance, held open the possibility that both claims would later be consolidated for trial.

The 1966 amendments make clear beyond any doubt that the desirable result is to be reached in situations like Christianson. Rule

12. Delman v. Federal Products Corp., C.A.1st, 1958, 251 F.2d 123; Mason v. Richmond Motor Co., D.C.Va.1986, 625 F.Supp. 883; Darwin v. Jess Hickey Oil Corp., D.C.Tex.1957, 153 F.Supp. 667.

13. 28 U.S.C.A. § 1367. See § 19 above.

14. D.C.Conn.1939, 26 F.Supp. 419.

15. See § 71 above.

16. For complete analysis of the cases under the former rule, see Wright, Joinder of Claims and Parties under Modern Pleading Rules, 1952, 36 Minn.L.Rev. 580, 604–611.

17. Kaplan, Continuing Work of the Civil Committee: 1966 Amendments of the Federal Rules of Civil Procedure (II), 1968, 81 Harv.L.Rev. 591, 595.

20(a) was amended to speak of "these persons" and of "defendants" rather than "of them," and thus the restrictions of that rule cannot even colorably be read as applying to the claims joined rather than the parties. But it was thought that the principle went beyond the precise situation involved in Christianson, in which unrelated claims are asserted affecting fewer than all parties permissively joined under Rule 20, and that it should apply to claims against any opposing party, no matter what the basis for joining that party. Accordingly Rule 18 was completely rewritten and now makes it clear that any party who has asserted a claim for relief against an opposing party or parties may join with it whatever other claims the party may have, regardless of their nature, against any opposing party.[18]

§ 79. Counterclaims [1]

The provisions of Rule 13 dealing with counterclaims permit any claim that defendant has against the plaintiff to be asserted as a counterclaim,[2] thereby avoiding multiplicity of actions. It is immaterial whether the counterclaim is legal or equitable, in contract or in tort, or even whether it has any connection with plaintiff's claim. As with the other joinder rules, the theory is to allow unlimited joinder at the pleading stage, with power in the court to order separate trial of a particular issue if this is in fact more convenient or desirable.[3] The rule does not interfere with the right of jury trial. Despite some fears expressed at the time Rule 13 was adopted, it is now settled that the pleading of a legal counterclaim, whether compulsory or permissive, in an equitable action does not waive defendant's right to jury trial on its counterclaim.[4]

The rules recognize two different kinds of counterclaims. If defendant's claim falls under Rule 13(a), it is a "compulsory counterclaim" and must be asserted as such or be forever barred. Any claim defendant has against plaintiff that does not fit the definition of Rule 13(a) is a

---

18. Id. at 595–598.

See First Nat. Bank of Cincinnati v. Pepper, C.A.2d, 1972, 454 F.2d 626, 635 (cross-claims); Schwab v. Erie Lackawanna R. Co., C.A.3d, 1971, 438 F.2d 62, 68–72 (additional claim against third-party defendant). Although the joinder of all of these claims is now proper as a pleading matter, there may be questions whether independent jurisdictional grounds are needed for the added claims. See U.S. for Use of Payne v. United Pac. Ins. Co., C.A.9th, 1973, 472 F.2d 792, certiorari denied 93 S.Ct. 2273, 411 U.S. 982, 36 L.Ed.2d 958. See also § 76 n. 15 above.

§ 79

1. 6 Wright, Miller & Kane, Civil 2d §§ 1401–1430, 1434–1437; Kennedy, Counterclaims Under Federal Rule 13, 1974, 11

Hous.L.Rev. 255; Wright, Estoppel by Rule: The Compulsory Counterclaim under Modern Pleading, 1954, 38 Minn.L.Rev. 423; Green, Federal Jurisdiction over Counterclaims, 1953, 48 Nw.U.L.Rev. 271.

2. Rule 13 actually allows as a counterclaim any affirmative claim for relief asserted by a pleader in the defensive pleadings against an opposing party. The overwhelming bulk of counterclaims, however, are by defendant against plaintiff.

3. Rules 13(i), 42(b): 6 Wright, Miller & Kane, Civil 2d § 1437.

4. Beacon Theatres, Inc. v. Westover, 1959, 79 S.Ct. 948, 359 U.S. 500, 3 L.Ed.2d 988; Beaunit Mills v. Eday Fabric Sales Corp., C.C.A.2d, 1942, 124 F.2d 563; 6 Wright, Miller & Kane, Civil 2d § 1405.

"permissive counterclaim"; Rule 13(b) permits defendant to assert such a claim as a counterclaim but does not compel it to do so.

In an action in personam [5] a claim defendant has against plaintiff is a compulsory counterclaim if it meets four conditions. It must: (1) arise "out of the transaction or occurrence that is the subject matter of the opposing party's claim;" (2) be matured and owned by the pleader at the time the pleading is served; [6] (3) not require for its adjudication the presence of third parties of whom the court cannot acquire personal jurisdiction; [7] and (4) not have been, at the time the original action was commenced, the subject matter of another pending action.[8]

Of these tests only the first, that the claim arise out of the transaction or occurrence that is the subject of the opposing party's claim, has given difficulty. It leaves at large the critical question of what is a "transaction or occurrence." The courts quite wisely have refrained from attempting to define this phrase; such definitions are so abstract as to be of little practical value.[9] Instead they have preferred to suggest tests by which the compulsory or permissive nature of a specific counterclaim can be determined.

It has been said that the test is whether the issues of fact and law on the counterclaim are largely the same.[10] Such a test would be unworkable, since it is impossible to know what the issues will be until after the plaintiff has replied to the counterclaim, if then. In addition, it would require discarding many authoritative decisions as wrongly decided. In the leading case of Moore v. New York Cotton Exchange,[11] the issue on plaintiff's claim was whether defendants were violating the antitrust

---

5. Under a 1963 amendment to Rule 13(a), a counterclaim is not compulsory if the plaintiff brought suit upon its claim by attachment or other process by which the court did not acquire jurisdiction to render a personal judgment on the claim.

6. Though not stated in terms, this requirement is fairly implied from Rule 13(e). Burlington N. R.R. Co. v. Strong, C.A.7th, 1990, 907 F.2d 707; Boston & M. Corp. v. United Transp. Union, D.C.Mass.1986, 110 F.R.D. 322; 6 Wright, Miller & Kane, Civil 2d § 1411, pp. 80–84.

If the court gives leave under Rule 13(e) to present a counterclaim maturing or acquired after pleading, and the counterclaim arises out of the same transaction or occurrence as the complaint, it will be treated as if it were a compulsory counterclaim for jurisdictional purposes. Harbor Ins. Co. v. Continental Bank Corp., C.A.7th, 1990, 922 F.2d 357, 360–361; 6 Wright, Miller & Kane, Civil 2d § 1429.

If the action is terminated before defendant serves a pleading, the compulsory-counterclaim rule never becomes operative. U.S. v. Snider, C.A.6th, 1985, 779 F.2d

1151, 1157; Lawhorn v. Atlantic Ref. Co., C.A.5th, 1962, 299 F.2d 353.

7. Rule 13(a) says only "cannot acquire jurisdiction." Some courts have held that the bringing in of additional parties to respond to a compulsory counterclaim does not destroy diversity jurisdiction, regardless of their citizenship, see note 69 below. Those courts therefore read the rule as having reference to personal jurisdiction. United Artists Corp. v. Masterpiece Productions, Inc., C.A.2d, 1955, 221 F.2d 213, 217.

8. Southern Constr. Co. v. Pickard, 1962, 83 S.Ct. 108, 371 U.S. 57, 9 L.Ed.2d 31; See Union Paving Co. v. Downer Corp., C.A.9th, 1960, 276 F.2d 468, 470.

9. See the definition attempted in Williams v. Robinson, D.C.D.C.1940, 1 F.R.D. 211, 213: " * * * whatever may be done by one person which affects another's rights and out of which a cause of action may arise."

10. See Nachtman v. Crucible Steel Co. of America, C.A.3d, 1948, 165 F.2d 997, 999.

11. 1926, 46 S.Ct. 367, 270 U.S. 593, 70 L.Ed. 750.

laws by refusing to give him ticker service, while the issue on the counterclaim was whether plaintiff was purloining quotations from defendant's exchange and using them for a "bucket shop" operation. Yet the Supreme Court held the counterclaim compulsory.

Again it is said that "everyone agrees" that the "acid test" in distinguishing compulsory from permissive counterclaims is whether the counterclaim would be barred by res judicata if there were no compulsory-counterclaim rule.[12] This is no test at all, for the authoritative doctrine is that, absent a compulsory-counterclaim rule, a pleader is not barred from suing independently on a claim that it refrained from pleading as a counterclaim in a prior action.[13]

A third test suggested by some courts is whether substantially the same evidence will support or refute the plaintiff's claim and the counterclaim.[14] It is hard to imagine a case where such an identity exists in which the counterclaim should not be held to be compulsory; indeed the purpose of compelling counterclaims, to prevent relitigation of the same set of facts, requires that the counterclaim be held compulsory where it does turn on the same evidence as plaintiff's claim. But the converse proposition is not equally obvious. Repeatedly a counterclaim has been held compulsory where it arises from the same events as does plaintiff's claim, even though the evidence needed to prove the opposing claims may be greatly different.[15] In the very simplest situation, a suit to void an insurance policy for fraud with a counterclaim for the amount of the loss, the evidence of fraud is likely to be entirely different from the evidence of the loss and amount; yet there can be no sound reason for permitting two suits to settle this one controversy between the parties.[16]

Finally there is what has been correctly called "the one compelling test of compulsoriness." [17] Any claim a party has against an opposing party that is logically related to the claim the opposing party is suing on, and that is not within the exceptions listed in the rule, is a compulsory

12. Frank, J., dissenting in Libbey–Owens–Ford Glass Co. v. Sylvania Indus. Corp., C.C.A.2d, 1946, 154 F.2d 814, 817; Big Cola Corp. v. World Bottling Co., C.C.A.6th, 1943, 134 F.2d 718; American Samec Corp. v. Florian, D.C.Conn.1949, 9 F.R.D. 718, 719; Non–Ferrous Metals, Inc. v. Saramar Aluminum Co., D.C.Ohio 1960, 25 F.R.D. 102, 105; see Beach v. KDI Corp., C.A.3d, 1974, 490 F.2d 1312, 1321 n. 16.

13. Painter v. Harvey, D.C.Va.1987, 673 F.Supp. 777, 781. The authoritative doctrine is stated in Restatement Second of Judgments, 1982, § 22. A very limited exception to the rule stated in the text is set forth in subsection (2)(b) of § 22. It applies when the relationship between the counterclaim and the plaintiff's claim is such that successful prosecution of the second action would nullify the initial judgment or impair rights established in the

initial action. See Henry v. Farmer City State Bank, C.A.7th, 1986, 808 F.2d 1228.

14. Williams v. Robinson, D.C.D.C.1940, 1 F.R.D. 211, 213; Kuster Laboratories v. Lee, D.C.Cal.1950, 10 F.R.D. 350, 351; American Samec Corp. v. Florian, D.C.Conn.1949, 9 F.R.D. 718, 719; Non–Ferrous Metals, Inc. v. Saramar Aluminum Co., D.C.Ohio 1960, 25 F.R.D. 102, 105; cf. Hoosier Cas. Co. of Indianapolis, Ind. v. Fox, D.C.Iowa 1952, 102 F.Supp. 214, 227.

15. See cases cited 6 Wright, Miller & Kane, Civil 2d § 1410 nn. 20–23.

16. Mercury Ins. Co. v. Verea, D.C.N.Y. 1949, 12 Fed.Rules Serv. 13a.11, case 2.

17. Rosenthal v. Fowler, D.C.N.Y.1952, 12 F.R.D. 388, 391. See also Pipeliners Local Union No. 798 v. Ellerd, C.A.10th, 1974, 503 F.2d 1193, 1199, where it is called "the most controlling" test.

counterclaim. Under the former equity rule from which Rule 13(a) is derived, the Supreme Court had said that " 'transaction' is a word of flexible meaning. It may comprehend a series of many occurrences, depending not so much upon the immediateness of their connection as upon their logical relationship." [18] There is now an immense body of decisions accepting this test of logical relation as controlling under the present rule.[19] Most other decisions, though not stating such a test in terms, seem entirely consistent with it.[20] There is one Supreme Court dictum that is difficult to reconcile with this test,[21] but it has been sharply criticized [22] and the lower courts have refused to regard it as precedent for other than its own limited facts.[23] Although a commentator has recently attempted to distinguish between a "narrow logical relationship test" and a "broad logical relationship test," [24] the differences seem to be nothing more than the various phrases courts use in explaining their application of what is necessarily a flexible test.[25]

It is entirely accepted that failure to assert a claim as a compulsory counterclaim precludes the party from later bringing an independent action on the claim,[26] though the rules nowhere so provide, and the theoretical basis of this result is not clear. There is talk in the literature

18. Moore v. New York Cotton Exchange, 1926, 46 S.Ct. 367, 371, 270 U.S. 593, 610, 70 L.Ed. 750.

19. Baker v. Gold Seal Liquors, Inc., 1974, 94 S.Ct. 2504, 2506 n. 1, 417 U.S. 467, 469 n. 1, 41 L.Ed.2d 243; and cases cited 6 Wright, Miller & Kane, Civil 2d § 1410 n. 10. But see Bose Corp. v. Consumers Union of the U.S., Inc., D.C.Mass. 1974, 384 F.Supp. 600, 603, where the logical-relation test is criticized for its uncertainty of application and potential overbreadth.

20. See generally 6 Wright, Miller & Kane, Civil 2d § 1410, and the cases discussed therein.

21. See Mercoid Corp. v. Mid–Continent Inv. Co., 1944, 64 S.Ct. 268, 273–274, 320 U.S. 661, 670–672, 88 L.Ed. 376, where the Supreme Court said, quite unnecessarily, that in an action for patent infringement, defendant's claim for damages for conspiracy to create a monopoly by means of the patents is not a compulsory counterclaim.

22. See Rohm & Haas Co. v. Brotech Corp., D.C.Del.1991, 770 F.Supp. 928, 931–933; Grumman Sys. Support Corp. v. Data General Corp., D.C.Cal.1988, 125 F.R.D. 160, 164; USM Corp. v. SPS Technologies, Inc., D.C.Ill.1984, 102 F.R.D. 167, 169; Lewis Mfg. Co. v. Chisholm–Ryder Co., D.C.Pa.1979, 82 F.R.D. 745, 750; Douglas v. Wisconsin Alumni Research Foundation, D.C.Ill.1948, 81 F.Supp. 167, 170; 6 Wright, Miller & Kane, Civil 2d § 1412, pp. 90–94.

23. U.S. v. Eastport S.S. Corp., C.A.2d, 1958, 255 F.2d 795, 805; Dolfi Music, Inc. v. Forest Inn, Inc., D.C.Wis.1973, 59 F.R.D. 5. See also Addressograph–Multigraph Corp. v. Cooper, C.C.A.2d, 1946, 156 F.2d 483, 488 (dissenting opinion).

24. Comment, Narrowing the Scope of Rule 13(a), 1993, 60 U.Chi.L.Rev. 141, 151–154.

25. There was a difference in view on whether, in a suit by a borrower under the Truth in Lending Act, 15 U.S.C.A. § 1601 et seq., the lender's claim for the underlying debt was a compulsory counterclaim. No: Maddox v. Kentucky Fin. Co., C.A.6th, 1984, 736 F.2d 380; Valencia v. Anderson Bros. Ford, C.A.7th, 1980, 617 F.2d 1278, 1290–1292, reversed on other grounds 1981, 101 S.Ct. 2266, 452 U.S. 205, 68 L.Ed.2d 783; Whigham v. Beneficial Fin. Co., C.A.4th, 1979, 599 F.2d 1322. Yes: Plant v. Blazer Financial Services, Inc., C.A.5th, 1979, 598 F.2d 1357, noted 1979, 10 Mem. St.L.Rev. 169; Olevares v. Viking Dodge, Inc., D.C.Ill.1985, 626 F.Supp.114. See 6 Wright, Miller & Kane, Civil 2d § 1410, pp. 76–78. This difference was closely tied to differences about whether to allow class actions in TILA cases. See 15 U.S.C.A. § 1640(a)(2)(B); 7B Wright, Miller & Kane, Civil 2d § 1804.

26. Baker v. Gold Seal Liquors, Inc., 1974, 94 S.Ct. 2504, 2506 n. 1, 417 U.S. 467, 469 n. 1, 41 L.Ed.2d 243.

of "res judicata," of "merger," of "bar," and of "waiver," [27] but the soundest analysis is that of a state court, interpreting rules virtually the same as the federal rules, which said that Rule 13 does not create the absolute bar of res judicata but is "a bar created by rule * * * which logically is in the nature of an estoppel arising from the culpable conduct of a litigant in failing to assert a proper counterclaim." [28] Such an analysis affords a means, if it be thought desirable, of extricating from the rigors of the compulsory rule the defendant who has never knowingly refrained from asserting its claim,[29] a situation that is particularly important where an insurance company has controlled the defense of the first action,[30] and it is a more flexible tool for handling the cases of a default judgment or a consent judgment or a dismissal after a compromise agreement.[31]

Considering the great number of jurisdictions that compel counterclaims, it is remarkable that there have been so few cases in which a party has actually been held to be barred because of failure to plead the claim as a counterclaim in a prior action.[32] The reason is obvious: jurisdictions that make some counterclaims compulsory almost invariably provide, as in the federal rules, that any other counterclaim, not compulsory, may be pleaded. Thus, the careful attorney can and will plead all the client's claims as counterclaims if there is any reason at all to think that they may be compulsory. Further, under Rule 13(f) the courts have power, which has been liberally exercised, to permit amendment to assert a compulsory counterclaim that has been omitted.[33] In a deserving case it is even possible to reopen the judgment, under Rule 60(b), and allow pleading of the omitted compulsory counterclaim after the first action has been terminated.[34]

Several cases have held that the bar created by the compulsory-counterclaim rule applies only after the first action has gone to judgment, and that the fact that a claim should have been asserted as a counterclaim in an action then pending is not ground for abatement of a

---

27. See 6 Wright, Miller & Kane, Civil 2d § 1417, nn. 5–7.

28. House v. Hanson, 1955, 72 N.W.2d 874, 877, 245 Minn. 466, 470. See also Dindo v. Whitney, C.A.1st, 1971, 451 F.2d 1, 3; Reynolds v. Hartford Acc. & Indem. Co., D.C.N.Y.1967, 278 F.Supp. 331, 332–333; Wright, note 1 above, at 428–436; Vestal, Claim Preclusion by Rule, 1968, 2 Ind.Leg.J. 25; Kennedy, note 1 above, at 260.

29. LaFollette v. Herron, D.C.Tenn. 1962, 211 F.Supp. 919.

30. Compare Reynolds v. Hartford Acc. & Indem. Co., D.C.N.Y.1967, 278 F.Supp. 331, with Kennedy v. Jones, D.C.Va.1968, 44 F.R.D. 52. See Dindo v. Whitney, C.A.1st, 1971, 451 F.2d 1.

31. Compare Benjamin v. U.S., Ct.Cl. 1965, 348 F.2d 502, and Douglas v. Wiscon-

sin Alumni Research Foundation, D.C.Ill. 1948, 81 F.Supp. 167, with Carteret Savs. & Loan Assn. v. Jackson, C.A.1st, 1987, 812 F.2d 36; Schott v. Colonial Baking Co., D.C.Ark.1953, 111 F.Supp. 13, and Firemen's Ins. Co. of Newark v. L.P. Steuart & Bro., Inc., D.C.Mun.App.1960, 158 A.2d 675.

32. The cases are listed in 6 Wright, Miller & Kane, § 1417 n. 22.

33. E.g., Safeway Trails v. Allentown & Reading Transit Co., C.A.4th, 1950, 185 F.2d 918 (lawyer had never read federal rules); 6 Wright, Miller & Kane, Civil 2d § 1430.

34. Williams v. Blitz, C.A.4th, 1955, 226 F.2d 463.

second action in which it is sued on independently.[35] These decisions seem inconsistent with the purposes of Rule 13(a), since they permit duplicative litigation of the sort the rule is intended to prevent, and most recent decisions are to the contrary.[36]

The compulsory-counterclaim rule is applicable even though state law has no such requirement.[37] A more difficult question is whether the states must refuse to hear a suit that would be barred in federal court for failure to have pleaded it as a compulsory counterclaim. It is held that a federal court may not enjoin prosecution in a state court of what should be a compulsory counterclaim in a pending federal action,[38] but this is because of the general reluctance of federal courts to enjoin state actions, and does not suggest that the states are free to disregard the failure of the pleader to put forward its federal counterclaim.

There are some cases in which state courts managed to find means of allowing the second suit, without passing on the general question of whether a federal procedure rule can bar a party from bringing a suit in state court.[39] And in one case a state court held that failure to plead what would plainly have been a compulsory counterclaim in federal court did not prevent later suit on the claim in state court, but did so on the basis of a quite erroneous notion that the pleader would not have been barred from independent suit in federal court.[40]

35. ACF Indus., Inc. v. Hecht, D.C.Kan. 1967, 284 F.Supp. 572; Local Union 499, Intl. Broth. of Elec. Workers, AFL–CIO v. Iowa Power & Light Co., D.C.Iowa 1964, 224 F.Supp. 731; Bellmore Sales Corp. v. Winfield Drug Stores, Inc., D.C.N.Y.1960, 187 F.Supp. 161.

36. Adam v. Jacobs, C.A.2d, 1991, 950 F.2d 89, 93 (second action dismissed); Asset Allocation & Management Co. v. Western Employers Ins. Co., C.A.7th, 1989, 892 F.2d 566, 572 (second action enjoined); Semmes Motors, Inc. v. Ford Motor Co., C.A.2d, 1970, 429 F.2d 1197, 1202–1203 (second action stayed). See 6 Wright, Miller & Kane, Civil 2d § 1418.

37. G & M Tire Co. v. Dunlop Tire & Rubber Corp., D.C.Miss.1964, 36 F.R.D. 440; Note, The Erie Doctrine and Federal Rule 13(a), 1962, 46 Minn.L.Rev. 913; cf. Sinkbeil v. Handler, D.C.Neb.1946, 7 F.R.D. 92; O'Donnell v. Archie's Motor Exp., D.C.Pa.1959, 176 F.Supp. 36. But cf. Intra–Mar Shipping (Cuba) S.A. v. John S. Emery & Co., D.C.N.Y.1951, 11 F.R.D. 284.

Indeed a counterclaim is compulsory under Rule 13 even though under relevant state law the party would lack capacity to bring an independent action on the claim. Tolson v. Hodge, C.A.4th, 1969, 411 F.2d 123; Avondale Shipyards, Inc. v. Propulsion Systems, Inc., D.C.La.1971, 53 F.R.D. 341, noted 1972, 26 Sw.L.J. 437, 18 Wayne L.Rev. 1619.

38. Aeroquip Corp. v. Chunn, D.C.Ala. 1981, 526 F.Supp. 1259; Carter v. Bedford, D.C.Ark.1976, 420 F.Supp. 927; Nolen v. Hammet Co., D.C.S.C.1972, 56 F.R.D. 361; L.F. Dommerich & Co. v. Bress, D.C.N.J. 1968, 280 F.Supp. 590, 599; Reines Distributors, Inc. v. Admiral Corp., D.C.N.Y.1960, 182 F.Supp. 226; Fantecchi v. Gross, D.C.Pa.1957, 158 F.Supp. 684, appeal dismissed C.A.3d, 1958, 255 F.2d 299; Red Top Trucking Corp. v. Seaboard Freight Lines, D.C.N.Y.1940, 35 F.Supp. 740. See 6 Wright, Miller & Kane, Civil 2d § 1418.

But if the federal action has gone to judgment, the federal court can enjoin a state action on what should have been a compulsory counterclaim under the exception to the Anti–Injunction Act, 28 U.S.C.A. § 2283, allowing a federal court to enjoin state proceedings where necessary to protect and effectuate its judgment. Brown v. McCormick, C.A.10th, 1979, 608 F.2d 410. See § 47 above.

39. Campbell v. Ashler, 1946, 70 N.E.2d 302, 320 Mass. 475, criticized 1948, 15 U.Chi.L.Rev. 446; Detroit, T. & I.R. Co. v. Pitzer, 1943, 61 N.E.2d 93, 42 Ohio Law Abs. 494.

40. Phoenix Ins. Co. v. Haney, 1959, 108 So.2d 227, 235 Miss. 60, certiorari denied 79 S.Ct. 1435, 360 U.S. 917, 3 L.Ed.2d 1534, criticized 1960, 73 Harv.L.Rev. 1410.

If Rule 13(a) is a mere rule of procedure, then, on well-understood principles of conflicts of laws, it should have no extra-territorial effect.[41] But if it defines the scope of the cause of action to which res judicata will apply, or if it sets up an estoppel against the party who does not comply with it, the defendant should be barred no matter where it attempts to sue. The effect of a judgment as res judicata is "substantive" and other jurisdictions must regard it as being as broad and conclusive as it would be in the jurisdiction in which it was rendered. And if a party so conducts itself as to erect an estoppel against prosecution of its claim, the estoppel is personal to it and may be asserted against it wherever it sues. On such reasoning a number of state courts have properly held a claim barred for failure to plead it as a counterclaim in a federal action.[42]

Any claim whatever that a party against whom a claim is made has against an opposing party may be pleaded as a permissive counterclaim, if its assertion is not compelled as a compulsory counterclaim.[43] There are a few apparent court-made exceptions. On grounds of a public policy in having such proceedings decided swiftly and without becoming ensnarled with counterclaims, it has been held that counterclaims are not permissible in an informer's qui tam action.[44] And there has been a variance of view about whether a counterclaim must or may be pleaded where it is a type of claim that is usually required to be asserted in an independent action.[45] Such decisions as these add to the confusion of the lawyer in understanding an essentially simple rule. They would not be necessary if it is remembered that the counterclaim rule affects only the pleadings; whatever advantages there may be in independent actions can be retained through the power of the court to order separate trials, and, if need be, to enter a final judgment on the plaintiff's claim before proceeding to consider the counterclaim. Here, as elsewhere, it is dangerous to push to the pleading stage a question that properly has to do only with the method of trial.[46]

---

41. In Chapman v. Aetna Fin. Co., C.A.5th, 1980, 615 F.2d 361, it was held that the Georgia compulsory-counterclaim rule is "essentially procedural," and that the Full Faith and Credit statute, 28 U.S.C.A. § 1738, does not require a federal court to dismiss a suit that would have been barred in state court for failure to interpose the claim as a counterclaim in an earlier state action. Nevertheless the court held that as a matter of comity the federal court should refuse to hear a suit that both under state law and under Rule 13(a) should have been a compulsory counterclaim in an earlier suit.

42. Nottingham v. Weld, 1989, 377 S.E.2d 621, 237 Va. 416; Schoeman v. New York Life Ins. Co., 1986, 726 P.2d 1, 106 Wash.2d 855; McDonald's Corp. v. Levine, 1982, 64 Ill.Dec. 224, 108 Ill.App.3d 732, 439 N.E.2d 475; and cases cited 6 Wright, Miller & Kane, Civil 2d § 1417 nn. 32, 34.

See Vestal, Claim Preclusion by Rule, 1968, 2 Indiana Leg.J. 25.

43. 6 Wright, Miller & Kane, Civil 2d §§ 1420, 1421.

44. U.S. ex rel. Rodriquez v. Weekly Publications, D.C.N.Y.1947, 74 F.Supp. 763. The same result has been reached in an action to recover short-swing profits from corporate insiders. Epstein v. Shindler, D.C.N.Y.1960, 26 F.R.D. 176.

45. Compare Jewish Consumptives Relief Soc'y v. Rothfeld, D.C.N.Y.1949, 9 F.R.D. 64 (action to test title to office), and Paxton v. Desch Bldg. Block Co., Inc., D.C.Pa.1956, 146 F.Supp. 32 (replevin), with John R. Alley & Co. v. Federal Nat. Bank of Shawnee, Shawnee County, Okl., C.C.A.10th, 1942, 124 F.2d 995 (usury).

46. 6 Wright, Miller & Kane, Civil 2d § 1425.

A similar approach would be desirable on the question, which has vexed the courts and led to a variety of conflicting decisions, of the capacity in which a party sues or is sued.[47] For example, in an action against the administrator of an estate for negligence of his decedent, may the defendant counterclaim for wrongful death of his intestate? A state court held that he cannot, reasoning that the administrator is sued in his capacity as the representative of the estate for the benefit of creditors, while he brings the wrongful death claim for the benefit of the statutory beneficiaries of such a claim.[48] All this is true, and can easily be taken care of in shaping the form of the judgment. But to reason from this to the conclusion that the administrator when sued is not the same person as the administrator when prosecuting a wrongful death claim, and to close with ringing declarations against "depriving of his cause of action a person who was never a party to litigation",[49] is, in the words of a commentator, "to pursue a legal fiction to an absurd extreme." [50] In this same situation other courts have refused to bemuse themselves with fiction, and have held the counterclaim permitted or compelled as the case might be.[51]

There is more reason to draw a distinction when one claim runs for or against a party in a representative capacity and that party is involved in the proposed counterclaim in an individual capacity. In those situations the counterclaim is not allowed.[52]

The rule allows a counterclaim only against an opposing party. Even one who is not formally a party of record has been found to be an opposing party within the rule,[53] but the courts are divided on whether a

---

47. 6 Wright & Miller, Civil § 1404, pp. 15–19.

48. Campbell v. Ashler, 1946, 70 N.E.2d 302, 320 Mass. 475.

49. 70 N.E.2d at 305, 320 Mass. at 481.

50. 1948, 15 U.Chi.L.Rev. 446, 447.

51. Sams v. Beech Aircraft Corp., C.A.9th, 1980, 625 F.2d 273; Moore–McCormack Lines, Inc. v. McMahon, C.A.2d, 1956, 235 F.2d 142; Newton v. Mitchell, Fla.1949, 42 So.2d 53, approved 1950, 4 Miami L.Q. 251; Morgan v. Rankin, 1938, 122 S.W.2d 555, 197 Ark. 119. See Tolson v. Hodge, C.A.4th, 1969, 411 F.2d 123.

See also Scott v. U.S., Ct.Cl.1965, 354 F.2d 292 (counterclaim against individual partner in suit by partnership); Matter of Penn Central Transp. Co., D.C.Pa.1976, 419 F.Supp. 1376 (similar).

52. E.g., Pioche Mines Consol., Inc. v. Fidelity–Philadelphia Trust Co., C.A.9th, 1953, 206 F.2d 336, certiorari denied 74 S.Ct. 225, 346 U.S. 899, 98 L.Ed. 400; North Carolina ex rel. Long v. Alexander &

Alexander, D.C.N.Y.1989, 711 F.Supp. 257, 263; and cases cited 6 Wright, Miller & Kane, Civil 2d § 1404 nn. 3–5.

Similarly in a suit against members of a school board as individuals it was said that a claim of the board itself against the plaintiff could not be asserted as a counterclaim. Dunham v. Crosby, C.A.1st, 1970, 435 F.2d 1177. The Third Circuit has properly reversed a district court that carried this to a fictional extreme. The lower court had held that a state Attorney General, sued on the fiction that he was acting as an individual in enforcing an allegedly unconstitutional statute—see § 48 above—could not counterclaim on behalf of the state for enforcement of the law. Aldens, Inc. v. Packel, C.A.3d, 1975, 524 F.2d 38, 50–51.

Except in the case of closely held corporations, a counterclaim will not lie against a stockholder who brings a derivative action. Twardzik v. Sepauley, D.C.Pa.1968, 45 F.R.D. 529.

53. Legate v. Maloney, C.A.1st, 1965, 348 F.2d 164; Automated Datatron, Inc. v. Woodcock, D.C.D.C.1979, 84 F.R.D. 408.

counterclaim will lie against members of a class who are not named as plaintiffs in a class action.[54] Even though a disinterested stakeholder is named as a plaintiff in an interpleader action, there is division on whether a counterclaim will lie against it.[55]

Another unsettled question is whether the filing of an action tolls the statute of limitations, so as to permit assertion of a counterclaim that would otherwise be barred. Probably this question is to be resolved by state law.[56] The usual doctrine, with respectable common-law origins, is that an unrelated counterclaim is barred by the statute of limitations.[57] A counterclaim that arises out of the transaction or occurrence on which the action is founded may be asserted for purposes of recoupment to prevent or reduce a judgment for plaintiff but affirmative relief will not be given on such a counterclaim.[58] There are conflicting decisions on whether a counterclaim under the Federal Tort Claims Act may be asserted against the government after the two-year statute has run; a majority of the decisions take the harsh view that the two-year limitation is a condition on the remedy and do not permit such a counterclaim, even for recoupment.[59] If the statute of limitations has not run on a counterclaim at the time suit is commenced, the counterclaim ought to be allowed for all purposes even though the statutory period expires between the filing of the claim and the assertion of the counterclaim.[60]

It has long been settled that a compulsory counterclaim requires no independent jurisdictional grounds and is to be considered within the

54. Counterclaim allowed: National Super Spuds, Inc. v. New York Mercantile Exchange, D.C.N.Y.1977, 75 F.R.D. 40; Herrmann v. Atlantic Richfield Co., D.C.Pa. 1976, 72 F.R.D. 182; Weit v. Continental Illinois Nat. Bank & Trust Co., D.C.Ill.1973, 60 F.R.D. 5; Partain v. First Nat. Bank of Montgomery, D.C.Ala.1973, 59 F.R.D. 56. Not allowed: Frederick County Fruit Growers Assn. v. Dole, D.C.D.C.1989, 709 F.Supp. 242, 246; Aamco Automatic Transmissions, Inc. v. Tayloe, D.C.Pa.1975, 67 F.R.D. 440; Donson Stores, Inc. v. American Bakeries Co., D.C.N.Y.1973, 58 F.R.D. 485, noted 1973, 87 Harv.L.Rev. 470; Cotchett v. Avis Rent A Car System, Inc., D.C.N.Y.1972, 56 F.R.D. 549.

55. Counterclaim allowed: Bell v. Nutmeg Airways Corp., D.C.Conn.1975, 66 F.R.D. 1. See also 7 Wright, Miller & Kane, Civil 2d § 1715, pp. 591–593. Not allowed: Erie Bank v. U.S. Dist. Court for Dist. of Colo., C.A.10th, 1966, 362 F.2d 539; First Nat. Bank in Dodge City v. Johnson County Nat. Bank & Trust Co., C.A.10th, 1964, 331 F.2d 325.

56. Bose Corp. v. Consumers Union of the U.S., Inc., D.C.Mass.1974, 384 F.Supp. 600; Azada v. Carson, D.C.Hawaii 1966,

252 F.Supp. 988; Keckley v. Payton, D.C.W.Va.1958, 157 F.Supp. 820. Contra: O'Donnell v. Archie's Motor Exp., D.C.Pa. 1959, 176 F.Supp. 36.

57. Employers Ins. of Wausau v. U.S., C.A.Fed.1985, 764 F.2d 1572; U.S. v. Southern Cal. Edison Co., D.C.Cal.1964, 229 F.Supp. 268; McGovern v. Martz, D.C.D.C.1960, 182 F.Supp. 343; Clark, Code Pleading, 2d ed. 1947, p. 666.

58. Stone v. White, 1937, 57 S.Ct. 851, 301 U.S. 532, 81 L.Ed. 1265; Distribution Servs., Ltd. v. Eddie Parker Interests, Inc., C.A.5th, 1990, 897 F.2d 811; ALI Study, pp. 258–259.

59. U.S. v. Wilkes–Barre Transit Corp., D.C.Pa.1956, 143 F.Supp. 413; U.S. v. Webb Trucking Co., D.C.Del.1956, 141 F.Supp. 573; U.S. v. W.H. Pollard Co., D.C.Cal.1954, 124 F.Supp. 495. Contra: U.S. v. Southern Pac. Co., D.C.Cal.1962, 210 F.Supp. 760; U.S. v. Capital Transit Co., D.C.D.C.1952, 108 F.Supp. 348.

60. Azada v. Carson, D.C.Hawaii 1966, 252 F.Supp. 988. See Hartford v. Gibbons & Reed Co., C.A.10th, 1980, 617 F.2d 567, 570; 6 Wright, Miller & Kane, Civil 2d § 1419, pp. 152–154.

ancillary jurisdiction, as it was then called, of the court.[61] It has been argued that permissive counterclaims should be similarly treated,[62] but the courts have not accepted this argument. They have required that a permissive counterclaim be supported by independent grounds of federal jurisdiction.[63] The one limited exception to this is that no independent jurisdictional grounds are required for a permissive counterclaim if it is in the nature of a set-off and is used to reduce plaintiff's judgment rather than as a basis of affirmative relief.[64] The codification of the rules of supplemental jurisdiction in 28 U.S.C.A. § 1367 in 1990 [65] have made no change in the jurisdictional rules for counterclaims.[66]

Venue is no problem with regard to counterclaims. The venue statutes speak of where a suit may be "brought." The courts construe this literally, holding that the suit is already brought by the plaintiff, and that defendant may assert its counterclaims even though the venue would not be proper if they were prosecuted in an independent action.[67]

Rule 13(h) permits bringing in additional parties to respond to a counterclaim if their joinder on the claim is required by Rule 19 or permitted by Rule 20. This is a revision of the rule made in 1966 to remove an implication in the prior rule that only those who would in the past have been called "indispensable" or "necessary" parties may be brought in as additional parties to a counterclaim.[68] Of course the rule does not alter ordinary requirements of jurisdiction or venue, but if the

61. Baker v. Gold Seal Liquors, Inc., 1974, 94 S.Ct. 2504, 2506, n. 1, 417 U.S. 467, 469 n. 1, 41 L.Ed.2d 243; Moore v. New York Cotton Exchange, 1926, 46 S.Ct. 367, 270 U.S. 593, 70 L.Ed. 750; and cases cited 6 Wright, Miller & Kane, Civil 2d § 1414 n. 1.

62. Green, Federal Jurisdiction over Counterclaims, 1953, 48 Nw.U.L.Rev. 271, 282–285. Another commentator suggests that a permissive counterclaim need not satisfy the requirement of amount in controversy. Fraser, Ancillary Jurisdiction and the Joinder of Claims in the Federal Courts, 1963, 33 F.R.D. 27, 28–31.

In a concurring opinion in U.S. for Use & Benefit of D'Agostino Excavators, Inc. v. Heyward–Robinson Co., C.A.2d, 1970, 430 F.2d 1077, 1088, Judge Friendly said that he "would now reject the conventional learning" and would hold that a permissive counterclaim does not require independent jurisdictional grounds. It is doubtful if Judge Friendly would renew that suggestion after Owen Equipment & Erection Co. v. Kroger, 1978, 98 S.Ct. 2396, 2403, 437 U.S. 365, 374–375, 57 L.Ed.2d 274. The Court there rejected the notion that a common nucleus of operative fact is enough for the exercise of ancillary jurisdiction. A permissive counterclaim would not even have such a common nucleus.

63. East–Bibb Twiggs Neighborhood Assn. v. Macon Bibb Planning & Zoning Commn., C.A.11th, 1989, 888 F.2d 1576; and cases cited 6 Wright, Miller & Kane, Civil 2d § 1422 n. 3.

64. Curtis v. J.E. Caldwell & Co., D.C.Pa.1980, 86 F.R.D. 454; Binnick v. Avco Financial Services of Nebraska, Inc., D.C.Neb.1977, 435 F.Supp. 359; and cases cited 6 Wright, Miller & Kane, Civil 2d § 1422 n. 8. See also Fraser, note 62 above, at 31–34.

65. See § 9 above.

66. Frumkin v. International Business Machines Corp., D.C.N.Y.1992, 801 F.Supp. 1029, 1045; Shamblin v. City of Colchester, D.C.Ill.1992, 793 F.Supp. 831, 833; Corsearch, Inc. v. Thomson & Thomson, D.C.N.Y.1992, 792 F.Supp. 305, 333; Teply & Whitten, Civil Procedure, 1991, pp. 106–112, 445–447; McLaughlin, The Federal Supplemental Jurisdiction Statute—A Constitutional and Statutory Analysis, 1992, 24 Ariz.St.L.J. 849, 920–925, 927–928. A contrary view—that supplemental jurisdiction is no longer limited to compulsory counterclaims—is taken in Comment, note 24 above, at 143, 148–149.

67. 6 Wright, Miller & Kane, Civil 2d §§ 1416, 1424.

68. 6 Wright, Miller & Kane, Civil 2d §§ 1434–1436.

counterclaim is compulsory, it has been treated in the past as within the ancillary jurisdiction of the court.[69] A contrary result was reached, and the ordinary rules of jurisdiction and venue applied, if the counterclaim was permissive only.[70] Under the 1990 supplemental jurisdiction statute it may be that Rule 13(h) can no longer be used, even with a compulsory counterclaim, to bring in additional parties whose citizenship would destroy complete diversity.[71] Additional persons can be made parties under Rule 13(h) only if the court is able to obtain personal jurisdiction over them by service of process.[72]

§ 80. Cross–Claims [1.]

A cross-claim is defined by Rule 13(g) as a "claim by one party against a co-party arising out of the transaction or occurrence that is the subject matter either of the original action or of a counterclaim therein or relating to any property that is the subject matter of the original action." The courts have not always distinguished clearly between a cross-claim and a counterclaim, and have used one name where the other is proper under the rules,[2] perhaps because in some states, and in the old equity practice, the term cross-complaint or cross-bill is used for what the rules regard as a counterclaim. Under Rule 13 a counterclaim is a claim against an opposing party, while a cross-claim is against a coparty. Further there is not the same freedom in asserting cross-claims that the rules provide for counterclaims. An unrelated claim against an opposing party may be asserted as a permissive counterclaim, but only claims related to the subject matter of the original action, or property involved therein, are appropriate as cross-claims. There is an obvious reason for this difference. When plaintiff brings suit against a defendant, there is no harm to plaintiff if defendant asserts some unrelated claim that he has against the plaintiff, but he or she could be prejudiced if defendants could raise in that action an unrelated claim that one defendant has against the other and in which plaintiff has no interest. Nevertheless

---

69. H.L. Peterson Co. v. Applewhite, C.A.5th, 1967, 383 F.2d 430; United Artists Corp. v. Masterpiece Productions, C.A.2d, 1955, 221 F.2d 213; Note, 1956, 56 Col. L.Rev. 130.

Professor Fraser is skeptical of this rule as applied to an additional party whose joinder is not compelled by Rule 19. Fraser, note 62 above, at 34–36.

70. Chance v. County Bd. of Sch. Trustees, C.A.7th, 1964, 332 F.2d 971; Reynolds v. Maples, C.A.5th, 1954, 214 F.2d 395.

71. Although Rule 13(h) is not mentioned in 28 U.S.C.A. § 1367(b), the clear purpose of the statute was to preserve the rule of complete diversity. See § 9 above.

72. Garfield Gas Gathering Co. v. Indiana–Ohio Pipe Co., D.C.Colo.1961, 29 F.R.D. 8. The 100–mile "bulge" provision of Rule 4(f) applies to service of process in this situation.

§ 80

1. 6 Wright, Miller & Kane, Civil 2d §§ 1431–1433.

2. E.g., Farr v. Detroit Trust Co., C.C.A.6th, 1941, 116 F.2d 807, 811; Keller Research Corp. v. Roquerre, D.C.Cal.1951, 99 F.Supp. 964, 965. If the parties use the wrong terminology, the court should disregard the error. Missouri–Kansas–Texas R. Co. v. Early, D.C.Okl.1977, 74 F.R.D. 60; Falciani v. Philadelphia Transp. Co., D.C.Pa.1960, 189 F.Supp. 203.

Courts have also confused a third-party claim, under Rule 14(a), with a cross-claim under Rule 13(g). E.g., Fogel v. United Gas Improvement Co., D.C.Pa.1963, 32 F.R.D. 202. The distinction is correctly stated in Schwab v. Erie Lackawanna R. Co., C.A.3d, 1971, 438 F.2d 62, 65–67.

the rule should be given a broad construction, and the test of logical relation, now authoritatively accepted as the measure of "transaction or occurrence" in Rule 13(a), should be equally applicable to that phrase where it appears in Rule 13(g).[3] As with the other joinder rules, it is more desirable to permit broad joinder at the pleading stage and to order separate trials if sound judicial administration so dictates. Even though the test for a cross-claim is similar to that for a compulsory counter-claim, it is always discretionary with a party to assert its claim as a cross-claim or to reserve it for later independent litigation.[4]

A cross-claim must state a claim for relief that the cross-claimant has against a coparty. Consider the various possibilities that may arise in a tort action against two defendants: if the parties are jointly liable, one of them may cross-claim against the other for contribution, provided that there is a substantive right to such relief under the relevant state law.[5] The rule specifically provides that a cross-claim will lie if the party against whom it is asserted "is or may be liable to the cross-claimant for all or part" of the original plaintiff's claim. The use of the words "may be" means, as with the same language in Rule 14 on impleader,[6] that the claim may be of a contingent nature, with the judgment shaped accordingly.[7] If one of the parties is only secondarily liable, it may cross-claim against the primarily liable defendant for indemnity against any amount the secondarily liable party may have to pay—the demand for indemnification is a "claim for relief."[8] But finally there is the situation, quite frequently encountered now that joinder in the alternative is permissible, where one defendant wishes to assert that it is blameless and that its codefendant is solely liable. In this circumstance a cross-claim will not be permissible, since it asks for no relief from the party against whom it is asserted.[9] Facts that show that the would-be cross-claimant is blameless will be a complete defense for that defendant, but they raise no issue between it and the other defendant.

Although the rule does not so provide in terms, it has been held that only parties against whom a claim has been made can cross-claim against each other. Thus, though two plaintiffs are coparties, and within the literal language of the rule, one plaintiff may not assert a cross-claim

3. LASA Per L'Industria Del Marmo Societa Per Azioni v. Alexander, C.A.6th, 1969, 414 F.2d 143; Allstate Ins. Co. v. Daniels, D.C.Okl.1978, 87 F.R.D. 1, 4–5; and cases cited 6 Wright, Miller & Kane, Civil 2d § 1432 nn. 3, 5.

See § 79 n. 19 above. But see Hoosier Cas. Co. of Indianapolis, Ind. v. Fox, D.C.Iowa 1952, 102 F.Supp. 214, 227.

4. U.S. v. Confederate Acres Sanitary Sewage & Drainage Sys., Inc., C.A.6th, 1991, 935 F.2d 796.

5. Dennler v. Dodge Transfer Corp., D.C.Conn.1962, 201 F.Supp. 431; cf. Linkenhoger v. Owens, C.A.5th, 1950, 181 F.2d 97.

6. See § 76 nn. 18–20 above.

7. Smith v. Whitmore, C.A.3d, 1959, 270 F.2d 741, 746; Providential Development Co. v. U.S. Steel Co., C.A.10th, 1956, 236 F.2d 277; Chicago, R.I. & P.R. Co. v. Chicago, B. & Q.R. Co., D.C.Ill.1972, 55 F.R.D. 209.

8. Callahan v. Cheramie Boats, Inc., D.C.La.1974, 383 F.Supp. 1217; Atlantic Aviation Corp. v. Estate of Costas, D.C.N.Y. 1971, 332 F.Supp. 1002.

9. Jones v. Illinois Dept.of Rehabilitation Servs., C.A.7th, 1982, 689 F.2d 724, 732.

against its fellow plaintiff.[10] Presumably the result would be different if there were a counterclaim against the two plaintiffs, and they then could cross-claim with regard to the subject matter of the counterclaim.

It is not yet settled whether a coparty necessarily must be a party at the same level of a multiparty action. Suppose, for example, that A sues B and C, and that B then asserts a third-party claim against D under Rule 14(a). A number of courts have held that in this situation C can file a cross-claim against D,[11] although the rule that best reflects the original intent of Rule 13(g) is that C and D are not coparties in this situation and that C must proceed the impleader rule in order to claim against D.[12]

The courts have disagreed about whether in a suit by a liability insurer for a declaratory judgment of noncoverage, brought against its insured and an injured person who is suing the insured, the injured person may assert a cross-claim against the insured for his or her injuries. Where the company is seeking to avoid the policy on the ground of fraud in its procurement, it is possible to argue that such a claim of fraud is not related to the injured person's claim of damages for negligence, and thus to hold that the cross-claim is not within Rule 13(g).[13] But a cross-claim to recover for damages is proper in a declaratory-judgment action if there is a logical relation between the claim and the cross-claim, as where the insurer is claiming non liability on the ground that the car in question was not under the control of its insured at the time of the accident, and the insured is raising the same defense as against the injured person.[14]

There is also a variety of views on whether cross-claims may be raised among the defendants in an action for condemnation.[15] To permit

10. Danner v. Anskis, C.A.3d, 1958, 256 F.2d 123. In 6 Wright, Miller & Kane, Civil 2d § 1432, pp. 249–251, this case is discussed and it is suggested that the result, though the one intended by the draftsmen of the rules, is contrary to the explicit and unqualified language of Rule 13(g).

11. Earle M. Jorgenson Co. v. T.I. United States, Ltd., D.C.Pa.1991, 133 F.R.D. 472; and cases cited 6 Wright, Miller & Kane, Civil 2d § 1431 n. 29. This view is supported in Note, 1991, 66 Ind.L.J. 549.

12. Hansen v. Shearson/American Express, Inc., D.C.Pa.1987, 116 F.R.D. 246, 248–249; Paur v. Crookston Marine, Inc., D.C.N.D.1979, 83 F.R.D. 466, 471–472; Murray v. Haverford Hospital Corp., D.C.Pa.1968, 278 F.Supp. 5. The problem is explored, and a change in the rule proposed to cure it, in Greenbaum, Jacks or Better to Open: Procedural Limitations on Co–Party and Third–Party Claims, 1990, 74 Minn.L.Rev. 507.

13. Allstate Ins. Co. v. Daniels, D.C.Okl. 1978, 87 F.R.D. 1; Fireman's Fund Ins. Co.

v. Trobaugh, D.C.Okl.1971, 52 F.R.D. 31; American Fidelity Fire Ins. Co. v. Hood, D.C.S.C.1965, 37 F.R.D. 17; Globe Indem. Co. v. Teixeira, D.C.Hawaii 1963, 230 F.Supp. 444; Hoosier Cas. Co. of Indianapolis, Ind. v. Fox, D.C.Iowa 1952, 102 F.Supp. 214; Temperance Ins. Exchange v. Carver, 1961, 365 P.2d 824, 83 Idaho 487. Contra: Allstate Ins. Co. v. Smith, D.C.Mich.1959, 169 F.Supp. 374, mandamus refused C.A.6th, 1959, 264 F.2d 38. See generally Note, Insurance Litigation: Counterclaims and Cross–Claims under the Federal Declaratory Judgment Act, 1967, 52 Iowa L.Rev. 671.

14. Collier v. Harvey, C.A.10th, 1949, 179 F.2d 664; cf. U.S. Fidelity & Guar. Co. v. Janich, D.C.Cal.1943, 3 F.R.D. 16; Plains Ins. Co. v. Sandoval, D.C.Colo.1964, 35 F.R.D. 293; cf. R.E. Linder Steel Erection Co., Inc. v. Alumisteel Systems, Inc., D.C.Md.1980, 88 F.R.D. 629.

15. Compare U.S. v. Merchants Matrix Cut Syndicate, Inc., C.A.7th, 1955, 219 F.2d 90, certiorari denied 75 S.Ct. 873, 349 U.S.

such procedure would be desirable, since it would avoid circuity of litigation, but it appears to be prohibited by Rule 71A(e).[16]

By definition cross-claims must be closely related to the existing action. Thus, they have always been treated as within the ancillary jurisdiction of the court. Independent jurisdictional grounds are not required and there can be no venue objection.[17] The 1990 supplemental-jurisdiction statute has made no change in this rule.[18] This assumes that the cross-claimant is stating a claim derived from the plaintiff's claim against him, as for liability over. But if the cross-claimant attempts to assert an independent claim on his own behalf, or in effect joins in the plaintiff's original claim, it may be necessary to realign the cross-claimant as a party plaintiff in determining whether diversity exists,[19] at least with regard to the cross-claim.[20]

E. DISCOVERY

Analysis

---

§ 81. The Scope of Discovery [1]

Discovery was the Cinderella of the changes in procedure made by the Civil Rules. Now there are those who are saying that the carriage

---

945, 99 L.Ed. 1271 (permitting cross-claim), with U.S. v. 76.15 Acres of Land, More or Less, D.C.Cal.1952, 103 F.Supp. 478 (refusing to permit cross-claim).

16. See 6 Wright, Miller & Kane, Civil 2d § 1432, p. 253.

17. LASA Per L'Industria Del Marmo Societa Per Azioni v. Alexander, C.A.6th, 1969, 414 F.2d 143; Scott v. Fancher, C.A.5th, 1966, 369 F.2d 842; and cases cited 6 Wright, Miller & Kane, Civil 2d § 1433 n. 1.

18. Meritor Savings Bank v. Camelback Canyon Investors, D.Ariz.1991, 783 F.Supp. 455; McLaughlin, The Federal Supplemental Jurisdiction Statute—A Constitutional

and Statutory Analysis, 1992, 24 Ariz.St. L.J. 849, 927–928.

19. See § 30 above.

20. Farr v. Detroit Trust Co., C.C.A.6th, 1941, 116 F.2d 807; Main v. Festa, D.C.Pa. 1965, 37 F.R.D. 227. But cf. Belcher v. Grooms, C.A.5th, 1968, 406 F.2d 14. The Main case is criticized at 6 Wright, Miller & Kane, Civil 2d § 1432, pp. 250–251.

§ 81

1. 8 Wright, Miller & Marcus, Civil 2d §§ 2007–2020, 2029–2034; Connolly, Holleman & Kuhlman, Judicial Controls and the Civil Litigative Process: Discovery, Federal Judicial Center 1978; Glaser, Pretrial Discovery and the Adversary Process, 1968.

has turned into a pumpkin, and that major changes are needed if it is to be a carriage again.

The broad and flexible provisions in Rules 26 to 37 for discovery were the most significant innovation in civil procedure when the rules were adopted in 1938. These rules rested on a philosophy that prior to trial every party to a civil action is entitled to the disclosure of all relevant information in the possession of any person, unless the information is privileged.[2] No longer are civil trials to be "carried on in the dark."[3] Use of the discovery rules is intended to "make a trial less a game of blind man's buff and more a fair contest with the basic issues and facts disclosed to the fullest practicable extent."[4] The "sporting theory of justice" was rejected.[5] Victory is intended to go to the party entitled to it, on all the facts, rather than to the side that best uses its wits. It was thought that surprise, dearly cherished by an earlier generation of trial lawyers, would be minimized or ended altogether.[6] The discovery rules complement the rules on pleadings. The pleadings are now not much emphasized, since the discovery rules provide better means for performing the functions formerly demanded of the pleadings.[7]

For more than three decades the discovery rules remained fundamentally unchanged. There continued to be controversy about them, and criticism from those who thought that the rules could be used to compel one lawyer to prepare the other's case or that elimination of surprise would open the door to perjury.[8] Despite these fears, the discovery rules were widely used and copied in many states, and the conclusion that "the present federal discovery rules enjoy the predominant support of the Bar"[9] seemed entirely justified.

Experience, however, did disclose details of the discovery rules that could be improved. In 1970 these rules were extensively amended. The amendments, which were based on an extensive empirical study of the operation of the discovery rules made by the Project for Effective Justice

---

2. 8 Wright, Miller & Marcus, Civil 2d § 2001.

3. Hickman v. Taylor, 1947, 67 S.Ct. 385, 388, 329 U.S. 495, 500, 91 L.Ed. 451.

4. U.S. v. Procter & Gamble Co., 1958, 78 S.Ct. 983, 987, 356 U.S. 677, 683, 2 L.Ed.2d 1077.

5. Tiedman v. American Pigment Corp., C.A.4th, 1958, 253 F.2d 803, 808.

6. Holtzoff, The Elimination of Surprise in Federal Practice, 1954, 7 Vand.L.Rev. 576; Frank, Pretrial Conferences and Discovery—Disclosure or Surprise, 1965 Ins. L.J. 661.

One study suggests that discovery does not reduce surprise and, if anything, may be associated with more surprise. Glaser, note 1 above, at pp. 105–109.

7. See § 68 above.

8. E.g., Hawkins, Discovery and Rule 34: What's So Wrong about Surprise?, 1953, 39 A.B.A.J. 1075; Knepper, Some Suggestions for Limiting Discovery, 1967, 34 Ins.Couns.J. 398; Gooch, Book Review, 1964, 42 Texas L.Rev. 764, 765.

9. Glaser, note 1 above, at p. 225. See also, e.g., Virtue, Sweet Are the Uses of Discovery: A Reply to Mr. Hawkins, 1954, 40 A.B.A.J. 303; Wright, Wegner & Richardson, The Practicing Attorney's View of the Utility of Discovery, 1952, 12 F.R.D. 97; Frost, The Ascertainment of Truth by Discovery, 1960, 28 F.R.D. 89.

at Columbia University, rearranged the rules and made a number of substantive changes in them.[10]

In the late 1970s, however, a new wave of criticism of discovery began, and this time the criticism was both more vigorous and from more influential sources. As the Supreme Court said in 1979: "There have been repeated expressions of concern about undue and uncontrolled discovery, and voices from this Court have joined the chorus."[11] For some in the profession it became an article of faith—though with little empirical proof—that discovery is being widely abused.[12] Others asserted that there is abuse of discovery, and that it is a serious thing when it occurs, but that it does not occur commonly.[13] From these conflicting viewpoints came contrasting suggestions on what, if anything, should be done. Some called for extensive changes in the rules,[14] or even the

---

10. The 1970 amendments, and the Advisory Committee Notes explaining them, are set out at 48 F.R.D. 459. The study by the Project for Effective Justice is described, and its findings set out, in Glaser, note 1 above.

Those amendments are discussed in Blair, A Guide To The New Federal Discovery Practice, 1971, 21 Drake L.Rev. 58, and in Cooper, Work Product of the Rulesmakers, 1969, 53 Minn.L.Rev. 1269.

11. Herbert v. Lando, 1979, 99 S.Ct. 1635, 1649, 441 U.S. 153, 177, 60 L.Ed.2d 115.

Bar dissatisfaction with discovery today is surveyed in Brazil, Civil Discovery: How Bad Are the Problems?, 1981, 67 A.B.A.J. 450.

See generally Louis Harris & Associates, Judges' Opinions on Procedural Issues, 1989, 69 B.U.L.Rev. 731, 737–738; Segal, Survey of Literature on Discovery From 1970 to the Present: Expressed Dissatisfactions and Proposed Reforms, Federal Judicial Center 1978.

There is an interesting attempt to apply game-theory analysis to discovery abuse in Setear, The Barrister and the Bomb: The Dynamics of Cooperation, Nuclear Deterrence, and Discovery Abuse, 1989, 69 B.U.L.Rev. 569. See also the comments on that paper in Easterbrook, Discovery as Abuse, 1989, 69 B.U.L.Rev. 635, and Weinstein, What Discovery Abuse?: A Comment on John Setear's The Barrister and The Bomb, 1989, 69 B.U.L.Rev. 649.

12. "Delay and excessive expense now characterize a large percentage of all civil litigation. The problems arise in significant part, as every judge and litigator knows, from abuse of the discovery procedures available under the Rules." Powell, J., joined by Stewart, J. and Rehnquist, J.,

dissenting from Order of April 29, 1980, Amending Civil Rules, 446 U.S. 997, 999.

See also, e.g., Brookings Institution Task Force, Justice for All: Reducing Costs and Delay in Civil Litigation, 1989, pp. 6–7; the two Reports of the ABA Special Committee for the Study of Discovery Abuse. October 1977 Report, reprinted 92 F.R.D. 149; November 1980 Report, reprinted 92 F.R.D. 137.

13. "The Committee believes that abuse of discovery, while very serious in certain cases, is not so general as to require such basic changes in the rules that govern discovery in all cases." Advisory Committee Note to 1980 amendment of Rule 26(f), 85 F.R.D. 521, 526.

See also, e.g., Weinstein, note 11 above; Levine, "Abuse" of Discovery: or Hard Work Makes Good Law, 1981, 67 A.B.A.J. 565; Friedenthal, A Divided Supreme Court Adopts Discovery Amendments to the Federal Rules of Civil Procedure, 1981, 69 Calif.L.Rev. 806, 813; Pollack, Discovery—Its Abuse and Correction, 1978, 80 F.R.D. 219, 222; Schroeder & Frank, The Proposed Changes in the Discovery Rules, 1978 Ariz. St.L.J. 475, 476–478, 492; Wright, New Civil Discovery Rules—A "No" Vote, Virginia Law Weekly, Oct. 13, 1978, pp. 1, 3–4.

14. See the dissent of Justice Powell and the two Reports of the ABA Special Committee, all cited note 12 above. See also Dudley, Discovery Abuse Revisited: Some Specific Proposals to Amend the Federal Rules of Civil Procedure, 1992, 26 U.S.F.L.Rev. 189; Schwarzer, The Federal Rules, the Adversary Process, and Discovery Reform, 1989, 50 U.Pitt.L.Rev.703; Flegal & Umin, Curbing Discovery Abuse in Civil Litigation: We're Not There Yet, 1981 B.Y.U.L.Rev. 597; Umin, Discovery Reform: A New Era or Business as Usual?, 1979, 65 A.B.A.J. 1050; Smith, The Con elimination of discovery,[15] while others argued that the rules already contain "ample powers of the district judge to prevent abuse"[16] and that strong judicial management of cases and use of the powers already there is an adequate answer to the problem.[17]

The term "discovery abuse" has been used as if it were a single concept, but it includes several different things. Thus, it is useful to subdivide "abuse" into "misuse" and "overuse." What is referred to as "misuse" would include not only direct violation of the rules, as by failing to respond to a discovery request within the stated time limit, but also more subtle attempts to harass or obstruct an opponent, as by giving obviously inadequate answers or by requesting information that clearly is outside the scope of discovery. By "overuse" is meant asking for more discovery than is necessary or appropriate to the particular case.[18] "Overuse," in turn, can be subdivided into problems of "depth" and of "breadth," with "depth" referring to discovery that may be relevant but is simply excessive and "breadth" referring to discovery requests that go into matters too far removed from the case.[19] Although most of the problems of abuse of discovery are discussed in a later section,[20] concerns about the breadth of discovery are related to the discussion in this section.

In 1980 some rather modest amendments to the discovery rules were adopted, over the objection of three Justices that the amendments "fall short of those needed to accomplish reforms in civil litigation that are long overdue" and that they were only "tinkering changes."[21]

cern Over Discovery, 1979, 28 Drake L.Rev. 51; Lundquist & Schechter, The New Relevancy: An End to Trial by Ordeal, 1978, 64 A.B.A.J. 59.

But see Easterbrook, note 11 above, at 647–648, arguing that discovery abuse "cannot be fixed by tinkering with Rule 26, Rule 37, or any of their companions, and that the source is in "the structure of legal rules (too much uncertainty), in the allocation of fees and costs (they should be borne by those who cause them to be incurred), and in the operation of the judicial system (there is room for more direction by judicial officers and less by litigants)."

15. Downey, Discoverectomy: A Proposal to Eliminate Discovery, 1992, 11 Rev.Litig. 475; Kieve, Discovery Reform, A.B.A.J., Dec. 1991, p. 79.

16. Herbert v. Lando, 1979, 99 S.Ct. 1635, 1649, 441 U.S. 153, 177, 60 L.Ed.2d 115.

17. Connolly, Holleman & Kuhlman, note 1 above; Weinstein, note 11 above; Brazil, note 11 above, at 456; Levine, note 13 above; Rosenberg & King, Curbing Discovery Abuse in Civil Litigation: Enough is Enough, 1981 B.Y.U.L.Rev. 579, 588–589; Sherman & Kinnard, Federal Court Discov-

ery in the 80s—Making the Rules Work, 1981, 2 Rev.Litig. 9; Pollack, note 13 above, at 227; Cutner, Discovery—Civil Litigation's Fading Light: A Lawyer Looks at the Federal Discovery Rules After Forty Years of Use, 1979, 52 Temp.L.Q. 933; Comment, Preventing Abuse of Discovery in Federal Courts, 1981, 30 Cath.U.L.Rev. 273.

But see Flegal & Umin, note 14 above, at 603–604; Nordenberg, The Supreme Court and Discovery Reform: The Continuing Need for an Umpire, 1980, 31 Syracuse L.Rev. 543.

18. This terminology, and the examples of its meaning, are borrowed from Lundquist & Flegal, Discovery Abuse—Some New Views About an Old Problem, 1981, 2 Rev.Litig. 1, and from Friedenthal, note 13 above, at 810–812.

19. This terminology is borrowed from Rosenberg & King, note 17 above, at 586–587. Those authors think that depth is the serious problem, while Flegal & Umin, note 14 above, at 601–603, argue that breadth is at least as serious a problem.

20. See § 83 below.

21. See the dissent, cited note 12 above, 446 U.S. at 997–998, 1000. The full text of the 1980 amendments, and of the dissent

Those amendments made changes in Rules 33 and 34 to prevent misuse of those rules [22] and also sought to strengthen judicial control of the discovery process by authorizing a discovery conference to frame a discovery plan for a particular case.[23]

Further amendments were made in 1983.[24] Rule 26(b) was amended to give the court broad power to limit the frequency or extent of use of discovery methods if the discovery is cumulative or duplicative or unduly burdensome or expensive. A new subdivision, Rule 26(g), was added at the same time, imposing an affirmative duty to engage in discovery in a responsible manner and encouraging use of sanctions, similar to those authorized that year in Rule 11, against those who abuse discovery.[25]

In 1993 the Supreme Court promulgated an extensive amendment of Rule 26, the central feature of which is a new duty of mandatory disclosure.[26] As is more fully discussed elsewhere, there was strong opposition from all sides of the bar to this amendment, but Congress allowed it to go into effect.[27]

The central notion of the discovery practice set out in the rules is that the right to take statements and the right to use them in court must be kept entirely distinct. In this way discovery at the pretrial stage is not fettered with the rules of admissibility that apply at a trial. The utmost freedom is allowed at the discovery stage, but restrictions are imposed on the use of the products of discovery in order to preserve traditional methods of trial.[28]

The rules provide a number of different procedures for compelling disclosure of information. These cannot be read in isolation, but are to

---

from their adoption, is reprinted also at 85 F.R.D. 521. For the history of those amendments, and of an earlier proposal by the Advisory Committee of more drastic changes, echoing those recommended in the October 1977 Report of the ABA Special Committee, cited note 12 above, see 8 Wright, Miller & Marcus, Civil 2d § 2002.

See generally Watkins, 1980 Amendments to the Federal Rules of Civil Procedure, 1980, 32 Baylor L.Rev. 533.

22. See §§ 86, 87 below.

23. Rule 26(f); 8 Wright, Miller & Marcus, Civil 2d § 2051. See Watkins, note 21 above, at 541–544; Sherman & Kinnard, note 17 above, at 38–39.

24. The full text of the 1983 amendments and the Advisory Committee Notes to them is reprinted at 97 F.R.D. 213–220. See Yager, Discovery Abuse: Have the 1983 Amendments to the Federal Rules Curbed the Problem?, 1987 Fed.Ind. & Corp. Couns.Q. 399; Comment, Recent Changes in the Federal Rules of Civil Procedure: Prescriptions to Ease the Pain?, 1984, 15 Texas Tech L.Rev. 887. The 1983 amend-

ments drew in large part on the recommendations in the November 1980 Report of the ABA Special Committee, cited note 12 above. For critical discussion of them see Schroeder & Frank, Discovery Reform: Long Road to Nowheresville, 1982, 68 A.B.A.J. 572; Rosenberg & King, note 16 above; Sherman & Kinard, note 17 above, at 46–56.

25. See § 69A above.

26. The text of the proposed amendment, and the Advisory Committee Note to it, is set out at 146 F.R.D. 606–644. The dissent of three Justices from this particular amendment, which they described as "potentially disastrous and certainly premature," appears at 146 F.R.D. 507, 510–512.

27. See § 83A below.

28. Independent Productions Corp. v. Loew's Inc., D.C.N.Y.1962, 30 F.R.D. 377, 381; Drum v. Town of Tonawanda, D.C.N.Y.1952, 13 F.R.D. 317, 319; Pike & Willis, The New Federal Deposition–Discovery Procedure, 1938, 38 Col.L.Rev. 1179, 1187.

be regarded as an integrated mechanism for narrowing the issues and ascertaining the facts.[29] To all of these devices Rule 26 is basic. It contains the central provisions on the scope of discovery, which, with one exception,[30] are incorporated by reference in the other discovery rules.

The scope of discovery contemplated by Rule 26 is extremely broad.[31] "No longer can the time-honored cry of 'fishing expedition' serve to preclude a party from inquiring into the facts underlying his opponent's case."[32] Discovery may extend to matters relating to the claim or defense of any party,[33] unlike the former equity practice that limited discovery to matters in support of the proponent's case. It is no objection that the examining party already knows the facts about which it seeks discovery, since one of the purposes of discovery is to ascertain the position of the adverse party on the controverted issues.[34]

Impeaching material has caused controversy. It should be clear that one party may obtain by discovery evidence that will impeach witnesses for the other party.[35] The controversy has been whether a party who has obtained on its own evidence that will impeach its adversary is required to disclose the existence of that evidence. Surveillance movies of an injured plaintiff that the defense has had made are the most common example. There is some support for the view that evidence of this kind is to be disclosed if the defendant intends to use it substantively but that defendant need not disclose it if defendant intends to use it only to impeach the plaintiff's testimony.[36] There are two difficulties with this. It ignores the fact that much evidence of this kind—and surveillance movies are an excellent example—has both impeaching and substantive aspects and that there is no way to prevent a jury from giving substantive effect to the evidence supposedly offered only for

29. Hickman v. Taylor, 1947, 67 S.Ct. 385, 391, 329 U.S. 495, 505, 91 L.Ed. 451; Clark, Special Problems in Drafting and Interpreting Procedural Codes and Rules, 1950, 3 Vand.L.Rev. 493, 502.

30. Rule 27, authorizing depositions before action is commenced or while an appeal is pending, is intended for perpetuation of testimony, rather than as a discovery device, and the scope of examination is less broad than under other discovery procedures. Ash v. Cort, C.A.3d, 1975, 512 F.2d 909, 912; Application of Checkosky, D.C.D.C.1992, 142 F.R.D. 4, 6–7; Petition of Gary Const., Inc., D.C.Colo.1983, 96 F.R.D. 432. But see Martin v. Reynolds Metals Corp., C.A.9th, 1961, 297 F.2d 49, 55, noted 1962, 41 Texas L.Rev. 330. See 8 Wright, Miller & Marcus, Civil 2d § 2071.

31. 8 Wright, Miller & Marcus, Civil 2d § 2007.

32. Hickman v. Taylor, 1947, 67 S.Ct. 385, 392, 329 U.S. 495, 507, 91 L.Ed. 451.

33. Rule 26(b); 8 Wright, Miller & Marcus, Civil 2d § 2011.

34. Weiner v. Bache Halsey Stuart, Inc., D.C.Fla.1977, 76 F.R.D. 624; Baim & Blank, Inc. v. Philco Distributors, Inc., D.C.N.Y.1957, 25 F.R.D. 86; 8 Wright, Miller & Marcus, Civil 2d § 2014.

35. E.g., Mellon v. Cooper–Jarrett, Inc., C.A.6th, 1970, 424 F.2d 499; Davidson Pipe Co. v. Laventhol & Horwath, D.C.N.Y.1988, 120 F.R.D. 455, 461–464; 8 Wright, Miller & Marcus, Civil 2d § 2015. But see Wharton v. Lybrand, Ross Bros. & Montgomery, D.C.N.Y.1966, 41 F.R.D. 177, 179.

36. Bogotay v. Montour R. Co., D.C.Pa. 1959, 177 F.Supp. 269; Leach v. Chesapeake & O. Ry. Co., D.C.Mich.1964, 35 F.R.D. 9; cf. Hikel v. Abousy, D.C.Md.1966, 41 F.R.D. 152; Mort v. A/S D/S Svendborg, D.C.Pa.1966, 41 F.R.D. 225; see Zimmerman v. Superior Court, 1965, 402 P.2d 212, 217, 98 Ariz. 85; Frank, Pretrial Conferences and Discovery—Disclosure or Surprise?, 1965 Ins.L.J. 661, 664–667; Comment, 1966, 7 Ariz.L.Rev. 283.

impeachment.[37] Further these proposals seem to assume that evidence used for impeachment is intrinsically more trustworthy than any other kind of evidence and therefore does not need the explanation or refutation that advance knowledge will permit.[38] For these reasons, it is thought that the better view is to read Rule 26 as it is written and not carve out of its broad scope any exception for impeaching material,[39] although many courts do require that the plaintiff submit to a deposition before discovery of the surveillance movies will be required.[40]

Rule 26(b) specifically allows discovery of the identity and location of persons having knowledge of discoverable matter. The traditional principle prior to the rules was that a party could not be required to disclose the names of its witnesses, in order that there should be no opportunity to tamper with them. The rules rest on the different premise that persons having knowledge of the relevant facts are not necessarily the witnesses of any particular party. Thus, it is routinely held that a party may be required to disclose the names of occurrence witnesses of whom it has knowledge.[41] A party cannot refuse, on the ground of attorney-client privilege, to divulge the names of witnesses its attorney has located.[42] To hold otherwise would defeat the purposes of the discovery rules.

A distinction had been drawn between witnesses to the occurrences in question and witnesses who will be called for trial by the adverse party. The names of occurrence witnesses could always be obtained by discovery. It had been usually held that a party was not entitled to find out, by discovery, which witnesses—other than expert witnesses—his opponent intends to call at the trial,[43] although the court could require

---

37. Zimmerman v. Superior Court, 1965, 402 P.2d 212, 98 Ariz. 85; Cooper, note 10 above, at 1317.

38. Boldt v. Sanders, 1961, 111 N.W.2d 225, 227–228, 261 Minn. 160; Cooper, note 10 above, at 1314–1315.

39. In addition to the cases cited note 40 below, see Boldt v. Sanders, 1961, 111 N.W.2d 225, 261 Minn. 160, noted 1962, 47 Minn.L.Rev. 289; Suezaki v. Superior Court, 1962, 23 Cal.Rptr. 368, 58 Cal.2d 166, 373 P.2d 432; Zimmerman v. Superior Court, 1965, 402 P.2d 212, 98 Ariz. 85, noted 1966, 51 Iowa L.Rev. 765; Cooper, note 10 above, at 1310–1318; Gourley, Effective Pretrial Must Be the Beginning of Trial, 1960, 28 F.R.D. 165, 169; Chandler, Discovery and Pre–Trial Procedure in Federal Courts, 1959, 12 Okla.L.Rev. 321, 324.

The issue is fully discussed in 8 Wright, Miller & Marcus, Civil 2d § 2015.

40. Martin v. Long Island R. Co., D.C.N.Y.1974, 63 F.R.D. 53; Blyther v. Northern Lines, Inc., D.C.Pa.1973, 61 F.R.D. 610; Snead v. American Export–Isbrandtsen Lines, Inc., D.C.Pa.1973, 59 F.R.D. 148, noted 1973, 18 How.L.J. 228; Smith v. Central Linen Serv. Co., D.C.Md. 1966, 39 F.R.D. 15; McCoy v. General Motors Corp., D.C.Pa.1963, 33 F.R.D. 354; Parla v. Matson Navigation Co., D.C.N.Y. 1961, 28 F.R.D. 348.

41. Bell v. Swift & Co., C.A.5th, 1960, 283 F.2d 407; Hikel v. Abousy, D.C.Md. 1966, 41 F.R.D. 152; 8 Wright, Miller & Marcus, Civil 2d § 2013.

42. Duffy v. Dier, C.A.8th, 1972, 465 F.2d 416; Harrison v. Prather, C.A.5th, 1968, 404 F.2d 267; Edgar v. Finley, C.A.8th, 1963, 312 F.2d 533; 8 Wright, Miller & Marcus, Civil 2d § 2013. Contra: Walczak v. Detroit–Pittsburgh Motor Freight, Inc., D.C.Ind.1956, 140 F.Supp. 10, criticized 1957, 45 Geo.L.J. 701.

43. Brennan v. Engineered Products, Inc., C.A.8th, 1974, 506 F.2d 299; Wirtz v. Continental Fin. & Loan Co. of West End, C.A.5th, 1964, 326 F.2d 561. But see U.S. EEOC v. Metropolitan Museum of Art, D.C.N.Y.1978, 80 F.R.D. 317.

disclosure of this information at a pretrial conference.[44] Under the 1993 amendments, however, a party is now required to identify, at least 30 days before trial, trial witnesses, specifying which witnesses it will call and which it may call and also designating which witnesses will have their testimony presented by deposition.[45]

Under Rule 26(b) discovery is also proper on the existence and location of books, documents, and other tangible things.[46] If the object itself is properly the subject of discovery, the party, having ascertained its location, may endeavor to require production under Rule 34, but the party is entitled to learn of the existence and location of tangible things even though the thing itself is one that he or she cannot compel to be produced.[47]

The extent to which the reports and opinions of experts are subject to discovery has undergone considerable change. The early cases, though divided, ordinarily refused to allow discovery, and in 1946 the Advisory Committee proposed an amendment, which the Supreme Court did not adopt, that would have created an absolute immunity from discovery for the conclusions of an expert. In later years the decisions, though still divided, were much more liberal in allowing discovery.[48] From 1970 to 1993 the subject was addressed in Rule 26(b)(4), as amended in 1970, which was a rather conservative codification of what were then the recent cases.[49] That rule spoke only to facts known and opinions held by experts that were "acquired or developed in anticipation of litigation or for trial." It distinguished sharply between those experts the opposing party expected to call as witnesses at the trial and those it did not expect to call. A party could learn by interrogatories the names of the experts its opponent expected to call, the subject matter on which the expert was expected to testify, and the substance of the facts and opinions to which the expert would testify. In addition, the discovering party was entitled to a summary of the grounds for each opinion.[50] It was further provided that the court on motion could order further discovery by other means, which ordinarily would be by taking the deposition of the expert.[51] If the court ordered further discovery of this

---

44. Wirtz v. Hooper–Holmes Bureau, Inc., C.A.5th, 1964, 327 F.2d 939; Globe Cereal Mills v. Scrivener, C.A.10th, 1956, 240 F.2d 330; Lloyd v. Cessna Aircraft Co., D.C.Tenn.1976, 434 F.Supp. 4.

45. Rule 26(a)(3). See § 83A below.

46. 8 Wright, Miller & Marcus, Civil 2d § 2012.

47. Cox v. E.I. DuPont de Nemours & Co., D.C.S.C.1965, 38 F.R.D. 396; Pressley v. Boehlke, D.C.N.C.1963, 33 F.R.D. 316; Harvey v. Eimco Corp., D.C.Pa.1961, 28 F.R.D. 380; Margeson v. Boston & M.R.R., D.C.Mass.1954, 16 F.R.D. 200.

48. 8 Wright, Miller & Marcus, Civil 2d § 2029. The later cases were heavily influenced by the arguments made in Frieden-

thal, Discovery and Use of an Adverse Party's Expert Information, 1962, 14 Stan. L.Rev. 455.

49. See McLaughlin, Discovery and Admissibility of Expert Testimony, 1988, 63 Notre Dame L.Rev. 760, 764.

50. Rule 26(b)(4)(A)(i). See Uresil Corp. v. Cook Group, Inc., D.C.Ill.1991, 135 F.R.D. 168; LeBarron v. Haverhill Co-op. School Dist., D.C.N.H.1989, 127 F.R.D. 38; 8 Wright, Miller & Marcus, Civil 2d § 2030.

51. Rule 26(b)(4)(A)(ii). Courts varied widely in how they applied this portion of the rule. 8 Wright, Miller & Marcus, Civil 2d § 2031; McLaughlin, note 49 above, at 765; Connors, A New Look at an Old Concern—Protecting Expert Information from kind, it could restrict the scope of the examination if it deemed this appropriate. Thus, it could restrict the deposition to the opinions that the expert was expected to give on direct examination at trial, and in this way prevent the discovering party from using the deposition to establish its own affirmative case,[52] but the court was not required to do so. If further discovery beyond the interrogatories was ordered, the court was authorized to make appropriate provision about paying for the expert's time and, if it chose, could require the discovering party to reimburse its opponent for a portion of the fee the opponent has paid to the expert.[53]

Although Rule 26(b)(4) was retained, with one change, in the 1993 amendments of Rule 26, the disclosure provisions adopted that year as Rule 26(a) make drastic alterations in the practice with regard to "any person who may be used at the trial" to present expert testimony.[54] At a time that ordinarily will be directed by the court, a party is required to identify these persons. The disclosure must include a written report if the expert is one retained or specially employed to provide testimony in the case or whose duties as a party's employee regularly involve giving expert testimony. The report must contain the opinions to be expressed and the reasons for them and give information about the qualifications and experience as a witness. After this report has been provided, a party may take the deposition of the expert.[55]

Expert witnesses who are not expected to testify are treated very differently under Rule 26(b)(4), and the 1993 amendments made no change in this regard. With the exception of an examining physician,[56] facts or opinions may be obtained from an expert who has been retained or specially employed by another party in anticipation of litigation or preparation for trial, but who is not expected to be called at the trial, only "upon a showing of exceptional circumstances under which it is impracticable for the party seeking discovery to obtain facts or opinions on the same subject by other means."[57] Most cases have refused to find the exceptional circumstances that will justify this discovery.[58] If a party

Discovery Under the Federal Rules, 1980, 18 Duq.L.Rev. 271; Notes, 1988, 66 Wash. U.L.Q. 787, 33 S.D.L.Rev. 331. In addition, there was evidence that full discovery, rather than the two-step procedure of the rule, was what normally happened in practice with regard to experts. See Graham, Discovery of Experts Under Rule 26(b)(4) of the Federal Rules of Civil Procedure: Part Two, An Empirical Study and a Proposal, 1977 U.Ill.L.F. 169. See Schwarzer, Guidelines for Discovery, Motion Practice and Trial, 1987, 117 F.R.D. 273, 276.

52. See Bailey v. Meister Brau, Inc., D.C.Ill.1972, 57 F.R.D. 11, 14; Connors, note 51 above, at 277–280.

53. Rule 26(b)(4)(C); Jochims v. Isuzu Motors, Ltd., D.C.Iowa 1992, 141 F.R.D. 493; Worley v. Massey–Ferguson, Inc.,

D.C.Miss.1978, 79 F.R.D. 534; 8 Wright, Miller & Marcus, Civil 2d § 2034.

54. Rule 26(a)(2).

55. Rule 26(b)(4)(A), as amended in 1993; 8 Wright, Miller & Marcus, Civil 2d § 2031.1.

56. Rule 35(b). See § 88 below.

57. Rule 26(b)(4)(B); 8 Wright, Miller & Marcus, Civil 2d § 2032; Notes, 1988, 33 S.D.L.Rev. 303, 56 U.Cin.L.Rev. 999; Comment, 1982, 67 Iowa L.Rev. 349.

58. Galella v. Onassis, C.A.2d, 1973, 487 F.2d 986; U.S. v. 215.7 Acres of Land, D.C.Del.1989, 719 F.Supp. 273; 8 Wright, Miller & Marcus, Civil 2d § 2302. But see Coates v. AC & S, Inc., D.C.La.1990, 133 F.R.D. 109; Roesberg v. Johns–Manville Corp., D.C.Pa.1980, 85 F.R.D. 292; Pearl Brewing Co. v. Jos. Schlitz Brewing Co., D.C.Tex.1976, 415 F.Supp. 1122.

merely seeks to obtain the names of experts retained by its opponent who will not be called at trial, and does not seek to obtain discovery from those experts, the better view is that the requirement of exceptional circumstances does not apply and the discovery should be allowed,[59] but there is significant authority to the contrary.[60] In the rare cases in which discovery is ordered with regard to a nontestifying expert, the court is normally required to make the party obtaining discovery reimburse the party who retained the expert for a portion of his fee.[61]

Rule 26(b)(4) makes no provision whatever for discovery with regard to an expert who was informally consulted in preparation for trial but who was never retained or specially employed. Therefore neither the names of these persons nor their information are subject to discovery.[62] On the other hand the rule does not limit discovery from an expert whose information was not acquired in preparation for trial but because he or she was an actor or viewer with respect to the transactions that are the basis of the lawsuit. The deposition of this kind of expert may be taken merely by notice, in the same fashion as with any other fact witness.[63]

The scope of discovery is governed entirely by the federal rules. State law on scope of discovery is of no force in federal court.[64]

The rules recognize only three limitations on the broad scope of discovery thus far indicated. The matter sought to be discovered must be relevant to the subject matter of the action, it must not be privileged, and it must not be the "work product" of an attorney.

59. Roesberg v. Johns–Manville Corp., D.C.Pa.1980, 85 F.R.D. 292, 303; In re Folding Carton Antitrust Litigation, D.C.Ill. 1979, 83 F.R.D. 256, 258; 8 Wright, Miller & Marcus, Civil 2d § 2032; Comment, 1985, 37 Hast.L.J. 201; Comment, 1982, 80 Mich.L.Rev. 514.

60. Ager v. Jane C. Stormont Hosp. & Training Sch. for Nurses, C.A.10th, 1980, 622 F.2d 496, 502–504; Perry v. W.S. Darley & Co., D.C.Wis.1971, 54 F.R.D. 278, 280; Graham, note 51 above, at 201.

61. Rule 26(b)(4)(C); 8 Wright, Miller & Marcus, Civil 2d § 2034.

62. Ager v. Jane C. Stormont Hosp. & Training Sch. for Nurses, C.A.10th, 1980, 622 F.2d 496, 501; 8 Wright, Miller & Marcus, Civil 2d § 2033. It is often difficult to decide whether an expert was "informally consulted" or was "retained or specially employed." See Comment, note 59 above, at 355–360.

63. Levingston v. Allis–Chalmers Corp., D.C.Miss.1985, 109 F.R.D. 546, 550; Keith v. Van Dorn Plastic Machinery Co., D.C.Pa. 1980, 86 F.R.D. 458; Note, Discovery and Testimony of Unretained Experts, 1987 Duke L.J. 140; 8 Wright, Miller & Marcus, Civil 2d § 2033.

Under a 1991 amendment, Rule 45(c)(3)(B)(ii) gives the court power to protect the intellectual property of nonparty witnesses. It calls for quashing a subpoena that "requires disclosure of an unretained expert's opinion or information not describing specific events or occurrences in dispute and resulting from the expert's study made not at the request of any party" unless there are assurances that the expert will be reasonably compensated.

64. Dixon v. 80 Pine St. Corp., C.A.2d, 1975, 516 F.2d 1278; Everitt v. Brezzel, D.C.Colo.1990, 750 F.Supp. 1063, 1065–1066; 8 Wright, Miller & Marcus, Civil 2d § 2005.

State law will be applicable, by virtue of Evidence Rule 501, in determining what information is privileged on those matters for which state law supplies the substantive rule of decision. State law is also available as an alternative to the federal rules for discovery in aid of execution after judgment. See Civil Rule 69.

The boundaries defining information that is relevant to the subject matter involved in the action are necessarily vague and it is practically impossible to state a general rule by which they can be drawn. Though some early decisions purported to require relevancy to "the issues" in the case, this is unduly restrictive, and it is clear that all that is required is relevancy to the "subject matter." Discovery cannot be limited to evidence that would be relevant at the trial. The concept at the discovery stage is much broader, as was made specific by a 1946 amendment to Rule 26(b), stating that it is not ground of objection that the testimony will be inadmissible at the trial if the testimony sought appears reasonably calculated to lead to the discovery of admissible evidence.[65] Certainly the requirement of relevancy should be construed liberally and with common sense, rather than in terms of narrow legalisms. Indeed in its most recent statement about this the Supreme Court said that the relevancy requirement "has been construed broadly to encompass any matter that bears on, or that reasonably could lead to other matter that could bear on, any issue that is or may be in the case." [66] The ABA Special Committee for the Study of Discovery Abuse thought that this broad definition of relevancy was a major source of discovery abuse. At one time the committee proposed that Rule 26(b) be amended to limit discovery to matters "relevant to the issues raised by the claim or defense of any party." [67] In a later report it proposed to eliminate the words "the subject matter involved in the pending action," so that the rule would then require relevance to the claims or defenses of any party.[68] These proposals never attracted a significant following. The general view has been that depth, rather than breadth, of discovery is more likely to be a problem,[69] and that if protection is needed against unduly broad discovery, it can better be provided by the discretionary powers of the court to issue protective orders rather than by a constricting concept of relevance.

A principal battleground on relevance had been whether the extent of defendant's liability insurance, if any, is subject to discovery. Though much was written on the question, the federal courts were hopelessly divided, as were also the state courts and the commentators.[70] An amendment adopted in 1970 resolved this long controversy by making

---

65. 8 Wright, Miller & Marcus, Civil 2d §§ 2008, 2009.

66. Oppenheimer Fund, Inc. v. Sanders, 1978, 98 S.Ct. 2380, 2389, 437 U.S. 340, 351, 57 L.Ed.2d 253. Justice Powell went on to write: "Consistently with the notice-pleading system established by the Rules, discovery is not limited to issues raised by the pleadings, for discovery itself is designed to help define and clarify the issues. * * * Nor is discovery limited to the merits of a case, for a variety of fact-oriented issues may arise during litigation that are not related to the merits."

67. October 1977 Report, reprinted 92 F.R.D. 149, 157. Compare with this what

the Supreme Court said in the Oppenheimer case, quoted note 66 above.

68. November 1980 Report, reprinted 92 F.R.D. 137, 140.

69. See note 19 above.

70. Compare, e.g., Hughes v. Groves, D.C.Mo.1969, 47 F.R.D. 52, and Jenkins, Discovery of Automobile Insurance Limits: Quillets of the Law, 1965, 14 Kan.L.Rev. 59, with Beal v. Zambelli Fireworks Mfg. Co., D.C.Pa.1969, 46 F.R.D. 449, and Frank, Discovery and Insurance Coverage, 1959 Ins.L.J. 281. The authorities are fully set out at 8 Wright, Miller & Marcus, Civil 2d § 2010.

the existence and contents of a liability insurance agreement subject to discovery.[71] The decision to adopt a rule permitting discovery was based on the view that knowledge of insurance limits will lead to more realistic negotiation and thus to more settlements.[72]

A second limitation on discovery is that it may extend only to matters "not privileged." Matter is privileged from discovery if it would be privileged at trial under the applicable rules of evidence.[73] On issues on which the court must look to the state law for the substantive rule of decision, it must apply also the state law of privilege.[74] If the arguably privileged communication was made, or the deposition is to be taken, in a state other than that in which the action is pending, it would seem that the federal court must apply whichever state's rule of privilege would be applied by the courts of the state in which the district court is held.[75] If, for example, in a diversity action pending in Pennsylvania there is a claim that a communication made in Ohio was privileged, the federal court must look to see whether the Pennsylvania state courts would apply their own rules of privilege to such a communication or would apply the Ohio notions of privilege.[76] On issues governed by federal law, the federal court applies the principles of the common law, as they have been modified in the light of reason and experience, in deciding questions of privilege.[77]

71. This was done in Rule 26(b)(2). In 1993 insurance was made one of the things that a party must disclose at the outset of a case, Rule 26(a)(1)(D), and the language about this in Rule 26(b)(2) was repealed as no longer necessary. See Wegner v. Cliff Viessman, Inc., D.C. Iowa 1994, 153 F.R.D. 154.

72. See Clauss v. Danker, D.C.N.Y.1967, 264 F.Supp. 246; Cook v. Welty, D.C.D.C. 1966, 253 F.Supp. 875; Glaser, Pretrial Discovery and the Adversary System, 1969, pp. 127–128.

The validity of the rule allowing discovery of the existence of insurance was upheld in Helms v. Richmond–Petersburg Turnpike Auth., D.C.Va.1971, 52 F.R.D. 530.

73. Evidence Rule 1101(c); U.S. v. Reynolds, 1953, 73 S.Ct. 528, 531, 345 U.S. 1, 6, 97 L.Ed. 727.

74. Evidence Rule 501. See § 93 below.

75. The Third Edition of this book took the view that the privilege rule should be that of the state whose substantive law is to govern. Wright, Federal Courts, 3d ed. 1976, p. 404. On further reflection the author became convinced that the view now stated in the text, which was stated also in 4th ed., 1983, p. 549, is the proper view. See Wellborn, The Federal Rules of Evidence and the Application of State Law in Federal Courts, 1977, 55 Texas L.Rev. 371, 448; 23 Wright & Graham, Evidence § 5435.

76. Samuelson v. Susen, C.A.3d, 1978, 576 F.2d 546. See also Gatewood v. U.S. Cellular Corp., D.C.D.C.1989, 124 F.R.D. 504, 505; and cases cited 23 Wright & Graham, Evidence § 5435 n. 24.

77. Evidence Rule 501. See § 93 below; 8 Wright, Miller & Marcus, Civil 2d §§ 2016–2020; 23 Wright & Graham, Evidence §§ 5425–5431.

The United States is subject to the discovery rules, but it has a number of privileges available to it that are not enjoyed by private litigants. 8 Wright, Miller & Marcus, Civil 2d § 2019. One point now settled in the cases is that income tax returns are not privileged, and their disclosure can be required in a civil case. Id. at § 2019.

The application of the privilege against self-incrimination to discovery in a civil case has caused confusion in the case law. Id. at § 2018. However, there is a dictum in Baxter v. Palmigiano, 1976, 96 S.Ct. 1551, 1558, 425 U.S. 308, 318, 47 L.Ed.2d 810, that "the Fifth Amendment does not forbid adverse inferences against parties to civil actions when they refuse to testify in response to probative evidence offered against them * * *." See the explanation of that dictum in Lefkowitz v. Cunningham, 1977, 97 S.Ct. 2132, 2137 n. 5, 431 U.S. 801, 808 n. 5, 53 L.Ed.2d 1. See also Note, Adverse Inferences Based on Nonparty Invocations: The Real Magic Trick in Fifth

Finally there is a court-made qualified immunity from discovery of matter gathered by a lawyer in anticipation of litigation or preparation for trial, known as the lawyer's "work product." In practice this is the most difficult and controversial of all the limits on discovery, and it is discussed in the following section.

Most of the law on discovery comes from the district courts, because there is little opportunity to obtain appellate review of discovery rulings. Such rulings are not final orders and are not appealable as such.[78] They can be reviewed on appeal from a final judgment, but by then the matter will probably be moot and in any event the broad discretion the discovery rules vest in the trial courts will bar reversal save under very unusual circumstances.[79] Occasionally there will be review from a sanction imposed under Rule 37,[80] and in a few instances an interlocutory appeal has been allowed under 28 U.S.C.A. § 1292(b),[81] although normally a question about discovery would not satisfy the rigid criteria of that statute.[82] In the states the writs of mandamus and prohibition are often used for this purpose and the federal courts have sometimes allowed them to be used to review a discovery order,[83] although this continues to be the exception rather than the rule.[84]

§ 82.   The Rule of Hickman v. Taylor [1]

The best-known, and most important, decision on discovery in

Amendment Civil Cases, 1985, 60 Notre Dame L.Rev. 370.

78. The fullest statement of the reason for the rule is in American Exp. Warehousing, Ltd. v. Transamerica Ins. Co., C.A.2d, 1967, 380 F.2d 277, 280. See also Browning Debenture Holders' Committee v. DASA Corp., C.A.2d, 1975, 524 F.2d 811, 817; and cases cited 15B Wright, Miller & Cooper, Jurisdiction 2d § 3914.23 nn. 2–15.

There are a few unusual situations in which the order is final and appealable. E.g., Republic Gear Co. v. Borg–Warner Corp., C.A.2d, 1967, 381 F.2d 551; U.S. v. McWhirter, C.A.5th, 1967, 376 F.2d 102; Martin v. Reynolds Metals Corp., C.A.9th, 1960, 297 F.2d 49. See 15B Wright, Miller & Cooper, Jurisdiction 2d § 3914.24.

79. See, e.g., Atlas Truck Leasing, Inc. v. First NH Banks, Inc., C.A.1st, 1987, 808 F.2d 902, 903; 8 Wright, Miller & Marcus, Civil 2d § 2006.

80. E.g., Hickman v. Taylor, 1947, 67 S.Ct. 385, 329 U.S. 495, 91 L.Ed. 451. See 15B Wright, Miller & Cooper, Jurisdiction 2d § 3914.23, pp. 133–140.

81. E.g., In re Showa Denko K.K. L–Tryptophan Prods. Liab. Lit.-II, C.A.4th, 1992, 953 F.2d 162, 165; Duplan Corp. v.

Moulinage et Retorderie de Chavanoz, C.A.4th, 1973, 487 F.2d 480; and cases cited 16 Wright, Miller & Cooper, Jurisdiction 2d § 3931 n. 7.

82. Xerox Corp. v. SCM Corp., C.A.2d, 1976, 534 F.2d 1031; U.S. v. Woodbury, C.A.9th, 1959, 263 F.2d 784.

83. Schlagenhauf v. Holder, 1964, 85 S.Ct. 234, 379 U.S. 104, 13 L.Ed.2d 152; In re Burlington N., Inc., C.A.5th, 1987, 822 F.2d 518. See also 16 Wright, Miller & Cooper, Jurisdiction § 3935, pp. 246–251.

84. Kerr v. U.S. Dist. Court of Northern Dist. of California, 1976, 96 S.Ct. 2119, 426 U.S. 394, 48 L.Ed.2d 725; In re Burlington N., Inc., C.A.8th, 1982, 679 F.2d 762. 8 Wright, Miller & Marcus, Civil 2d § 2006.

§ 82

1. 8 Wright, Miller & Marcus, Civil 2d §§ 2021–2028; Restatement Third of the Law Governing Lawyers, Tent.Dr.No. 6, 1993, §§ 136–141; Thornburg, Rethinking Work Product, 1991, 77 Va.L.Rev. 1515; McFatridge, The Work Product Doctrine Revisited, 1987, 23 Tulsa L.J. 105; Cooper, Work Product of the Rulesmakers, 1969, 53 Minn.L.Rev. 1269; Special Project, The Work Product Doctrine, 1983, 68 Cornell L.Rev. 760.

federal court is that of the Supreme Court in Hickman v. Taylor.[2] The tug "John M. Taylor" sank on February 7, 1943, while helping to tow a car float across the Delaware River at Philadelphia. Five of the nine crewmen, including Norman Hickman, drowned. Three days later the owners of the tug retained a lawyer to defend them in whatever litigation might arise. On March 4th a public hearing was held before the United States Steamboat Inspectors, at which the four survivors testified. This testimony was recorded and made available to all interested parties. Shortly thereafter the lawyer interviewed the survivors privately, and obtained statements from them about the sinking, which they signed on March 29th. He also interviewed other persons believed to have some information relating to the accident and in some cases he made memoranda of what they told him. Seven months after the sinking Hickman's administrator brought suit under the Jones Act against the tugowners and the owner of the car float.

One year after this lawsuit was commenced plaintiff served 39 interrogatories upon the tugowners. All of these were answered except one, interrogatory 38, which read: "State whether any statements of the members of the crews of the Tugs 'J.M. Taylor' and 'Philadelphia' or of any other vessel were taken in connection with the towing of the car float and the sinking of the Tug 'John M. Taylor.' Attach hereto exact copies of all such statements if in writing, and if oral, set forth in detail the exact provisions of any such oral statements or reports." The defendants also refused to answer certain supplemental interrogatories that called for copies of any other oral or written statements defendants had obtained about the accident.

The five judges of the district court, sitting en banc, overruled defendants' objection to interrogatory 38 and the supplemental interrogatories, and ordered them answered.[3] The court held that statements of a third party obtained by an attorney are not within the attorney-client privilege, and that discovery of nonprivileged material would be granted when asked unless under the circumstances of a particular case the court was satisfied that the administration of justice would be in some way impeded. It did agree that the lawyer's memoranda of oral statements made to him could be submitted to the court, and so much of those memoranda as contained his mental impressions, opinions, legal theories, or other collateral matter would be deleted.

The tugowners and the lawyer refused to produce these statements, and the court ordered them imprisoned for contempt of court. Their appeal from the contempt conviction was twice heard by the Court of Appeals for the Third Circuit, sitting en banc. It unanimously held that the order of production was improper and that the contempt conviction

---

2. 1947, 67 S.Ct. 385, 329 U.S. 495, 91 L.Ed. 451. See also the account of the case by plaintiff's lawyer, Freedman, Discovery as an Instrument of Justice, 1948, 22 Temp. L.Q. 174.

3. Hickman v. Taylor, D.C.Pa.1945, 4 F.R.D. 479.

should be reversed.[4] It created a broadened attorney-client privilege, applicable in discovery proceedings, and held that the "work product of the lawyer," the results of his use of his tongue, his pen, and his head, for his client, fell within this broadened privilege.

The Supreme Court unanimously affirmed the holding of the court of appeals that the discovery ordered, and the resulting contempt conviction, were improper, but it did so on a rather different analysis from that employed by either of the lower courts. In a sweeping opinion by Justice Murphy, the Court illuminated many of the dark and controversial areas of the discovery rules.

In a much-quoted passage, the Court called for a broad and liberal treatment of the discovery rules.[5] And it agreed with the plaintiff that the materials sought were not protected by the attorney-client privilege,[6] apparently considering, as it later explicitly held,[7] that "privilege" in the discovery rules is to be given the same meaning as it has generally in the law of evidence. Even though the material sought was not privileged, the Court held that discovery was not proper. "Here is simply an attempt, without purported necessity or justification, to secure written statements, private memoranda and personal recollections prepared or formed by an adverse party's counsel in the course of his legal duties. As such, it falls outside the arena of discovery and contravenes the public policy underlying the orderly prosecution and defense of legal claims. Not even the most liberal of discovery theories can justify unwarranted inquiries into the files and the mental impressions of an attorney." [8]

This did not mean, the Court said, that all written materials obtained or prepared by a lawyer with an eye to litigation are necessarily free from discovery in all cases. "Where relevant and non-privileged facts remain hidden in an attorney's file and where production of those facts is essential to the preparation of one's case, discovery may properly be had. Such written statements and documents might, under certain circumstances, be admissible in evidence or give clues to the existence or location of relevant facts. Or they might be useful for purposes of impeachment or corroboration. And production might be justified where the witnesses are no longer available or can be reached only with difficulty." [9] The burden, though, was on the party seeking discovery of the lawyer's "work product" to establish adequate reasons to justify such production.

A different rule was said to apply to the oral statements made by witnesses to the lawyer. To require him to state what he remembers or

---

4. Hickman v. Taylor, C.C.A.3d, 1945, 153 F.2d 212.

It has been commonly supposed that the order was for criminal contempt and appealable on that ground. See § 101 below. But see Southern Ry. Co. v. Lanham, C.A.5th, 1969, 408 F.2d 348, 350 n. 2 (Brown, J., dissenting).

5. 67 S.Ct. at 392, 329 U.S. at 507. See also Herbert v. Lando, 1979, 99 S.Ct. 1635, 1649, 441 U.S. 153, 177, 60 L.Ed.2d 115.

6. 67 S.Ct. at 392, 329 U.S. at 508.

7. U.S. v. Reynolds, 1953, 73 S.Ct. 528, 531, 345 U.S. 1, 6, 97 L.Ed. 727.

8. 67 S.Ct. at 393, 329 U.S. at 510.

9. 67 S.Ct. at 394, 329 U.S. at 511.

what he saw fit to write down about the remarks of a witness would carry additional dangers not involved when the lawyer is merely asked to turn over a statement that the witness has signed. Thus, as to such oral statements, the Court said, "we do not believe that any showing of necessity can be made under the circumstances of this case so as to justify production." [10]

Finally, on the facts before it the Court noted that searching interrogatories had been directed to defendants and that full and honest answers to such broad inquiries would necessarily have included all pertinent information gleaned by the lawyer through his interviews with the witnesses. Thus, plaintiff already had the facts that he needed, and his stated reason for seeking production of the statements, that he wanted them to help prepare himself to examine witnesses and to make sure that he had overlooked nothing, was an insufficient showing of necessity and justification for the discovery sought.[11]

Hickman v. Taylor adopted a middle position between that of the district court, which would have made the work product of lawyers normally subject to discovery, and that of the court of appeals, which, by calling such material privileged, would have barred all discovery no matter how pressing the need. The Supreme Court gave the lawyer's work product a qualified immunity from discovery. Such material was discoverable only on a substantial showing of "necessity or justification." [12] The Court also made a distinction, presaged both by the decision of the district court and by an amendment to Rule 30(b) proposed by the Advisory Committee in 1946 but never adopted, by which so much of the work product as may reflect the mental impressions or opinions of the lawyer was for practical purposes, absolutely immune from discovery.

An absolute rule, either permitting or barring all discovery, would be simple to administer. A qualified rule, which requires a balancing of competing interests in each case, necessarily is not. Thus, there was much litigation and many reported decisions subsequent to Hickman v. Taylor in which courts sought to apply that qualified rule.

It is probably no exaggeration to say, as one court did, that Hickman v. Taylor had opened "a veritable Pandora's Box." [13] Many states, otherwise adopting the federal discovery rules, had undertaken to solve the problems raised by the decision in a detailed rule,[14] but for more than 20 years the matter was left in the federal system to adjudication on a case-by-case basis. It was not until 1970 that a new Rule 26(b)(3) was adopted in the federal system to cover this problem. That rule accepts

10. 67 S.Ct. at 394, 329 U.S. at 512–513.

11. 67 S.Ct. at 395, 329 U.S. at 513.

12. 67 S.Ct. at 393, 329 U.S. at 510.

13. Viront v. Wheeling & L.E. Ry. Co., D.C.Ohio 1950, 10 F.R.D. 45, 47.

"No subject had been more disputed or had received more conflicting judicial interpretation than the discovery of lawyers' work product * * *." Glaser, Pretrial Discovery and the Adversary System, 1968, p. 128.

14. The state provisions are cited in 8 Wright, Miller & Marcus, Civil 2d § 2022.

the notion of a qualified immunity for work product, as the Hickman case had announced,[15] but it speaks to details on which Hickman was silent and has resolved questions on which the lower courts were in disagreement.

Thus, Hickman's holding that the work product of a lawyer has a qualified immunity from discovery can be applied only when it is known what constitutes a lawyer's work product. Prior to the 1970 amendment there were repeated questions about who is a "lawyer" for purposes of the work-product immunity, and about what classes of materials obtained by such persons are entitled to this qualified immunity.[16]

One question of much practical importance is whether the work-product immunity extends only to statements and other material obtained by trial counsel, or whether it gives a qualified protection also to statements obtained by claim agents or investigators, which may ultimately be used by counsel. In the Hickman case the Court was concerned only with statements obtained by the defendants' lawyer. The holding of Hickman necessarily went only that far. The Third Circuit, however, in the important Alltmont case, said that "its rationale has a much broader sweep and applies to all statements of prospective witnesses which a party has obtained for his trial counsel's use." [17] There is obvious force to the arguments made in Alltmont, but arguments could be made for an opposite result and the lower court decisions were quite divided.[18] Rule 26(b)(3) resolves this conflict in the direction taken by Alltmont. It defines work product as "documents and tangible things * * * prepared in anticipation of litigation or for trial by or for another party or by or for that other party's representative (including his attorney, consultant, surety, indemnitor, insurer, or agent) * * *." [19] Thus, it is now clear that the immunity, when it is otherwise applicable, does not turn on whether an attorney obtained a document but extends to material obtained by anyone representing a party,[20] including the party's insurer.[21]

15. A recent scholar does not. "Work product immunity is unsound in theory, unfair in operation, and immensely costly to litigants and society. Legitimate concerns about the timing of litigation, cost-sharing, or attorney behavior can be addressed directly, but the current draconian work product doctrine must go." Thornburg, note 1 above, at 1517.

16. 8 Wright, Miller & Marcus, Civil 2d § 2024.

17. Alltmont v. U.S., C.C.A.3d, 1949, 177 F.2d 971, 976, certiorari denied 70 S.Ct. 999, 339 U.S. 967, 94 L.Ed. 1375.

18. See cases cited 8 Wright, Miller & Marcus, Civil 2d § 2024.

19. "The sole issue in Hickman related to materials prepared by an attorney, and courts thereafter disagreed over whether the doctrine applied as well to materials prepared on his behalf. * * * Necessarily, it must. This view is reflected in the Federal Rules of Civil Procedure, see Rule 26(b)(3) * * *." U.S. v. Nobles, 1975, 95 S.Ct. 2160, 2170 n. 13, 422 U.S. 225, 239 n. 13, 45 L.Ed.2d 141. See also Cooper, note 1 above, at 1327.

20. Almaguer v. Chicago, R.I. & P.R. Co., D.C.Neb.1972, 55 F.R.D. 147; Bunting v. Gainsville Machine Co., D.C.Del.1971, 53 F.R.D. 594; U.S. v. Maryland Shipbuilding & Drydock Co., D.C.Md.1970, 51 F.R.D. 159; Dingler v. Halcyon Lijn N.V., D.C.Pa. 1970, 50 F.R.D. 211.

21. Bondy v. Brophy, D.C.Mass.1989, 124 F.R.D. 517; Basinger v. Glacier Carriers, Inc., D.C.Pa.1985, 107 F.R.D. 771.

The one area to which the work-product immunity had always clearly applied was to material obtained by a lawyer. Even here it was thought that there was a qualified immunity only if the material was the result of a basic professional relationship between the lawyer who obtained the material and the party, or that it required the training, skill, and knowledge of a lawyer, or the essential integrity implicit in the lawyer-client relationship.[22] These limitations are ended under Rule 26(b)(3) since it reaches any representative of the party.

Rule 26(b)(3) codifies the prior decisions in providing that no matter who has obtained the material, the immunity attaches only if the material was "prepared in anticipation of litigation or for trial." Some of the prior cases had attached significance to whether a document was obtained before or after litigation was commenced, but this cannot be sound. Prudent parties anticipate litigation and begin preparation prior to the formal commencement of an action. Thus, the test should be whether, in light of the nature of the document and the factual situation in the particular case, the document can fairly be said to have been prepared or obtained because of the prospect of litigation.[23] But the converse of this is that even though litigation is already in prospect, there is no work-product immunity for documents prepared in the regular course of business rather than for purposes of the litigation.[24] Although the earlier decisions are not wholly consistent, and to the extent that the amended rule seems to speak to the question it gives unsatisfactory answers,[25] it ought to be held, as the Fourth Circuit has in an important decision, that material prepared in anticipation of one lawsuit enjoys the qualified immunity even in another unrelated lawsuit.[26]

Even if the work-product doctrine applies, it protects only documents and tangible things. It does not protect facts learned from the documents or things. There is no shield against discovery, by interrogatories or by deposition, of the facts that the opponent has acquired, or the persons from whom he or she obtained the facts, or the existence or

22. U.S. v. Anderson, D.C.Colo.1963, 34 F.R.D. 518, 521; Bifferato v. States Marine Corp. of Delaware, D.C.N.Y.1951, 11 F.R.D. 44, 46.

23. National Union Fire Ins. Co. v. Murray Sheet Metal Co., C.A.4th, 1992, 967 F.2d 980, 984; In re Grand Jury Proceedings, C.A.3d, 1979, 604 F.2d 798, 803; 8 Wright, Miller & Marcus, Civil 2d § 2024. See also Note, 1981, 66 Iowa L.Rev. 1277.

24. Binks Mfg. Co.v. National Presto Industries, Inc., C.A.7th, 1983, 709 F.2d 1109, 1119–1120; Harper v. Auto–Owners Ins. Co., D.C.Ind.1991, 138 F.R.D. 655, 661; 8 Wright, Miller & Marcus, Civil 2d § 2024. But see Special Project, note 1 above, at 848–855, arguing that there ought be no

exception for documents prepared in the ordinary course of business.

25. See 8 Wright, Miller & Marcus, Civil 2d § 2024.

26. Duplan Corp. v. Moulinage et Retorderie de Chavanoz, C.A.4th, 1973, 487 F.2d 480, noted 1974, 27 Vand.L.Rev. 826.

See also Duplan Corp. v. Moulinage et Retorderie de Chavanoz, C.A.4th, 1974, 509 F.2d 730, certiorari denied 95 S.Ct. 1438, 420 U.S. 997, 43 L.Ed.2d 680; Hercules Inc. v. Exxon Corp., D.C.Del.1977, 434 F.Supp. 136, 153; Note, The Work Product Doctrine in Subsequent Litigation, 1983, 83 Col. L.Rev. 412; cf. FTC v. Grolier, Inc., 1983, 103 S.Ct. 2209, 2213–2214, 462 U.S. 19, 25–26, 76 L.Ed.2d 387.

nonexistence of documents, even though the documents themselves have a qualified immunity from discovery.[27]

Even if, on the tests just described, a document or other tangible thing is found to be a part of the work product, this does not mean that it is not subject to discovery. Rule 26(b)(3), like the Hickman decision, creates only a qualified immunity and allows discovery of work-product material if "the party seeking discovery has substantial need of the materials in the preparation of the party's case and * * * the party is unable without undue hardship to obtain the substantial equivalent of the materials by other means." [28]

Undoubtedly the single most important factor in determining whether to allow discovery of work-product information is whether the information in question is otherwise available to the party seeking discovery. This factor is deftly captured in the formula of Rule 26(b)(3). On this principle discovery of the statements of witnesses is usually denied if it is possible for the party to interview the witnesses himself or to take their depositions.[29] The fact that this will cause added expense for the party seeking discovery is not usually, in itself, enough to constitute necessity or justification for discovery.[30] The corollary is that if the witness is no longer available, so that the moving party cannot obtain his version of the facts, production of his statements will be required.[31]

The fact that the witness is available does not bar a finding that discovery should be had. As one important decision put it, "the real question is whether the movant can obtain the facts without production of the documents containing the original statements. Therefore, the likelihood that the movant, even though he presently can obtain statements from the witnesses by deposition, will not obtain the substantial equivalent of the prior statements he seeks to obtain through production should also be considered." [32] This view is accepted in Rule 26(b)(3).

The party cannot obtain the substantial equivalent of a prior statement of a witness, and discovery must be allowed, if by the time the party interviews him or takes his deposition his memory is faulty and he no longer recalls details of the event.[33] Indeed, though there are cases to

27. Hickman v. Taylor, 1947, 67 S.Ct. 385, 390, 329 U.S. 495, 504, 91 L.Ed. 451; In re Six Grand Jury Witnesses, C.A.2d, 1992, 979 F.2d 939, 945; Bogosian v. Gulf Oil Corp., C.A.3d, 1984, 738 F.2d 587, 595.

28. See Special Project, note 1 above, at 798–811.

29. In re International Systems & Controls Corp., C.A.5th, 1982, 693 F.2d 1235, 1240; Miles v. Bell Helicopter Co., D.C.Ga. 1974, 385 F.Supp. 1029, 1032; and cases cited 8 Wright, Miller & Marcus, Civil 2d § 2025.

30. See 8 Wright, Miller & Marcus, Civil 2d § 2025.

31. In re Grand Jury Investigation, C.A.3d, 1979, 599 F.2d 1224, 1231–1232; McNulty v. Bally's Park Place, Inc., D.C.Pa. 1988, 120 F.R.D. 27; and cases cited 8 Wright, Miller & Marcus, Civil 2d § 2025.

32. Southern Ry. Co. v. Lanham, C.A.5th, 1968, 403 F.2d 119, 127.

33. McDougall v. Dunn, C.A.4th, 1972, 468 F.2d 468, 474; Phillips v. Dallas Carriers Corp., D.C.N.C.1990, 133 F.R.D. 475; and cases cited 8 Wright, Miller & Marcus, Civil 2d § 2025.

the contrary,[34] there is now substantial authority for the proposition that statements taken from witnesses close to the time of the occurrence are unique, in that they provide an immediate impression of the facts. On this view, mere lapse of time is in itself enough to justify discovery.[35] On the face of it, the Hickman case itself might seem to the contrary, since the statements sought unsuccessfully in that case were contemporaneous statements. But Hickman may be distinguishable on this point, since in Hickman plaintiff did have access to the testimony of the survivors before an investigating board, and this testimony was even closer to the date of the accident sued for than were the statements obtained by defendants' lawyer. Thus, in Hickman both parties did have access to a more-or-less contemporaneous record of events.[36] The notion that the statement taken nearest to the event will most accurately reflect the perception the witness had of the event is amply supported by psychological studies,[37] as well as by common sense. This fact lends strong support to the argument that lapse of time in itself creates necessity or justification for the production of statements taken near the time of the event.

It is not enough to obtain discovery of work-product material that the party cannot get the information it is seeking by other means. It must also satisfy the court that it has "substantial need of the materials in the preparation of his case."[38] A mere surmise that the material sought may be useful is not a sufficient showing.[39]

If information that otherwise is subject to discovery may be obtained in no other way, it may be had from the opposing party's attorney.[40] In ordering discovery, however, Rule 26(b)(3) codifies the teaching of the cases when it says that the court "shall protect against disclosure of the mental impressions, conclusions, opinion, or legal theories of an attorney

---

34. First Wisconsin Mortg. Trust v. First Wisconsin Corp., D.C.Wis.1980, 86 F.R.D. 160, 166–167; and cases cited 8 Wright, Miller & Marcus, Civil 2d § 2025.

35. McDougall v. Dunn, C.A.4th, 1972, 468 F.2d 468, 474; Southern R. Co. v. Lanham, C.A.5th, 1968, 403 F.2d 119, 127–131; Advisory Committee Note, 48 F.R.D. 485, 501; and cases cited 8 Wright, Miller & Marcus, Civil 2d § 2025.

36. See Guilford Nat. Bank of Greensboro v. Southern Ry. Co., C.A.4th, 1962, 297 F.2d 921, 926.

37. Gray et al., Psychology in Use, 2d ed. 1951, p. 242; Dallenbach, The Relation of Memory Error to Time Interval, 1913, 20 Psych.Rev. 323; Hutchins & Schlesinger, Some Observations on the Law of Evidence—Memory, 1928, 41 Harv.L.Rev. 860, 864–867; Gardner, The Perception and Memory of Witnesses, 1933, 18 Cornell L.Q. 391, 393–394. See Southern Ry. Co. v. Lanham, C.A.5th, 1968, 403 F.2d 119, 128 n. 7.

This point is subject to the qualification, however, stated by Judge Rubin in Hamilton v. Canal Barge Co., Inc., D.C.La.1974, 395 F.Supp. 975, 977–978, that only statements taken almost immediately after an event have this unique value.

38. Castle v. Sangamo Weston, Inc., C.A.11th, 1984, 744 F.2d 1464, 1467; Henderson v. Zurn Indus., Inc., D.C.Ind. 1990, 131 F.R.D. 560, 572. See 8 Wright, Miller & Marcus, Civil 2d § 2025.

39. Stephens Produce Co. v. NLRB, C.A.8th, 1975, 515 F.2d 1373, 1377; Hauger v. Chicago, R.I. & P.R. Co., C.A.7th, 1954, 216 F.2d 501, 508; U.S. v. Chatham City Corp., D.C.Ga.1976, 72 F.R.D. 640, 643.

40. Xerox Corp. v. International Business Machines Corp., D.C.N.Y.1974, 64 F.R.D. 367; In re Penn Central Commercial Paper Litigation, D.C.N.Y.1973, 61 F.R.D. 453; 8 Wright, Miller & Marcus, Civil 2d § 2026.

or other representative of a party concerning the litigation."[41] Some cases hold that this protection is absolute and "no showing of relevance, substantial need or undue hardship should justify compelled disclosure of an attorney's mental impressions, conclusions, opinions or legal theories."[42] This view is not universally accepted, however. One court has announced what it terms "an abecedarian verity" that "not every item which may reveal some inkling of a lawyer's mental impressions, conclusions, opinions, or legal, theories is protected as opinion work product."[43] Even if something is opinion work product, the courts have recognized a crime-fraud exception to the work-product immunity, similar to the exception for attorney-client privilege.[44] It has also been held that opinion work product is discoverable if the strategy and mental impressions of a party's agents and attorneys are directly at issue in the case and the information could not be obtained elsewhere.[45]

Although there was considerable confusion on the matter, prior to 1970 the courts had come increasingly to the view that a statement given by the party to his or her opponent stood in a different category from other work-product material and that the party should be allowed to obtain a copy of his or her own statement without making any special showing.[46] The statement of a party differs significantly from the statement of an ordinary witness. The statement of the witness is hearsay, normally usable at the trial, if at all, only for purposes of impeachment. The statement of the party, on the other hand, may be introduced as substantive evidence by the party's opponent as an admission. Decisions that had refused to require production of a party's statement had failed to give full effect to the important principle, stated by Justice Jackson in his concurring opinion in the Hickman case, that "it seems clear and long has been recognized that discovery should provide a party access to anything that is evidence in his case."[47]

---

41. Hickman v. Taylor, 1947, 67 S.Ct. 385, 394–395, 329 U.S. 495, 512–513, 91 L.Ed. 451; 8 Wright, Miller & Marcus, Civil 2d § 2026.

42. Duplan Corp. v. Moulinage et Retorderie de Chavanoz, C.A.4th, 1974, 509 F.2d 730, 734, certiorari denied 95 S.Ct. 1438, 420 U.S. 997, 43 L.Ed.2d 680. See also Upjohn Co. v. U.S., 1981, 101 S.Ct. 677, 686–689, 449 U.S. 383, 397–402, 66 L.Ed.2d 584; Comment, The Potential for Discovery of Opinion Work Product under Rule 26(b)(3), 1978, 64 Iowa L.Rev. 103; Note, Protection of Opinion Work Product under the Federal Rules of Civil Procedure, 1978, 64 Va.L.Rev. 333.

43. In re San Juan Dupont Plaza Hotel Fire Litigation, C.A.1st, 1988, 859 F.2d 1007, 1015.

The following definition of "abecedarian" is taken from Random House Dictionary of the English Language, 2d ed. 1987: "—adj. 3. of or pertaining to the alphabet. 4.

arranged in alphabetical order. 5. rudimentary; elementary; primary."

44. Restatement Third, note 1 above, § 142; In re Sealed Case, C.A.D.C.1982, 676 F.2d 793, 811–816; In re Special Sept. 1978 Grand Jury (II), C.A.7th, 1980, 640 F.2d 49, 62–63; In re Murphy, C.A.8th, 1977, 560 F.2d 326.

45. Restatement Third, note 1 above, § 141A; Holmgren v. State Farm Mut. Auto Ins. Co., C.A.9th, 1992, 976 F.2d 573, 577; Bio–Rad Laboratories, Inc. v. Pharmacia, Inc., D.C.Cal.1990, 130 F.R.D. 116, 122; Boring v. Keller, D.C.Colo.1983, 97 F.R.D. 404, 407; Handgards, Inc. v. Johnson & Johnson, D.C.Cal.1976, 413 F.Supp. 926, 931; Special Project, note 1 above, at 831–837.

46. 8 Wright, Miller & Marcus, Civil 2d § 2027.

47. 67 S.Ct. at 396, 329 U.S. at 515.

The 1970 amendments wrote the better view on this question into the rules. Under the second paragraph of Rule 26(b)(3) a party may obtain as a matter of right a statement concerning the action or its subject matter that he or she has previously made.[48]

The 1970 rule, however, goes even farther. In addition to allowing a party access to a copy of his own statement it also creates a procedure by which any person who has given a statement concerning the action or its subject matter may request a copy from the person to whom it was given and may obtain a court order compelling delivery of the copy if the request is refused.[49] The compelling arguments for requiring discovery of a party's statement are applicable only in part to a statement of a person not a party. The strongest argument for this new procedure is one simply of fairness, that it is unfair to take a statement from a person without providing him with a copy of it. It must be emphasized that this provision creates a right only in the person who gave the statement and does not allow a party to the lawsuit to obtain, as of right, the statement of some other person.[50] It well may be, however, that this portion of Rule 26(b)(3) is a step in the direction of ultimately making all statements of witnesses freely discoverable.[51] If the rulemakers should ever go all the way in that direction, it would greatly reduce the controversy about the work-product doctrine and the bulk of the litigation it has caused.

The Supreme Court has recently said that "the concerns reflected in the work-product doctrine do not disappear once trial has begun. Disclosure of an attorney's efforts at trial, as surely as disclosure during pretrial discovery, could disrupt the orderly development and presentation of his case."[52] The Court found it unnecessary in that case to delineate the scope of the doctrine at trial, but the very suggestion that the doctrine applies at trial was surprising to two concurring Justices who had shared the common understanding that the Hickman rule is solely a limitation on pretrial discovery.[53]

---

48. Miles v. M/V Mississippi Queen, C.A.5th, 1985, 753 F.2d 1349, 1351.

49. 8 Wright, Miller & Marcus, Civil 2d § 2028; Special Project, note 1 above, at 814–816.

50. But the nonparty witness cannot be barred by a protective order from turning the copy of the statement over to a party. Hirstein v. American Motors Corp., D.C.Ind.1986, 112 F.R.D. 436.

51. See Restatement Third, note 1 above, § 136(3); Waits, Work Product Protection for Witness Statements: Time for Abolition, 1985 Wis.L.Rev. 305; Cooper, note 1 above, at 1318–1328; Miller v. Harpster, Alaska, 1964, 392 P.2d 21; Monier v. Chamberlain, 1966, 221 N.E.2d 410, 35 Ill.2d 351.

52. U.S. v. Nobles, 1975, 95 S.Ct. 2160, 2170, 422 U.S. 225, 239, 45 L.Ed.2d 141. The holding of the case is that the work-product doctrine applies in criminal litigation as well as civil.

53. 95 S.Ct. at 2172–2176, 422 U.S. at 242–254 (White, J., joined by Rehnquist, J., concurring).

§ 83.　Preventing Abuse of Discovery [1]

Liberal discovery procedures are an important advance in the litigation process but it cannot be thought that they are an unmixed blessing. Any device, however salutary, can be abused and there are undoubtedly instances in which a party will seek to use discovery in a way that will oppress its opponent,[2] although studies have shown that these instances are relatively uncommon.[3]

The rules provide remedies against abuse of discovery. Rule 26(c) authorizes the court to make orders for the protection of parties and persons from whom discovery is being sought.[4] The Supreme Court has said that this provides "ample powers of the district judge to prevent abuse" and that "[w]ith this authority at hand, judges should not hesitate to exercise appropriate control over the discovery process."[5]

A motion for a protective order may be made by any party to the case or by the person from whom discovery is sought.[6] Ordinarily the

---

§ 83

1.　8 Wright, Miller & Marcus, Civil 2d §§ 2035–2044; Dudley, Discovery Abuse Revisited: Some Specific Proposals to Amend the Federal Rules of Civil Procedure, 1992, 26 U.S.F.L.Rev. 189; Marcus, Myth and Reality in Protective Order Litigation, 1983, 69 Cornell L.Rev. 1; Levine, "Abuse" of Discovery: or Hard Work Makes Good Law, 1981, 67 A.B.A.J. 565; Pollack, Discovery—Its Abuse and Correction, 1979, 80 F.R.D. 219; Note, Trends in Protective Orders Under Federal Rule of Civil Procedure 26(c): Why Some Cases Fumble While Others Score, 1991, 60 Fordham L.Rev. 541; Comment, Preventing Abuse of Discovery in Federal Courts, 1981, 30 Cath.U.L.Rev. 273.

2.　In a 1975 securities case, the Supreme Court said: "The potential for possible abuse of the liberal discovery provisions of the federal rules may likewise exist in this type of case to a greater extent than they do in other litigation. The prospect of extensive deposition of the defendant's officers and associates and the concomitant opportunity for extensive discovery of business documents, is a common occurrence in this and similar types of litigation. To the extent that this process eventually produces relevant evidence which is useful in determining the merits of the claims asserted by the parties, it bears the imprimatur of the Federal Rules of Civil Procedure and of the many cases liberally interpreting them. But to the extent that it permits a plaintiff with a largely groundless claim to simply take up the time of a number of other people, with the right to do so representing an *in terrorem* increment of the settlement value rather than a reasonably founded

hope that the process will reveal relevant evidence, it is a social cost rather than a benefit." Blue Chip Stamps v. Manor Drug Stores, 1975, 95 S.Ct. 1917, 1928, 421 U.S. 723, 741, 44 L.Ed.2d 539.

3.　Connolly, Holleman & Kuhlman, Judicial Controls and the Civil Litigative Process: Discovery, Federal Judicial Center 1978, p. 35; Glaser, Pretrial Discovery and the Adversary System, 1968, pp. 117–123, 129–134; Schroeder & Frank, The Proposed Changes in the Discovery Rules, 1978 Ariz.St.L.J. 475, 476–478, 492.

4.　Prior to the 1970 amendments what is now Rule 26(c) was Rule 30(b), and purported to apply only to oral depositions, though it was incorporated by reference in some other discovery rules and had been read by the courts into the others.

5.　Herbert v. Lando, 1979, 99 S.Ct. 1635, 1649, 441 U.S. 153, 177, 60 L.Ed.2d 115.

"An examination of the evolution of civil procedure since 1938 demonstrates the need for active judicial management of pretrial discovery and shows that retaining judicial discretion to grant protective orders is consistent with that active management." Miller, Confidentiality, Protective Orders, and Public Access to the Courts, 1991, 105 Harv.L.Rev. 427, 447.

6.　Caisson Corp. v. County West Bldg. Corp., D.C.Pa.1974, 62 F.R.D. 331; Norris Mfg. Co. v. R.E. Darling Co., D.C.Md.1961, 29 F.R.D. 1; Central Hide & Rendering Co. v. B–M–K Corp., D.C.Del.1956, 19 F.R.D. 296. Other parties have no standing to claim protection of a purely personal nature for a witness or party who makes no such claim for himself or herself. In re Westingmotion must be addressed to the court in which the action is pending, though Rule 26(c) also allows application to the court in the district where a deposition is to be taken on matters relating to that deposition.[7] The motion should be timely, a limitation that is interpreted with reference to the circumstances of the particular case and the discovery sought.[8] The moving party must show good cause for a protective order, which puts the burden on that party to show some adequate reason for the order.[9]

Rule 26(c) provides that the court may make any order that justice requires to protect from annoyance, embarrassment, oppression, or undue burden or expense. It then specifies eight particular types of protective orders that a court may make. The court may order that the discovery not be had, although in view of the freedom of discovery that the rules provide, motions for such relief are usually denied.[10] Witnesses cannot ordinarily escape examination by claiming that they have no knowledge of any relevant facts, since the party seeking to take the deposition is entitled to test their lack of knowledge.[11]

The court may order that discovery be had only on specified terms

house Elec. Corp. Uranium Contracts Litigation, D.C.Pa.1977, 76 F.R.D. 47.

Under a 1993 amendment of Rule 26(c), a motion for a protective order must be accompanied by a certification that the movant has in good faith conferred or attempted to confer with other affected parties in an effort to resolve the dispute without court action.

7. The courts prefer to have the court in which the action is pending pass on these matters. Socialist Workers Party v. Attorney Gen. of U.S., D.C.Md.1977, 73 F.R.D. 699; E.I. Dupont De Nemours & Co. v. Deering Milliken Research Corp., D.C.Del. 1976, 72 F.R.D. 440.

8. Until 1970 the rule required that the motion be "seasonably" made. The present form of the rule does not include that requirement, but the courts continue to look to the timeliness of the motion. See 8 Wright, Miller & Marcus, Civil 2d § 2035.

Rule 30(a)(3), as amended in 1993, provides that if a party has received less than 11 days notice of a deposition and has promptly moved for a protective order that the deposition not be held or be held at different time or place, and the motion is still pending at the time the deposition is held, the deposition cannot be used against that party.

9. Cipollone v. Liggett Group, Inc., C.A.3d, 1986, 785 F.2d 1108, 1121, certiorari denied 107 S.Ct. 907, 479 U.S. 1043, 93 L.Ed.2d 857; In re Halkin, C.A.D.C.1979,

598 F.2d 176, 183. See Comment, note 1 above, at 285–297, for discussion of how courts decide whether this burden has been carried.

10. Salter v. Upjohn Co., C.A.5th, 1979, 593 F.2d 649, 651; Fann v. Giant Food, Inc., D.C.D.C.1987, 115 F.R.D. 593, 597; 8 Wright, Miller & Marcus, Civil 2d § 2037.

In suits by AIDS victims, claiming that the Red Cross has failed to screen blood donors adequately, the Red Cross has resisted discovery, on the ground that information about blood donors is protected by the donors' rights to privacy and that allowing discovery about donors would deter some people from donating blood. The Fourth Circuit has held that this discovery should be allowed, subject to stringent protection against disclosure of the donor's identity. Watson v. Lowcrounty Red Cross, C.A.4th, 1992, 974 F.2d 482, 489. See also Note, 1991, 76 Cornell L.Rev. 927. Discovery was refused in Coleman v. American Red Cross, D.C.Mich.1990, 130 F.R.D. 360.

11. Amherst Leasing Corp. v. Emhart Corp., D.C.Conn.1974, 65 F.R.D. 121; Less v. Taber Instrument Corp., D.C.N.Y.1971, 53 F.R.D. 645; 8 Wright, Miller & Marcus, Civil 2d § 2037.

A different result is often reached if the proposed deponent is a busy government official or high corporate officer. U.S. v. Miracle Recreation Equipment Co., D.C.Iowa 1987, 118 F.R.D. 100; Mulvey v. Chrysler Corp., D.C.R.I.1985, 106 F.R.D.

and conditions, and may designate the time or place for discovery.[12] As a normal rule plaintiff will be required to submit to a deposition in the district in which he or she has brought suit.[13] Since plaintiff has selected the forum, he or she will not be heard to complain about having to appear there for a deposition. But this is at best a general rule, and is not adhered to if the plaintiff can show good cause for not being required to come to the district where the action is pending. Thus, a protective order will be granted if the plaintiff is physically or financially unable to come to the forum,[14] or if to do so would cause unusual and serious hardship to the plaintiff.[15] The general principle that the plaintiff must come to the forum it has chosen loses force if there was no choice of forum to begin with.[16] Commonly if a sufficient showing is made that examination at the designated place will cause undue hardship, the court makes an order in the alternative, providing that the examination be held at some other place or that the party seeking the examination pay travel expenses for the deponent to the place he has chosen, or that the deposition be taken on written questions rather than orally, or that the deposition be taken by telephone, thus leaving the choice of method to the party who wishes the examination.[17]

The court has power, however, in any case to order that discovery be had only by a method of discovery other than that selected by the party seeking discovery. In the past this has most often involved a motion asking that a deposition be taken only on written questions rather than by oral examination. Usually the court will not interfere with the choice made by the party seeking discovery,[18] but if the examination will be brief or simple, or there are other reasons why written questions will suffice in the particular case, the court will order that the deposition be taken in that fashion.[19]

The court may order that certain matters not be inquired into, or that the scope of the discovery be limited to certain matters. Ever since the days of the former equity bill of discovery there has been applied to discovery "the principle of judicial parsimony," by which, where one

---

364; 8 Wright, Miller & Marcus, Civil 2d § 2037.

12. Rule 26(c)(2); 8 Wright, Miller & Marcus, Civil 2d §§ 2038, 2111, 2112.

13. Collins v. Wayland, C.C.A.9th, 1944, 139 F.2d 677, certiorari denied 64 S.Ct. 1151, 322 U.S. 744, 88 L.Ed. 1576; Hunter v. Riverside Community Memorial Hosp., D.C.Wis.1972, 58 F.R.D. 218; 8 Wright, Miller & Marcus, Civil 2d § 2112.

14. Sullivan v. Southern Pac. Co., D.C.N.Y.1947, 7 F.R.D. 206; cf. Rifkin v. United States Lines Co., D.C.N.Y.1959, 177 F.Supp. 875. The showing of inability was held insufficient in de Dalmady v. Price Waterhouse & Co., D.C.Puerto Rico 1973, 62 F.R.D. 157.

15. Hyam v. American Export Lines, C.A.2d 1954, 213 F.2d 221; Powell v. Inter-

national Foodservice System, Inc., D.C.Puerto Rico 1971, 52 F.R.D. 205; and cases cited 8 Wright, Miller & Marcus, Civil 2d § 2112.

16. Ellis Air Lines v. Bellanca Aircraft Corp., D.C.Del.1955, 17 F.R.D. 395; Endte v. Hermes Export Corp., D.C.N.Y.1957, 20 F.R.D. 162; cf. O'Hara v. United States Lines Co., D.C.N.Y.1958, 164 F.Supp. 549.

17. E.g., DePetro v. Exxon, Inc., D.C.Ala.1988, 118 F.R.D. 523; Boone v. Wynne, D.C.D.C.1947, 7 F.R.D. 22; 8 Wright, Miller & Marcus, Civil 2d § 2112.

18. E.g., National Life Ins. Co. v. Hartford Acc. & Indem. Co., C.A.3d, 1980, 615 F.2d 595, 599–600.

19. Rule 26(c)(3); Colonial Capital Co. v. General Motors Corp., D.C.Conn.1961, 29 F.R.D. 514; Moore v. George A. Hormel &

issue may be determinative of a case, the court has discretion to stay discovery on other issues until the critical issue has been decided.[20] An obvious application of this principle—salutary if applied sparingly and with real discretion rather than as an absolute rule—is that courts may stay discovery on the merits of an action until challenges to jurisdiction have been resolved.[21] Similarly where an issue is to be tried separately the court may limit discovery to that issue.[22] But in many instances such a limitation could lead to wasted effort, by requiring two depositions from the same witness, and the court is well justified in refusing such a limitation.[23] The scope of depositions in a federal civil action may also be limited in cases where it is contended that the depositions are intended for discovery in another case, such as a closely related criminal action[24] or an action in state court.[25] Again if the information sought is relevant to the pending action and the transactions involved are so interrelated that a limitation of examination to specific matters would frustrate the inquiry, limitation should be denied.[26]

The court may order that discovery be conducted with no one present except persons designated by the court.[27] Under the pre–1970 rule the court lacked power to order the exclusion of a party or an officer of a corporate party, but this language was not carried into the 1970 amendment and courts now hold that they can exclude a party.[28] A

Co., D.C.N.Y.1942, 2 F.R.D. 340; 8 Wright, Miller & Marcus, Civil 2d § 2039.

20. Sinclair Ref. Co. v. Jenkins Petroleum Process Co., 1933, 53 S.Ct. 736, 289 U.S. 689, 77 L.Ed. 1449.

21. Investment Properties Intl., Ltd. v. IOS, Ltd., C.A.2d, 1972, 459 F.2d 705; McDonnell Douglas Corp. v. Polin, C.A.3d, 1970, 429 F.2d 30; and cases cited 8 Wright, Miller & Marcus, Civil 2d § 2040.

22. Maxey by Maxey v. Fulton, C.A.10th, 1989, 890 F.2d 279; Kutilek v. Gannon, D.C.Kan.1990, 132 F.R.D. 296; and cases cited 8 Wright, Miller & Marcus, Civil 2d § 2040.

23. Vollert v. Summa Corp., D.C.Hawaii 1975, 389 F.Supp. 1348; Technitrol Inc. v. Digital Equipment Corp., D.C.Ill.1973, 62 F.R.D. 91; and cases cited 8 Wright, Miller & Marcus, Civil 2d § 2040.

24. Campbell v. Eastland, C.A.5th, 1962, 307 F.2d 478, certiorari denied 83 S.Ct. 502, 371 U.S. 955, 9 L.Ed.2d 502; Dienstag v. Bronsen, D.C.N.Y.1970, 49 F.R.D. 327; Hiss v. Chambers, D.C.Md. 1948, 8 F.R.D. 480; cf. McSurely v. McClellan, C.A.D.C.1970, 426 F.2d 664. See Note, 1968, 66 Mich.L.Rev. 738.

25. Sperry Rand Corp. v. Rothlein, C.A.2d, 1961, 288 F.2d 245, noted 1962, 110 U.Pa.L.Rev. 751; In re Coronet Metal Products Corp., D.C.N.Y.1948, 81 F.Supp. 500. See also 8 Wright, Miller & Marcus, Civil 2d § 2040.

26. E.g., Waldbaum v. Worldvision Enterprises, Inc., D.C.N.Y.1979, 84 F.R.D. 95; Johnson Foils, Inc. v. Huyuck Corp., D.C.N.Y.1973, 61 F.R.D. 405; 8 Wright, Miller & Marcus, Civil 2d § 2040. See Comment, Federal Discovery in Concurrent Criminal and Civil Proceedings, 1978, 52 Tul.L.Rev. 769.

27. Rule 26(c)(5); 8 Wright, Miller & Marcus: Civil 2d § 2041.

Neither the public nor representatives of the press have a right to be present at the taking of a deposition. Grundberg v. Upjohn Co., D.C.Utah 1991, 140 F.R.D. 459, 466; Times Newspapers Ltd. (of Great Britain) v. McDonnell Douglas Corp., D.C.Cal. 1974, 387 F.Supp. 189. But there must be compelling reasons for denying access to the public. American Tel. & Tel. Co. v. Grady, C.A.7th, 1978, 594 F.2d 594, certiorari denied 99 S.Ct. 1533, 440 U.S. 971, 59 L.Ed.2d 787.

28. Galella v. Onassis, C.A.2d, 1973, 487 F.2d 986; Beacon v. R.M. Jones Apartment Rentals, D.C.Ohio 1978, 79 F.R.D. 141. This result continued to be reached despite Evidence Rule 615, which precludes barring a party or the officer of a corporate party from being present at the trial. In re Shell Oil Co., D.C.La.1991, 136 F.R.D. 615. In 1993 Rule 30(c) was amended to provide that Evidence Rules 103 and 615 do not apply at the taking of a deposition.

related provision permits an order that after being sealed, as required by Rule 30(f), the deposition shall be opened only by order of court.[29] In the absence of such a protective order the deposition is a public document; it is freely open to inspection after it is filed by the clerk [30] and a party that has received discovery materials may make them public.[31]

The court may order that a trade secret or other confidential research, development, or commercial information not be disclosed or be disclosed only in a designated way.[32] There is no true privilege for trade secrets [33] and disclosure will be ordered if the issues cannot be fairly adjudicated without such information,[34] but the court must exercise its discretion to avoid unnecessary disclosure of the information, and it may make conditions about the disclosure in order to protect the party compelled to disclose.[35]

The court may order that the parties simultaneously file specified documents or information enclosed in sealed envelopes to be opened as directed by the court.[36]

Some courts and commentators had thought that an order limiting access to and use of material obtained by discovery is a form of prior restraint that must be justified by First Amendment standards.[37] This view was rejected by the Supreme Court in a 1984 case holding that where "a protective order is entered on a showing of good cause as required by Rule 26(c), is limited to the context of pretrial civil discovery, and does not restrict the dissemination of the information if gained from

29. Martindell v. International Tel. & Tel. Corp., C.A.2d, 1979, 594 F.2d 291; OKC Corp. v. Williams, D.C.Tex.1978, 461 F.Supp. 540. Such an order was refused in Teplitzky v. Boston Ins. Co., D.C.Pa.1971, 52 F.R.D. 160.

30. See Avirgan v. Hull, D.C.D.C.1987, 118 F.R.D. 252, 255; 8 Wright, Miller & Marcus, Civil 2d § 2042.

Rules 5(d) and 30(f)(1) were amended in 1980 to allow the court, on motion of a party or on its own initiative, to provide that discovery materials not be filed. See 4A Wright & Miller, Civil 2d § 1152.

31. Public Citizen v. Liggett Group, Inc., C.A.1st, 1988, 858 F.2d 775, 790, certiorari denied 109 S.Ct. 838, 488 U.S. 1030, 102 L.Ed.2d 970; Wilk v. American Medical Assn., C.A.7th, 1980, 635 F.2d 1295, 1299.

32. Rule 26(c)(7); 8 Wright, Miller & Marcus: Civil 2d § 2043; Note, The White Knight Privilege in Litigated Takeovers: Leveling the Playing Field in Discovery, 1991, 43 Stan.L.Rev. 1991.

33. Federal Open Market Committee v. Merrill, 1979, 99 S.Ct. 2800, 2813, 443 U.S. 340, 362, 61 L.Ed.2d 587.

34. Centurion Industries, Inc. v. Warren Steurer and Associates, C.A.10th, 1981, 665 F.2d 323, 326; Carter Products, Inc. v. Eversharp, Inc., C.A.7th, 1966, 360 F.2d 868; Covey Oil Co. v. Continental Oil Co., C.A.10th, 1965, 340 F.2d 993, certiorari denied 85 S.Ct. 1110, 380 U.S. 964, 14 L.Ed.2d 155; Olympic Ref. Co. v. Carter, C.A.9th, 1964, 332 F.2d 260, certiorari denied 85 S.Ct. 186, 379 U.S. 900, 13 L.Ed.2d 175; 8 Wright, Miller & Marcus, Civil 2d § 2043.

35. Brown Bag Software v. Symantec Corp., C.A.9th, 1992, 960 F.2d 1465, certiorari denied 113 S.Ct. 198, ___ U.S. ___, 121 L.Ed.2d 141; Donald v. Rast, C.A.8th, 1991, 927 F.2d 379, certiorari denied 112 S.Ct. 96, ___ U.S. ___, 116 L.Ed.2d 68; Quotron Systems, Inc. v. Automatic Data Processing, Inc., D.C.N.Y.1992, 141 F.R.D. 37, 40.

36. Rule 26(c)(8); 8 Wright, Miller & Marcus, Civil 2d § 2044.

37. In re Halkin, C.A.D.C.1979, 598 F.2d 176. See also In re San Juan Star Co., C.A.1st, 1981, 662 F.2d 108; Notes, 1981, 94 Harv.L.Rev. 1085; 1980, 80 Col.L.Rev. 1465. But see Marcus, note 1 above.

other sources, it does not offend the First Amendment."[38]   That it is constitutional to limit access to discovery materials does not mean that it is wise to do so.   There have been proposals that there ought to be a rule of general public access to discovery, and some states have adopted statutes or rules that go a long way in that direction.   But two of the most respected scholars in this area of the law have argued against this kind of shift from the traditional rule that discovery is essentially a private affair; in their view current legal doctrine is working well and radical changes would be risky.[39]

The eight specific types of orders listed in Rule 26(c) are merely illustrative of the general power of the court to make any order justice requires to protect from annoyance, embarrassment, oppression, or undue burden or expense.[40]   This emphasizes the complete control that the court has over the discovery process.   It is impossible to set out in a rule all the circumstances that may require limitations on discovery or the kinds of limitations that may be needed.   The rules, instead, permit the broadest scope of discovery and leave it to the enlightened discretion of the district court to decide what restrictions may be necessary in a particular case.   The harassment or oppression should be unreasonable to justify restriction on discovery,[41] but even very slight inconvenience may be unreasonable if there is no showing of need for the discovery sought.[42]

A provision appearing for the first time in 1970 in Rule 26(c) authorizes the court, in denying a motion for a protective order, to go a step further and issue an affirmative order compelling the discovery objected to.   This will bring into play the sanctions of Rule 37 if the party against whom discovery is sought continues to refuse to provide it.[43]   In addition the court has discretion under proposed Rules 26(c) and 37(a)(4) to require the losing party on the motion to pay expenses incurred in relation to the motion.

In 1983, as part of an attack on the problem of overuse of discovery in terms of depth,[44] Rule 26 was amended.   A sentence in Rule 26(a)

---

38. Seattle Times Co. v. Rhinehart, 1984, 104 S.Ct. 2199, 2210, 467 U.S. 20, 37, 81 L.Ed.2d 17.

This does not mean that the First Amendment has been entirely eliminated from consideration in issuing protective orders. It comes in within the framework of the "good cause" requirement of Rule 26(c). James, Hazard & Leubsdorf, Civil Procedure, 4th ed. 1992, p. 265; Anderson v. Cryovac, Inc., C.A.1st, 1986, 805 F.2d 1. See generally Campbell, The Protective Order in Products Liability Litigation: Safeguard of Misnomer?, 1990, 31 B.C.L.Rev. 771.

39. Miller, note 5 above; Marcus, The Discovery Confidentiality Controversy, 1991 U.Ill.L.Rev. 457.

40. Herbert v. Lando, 1979, 99 S.Ct. 1635, 1649, 441 U.S. 153, 177, 60 L.Ed.2d 115.

41. U.S. v. International Business Machines Corp., D.C.N.Y.1979, 83 F.R.D. 92; Alliance to End Repression v. Rochford, D.C.Ill.1977, 75 F.R.D. 441; 8 Wright, Miller & Marcus, Civil 2d § 2036.

42. United Air Lines, Inc. v. U.S., D.C.Del.1960, 26 F.R.D. 213.

Courts also have ample power to modify an earlier protective order. 8 Wright, Miller & Marcus, Civil 2d § 2044.1.

43. See § 90 below.

44. See § 81 above at notes 11 to 24.

providing that in the absence of a court order the frequency of use of discovery was not limited was deleted. A new paragraph was added to Rule 26(b)(1). It provides that the court, on its own initiative or pursuant to a motion, can limit discovery when it is unreasonably cumulative or duplicative, when the information can be obtained more conveniently or economically elsewhere, when there has been ample opportunity for the discovery, and when the discovery is unduly burdensome or expensive, taking into account the needs of the case, the amount in controversy, limitations on the parties' resources, and the importance of the issue.[45] Although this is put in terms of a limit on the scope of discovery, an order of this kind is similar in purpose and operation to the protective orders with which the courts have long been familiar.[46]

§ 83A. Required Disclosures [1]

On December 1, 1993, significant and highly controversial amendments to the Federal Rules of Civil Procedure regarding discovery became effective.[2] The most dramatic change in the Federal Rule of Civil Procedure 26 is the imposition of a new disclosure regime. The adoption of the disclosure system came unexpectedly.[3] The revisions to Rule 26 were adopted before the experiments called for by the Civil Justice Reform Act of 1990[4] could be completed, and thus before empirical evidence could be gathered from testing on the local level.[5] The Advisory Committee intimated that the delays incurred by awaiting the returns of the experiments were too lengthy.[6] The important fact is

---

45. 8 Wright, Miller & Marcus, Civil 2d § 2036. The 1983 amendments and the Advisory Committee Notes to them are reprinted 97 F.R.D. 213–220.

46. Indeed if a party moves for a limit under Rule 26(b)(1), the rule itself provides that the motion is to be made under Rule 26(c), the protective-order subdivision.

§ 83A

1. 8 Wright, Miller & Marcus, Civil 2d §§ 2053, 2054. See also Mayer, Prescribing Cooperating: The Mandatory Pretrial Disclosure Requirement of Proposed Rules 26 and 37 of the Federal Rules of Civil Procedure, 1992, 12 Rev.Litig. 77.

The author is indebted to Scott P. Baker for his valuable assistance in the preparation of this section.

2. Samborn, New Discovery Rules Take Effect, Natl.L.J., Dec. 6, 1993, at 3. The House of Representatives had passed a bill that would have disapproved all of the required-disclosure provisions of Rule 26(a) except for what is now Rule 26(a)(1)(D), calling for disclosure of insurance agreements. Although this bill was supported by a remarkable coalition of groups from both sides of the bar, as well as by the Justice Department, it never came to a vote in the Senate in the closing days of the congressional session because some civil-rights groups thought that it should also have disapproved the portions of the 1993 amendments that limit the number of depositions and interrogatories.

3. Id. at 3.

4. See § 63A above.

5. See the dissent of Justices Scalia, Souter, and Thomas from the Order of April 22, 1993 adopting amendments to the Civil Rules. 146 F.R.D. 507, 510–513. The dissenting justices harshly criticize the imposition of "such a radical alteration" without the support of empirical evidence. 146 F.R.D. at 511. See also Mullenix, Hope Over Experience: Mandatory Informal Discovery And the Politics of Rulemaking, 1991, 69 N.C.L.Rev. 795, 810. But see id. at 798 n. 4, 810 n. 75.

6. See the Advisory Committee Note to the 1993 amendments of Rule 26(a), reprinted 146 F.R.D. at 627–638. The statement in the text is supported by what the Note says at 629–630.

Members of the Standing Committee are reported to have believed "that the Rules Committee will be in hot water if nothing is done to reform discovery. Critics like Vice President Dan Quayle are pushing for mathat the amendments have gone into effect [7] and are the rule in federal court (except for the many districts that have taken advantage of the possibility to "opt out" of them by local rule). It is worthy of note, however, that the disclosure provisions were recommended by the Advisory Committee on Civil Rules, the Standing Committee, and the Judicial Conference of the United States, were promulgated by the Supreme Court, and were allowed to go into effect by Congress "in the face of nearly universal criticism from every conceivable sector of our judicial system, including judges, practitioners, litigants, academics, public interest groups, and national, state, and local bar and professional groups." [8] In the 1988 Judicial Improvements Act, Congress mandated that the Advisory Committee open its process to enhanced participation. [9] Despite the new openness of the rulemaking process, amended Rule 26 appears strongly at odds with majority opinion of the profession. [10]

The impetus for the disclosure regime was the dissatisfaction with the traditional system of discovery. [11] The complaints regarding discovery largely focus on its failure to achieve "the just, speedy, and inexpensive determination of every action," [12] the stated objective of the Federal Rules of Civil Procedure. Although the complaints regarding discovery's ills lack the support of empirical data, widespread perceptions and anecdotal evidence do suggest that the current system contains flaws. [13] A major purpose of the revision of Rule 26 is to accelerate the exchange of basic information about a case and to eliminate the paper work involved in requesting such information. [14]

The complaints about the system of discovery, and the proposals of a

jor change, and Sen. Joseph Biden Jr. (D–Del.) has already pushed through the Civil Justice Reform Act, which requires civil-justice reform plans in every district. Waiting any longer, the other committee members reason, could leave the judiciary and its rule-making process in the dust." Pelham, A Legend Worries, Legal Times, June 29, 1993, p. 6.

7. A discussion of the procedure of the amendments' passage is outside the scope of this section. For a detailed analysis of this process, see the statement of Justice White in connection with adoption of the amendments, reprinted 146 F.R.D. at 501–506, and Bell, Varner & Gottschalk, Automatic Discovery—The Rush to Reform, 1993, 27 Ga.L.Rev. 1, 24–39.

8. 146 F.R.D. at 512 (Scalia, J., dissenting). See also Cortese & Blaner, A Change In the Rules Draws Fire, Natl.L.J., Oct. 18, 1993, at 25, 26 (widespread opposition to disclosure).

"The reaction of the organized bar to the prospect of disclosure, however, can best be described as sheer horror." Mayer, note 1 above, at 81.

Since it is a matter of public record, Pelham, note 6 above, the present author should note that as a member of the Standing Committee he voted against the disclosure amendments.

9. 28 U.S.C.A. § 2073. See § 62 above; Mullenix, note 5 above, at 836; Bell, Varner & Gottschalk, note 7 above, at 1, 21–23.

10. See, e.g., Samborn, note 2 above, at 4 ("In most cases it [disclosure] isn't necessary and creates more problems than it resolves").

11. See § 81 above.

12. Rule 1, Federal Rules of Civil Procedure.

13. A detailed analysis of the criticisms of discovery is outside the scope of this section. Criticism of the traditional discovery system has spawned a large amount of literature. See, e.g., Frankel, Disclosure in the Federal Courts: A Cure for the Discovery Ills?, 1993, 25 Ariz.St.L.J. 249, 253–264. See also the materials cited in § 81 nn. 11–13 above.

14. See the Advisory Committee Note, 146 F.R.D. at 628.

disclosure regime, are not novel ideas.[15] Moreover, several of the Federal Rules of Civil Procedure seem to support the ideas for which the proponents of disclosure stand.[16] Whether amended Rule 26 will alleviate the problems of discovery and help achieve the objectives of the Federal Rules is the center of much debate.

The theories of discovery and disclosure are inherently different.[17] Under a system of discovery, advocates must attempt to discover evidence from their opponent; the party seeking the evidence controls the process. The evidence-seeking party must affirmatively ask for evidence and specify what information it wishes the evidence-possessor to produce. Conversely, under a system of disclosure, advocates must disclose all relevant information of which they are aware. Here, the evidence-possessor has principal control over the process. Between these two opposing regimes lies a broad middle ground. A system of exchanging evidence may combine elements of both systems by supplementing initial disclosures by further discovery. Amended Rule 26 adopts this relatively moderate, or middle-ground, approach.[18] Note, however, that there are proponents of a more dramatic shift toward a system of disclosure.[19]

"Required disclosures," the name used in Rule 26(a), is a descriptive label; however, the same idea that such a name embodies has many aliases. "Voluntary disclosure," [20] "informal discovery," [21] "cooperative lawyering," [22] and "show and tell" [23] are a few examples. Whatever the label, disclosure embodies a goal of requiring attorneys to exchange certain documents and other information without a prior request and without interference from the court.

Rule 26(a), as amended in 1993, calls for three waves of disclosures. In the initial disclosures each party must provide to its opponent: (1) names of individuals likely to have information relevant to disputed facts alleged with particularity in the pleadings; [24] (2) a copy of, or a descrip-

---

15. See, e.g., Brazil, The Adversary Character of Civil Discovery: A Critique and Proposals for Change, 1978, 31 Vand. L.Rev. 1296; Schwarzer, The Federal Rules, The Adversary Process, and Discovery Reform, 1989, 50 U.Pitt.L.Rev. 703; Schwarzer, Slaying the Monsters of Cost and Delay: Would Disclosure Be More Effective than Discovery?, 1991, 74 Judicature 178; Manual For Complex Litigation, 2d ed. 1985, § 21.422 (informal discovery recommended in complex cases).

16. Mullenix, note 5 above, at 809.

17. Frankel, note 13 above, at 252–253.

18. See generally Rules 26(a)(5), 26(b), and the Advisory Committee's Notes to those rules.

19. See the articles by Judge Schwarzer, note 15 above.

20. Frankel, note 13 above, at 249.

21. Mullenix, note 5 above, at 797.

22. Id. at 811.

23. Ibid.

24. Rule 26(a)(1)(A). The Chairman of the Advisory Committee on Civil Rules, Judge Patrick E. Higginbotham, and the Reporter for the Committee, Dean Edward H. Cooper, prepared a Summary of Recent Amendments that was widely distributed in December 1993. Among other places it is published in Legal Times, Dec. 6, 1993, p. 12. With regard to the critical language about "disputed facts alleged with particularity" they say: "Disclosure relates to disputed facts, not admitted facts. The reference to particular pleading responds to the concern that broad notice pleading allegations may suggest a scope of disclosure out of proportion to any real need or use. The Note states that the greater the specificity and clarity of the pleadings, the more complete should be the listing of witnesses and documents."

tion and the location of, all documents, data compilations, and tangible things that are relevant to the disputed facts alleged with particularity in the pleadings;[25] (3) a computation of any damages claimed by the disclosing party;[26] and (4) any insurance agreements that indicate that an insurer will satisfy all or part of a judgment.[27] The deadline for these initial disclosures is ten days after the parties have the meeting required by Rule 26(f).[28]

A second wave requires a party to disclose the identity of experts that the party may use at trial, the opinions that such experts will express, and the basis of such expert opinions. Normally the court will specify the timing for these disclosures.[29]

A final wave requires disclosures shortly before trial of information regarding evidence that may be used at trial "other than solely for impeachment purposes." A party must identify each witness that it expects to call,[30] witnesses whose testimony is expected to be presented by means of a deposition,[31] and each document or other exhibit that the party expects to offer in evidence.[32] Unless otherwise ordered by the court, these final disclosures must be made at least 30 days before trial.

Within 14 days of these final disclosures, a party may submit objections to the use of depositions or to the admissibility of documents or exhibits that have been listed in the final disclosures. Objections not made at that time, other than objections under Evidence Rules 402 and 403, are waived unless excused by the court for good cause.[33] Amended Rule 26 also imposes a duty upon parties to supplement its disclosures made under Rule 26(a) if the party either learns of incorrect prior

---

Mayer, note 1 above, at 113, argues that the new rules "present several difficult threshold interpretative issues, such as the meaning of 'particularity' and 'relevant.'" See his general discussion of these issues, id. at 112–116, and his particular discussion of "relevant", id. at 112 n. 97.

25. Rule 26(a)(1)(B). "The choice whether to produce copies or a description is made by the disclosing party." Summary, note 24 above.

26. Rule 26(a)(1)(C). The Advisory Committee Note says that "a party would not be expected to provide a calculation of damages which, as in many patent infringement actions, depends on information in the possession of another party or person." 146 F.R.D. at 631–632.

27. Rule 26(a)(1)(D).

28. "That section calls for a mandatory pre-disclosure conference of the parties to discuss the claims and defenses and develop a plan for disclosure and discovery, followed by the mandatory Rule 16 scheduling conference at which the judge takes appropriate action for the management of the case,

including making orders governing discovery and disclosure. In this way, courts will adapt the disclosure obligation to the needs and circumstances of particular cases, such as complex cases in which the issues may not be clearly defined at the outset of the litigation." Schwarzer, In Defense of "Automatic Disclosure in Discovery", 1993, 27 Ga.L.Rev. 655, 657.

See 8 Wright, Miller & Marcus, Civil 2d § 2051.1.

29. Rule 26(a)(2). There are timing provisions in (2)(C) if the court has not specified when the disclosures about experts are to be made.

30. Rule 26(a)(3)(A).

31. Rule 26(a)(3)(B).

32. Rule 26(a)(3)(C).

33. Rule 26(a)(3). Evidence Rule 402 makes irrelevant evidence inadmissible. Evidence Rule 403 provides for the exclusion of relevant evidence if its probative value is outweighed by the danger of prejudice, confusion, or waste of time.

disclosures or has become aware of additional relevant information.[34] Finally, to put teeth into all of its previous provisions, Rule 26(g) provides for sanctions for violations of discovery or disclosure.[35]

The introductory clause of Rule 26 permits a court, by local rule or order, to exempt certain types of cases from the disclosure requirements, to modify the nature of information to be disclosed, or to eliminate or modify the disclosure requirements in a particular case when the circumstances warrant.[36] Many districts have taken advantage of that provision and have chosen to "opt out" of Rule 26(a) in whole or in part. Other districts by local rule have adopted their own requirements for disclosure, and often these are different from what is set out in Rule 26(a).[37]

Much debate has occurred, and will continue to occur, regarding the wisdom of a disclosure regime.[38] Many feel that amended Rule 26 will not cure the ills that are now thought to come from discovery. Critics of disclosure argue that the new system will only exacerbate current problems, while creating new ones. Among the problems that the critics foresee are overdisclosure, underdisclosure resulting in sanctions, disclosure disputes due to vague standards of "relevant facts" and "particularity in the pleadings," and harm to the adversary system of justice, the attorney-client relationship, and the work-product doctrine.[39] Only time

34. Rule 26(e). See § 86 nn. 52 to 60 below.

35. Rule 26(g). See § 90 below.

36. The rule also allows the parties, unless prohibited by local rule, to stipulate to eliminate or modify the disclosure requirements.

"It is expected that courts would, for example, exempt cases like Social Security reviews and government collection cases in which discovery would not be appropriate or would be unlikely. * * * The disclosure obligations specified in paragraph (1) will not be appropriate for all cases, and it is expected that changes in these obligations will be made by the courts or parties when the circumstances warrant." Advisory Committee Note to the 1993 amendment of Rule 26(a)(1), 146 F.R.D. at 629.

37. See Half of Districts Opt Out of New Civil Rules, Natl.L.J., Feb. 28, 1994, p. 5. Samborn, Rules for Discovery Uncertain, Natl.L.J., Dec. 20, 1993, pp. 1, 26. Thus, the Southern District of New York has chosen not to require disclosure while the Eastern District of New York has a disclosure rule that is based on an earlier draft of Rule 26(a)(1) and differs significantly from what is now in the national rule.

The Advisory Committee Note says: "Authorization of these local variations is, in large measure, included in order to accom-

modate the Civil Justice Reform Act of 1990, which implicitly directs districts to experiment during the study period with differing procedures to reduce the time and expense of civil litigation. The civil justice delay and expense reduction plans adopted by the courts under the Act differ as to the type, form, and timing of disclosures required." 146 F.R.D. at 629.

38. For a detailed analysis regarding the drawbacks and benefits of a disclosure regime; and whether such a regime will aid problems of discovery, see Mayer, note 1 above, at 109–135, and Frankel, note 13 above, at 249. For spirited presentation of the arguments against and for disclosure, compare Mengler, Eliminating Abusive Discovery Through Disclosure: Is It Again Time for Reform?, 1991, 138 F.R.D. 155, Bell, Varner & Gottschalk, note 7 above, and Koski, Mandatory Disclosure, A.B.A.J., Feb. 1994, p. 85, with Schwarzer, note 28 above. A more guarded view is expressed in Tobias, In Defense of Experimentation with Automatic Disclosure, 1993, 27 Ga. L.Rev. 665.

39. "[T]he new rule is fraught with mischief because it ignores both the work product doctrine and attorney-client privileges, as well as the practical realities of notice pleading." Bell, Varner & Gottschalk, note 7 above, at 5. The same authors also anticipate increased motions practice, overproduction of marginally relevant information, will tell whether the new system of required disclosure is as bad as its critics have contended or as beneficial as its advocates have hoped.

§ 84. Oral Depositions [1]

The most important of the discovery devices is the oral deposition. It is used far more often than any other device, despite the fact that it is the most expensive, because lawyers can accomplish more purposes by oral depositions than by the other devices.[2] It is the only significant discovery device that may be directed against any person and is not confined to parties to the action. It is the only discovery device that permits examination and cross-examination of a live witness by counsel, where there is no opportunity to reflect and carefully shape the information given. Thus, despite its expense, it is the most valuable device if the deponent has important information.

When the rules were originally adopted, the basic rule governing oral depositions was Rule 26. As a part of the rearrangement of the discovery rules in 1970, Rule 26 was made a general rule on the scope of discovery and the provisions for depositions were transferred, with very little change in substance, so that Rule 30 now contains the provisions dealing with the procedure for taking an oral deposition while Rule 32 has the provisions on use of a deposition.

An oral deposition may be taken in any civil action, and any person, whether or not a party to the suit, may be required to give such a deposition. Indeed a party may even take his or her own deposition.[3] When an oral deposition is sought, the party wishing to take such a deposition must give reasonable notice in writing to every other party to the action, stating the time and place where the deposition is to be taken and the name and address of the deponent.[4] If the deposition is to be of a party, this notice is sufficient to compel the party's attendance.[5] A subpoena must be served on a person not a party whose deposition is to be taken.[6]

---

and increased cost. Id. at 41–46. See also Cortese & Blaner, note 8 above, at 25–26, Koski, note 38 above, pp. 86–87, and Samborn, note 2 above, at 3.

Many of these specific criticisms are answered in Schwarzer, note 28 above, at 656–664.

§ 84

1. 8 Wright, Miller & Marcus, Civil 2d §§ 2101–2120, 2141–2157.

2. Glaser, Pretrial Discovery and the Adversary System, 1968, pp. 52–54, 63–67. This is confirmed by a more recent study. It shows that oral depositions were used in 43.1% of all cases in which any kind of discovery was employed, while interrogatories were used in 35.4% and requests for production in 14.5%. Connolly, Holleman & Kohlman, Judicial Controls and the Civil Litigative Process: Discovery, Federal Judi-

cial Center 1978, p. 30. The same authors say, at 32, that "the average case had about three notices of depositions, two interrogatories, and one request for documents; the remaining types of requests were far less frequently used."

3. Richmond v. Brooks, C.A.2d, 1955, 227 F.2d 490; Van Sciver v. Rothensies, C.C.A.3d, 1941, 122 F.2d 697; 8 Wright, Miller & Marcus, Civil 2d § 2102.

4. Rule 30(b)(1); 8 Wright, Miller & Marcus, Civil 2d § 2106.

5. E.g., Chages v. U.S., C.A.5th, 1966, 369 F.2d 643; 8 Wright, Miller & Marcus, Civil 2d § 2107.

6. El Salto, S.A. v. PSG Co., C.A.9th, 1971, 444 F.2d 477, certiorari denied 92 S.Ct. 273, 404 U.S. 940, 30 L.Ed.2d 253; Cleveland v. Palmby, D.C.Okl.1977, 75 F.R.D. 654. Subpoenas to a witness for the

Obviously it is not literally possible to take the deposition of a corporation; instead, where a corporation is involved, the information sought must be obtained from natural persons who can speak for the corporation. It is equally obvious that, since the deposition of any person can be taken, any person connected with the corporation or acquainted with the facts may be examined. A problem that has arisen frequently in the cases is the extent to which the corporation is responsible for producing those persons to have their deposition taken, and whether what they say may be used against the corporation.[7]

These questions are not specifically answered in the rules but the courts have worked out satisfactory answers from other rules. An action may be dismissed, or a default judgment entered, if a party or an officer, director, or managing agent of a party fails to appear for the taking of his or her deposition after being served with proper notice.[8] Thus, the corporation is responsible for producing its officers, directors, and managing agents if notice is given, a subpoena for their appearance is unnecessary, and sanctions may be imposed against the corporation if one of these persons fails to appear. Another provision allows introduction into evidence by an adverse party of the deposition of any one who at the time of taking the deposition was an officer, director, or managing agent of a corporation, partnership, or association.[9] Thus, the depositions of persons who fit these categories may be used against the corporate party. It is in this sense, in respect of the responsibility to produce the deponent and of the usability of the deposition, that it is said that the deposition of the corporation is "taken through" the particular individual.

The meaning of the terms "officer" and "director" has caused no difficulty, but "managing agent" has required definition. Though the question of whether a particular person is a "managing agent" is to be answered pragmatically on an ad hoc basis,[10] the courts look to see if the individual involved is invested by the corporation with general powers to exercise discretion and judgment in dealing with corporate matters,[11] whether the person can be depended upon to carry out the employer's direction to give testimony at the demand of a party engaged in litigation with the employer,[12] and whether the person can be expected to identify with the interests of the corporation rather than with those of the other parties.[13] The determination will be made by the trial court, when the

taking of a deposition are regulated by Rule 45. See 9 Wright & Miller, Civil § 2458; Siegel, Federal Subpoena Practice Under The New Rule 45 of the Federal Rules of Civil Procedure, 1991, 139 F.R.D. 197.

7. Massey, Depositions of Corporations: Problems and Solutions, 1986 Ariz.St.L.J. 81.

8. Rule 37(d). This differs from the former rule only by including "director."

9. Rule 32(a)(2).

10. Petition of Manor Inv. Co., D.C.N.Y. 1967, 43 F.R.D. 299; U.S. v. The Dorothy McAllister, D.C.N.Y.1959, 24 F.R.D. 316.

11. Kolb v. A.H. Bull S.S. Co., D.C.N.Y. 1962, 31 F.R.D. 252; Krauss v. Erie R. Co., D.C.N.Y.1954, 16 F.R.D. 126.

12. Bernstein v. N.V. Nederlandsche– Amerikaansche Stoomvaart–Maatschappij, D.C.N.Y.1953, 15 F.R.D. 37.

13. Independent Productions Corp. v. Loew's, Inc., D.C.N.Y.1959, 24 F.R.D. 19;

deposition is sought to be introduced or sanctions are asked because the person failed to appear for the taking of the deposition,[14] on the basis of these three tests.[15] Normally the corporation is accountable only for a person who was an officer, director, or managing agent at the time the deposition was taken. This is to protect the party from the admissions of disgruntled former officers or agents,[16] and is applied in the light of its purpose where the person retains such a connection with the corporation as to be loyal to it.[17]

There is frequent difficulty in designating in the notice the name of the deponent where the party is a corporation, and the opposing party does not know which corporate officer or agent has the needed information. Most cases had refused to permit a notice that called on the corporation to produce such of its officers and managing agents as have knowledge of the facts.[18] Here it would seem that the corporate party is much better able to make this determination than is its opponent, and that the requirement that the party seeking the deposition make a specific designation is a technical and unnecessary stumbling block, serving only to delay and make more expensive the discovery to which the party is entitled.

Rule 30(b)(6), added in 1970 and amended in 1971, provides a procedure to meet this problem. A party seeking the deposition of a corporation or other organization may still name a particular deponent and proceed as before, but the new rule makes an alternative available. The party seeking discovery may simply name the corporation, or other organization, as the deponent and designate with reasonable particularity the matters on which examination is requested.[19] It is then the duty of the corporation to name one or more persons who consent to testify on its behalf and these persons must testify about matters known or reasonably available to the corporation. This new procedure applies to corporations and other organizations whether or not they are a party to

Rubin v. General Tire & Rubber Co., D.C.N.Y.1955, 18 F.R.D. 51.

14. Dunn v. Standard Fire Ins. Co., D.C.Tenn.1981, 92 F.R.D. 31; Hughes Bros., Inc. v. Callanan Road Improvement Co., D.C.N.Y.1967, 41 F.R.D. 450.

15. Terry v. Modern Woodmen of America, D.C.Mo.1972, 57 F.R.D. 141; Newark Ins. Co. v. Sartain, D.C.Cal.1957, 20 F.R.D. 583, 586; 8 Wright, Miller & Marcus, Civil 2d § 2103.

16. Curry v. States Marine Corp. of Delaware, D.C.N.Y.1954, 16 F.R.D. 376; Independent Productions Corp. v. Loew's, Inc., D.C.N.Y.1959, 24 F.R.D. 19; Sykes Intl., Ltd. v. Pilch's Poultry Breeding Farms, Inc., D.C.Conn.1972, 55 F.R.D. 138; see Cameo–Parkway Records, Inc. v. Premier

Albums, Inc., D.C.N.Y.1967, 43 F.R.D. 400, 401.

17. Independent Productions Corp. v. Loew's, Inc., D.C.N.Y.1962, 30 F.R.D. 377; Fay v. U.S., D.C.N.Y.1958, 22 F.R.D. 28. Compare Proseus v. Anchor Line, Ltd., D.C.N.Y.1960, 26 F.R.D. 165, with U.S. v. The Dorothy McAllister, D.C.N.Y.1959, 24 F.R.D. 316.

18. E.g., Budget Dress Corp. v. Joint Bd. of Dress and Waistmakers' Union of Greater New York, D.C.N.Y.1959, 24 F.R.D. 506; U.S. v. Gahagan Dredging Corp., D.C.N.Y.1958, 24 F.R.D. 328; 8 Wright, Miller & Marcus, Civil 2d § 2110.

19. Marker v. Union Fidelity Life Ins. Co., D.C.N.C.1989, 125 F.R.D. 121; Volz, Depositions of Organizations: The Designation Procedure Under the Federal Rules, 1988, 33 S.D.L.Rev. 236.

the suit, but if the organization is not a party mere notice is not enough and it must be served with a subpoena.[20]

Rule 30(a)(2)(C) provides that leave of court must ordinarily be obtained if a deposition is to be taken by a party before the parties have met to develop a proposed discovery plan, as required by Rule 26(f). This is a 1993 revision of narrower provisions for leave that had previously been in the rules.[21]   In addition, leave is now required if a proposed deposition would result in more than ten depositions being taken by the plaintiffs, or by the defendants, or by third-party defendants, or if the person to be examined already has been deposed in the case.[22]

As originally adopted, the rules were silent about the order in which depositions were to be taken or other discovery was to be had.   There developed, however, very substantial case authority for the proposition that, as a general rule, the party who first made service of a notice of taking depositions was entitled to priority.[23]   The rule of priority led to a race of diligence in serving notice, though how frequently such a race occurred was a matter of dispute.[24]   The courts have always had ample power in this regard—though they often seemed reluctant to use it—and Rule 26(d), adopted in 1970, codifies that power and allows both sides to proceed with discovery unless the court has otherwise ordered.

Under the new rule, as formerly, the courts may give priority as the circumstances of a particular case require.[25]   They may stay the beginning of one examination until after the completion of another.[26]   They may provide that each party examine the other for alternating periods of

---

20. Cates v. LTV Aerospace Corp., C.A.5th, 1973, 480 F.2d 620. The subpoena to a nonparty organization must advise the organization of its duty to designate someone to testify for it. See 8 Wright, Miller & Marcus, Civil 2d § 2103.

21. 8 Wright, Miller & Marcus, Civil 2d §§ 2046.1, 2104. Leave is not required if the person to be deposed is expected to leave the United States and be unavailable for examination in this country.

22. Rules 30(a)(2)(A), (B). The numerical limit on depositions per side that can be taken without leave of court can be altered by court order or by local rule. Rule 26(b)(2).

23. 8 Wright, Miller & Marcus, Civil 2d § 2045; Younger, Priority of Pretrial Examinations in the Federal Courts—A Comment, 1959, 34 N.Y.U.L.Rev. 1271.

24. E.g., Stover v. Universal Moulded Products Corp., D.C.Pa.1950, 11 F.R.D. 90;

Sanib Corp. v. United Fruit Co., D.C.N.Y. 1955, 19 F.R.D. 9.

The extent of this problem is minimized in Glaser, Pretrial Discovery and the Adversary System, 1969, pp. 212–219.

25. E.g., Boxer v. Smith, Kline and French Laboratories, D.C.N.Y.1967, 43 F.R.D. 25; G.A. Kaeppler & Son v. Jas. H. Matthews & Co., D.C.Pa.1961, 200 F.Supp. 229; Deep South Oil Co. of Texas v. Metropolitan Life Ins. Co., D.C.N.Y.1958, 21 F.R.D. 340; Morrison Export Co. v. Goldstone, D.C.N.Y.1952, 12 F.R.D. 258.

The lower court was criticized, however, in George C. Frey Ready–Mixed Concrete, Inc. v. Pine Hill Concrete Mix Corp., C.A.2d, 1977, 554 F.2d 551, for giving priority to defendant rather than allowing both parties to proceed simultaneously.

26. Kahn v. Eaststates Gas Producing Co., D.C.Ohio 1973, 59 F.R.D. 132. A stay was refused in Black v. Sheraton Corp. of America, D.C.D.C.1974, 371 F.Supp. 97.

equal duration.[27] In the absence of a court order the parties will be free to proceed when and how they choose.

A deposition may be taken before any person authorized to administer oaths who has no disqualifying interest in the case.[28] Normally a court reporter will be selected by the party giving notice of the deposition, and the reporter will administer the oath to the deponent as well as record the testimony. But Rule 30(b)(4), added in 1970, permits the court on motion to order that the testimony be recorded by other than stenographic means, as by videotape or a tape recorder. An important decision of the District of Columbia Circuit held that experimentation with this new procedure should be encouraged rather than blocked and that the discretion of the trial court in passing on a motion to record the testimony by nonstenographic means is limited to those actions needed to ensure accuracy and trustworthiness.[29] The Advisory Committee on Civil Rules was persuaded. It proposed, and in 1993 the Supreme Court promulgated, an amendment to Rule 30(b)(2) that allows a party, without a court order, to specify the method by which the testimony was to be recorded: by sound, sound-and-visual, or stenographic means. Any party can then designate another method to record the testimony, at that party's expense, in addition to the method specified by the person taking the deposition.[30] The court reporters lobbied hard against this amendment and the House of Representatives passed a bill that would have prevented it, and the required-disclosure provisions of Rule 26(a), from going into effect, but that bill never came to a vote in the Senate and the amendment therefore became effective.[31]

At the taking of a deposition, the witness will be examined and cross-examined by counsel for the parties in the same fashion as at a trial,[32] but with one important exception. If there is objection to a question, the reporter will simply note the objection in the transcript and the witness will answer the question despite the objection.[33] The

---

27. Planning and Investing Co., S.A. v. Hemlock, D.C.N.Y.1970, 50 F.R.D. 48; Caldwell–Clements, Inc. v. McGraw–Hill Pub. Co., D.C.N.Y.1951, 11 F.R.D. 156.

28. Rule 28; 8 Wright, Miller & Marcus, Civil 2d §§ 2081–2084. See, also the provision about stipulations in Rule 29; 8 Wright, Miller & Marcus, Civil 2d §§ 2091–2094.

29. Colonial Times, Inc. v. Gasch, C.A.D.C.1975, 509 F.2d 517, noted 1975, 26 S.C.L.Rev. 753. See also Weiss v. Wayes, D.C.Pa.1990, 132 F.R.D. 152, 154.

But see United Auto., Aerospace & Agr. Implement Workers of America v. National Caucus of Labor Committees, C.A.2d, 1975, 525 F.2d 323; Barham v. IDM Corp., D.C.Ohio 1978, 78 F.R.D. 340.

See generally 8 Wright, Miller & Marcus, Civil 2d § 2115.

In another triumph of modern technology, Rule 30(b)(7) was amended in 1980 to

allow the taking of testimony at a deposition by telephone, if the court so orders or on stipulation by the parties.

30. The text of the amendment and the Committee Note to it appear 146 F.R.D. at 652–654, 663.

31. See § 83A n. 2 above.

32. Private conferences between deponents and their attorneys during the taking of a deposition are improper unless the conferences are for the purpose of determining whether a privilege should be asserted. Hall v. Clifton Precision, D.C.Pa. 1993, 150 F.R.D. 525. See also Van Pilsum v. Iowa State University of Science & Technology, D.C.Iowa 1993, 152 F.R.D. 179.

33. Rule 30(c); 8 Wright, Miller & Marcus, Civil 2d § 2113.

Under Rule 30(d)(1), as amended in 1993, objections are to be stated concisely and in a nonargumentative and nonsuggestive court can consider the objection if the deposition is offered at the trial, and at that time will refuse to allow reading of the answer to any question that was properly objectionable. If the witness refuses to answer a question put at a deposition, the examination may be adjourned, or completed on other matters, and application then made to the court to compel an answer. This is undesirable, since it delays the deposition and brings the court into a process that is intended to work largely without judicial supervision. For this reason, it is provided that expenses and attorneys' fees may be assessed if the refusal to answer was unjustified, or if there was no substantial justification for the motion to compel an answer.[34]

Most errors and irregularities in the taking of a deposition are waived unless prompt objection is made.[35] This gives the erring party an opportunity to correct the mistake; it also prevents waste of time and money by a subsequent claim to suppress a deposition because of some technical error long before. But objections to competency, relevancy, or materiality that could not have been corrected if made at the time need not be made and are not waived.[36] They may be made for the first time at the trial.[37]

The provision for protective orders gives the parties and witnesses protection before a deposition begins.[38] Continued protection during the course of the examination is provided by Rule 30(d). At any time during the taking of the deposition, on motion of the deponent or of any party[39] and upon a showing that the examination is being conducted in bad faith or in such manner as unreasonably to annoy, embarrass, or oppress the deponent or party, the court may order the termination of the examination, or may limit the scope and manner of the taking of the deposition.[40] The order may be made either by the court in which the action is pending or by the court for the district where the deposition is being taken.[41] On such a motion the only question is whether the examination is being conducted properly, and the fact that counsel did not wish further cross-examination of the deponent is not a ground for termination of the examination.[42] Grounds for terminating or limiting an

---

manner. A party may instruct a deponent not to answer only when necessary to preserve a privilege, to enforce a limitation on evidence directed by the court, or to present a motion to terminate or limit the examination.

34. Rule 37(a)(4); 8 Wright, Miller & Marcus, Civil 2d § 2288.

35. Rule 32(d); 8 Wright, Miller & Marcus, Civil 2d §§ 2153–2157.

36. Rule 32(d)(3)(A); Glenwillow Landfill, Inc. v. City of Akron, D.C.Ohio 1979, 485 F.Supp. 671, 674; 8 Wright, Miller & Marcus, Civil 2d § 2156.

37. Rule 32(b); Jordan v. Medley, C.A.D.C.1983, 711 F.2d 211.

38. See § 83 above.

39. De Wagenknecht v. Stinnes, C.A.D.C.1957, 243 F.2d 413, certiorari denied 78 S.Ct. 44, 355 U.S. 830, 2 L.Ed.2d 43.

40. 8 Wright, Miller & Marcus, Civil 2d § 2116.

41. Shawmut, Inc. v. American Viscose Corp., D.C.N.Y.1951, 11 F.R.D. 562.

42. Broadbent v. Moore McCormack Lines, Inc., D.C.Pa.1946, 5 F.R.D. 220.

Motions to terminate depositions were also denied in In re Master Key Litigation, C.A.9th, 1974, 507 F.2d 292, and in Paiewonsky v. Paiewonsky, D.C.V.I.1970, 50 F.R.D. 379.

examination include insistent questioning on privileged matters,[43] or that the examination has gone too far afield,[44] or that unwarranted attempts are being made to pry into a party's preparation for trial.[45] The physical condition of the witness and the adequacy of the examination which has already taken place are other factors that may be considered.[46]

A deposition must be transcribed, submitted to the witness for examination and signature, certified by the officer before whom the deposition was taken, and, unless otherwise ordered by the court, filed with the court.[47]

The provisions governing the use of a deposition at a trial or hearing are in Rule 32(a). Even if the requirements of that rule are met the deposition can be used only to the extent that the matters contained in it are admissible under the rules of evidence "applied as though the witness were then present and testifying." The quoted language did not appear in the pre–1970 rule. It recognizes that the rule for use of depositions is itself an exception to the hearsay rule. Thus, a deposition that satisfies Rule 32(a) is not objectionable on the ground that it is hearsay. Instead it is tested as if the witness were giving the answers orally. An answer that itself contains hearsay would be subject to that rule of evidence, but the fact that the witness himself was not testifying in court would not permit a hearsay objection.[48]

Rule 32(a)(1) permits use of any deposition by any party to contradict or impeach the testimony of deponent as a witness.[49] As amended in 1980 it also allows use of the deposition for any other purpose permitted by the Federal Rules of Evidence.[50]

43. Magida on Behalf of Vulcan Detinning Co. v. Continental Can Co., D.C.N.Y. 1951, 12 F.R.D. 74; Lever Bros. Co. v. Proctor & Gamble Mfg. Co., D.C.Md.1941, 38 F.Supp. 680; Lewis v. United Air Lines Transport Corp., D.C.Pa.1940, 32 F.Supp. 21.

44. Pittsburgh Plate Glass Co. v. Allied Chem. Alkali Workers of America, Local Union No. 1, D.C.Ohio 1951, 11 F.R.D. 518; Macrina v. Smith, D.C.Pa.1955, 18 F.R.D. 254.

45. Schweinert v. Insurance Co. of North America, D.C.N.Y.1940, 1 F.R.D. 247.

46. De Wagenknecht v. Stinnes, C.A.D.C.1957, 243 F.2d 413, certiorari denied 78 S.Ct. 44, 355 U.S. 830, 2 L.Ed.2d 43.

47. Rule 30(c), (e), (f); 8 Wright, Miller & Marcus, Civil 2d §§ 2117–2119. See Bernstein v. Brenner, D.C.D.C.1970, 51 F.R.D. 9.

The witness may change his or her answers when the transcript is presented for signing but the original answers must remain part of the record. Rogers v. Roth, C.A.10th, 1973, 477 F.2d 1154. The witness must state the reasons for making the changes. Sanford v. CBS, Inc., D.C.Ill. 1984, 594 F.Supp. 713.

Rules 5(d) and 30(f)(1) were amended in 1980 to give the court power to order that a deposition need not be filed. However the tempestuous history of this amendment strongly suggests that this is a power to be exercised only in a particular case when strong public or private interests compel waiving the filing requirement. See 4 Wright & Miller, Civil § 1152.

48. 8 Wright, Miller & Marcus, Civil 2d § 2143. See also Evidence Rules 802 and 804(b)(1).

49. Merchants Motor Freight v. Downing, C.A.8th, 1955, 227 F.2d 247; Lewis v. United Air Lines Transport Corp., D.C.Conn.1939, 27 F.Supp. 946; 8 Wright, Miller & Marcus, Civil 2d § 2144.

50. Evidence Rule 801(d)(1)(A) excludes a deposition of a witness who testifies at the trial from the definition of hearsay, and thus the contradictory statements in the deposition may be given substantive effect. In addition, Evidence Rule 801(d)(2) makes the statement of an agent or servant admis-

Under Rule 32(a)(2) the deposition of a party, the officer, director, or managing agent of a party, or of a person designated by an organization to testify on its behalf, may be used by an adverse party for any purpose.[51]

Rule 32(a)(3) authorizes use of the deposition of any witness, whether a party or not, by any party for any purpose if one of five conditions is met.[52] Such use is permitted if the witness is dead, or if the witness is more than 100 miles from the place of trial and the absence was not procured by the party offering the deposition, or if the witness is unable to attend or testify because of age, sickness, infirmity or imprisonment, or if the party offering the deposition has been unable to procure the attendance of the witness by subpoena. The fifth of the conditions permitted by this rule is that a deposition may be used if, upon application and notice, the court finds that such exceptional circumstances exist as to make it desirable, in the interest of justice and with due regard to the importance of presenting the testimony of witnesses orally in open court, to admit the deposition. This provision has been regarded as an attempt at liberalization of the hearsay rule[53] but it has hardly ever been used.[54] Rule 32(a)(3)(B), allowing a party who is more than 100 miles from the place of trial to introduce his own deposition,[55] is also a liberalization of traditional notions of the hearsay rule.

Rule 32(a) has always purported to state the circumstances in which a deposition taken in one action can be used in another action. In fact, the rule was quite misleading and the courts allowed depositions to be used in these circumstances more broadly than the rule seemed to indicate. Since 1975 this matter has been covered also by Evidence Rule 804(b)(1), which allowed depositions taken in other actions to be used more often than Civil Rule 32(a) had seemed to permit, though arguably less often than what the courts had been allowing in practice. Rule 32(a) was amended in 1980 to make it as broad as the Evidence Rule.[56]

sible against the principal under the circumstances stated in that rule.

51. Coughlin v. Capitol Cement Co., C.A.5th, 1978, 571 F.2d 290, 308; Fey v. Walston & Co., Inc., C.A.7th, 1974, 493 F.2d 1036; 8 Wright, Miller & Marcus, Civil 2d § 2145. Under Evidence Rule 801(d)(2) this use of a deposition is defined as not being hearsay.

52. 8 Wright, Miller & Marcus, Civil 2d § 2146.

53. Weinstein, Probative Force of Hearsay, 1961, 46 Iowa L.Rev. 331, 340.

54. Huff v. Marine Tank Testing Corp., C.A.4th, 1980, 631 F.2d 1140; Borchardt v. U.S., D.C.Wis.1991, 133 F.R.D. 547; Reber v. General Motors Corp., D.C.Pa.1987, 669 F.Supp. 717; Lebeck v. William A. Jarvis, Inc., D.C.Pa.1956, 145 F.Supp. 706, 724–725, reversed in part on other grounds C.A.3d, 1957, 250 F.2d 285; Hart v. Fried-

man, D.C.Pa.1961, 29 F.R.D. 2. Hostility of a witness was held insufficient for application of this provision. Klepal v. Pennsylvania R. Co., C.A.2d, 1956, 229 F.2d 610.

55. E.g., Stewart v. Meyers, C.A.7th, 1965, 353 F.2d 691; Richmond v. Brooks, C.A.2d, 1955, 227 F.2d 490; Glaverbel Societe Anonyme v. Northlake Marketing & Supply, Inc., D.C.Ind.1991, 139 F.R.D. 368, 370; F. S. Sinkwich, Inc. v. Texaco Refining & Marketing, Inc. D.C.Ga.1988, 120 F.R.D. 540, 541–542. But cf. Vevelstad v. Flynn, C.A.9th, 1956, 230 F.2d 695, certiorari denied 77 S.Ct. 40, 352 U.S. 827, 1 L.Ed.2d 49. See Note, Offering Plaintiff's Deposition in Evidence, 1956, 69 Harv.L.Rev. 1503; 8 Wright, Miller & Marcus, Civil 2d § 2147.

56. See 8 Wright, Miller & Marcus, Civil 2d § 2150.

If one party offers in evidence part of a deposition, an adverse party may require him or her to introduce any other part of it that ought in fairness to be considered with the part introduced, and any party may introduce any other parts.[57] This guards against giving a distorted picture of the deponent's testimony by introducing only a part of it.

Until 1975 Rule 32(c) provided that a party did not make a person its own witness for any purpose by taking the person's deposition.[58] This was repealed in 1975, on the ground that it was no longer needed in the light of the adoption of the Evidence Rules that year. This overlooked the fact that the Evidence Rules were substantially changed in Congress, and, as finally adopted, continued to recognize state rules of incompetency such as Dead Man's Acts in many cases.[59] Thus, to the extent that Rule 32(c) had been significant with regard to incompetency, it should not have been repealed. The saving grace with regard to the mistaken repeal of Rule 32(c) is that it shed almost no light on questions of waiver of incompetency, and, in particular, it was not settled whether the estate of a deceased party waived the protection of a Dead Man's Act by taking a deposition of the survivor. A powerful argument can be made in favor of waiver in this situation,[60] but the fact is that the rules are silent on the question and incompetency, when it exists at all under Rule 601, exists only because of a state rule of incompetency. Since the initial protection comes solely from state law, the conditions on which it is waived must also depend on state law.[61]

§ 85. Depositions on Written Questions [1]

Rule 31 specifies the procedure to be followed in taking depositions by written questions. This is an alternative to the taking of depositions by oral examination provided by Rule 30. The advantage of a deposition on written questions is that counsel for the parties need not go to some distant place to be present at the taking of the deposition. Instead they serve on each other questions and cross questions—and even redirect and recross questions—that they wish to have put to the deponent.[2] These are then sent to the officer who is to take the deposition. The officer puts the questions to the witness, records the answers, and

---

57. Rule 32(a)(4); Ikerd v. Lapworth, C.A.7th, 1970, 435 F.2d 197; Mangual v. Prudential Lines, Inc., D.C.Pa.1971, 53 F.R.D. 301; 8 Wright, Miller & Marcus, Civil 2d § 2148.

The otherwise similar provision of Evidence Rule 106 says "which ought in fairness to be considered contemporaneously with it." The word "contemporaneously" does not appear in Civil Rule 32(a)(4).

58. 8 Wright, Miller & Marcus, Civil 2d § 2152; Keeton, Proprietorship over Deponents, 1955, 68 Harv.L.Rev. 600.

59. Evidence Rule 601. See § 93 below.

60. Degnan, The Evidence Law of Discovery: Exclusion of Evidence Because of Fear of Perjury, 1965, 43 Texas L.Rev. 435.

61. Prior to the repeal of Rule 32(c) and the adoption of the Evidence Rules, the cases were divided on this point. See 8 Wright, Miller & Marcus, Civil 2d § 2152.

§ 85

1. 8 Wright, Miller & Marcus, Civil 2d §§ 2131–2133; Schmertz, Written Depositions under Federal and State Rules as Cost–Effective Discovery at Home and Abroad, 1970, 16 Vill.L.Rev. 7.

2. Rule 31(a); 8 Wright, Miller & Marcus, Civil 2d § 2132.

transcribes and files the deposition as with an oral deposition.[3] The officer is merely to record what the witness says in response to the various questions propounded to him or her. Comments by the officer about the demeanor of the witness or about remarks he or she made before the questions were put are improper and will be stricken.[4]

Though Rule 31 appears to offer a saving in expense where the deposition is to be taken at some faroff place,[5] its advantages are largely illusory. The procedure is more cumbersome than an oral examination, and is less suitable for a complicated inquiry, or for a searching interrogation of a hostile or reluctant witness. Thus, Justice Whittaker, while still a district judge, commented: "From my long experience at the Bar, I can readily agree that the device of taking a deposition upon written interrogatories under Rule 31, except for the proof of formal matters, is a tool of discovery very inferior to oral examination." [6]

The court may make protective orders where a deposition is to be taken on written questions, and in particular may order that the deposition not be taken except upon oral examination.[7] It also may authorize oral cross-examination though the deposition is otherwise to be taken on written questions.[8] Usually such authorization is denied and the party is required to attempt first to conduct his examination by cross-questions, with leave to apply for oral examination if it appears that further cross-examination is necessary.[9]

As originally adopted the procedure provided by Rule 31 was known as a "deposition upon written interrogatories." This was an invitation to confusion with Rule 33, providing for the use of interrogatories to parties. These are quite different devices, with different purposes and different procedures and they are applicable to different persons.[10] Rule 31, as it was amended in 1970, changed the name of the device to "deposition upon written questions" and thus avoided this confusion.

§ 86. Interrogatories to Parties [1]

Rule 33 provides a procedure by which a party may require another party to give written answers under oath to written questions relevant

---

3. Rule 31(b); 8 Wright, Miller & Marcus, Civil 2d § 2133.

4. Gill v. Stolow, D.C.N.Y.1954, 16 F.R.D. 9.

5. See J.C. Nichols Co. v. Mid–States Freight Lines, D.C.Mo.1949, 9 F.R.D. 553, 554.

6. Perry v. Edwards, D.C.Mo.1954, 16 F.R.D. 131, 133. See also Mill–Run Tours, Inc. v. Khashoggi, D.C.N.Y.1989, 124 F.R.D. 547, 549.

7. Rule 26(c)(3); Smith v. Morrison–Knudsen Co., D.C.N.Y.1958, 22 F.R.D. 108; Lago Oil & Transport Co. v. U.S., D.C.N.Y. 1951, 97 F.Supp. 438. But cf. J.C. Nichols Co. v. Mid–States Freight Lines, D.C.Mo. 1949, 9 F.R.D. 553; Kiachif v. Philco Intl.

Corp., D.C.N.Y.1950, 10 F.R.D. 277; 8 Wright, Miller & Marcus, Civil 2d § 2039.

8. Winograd Bros. v. Chase Bank, D.C.N.Y.1939, 31 F.Supp. 91.

9. Wheeler v. West India S.S. Co., D.C.N.Y.1951, 11 F.R.D. 396; U.S. v. National City Bank of New York, D.C.N.Y. 1940, 1 F.R.D. 367.

10. Smith v. Morrison–Knudsen Co., D.C.N.Y.1958, 22 F.R.D. 108. See § 86 below.

§ 86

1. 8 Wright, Miller & Marcus, Civil 2d §§ 2161–2182; Haydock & Herr, Interrogatories: Questions and Answers, 1981, 1 Rev.Litig. 263.

to the subject matter of the action. Where the person who has the information sought is a party, whether to use interrogatories or to take the party's deposition is a choice dependent on practical considerations.[2]

Inevitably much of the efficacy that attaches to oral examination on deposition is lost when Rule 33 interrogatories are used. At the very outset, the interrogated party is fully apprised of all the questions that will be addressed to him. He is accorded time to ponder and reflect on his answers and to formulate them in writing with exactness and caution. He may take the advice of counsel and secure the assistance of other persons in framing his replies, benefits that he does not enjoy at a rapid oral examination. Moreover, the examining party is handicapped by the fact that it is required to formulate all of its questions in advance of receiving answers to any of them. Attempts at evasion, which might be met by a persistent oral examination, cannot be easily dealt with. The flexibility and the potency of oral depositions is in large part lacking in written interrogatories to an adverse party.

Nevertheless, Rule 33 interrogatories fulfill important functions. They are much less expensive than a deposition, either orally or on written questions, where the answers must be stenographically recorded and transcribed. They are useful in narrowing the issues about items that though formally denied in the pleadings are not seriously disputed. Resort may successfully be had to Rule 33 for the purpose of obtaining details on matters concerning which the allegations of the pleadings are general in character. Interrogatories had been a simple mode of obtaining names and addresses of persons having knowledge of pertinent facts, and information about the existence of documentary evidence. Now that information will normally come by required disclosures under Rule 26(a)(1). An attempt may even be made to secure damaging admissions by taking the depositions of a party whose answers to interrogatories are disingenuous. The replies to interrogatories may be used for purposes of impeachment if the oral examination leads to contradiction.

Despite these advantages, "interrogatories are the most unpopular device because they can embody either the best or worst qualities of discovery: some pursue information too skillfully, others too crudely."[3] Disputes over interrogatories frequently must be resolved by the court and this has been burdensome and irritating to the judges. The amendments to Rule 33 adopted in 1970 were intended to remedy some of the defects in the prior rule and to reduce the number of cases involving interrogatories that the courts must pass upon.

2. 8 Wright, Miller & Marcus, Civil 2d § 2163; Haydock & Herr, note 1 above, at 264–265.

3. Glaser, Pretrial Discovery and the Adversary System, 1968, p. 149. The reasons for this are spelled out, id. at pp. 149–153. See also Flegal & Umin, Curbing Discovery Abuses in Civil Litigation: We're Not There Yet, 1981 B.Y.U.L.Rev. 597, 604–606.

But compare Haydock & Herr, note 1 above, at 307: "We do know that rule 33 provides an efficient, effective, and economical discovery tool. Implementations of this system requires attorneys to submit only those interrogatories necessary to obtain essential information and to respond in good faith to properly submitted interrogatories."

The scope of examination under Rule 33 is the same as that for the other discovery devices, as defined in Rule 26 and already discussed.[4] The only problems of scope that are peculiar to Rule 33 are whether interrogatories may be used to ascertain opinions, contentions, and conclusions of the adverse party, and whether the party may be required to answer interrogatories where it lacks personal knowledge of the matter or is required to do research to prepare its answers.

Prior to the 1970 amendments of Rule 33, the decisions on the propriety of interrogatories inquiring about opinions, contentions, and conclusions had been extremely numerous and quite inconsistent.[5] The better view, however, was that "the line between fact and conclusion is frequently an uncertain and illogical one," [6] and that an interrogatory was proper, regardless of its label, if it would serve any substantial purpose, either in leading to evidence or in clarifying the issues in the case.[7]

This better view was written into the rules in 1970 in what is now Rule 33(c).[8] It provides that an otherwise proper interrogatory "is not necessarily objectionable merely because an answer to the interrogatory involves an opinion or contention that relates to fact or the application of law to fact * * *." The word "merely" is significant and should not be overlooked. The interrogatory may still be objectionable because in the circumstances of the particular case an answer to the interrogatory will not serve any useful purpose.[9] But there is no longer any automatic rule that an interrogatory must be disallowed merely because it calls for an opinion or a contention.

The rule is limited to opinions and contentions that relate to "fact or the application of law to fact." It does not authorize interrogatories calling for legal conclusions as such.[10] But many legal conclusions do require the application of law to fact and are the proper subject of interrogatories under the amended rule.[11]

The more liberal cases permitting interrogatories about the contentions of the opponent are not always an unmixed blessing. To the extent that they put an end to attempted distinctions between facts and conclusions, they are desirable. But an argument has been made by a distinguished critic that the cases allowing interrogatories about conten-

4. See § 81 above.

5. 8 Wright, Miller & Marcus, Civil 2d § 2167.

6. B. & S. Drilling Co. v. Halliburton Oil Well Cementing Co., D.C.Tex.1959, 24 F.R.D. 1, 7.

7. Hartsfield v. Gulf Oil Corp., D.C.Pa. 1962, 29 F.R.D. 163, 165; and cases cited 8 Wright, Miller & Marcus, Civil 2d § 2167.

8. From 1970 to 1993 this was Rule 33(b).

9. Scovill Mfg. Co. v. Sunbeam Corp., D.C.Del.1973, 357 F.Supp. 943; Comment, Civil Procedure—Opinion Interrogatories After the 1970 Amendment to Federal Rule 33(b), 1975, 53 N.C.L.Rev. 695, 705.

10. Advisory Committee Note, 48 F.R.D. 487, 524; O'Brien v. International Broth. of Elec. Workers, D.C.Ga.1977, 443 F.Supp. 1182; Union Carbide Corp. v. Travelers Indem. Co., D.C.Pa.1973, 61 F.R.D. 411; Sargent–Welch Scientific Co. v. Ventron Corp., D.C.Ill.1973, 59 F.R.D. 500.

11. Schaap v. Executive Industries, Inc., D.C.Ill.1990, 130 F.R.D. 384, 387–388; Donovan v. Porter, D.C.Md.1984, 584 F.Supp. 202, 209–210. See Haydock & Herr, note 1 above, at 283–286.

tions have revived, under a different name, the unlamented bill of particulars, which was abolished in 1948.[12] The generalized pleading permitted by the rules has significance beyond the pleading rules themselves. It represents a broad determination that it is not desirable or feasible to tie a party down at an early stage to a particular theory of the case, and that judgment must be allowed to go according to the facts as they develop at the trial, not limited by the belief of the party before the trial about what the facts may be.

Amended Rule 33(c) seeks to meet this objection by providing that the court may order that an interrogatory calling for an opinion or contention need not be answered until after designated discovery has been completed, or at a pretrial conference, or at some other later time. Thus, if a malpractice plaintiff is sent an interrogatory asking her to specify the respects in which she claims defendant was negligent, and she does not know as yet because she was under anesthesia at the time, she should not be required to answer the interrogatory until she has ample opportunity through discovery of her own to see if she can prove specific acts of negligence.[13] The power to defer answers is useful, since it enables the court to protect a party from being tied down before the party has had an opportunity fully to explore the case,[14] but it is a power that should not be exercised automatically but only in appropriate cases.[15]

As a general rule a party in answering interrogatories must furnish information that is in its possession and can be given without undue labor and expense.[16] It cannot generally be forced to prepare its opponent's case.[17] Consequently interrogatories that require a party to make investigations, research, or compilation of data are in many circumstances improper.[18] Even if the records containing the desired information are in the possession of the interrogated party, its adversary cannot use interrogatories to evade the burden of compiling data at its own expense if the records are available for its inspection under Rule 34 or with the consent of the interrogated party.[19] What is now Rule 33(d)[20] gives the party on whom an interrogatory is served the option to make

12. James, The Revival of Bills of Particulars under the Federal Rules, 1958, 71 Harv.L.Rev. 1473.

13. A rather different result was reached on these facts under the former rule in Bynum v. U.S., D.C.La.1964, 36 F.R.D. 14.

14. Dow Corning Corp. v. Surgitek, Inc., D.C.Wis.1973, 61 F.R.D. 578; Diamond Crystal Salt Co. v. Package Masters, Inc., D.C.Del.1970, 319 F.Supp. 911. See James, Hazard & Leubsdorf, Civil Procedure, 4th ed. 1992, § 5.12.

15. In re One Bancorp Securities Litigation, D.C.Me.1991, 134 F.R.D. 4, 7–8; Diversified Products Corp. v. Sports Center Co., D.C.Md.1967, 42 F.R.D. 3, 5.

16. Flour Mills of America, Inc. v. Pace, D.C.Okl.1977, 75 F.R.D. 676; Cinema Amusements v. Loew's Inc., D.C.Del.1947, 7 F.R.D. 318.

17. Olmert v. Nelson, D.C.D.C.1973, 60 F.R.D. 369; La Chemise Lacoste v. Alligator Co., Inc., D.C.Del.1973, 60 F.R.D. 164; Kainz v. Anheuser–Busch, Inc., D.C.Ill. 1954, 15 F.R.D. 242.

18. E.g., Deering Milliken Research Corp. v. Tex–Elastic Corp., D.C.S.C.1970, 320 F.Supp. 806; 8 Wright, Miller & Marcus, Civil 2d § 2174.

19. See 8 Wright, Miller & Marcus, Civil 2d § 2174.

20. From 1970 to 1993 this provision was Rule 33(c).

available its records from which an answer can be found [21] in any case in which the burden of finding the answer is substantially the same for the party serving the interrogatory as for the party served.[22] That provision was amended in 1980 to provide that a party exercising this option must specify the records from which the answer can be found in sufficient detail to permit the interrogating party to locate and to identify them as readily as can the party served.[23]

The objection that preparing an answer would require research by the interrogated party is not enough to bar interrogatories in every case. In order to justify sustaining an objection to such an interrogatory— except where the option provided by Rule 33(d) has been used—it must be shown that the research is unduly burdensome and oppressive.[24] The party seeking to avoid answering the interrogatories carries the burden of showing that the information sought is not readily available to it,[25] and where there is conflict the court will make its own determination of the cost and inconvenience of answering the interrogatories, rather than relying on bare assertions about this by the party.[26]

Some cases say that a party who has no personal knowledge of an incident may not be required to search out information and answer interrogatories on the basis of such hearsay,[27] but such statements are too broad. A party is charged with knowledge of what its agents know, or what is in records available to it, or even, for purposes of Rule 33, what others have told it on which it intends to rely in its suit.[28] Nor can it refuse to answer interrogatories on the ground that the information sought is solely within the knowledge of its attorney.[29]

21. 8 Wright, Miller & Marcus, Civil 2d § 2178. See Harlem River Consumers Co-op., Inc. v. Associated Grocers of Harlem, Inc., D.C.N.Y.1974, 64 F.R.D. 459; Concept Indus. Inc. v. Carpet Factory, Inc., D.C.Wis. 1973, 59 F.R.D. 546; Ballard v. Allegheny Airlines, Inc., D.C.Pa.1972, 54 F.R.D. 67.

22. Daiflon, Inc. v. Allied Chem. Corp., C.A.10th, 1976, 534 F.2d 221, certiorari denied 97 S.Ct. 239, 429 U.S. 886, 50 L.Ed.2d 168; Mid–America Facilities, Inc. v. Argonaut Ins. Co., D.C.Wis.1978, 78 F.R.D. 497.

23. Rainbow Pioneer No. 44–18–04A v. Hawaii–Nevada Inv. Corp., C.A.9th, 1983, 711 F.2d 902; Avramidis v. Atlantic Richfield Co., D.C.Mass.1988, 120 F.R.D. 450. This does not mean that exact documents must be identified. See Sherman & Kinnard, Federal Court Discovery in the 80s— Making the Rules Work, 1981, 2 Rev.Litig. 9, 14–21.

24. Roesberg v. Johns–Manville Corp., D.C.Pa.1980, 85 F.R.D. 292; Rogers v. Tri-State Materials Corp., D.C.W.Va.1970, 51 F.R.D. 234; 8 Wright, Miller & Marcus, Civil 2d § 2174.

25. Sherman Park Community Assn. v. Wauwatosa Realty Co., D.C.Wis.1980, 486 F.Supp. 838; Martin v. Easton Pub. Co., D.C.Pa.1980, 85 F.R.D. 312.

26. Tivoli Realty v. Paramount Pictures, D.C.Del.1950, 10 F.R.D. 201; State ex rel. Gamble Constr. Co. v. Carroll, Mo. 1966, 408 S.W.2d 34.

27. E.g., Robinson v. Tracy, D.C.Mo. 1954, 16 F.R.D. 113; Bullard v. Universal Millwork Corp., D.C.N.Y.1960, 25 F.R.D. 342.

28. Miller v. Doctor's General Hosp., D.C.Okl.1977, 76 F.R.D. 136; Stonybrook Tenants Assn., Inc. v. Alpert, D.C.Conn. 1961, 29 F.R.D. 165; and cases cited 8 Wright, Miller & Marcus, Civil 2d § 2177.

29. Hickman v. Taylor, 1947, 67 S.Ct. 385, 390, 329 U.S. 495, 504, 91 L.Ed. 451; General Dynamics Corp. v. Selb Mfg. Co., C.A.8th, 1973, 481 F.2d 1204, certiorari denied 94 S.Ct. 926, 414 U.S. 1162, 39 L.Ed.2d 116; Shapiro, Some Problems of Discovery in an Adversary System, 1979, 63 Minn.L.Rev. 1055, 1071–1072.

It is clear, from Rule 26(b)(1), that interrogatories may properly be used to ascertain the existence and location of documents or tangible things.[30] In the past it was not clear whether these interrogatories might require that copies of documents be attached to the answers, or whether a subsequent Rule 34 motion was required for production. A 1949 decision said, correctly at the time, that there was "irreconcilable conflict" among the decisions on this point.[31] The conflict has vanished in the more recent decisions, which are in agreement that copies of documents may not be obtained by interrogatories.[32]

Amendments to Rule 33 were made in 1948 to resolve two questions on which the decisions had been conflicting. Some courts had set an arbitrary limit on the number of interrogatories a party might submit. The amendment provided that "the number of interrogatories or of sets of interrogatories to be served is not limited except as justice requires to protect the party from annoyance, expense, embarrassment, or oppression." [33] Another amendment made at the same time provided that interrogatories may be served after a deposition has been taken, and a deposition may be sought after interrogatories have been answered, subject to the power of the court to make a protective order if justice so requires.[34] Thus, under the amended rules the two procedures were clearly regarded as complementary. A party could use both depositions and interrogatories, either consecutively or simultaneously, so long as the other party could not show some hardship or injustice from use of the two procedures. These 1948 amendments were dropped from Rule 33 when it was further amended in 1970, on the ground that they were now covered by general provisions, applicable to all discovery devices. At that time Rule 26(a) said that in the absence of a protective order "the frequency of use of these methods is not limited," and Rule 26(d) permitted methods of discovery to be used in any sequence.[35] Rule 26(d) has remained unchanged, but in 1993 what had been Rule 26(a) was repealed, numerical limits were put on the number of depositions and interrogatories, and courts were authorized, either by order or by local rule, to alter those limits.[36] Rule 33(a) now provides that except with leave of court or by written stipulation, a party may not serve more than 25 interrogatories, including all discrete subparts, on an adverse party.[37]

---

30. U.S. v. Becton–Dickinson & Co., D.C.N.J.1962, 30 F.R.D. 132; Chatman v. American Export Lines, D.C.N.Y.1956, 20 F.R.D. 176; Gaynor v. Atlantic Greyhound Corp., D.C.Pa.1948, 8 F.R.D. 302.

31. Alfred Pearson & Co. v. Hayes, D.C.N.Y.1949, 9 F.R.D. 210.

32. Alltmont v. U.S., C.A.3d, 1949, 177 F.2d 971, certiorari denied 70 S.Ct. 999, 339 U.S. 967, 94 L.Ed. 1375; Miller v. Doctor's Hosp., D.C.Okl.1977, 76 F.R.D. 136; and cases cited 8 Wright, Miller & Marcus, Civil 2d § 2166 n. 82.

33. 8 Wright, Miller & Marcus, Civil 2d § 2168.1.

34. E.g., Rogers v. Tri–State Materials Corp., D.C.W.Va.1970, 51 F.R.D. 234, 241. See 8 Wright, Miller & Marcus, Civil 2d § 2169.

35. Advisory Committee Note, 48 F.R.D. 487, 524. See Hine v. Superior Court, 1972, 504 P.2d 509, 18 Ariz.App. 568.

36. Rule 26(b)(2), as amended in 1993.

37. The Advisory Committee had circulated in 1978 a proposal that would have authorized districts to adopt local rules limiting the number of interrogatories. In 1979 it withdrew that proposal, explaining that it had attracted virtually no support. See 85 F.R.D. 521, 543–544; 8 Wright, Miller & Marcus, Civil 2d § 2168.1. Despite

Until 1970 Rule 33 provided that interrogatories could be served only on an "adverse party." Presumably this requirement of adversity was intended to compensate for the absence from Rule 33 of any provision for notice or opportunity for cross-examination.[38] This limitation to "adverse" parties was an undesirable one. It was difficult to apply,[39] and in many circumstances barred use of the least expensive and most convenient means of discovery. The decision in the 1970 amendments to drop the word "adverse" and thus to allow a party to serve interrogatories on any other party was a sound one.[40] Under the rule as it had been in the past, answers to interrogatories had always been admissible at trial when offered by the interrogating party, as an admission of a party opponent.[41] Now that it is possible to have interrogatories answered by someone who is not a party opponent it will be necessary to see if the answers fall into some other exception to the hearsay rule, since what is now Rule 33(c) states that answers are admissible "to the extent permitted by the rules of evidence."

The procedure for using interrogatories was changed by amendments in 1970 and 1993. Leave of court is generally unnecessary.[42] The party interrogated ordinarily has 30 days in which to serve his answers and his objections, if any.[43] Objections to interrogatories must be stated with specificity and they are waived if they are not timely [44] or if the party has voluntarily answered the interrogatory.[45] If a party fails to answer, or objects to an interrogatory, the burden is now put on the party serving the interrogatory to make a motion under Rule 37(a) to

---

this, many districts adopted local rules of this kind. On the merits of numerical limits, compare Schroeder & Frank, Discovery Reform: Long Road to Nowheresville, 1982, 68 A.B.A.J. 572, 574, with Sherman & Kinnard, note 23 above, at 31–38.

38. In re City of Coral Gables, D.C.Fla. 1941, 1 F.R.D. 600; Cooke v. Kilgore Mfg. Co., D.C.Ohio 1954, 15 F.R.D. 465.

39. See Powell v. Willow Grove Amusement Park, D.C.Pa.1968, 45 F.R.D. 274; Carey v. Schuldt, D.C.La.1967, 42 F.R.D. 390; 8 Wright, Miller & Marcus, Civil 2d § 2171.

40. Carey v. Schuldt, D.C.La.1967, 42 F.R.D. 390, 396; Friedenthal, Kane & Miller, Civil Procedure, 2d ed. 1993, § 7.9, pp. 401–402.

There has been some disagreement on whether members of a class who are not named as parties can be required to respond to discovery under Rules 33 and 34. A consensus seems now to have developed that if discovery from absent members of the class is permissible at all, it should be sharply limited and allowed only on a strong showing of justification. Dellums v. Powell, C.A.D.C.1977, 566 F.2d 167, 187, certiorari denied 1978, 98 S.Ct. 3146, 438 U.S. 916, 57 L.Ed.2d 1161; Clark v. Univer-

sal Builders, Inc., C.A.7th, 1974, 501 F.2d 324, 340, certiorari denied 95 S.Ct. 657, 419 U.S. 1070, 42 L.Ed.2d 666; Transamerican Refining Co. v. Dravo Corp., D.C.Tex.1991, 139 F.R.D. 619, 621–622; Note, Obtaining Discovery from Absent Class Members in Federal Rule of Civil Procedure 23(b)(3) Class Actions, 1981, 30 Drake L.Rev. 347.

41. 8 Wright, Miller & Marcus, Civil 2d § 2180.

It is held in Treharne v. Callahan, C.A.3d, 1970, 426 F.2d 58, that there are circumstances in which a party may introduce its own answers to interrogatories submitted to it by its opponent.

42. Rule 33(a).

43. Rule 30(b)(3). This is a longer period than the unrealistic times formerly set prior to 1970 for objections and for answers. See Glaser, Pretrial Discovery and the Adversary System, 1968, pp. 222–224.

44. Rule 33(b)(4). Godsey v. U.S., D.C.Miss.1990, 133 F.R.D. 111; 8 Wright, Miller & Marcus, Civil 2d § 2173.

45. Meese v. Eaton Mfg. Co., D.C.Ohio 1964, 35 F.R.D. 162; Cardox Corp. v. Olin Mathieson Chem. Corp., D.C.Ill.1958, 23 F.R.D. 27, approved 1959, 6 Utah L.Rev. 429.

compel an answer, and the expense sanction of that rule is applicable. But an objecting party must answer the interrogatory to the extent that it is not objectionable.[46]

Interrogatories must be answered separately and fully under oath and signed by the person making the answers.[47] If a party fails entirely to serve answers or objections it is subject to the sanctions provided by Rule 37(d).[48] The rules had made no explicit provision for a remedy against incomplete, evasive, or false answers, but the courts uniformly and properly held that a motion would lie to compel further answers in such a case.[49] This is now dealt with explicitly in Rules 33(b)(5) and 37(a)(3), which allow a motion under Rule 37(a) in these circumstances.

Although answers to interrogatories may limit the issues and define the contentions of the parties, the party should not be held irrevocably to them. The court has discretion to limit the proof in the light of the answers to the interrogatories,[50] but this is a discretion that should be exercised with attention to the fact that the great goal of the rules is that judgment be given on the facts as they actually exist. A party may be embarrassed by its answer to a pretrial interrogatory in which it took a position different from that it asserts at the trial, and it is right that the party should have to explain its change of position, but the answer to the interrogatory should not be a conclusive bar to asserting a different view at the trial.[51]

Not infrequently it will happen that an answer to an interrogatory, though full and truthful to the best of the party's knowledge at the time it is made, will become incomplete or misleading in the light of later information the answering party finds. Is the party under any duty to amend the answer and advise the party who submitted the interrogatory of the new information? This question had caused the courts difficulty.[52] For a party to sit idly by, knowing that a previous answer it has given to an interrogatory is not truthful in the light of its present information, seems inconsistent with the purpose of the rules to avoid surprise and with the standards expected of a learned and honorable profession.[53] At

---

46. Rule 33(b)(1). This was added to the rule in 1993.

47. Rule 33(b)(1); McDougall v. Dunn, C.A.4th, 1972, 468 F.2d 468; 8 Wright, Miller & Marcus, Civil 2d §§ 2172, 2177.

48. See § 90 below. 8 Wright, Miller & Marcus, Civil 2d § 2291.

49. E.g., Robinson v. Jordan, D.C.Mass. 1961, 27 F.R.D. 493; Brown v. United States Lines Co., D.C.N.Y.1953, 15 F.R.D. 127; Kraft v. Washington & Jefferson College, D.C.Pa.1951, 11 F.R.D. 503; 8 Wright, Miller & Marcus, Civil 2d §§ 2177, 2285.

50. Maryland to Use of Summerlin v. Kemp, D.C.Md.1961, 194 F.Supp. 838; Zielinski v. Philadelphia Piers, Inc., D.C.Pa. 1956, 139 F.Supp. 408; Newsum v. Pennsylvania R. Co., D.C.N.Y.1951, 97 F.Supp. 500.

51. Marcoin, Inc. v. Edwin K. Williams & Co., C.A.4th, 1979, 605 F.2d 1325, 1328; Victory Carriers, Inc. v. Stockton Stevedoring Co., C.A.9th, 1968, 388 F.2d 955, 959; Ray v. J.C. Penney Co., C.A.10th, 1959, 274 F.2d 519, 521; Mangual v. Prudential Lines, Inc., D.C.Pa.1971, 53 F.R.D. 301; Pressley v. Boehlke, D.C.N.C.1963, 33 F.R.D. 316, 317; 8 Wright, Miller & Marcus, Civil 2d § 2181.

52. 8 Wright, Miller & Marcus, Civil 2d § 2048.

53. Comment, The "Continuing" Nature of Discovery Techniques, 1957, 42 Iowa L.Rev. 579.

Texas & P. Ry. v. Buckles, C.A.5th, 1956, 232 F.2d 257, 260, certiorari denied 76 S.Ct. 1052, 351 U.S. 984, 100 L.Ed. 1498; Abbathe same time it must be recognized that in a large and busy law practice the lawyer may honestly not realize that information he or she had just acquired is inconsistent with an answer given months or years before to an interrogatory.

A compromise was originally struck in 1970 in Rule 26(e), which applies to all discovery devices but is most important with regard to interrogatories.[54] This was substantially revised in 1993. As it now stands, a party is under a duty to supplement its response in two situations. A party is required at appropriate intervals to supplement its disclosures under Rule 26(a)[55] if the party learns that in some material respect the information disclosed is incomplete or incorrect and if the additional or corrective information has not otherwise been made known to the other parties during the discovery process or in writing. There is a similar duty seasonably to amend a prior response to an interrogatory, request for production, or request for admission. If a party fails to give its opponent added information when it is under a duty to do so, the court may refuse to allow an unnamed witness to testify, or may grant a continuance or a new trial, or otherwise follow whatever course seems just.[56]

§ 87. Production of Documents [1]

Rule 34 authorizes the broadest sweep of access, inspection, examination, copying, and photographing of documents or objects in the possession or control of another party.[2] The scope of discovery under this rule is the same as that under the discovery rules generally.[3] The rule includes production of documents and things so that the other party may inspect them,[4] allowing a party to make drawings or photographs of

---

temarco v. Colton, 1954, 106 A.2d 12, 31 N.J.Super. 181; D'Agostino v. Schaffer, 1957, 133 A.2d 45, 45 N.J.Super. 395.

54. See Rogers v. Tri–State Materials Corp., D.C.W.Va.1970, 51 F.R.D. 234, 244–245; 8 Wright, Miller & Marcus, Civil 2d §§ 2049, 2050.

55. See § 83A above.

56. Voegeli v. Lewis, C.A.8th, 1977, 568 F.2d 89 (new trial); Jefferson v. Davis, D.C.Ill.1990, 131 F.R.D. 522, 528 (testimony excluded); Frankel v. Stake, D.C.Pa.1963, 33 F.R.D. 1 (statement suppressed); Freeman v. Minnesota Min. & Mfg. Co., D.C.Del.1987, 675 F.Supp. 877, 889 n. 5 (continuance). See 8 Wright, Miller & Marcus, Civil 2d §§ 2049.1, 2050.

But the court always has discretion in the matter and may allow an unnamed witness to testify or otherwise refuse to impose a sanction. See, e.g., Outley v. City of New York, C.A.2d, 1988, 837 F.2d 587, 590;

Murphy v. Magnolia Elec. Power Assn., C.A.5th, 1981, 639 F.2d 232, 235.

§ 87

1. 8 Wright, Miller & Marcus, Civil 2d §§ 2201–2218.

2. Morales v. Turman, D.C.Tex.1972, 59 F.R.D. 157.

3. See § 81 above. For application of the principles there developed to Rule 34, see 8 Wright, Miller & Marcus, Civil 2d § 2206.

4. Even the taking of urine specimens from cattle and doing postmortems on dead cattle had been said to be within the concept of "inspection." Martin v. Reynolds Metals Corp., C.A.9th, 1961, 297 F.2d 49, noted 1962, 41 Texas L.Rev. 330. This result was made explicit by the inclusion in amended Rule 34(a) of the words "test, or sample." See Sladen v. Girltown, Inc., C.A.7th, 1970, 425 F.2d 24; Sperberg v. Firestone Tire & Rubber Co., D.C.Ohio 1973, 61 F.R.D. 80.

the objects in question,[5] and entry upon premises for inspection of objects.[6] As amended in 1970, the rule even makes provision for production or inspection of computerized information.[7]

Rule 34 runs only against a party to a pending action,[8] though production and inspection can be had against a person not a party in many instances by a subpoena duces tecum,[9] and Rule 34(c) makes it clear that the rule does not have a preemptive effect and does not bar an independent action in the nature of a bill of discovery against a person not a party.[10]

A party can be required to produce only such documents or things as "are in his possession, custody, or control." [11] The basic test of the rule is "control." [12] Frequently inspection will be ordered where the party against whom the order runs has the legal right to obtain the document, even though in fact he has no copy,[13] and regardless of whether the document is beyond the jurisdiction of the court.[14] Thus, a party cannot

5. Diapulse Corp. of America v. Curtis Pub. Co., C.A.2d, 1967, 374 F.2d 442; Rosenthal v. Compagnie–Generale Transatlantique, D.C.N.Y.1953, 14 F.R.D. 336; Prosperity Co. v. St. Joe Machines, D.C.Mich. 1942, 2 F.R.D. 299.

6. A sufficient showing for entry on land was held not to have been made in Belcher v. Bassett Furniture Indus., Inc., C.A.4th, 1978, 588 F.2d 904. Inspection was allowed in, e.g., Lubrin v. Hess Oil Virgin Islands Corp., D.C.V.I.1986, 109 F.R.D. 403. See generally Hughes & Anderson, Discovery: A Competition Between the Right of Privacy and the Right to Know, 1971, 23 U.Fla.L.Rev. 289.

7. National Union Elec. Corp. v. Matsushita Elec. Indus. Co., Ltd., D.C.Pa.1980, 494 F.Supp. 1257; Pearl Brewing Co. v. Jos. Schlitz Brewing Co., D.C.Tex.1976, 415 F.Supp. 1122; Adams v. Dan River Mills, Inc., D.C.Va.1972, 54 F.R.D. 220; Sherman & Kinnard, The Development, Discovery, and Use of Computer Support Systems in Achieving Efficiency in Litigation, 1979, 73 Col.L.Rev. 267; 8 Wright, Miller & Marcus, Civil 2d § 2218.

8. Hickman v. Taylor, 1947, 67 S.Ct. 385, 390, 329 U.S. 495, 504, 91 L.Ed. 451; In re Franklin Nat. Bank Securities Litigation, C.A.2d, 1978, 574 F.2d 662; 8 Wright, Miller & Marcus, Civil 2d § 2208.

In Henderson v. Zurn Industries, Inc., D.C.Ind.1990, 131 F.R.D. 560, 565–567, a party's insurer was held not to be a "party" within Rule 34. But in that case the documents were found to be under the control of a party, since the insured could require the insurer to make them available.

For possible application of Rule 34 to unnamed members of a class, see § 86 n. 36 above.

A person who expects to be a party to an action may proceed under Rule 27 and obtain any relief that would be proper in a pending action under Rule 34. Martin v. Reynolds Metals Corp., C.A.9th, 1961, 297 F.2d 49, noted 1962, 41 Texas L.Rev. 330.

9. Rule 45(a)(1)(C). Until 1991 it was necessary to issue a subpoena duces tecum for the taking of the deposition of a nonparty from whom production and inspection were sought. Since 1991 that is not necessary and the subpoena may command the person to whom it is directed to produce things or to permit inspection of premises at a specified time and place. See Siegel, Federal Subpoena Practice Under The New Rule 45 of the Federal Rules of Civil Procedure, 1991, 139 F.R.D. 197, 205–207.

10. See 8 Wright, Miller & Marcus, Civil 2d § 2209; Note, Rule 34(c) and Discovery of Nonparty Land, 1975, 85 Yale L.J. 112.

11. 8 Wright, Miller & Marcus, Civil 2d § 2210.

12. Bifferato v. States Marine Corp. of Delaware, D.C.N.Y.1951, 11 F.R.D. 44, 46; Note, Meaning of "Control" in F.R.C.P. 34, 1958, 107 U.Pa.L.Rev. 103.

13. E.g., Haseotes v. Abacab Intern. Computers, Inc., D.C.Mass.1988, 120 F.R.D. 12, 15 (corporate documents in hands of officers and directors); Herbst v. Able, D.C.N.Y.1972, 63 F.R.D. 135 (SEC testimony); Schwartz v. Travelers Ins. Co., D.C.N.Y.1954, 17 F.R.D. 330 (hospital records); Scott v. Arex, Inc., D.C.Conn.1989, 124 F.R.D. 39 (income tax returns).

14. First Nat. City Bank of New York v. IRS, C.A.2d, 1959, 271 F.2d 616, certiorari denied 80 S.Ct. 402, 361 U.S. 948, 4 L.Ed.2d 381.

escape discovery by turning the document over to his attorney or his insurer.[15] Where the party has no legal right to the thing in question, he has been held not required to produce,[16] even though the thing was in his possession.[17] The Supreme Court has held, however, that a foreign corporation is in "control" of certain records, and thus may be ordered to produce them, even though penal laws of the country where it is located limit its ability to satisfy the production order.[18] The effect of those laws is considered in determining what sanction to impose for noncompliance with the order, rather than regarded as a reason for refusing to order production.[19]

As originally adopted in 1938 Rule 34 required a court order on a showing of "good cause." Rule 34(b), as it was amended in 1970, changed this and provided a mechanism that is intended ordinarily to operate extrajudicially. This simply recognizes what was in fact happening under the former rule. In practice lawyers rarely went to court to invoke Rule 34 and proceeded instead by informal agreement. Thus, the amended rule permits the party seeking inspection to proceed by a simple request, describing what it is it wishes to see and specifying a reasonable time, place, and manner for this to be accomplished.[20] The party on whom the request is served must respond, ordinarily within 30 days, either saying that inspection will be permitted or stating reasons for objections to the request.[21] If objection is made, the party seeking discovery may move under Rule 37(a) to compel the inspection sought.

In a request for inspection under amended Rule 34, just as in a motion under the prior rule, the party seeking discovery must designate the things it wishes to inspect. There has been considerable discussion about how specifically these must be designated.[22] The discussion has

15. Bingle v. Liggett Drug Co., D.C.Mass.1951, 11 F.R.D. 593; Simper v. Trimble, D.C.Mo.1949, 9 F.R.D. 598; Kane v. News Syndicate Co., D.C.N.Y.1941, 1 F.R.D. 738; State Farm Ins. Co. v. Roberts, 1965, 398 P.2d 671, 97 Ariz. 169; cf. Wilson v. David, D.C.Mich.1957, 21 F.R.D. 217.

16. Gerling Intern. Ins. Co. v. C.I.R., C.A.3d, 1988, 839 F.2d 131, 140; Fisher v. U.S. Fidelity & Guar. Co., C.A.7th, 1957, 246 F.2d 344.

17. U.S. v. Kyle, D.C.N.Y.1957, 21 F.R.D. 163; In re Harris, D.C.N.Y.1939, 27 F.Supp. 480.

18. Societe Internationale Pour Participations Industrielles et Commerciales, S.A. v. Rogers, 1958, 78 S.Ct. 1087, 357 U.S. 197, 2 L.Ed.2d 1255, noted 1958, 107 U.Pa. L.Rev. 103.

19. Richmark Corp. v. Timber Falling Consultants, C.A.9th, 1992, 959 F.2d 1468; In re Westinghouse Elec. Corp. Uranium Contracts Litigation, C.A.10th, 1977, 563 F.2d 992, noted 1978 Utah L.Rev. 361; Compagnie Francaise d'Assurance Pour le

Commerce Exterieur v. Phillips Petroleum Co., D.C.N.Y.1984, 105 F.R.D. 16; SEC v. Banca Della Svizzera Italiana, D.C.N.Y. 1981, 92 F.R.D. 111. The American Law Institute has proposed a balancing test to deal with issues of this kind. Restatement Third of the Foreign Relations Law of the United States, 1987, § 442(1)(c). That test is endorsed by the Supreme Court in Societe National Industrielle Aerospatiale v. U.S. District Court, 1987, 107 S.Ct. 2542, 2556 n. 28, 482 U.S. 522, 544 n. 28, 96 L.Ed.2d 461.

20. 8 Wright, Miller & Marcus, Civil 2d § 2212. See proposed Official Form 24 for the form of such a request.

21. If objection is made only to part of an item or category, that part must be specified and inspection permitted of the remaining parts. Rule 34(b), as amended in 1993.

22. 8 Wright, Miller & Marcus, Civil 2d § 2211; Roman, Designation of Documents under Rule 34, 1958, 25 Ins.Couns.J. 313; Newport, "Designation" as used in Rule 34

centered on two familiar cases that seem to reflect varying views on this point. In one case Judge Woolsey said that a "designation in a motion under Rule 34 must be sufficiently precise in respect to each document or item of evidence sought to enable the defendant to go to his files and, without difficulty, to pick the document or other item requested out and turn to the plaintiff saying 'Here it is.' "[23] In a later case Judge Rifkind held that it is sufficient to demand all the documents under defendant's control pertaining to a particular subject matter.[24]

It is not unnatural, in the light of these differing constructions of the rule, that commentators and courts should speak of the cases as if they represent a narrow view and a broad view on the specificity of designation.[25] Yet it is not clear that the decisions cannot be reconciled. As many cases have said, and probably all courts would agree, the things to be produced for inspection must be described with reasonable particularity.[26] Particularity of designation, however, like so many other matters in life and law, is a matter of degree, dependent upon a pragmatic consideration of the circumstances in each case. Necessarily the test must be a relative one, turning on the amount of knowledge that a party has about the documents he requests.[27] In some cases the party seeking production has such exact and definite knowledge that it can designate, identify, and enumerate with precision the documents to be produced, in which event it should do so. This is the ideal designation, but the ideal is not always attainable, and the rule does not require the impossible. The goal is that the description be sufficient to apprise a man or woman of ordinary intelligence what documents are required, and that the court be able to ascertain whether the request has been complied with.[28] This notion is well captured in amended Rule 34(b); it provides that the request may describe either individual items or categories and that it must "describe each item and category with reasonable particularity."

Easily the most difficult and controversial requirement of Rule 34 as originally adopted was the showing of "good cause." It was clear, as the Supreme Court said, that the requirement was "not a mere formality" but rather "a plainly expressed limitation on the use of that Rule."[29]

---

of the Federal Rules of Civil Procedure on Discovery and Production of Documents, 1950, 35 Iowa L.Rev. 422.

23. U.S. v. American Optical Co., D.C.N.Y.1942, 2 F.R.D. 534, 536.

24. U.S. v. U.S. Alkali Export Assn., Inc., D.C.N.Y.1946, 7 F.R.D. 256.

25. See U.S. v. National Steel Corp., D.C.Tex.1960, 26 F.R.D. 607, 611.

26. Roebling v. Anderson, C.A.D.C.1958, 257 F.2d 615, 620; In re IBM Peripheral EDP Devices Antitrust Litigation, D.C.Cal. 1977, 77 F.R.D. 39; Olson Transp. Co. v. Socony–Vacuum Oil Co., D.C.Wis.1944, 7 F.R.D. 134, 136.

27. Tiedman v. American Pigment Corp., C.A.4th, 1958, 253 F.2d 803, 809; Taylor v. Florida Atlantic University, D.C.Fla.1990, 132 F.R.D. 304, 305; Mitsui & Co. (U.S.A.) Inc. v. Puerto Rico Water Resources Auth., D.C.Puerto Rico 1978, 79 F.R.D. 72.

28. Scuderi v. Boston Ins. Co., D.C.Del. 1964, 34 F.R.D. 463, 466; U.S. v. National Steel Corp., D.C.Tex.1960, 26 F.R.D. 607, 610; Dean v. Superior Court, 1958, 324 P.2d 764, 84 Ariz. 104.

29. Schlagenhauf v. Holder, 1964, 85 S.Ct. 234, 242, 379 U.S. 104, 118, 13 L.Ed.2d 152.

The requirement was certainly plainly expressed, but its meaning was far from plain and its application was uncertain.[30]

Probably the principal accomplishment of amended Rule 34 was that it eliminated the requirement of good cause. This was possible because an empirical study showed that the "good cause" requirement in fact had little effect on the use of inspections.[31] The cases in which its meaning had been litigated dealt almost exclusively with trial-preparation materials, in which the work-product concept was close to the surface even if technically the documents did not come within the concept. Inspection of documents and things not obtained in anticipation of litigation or preparation for trial was routinely granted. The 1970 amendments brought the rules into conformance with actual practice. Rule 26(b)(3) gives substantial protection to trial-preparation materials[32] while amended Rule 34 allows inspection, without any showing of good cause, of other documents and things that are relevant to the subject matter of the action and not privileged.[33]

A minor amendment to Rule 34 was made in 1980. It provides that a party who produces documents for inspection shall produce them as they are kept in the usual course of business or shall organize and label them to correspond with the categories in the request.[34] Although the amendment is ambiguous on this point, it should not be read as giving the party from whom the discovery is sought an absolute option to produce records as kept in the usual course of business. The party should be required to produce them in a form that will make reasonable use of them possible.[35]

§ 88. Physical Examination[1]

Under Rule 35, whenever the physical or mental condition of a party is in controversy, the court in which the action is pending may require him to submit to an examination by a suitably licensed or certified examiner.[2] Prior to the adoption of the rules a federal court could not order such an examination unless express authority therefor was granted

---

30. See 8 Wright, Miller & Marcus, Civil 2d § 2205, discussing the varying views of good cause taken in the pre–1970 cases and the elimination of that requirement by the amendments in that year.

31. Glaser, Pretrial Discovery and the Adversary System, 1968, p. 221.

32. See § 82 above.

33. Galambus v. Consolidated Freightways Corp., D.C.Ind.1974, 64 F.R.D. 468, 474; Mallinckrodt Chem. Works v. Goldman, Sachs & Co., D.C.N.Y.1973, 58 F.R.D. 348, 354; Herbst v. Able, D.C.N.Y.1972, 63 F.R.D. 135.

34. Board of Educ. of Evanston Tp. High School v. Admiral Heating and Ventilating, Inc., D.C.Ill.1984, 104 F.R.D. 23.

35. Sherman & Kinnard, Federal Court Discovery in the 80s—Making the Rules Work, 1981, 1 Rev.Litig. 9, 21–25; Watkins, 1980 Amendments to the Federal Rules of Civil Procedure, 1980, 32 Baylor L.Rev. 533, 550.

§ 88

1. 8 Wright, Miller & Marcus, Civil 2d §§ 2231–2239; Note, Court–Ordered Mental and Physical Examinations: A Survey of Federal Rule 35 and Illinois Rule 215, 1980, 11 Loy.U.L.J. 725.

2. For 50 years the rule spoke of examination by a "physician". In 1988 an Act of Congress added "or psychologist" as well as a subdivision (c) defining "psychologist". In 1991 subdivision (c) was deleted and more general language about "examiner" was substituted in (a).

by the laws of the state in which the court sat.[3] The leading Supreme Court decision so holding posed the issue squarely. To the majority the issue was one of sanctity of the person, which it thought as much invaded by a compulsory stripping, and exposure, as by a blow,[4] while the dissenters considered "truth and justice * * * more sacred than any personal consideration."[5] Most of the states believed that the invasion of the person involved in a physical examination was outweighed by the need for such examinations in the interest of truth and justice.[6] Relying on this experience, Rule 35 was adopted, providing for such examinations in federal court. The Supreme Court, by a five-to-four vote, held the rule valid and applicable regardless of the law of the state in which the district court was sitting,[7] and in the more recent case of Schlagenhauf v. Holder,[8] though the Court was divided on other issues, there was no dissent from the proposition that "Rule 35, as applied to either plaintiffs or defendants to an action, is free of constitutional difficulty and is within the scope of the Enabling Act."[9]

The rule purports to apply to any action in which the mental or physical condition of a party is in controversy.[10] An early case refused to allow an examination in a libel action, where defendant was claiming he had spoken truthfully in attributing various physical and mental conditions to the plaintiff.[11] The court thought that the rule looked only to personal-injury litigation where the condition was in issue "immediately and directly" rather than "incidentally and collaterally." Fortunately such a restrictive construction did not long prevail. The rule was soon held to permit blood tests in a paternity action,[12] and since then it has not been doubted that the rule applies to any action.

The rule authorizes examination only of a "party." In the Schlagenhauf case the Supreme Court said that this means what it says: it authorizes examination either of a plaintiff or a defendant and there is no requirement that the examination be sought by a party who is opposed to the party to be examined.[13] The Court found it unnecessary to determine "to what extent, if any, the term 'party' includes one who is a 'real party in interest' although not a named party to the action."[14]

---

3. Union Pac. R. Co. v. Botsford, 1891, 11 S.Ct. 1000, 141 U.S. 250, 35 L.Ed. 734; Camden & Suburban R. Co. v. Stetson, 1900, 20 S.Ct. 617, 177 U.S. 172, 44 L.Ed. 721.

4. Union Pac. R. Co. v. Botsford, 1891, 11 S.Ct. 1000, 1001, 141 U.S. 250, 251–252, 35 L.Ed. 734.

5. 11 S.Ct. at 1004, 141 U.S. at 259.

6. The almost universal acceptance of physical examinations in the states is discussed in 8 Wright, Miller & Marcus, Civil 2d § 2231.

7. Sibbach v. Wilson & Co., Inc., 1941, 61 S.Ct. 422, 312 U.S. 1, 85 L.Ed. 479.

8. 1964, 85 S.Ct. 234, 379 U.S. 104, 13 L.Ed.2d 152.

9. 85 S.Ct. at 240, 379 U.S. at 114.

10. 8 Wright, Miller & Marcus, Civil 2d § 2232.

11. Wadlow v. Humberd, D.C.Mo.1939, 27 F.Supp. 210.

12. Beach v. Beach, C.C.A.D.C.1940, 114 F.2d 479. This result was codified in a 1970 amendment of Rule 37(a). The rule does not apply if no action is pending. Tarlton v. U.S., C.A.5th, 1970, 430 F.2d 1351.

13. 85 S.Ct. at 239–242, 379 U.S. at 112–116.

14. 88 S.Ct. at 241 n. 12, 379 U.S. at 115 n. 12. As an example of the situation it had in mind, the Court cited Beach v. Beach, C.C.A.D.C.1940, 114 F.2d 479, in

As amended in 1970, Rule 37(a) allows examination of "a person in the custody or under the legal control of a party,"[15] but it now seems clear that examination of strangers to an action is not authorized, no matter how useful the examination might be in deciding a case.[16]

An order under Rule 35 may be made only on motion and a showing of good cause. In practice, the showing is very perfunctory, in personal injury cases at least, and in almost all cases the examination is arranged by stipulation of the attorneys.[17] The Supreme Court said in Schlagenhauf that the requirements that the condition be "in controversy" and that "good cause" for the examination be shown are satisfied from the pleadings alone if a plaintiff claims mental or physical injury or a defendant asserts his or her mental or physical condition as a defense to a claim.[18] But if a party does not put his or her own condition in issue, and the issue is raised by some other party who seeks an examination, a more discriminating decision is required. In this instance neither conclusory allegations of the pleadings nor mere relevance to the case are enough. Instead there must be "an affirmative showing by the movant that each condition as to which the examination is sought is really and genuinely in controversy and that good cause exists for ordering each particular examination."[19]

Examination by more than one doctor is permissible,[20] and more than one examination may be ordered, though the court will require a stronger showing of necessity before ordering repeated examinations.[21] Usually the court will name a doctor suggested by the moving party to

which a blood test was ordered on an infant who would benefit from her mother's separate maintenance action.

15. In re Certain Asbestos Cases, D.C.Tex.1986, 112 F.R.D. 427 (decedent in wrongful-death action is under the legal control of the party and an autopsy could be ordered); Beckwith v. Beckwith, D.C.App. 1976, 355 A.2d 537 (child in custody of defendant in a divorce action).

16. Scharf v. U.S. Attorney Gen., C.A.9th, 1979, 597 F.2d 1240 (parents of person claiming citizenship); Schuppin v. Unification Church, D.C.Vt.1977, 435 F.Supp. 603 (adult child of party), affirmed C.A.2d, 573 F.2d 1295; Kropp v. General Dynamics Corp., D.C.Mich.1962, 202 F.Supp. 207 (employee). See 8 Wright, Miller & Marcus, Civil 2d § 2233.

17. Liechty v. Terrill Trucking Co., D.C.Tenn.1971, 53 F.R.D. 590; Glaser, Pretrial Discovery and the Adversary System, 1968, pp. 54–55. See generally 8 Wright, Miller & Marcus, Civil 2d § 2234.1.

18. 85 S.Ct. at 243, 379 U.S. at 119.

19. 88 S.Ct. at 242–243, 379 U.S. at 118. See Stuart v. Burford, D.C.Okl.1967, 42

F.R.D. 591. Plaintiff's physical and mental condition were held not in controversy in Acosta v. Tenneco Oil Co., C.A.5th, 1990, 913 F.2d 205, and in Winters v. Travia, C.A.2d, 1974, 495 F.2d 839. A sufficient showing for an examination was not made in Stinchcomb v. U.S., D.C.Pa.1990, 132 F.R.D. 29, or in Marroni v. Matey, D.C.Pa. 1979, 82 F.R.D. 371.

It is held in Bodnar v. Bodnar, C.A.5th, 1971, 441 F.2d 1103, that a court has power to order mental examination of a plaintiff to determine if plaintiff is mentally competent to understand the nature and effect of the litigation.

20. Little v. Howey, D.C.Mo.1963, 32 F.R.D. 322, 323; Marshall v. Peters, D.C.Ohio 1962, 31 F.R.D. 238, 239; cf. Stuart v. Burford, D.C.Okl.1967, 42 F.R.D. 591, 593.

21. Moore v. Calavar Corp., D.C.La. 1992, 142 F.R.D. 134; Ishler v. Cook, C.A.7th, 1962, 299 F.2d 507; Benning v. Phelps, C.A.2d, 1957, 249 F.2d 47; Vopelak v. Williams, D.C.Ohio 1967, 42 F.R.D. 387; cf. Rutherford v. Alben, D.C.W.Va.1940, 1 F.R.D. 277.

make the examination.[22] The court has the power to make the ultimate decision, however,[23] and will consider any serious objection that the person to be examined may have to the doctor suggested by the moving party.[24]

In determining what kinds of examination to permit, the court must balance the desire to insure the safety and freedom from pain of the party to be examined against the need for the facts in the interest of truth and justice. The showing of the medical acceptance and safety of the particular procedure is important. Where an adequate foundation is laid about the need for the procedure and its safety, even novel and painful procedures may be ordered.[25] It is commonly provided that the examined party may have his own physician present during the examination if he wishes to do so.[26] In some states the person may also have his attorney present, but this is hardly necessary under ordinary circumstances, and a more sensible rule is that the attorney cannot be present as a matter of right, but only with permission of the court granted for good reason.[27]

Under Rule 35(b)(1) the party examined has an absolute right to receive from the party who caused the examination to be made a copy of the report of the findings of the examiner. Not infrequently a party submits to an examination voluntarily, prior to retaining counsel, and does not stipulate that he or she is to receive a copy of the report. Rule 35(b)(3), added in 1970, codifies a result the courts had already reached and provides that the same right to receive, on a request, a copy of the report of the findings exists in this situation as exists when the examination is pursuant to a court order.[28]

Rule 35(b)(2) provides that by requesting and obtaining a report of the examination made pursuant to Rule 35, the party examined waives any privilege he may have in that action regarding the testimony of

---

22. Looney v. National Railroad Passenger Corp., D.C.Mass.1992, 142 F.R.D. 264; and cases cited 8 Wright, Miller & Marcus, Civil 2d § 2234.1.

23. 8 Wright, Miller & Marcus, Civil 2d § 2234.2; Stinchcomb v. U.S., D.C.Pa.1990, 132 F.R.D. 29, 30; Comment, Rule 35: Is There a Right to Choice of Physician?, 1988, 14 N.Ky.L.Rev. 447. Contra: Wasmund v. Nunamaker, 1967, 151 N.W.2d 577, 277 Minn. 52.

24. Stuart v. Burford, D.C.Okl.1967, 42 F.R.D. 591; Gitto v. Societá Anonima Di Navigazione, Genova, D.C.N.Y.1939, 27 F.Supp. 785.

25. E.g., Klein v. Yellow Cab Co., D.C.Ohio 1944, 7 F.R.D. 169 (cystoscopy and phylegrams); 8 Wright, Miller & Marcus, Civil 2d § 2235.

26. Dziwanoski v. Ocean Carriers Corp., D.C.Md.1960, 26 F.R.D. 595; Klein v. Yel-

low Cab Co., D.C.Ohio, 1944, 7 F.R.D. 169; see Warrick v. Brode, D.C.Del.1969, 46 F.R.D. 427, 428. But see Sanden v. Mayo Clinic, C.A.8th, 1974, 495 F.2d 221; Swift v. Swift, D.C.N.Y.1974, 64 F.R.D. 440.

27. Cline v. Firestone Tire & Rubber Co., D.C.W.Va.1988, 118 F.R.D. 588; Brandenberg v. El Al Israel Airlines, D.C.N.Y. 1978, 79 F.R.D. 543; 8 Wright, Miller & Marcus, Civil 2d § 2236. But see Ewing v. Ayres Corp., D.C.Miss.1989, 129 F.R.D. 137, 140.

28. 8 Wright, Miller & Marcus, Civil 2d § 2237.

Even if the examining physician has not made a written report, the court can require the party who moved for the examination to obtain a report to give to the party examined. Salvatore v. American Cyanamid Co., D.C.R.I.1982, 94 F.R.D. 156.

every other person who has examined or may thereafter examine him with regard to the same mental or physical condition. He must turn over to his adversary his own medical reports.[29] Literally the rule applies only if the person examined has requested a copy of the report,[30] but if the physician-patient privilege is not applicable, the examined person's reports may be subject to discovery under Rule 34 or otherwise,[31] and the deposition of the doctor can be taken if the requirements of Rule 26(b)(4) are satisfied.[32]

If a party fails to comply with a court order requiring it to submit to a physical examination, all of the sanctions of Rule 37(b)(2) are available,[33] with the important exception that the party may not be imprisoned for contempt.[34]

There has been interest in comparatively recent years in proposals to provide for impartial medical examinations in appropriate cases,[35] and some federal courts had followed the lead of certain state courts in providing by local rule for such examinations. Such rules appear to codify the common-law power of the court to call its own witnesses where this is necessary.[36] Although there has been controversy about the idea of impartial medical examinations,[37] the issue is now resolved by Evidence Rule 706, effective in 1975. It authorizes court appointment of expert witnesses on any subject, not merely for medical matters, and makes provision for the compensation of experts so appointed. The court is given discretion to authorize disclosure to the jury of the fact that the court appointed the expert witness.[38]

29. Weir v. Simmons, D.C.Neb.1964, 233 F.Supp. 657; Lindsay v. Prince, D.C.Ohio, 1948, 8 F.R.D. 233; 8 Wright, Miller & Marcus, Civil 2d § 2237.

30. Sher v. De Haven, C.A.D.C.1952, 199 F.2d 777, certiorari denied 73 S.Ct. 797, 345 U.S. 936, 97 L.Ed. 1363; Galloway v. National Dairy Products Corp., D.C.Pa. 1959, 24 F.R.D. 362; Shepherd v. Castle, D.C.Mo.1957, 20 F.R.D. 184; cf. Benning v. Phelps, C.A.2d, 1957, 249 F.2d 47.

31. Rule 35(b)(3), added in 1970; Buffington v. Wood, C.A.3d, 1965, 351 F.2d 292; Leszynski v. Russ, D.C.Md.1961, 29 F.R.D. 10; see Cox v. Fennelly, D.C.N.Y.1966, 40 F.R.D. 1, 2.

It is held in Hardy v. Riser, D.C.Miss. 1970, 309 F.Supp. 1234, that testimony of a physician who has examined a party under Rule 35 is admissible even though the state would recognize a physician-patient privilege and there has been no waiver of the privilege.

32. See the discussion of Rule 26(b)(4) in § 81 above. See also Brown v. Ringstad, D.C.Iowa 1992, 142 F.R.D. 461; Comment, Discovery and the Doctor: Expansion of Rule 35(b), 1973, 34 Mont.L.Rev. 257.

33. See § 90 below.

34. See Rule 37(b)(2)(D), (E). See also Sibbach v. Wilson & Co., Inc., 1941, 61 S.Ct. 422, 312 U.S. 1, 85 L.Ed. 479; 8 Wright, Miller & Marcus, Civil 2d § 2238.

35. 8 Wright, Miller & Marcus, Civil 2d § 2239; Comment, The Doctor in Court: Impartial Medical Testimony, 1967, 40 So. Cal.L.Rev. 728; Symposium on the Impartial Medical Expert, 1961, 34 Temp.L.Q. 357; Comment, Impartial Medical Testimony Plans, 1961, 55 Nw.U.L.Rev. 700; Comment, Impartial Medical Testimony—A New Horizon, 1959, 32 Temp.L.Q. 193; Peck, Impartial Medical Testimony: A Way to Better and Quicker Justice, 1958, 22 F.R.D. 21; Association of the Bar of the City of New York, Impartial Medical Testimony, 1956.

36. Scott v. Spanjer Bros., Inc., C.A.2d, 1962, 298 F.2d 928; McCormick, Evidence, Cleary et al. ed. 1972, § 17.

37. See Levy, The Impartial Medical Expert System: The Plaintiff's Point of View, 1961, 34 Temp.L.Q. 416.

38. Evidence Rule 706(c).

§ 89. Requests for Admissions [1]

Rule 36(a) provides that a party to an action may serve upon any other party a written request for the admission by the latter of the genuineness of any relevant documents described in the request or of the truth of any matter set forth in the request that is within the general scope of discovery defined in Rule 26(b).[2] The party on whom such a request is served may file written objections to the request, if it thinks the request improper under the rule, or it may file an answer denying specifically the matters of which an admission is requested or setting forth in detail the reasons why it cannot truthfully admit or deny those matters.[3] If the party fails to respond to the request, the matters set out in the request are deemed admitted,[4] though the court has discretion to avoid the admission if there is an untimely answer.[5] If the party fails to admit the matters set out in the request, and the party requesting the admission later proves the truth of the matter, the court, on application, will order the party failing to admit to pay the reasonable expenses incurred in proving the matter, including reasonable attorney's fees, unless the court has previously sustained an objection to the request, or the court finds that the admission was not of substantial importance, or the party failing to admit had reasonable ground to believe that it might prevail on the matter, or there was some other good reason for the failure to admit.[6]

An admission is for the purpose of Rule 36 only and cannot be used against the party in any other proceeding.[7] It is a binding admission in that proceeding, however, except insofar as the court permits the admission to be amended or withdrawn.[8] District courts have considerable discretion about this, but are to allow amendment or withdrawal only if the presentation of the merits will be subserved by allowing this and the party that obtained the admission will not be prejudiced by the withdrawal.[9]

§ 89

1. 8 Wright, Miller & Marcus, Civil 2d §§ 2251–2265.

2. On the general scope of discovery, see § 81 above.

3. 8 Wright, Miller & Marcus, Civil 2d §§ 2260–2262.

4. Luick v. Graybar Elec. Co., Inc., C.A.8th, 1973, 473 F.2d 1360; 8 Wright, Miller & Marcus, Civil 2d § 2259.

5. U.S. v. Lake Killarney Apartments, Inc., C.A.5th, 1971, 443 F.2d 1170; Hadra v. Herman Blum Consulting Engineers, D.C.Tex.1977, 74 F.R.D. 113; 8 Wright, Miller & Marcus, Civil 2d § 2257.

6. Rule 37(c); 8 Wright, Miller & Marcus, Civil 2d § 2290. Sanctions have not often been imposed in the past. Glaser, Pretrial Discovery and the Adversary System, 1968, pp. 211–212. Payment of costs was ordered in Bradshaw v. Thompson, C.A.6th, 1972, 454 F.2d 75, certiorari denied 93 S.Ct. 130, 409 U.S. 878, 34 L.Ed.2d 131.

7. Rule 36(b).

8. The language to this effect in amended Rule 36(b) codified what the courts were already holding. See McSparran v. Hanigan, D.C.Pa.1963, 225 F.Supp. 628, affirmed C.A.3d, 1966, 356 F.2d 983; 8 Wright, Miller & Marcus, Civil 2d § 2264; Finman, The Request for Admissions in Federal Civil Procedure, 1962, 71 Yale L.J. 371, 418–426.

9. American Auto. Assn. (Inc.) v. AAA Legal Clinic of Jefferson Crooke, P.C., C.A.5th, 1991, 930 F.2d 1117; Farr Man & Co. v. M/V Rozita, C.A.1st, 1990, 903 F.2d 871.

Strictly speaking Rule 36 is not a discovery procedure at all, since it presupposes that the party proceeding under it knows the facts or has the document and merely wishes his opponent to concede their genuineness.[10] Thus, the purpose of this rule is to expedite the trial and to relieve the parties of the cost of proving facts that will not be disputed at the trial and the truth of which can be ascertained by reasonable inquiry.[11]

As originally adopted Rule 36 spoke of admissions about "relevant" documents and "relevant" matters of fact. It was generally agreed that this was to be given the same broad meaning as in the other discovery rules, and that relevancy to the subject matter of the action, rather than admissibility in evidence, was the test.[12] There was some authority taking a different view, and suggesting that admissibility was the key,[13] but this was doubtful at the time and such a construction cannot survive the amendments of Rule 36 adopted in 1970 in which the word "relevant" was deleted and requests allowed of any matters within the scope of proposed Rule 26(b), the general rule on scope of discovery.

Some cases had refused to recognize the privilege against self-incrimination because of the provision of Rule 36(b) that an answer to a request for admission may not be used in any other proceeding.[14] This seems to overlook the possibility that the answer, though not usable in itself, may be a link in an incriminating chain. Thus, the better, and now accepted, view is that a party in answering a request for admissions is entitled to the same constitutional protection as if he or she were called as a witness.[15]

As amended in 1970, Rule 36(a) speaks directly to several points on which there were differences of view under the original rule. Thus, it allows a request to go to any matters "that relate to statements or opinions of fact or of the application of law to fact." This recognizes that the test should be whether a response will assist in narrowing the proof, rather than a nice exercise in probing the shadowy borderline of

---

10. McHugh v. Reserve Min. Co., D.C.Ohio, 1961, 27 F.R.D. 505; Driver v. Gindy Mfg. Corp., D.C.Pa.1959, 24 F.R.D. 473; Knowlton v. Atchison, T. & S.F. Ry. Co., D.C.Mo.1951, 11 F.R.D. 62.

11. Langer v. Monarch Life Ins. Co., C.A.3d, 1992, 966 F.2d 786, 803; Rabil v. Swafford, D.C.D.C.1989, 128 F.R.D. 1. See Shapiro, Some Problems of Discovery in an Adversary System, 1979, 63 Minn.L.Rev. 1055, 1079.

12. Goldman v. Mooney, D.C.Pa.1959, 24 F.R.D. 279; Knowlton v. Atchison, T. & S.F. Ry. Co., D.C.Mo.1951, 11 F.R.D. 62; Finman, note 8 above, at 386–394; Developments in the Law—Discovery, 1961, 74 Harv.L.Rev. 940, 969.

13. U.S. v. Watchmakers of Switzerland Information Center, Inc., D.C.N.Y.1960, 25 F.R.D. 203; Johnstone v. Cronlund, D.C.Pa.

1960, 25 F.R.D. 42; Waider v. Chicago, R.I. & P.R. Co., D.C.Iowa, 1950, 10 F.R.D. 376.

14. Woods v. Robb, C.A.5th, 1948, 171 F.2d 539; U.S. v. La Fontaine, D.C.R.I. 1952, 12 F.R.D. 518; U.S. v. Lewis, D.C.N.J.1950, 10 F.R.D. 56.

15. Gordon v. FDIC, C.A.D.C.1970, 427 F.2d 578, 581; LeBlanc v. Spector, D.C.Conn.1974, 378 F.Supp. 310; FDIC v. Logsdon, D.C.Ky.1955, 18 F.R.D. 57; U.S. v. Fishman, D.C.N.Y.1953, 15 F.R.D. 151; In re Stein, D.C.Ill.1942, 43 F.Supp. 845; see Village of Brookfield v. Pentis, C.C.A.7th, 1939, 101 F.2d 516, 522; Finman, note 8 above, at 383–386; Note, The Constitutional Limits of Discovery, 1960, 35 Ind.L.J. 337, 346.

what is a "fact." [16] Though the earlier cases were surely not all one way, and many decisions held objectionable requests calling for admissions of opinions or conclusions of law, admissions about factual conclusions had frequently been required, as were requests calling for the admission of facts that would support legal conclusions. [17] Under the amended rule, it is still not proper to request an admission of a pure matter of law, [18] but admissions can be requested on matters of factual opinions and the application of law to fact. [19]

Again amended Rule 36(a) provides that a request is not objectionable solely on the ground that the party on whom it is served thinks that it presents a genuine issue for trial. If this is the situation the party is to deny the matter or set forth reasons why it cannot admit or deny. This accords with the view of some of the earlier cases [20] and the commentators [21] that Rule 36 is not confined to securing admissions of peripheral facts and may properly be addressed to matters that are crucial to the outcome of the case or are "controversial" or "disputed." There were cases to the contrary under the original rule, [22] but these seemed too confining since when a request is served it cannot be told whether a particular fact is actually disputed, and a party should not be able to avoid an answer, simply because a matter is disputable, if the party has no intention of disputing it.

Finally, amended Rule 36(a) states that a party may not give lack of information or knowledge as a reason for failure to admit or deny unless the party has made reasonable inquiry and the information known or readily obtainable by it is insufficient for it to admit or deny. [23] Some cases had imposed no duty on a party in this circumstance, but the better view had been that a good-faith effort to ascertain the truth of the

---

16. Photon, Inc. v. Harris Intertype, Inc., D.C.Mass.1961, 28 F.R.D. 327, 328; Finman, note 8 above, at 409–418.

17. 8 Wright, Miller & Marcus, Civil 2d § 2255.

18. Williams v. Krieger, D.C.N.Y.1973, 61 F.R.D. 142.

19. Lumpkin v. Meskill, D.C.Conn.1974, 64 F.R.D. 673. See the earlier cases cited 8 Wright, Miller & Marcus, Civil 2d § 2255.

20. U.S. ex rel. Seals v. Wiman, C.A.5th, 1962, 304 F.2d 53, 61–64; Ranger Ins. Co. v. Culberson, D.C.Ga.1969, 49 F.R.D. 181, 182–183; Tillman v. Fickencher, D.C.Pa. 1960, 27 F.R.D. 512, 513; and cases cited 8 Wright, Miller & Marcus, Civil 2d § 2256.

Under the amended rule an admission may be requested on "ultimate facts." City of Rome v. U.S., D.C.D.C.1978, 450 F.Supp. 378, 383, affirmed 1980, 100 S.Ct. 1548, 446 U.S. 156, 64 L.Ed.2d 119, rehearing denied 100 S.Ct. 3003, 447 U.S. 916, 64 L.Ed.2d 865.

21. Finman, note 8 above, at 394–402; Comment, The Dilemma of Rule 36, 1961, 56 Nw.U.L.Rev. 679, 684–685.

22. Pickens v. Equitable Life Assur. Socy., C.A.5th, 1969, 413 F.2d 1390, 1393–1394; Syracuse Broadcasting Corp. v. Newhouse, C.A.2d, 1959, 271 F.2d 910, 917; and cases cited 8 Wright, Miller & Marcus, Civil 2d § 2256.

23. Diederich v. Department of Army, D.C.N.Y.1990, 132 F.R.D. 614; Lumpkin v. Meskill, D.C.Conn.1974, 64 F.R.D. 673; Alexander v. Rizzo, D.C.Pa.1971, 52 F.R.D. 235.

It has been persuasively argued, however, that regardless of what a party believes or should believe, it is not required to make an admission if there is reasonable ground for concluding, on the basis of all the admissible evidence known to it, that the party who is seeking the admission may not prevail at trial. Shapiro, note 11 above, at 1078–1092.

matter was required of a litigant when the sources of corroboration were readily at hand.[24]

Requests under Rule 36 should be simple and direct, so that the answering party in a few words can admit, deny, or explain why it can do neither.[25] Similarly answers should fairly meet the substance of the requested admission,[26] and an evasive denial or an insufficient statement of reasons why the party cannot either admit or deny will have the effect of an admission.[27] An alternative remedy is for the court, on motion of the party making the request, to order further answers if the original answers are inadequate. This is now expressly authorized by amended Rule 36(a). It provides that if, on motion, the court finds that an answer does not comply with the requirements of the rule it may order either that the matter is admitted or that an amended answer be served.[28]

§ 90. Sanctions for Failure to Make Discovery [1]

Rule 37 deals with the consequences of failure to make discovery. It refers back to all the rules relating to disclosure, depositions, and discovery. The general scheme of the rule is that sanctions can be imposed only for failure to comply with an order of the court. Thus, where the discovery procedure itself requires a court order, as under Rule 35, or permits a court order, as when there has been a discovery conference under Rule 26(f) or a protective order has been denied under Rule 26(c), failure to obey the order can be punished immediately by any of the sanctions listed in Rule 37(b)(2). Where the discovery procedure is one set in motion by the parties themselves without court order, the party seeking discovery must first obtain an order under Rule 37(a) requiring the recalcitrant party or witness to make the discovery sought;[2] it is only violation of this order that is punishable under Rule

24. Veranda Beach Club Ltd. Partnership v. Western Sur. Co., C.A.1st, 1991, 936 F.2d 1364, 1374; 8 Wright, Miller & Marcus, Civil 2d § 2261.

25. Dubin v. E.F. Hutton Group, Inc., D.C.N.Y.1989, 125 F.R.D. 372, 375; 8 Wright, Miller & Marcus, Civil 2d § 2258.

26. U.S. v. American Tel. & Tel. Co., D.C.D.C.1979, 83 F.R.D. 323, 333; 8 Wright, Miller & Marcus, Civil 2d § 2260.

27. U.S. ex rel. Seals v. Wiman, C.A.5th, 1962, 304 F.2d 53, 64; Southern Ry. Co. v. Crosby, C.A.4th, 1953, 201 F.2d 878, 880. But see Finman, note 8 above, at 404–409.

28. Thalheim v. Eberheim, D.C.Conn. 1988, 124 F.R.D. 34; Alexander v. Rizzo, D.C.Pa.1971, 52 F.R.D. 235. See 8 Wright, Miller & Marcus, Civil 2d § 2263.

§ 90

1. 8 Wright, Miller & Marcus, Civil 2d §§ 2281–2293; Rodes, Ripple & Mooney, Sanctions Imposable for Violations of the Federal Rules of Civil Procedure, Federal Judicial Center 1981; Dudley, Discovery Abuse Revisited: Some Specific Proposals to Amend the Federal Rules of Civil Procedure, 1992, 26 U.S.F.L.Rev. 189; Renfrew, Discovery Sanctions: A Judicial Perspective, 1981, 1 Rev.Litig. 71; Werner, Survey of Discovery Sanctions, 1979 Ariz.St.L.J. 229; Epstein et al., An Up–Date on Rule 37 Sanctions, 1979, 84 F.R.D. 145; Comment, Preventing Abuse of Discovery in Federal Courts, 1981, 30 Cath.U.L.Rev. 273, 298–305.

2. An order of this kind can only be obtained on motion, and the moving party must certify that it has in good faith conferred or attempted to confer with the person or party failing to make the discovery in an effort to secure the information without court action. Rule 37(a)(2)(B), as amended in 1993. Similar provisions were made in that year in Rules 26(c), 37(a)(4)(A) and 37(c)(2).

37(b).[3] There are four exceptions to this general scheme: Rule 37(d) permits an immediate sanction against parties, and those who speak for corporate or other organization parties, for a willful failure to appear for a deposition or to answer interrogatories or to respond to a request for inspection under Rule 34; Rule 37(c)(2) authorizes imposition of expenses for an unjustified refusal to admit under Rule 36; and Rule 37(g) authorizes imposition of expenses for failure to participate in good faith in the framing of a discovery plan when required to do so under Rule 26(f). Finally, Rule 37(c)(1) provides a self-executing sanction for failure to make a disclosure required, since 1993, under Rule 26(a): unless the failure was harmless or there was substantial justification for it, the party may not use as evidence any witnesses or information that should have been disclosed.[4]

Without adequate sanctions, the procedure for discovery would be ineffectual. Under Rule 37 a party who seeks to evade or thwart a full and candid discovery incurs the risk of serious consequences that may include imprisonment for contempt of court,[5] the entry of an order that designated facts be taken to be established,[6] the entry of an order refusing the disobedient party the right to support or oppose designated claims or defenses,[7] striking out pleadings or parts of pleadings,[8] rendering judgment by default,[9] dismissal of claims or defenses,[10] or assessment of costs and attorneys' fees.[11]

The rule is flexible. Under Rule 37(b) the court makes such orders "as are just." The addition of this language in amended Rule 37(d) only

---

3. Daval Steel Products v. M/V Fakredine, C.A.2d, 1991, 951 F.2d 1357, 1364–1365; R.W. Intern. Corp. v. Welch Foods, Inc., C.A.1st, 1991, 937 F.2d 11, 15; Dorey v. Dorey, C.A.5th, 1980, 609 F.2d 1128, 1135. Contra: Airtex Corp. v. Shelley Radiant Ceiling Co., C.A.7th, 1976, 536 F.2d 145, 155.

4. Rule 37(c)(1). See 8 Wright, Miller & Marcus, Civil 2d § 2289.1. The court on motion may also impose other appropriate sanctions, including informing the jury of the failure to make the disclosure.

5. Rules 37(b)(1), 37(b)(2)(D); Lamar Financial Corp. v. Adams, C.A.5th, 1990, 918 F.2d 564; and cases cited 8 Wright, Miller & Marcus, Civil 2d § 2289 n. 71.

Contempt requires a court order and is not available as a sanction under Rule 37(d). Schleper v. Ford Motor Co., C.A.8th, 1978, 585 F.2d 1367, 1371 n. 3. The elaborate argument to the contrary in the dissent in that case founders not only on the absence of a court order but also on the fact that Rule 37(d) incorporates by reference the sanctions available under paragraphs (A), (B), and (C) of Rule 37(b)(2) and does not incorporate paragraph (D), which provides for contempt.

6. Rule 37(b)(2)(A); Insurance Corp. of Ireland, Ltd. v. Compagnie des Bauxites de Guinee, 1982, 102 S.Ct. 2099, 456 U.S. 694, 72 L.Ed.2d 492, noted 1982, 70 Calif.L.Rev. 1446.

7. Rule 37(b)(2)(B); Update Art, Inc. v. Modiin Pub., Ltd., C.A.2d, 1988, 843 F.2d 67, 71. This sanction was applied on unusually colorful facts in Rubenstein v. Kleven, D.C.Mass.1957, 150 F.Supp. 47.

8. Rule 37(b)(2)(C); Comdyne I, Inc. v. Corbin, C.A.3d, 1990, 908 F.2d 1142.

9. Rule 37(b)(2)(C); McLeod, Alexander, Power & Apffel, P.C. v. Quarles, C.A.5th, 1990, 894 F.2d 1482; Anderson v. Air West, Inc., C.A.9th, 1976, 542 F.2d 1090.

10. Rule 37(b)(2)(C); National Hockey League v. Metropolitan Hockey Club, Inc., 1976, 96 S.Ct. 2778, 427 U.S. 639, 49 L.Ed.2d 747; Bobal v. Rensselaer Polytechnic Institute, C.A.2d, 1990, 916 F.2d 759, certiorari denied 111 S.Ct. 1404, 499 U.S. 943, 113 L.Ed.2d 459.

11. Rule 37(a)(4). See also Rules 37(b), (c), and (d); David v. Hooker, Ltd., C.A.9th, 1977, 560 F.2d 412; In re Air Crash Disaster at Detroit Metropolitan Airport, D.C.Mich.1989, 130 F.R.D. 627; 8 Wright, Miller & Marcus, Civil 2d §§ 2288, 2289.

codifies a result that the courts had already reached and that the Constitution would in any event require.[12]   Amended Rule 37(d) eliminated the former stated requirement [13] that a failure be willful.   Even a negligent failure may be ground for imposition of sanctions though the willfulness of the failure is a role in the choice of sanctions.   This is in accord with the construction that the Supreme Court had previously given Rule 37(b).   It held that a mere failure, whether or not willful, was a "refusal," in the language of the rule as it then stood, but that if the failure to comply is because of inability to do so, rather than because of willfulness, bad faith, or any fault of the party, the action should not be dismissed and less drastic sanctions provided by the rule should be invoked.[14]

It had been the custom for the courts to give a delinquent party another opportunity to comply with the rules and the orders of the court. This still happens,[15] but it is less common as a result of the Supreme Court's decision in 1976 in National Hockey League v. Metropolitan Hockey Club, Inc.[16]   The important holding of the case is that in reviewing sanctions appellate courts are not to ask whether the sanction is one that they as an original matter would have imposed but only whether the district court abused its discretion in imposing the sanction.[17]   In an important dictum the Court spoke to the purposes of sanctions, saying that "the most severe in the spectrum of sanctions provided by statute or rule must be available to the district court in appropriate cases, not merely to penalize those whose conduct may be

---

12. The requirement that any sanction must be just "represents the general due process restrictions on the court's discretion." Insurance Corp. of Ireland, Ltd. v. Compagnie des Bauxites de Guinee, 1982, 102 S.Ct. 2099, 2107, 456 U.S. 694, 707, 72 L.Ed.2d 492.

13. E.g., Patterson v. C.I.T. Corp., C.A.10th, 1965, 352 F.2d 333, 336; U.S. v. 3963 Bottles, C.A.7th, 1959, 265 F.2d 332, 337, certiorari denied 79 S.Ct. 1448, 360 U.S. 931, 3 L.Ed.2d 1544. But cf. Milewski v. Schneider Transp. Co., C.A.6th, 1956, 238 F.2d 397.

14. Societe Internationale Pour Participations Industrielles et Commerciales, S.A. v. Rogers, 1958, 78 S.Ct. 1087, 357 U.S. 197, 2 L.Ed.2d 1255. This is reaffirmed in National Hockey League v. Metropolitan Hockey Club, Inc., 1976, 96 S.Ct. 2778, 2779, 427 U.S. 639, 640, 49 L.Ed.2d 747.

Simple negligence does not warrant dismissal. Marshall v. Segona, C.A.5th, 1980, 621 F.2d 763. Gross professional negligence may. Cine Forty–Second St. Theatre Corp. v. Allied Artists Pictures Corp., C.A.2d, 1979, 602 F.2d 1062. See Note, Defining a Feasible Culpability Threshold for the Imposition of Severe Discovery Sanctions, 1980, 65 Minn.L.Rev. 137.

15. E.g., Porter v. Martinez, C.A.9th, 1991, 941 F.2d 732; Diehl v. H.J. Heinz Co., C.A.7th, 1990, 901 F.2d 73, 75–76; U.S. v. Klimavicius, D.C.Me.1987, 116 F.R.D. 54; 8 Wright, Miller & Marcus, Civil 2d § 2284.

"The typical pattern of sanctioning that emerges from the reported cases is one in which the delay, obfuscation, contumacy, and lame excuses on the part of litigants and their attorneys are tolerated without any measured remedial action until the court is provoked beyond endurance. At that point the court punishes one side or the other with a swift and final termination of the lawsuit by dismissal or default. This 'all or nothing' approach to sanctions results in considerable laxity in the day-to-day application of the rules. Attorneys are well aware that sanctions will be imposed only in the most flagrant situations." Rodes, Ripple & Mooney, note 1 above, at 85.

16. 1976, 96 S.Ct. 2778, 427 U.S. 639, 49 L.Ed.2d 747.

17. 96 S.Ct. at 2780, 427 U.S. at 642. See also Insurance Corp. of Ireland, Ltd. v. Compagnie des Bauxites de Guinee, 1982, 102 S.Ct. 2099, 2107, 456 U.S. 694, 2107, 72 L.Ed.2d 492.

deemed to warrant such a sanction, but to deter those who might be tempted to such conduct in the absence of such a deterrent. If the decision of the Court of Appeals remained undisturbed in this case, it might well be that *these* respondents would faithfully comply with all future discovery orders entered by the District Court in this case. But other parties to other lawsuits would feel freer than we think Rule 37 contemplates they should feel to flout other discovery orders of other district courts." [18] There is evidence, though not yet conclusive, that the emphasis in National Hockey on the deterrent effect of sanctions on other litigants has caused courts to impose sanctions more readily, and to impose more severe sanctions than in the past.[19] As one court put it, "[a] district court is not required to fire a warning shot." [20] There is also evidence, however, that some courts of appeals have not fully heeded the holding of National Hockey and continue to exercise considerable freedom in setting aside or altering sanctions imposed by the district courts.[21]

In applying the sanctions permitted by Rule 37, it must be remembered that there are constitutional limitations upon the power of courts, even in aid of their own valid processes, to dismiss an action without affording a party the opportunity for a hearing on the merits of his cause.[22] In the early case of Hovey v. Elliott [23] it was held that due process had been denied a defendant where, because of his refusal to obey a court order pertinent to the suit, his answer was stricken and a decree pro confesso entered against him. This holding was substantially modified 12 years later in Hammond Packing Co. v. Arkansas.[24] There it was held not to be a denial of due process to strike defendant's answer, and render a default judgment against it, where it refused to produce documents in accordance with a pretrial order. In Hammond the Court explained the Hovey case on the basis that there defendant had been denied his right to defend "as a mere punishment," while in Hammond, it reasoned, the state was merely relying on a reasonable presumption that defendant's failure to produce the documents was an admission that there was no merit to its defense. The modern Court reads the two cases as showing that it would at least raise "substantial constitutional

18. 96 S.Ct. at 2781, 427 U.S. at 643.

19. Werner, note 1 above, at 316. See Rodes, Ripple & Mooney, note 1 above, at 31.

See also Cine Forty–Second St. Theatre Corp. v. Allied Artists Pictures Corp., C.A.2d, 1979, 602 F.2d 1062, 1066, noted 1980, 53 Temp.L.Q. 140; G–K Properties v. Redevelopment Agency of City of San Jose, C.A.9th, 1978, 577 F.2d 645, 647; and cases cited 8 Wright, Miller & Marcus, Civil 2d § 2284; Note, The Emerging Deterrence Orientation in the Imposition of Discovery Sanctions, 1978, 91 Harv.L.Rev. 1033.

20. Hal Commodity Cycles Management Co. v. Kirsh, C.A.7th, 1987, 825 F.2d 1136, 1139 (per Manion, J.). See also Daval Steel

Products v. M/V Fakredine, C.A.2d, 1991, 951 F.2d 1357, 1366.

21. See Epstein et al., note 1 above, at 169–170.

22. 8 Wright, Miller & Marcus, Civil 2d § 2283; Rodes, Ripple & Mooney, note 1 above, at 80–84; Note, cited note 19 above, at 1041–1043, 1052–1055; Note, Sanctions for Enforcement of Discovery—Constitutionality of Rule 37, 1962, 37 Wash.L.Rev. 175; Note, The Constitutional Limits of Discovery, 1960, 35 Ind.L.J. 337, 348–350.

23. 1897, 17 S.Ct. 841, 167 U.S. 409, 42 L.Ed. 215.

24. 1909, 29 S.Ct. 370, 212 U.S. 322, 53 L.Ed. 530.

questions" were a pleading to be stricken for noncompliance with a discovery order where the party had made a good faith effort to comply.[25] Thus, an adequate excuse for noncompliance, barring dismissal, was found where, under foreign law, controlling on the party in the case before the Court, it would be committing a crime if it made the disclosure sought. More recently the Court has said that due process is violated only if the behavior of the defendant will not support the Hammond presumption, and that a proper application of Rule 37(b)(2) will, as a matter of law, support such a presumption.[26] Even so, it emphasized what the Hammond rule requires: "the sanction must be specifically related to the particular 'claim,' which was at issue in the order to provide discovery."[27] Although Rule 37 sweeps broadly, some courts had looked to other sources, such as Rule 41, or local rules, or inherent power, to justify imposition of sanctions for failure to disclose. Usually this resort to other authority is unnecessary, and in 1958 the Court held that Rule 37 is the exclusive authority for sanctions for the discovery procedures.[28] There are other rules with their own provisions for sanctions[29] and there are some violations of the discovery rules that are not within the compass of Rule 37. For these latter matters courts continue to exercise inherent power.[30]

When the discovery rules were amended in 1970, it was thought that one reason courts had been reluctant to impose sanctions was that the sanctions then described in the rule were so drastic. Amended Rule 37 sought to alter this by making more generally available the sanction of requiring a party or its attorney to pay to its opponent the reasonable expenses incurred by the failure to make discovery.[31] This broadened a provision long in the rules with regard to an unjustified refusal to answer questions at a deposition or an unjustified attempt to obtain an order to compel answers to questions. The amended rule made this generally available for many discovery devices and shifted the emphasis by saying that the court "shall" order payment of expenses unless it

25. Societe Internationale Pour Participations Industrielles et Commerciales, S.A. v. Rogers, 1958, 78 S.Ct. 1087, 1095, 357 U.S. 197, 210, 2 L.Ed.2d 1255.

26. Insurance Corp. of Ireland, Ltd. v. Compagnie des Bauxites de Guinee, 1982, 102 S.Ct. 2099, 2105–2106, 456 U.S. 694, 705–707, 72 L.Ed.2d 492.

27. 102 S.Ct. at 2107, 456 U.S. at 707.

28. Societe Internationale Pour Participations Industrielles et Commerciales, S.A. v. Rogers, 1958, 78 S.Ct. 1087, 1093, 357 U.S. 197, 207, 2 L.Ed.2d 1255.

29. Rules 7(b)(3), 11(c), 16(f), 26(g)(3), 30(g), 45(f). See § 69A above.

30. See Chambers v. NASCO, Inc., 1991, 111 S.Ct. 2123, 501 U.S. 32, 115 L.Ed.2d 27, discussed § 69A above.

Courts have considered that they have inherent power to devise a sanction against

a party who has ignored the duty under Rule 26(e) to supplement answers. See 8 Wright, Miller & Marcus, Civil 2d § 2050.

In narrowly defined circumstances federal courts have inherent power to assess attorney's fees against counsel. Roadway Exp., Inc. v. Piper, 1980, 100 S.Ct. 2455, 2463–2464, 447 U.S. 752, 764–767, 65 L.Ed.2d 488.

31. Rules 37(a)(4), 37(b), 37(d). A very similar expense sanction was made available by Rule 37(g), added in 1980, for failure to participate in good faith in the framing of a discovery plan when required by Rule 26(f), by Rule 26(g), added in 1983, for making a certification in violation of the rule on a discovery request, response, or objection, and by Rule 30(d)(2), added in 1993, for impeding or delaying the examination of a deponent.

finds that the failure to make discovery or the attempt to secure an order compelling discovery was substantially justified or that other circumstances make an award of expenses unjust. Although an award of expenses has been made in many cases,[32] there are those who think that the award of expenses should be made almost automatic.[33]

A motion for imposition of sanctions should not provide an occasion to test the propriety of the discovery sought. Amended Rule 37(d) is explicit that sanctions under that subsection cannot be avoided on the ground that the discovery sought was objectionable unless the party failing to act has a pending motion for a protective order as provided by Rule 26(c). This had already been the usual view of the courts prior to the amendment.[34] This result seems implicit also in Rule 37(b), since the sanctions there provided for come into play only when a party has failed to comply with a court order to allow discovery. Any question of the propriety of the discovery will have been resolved when the court entered its order.[35] Though it is less clear, this would seem the proper result also under amended Rule 37(c)(2), dealing with requests for admissions. Since Rule 36 was amended in 1970 to provide a mechanism for judicial determination of the sufficiency of answers or objections to requests, a party should be required to use that procedure rather than contending after trial that its objection was a good one. It may be that there will be a different result with regard to the sanction provided in Rule 37(c)(1) for failure to disclose information required by Rule 26(a) or Rule 26(e)(1). That provision, added in 1993, imposes the sanction only on a party that "without substantial justification" has failed to make disclosure.[36]

---

32. E.g., Coane v. Ferrara Pan Candy Co., C.A.5th, 1990, 898 F.2d 1030; and cases cited 8 Wright, Miller & Marcus, Civil 2d § 2288.

There have also been cases in which the courts have exercised their power to make an award personally against the delinquent attorney. Shipes v. Trinity Industries, C.A.5th, 1993, 987 F.2d 311, 323, certiorari denied 114 S.Ct. 548, ___ U.S. ___, 126 L.Ed.2d 450; and cases cited 8 Wright, Miller & Marcus, Civil 2d § 2288. The court may even make this award against government attorneys and prohibit them from seeking reimbursement from the government. Chilcutt v. U.S., C.A.5th, 1993, 4 F.3d 1313, 1325–1327; Derechin v. State University of New York, C.A.2d, 1992, 963 F.2d 513, 519–520. See Comment, Sanctions Imposed by Courts on Attorneys Who Abuse the Judicial Process, 1977, 44 U.Chi. L.Rev. 619. Rules 37(a)(4), 37(b)(2), 37(d), and 37(g) authorize the award to be made against the party or the attorney or both. But Rule 37(c)(2) authorizes an award only against "the other party" and does not permit sanctions against the party's attorney. Apex Oil Co. v. Belcher Co. of New York, Inc., C.A.2d, 1988, 855 F.2d 1009, 1013–1014. Rule 37(c)(1) appears to be similarly limited.

33. Schroeder & Frank, Discovery Reform: Long Road to Nowheresville, 1982, 68 A.B.A.J. 572, 574.

34. Collins v. Wayland, C.C.A.9th, 1944, 139 F.2d 677, certiorari denied 64 S.Ct. 1151, 322 U.S. 744, 88 L.Ed. 1576; and cases cited 8 Wright, Miller & Marcus, Civil 2d § 2291.

35. Interstate Cigar Co. v. Consolidated Cigar Co., C.A.2d, 1963, 317 F.2d 744, 746; Kozlowski v. Sears, Roebuck & Co., D.C.Mass.1976, 71 F.R.D. 594, 597, motion denied 73 F.R.D. 73. Independent Productions Corp. v. Loew's, Inc., D.C.N.Y.1962, 30 F.R.D. 377, 380. But see Roberson v. Christoferson, D.C.N.D.1975, 65 F.R.D. 615, 620.

36. See 8 Wright, Miller & Marcus, Civil 2d § 2289.1.

F.   TRIALS

Analysis

---

§ 91.   Pretrial Conference [1]

Rule 16, authorizing the pretrial conference, was easily the most popular of the rules. Similar provisions have been adopted in almost all of the states. The original concept was to provide a means by which the court and counsel could confer about a case in advance. They would endeavor to eliminate unnecessary issues, analyze and settle the pleadings by amendments if desirable or necessary, eliminate matters of proof by admissions or stipulations, limit the number of expert witnesses, ascertain whether issues in jury cases might be referred to a master for findings, and discuss other matters that might expedite the disposition of the action.[2]

The pretrial conference was and is an important adjunct of the other procedural devices provided by the rules. The simplified pleading permitted by Rule 8 is possible because the issues can be defined at the pretrial conference. The unlimited joinder of claims and parties that other rules allow is made workable by the availability of a pretrial conference at which the court can decide on the form and order of the trial.

But the changes in Rule 16 since 1938 are a striking example of what has happened in federal litigation, and in federal rulemaking, since the Civil Rules were first adopted. The original rule was two paragraphs and filled only half a page. As extensively rewritten and enlarged, first in 1983 and again in 1993, the rule is three-pages long,[3] and it is divided into six subdivisions and 32 numbered paragraphs.[4]

---

§ 91

1.   6A Wright, Miller & Kane, Civil 2d §§ 1521–1530; Richey, Rule 16 Revisited: Reflections for the Benefit of Bench and Bar, 1992, 139 F.R.D. 525; Shapiro, Federal Rule 16: A Look at the Theory and Practice of Rulemaking, 1989, 137 U.Pa.L.Rev. 1969. There is important data, though it is now old, in the study by the Project for Effective Justice reported in Rosenberg, The Pretrial Conference and Effective Justice, 1964.

2.   6A Wright, Miller & Kane, Civil 2d § 1522.

3.   "The 1983 amendment of Rule 16, like many amendments of other Rules over the years, made the text a good deal longer." Shapiro, note 1 above, at 1984.

4.   The Advisory Committee Note to the original rule was two short paragraphs. The Note to the 1983 amendments fills four pages of small type, while the Note to the 1993 amendments is slightly more than four pages long.

Though the pretrial conference had been promoted on the ground that it will improve the quality of the trial, the main reason for its wide popularity had been a belief that it would help reduce court congestion by increasing the number of cases that are settled and by shortening the trial in those cases that are tried. In an eloquent tribute to the device of the pretrial conference, the Second Circuit, speaking through Judge Clark, said that it leads to "better justice more shortly and efficiently obtained."[5] This would be marvelous if true—but there was convincing evidence suggesting that it was not wholly true. An exhaustive empirical study by Professor Maurice Rosenberg showed that pretrial did indeed improve the quality of those cases that were tried, but that to require a pretrial conference in every case led to a net loss in judicial time because there was no saving in the trial-time demands a case made to compensate for the time required to conduct conferences.[6] Thus, pretrial should be justified on the ground that it leads to better justice rather than because justice will be more shortly and efficiently obtained.

This was a major reason for the 1983 amendments. The Advisory Committee Note to them said that "there is evidence that pretrial conferences may improve the quality of justice rendered in the federal courts by sharpening the preparation and presentation of cases, tending to eliminate trial surprise, and improving, as well as facilitating, the settlement process."[7] But the Note went on to say that with regard to case management the rule had not always been as helpful as it might have been. The rule was rewritten to make scheduling and case management an express goal of pretrial procedure. This was done "by shifting the emphasis away from a conference focused solely on the trial and toward a process of judicial management that embraces the entire pretrial phase, especially motions and discovery."[8]

Rule 16 does not make a pretrial conference compulsory in every case in federal court.[9] In some districts only selected cases are pretried, generally on the application of counsel, though many districts do provide by local rule for pretrial as a matter of routine in every case.[10] There is, however, a widespread belief that mandatory use of pretrial conferences is a bad idea: "a conference is a waste of time in simple cases and the procedure will not work unless the judge believes it will be useful."[11] This feeling extends also to the case-management techniques that were added to the rule in 1983. As one commentator put it: "The procedures of amended Rule 16 are cumbersome and unnecessary in most smaller

5. Padovani v. Bruchhausen, C.A.2d, 1961, 293 F.2d 546, 550.

6. Rosenberg, note 1 above, at 28–29. See also Friedenthal, Kane & Miller, Civil Procedure, 2d ed. 1993, p. 429.

7. 97 F.R.D. at 205, 205–206.

8. 97 F.R.D. at 205, 207.

9. McCargo v. Hedrick, C.A.4th, 1976, 545 F.2d 393; Sleek v. J. C. Penney Co., C.A.3d, 1963, 324 F.2d 467.

10. Note, Pretrial Conference: A Critical Examination of Local Rules Adopted in Federal District Courts, 1978, 64 Va.L.Rev. 467.

11. Friedenthal, Kane & Miller, note 6 above, at 429.

lawsuits. Micro-management of even modestly complex litigation is enormously time-consuming."[12]

Rule 16(b), added in 1983 and expanded in 1993, does make the entry of a scheduling order mandatory,[13] except in categories of actions exempted by district-court rule as inappropriate.[14] The order is to issue as soon as practicable, but in any event within 90 days after the appearance of a defendant and within 120 days after the complaint has been served on a defendant. The scheduling order must set time limits for adding parties, amending pleading, and completing discovery[15] and may also include modification of the times for disclosures under Rules 26(a) and 26(e)(1) and of the extent of discovery to be permitted, the dates of pretrial conferences and the trial itself, and other appropriate matters.[16]

It is left to the court to determine at what time to have the pretrial conference or conferences. The rule speaks to this only in saying that any final pretrial conference shall be held as close to the time of trial as reasonable under the circumstances.[17] There is no limit on the number of conferences that may be ordered in a particular case. In one "big" case, the court noted that it had held 23 pretrial conferences.[18]

At least one of the attorneys for each party participating in any pretrial conference must have authority to enter into stipulations and to make admissions regarding all matters that the participants may reasonably anticipate may be discussed.[19] Any final pretrial conference must be attended by at least one attorney on each side who will participate in the trial.[20] While it is not compulsory upon the court to call a pretrial conference, it is compulsory upon counsel to attend when the court does call one. A divided Supreme Court has held that where the excuse of counsel for failure to attend a pretrial conference was inadequate, and the history of the litigation suggested that plaintiff had been deliberately proceeding in a dilatory fashion, the court has inherent power to dismiss

---

12. Dudley, Discovery Abuse Revisited: Some Specific Proposals to Amend the Federal Rules of Civil Procedure, 1992, 26 U.S.F.L.Rev. 189, 190. See also Shapiro, note 1 above, at 1995.

13. Though the order is mandatory, a scheduling conference is not. The judge—or magistrate judge, if authorized by local rule—may enter the scheduling order after receiving the report from the parties required in most cases by Rule 26(f) or after consulting with the attorneys for the parties, either at a scheduling conference or by telephone, mail, or other suitable means.

14. For the kinds of exemptions that districts created, see Weeks, District Court Implementation of Amended Federal Civil Rule 16: A Report on New Local Rules, 1984, p. 17.

15. These limits cannot be modified except on a showing of good cause. See Sil–Flo, Inc. v. SFHC, Inc., C.A.10th, 1990, 917 F.2d 1507; and cases cited 6A Wright, Miller & Kane, Civil 2d § 1522.1 n. 14. See also Richey, note 1 above, at 528–530.

16. 6A Wright, Miller & Kane, Civil 2d § 1522.1.

17. Rule 16(d).

18. See Life Music, Inc. v. Broadcast Music, Inc., D.C.N.Y.1962, 31 F.R.D. 3, 4.

See also Manual for Complex Litigation, Second, 1985, § 21.21.

19. Rule 16(c).

20. Rule 16(d).

because of the failure to attend.[21] This is now written into Rule 16(f), which authorizes sanctions for failure to obey a scheduling or pretrial order, or failing to appear at a conference, or appearing unprepared, or failing to participate in good faith.[22]

Rule 16(c) now lists 16 subjects that may be considered, and concerning which the court may take appropriate action, at a pretrial conference.[23] Counsel must make full and fair disclosure of their views about what the real issues of the trial will be.[24] They may be required at that time to disclose the names of the witnesses they plan to call at the trial.[25] In many districts, local rules require parties to exchange pretrial memoranda prior to the conference, which commonly are expected to contain a very detailed statement of the case from each party's point of view.[26]

How pretrial is carried on varies from court to court, indeed from judge to judge. Some are extremely formal, with elaborate hearings in open court attended by litigants and counsel resulting in a memorial order wrapping up the whole proceeding. Some are carried on in chambers, with no record kept save the final pretrial order, which may be simple or may be complex, while others are in chambers with a court reporter present. There is still much difference of view on whether the judge should take part directly in seeking to achieve a settlement of the case at the pretrial conference.[27] But the 1983 amendments stated "facilitating the settlement of the case" as one of the purposes of pretrial conferences [28] and settlement is one of the things that may be considered at the conference.[29] In addition, the rule was amended in 1993 to give the court power to require that a party or its representative be present or reasonably available by telephone to consider possible settlement.[30]

21. Link v. Wabash R. Co., 1962, 82 S.Ct. 1386, 370 U.S. 626, 8 L.Ed.2d 734.

22. 6A Wright, Miller & Kane, Civil 2d § 1631.

23. 6A Wright, Miller & Kane, Civil 2d § 1525.

24. Payne v. S.S. Nabob, C.A.3d, 1962, 302 F.2d 803; Marble v. Batten & Co., D.C.D.C.1964, 36 F.R.D. 693.

25. Rule 16(c)(7); Brock v. R.J. Auto Parts & Serv., Inc., C.A.10th, 1988, 864 F.2d 677; and cases cited 6A Wright, Miller & Kane, Civil 2d § 1525 n. 12.

26. 6A Wright, Miller & Kane, Civil 2d § 1524, p. 238, § 1527, pp. 291–292.

27. Shapiro, note 1 above, at 1989–1991; Brennan, Introduction to the Problem of the Protracted Case, 1958, 23 F.R.D. 276, 278–279; Clark, Objectives of Pre–Trial Procedure, 1956, 17 Ohio St.L.J. 163, 167. The view that the court should take an active role in settlement negotiations is stated by Judge Charles R. Richey, note 1 above, at 538–539, and by Judge J. Skelly

Wright in The Pre–Trial, Conference, 1960, 28 F.R.D. 141, 145–147.

28. Rule 16(a)(5).

29. Rule 16(c)(9). As amended in 1993, this provision allows consideration of "settlement or the use of special procedures to assist in resolving the dispute when authorized by statute or local rule". The Advisory Committee Note says that the rule "does not attempt to resolve questions as to the extent a court would be authorized to require such proceedings as an exercise of its inherent powers." 146 F.R.D. at 604. It has been held that compelling participation in a summary jury trial under threat of sanctions is clearly erroneous as a matter of law. In re NLO, Inc., C.A.6th, 1993, 5 F.3d 154; Strandell v. Jackson County, C.A.7th, 1987, 838 F.2d 884.

30. Rule 16(c). See the Advisory Committee Note to this addition, 146 F.R.D. at 604–605. A controversial case had held that courts have inherent power to order parties, even though they are represented by counsel, to attend personally a pretrial

Stipulations and statements of counsel at a pretrial conference are binding on the parties,[31] but if the court should relieve the party of the statement, as Rule 16 permits, the statement is out of the case and is neither binding nor admissible as evidence of the facts stated.[32]

After the pretrial conference, the court makes an order reciting the action taken at the conference. This order, unless modified, controls the subsequent course of the case.[33] A final pretrial order may be modified by the court to prevent manifest injustice,[34] and it will be deemed modified to conform to evidence admitted without objection.[35] It is discretionary with the court whether to permit modification of the order. Particularly when the pretrial conference is held shortly before trial and at a time when each side should know what it intends to prove, the court may, if it thinks it best, refuse to permit modification.[36] But as with all rules problems, the dominant purpose of the courts must be to do justice rather than to vindicate procedural rules, and an unswerving insistence upon every provision of a pretrial order may, under certain circumstances, cause injustice.[37]

§ 92. The Right to Jury Trial [1]

The Seventh Amendment to the Constitution provides: "In suits at common law, where the value in controversy shall exceed twenty dollars,

settlement conference. G. Heileman Brewing Co. v. Joseph Oat Corp., C.A.7th, 1989, 871 F.2d 648, noted 1990, 39 DePaul L.Rev. 931, 23 J.Marshall L.Rev. 517, 58 U.Cin. L.Rev. 1421, 15 U.Dayton L.Rev. 343. See also Note, Rule 16 and Pretrial Conferences: Have We Forgotten the Most Important Ingredient?, 1990, 63 S.Cal.L.Rev. 1449.

31. Air–Exec, Inc. v. Two Jacks, Inc., C.A.10th, 1978, 584 F.2d 942; Gaztambide Barbosa v. Torres Gaztambide, D.C.Puerto Rico 1991, 776 F.Supp. 52, 57; and cases cited 6A Wright, Miller & Kane, Civil 2d § 1527 nn. 1–3.

32. Hunt v. Marchetti, C.A.11th, 1987, 824 F.2d 916, 918; Laird v. Air Carrier Engine Serv., Inc., C.A.5th, 1959, 263 F.2d 948, 954.

In an extreme case it is an abuse of discretion not to relieve a party from pretrial stipulations. U.S. v. Texas, C.A.5th, 1982, 680 F.2d 356, 370.

33. Rule 16(e); Valley Ranch Dev. Co. v. FDIC, C.A.5th, 1992, 960 F.2d 550; Hullman v. Board of Trustees of Pratt Community College, C.A.10th, 1991, 950 F.2d 665; and cases cited 6A Wright, Miller & Kane, Civil 2d § 1527 nn. 12–18. See also Richey, note 1 above, at 530–531.

34. Rule 16(e); Coastal States Marketing, Inc. v. Hunt, C.A.5th, 1983, 694 F.2d 1358; Clark v. Pennsylvania R. Co., C.A.2d, 1964, 328 F.2d 591, 593–595, certiorari denied 84 S.Ct. 1943, 377 U.S. 1006, 12 L.Ed.2d 1054; 6A Wright, Miller & Kane, Civil 2d § 1527, pp. 279–290.

35. Frank Music Corp. v. Metro–Goldwyn–Mayer, Inc., C.A.9th, 1985, 772 F.2d 505, 515 n. 9; Perfection–Cobey Co., Div. of Harsco Corp. v. City Tank Corp., C.A.4th, 1979, 597 F.2d 419; and cases cited 6A Wright, Miller & Kane, Civil 2d § 1527 nn. 30–33.

36. Walker v. Anderson Elec. Connectors, C.A.11th, 1991, 944 F.2d 841; Payne v. S.S. Nabob, C.A.3d, 1962, 302 F.2d 803, noted 1962, 36 Temp.L.Q. 101; Stukey v. U.S. Air Force, D.C.Ohio 1992, 790 F.Supp. 165.

37. Sill Corp. v. U.S., C.A.10th, 1965, 343 F.2d 411, 420, certiorari denied 86 S.Ct. 88, 382 U.S. 840, 15 L.Ed.2d 81; Scott v. Spanjer Bros., Inc., C.A.2d, 1962, 298 F.2d 928, 931.

§ 92

1. 9 Wright & Miller, Civil §§ 2301–2307; Landsman, The Civil Jury in America: Scenes from an Unappreciated History, 1993, 44 Hastings L.J. 579; Rendleman, Chapters of the Civil Jury, 1977, 65 Ky.L.J. 769; Redish, Seventh Amendment Right to Jury Trial: A Study in the Irrationality of Rational Decision Making, 1975, 70 Nw. U.L.Rev. 486; McCoid, Procedural Reform and the Right to Jury Trial: A Study of the right of trial by jury shall be preserved, and no fact tried by a jury shall be otherwise re-examined in any Court of the United States, than according to the rules of the common law." [2] Rule 38(a) states that the right of trial by jury as declared by the Seventh Amendment, or as given by a federal statute, "shall be preserved to the parties inviolate."

The right of trial by jury is of ancient origin.[3] To Blackstone it was "the glory of the English law" and "the most transcendent privilege which any subject can enjoy." [4] In Justice Story's view "the Constitution would have been justly obnoxious to the most conclusive objection if it had not recognized and confirmed it in the most solemn terms." [5] The Supreme Court itself has voiced similar eulogies to the jury.[6]

Today these views are not universally accepted. Assertions are made that trial by jury is "expensive and dilatory—perhaps anachronistic." [7] In federal courts, at least, the Seventh Amendment writes into the basic charter the belief that trial by jury is the normal and preferable mode of disposing of issues of fact in civil cases involving legal relief as well as in criminal cases. Despite the critics, there is still a general professional view that maintenance of the jury as a factfinding body is of such importance and occupies so firm a place in our history and jurisprudence that any seeming curtailment of the right to jury trial should be scrutinized with the utmost care.[8] The Supreme Court has been zealous to safeguard, perhaps even to enlarge, the function of the jury.

Beacon Theatres, Inc. v. Westover, 1967, 116 U.Pa.L.Rev. 1; Rothstein, Beacon Theatres and the Constitutional Right to Jury Trial, 1965, 51 A.B.A.J. 1145; James, Right to a Jury Trial in Civil Actions, 1963, 72 Yale L.J. 655; Comment, From Beacon Theatres to Dairy Queen to Ross: The Seventh Amendment, The Federal Rules, and a Receding Law–Equity Dichotomy, 1971, 48 J.Urban Law 459. There is a large literature on this subject, but, with the exception of the authorities just cited, and of those cited note 45 below, it antedates recent Supreme Court decisions that have made all that was written before obsolete and probably misleading.

2. Wolfram, The Constitutional History of the Seventh Amendment, 1973, 57 Minn. L.Rev. 639. Professor Wolfram shows that the Seventh Amendment was a concession the Federalists had to promise in order to secure ratification of the Constitution.

3. Henderson, The Background of the Seventh Amendment, 1966, 80 Harv.L.Rev. 289.

4. 3 Bl.Comm. * 379.

5. 2 Story, Commentaries on the Constitution, 1833, § 1779.

6. E.g., Sioux City & P. Ry. Co. v. Stout, 1874, 17 Wall. 657, 664, 21 L.Ed.2d 745.

7. James, Trial by Jury and the New Federal Rules of Procedure, 1936, 45 Yale L.J. 1022, 1026. See also, e.g., Symposium, The Role of the Jury in Civil Dispute Resolution, 1990 U.Chi.Legal F.; Frank, Courts on Trial, 1949; Devitt, Should Jury Trial Be Required in Civil Cases? A Challenge to the Seventh Amendment, 1982, 47 J.Air L. & Comm. 495; Redish, note 1 above, at 502–508; Shapiro & Coquillette, The Fetish of Jury Trial in Civil Cases: A Comment on Rachal v. Hill, 1971, 85 Harv.L.Rev. 442; Peck, Do Juries Delay Justice?, 1956, 18 F.R.D. 455.

8. Dimick v. Schiedt, 1934, 55 S.Ct. 296, 300, 293 U.S. 474, 485, 79 L.Ed. 603.

"Over the past quarter century * * * support for the civil jury has become nearly unanimous." Priest, The Role of the Civil Jury in a System of Private Litigation, 1990 U.Chi.Legal F. 162; See also Verdict: Assessing the Civil Jury System, Litan ed. 1993; Landsman, note 1 above; Kalven, The Dignity of the Civil Jury, 1964, 50 Va.L.Rev. 1055; Summers, Some Merits of Civil Jury Trials, 1964, 39 Tul.L.Rev. 3; DeParcq, Thoughts on the Civil Jury, 1965, 3 Tulsa L.J. 1.

Though there had been some divergence of opinion on this point,[9] it is now wholly clear that the right of jury trial in federal court is governed entirely by federal law, and that state law may be disregarded. Three different situations may exist. State law may deny a jury trial in a case where the Seventh Amendment requires a jury trial. In this situation the federal court must allow a jury trial.[10] The language of the Rules of Decision Act[11] cannot prevail over the clear command of the Seventh Amendment. Even if Justice Brandeis's controversial view that the Erie holding was constitutionally required be accepted,[12] it cannot alter the result in this situation, for Congress not only has explicit constitutional authority to provide a jury trial in common law cases but indeed is prohibited from denying such a trial.

The second situation is that in which the state law denies jury trial, but federal courts customarily permit such trial though not required to do so by the Seventh Amendment. The Court decided Byrd v. Blue Ridge Rural Electric Cooperative[13] as if it were such a case, expressly refusing to determine whether the right of jury trial there involved was constitutionally protected,[14] and held that, at least where the state rule is not bound up with rights and obligations, the federal policy favoring jury decisions of disputed fact questions should prevail over the contrary state rule.

Finally there is the situation in which state law would provide trial by jury on an issue that, in the federal system, would normally be decided by the judge. This was essentially the situation involved in Herron v. Southern Pacific Co.,[15] where a unanimous Court held that a federal court might direct a verdict on the ground of contributory negligence despite a state constitutional provision that that defense "shall, in all cases whatsoever, be a question of fact and shall, at all times, be left to the jury." There was room to doubt whether the Herron rule had survived the subsequent announcement of the Erie doctrine, but the holding and language of Herron were heavily relied on in the post-Erie decision of Byrd v. Blue Ridge, and it now seems established that in this third situation trial should be to the judge in a federal court regardless of the contrary state rule.[16]

The same result should be reached, and state law disregarded, in determining the sufficiency of the evidence to go to the jury. The state

---

9. See authorities cited 9 Wright & Miller, Civil § 2303 nn. 64–66.

10. Simler v. Conner, 1963, 83 S.Ct. 609, 610–611, 372 U.S. 221, 222, 9 L.Ed.2d 691; Parsons v. Bedford, Breedlove & Robeson, 1830, 3 Pet. 433, 7 L.Ed. 732; U.S. v. Williams, C.A.5th, 1971, 441 F.2d 637, 643–644; Green, Protection of Jury Trial in Diversity Cases against State Invasions, 1957, 35 Texas L.Rev. 768. This is true also of particular issues within a case. E.g., Agfa–Gevaert, A.G. v. A.B. Dick Co., C.A.7th, 1989, 879 F.2d 1518, 1521.

11. 28 U.S.C.A. § 1652.

12. See § 56 above.

13. 1958, 78 S.Ct. 893, 356 U.S. 525, 2 L.Ed.2d 953. See § 55 above.

14. 78 S.Ct. at 901 n. 10, 356 U.S. at 537 n. 10.

15. 1931, 51 S.Ct. 383, 283 U.S. 91, 75 L.Ed. 857.

16. E.g., Goar v. Compania Peruana de Vapores, C.A.5th, 1982, 688 F.2d 417, 423–424.

may have a more liberal standard than the federal courts in permitting an issue to go to the jury. It may be that a certain issue in state practice is always for the jury, as with the Arizona constitutional provision involved in the Herron case, or the state rule may be, as in Alabama, that a scintilla of evidence is enough to create a jury issue. The Herron case would seem to have settled that the state rule is not controlling in such circumstances. Conversely the state may demand a higher quantum of proof than would the federal court, and may authorize a directed verdict where a federal court would normally submit the matter to a jury. The Seventh Amendment itself would seem to bar resort to state law here, since to follow the state rule would deprive the party of the verdict of a jury under circumstances where, at common law, it would have been entitled to go to the jury.

Doubt was cast upon this analysis by the decision of the Supreme Court in Stoner v. New York Life Ins. Co.[17] A federal trial judge, sitting without a jury, held that a person was totally disabled within the meaning of an insurance policy. The circuit court of appeals reversed, finding that the evidence established that the person was not totally disabled. In two actions still pending, the state intermediate appellate court had held, with regard to the same evidence and the same parties, that there was sufficient evidence to create a jury issue on total disability. In this situation the Supreme Court held that the Erie doctrine required the federal courts to accept the state holdings that the evidence would support a finding of total disability.

In Byrd v. Blue Ridge, in 1958, the Supreme Court referred to its decision in Stoner as having "held that the federal court should follow the state rule defining the evidence sufficient to raise a jury question whether the state-created right was established."[18] Some courts of appeals had read Stoner in this same way, though a majority were to the contrary and applied the federal standard of sufficiency of the evidence.[19] It is hard to believe that Stoner held what the Court later said it held. The Stoner decision may be regarded as merely a peculiar application of the doctrine of "law of the case."[20] Or it may be thought that the state-court decisions defined what constituted total disability under the law of that state, and that the circuit court of appeals had erred in applying a different definition.[21] The one thing that Stoner did not hold is that state law controls on when a verdict may be directed. In Stoner itself trial was to the court and no jury problem arose. Neither the circuit court, the Supreme Court, nor the parties in their briefs in Stoner ever mentioned the Herron case or the Seventh Amendment.

The Court, which thought the question settled in 1958, spoke more fully to the point in 1959, and in rather a different tone. Without even

17. 1940, 61 S.Ct. 336, 311 U.S. 464, 85 L.Ed. 284.

18. 78 S.Ct. at 902 n. 15, 356 U.S. at 540 n. 15.

19. See cases cited 9 Wright & Miller, Civil § 2525 n. 69.

20. See Note, 1953, 66 Harv.L.Rev. 1516, 1524.

21. See Notes, 1956, 51 Nw.U.L.Rev. 338, 348–350, 1953, 66 Harv.L.Rev. 1516, 1524–1525.

referring to Stoner, the Court called the issue here discussed—the effect of state law in defining the sufficiency of the evidence—an "important question" that should be left for decision to a case in which it was properly briefed and argued.[22] Thus, the question is now explicitly an open one in the federal system, but, for reasons already indicated, it would be very surprising if state law were held controlling on this point.[23]

The Seventh Amendment creates a historical test for trial by jury.[24] The practice of the common law in 1791, when the amendment was adopted, is made the standard, although this practice must be read in the light of the decisions between 1791 and 1938, when law and equity were merged. This historical test does not exhaust the situations in which trial by jury can be had. Congress has given a right to jury trial in certain matters not within the Seventh Amendment, and it seems quite settled that there is no constitutional right to a nonjury trial in a case outside the Seventh Amendment.[25]

Because the test under the Seventh Amendment is historical, it will not always be easy to apply. Courts have complained of being held in "historical bondage," [26] and have apologized for an analysis that "may seem to reek unduly of the study." [27] But the number of cases in which existence of a jury right will be difficult to determine is very small. In many cases jury trial will not be demanded. Where it is demanded, in

22. Dick v. New York Life Ins. Co., 1959, 79 S.Ct. 921, 926, 359 U.S. 437, 444–445, 3 L.Ed.2d 935. The Court also left the question open in Mercer v. Theriot, 1964, 84 S.Ct. 1157, 377 U.S. 152, 12 L.Ed.2d 206.

23. 9 Wright & Miller, Civil § 2525; 19 Wright, Miller & Cooper, Jurisdiction § 4511, pp. 177–178; Childress, Judicial Review and Diversity Jurisdiction: Solving an Irrepressible Erie Mystery, 1994, 47 SMU L.Rev. 271; cf. Cooper, Directions for Directed Verdicts: A Compass for Federal Courts, 1971, 55 Minn.L.Rev. 903, 972–989. Contra: Moore, A Century Old Problem: Federal or State Law as Determinative of a Directed Verdict in a Federal Court, 1970, 4 U.Rich.L.Rev. 282; Comment, Arizona Constitutional Law Derailed in Federal Diversity Court: A Reevaluation of Herron v. Southern Pacific Co., 1974, 16 Ariz.L.Rev. 208.

Although the lower courts are not yet in agreement on the point, there are especially forceful statements of the arguments for a federal test by Chief Judge Haynsworth in Wratchford v. S.J. Groves & Sons Co., C.A.4th, 1969, 405 F.2d 1061, 1064–1066, and by Chief Judge Tuttle in Planters Mfg. Co. v. Protection Mut. Ins. Co., C.A.5th, 1967, 380 F.2d 869, 870–871, certiorari denied 88 S.Ct. 293, 389 U.S. 930, 19 L.Ed.2d 282.

See also Browning–Ferris Indus. of Vermont, Inc. v. Kelco Disposal Inc., 1989, 109 S.Ct. 2909, 2922, 492 U.S. 257, 278–279, 106 L.Ed.2d 219: "Federal law * * * will control on those issues involving the proper review of the jury award by a federal district court and court of appeals."

The Sixth and Seventh Circuits are the last to adhere to a general rule that state law controls. Gafford v. General Elec. Co., C.A.6th, 1993, 997 F.2d 150, 170; Pro Football Weekly, Inc. v. Gannett Co., C.A.7th, 1993, 988 F.2d 723, 726.

24. This has long been accepted by the Supreme Court and by almost all commentators. For an elaborate attempt to argue to the contrary, suggesting that a functional test was intended, see Klein, The Myth of How to Interpret the Seventh Amendment Right to a Civil Jury Trial, 1992, 53 Ohio St.L.J. 1005.

25. Beacon Theatres, Inc. v. Westover, 1958, 79 S.Ct. 948, 956, 359 U.S. 500, 510, 3 L.Ed.2d 988; Note, The Right to a Non-jury Trial, 1961, 74 Harv.L.Rev. 1176.

26. Gefen v. U.S., C.A.5th, 1968, 400 F.2d 476, 479, certiorari denied 89 S.Ct. 990, 393 U.S. 1119, 22 L.Ed.2d 123.

27. Damsky v. Zavatt, C.A.2d, 1961, 289 F.2d 46, 48. A dissenter would have added "if not of the museum." Id. at 59.

most instances it will be obvious that there is or is not a right to trial by jury. Thus, the vast and controversial literature that has developed about the scope of the jury right is, fortunately, not in proportion to the practical importance of the problem in the actual working of the courts.

In general there is no right to a trial by jury of claims that historically were "equitable," such as actions for injunction, specific performance, and the like.[28] There is a right to trial by jury in actions that historically would have been considered "legal," of which actions for money damages for tort or breach of contract are the most familiar examples.[29] If new causes of action are created unknown at common law, the courts must look to the nearest historical analogy and characterize the remedy sought to decide whether there is a right to a jury.[30]

The discussion thus far has assumed, as has been common in the literature, that the test of jury trial is entirely historical, and that the task of the court is to determine whether the claim is, or may be considered analogous to, a claim that would have been triable to a jury

28. 9 Wright & Miller, Civil §§ 2302, 2308, 2309.

29. 9 Wright & Miller, Civil §§ 2302, 2316.

30. E.g., right to jury: Wooddell v. International Broth. of Elec. Workers, Local 71, 1991, 112 S.Ct. 494, ___ U.S. ___, 116 L.Ed.2d 419; (suit for money damages and injunctive relief by a union member claiming that the union discriminated against him in job referrals); Chauffeurs, Teamsters & Helpers Local No. 391 v. Terry, 1990, 110 S.Ct. 1339, 494 U.S. 558, 108 L.Ed.2d 519 (employee seeking back pay for union's breach of duty of fair representation); Granfinanciera, S.A. v. Nordberg, 1989, 109 S.Ct. 2782, 492 U.S. 33, 106 L.Ed.2d 26 (suit for money damages for a fraudulent monetary transfer); Lorillard v. Pons, 1978, 98 S.Ct. 866, 434 U.S. 575, 55 L.Ed.2d 40, noted 1978, 62 Harv.L.Rev. 270 (suit for lost wages under the Age Discrimination in Employment Act); Pernell v. Southall Realty, 1974, 94 S.Ct. 1723, 416 U.S. 363, 40 L.Ed.2d 198 (summary action for repossession of real property); Curtis v. Loether, 1974, 94 S.Ct. 1005, 415 U.S. 189, 39 L.Ed.2d 260 (action for damages and injunctive relief for violation of fair housing provisions of the Civil Rights Act of 1968); Fleitmann v. Welsbach Street Lighting Co., 1916, 36 S.Ct. 233, 240 U.S. 27, 60 L.Ed. 505 (private antitrust actions).

No right to jury: Lehman v. Nakshian, 1981, 101 S.Ct. 2698, 2702 n. 9, 453 U.S. 156, 162 n. 9, 69 L.Ed.2d 548 (suit against the United States); Katchen v. Landy, 1966, 86 S.Ct. 467, 382 U.S. 323, 15 L.Ed.2d 391 (summary action in bankruptcy court);

Luria v. U.S., 1913, 34 S.Ct. 10, 15, 231 U.S. 9, 27–28, 58 L.Ed. 101 (statutory action to cancel naturalization).

Several of the recent cases have emphasized that characterization of the remedy is "the more important". Wooddell, 112 S.Ct. at 497, ___ U.S. at ___; and cases there cited.

The Seventh Amendment does not prevent Congress from creating new statutory public rights and allowing an administrative agency to enforce them by civil penalties without jury trial. Atlas Roofing Co. v. Occupational Safety and Health Review Commn., 1977, 97 S.Ct. 1261, 430 U.S. 442, 51 L.Ed.2d 464; NLRB v. Jones & Laughlin Steel Co., 1937, 57 S.Ct. 615, 629, 301 U.S. 1, 48, 81 L.Ed. 893. See Kirst, Administrative Penalties and the Civil Jury: The Supreme Court's Assault on the Seventh Amendment, 1978, 126 U.Pa.L.Rev. 1281. And Congress can fix the amount of a statutory penalty, or allow a judge to determine it, even if there is a Seventh Amendment right to determine liability on the legal claims. Tull v. U.S., 1987, 107 S.Ct. 1831, 481 U.S. 412, 95 L.Ed.2d 365. But Congress "lacks the power to strip parties contesting matters of private right of their constitutional right to a trial by jury." Granfinanciera, 109 S.Ct. at 2795, 492 U.S. at 52–53.

The lower courts have held that a suit against a foreign sovereign pursuant to the Foreign Sovereign Immunities Act is not a suit at common law and that the statute barring jury trial in such actions, 28 U.S.C.A. § 1330(a), is valid. See Arango v. Guzman Travel Advisors, C.A.11th, 1985, prior to the merger of law and equity and the adoption of the rules.   The Supreme Court has cast doubt on this assumption.   In Beacon Theatres, Inc. v. Westover,[31] the Court said: "Since in the federal courts equity has always acted only when legal remedies were inadequate, the expansion of adequate legal remedies provided by the Declaratory Judgment Act and the Federal Rules necessarily affects the scope of equity.   Thus, the justification for equity's deciding legal issues once it obtains jurisdiction, and refusing to dismiss a case, merely because subsequently a legal remedy becomes available, must be re-evaluated in the light of the liberal joinder provisions of the Federal Rules which allow legal and equitable causes to be brought and resolved in one civil action.   Similarly the need for, and therefore, the availability of such equitable remedies as Bills of Peace, Quia Timet and Injunction must be reconsidered in view of the existence of the Declaratory Judgment Act as well as the liberal joinder provision of the Rules.   This is not only in accord with the spirit of the Rules and the Act but is required by the provision in the Rules that '(t)he right to trial by jury as declared by the Seventh Amendment to the Constitution or as given by a statute of the United States shall be preserved * * * inviolate.' "

The historical test, to the extent it is still applicable, works without undue difficulty where the case presents but a single claim for relief.   The jurisdictional line that divided Westminster Hall was drawn largely, if not exclusively, in terms of the remedy sought.   If but a single claim is presented and a single remedy demanded, the action can rationally be classified as one that historically would have been either legal or equitable.   Modern procedure, however, not only permits but encourages more complicated actions that had no precise analogue in the ancient practice, and it is these that pose the most complex problems about a jury right.

One kind of case is that in which the parties, by joinder of claims and counterclaims, are asserting several claims for relief, or are demanding several remedies arising out of a single claim for relief.   If the claims, or the remedies, are either all legal or all equitable, the matter is no more difficult than in a simple suit.   If the matters raised are entirely independent, again there is no difficulty.   There is no waiver of jury trial by joining "legal" and "equitable" claims and counterclaims in one

---

761 F.2d 1527, 1533–1534, and cases there cited.

31.   1959, 79 S.Ct. 948, 956, 359 U.S. 500, 509–510, 3 L.Ed.2d 988.   Professor James finds the Beacon Theatres case "cloudy and ambiguous and susceptible of an interpretation which would go far to abolish the historical test altogether and extend jury trial over most of the former domain of equity."   James, note 1 above, at 687.   See also James, Hazard & Leubsdorf, Civil Procedure, 4th ed.1992, § 8.11.   Professors Rothstein and McCoid, in the articles cited note 1 above, find these fears

unjustified and take a favorable view of Beacon Theatres.

"In the end, unless we are prepared for the major re-definition of the role of juries that might come from a re-drafting of the constitutional guarantees, it would seem that the rule of Beacon Theatres is the best, or least worse available solution to the problem of preserving the role of jury trials in modern litigation."   Gelfand, Smith v. University of Detroit: Is There a Viable Alternative to Beacon Theatres?, 1988, 45 Wash. & Lee L.Rev. 159.   The case referred to in the title of Professor Gelfand's article action.[32] Those claims historically legal will be tried to a jury; those claims historically equitable will be tried to the court. Frequently, however, the matters will not be independent; there will be, instead, one or more issues common to both the legal and equitable claims and determinative of each. In this instance the order of trial becomes important, for the determination of the first factfinder, whether court or jury, will be binding on the other. The clear holding of Beacon Theatres is that, in all conceivable situations of this sort, the legal claim should be tried first, in order to avoid depriving the party of a determination by a jury on the common issue.[33]

Another difficult situation is where a party has a single claim for relief, but demands various remedies, some available at law and some available only in equity. Thus, a party may ask damages for past harm and an injunction against continuing the wrongful conduct in the future, or it may pray alternatively for specific performance of a contract or for damages for its breach. In some of these situations there is historical precedent by which equity took the whole case and awarded damages in addition to or in lieu of the equitable relief demanded.[34] Such precedent is fairly limited, and in any event it is not clear that this practice, which was justified historically only to avoid multiplicity of litigation, should be continued in a system where such multiplicity can be avoided without depriving the parties of a jury.

This problem had perplexed the courts and bemused the commentators. They suggested variously that the whole case should be labeled as "basically legal" or "basically equitable," or that the court should be guided by plaintiff's preferred remedy, or that history should be resorted to for a determination of which party could have controlled whether the case would have gone to a jury in the old practice, or that a certain issue should be identified as "basic" and the right to a jury trial made to turn on its characteristics.[35]

All such tests must fail. They attempt to use a historical test, of one form or another, to classify a hybrid form of lawsuit that could never have existed in the ancient days. If the problem cannot be solved by history, resort must be had to policy, and the relevant policy, expressed in the Seventh Amendment, is favorable to jury trial. This was clearly

is Smith v. University of Detroit, 1985, 378 N.W.2d 511, 145 Mich.App. 468.

32. Kennedy v. Lakso Co., Inc., C.A.3d, 1969, 414 F.2d 1249; Thermo–Stitch, Inc. v. Chemi–Cord Processing Corp., C.A.5th, 1961, 294 F.2d 486; Ring v. Spina, C.C.A.2d, 1948, 166 F.2d 546, certiorari denied 69 S.Ct. 30, 335 U.S. 813, 93 L.Ed. 368; 9 Wright & Miller, Civil § 2305.

33. 9 Wright & Miller, Civil § 2338.

If the trial court erroneously dismisses a legal claim and tries without a jury an equitable claim that is joined with it, the appellate court must order a new trial rather than allowing the trial court's findings on the equitable claim to bar the legal claim as a matter of issue preclusion. Lytle v. Household Mfg., Inc., 1990, 110 S.Ct. 1331, 494 U.S. 545, 108 L.Ed.2d 504.

34. E.G., Denton v. Stewart, Ch. 1786, 1 Cox Ch. 258, 29 Eng.Rep. 1156; Gulbenkian v. Gulbenkian, C.C.A.2d, 1945, 147 F.2d 173; Levin, Equitable Clean–Up and the Jury: A Suggested Orientation, 1951, 100 U.Pa.L.Rev. 320.

35. E.g., Fraser v. Geist, D.C.Pa.1940, 1 F.R.D. 267; Innersprings, Inc. v. Joseph Aronauer, Inc., D.C.N.Y.1961, 27 F.R.D. 32; and articles cited 9 Wright & Miller, Civil § 2302 n. 35.

indicated by the Supreme Court in Dairy Queen, Inc. v. Wood,[36] in which it carried further the doctrines first suggested in Beacon Theatres. The theory of the complaint in Dairy Queen was not clear. Defendant had been licensed by contract to use plaintiffs' trademark, and continued to do so after plaintiffs, claiming material breach of the contract, told it to desist. The complaint could be read as one for breach of contract, or for infringement of trademark, or both, but in any event plaintiffs wished to enjoin defendant from doing business using plaintiffs' mark, and they sought a money judgment, styled a demand for an "accounting," for sums due them in the past. The district court regarded the claim for a money judgment as "incidental" to the injunctive relief sought, and struck defendant's demand for jury trial. The Supreme Court held that the court of appeals erred in refusing to grant a writ of mandamus to require jury trial.

The Court first laid to rest the erroneous notion that if a "basic" equitable issue can be discovered, there is no right to jury trial on other legal issues. "Our previous decisions," it said, "make it plain that no such rule may be applied in the federal courts."[37] In particular it read Beacon Theatres as requiring that any legal issue for which a trial by jury is timely and properly demanded be submitted to a jury, and said: "That holding, of course, applies whether the trial judge chooses to characterize the legal issues presented as 'incidental' to equitable issues or not."[38]

Thus, if the claim for a money judgment was triable to a jury, it must still be so tried although it was asserted in a suit where the basic relief sought was equitable. The Court then had to consider whether there was a right to jury trial on the money claim. It held that whether the claim be construed as one for debt allegedly due on a contract, or for damages based on a charge of trademark infringement, it was a legal claim, triable to a jury. The fact that the complaint styled the claim as one for an accounting was held not controlling, for "the constitutional right to trial by jury cannot be made to depend upon the choice of words used in the pleadings."[39] Citing Beacon Theatres, the Court restated the rule that equitable relief is available only where the remedy at law is inadequate, and it repeated the accepted proposition that the legal remedy is inadequate, and an equitable accounting available, only where the accounts are of such a complicated nature that a court of equity alone is able satisfactorily to unravel them.[40] The Court noted the procedure under Rule 53(b) by which a master can be appointed to assist the jury in those exceptional cases that are too complicated for the jury,[41] and said that in view of this the burden of showing that the legal remedy is inadequate and that an equitable accounting is required "is consider-

---

36. 1962, 82 S.Ct. 894, 369 U.S. 469, 8 L.Ed.2d 44.

37. 82 S.Ct. at 896, 369 U.S. at 470.

38. 82 S.Ct. at 897, 369 U.S. at 473.

39. 82 S.Ct. at 900, 369 U.S. at 477–478. See 9 Wright & Miller, Civil § 2304.

40. See Kirby v. Lake Shore & M.S.R. Co., 1887, 7 S.Ct. 430, 432, 120 U.S. 130, 134, 30 L.Ed. 569.

41. See § 97 below.

ably increased and it will indeed be a rare case in which it can be met." [42] The case before it was not such a rare case, and defendant was entitled to a trial by jury on the issues involved in the claim for a money judgment. Since those issues were common to the plaintiffs' claim for equitable relief, the Beacon Theatres rule was held to require that the legal claims be determined prior to any final court determination of the equitable claims.

Still another variant of the problem arises when a party is seeking relief that would by itself be legal in nature but he or she invokes a procedural device, such as interpleader, a class suit, or a derivative action, that had been available only in equity. This came to the Court in 1970 in Ross v. Bernhard.[43] The holding there is that in a stockholders' derivative action, a type of action that historically could only have been brought in equity, there is now a right to jury trial on those issues on which the corporation, if it had been suing in its own right, would have been entitled to a jury. This seems a necessary result from the doctrines announced in Beacon Theatres and Dairy Queen, and it is the result that should be reached in all situations in which a party is seeking relief that would by itself pose legal issues but is doing so by a procedural device historically available only in equity.[44] Indeed the Court itself seemed to indicate this when it said in the Ross opinion that "nothing turns now upon * * * the procedural devices by which the parties happen to come before the court." [45]

The Court did make one surprising statement in Ross. In a footnote, in which it cited no authority for this proposition, it said: "As our cases indicate, the 'legal' nature of an issue is determined by considering, first, the pre-merger custom with reference to such questions; second, the remedy sought; and third, the practical abilities and limitations of juries." [46] The third of the factors mentioned in that footnote was surprising since it seems to invite a balancing approach to the right to jury trial, while the accepted learning has been that that balance was already struck by the Seventh Amendment. But "the footnote is so cursory, conclusory and devoid of cited authority or reasoned analysis that it is difficult to believe it could have been intended to reject such established historical practice or Supreme Court precedent." [47] The lower courts have ignored the Ross footnote, or cited it as a makeweight reference to support results that would have been reached had the footnote never been written. It now seems clear that they were right in

---

42. 82 S.Ct. at 900, 369 U.S. at 478.

43. 1970, 90 S.Ct. 733, 396 U.S. 531, 24 L.Ed.2d 729. See Note, Ross v. Bernhard: The Uncertain Future of the Seventh Amendment, 1971, 81 Yale L.J. 112.

44. 9 Wright & Miller, Civil § 2307.

See 7 Wright & Miller, Civil § 1718 (interpleader); 7A id. §§ 1801 (class actions), 1837 (derivative suits), 1910 (intervention).

This principle was recognized in Hyde Properties v. McCoy, C.A.6th, 1974, 507 F.2d 301, but it was held that there was no right to a jury when the underlying issue in an interpleader action was equitable in nature.

45. 90 S.Ct. at 739, 396 U.S. at 540.

46. 90 S.Ct. at 738 n. 10, 396 U.S. at 538 n. 10.

47. Redish, note 1 above, at 526. See also Wolfram, note 2 above, at 644–645; Note, 1971, 81 Yale L.J. 112, 126–130.

doing so, since the Supreme Court has explained, in very narrow terms, what that language meant.[48]

The Ross footnote did help to fire one very lively controversy that is still not resolved. As part of the general questioning of the utility of the civil jury, there has been a narrower argument that juries should not be used in the complex cases of great duration that are a part of contemporary litigation. Much has been written on every side of this argument.[49] The case for a "complexity exception" to the Seventh Amendment has proceeded on three fronts. First, it has been sought to justify such an exception on historical grounds. Scholars have searched the pre–1791 English precedents and some of them believe that they have found there evidence that cases otherwise legal were given to the chancellor for trial if the issues were too complex for a jury. Other scholars disagree. Second, there is an argument from the Ross footnote. It is claimed that regardless of what may have been the historical practice, "the practical abilities and limitations of juries" dictate that trial be to the court in complex patent or antitrust cases and other litigation of this scope. Finally, it is claimed that a party is denied due process of law if its rights are decided by a jury unable to understand the case and decide it rationally, and that the Due Process Clause of the Fifth Amendment overrides the Seventh Amendment when the two are in conflict.

The Ninth Circuit has rejected all of these arguments and held that there is no complexity exception.[50] The Third Circuit rejected the historical argument and the argument from the Ross footnote, but accepted, in guarded form, a complexity exception based on the due-process argument.[51] Finally, the Fifth Circuit has expressed no opinion on whether there can be a complexity exception, but has held that if such an exception exists, it cannot reach a case where the trial court finds only that "it would be most difficult, if not impossible, for a jury to

---

48. In Granfinanciera, S.A. v. Nordberg, 1989, 109 S.Ct. 2782, 2790 n. 4, 492 U.S. 33, 42 n. 4, 106 L.Ed.2d 26, the Court said that Ross's language about "the practical abilities and limitations of juries" is addressed to "whether Congress has permissibly entrusted the resolution of certain disputes to an administrative agency or specialized court of equity, and whether jury trials would impart the functioning of the legislative scheme."

49. See, e.g., Campbell, The Current Understanding of the Seventh Amendment: Jury Trials in Modern Complex Litigation, 1988, 66 Wash.U.L.Q. 63; Lempert, Civil Juries and Complex Cases: Taking Stock after Twelve Years, in Verdict, note 7 above, at p. 181; Lempert, Civil Juries and Complex Cases: Let's Not Rush to Judgment, 1981, 80 Mich.L.Rev. 68; and the many other articles cited 9 Wright & Miller, § 2301 n. 10.

50. In re U.S. Financial Securities Litigation, C.A.9th, 1979, 609 F.2d 411, certiorari denied 100 S.Ct. 1866, 446 U.S. 929, 64 L.Ed.2d 281. Judge Kilkenny dissented, but without indicating which of the arguments for an exception persuaded him. 609 F.2d at 432.

51. "The complexity of a suit must be so great that it renders the suit beyond the ability of a jury to decide by rational means with a reasonable understanding of the evidence and applicable legal rules." In re Japanese Electronic Products Antitrust Litigation, C.A.3d, 1980, 631 F.2d 1069, 1088. Judge Gibbons dissented, arguing that "there is no case in which properly separated claims for relief cognizable at common law would be so complex that trial by jury would amount to a violation of due process." 631 F.2d at 1093.

reach a rational decision." [52]   It is obvious that this is an issue that the Supreme Court will have to resolve, but it may be wise for the Court to refrain from doing so until there has been more discussion of the issue in the lower courts.

In Fitzgerald v. United States Lines Co.[53] a suit was brought seeking money damages under the Jones Act and also for maintenance and cure. The Jones Act remedy is "legal" and there is a right of trial by jury. The remedy of maintenance and cure is of admiralty origin, and by itself would not be tried to a jury.[54]   In practice, however, injured seamen routinely join both claims, as well as an admiralty claim for unseaworthiness.   The Supreme Court held that when the claims arise from a single set of facts, practical convenience requires that they be submitted to a single trier of fact, and since a jury must hear the Jones Act claim, the other claims must therefore also be submitted to the jury.[55]   In the opinion the Court made the suggestive statement that: "Only one trier of fact should be used for the trial of what is essentially one lawsuit to settle one claim split conceptually into separate parts because of historical developments." [56]   This would suggest that where legal and equitable claims arise from a single set of facts, it may be held not only that the legal claim must be tried first, as previously required by Beacon Theatres, but also that the whole case must be submitted to the jury. However the Fitzgerald case has had no generative force outside the maritime area and it is doubtful that the Court meant to go beyond the particular issue the case presented.

There can be no right to trial by jury if there are no issues of fact to be tried.[57]   This principle was controlling in Parklane Hosiery Co. v. Shore.[58]   A class action for damages was brought against Parklane and some of its officers and directors for issuing false proxy statements. The Securities and Exchange Commission brought a separate action against the same defendants for a declaratory judgment, and it was successful. Plaintiffs in the class action then claimed Parklane was precluded from

---

52. Cotten v. Witco Chem. Corp., C.A.5th, 1981, 651 F.2d 274, 276. Judge Tate, concurring, thought that the result should have been based on a square holding that the constitutional right of jury trial cannot be abrogated on the grounds of complexity of inconvenience. 651 F.2d at 277.

53. 1963, 83 S.Ct. 1646, 374 U.S. 16, 10 L.Ed.2d 720. The author is indebted to Professor David J. Sharpe for pointing out that Justice Black, the author of the Fitzgerald opinion, was persuaded on motion for rehearing that his opinion needed clarification, but the Court denied the motion. 1964, 84 S.Ct. 655, 376 U.S. 901, 11 L.Ed.2d 604.

54. The strange distinctions governing right to a jury in actions arising from a maritime transaction were preserved when

admiralty and civil procedure were unified. See Rules 9(h), 38(e); 9 Wright & Miller, Civil § 2315. The American Law Institute proposed a simpler and more rational standard to govern the right to jury, but these have not been adopted. See ALI Study, § 1319 and Commentary thereto.

55. Federal judges try to prevent overlap between maintenance and lost wages, and between cure and hospital expenses, by using special interrogatories and by moulding the judgment.

56. 83 S.Ct. at 1650, 374 U.S. at 21.

57. Ex parte Peterson, 1920, 40 S.Ct. 543, 547, 253 U.S. 300, 310, 64 L.Ed. 919.

58. 1979, 99 S.Ct. 645, 439 U.S. 322, 58 L.Ed.2d 552.

relitigating in their action the issues that had been determined adversely to it in the SEC action. The Supreme Court agreed, rejecting Parklane's argument that to do so deprived it of its right to trial by jury on these issues. At common law a litigant was not entitled to have a jury determine issues that had previously been adjudicated by a chancellor in equity, and it is immaterial that the scope of collateral estoppel, or issue preclusion as it is now called,[59] has recently been greatly broadened. In 1791 a litigant could not have been precluded unless the parties were the same in both actions. Today's notions of issue preclusion allow preclusion against Parklane, since it was a party to both suits, even though it is the stockholders, who were not parties to the SEC suit, who are now claiming the benefit of preclusion. "[M]any procedural devices developed since 1791 that have diminished the civil jury's historic domain have been found not to be inconsistent with the Seventh Amendment,"[60] and the broadened concept of issue preclusion is merely one of these.

The provision for a jury trial preserved by Rule 38 is not self-executing. A party desiring trial by jury must serve a timely written demand therefor not later than ten days after the service of the last pleading directed to the issue the party wishes tried to a jury.[61] Once such a demand has been made, other parties may rely on it, and it cannot be withdrawn without the consent of all parties.[62] Failure to make a timely demand for jury trial waives the right to this form of trial,[63] though the court has discretion, on motion,[64] to order jury trial despite the waiver.[65] A considerable number of decisions take a very strict view, and refuse to relieve a party from its waiver of jury trial unless there are special circumstances excusing the failure to make a timely demand. Thus, one court boasts that "it has been the unbending practice of this Court for many years not to order a jury trial once it has been waived."[66] Such decisions put the emphasis in the wrong place. Technical insistence upon imposing a penalty for inadvertence by denying a jury trial is not in the spirit of the rules. If the issue is one that normally should be tried by a jury, the court should consider the motion with an open mind and an eye to the factual situation in that particular case, rather than with a preconceived notion that motions of this kind

59. See § 100A below.

60. 99 S.Ct. at 654, 439 U.S. at 336.

61. Rule 38(b), (c); 9 Wright & Miller, Civil §§ 2318–2320. The demand must also be filed within a reasonable time after service. Rule 5(d).

62. In re N–500L Cases, C.A.1st, 1982, 691 F.2d 15; and cases cited 9 Wright & Miller, Civil § 2318 nn. 8, 12. But participation in a bench trial without objection waives the jury-trial right previously demanded. Cooper v. Loper, C.A.3d, 1991, 923 F.2d 1045, 1048; and cases there cited.

63. Rule 38(d); 9 Wright & Miller, Civil § 2321. "Waiver by failure to make a time-

ly demand is complete even though it was inadvertent, unintended and regardless of the explanation or excuse." Scharnhorst v. Independent School Dist. No. 710, C.A.8th, 1982, 686 F.2d 637, 641.

64. Mesa Petroleum Co. v. Coniglio, C.A.5th, 1980, 629 F.2d 1022; and cases cited 9 Wright & Miller, Civil § 2334 nn. 27, 28.

65. 9 Wright & Miller, Civil § 2334.

66. Ligouri v. New York, N.H. & H.R. Co., D.C.Conn.1961, 26 F.R.D. 565, 568, criticized 1962, 47 Iowa L.Rev. 759; and cases cited 9 Wright & Miller, Civil § 2334 nn. 33–37.

are usually to be denied.[67]

In the absence of a demand for jury trial, or if there has been a demand but the case is not one triable to a jury as of right, the case will be tried to the court.[68] The court may, if it wishes, submit an issue to an advisory jury on its own initiative, but the verdict of such a jury is advisory only, and the ultimate responsibility for finding the facts remains with the court.[69] In an action not triable to a jury as of right, the court may, with the consent of both parties, order a trial with a jury whose verdict has the same effect as if trial by jury had been a matter of right.[70]

§ 93. Evidence [1]

The Federal Rules of Evidence became effective on July 1, 1975.[2] They have such a wide impact that it is not possible to discuss them comprehensively in the present work. Instead resort must be had to the standard textbooks on evidence [3] and to the writing that has been produced and will be produced in direct response to the Evidence Rules.[4] No more can be attempted here than to describe the background of the new rules and to suggest one or two problems raised by the new rules that have general implications on the law applied in the federal courts.

Prior to 1975, Criminal Rule 26 had provided for uniform rules of evidence in federal criminal cases. The admissibility of evidence and the competency and privileges of witnesses were governed, in the absence of a federal statute providing otherwise, "by the principles of the common law as they may be interpreted by the courts of the United States in the light of reason and experience." [5] There is empirical evidence that the courts were faithful to this principle and made almost no use of state rules of evidence in criminal cases.[6]

---

67. Daniel Intern. Corp. v. Fischbach & Moore, Inc., C.A.5th, 1990, 916 F.2d 1061, 1066; Merritt v. Faulkner, C.A.7th, 1983, 697 F.2d 761, 767, certiorari denied 104 S.Ct. 434, 464 U.S. 986, 78 L.Ed.2d 366; Credit Bureau of Council Bluffs, Inc., v. Credit Bureau Data Centers, Inc., D.C.Iowa 1992, 143 F.R.D. 206, 212–213; Carr v. Wal–Mart Stores, Inc., D.C.La.1991, 138 F.R.D. 80, 81; and cases cited 9 Wright & Miller, Civil § 2334 nn. 32, 38–40.

68. See § 96 below.

69. Rule 39(c); Hyde Properties v. McCoy, C.A.6th, 1974, 507 F.2d 301; Hurwitz v. Hurwitz, C.C.A.D.C.1943, 136 F.2d 796; (American) Lumbermens Mut. Cas. Co. v. Timms & Howard, Inc., C.C.A.2d, 1939, 108 F.2d 497; 9 Wright & Miller, Civil § 2335.

70. Rule 39(c); 9 Wright & Miller, Civil § 2333. If the court does not agree to a nonadvisory jury, it must so advise the parties before jury selection begins. Bereda v.

Pickering Creek Indus. Park, Inc., C.A.3d, 1989, 865 F.2d 49.

§ 93

1. 21–26A Wright & Graham, Evidence; 27–28 Wright & Gold, Evidence.

2. The text of the rules as finally adopted appears at 65 F.R.D. 131, but there have been amendments since that time.

3. E.g., McCormick, Evidence, Strong et al. eds., 4th ed. 1992; Graham, Federal Evidence, 3d ed. 1991.

4. E.g., Wright & Graham, note 1 above; Wright & Gold, note 1 above; Weinstein, Evidence: United States Rules: Commentary on Rules of Evidence for the United States Courts and Magistrates.

5. 2 Wright, Criminal 2d § 402.

6. Sherman, Appendix, 1969, 69 Col. L.Rev. 377.

The situation in civil cases was very different prior to 1975. Although the Civil Rules made some provisions on evidentiary matters—and a few of these, including Rule 43(e) on evidence on motions,[7] Rule 44 on proof of official records,[8] and Rule 44.1 on determination of foreign law,[9] have survived the adoption of the Evidence Rules—the basic provision was former Rule 43(a). It created a three-pronged test, allowing the admission of evidence if it fell into any one of the three categories described in the rule:

(1) Evidence was admissible if statutes of the United States so provided. There were not many such statutes.[10]

(2) Evidence was admissible "under the rules of evidence heretofore applied in the courts of the United States on the hearing of suits in equity." Read literally, this was of limited usefulness, because there were very few decisions on the admissibility of evidence under the old equity procedure.[11] However the courts showed considerable inventiveness, holding that the federal judge could put himself or herself in the shoes of a chancellor prior to 1938 and search the sources for guidance that a chancellor of that day would have used.[12] Another formulation was that a rule could be deduced from general principles and related federal decisions, although there was no stated equity precedent available.[13]

(3) Evidence was admissible "under the rules of evidence applied in the courts of general jurisdiction of the state in which the United States court is held."

Thus, unless evidence fell under one of the first two branches of Rule 43(a)—or could be brought by an inventive view of what the federal equity rule had been into the second of those branches—admissibility was dependent on the rules of evidence of the state in which the federal court was sitting. The courts disagreed on whether they could admit evidence if it would not come in under any of the three prongs of Rule

---

7. 9 Wright & Miller, Civil § 2416.

8. 9 Wright & Miller, Civil §§ 2431–2437.

9. 9 Wright & Miller, Civil §§ 2241–2247; Brown, 44.1 Ways to Prove Foreign Law, 1984, 9 Mar.L. 179; Sass, Foreign Law in Federal Courts, 1981, 1 Amer. J.Comp.L. 97; Baade, Proving Foreign and International Law in Domestic Tribunals, 1978, 18 Va.J.Intl.L. 619; Miller, Federal Rule 44.1 and the "Fact" Approach to Determining Foreign Law: Death Knell for a Die–Hard Doctrine, 1967, 65 Mich.L.Rev. 613; Comment, Determination of Foreign Law Under Rule 44.1, 1975, 10 Texas Intl. L.J. 67.

10. The most important was the Business Records Act, 28 U.S.C.A. § 1732, now superseded by Evidence Rule 803(6).

11. Callahan & Ferguson, Evidence and the New Federal Rules of Civil Procedure: I, 1936, 45 Yale L.J. 622, 625.

12. Monarch Ins. Co. of Ohio v. Spach, C.A.5th, 1960, 281 F.2d 401, 411; Hope v. Hearst Consol. Publications, Inc., C.A.2d, 1961, 294 F.2d 681, 684, certiorari denied 82 S.Ct. 399, 368 U.S. 956, 7 L.Ed.2d 388, noted 1962, 15 Vand.L.Rev. 1330; New York Life Ins. Co. v. Harrington, C.A.9th, 1962, 299 F.2d 803, 808; United Services Auto. Assn. v. Wharton, D.C.N.C.1965, 237 F.Supp. 255.

13. Butler v. Southern Pac. Co., C.A.5th, 1970, 431 F.2d 77; Treharne v. Callahan, C.A.3d, 1970, 426 F.2d 58; 9 Wright & Miller, Civil § 2403.

43(a),[14] but that disagreement is a matter of ancient history in the light of the adoption of the Evidence Rules. There were also problems of the application of the Erie doctrine in a diversity case if evidence would be excluded in a state court but could be admitted under the first or second branches of Rule 43(a).[15] This problem, too, takes on such a different form with the adoption of the Evidence Rules that it would be unprofitable to examine the former views about it.

Rule 43(a) was a stopgap.[16] It was intended to provide a liberal and flexible rule for the admissibility of evidence, pending the adoption of a detailed set of Evidence Rules for the federal courts. There was dispute about how successful it was as a stopgap.[17] Although the desirability of a uniform set of federal Evidence Rules, to be applied in all cases, civil or criminal, continued to be recognized,[18] and distinguished authorities concluded that the task was a feasible one,[19] it was not until 1965 that Chief Justice Warren appointed an advisory committee to formulate these rules. In 1972 the Supreme Court reported to Congress a set of Federal Rules of Evidence, to take effect in 1973.[20] These provoked considerable controversy, with disagreement about the power of the Supreme Court to adopt rules of evidence, about the utility of uniform federal rules of evidence, and about the desirability of particular provisions in the rules as approved by the Supreme Court, with particular emphasis on the proposed rules of privilege.[21] Prior to the date on which the rules were to have taken effect, Congress adopted a statute providing that the rules should have no effect except as they might be expressly approved by Act of Congress.[22] The proposed rules were carefully studied in both Houses, and many significant changes were made in the draft the Supreme Court had approved before Congress adopted the Federal Rules of Evidence by statute, effective July 1, 1975.[23]

The aspect of the Evidence Rules, as finally adopted, that is within the scope of the present work is their impact on state law, particularly in

14. Compare, e.g., Wright v. Wilson, C.C.A.3d, 1946, 154 F.2d 616, 619, certiorari denied 67 S.Ct. 50, 329 U.S. 743, 91 L.Ed. 640, with Dallas County v. Commercial Union Assur. Co., Ltd., C.A.5th, 1961, 286 F.2d 388. See 9 Wright & Miller, Civil § 2404.

15. 9 Wright & Miller, Civil § 2405.

16. Clark, Foreword to Symposium on the Uniform Rules of Evidence, 1956, 10 Rutgers L.Rev. 479, 482.

17. 9 Wright & Miller, Civil § 2401.

18. Estes, The Need for Uniform Rules of Evidence in the Federal Courts, 1960, 24 F.R.D. 331; Joiner, Uniform Rules of Evidence for the Federal Courts, 1957, 20 F.R.D. 429.

19. Rules of Evidence: A Preliminary Report on the Advisability and Feasibility of Developing Uniform Rules of Evidence for the United States District Courts, 1962, 30 F.R.D. 73; Degnan, The Law of Federal Evidence Reform, 1962, 76 Harv.L.Rev.

275; Degnan, The Feasibility of Rules of Evidence in Federal Courts, 1960, 24 F.R.D. 341; Ladd, Uniform Evidence Rules in the Federal Courts, 1963, 49 Va.L.Rev. 692. Morgan, Rules of Evidence—Substantive or Procedural, 1957, 10 Vand.L.Rev. 467.

20. 56 F.R.D. 183.

21. E.g., Moore & Bendix, Congress, Evidence and Rulemaking, 1974, 84 Yale L.J. 9; Weinberg, Choice of Law and the Proposed Federal Rules of Evidence: New Perspectives, 1974, 122 U.Pa.L.Rev. 594; Note, Separation of Powers and the Federal Rules of Evidence, 1975, 26 Hast.L.J. 1059; Comment, Rules of Evidence and the Federal Practice: Limits on the Supreme Court's Rulemaking Power, 1974 Ariz.St.L.J. 77.

22. Act of March 30, 1973, Pub.L. 93–12, 87 Stat. 9.

23. Act of Jan. 2, 1975, Pub.L. 93–595, 88 Stat. 1926.

diversity cases and in other cases in which state law provides the substantive rule of decision. Since the rules were finally adopted by Act of Congress rather than by the Supreme Court, any question whether rules of evidence were within the scope of the Enabling Act was mooted.[24] In Hanna v. Plumer,[25] the Court said: "Erie and its offspring cast no doubt on the long-recognized power of Congress to prescribe housekeeping rules for federal courts even though some of those rules will inevitably differ from comparable state rules."[26] Thus, it would seem that the Evidence Rules are to be applied without regard to the Erie doctrine, although the Court in Hanna did add the caution that in determining the validity of a particular rule, a court "need not wholly blind itself to the degree to which the Rule makes the character and result of the federal litigation stray from the course it would follow in state courts * * *."[27]

At the same time, the implication of Hanna is not that the federal rules are valid because wise men made them, but because wise men thought carefully before making them.[28] A major reason for the critical reaction in Congress to the draft prepared by the advisory committee and approved by the Court was a feeling that insufficient thought had been given to the presuppositions of federalism, and to the value of deference to state policies, in the formulation of that draft.

As Judge Weinstein and Professor Degnan had most fully developed,[29] Evidence Rules are of three kinds. Most rules are of a housekeeping nature and are merely intended to make efficient use of the court's time and to assist in reaching the truth by preventing the jury from being confused or mislead. These matters should be settled by the federal courts for themselves. They commonly had been in diversity cases [30] and there was no reason to defer to state practices in formulating rules of this kind for the future.

Next there are rules that in form only regulate evidence but in fact are closely associated with substantive rights. The most obvious of these are rules dealing with burden of proof and presumptions respect-

---

24. 19 Wright, Miller & Cooper, Jurisdiction § 4512. This question was probably insubstantial in any event. See note 19 above. Some of the authorities cited note 21 above took a different view.

25. 1965, 85 S.Ct. 1136, 380 U.S. 460, 14 L.Ed.2d 8. See § 59 above.

26. 85 S.Ct. at 1145, 380 U.S. at 473.

27. Id.

28. The phrase was suggested to the author by Professor Ronan E. Degnan.

29. Weinstein, The Uniformity–Conformity Dilemma Facing Draftsmen of Federal Rules of Evidence, 1969, 69 Col.L.Rev. 353; Degnan, The Law of Federal Evidence Reform, 1962, 76 Harv.L.Rev. 275.

This subject is brilliantly explored in a later article, Wellborn, The Federal Rules of Evidence and the Application of State Law in the Federal Courts, 1977, 55 Texas L.Rev. 371.

30. E.g., Haddigan v. Harkins, C.A.3d, 1970, 441 F.2d 844, 851–852 (admissibility of expert testimony); U.S. v. 60.14 Acres of Land, C.A.3d, 1966, 362 F.2d 660 (competency of expert witness); Croom v. Fiedler, C.A.6th, 1965, 341 F.2d 909 (hearsay); Hambrice v. F.W. Woolworth Co., C.A.5th, 1961, 290 F.2d 557 (relevancy); United Services Auto. Assn. v. Wharton, D.C.N.C. 1965, 237 F.Supp. 255 (hearsay); Een v. Consolidated Freightways, D.C.N.D.1954, 120 F.Supp. 289, affirmed C.A.8th, 1955, 220 F.2d 82. See generally 9 Wright & Miller, Civil § 2405.

ing facts that are elements of a claim or defense. The federal courts had always applied state rules on these matters in diversity cases in the past,[31] and the rules wisely continue to do so.[32] Here, however, there are grey areas. Is a dead man's statute, for example, intended to provide substantive protection for estates or to guard against misleading the jury by untruthful testimony of an interested party that cannot be rebutted? The cases had held that a state statute of this kind must be followed.[33] It would not have been followed under the rules as proposed by the Court but Congress restored the former understanding on this point.[34] Other situations are even more murky. A state rule prohibiting opinion evidence on whether a defamatory article was understood to refer to a particular person appears to be a routine rule of evidence but it may reflect a state policy to discourage this kind of disfavored action.[35]

This grey area is illustrated by Conway v. Chemical Leaman Tank Lines, Inc.,[36] one of the first decisions of significance to apply the Evidence Rules. That was a Texas wrongful-death case, brought in federal court on the basis of diversity. A Texas statute provides that in a wrongful-death action evidence of the remarriage of the surviving spouse is admissible, but the Texas courts continue to hold that the fact of the remarriage may not be considered in mitigation of damages.

The Fifth Circuit held that the evidence of the plaintiff's remarriage was admissible in Conway, not because of the Texas statute but because of the Evidence Rules. Rules 401 and 402 on relevancy, it said, were specifically intended to provide that background evidence is admissible.[37] But the court, with obvious regret, held that since under Erie state law governs the measures of damages, including admissibility and jury

31. Cities Serv. Oil Co. v. Dunlap, 1939, 60 S.Ct. 201, 308 U.S. 208, 84 L.Ed. 196 (burden of proof); Dick v. New York Life Ins. Co., 1959, 79 S.Ct. 921, 359 U.S. 437, 3 L.Ed.2d 935 (presumptions).

The misnamed "parol evidence rule" is not a rule of evidence at all, and state doctrine must be followed. Freeman v. Continental Gin Co., C.A.5th, 1967, 381 F.2d 459. This continues to be true under the Evidence Rules. E.g., Southern Stone Co., Inc. v. Singer, C.A.5th, 1982, 665 F.2d 698; Betz Labs., Inc. v. Hines, C.A.3d, 1981, 647 F.2d 402.

32. Evidence Rule 302.

33. First Nat. Bank & Trust Co. v. McKeel, C.A.10th, 1967, 387 F.2d 741; Wright v. Wilson, C.C.A.3d, 1946, 154 F.2d 616, certiorari denied 67 S.Ct. 50, 329 U.S. 743, 91 L.Ed. 640.

34. Evidence Rule 601 makes state law govern questions of the competency of a witness in civil actions with respect to which state law supplies the substantive rule of decision. See 27 Wright & Gold, Evidence § 6005, pp. 59–62, § 6006, pp. 66–70, § 6009, pp. 85–93; Equitable Life As-

sur. Soc. of U.S. v. McKay, C.A.9th, 1988, 837 F.2d 904.

35. Both Weinstein, note 29 above, at 367–368, and Degnan, note 29 above, at 294, raise questions on this ground about Hope v. Hearst Consol. Publications, Inc., C.A.2d, 1961, 294 F.2d 681, certiorari denied 82 S.Ct. 399, 368 U.S. 956, 7 L.Ed.2d 388, in which this kind of evidence was held admissible though the state would have excluded it.

36. C.A.5th, 1976, 525 F.2d 927, on rehearing C.A.5th, 1976, 540 F.2d 837, noted 1977, 55 Texas L.Rev. 557. See 22 Wright & Graham, Evidence § 5201, pp. 235–237; Wellborn, note 29 above, at 376–384, 415–417.

37. "Although the Rules do not deal specifically with proof of a surviving spouse's remarriage, their treatment of comparable issues suggests that the evidence is admissible for background and perhaps various other limited purposes. See Fed.R.Evid. 407 (admissibility of subsequent remedial measures); Fed.R.Evid. 411 (admissibility of liability insurance coverage)." 525 F.2d at 930.

consideration of particular issues, the jury must be instructed that it could not consider plaintiff's remarriage for the purpose of mitigating damages.

This clearly seemed to mean that evidence of remarriage would be admissible in a wrongful-death case, not only in Texas, which has so provided by statute, but in each of the states of the Fifth Circuit, even though other states have no such statute. The rule that the spouse's remarriage is not to be considered in mitigation of damages is plainly a rule of substantive law that must be honored in a diversity case. Yet if a state considers this policy so important that it enforces it by not allowing the evidence for any purpose, and thus avoids the considerable risk that a jury would disregard a limiting instruction, the federal diversity court, by virtue of the Evidence Rules, would give the policy less protection than the state thinks it merits. To achieve this under the guise of a housekeeping rule on relevancy would be a severe blow to the values of federalism.

Fortunately the panel of the Fifth Circuit that had decided Conway wrote again on the case on an application for rehearing. There the court held that the evidence of remarriage is admissible because the Texas statute was more than a rule of evidence; it was a part of the state law of wrongful death, which federal courts must follow under Erie.[38] Evidence Rule 402 was not mentioned. This strongly suggests that a federal court should exclude the evidence in a state that would do so,[39] and this appears to be the desirable result.[40]

Finally there are state rules of evidence that are deliberately adopted to effectuate some extrinsic policy of the state. The problem is seen most clearly where the state has adopted an evidentiary privilege for confidential communications that was unknown at common law, or it has given an established privilege greater scope than it traditionally has had.

Prior to 1975 there was considerable confusion on the applicability of state privileges in federal actions, with both the decisions and the commentators divided.[41] Though there were many variations and incon-

---

38. "These determinations, though in a sense matters of evidence-law, are embedded in Texas substantive law and policy, and we adopt them as part of the Texas wrongful-death act for application in federal trials of actions brought thereunder." 540 F.2d at 839.

39. In Estate of Spinosa, C.A.1st, 1980, 621 F.2d 1154, the district court was affirmed in excluding evidence of remarriage of the spouse in a diversity wrongful-death case. The appellate court looked only to the fact that it believed this evidence would be excluded in state court. It made no reference to the Evidence Rules.

40. Wellborn, note 29 above, at 416–417; Case Note, 1977, 55 Texas L.Rev. 557, 566–567.

A state rule forbidding evidence of an arrest without conviction was followed in a diversity case because the rule was meant to prescribe rights and obligations of the parties not related to factfinding. Penfield v. Venuti, D.C.Conn.1984, 589 F.Supp. 250, 253 n. 1. See also Hemingway v. Ochsner Clinic, C.A.5th, 1984, 722 F.2d 1220, 1225 n. 10; DiAntonio v. Northampton–Accomack Memorial Hosp., C.A.4th, 1980, 628 F.2d 287, 291; D'Orio v. West Jersey Health Systems, D.C.N.J.1992, 797 F.Supp. 371, 376.

41. 9 Wright & Miller, Civil § 2408.

sistencies, in general the courts applied state privileges in diversity cases [42] but did not do so in actions in which the United States was seeking to enforce federal law.[43]   In private federal-question cases the situation was quite unclear.[44]

As a matter of policy it seems appropriate that the states should not be permitted to say when the federal courts must refrain from hearing useful testimony in a matter involving federal law.   A different result seems most tenable in diversity litigation.   Privileges for confidential communications are created because the state thinks a particular relationship—attorney-client, husband-wife, journalist-source—is sufficiently important that it should be fostered by preserving confidentiality in the relationship even at the cost of losing evidence that would help to determine the truth in later litigation.[45]   Thus, privilege differs from most rules of evidence, which are intended to facilitate getting at the truth of a matter, not deliberately block it.   The state's effort to encourage these relationships will be hampered if the secrets of the marriage bed or the attorney's office can be kept secret in state court but disclosed if, because of the accident of diversity, suit is brought in the federal court a block away.   Since the litigation is on a state-created right, there is no federal interest that justifies such an interference with the state's decision that the relation is more important than the litigation.

The Advisory Committee on Rules of Evidence reached a contrary conclusion.   In its proposed rules it defined those privileges it thought should be recognized and expressly refused to honor broader state privileges.[46]   The wisdom of making such a serious intrusion on state policies was highly doubtful,[47] and this treatment of privilege was a major factor in the controversy that developed about the proposed rules as they were approved by the Supreme Court.

As finally adopted by Congress, the detailed set of rules of privilege that had been proposed for the Evidence Rules was scrapped, and the subject is covered by Rule 501, which provides: "Except as otherwise required by the Constitution of the United States or provided by Act of Congress or in rules prescribed by the Supreme Court pursuant to statutory authority, the privilege of a witness, person, government,

---

42. See cases cited 9 Wright & Miller, Civil § 2408 nn. 2–5.

43. See cases cited 9 Wright & Miller, Civil § 2408 n. 94.

There was some reason for believing that more deference was paid to state privileges in the courtroom than in the reported decisions.   See Weinstein, note 29 above, at 372 n. 82.

44. The fullest examination of the problem was in Garner v. Wolfinbarger, C.A.5th, 1970, 430 F.2d 1093, 1098–1100.

45. 8 Wigmore, Evidence, McNaughton rev. 1961, § 2285.

46. Proposed Evidence Rule 501.   The Committee Note defending this course is set out at 51 F.R.D. 356–360.   For a full examination of this history, see 23 Wright & Graham, Evidence § 5421.

47. See the articles by Judge Weinstein and Professor Degnan cited note 29 above. See also Wright, Procedural Reform: Its Limitations and Its Future, 1967, 1 Ga. L.Rev. 563, 571–574; Note, The Constitutionality of Federal Abrogation of State Created Rules of Privilege in Diversity Cases: Proposed Federal Rule of Evidence 501, 1973, 34 Ohio St.L.J. 400.

State, or political subdivision thereof shall be governed by the principles of the common law as they may be interpreted by the courts of the United States in the light of reason and experience. However, in civil actions and proceedings, with respect to an element of a claim or defense as to which State law supplies the rule of decision, the privilege of a witness, person, government, State, or political subdivision thereof shall be determined in accordance with State law." [48]

Evidence Rule 501, as rewritten by Congress, adopts what had been the common understanding prior to enactment of the rules. On matters governed by federal substantive law—and this will generally be true in criminal cases, civil actions brought by the United States, and private federal-question cases—federal courts are to apply and develop a federal common law of privilege.[49] In determining what this is to be, the federal courts may consider state privilege law [50] but are not bound by it,[51] and may look also for guidance to the rules of privilege that were proposed by the Advisory Committee on Rules of Evidence but not adopted.[52] The Supreme Court has recognized that Rule 501 was not intended to freeze the law of privilege, and that Congress gave the courts flexibility to develop rules of privilege on a case-by-case basis, but it said "we are disinclined to exercise this authority expansively. We are especially reluctant to recognize a privilege in an area where it appears that Congress has considered the relevant competing concerns but has not provided the privilege itself." [53]

With regard to elements of a claim or defense for which state law supplies the rule of decision, the state law of privilege must be applied.[54] To the extent that federal law provides the rule of decision in federal-question cases and state law provides the rule of decision in diversity cases, Evidence Rule 501 will work without difficulty. But though the pattern just described is usually true, it is not always true. At times state law is looked to in federal-question cases and at times federal law is controlling on some issues in diversity cases.[55] Thus, the application of Rule 501 depends on the rule of decision that applies to a particular

---

48. The rule as finally adopted is analyzed in 23 Wright & Graham, Evidence §§ 5421–5438.

49. U.S. v. Gillock, 1980, 100 S.Ct. 1185, 445 U.S. 360, 63 L.Ed.2d 454; Trammel v. U.S., 1980, 100 S.Ct. 906, 445 U.S. 40, 63 L.Ed.2d 186; 23 Wright & Graham, Evidence § 5425.

50. E.g., Socialist Workers Party v. Grubusic, C.A.7th, 1980, 619 F.2d 641, 643; Riley v. City of Chester, C.A.3d, 1979, 612 F.2d 708, 715; U.S. v. H.E. Crain, C.A.9th, 1979, 589 F.2d 996, 999.

51. U.S. v. Gillock, 1980, 100 S.Ct. 1185, 1191, 445 U.S. 360, 368, 63 L.Ed.2d 454; U.S. v. One Parcel of Property at 31–33 York Street, C.A.2d, 1991, 930 F.2d 139, 141.

52. U.S. v. Meagher, C.A.5th, 1976, 531 F.2d 752, 753; U.S. v. Allery, C.A.8th, 1975, 526 F.2d 1362, 1365–1367. See 23 Wright & Graham, Evidence § 5422, pp. 691–693.

53. University of Pennsylvania v. EEOC, 1990, 110 S.Ct. 577, 582, 493 U.S. 182, 189, 107 L.Ed.2d 571. In that case the Court refused to create a privilege for peer-review materials pertinent to a charge of discrimination in a tenure decision. This case is relied on in Linde Thomson Langworthy Kohn & Van Dyke v. RTC, C.A.D.C. 1993, 5 F.3d 1508, 1514–1515, where the court refused to recognize an insured-insurer privilege.

54. 23 Wright & Graham, Evidence §§ 5432–5434.

55. See § 60 above at notes 49 to 55.

issue in a particular case and cannot be mechanically resolved by looking to the basis for jurisdiction of the case.[56]

In federal-question cases in which a federal court adopts or incorporates state law to fill interstices in federal statutory phrases, federal privilege law will be applied. In these cases in which a federal court chooses to absorb state law, it is applying the state law as a matter of federal common law. Thus, the rule of decision is not state law, even though the rule may be derived from state decisions.[57]

There are instances in which federal statutes or common law provide the rule of decision in diversity cases.[58] In those instances the federal common law of privilege will be applied.

Finally, there are federal-question cases in which the court hears a related state-law claim as pendent to a federal claim.[59] In these instances the federal law of privilege would apply on the federal claim and the state law of privilege on the state claim.[60] Often the federal and state rules of privilege will be the same, and no problem will be created. If the privilege rules differ, it would be anomalous if evidence were held admissible on one claim and privileged on the related claim. But the possibility of jury confusion had been a recognized reason for refusing to exercise jurisdiction over a pendent state claim,[61] and this is the course

56. The version of Rule 501 approved in the Senate would have made privilege turn on the jurisdictional basis of the suit. It was wisely rejected by the conference committee in favor of the House version, which appears in the rule as finally adopted. See Federal Judicial Center, Federal Rules of Evidence Annotated, 1975, pp. 45–46.

57. E.g., De Sylva v. Ballentine, 1956, 76 S.Ct. 974, 351 U.S. 570, 100 L.Ed. 1415; Holmberg v. Armbrecht, 1946, 66 S.Ct. 582, 327 U.S. 392, 90 L.Ed. 743; D'Oench, Duhme & Co. v. Federal Deposit Ins. Corp., 1942, 62 S.Ct. 676, 686, 315 U.S. 447, 471–472, 86 L.Ed. 956 (Jackson, J., concurring).

58. E.g., Francis v. Southern Pac. Co., 1948, 68 S.Ct. 611, 333 U.S. 445, 92 L.Ed. 798; Sola Elec. Co. v. Jefferson Elec. Co., 1942, 63 S.Ct. 172, 317 U.S. 173, 87 L.Ed. 165; Huber Baking Co. v. Stroehmann Bros. Co., C.A.2d, 1958, 252 F.2d 945, certiorari denied 79 S.Ct. 50, 358 U.S. 829, 3 L.Ed.2d 69.

59. See § 19 above.

60. 2 Louisell & Mueller, Federal Evidence, 1978, pp. 503–504; see Cunningham v. Southlake Center for Mental Health, D.C.Ind.1989, 125 F.R.D. 474, 475–476; Scott v. McDonald, D.C.Ga.1976, 70 F.R.D. 568, 571. But cf. 23 Wright & Graham, Evidence § 5434, where it is recognized that Professor Graham and the present author differ on this issue.

In Wm. T. Thompson Co. v. General Nutrition Corp., C.A.3d, 1982, 671 F.2d 100, 104, the court held that "when there are federal law claims in a case also presenting state law claims, the federal rule favoring admissibility, rather than any state law privilege, is the controlling rule. * * * [O]ur holding is consistent with the legislative history of Rule 501 and the decisions of a number of trial courts." In support of its reference to legislative history, the court quoted the Senate Report, apparently overlooking that the Conference Committee deliberately rejected the Senate version of Rule 501, which would have made the question of privilege turn on the jurisdictional basis of the action rather than which body of law furnishes the rule of decision. See note 57 above. The same mistaken reliance on the Senate Report occurred in von Bulow by Auersperg v. von Bulow, C.A.2d, 1987, 811 F.2d 136, 141.

61. United Mine Workers v. Gibbs, 1966, 86 S.Ct. 1130, 1139, 383 U.S. 715, 727, 16 L.Ed.2d 218.

This is not one of the stated grounds on which 28 U.S.C.A. § 1367(c) allows a federal court to decline to exercise supplemental jurisdiction. See § 9 above. But the problem should arise so rarely that this fairly could be regarded as one of the "exceptional circumstances" in which "there are other compelling reasons for declining jurisdiction." 28 U.S.C.A. § 1367(c)(4).

the court should follow when contradictory rules of privilege will apply to the two claims.[62]

Rule 501 has raised another interesting problem, one that was never considered by the Advisory Committee or by Congress. If state law is to furnish the rule of privilege under the proviso to the rule, to which state's law is the federal court to look if it is sitting in one state but the arguably privileged communication was made in some other state? Although there are several answers to this question for which reasonable arguments can be made,[63] the wisest course seems to be to hold that the general principle of the Klaxon case[64] applies, and that the federal court is to do whatever the courts of the state in which it is sitting would do under that state's notions of conflict of laws.[65]

§ 94. Submission to the Jury[1]

The Seventh Amendment preserves the essential elements of trial by jury, rather than particular details.[2] Among the essential elements that are preserved is the requirement that the jury must be an impartial cross-section of the community, without systematic and intentional exclusion of any economic, social, religious, racial, political, or geographical group.[3] Although it had long been supposed that another of these essential elements of trial by jury was, except as waived by the parties, a unanimous verdict of 12 jurors, the Supreme Court has upheld local rules providing for civil juries of fewer than 12,[4] and whether a unanimous verdict is constitutionally required is now a matter of doubt.[5] Rule

---

62. See Walker v. Lewis, D.C.N.C.1989, 127 F.R.D. 466, 470; R.I.M.A.C. v. W.A.R.F., D.C.Wis.1987, 114 F.R.D. 672, 675 n. 2.

63. See 23 Wright & Graham, Evidence § 5435.

64. Klaxon v. Stentor Elec. Mfg. Co., 1941, 61 S.Ct. 1020, 313 U.S. 487, 85 L.Ed. 1477. See § 57 above.

65. Miller v. Transamerican Press, Inc., C.A.5th, 1980, 621 F.2d 721, certiorari denied 101 S.Ct. 1759, 450 U.S. 1041, 68 L.Ed.2d 238; Samuelson v. Susen, C.A.3d, 1978, 576 F.2d 546; Gatewood v. U.S. Cellular Corp., D.C.D.C.1989, 124 F.R.D. 504, 506; and cases cited 23 Wright & Graham, Evidence § 5435 n. 24.

In the Third Edition of the present work, the author took the view that the law of privilege of the state whose substantive law is being applied should be the applicable law. Wright, Federal Courts, 3d ed. 1976, p. 462. This would have the advantage that in a single sentence of the rule in which "State law" is used twice, it would not mean two different things. Further reflection persuaded him, however, that the more complicated Klaxon approach is the proper one.

§ 94

1. 9 Wright & Miller, Civil §§ 2481–2485, 2491–2492, 2501–2513, 2521–2536, 2551–2558.

2. Parklane Hosiery Co., Inc. v. Shore, 1979, 99 S.Ct. 645, 654, 439 U.S. 322, 336–337, 58 L.Ed.2d 552.

3. Thiel v. Southern Pac. Co., 1946, 66 S.Ct. 984, 328 U.S. 217, 90 L.Ed. 1181; Ballard v. U.S., 1946, 67 S.Ct. 261, 329 U.S. 187, 91 L.Ed. 181. This is implemented by the careful procedures required by the Jury Selection and Service Act of 1968, as amended, 28 U.S.C.A. §§ 1861–1878. See 2 Wright, Criminal 2d § 375.

4. Colgrove v. Battin, 1973, 93 S.Ct. 2448, 413 U.S. 149, 37 L.Ed.2d 522. See Bieser & Varrin, Six-member Juries in the Federal Courts, 1975, 58 Judicature 425; Zeisel & Diamond, "Convincing Empirical Evidence" on the Six–Member Jury, 1974, 41 U.Chi.L.Rev. 281; Fisher, The Seventh Amendment and the Common Law: No Magic in Numbers, 1973, 56 F.R.D. 507; 9 Wright & Miller, Civil § 2491.

5. The Seventh Amendment was held to require a unanimous verdict in American Pub. Co. v. Fisher, 1897, 17 S.Ct. 618, 619, 166 U.S. 464, 468, 41 L.Ed. 1079. More

48 was amended in 1991 and now allows the court to seat a jury of not fewer than six and not more than 12, but the amended rule requires a unanimous verdict unless the parties stipulate otherwise.

The case need not be submitted to the jury at all. The court has the power to direct a verdict [6] if the evidence is such that reasonable persons could not differ about the result. A verdict may be directed for the plaintiff, though this is much less common than a directed verdict for the defendant.[7] A 1963 amendment to the rules put an end to the embarrassing practice by which the jurors were required to sign a directed verdict, though it was in no sense their own free act.[8] Even the terminology was changed by a 1991 amendment; instead of directing a verdict the court now grants a motion for judgment as a matter of law. But the old term is so convenient, and appears so often in the cases and the literature, that it is still used here. In most circumstances the court wisely will reserve decision on the motion for directed verdict, submit the case to the jury, and then pass on the legal sufficiency of the evidence on a motion for judgment notwithstanding verdict. This course avoids the need for a second trial if an appellate court should hold, contrary to the view of the trial court, that the evidence was sufficient to raise a jury issue.[9] The standard of sufficiency of the evidence is the same whether on a motion for directed verdict or a motion for judgment notwithstanding the verdict, and is discussed in the following section.

In the manner and method of instructing the jury, federal courts follow their own rules, regardless of state practice and legislation. Substantially the federal courts follow the common-law practice inherited from the English courts, where it still prevails. The judge instructs the jury orally at the conclusion of the trial after the summing up arguments of counsel to the jury. Where a state-created right is to be

recently the Court has held that the Fourteenth Amendment does not require a unanimous verdict in a state criminal case, Apodaca v. Oregon, 1972, 92 S.Ct. 1628, 406 U.S. 404, 32 L.Ed.2d 184, but that the Sixth Amendment requires a unanimous verdict in a federal prosecution. 92 S.Ct. at 1635, 406 U.S. at 366 (Powell, J., concurring). There are no recent opinions on the requirement of unanimity in civil cases, but if the issue should arise, it seems very likely that the Court would hold that unanimity is not required.

6. Galloway v. U.S., 1943, 63 S.Ct. 1077, 319 U.S. 372, 87 L.Ed. 1458; Blume, Origin and Development of the Directed Verdict, 1950, 48 Mich.L.Rev. 555; Chadbourn, Trial by Jury under the Seventh Amendment, 1943, 92 U.Pa.L.Rev. 92.

On the problems of a directed verdict generally, see the helpful article, Cooper, Directions for Directed Verdicts: A Compass for Federal Courts, 1971, 55 Minn. L.Rev. 903.

7. Delaware, L. & W.R. Co. v. Converse, 1890, 11 S.Ct. 569, 139 U.S. 469, 35 L.Ed.

213; Chesapeake & O.R. Co. v. Martin, 1931, 51 S.Ct. 453, 283 U.S. 209, 75 L.Ed. 983; Service Auto Supply Co. of Puerto Rico v. Harte & Co., Inc., C.A.1st, 1976, 533 F.2d 23; Comment, Directing the Verdict in Favor of the Party with the Burden of Proof, 1972, 50 N.C.L.Rev. 843; 9 Wright & Miller, Civil § 2535.

The 1991 amendments of Rule 50 seemed inadvertently to have ended the possibility of entering a judgment as a matter of law for plaintiffs. See Waggoner, New Rule 50 May End Directed Verdicts for Plaintiffs, 1993, 22 Sw.U.L.Rev. 389. It was necessary to amend Rule 50(a) again in 1993 to make it clear that this was not the case.

8. Rule 50(a); 9 Wright & Miller, Civil § 2533, p. 583.

9. Mattivi v. South African Marine Corp., "Huguenot", C.A.2d, 1980, 618 F.2d 163, 166 n. 2; Tackett v. Kidder, C.A.8th, 1980, 616 F.2d 1050, 1052–1053; and cases cited 9 Wright & Miller, Civil § 2533 n. 98.

enforced, of course the state law must be looked to for the substance of the instructions, but the form of instructions and the method of objecting to them are procedural questions on which the federal court is not bound by state concepts.[10] Thus, the federal judge retains the common-law power to comment on the evidence, which in many of the states is no longer available.[11] He is not limited to summarizing the applicable rules of law, but may also summarize, discuss, and comment on the facts and the evidence, provided he indicates to the jury that they are not bound by his discussion of the evidence. The power to comment on the evidence has its own inherent limitations. The judge's discretion is not unbridled but is a judicial discretion to be exercised in conformity with the standards governing the judicial office. In commenting upon the testimony the judge may not assume the role of a witness. He may analyze and dissect the evidence, but may not destroy it or add to it.[12] He should not hesitate to clear away false issues and lead the jury to a proper understanding of the facts. His comments, however, should be fair and not arguments for either party. He should not assume the role of counsel or say anything that might prejudice either party.[13]

In another respect the federal practice on instructions differs from that common in the states. Rule 51 precludes a claim of error for giving an improper instruction, or failure to give a proper one, unless an objection has been taken, stating distinctly the grounds of the objection, before the jury retires.[14] Thus, the judge is made aware of the supposed defect in the instructions while he or she still has an opportunity to correct it. This avoids the necessity of a retrial where by design or through oversight a party has remained silent despite error in the instructions.[15] There is a good deal of dicta from appellate courts that they have power to consider "plain error" in the instructions, even though the instructions were not objected to.[16] In recent years there has

10. Nudd v. Burrows, 1875, 91 U.S. 426, 23 L.Ed. 286; Barrett v. Virginian R. Co., 1919, 39 S.Ct. 540, 250 U.S. 473, 63 L.Ed. 1092; Barger v. Charles Machine Works, Inc., C.A.8th, 1981, 658 F.2d 582, 586; Batesole v. Stratford, C.A.6th, 1974, 505 F.2d 804, 807; 9 Wright & Miller, Civil § 2555, pp. 651–652.

11. Vicksburg & M.Ry. v. Putnam, 1886, 7 S.Ct. 1, 2, 118 U.S. 545, 553, 30 L.Ed. 257; Capital Traction Co. v. Hof, 1899, 19 S.Ct. 580, 174 U.S. 1, 43 L.Ed. 873; Evans v. Wright, C.A.4th, 1974, 505 F.2d 287; County of Todd, Minnesota v. Loegering, C.A.8th, 1961, 297 F.2d 470, 480–481; Chesnut, Instructions to the Jury, 1943, 3 F.R.D. 113, 117.

12. Quercia v. U.S., 1933, 53 S.Ct. 698, 289 U.S. 466, 77 L.Ed. 1321; McCullough v. Beech Aircraft Corp., C.A.5th, 1979, 587 F.2d 754.

13. Callen v. Pennsylvania R. Co., 1947, 68 S.Ct. 296, 332 U.S. 625, 92 L.Ed. 242; 9 Wright & Miller, Civil § 2557.

14. 9 Wright & Miller, Civil §§ 2553, 2554.

Even though it is reversible error in Colorado state courts not to instruct that plaintiff can recover nothing under the comparative negligence statute if it is found to be more than 50% negligent, it is not error to omit this instruction in federal court if plaintiff fails to object. Platis v. Stockwell, C.A.7th, 1980, 630 F.2d 1202.

15. Atlantic Coast Line R. Co. v. Bennett, C.A.4th, 1958, 251 F.2d 934; Paschal, A Plea for a Return to Rule 51 of the Federal Rules of Civil Procedure in North Carolina, 1957, 36 N.C.L.Rev. 1.

16. E.g., Shearson Hayden Stone, Inc. v. Leach, C.A.7th, 1978, 583 F.2d 367, 370; Batesole v. Stratford, C.A.6th, 1974, 505 F.2d 804, 808; and cases cited 9 Wright & Miller, Civil § 2558 n. 40.

been an increased number of cases in which such power has been exercised, and a reversal ordered.[17] To allow reversal for plain error in the instructions is not only inconsistent with what Rule 51 says,[18] but burdens the appellate courts with having to review afterthought claims of error, which counsel parade forward under the banner of plain error. If there is to be an exception of this kind, it should be confined to the exceptional case where the error has seriously affected the fairness, integrity, or public reputation of judicial proceedings.[19]

In most federal cases, the traditional general verdict is used, by which the jury merely finds for one or the other of the parties. Two other procedures are made available by the rules. Under Rule 49(b) the court may, in its discretion, submit along with the general verdict one or more issues of fact upon which the verdict necessarily depends. This course requires the jury to give close attention to the more important issues and their answers serve to check the propriety of the general verdict.[20]

A more drastic, and controversial, procedure is made available by Rule 49(a). When this is used, the jury returns no general verdict at all but makes special written findings on each issue of fact. Special verdicts were known at common law, but rarely used, because of a rigid rule that the findings of the jury had to cover every material issue, at pain of judgment against the party carrying the burden of proof.[21] Rule 49(a), building on experience in North Carolina, Wisconsin, and Texas, avoids this particular pitfall by providing that a party waives its right to jury trial of any omitted issue unless it demands submission before the jury retires. The judge may make a finding on such an omitted issue, or if no

17. Rodrigue v. Dixilyn Corp., C.A.5th, 1980, 620 F.2d 537, certiorari denied 1981, 101 S.Ct. 923, 449 U.S. 1113, 66 L.Ed.2d 842; MacEdward v. Northern Elec. Co., Ltd., C.A.2d, 1979, 595 F.2d 105; Pritchard v. Liggett & Myers Tobacco Co., C.A.3d, 1965, 350 F.2d 479, certiorari denied 1966, 86 S.Ct. 549, 382 U.S. 987, 15 L.Ed.2d 475, amended C.A.3d, 1966, 370 F.2d 95, certiorari denied 1967, 87 S.Ct. 1350, 386 U.S. 1009, 18 L.Ed.2d 436; and cases cited 9 Wright & Miller, Civil § 2558 n. 41.

18. Compare the third sentence of Civil Rule 51 with Criminal Rule 52(b), which specifically permits a consideration of "plain errors."

19. Liner v. J.B. Talley and Co., Inc., C.A.5th, 1980, 618 F.2d 327, 329; Cohen v. Franchard Corp., C.A.2d, 1973, 478 F.2d 115, 125, certiorari denied 94 S.Ct. 161, 414 U.S. 857, 38 L.Ed.2d 106; Sowizral v. Hughes, C.A.3d, 1964, 333 F.2d 829, 837; Figge Auto Co. v. Taylor, C.A.8th, 1964, 325 F.2d 899, 907; Troupe v. Chicago, Duluth & Georgia Bay Transit Co., C.A.2d, 1956, 234 F.2d 253, 260. See U.S. v. Atkinson,

1936, 56 S.Ct. 391, 392, 297 U.S. 157, 160, 80 L.Ed. 555.

Nor can a party claim that an instruction was plain error if the party invited the error by requesting that instruction. Herman v. Hess Oil Virgin Islands Corp., C.A.3d, 1975, 524 F.2d 767, 771.

20. Guinn, The Jury System and Special Verdicts, 1970, 2 St. Mary's L.J. 175; Note, The Case for Interrogatories Accompanying a General Verdict, 1964, 52 Ky.L.J. 852; 9 Wright & Miller, Civil §§ 2511–2513.

The Fifth Circuit, however, believes that use of Rule 49(b) is "fraught with many pitfalls." Weymouth v. Colorado Interstate Gas Co., C.A.5th, 1966, 367 F.2d 84, 93 n. 1.

21. Graham v. Bayne, 1855, 18 How. 60, 15 L.Ed. 265; Stinson, Special Verdicts and Interrogatories, 1942, 7 Mo.L.Rev. 105, 142.

There is an excellent discussion of the background and application of the rule in Comment, Special Verdicts: Rule 49 of the Federal Rules of Civil Procedure, 1965, 74 Yale L.J. 483.

finding is made, he or she will be deemed to have made a finding in accord with the judgment the judge orders entered.[22]

The use of special verdicts is intended to emphasize the facts, prevent the jury from acting on bias, and make the law more scientific.[23] Little is gained, however, by making the law more scientific if, in the process, it becomes harder to achieve substantial justice. Some of the most famous students of the judicial process have argued that one of the purposes of the jury system is to permit the jury to temper strict rules of law by the demands and necessities of substantial justice, thereby adding a much needed element of flexibility.[24] Those who share this conception of the role of the jury rightly fear that it will be limited or defeated by the special-verdict practice, and thus oppose widespread use of special verdicts.

The use of special verdicts is always in the discretion of the trial judge.[25] The use he makes of this procedure is likely to depend on his view of its utility, and his conception of the role of the jury. At one extreme, the late Judge Jerome N. Frank, a brilliant and outspoken critic of the jury system, hailed the special verdict as "usually preferable to the opaque general verdict," and urged that the use of Rule 49 be made compulsory in all civil cases.[26] At the other extreme, those who look on the jury as a means by which the law is made to speak the voice of the man in the street urge that the special verdict should be used rarely.[27] Indeed Justices Hugo L. Black and William O. Douglas called Rule 49 "but another means utilized by courts to weaken the constitutional power of juries" and argue for its repeal.[28]

Many experienced judges take a middle position, holding that special verdicts may often be useful, but pointing out that in some areas they

---

22. Hyde v. Land–of–Sky Regional Council, C.A.4th, 1978, 572 F.2d 988; John R. Lewis Inc. v. Newman, C.A.5th 1971, 446 F.2d 800; 9 Wright & Miller, Civil § 2507.

23. Driver, The Special Verdict—Theory and Practice, 1951, 26 Wash.L.Rev. 21; Driver, A Consideration of the More Extended Use of the Special Verdict, 1950, 25 Wash.L.Rev. 43; Rossman, The Judge–Jury Relationship, 1943, 3 F.R.D. 98; Lipscomb, Special Verdicts Under The Federal Rules, 1940, 25 Wash.U.L.Q. 185. See 9 Wright & Miller, Civil § 2503.

24. Wigmore, A Program For the Trial of a Jury Trial, 1929, 12 J.Am.Jud.Soc. 166, 170; Pound, Law in Books and Law in Action, 1910, 44 Am.L.Rev. 12, 18–19; Wyzanski, A Trial Judge's Freedom and Responsibility, 1952, 65 Harv.L.Rev. 1281, 1286; Traynor, Fact Skepticism and the Judicial Process, 1958, 106 U.Pa.L.Rev. 635, 640; Holmes, Collected Legal Papers, 1920, pp. 237–238. See also Comment, 1965, 74 Yale L.J. 483, 495–497.

25. Landes Const. Co. v. Royal Bank of Canada, C.A.9th, 1987, 833 F.2d 1365,

1374; 9 Wright & Miller, Civil § 2505. But see Comment, note 24 above, at 508, 517–522, which is critical of the broad discretion given the trial courts.

26. Skidmore v. Baltimore & O.R. Co., C.A.2d, 1948, 167 F.2d 54, 67, certiorari denied 69 S.Ct. 34, 335 U.S. 816, 93 L.Ed. 371.

Chief Judge John R. Brown, though recognizing that there are pitfalls in Rule 49(a), has enthusiastically praised the rule and called for its more frequent use. Brown, Federal Special Verdicts: The Doubt Eliminator, 1967, 44 F.R.D. 245.

27. Thayer, A Preliminary Treatise on Evidence at the Common Law, 1898, p. 218; James, Sufficiency of the Evidence and Jury–Control Devices Available Before Verdict, 1961, 47 Va.L.Rev. 218, 246–248.

28. 1963, 83 S.Ct. 43, 45, 31 F.R.D. 617, 619 (dissenting from adoption of the 1963 amendments to the Civil Rules).

cause more difficulties than they solve. Thus, Judge Learned Hand, in a concurring opinion in the case in which Judge Frank called for compulsory use of Rule 49, was willing to say only that "it would be desirable to take special verdicts more often." [29] The draftsman of the Federal Rules, Judge Charles E. Clark, observed that "this often-desirable practice should be resorted to with discrimination and foresight; it should never be used for mere cross-examination of the jury to create error for the record. Its purpose and best achievement is to enable errors already potential because of confusions of fact or law 'to be localized so that the sound portions of the verdict may be saved.' * * * It is hence best available, when, as the judge can foresee, the issues can be thus clearly and simply differentiated, to save an appeal on at least that portion which cannot be questioned; it is of more doubtful value in a relatively simple factual situation * * * where the details asked for may not be the whole story." [30]

§ 95. Attacks on a Verdict [1]

The party dissatisfied with a jury verdict, as the losing party usually is, may attack it in either of two ways. The party may assert that the proceeding was in some fashion so tainted with error that the party should be given a new trial, or it may assert that its opponent's evidence failed to create an issue on which reasonable persons could differ, and that as a matter of law the dissatisfied party should be awarded judgment as a matter of law.[2] Though these two motions are very different in what they seek, and in the standard to be applied in passing on them, the losing party may, and usually does, move in the alternative for both kinds of relief.

Rule 59 does not list the grounds for which a new trial may be granted, but says only that this action may be taken for any of the reasons for which new trials have heretofore been granted in actions at law in federal courts. The usual grounds for a new trial are that the verdict is against the weight of the evidence, that the damages are

29. Skidmore v. Baltimore & O.R. Co., C.A.2d, 1948, 167 F.2d 54, 70, certiorari denied 69 S.Ct. 34, 335 U.S. 816, 93 L.Ed. 371.

30. Morris v. Pennsylvania R. Co., C.A.2d, 1951, 187 F.2d 837, 841. See also Wright, The Use of Special Verdicts in Federal Court, 1965, 38 F.R.D. 199. The same philosophic difference that causes varying views on how frequently special verdicts should be used leads to differing opinions on whether the court should advise the jury of the legal effect of its answers. See Comment, Informing the Jury of the Legal Effect of Special Verdict Answers in Comparative Negligence Actions, 1981 Duke L.J. 824; Note, Informing the Jury of the Effect of Its Answers to Special Verdict Questions—The Minnesota Experience, 1974, 58

Minn.L.Rev. 903; 9 Wright & Miller, Civil § 2509.

§ 95

1. 9 Wright & Miller, Civil §§ 2521–2532, 2537–2540; 11 id., §§ 2801–2821; Cooper, Directions for Directed Verdicts: A Compass for Federal Courts, 1971, 55 Minn. L.Rev. 903.

2. Rule 50 was amended in 1991 so that the single name "judgment as a matter of law" is now used for what formerly had been known as "directed verdict" and also for what had been "judgment notwithstanding the verdict", or "judgment n.o.v." as it was often written with the letters abbreviating the Latin name "non obstante veredicto". The older terminology is generally used in this section.

excessive, or that, for other reasons, the trial was not fair, and the motion may also raise questions of law arising out of substantial errors in the admission or rejection of evidence or the giving or refusal of instructions.[3] As to most of these grounds there is little controversy.

The power to order a new trial because the judge deems the verdict to be against the weight of the evidence—or the very similar power to order a new trial because the damages are excessive—is more controversial. The power is supported by clear precedent at common law and has long been regarded as an integral part of trial by jury. In a famous passage, Justice Gray long ago said: " 'Trial by jury,' in the primary and usual sense of the term at the common law and in the American constitutions * * * is a trial by a jury of twelve men in the presence and under the superintendence of a judge empowered to instruct them on law and to advise them on the facts, and (except on acquittal of a criminal charge) to set aside their verdict if, in his opinion, it is against the law or the evidence."[4] It has long been understood that if the trial judge is not satisfied with the verdict of a jury, he has the right—and indeed the duty—to set the verdict aside and order a new trial.[5]

Despite the historical background, there is still some feeling that when the trial court grants a new trial because of dissatisfaction with the verdict, it has, to an extent, substituted its judgment of the facts and the credibility of the witnesses for that of the jury, and that "such an action effects a denigration of the jury system and to the extent that new trials are granted the judge takes over, if he does not usurp, the prime function of the jury as the trier of the facts."[6] This uneasiness about such grants of a new trial is reflected in the varying views as to the standard a trial court should apply in passing on a motion seeking such relief. At one extreme is a decision saying that a new trial should not ordinarily be granted on the ground that the verdict was against the weight of the evidence if the evidence was conflicting and the jury might

---

3. Montgomery Ward & Co. v. Duncan, 1940, 61 S.Ct. 189, 194, 311 U.S. 243, 251, 85 L.Ed. 147; 11 Wright & Miller, Civil §§ 2805–2810.

4. Capital Traction Co. v. Hof, 1899, 19 S.Ct. 580, 585, 174 U.S. 1, 13–14, 43 L.Ed. 873.

5. A leading case is Aetna Cas. & Sur. Co. v. Yeatts, C.C.A.4th, 1941, 122 F.2d 350, 352–354. See also Tidewater Oil Co. v. Waller, C.A.10th, 1962, 302 F.2d 638, 643; Riddell, New Trial at the Common Law, 1916, 26 Yale L.J. 49.

If the judge considers a verdict excessive he need not grant a new trial but may deny it on condition that plaintiff consent to a remittitur of the excess. Dimick v. Schiedt, 1935, 55 S.Ct. 296, 293 U.S. 474, 79 L.Ed. 603; 11 Wright & Miller, Civil § 2815. However the Dimick case held that the Seventh Amendment prohibits a conditional

additur if the judge thinks the verdict inadequate. 11 Wright & Miller, Civil § 2816. Contra: McCoy v. Wean United, Inc., D.C.Tenn.1975, 67 F.R.D. 495. See Sann, Remittiturs (and Additurs) in the Federal Courts: An Evaluation with Suggested Alternatives, 1988, 38 Case W.Res.L.Rev. 157.

The Supreme Court has resolved a conflict in the circuits by holding that a plaintiff who has consented to a remittitur under protest cannot obtain appellate review of the remittitur order. Donovan v. Penn Shipping Co., Inc., 1977, 97 S.Ct. 835, 429 U.S. 648, 51 L.Ed.2d 112. See generally Comment, Remittitur Practice in the Federal Courts, 1976, 76 Col.L.Rev. 299.

6. Lind v. Schenley Indus. Inc., C.A.3d, 1960, 278 F.2d 79, 90, certiorari denied 81 S.Ct. 58, 364 U.S. 835, 5 L.Ed.2d 60, criticized 1961 Duke L.J. 308.

have found for either party.[7] If this is right, a new trial can never be granted on this ground, since unless the jury could reasonably have found for either party, the court should enter judgment as a matter of law. At the other extreme are cases that seem to give the trial court virtually unlimited discretion in granting or denying a new trial.[8] In the middle is a large group of cases that use varying adjectives, but agree in general that the trial court should not interfere with the verdict unless it is quite clear that the jury has reached a seriously erroneous result, and that it should not set the verdict aside merely because the court, as finder of fact, would have come to a different conclusion.[9] It may be doubted whether there is any verbal formula that will be of much use to trial courts in passing on motions of this type. Necessarily all such formulations are couched in broad and general terms that furnish no unerring litmus for a particular case. On the one hand, the trial judge does not sit to approve miscarriages of justice. On the other hand, a decent respect for the collective wisdom of the jury, and for the function entrusted to it in our system, certainly suggests that in most cases the judge should accept the findings of the jury, regardless of his or her own doubts in the matter. Probably all that the judge can do is to balance these conflicting principles in the light of the facts of the particular case. If, having given full respect to the jury's findings, the judge on the entire evidence is left with the definite and firm conviction that a mistake has been committed, it is to be expected that he or she will grant a new trial.[10]

In theory the trial court could continue to set aside verdicts for the same party until the case finally went to a jury that agreed with the judge. This is almost entirely theoretical. When two juries have reached substantially the same result, the possibility of a miscarriage of justice is very slight, and thus "courts rarely grant a new trial after two verdicts upon the facts in favor of the same party." [11]

A motion for a new trial, stating grounds therefore, must be made within ten days after the entry of judgment.[12] Though the tendency has been to apply this strictly, and to hold that neither waiver nor estoppel

---

7. Snyder v. Macaluso, D.C.Pa.1962, 204 F.Supp. 370, 373.

8. Murphy v. U.S. District Court, C.C.A.9th, 1944, 145 F.2d 1018, 1020; Grayson v. Deal, D.C.Ala.1949, 85 F.Supp. 431.

9. E.g., Conway v. Chemical Leaman Tank Lines, Inc., C.A.5th, 1980, 610 F.2d 360, 362–363; Fireman's Fund Ins. Co. v. Aalco Wrecking Co., Inc., C.A.8th, 1972, 466 F.2d 179, 187, certiorari denied 93 S.Ct. 1371, 410 U.S. 930, 35 L.Ed.2d 592; Werthan Bag Corp. v. Agnew, C.A.6th, 1953, 202 F.2d 119, 122; 11 Wright & Miller, Civil § 2806.

10. Kearns v. Keystone Shipping Co., C.A.1st, 1988, 863 F.2d 177, 181; Landes Const. Co. v. Royal Bank of Canada,

C.A.9th, 1987, 833 F.2d 1365, 1372; Brown by Brown v. Syntex Laboratories, Inc., C.A.8th, 1985, 755 F.2d 668.

11. Louisville & N.R. Co. v. Woodson, 1890, 10 S.Ct. 628, 631, 134 U.S. 614, 623, 33 L.Ed. 1032. See also Massey–Ferguson Credit Corp. v. Webber, C.A.4th, 1988, 841 F.2d 1245, 1250; Frank v. Atlantic Greyhound Corp., D.C.D.C.1959, 177 F.Supp. 922, affirmed C.A.D.C.1960, 280 F.2d 628.

12. Rules 59(b), (d); 11 Wright & Miller, Civil §§ 2812, 2813.

It is the time of service of the motion, not the time of filing, that is critical. Peake v. First Nat. Bank & Trust Co. C.A.6th, 1983, 717 F.2d 1016, 1019 n. 5.

nor acquiescence by the opposing party can permit the court to act on an untimely motion,[13] a doctrine has developed allowing relief where a party has been misled by action of the court purporting to enlarge the time, even though the court lacks power to make such an order.[14] It is held also that the court cannot grant new trial on its own initiative more than ten days after judgment,[15] and, until 1966, it was the law that even if there was a timely motion the court could not grant the new trial on a ground not stated in the motion.[16] These restrictions caused the new trial rule to be buried under confusing technicalities. It is right that there should be only a brief period in which to attack a verdict. The difficulty came from confusion as to the specificity with which grounds for a new trial had to be stated. Where counsel has made a good faith attempt to state the grounds on which they are seeking a new trial, and have put the grounds as specifically as their trial notes or their memory of the supposed errors permits, there is no reason for the court to view the motion with the hostile eye of a Baron Parke in deciding what it is the moving party sought to allege. The motion should be given a broad construction, and reasonable specification of grounds held sufficient.[17] The problem is greatly eased by a 1966 amendment to Rule 59(d) providing that if there is a timely motion, the court may grant a new trial on a ground not stated in the motion.[18]

The law as to the reviewability of orders granting or denying a new trial is in a state of flux. Normally an order granting a new trial is not appealable,[19] except where the trial court has lacked power to grant the new trial.[20] The order is reviewable, however, and on appeal from the

13. Leishman v. Associated Wholesale Elec. Co., 1943, 63 S.Ct. 543, 318 U.S. 203, 87 L.Ed. 714; Hulson v. Atchison, T. & S.F. Ry. Co., C.A.7th, 1961, 289 F.2d 726, certiorari denied 82 S.Ct. 61, 368 U.S. 835, 7 L.Ed.2d 36; Nugent v. Yellow Cab Co., C.A.7th, 1961, 295 F.2d 794, certiorari denied 82 S.Ct. 844, 369 U.S. 828, 7 L.Ed.2d 793.

14. Thompson v. Immigration and Naturalization Service, 1964, 84 S.Ct. 397, 375 U.S. 384, 11 L.Ed.2d 404; Wolfsohn v. Hankin, 1964, 84 S.Ct. 699, 376 U.S. 203, 11 L.Ed.2d 636; Agola v. Hagner, D.C.N.Y. 1987, 678 F.Supp. 988.

15. Tarlton v. Exxon, C.A.5th, 1982, 688 F.2d 973, certiorari denied 103 S.Ct. 3536, 463 U.S. 1206, 77 L.Ed.2d 1387; Peterman v. Chicago, R.I. & P.R. Co., C.A.8th, 1974, 493 F.2d 88, certiorari denied 94 S.Ct. 3072, 417 U.S. 947, 41 L.Ed.2d 667; and authorities cited note 16 below.

16. Russell v. Monongahela R. Co., C.A.3d, 1958, 262 F.2d 349; 11 Wright & Miller, Civil § 2813.

17. Tsai v. Rosenthal, C.A.8th, 1961, 297 F.2d 614, 619; General Motors Corp. v. Perry, C.A.7th, 1962, 303 F.2d 544.

18. Since the court can now grant a new trial on a ground not stated in the motion, it is difficult to understand recent cases that have said that a new trial motion cannot be amended more than ten days after judgment. See the cases cited in Maylie v. National R.R. Passenger Corp., D.C.Pa. 1992, 791 F.Supp. 477, 480 n. 3, affirmed C.A.3d, 1992, 983 F.2d 1051. "[I]t would be a strange rule which deprived a judge of power to do what was asked when made by the person most concerned, and yet allowed him to act without petition." U.S. v. Smith, 1947, 67 S.Ct. 1330, 1333, 331 U.S. 469, 474–475, 91 L.Ed. 1610. The better view, allowing the court to allow the motion to be amended, is adopted in Pate v. Seaboard R.R., Inc., C.A.11th, 1987, 819 F.2d 1074, 1084–1086.

19. Allied Chem. Corp. v. Daiflon, Inc., 1980, 101 S.Ct. 188, 190, 449 U.S. 33, 34, 66 L.Ed.2d 193. This case holds also that such an order will rarely, if ever, justify issuance of mandamus.

20. Phillips v. Negley, 1886, 6 S.Ct. 901, 117 U.S. 665, 29 L.Ed. 1013; and cases cited 11 Wright & Miller, Civil § 2818 n. 39. See Baron, The Appeal of the Grant of final judgment following the second trial, the appellant may claim error in the grant of the new trial and seek reinstatement of the verdict at the first trial.[21] An order denying a new trial is technically not appealable. Appeal must be taken from the final judgment and on that appeal the erroneous denial of the new trial, if reviewable at all, may be considered.[22] However if the party mistakenly purports to appeal from denial of the new trial, the appeal will be considered as if from the final judgment.[23]

Where the grant or denial of a new trial is claimed as error in an appeal from an appealable judgment, it is reviewable, and the order below can be reversed, if the trial court has made an error of law. There is vast disagreement, however, about the power of an appellate court to review the trial court's exercise of discretion with regard to such factual issues as whether the verdict is excessive or against the weight of the evidence.[24]

As recently as 1945 the Third Circuit said: "The members of the Court think the verdict is too high. But they also feel very clear there is nothing the Court can do about it." [25] This was the accepted view, supported by famous opinions of Justices Holmes and Brandeis,[26] which have never been overruled. Yet by 1962, when the Eighth Circuit, which had been the last to cling to the accepted view, succumbed,[27] every one of the eleven courts of appeals had either held or said that it had power to do something about excessive verdicts.[28] Such power has been claimed far more often than it has been exercised, and the Supreme Court has made it clear that it is a power to be exercised, if at all, only in the most extreme case.[29]

Both on the issue of the size of the verdict and on the related issue whether the verdict is against the weight of the evidence a distinction

a New Trial in Federal Court, 1988, 62 St. John's L.Rev. 617.

21. Conway v. Chemical Leaman Tank Lines, Inc., C.A.5th, 1980, 610 F.2d 360; and cases cited 11 Wright & Miller, Civil § 2818 nn. 41, 42. For the interesting sequels to the Conway case, see C.A.5th, 1981, 644 F.2d 1059, and C.A.5th, 1982, 687 F.2d 108.

22. Mattox v. U.S., 1892, 13 S.Ct. 50, 146 U.S. 140, 36 L.Ed. 917; Montgomery Ward & Co. v. Duncan, 1940, 61 S.Ct. 189, 311 U.S. 243, 85 L.Ed. 147.

23. Foman v. Davis, 1962, 83 S.Ct. 227, 371 U.S. 178, 9 L.Ed.2d 222; Osterberger v. Relocation Realty Service Corp., C.A.5th, 1991, 921 F.2d 72; and cases cited 11 Wright & Miller, Civil § 2818 n. 46.

24. Compare Carrington, The Power of District Judges and the Responsibility of Courts of Appeals, 1969, 3 Ga.L.Rev. 507, 524–526, and Note, Appealability of Rulings on Motion for New Trial in the Federal Courts, 1950, 98 U.Pa.L.Rev. 575, with Schnapper, Judges Against Juries—Appel-

late Review of Federal Civil Jury Verdicts, 1989 Wis.L.Rev. 237, and Wright, The Doubtful Omniscience of Appellate Courts, 1957, 41 Minn.L.Rev. 751. See 11 Wright & Miller, Civil §§ 2819, 2820.

25. Scott v. Baltimore & O.R. Co., C.C.A.3d, 1945, 151 F.2d 61, 64.

26. Southern Ry.—Carolina Div. v. Bennett, 1914, 34 S.Ct. 566, 233 U.S. 80, 58 L.Ed. 860; Fairmount Glass Works v. Cub Fork Coal Co., 1933, 53 S.Ct. 252, 287 U.S. 474, 77 L.Ed. 439.

27. Bankers Life & Cas. Co. v. Kirtley, C.A.8th, 1962, 307 F.2d 418. See Solomon Dehydrating Co. v. Guyton, C.A.8th, 1961, 294 F.2d 439, 446–448.

28. See cases cited 11 Wright & Miller, Civil § 2820 n. 84.

29. Grunenthal v. Long Island R. Co., 1968, 89 S.Ct. 331, 393 U.S. 156, 21 L.Ed.2d 309; Neese v. Southern Ry. Co., 1955, 76 S.Ct. 131, 350 U.S. 77, 100 L.Ed. 60.

should be recognized between an order denying a new trial and one granting a new trial. If a new trial is denied, the trial judge has accepted the verdict of the jury and there are the most compelling reasons for an appellate court not to interfere. But if a new trial is granted, the verdict of the jury has gone for naught and the appellate court can interfere more freely to resolve the difference between the judge and the jury.[30]

There is a developing body of dicta claiming a power to set aside the determination of the trial judge that a verdict is not against the weight of the evidence, and at least two cases in which an appellate court has actually reversed on this ground.[31] Again this is in the face of a long line of authority from the Supreme Court and elsewhere that the action of the trial judge on a motion for a new trial on the ground that the verdict was against the weight of the evidence "would not be subject to review." [32] The recent claims that there can be such review are probably also in the face of the Seventh Amendment, which prohibits reexamination of any "fact tried by jury * * * than according to the rules of the common law."

Various attempts have been made to reconcile appellate review of the weight of the evidence with the Seventh Amendment.[33] The most popular argument rests on the practice, at common law, by which the trial was conducted by a single judge at nisi prius, while motions for a new trial were heard by the court sitting en banc at Westminster. It is argued that this review by the court en banc, though it was not appellate review, is more like present American appellate practice than it is like our motion for a new trial, addressed to the single judge who presided at the trial.[34] The argument oversimplifies the historical data. An exhaustive examination of the early English cases has led one writer to conclude that there is not a single reported case where an English court at common law ever granted a new trial, as being against the weight of the evidence, unless the judge or judges who sat with the jury stated in open court, or certified, that the verdict was against the evidence and that he was dissatisfied with the verdict.[35] Assuming the accuracy of the

---

30. de Perez v. Hospital del Maestro, C.A.1st, 1990, 910 F.2d 1004, 1006; Matter of Innovative Const. Systems, Inc.,C.A.7th, 1986, 793 F.2d 875, 888; Lind v. Schenley Indus., Inc., C.A.3d, 1960, 278 F.2d 79, 90, certiorari denied 81 S.Ct. 58, 364 U.S. 835, 5 L.Ed.2d 60; and cases cited 11 Wright & Miller, Civil § 2819 n. 70, § 2820 n. 4.

31. U.S. v. Simmons, C.A.5th, 1965, 346 F.2d 213; Georgia–Pacific Corp. v. U.S., C.A.5th, 1959, 264 F.2d 161.

The dicta asserting a power to reverse but not exercising it are collected in 11 Wright & Miller, Civil § 2819 n. 59.

32. U.S. v. Socony–Vacuum Oil Co., 1940, 60 S.Ct. 811, 856, 310 U.S. 150, 248, 84 L.Ed. 1129; U.S. v. Laub, 1838, 12 Pet. 1, 4, 9 L.Ed. 977; Green v. American Air-

lines, Inc., C.A.8th, 1986, 804 F.2d 453, 455–456.

33. 11 Wright & Miller, Civil § 2819, pp. 123–125.

34. Blume, Review of Facts in Jury Cases—The Seventh Amendment, 1936, 20 J.Am.Jud.Soc. 130, 131; Notes, 1951, 30 Tex.L.Rev. 242, 1950, 98 U.Pa.L.Rev. 575, 579; Corcoran v. City of Chicago, 1940, 27 N.E.2d 451, 373 Ill. 567; see Dagnello v. Long Island R. Co., C.A.2d, 1961, 289 F.2d 797, 802–805.

35. Weisbrod, Limitations on Trial by Jury in Illinois, 1940, 19 Chi.–Kent L.Rev. 91, 92.

historical conclusion, the common-law system was one in which the verdict could be set aside only if the judge who had presided at the trial and heard the witnesses deemed the verdict to be unjustified, and even then, only if he could persuade his brethren at Westminster to this view. Thus, we have already liberalized the granting of new trials beyond that known at common law, since under the present American system the trial judge can set aside the verdict on this ground without getting the approval of any other judge. To allow appellate review of his or her refusal to do so would mean that the verdict could be set aside solely by judges who were not present at the trial even though the trial judge, by denying the motion for a new trial, has found that the verdict is not contrary to the clear weight of the evidence. This would be a complete reversal of the common-law practice, and does not seem consistent with the Seventh Amendment.[36]

Though the power to order a new trial is based on a long historical foundation, the power to order judgment notwithstanding the verdict is not. In the much-criticized case of Slocum v. New York Life Insurance Co.,[37] the Supreme Court in 1913 held that entry of a judgment contrary to the verdict was a violation of the Seventh Amendment. That rule was qualified in 1935 in Baltimore & Carolina Line v. Redman.[38] In the Redman case the district court had expressly reserved its decision on motions for directed verdicts and had submitted the case to the jury subject to its opinion on the questions reserved, without objection by either party. The Supreme Court held that this practice was recognized at common law and that on appeal from a judgment entered on the verdict the circuit court of appeals might reverse the judgment and direct the entry of a judgment notwithstanding the verdict. This case was distinguished from the Slocum case on the ground that in Slocum the submission to the jury had been absolute and not subject to the court's reservation of decision of the question of law raised by the motion for directed verdict. Rule 50(b) substituted a fiction for the reservation that was held to distinguish Slocum from Redman. Under that rule whenever a motion for a directed verdict made at the close of all the evidence is denied or for any reason is not granted, the court is deemed to have submitted the action to the jury subject to a later determination of the legal questions raised by the motion, and the court can subsequently order judgment notwithstanding the verdict, or can order judgment if the jury fails to agree.[39] The motion for a directed

---

36. See also Schnapper, note 24 above. The author argues that for the last 20 years there has been a de-facto suspension of the Seventh Amendment. The Supreme Court has taken no cases on scope of review of jury verdicts and the courts of appeals have been free to do what they want. "[L]eft to their own devices, a large number of appellate judges simply cannot resist acting like superjurors, reviewing and revising civil verdicts to assure that the result is precisely the verdict they would have returned had they been in the jury box." 1989 Wis. L.Rev. at 354.

37. 1913, 33 S.Ct. 523, 228 U.S. 364, 57 L.Ed. 879.

38. 1935, 55 S.Ct. 890, 295 U.S. 654, 79 L.Ed. 1636.

39. 9 Wright & Miller, Civil § 2522. Although the 1991 amendments changed the terminology of this procedure, see note 2 above, they preserved the "deemed to have submitted" fiction.

verdict is an absolute prerequisite to a subsequent grant of judgment n.o.v. If no motion for a directed verdict was made, neither the trial nor the appellate court can order judgment n.o.v.[40] It is not necessary that the trial court expressly reserve decision on the motion for a directed verdict. It can do so if it wishes, but the fiction that it has reserved decision is held sufficient to permit the postverdict motion even though the motion for a directed verdict was expressly denied.[41] A motion must be made after verdict, however, for judgment n.o.v. Even where the trial court had expressly reserved decision on the motion for a directed verdict, it was held that the appellate court was powerless to order judgment n.o.v. where the moving party had failed to make a specific motion for such judgment after the verdict.[42] Where proper motions have been made, the court is not required to order judgment n.o.v., even though the case is appropriate for such an order, but has discretion to order a new trial instead if it believes that this, rather than a final termination of the case, would better serve the ends of justice.[43]

The motion for judgment n.o.v., like the motion for directed verdict, raises only a legal question. It can be granted only if there was "no legally sufficient evidentiary basis for a reasonable jury to have found for" the moving party.[44] It differs from the motion for a new trial, where the court has discretion to set aside a verdict and grant a new trial even if the verdict is supported by substantial evidence. The motion for judgment n.o.v., on the other hand, must be denied if there is any substantial evidence supporting the verdict. The credibility of witnesses and weight of the evidence, proper considerations on a motion for a new trial, are not the concern of the court on a motion for a directed verdict or for judgment n.o.v. The evidence must be viewed in the light most favorable to the party against whom the motion is made, that party must be given the benefit of all legitimate inferences that may be drawn in its favor from that evidence, and the motion must be denied if, so viewed, reasonable persons might differ as to the conclusions of fact to be drawn.

The rules set out in the foregoing paragraph have been stated and restated, in many forms, by the courts.[45] Though the matter is not yet

---

40. E.g., Austin–Westshore Const. Co. v. Federated Dept. Stores, Inc., C.A.11th, 1991, 934 F.2d 1217; Yohannon v. Kenne Corp., C.A.3d, 1991, 924 F.2d 1255, 1261; and cases cited 9 Wright & Miller, Civil § 2537 nn. 31–33.

41. E.g., Lowden v. Denton, C.C.A.8th, 1940, 110 F.2d 274, certiorari denied 60 S.Ct. 1100, 310 U.S. 652, 84 L.Ed. 1417.

42. Johnson v. New York, N.H. & H.R. Co., 1952, 73 S.Ct. 125, 344 U.S. 48, 97 L.Ed. 77. Accord: Cone v. West Virginia Pulp & Paper Co., 1947, 67 S.Ct. 752, 330 U.S. 212, 91 L.Ed. 849; Globe Liquor Co. v. San Roman, 1948, 68 S.Ct. 246, 332 U.S. 571, 92 L.Ed. 177.

43. Cone v. West Virginia Pulp & Paper Co., 1947, 67 S.Ct. 752, 755, 330 U.S. 212, 215, 91 L.Ed. 849; cf. Iacurci v. Lummus Co., 1967, 87 S.Ct. 1423, 387 U.S. 86, 18 L.Ed.2d 581. See 9 Wright & Miller, Civil § 2539.

44. Rule 50(a)(1), as amended in 1991. The statement of it in the rule made no change in the previous standard.

45. 9 Wright & Miller, Civil § 2524.

As good a statement of the test as any is in Simblest v. Maynard, C.A.2d, 1970, 427 F.2d 1, 4: "Simply stated, it is whether the evidence is such that, without weighing the credibility of the witnesses or otherwise considering the weight of the evidence, definitely settled, the better view is that they represent a federal test of sufficiency of evidence that must be followed even if state law sets up some other standard.[46] No one disagrees with the rules but only as to their application in a particular case. There are three questions about the rules, however, that are not yet resolved.

It is said that a party is entitled to the benefit of all "legitimate" inferences that may be drawn in his favor from the evidence, and that even if the facts are undisputed, the case must go to the jury if conflicting inferences may legitimately be drawn from the facts. Unfortunately there is no sure test to distinguish between the legitimate inference, to which the party opposing the motion is entitled, and the unreasonable inference, to which the party is not entitled. Courts endeavor to state a test for distinguishing the two in terms of probability. They say that the inference is legitimate only where the evidence offered makes the existence of the fact to be inferred more probable than the nonexistence of the fact, and they warn that any lesser test would permit the jury to rest its verdict on speculation and conjecture.[47] Any attempt to suggest mathematical precision in the weighing of probabilities is spurious; rarely does the court have any way of knowing what the mathematical probabilities are.[48] And it may be that the purported test overstates the quantum of proof required, as one court has suggested.[49] The Supreme Court itself has said that "whenever facts are in dispute or the evidence is such that fair-minded men may draw different inferences, a measure of speculation and conjecture is required on the part of those whose duty it is to settle the dispute by choosing what seems to them to be the most reasonable inference."[50]

In determining whether there is a submissible issue, it is not settled whether the court is to look only to the evidence favorable to the party against whom the motion is made, or whether it is to consider all the evidence. A party may have produced weak evidence that, in itself, would be sufficient for a finding in his favor, but that is overwhelmed by his opponent's evidence to the contrary. The earlier cases reflect a practice of examining all the evidence in order to affirm direction of a verdict or grant of judgment n.o.v. in these circumstances,[51] and this

there can be but one conclusion as to the verdict that reasonable men could have reached."

46. See § 92 above at notes 17 to 23.

47. E.g., Lamb by Shepard v. Sears, Roebuck & Co., C.A.11th, 1993, 1 F.3d 1184, 1190; Frankel v. Slotkin, C.A.2d, 1993, 984 F.2d 1328, 1335; Resare v. Raytheon Co., C.A.1st, 1992, 981 F.2d 32, 34; Ford Motor Co. v. McDavid, C.A.4th, 1958, 259 F.2d 261, certiorari denied 79 S.Ct. 234, 358 U.S. 908, 3 L.Ed.2d 229.

48. James, Sufficiency of the Evidence and Jury–Control Devices Available Before Verdict, 1961, 47 Va.L.Rev. 218, 221–222.

49. Gutierrez v. Public Serv. Interstate Transp. Co., C.A.2d, 1948, 168 F.2d 678, 680.

50. Lavender v. Kurn, 1946, 66 S.Ct. 740, 744, 327 U.S. 645, 653, 90 L.Ed. 916. See also Cooper, note 1 above, at 955–958; 9 Wright & Miller, Civil § 2528, pp. 565–569.

51. Pennsylvania R. Co. v. Chamberlain, 1933, 53 S.Ct. 391, 288 U.S. 333, 77 L.Ed. 819; Southern Ry. Co. v. Walters, 1931, 52 S.Ct. 58, 284 U.S. 190, 76 L.Ed. 239.

practice has scholarly support.[52]   The Supreme Court has apparently adopted a different rule, though without expressly rejecting the older cases.   Thus, in one case it noted that there was evidence from which a jury could have reached a contrary conclusion, but said: "There was evidence from which a jury could reach the conclusion that petitioner was totally and permanently disabled.   That was enough."[53]   In a later case the Court said: "it is the established rule that in passing upon whether there is sufficient evidence to submit an issue to the jury we need look only to the evidence and reasonable inferences which tend to support the case of a litigant against whom a peremptory instruction has been given."[54]   Despite these decisions from the Supreme Court, many lower courts continue to follow the older practice.[55]

The correct rule seems to be that the court may consider all of the evidence favorable to the position of the party opposing the motion as well as any unfavorable evidence that the jury is required to believe. Thus, it may take into account evidence supporting the moving party that is uncontradicted and unimpeached, at least to the extent that this evidence comes from disinterested witnesses.[56]

Finally, consideration must be given to the well-known, and highly controversial, series of decisions in which the Supreme Court has reversed judgments of lower courts that have taken cases away from the jury in actions arising under the Federal Employers' Liability Act and the Jones Act.   Although these decisions do not clearly articulate the test of sufficiency of the evidence that the Court is applying, it appears that the Court is holding that so long as there is evidence from which an inference might rationally be drawn, whether about how the accident happened or whether defendant's conduct was negligent, it is for the jury to accept or reject that inference, even though the inference may be quite an improbable one and some other inference highly probable.[57]   It

52.   Blume, Origin and Development of the Directed Verdict, 1950, 48 Mich.L.Rev. 555, 576–581; Comment, 1949, 47 Mich. L.Rev. 974.   But see Comment, 1964, 42 Texas L.Rev. 1053, 1060–1061.

53.   Berry v. U.S., 1941, 61 S.Ct. 637, 640, 312 U.S. 450, 456, 85 L.Ed. 945.

54.   Wilkerson v. McCarthy, 1949, 69 S.Ct. 413, 415, 336 U.S. 53, 57, 93 L.Ed. 497.

55.   Barnett v. I.R.S., C.A.5th, 1993, 988 F.2d 1449, 1453; Connell v. Sears, Roebuck & Co., C.A.Fed.1983, 722 F.2d 1542, 1546; Lovelace v. Sherwin–Williams Co., C.A.4th, 1982, 681 F.2d 230, 243 n. 14; Oldenburg v. Clark, C.A.10th, 1974, 489 F.2d 839, 841; Boeing Co. v. Shipman, C.A.5th, 1969, 411 F.2d 365, 375 n. 16; and cases cited 9 Wright & Miller, Civil § 2529 n. 49.

Contra: Dace v. ACF Industries, Inc., C.A.8th, 1983, 722 F.2d 374, 375–377, opinion supplemented C.A.8th, 1984, 728 F.2d 976; Lohr v. Tittle, C.A.10th, 1960, 275

F.2d 662, 664 n. 1; Weir v. Chicago Plastering Institute, C.A.7th, 1959, 272 F.2d 883, 885; and cases cited 9 Wright & Miller, Civil § 2529 n. 48.

56.   County of Suffolk v. Long Island Lighting Co., C.A.2d, 1990, 907 F.2d 1295, 1314; St. Paul Fire & Marine Ins. Co. v. Vaughan, C.A.4th, 1985, 779 F.2d 1003, 1008; Simblest v. Maynard, C.A.2d, 1970, 427 F.2d 1, 5; Negron v. Ward, D.C.N.Y. 1978, 458 F.Supp. 748, 756; Cooper, note 1 above, at 948–953; 9 Wright & Miller, Civil § 2529.

57.   E.g., Lavender v. Kurn, 1946, 66 S.Ct. 740, 743–744, 327 U.S. 645, 652–653, 90 L.Ed. 916; Tennant v. Peoria & P.U. Ry. Co., 1944, 64 S.Ct. 409, 412, 321 U.S. 29, 35, 88 L.Ed. 520; Rogers v. Missouri Pac. R. Co., 1957, 77 S.Ct. 443, 448, 352 U.S. 500, 506, 1 L.Ed.2d 493.   See 9 Wright & Miller, Civil § 2526.

For a suggestion that in later years the Court took a more conservative approach to is of much practical importance to know whether these decisions are confined to the particular statutory actions in which they have been handed down, or whether they represent a construction of the Seventh Amendment that is controlling in all jury cases in federal courts. Arguments can be made that these decisions are to be confined to FELA and Jones Act litigation, and many lower courts and commentators have so understood them.[58] The most powerful argument to the contrary is that the opinions announcing the rule as to sufficiency of the evidence in these cases refer to "the jury's historic function" [59] and to the Seventh Amendment,[60] and the Supreme Court itself has cited these cases as representing the "federal test of sufficiency of the evidence to support a jury verdict where federal jurisdiction is rested on diversity of citizenship." [61] For these reasons other courts and commentators have held the test laid down in the FELA cases applicable in all cases.[62]

Rule 50(b) permits a party to move in the alternative for judgment n.o.v. or for a new trial. In such a case if the trial court grants the motion for judgment n.o.v. but fails to rule upon the alternative motion for a new trial, and the appellate court finds that the entry of judgment n.o.v. was erroneous, it is necessary to remand the case to the trial court for a decision on the motion for a new trial. In Montgomery Ward & Co. v. Duncan [63] the Supreme Court pointed out this difficulty and held that in such a case the trial court should rule upon both motions, making its grant or denial of a new trial conditional upon reversal of its decision on

FELA cases, see Note, Federal Employers' Liability Act: Apostasy of Sufficiency of Evidence Policy, 1971, 42 Miss.L.J. 418.

58. E.g., Clark v. Kentucky & Indiana Term. R.R., C.A.6th, 1984, 728 F.2d 307, 310; Missouri–K.–T. Ry. v. Hearson, C.A.10th, 1970, 422 F.2d 1037, 1040; Boeing Co. v. Shipman, C.A.5th, 1969, 411 F.2d 365, 370–373; Dehydrating Process Co. v. A.O. Smith Corp., C.A.1st, 1961, 292 F.2d 653, 656 n. 6, certiorari denied 82 S.Ct. 368, 368 U.S. 931, 7 L.Ed.2d 194; Zegan v. Central R. Co. of N.J., C.A.3d, 1959, 266 F.2d 101, 104; Gibson v. Elgin, J. & E. R. Co., C.A.7th, 1957, 246 F.2d 834, 840, certiorari denied 78 S.Ct. 270, 355 U.S. 897, 2 L.Ed.2d 193; Cahill v. New York, N.H. & H.R. Co., C.A.2d, 1955, 224 F.2d 637, 640 (Frank, J., dissenting); Cooper, note 1 above, at 924–927; Note, 58 Col.L.Rev. 517, 523 n. 47.

59. Lavender v. Kurn, 1946, 66 S.Ct. 740, 744, 327 U.S. 645, 652, 90 L.Ed. 916. See also Davis v. Virginian R. Co., 1960, 80 S.Ct. 387, 389, 361 U.S. 354, 356–357, 4 L.Ed.2d 366.

60. Atlantic and Gulf Stevedores, Inc. v. Ellerman Lines, Ltd., 1962, 82 S.Ct. 780, 784, 369 U.S. 355, 360, 7 L.Ed.2d 798; Harris v. Pennsylvania R. Co., 1959, 80 S.Ct. 22, 24, 361 U.S. 15, 17, 4 L.Ed.2d 1 (Douglas, J., concurring). See also Rogers v. Missouri Pac. R. Co., 1957, 77 S.Ct. 443,

449–450 n. 18, 352 U.S. 500, 508 n. 18, 1 L.Ed.2d 493.

61. Dick v. New York Life Ins. Co., 1959, 79 S.Ct. 921, 926 n. 8, 359 U.S. 437, 445 n. 8, 3 L.Ed.2d 935; Continental Ore Co. v. Union Carbide & Carbon Corp., 1962, 82 S.Ct. 1404, 1409 n. 6, 370 U.S. 690, 696 n. 6, 8 L.Ed.2d 777.

62. Scavens v. Macks Stores, Inc., C.A.4th, 1978, 577 F.2d 870, 873 n. 5; Wratchford v. S.J. Groves & Sons Co., C.A.4th, 1969, 405 F.2d 1061, 1066 n. 14; Lones v. Detroit, Toledo & Ironton R. Co., C.A.6th, 1968, 398 F.2d 914, 919; see Bruce Lincoln–Mercury, Inc. v. Universal C.I.T. Credit Corp., C.A.3d, 1963, 325 F.2d 2, 22; Anglen v. Braniff Airways, C.A.8th, 1956, 237 F.2d 736, 740; Radio v. Chernack, D.C.R.I.1963, 217 F.Supp. 33, 35.

See also Green, Jury Trial and Mr. Justice Black, 1956, 65 Yale L.J. 482, 490 n. 17; Green, Protection of Jury Trial in Diversity Cases Against State Invasions, 1957, 35 Tex.L.Rev. 768; DeParcq, The Supreme Court and the Federal Employers' Liability Act, 1958–1959 Term, 44 Minn.L.Rev. 707, 716–717; Comment, 1964, 42 Texas L.Rev. 1053, 1064–1071.

63. 1940, 61 S.Ct. 189, 195, 311 U.S. 243, 253, 85 L.Ed. 147.

the motion for judgment n.o.v. Though this practice is desirable in avoiding an unnecessary remand, it is extremely unrealistic in asking the trial judge to make a conditional ruling on the assumption that, for reasons that the judge cannot know, the ruling on the motion for judgment is held to be erroneous.[64] Further, with all the possibilities present when the court may either grant or deny either or both branches of the alternative motion, the practice is necessarily very complicated, and has often been misunderstood by courts and counsel.[65] In 1963 subdivisions (c) and (d) were added by amendment to Rule 50, spelling out the procedure to be followed for conditional rulings on the alternative motion. The amendment has lessened the confusion in applying this procedure, but it could not lessen the unreality of it. And Supreme Court decisions construing the 1963 additions[66] have received sharp criticism from the commentators, who assert that they have created new uncertainty about the procedure and that they have decreased the protection formerly provided for the party in whose favor the verdict had run.[67]

§ 96.   Trial to the Court[1]

Fewer than 10% of the civil actions commenced in federal court are actually disposed of by trial. Of those that do go to trial, about half are tried to a judge, rather than to a jury,[2] either because no right of jury trial exists or because the parties have waived such right. Though trial to the court is statistically a common method of disposing of cases, it raises many fewer procedural problems than does trial to a jury.

Consider, for example, the question of evidence. The rules of evidence are, in large part, the product of the jury system. They apply, nevertheless, in nonjury actions as well.[3] Rules of privilege, which represent an extrinsic policy determination that protection of a confidential relation is more important than obtaining all relevant evidence in the particular case, are applied in nonjury cases with as much vigor as in jury cases. The importance of such other rules as the hearsay rule, the misnamed "best evidence" rule, and the rule against opinions, is minimized in nonjury cases, though the rules remain applicable. The errone-

---

64. See Momand v. Universal Film Exchange, Inc., D.C.Mass.1947, 72 F.Supp. 469, 483.

65. See 9 Wright & Miller, Civil §§ 2539, 2540.

66. Neely v. Martin K. Eby Constr. Co., 1967, 87 S.Ct. 1072, 386 U.S. 317, 18 L.Ed.2d 75; Iacurci v. Lummus Co., 1967, 87 S.Ct. 1423, 387 U.S. 86, 18 L.Ed.2d 581.

67. Note, Post–Verdict Motions Under Rule 50: Protecting the Verdict Winners, 1968, 53 Minn.L.Rev. 358; Note, Disposition of Cases by the Court of Appeals after Granting Judgment Notwithstanding the Verdict, 1968, 47 N.C.L.Rev. 162.

These decisions are defended in Louis, Post–Verdict Rulings on the Sufficiency of the Evidence: Neely v. Martin K. Eby Construction Co. Revisited, 1975 Wis.L.Rev. 503.

§ 96

1. 9 Wright & Miller, Civil §§ 2371, 2412, 2571–2591.

2. In the fiscal year 1992, of 230,750 civil actions terminated in district courts, only 8,038 were disposed of by trial. Of these, 3,751, or 47%, were tried to a judge, while 4,287 were tried to a jury. Ann.Rep. of the Director of the Administrative Office of the U.S. Courts, 1992, Table C–4.

3. On evidence in federal court, see § 93 above.

ous admission of evidence will not often be the basis of reversal, since the appellate courts indulge the gracious presumption that the trial judge relied only on the evidence that was properly admitted in making his or her findings.[4] Thus, in a nonjury case the court should be slow to keep out evidence challenged under one of the exclusionary rules. The attitude now governing has been strongly stated by the Eighth Circuit: "In the trial of a nonjury case, it is virtually impossible for a trial court to commit reversible error by receiving incompetent evidence, whether objected to or not. * * * On the other hand, a trial judge, who, in the trial of a nonjury case, attempts to make strict rulings on the admissibility of evidence, can easily get his decision reversed by excluding evidence which is objected to but which, on review, the appellate court believes should have been admitted."[5]

Until 1991 a motion for dismissal for insufficiency of the evidence, under Rule 41(b), took the place in a nonjury case of the motion for a directed verdict in a jury case. That has been changed and the relevant motion, which may be made by either party, is for judgment as a matter of law under Rule 52(c). In a jury case, when a motion for a directed verdict is made, the judge is required to consider the evidence in the light most favorable to the party against whom the motion is directed, in order to prevent any infringement on the function of the jury.[6] No such limitation applies in a nonjury case.[7]

When the judge decides the case, either on a motion for judgment as a matter of law or at the close of all the evidence, he or she must make findings of fact and state separately the conclusions of law, though these may be contained in an opinion if one is written.[8] Such findings are intended to aid the appellate court by affording it a clear understanding of the basis of the trial court's decision, and to make definite what was decided for purposes of claim and issue preclusion. Finally, the requirement of findings should evoke care on the part of the trial judge in ascertaining the facts.[9] Some judges prepare their own findings, while others ask winning counsel to submit proposed findings for the court to adopt.[10] Though it is settled that findings do not carry less weight on appeal because they were prepared in the first instance by counsel rather

---

4. See Plummer v. Western Intl. Hotels Co., C.A.9th, 1981, 656 F.2d 502, 505; and cases cited 9 Wright & Miller, Civil § 2412 n. 89. See also Davis, Hearsay in Nonjury Cases, 1970, 83 Harv.L.Rev. 1362.

5. Builders Steel Co. v. C.I.R., C.A.8th, 1950, 179 F.2d 377, 379. See also Eagle–Picher Industries, Inc. v. Liberty Mut. Ins. Co., C.A.1st, 1982, 682 F.2d 12, 18, certiorari denied 103 S.Ct. 1279, 460 U.S. 1028, 75 L.Ed.2d 500; U.S. ex rel. Placek v. Illinois, C.A.7th, 1976, 546 F.2d 1298, 1307 n. 9. See generally Davis, An Approach to Rules of Evidence for Nonjury Cases, 1964, 50 A.B.A.J. 723. A contrary view is stated in Note, Improper Evidence in Nonjury Trials:

Basis for Reversal, 1965, 79 Harv.L.Rev. 407.

6. See § 95 above.

7. 9 Wright & Miller, Civil § 2371. See Steffen, The Prima Facie Case in Non–Jury Trials, 1959, 27 U.Chi.L.Rev. 94.

8. Rule 52(a); 9 Wright & Miller, Civil §§ 2571–2582.

9. Snyder v. U.S., C.A.10th, 1982, 674 F.2d 1359, 1362–1363; Lemelson v. Kellogg Co., C.A.2d, 1971, 440 F.2d 986, 988; Nordbye, Improvements in Statement of Findings of Fact and Conclusions of Law, 1940, 1 F.R.D. 25.

10. 9 Wright & Miller, Civil § 2578.

than the court,[11] findings that represent the independent study of the district judge are more helpful to the appellate court.[12]

A motion to amend the findings is authorized by Rule 52(b) and may be joined with a motion for a new trial. Though this bears a surface similarity to the motion for new trial in a jury case, in practice it is not much used and has a different function. Such a motion is not required as a prerequisite to appeal.[13] In a jury case, a new trial will be before a different, and, it is hoped, more favorable, jury, while in the nonjury case the motion to amend or for a new trial goes to the same judge who has already decided the case. Thus, the primary purpose of Rule 52(b) is to enable the appellate court to obtain a correct understanding of the factual issues determined by the trial court.[14]

Probably no provision of the federal rules has been quoted and cited more often than the famous sentence in Rule 52(a) that, as originally adopted, said: "Findings of fact shall not be set aside unless clearly erroneous, and due regard shall be given to the opportunity of the trial court to judge of the credibility of the witnesses." [15] This provision represents a statement of what was considered to be the federal equity practice in the years just prior to merger of law and equity. Before adoption of the rules, in a legal action in which jury trial was waived the findings of fact of the court were not reviewable,[16] just as the fact determination of a jury could not be reviewed. Equity practice had departed from the broad de novo review of ancient chancery, and the rule had developed that the findings of the trial court had great weight with the appellate court, though they were not conclusive.[17] It was thought desirable to have a single standard of review apply to all nonjury cases, whether historically legal or equitable, and the broader equity review was adopted.[18] Thus, findings of fact by the trial court are not conclusive on appeal, but there is a heavy burden on the party who seeks to overturn them.[19] In the colorful phrase of one court, the findings

11. Anderson v. City of Bessemer City, 1985, 105 S.Ct. 1504, 1510–1511, 470 U.S. 564, 572–573, 84 L.Ed.2d 518.

12. Ibid; U.S. v. El Paso Natural Gas Co., 1964, 84 S.Ct. 1044, 1047, 376 U.S. 651, 656–657, 12 L.Ed.2d 12; Berger v. Iron Workers Reinforced Rodmen Local 201, C.A.D.C.1988, 843 F.2d 1395, 1407, certiorari denied 109 S.Ct. 3155, 490 U.S. 1105, 104 L.Ed.2d 1018; Roberts v. Ross, C.A.3d, 1965, 344 F.2d 747, 752, noted 1966, 51 Corn.L.Q. 567; and cases cited 9 Wright & Miller, Civil § 2578 nn. 18–20.

13. E.g., Twentieth Century Fox Film Corp. v. Goldwyn, C.A.9th, 1964, 328 F.2d 190, certiorari denied 85 S.Ct. 143, 379 U.S. 880, 13 L.Ed.2d 87; 9 Wright & Miller, Civil § 2582.

14. U.S. v. Carolina Eastern Chemical Co., D.C.S.C.1986, 639 F.Supp. 1420; Heikkila v. Barber, D.C.Cal.1958, 164 F.Supp. 587.

15. See Cooper, Civil Rule 52(a): Rationing and Rationalizing the Resources of Appellate Review, 1988, 63 Notre Dame L.Rev. 645. Dean Cooper suggests, at 645, that the success of the rule "is due to the fact that the 'clearly erroneous' phrase has no intrinsic meaning. It is elastic, capacious, malleable, and above all variable. Because it means nothing, it can mean anything and everything that it ought to mean."

16. Dooley v. Pease, 1900, 21 S.Ct. 329, 331, 180 U.S. 126, 131, 45 L.Ed. 457.

17. U.S. v. United States Gypsum Co., 1948, 68 S.Ct. 525, 542, 333 U.S. 364, 395, 92 L.Ed. 746.

18. 9 Wright & Miller, Civil § 2571; Cooper, note 15 above, at 647–648.

19. 9 Wright & Miller, Civil § 2585.

"come here well armed with the buckler and shield" of Rule 52(a).[20] The rule is usually cited to justify refusal to interfere with the fact findings made in the trial court. It is settled that a finding is clearly erroneous, within the meaning of Rule 52(a), when "although there is evidence to support it, the reviewing court on the entire evidence is left with the definite and firm conviction that a mistake has been committed."[21]

The Supreme Court quoted that formulation with approval in 1985 in the leading case of Anderson v. City of Bessemer City.[22] It went on to emphasize what a restrictive standard of review that is. As Justice White put it: "If the district court's account of the evidence is plausible in light of the record viewed in its entirety, the court of appeals may not reverse it even though convinced that had it been sitting as the trier of fact, it would have weighed the evidence differently. Where there are two permissible views of the evidence, the factfinder's choice between them cannot be clearly erroneous."[23]

On one question of construction of Rule 52(a), the authorities for many years were indescribably confused. Even within a single circuit, decisions vacillated inexplicably from one position to another. This question is whether the deference that must normally be paid to the findings by the trial court applies where the finding rests on an inference drawn from documentary evidence or undisputed facts.[24]

Where the trial judge has seen and heard the witnesses, he or she has the benefit, which the appellate court does not, of being able to observe their demeanor, and the rule has always recognized this by adding to the "clearly erroneous" test the statement "and due regard shall be given to the opportunity of the trial court to judge of the credibility of the witnesses." But some courts had reasoned from this that if the trial court did not see the witnesses the appellate court can more readily hold the trial court's finding to be clearly erroneous.[25] Other decisions had gone on to reason from this gloss, rather than from the rule itself, and to say that the appellate court is not bound at all, and that review is de novo with no presumption in favor of the trial court's findings, where the evidence below was not oral.[26] This process was carried to its ultimate in an opinion by the late Judge Jerome N. Frank in which he set out a number of narrowly-defined classes, turning on the kind of case and the proportion of testimony that was oral, and asserted

20. Horton v. U.S. Steel Corp., C.A.5th, 1961, 286 F.2d 710, 713.

21. U.S. v. United States Gypsum Co., 1948, 68 S.Ct. 525, 542, 333 U.S. 364, 395, 92 L.Ed. 746. See also Sawyer v. Whitley, 1992, 112 S.Ct. 2514, 2522 n. 14, ___ U.S. ___, ___ n. 14, 120 L.Ed.2d 269.

22. 1985, 105 S.Ct. 1504, 470 U.S. 564, 84 L.Ed.2d 518.

23. 105 S.Ct. at 1511, 470 U.S. at 573–574. See also Amadeo v. Zant, 1988, 108 S.Ct. 1771, 486 U.S. 214, 100 L.Ed.2d 249.

24. 9 Wright & Miller, Civil § 2587.

25. See cases cited 9 Wright & Miller, Civil § 2587 n. 29.

26. See cases cited 9 Wright & Miller, Civil § 2587 n. 30.

that the freedom of review is dependent upon the class in which a particular case falls.[27]

Many other cases, however, held that the "clearly erroneous" test was applicable even though the trial judge has not had the opportunity to judge the credibility of the witnesses.[28] Despite the confusion in the case law, it should have been clear that this was the correct construction of the rule. It was supported by the language of the rule itself and the Committee Notes to the rule.[29] It is supported also by the essential nature of trial courts as distinguished from appellate courts. Even in instances where an appellate court is in as good a position to decide as the trial court, it should not disregard the trial court's finding, for to do so impairs confidence in the trial courts and multiplies appeals with attendant expense and delay.[30] The matter was clearly stated by Judge John B. Sanborn for the Eighth Circuit: "The entire responsibility for deciding doubtful fact questions in a nonjury case should be, and we think it is, that of the district court. The existence of any doubt about whether the trial court or this Court is the ultimate trier of fact issues in nonjury cases is, we think, detrimental to the orderly administration of justice, impairs the confidence of litigants and the public in the decisions of the district courts, and multiplies the number of appeals in such cases." [31]

The matter was put to rest, by both a Supreme Court decision and a rule amendment, in 1985. The words "whether based on oral or documentary evidence" were added to the crucial sentence of Rule 52(a) by amendment in that year. Even earlier in the year, the Supreme Court held in the Anderson case that the "clearly erroneous" test applies "even when the district court's findings do not rest on credibility determination, but are based instead on physical or documentary evidence or inferences from other facts." [32] But "[w]hen findings are based on determinations regarding the credibility of witnesses, Rule 52(a)

---

27. Orvis v. Higgins, C.A.2d 1950, 180 F.2d 537, 539–540, certiorari denied 71 S.Ct. 37, 340 U.S. 810, 95 L.Ed. 595, criticized 1950, 2 Stan.L.Rev. 784.

28. A leading case to this effect was Lundgren v. Freeman, C.A.9th, 1962, 307 F.2d 104, 113–115, noted 1963, 41 Texas L.Rev. 935. See also the cases cited 9 Wright & Miller, Civil § 2587 n. 33.

29. The Committee Note to the original rule, reprinted 12 Wright & Miller, Civil pp. 490–491, said that the "clearly erroneous" test applied "whether the finding is of a fact concerning which there was conflict of testimony, or of a fact deduced or inferred from uncontradicted testimony." See also the 1955 note to Rule 52(a), id. at pp. 609–611.

30. Lundgren v. Freeman, C.A.9th, 1962, 307 F.2d 104, 114; Wright, The Doubtful Omniscience of Appellate Courts, 1957, 41 Minn.L.Rev. 751, 764–771, 778–782. But see Godbold, Fact Finding by

Appellate Courts—An Available and Appropriate Power, 1982, 12 Cum.L.Rev. 365; Carrington, The Power of District Judges and the Responsibility of Courts of Appeals, 1969, 3 Ga.L.Rev. 507.

31. Pendergrass v. New York Life Ins. Co., C.A.8th, 1950, 181 F.2d 136, 138.

32. 105 S.Ct. at 1511–1512, 470 U.S. at 574. The Court then said: "The rationale for deference to the original finder of fact is not limited to the superiority of the trial judge's position to make determinations of credibility. The trial judge's major role is the determination of fact, and with experience in fulfilling that role comes expertise. Duplication of the trial judge's efforts in the court of appeals would very likely contribute only negligibly to the accuracy of fact determination at a huge cost in diversion of judicial resources." 105 S.Ct. at 1512, 470 U.S. at 574–575.

demands even greater deference to the trial court's findings; for only the trial judge can be aware of the variations in demeanor and tone of voice that bear so heavily on the listener's understanding of and belief in what is said. * * * "[33]

It is well understood that the "clearly erroneous" rule applies on issues of fact,[34] but not on questions of law,[35] and there is much authority that it does not apply to rulings on mixed questions of law and fact.[36] Such expressions may be misleading. If an error of law has impaired the judgment of the trial judge on such a mixed question, then the finding should be set aside,[37] but this should not be true where the finding involves the application of a correct principle of law to the facts.[38] Thus, the Supreme Court has held that the "clearly erroneous" test applies to a finding of negligence,[39] to the determination of whether a payment to a taxpayer was a "gift,"[40] and to whether an employer had a discriminatory intent.[41] Lower courts have held Rule 52(a) applicable on many questions that surely have elements of law involved in them.[42] In view of this array of precedent any attempt to make nice distinctions between fact and law, so as to broaden the scope of review of determinations that can better be made by the trial court, seems doomed to fail. The "clearly erroneous" test ordinarily should apply whenever the finding is based on the "fact-finding tribunal's experience with the mainsprings of human conduct."[43] But if a fact is of constitutional significance, such as "actual malice" in a defamation case, independent review is required in

33. 105 S.Ct. at 1512, 470 U.S. at 575. The Court went on to add that "when a trial judge's finding is based on his decision to credit the testimony of one of two or more witnesses, each of whom has told a coherent and facially plausible story that is not contradicted by extrinsic evidence, that finding, if not internally inconsistent, can virtually never be clear error."

34. "It does not divide facts into categories; in particular, it does not divide findings of fact into those that deal with 'ultimate' and those that deal with 'subsidiary' facts." Pullman–Standard v. Swint, 1982, 102 S.Ct. 1781, 1789, 456 U.S. 273, 72 L.Ed.2d 66.

35. 9 Wright & Miller, Civil § 2588.

36. See Pullman–Standard v. Swint, 1982, 102 S.Ct. 1781, 1790 n. 19, 456 U.S. 273, 289 n. 19, 72 L.Ed.2d 66; and cases cited 9 Wright & Miller, Civil § 2589 nn. 55–61.

37. U.S. v. Singer Mfg. Co., 1963, 83 S.Ct. 1773, 1784 n. 9, 374 U.S. 174, 194 n. 9, 10 L.Ed.2d 823; and cases cited 9 Wright & Miller, Civil § 2585 n. 7. See also the discerning treatment of Rule 52(a) and law application in Cooper, note 15 above, at 657–670.

38. A contrary view is taken in Karavos Compania Naviera S.A. v. Atlantica Export

Corp., C.A.2d, 1978, 588 F.2d 1, 7–9, and in Weiner, The Civil Nonjury Trial and the Law–Fact Distinction, 1967, 55 Calif.L.Rev. 1020.

39. McAllister v. U.S., 1954, 75 S.Ct. 6, 348 U.S. 19, 99 L.Ed. 20.

A few of the courts of appeals have been reluctant to accept this. See 9 Wright & Miller, Civil § 2590.

40. C.I.R. v. Duberstein, 1960, 80 S.Ct. 1190, 363 U.S. 278, 4 L.Ed.2d 1218, criticized as typical of "excessive deference to triers of fact." Griswold, Of Time and Attitudes—Professor Hart and Judge Arnold, 1960, 74 Harv.L.Rev. 81, 86–91. The decision is criticized also in Carrington, note 30 above, at 521–523 and in Cooper, note 15 above, at 662–664.

41. Pullman–Standard v. Swint, 1982, 102 S.Ct. 1781, 1790–1791, 456 U.S. 273, 289–290, 72 L.Ed.2d 66.

42. See generally 9 Wright & Miller, Civil § 2589. On the review of findings in patent cases, see id. at § 2591.

43. C.I.R. v. Duberstein, 1960, 80 S.Ct. 1190, 1198, 363 U.S. 278, 289, 4 L.Ed.2d 1218.

order to preserve constitutional rights.[44]

§ 97. Control by the Judge [1]

A federal judge is a puissant figure. "In a trial by jury in a federal court, the judge is not a mere moderator, but is the governor of the trial for the purpose of assuring its proper conduct and of determining questions of law."[2] He retains the powers that judges had at common law, including notably the power to comment on the evidence,[3] though one of the results of Jacksonian democracy was to deny such powers to judges in most states. He is appointed for life, and need not justify his record to the electorate at regular intervals. In many respects he is given power unknown at common law, because one of the principal ideas embodied in the rules is that it is wise to leave many details of procedure to the informed discretion of the judge, acting in the circumstances of the particular case, rather than regulating such details by rigid provisions.

Joinder of claims and parties is a good example of this thesis. At common law and under the codes joinder was measured by conceptual tests and was narrowly confined. Under the rules joinder is virtually unlimited. But Rule 42(b) then gives the judge power to order a separate trial of any claim or issue, as seems necessary to further convenience, to avoid prejudice, and to promote expedition and economy.[4] The judge, acting with an eye to all the circumstances of the particular case, has been able to regulate the joint or separate trial of issues far better than was done under the former systems.

There is still some question whether issues can be ordered tried before different juries. There is no doubt that the court can order separate trials of issues, with the same jury sitting in each trial,[5] and it seems to be accepted that the better and preferred practice is to use the same jury for all issues, even though it may hear the issues at different

---

44. Bose Corp. v. Consumers Union of U.S., Inc., 1984, 104 S.Ct. 1949, 1958–1965, 466 U.S. 485, 498–511, 80 L.Ed.2d 502. See also Harte–Hanks Communications, Inc. v. Connaughton, 1989, 109 S.Ct. 2678, 2695, 491 U.S. 657, 686, 105 L.Ed.2d 562; In re Capital Cities/ABC, Inc.'s Application for Access to Sealed Transcripts, C.A.3d, 1990, 913 F.2d 89, 92; Note, Constitutional Fact Review: An Essential Exception to Anderson v. Bessemer, 1987, 67 Ind.L.J. 1209.

§ 97

1. 9 Wright & Miller, Civil §§ 2361–2376 (dismissal of actions), 2381–2392 (consolidation or separate trials), 2601–2615 (reference to master).

2. Herron v. Southern Pac. Co., 1931, 51 S.Ct. 383, 384, 283 U.S. 91, 95, 75 L.Ed. 857.

The Fourth Circuit has restated this somewhat less elegantly in saying that "a United States district judge is not a bump on a log. Nor is he a referee at a prize fight." Evans v. Wright, C.A.4th, 1974, 505 F.2d 287, 289.

3. See § 94 above.

4. 9 Wright & Miller, Civil §§ 2388–2389; Schwartz, Severance—A Means of Minimizing the Role of Burden and Expense in Determining the Outcome of Litigation, 1967, 20 Vand.L.Rev. 1197; Note, Liberal Joinder of Issues and the Sequence of Trial, 1958, 34 Ind.L.J. 97; Note, Separate Trial of a Claim or Issue in Modern Pleading: Rule 42(b) of the Federal Rules of Civil Procedure, 1955, 39 Minn.L.Rev. 743.

5. Moss v. Associated Transport, Inc., C.A.6th, 1965, 344 F.2d 23; Burlington N. R. Co. v. JMC Transport, Inc., D.C.Ill.1983, 567 F.Supp. 389, 394.

times.[6] The issue can thus be narrowed to whether the preferred procedure is constitutionally required. It has been held, on sound ground, that the Seventh Amendment is not violated by the separate submission of the issues to a single jury.[7] Is there a violation of the constitutional provision if issues are separately submitted to separate juries? The answer rather clearly must be in the negative. Where a single jury has passed on all issues, but error has tainted its verdict on one of the issues, it is quite settled that there may be a new trial before a second jury limited to that single issue, provided that the error requiring a new trial has not affected the determination of any other issue.[8] In this instance the result is that different juries ultimately resolve the issues. An argument that two juries may be used if one jury has first passed on all the issues—though its verdict on one of them has gone out of the case—but that two juries may not be used in the first instance, seems untenable.[9] The great guaranty of the Seventh Amendment will hardly support such a gossamer distinction.

There is a limitation that must not be overlooked. In the case stating that a partial new trial may under some circumstances be used, the Supreme Court held that this practice cannot be resorted to unless it clearly appears that the issue to be retried is so distinct and separable from the others that a trial of it alone may be had without injustice.[10] Similarly separate trial of a particular issue cannot be ordered in the first instance where the issue is so interwoven with the other issues that it cannot be submitted to the jury independently of the others without confusion and uncertainty that would amount to a denial of a fair trial.[11] But this problem goes beyond the question of whether two juries are to be used. In the circumstances described, separate trial, even to the same jury, would be erroneous. Applying these principles to a matter that is of much current interest, separate trial of the issues of damages and of liability in a personal injury case, even to separate juries, is not improper where the two issues are distinct and separate. Whether such

---

6. Dunn v. Sears, Roebuck & Co., C.A.5th, 1981, 639 F.2d 1171, 1174; Martin v. Bell Helicopter Co., D.C.Colo.1980, 85 F.R.D. 654, 659; O'Donnell v. Watson Bros. Transp. Co., D.C.Ill.1960, 183 F.Supp. 577, 580.

7. Hosie v. Chicago & N.W.R. Co., C.A.7th, 1960, 282 F.2d 639, 642–643, certiorari denied 81 S.Ct. 695, 365 U.S. 814, 5 L.Ed.2d 693, noted 1961, 74 Harv.L.Rev. 781, 1961 U.Ill.L.Forum 194.

8. Gasoline Products Co., Inc. v. Champlin Refining Co., 1931, 51 S.Ct. 513, 283 U.S. 494, 75 L.Ed. 1188; Dopp v. HTP Corp., C.A.1st, 1991, 947 F.2d 506, 519; Pritchard v. Liggett & Myers Tobacco Co., C.A.3d, 1966, 370 F.2d 95, certiorari denied 87 S.Ct. 1350, 386 U.S. 1009, 18 L.Ed.2d 436. See 11 Wright & Miller, Civil § 2814.

9. Arthur Young & Co. v. U.S. District Court, C.A.9th, 1977, 549 F.2d 686, certiorari denied 98 S.Ct. 109, 434 U.S. 829, 54 L.Ed.2d 88; In re Shell Oil Refinery, D.C.La.1991, 136 F.R.D. 588, 596; Wilson v. Johns–Manville Sales Corp., D.C.Tex. 1985, 107 F.R.D. 250; Martin v. Bell Helicopter Co., D.C.Colo.1980, 85 F.R.D. 654.

10. Gasoline Products Co., Inc. v. Champlin Ref. Co., 1931, 51 S.Ct. 513, 515, 283 U.S. 494, 500, 75 L.Ed. 1188. See 11 Wright & Miller, Civil § 2814.

11. Franchi Constr. Co. v. Combined Ins. Co. of America, C.A.1st, 1978, 580 F.2d 1, 7–8; United Air Lines, Inc. v. Wiener, C.A.9th, 1961, 286 F.2d 302, certiorari denied 81 S.Ct. 1352, 366 U.S. 924, 6 L.Ed.2d 384; McClain v. Socony–Vacuum Oil Co., D.C.Mo.1950, 10 F.R.D. 261; U.S. ex rel. Rodriguez v. Weekly Publications, Inc., D.C.N.Y.1949, 9 F.R.D. 179.

separate trials should be ordered as a routine matter is a different, and highly controversial, question.[12] When it is seen that defendants win 42% of the cases tried routinely, but that they win 79% of the cases in which the liability issue is submitted alone, there is reason to believe that this procedural reform, though it does alleviate court congestion, has made a drastic change in the nature of jury trial itself.[13]

Just as the judge may order separate trials of the issues in a single case under Rule 42(b), he is empowered by Rule 42(a) to order joint trial of two separate actions, and may even order such actions consolidated.[14] Here again he has a broad discretion, and efficient judicial administration is the principal goal, but in one respect his discretion to order joint trial or consolidation is limited. He may do this only if the actions involve a common question of law or fact.[15] Thus, the power of the judge to order consolidation is narrower than the power of the parties to join claims against each other, where the claims may be entirely unrelated, but it is broader than the power to join parties to an action, where both a common question of law or fact and some claim arising out of the same transaction or occurrence must be present.[16]

The judge also has considerable power over the taking of a voluntary dismissal, or nonsuit, by the plaintiff. The right to take a nonsuit was far-reaching at common law. It is limited by Rule 41(a) to the period before defendant has answered or moved for summary judgment, although a few cases suggest that if the parties have joined issue on the merits of the controversy, regardless of the formal status of the pleadings, plaintiff's right to dismiss is ended.[17] After the period for dismissal

12. The following commentators are critical of such practice: Weinstein, Routine Bifurcation of Jury Negligence Trial: An Example of the Questionable Use of Rule Making, 1961, 14 Vand.L.Rev. 831; Comment, 1961, 46 Iowa L.Rev. 815; Notes, 1961, 36 Notre Dame Law. 388; 1955, 39 Minn.L.Rev. 743, 760–761. But see: Miner, A New Approach to Court Congestion, 1959, 45 A.B.A.J. 1265; Zeisel & Callahan, Split Trials and Time Saving: A Statistical Analysis, 1963, 76 Harv.L.Rev. 1606; Notes 1964, 26 U.Pitt.L.Rev. 99; 1962, 48 Va. L.Rev. 99, 46 Minn.L.Rev. 1059.

See generally 9 Wright & Miller, Civil § 2390.

13. Rosenberg, Court Congestion: Status, Causes, and Proposed Remedies, in The Courts, The Public, and The Law Explosion, 1965, pp. 29, 45; Wright, Procedural Reform: Its Limitations and Its Future, 1967, 1 Ga.L.Rev. 563, 569–570.

14. 9 Wright & Miller, Civil §§ 2382–2386; Comment, Consolidation in Mass Tort Litigation, 1963, 30 U.Chi.L.Rev. 373; Note, Federal District Court Consolidation Orders and the Final Judgment Rules, 1962, 38 Ind.L.J. 86.

15. St. Paul Fire & Marine Ins. Co. v. King, D.C.Okl.1968, 45 F.R.D. 519; Holiday Inns of America, Inc. v. Lussi, D.C.N.Y. 1967, 42 F.R.D. 27; Olivier v. Humble Oil & Ref. Co., D.C.La.1963, 225 F.Supp. 536.

16. Ringwald v. Harris, C.A.5th, 1982, 675 F.2d 768, 771 n. 5. See Stanford v. Tennessee Val. Auth., D.C.Tenn.1955, 18 F.R.D. 152, ordering consolidation on the basis of a common question though the court had found misjoinder of parties since independent transactions were involved.

17. Harvey Aluminum, Inc. v. American Cyanamid Co., C.A.2d, 1953, 203 F.2d 105, certiorari denied 73 S.Ct. 949, 345 U.S. 964, 97 L.Ed. 1383; Tele–Views News Co. v. S.R.B. TV Pub. Co., D.C.Pa.1961, 28 F.R.D. 303; Robertson v. Limestone Mfg. Co., D.C.S.C.1957, 20 F.R.D. 365. See Note, Absolute Dismissal under Federal Rule 41(a): The Disappearing Right of Voluntary Nonsuit, 1954, 63 Yale L.J. 738; Note, Right of a Plaintiff to Take a Voluntary Nonsuit or to Dismiss His Action Without Prejudice, 1951, 37 Va.L.Rev. 969.

Most cases have refused to write a judge-made exception into the rule and have held that until an answer or motion for sum-as of right has expired, plaintiff, except on stipulation with the other parties, can dismiss without prejudice only with the consent of the court and upon such terms and conditions as are just. The discretion of the court does not go merely to the terms and conditions, but extends to whether to permit a nonsuit at all.[18] Dismissal will normally be allowed unless the defendant will suffer some plain legal prejudice other than the mere prospect of a second lawsuit.[19] It is no bar to dismissal that plaintiff may obtain some tactical advantage thereby,[20] but it will not be permitted to dismiss where this is unjust, as where the evidence has been concluded and the judge has indicated the ruling will be for the defendant.[21] It has been held that voluntary dismissal under Rule 41 applies only to dismissal of an entire controversy, and that Rule 15(a) or 21 must be used for dismissal of particular parties or fewer than all of the claims.[22] The same considerations apply, however, no matter which of these rules is invoked,[23] and more recent cases have not applied this limitation on Rule 41.[24]

The judge also has the power to dismiss the case involuntarily for want of prosecution by the plaintiff, or for failure of the plaintiff to comply with the rules or any order of court.[25] Such a dismissal is normally with prejudice. This is a drastic sanction, and though the courts have the power and must have the power if they are to discharge their responsibility to prevent undue delay in litigation, it was once thought that this is a power that should be exercised only in extreme

mary judgment has been filed plaintiff has an absolute right to dismiss. See cases cited 9 Wright & Miller, Civil § 2363 n. 38. Indeed the Second Circuit itself has noted that Harvey Aluminum "has not been well received" and has refused to extend it beyond its own extreme facts. Thorp v. Scarne, C.A.2d, 1979, 599 F.2d 1169, 1174–1176. See also U.S. v. United States Trust Co., D.C.Mass.1985, 106 F.R.D. 474, 477 n. 3.

18. E.g., Grivas v. Parmalee Transp. Co., C.A.7th, 1953, 207 F.2d 334, 336–337, overruling an earlier decision of the same court to the contrary.

The court cannot prevent plaintiff from dismissing with prejudice if dismissal will dispose of all aspects of the action. Compare Smoot v. Fox, C.A.6th, 1964, 340 F.2d 301, with Hudson Engineering Co. v. Bingham Pump Co., D.C.N.Y.1969, 298 F.Supp. 387.

19. Ex parte Skinner & Eddy Corp., 1924, 44 S.Ct. 446, 265 U.S. 86, 68 L.Ed. 912; Cone v. West Virginia Pulp & Paper Co., 1947, 67 S.Ct. 752, 755, 330 U.S. 212, 217, 91 L.Ed. 849; Note, Voluntary Dismissal by Order of Court—Federal Rules of Civil Procedure Rule 41(a)(2) and Judicial Discretion, 1972, 48 Notre Dame Law. 446; 9 Wright & Miller, Civil § 2364.

20. E.g., Templeton v. Nedlloyd Lines, C.A.5th, 1990, 901 F.2d 1273; and cases cited 9 Wright & Miller, Civil § 2364 nn. 70–76. But cf. Noonan v. Cunard S.S. Co., C.A.2d, 1967, 375 F.2d 69, noted 1967, 36 U.Cin.L.Rev. 714.

21. Piedmont Interstate Fair Assn. v. Bean, C.A.4th, 1954, 209 F.2d 942; International Shoe Co. v. Cool, C.C.A.8th, 1946, 154 F.2d 778.

22. Harvey Aluminum, Inc. v. American Cyanamid Co., C.A.2d, 1953, 203 F.2d 105, certiorari denied 73 S.Ct. 949, 345 U.S. 964, 97 L.Ed. 1383; Kerr v. Compagnie De Ultramar, C.A.2d, 1958, 250 F.2d 860; Robertson v. Limestone Mfg. Co., D.C.S.C.1957, 20 F.R.D. 365. Contra: Young v. Wilky Carrier Corp., C.C.A.3d, 1945, 150 F.2d 764, certiorari denied 66 S.Ct. 470, 326 U.S. 786, 90 L.Ed. 477.

23. Johnston v. Cartwright, C.A.8th, 1966, 355 F.2d 32, 39; Altman v. Liberty Equities Corp., D.C.N.Y.1972, 54 F.R.D. 620; Note, 1961 Wis.L.Rev. 160.

24. Leroux v. Lomas & Nettleton Co., D.C.Mass.1986, 626 F.Supp. 962, 966; and cases cited 9 Wright & Miller, Civil § 2362 n. 10.

25. Rule 41(b); 9 Wright & Miller, Civil §§ 2369–2373.

situations.[26]   Thus, in one case dismissal with prejudice was held to be an abuse of discretion where plaintiff had delayed for more than two years in making service on a defendant who was at all times amenable to service, the court saying that "the doom entered below seems altogether too final and definitive" and that plaintiff should not "face a permanent bar for a delay which in our congested trial courts is hardly unusual." [27] But in recent years courts have made much more use of sanctions [28] and involuntary dismissal has been used more frequently.[29]

Where the judge requires help in a case, he may refer it to a master, under Rule 53, but this is a power to be exercised only in rare cases.[30] The procedural advantage from a reference must be weighed against the fact that it deprives litigants of their traditional right to have their case passed upon, in the first instance, by a court or jury.   And even the supposed procedural advantage must be considered in the light of the "unbelievably long" delay and the increased expense to which the litigants will be subjected by a reference.[31]   In a jury case Rule 53 purports to make it sufficient for reference that the issues are complicated, since the report of the master is merely evidence, which the jury is free to disregard, and there is no danger that the master will displace the court in making the decision.   Reference is as expensive and as time-consuming in a jury case as in any other, it is always disfavored for that reason, and the Supreme Court has indicated that it represents an inroad on trial by jury that should be made, if at all, only when unusual circumstances exist.[32]

In a nonjury case the findings of the master must be accepted by the court unless they are clearly erroneous, and thus there is added reason to refuse reference in such a case.   Accordingly the rule has always required an "exceptional condition" to justify reference in a nonjury case.   In La Buy v. Howes Leather Co.[33] the Court held that neither calendar congestion, nor complexity of the issues, nor the great length of time trial would take were exceptional conditions justifying reference. With a few minor exceptions, it is hard to conceive of any reference of a nonjury case that will meet the rigid standard of the La Buy decision.[34]

---

26. Moore v. St. Louis Music Supply Co., Inc., C.A.8th, 1976, 539 F.2d 1191; Syracuse Broadcasting Corp. v. Newhouse, C.A.2d, 1959, 271 F.2d 910; and cases cited 9 Wright & Miller, Civil § 2369 nn. 67–75. See also Comment, The Demise (Hopefully) of an Abuse: The Sanction of Dismissal, 1971, 7 Calif.West.L.Rev. 438.

27. Lyford v. Carter, C.A.2d, 1960, 274 F.2d 815, 816.

28. See § 69A above.

29. A leading case is Link v. Wabash R. Co., 1962, 82 S.Ct. 1386, 370 U.S. 626, 8 L.Ed.2d 734.   See Frank, Book Review, 1963, 76 Harv.L.Rev. 1704, 1707–1708.

30. 9 Wright & Miller, Civil §§ 2601–2615.

31. Adventures in Good Eating v. Best Places to Eat, C.C.A.7th, 1942, 131 F.2d 809, 815; Vanderbilt, Cases and Materials on Modern Procedure and Judicial Administration, 1952, pp. 1240–1241; Kaufman, Masters in the Federal Courts: Rule 53, 1958, 58 Col.L.Rev. 452; 9 Wright & Miller, Civil § 2603.

32. Dairy Queen, Inc. v. Wood, 1962, 82 S.Ct. 894, 900, 369 U.S. 469, 478, 8 L.Ed.2d 44.

33. 1957, 77 S.Ct. 309, 352 U.S. 249, 1 L.Ed.2d 290.

34. See In re Armco, Inc., C.A.8th, 1985, 770 F.2d 103, 105; Kaufman, note 29 above, at 459.   For cases in which a reference has been found proper, see 9 Wright & Miller, Civil § 2605 n. 56.

Recently new uses have developed for masters that are quite different from what was contemplated when Rule 53 was written. New kinds of complex litigation that are now coming to the courts have emphasized the need for aggressive management of the case on behalf of the court at the pretrial stages. In some cases of this kind, the use of a master to supervise discovery or otherwise act as a class manager has been found helpful.[35] And in cases in which the court has found that an institution has committed constitutionally impermissible practices, it may use a special master to monitor compliance with its remedial decree.[36] But there are limits on the proper use of masters. As it was put by then-Judge Ruth Bader Ginsburg, "[t]he judge may not impose on the parties, over the objection of at least one of them, a magistrate or master as 'a surrogate judge' to try the controversy and determine liability." [37]

Because the federal judge is given such extensive power over litigation before him, it is especially important that he not only be but seem impartial. To be sure that this is the case, there are statutory provisions requiring the judge to disqualify himself if a timely and sufficient affidavit has been filed that he has a personal bias or prejudice against a party or in favor of an adverse party.[38] Another statute, which was completely rewritten in 1974, requires a judge to disqualify himself in any proceeding in which his impartiality might reasonably be questioned, or if he is related to the case in any of a number of ways specified in the statute.[39]

G. JUDGMENT

Analysis

Sec.
98. Judgments in General.
99. Summary Judgment.
100. Declaratory Judgment.
100A. Effect of a Prior Judgment.

The Supreme Court has held that reference of all Social Security benefit cases to United States magistrates for preparation of a recommended decision is permissible. It was at pains to distinguish the La Buy case and to say that "the important premises from which the La Buy decision proceeded are not threatened here." Mathews v. Weber, 1976, 96 S.Ct. 549, 556, 423 U.S. 261, 275, 46 L.Ed.2d 483.

35. See In re U.S. Dept. of Defense, C.A.D.C.1988, 848 F.2d 232, 236; In re "Agent Orange" Product Liab. Litigation, D.C.N.Y.1982, 94 F.R.D. 173; Brazil, Special Masters in the Pretrial Development of Big Cases: Potential and Problems, 1982 A.B.A.Res.J. 287; Hazard & Rice, Judicial Management of the Pretrial Process in Massive Litigation: Special Masters as Case Managers, 1982 A.B.A.Res.J. 375.

36. See Note, Rule 53, Inherent Powers, and Institutional Reform: The Lack of Lim-

its on Special Masters, 1991, 66 N.Y.U.L.Rev. 600, pointing out both the potentialities and the problems of this use of masters.

37. In re Bituminous Coal Operators' Assn., Inc., C.A.D.C.1991, 949 F.2d 1165, 1169.

38. 28 U.S.C.A. § 144; 13 Wright, Miller & Cooper, Jurisdiction § 3551.

39. 28 U.S.C.A. § 455; 13 Wright, Miller & Cooper, Jurisdiction §§ 3541–3544, 3546–3550, 3552–3553.

Another statute, 28 U.S.C.A. § 47, prohibits a judge from sitting on an appeal from the decision of a case or issue tried by him. See Swann v. Charlotte–Mecklenburg Bd. of Educ., C.A.4th, 1970, 431 F.2d 135 (memorandum of Craven, J.); 13 Wright, Miller & Cooper, Jurisdiction § 3545.

§ 98. Judgments in General [1]

A judgment, as defined by Rule 54(a), "includes a decree and any order from which an appeal lies." It is the final decisive act of a court defining the rights of the parties.[2] The rule contemplates "a simple form of judgment * * * eschewing the lengthy recitals familiar in state practice,"[3] and Official Forms 31 and 32 illustrate the simplicity that is permissible.

Where judgment is by default, the relief given cannot be different from or in excess of that demanded in the complaint. This is the traditional view, based on the fundamental unfairness of giving greater or different relief in a judgment from that of which the defendant was given notice by the complaint, in cases where defendant does not appear and defend against the action.[4] A different principle is stated, however, in Rule 54(c), for nondefault cases. Here the judgment is not limited in kind or amount by the demand for relief, but may include whatever relief the successful party is entitled to, regardless of the demand. This is in accord with the general theory of Rule 15(b), that in a contested case the judgment is to be based on what has been proved rather than what has been pleaded. It is a necessary rule in a merged system of law and equity; indeed the difficulties some states have had in implementing such a merger stems from a failure to grasp and to apply this principle.[5] Any rule other than that stated in the second sentence of Rule 54(c) would mean preservation of the distinctions between law and equity and of the various forms of action that these rules are intended to abolish.

§ 98

1. 10 Wright, Miller & Kane, Civil 2d §§ 2651–2664, 2681–2702; 11 Wright & Miller, Civil §§ 2781–2787, 2851–2873.

2. A consent judgment or consent decree is a settlement that includes an injunction, or some other form of specific relief, and that is formally entered by the court and enforceable by contempt. "A consent decree no doubt embodies an agreement of the parties and thus in some respects is contractual in nature. But it is an agreement that the parties desire and expect will be reflected in and be enforceable as a judicial decree that is subject to the rules generally applicable to other judgments and decrees." Rufo v. Inmates of the Suffolk County Jail, 1992, 112 S.Ct. 748, 757, — U.S. —, —, 116 L.Ed.2d 867. Issues raised by these are explored in an informative Symposium, Consent Decrees: Practical Problems and Legal Dilemmas, 1987 U.Chi.L.F. 1. On the preclusive effect of a consent judgment, see 18 Wright, Miller & Cooper, § 4443.

3. U.S. v. Wissahickon Tool Works, C.A.2d, 1952, 200 F.2d 936, 938. See 10 Wright, Miller & Kane, Civil 2d § 2652.

4. Thomson v. Wooster, 1885, 5 S.Ct. 788, 114 U.S. 104, 29 L.Ed. 105; Fong v. U.S., C.A.9th, 1962, 300 F.2d 400, 412–413, certiorari denied 82 S.Ct. 1584, 370 U.S. 938, 8 L.Ed.2d 807; National Discount Corp. v. O'Mell, C.A.6th, 1952, 194 F.2d 452, 455–456. See 10 Wright, Miller & Kane, Civil 2d § 2663.

5. Note, Law and Equity in New York— Still Unmerged, 1946, 55 Yale L.J. 826; Clark & Wright, The Judicial Council and the Rule–Making Power: A Dissent and a Protest, 1950, 1 Syracuse L.Rev. 346, 353–357. See Rosden v. Leuthold, C.A.D.C. 1960, 274 F.2d 747, 750; Fitzharris v. Phillips, 1958, 333 P.2d 721, 723, 74 Nev. 371.

Thus, the rule provides that the demand for judgment loses much of its restrictive force if the case is at issue.[6] Particular legal theories of counsel then are subordinated to the court's right and duty to grant the relief to which the prevailing party is entitled whether demanded or not.[7] The party may be awarded damages in excess of those it demanded in its pleading,[8] or may be awarded a different kind of relief than it requested.[9] This does not mean that the court will force relief on the parties against their wishes where there is nothing in the case to indicate a need therefor,[10] nor will it give the successful party relief, though the party may be entitled to it, where the propriety of such relief was not litigated and the opposing party had no opportunity to assert defenses to that kind of relief.[11]

The federal statute makes mandatory the allowance of interest, at a rate tied to the yield on Treasury bills, from the date of entry of the judgment, and the judgment must make provision for such interest regardless of whether it was demanded in the complaint.[12] Whether the judgment is to include interest from the time of the wrong to the entry of judgment is a question of the measure of damages, to be resolved by state law or by any applicable federal statute or in the discretion of the court, as the case may be.[13]

Rule 54(d) provides that, except as against the United States or when a statute or the rules are otherwise controlling, costs shall be allowed as of course to the prevailing party unless the court otherwise directs. The court retains a considerable discretion on whether costs

6. Bowles v. J.J. Schmitt & Co., C.A.2d, 1948, 170 F.2d 617.

7. Hoston v. Silbert, C.A.D.C.1982, 681 F.2d 876, 878 n. 3; Massachusetts Bonding & Ins. Co. v. State of New York, C.A.2d, 1958, 259 F.2d 33, 40; and cases cited 10 Wright, Miller & Kane, Civil 2d § 2664 n. 2. But see In re Linda Coal & Supply Co., C.A.3d, 1958, 255 F.2d 653, 656–657.

8. E.g., Menne v. Celotex Corp., C.A.10th, 1988, 861 F.2d 1453, 1474; Riggs, Ferris & Geer v. Lillibridge, C.A.2d, 1963, 316 F.2d 60; Bergeson v. Dilworth, D.C.Kan.1990, 738 F.Supp. 1361, 1364; and cases cited 10 Wright, Miller & Kane, Civil 2d § 2664 nn. 10–13. Though the rule is thoroughly settled, its desirability is questioned in Frank, Book Review, 1963, 76 Harv.L.Rev. 1704, 1707.

9. E.g., Fitzgerald v. Sirloin Stockade, Inc., C.A.10th, 1980, 624 F.2d 945 (reinstatement ordered though only monetary relief sought); Blazer v. Black, C.A.10th, 1952, 196 F.2d 139 (constructive trust where damages asked); Garland v. Garland, C.C.A.10th, 1947, 165 F.2d 131 (specific performance where rescission demanded); Truth Seeker Co. v. Durning, C.C.A.2d,

1945, 147 F.2d 54 (damages where injunction demanded).

10. Mercury Oil Ref. Co. v. Oil Workers Intl. Union, C.I.O., C.A.10th, 1951, 187 F.2d 980.

11. International Harvester Credit Corp. v. East Coast Truck, C.A.5th, 1977, 547 F.2d 888, 891; Atlantic Purchasers, Inc. v. Aircraft Sales, Inc., C.A.4th, 1983, 705 F.2d 712, 716–717, certiorari denied 104 S.Ct. 155, 464 U.S. 848, 78 L.Ed.2d 143.

12. 28 U.S.C.A. § 1961(a), as amended by Act of April 2, 1982, Pub.L. 97–164, § 301, 96 Stat. 55. See Comment, Post–Judgment Interest in Federal Courts, 1988, 37 Emory L.J. 495.

13. Lytle v. Freedom Intl. Carrier, S.A., C.A.6th, 1975, 519 F.2d 129; Phillips Petroleum Co. v. Adams, C.A.5th, 1975, 513 F.2d 355; and cases cited 10 Wright, Miller & Kane, Civil 2d § 2664 nn. 15–18.

Interest cannot be recovered in a suit against the United States in the absence of an express waiver of sovereign immunity from an award of interest. Library of Congress v. Shaw, 1986, 106 S.Ct. 2957, 478 U.S. 310, 92 L.Ed.2d 250.

should be allowed,[14] and on review of taxation of the costs by the clerk, may pass on whether particular items are properly included as costs, and the amounts to be allowed for them. The Supreme Court has said that the courts should exercise their discretion sparingly in taxing as costs expenses not specifically allowed by statute.[15]

Many important matters, including notably the time in which to appeal or to make post-trial motions, turn on the date of entry of the judgment. This had been a source of considerable confusion.[16] Rule 58 was amended in 1963 to remove that confusion. The amended rule recognizes two classes of cases. Where there is a general verdict of a jury, or where the court has decided that a party shall recover only money or costs or that all relief shall be denied, the clerk, unless otherwise ordered by the court, will forthwith prepare, sign, and enter the judgment without awaiting any direction by the court. On the other hand, where the court orders some other relief, or there is a special verdict or a general verdict accompanied by answers to interrogatories, the court must promptly approve the form of the judgment, and the clerk will then enter it. The amended rule states specifically that the judgment is to be set forth on a separate document,[17] and declares that entry of judgment is not to be delayed for the taxing of costs and that "attorneys shall not submit forms of judgment except upon direction of the court, and these directions shall not be given as a matter of course."

The amended rule has much to commend it, and has operated without difficulty in practice. The requirement of a separate document gives a readily determinable date for when judgment was entered, while the requirements that the clerk act "forthwith," where the clerk has power to act, and that the court act "promptly," where it must approve the form of judgment, indicate that the process is not to be a dilatory

14. Fishgold v. Sullivan Drydock & Repair Corp., 1946, 66 S.Ct. 1105, 1110, 328 U.S. 275, 283–284, 90 L.Ed. 1230; 10 Wright, Miller & Kane, Civil 2d § 2668.

Costs and attorneys' fees can be taxed against the United States as provided by 28 U.S.C.A. § 2412. See 10 Wright, Miller & Kane, Civil 2d § 2672.

Rule 68 allows a defending party to cut off the further running of costs against it if it makes an offer of judgment and the judgment ultimately obtained by its opponent is not more favorable than the offer. The rule does not come into play if the judgment is for the defending party rather than for its opponent but in an amount less than the offer. Delta Air Lines, Inc. v. August, 1981, 101 S.Ct. 1146, 450 U.S. 346, 67 L.Ed.2d 287. See generally Schwarzer, Fee–Shifting Offers of Judgment—An Approach to Reducing the Cost of Litigation, 1992, 76 Judicature 147.

15. Farmer v. Arabian American Oil Co., 1964, 85 S.Ct. 411, 416, 379 U.S. 227, 235, 13 L.Ed.2d 248. The relevant statute

is 28 U.S.C.A. § 1920. See generally 10 Wright, Miller & Kane, Civil 2d §§ 2675–2678.

16. E.g., U.S. v. F. & M. Schaefer Brewing Co., 1958, 78 S.Ct. 674, 356 U.S. 227, 2 L.Ed.2d 721; Jung v. K. & D. Mining Co., 1958, 78 S.Ct. 764, 356 U.S. 335, 2 L.Ed.2d 806; 11 Wright & Miller, Civil §§ 2781, 2782.

17. The 1963 amendment requiring the judgment to be on a separate document is "a 'mechanical change' that must be mechanically applied * * *." U.S. v. Indrelunas, 1973, 93 S.Ct. 1562, 1565, 411 U.S. 216, 222, 36 L.Ed.2d 202. For that reason, as the cited case held, a party need not file a notice of appeal until a judgment on a separate document has been filed and ended. But the parties are free to waive the requirement of a separate document, and if by error a separate judgment is not filed before a party appeals, this does not defeat jurisdiction of the court of appeals. Bankers Trust Co. v. Mallis, 1978, 98 S.Ct. 1117, 435 U.S. 381, 55 L.Ed.2d 357.

one. Finally the provision that attorneys are not to submit forms of judgment bars a practice, formerly followed by custom in some districts and required by local rules in others, that had served only to delay the end of litigation.[18]

Under the 1963 amendment, as before, a judgment is not effective until it has been noted on the docket.[19] Ample power is given the trial court and the appellate court to stay the effectiveness of the judgment after that date on proper conditions.[20] When the court has made a final decision with regard to fewer than all of the parties or the claims in a case that involves multiple parties or claims, it may order judgment on the part that it has decided, without awaiting decision of the remainder of the case, but must make an express determination that there is no just reason for delay and an express direction for the entry of judgment.[21]

If a party against whom a claim has been asserted fails to plead or otherwise defend as provided in the rules, the clerk, on a showing of this fact, will enter a default.[22] Thereafter a default judgment may be entered. In some situations the clerk may enter the default judgment, as where the claim is for a sum certain or a sum that can be made certain by computation,[23] but in most cases application for judgment to be entered on the default must be to the court, and proof will be required of the damages sought or other relief to be given.[24] The rules provide for setting aside a default, or a judgment entered thereon, in the discretion of the court.[25] In exercising this discretion the court will be guided by the fact that default judgments are not favored in the law.[26] Courts exist to do justice, and are properly reluctant to lend their processes to the enforcement of an unjust judgment. At the same time, the rules that require responsive pleadings within a limited time serve important social goals, and a party should not be permitted to flout them with impunity. In balancing these policies, the court will not reopen a default judgment merely because the party in default requests it, but

18. Roberts v. Ross, C.A.3d, 1965, 344 F.2d 747, 753; Matteson v. U.S., C.A.2d, 1956, 240 F.2d 517, 518–519. See 11 Wright & Miller, Civil § 2786.

19. Brown v. U.S., C.A.8th, 1955, 225 F.2d 861; McAlister v. C.J. Dick Towing Co., C.A.3d, 1949, 175 F.2d 652. See Rule 79(a); 12 Wright & Miller, Civil §§ 3102, 3103.

20. Rule 62; 11 Wright & Miller, Civil §§ 2901–2909.

21. Rule 54(b); 10 Wright, Miller & Kane, Civil 2d §§ 2653–2661. See § 101 below.

22. Rule 55(a); Systems Indus., Inc. v. Han, D.C.Pa.1985, 105 F.R.D. 72, 74; 10 Wright, Miller & Kane, Civil 2d § 2682.

23. Rule 55(b)(1); Thorpe v. Thorpe, C.A.D.C.1966, 364 F.2d 692; FDIC v. Spartan Mining Co., D.C.W.Va.1983, 96 F.R.D.

677, 683; 10 Wright, Miller & Kane, Civil 2d § 2683.

It has been held that the clerk cannot enter a judgment by confession and that court approval is required where defendant confesses judgment rather than defaulting. Virgin Islands Nat. Bank v. Tropical Ventures, Inc., D.C.V.I.1973, 358 F.Supp. 1203.

24. Rule 55(b)(2); 10 Wright, Miller & Kane, Civil 2d §§ 2684–2688.

25. Rules 55(c), 60(b); American & Foreign Ins. Assn. v. Commercial Ins. Co., C.A.1st, 1978, 575 F.2d 980, 982 n. 3; 10 Wright, Miller & Kane, Civil 2d § 2693.

26. Coon v. Grenier, C.A.1st, 1989, 867 F.2d 73, 76; and cases cited 10 Wright, Miller & Kane, Civil 2d § 2693 nn. 18, 20.

should require the party to show both that there was good reason for the default and that it has a meritorious defense to the action.[27]

Any judgment, whether by default or after trial, may be altered or amended by the court on motion made and served within 10 days after entry of the judgment.[28] Thereafter the judgment may be attacked, other than by appeal, only as provided in Rule 60. That rule allows clerical mistakes arising from oversight or omission to be corrected at any time, either on motion or at the court's initiative.[29] The rule is more restrictive on other grounds for relief from a judgment. Where relief is sought because of mistake, inadvertence, surprise, or excusable neglect, or because of newly-discovered evidence that could not have been discovered in time to be brought forward on motion for a new trial, or because of fraud or other misconduct of the adverse party, the motion must be made within a reasonable time, and in any event not more than one year after the judgment.[30] This time limit does not apply if it is claimed that the judgment is void [31], or that it is no longer equitable,[32] or if the claim is based on "any other reason justifying relief from the

---

27. McGrady v. D'Andrea Elec., Inc., C.A.5th, 1970, 434 F.2d 1000, 1001; Gomes v. Williams, C.A.10th, 1970, 420 F.2d 1364, 1366; Consolidated Masonry & Fireproofing, Inc. v. Wagman Constr. Corp., C.A.4th, 1967, 383 F.2d 249; Zaro v. Strauss, C.C.A.5th, 1948, 167 F.2d 218; Project, Relief from Default Judgments under Rule 60(b), 1981, 49 Ford.L.Rev. 956.

28. Rule 59(e); Boaz v. Mutual Life Ins. Co. of New York, C.C.A.8th, 1944, 146 F.2d 321; Scola v. Boat Frances, R., Inc., C.A.1st, 1980, 618 F.2d 147; 11 Wright & Miller, Civil § 2817.

A post-judgment request for an attorney's fee under 42 U.S.C.A. § 1988 or for costs under Rule 54(d) is not a motion to alter or amend a judgment and need not be made within the time limit of Rule 59(e). White v. New Hampshire Dept. of Employment Sec., 1982, 102 S.Ct. 1162, 455 U.S. 445, 71 L.Ed.2d 325; Buchanan v. Stanships, Inc., 1988, 108 S.Ct. 1130, 485 U.S. 265, 99 L.Ed.2d 289. But a motion for discretionary prejudgment interest is a Rule 59(e) motion. Osterneck v. Ernst & Whinney, 1989, 109 S.Ct. 987, 489 U.S. 169, 103 L.Ed.2d 146. These distinctions are significant also in terms of Appellate Rule 4(a)(4), which provides that a timely motion under Rule 59(e) suspends the effectiveness of the judgment and postpones the time in which to give notice of appeal.

29. Rule 60(a); Fluoro Elec. Corp. v. Branford Associates, C.A.2d, 1973, 489 F.2d 320; Jackson v. Jackson, C.A.D.C.1960, 276 F.2d 501; 11 Wright & Miller, Civil §§ 2854–2856.

30. Rule 60(b); 11 Wright & Miller, Civil §§ 2858–2861, 2866. See Morgan, Delayed Attacks on Final Judgments, 1980, 33 Okla.L.Rev. 45; Note, Relief from Fraudulent Judgments in the Federal Courts: Motion to Vacate or Independent Action—Opposite Sides of the Same Coin, 1987, 36 Drake L.Rev. 389; Comment, Rule 60(b): Survey and Proposal for General Reform, 1972, 60 Calif.L.Rev. 531.

31. It should be noted, however, that a court has jurisdiction to determine its own jurisdiction. See § 16 above. A court's determination that it has jurisdiction of the subject matter is res judicata on that issue, and the judgment cannot be attacked as void, if the jurisdictional question actually was litigated and decided or if the party had an opportunity to contest subject-matter jurisdiction and failed to do so. See 11 Wright & Miller, Civil § 2862.

32. The traditional rule has been that a consent judgment—see note a above—can be modified only on a "clear showing of grievous wrong evoked by new and unforeseen conditions." U.S. v. Swift & Co., 1932, 52 S.Ct. 460, 464, 286 U.S. 106, 119, 76 L.Ed. 999. But a more flexible standard applies to institutional-reform litigation. Modification in those cases is proper if there has been a significant change in facts or law and the proposed modification is suitably tailored to the changed circumstance. Rufo v. Inmates of Suffolk County Jail, 1992, 112 S.Ct. 748, ___ U.S. ___, 116 L.Ed.2d 867.

operation of the judgment." [33] It is now settled that the language just quoted and the other reasons stated in Rule 60(b) are mutually exclusive, and that that language cannot without more be used as an escape from the time limits that usually apply to such a motion. [34] At the same time the concepts involved are sufficiently flexible that a court that finds the equities so compelling that it wishes to reopen the judgment will have little difficulty in discerning that the moving party has presented "something more" than the grounds stated in the first three clauses of Rule 60(b), and that the party has brought itself within the broad reach of Rule 60(b)(6). [35]

The court has considerable discretion in motions for relief from judgments, and the teaching of experience is that the courts will not permit technicalities to prevent them from remedying injustice. Laudable as this goal is, the rule requires the courts to balance it against the desire to achieve finality in litigation. [36] The cases show that the courts have exercised their discretion under the rule with a scrupulous regard for the aims of finality. [37] They have required that the motion be made within a "reasonable time," even though the stated time limit has not expired. [38] They have prevented the needless protraction of litigation by requiring the moving party to show a good claim or defense. [39] They have been astute to consider the hardship that a reopening of the judgment might cause to other persons. [40]

A district court cannot grant relief from a judgment while a case is pending on appeal. There are some older holdings that where grounds for relief appear while the appeal is pending, the party should present them to the appellate court, which may then remand the case for consideration of the motion for relief from the judgment. [41] Recent cases have suggested a different, and preferable procedure, by which the application is made to the district court. If it indicates that it would

---

33. Rule 60(b); 11 Wright & Miller, Civil §§ 2862–2864, 2866.

34. Liljeberg v. Health Services Acquisition Corp., 1988, 108 S.Ct. 2194, 2204 n. 11, 486 U.S. 847, 862 n. 11, 100 L.Ed.2d 855; Klapprott v. U.S., 1949, 69 S.Ct. 384, 335 U.S. 601, 93 L.Ed. 266.

35. Compare the two opinions in U.S. v. Karahalias, C.A.2d, 1953, 205 F.2d 331. See also 11 Wright & Miller, Civil § 2864, pp. 218–223. But cf. Kane, Relief from Federal Judgments: A Morass Unrelieved by a Rule, 1978, 30 Hastings L.J. 41.

36. Lussier v. Dugger, C.A.11th, 1990, 904 F.2d 661, 667; Kotlicky v. U.S. Fid. & Guar. Co., C.A.2d, 1987, 817 F.2d 6, 9; 11 Wright & Miller, Civil § 2857.

37. See Kane, note 35 above, at 67.

Indeed it has been argued that the courts have been too strict. Wham, Federal District Court Rule 60(b): A Humane Rule Gone Wrong, 1963, 49 A.B.A.J. 566.

38. Federal Land Bank of St. Louis v. Cupples Bros., C.A.8th, 1989, 889 F.2d 764; Schildhaus v. Moe, C.A.2d, 1964, 335 F.2d 529; Goldfine v. U.S., C.A.1st, 1964, 326 F.2d 456; and cases cited 11 Wright & Miller, Civil § 2866 nn. 70, 72.

39. Boyd v. Bulala, C.A.4th, 1990, 905 F.2d 764, 769; and cases cited 11 Wright & Miller, Civil § 2857 n. 85.

40. Menashe v. Sutton, D.C.N.Y.1950, 90 F.Supp. 531; McCawley v. Fleischmann Transp. Co., D.C.N.Y.1950, 10 F.R.D. 624; Albion–Idaho Land Co. v. Adams, D.C.Idaho, 1945, 58 F.Supp. 579.

41. Baruch v. Beech Aircraft Corp., C.A.10th, 1949, 172 F.2d 445; Zig Zag Spring Co. v. Comfort Spring Corp., C.A.3d, 1953, 200 F.2d 901; Schempp v. Sch. Dist. of Abington Twp., Pennsylvania, D.C.Pa. 1960, 184 F.Supp. 381, remand ordered 1960, 81 S.Ct. 268, 364 U.S. 298, 5 L.Ed. 89.

grant the motion, the appellate court will then remand for that purpose.[42]

After the appellate court has decided a case, a lower court has no power to deviate from the decision of the appellate court so far as it goes.[43] This does not bar the district court, however, from entertaining a Rule 60(b) motion. Although a number of lower courts had said that leave from the appellate court was required before a Rule 60(b) motion could be considered to set aside a judgment that had been affirmed by the appellate court, the Supreme Court has wisely ruled to the contrary, saying that a requirement of appellate leave "adds to the delay and expense of litigation and also burdens the increasingly scarce time of the federal appellate courts."[44]

§ 99. Summary Judgment [1]

Rule 56 permits any party to a civil action to move for a summary judgment upon a claim, counterclaim, or cross-claim on which there is no genuine issue of material fact and upon which the moving party is entitled to prevail as a matter of law. The motion may be made on all or a part of a claim or defense. It may be made on the pleadings or the information produced by discovery or it may be supported by affidavits. The motion strikes at the heart of the claim. In effect it argues that as a matter of law upon admitted or established facts the moving party is entitled to prevail.

The motion lies whenever there is no genuine issue about any material fact. It follows that a formal denial in an answer should not necessarily defeat such a motion as otherwise the rule could be rendered nugatory. To take a simple example, in an action on a promissory note the defendant in his answer denies the making of the note. Plaintiff moves for summary judgment, accompanying her motion with an affidavit of a person who swears that she saw the defendant sign the note. If the defendant does not file an opposing affidavit, raising a genuine issue

42. Winter v. Cerro Gordo County Conservation Bd., C.A.8th, 1991, 925 F.2d 1069, 1073; Textile Banking Co. v. Rentschler, C.A.7th, 1981, 657 F.2d 844, 849–850; Smith v. Pollin, C.A.D.C.1952, 194 F.2d 349; 11 Wright & Miller, Civil § 2873, pp. 265–266.

43. Briggs v. Pennsylvania R. Co., 1948, 68 S.Ct. 1039, 334 U.S. 304, 92 L.Ed. 1403; U.S. v. Cato Bros. Inc., C.A.4th, 1959, 273 F.2d 153, certiorari denied 80 S.Ct. 753, 362 U.S. 927, 4 L.Ed.2d 746.

44. Standard Oil Co. of California v. U.S., 1976, 97 S.Ct. 31, 32, 429 U.S. 17, 19, 50 L.Ed.2d 21.

§ 99

1. 10 and 10A Wright, Miller & Kane, Civil 2d §§ 2711–2742; Schwarzer, Hirsch & Barrans, The Analysis and Decision of Summary Judgment Motions, 1992, 139 F.R.D. 441; Issacharoff & Lewenstein, Second Thoughts About Summary Judgment, 1990, 100 Yale L.J. 73; Friedenthal, Cases on Summary Judgment: Has There Been a Material Change in Standards?, 1988, 63 Notre Dame L.Rev. 770; Nelken, One Step Forward, Two Steps Back: Summary Judgment After Celotex, 1988, 40 Hastings L.J. 53; Risinger, Another Step in the Counter-Revolution: A Summary Judgment on the Supreme Court's New Approach to Summary Judgment, 1988, 54 Brooklyn L.Rev. 35; McLauchlan, An Empirical Study of the Federal Summary Judgment Rule, 1977, 6 J.Legal Studies 427; Louis, Federal Summary Judgment Doctrine; A Critical Analysis, 1974, 83 Yale L.J. 745; Note, Summary Judgment in Federal Court: New Maxims for a Familar Rule, 1989, 34 N.Y.L.Sch. L.Rev. 201.

about this fact, summary judgment should be rendered for plaintiff. On the other hand, if the defendant files an affidavit to the effect that his purported signature is a forgery, or that it was affixed by a person who was not authorized to do so, a genuine issue pn a material fact is created, and the case must go to trial.[2]

Summary judgment procedure "is not a catch-penny contrivance to take unwary litigants into its toils and deprive them of a trial, it is a liberal measure, liberally designed for arriving at the truth. Its purpose is not to cut litigants off from their right of trial by jury if they really have evidence which they will offer on a trial, it is to carefully test this out, in advance of trial by inquiring and determining whether such evidence exists."[3] On a motion for summary judgment the court cannot try issues of fact. It can only determine whether there are issues to be tried. So conceived, it is a salutary and efficient instrumentality for expedition of the business of the courts.[4] Rule 56 builds on a procedure that had been used in England for more than 50 years and adopted in a number of states.[5] It goes beyond earlier procedures of this sort in that it is available to both plaintiffs and defendants in all forms and kinds of civil actions to which the Civil Rules apply.[6]

Though the procedure is freely available in all types of litigation, it is obvious that some kinds of cases lend themselves more readily to summary adjudication than do others. It is as much for functional reasons as for historical that statistics show motions for summary judgment granted more frequently in actions on notes, and for debts than in other kinds of cases.[7] Thus, summary judgment will not usually be as feasible in negligence cases, where the standard of the reasonable person must be applied to conflicting testimony, as it is in other kinds of litigation, but there have been unusual cases in which grant of summary judgment, either for defendant or for plaintiff, has been held proper in a negligence case.[8] It is probably true, as five members of the Supreme

---

2. See Fugate v. Mayor & City Council of Town of Buffalo, Wyo.1959, 348 P.2d 76, 81; Epps v. Remmel, 1963, 373 S.W.2d 141, 237 Ark. 391; New Hampshire York Co. v. Titus Constr. Co., 1966, 219 A.2d 708, 710, 107 N.H. 223.

3. Whitaker v. Coleman, C.C.A.5th, 1940, 115 F.2d 305, 307 (per Hutcheson, J.).

4. Freeman v. Continental Gin Co., C.A.5th, 1967, 381 F.2d 459, 469; Minnesota Mining & Mfg. Co. v. U.S. Rubber Co., C.A.4th, 1960, 279 F.2d 409, 415.

5. Clark & Samenow, The Summary Judgment, 1929, 38 Yale L.J. 423; Bauman, Evolution of the Summary Judgment Procedure, 1956, 31 Ind.L.J. 329; see Weather-Rite Sportswear Co. v. U.S., Customs Ct. 1969, 298 F.Supp. 508, 510–516.

6. Engl v. Aetna Life Ins. Co., C.C.A.2d, 1943, 139 F.2d 469.

7. Note, Use of Summary Judgment by Type of Case, 1952, 36 Minn.L.Rev. 515.

The statistics are more varied in a more recent study. See McLauchlan, note 1 above, at 435–442.

8. Hydrogen Technology Corp. v. U.S., C.A.1st, 1987, 831 F.2d 1155, 1164, certiorari denied 108 S.Ct. 1995, 486 U.S. 1022, 100 L.Ed.2d 227; Nelson v. International Paint Co., C.A.5th, 1984, 734 F.2d 1084, 1094; Flying Diamond Corp. v. Pennaluna & Co., Inc., C.A.9th, 1978, 586 F.2d 707; Crum v. Continental Oil Co., C.A.5th, 1973, 471 F.2d 784; Littleton v. Mardigan, C.A.7th, 1972, 458 F.2d 251; Bland v. Norfolk & S.R. Co., C.A.4th, 1969, 406 F.2d 863; Marsden v. Patane, C.A.5th, 1967, 380 F.2d 489; Berry v. Atlantic Coast Line R. Co., C.A.4th, 1960, 273 F.2d 572, certiorari denied 80 S.Ct. 1060, 362 U.S. 976, 4 L.Ed.2d 1011; American Airlines, Inc. v. Ulen, C.A.D.C.1949, 186 F.2d 529.

See 10A Wright, Miller & Kane, Civil 2d § 2729; Forkosch, Summary Judgment in

Court said over a strong dissent, that summary judgment "should be used sparingly in complex antitrust litigation where motive and intent play leading roles, the proof is largely in the hands of the alleged conspirators, and hostile witnesses thicken the plot." [9] Yet there are decisions, including some from the Supreme Court, in which summary judgment has been granted in cases of this type.[10] Probably it usually is not feasible to resolve on motion for summary judgment cases involving state of mind, or in which the facts are peculiarly within the knowledge of the moving party, but it would be wrong to generalize from this and say that summary judgment never can be granted in such cases.[11] The rule permits summary judgment in any case, and the inquiry must be whether such a judgment is appropriate in the particular case, a question that cannot be resolved by some broad judicial gloss on the rule.

The rule requires that the moving party show that it "is entitled to judgment as a matter of law." One court made the mistake of reasoning

Automobile Negligence Cases: A Procedural Analysis and Suggestions, 1968, 53 Corn. L.Q. 814.

9. Poller v. Columbia Broadcasting System, Inc., 1962, 82 S.Ct. 486, 491, 368 U.S. 464, 473, 7 L.Ed.2d 458. The view of the dissenters on this point is stated 82 S.Ct. at 493, 368 U.S. at 478. See also Fortner Enterprises, Inc. v. United States Steel Corp., 1969, 89 S.Ct. 1252, 1257, 394 U.S. 495, 500, 22 L.Ed.2d 495.

In a later case the Court said: "Summary judgments have a place in the anti-trust field, as elsewhere, though as we warned in Poller v. Columbia Broadcasting System, * * * they are not appropriate 'where motive and intent play leading roles.' Some of the law in this area is so well developed that where, as here, the gist of the case turns on documentary evidence, the rule at times can be divined without a trial." White Motor Co. v. U.S., 1963, 83 S.Ct. 696, 700, 372 U.S. 253, 259, 9 L.Ed.2d 738.

See also Eastman Kodak Co. v. Image Technical Services, Inc., 1992, 112 S.Ct. 2072, ___ U.S. ___, 119 L.Ed.2d 265. In that case the Supreme Court affirmed reversal of a summary judgment for defendant in an antitrust case. Distinguished commentators have compared the Kodak case to the Matsushita case cited note 10 below. "One lesson of Kodak, which perhaps should have been apparent all along, is that summary judgment motions based on the 'implausibility' of the opponent's claim will rarely succeed. * * * Matsushita, * * * rather than making a statement about implausible inferences in summary judgment motions generally, rests on a specific point of antitrust law: Plaintiffs cannot prevail if their case requires inferring a price-fixing conspiracy from normal business activity (specifically price cutting) that, standing alone, is consistent with lawful competition." Schwarzer & Hirsch, Summary Judgment After Eastman Kodak, 1993, 45 Hastings L.J. 1, 6–7.

10. E.g., Matsushita Electric Industrial Co. v. Zenith Radio Corp., 1986, 106 S.Ct. 1348, 475 U.S. 574, 89 L.Ed.2d 538; First Nat. Bank of Arizona v. Cities Serv. Co., 1968, 88 S.Ct. 1575, 391 U.S. 253, 20 L.Ed.2d 569; Morton Salt Co. v. G.S. Suppiger Co., 1942, 62 S.Ct. 402, 314 U.S. 488, 315 U.S. 788, 86 L.Ed. 363; and cases cited 10A Wright, Miller & Kane, Civil 2d § 2732.1. See also Calkins, Summary Judgment, Motions to Dismiss, and Other Examples of Equilibrating Tendencies in the Antitrust System, 1986, 74 Geo.L.J. 1065, 1120.

11. See 10A Wright, Miller & Kane, Civil 2d § 2730; Sonenshein, State of Mind and Credibility in the Summary Judgment Context: A Better Approach, 1983, 78 Nw. U.L.Rev. 774.

In an important recent case the Court rejected the notion that a plaintiff may defeat a defendant's properly supported motion for summary judgment in a conspiracy or libel case, for example, without offering any concrete evidence from which a reasonable juror could return a verdict in plaintiff's favor and by merely asserting that the jury might, and legally could, disbelieve the defendant's denial of a conspiracy or of legal malice. "The movant has the burden of showing that there is no genuine issue of fact, but the plaintiff is not thereby relieved of his own burden of producing in turn evidence that would support a jury verdict." Anderson v. Liberty Lobby, Inc., 1986, 106 from this that summary judgment is never proper in an equitable action, where judgment is in the discretion of the court rather than a matter of right.[12] This is an obvious misconstruction of the rule, contrary to a multitude of cases in which summary judgment for specific performance or injunction has been granted without comment,[13] and it has been expressly repudiated several times by other courts.[14]

It is frequently said that summary judgment should not be granted if there is the "slightest doubt" of the facts.[15] Such statements are a rather misleading gloss on a rule that speaks in terms of "genuine issue as to any material fact," and would, if taken literally, mean that there could hardly ever be a summary judgment, for at least a slight doubt can be developed about practically all things human.[16] A better formulation would be that the party opposing the motion is to be given the benefit of all reasonable doubts in determining whether a genuine issue exists.[17] Again it is sometimes said, rather opprobriously, that Rule 56 does not permit "trial by affidavits." [18] The correct principle, which the epithet tends to conceal, is that affidavits may be used on a motion for summary judgment, but that the court may not resolve disputed fact issues by reference to the affidavits.[19] Affidavits, both in support of and in

S.Ct. 2505, 2514, 477 U.S. 242, 256, 91 L.Ed.2d 202.

12. Seaboard Sur. Co. v. Racine Screw Co., C.A.7th, 1953, 203 F.2d 532.

13. E.g., U.S. v. W.T. Grant Co., 1953, 73 S.Ct. 894, 345 U.S. 629, 97 L.Ed. 1303; 10A Wright, Miller & Kane, Civil 2d § 2731.

14. Booth v. Barber Transp. Co., C.A.8th, 1958, 256 F.2d 927, 931; Holmes v. Government of the Virgin Islands, D.C.V.I.1974, 370 F.Supp. 715, 718; Moore v. Texas Reserve Life Ins. Co., D.C.Tex. 1962, 214 F.Supp. 925, 928, affirmed C.A.5th, 1963, 314 F.2d 948; Thickman v. Schunk, Wyo.1964, 391 P.2d 939, 944; Elias v. Manis, Tex.Civ.App.1956, 292 S.W.2d 836, 838, error refused.

15. E.g., Clark v. West Chemical Products, Inc., C.A.5th, 1977, 557 F.2d 1155, 1157; Doehler Metal Furniture Co. v. U.S., C.C.A.2d, 1945, 149 F.2d 130, 135; and cases cited 10A Wright, Miller & Kane, Civil 2d § 2727 nn. 24, 25.

16. See De Luca v. Atlantic Ref. Co., C.A.2d, 1949, 176 F.2d 421, 423, certiorari denied 70 S.Ct. 423, 338 U.S. 943, 94 L.Ed. 581; Carlander v. Dubuque Fire & Marine Ins. Co., D.C.Ark.1949, 87 F.Supp. 65, 69; Clark, Special Problems in Drafting and Interpreting Procedural Code and Rules, 1950, 3 Vand.L.Rev. 493, 504.

"Since courts are composed of mere mortals they can decide matters only on the basis of probability, never on certainty.

The 'slightest doubt' test, if it is taken seriously, means that summary judgment is almost never to be used—a pity in this critical time of overstrained legal resources." Chubbs v. City of New York, D.C.N.Y.1971, 324 F.Supp. 1183, 1189.

See also Frank, American Law: The Case for Radical Reform, 1969, pp. 146–152.

17. E.g., U.S. v. Farmers Mut. Ins. Assn. of Kiron, Iowa, C.A.8th, 1961, 288 F.2d 560, 562; Chesapeake & O. Ry. Co. v. International Harvester Co., C.A.7th, 1959, 272 F.2d 139, 142; Heyward v. Public Housing Adm'n, C.A.5th, 1956, 238 F.2d 689, 696; Begnaud v. White, C.A.6th, 1948, 170 F.2d 323, 327; Mickle v. Lipstock, D.C.S.C.1965, 39 F.R.D. 58, 61.

"Appellate courts should not look the other way to ignore the existence of the genuine issues of material facts, but neither should they strain to find the existence of such genuine issues where none exist." Mintz v. Mathers Fund, Inc., C.A.7th, 1972, 463 F.2d 495, 498.

18. Poller v. Columbia Broadcasting System, Inc., 1962, 82 S.Ct. 486, 491, 368 U.S. 464, 473, 7 L.Ed.2d 458; Redman v. Warrener, C.A.1st, 1975, 516 F.2d 766, 768; Colby v. Klune, C.A.2d, 1949, 178 F.2d 872, 873; Turner v. McWhirter Material Handling Co., D.C.Ga.1964, 35 F.R.D. 560, 563.

19. E.g., U.S. ex rel. Jones v. Rundle, C.A.3d, 1971, 453 F.2d 147, 150; F.A.R. Liquidating Corp. v. Brownell, C.A.3d, 1954, 209 F.2d 375; Lane Bryant, Inc. v.

opposition to the motions may be considered only if they are made on personal knowledge, set forth facts that would be admissible in evidence, and show affirmatively that the affiant is competent to testify to the matters stated in the affidavits.[20]

Allegations in the pleadings do not create an issue as against a motion for summary judgment supported by affidavits. The very object of the summary judgment procedure, as then-Judge Cardozo said long ago, is "to separate what is formal or pretended in denial or averment from what is genuine and substantial, so that only the latter may subject a suitor to the burden of a trial." [21] Indeed there would be no point to Rule 56 if it did not permit a party to pierce the allegations of fact in the opponent's pleadings, for it would then merely duplicate the old common-law demurrer. Though this principle was accepted in every other circuit,[22] the Third Circuit held resolutely to the rule that pleading allegations did create an issue barring summary judgment,[23] and it was necessary to amend Rule 56(e), in 1963, to state explicitly that when the moving party has supported its motion with proper affidavits or other materials, its opponent, to defeat summary judgment, must set forth by affidavits or otherwise specific facts showing that there is a genuine issue for trial.[24]

The obligation created by amended Rule 56(e) exists only if the papers submitted by the moving party show initially the absence of a genuine issue concerning any material fact.[25] The moving party is not required, however, to support its motion with affidavits or other materials negating its opponent's claim. It can also satisfy its burden by demonstrating to the court that the nonmoving party is unable to prove an essential element of the claim.[26] It is only after this initial showing

---

Maternity Lane, Ltd. of California, C.A.9th, 1949, 173 F.2d 559.

20. Rule 56(e); Automatic Radio Mfg. Co. v. Hazeltine Research, 1950, 70 S.Ct. 894, 339 U.S. 827, 94 L.Ed. 1312; Pension Benefit Guar. Corp. v. Heppenstall Co., C.A.3d, 1980, 633 F.2d 293; Dyer v. MacDougall, C.A.2d, 1952, 201 F.2d 265; 10A Wright, Miller & Kane, Civil 2d § 2738. See generally Brunet, Summary Judgment Materials, 1993, 147 F.R.D. 647.

Facts in an affidavit must be specifically averred. Lujan v. National Wildlife Federation, 1990, 110 S.Ct. 3177, 3188–3189, 497 U.S. 871, 888–889, 111 L.Ed.2d 695.

21. Richard v. Credit Suisse, 1926, 152 N.E. 110, 111, 242 N.Y. 346, 350.

22. See cases cited 10 Wright, Miller & Kane, Civil 2d § 2711 n. 19.

23. Frederick Hart & Co. v. Recordgraph Corp., C.C.A.3d, 1948, 169 F.2d 580; Reynolds Metals Co. v. Metals Disintegrating Co., C.A.3d, 1949, 176 F.2d 90; Bragen v. Hudson County News Co., C.A.3d, 1960, 278 F.2d 615.

24. First Nat. Bank of Arizona v. Cities Serv. Co., 1968, 88 S.Ct. 1575, 1592–1593, 391 U.S. 253, 289, 20 L.Ed.2d 569; Dressler v. MV Sandpiper, C.A.2d, 1964, 331 F.2d 130, 131–135; Robin Constr. Co. v. U.S., C.A.3d, 1965, 345 F.2d 610, 614–615; Wright, Rule 56(e): A Case Study on the Need for Amending the Federal Rules, 1956, 69 Harv.L.Rev. 839; Note, Summary Judgment Under Federal Rule of Civil Procedure 56—A Need for a Clarifying Amendment, 1963, 48 Iowa L.Rev. 453.

25. Adickes v. S.H. Kress & Co., 1970, 90 S.Ct. 1598, 398 U.S. 144, 26 L.Ed.2d 142. See the discussion of this case in 10A Wright, Miller & Kane, Civil 2d § 2739, and the cases there cited.

26. Celotex Corp. v. Catrett, 1986, 106 S.Ct. 2548, 2553, 477 U.S. 317, 323–324, 91 L.Ed.2d 265. See also Lujan v. National Wildlife Federation, 1990, 110 S.Ct. 3177, 3186–3187, 497 U.S. 871, 883–885, 111 L.Ed.2d 695. This principle was applied in an interesting factual situation in Brazinski v. Amoco Petroleum Additives Co., C.A.7th, 1993, 6 F.3d 1176, 1182–1184.

has been made by the movant that the party opposing the motion has a duty to respond.[27] A continuance can be ordered to permit the opposing party to obtain additional facts, or it can defeat the motion by demonstrating that evidence exists that it would have at the trial but cannot, for some good reason, produce on the motion.[28] Despite all that may be shown, the court always has the power to deny summary judgment if, in its sound judgment, it believes for any reason that the fair and just course is to proceed to trial rather than to resolve the case on a motion.[29]

Finally, it is always true that, whether or not the nonmoving party has submitted affidavits or similar material, the burden is on the moving party to establish that there is no genuine issue about any material fact, or that there is an absence of evidence to support the nonmoving party's case, and that the moving party is entitled to judgment as a matter of law.[30] The standard mirrors that used for a directed verdict under Rule 50(a). The court must determine whether there is a genuine issue for trial and there is no issue for trial unless there is sufficient evidence favoring the nonmoving party for a jury to return a verdict for that party.[31] The moving party is not entitled to the benefit of favorable inferences to be drawn from its moving papers.[32] Instead the matters presented in connection with the motion must be construed most favorably to the party opposing the motion.[33] That it may be surmised that the nonmoving party is unlikely to prevail at the trial is not sufficient to authorize summary judgment against that party.[34]

Much of the confusion in the case law about the showing required to defeat a motion for summary judgment stems from the differing views various judges have about the utility and application of this procedural device. These differences are most dramatically illustrated by divergent opinions from the Court of Appeals for the Second Circuit, with Judge Charles E. Clark, the principal draftsman of the federal rules, the spokesman for those sympathetic to Rule 56, and Judge Jerome N.

---

27. In the Celotex case, note 26 above, the Court said: "We do not mean that the nonmoving party must produce evidence in a form that would be admissible at trial in order to avoid summary judgment." 106 S.Ct. at 2553, 477 U.S. at 324.

28. Rule 56(f); Washington v. Allstate Ins. Co., C.A.5th, 1990, 901 F.2d 1281, 1284–1286; Taylor v. Rederi A/S Volo, C.A.3d, 1967, 374 F.2d 545; 10A Wright, Miller & Kane, Civil 2d §§ 2740, 2741.

29. Kennedy v. Silas Mason Co., 1948, 68 S.Ct. 1031, 334 U.S. 249, 92 L.Ed. 1347; Forest Hills Early Learning Center, Inc. v. Lukhard, C.A.4th, 1984, 728 F.2d 230, 245; 10A Wright, Miller & Kane, Civil 2d § 2728.

30. Celotex Corp. v. Catrett, 1986, 106 S.Ct. 2548, 2553–2554, 477 U.S. 317, 325, 91 L.Ed.2d 265; and cases cited 10A Wright, Miller & Kane, Civil 2d § 2727 n. 1.

31. Anderson v. Liberty Lobby, Inc., 1986, 106 S.Ct. 2505, 2510–2511, 477 U.S. 242, 249–251, 91 L.Ed.2d 202. See 10 Wright, Miller & Kane, Civil 2d § 2713.1.

32. Cochran v. U.S., D.C.Conn.1954, 123 F.Supp. 362, noted 1956, 41 Iowa L.Rev. 452.

33. E.g., U.S. v. Diebold, Inc., 1962, 82 S.Ct. 993, 369 U.S. 654, 8 L.Ed.2d 176; Natural Resources Defense Council, Inc. v. Jamison, D.C.D.C.1990, 787 F.Supp. 231, 237; Johnson v. Doherty, D.C.N.Y.1989, 713 F.Supp. 69, 70; and cases cited 10A Wright, Miller & Kane, Civil 2d § 2727 n. 5.

34. E.g., Hayden v. First Nat. Bank of Mt. Pleasant, C.A.5th, 1979, 595 F.2d 994, 997; Jobson v. Henne, C.A.2d, 1966, 355 F.2d 129, 133; Harl v. Acacia Mut. Life Ins. Co., C.A.D.C.1963, 317 F.2d 577.

Frank representing the point of view of the rule's critics.[35] The conflict appeared most sharply in the well-known case of Arnstein v. Porter,[36] a copyright-infringement action termed by a historian of the art "one of the most absurd plagiarism suits on record."[37] There was an issue whether defendant could have had access in order to copy plaintiff's composition. Each party took the deposition of the other. The defendant categorically denied access or copying and the plaintiff admitted that he had no evidence to support his contention on this point. The court, speaking through Judge Frank, characterized much of plaintiff's testimony as "fantastic,"[38] but held nevertheless that the grant of summary judgment for defendant was error, since defendant's credibility was a question of fact and plaintiff might be able to discredit defendant's denial by cross-examination before a jury. In a vigorous dissent Judge Clark spoke of "the anti-intellectual and book-burning nature" of the majority opinion, which, in his view, amounted to a "novel method of amending" Rule 56. He said: "Of course it is error to deny trial when there is a genuine dispute of facts; but it is just as much error—perhaps more in cases of hardship, or where impetus is given to strike suits—to deny or postpone judgment where the ultimate legal result is clearly indicated."[39]

The Arnstein decision is difficult to reconcile with earlier decisions from the Second Circuit, in which, however, Judge Frank either dissented or did not participate. It is even more difficult to reconcile it with the later case of Dyer v. MacDougall,[40] a slander action in which defendant presented affidavits from the persons to whom the slanders were supposedly uttered, denying that the slanderous remarks were made. Judge Frank concurred in affirmance of the grant of summary judgment on this showing. Although subsequent cases from the Second Circuit seemed for years to echo Judge Frank's views on summary judgment, that court has now made it clear that it is not unsympathetic to summary-judgment motions.[41]

The views of judges of a court of appeals are now largely of intellectual interest. In three decisions in 1986 the Supreme Court showed its enthusiasm for summary judgments.[42] Taken together the

---

35. See 10A Wright, Miller & Kane, Civil 2d § 2727.

36. C.C.A.2d, 1946, 154 F.2d 464, noted 1946, 55 Yale L.J. 810.

37. Spaeth, A History of Popular Music, 1948, p. 553.

38. 154 F.2d at 469.

39. 154 F.2d at 478, 479, 480.

40. C.A.2d, 1952, 201 F.2d 265.

41. Knight v. U.S. Fire Ins. Co., C.A.2d, 1986, 804 F.2d 9, certiorari denied 107 S.Ct. 1570, 480 U.S. 932, 94 L.Ed.2d 762. In order to correct the "widespread misperception" regarding its attitude toward summary judgment, the court cited a study by Professor Maurice Rosenberg showing that over a two-year period its affirmance rate of grants of summary judgment was 79%, as compared with its 84% affirmance rate in civil cases generally. 804 F.2d at 11–12.

42. Celotex Corp. v. Catrett, 1986, 106 S.Ct. 2548, 477 U.S. 317, 91 L.Ed.2d 265; Anderson v. Liberty Lobby, Inc., 1986, 106 S.Ct. 2505, 477 U.S. 242, 91 L.Ed.2d 202; Matsushita Elec. Industrial Co. v. Zenith Radio Corp., 1986, 106 S.Ct. 1348, 475 U.S. 574, 89 L.Ed.2d 538. The specific holdings of these cases have been cited in this section where appropriate. Much of the scholarly commentary cited in note 1 above is devoted to these cases and their implications.

three cases signal to the lower courts that summary judgment can be relied upon more so than in the past to weed out frivolous lawsuits and avoid wasteful trials.[43]

On a motion for summary judgment, it may appear that there is some genuine issue about a material fact, which requires denial of the motion, but that there is no substantial controversy on a number of other material facts. In that situation the court may make an entry specifying the facts that appear without substantial controversy, and these facts will be deemed established on the trial of the action.[44] Such an order is frequently referred to as a "partial summary judgment." This phrase is misleading, since a "judgment" is, by definition, appealable,[45] while the order here contemplated is not appealable unless it makes final disposition of some claim or party and is certified as final by the court under Rule 54(b).[46]

§ 100. Declaratory Judgment [1]

In an earlier section, it was seen that for some years the Supreme Court had raised serious doubts about whether an action for a declaratory judgment was a "case or controversy" within the jurisdiction of the federal courts.[2] The Court changed its view in 1933, and this was followed immediately in 1934 by the adoption of the Federal Declaratory Judgment Act, now 28 U.S.C.A. §§ 2201, 2202. Rule 57 implements the provisions of that Act and specifies that the procedure in an action for a declaratory judgment is to be in accord with the rules. The validity of the Act was settled quite early.[3]

Actions for declaratory judgments represent a comparatively recent development in American jurisprudence. Much of the credit for this

---

43. But see McLauchlan, note 1 above, at 458: "[T]he summary judgment rule does not dispose of a very large proportion of cases filed in the federal district courts. In fact, it is a very weak reed upon which to rely for decreasing much of the workload with which courts are faced." The empirical data on which this conclusion is based comes from a period well before the 1986 Supreme Court decisions.

44. Rule 56(d); National Life Ins. Co. v. Silverman, C.A.D.C.1971, 454 F.2d 899; Parmelee v. Chicago Eye Shield Co., C.C.A.8th, 1946, 157 F.2d 582; Brager & Co. v. Leumi Securities Corp., D.C.N.Y. 1979, 84 F.R.D. 220; Hedrick v. S. Bonaccurso & Sons, Inc., D.C.Pa.1978, 466 F.Supp. 1025; 10A Wright, Miller & Kane, Civil 2d § 2737.

45. Rule 54(a). See § 98 above.

46. Liberty Mut. Ins. Co. v. Wetzel, 1976, 96 S.Ct. 1202, 424 U.S. 737, 47 L.Ed.2d 435; Wolf v. Banco Nacional de Mexico, C.A.9th, 1983, 721 F.2d 660, certiorari denied 105 S.Ct. 784, 469 U.S. 1108, 83 L.Ed.2d 778; and cases cited 10 Wright, Miller & Kane, Civil 2d § 2715 nn. 14–23.

Under appropriate circumstances the order might be certified under Rule 54(b). Continental Airlines, Inc. v. Goodyear Tire & Rubber Co., C.A.8th, 1987, 819 F.2d 1519.

§ 100

1. 10A Wright, Miller & Kane, Civil 2d §§ 2751–2771; Borchard, Declaratory Judgments, 2d ed. 1941; Zamir, The Declaratory Judgment Revisited, 1977, 30 Current Legal Problems 43.

2. See § 12 above, discussing the cases of Liberty Warehouse Co. v. Grannis, 1927, 47 S.Ct. 282, 273 U.S. 70, 71 L.Ed. 541, and Willing v. Chicago Auditorium Assn., 1928, 48 S.Ct. 507, 277 U.S. 274, 72 L.Ed. 880, raising such doubts, and Nashville, C. & St. L. Ry. Co. v. Wallace, 1933, 53 S.Ct. 345, 288 U.S. 249, 77 L.Ed. 730, which resolved them.

3. Aetna Life Ins. Co. v. Haworth, 1937, 57 S.Ct. 461, 300 U.S. 227, 81 L.Ed. 617.

development is due to Professors Edwin Borchard, of Yale, and Edson Sunderland, of Michigan, who crusaded for more than 30 years for a uniform state and federal declaratory-relief procedure,[4] a goal that has now been substantially achieved.   The traditional and conventional concept of the judicial process had been that the courts may act only in case a litigant is entitled to coercive relief, such as a judgment for damages or an injunction.[5]   Until a controversy had matured to a point at which such relief was appropriate and the person entitled thereto sought to invoke it, the courts were powerless to act.   At times, however, there may be an actual dispute about the rights and obligations of the parties, and yet the controversy may not have ripened to a point at which a coercive remedy is needed.   Or this stage may have been reached, but the party entitled to seek the remedy may fail to take the necessary steps.   For example, the maker of a promissory note may have stated to the payee that the instrument would not be honored at maturity, because, perhaps, his signature is claimed to have been forged or procured by fraud or affixed without his authority.   The payee had to wait until payment was due before appealing to the courts.   It might well have been important for her to ascertain in advance whether the note was a binding obligation and whether she might rely on it and list it among her assets.   Nevertheless, she could receive no judicial relief until the instrument became due and was dishonored.   Or it might have been necessary for a person to determine whether he was bound by some contractual provision that he deemed void.   In that event, if he desired to contest the matter, he had to assume the risk and to hazard the consequences of committing a breach and then await a suit.[6]   Or the owner of a patent might assert that a manufacturer was infringing its monopoly, while the latter contended that its product was not an infringement or that the patent was invalid.   The manufacturer was helpless, however, to secure an adjudication of the issue, but had to pursue its course of action and await suit for infringement, unless it preferred to yield and discontinue its activity.

In all of these situations the declaratory-judgment procedure provides a useful solution.   It creates a means by which rights and obligations may be adjudicated in cases involving an actual controversy that has not reached the stage at which either party may seek a coercive

---

4. Clark, Code Pleading 2d ed. 1947, § 53, p. 333.   See Sunderland, A Modern Evolution in Remedial Rights, 1917, 16 Mich.L.Rev. 69; Borchard, The Declaratory Judgment—A Needed Procedural Reform, 1918, 28 Yale L.J. 1, 105.

5. The term "coercive relief" is commonly used to distinguish these kinds of remedies from a declaratory judgment. E.g., Powell v. McCormack, 1969, 89 S.Ct. 1944, 1962, 395 U.S. 486, 517, 23 L.Ed.2d 491; Franklin v. Massachusetts, 1992, 112 S.Ct. 2767, 2790 n. 3, ___ U.S. ___, ___ n. 3, 120 L.Ed.2d 636 (Scalia, J., concurring);

Baker v. Carr, 1962, 82 S.Ct. 691, 770, 369 U.S. 186, 328, 7 L.Ed.2d 663 (Frankfurter, J., dissenting).

6. This is strikingly illustrated by Willing v. Chicago Auditorium Assn., 1928, 48 S.Ct. 507, 277 U.S. 274, 72 L.Ed. 880, in which the lessee under a long-term lease was not able to get any judicial declaration whether he would forfeit the lease if he tore down an unprofitable auditorium and built an office building.   Compare the use of a declaratory judgment in such a situation in the cases cited note 12 below.

remedy, or in which the party entitled to such a remedy fails to sue for it.

The critical question in each case is whether the facts averred under the existing circumstances present a real controversy between parties having adverse legal interests of such immediacy and reality as to warrant a declaratory judgment.[7] The Act, as required by the Constitution, is limited to cases that present an "actual" controversy.[8] Necessarily the difference between an abstract question and an actual controversy is one of degree, and where there is a substantial dispute touching some real and proximate interest of the party, the fact that it has taken action in order to provoke a test case does not make the case inappropriate for a declaratory judgment.[9]

It has been suggested by distinguished scholars that there may be a difference between suit for a declaration about the legal consequences of past conduct and a suit in which a declaration is sought about the legal consequences of future conduct. The latter situation, it is said, is "doubly contingent," [10] since the future conduct may not take place and if it does the other party may not challenge it. Of course a court should not "express legal opinions on academic theoreticals which might never come to pass." [11] But the number of contingencies that can be found in a particular situation seems largely a verbal matter, and the practical likelihood that the contingencies will occur and that the controversy is a real one should be decisive in determining whether an actual controversy exists. The courts have ordinarily not used the language of single or double contingency and they have issued declaratory judgments about the legal consequences of future conduct.[12]

7. Lake Carriers' Assn. v. MacMullan, 1972, 92 S.Ct. 1749, 406 U.S. 498, 32 L.Ed.2d 257; Golden v. Zwickler, 1969, 89 S.Ct. 956, 394 U.S. 103, 22 L.Ed.2d 113; Altvater v. Freeman, 1943, 63 S.Ct. 1115, 319 U.S. 359, 87 L.Ed. 1450; Maryland Cas. Co. v. Pacific Coal & Oil Co., 1941, 61 S.Ct. 510, 312 U.S. 270, 85 L.Ed. 826.

8. Aetna Life Ins. Co. v. Haworth, 1937, 57 S.Ct. 461, 300 U.S. 227, 81 L.Ed. 617; Eccles v. Peoples Bank of Lakewood Village, 1948, 68 S.Ct. 641, 333 U.S. 426, 92 L.Ed. 784; Golden v. Zwickler, 1969, 89 S.Ct. 956, 394 U.S. 103, 22 L.Ed.2d 113; 10A Wright, Miller & Kane, Civil 2d § 2757.

9. Evers v. Dwyer, 1958, 79 S.Ct. 178, 358 U.S. 202, 3 L.Ed.2d 222, noted 1959, 30 Miss.L.J. 329. See also International Longshoremen's Assn. v. Seatrain Lines, Inc., C.A.2d, 1964, 326 F.2d 916, 918–919.

10. Hart & Wechsler, The Federal Courts and the Federal System, Bator, Meltzer, Mishkin & Shapiro 3d ed. 1988, p. 238.

11. American Fidelity & Cas. Co. v. Pennsylvania Threshermen & Farmers'

Mut. Cas. Ins. Co., C.A.5th, 1960, 280 F.2d 453, 461. See also Hendrix v. Poonai, C.A.11th, 1981, 662 F.2d 719, 722; Bellefonte Reinsurance Co. v. Aetna Cas. & Sur. Co., D.C.N.Y.1984, 590 F.Supp. 187, 192.

12. E.g., Steffel v. Thompson, 1974, 94 S.Ct. 1209, 415 U.S. 452, 39 L.Ed.2d 505; Browning–Ferris Indus. of Alabama, Inc. v. Alabama Dept. of Environmental Mgmt., C.A.11th, 1986, 799 F.2d 1473; Interdynamics, Inc. v. Firma Wolf, C.A.3d, 1982, 698 F.2d 157; Keene Corp. v. Insurance Co. of Northern America, C.A.D.C.1981, 667 F.2d 1034, 1039–1040, certiorari denied 102 S.Ct. 1644, 455 U.S. 1007, 71 L.Ed.2d 875; Super Products Corp. v. D P Way Corp., C.A.7th, 1976, 546 F.2d 748; Technical Tape Corp. v. Minnesota Mining & Mfg. Co., C.A.2d, 1952, 200 F.2d 876.

Courts have refused to entertain the case if the future events are not sufficiently real or immediate. E.g., Zimmerman v. HBO Affiliate Group, C.A.3d, 1987, 834 F.2d 1163; International Harvester Co. v. Deere & Co., C.A.7th, 1980, 623 F.2d 1207, 1215–1217; Wembley, Inc. v. Superba Cravats, Inc., C.A.2d, 1963, 315 F.2d 87; Enka B.V.

Declaratory judgments are probably sought most often in insurance and patent litigation,[13] but they are available and are used in all types of civil litigation[14] with two exceptions. Controversies over most federal taxes are expressly excluded from the Declaratory Judgment Act,[15] while the Tax Injunction Act,[16] though in terms only prohibiting federal courts from enjoining the collection of state taxes if a plain, speedy, and efficient remedy is available in the courts of the state, is read as also barring declaratory judgments about state taxes if an injunction would be barred.[17]

It is always discretionary with the court whether to entertain an action for a declaratory judgment.[18] It may refuse to give such relief where the judgment sought would not settle the controversy between the parties,[19] or would cause inconvenience to some of them,[20] or where the declaratory-judgment action is being used for "procedural fencing."[21]

of Arnhem, Holland v. E.I. duPont de Nemours & Co., D.C.Del.1981, 519 F.Supp. 356.

The "doubly contingent" language is used in McCahill v. Borough of Fox Chapel, C.A.3d, 1971, 438 F.2d 213, 218.

13. 10A Wright, Miller & Kane, Civil 2d §§ 2760, 2761; Comment, Intellectual Property Protection or Protectionism? Declaratory Judgment Use by Patent Owners Against Prospective Infringers, 1992, 42 Am.U.L.Rev. 239. The Comment is primarily concerned with recent cases allowing the use of declaratory judgment by a patent owner as a preemptive measure against potential future infringers. E.g., Lang v. Pacific Marine & Supply Co., C.A.Fed.1990, 895 F.2d 761.

Affirmance by the Court of Appeals for the Federal Circuit of a finding that a patent has not been infringed is not per se a sufficient reason for vacating a declaratory judgment holding the patent invalid. Cardinal Chemical Co. v. Morton Intl., Inc., 1993, 113 S.Ct. 1967, ___ U.S. ___, 124 L.Ed.2d 1.

14. 10A Wright, Miller & Kane, Civil 2d §§ 2760–2765.

15. See Bob Jones Univ. v. Simon, 1974, 94 S.Ct. 2038, 2045 n. 7, 416 U.S. 725, 732 n. 7, 40 L.Ed.2d 496; and cases cited 10A Wright, Miller & Kane, Civil 2d § 2762 nn. 3, 4.

16. 28 U.S.C.A. § 1341. See § 51 above.

17. California v. Grace Brethren Church, 1982, 102 S.Ct. 2498, 457 U.S. 393, 73 L.Ed.2d 93.

18. Brillhart v. Excess Ins. Co. of America, 1942, 62 S.Ct. 1173, 1175, 316 U.S. 491, 494, 86 L.Ed. 1620; Public Affairs Associates, Inc. v. Rickover, 1962, 82 S.Ct. 580, 582, 369 U.S. 111, 112, 7 L.Ed.2d 604;

Borchard, Discretion to Refuse Jurisdiction of Actions for Declaratory Judgments, 1942, 26 Minn.L.Rev. 677; 10A Wright, Miller & Kane, Civil 2d § 2759.

"In the exercise of their sound discretion to entertain declaratory actions the district courts may not decline on the basis of whim or personal disinclination; but they may take into consideration the speculativeness of the situation before them and the adequacy of the record for the determination they are called upon to make, as well as other factors, such as whether there is a pending procedure in state court in which the matters in controversy between the parties may be fully litigated." Hollis v. Itawamba County Loans, C.A.5th, 1981, 657 F.2d 746, 750.

19. Aetna Cas. & Sur. Co. v. Quarles, C.C.A.4th, 1937, 92 F.2d 321; Williams v. Ball, C.A.2d, 1961, 294 F.2d 94, certiorari denied 82 S.Ct. 598, 368 U.S. 990, 7 L.Ed.2d 526.

20. Kozol v. Lumbermens Mut. Cas. Co., D.C.Mass.1962, 201 F.Supp. 718; Ohio Cas. Ins. Co. v. Richards, D.C.Or.1939, 27 F.Supp. 18; Lumbermens Mut. Cas. Co. of Illinois, (American) v. Cieri, D.C.Pa.1938, 23 F.Supp. 435.

21. Torch, Inc. v. LeBlanc, C.A.5th, 1991, 947 F.2d 193; Grand Trunk W. R.R. Co. v. Consolidated Rail Corp., C.A.6th, 1984, 746 F.2d 323, 326; Franklin Life Ins. Co. v. Johnson, C.C.A.10th, 1946, 157 F.2d 653, 656; Republic Ins. Co. v. Sinclair Oil Corp., D.C.Utah 1992, 791 F.Supp. 278.

It has been held that a prospective negligence-action defendant should not be able to obtain a declaratory judgment of nonliability since this would force the injured party to litigate his or her claim at a time and place of the alleged tortfeasor's choos-

At the same time, as Rule 57 specifically provides, the existence of another adequate remedy,[22] or even the pendency of another suit in state or federal court,[23] does not bar an otherwise appropriate action for a declaratory judgment. The determinative factor is whether the declaratory action will probably result in a just and more expeditious and economical determination of the entire controversy.[24]

Two issues of considerable importance concerning the discretion of district courts in deciding whether to entertain declaratory-judgment actions remain unresolved. The lower courts are divided on whether this discretion is limited to situations in which "Colorado River abstention"[25] would be permissible.[26] There is also much division among the circuits on the scope of review of the district court's exercise of this discretion, with some circuits reviewing de novo while others use an abuse-of-discretion standard or some variation on that standard.[27]

ing. Cunningham Bros., Inc. v. Bail, C.A.7th, 1969, 407 F.2d 1165; Southern Ins. Co. v. Bennett, D.C.Ga.1988, 680 F.Supp. 387, 389; UNC Resources, Inc. v. Benally, D.C.Ariz.1981, 518 F.Supp. 1046, 1049; Frito–Lay, Inc. v. Dent, D.C.Miss. 1974, 373 F.Supp. 771. But an interesting state-court case shows that there are circumstances in which a declaratory judgment may be useful in negligence litigation. Ditzler v. Spee, 1970, 180 N.W.2d 178, 288 Minn. 314. See 10A Wright, Miller & Kane, Civil 2d § 2765, pp. 729–731.

22. E.g., Scott–Burr. Stores Corp. v. Wilcox, C.A.5th, 1952, 194 F.2d 989; Mutual Life Ins. Co. of New York v. Krejci, C.C.A.7th, 1941, 123 F.2d 594; U.S. Fidelity & Guar. Co. v. Koch, C.C.A.3d, 1939, 102 F.2d 288; New York Life Ins. Co. v. Roe, C.C.A.8th, 1939, 102 F.2d 28.

23. E.g., Provident Tradesmens Bank & Trust Co. v. Patterson, 1968, 88 S.Ct. 733, 746–747, 390 U.S. 102, 125–128, 19 L.Ed.2d 936; Travelers Ins. Co. v. Louisiana Farm Bureau Federation, Inc., C.A.5th, 1993, 996 F.2d 774; Metropolitan Property & Liab. Ins. Co. v. Kirkwood, C.A.1st, 1984, 729 F.2d 61; Tyrill v. Alcoa S.S. Co., D.C.N.Y. 1958, 172 F.Supp. 363, affirmed C.A.2d, 1959, 266 F.2d 27.

But see Continental Cas. Co. v. Robsac Indus., C.A.9th, 1991, 947 F.2d 1367, 1374, holding that courts "should generally decline to assert jurisdiction in insurance coverage and other declaratory relief actions presenting only issues of state law during the pendency of parallel proceedings in state court."

24. Maryland Cas. Co. v. Boyle Constr. Co., C.C.A.4th, 1941, 123 F.2d 558, 565. See also Guardian Life Ins. Co. of America v. Kortz, C.C.A.10th, 1945, 151 F.2d 582,

586; Smith v. Vowell, D.C.Tex.1974, 379 F.Supp. 139, 162, affirmed without opinion C.A.5th, 504 F.2d 759; Western v. McGehee, D.C.Md.1962, 202 F.Supp. 287, 294; 10A Wright, Miller & Kane, Civil 2d § 2758.

The factors to be considered are enlighteningly discussed in: Rowan Cos., Inc. v. Griffin, C.A.5th, 1989, 876 F.2d 26, 28–29; Grand Trunk W. R.R. Co. v. Consolidated Rail Corp., C.A.6th, 1984, 746 F.2d 323, 326–327; Metropolitan Prop. & Liab. Ins. Co. v. Kirkwood, C.A.1st, 1984, 729 F.2d 61, 62–63.

25. Two cases, Colorado River Water Conservation Dist. v. U.S., 1976, 96 S.Ct. 1236, 424 U.S. 800, 47 L.Ed.2d 483, and Moses H. Cone Memorial Hospital v. Mercury Construction Corp., 1983, 103 S.Ct. 927, 460 U.S. 1, 74 L.Ed.2d 765, identified six factors to be considered in determining whether a federal court is permitted to abstain in favor of a state-court proceeding concerning the same matter. See § 52 above.

26. Most cases hold that the discretion in declaratory-judgment actions is not limited by Colorado River. E.g., Chamberlain v. Atlantic Ins. Co., C.A.9th, 1991, 931 F.2d 1361, 1366. Contra: Insurance Co. of Pa. v. Syntex Corp., C.A.8th, 1992, 964 F.2d 829, 833–834. See cases cited 17A Wright, Miller & Cooper, Jurisdiction 2d § 4247 n. 5. The Supreme Court granted certiorari to resolve this controversy, but dismissed the writ after argument when the parties settled the case. Granite State Ins. Co. v. Tandy Corp., 1993, 113 S.Ct. 1836, ___ U.S. ___, 123 L.Ed.2d 463.

27. Cases from various circuits are collected in Charter Federal Savings Bank v. Office of Thrift Supervision, C.A.4th, 1992,

The Supreme Court has frequently, although not invariably, indicated a marked reluctance to have important issues of public law resolved by declaratory judgments.[28] It has said that declaratory-judgment procedure should not be used to preempt and prejudge issues that are committed for initial decision to an administrative body or special tribunal,[29] and warned against grant of a declaratory judgment involving an important question of public law on the basis of a sparse and inadequate record.[30] The Court has said also that questions of the scope and constitutionality of legislation must not be decided "in advance of its immediate adverse effect in the context of a concrete case."[31]

Despite these repeated cautions, it is clear that declaratory judgments play an important part in litigation of constitutional issues and other issues of public law. The Supreme Court has held that declaratory relief was appropriate in a case raising a constitutional issue of the utmost importance and sensitivity[32] and it has expressed a willingness to have declaratory actions used to challenge the constitutionality of state laws if no state proceeding is pending.[33]

The Declaratory Judgment Act is not a grant of jurisdiction to the federal courts. It merely makes available an additional remedy in cases of which they have jurisdiction by virtue of diversity and the requisite amount in controversy, or because of a federal question.[34] Similarly the procedure in a declaratory-judgment action is the same as that in any other action. Only two difficult procedural questions have arisen. These concern the effect of a declaratory action on the burden of proof and on the right to jury trial.

The answer to the question about jury trial is now clear. Although it is sometimes said that an action for a declaratory judgment is

976 F.2d 203, 208 n. 8, certiorari denied 113 S.Ct. 1643, ___ U.S. ___, 123 L.Ed.2d 265. See also 10A Wright, Miller & Kane, Civil 2d § 2759 n. 22.

28. E.g., United Public Workers v. Mitchell, 1947, 67 S.Ct. 556, 330 U.S. 75, 91 L.Ed. 754; Eccles v. Peoples Bank of Lakewood Village, 1948, 68 S.Ct. 641, 333 U.S. 426, 92 L.Ed. 784; Golden v. Zwickler, 1969, 89 S.Ct. 956, 394 U.S. 103, 22 L.Ed.2d 113; 10A Wright, Miller & Kane, Civil 2d § 2763.

29. Public Serv. Comm. of Utah v. Wycoff Co., 1952, 73 S.Ct. 236, 344 U.S. 237, 97 L.Ed. 291, noted 1953, 3 Utah L.Rev. 388; cf. A.L. Mechling Barge Lines, Inc. v. U.S., 1961, 82 S.Ct. 337, 368 U.S. 324, 7 L.Ed.2d 317. Compare Toilet Goods Assn. v. Gardner, 1967, 87 S.Ct. 1520, 387 U.S. 158, 18 L.Ed.2d 697, with Abbott Laboratories v. Gardner, 1967, 87 S.Ct. 1507, 387 U.S. 136, 18 L.Ed.2d 681.

30. A.L. Mechling Barge Lines, Inc. v. U.S., 1961, 82 S.Ct. 337, 368 U.S. 324, 7 L.Ed.2d 317; Public Affairs Associates, Inc.

v. Rickover, 1962, 82 S.Ct. 580, 369 U.S. 111, 7 L.Ed.2d 604; Askew v. Hargrave, 1971, 91 S.Ct. 856, 401 U.S. 476, 28 L.Ed.2d 196.

31. International Longshoremen's and Warehousemen's Union v. Boyd, 1954, 74 S.Ct. 447, 448, 347 U.S. 222, 224, 98 L.Ed. 650.

See also Zemel v. Rusk, 1965, 85 S.Ct. 1271, 381 U.S. 1, 14 L.Ed.2d 179; McCahill v. Borough of Fox Chapel, C.A.3d, 1971, 438 F.2d 213; Dickson, Declaratory Remedies and Constitutional Change, 1971, 24 Vand. L.Rev. 257.

32. Powell v. McCormack, 1969, 89 S.Ct. 1944, 395 U.S. 486, 23 L.Ed.2d 491.

33. Steffel v. Thompson, 1974, 94 S.Ct. 1209, 415 U.S. 452, 39 L.Ed.2d 505. See § 52A above and Note, Federal Declaratory Relief and the Non-pending State Criminal Suit, 1974, 34 Md.L.Rev. 87.

34. 10A Wright, Miller & Kane, Civil 2d §§ 2766, 2767. The jurisdictional questions are particularly complex in a federal-question case. See § 18 above.

"equitable in nature," [35] other cases have spoken of an action for a declaratory judgment as "essentially legal." [36] The truth is that "a declaratory judgment action is a statutory creation, and by its nature is neither fish nor fowl, neither legal nor equitable." [37] The new remedy may be sought both in cases that historically would have been legal and those that historically would have been equitable. Of course the availability of this new procedure cannot be used to erode a constitutional right to a jury that would have existed if there were no such procedure.[38] The solution the courts have worked out is to look to the kind of action in which the issue involved would have been decided if there were no declaratory-judgment procedure.[39] Thus, in one typical case an insurance company sought a declaratory judgment that an accident in which its insured was involved was not within the coverage of the policy. There were three ways in which this issue of coverage could have been litigated were there no declaratory-judgment procedure. The insured could have paid a judgment against him and sued the insurer for the amount due him by way of indemnity. This would be a simple action for the recovery of money only, which at common law would have been tried in debt or assumpsit and which thus would be triable to a jury today. If the insured failed to pay the judgment, the injured person, under the relevant state statutes, could have brought an independent action against the insurer for the amount of the judgment, which would be triable to a jury, or at his option he could have garnished the insurer, and the garnishment proceeding would be tried, in the state in question, without a jury. Since the issues of coverage would, then, usually be tried to a jury, and would only be tried without a jury if the injured person so elected by using garnishment rather than bringing an independent action, the court held that in the declaratory-judgment action it was error to deny trial by jury over a demand for jury trial by the injured person.[40]

The question of burden of proof is not yet settled. It arises when, as in the example just described, the parties are reversed by virtue of the declaratory judgment action. If there were no declaratory-judgment procedure, the issue of policy coverage would come up when the injured person or the insured sued the insurer, and in such a suit that person, as

---

35. Abbott Laboratories v. Gardner, 1967, 87 S.Ct. 1507, 1519, 387 U.S. 136, 155, 18 L.Ed.2d 681.

36. Simler v. Conner, 1963, 83 S.Ct. 609, 611, 372 U.S. 221, 223, 9 L.Ed.2d 691.

37. American Safety Equipment Corp. v. J.P. Maguire & Co., C.A.2d, 1968, 391 F.2d 821, 824. In this case the right of interlocutory appeal depended on whether the action was regarded as legal or equitable. See also Mowbray v. Moseley, Hallgarten, Estabrook & Weeden, Inc., C.A.1st, 1986, 795 F.2d 1111, 1114.

38. Simler v. Conner, 1963, 83 S.Ct. 609, 611, 372 U.S. 221, 223, 9 L.Ed.2d 691; Beacon Theatres v. Westover, 1959, 79 S.Ct.

948, 359 U.S. 500, 3 L.Ed.2d 988; Fraser, Jury Trials in Declaratory Judgment Actions, 1967, 52 Iowa L.Rev. 609; Comment, The Right to Trial by Jury in Declaratory Judgment Actions, 1971, 3 Conn.L.Rev. 564; 9 Wright & Miller, Civil § 2313.

39. Pacific Indem. Co. v. McDonald, C.C.A.9th, 1939, 107 F.2d 446, 448, 131 A.L.R. 208; (American) Lumbermens Mut. Cas. Co. of Illinois v. Timms & Howard, Inc., C.C.A.2d, 1939, 108 F.2d 497; James v. Pennsylvania General Ins. Co., C.A.D.C. 1965, 349 F.2d 228.

40. Johnson v. Fidelity & Cas. Co. of New York, C.A.8th, 1956, 238 F.2d 322.

plaintiff, would have the burden of proof on this issue. There is strong support for the view that it still has the burden of proof even though the insurer has instituted the action.[41] Though this is consistent with the result about jury trial just described, the case law is in much confusion,[42] and there is a good deal to be said for the view that the party who brings a law suit—in the example given, the insurer—should carry the burden.[43] Even if the view first described should prevail, it is substantially qualified in practice by a well-developed line of authority that holds that if the plaintiff in the declaratory-judgment action voluntarily goes forward and attempts to prove its case, it will be held to have assumed the risk of nonpersuasion.[44]

There is not much law on whether the availability of a declaratory judgment in a diversity case should depend on state law, probably because virtually all states have statutes similar to the federal act. If a state simply does not provide for declaratory judgments, it would seem that a federal court is nevertheless free to grant such relief, which may be regarded as "procedural" and is expressly authorized by Act of Congress.[45] It has been held, however, that where a state, though permitting declaratory judgments generally, refuses to permit them in one particular situation in order to further a unique state policy, the state rule must be followed and similar declaratory judgments refused in federal courts in that state in diversity actions.[46] That decision was questionable when it was handed down, and its authority has been eroded by the later decision in Hanna v. Plumer.[47] The fact that the right of action is state-created, and that the state would not allow a declaratory-judgment suit under the circumstances, may, however, be an

---

41. Fireman's Fund Ins. Co. v. Videfreeze Corp., C.A.3d, 1976, 540 F.2d 1171, certiorari denied 97 S.Ct. 767, 429 U.S. 1053, 50 L.Ed.2d 770; Preferred Acc. Ins. Co. of New York v. Grasso, C.A.2d, 1951, 186 F.2d 987; Travelers Ins. Co. v. Greenough, 1937, 190 A. 129, 88 N.H. 391; Borchard, note 1 above, at pp. 404–409; cf. Royal Indem. Co. v. Wingate, D.C.Md.1973, 353 F.Supp. 1002, affirmed without opinion C.A.4th, 1973, 487 F.2d 1398.

42. See the cases cited 10A Wright, Miller & Kane, Civil 2d § 2770.

43. See Developments in the Law—Declaratory Judgments, 1949, 62 Harv.L.Rev. 787, 836–838.

44. Liberty Mut. Ins. Co. v. Sweeney, C.A.3d, 1954, 216 F.2d 209, 210; Pacific Portland Cement Co. v. Food Machinery & Chem. Corp., C.A.9th, 1949, 178 F.2d 541, 547; Bauer v. Clark, C.C.A.7th, 1947, 161 F.2d 397, 401; Hartford Acc. & Indem. Co. v. Lougee, 1938, 196 A. 267, 89 N.H. 222.

45. See M. Swift & Sons, Inc. v. Lemon, D.C.N.Y.1959, 24 F.R.D. 43, 45. There is also a dictum to this effect in Skelly Oil Co. v. Phillips Petroleum Co., 1950, 70 S.Ct. 876, 880, 339 U.S. 667, 674, 94 L.Ed. 1194.

46. Allstate Ins. Co. v. Charneski, C.A.7th, 1960, 286 F.2d 238. See § 59 above. For varying views of this decision, compare Comment, The Constitutional Power of Congress to Control Procedure in the Federal Courts, 1961, 56 Nw.U.L.Rev. 560, with Smith, Blue Ridge and Beyond: A Byrd's Eye View of Federalism in Diversity Litigation, 1962, 36 Tul.L.Rev. 443.

47. 1965, 85 S.Ct. 1136, 380 U.S. 460, 14 L.Ed.2d 8. See § 55 above.

Post–Hanna cases have held that federal law determines whether a federal court can give a declaratory judgment. Cincinnati Ins. Co. v. Holbrook, C.A.11th, 1989, 867 F.2d 1330, 1332–1333; Farmers Alliance Mut. Ins. Co. v. Jones, C.A.10th, 1978, 570 F.2d 1384, certiorari denied 99 S.Ct. 97, 439 U.S. 826, 58 L.Ed.2d 119; Beacon Constr. Co. v. Matco Elec. Co., Inc., C.A.2d, 1975, 521 F.2d 392, 397–399; Nationwide Mut. Ins. Co. v. Welker, D.C.Md.1992, 792 F.Supp. 433, 439–440; American Motorists Ins. Co. v. Mack, D.C.Pa.1965, 248 F.Supp. 1016.

appropriate factor for the court to consider in exercising its discretion whether to hear the declaratory action.

A judgment in a declaratory-judgment action is conclusive in a subsequent action between the parties about the matters declared and, in accordance with the usual rules of issue preclusion, on any issues actually litigated and determined.[48] Further necessary or proper relief based on a declaratory judgment may be granted, after reasonable notice and hearing, against any adverse party whose rights have been determined by the judgment.[49] Although the Supreme Court has voiced some uncertainty about the res judicata effect to be given to a federal declaratory judgment by a state court,[50] the Court's concern apparently is limited to the special situation in which a federal declaration that a state statute is unconstitutional may interfere with state law enforcement.[51]

§ 100A. Effect of a Prior Judgment [1]

"The defense of res judicata is universally respected, but actually not very well liked." [2] So wrote one of America's greatest proceduralists, Judge Charles E. Clark, in a 1945 dissent. Compare with that a 1981 decision in which a court of appeals had held that "simple justice" dictated that it should not hold a party barred by res judicata. Justice Rehnquist answered for the Supreme Court that "we do not see the grave injustice which would be done by the application of accepted principles of res judicata. 'Simple justice' is achieved when a complex body of law developed over a period of years is evenhandedly applied. The doctrine of res judicata serves vital public interests beyond any individual judge's ad hoc determination of the equities in a particular case." [3]

The new attitude toward res judicata, toward the various ways in which a judgment in one action will have a binding effect in another, has certainly been influenced by the flood of cases that have come into the

---

48. Restatement Second of Judgments, 1982, § 33; 18 Wright, Miller & Cooper, Jurisdiction, § 4446; Note, The Res Judicata Effect of Declaratory Relief in the Federal Courts, 1973, 45 S.Cal.L.Rev. 803.

49. 28 U.S.C.A. § 2202; Powell v. McCormack, 1969, 89 S.Ct. 1944, 1952, 395 U.S. 486, 499, 23 L.Ed.2d 491; 10A Wright, Miller & Kane, Civil 2d § 2771.

50. Steffel v. Thompson, 1974, 94 S.Ct. 1209, 1221, 415 U.S. 452, 470–471, 39 L.Ed.2d 505. See also id., 94 S.Ct. at 1224–1225, 415 U.S. at 477 (White, J., concurring); 94 S.Ct. at 1227 n. 3, 415 U.S. at 482 n. 3 (Rehnquist, J., concurring).

See also U.S. ex rel. Lawrence v. Woods, C.A.7th, 1970, 432 F.2d 1072, certiorari denied 91 S.Ct. 1658, 402 U.S. 983, 29 L.Ed.2d 148; Comment, The Binding Effect of Federal Declaratory Judgments on State Courts, 1973, 51 Texas L.Rev. 743.

51. Shapiro, State Courts and Federal Declaratory Judgments, 1979, 74 Nw. U.L.Rev. 759; Restatement Second of Judgments, Reporter's Note to § 33 comm. b.

§ 100A

1. 18 Wright, Miller & Cooper, Jurisdiction, c. 13; Restatement Second of Judgments, 1982 (cited hereafter in this section as "Restatement Second"); James, Hazard & Leubsdorf, Civil Procedure, 4th ed. 1992, c. 11; Casad, Res Judicata in a Nutshell, 1976.

2. Riordan v. Ferguson, C.C.A.2d, 1945, 147 F.2d 983, 988.

3. Federated Department Stores, Inc. v. Moitie, 1981, 101 S.Ct. 2424, 2429, 452 U.S. 394, 401, 69 L.Ed.2d 103.

courts. Courts today are having difficulty giving a litigant one day in court. To allow that litigant a second day is a luxury that cannot be afforded.[4] But "it is clear that more than crowded dockets is involved."[5] Modern scholarship had looked hard at the rules of res judicata and found that they had failed to keep pace with the rules of procedure that they complement.[6]

The central proposition of res judicata remains, as it has always been, that "a party who has had a full opportunity to present a contention in court ordinarily should be denied permission to assert it on some subsequent occasion."[7] What has only recently been grasped is that the traditional rules of res judicata had developed at a time when the common-law system of pleading and procedure was still in vogue. Modern procedural notions, found in the Federal Rules of Civil Procedure and in most of the states, have greatly expanded the opportunity to present all of the contentions a party has in a single action. Joinder of claims is no longer restricted by the forms of action and the separation of law and equity. Joinder of parties has been liberalized so that a lawsuit need not be merely a two-party matter but can include persons interested in a controversy from many sides. Pleadings no longer must be precise, and modern rules on amendment allow them to be changed as the case develops. The rules on discovery give a party the ability to learn fully about the case. Modern procedure has expanded the scope of the initial opportunity to litigate and this has made inevitable the narrowing of the situations in which a second opportunity to litigate need be given.[8]

This modern thinking about res judicata has not only produced new and more restrictive rules on when relitigation will be allowed, but it has

---

4. National Treasury Employees Union v. I.R.S., C.A.D.C.1985, 765 F.2d 1174, 1176.

5. Blonder–Tongue Laboratories, Inc. v. University of Illinois Foundation, 1971, 91 S.Ct. 1434, 1442, 402 U.S. 313, 328, 28 L.Ed.2d 788.

"To preclude parties from contesting matters that they have had a full and fair opportunity to litigate protects their adversaries from the expense and vexation attending multiple lawsuits, conserves judicial resources, and fosters reliance on judicial action by minimizing the possibility of inconsistent decisions." Montana v. U.S., 1979, 99 S.Ct. 970, 973–974, 440 U.S. 147, 153–154, 59 L.Ed.2d 210.

It is argued in Hay, Some Settlement Effects of Preclusion, 1993 U.Ill.L.Rev. 21, that preclusion rules encourage parties to settle disputes for amounts close to the expected judicial valuation of the plaintiff's claim, since without preclusion parties would be more likely to extract settlements unrelated to the merits of a dispute by threatening their opponents with multiple rounds of litigation.

6. Vestal, Res Judicata/Preclusion, 1969; Hazard, Res Nova in Res Judicata, 1971, 44 S.Cal.L.Rev. 1036; Cleary, Res Judicata Reexamined, 1948, 57 Yale L.J. 339.

7. Hazard, note 6 above, at 1043.

8. James, Hazard & Leubsdorf, note 1 above, at 580–581.

The relation is neatly put in Restatement Second, c. 1, at p. 10: "The rules of res judicata in modern procedure therefore may fairly be characterized as illiberal toward the opportunity for relitigation. Their rigor contrasts sharply with the liberality of the rules governing the original event, which is the theme of the Federal Rules of Civil Procedure and similar systems. * * *

"That difference does not represent a contradiction or ambivalence in procedural policy. Rather, it reflects the relationship between rules of original procedure and rules of res judicata. Inasmuch as the former are now generally permissive, the latter are correspondingly restrictive."

also produced rules that are cast in practical and empirical terms. It is no longer necessary to resort to "the question-begging and illusorily definite conceptual categories of 'cause of action,' 'privity,' and 'on the merits.' "[9] The new approach has been enthusiastically accepted by the United States Supreme Court and by many state courts.[10] The acceptance this approach has had in the courts has made it possible to bring together the current analysis of problems of preclusion in an elegant Restatement Second of Judgments, which has already been immensely influential.[11]

It has been said that the changes in this area of the law "are clearly evolutionary rather than revolutionary."[12] This may be true; but only those who cannot distinguish between a monkey and a man will think that the changes are less marked for that reason.

Space limitations make it impossible to give here any kind of comprehensive overview of res judicata.[13] The present section can do no more than to inform the reader that this is now a lively and important part of adjective law, to explain the new terminology that is now being used, and to mention a few of the special problems that come from having parallel systems of state and federal courts.

"Res judicata" has been used in this section as a general term referring to all of the ways in which one judgment will have a binding effect on another. That usage is and doubtless will continue to be common, but it lumps under a single name two quite different effects of judgments. The first is the effect of foreclosing any litigation of matters that never have been litigated, because of the determination that they should have been advanced in an earlier suit. The second is the effect of foreclosing relitigation of matters that have once been litigated and decided. The first of these, preclusion of matters that were never litigated, has gone under the name, "true res judicata,"[14] or the names, "merger" and "bar."[15] The second doctrine, preclusion of matters that

---

9. Hazard, note 6 above, at 1043.

10. Indeed a principal impetus toward the new way of thinking was the pathbreaking opinion by Chief Justice Roger J. Traynor in Bernhard v. Bank of America Nat. Trust & Sav. Assn., 1942, 122 P.2d 892, 19 Cal.2d 807. See below at note 58.

11. There is a useful Symposium on Restatement Second, 1981, 66 Cornell L.Rev. 401. See also Casad, Two Important Books on Res Judicata, 1982, 80 Mich.L.Rev. 664.

As of March 1, 1993, Restatement Second had been cited 7539 times by the courts. Even before it was finally approved, courts had often cited and followed formulations contained in Tentative Drafts of that project. The numbering of sections is not the same in the Official Draft as in the Tentative Drafts. Helpful tables in the rear of the second volume of the Official Draft make it easy to identify provisions there

with their counterparts in a Tentative Draft.

12. Martin, The Restatement (Second) of Judgments: An Overview, 1981, 66 Cornell L.Rev. 404, 405.

13. Volume 18 of Wright, Miller & Cooper, Jurisdiction devotes 801 pages to current federal law on the subject without purporting to get into the rich and often divergent strands of state law.

14. E.g., White v. World Fin. of Meridian, Inc., C.A.5th, 1981, 653 F.2d 147, 150 n. 5; Ross v. International Broth. of Elec. Workers, C.A.9th, 1980, 634 F.2d 453, 457 n. 6.

15. Restatement Second, Introductory Note before § 24; Kaspar Wire Works, Inc. v. Leco Engineering & Machine, Inc., C.A.5th, 1978, 575 F.2d 530, 535. The Kaspar case has a highly useful summary of the major variations in terminology.

have once been decided, has usually been called "collateral estoppel."[16] Professor Allan Vestal has long argued for use of the names "claim preclusion" and "issue preclusion" for these two doctrines,[17] and this usage is increasingly employed by the courts as it is by Restatement Second of Judgments.[18]

The general rule of claim preclusion is that a valid and final judgment on a claim precludes a second action on that claim or any part of it.[19] The judgment must be final,[20] but an otherwise final judgment of a trial court is regarded as final even though an appeal from it is pending.[21] Cases continue to say that the judgment has a preclusive effect only if it is "on the merits,"[22] but that terminology has been avoided in Restatement Second "because of its possibly misleading connotations."[23] It is sufficient that in the first litigation there was an opportunity to get to the merits. Those situations in which plaintiff was unable to litigate the merits in the first action because of some procedural barrier are now identified and made exceptions to the general rule of claim preclusion.[24]

Claim preclusion applies "not only as to every matter which was offered and received to sustain or defeat the claim or demand, but as to any other admissible matter which might have been offered for that purpose."[25] Indeed the principal distinction between claim preclusion and issue preclusion is, as noted earlier, that the former forecloses litigation of matters that never have been litigated. This makes it important to know the dimensions of the "claim" that is foreclosed by bringing the first action, but unfortunately no precise definition is possible. Restatement Second has taken a pragmatic approach that looks to the transaction from which the action arose. The claim extinguished "includes all rights of the plaintiff to remedies against the defendant with respect to all or any part of the transaction, or series of connected transactions, out of which the action arose," and what constitutes a "transaction" or a "series" is "to be determined pragmatically,

---

16. E.g., Lawlor v. National Screen Serv. Corp., 1955, 75 S.Ct. 865, 867, 349 U.S. 322, 326, 99 L.Ed. 1122.

17. E.g., Vestal, Rationale of Preclusion, 1964, 9 St.L.U.L.J. 29.

18. 18 Wright, Miller & Cooper, Jurisdiction § 4402. E.g., Migra v. Warren City School Dist., 1984, 104 S.Ct. 892, 894 n. 1, 465 U.S. 75, 77 n. 1, 79 L.Ed.2d 56.

19. Restatement Second, §§ 18, 19; 18 Wright, Miller & Cooper, Jurisdiction §§ 4406–4409.

20. Restatement Second, § 13; 18 Wright, Miller & Cooper, Jurisdiction § 4432.

21. Restatement Second, § 13, comm. f; 18 Wright, Miller & Cooper, Jurisdiction § 4433. Even if the first judgment is ultimately reversed, this does not automatically mean nullification of the judgment in a second action in which the first judgment

was given preclusive effect. Reed v. Allen, 1932, 52 S.Ct. 532, 286 U.S. 191, 76 L.Ed. 1054; Restatement Second, § 16.

22. E.g., Kremer v. Chemical Constr. Corp., 1982, 102 S.Ct. 1883, 1889 n. 6, 456 U.S. 461, 467 n. 6, 72 L.Ed.2d 262.

23. Restatement Second, § 19, comm. a. See James, Hazard & Leubsdorf, note 1 above, § 11.16.

24. Restatement Second, § 20, listing such situations as where the first judgment was for lack of jurisdiction, improper venue, nonjoinder or misjoinder of parties, prematurity, failure to satisfy a precondition to suit, or dismissal without prejudice. See 18 Wright, Miller & Cooper, Jurisdiction §§ 4435–4447.

25. Cromwell v. County of Sac, 1877, 94 U.S. 351, 352, 24 L.Ed. 195.

giving weight to such considerations as whether the facts are related in time, space, origin, or motivation, whether they form a convenient trial unit, and whether their treatment as a unit conforms to the parties' expectations or business understanding or usage." [26] That formulation defines a process rather than an absolute concept. The test thus stated is fully consistent with the clear rules that control the vast run of ordinary litigation and suggests the approach that should be taken in unusual litigation.[27] It applies to extinguish a claim by the plaintiff against the defendant even though the plaintiff is prepared in the second action to present evidence or grounds or theories of the case not presented in the first action, or to seek remedies or forms of relief not demanded in the first action.[28] For many common kinds of cases the rules on what is or is not a single claim are already well worked out in the decisions.[29] For those situations where this is not true, the test is imprecise, but no more so than the test for determining which counterclaims are compulsory.[30] Here, as with the compulsory counterclaim rule, the safe course is to bring forward in the first action anything that might later be thought to have arisen out of the same transaction. There are also a number of exceptions to the general rule of claim preclusion, such as consent or acquiescence by the defendant to the bringing of two actions, limitations on the first proceeding that made it impossible to sue on the entire claim, and conflict with other public policies.[31]

The general rule of issue preclusion is that if an issue of fact or law was actually litigated and determined by a valid and final judgment, the determination is conclusive in a subsequent action between the parties, whether on the same or a different claim.[32] The determination must have been essential to the first judgment, however, and if the court has determined two issues, either of which standing independently would be sufficient to support the result, it cannot be said that either determination was essential to the judgment and thus it will not be conclusive with

---

26. Restatement Second, § 24.

27. 18 Wright, Miller & Cooper, Jurisdiction § 4407.

28. Restatement Second, § 25; Comment, The Res Judicata Implications of Pendent Jurisdiction, 1981, 66 Cornell L.Rev. 608.

29. 18 Wright, Miller & Cooper, Jurisdiction §§ 4408–4411; Casad, note 1 above, §§ 3–9 to 3–25; James, Hazard & Leubsdorf, note 1 above, §§ 11.10–11.13. The illustrations to §§ 24 and 25 of Restatement Second also show many of the areas for which there are clear rules.

30. See § 59 above.

31. Restatement Second, § 26; 18 Wright, Miller & Cooper, Jurisdiction §§ 4412, 4413, 4415; Casad, note 1 above, §§ 3–19 to 3–24.

32. Restatement Second, § 27; 18 Wright, Miller & Cooper, Jurisdiction §§ 4416–4419.

An often-difficult question in issue preclusion, the existence of which can only be noted here, is defining the dimensions of the issue that is precluded. There need not be total identity between the particular matter presented in the second action and that presented in the first. Restatement Second, § 27 comm. c; 18 Wright, Miller & Cooper, Jurisdiction § 4417. Thus, if A claims that B was negligent in driving at an excessive rate of speed and that issue is determined in B's favor, then in a subsequent suit by B against A, A is precluded from defending on the ground of contributory negligence, even though A now wishes to claim negligence in respects other than excessive speed. Restatement Second, § 27, ill. 4.

respect to either issue.[33] The requirement that there have been a final judgment in the first action is applied less rigidly to issue preclusion than to claim preclusion. For purposes of issue preclusion, a final judgment includes any prior adjudication of an issue in another action that is "determined to be sufficiently firm to be accorded conclusive effect." [34]

Suppose, by way of example, that Paul sues Davis, claiming that a widget manufactured by Davis infringes a patent held by Paul. The court finds that Paul's patent is valid and that it is being infringed, and gives judgment for Paul. Subsequently Davis retools the plant and begins manufacture and sale of "New! Improved! Widget II." Paul thinks that this is as much an infringement of the patent as was the original device and brings a second suit. Claim preclusion does not apply, since Widget II did not exist at the time of the first action.[35] Davis is fully free to litigate in the second suit whether Widget II infringes the patent. That issue has never been litigated, and there is no issue preclusion with regard to it. As between Paul and Davis, however, it has been determined that Paul's patent is valid. That issue was actually litigated and determined in the first suit, and that determination was essential to the judgment. Therefore Davis cannot again contest the validity of the patent.

The situation would be quite different if judgment had gone for Davis in the first suit, with the court finding that Paul's patent was invalid, but also that it was not infringed. If Paul then brings a second action concerning Widget II, no issue is precluded. There has never been a determination whether Widget II infringes, and although it was determined in the first action that Paul's patent was not valid, that was only an alternative determination by a court of first instance. Since the judgment for Davis could have rested solely on the finding that the device did not infringe the patent, the further holding that the patent was invalid was not essential to the judgment and has no preclusive effect.[36]

---

33. Restatement Second, § 27 comm. h, i, j. The result is different, however, and both of the alternative determinations are conclusive, if an appellate court upholds both of those determinations. Id., § 27 comm. o. See 18 Wright, Miller & Cooper, Jurisdiction § 4421.

34. Restatement Second, § 13; 18 Wright, Miller & Cooper, Jurisdiction § 4434; Abbott Laboratories v. Thermo Chem, Inc., D.C.Mich.1991, 790 F.Supp. 135, 139–140.

35. Cf. illustrations 7 and 8 to Restatement Second, § 24. If Davis had been manufacturing both devices at the time of the original suit, Paul might have been required by the rules of claim preclusion to assert that each was infringing. See 18

Wright, Miller & Cooper, Jurisdiction § 4409.

36. Restatement Second, § 27 ill. 14. But if the first judgment had been appealed, and the appellate court upheld both determinations by the trial court, the determination of invalidity of the patent would be preclusive in the second suit. See note 33 above.

Although the position taken in the text is supported by Restatement Second, the federal cases on the point are in disarray. See 18 Wright, Miller & Cooper, Jurisdiction, § 4421, pp. 203–209. The Restatement Second position is criticized in Lucas, The Direct and Collateral Estoppel Effect of Alternative Holdings, 1993, 50 U.Chi.L.Rev. 701.

Neither claim preclusion nor issue preclusion can apply unless the party against whom preclusion is asserted had a "full and fair opportunity" to litigate the claim or issue in the first action.[37] This is recognized in the exceptions to the rule of claim preclusion.[38] There are also exceptions to the rule of issue preclusion, and these are somewhat more flexible than are the exceptions to claim preclusion, although it is not often that they need to be applied. There is no issue preclusion if appellate review could not have been obtained of the judgment in the first action,[39] or the issue is one of law and there has been a change in the legal context or the claims are substantially unrelated,[40] or because a new determination of the issue is warranted by differences in the quality or extensiveness of the procedure followed in the two courts[41] or there is a significant difference in the burden of persuasion on the issue in the two actions.[42] Finally, in exceptional cases a new determination may be needed because of considerations of the public interest or of fairness to persons who were not parties to the first action, or because it was not sufficiently foreseeable at the time of the initial action that the issue would arise in the context of a subsequent action.[43]

Once the basic rules are mastered, it remains necessary to identify the persons affected by preclusion. This question arises in determining both who is bound by a judgment and who may take advantage of it. Analysis begins with the proposition that parties are bound and that ordinarily nonparties are not bound.[44] Even actual parties may escape preclusion, however, if they appear in a different capacity in the second action than in the first.[45] Parties who were on the same side in the first

37. Kremer v. Chemical Constr. Corp., 1982, 102 S.Ct. 1883, 1897 n. 22, 456 U.S. 461, 481 n. 22, 72 L.Ed.2d 262 (claim preclusion); Allen v. McCurry, 1980, 101 S.Ct. 411, 415, 449 U.S. 90, 95, 66 L.Ed.2d 308 (issue preclusion).

38. See note 31 above.

39. Restatement Second, § 28(1); Harris Trust & Savings Bank v. John Hancock Mut. Life Ins. Co., C.A.2d, 1992, 970 F.2d 1138.

40. Restatement Second, § 28(2); 18 Wright, Miller & Cooper, Jurisdiction § 4425.

This exception is recognized, but found inapplicable, in Montana v. U.S., 1979, 99 S.Ct. 970, 978, 440 U.S. 147, 162–163, 59 L.Ed.2d 210.

41. Restatement Second, § 28(3); 18 Wright, Miller & Cooper, Jurisdiction § 4423.

"Redetermination of issues is warranted if there is reason to doubt the quality, extensiveness, or fairness of procedures followed in prior litigation." Montana v. U.S., 1979, 99 S.Ct. 970, 979 n. 11, 440 U.S. 147, 164 n. 11, 59 L.Ed.2d 210.

That the second action will be tried to a jury and the first action was tried to the court is not sufficient to bring this exception into play. Parklane Hosiery Co., Inc. v. Shore, 1979, 99 S.Ct. 645, 652 n. 19, 439 U.S. 322, 332 n. 19, 58 L.Ed.2d 552.

42. Restatement Second, § 28(4); 18 Wright, Miller & Cooper, Jurisdiction § 4422.

Thus, an acquittal in a criminal case does not have a preclusive effect against the government in a civil forfeiture proceeding, where the government must prove its case only by a preponderance of the evidence. One Lot Emerald Cut Stones and One Ring v. U.S., 1972, 93 S.Ct. 489, 492, 409 U.S. 232, 234–235, 34 L.Ed.2d 438.

43. Restatement Second, § 28(5); 18 Wright, Miller & Cooper, Jurisdiction §§ 4424, 4426; James, Hazard & Leubsdorf, note 1 above, § 11.31.

44. Restatement Second, § 34; 18 Wright, Miller & Cooper, Jurisdiction § 4449.

45. E.g., Conte v. Justice, C.A.2d, 1993, 996 F.2d 1398 (mother's appearance in a representative capacity on behalf of her infant son did not preclude her from bringing litigation ordinarily are not bound if they are adversaries in the second suit, but issue preclusion will apply if the issue was actually litigated between them in the first suit.[46]

There are many situations in which a nonparty will be bound. Traditionally it was said that a judgment bound the parties and persons in "privity" with them. Current decisions look directly to the reasons for holding a nonparty bound by a judgment. The most obvious justification for preclusion of a nonparty is that the person was a nonparty in name only, and participated so actively in the first litigation that he or she assumed a de facto role as an actual party.[47] A more attenuated justification is found in the slowly emerging possibility that nonparties may at times be precluded because they had some duty either to become a party or to give notice that they intended to pursue separate litigation.[48] A second major concept is found in a variety of rules that extend preclusion to persons who somehow were represented in the first litigation. Thus, trust beneficiaries are bound by the judgment in a suit by the trustee, and absent members of a class are bound by the judgment in a class action.[49] Finally, there is a third set of rules defining when preclusion results because of some substantive legal relationship between the person who was a party to the suit and the person who was not. Persons holding successive interests in the same property or claim can often preclude each other, while persons holding concurrent interests in the same property ordinarily do not. These rules apply in a variety of commercial and property law contexts, and arise as much from the needs of the substantive branches of law involved as they do from the values of preclusion by judgment.[50]

These various kinds of rules on when nonparties are bound are, for the most part, quite well settled. It is highly likely that courts and lawyers will continue to use the term "privity" when speaking of them. There is no reason why they should not do so, just as the terms "substance" and "procedure" are still used in an Erie context[51] and the label "indispensable" is still used in connection with compulsory joinder

---

her own suit arising out of the same accident). See Restatement Second, § 36; 18 Wright, Miller & Cooper, Jurisdiction § 4454.

46. Restatement Second, § 38; 18 Wright, Miller & Cooper, Jurisdiction § 4450.

47. Restatement Second, § 39; 18 Wright, Miller & Cooper, Jurisdiction § 4451.

The United States directed a federal contractor to bring suit challenging a state tax. The United States paid the attorneys' fees and costs and directed the course of the litigation. After the highest state court upheld the tax, and the contractor, at the instance of the United States, dropped an appeal to the Supreme Court, the United

States was bound by the judgment and issue preclusion prevented it from again challenging the tax. Montana v. U.S., 1979, 99 S.Ct. 970, 440 U.S. 147, 59 L.Ed.2d 210.

48. Restatement Second, § 62; James, Hazard & Leubsdorf, note 1 above, § 11.32. A guarded view is taken of this development in 18 Wright, Miller & Cooper, Jurisdiction §§ 4452–4453.

49. Restatement Second, §§ 41–42; 18 Wright, Miller & Cooper, Jurisdiction §§ 4454–4458.

50. Restatement Second, §§ 43–61; 18 Wright, Miller & Cooper, Jurisdiction §§ 4459–4462.

51. See § 59 above.

of parties.[52] The old names are harmless so long as they are recognized for what they are, a convenient means of expressing conclusions that are supported by independent analysis. So it is with "privity."

There has not been much major change in the rules on who is bound by a judgment. There has been a great deal of change in the rules on when a nonparty can take advantage of a judgment. At one time the Supreme Court could accurately describe the usual rule when it said: "It is a principle of general elementary law that the estoppel of a judgment must be mutual."[53] This meant that if the circumstances were such that a nonparty was not bound by a previous judgment, it could not assert the judgment as preclusive against one who was bound by it. Although Jeremy Bentham long ago had made the scathing comment that the rule of mutuality was "a maxim which one would suppose to have found its way from the gaming-table to the bench,"[54] and though no satisfactory rationalization was ever offered for the rule, it was widely followed for many years.[55]

Thus, suppose that in Paul's suit against Davis for patent infringement, described earlier in this section, judgment goes for Davis solely on the ground that Paul's patent is invalid. That determination will have preclusive effect in any future suit between Paul and Davis involving that same patent. But what if Paul brings suit for infringement of that same patent against another widget manufacturer, Triplett? If Paul's suit against Davis had resulted in a finding of validity, that could not be preclusive against Triplett.[56] The rule of mutuality meant that since

52. See § 70 above.

53. Bigelow v. Old Dominion Copper Mining & Smelting Co., 1912, 32 S.Ct. 641, 642, 225 U.S. 111, 127, 56 L.Ed. 1009.

54. 3 Bentham, Rationale of Judicial Evidence, 1827, p. 579, reprinted in 7 Bowring, Works of Jeremy Bentham, 1843, p. 171.

See also the witty, but also penetrating, opinion by the then-Master of the Rolls, Lord Denning, in McIlkenny v. Chief Constable, [1980] 1 Q.B. 283, 317–318 (C.A.): "Today we go into a room described as estoppel per rem judicatam: in which there is an alcove which has sometimes passed unnoticed. It is called issue estoppel. In this room there are several chairs to sit on. One is called the doctrine of privity. The other is the doctrine of mutuality. The two look all right but they are both a bit rickety. * * *

"Now although those two chairs look all right to start with, you will soon find that they are quite unsafe. Jeremy Bentham as long ago as 1827 told people not to rely on them. * * *

"Our friends in the United States have been just as scathing as Jeremy Bentham. They have rejected the doctrine of mutuality altogether: and they have limited the doctrine of privity."

Lord Denning's result was affirmed, but on grounds of abuse of process rather than issue estoppel, in Hunter v. Chief Constable of the West Midlands Police, 1981, [1982] App.Cas. 529.

55. 18 Wright, Miller & Cooper, Jurisdiction § 4463. See 18 id. § 4464, pp. 581–585, for citations to the literature on the subject and for consideration of the arguments for and against mutuality in modern litigation, when opportunities for complex litigation among multiple parties in disparate forums are commonly available.

Rules about mutuality were a favorite with 19th-century legal thinkers. The announcement by one commentator that there is a requirement of mutuality for specific performance of a contract led to what has been described as "one of the most hilarious misadventures in legal history." Wright, Cases on Remedies, 1955, p. 234.

56. "Due process prohibits estopping them despite one or more existing adjudications of the identical issue which stand squarely against their position." Blonder–Tongue Laboratories, Inc. v. University of Illinois Foundation, 1971, 91 S.Ct. 1434, 1443, 402 U.S. 313, 329, 28 L.Ed.2d 788.

Triplett could not be bound by an adverse determination in the first action, he could not take advantage of a favorable determination there.[57] This permitted the unattractive result that the patent might be found valid and enforceable against Triplett though invalid and unenforceable against Davis. It also meant that Paul, who had had a full and fair opportunity to litigate the issue in the suit against Davis, was now given a second opportunity to litigate the same issue all over again.

It is rare that a major change in established legal doctrine can be identified with a single decision and judge, but there is no doubt that Chief Justice Traynor's decision in Bernhard v. Bank of America[58] was the turning point that brought about the demise of mutuality. His powerful reasoning proved persuasive to other courts and, in 1971 in the Blonder–Tongue case,[59] the United States Supreme Court joined the courts that had abandoned the requirement of mutuality. The Supreme Court did so in a patent setting similar to that of the example just given, holding that the determination in Paul's suit against Davis that Paul's patent was invalid could be used defensively by Triplett in the subsequent suit.

The Blonder–Tongue decision could have been limited to patent cases, but there was language in the opinion that seemed to indicate that the Court was announcing a broader principle, applicable in any lawsuit. Subsequent Supreme Court decisions have proved that this is true. In addition, Blonder–Tongue involved "defensive" use of issue preclusion, meaning that a plaintiff was precluded from asserting a claim that it had previously litigated and lost against another defendant. There was more hesitation about "offensive" use of issue preclusion, in which a plaintiff is seeking to preclude a defendant from relitigating the issues that the defendant had previously litigated and lost against another plaintiff. In the case of a mass disaster, for example, if one plaintiff sues the common defendant and loses, this would have no preclusive effect in a suit by another plaintiff, while if offensive use of issue preclusion is proper, a victory by any plaintiff effectively establishes defendant's liability to all the remaining plaintiffs. It has been pointed out that this means that each case is essentially a test case for the defendant, but not for the remaining plaintiffs, and leads to great disparity in litigating risks.[60]

The Supreme Court was not unaware of these concerns in 1979 in the Parklane Hosiery case.[61] Nevertheless it held that "the preferable

---

57. Triplett v. Lowell, 1936, 56 S.Ct. 645, 297 U.S. 638, 80 L.Ed. 949.

58. 1942, 122 P.2d 892, 19 Cal.2d 807.

But see Waggoner, Fifty Years of Bernhard v. Bank of America Is Enough: Collateral Estoppel Should Require Mutuality But Res Judicata Should Not, 1993, 12 Rev.Litig. 391.

59. Blonder–Tongue Laboratories, Inc. v. University of Illinois Foundation, 1971, 91 S.Ct. 1434, 402 U.S. 313, 28 L.Ed.2d 788.

60. James, Hazard & Leubsdorf, note 1 above, § 11.25, at pp. 621–622.

61. Parklane Hosiery Co. v. Shore, 1979, 99 S.Ct. 645, 439 U.S. 322, 58 L.Ed.2d 552. See Kempkes, Issue Preclusion: Parklane Hosiery Co. v. Shore Revisited, 1981, 31 Drake L.Rev. 111; Callen & Kadue, To Bury Mutuality Not to Praise It: An Analysis of Collateral Estoppel After Parklane Hosiery Co. v. Shore, 1980, 31 Hastings L.J. 755.

approach for dealing with these problems in the federal courts is not to preclude the use of offensive collateral estoppel, but to grant trial courts broad discretion to determine when it should be applied." [62] This is also the approach taken in Restatement Second. It abandons mutuality across the board by stating that a party precluded from relitigating an issue with an opposing party is also precluded from doing so with another person unless the fact that the party lacked full and fair opportunity to litigate the issue in the first action or other circumstances justify according it an opportunity to relitigate the issue. [63] Any of the circumstances that would justify an exception to the issue preclusion if the second suit were between the parties to the first suit [64] will also justify an exception to the nonmutual use of issue preclusion, by one who was not a party to the prior suit, but in addition there are many other factors that may tip the scales against nonmutual preclusion, and especially against offensive nonmutual preclusion, that would not apply to defeat preclusion between the original parties. [65] No clear logical ordering can be found for the various factors that Restatement Second lists or that courts have considered in particular cases, but they run from broad concerns about such general matters as choice of forum, party joinder, incentive to litigate, and foreseeability, through more pointed inquiries about the nature of the initial forum and litigation, and into very individualized concerns with the competence of counsel, appearance of compromise, and the like. [66] The burden of avoiding preclusion is on the party who asserts lack of a full and fair opportunity to litigate in the first action. [67]

The problems discussed thus far in this section are matters that could arise within a single legal system. They take on an added dimension because of the special problems that come from having two systems of courts, state and federal. What rules of claim and issue preclusion is a federal court to apply if a state-court judgment is the source of the supposed preclusion? What preclusion rules apply to a federal judgment in a second federal action? What preclusion rules apply to a federal judgment in a state-court action? The recent change in thinking about preclusion generally has been paralleled by an even more recent change in thinking, both scholarly and judicial, on these questions, a change that has been heavily influenced by Professor Degnan's seminal article. [68]

Both the Constitution and a statute enacted so near in time to the Constitution that it has been described as "contemporaneous" [69] are important in approaching these questions. Article IV, § 1, of the Constitution says: "Full Faith and Credit shall be given in each State to the

62. 99 S.Ct. at 651, 439 U.S. at 331.

63. Restatement Second, § 29.

64. Restatement Second, § 28. See text above at notes 39 to 43.

65. Restatement Second, § 29.

66. See 18 Wright, Miller & Cooper, Jurisdiction § 4465.

67. The Blonder–Tongue case so held, 91 S.Ct. at 1443, 402 U.S. at 329.

68. Degnan, Federalized Res Judicata, 1976, 85 Yale L.J. 741.

69. McElmoyle for Use of Bailey v. Cohen, 1839, 13 Pet. 312, 325, 10 L.Ed. 177.

public Acts, Records, and judicial Proceedings of every other State. And the Congress may by general Laws prescribe the Manner in which such Acts, Records and Proceedings shall be proved, and the Effect thereof." The statute, first adopted in 1790 and not significantly altered since then in the matters here relevant,[70] provides that "[t]he records and judicial proceedings of any court" of "any State, Territory, or Possession of the United States" shall have "the same full faith and credit in every court within the United States and its Territories and Possessions as they have by law or usage in the courts of such State, Territory or Possession from which they are taken."[71] It is worth noting that the Constitution speaks only of the effect "in each State" of the "Proceedings of every other State." Probably because it was not clear when the Constitution was drawn that there would be lower federal courts,[72] Article IV, § 1, says nothing about them. By 1790 Congress had created a system of lower federal courts. A lower federal court is surely a "court within the United States" that is required to give full faith and credit, but only the proceedings of courts of a state, territory, or possession are listed as those to which full faith and credit must be given. Thus, the statute speaks to the effect in a federal court of a state-court judgment, but it says nothing about the effect in a state court of a federal court judgment.

To the first question, what rules of claim and issue preclusion is a federal court to apply if a state-court judgment is the source of the supposed preclusion, the basic answer is clear. It is to give the state-court judgment the same full faith and credit as it would have in the courts of the state in which it was entered. This is the command of the 1790 statute, now 28 U.S.C.A. § 1738.[73] The Supreme Court merely stated what had long been well settled when it said in Allen v. McCurry[74] that "though the federal courts may look to the common law or to the policies supporting res judicata and collateral estoppel in assessing the preclusive effect of decisions of other federal courts, Congress has specifically required all federal courts to give preclusive effect to state-court judgments whenever the courts of the State from which the judgments emerged would do so."[75] All that was involved in Allen was issue preclusion, and the Court was careful to limit its decision to that, but two years later, in Kremer v. Chemical Construction Corporation.,[76] the Court was speaking also of claim preclusion when it said: "It has

70. Act of May 26, 1790, c. XI, 1 Stat. 122. The language in the statute on how the first judgment should be proved was added in 1804.

71. 28 U.S.C.A. § 1738.

72. See § 1 above.

73. See generally Shreve, Preclusion and Federal Choice of Law, 1986, 64 Texas L.Rev. 1209.

Arguments that the rule ought be something other than this are made in Burbank, Federal Judgments Law: Sources of Authority and Sources of Rules, 1992, 70 Texas L.Rev. 1551; Braveman & Goldsmith, Rules of Preclusion and Challenges to Official Action: An Essay on Finality, Fairness and Federalism, All Gone Awry, 1988, 39 Syracuse L.Rev. 599; Luneberg, The Opportunity to be Heard and the Doctrines of Preclusion: Federal Limits on State Law, 1986, 31 Vill.L.Rev. 81.

74. 1980, 101 S.Ct. 411, 449 U.S. 90, 66 L.Ed.2d 308.

75. 101 S.Ct. at 415, 449 U.S. at 96.

76. 1982, 102 S.Ct. 1883, 456 U.S. 461, 72 L.Ed.2d 262.

long been established that § 1738 does not allow federal courts to employ their own rules of res judicata in determining the effect of state judgments. Rather, it goes beyond the common law and commands a federal court to accept the rules chosen by the state from which the judgment is taken." [77] Neither issue nor claim preclusion can attach to a judgment unless there was a "full and fair opportunity" to litigate the claim or issue,[78] but in the context of a state-court judgment being relied on in a federal action, this apparently means very little. State rules on what is a "full and fair opportunity," and on any of the other usual exceptions to preclusion,[79] will be applied, but beyond that, as Kremer put it, "where we are bound by the statutory directive of § 1738, state proceedings need no more than satisfy the minimum procedural requirements of the Fourteenth Amendment's Due Process Clause in order to qualify for the full-faith-and-credit guaranteed by federal law." [80]

There is still room to argue that full faith and credit embraces the central doctrines of claim and issue preclusion but that it does not incorporate every minute detail. On this view full faith and credit would be limited to the rules that support the core values of finality, repose, and reliance, as well as some of the rules that facilitate control by the first court over its own procedure, but the statute would not demand obeisance to other aspects of preclusion doctrine that are incidental to the central role of preclusion and that may intrude on substantial interests of later courts.[81] Such arguments have been made more difficult, however, by Allen and Kremer.

It is generally assumed that the command of § 1738 "is to give to the state judgment the same effect—no more and no less—that the state courts would give it." [82] Nevertheless the central purpose of § 1738 seems to be to assure that state judgments are respected elsewhere, and it would not offend this policy to give the judgment greater effect than it would have in the rendering state.[83] A testing case of current importance is where the judgment is from a state that retains the old rule that mutuality is required for issue preclusion. The federal courts, to the extent that they are free to decide these matters independently, have

---

77. 102 S.Ct. at 1898, 456 U.S. at 481–482. See generally 18 Wright, Miller & Cooper, Jurisdiction § 4469.

78. Allen, 101 S.Ct. at 415, 449 U.S. at 95; Kremer, 102 S.Ct. at 1897 n. 22, 456 U.S. at 481 n. 22.

79. Allen, 101 S.Ct. at 415 n. 7, 449 U.S. at 95 n. 7.

80. 102 S.Ct. at 1897–1898, 456 U.S. at 481.

81. 18 Wright, Miller & Cooper, Jurisdiction § 4467, pp. 636–648.

82. Restatement Second, § 86, comm. g; Parsons Steel, Inc. v. First Alabama Bank, 1986, 106 S.Ct. 768, 773, 474 U.S. 518, 525–526, 88 L.Ed.2d 877; and see the same case on remand C.A.11th, 1987, 825 F.2d 1475,

certiorari denied 108 S.Ct. 1015, 484 U.S. 1060, 98 L.Ed.2d 980; Wozniak v. DuPage County, C.A.7th, 1988, 845 F.2d 677, 680.

"As the judgment pleaded had no force or effect in the Tennessee state courts other than as a bar to the identical taxes litigated in the suit, the courts of the United States can accord it no greater efficacy." Union & Planters' Bank of Memphis v. City of Memphis, 1903, 23 S.Ct. 604, 606, 189 U.S. 71, 75, 47 L.Ed. 712.

83. Currie, Res Judicata: The Neglected Defense, 1978, 45 U.Chi.L.Rev. 317, 326–327. This possibility is noted, but no position taken on it, in Restatement Second, § 86 comm. g.

abandoned that rule and now allow both offensive and defensive use of nonmutual preclusion.[84] The few cases in point are divided on whether the federal court could hold a party bound by nonmutual preclusion if it would not be bound in the state from which the judgment comes,[85] but the better view is that the interest of the federal court in this situation in avoiding relitigation is not sufficient to impose preclusion at the expense of the state court's interest in limiting the effect of its own proceedings.[86]

That all states have not yet abandoned mutuality illustrates another aspect of the problem that has given the courts unnecessary difficulty. Suppose that Nebraska has abandoned mutuality but that South Carolina has not. Suppose further that a diversity action is brought in federal court in South Carolina in which one party urges that the other party is precluded by a determination adverse to it in a Nebraska state-court proceeding to which the other was a party. Some courts have supposed that this is an Erie problem and that it must look to see whether a South Carolina state court would apply its own rule denying preclusion or the Nebraska rule allowing preclusion to a Nebraska judgment.[87] This approach is incorrect. Section 1738 requires both the South Carolina state courts and the federal court to give the Nebraska judgment the effect it would have in Nebraska.[88] Erie has no application, since it rests on the Rules of Decision Act[89] and that Act does not apply when an Act of Congress otherwise requires or provides. Section 1738 is such an Act of Congress and it is its command, not that of the Rules of Decision Act, that must be honored.[90]

The American Law Institute completed action on Restatement Second of Judgments in June 1980. It stated the general rule on the effect of a state-court judgment in a subsequent action in federal court as it has been described here, but it noted that claim preclusion does not apply if the federal claim arises under a scheme of federal remedies that contemplates that the federal claim may be asserted notwithstanding the adjudication in state court, and that issue preclusion does not apply if it would be incompatible with a scheme of federal remedies that contemplates that the federal court may make an independent determination of

---

84. See above at notes 53 to 67.

85. Compare Clyde v. Hodge, C.A.3d, 1969, 413 F.2d 48, 50 (denying non-mutual preclusion), with In re TransOcean Tender Offer Securities Litigation, D.C.Ill.1978, 455 F.Supp. 999, 1005–1006 (allowing preclusion.)

86. See 18 Wright, Miller & Cooper, Jurisdiction § 4465, pp. 616–617, and § 4467, pp. 647–648.

87. E.g., Adzigian v. Harron, D.C.Pa. 1969, 297 F.Supp. 1317, 1323; Eisel v. Columbia Packing Co., D.C.Mass.1960, 181 F.Supp. 298, 299; and cases cited Degnan, note 68 above, at 753 n. 49.

88. E.g., Braselton v. Clearfield State Bank, C.A.10th, 1979, 606 F.2d 285, 287 n. 1; Hazen Research, Inc. v. Omega Minerals, Inc., C.A.5th, 1974, 497 F.2d 151, 153 n. 1; J. Aron & Co., Inc. v. Service Transp. Co., D.C.Md.1981, 515 F.Supp. 428, 435–439; 18 Wright, Miller & Cooper, Jurisdiction § 4472 n. 13.

89. 28 U.S.C.A. § 1652. See § 54 above.

90. Degnan, note 68 above, at 750–755; J. Aron & Co., Inc. v. Service Transp. Co., D.C.Md.1981, 515 F.Supp. 428, 438–439.

the issue in question.[91] The Comment said: "Whether a scheme of federal remedies implies an exception to 28 U.S.C. § 1738 in any particular case is a matter of statutory interpretation. However, the intention of Congress to make such an exception should not be readily inferred." [92] Decisions in the next two years showed that the Institute was wise to take so guarded a position on possible exceptions to the general rule.

There had been extensive arguments in the literature in the 1970s on why there should be an exception to issue preclusion or claim preclusion or both in federal civil rights actions under 42 U.S.C.A. § 1983, and some lower courts, though they were distinctly in the minority, had so held.[93] Allen v. McCurry, decided six months after the Institute acted, rejected those arguments. The Court there could find nothing in the language or the legislative history of § 1983 that "in any clear way suggests that Congress intended to repeal or restrict the traditional doctrines of preclusion." [94] A supposed analogy to habeas corpus, where usual notions of preclusion do not apply, was dismissed.[95] Finally, the argument that every person asserting a federal right is entitled to one unencumbered opportunity to litigate that right in a federal district court, regardless of the legal posture in which the federal claim arises, was found unsupported by authority, and to rest on what is "hardly a legal basis at all, * * * a general distrust of the capacity of the state courts to render correct decisions on constitutional issues." [96] The Court made it clear it did not share this distrust.

It was possible after Allen to suppose that even though § 1983 did not create an implied exception to § 1738, perhaps modern, more specific, civil rights statutes do. The provisions against employment discrimination in Title VII of the Civil Rights Act of 1964 [97] were thought to be a likely candidate.[98] The Supreme Court rejected that possibility in Kremer. The Kremer Court relied on Allen for the proposition that an exception to § 1738 will not be recognized unless a later statute contains an express or implied partial repeal.[99] Title VII does not expressly repeal

---

91. Restatement Second, § 86.

92. Restatement Second, § 86, comm. d.

93. The literature and the cases are discussed in 18 Wright, Miller & Cooper, Jurisdiction § 4471.

94. 101 S.Ct. at 416–417, 449 U.S. at 97–98.

95. 101 S.Ct. at 417 n. 12, 449 U.S. at 98 n. 12.

The rule announced in England v. Louisiana State Bd. of Medical Examiners, 1964, 84 S.Ct. 461, 375 U.S. 411, 11 L.Ed.2d 440, that when the parties are required to go to state court for decision of an issue of state law after Pullman-type abstention has been ordered, either party may reserve the federal issue and return to federal court for its determination—see § 52 above—was distinguished as based on the purposes of absten-

tion and as having "no bearing in the present case." 101 S.Ct. at 418 n. 17, 449 U.S. at 101 n. 17.

96. 101 S.Ct. at 420, 449 U.S. at 105.

97. 42 U.S.C.A. § 2000e et seq.

98. See 18 Wright, Miller & Cooper, Jurisdiction § 4471, pp. 721–725.

99. 102 S.Ct. at 1890, 456 U.S. at 468.

The third exception to the Anti–Injunction Act, 28 U.S.C.A. § 2283, allows a federal court to enjoin state-court proceedings "to protect or effectuate its judgment." See § 47 above. This is not an implied repeal of § 1738. Parsons Steel, Inc. v. First Alabama Bank, 1986, 106 S.Ct. 768, 474 U.S. 518, 88 L.Ed.2d 877.

§ 1738 and the Court could not find in Title VII or in the legislative debates giving rise to it the "clear and manifest" intention of Congress that is required before an implied repeal will be found.[100]

There is one area of uncertainty still remaining after Allen and Kremer. This is whether a state-court defendant will be precluded from bringing a federal civil rights action based on constitutional arguments that he could have used as a defense, but did not, in state court. The notion that there may be a third kind of preclusion, defendant preclusion, that bars later litigation of matters that could have been used as a defense but in fact were not litigated is still in embryonic form.[101] If there is not to be preclusion here, however, special care must be taken to avoid later federal actions that will jeopardize the stability of the state judgment in any significant way.[102] The case law is still in a very unsatisfactory condition on the related question of whether anything is "actually litigated," so that issue preclusion will follow, by plea of guilty.[103]

Another issue that was considered by the American Law Institute when it took its guarded position in 1980 on possible exceptions to the usual rules of preclusion was whether an exception is justified because the federal courts have exclusive jurisdiction of the proceeding in which it is argued that a state-court judgment has some preclusive effect. As recently as 1978 three members of the Supreme Court had joined in a dissent in which Justice Brennan, though calling it "an unresolved and difficult issue," had said: "For myself, I confess to serious doubt that it is ever appropriate to accord res judicata effect to a state court determination of a claim over which the federal courts have exclusive jurisdiction; for surely state court determinations should not disable federal courts from ruling de novo on purely legal questions surrounding such federal claims."[104] Such case law as there was on the point has been divided and inconclusive.[105] The Supreme Court addressed, but did not resolve, this issue in 1985 in Marrese v. American Academy of Ortho-

---

100. 102 S.Ct. at 1890–1896, 456 U.S. at 468–478.

101. 18 Wright, Miller & Cooper, Jurisdiction § 4414. See, e.g., Southern Jam, Inc. v. Robinson, C.A.5th, 1982, 675 F.2d 94.

102. Wright, Miller & Cooper, Jurisdiction § 4471, pp. 716–717.

103. 18 Wright, Miller & Cooper, Jurisdiction § 4474, pp. 759–761; Restatement Second, § 85 comm. b; Haring v. Prosise, 1983, 103 S.Ct. 2368, 462 U.S. 306, 76 L.Ed.2d 595. Compare Vestal, The Restatement (Second) of Judgments: A Modest Dissent, 1981, 66 Cornell L.Rev. 464, 478–483, with Hazard, Revisiting the Second Restatement of Judgments: Issue Preclusion and Related Problems, 1981, 66 Cornell L.Rev. 564, 576–584.

104. Will v. Calvert Fire Ins. Co., 1978, 98 S.Ct. 2552, 2563–2564, 437 U.S. 655,

675–676, 57 L.Ed.2d 504. Justices Marshall and Powell joined in the dissent. Chief Justice Burger joined the dissent generally, but wrote separately to note that he thought it unnecessary to determine how preclusion applies in cases of exclusive jurisdiction.

105. See 18 Wright, Miller & Cooper, Jurisdiction § 4470; House, Preclusion by State Judgment in Cases Involving Exclusive Jurisdiction, 1986, 13 Western St. U.L.Rev. 435; Comment, Exclusive Federal Court Jurisdiction and State Judgment Finality—The Dilemma Facing the Federal Courts, 1980, 10 Seton Hall L.Rev. 848; Note, The Collateral Estoppel Effects of Prior State Court Findings in Cases Within Exclusive Federal Jurisdiction, 1978, 91 Harv.L.Rev. 1281.

paedic Surgeons.[106] It held that a federal court must look first to state preclusion law. If it says that claim or issue preclusion does not apply to foreclose a claim beyond the jurisdiction of the rendering court, a state judgment would not bar federal relitigation of matters of which the federal courts have exclusive jurisdiction.[107] "[O]nly if state law indicates that litigation of a particular claim or issue should be barred in the subsequent federal proceeding" will it be necessary to decide whether a grant of exclusive jurisdiction to the federal courts is an implied partial repeal of § 1738.[108]

The second of the special problems of preclusion that arise from having two systems of courts was what preclusion rules apply to a federal judgment in a second federal action. The third asked what rules apply to a federal judgment in a state-court action. They may usefully be considered together, since it turns out that there is a single answer to both questions, although the means of reaching that answer differ. Restatement Second of Judgments declares the answer as a matter of black-letter law: "Federal law determines the effects under the rules of res judicata of a judgment of a federal court." [109]

If the judgment was in federal court, and the second action is also in federal court, full faith and credit does not apply but res judicata does.[110] It has been less clear what gives a federal judgment preclusive effect if the second action is in state court. The suggestion that state courts should be free to disregard the judgments of federal courts is so unthinkable that the rule rejecting any such suggestion has been stated in an unbroken line of cases that do not offer any clear judicial thought or explanation. Many of the cases talk as if § 1738 requires state courts to honor federal judgments, but as was noted at the outset of this discussion, the face of the statute itself makes this conclusion preposterous. Perhaps what these cases are saying is that this is something that Congress would have intended when it enacted § 1738 if only it had thought about it.[111]

There is a better explanation for why state courts are bound. Article III limits the federal judicial power to cases and controversies. To decide a case or controversy implies some binding effect. Proceedings that do not have at least the potential effect of precluding later relitigation of the same claims and issues would constitute something other than the exercise of the judicial power. Once it is accepted that

---

106. 1985, 105 S.Ct. 1327, 470 U.S. 373, 84 L.Ed.2d 274. See Shreve, note 73 above.

107. 105 S.Ct. at 1332–1333, 470 U.S. at 381–382. On remand in Marrese it was held that the Illinois courts would deny claim preclusion because the federal claim could not be joined with the state claims in state court. "Our task is an exercise in extrapolation because, of course, the Illinois courts never address issues pertaining to exclusively federal lawsuits." D.C.Ill.1986, 628 F.Supp. 918.

108. 105 S.Ct. at 1333, 470 U.S. at 383.

109. Restatement Second, § 87.

110. Baldwin v. Iowa State Traveling Men's Assn., 1931, 51 S.Ct. 517, 517, 283 U.S. 522, 524, 75 L.Ed. 1244. See 18 Wright, Miller & Cooper, Jurisdiction § 4466.

111. See 18 Wright, Miller & Cooper, Jurisdiction § 4468, pp. 648–654.

Article III and its implementing legislation have created courts with the power to issue judgments that will have preclusive effects in other litigation, the Supremacy Clause of Article VI mandates that those preclusive effects are binding on state courts.[112]

The conclusion that both federal and state courts are obliged to honor the preclusive effects of federal-court judgments does not automatically identify the body of rules that measure those effects. The early cases often said that a federal-court judgment had the same effect as would judgments of the state in which the federal court was sitting in a like case and under similar circumstances.[113] These cases were decided at a time when the Conformity Act required federal courts to conform to state procedure.[114] Language from those older cases has been repeated by modern courts without taking into account the facts that the Conformity Act has long since been repealed and federal courts are now governed by their own independent system of procedure. Thus, the scope of the preclusive effect to be given to a judgment today should be recognized as a question of federal law, on which the federal courts are free to adopt their own doctrines.[115]

This is now well recognized if the federal judgment has decided some question of federal law.[116] There are still many cases that say that when the federal court is exercising its diversity jurisdiction, the law of the state where it sits determines the preclusive effect of its judgment.[117] This is wrong on two counts. If there is to be a distinction of this kind, it should have nothing to do with the jurisdictional basis of the suit, but with whether the particular issue is one on which state law or federal law provides the rule for decision.[118] Those decisions are more fundamentally wrong because there ought not be such a distinction. As Judge Medina wrote in a well-known decision: "One of the strongest policies a court can have is that of determining the scope of its own judgments. * * * It would be destructive of the basic principles of the Federal Rules of Civil Procedure to say that the effect of a judgment of a federal court was governed by the law of the state where the court sits simply because the source of federal jurisdiction is diversity. * * * [W]e think it would be strange doctrine to allow a state to nullify the judgments of federal courts constitutionally established and given power also to enforce state

112. Degnan, note 68 above, at 742–749, 768–769; 18 Wright, Miller & Cooper, Jurisdiction § 4468, pp. 649–650. There is an illuminating discussion of the point in Watkins v. Resorts Intl. Hotel & Casino, Inc., 1991, 591 A.2d 592, 598–599, 124 N.J. 398, 410–412.

113. Dupasseur v. Rochereau, 1874, 21 Wall. 130, 135, 22 L.Ed. 588; and cases cited 18 Wright, Miller & Cooper, Jurisdiction § 4468 n. 24.

114. See § 61 above.

115. Degnan, note 68 above, at 760–773.

116. Blonder–Tongue Laboratories, Inc. v. University of Illinois Foundation, 1971, 91 S.Ct. 1434, 1440 n. 12, 402 U.S. 313, 324 n. 12, 28 L.Ed.2d 788; and cases cited 18 Wright, Miller & Cooper, Jurisdiction § 4466 nn. 8, 9.

117. Bates v. Union Oil Co., C.A.9th, 1991, 944 F.2d 647, 649, certiorari denied 112 S.Ct. 1761, ___ U.S. ___, 118 L.Ed.2d 424; Lane v. Sullivan, C.A.8th, 1990, 900 F.2d 1247, 1249–1250, certiorari denied 111 S.Ct. 134, 498 U.S. 847, 112 L.Ed.2d 101; and cases cited 18 Wright, Miller & Cooper, Jurisdiction § 4472 n. 27.

118. 18 Wright, Miller & Cooper, Jurisdiction § 4466, pp. 623–624.

created rights. The Erie doctrine * * * is not applicable here * * *."[119] Many cases have now taken the view that state law cannot control the preclusive effects of a federal-court judgment, regardless of the nature of the case the federal court was deciding.[120]

To say this is not to suggest that federal courts are to ignore important state interests or that the preclusive effect of federal judgments is monolithic. It has become very common in other areas to hold that a particular subject matter is governed by federal law, but that a uniform national rule is not necessary and state law is to be looked to so long as it is not discriminatory or in conflict with federal statutes.[121] Some aspects of preclusion reflect primarily procedural policies and go to the essence of the judicial function. These aspects of preclusion should be governed by a single uniform federal rule. Other aspects of preclusion reflect policies that seem more distinctively substantive. It was pointed out earlier that many of the rules on when nonparties are bound turn on substantive legal relationships stemming from property law and commercial law.[122] If state law governs the substantive relationship, then it would be appropriate to adopt the law of the state as the federal rule for determining the effect of the judgment on others. This is the position taken in Restatement Second of Judgments.[123] The implications of this will have to be worked out as the courts become more familiar with the notion that federal law governs the effect of federal judgments.

---

119. Kern v. Hettinger, C.A.2d, 1962, 303 F.2d 333, 340. See also Aerojet–General Corp. v. Askew, C.A.5th, 1975, 511 F.2d 710, 717, certiorari denied 96 S.Ct. 210, 423 U.S. 908, 46 L.Ed.2d 137.

120. See cases cited 18 Wright, Miller & Cooper, Jurisdiction § 4472 nn. 32, 36, 42.

121. See § 60 above.

122. See above at note 50.

123. Restatement Second, § 87, comm. b. See also 18 Wright, Miller & Cooper, Jurisdiction § 4472, pp. 733–741.

Chapter 11

THE APPELLATE JURISDICTION OF THE COURTS OF APPEALS

Analysis

§ 101. Review of Final Decisions [1]

The historic policy of the federal courts has been that appeal will lie only from a final decision.[2] This policy was first declared in the Judiciary Act of 1789, and is carried forward today in the provision of the Judicial Code giving the courts of appeals "jurisdiction of appeals from all final decisions of the district courts * * *."[3] Though there are varying judgments about the wisdom of this policy,[4] in general it has

---

§ 101

1. 15A Wright, Miller & Cooper, Jurisdiction 2d §§ 3905–3914.14 and 15B id. §§ 3914.15–3917; Tigar, Federal Appeals: Jurisdiction and Practice, 2d ed. 1993; Redish, The Pragmatic Approach to Appealability in the Federal Courts, 1975, 75 Col. L.Rev. 89; Note, Toward a More Rational Final Judgment Rule: A Proposal to Amend 28 U.S.C. § 1292, 1979, 67 Geo.L.J. 1025. There is also an important two-part Symposium on Civil Appellate Jurisdiction in 47 Law & Contemp.Probs., Spring 1984 and Summer 1984.

2. Cobbledick v. U.S., 1940, 60 S.Ct. 540, 541, 309 U.S. 323, 324, 84 L.Ed. 783; Andrews v. U.S., 1963, 83 S.Ct. 1236, 1240, 373 U.S. 334, 340, 10 L.Ed.2d 383. See 15A Wright, Miller & Cooper, Jurisdiction 2d § 3906.

3. 28 U.S.C.A. § 1291.

But if a direct appeal will lie to the Supreme Court—see § 105 below—the courts

of appeals lack jurisdiction to hear an appeal. Donovan v. Richland County Assn. for Retarded Citizens, 1982, 102 S.Ct. 713, 454 U.S. 389, 70 L.Ed.2d 570.

Section 1291 is not limited to civil actions and includes appeals by defendants from final decisions in criminal cases. See 15B Wright, Miller & Cooper, Jurisdiction 2d § 3918–3918.10. The government may also appeal to the courts of appeals in criminal cases. It may appeal from interlocutory orders suppressing or excluding evidence, and also from any order dismissing an indictment or information "as to any one or more counts, except that no appeal shall lie where the double jeopardy clause of the United States Constitution prohibits further prosecution." 18 U.S.C.A. § 3731. See 15B Wright, Miller & Cooper, Jurisdiction 2d § 3919–3919.10.

4. See 15A Wright, Miller & Cooper, Jurisdiction 2d § 3907; Redish, note 1 above; Crick, The Final Judgment as a Basis for Appeal, 1932, 41 Yale L.J. 539.

seemed to be sound. Interlocutory appeals add to the delay of litigation. This delay can be justified only if it is outweighed by the advantage of settling prior to final decision an important issue in the case. In most cases such an advantage is not present; the interlocutory issue that seems crucial at the time may fade into insignificance as the case progresses, and in any event the district courts are right in their resolution of most such issues.

Nevertheless, it is not feasible to bar all appeals save from final decisions. In some cases important rights of a party will be irremediably destroyed if he or she is unable to secure prompt review, and in others an issue is so readily separable from the balance of the case that there is no advantage in postponing review of that issue, and thus holding in abeyance the trial court's resolution of it, until the remainder of the case has been decided. For these reasons there are certain statutory provisions, discussed in the next section, permitting review of interlocutory orders, and there are a variety of court-made rules by which particular orders are treated as "final" and appealable as such.

Indeed even if it were to be agreed that only "final" orders might be reviewed, there would be no sure test for what is meant by "final." It is said that "a 'final decision' generally is one which ends the litigation on the merits and leaves nothing for the court to do but execute the judgment." [5] It is hardly clear from such a definition that an order in a condemnation case decreeing title in the United States but leaving open the question of compensation is not "final" and not appealable,[6] while an order in an antitrust case finding a violation of the statutes and ordering divestiture, though leaving open the question of how such divestiture would be accomplished, is "final" and thus appealable.[7] It is not surprising that the Court should have said long ago that the cases on finality "are not altogether harmonious",[8] nor that more than eighty years later it should have said: "No verbal formula yet devised can explain prior finality decisions with unerring accuracy or provide an utterly reliable guide for the future." [9] The source of the difficulty is that the Court, torn between the usual wisdom of the final-judgment

---

In Firestone Tire & Rubber Co. v. Risjord, 1981, 101 S.Ct. 669, 673, 449 U.S. 368, 374, 66 L.Ed.2d 571, the Court said that the finality requirement preserves the independence and the special role of the district judge, avoids the potential harassment and cost of a succession of separate appeals, and "serves the important purpose of promoting efficient judicial administration." See also Stringfellow v. Concerned Neighbors in Action, 1987, 107 S.Ct. 1177, 1184, 480 U.S. 370, 380, 94 L.Ed.2d 389.

5. Catlin v. U.S., 1945, 65 S.Ct. 631, 633, 324 U.S. 229, 233, 89 L.Ed. 911. This formulation has been much quoted. E.g., Lauro Lines S.R.L. v. Chasser, 1989, 109 S.Ct. 1976, 1978, 490 U.S. 495, 497, 104 L.Ed.2d 548.

6. Catlin v. U.S., 1945, 65 S.Ct. 631, 324 U.S. 229, 89 L.Ed. 911; cf. The Palmyra, 1825, 10 Wheat. 502, 6 L.Ed. 375.

7. Brown Shoe Co. v. U.S., 1962, 82 S.Ct. 1502, 370 U.S. 294, 8 L.Ed.2d 510, noted 1962, 42 B.U.L.Rev. 559.

8. McGourkey v. Toledo & O. Central R. Co., 1892, 13 S.Ct. 170, 172, 146 U.S. 536, 545, 36 L.Ed. 1079.

9. Eisen v. Carlisle & Jacquelin, 1974, 94 S.Ct. 2140, 2149, 417 U.S. 156, 170, 40 L.Ed.2d 732. See also Dickinson v. Petroleum Conversion Corp., 1950, 70 S.Ct. 322, 338 U.S. 507, 508, 94 L.Ed. 299.

rule and its inappropriateness in certain unusual situations, has followed "a pragmatic approach to the question of finality." [10]   In general this has worked out well in practice, whatever theoretical problems it may raise, though it is hard not to feel sympathy for the litigant that appeals from what is styled "Final Decree," only to learn that a decree a year earlier, on its face only a partial disposition of the case, was final for that particular litigant, and thus its later appeal was untimely.[11]   The saving grace of the imprecise rule of finality is that in almost all situations it is entirely clear, either from the nature of the order or from a crystallized body of decisions, that a particular order is or is not final.[12]   No one would doubt that a judgment awarding money damages to plaintiff on the only claim involved in the case is a final judgment.   No one would doubt that an order denying a motion to dismiss under Rule 12(b)(6) is interlocutory and not final.[13]   The case in which there is real doubt about the finality of an order is extremely rare, although recent cases broadening the concept of finality have created new uncertainties.   A 1990 statute amended the general rulemaking statute to provide that rules promulgated by the Supreme Court "may define when a ruling of a district court is final for the purposes of appeal" under § 1291.[14]   No rules of this kind have yet been adopted.

Rule 54(b) contributes clarity in one recurring situation that, absent the rule, would be either confusing, or unworkable, or both.   Before the adoption of the federal rules, a judgment was thought appealable only if it made final disposition with regard to all the parties and all the claims involved in the suit.[15]   The rules have liberalized joinder of claims and of parties, and there now are cases in which it is desirable to put into effect, or to permit appeal from, an order that disposes of some of the claims or parties, without waiting for decision of the remainder of the case.   If this is to be done, it must be clear when the decision is final on

---

10. Brown Shoe Co. v. U.S., 1962, 82 S.Ct. 1502, 1513, 370 U.S. 294, 306, 8 L.Ed.2d 510.   See Freeman v. Califano, C.A.5th, 1978, 574 F.2d 264, 266–267; Redish, note 1 above.

11. Dickinson v. Petroleum Conversion Corp., 1950, 70 S.Ct. 322, 338 U.S. 507, 94 L.Ed. 299.   Later amendments to Rule 54(b) will prevent recurrence of this particular problem, but others like it will surely arise.   E.g., Howze v. Arrow Transp. Co., C.A.5th, 1960, 280 F.2d 403, certiorari denied 81 S.Ct. 285, 364 U.S. 920, 5 L.Ed.2d 260, criticized 1961, 35 Tul.L.Rev. 444.

12. See Note, Appealability in the Federal Courts, 1961, 75 Harv.L.Rev. 351, 354.

But see the dissent of Chief Judge Gibbons in Beckwith Machinery Co. v. Travelers Indem. Co., C.A.3d, 1987, 815 F.2d 286, 292–295.   He argues that rules of appellate jurisdiction should be clear, provide workable results, and avoid frequent and protracted dispute over appealability.   "The monstrous edifice which the federal judicia-

ry has erected as a temple to that great white whale, the final judgment rule, satisfies none of these criteria."

13. See Catlin v. U.S., 1945, 65 S.Ct. 631, 635, 324 U.S. 229, 236, 89 L.Ed. 911; and cases cited 15A Wright, Miller & Cooper, Jurisdiction 2d § 3914.6 n. 4.

14. 28 U.S.C.A. § 2072(c), as amended by Act of Dec. 1, 1990, Pub.L. 101–650, 104 Stat. 5115.

This amendment—like an amendment of 28 U.S.C.A. § 1292(e) adopted two years later—came from a recommendation of the Federal Courts Study Committee, April 2, 1990, pp. 95–96.   These statutes are criticized in Martineau, Defining Finality and Appealability by Court Rule: Right Problem, Wrong Solution, 1993, 54 U.Pitt.L.Rev. 717, and defended in a Reply by Rowe, 1993, 54 U.Pitt.L.Rev. 795.

15. Collins v. Miller, 1920, 40 S.Ct. 347, 252 U.S. 364, 64 L.Ed. 616.

the partial disposition, in order that an unwary litigant will not let the time for appeal go by without action. This is accomplished by Rule 54(b), though it has taken two amendments of the rule to perfect it. Under the rule as it now stands, when more than one claim for relief is presented in an action, or when multiple parties are involved, the court may direct the entry of judgment as to one or more but fewer than all of the claims or parties only upon (1) an express determination that there is no just reason for delay, and (2) an express direction for the entry of judgment. A partial disposition of the case is not final in the absence of such a determination and direction by the court.[16]

The rule lends a welcome certainty to the appellate procedure. In cases within the scope of the rule, a litigant need not appeal an interlocutory order that has not been certified as required by Rule 54(b) to guard against the possibility that it may be held to have been a final decision. When the court does make the requisite certificate, the litigant is put on notice that it is time to take the appeal.

A Rule 54(b) certificate is not conclusive on the finality of the order below. If an order is in fact interlocutory, and does not actually make a final disposition of some of the claims or as to some of the parties, appeal from it will be dismissed even though the trial court has certified the order as final.[17] Further, the certificate of the trial judge does not conclude the appellate court on whether there were actually multiple claims presented, and thus on whether Rule 54(b) has any application. If the complaint presents only variants of a single claim, appeal cannot be taken from an order dealing with some of these variants, even though the order has been duly certified.[18] The determination of whether there are multiple claims rests on whether the underlying factual bases for recovery state a number of different claims, not mutually exclusive, that could have been separately enforced.[19]

The appellate court is not limited to determining whether the order actually falls within Rule 54(b). It may also consider whether the trial court abused its discretion in finding that there was no just reason for delay. On this point, however, the discretionary judgment of the trial court must be given substantial deference and the reviewing court may disturb the trial court's assessment of the equities only if it can say that the judge's conclusion was clearly unreasonable.[20]

16. 10 Wright, Miller & Kane, Civil 2d § 2654.

17. E.g., Monument Management Ltd. Partnership I v. City of Pearl, C.A.5th, 1992, 952 F.2d 883; Haverhill Gazette Co. v. Union Leader Corp., C.A.1st, 1964, 333 F.2d 798, certiorari denied 85 S.Ct. 329, 379 U.S. 931, 13 L.Ed.2d 343; and cases cited 10 Wright, Miller & Kane, Civil 2d § 2655 n. 6.

18. Liberty Mut. Ins. Co. v. Wetzel, 1976, 96 S.Ct. 1202, 424 U.S. 737, 47

L.Ed.2d 435; Spiegel v. Trustees of Tufts College, C.A.1st, 1988, 843 F.2d 38.

19. This test was first enunciated in Rieser v. Baltimore & O. R. Co., C.A.2d, 1955, 224 F.2d 198, 199, affirmed 228 F.2d 563, certiorari denied 1956, 76 S.Ct. 651, 350 U.S. 1006, 100 L.Ed. 868, and has since been followed in many cases. See 10 Wright, Miller & Kane, Civil 2d § 2657.

20. Curtiss–Wright Corp. v. General Elec. Co., 1980, 100 S.Ct. 1460, 446 U.S. 1, 64 L.Ed.2d 1. In that case the Court rejected, as neither workable nor entirely reliable

If a case falls within Rule 54(b), an appeal must be dismissed if the trial court has not made the requisite certificate.[21] If the case is not within Rule 54(b), as where the court has ordered entry of judgment on all the claims and parties involved in the action, or there has been judgment on the only claim in a case not involving multiple parties, the judgment is appealable without such a certificate.[22]

For many years there was controversy about the validity of Rule 54(b). No one doubted the validity of the "negative aspect" of the rule, by which the refusal to certify barred appeal from orders which would have been appealable before the adoption of the rule. The controversy centered about the other aspect of the rule, by which the court, through issuance of its certificate, made its order final and appealable though that order might not have been regarded as a final decision before the rules.[23] It was thought by some that this was an impermissible extension by rule of the jurisdiction of the appellate courts. This argument was rejected by the Supreme Court, which held that the rule scrupulously recognizes the statutory requirement of a "final decision" as a basic requirement for an appeal, and merely provides a practical means of permitting an appeal to be taken from one or more final decisions on individual claims without waiting for final decisions to be rendered on all the claims in the case.[24] Thus, the validity of the rule is now clearly settled.

The Supreme Court has long recognized, though it defined only in 1949, a small class of orders, now referred to as "collateral orders," which are offshoots from the principal litigation in which they are issued, and which are immediately appealable, as "final decisions," without regard to the posture of the principal litigation. The leading case is Cohen v. Beneficial Industrial Loan Corporation.[25] That case was a stockholders' suit in which the defendant corporation, pursuant to

---

as a benchmark for appellate review, expressions that had appeared in some lower court decisions that Rule 54(b) is to be reserved for "the infrequent harsh case." 100 S.Ct. at 1466, 446 U.S. at 9. See 10 Wright, Miller & Kane, Civil 2d § 2659; Hogan v. Consolidated Rail Corp., C.A.2d, 1992, 961 F.2d 1021.

21. See Borne v. A & P Boat Rentals No. 4, Inc., C.A.5th, 1985, 755 F.2d 1131; and cases cited 10 Wright, Miller & Kane, Civil 2d § 2660 nn. 5, 6. But cf. Riggle v. California, C.A.9th, 1978, 577 F.2d 579, 581 n. A; Browning Debenture Holders' Committee v. DASA Corp., C.A.2d, 1975, 524 F.2d 811, 814 n. 4.

22. Shafer v. Children's Hosp. Soc'y of Los Angeles, C.A.D.C.1959, 265 F.2d 107; General Time Corp. v. Padua Alarm Systems, C.A.2d, 1952, 199 F.2d 351, certiorari denied 73 S.Ct. 728, 345 U.S. 917, 97 L.Ed. 1351.

23. Compare the several opinions in Pabellon v. Grace Line, C.A.2d, 1951, 191 F.2d 169, certiorari denied 72 S.Ct. 201, 342 U.S. 893, 96 L.Ed. 669, and Bendix Aviation Corp. v. Glass, C.A.3d, 1952, 195 F.2d 267.

24. Sears, Roebuck & Co. v. Mackey, 1956, 76 S.Ct. 895, 899–901, 351 U.S. 427, 435–438, 100 L.Ed. 1297; 10 Wright, Miller & Kane, Civil 2d § 2653.

25. 1949, 69 S.Ct. 1221, 337 U.S. 541, 93 L.Ed. 1528. See 15A Wright, Miller & Cooper, Jurisdiction 2d § 3911. The case was argued by Philip B. Kurland, later a professor at the University of Chicago Law School, for Cohen, and by John M. Harlan, later a justice of the United States Supreme Court, for Beneficial Loan.

If the "collateral orders" doctrine is applicable, the better view is that a certificate under Rule 54(b) is not required. 10 Wright, Miller & Kane, Civil 2d § 2658.4, pp. 89–95.

New Jersey law, moved to require plaintiff to post security for defendant's costs, including attorney's fees, and appealed from denial of the motion. The Supreme Court held unanimously that the order denying the motion was appealable, saying that it fell within "that small class which finally determine claims of right separable from, and collateral to, rights asserted in the action, too important to be denied review and too independent of the cause itself to require that appellate consideration be deferred until the whole case is adjudicated. * * * We hold this order appealable because it is a final disposition of a claimed right which is not an ingredient of the cause of action and does not require consideration with it."[26] The Court emphasized also that the new doctrine does not permit appeal of orders that are "tentative, informal or incomplete,"[27] and that it was applicable only if the issue raised by appeal "presents a serious and unsettled question."[28]

The Court reviewed the "collateral order" doctrine again in 1978 in Coopers & Lybrand v. Livesay.[29] The holding there was that a determination that an action may not go forward as a class action is not appealable as a matter of right, either under the "collateral order" doctrine or any other. "To come within the 'small class' of decisions excepted from the final-judgment rule by Cohen, the order must conclusively determine the disputed question, resolve an important issue completely separate from the merits of the action, and be effectively unreviewable on appeal from a final judgment."[30] An order decertifying a previously certified class action met none of those requirements. It is inherently nonfinal and subject to revision before final judgment, it is inherently enmeshed in the facts of the individual case, and it is subject to effective review after final judgment either at the behest of the named plaintiff or of intervening class members.

The Coopers & Lybrand formulation was repeated by the Court three years later, in the course of holding that an order refusing to disqualify opposing counsel in a civil case, is not appealable.[31] The Court thought that the order before it met the first part of the test, since it conclusively determined the question, and it assumed that this is an important issue separate from the merits, but it held that the order failed the third part of the Coopers & Lybrand test, since the order was

---

26. 69 S.Ct. at 1225–1226, 337 U.S. at 546–547.

27. 69 S.Ct. at 1225, 337 U.S. at 546.

28. 69 S.Ct. at 1226, 337 U.S. at 547.

29. 1978, 98 S.Ct. 2454, 437 U.S. 463, 57 L.Ed.2d 351.

30. 98 S.Ct. at 2458, 437 U.S. at 468.

The general requirements for a "collateral order" appeal have been neatly summarized as "separability, finality, urgency, and importance." U.S. v. Alcon Labs., C.A.1st, 1981, 636 F.2d 876, 884, certiorari denied 101 S.Ct. 3005, 451 U.S. 1017, 69 L.Ed.2d 388.

It is not yet resolved whether the "collateral order" doctrine requires an important and unsettled question of controlling law rather than a mere matter of trial-court discretion. See Justice Scalia's concurring opinion in Gulfstream Aerospace Corp. v. Mayacamas Corp., 1988, 108 S.Ct. 1133, 1144–1145, 485 U.S. 271, 290–291, 99 L.Ed.2d 296; 15A Wright, Miller & Cooper, Jurisdiction 2d § 3911.5.

31. Firestone Tire & Rubber Co. v. Risjord, 1981, 101 S.Ct. 669, 674, 449 U.S. 368, 375, 66 L.Ed.2d 571.

one that could be effectively reviewed after a final judgment. In later cases it held that the grant of disqualification is not appealable as a "collateral order." The disqualification order is not separable from the merits if actual prejudice must be shown, and it can be reviewed effectively on appeal from a final judgment if there is no need to show prejudice.[32]

The three-part test of Coopers & Lybrand leads to a different result if the lower court has denied a claim of immunity from suit. An immunity from suit, unlike a mere defense to liability, is effectively lost if a case is erroneously permitted to go to trial, and this loss cannot be remedied on appeal from a final judgment.[33]

There had been a tendency to expand the "collateral order" doctrine, but more recently the courts have been emphasizing the need to use the doctrine sparingly, lest an expanded "collateral order" doctrine swallow the basic finality requirement and the courts become swamped with appeals.[34] Recent Supreme Court decisions reinforce this stricter approach.[35]

Another, though related, court-made exception to the usual requirement of finality, although not stated as such, is that a judgment directing immediate delivery of physical property is appealable, if necessary in order to avoid irreparable injury, even though the court has also ordered an accounting that has not yet taken place.[36] Civil-contempt orders against a person not a party to the case are considered final and

32. Flanagan v. U.S., 1984, 104 S.Ct. 1051, 465 U.S. 259, 79 L.Ed.2d 288 (criminal case); Richardson–Merrell, Inc. v. Koller, 1985, 105 S.Ct. 2757, 472 U.S. 424, 86 L.Ed.2d 340 (civil action). In a criminal case there can of course be no appeal if defendant is acquitted, but in Flanagan the Court reasoned that the defendant's interests are sufficiently protected by the acquittal and the interests of disqualified counsel are not important enough to justify immediate appeal.

33. Puerto Rico Aqueduct & Sewer Authority v. Metcalf & Eddy, 1993, 113 S.Ct. 684, ___ U.S. ___, 121 L.Ed.2d 605 (Eleventh Amendment immunity); Mitchell v. Forsyth, 1985, 105 S.Ct. 2806, 472 U.S. 511, 86 L.Ed.2d 411 (qualified official immunity); Nixon v. Fitzgerald, 1982, 102 S.Ct. 2690, 457 U.S. 731, 73 L.Ed.2d 349 (absolute official immunity).

34. E.g., Rolo v. General Development Corp., C.A.3d, 1991, 949 F.2d 695, 700; Germain v. Connecticut Nat. Bank, C.A.2d, 1991, 930 F.2d 1038, 1040; Dardar v. Lafourche Realty Co., C.A.5th, 1988, 849 F.2d 955, 958–959; Borden Co. v. Sylk, C.A.3d, 1969, 410 F.2d 843, 845–846. See 15A Wright, Miller & Cooper, Jurisdiction 2d § 3911–3911.5.

The circuits are divided on whether an appeal of a "collateral order" carries with it power to address additional orders of the trial court that would not themselves qualify for immediate review. See Note, The Proper Scope of Pendent Appellate Jurisdiction in the Collateral Order Context, 1990, 100 Yale L.J. 511; 16 Wright, Miller & Cooper, Jurisdiction § 3937.

35. Gulfstream Aerospace Corp. v. Mayacamas Corp., 1988, 108 S.Ct. 1133, 485 U.S. 271, 99 L.Ed.2d 296 (denial of a stay on Colorado River grounds not appealable since it is not a conclusive determination of that question); Van Cauwenberghe v. Biard, 1988, 108 S.Ct. 1945, 486 U.S. 517, 100 L.Ed.2d 517 (denial of a claim that an extradited person is immune from civil process is effectively reviewable on appeal from a final judgment and refusal to dismiss on the ground of forum non conveniens is not completely separate from the merits).

36. Forgay v. Conrad, 1848, 6 How. 201, 12 L.Ed. 404; Radio Station WOW v. Johnson, 1945, 65 S.Ct. 1475, 1478–1480, 326 U.S. 120, 124–127; 89 L.Ed. 2092; King Instrument Corp. v. Otari Corp., C.A.Fed. 1987, 814 F.2d 1560, 1562–1563; Kasishke v. Baker, C.C.A.10th, 1944, 144 F.2d 384; 15A Wright, Miller & Cooper, Jurisdiction 2d § 3910.

appealable, since that person could not appeal a final judgment in the case.[37] Criminal-contempt orders also are regarded as severable from the main action and appealable before final judgment in that action.[38]

Decisions granting or denying class-action status have caused pressure for immediate review that had led some courts to accept a "death knell" doctrine as a new expansion of the requirement of finality. In an important early case the Second Circuit held that appeal would lie from an order denying class-action status in a case in which the individual plaintiff's claim was only for $70 and if the action were not permitted to proceed on a class basis it surely would not proceed at all. "Where the effect of a district court's order, if not reviewed, is the death knell of the action, review should be allowed."[39] This doctrine had been accepted in some circuits though rejected in others. A few cases had even reasoned by analogy to the "death knell" doctrine to hold that an order granting class action status was appealable, even though such an order plainly does not bring an action to an end.[40]

It was pointed out earlier that in the Coopers & Lybrand case the Court held that refusal to allow a suit to be maintained as a class action could not be appealed as a "collateral order." In that same case the Court sounded the death knell for the "death knell" doctrine. "A threshold inquiry of this kind," it said, "may, it is true, identify some orders that would truly end the litigation prior to final judgment; allowing an immediate appeal from those orders may enhance the quality of justice afforded a few litigants. But this incremental benefit is outweighed by the impact of such an individualized jurisdictional inquiry on the judicial system's overall capacity to administer justice."[41] It held, therefore, that the fact that an interlocutory order may induce a party to abandon its claim before final judgment is not a sufficient reason for considering it a "final decision" within the meaning of the statute.[42] If there is to be immediate review of a class-certification

37. U.S. Catholic Conference v. Abortion Rights Mobilization, Inc., 1988, 108 S.Ct. 2268, 2271, 487 U.S. 72, 76, 101 L.Ed.2d 69; Lamb v. Cramer, 1932, 52 S.Ct. 315, 285 U.S. 217, 76 L.Ed. 715.

The rule is otherwise if a party is found in civil contempt. McCrone v. U.S., 1939, 59 S.Ct. 685, 307 U.S. 61, 83 L.Ed. 1108. For criticism of this view, see 15B Wright, Miller & Cooper, Jurisdiction 2d § 3917.

38. Bray v. U.S., 1975, 96 S.Ct. 307, 423 U.S. 73, 46 L.Ed.2d 215; Bessette v. W.B. Conkey Co., 1904, 24 S.Ct. 665, 194 U.S. 324, 48 L.Ed. 997. This is true even if it is a party who is found guilty of criminal contempt. Marrese v. American Academy of Orthopaedic Surgeons, 1985, 105 S.Ct. 1327, 1331, 470 U.S. 373, 379, 84 L.Ed.2d 274.

On the distinction between civil contempt and criminal contempt, see 3 Wright Criminal 2d § 704.

39. Eisen v. Carlisle & Jacquelin, C.A.2d, 1966, 370 F.2d 119, 120–121, certiorari denied 87 S.Ct. 1487, 386 U.S. 1035, 18 L.Ed.2d 598.

40. 15A Wright, Miller & Cooper, Jurisdiction 2d § 3912.

41. 98 S.Ct. at 2460, 437 U.S. at 473.

42. 98 S.Ct. at 2462, 437 U.S. at 477.

On the same day as the Coopers & Lybrand decision, the Court also held that denial of class-action status cannot be appealed under 28 U.S.C.A. § 1292(a)(1) on the theory that the refusal to allow class status restricted the permanent injunctive relief that might ultimately be awarded. Gardner v. Westinghouse Broadcasting Co., 1978, 98 S.Ct. 2451, 437 U.S. 478, 57 L.Ed.2d 364.

ruling, it must be by allowance of an interlocutory appeal under 28 U.S.C.A. § 1292(b).[43] It is true that this requires a certificate from the trial judge but few district judges are likely to be so eager to suffer the burdens of class-action litigation that they will deny certification of orders that offer a genuine basis for a plausible appeal.[44]

Generalizing from the various situations in which the courts have treated as "final" an order that is not a complete disposition of a case, the Fifth Circuit once said that "an order, otherwise nonappealable, determining substantial rights of the parties which will be irreparably lost if review is delayed until final judgment may be appealed immediately under section 1291."[45] Though the Supreme Court has never said as much in terms, its decisions do point in such a direction. In recent years the Court has relaxed considerably the requirement of finality. Although the most striking of these decisions have come in considering what is a "final judgment" for purposes of review in the Supreme Court of a state-court decision,[46] and it should be plain that decisions in one area cannot be binding precedent in the other,[47] the Court often acts as if a "final judgment" is the same thing in all contexts and treats precedents under the various statutes that use those words as interchangeable.[48]

The sharpest departure from traditional notions of finality for review by a court of appeals of a district court decision came in Gillespie

---

43. See § 102 below.

"[O]ur ruling in Livesay was not intended to preclude motions under 28 U.S.C. § 1292(b) seeking discretionary interlocutory appeal for review of the certification ruling. * * * In some cases such an appeal would promise substantial savings of time and resources or for other reasons should be viewed hospitably." Deposit Guar. Nat. Bank v. Roper, 1980, 100 S.Ct. 1166, 1173 n. 8, 445 U.S. 326, 336 n. 8, 63 L.Ed.2d 427.

44. Hackett v. General Host Corp., C.A.3d, 1972, 455 F.2d 618, 624, certiorari denied 92 S.Ct. 2460, 407 U.S. 925, 32 L.Ed.2d 812.

45. U.S. v. Wood, C.A.5th, 1961, 295 F.2d 772, 778, certiorari denied 82 S.Ct. 933, 369 U.S. 850, 8 L.Ed.2d 9. See 15A Wright, Miller & Cooper, Jurisdiction 2d § 3912, pp. 446–450.

46. See § 107 below.

47. 15A Wright, Miller & Cooper, Jurisdiction 2d § 3908. See Flanagan v. U.S., 1984, 104 S.Ct. 1051, 1055 n. 3, 465 U.S. 259, 265 n. 3, 79 L.Ed.2d 288.

48. Thus, at one key point in Brown Shoe Co. v. U.S., 1962, 82 S.Ct. 1502, 1515, 370 U.S. 294, 309, 8 L.Ed.2d 510, on direct appeal from a district court to the Supreme Court, the Court, in determining what was a "final judgment" within the meaning of the Expediting Act, 15 U.S.C.A. § 29, cited three cases. Two of the cases were concerned with whether there was a "final judgment" of a district court within 28 U.S.C.A. § 1291 permitting appeal to a court of appeals, while the third involved the meaning of "final judgment" in 28 U.S.C.A. § 1257, providing for review of state-court decisions in the Supreme Court. And in determining whether a state-court decision is final for purposes of review the Court commonly cites decisions on finality for review of district-court decisions by a court of appeals. E.g., Local No. 438 Constr. & Gen. Laborers' Union, AFL–CIO v. Curry, 1963, 83 S.Ct. 531, 536, 371 U.S. 542, 549, 9 L.Ed.2d 514; Cox Broadcasting Corp. v. Cohn, 1975, 95 S.Ct. 1029, 1037 n. 7, 420 U.S. 469, 478 n. 7, 43 L.Ed.2d 328; National Socialist Party of America v. Village of Skokie, 1977, 97 S.Ct. 2205, 2206, 432 U.S. 43, 44, 53 L.Ed.2d 96. In Smalis v. Pennsylvania, 1986, 106 S.Ct. 1745, 1748 n. 4, 476 U.S. 140, 143 n. 4, 90 L.Ed.2d 116, the Court cited a decision allowing a federal defendant to appeal to support its holding that a state-court judgment was final for purposes of § 1257.

v. United States Steel Corp.[49] In a Jones Act case the district court struck portions of the complaint adding claims under state law and also struck all references in the complaint to recovery for the benefit of relatives of the decedent other than his mother. The court refused to certify its order for interlocutory appeal under 28 U.S.C.A. § 1292(b). Plaintiff took an appeal despite this and the court of appeals decided the appeal on its merits. It found that it had jurisdiction to decide the case on the intriguing theory that the plaintiff had sought such a decision, by taking the appeal, and defendant was not harmed by it, since the appellate court agreed with the defendant on the merits.[50] The Supreme Court also reached the merits, though on a different theory than that of the court of appeals. It thought that the appeal raised questions fundamental to the further conduct of the case, that it would save time and money to have them settled, and that "the Court of Appeals properly implemented the same policy Congress sought to promote in § 1292(b) by treating this obviously marginal case as final and appealable under 28 U.S.C.A. § 1291." [51]

Even a commentator who favors a pragmatic approach to appealability has said that the Gillespie opinion "is astounding for its clouded reasoning and enigmatic conclusions. It is unfortunate that a decision which may represent a truly significant adjustment of the entire philosophy of appealability is so devoid of any persuasive analysis." [52] The explanation offered by the Court in Gillespie for holding the order appealable suggests at least two positive and two negative justifications for finding that a fundamental change had been wrought in all prior approaches to finality. The positive justifications lie in the apparent invitation to weigh the benefits and costs of immediate appeal on an individualized basis, and the statement that appeal should be available from orders fundamental to the further conduct of the case. The negative justifications were in the assertion of a fictitious severability analogy, and in the incredible suggestion that the purposes of § 1292(b) were fulfilled by simply ignoring the deliberate statutory choice to require a certificate from the district court.

There are lower-court cases that have seized on each of these four justifications of the Gillespie opinion as a basis for permitting review.[53]

49. 1964, 85 S.Ct. 308, 379 U.S. 148, 13 L.Ed.2d 199.

50. Gillespie v. United States Steel Corp., C.A.6th, 1963, 321 F.2d 518, 520–522.

51. 85 S.Ct. at 312, 379 U.S. at 154.

52. Redish, note 1 above, at 118.

53. Balancing approach: Mallory v. Eyrich, C.A.6th, 1991, 922 F.2d 1273, 1276–1279; Mahaley v. Cuyahoga Metropolitan Housing Auth., C.A.6th, 1974, 500 F.2d 1087, 1090 n. 3, certiorari denied 95 S.Ct. 781, 419 U.S. 1108, 42 L.Ed.2d 805; Fox v. City of West Palm Beach, C.A.5th, 1967, 383 F.2d 189. Fundamental to further conduct: Thoms v. Heffernan, C.A.2d, 1973, 473 F.2d 478, 481–482, vacated on other grounds 1974, 94 S.Ct. 3199, 418 U.S. 908, 41 L.Ed.2d 1154. Severability: Wescott v. Impresas Armadoras, S.A. Panama, C.A.9th, 1977, 564 F.2d 875, 879–881; Jet-co Electronic Indus., Inc. v. Gardiner, C.A.5th, 1973, 473 F.2d 1228, 1231. Policies of § 1292(b): Nelson v. Heyne, C.A.7th, 1974, 491 F.2d 352, 354 n. 2, certiorari denied 94 S.Ct. 3183, 417 U.S. 976, 41 L.Ed.2d 1146.

Nevertheless, for the most part Gillespie has been left in a dismal limbo. It has either been ignored by the courts of appeals or invoked to justify appeals that could have been explained on more traditional notions of finality.[54]   Indeed in Coopers & Lybrand the Court itself said: "If Gillespie were extended beyond the unique facts of that case, § 1291 would be stripped of all significance."[55]

Justice Harlan was a consistent, and usually a lonely, dissenter from the line of cases expanding the notion of finality.   There is surely force in his remark in one of his dissents that these decisions throw "the law of finality into a state of great uncertainty and will, I am afraid, tend to increase further efforts at piecemeal review."[56]

§ 102.   Review of Interlocutory Orders [1]

There are three situations, by now well-established, in which the courts of appeals have statutory jurisdiction to review interlocutory orders of the district court.   They may review:

1.   Interlocutory orders granting, continuing, modifying, refusing, or dissolving injunctions, or refusing to dissolve or modify injunctions, except where a direct review may be had in the Supreme Court.[2]

2.   Interlocutory orders appointing receivers, or refusing orders to wind up receiverships or to take steps to accomplish purposes of a receivership, such as directing sales or other disposals of property.[3]

3.   Interlocutory decrees determining the rights and liabilities of the parties to admiralty cases in which appeals from final decrees are allowed.[4]

A 1992 statute gives the Supreme Court power to prescribe rules to provide for an appeal of an interlocutory decision that is not provided for in the three categories just listed.[5]   To date this authority has not been used.

---

54.   15A Wright, Miller & Cooper, Jurisdiction 2d § 3913; Redish, note 1 above, at 120–124.

55.   98 S.Ct. at 2462 n. 30, 437 U.S. at 477 n. 30.

Nevertheless in American Export Lines, Inc. v. Alvez, 1980, 100 S.Ct. 1673, 446 U.S. 274, 64 L.Ed.2d 284, the Court relied on Gillespie to establish finality for review of a state court in circumstances that stretch the finality doctrine to or beyond the limit. See 16 Wright, Miller & Cooper, Jurisdiction § 4010.

56.   Mercantile Nat. Bank at Dallas v. Langdeau, 1963, 83 S.Ct. 520, 531, 371 U.S. 555, 575, 9 L.Ed.2d 523.

§ 102

1.   16 Wright, Miller & Cooper, Jurisdiction §§ 3920–3936.

2.   28 U.S.C.A. § 1292(a)(1).   See 16 Wright, Miller & Cooper, Jurisdiction §§ 3921–3924.   With regard to the exception, see § 105 below.

3.   28 U.S.C.A. § 1292(a)(2).   See 16 Wright, Miller & Cooper, Jurisdiction § 3925.

4.   28 U.S.C.A. § 1292(a)(3); Rule 9(h). See Slatton v. Martin K. Eby Constr. Co., C.A.8th, 1974, 491 F.2d 707; 16 Wright, Miller & Cooper, Jurisdiction § 3927.   The admiralty bar continues to find interlocutory appeals from the determination of liability useful although, as the Slatton case shows, the courts of appeals do not like them.

5.   28 U.S.C.A. § 1292(e).   See § 101 n. 14 for discussion of this and of a 1990 statute allowing the Supreme Court to prescribe rules defining finality for purposes of 28 U.S.C.A. § 1291.

Until recently the courts of appeals also could review either interlocutory or final judgments, orders, or decrees in bankruptcy, but the 1978 Bankruptcy Act has provided a new, and virtually incomprehensible, scheme for appellate review of bankruptcy matters, and though these provisions were improved by 1984 legislation, the new statute does not address any of the most troubling ambiguities of the 1978 provisions.[6] Also until 1982 the courts of appeals could review judgments in civil actions for patent infringement that are final except for accounting. These are still reviewable, but now only by the Court of Appeals for the Federal Circuit.[7]

These exceptions from the usual requirement of finality, the Court has said, "seem plainly to spring from a developing need to permit litigants to effectually challenge interlocutory orders of serious, perhaps irreparable consequence. When the pressure rises to a point that influences Congress, legislative remedies are enacted."[8] Of these traditional grounds for interlocutory appeals, that involving injunctions is of the most general interest and has caused the most difficulty.

Ordinarily the scope of appellate review under 28 U.S.C.A. § 1292(a)(1) of an order granting or refusing an injunction is confined to the issues necessary to determine the propriety of the interlocutory order itself. Nevertheless, review quite properly extends to all matters inextricably bound up with the remedial decision and the court, if it sees fit, may consider and decide the merits of the case and may order dismissal of the action.[9]

Orders specifically granting or denying injunctions are appealable as a matter of right.[10] Orders granting or denying a preliminary injunction

---

6. 28 U.S.C.A. § 158. See 16 Wright, Miller & Cooper, Jurisdiction § 3926.

7. 28 U.S.C.A. § 1292(c)(2). Under this provision, appeal will lie only if a judgment has been entered pursuant to Civil Rules 58 and 79. Marsh–McBirney, Inc. v. Montedoro–Whitney Corp., C.A.Fed.1989, 882 F.2d 498. See 16 Wright, Miller & Cooper, Jurisdiction § 3928.

8. Baltimore Contractors v. Bodinger, 1955, 75 S.Ct. 249, 252, 348 U.S. 176, 181, 99 L.Ed. 233.

A modern example of congressional response to pressures of this kind was the 1968 amendment of 18 U.S.C.A. § 3731 allowing the United States to appeal from an order suppressing or excluding evidence or requiring the return of seized property in a criminal proceeding. See 3 Wright, Criminal 2d § 678.

9. Smith v. Vulcan Iron Works, 1897, 17 S.Ct. 407, 165 U.S. 518, 41 L.Ed. 810; Myers v. Bethlehem Shipbuilding Corp., 1938, 58 S.Ct. 459, 303 U.S. 41, 82 L.Ed.

638; Aerojet–General Corp. v. American Arbitration Assn., C.A.9th, 1973, 478 F.2d 248, 252–253; 16 Wright, Miller & Cooper, Jurisdiction § 3921.

Jurisdiction of the interlocutory appeal is in large measure jurisdiction to deal with all aspects of the case that have been sufficiently illuminated to enable decision by the court of appeals without further trial court development. Thornburgh v. American College of Obstetricians & Gynecologists, 1986, 106 S.Ct. 2169, 2176–2177, 476 U.S. 747, 756–757, 90 L.Ed.2d 779; U.S. v. Michigan, C.A.6th, 1991, 940 F.2d 143, 151–152.

For cases in which the appellate court follows the more usual practice of limiting itself to review of the order concerning the injunction, see 11 Wright & Miller, Civil § 2962 n. 28.

10. U.S. v. Bayshore Associates, C.A.6th, 1991, 934 F.2d 1391, 1395–1396; EEOC v. Kerrville Bus Co., C.A.5th, 1991, 925 F.2d 129, 132.

are appealable,[11] while similar orders involving a temporary restraining order are not.[12] In applying this distinction the label put on the order by the trial court is not decisive.[13] Instead the courts look to such factors as the duration of the order, whether it was issued after notice and hearing, and the type of showing made in obtaining the order.[14] Application of these tests is not easy to fathom. In one case an order labelled "temporary restraining order" was issued after a hearing at which both parties were represented, on a showing similar to what would have been made to obtain a preliminary injunction, and was to last for 28 days. But the appellate court held that since it "barely extended" beyond the 20–day limit for temporary restraining orders [15] it was not a preliminary injunction and was not appealable.[16]

The cases seem to be edging slowly toward a principle that rulings with respect to temporary restraining orders are appealable on a sufficiently strong showing of potentially irreparable injury.[17] It has been held also that the trial court may not avoid review of its determination that a preliminary injunction should not issue merely by refusing to make a formal ruling on the motion for such an injunction. Its refusal to act will be held equivalent to denial of the preliminary injunction, and appealable as such.[18]

An order need not refuse an injunction in terms in order to be immediately appealable under § 1292(a)(1). But if the order has the practical effect of refusing an injunction, it is only appealable if the order has serious, perhaps irreparable, consequences that can be effectually challenged only by immediate appeal. On this analysis appeal was allowed from a refusal to approve a consent decree that would have

11. Deckert v. Independence Shares Corp., 1940, 61 S.Ct. 229, 311 U.S. 282, 85 L.Ed. 189.

12. In re Champion, C.A.8th, 1990, 895 F.2d 490, 492; Schainmann v. Brainard, C.C.A.9th, 1925, 8 F.2d 11; and cases cited 16 Wright, Miller & Cooper, Jurisdiction § 3922 n. 10.

13. Sampson v. Murray, 1974, 94 S.Ct. 937, 951, 415 U.S. 61, 86–87, 39 L.Ed.2d 166; Western Union Tel. Co. v. U.S. & Mexican Trust Co., C.C.A.8th, 1915, 221 F. 545, 553.

14. Sampson v. Murray, 1974, 94 S.Ct. 937, 951, 415 U.S. 61, 86–87, 39 L.Ed.2d 166; In re Bowoon Sangsa Co., C.A.9th, 1983, 720 F.2d 595, 597; Dilworth v. Riner, C.A.5th, 1965, 343 F.2d 226, 229; Austin v. Altman, C.A.2d, 1964, 332 F.2d 273, 275.

15. Rule 65(b); 11 Wright & Miller, Civil § 2953.

16. Connell v. Dulien Steel Products, Inc., C.A.5th, 1957, 240 F.2d 414, noted 1958, 71 Harv.L.Rev. 550. Cf. Pennsylva-nia Motor Truck Assn. v. Port of Philadelphia Marine Terminal Assn., C.A.3d, 1960, 276 F.2d 931.

17. In some instances the order is considered a final decision and appealable under 28 U.S.C.A. § 1291. See § 101 n. 50 above. Other cases consider that the effect of the ruling on the temporary restraining order is sufficiently grave to make it, in effect, the grant or denial of a preliminary injunction and thus appealable under 28 U.S.C.A. § 1292(a)(1). E.g., Doe v. Village of Crestwood, C.A.7th, 1990, 917 F.2d 1476, 1477; Religious Technology Center v. Scott, C.A.9th, 1989, 869 F.2d 1306, 1308–1309. See 16 Wright, Miller & Cooper, Jurisdiction § 3922 at nn. 24–28.

18. Rolo v. General Devel. Corp., C.A.3d, 1991, 949 F.2d 695, 703; U.S. v. Lynd, C.A.5th, 1962, 301 F.2d 818, certiorari denied 83 S.Ct. 187, 371 U.S. 893, 9 L.Ed.2d 125; McCoy v. Louisiana State Bd. of Educ., C.A.5th, 1964, 332 F.2d 915. But cf. Overton v. City of Austin, C.A.5th, 1984, 748 F.2d 941, 951–952.

barred racial discrimination in hiring,[19] but appeal was not allowed from denial of a plaintiff's motion for summary judgment in a case seeking permanent injunctive relief[20] nor was it allowed from denial of class certification in a similar case.[21]

In Enelow v. New York Life Insurance Co.,[22] decided before law and equity were merged by adoption of the federal rules, and, more surprisingly, in Ettelson v. Metropolitan Life Insurance Co.,[23] decided after adoption of the rules, the Supreme Court held that if an action is brought that is triable to a jury, and defendant asserts a defense or a counterclaim not triable to a jury, the decision of the trial court to try the nonjury issues before the jury issues is appealable. The theory was that such an order had the effect of an injunction staying prosecution of the legal action, a theory that bore little resemblance to reality in 1935 and none in 1942, when the merger of law and equity had been completed. A converse situation arose a few years later in City of Morgantown v. Royal Insurance Co.[24] There it was the plaintiff who sued for reformation of an insurance policy, a claim not triable to a jury, and the defendant who counterclaimed to recover on the policy, a claim on which there is a right of jury trial. The court struck defendant's demand for a jury and ordered trial to the court. This order was held not to be appealable. The Court refused to accept analogies to premerger practice, and said that this was not an injunction, but simply "a judge making a ruling as to the manner in which he will try one issue in a civil action pending before himself." [25] The dissenters complained that the decision was a silent overruling of Enelow and Ettelson. Indeed the theory of the Court seemed to have this effect, and the commentators were hopeful that this was the result. Unfortunately the Enelow and Ettelson decisions were resuscitated in Baltimore Contractors, Inc. v. Bodinger.[26] The result there is surely sound. It was held that the refusal, in a nonjury case, to order a stay for arbitration "was simply a ruling in the only suit pending, actual or fictional. It was a mere order and not an injunction as that word is understood through the Enelow and the Ettelson cases as a stay through equitable principles of a common-law action." [27] In its reasoning, however, the Court accepted a distinction that had been offered by one concurring justice in the City of Morgantown case, by which a stay of the jury issues is appealable where

---

19. Carson v. American Brands, Inc., 1981, 101 S.Ct. 993, 450 U.S. 79, 67 L.Ed.2d 59. See 16 Wright, Miller & Cooper, Jurisdiction § 3924.

20. "Orders that in no way touch on the merits of the claim but only relate to pretrial procedures are not in our view 'interlocutory' within the meaning of § 1292(a)(1)." Switzerland Cheese Assn., Inc. v. E. Horne's Market, Inc., 1966, 87 S.Ct. 193, 195, 385 U.S. 23, 25, 17 L.Ed.2d 23.

21. Gardner v. Westinghouse Broadcasting Co., 1978, 98 S.Ct. 2451, 437 U.S. 478, 57 L.Ed.2d 364.

22. 1935, 55 S.Ct. 310, 293 U.S. 379, 79 L.Ed. 440.

23. 1942, 63 S.Ct. 163, 317 U.S. 188, 87 L.Ed. 176.

24. 1949, 69 S.Ct. 1067, 337 U.S. 254, 93 L.Ed. 1347.

25. 69 S.Ct. at 1069, 337 U.S. at 257.

26. 1955, 75 S.Ct. 249, 348 U.S. 176, 99 L.Ed. 233.

27. 75 S.Ct. at 254, 348 U.S. at 184.

the "law" action is brought first but not where the original action is "equitable" and the "legal" claim comes in as a counterclaim. The Court recognized the "incongruity" of such a distinction, and said that it "has elements of fiction" and "springs from the persistence of outmoded procedural differentiations," [28] but felt that any change must come from Congress.

If Congress had been aware of the travail this obsolete and fictional distinction was causing the courts of appeals, relief would surely have been forthcoming. But fortunately when Congress did not act, the Court did. In 1988, in Gulfstream Aerospace Corporation v. Mayacamas Corporation,[29] Justice Marshall spoke for a unanimous Court in saying that the Enelow–Ettelson rule "is unsound in theory, unworkable and arbitrary in practice, and unnecessary to achieve any legitimate goals." [30] The Court expressly overruled the cases establishing the rule and held that orders granting or denying stays of "legal" proceedings on "equitable" grounds are no longer automatically appealable under § 1292(a)(1). Denial of an express request for an injunction is appealable, and appeal also can be taken if an order has the practical effect of granting or denying an injunction and threatens serious, perhaps irreparable consequence.[31]

In addition to the situations in which the statute has for years permitted interlocutory review, the potential availability of such review by means of the so-called "extraordinary writs" of mandamus and prohibition has been an additional avenue of escape from the final-judgment rule. Traditionally the use of these writs in the federal courts has been sharply limited.[32] In one case the Court said: "We are unwilling to utilize them as substitutes for appeals. As extraordinary remedies, they are reserved for really extraordinary cases." [33] Though their use was said to be in the sound discretion of the courts of appeals, the Supreme Court would not hesitate to reverse, without reference to any discretion below, if it considered that a writ had been used as a substitute for appeal.[34] The usual federal doctrine was summarized as follows by the Supreme Court in 1956: "Such writs may go only in aid of

28. Ibid.

29. 1988, 108 S.Ct. 1133, 485 U.S. 271, 99 L.Ed.2d 296.

30. 108 S.Ct. at 1140, 485 U.S. at 283.

31. 108 S.Ct. at 1142–1143, 485 U.S. at 287–288. The Court also noted that in appropriate circumstances review will remain available by "collateral order" appeal under § 1291—see § 101 above—or by permissive interlocutory appeal under § 1292(b) or by extraordinary writ. See 16 Wright, Miller & Cooper, Jurisdiction § 3923.

The Enelow–Ettelson rule had been used to determine appealability of orders regulating the relationships between litigation and arbitration. This is now covered by a 1988 statute, 9 U.S.C.A. § 16, which permits appeals from orders that give litigation precedence over arbitration and generally denies appeals from interlocutory orders that give arbitration precedence over litigation. See 15B Wright, Miller & Cooper, Jurisdiction 2d § 3914.17.

32. 16 Wright, Miller & Cooper, Jurisdiction §§ 3932, 3933. See also Tigar, Federal Appeals: Jurisdiction and Practice, 2d ed. 1993, §§ 3.01–3.17.

33. Ex parte Fahey, 1947, 67 S.Ct. 1558, 1559, 332 U.S. 258, 260, 91 L.Ed. 2041.

34. Roche v. Evaporated Milk Assn., 1943, 63 S.Ct. 938, 319 U.S. 21, 87 L.Ed. 1185.

appellate jurisdiction. 28 U.S.C.A. § 1651. The power to issue them is discretionary and it is sparingly exercised. * * * This is not a case where a court has exceeded or refused to exercise its jurisdiction, see Roche v. Evaporated Milk Ass'n, 319 U.S. 21, 26, 63 S.Ct. 938, 941, 87 L.Ed. 1185, nor one where appellate review will be defeated if a writ does not issue, cf. Maryland v. Soper, 270 U.S. 9, 29–30, 46 S.Ct. 185, 189, 70 L.Ed. 449. Here the most that could be claimed is that the district courts have erred in ruling on matters within their jurisdiction. The extraordinary writs do not reach to such cases; they may not be used to thwart the congressional policy against piecemeal appeals." [35]

A bare majority of the Supreme Court found these principles inapplicable, however, in a 1957 case, and held that a writ of mandamus was properly issued by a court of appeals to overrule the determination of a district judge that "exceptional conditions" existed, within the meaning of Rule 53(b), justifying appointment of a master.[36] Though the Court cautioned that by its holding it did not intend "to authorize the indiscriminate use of prerogative writs as a means of reviewing interlocutory orders," [37] its conclusion that "supervisory control of the District Courts by the Courts of Appeals is necessary to proper judicial administration in the federal system" [38] certainly appeared to make the writs more freely available.[39]

Mandamus is now routinely used to require jury trial where it has been improperly denied.[40] The writ has been held appropriate also where there was a substantial allegation of usurpation of power by the trial court and the issue was one of first impression requiring application of one of the Civil Rules in a new context.[41] It has been held appropriate also where a district court remanded a case removed from state court on improper grounds.[42] On the other hand, the Court has held that mandamus will not issue to test a pretrial discovery order in a criminal case.[43] Although there is much emphasis in the opinion on the "extraor-

---

35. Parr v. U.S., 1956, 76 S.Ct. 912, 917, 351 U.S. 513, 520, 100 L.Ed. 1377.

36. La Buy v. Howes Leather Co., 1957, 77 S.Ct. 309, 352 U.S. 249, 1 L.Ed.2d 290. See the critical discussion of this case in Wright, The Doubtful Omniscience of Appellate Courts, 1957, 41 Minn.L.Rev. 751, 771–778. A favorable view is taken in Carrington, The Power of District Judges and the Responsibility of Courts of Appeals, 1969, 3 Ga.L.Rev. 507, 508–517.

37. 77 S.Ct. at 314, 352 U.S. at 255.

38. 77 S.Ct. at 315, 352 U.S. at 259–260. See 16 Wright, Miller & Cooper, Jurisdiction § 3934; Note, Supervisory and Advisory Mandamus Under the All Writs Act, 1973, 86 Harv.L.Rev. 595.

39. See 16 Wright, Miller & Cooper, Jurisdiction § 3935.

40. Beacon Theatres, Inc. v. Westover, 1959, 79 S.Ct. 948, 957, 359 U.S. 500, 511, 3 L.Ed.2d 988; Dairy Queen, Inc. v. Wood, 1962, 82 S.Ct. 894, 901, 369 U.S. 469, 480, 8 L.Ed.2d 44; Gulfstream Aerospace Corp. v. Mayacamas Corp., 1988, 108 S.Ct. 1133, 1143 n. 13, 485 U.S. 271, 288 n. 13, 99 L.Ed.2d 296. The extraordinary decision to the contrary in First Nat. Bank of Waukesha v. Warren, C.A.7th, 1986, 796 F.2d 999, can hardly have survived the explicit dictum in the Gulfstream case.

41. Schlagenhauf v. Holder, 1964, 85 S.Ct. 234, 238–239, 379 U.S. 104, 109–112, 13 L.Ed.2d 152.

See also Colonial Times, Inc. v. Gasch, C.A.D.C.1975, 509 F.2d 517.

42. Thermtron Products, Inc. v. Hermansdorfer, 1976, 96 S.Ct. 584, 423 U.S. 336, 46 L.Ed.2d 542.

43. Will v. U.S., 1967, 88 S.Ct. 269, 389 U.S. 90, 19 L.Ed.2d 305.

dinary" nature of the writ and the reluctance with which it should be used, the particular case was heavily influenced by the fact that it was a criminal case and that normally the government has no right to appeal in a criminal matter.[44] However later cases have relied on that decision in a civil context,[45] and most recently, in the course of holding that the grant of a new trial by the district court will rarely, if ever, justify the issuance of a writ of mandamus, the Court said that "[o]nly exceptional circumstances, amounting to a judicial usurpation of power, will justify the invocation of this extraordinary remedy."[46] And in the Gulfstream case the Court refused to allow mandamus to be used to review a district court's refusal to stay or dismiss an action in favor of a pending state action. In doing so the Court repeated the traditional formulas that mandamus is "to be reserved for extraordinary situations," that only "exceptional circumstances amounting to a judicial 'usurpation of power' " will justify it, and that the party seeking the writ has the burden of showing that its right to it is "clear and indisputable."[47] Thus, the Court has retreated from the expanded use of mandamus that it had seemed to sanction in 1957.[48]

The entire pattern of interlocutory review in federal civil cases was drastically altered by the Interlocutory Appeals Act of 1958, which grants discretion to the courts of appeals to review any interlocutory order whatever in a civil case if the trial judge, in making the order, has stated in writing that the order involves a controlling question of law about which there is substantial ground for difference of opinion and that an immediate appeal from the order may materially advance the ultimate termination of the litigation.[49] This statute, 28 U.S.C.A. § 1292(b), was recommended by the Judicial Conference of the United States as a compromise between those who opposed any broadening of interlocutory review and those who favored giving the appellate courts discretion to entertain any interlocutory appeal they wished regardless of

---

44. 88 S.Ct. at 274–275, 389 U.S. at 96–98. But see 16 Wright, Miller & Cooper, Jurisdiction § 3936.

45. Kerr v. U.S. Dist. Court, 1976, 96 S.Ct. 2119, 426 U.S. 394, 48 L.Ed.2d 725; Will v. Calvert Fire Ins. Co., 1978, 98 S.Ct. 2552, 437 U.S. 655, 57 L.Ed.2d 504 (plurality opinion).

46. Allied Chem. Corp. v. Daiflon, Inc., 1980, 101 S.Ct. 188, 190, 449 U.S. 33, 35, 66 L.Ed.2d 193.

47. 108 S.Ct. at 1143–1144, 485 U.S. at 288–290.

48. "La Buy is defunct. Although the Court has not yet erected the tombstone, it has ordered flowers. The dissenting Justices in La Buy argued that mandamus should be reserved for truly extraordinary cases and should not be used when an issue

is reviewable on appeal. * * * In the last 20 years this view has prevailed." First Nat. Bank of Waukesha v. Warren, C.A.7th, 1986, 796 F.2d 999, 1004 (per Easterbrook, J.).

See Berger, The Mandamus Power of the United States Courts of Appeals: A Complex and Confused Means of Appellate Control, 1982, 31 Buffalo L.Rev. 37.

49. 16 Wright, Miller & Cooper, Jurisdiction §§ 3929–3931; Solomine, Revitalizing Interlocutory Appeals in the Federal Courts, 1990, 58 Geo.Wash.L.Rev. 1165.

Section 1292(b) has no application in a criminal case. General Motors Corp. v. U.S., C.A.6th, 1978, 584 F.2d 1366, certiorari denied 99 S.Ct. 1277, 440 U.S. 934, 59 L.Ed.2d 492, criticized Note, 1979, 92 Harv. L.Rev. 931, 939–942.

certification by the trial judge.[50]

The 1958 statute is an addition to prior methods of securing interlocutory review; it does not replace them. Thus, orders of the types already described, which were appealable by statute prior to 1958, are still appealable without the certificate required by § 1292(b). Matters previously appealable as "final decisions," such as "collateral orders," judgments in multiple claims cases certified as final under Rule 54(b), and the like,[51] are still appealable as final decisions under § 1291 and do not require a § 1292(b) certificate. Although it is preferable to use Rule 54(b) rather than § 1292(b) in those cases within the rule, an order that disposes of fewer than all of the parties or claims is interlocutory in the absence of a Rule 54(b) certificate. Thus, it is within the terms of the statute, and the appellate court can take the case if a § 1292(b) certificate is made.[52] The statute should reduce the number of cases in which the extraordinary writs are used, since a condition for issuance of those writs has been the absence of any other adequate remedy,[53] but the writs remain available in the extraordinary cases where the trial judge has refused to give a § 1292(b) certificate and the case is of that rare sort that is properly reviewable by mandamus or prohibition.[54]

For the statute to apply there must be a "controlling question of law." Many cases have held a § 1292(b) appeal not proper on matters that lie within the discretion of the district court.[55] Ordinarily a district court should refuse to certify such matters, not only because of the low probability of reversal, but also because the recognition of discretion results from a studied determination that appellate courts should not generally interfere. But the key consideration is not whether the order involves the exercise of discretion, but whether it truly implicates the policies underlying § 1292(b).[56]

---

50. See Gottesman v. General Motors Corp., C.A.2d, 1959, 268 F.2d 194, 196.

51. See § 101 above.

52. Demelo v. Woolsey Marine Indus., Inc., C.A.5th, 1982, 677 F.2d 1030; Local P–171, Amalgamated Meat Cutters and Butcher Workmen of North America v. Thompson Farms Co., C.A.7th, 1981, 642 F.2d 1065, 1069 n. 4; Sass v. District of Columbia, C.A.D.C.1963, 316 F.2d 366; 16 Wright, Miller & Cooper, Jurisdiction § 3929.

53. In re Centrotextil, C.A.8th, 1980, 620 F.2d 690; Mohasco Indus., Inc. v. Lydick, C.A.9th, 1972, 459 F.2d 959; Ex parte Watkins, C.A.5th, 1958, 260 F.2d 548; and cases cited 16 Wright, Miller & Cooper, Jurisdiction § 3929 n. 54.

54. Japan Line Ltd. v. Sabre Shipping Corp., C.A.2d, 1969, 407 F.2d 173, certiorari denied 89 S.Ct. 1774, 395 U.S. 922, 23 L.Ed.2d 239; Holub Indus., Inc. v. Wyche,

C.A.4th, 1961, 290 F.2d 852; In re Watkins, C.A.5th, 1959, 271 F.2d 771, 76 A.L.R.2d 1113. But see Roach v. Churchman, C.A.8th, 1972, 457 F.2d 1101, 1105.

55. E.g., Phelps v. Burnham, C.A.2d, 1964, 327 F.2d 812 (setting amount of security for costs); City of Burbank v. General Elec. Co., C.A.9th, 1963, 329 F.2d 825 (refusal to strike portion of a pleading); Standard v. Stoll Packing Corp., C.A.3d, 1964, 315 F.2d 626 (refusal to change venue); Herold v. Braun, D.C.N.Y.1987, 671 F.Supp. 936 (discovery sanctions); Rippey v. Denver U.S. Nat. Bank, D.C.Colo.1966, 260 F.Supp. 704 (determination parties not "indispensable"); Seven–Up Co. v. O–So Grape Co., D.C.Ill.1959, 179 F.Supp. 167 (separate trial of a particular issue).

56. Katz v. Carte Blanche Corp., C.A.3d, 1974, 496 F.2d 747, 756, certiorari denied 95 S.Ct. 152, 419 U.S. 885, 42 L.Ed.2d 125; and cases cited 16 Wright, Miller & Cooper, Jurisdiction § 3930 nn. 18–20.

There must also be "substantial ground for difference of opinion" about the controlling question of law. One court held that this precluded it from certifying a question governed by clear precedent in its own circuit, though five other circuits were to the contrary.[57] The better view, however, is that a clear ruling in the local circuit is a strong reason for not certifying, but that this cannot be dispositive.[58]

Finally, it must be thought that immediate appeal "may materially advance the ultimate termination of the litigation." On this theory interlocutory appeal has been held inappropriate from orders involving sufficiency of the pleadings, since if the pleading were held insufficient it could be amended.[59] Also appeal has not been allowed where the case must go to trial in any event against other parties regardless of the correctness of the challenged ruling.[60] Generalizing from this statutory language, and from the legislative history of the statute, there is a good deal of authority for the proposition that § 1292(b) should not be used in "run-of-the-mill" cases and is intended for "exceptional cases" where appeal may avoid "protracted and expensive litigation."[61] The Fifth Circuit, however, has expressly disapproved statements from other courts calling for a strict construction of § 1292(b), or suggesting that it should be restricted to exceptional cases,[62] though in later cases it has taken a narrower view of when the statute is properly used.[63]

If the district court believes that the criteria of § 1292(b) are satisfied, it is to state this in writing in its order. Within ten days of entry of the order the party wishing to appeal then must petition the court of appeals for leave to appeal.[64] It is discretionary with the court

57. Berger v. U.S., D.C.N.Y.1959, 170 F.Supp. 795, noted 1960, 108 U.Pa.L.Rev. 601.

58. Giglio v. Farrell Lines, Inc., D.C.N.Y.1977, 424 F.Supp. 927. See also Corabi v. Auto Racing, Inc., C.A.3d, 1959, 264 F.2d 784 (appeal allowed where other circuits held a view contrary to that of court allowing appeal on controlling question of law).

59. City of Burbank v. General Elec. Co., C.A.9th, 1964, 329 F.2d 825; Gottesman v. General Motors Corp., C.A.2d, 1959, 268 F.2d 194, noted 1959, 45 Va.L.Rev. 1236, 48 Geo.L.J. 594; Urbach v. Sayles, D.C.N.J.1991, 779 F.Supp. 351, 364–365.

60. Bowling Machines, Inc. v. First Nat. Bank of Boston, C.A.1st, 1960, 283 F.2d 39; Speir v. Robert C. Herd & Co., D.C.Md. 1960, 189 F.Supp. 436. Contra: Schnell v. Peter Eckrich & Sons, Inc., C.A.7th, 1960, 279 F.2d 594.

61. Lear Siegler, Inc. v. Adkins, C.A.9th, 1964, 330 F.2d 595, 598. See also In re Cement Antitrust Litigation, C.A.9th, 1981, 673 F.2d 1020, 1026, affirmed 1983, 103 S.Ct. 1173, 459 U.S. 1190, 75 L.Ed.2d 425; Bruce v. Martin, D.C.N.Y.1989, 712 F.Supp.

442, 445; and cases cited 16 Wright, Miller & Cooper, Jurisdiction § 3929 nn. 3, 7.

But see Solomine, note 49 above; Note, Interlocutory Appeals in the Federal Courts under 28 U.S.C.A. § 1292(b), 1975, 88 Harv.L.Rev. 607; 16 Wright, Miller & Cooper, Jurisdiction § 3929.

62. Hadjipateras v. Pacifica, S.A., C.A.5th, 1961, 290 F.2d 697, 702–703.

63. Alabama Labor Council v. Alabama, C.A.5th, 1972, 453 F.2d 922, 924; Garner v. Wolfinbarger, C.A.5th, 1970, 433 F.2d 117. In the Garner case even the dissenting judge expressed "concern that we have been too lax in allowing § 1292(b) appeals." 433 F.2d at 123.

64. Appellate Rule 5. The ten-day time limit is ordinarily jurisdictional, but under unusual circumstances the district court may vacate its order and enter a new order so that a new ten-day period can begin running. Compare In re Benny, C.A.9th, 1987, 812 F.2d 1133, 1136–1137, with Braden v. University of Pittsburgh, C.A.3d, 1977, 552 F.2d 948, 949–955.

of appeals whether to permit the appeal and it may deny the appeal for any reason.[65]

If the appellate court agrees to hear a case that the district court has certified under § 1292(b), the appellate court is not limited to the question or questions the district court has certified. The appeal is from the order, not the questions, and though the jurisdiction of the appellate court is confined to the particular order appealed from, all questions material to that order are properly before the court.[66]

Though a great deal has been written about § 1292(b), numerically the statute has not been of great importance. In the fiscal year 1992 47,013 appeals were taken to the twelve courts of appeals.[67] By contrast trial-court certificates under § 1292(b) are made in only about 100 cases a year and the courts of appeals allow interlocutory appeal in about half of those 100 cases.[68]

§ 103. Review of Administrative Determinations [1]

Two principal statutory patterns for judicial review of orders of federal administrative agencies have been commonly employed in the past, in addition to the "nonstatutory" review available by suit in the district court against the officer or agency involved.[2] The first pattern, originally adopted for the Interstate Commerce Commission in the Hepburn Act of 1906[3] and reenacted as the Urgent Deficiencies Act of 1913,[4] permitted suit to enjoin a commission order before a three-judge district court, with such suit given precedence over all other cases, and appeal as of right to the Supreme Court. The other pattern is that of the Federal Trade Commission Act of 1914.[5] It gave exclusive jurisdiction to affirm, enforce, modify, or set aside orders of that commission to the then-circuit courts of appeals, with discretionary review in the Supreme Court by certiorari.

In subsequent years each pattern of review was chosen by Congress for particular agencies. Review of some or all orders of the Federal Communications Commission, the Maritime Commission, the Packers and Stockyards Administration, and the Perishable Agricultural Com-

---

65. Coopers & Lybrand v. Livesay, 1978, 98 S.Ct. 2454, 2461, 437 U.S. 463, 475, 57 L.Ed.2d 351; In re Convertible Rowing Exerciser Patent Litigation, C.A.Fed.1990, 903 F.2d 822.

66. U.S. v. Stanley, 1987, 107 S.Ct. 3054, 3060, 483 U.S. 669, 677, 97 L.Ed.2d 550; Ivy Club v. Edwards, C.A.3d, 1991, 943 F.2d 270, 275, certiorari denied 112 S.Ct. 1282, ___ U.S. ___, 117 L.Ed.2d 507; Nuclear Engineering Co. v. Scott, C.A.7th, 1981, 660 F.2d 241, 245–246; 16 Wright, Miller & Cooper, Jurisdiction § 3929 at nn. 31–36.

67. Ann.Rep. of the Director of the Administrative Office of the U.S. Courts, 1992, Table B–1. This figure does not include the Court of Appeals for the Federal Circuit.

68. Note, note 61 above, at 607 n. 5.

§ 103

1. 16 Wright, Miller & Cooper, Jurisdiction §§ 3940–3944.

2. The scope of "nonstatutory" review was greatly broadened when 5 U.S.C.A. §§ 702, 703, were amended in 1976. See 14 Wright, Miller & Cooper, Jurisdiction 2d § 3655.

3. Act of June 29, 1906, c. 3591, § 5, 34 Stat. 584, 590.

4. Act of Oct. 22, 1913, c. 32, 38 Stat. 219; 28 U.S.C.A. §§ 1336, 2321–2325.

5. Act of Sept. 26, 1914, c. 311, § 5, 38 Stat. 717, 720; 15 U.S.C.A. § 45.

modities Administration was by a three-judge district court, under the procedure of the Urgent Deficiencies Act. Review by a court of appeals, under the pattern of the Federal Trade Commission Act, was written into most other regulatory statutes. Often it was difficult to fathom why Congress chose one form of review rather than another. Thus, in the Packers and Stockyards Act of 1921 it was provided that orders of the Secretary of Agriculture under the "Packers" part of the act were to be reviewed in the court of appeals, while those under the "Stockyards" part of the act were to be reviewed by a three-judge district court.[6]

There were substantial reasons for preferring review by a court of appeals to review by a three-judge district court. It was always difficult to bring together two district judges and a judge of the court of appeals to make up a statutory three-judge district court,[7] while the court of appeals was readily available for review. In addition, the direct appeal to the Supreme Court from three-judge courts forced that Court to review many cases where the questions involved were of only minor importance, but where lengthy records and extreme technicalities added heavily to the burden of the Court. Accordingly in 1950 Congress, recognizing that review by a court of appeals "is the more modern method and is generally considered to be the best method for the review of orders of administrative agencies," [8] adopted that means of review for all agencies except the Interstate Commerce Commission.[9] Review is obtained under the 1950 statute by filing a petition for review with the court of appeals for the circuit where the party or parties seeking review reside or have their principal office, or with the Court of Appeals for the District of Columbia.[10] Review will ordinarily be on the record made at the hearing before the administrative agency,[11] with the findings of fact by the agency accepted if they are supported by substantial evidence in the light of the whole record.[12]

It was wholly anomalous that Interstate Commerce Commission orders were not made reviewable in the courts of appeals when this was accomplished for other agencies in the 1950 legislation.[13] Fortunately

6. Act of Aug. 15, 1921, c. 64, §§ 204, 316, 42 Stat. 159, 162, 168.

7. See § 50 above.

8. H.Rep. No. 2122, 81st Cong., 2d Sess. 1950; 1950 U.S.Code Cong.Serv., pp. 4303, 4306. See also D.L. Piazza Co. v. West Coast Line, Inc., C.A.2d, 1954, 210 F.2d 947, 949.

9. Act of Dec. 29, 1950, c. 1189, 64 Stat. 1129; 28 U.S.C.A. §§ 2341–2352. The act is not all-inclusive. Other statutes providing for review by a court of appeals remain, and are not superseded by the 1950 statute. For such other statutes, see 16 Wright, Miller & Cooper, Jurisdiction § 3941.

10. 28 U.S.C.A. §§ 2342, 2343. There is a provision for transfer if petitions for review of the same order are filed in several courts of appeals. 28 U.S.C.A. § 2112(a).

See 16 Wright, Miller & Cooper, Jurisdiction § 3944. The statute was amended in 1988 to put an end to the unseemly race to the courthouse that had often been spurred by the "first to file" rule. See McGarity, Multi–Party Forum Shopping for Appellate Review of Administrative Action, 1980, 129 U.Pa.L.Rev. 302.

11. 28 U.S.C.A. § 2347. See also Appellate Rules 15–20.

12. 5 U.S.C.A. § 706(2)(E); Universal Camera Corp. v. N.L.R.B., 1951, 71 S.Ct. 456, 340 U.S. 474, 95 L.Ed. 456.

13. Report of the Study Group on the Caseload of the Supreme Court, 1972, 57 F.R.D. 573, 597. The Supreme Court had said that the statutes on review of ICC orders were "an historical patchwork * * * surely ripe for congressional consideration this reform was finally accomplished in 1975.[14]   Actions to enforce an ICC order or to enjoin or suspend an order of the ICC for the payment of money or the collection of fines, penalties, or forfeitures are heard by a single judge in the district court.[15]   All other review of ICC orders is now in the courts of appeals to be handled in the same fashion as review of other agencies.[16]

On occasion Congress will seek to preclude review.   The Comprehensive Environmental Response, Compensation, and Liability Act ("CERCLA"), for example, uses broad and categorical language to foreclose federal judicial review of CERCLA cleanups unless the review action falls within several narrowly defined exceptions.[17]   Many litigants have turned to the courts, claiming that immediate review should be available to them.   The courts have responded in a variety of ways, and often have allowed review despite what seems the plain meaning of the statute.[18]

§ 104.   Appellate Procedure [1]

One of the most striking achievements in the federal rules from the first has been the simplified procedures they introduced for taking appeals.   These matters were dealt with until 1968 by Civil Rules 73 to 76 and Criminal Rules 37 to 39.   In that year the Federal Rules of Appellate Procedure were adopted, applicable to all cases, and the former civil and criminal provisions were repealed.   The Appellate Rules incorporate in general the portions of the Civil Rules and Criminal Rules that they replaced but they also make uniform provision for a number of other matters of appellate practice that prior to 1968 were dealt with in varying ways by the rules of the eleven courts of appeals, though the uniformity that was hoped for has been greatly compromised by the proliferation of local rules for particular circuits.

Under the rules the timely filing of a simple notice of appeal is the only step required to take an appeal.   Such former devices as writs of errors, bills of exceptions, summons and severance, petitions for allowance of appeal, citations, assignments of errors, and similar vestiges of

* * *."   Interstate Commerce Comm. v. Atlantic Coast Line R. Co., 1966, 86 S.Ct. 1000, 1007 n. 4, 383 U.S. 576, 586 n. 4, 16 L.Ed.2d 109.

14. Act of Jan. 2, 1975, Pub.L. 93–584, 88 Stat. 1917; Boskey & Gressman, Recent Reforms in the Federal Judicial Structure— Three–Judge District Courts and Appellate Review, 1975, 67 F.R.D. 135, 154–156.

15. 28 U.S.C.A. § 1336(a).

16. 28 U.S.C.A. §§ 2321–2323, 2342(5).

17. This is § 113(h) of CERCLA, 42 U.S.C.A. § 9613(h).

18. See Healy, Judicial Review and CERCLA Response Actions: Interpretive Strategies in the Face of Plain Meaning, 1993, Harv.Envtl.L.Rev. 1.

§ 104

1. 16 Wright, Miller & Cooper, Jurisdiction §§ 3945–3994. The principal author of this portion of volume 16 was Professor Eugene Gressman of the University of North Carolina Law School. See also Tigar, Federal Appeals: Jurisdiction and Practice, 2d ed. 1993, cc. 6–11; Knibb, Federal Courts of Appeals Manual, 2d ed. 1990, cc. 13–28; Ward, The Federal Rules of Appellate Procedure, 1968, 28 Fed.B.J. 100.

procedural antiquity have been "consigned, without mourners, to the legal limbo."[2]

It is true that an appellant who has filed a notice of appeal cannot then sit back and do nothing until its case is called for argument. It must pay the required fees,[3] give security for costs, if the court so requires in a civil case,[4] file the record on appeal,[5] and file its brief and appendix,[6] but none of these steps is jurisdictional.[7] The appeal may be dismissed for failure to take these further steps at the proper time, but the matter is within the discretion of the court of appeals. It need not dismiss the appeal and ordinarily will not do so in the absence of prejudice to the appellee.[8]

The only exceptions to this general pattern are interlocutory appeals under 28 U.S.C.A. § 1292(b) and appeals from the order of a district court on appeal from a magistrate judge. In these instances the party seeking to appeal must petition the appellate court and its petition must be allowed before the appeal may proceed further.[9]

The notice of appeal, as described in Appellate Rule 3(c), is an extremely simple document.[10] Some notice of appeal, regarded as sufficient by the appellate court, must be filed, for the notice of appeal is the one jurisdictional prerequisite to an appeal.[11] The courts are very liberal, however, in entertaining an appeal even where the notice fails to comply with the rule. The notice should not be used as a technical trap for the unwary draftsman, and a defective notice of appeal should not warrant dismissal for want of jurisdiction if the intention to appeal from a specific judgment may be reasonably inferred from the text of the notice and the defect has not materially misled the appellee.[12] This has been fully understood by the courts. As noted by the Ninth Circuit, "there is a considerable body of authority indicating that in determining whether an attempted appeal has been accomplished, most informally drawn papers and improperly labeled documents have been held sufficient to accomplish the apparent objective of taking an appeal. * * *

---

2. Cf. Wiener, The Supreme Court's New Rules, 1954, 68 Harv.L.Rev. 20, 59.

3. Appellate Rule 3(e).

4. Appellate Rule 7.

5. Appellate Rules 10, 11.

6. Appellate Rules 28, 30–32.

7. Appellate Rule 3(a).

8. Compare Savard v. Marine Contracting Inc., C.A.2d, 1972, 471 F.2d 536, 543, certiorari denied 93 S.Ct. 2778, 412 U.S. 943, 37 L.Ed.2d 404, and Mikkelson v. Young Men's Christian Assn. of Chicago, C.A.7th, 1963, 317 F.2d 78, 80, with Paac v. Rizzo, C.A.3d, 1974, 502 F.2d 306, 309 n. 3, certiorari denied 95 S.Ct. 780, 419 U.S. 1108, 42 L.Ed.2d 804, and Johnson v. Danielson, C.A.9th, 1961, 295 F.2d 12.

9. The procedure for petitioning for a § 1292(b) appeal is set out in Appellate Rule 5 and for an appeal from a magistrate judge under 28 U.S.C.A. § 636(c)(5) in Appellate Rule 6. See 16 Wright, Miller & Cooper, Jurisdiction §§ 3951, 3951.1. The former practice requiring permission for bankruptcy appeals has been eliminated. See Appellate Rule 6; 16 Wright, Miller & Cooper, Jurisdiction § 3952.

10. See Official Form 1 of the Appellate Rules.

11. U.S. v. Robinson, 1960, 80 S.Ct. 282, 285, 361 U.S. 220, 224, 4 L.Ed.2d 259; Federal Deposit Ins. Corp. v. Congregation Poiley Tzedeck, C.C.A.2d, 1946, 159 F.2d 163, 166.

12. See the many cases cited 16 Wright, Miller & Cooper, Jurisdiction § 3949 nn. 2, 15.

The rationale of the cases relating to informal or irregular appeals is that notwithstanding the papers filed were inaptly worded, or labeled, or even failed to use the word 'appeal,' or were filed in the wrong court, yet they sufficed to show the party intended to appeal." [13] The Supreme Court has endorsed this liberality in passing on the sufficiency of a notice of appeal. [14]

There has been one striking exception to this pattern of liberality. The Supreme Court held that a notice of appeal that omitted the name of a particular appellant, through a clerical error by a secretary in his attorney's office, was ineffective to take an appeal for that party, and it did not remedy the situation that the notice of appeal had said "et al." "Although a court may construe the Rules liberally in determining whether they have been complied with, it may not waive the jurisdictional requirements of Rules 3 and 4, even for 'good cause shown' under Rule 2." [15] This has been remedied by an elaborate amendment of Rule 3(c) adopted in 1993. The amendment allows the use of general terms in designating the parties who are appealing and provides also that an appeal will not be dismissed for failure to name a party whose intent to appeal is otherwise clear from the notice. [16]

In civil cases the notice of appeal must be filed within 30 days after entry of judgment except where the United States is a party to the suit, in which case 60 days is allowed. [17] In a criminal case the notice must be filed within ten days by the defendant and within 30 days by the government if it is authorized to appeal. [18] Prior to 1966 the time could be extended for 30 days in a civil case only because the party, through excusable neglect, had failed to learn of the entry of the judgment. [19] In criminal cases there could be no extension for any reason. [20] These

13. Yanow v. Weyerhaeuser S.S. Co., C.A.9th, 1958, 274 F.2d 274, 282–283, certiorari denied 80 S.Ct. 671, 362 U.S. 919, 4 L.Ed.2d 739.

14. Foman v. Davis, 1962, 83 S.Ct. 227, 371 U.S. 178, 9 L.Ed.2d 222. See also Smith v. Barry, 1992, 112 S.Ct. 678, ___ U.S. ___, 116 L.Ed.2d 678; Sanabria v. U.S., 1978, 98 S.Ct. 2170, 2180 n. 21, 437 U.S. 54, 67 n. 21, 57 L.Ed.2d 43.

15. Torres v. Oakland Scavenger Co., 1988, 108 S.Ct. 2405, 2409, 487 U.S. 312, 317, 101 L.Ed.2d 285.

16. See the Advisory Committee Note to the 1993 amendment of Rule 3(c), reprinted 147 F.R.D. at 346–348.

That a party is named in the notice of appeal does not mean that the party has standing to take an appeal. A member of a school board who dissented from the board's decision not to appeal a decision adverse to it had no standing to appeal the decision. Bender v. Williamsport Area School Dist., 1986, 106 S.Ct. 1326, 475 U.S. 534, 89 L.Ed.2d 501. Nor may a private citizen who has intervened in the district court appeal a decision holding a state statute unconstitutional in part if the state has decided not to appeal. Diamond v. Charles, 1986, 106 S.Ct. 1697, 476 U.S. 54, 90 L.Ed.2d 48. Someone who was party to a case only in an official capacity lacks standing to appeal in an individual capacity. Karcher v. May, 1987, 108 S.Ct. 388, 484 U.S. 72, 98 L.Ed.2d 327. On standing to appeal, see 15A Wright, Miller & Cooper, Jurisdiction 2d §§ 3902, 3902.1.

17. Appellate Rule 4(a)(1).

The time limit was rigidly applied in Budinich v. Becton Dickinson & Co., 1988, 108 S.Ct. 1717, 486 U.S. 196, 100 L.Ed.2d 178.

18. Appellate Rule 4(b).

19. E.g., Watson v. Providence Washington Ins. Co., C.A.4th, 1953, 201 F.2d 736.

20. Berman v. U.S., 1964, 84 S.Ct. 1895, 378 U.S. 530, 12 L.Ed.2d 1012; U.S. v. Robinson, 1960, 80 S.Ct. 282, 361 U.S. 220, 4 L.Ed.2d 259.

provisions were changed in 1966 and in both civil and criminal cases the time for noticing the appeal may now be extended an additional 30 days for "excusable neglect" of any kind.[21] If the trial court finds excusable neglect, and grants an extension, the appellate court should not second-guess this determination and thus defeat the appeal, though some courts have done so.[22]

It is important to observe that it is the "filing" of the notice within the designated time that is required. Service on the opposing party will not do.[23] Neither will deposit in the mail if the notice is not actually received in the clerk's office within the designated time,[24] though an exception has been made in extreme cases.[25] If the clerk actually receives the notice, however, he cannot refuse to file it on the ground that his fee has not been paid.[26]

Certain posttrial motions suspend the finality of the judgment and the time for giving notice of appeal runs from the entry of the order granting or denying the motions. In criminal cases a motion for judgment of acquittal under Criminal Rule 29, a motion for a new trial under Rule 33, or a motion for arrest of judgment under Rule 34, has this effect.[27] In civil cases the time is extended by: a motion for judgment under Civil Rule 50(b); a motion to amend the findings under Rule 52(b); a motion for a new trial under Rule 59; a motion to alter or amend the judgment under Rule 59(e); or a motion for relief under Rule 60.[28] A motion for attorney's fees under Rule 54 also has this effect, but

21. The provision for extension in a civil case has since been broadened in two other ways. As further amended in 1979, Rule 4(a)(5) allows extension of time in a civil case for either excusable neglect or good cause. Appellate Rule 4(a)(5). And in 1991 a new provision was added as Appellate Rule 4(a)(6) (now mirrored also in 28 U.S.C.A. § 2107). This gives the court discretion, possibly for as long as 180 days after entry of judgment, to reopen the time for appeal for a party who did not receive notice of the entry of judgment from the clerk or from any party. Only excusable neglect will suffice in a criminal case. Appellate Rule 4(b). See 16 Wright, Miller & Cooper, Jurisdiction § 3950.

22. Cange v. Stotler & Co., C.A.7th, 1990, 913 F.2d 1204, 1212–1213; Allied Steel v. City of Abilene, C.A.5th, 1990, 909 F.2d 139, 142–143; and cases cited 16 Wright, Miller & Cooper, Jurisdiction § 3950 n. 15.

23. Federal Deposit Ins. Corp. v. Congregation Poiley Tzedeck, C.C.A.2d, 1946, 159 F.2d 163.

24. See Houston v. Lack, 1988, 108 S.Ct. 2379, 2384, 487 U.S. 266, 274, 101 L.Ed.2d 245, and cases there cited.

25. Fallen v. U.S., 1964, 84 S.Ct. 1689, 378 U.S. 139, 12 L.Ed.2d 760; Da'Ville v.

Wise, C.A.5th, 1973, 470 F.2d 1364, certiorari denied 94 S.Ct. 40, 414 U.S. 818, 38 L.Ed.2d 50; Hegler v. Board of Educ. of Bearden Sch. Dist., C.A.8th, 1971, 447 F.2d 1078.

Rule 4(c), added in 1993, makes special provision for notices of appeal filed by inmates in an institution. It codifies, and regularizes, the Supreme Court's holding in Houston v. Lack, 1988, 108 S.Ct. 2379, 487 U.S. 266, 101 L.Ed.2d 245.

26. Parissi v. Telechron, Inc., 1955, 75 S.Ct. 577, 349 U.S. 46, 99 L.Ed. 867. But see Stirling v. Chem. Bank, C.A.2d, 1975, 511 F.2d 1030.

See also Aldabe v. Aldabe, C.A.9th, 1980, 616 F.2d 1089, holding the appeal timely where the notice was received by the clerk on the last day even though it was not "filed" for another two weeks.

27. Appellate Rule 4(b). A motion for a new trial on the ground of newly discovered evidence has this effect only if the motion is made before or within ten days after entry of the judgment. Appellate Rule 4(b)(4).

28. Appellate Rule 4(a)(4). A Rule 60 motion has this effect only if it is served within ten days after the entry of judgment. Prior to amendment of this rule in 1993, a motion under Rule 60 did not affect the finality of the judgment.

only if the district court has extended the time for appeal, as it may do under a 1993 amendment of Rule 58.[29] A posttrial motion must itself be timely if it is to extend the time for appeal.[30]

Unfortunately an amendment of Appellate Rule 4(a)(4) in 1979 turned it into what one court called "a trap for the unwary into which many appellants * * * have fallen * * *."[31] The rule, as it stood from 1979 to 1993, not only provided that the specified motions suspended the finality of a judgment, but it said also that a new notice of appeal filed before the disposition of one of those motions had no effect. The Supreme Court had no choice except to apply this literally.[32] A litigant might file a timely notice of appeal, only to lose the right to appeal because of failure to file a second notice of appeal after one of the motions specified in Rule 4(a)(4) was decided. Many litigants were unaware of the requirement of a second notice, buried as it was in the middle of a complicated rule, and even where litigants knew about the rule they often failed to recognize that a motion that seemed to be for some other form of relief was in fact a Rule 4(a)(4) motion. This trap was finally corrected by amendments in 1993. The rule now provides that a notice of appeal filed before the disposition of one of the specified posttrial motions becomes effective upon disposition of the motion. Thus, a notice filed before the filing of one of the specified motions, or after the filing of a motion but before its disposition, is in effect suspended until the motion is disposed of, whereupon the previously filed notice effectively places jurisdiction in the court of appeals. That earlier notice brings the underlying case, as well as any orders specified in that notice, to the court of appeals. If a party wishes to appeal from the disposition of the motion, or from any alteration of the judgment made as a result of the motion, the party must amend the earlier notice of appeal—or file a notice of appeal if the party has not appealed earlier—to indicate this.[33]

An appellee may defend a judgment on any ground consistent with the record, even if rejected in the lower court.[34] But it cannot attack the decree with a view either to enlarging its own rights thereunder or to

---

29. In the absence of such an order under Rule 58, neither a motion for attorney's fees nor a motion for costs affects the finality of the judgment or extends the time in which to appeal. White v. New Hampshire Dept. of Employment Security, 1982, 102 S.Ct. 1162, 455 U.S. 445, 71 L.Ed.2d 325; Budinich v. Becton Dickinson & Co., 1988, 108 S.Ct. 1717, 486 U.S. 196, 100 L.Ed.2d 178. See 15B Wright, Miller & Cooper, Jurisdiction 2d § 3915.6.

30. Browder v. Director, Dept. of Corrections, 1978, 98 S.Ct. 556, 434 U.S. 257, 54 L.Ed.2d 521; Knapp v. Dow Corning Corp., C.A.5th, 1991, 941 F.2d 1336; Hulson v. Atchison, T. & S.F. Ry. Co., C.A.7th, 1961, 289 F.2d 726, certiorari denied 82 S.Ct. 61, 368 U.S. 835, 7 L.Ed.2d 36; John

E. Smith's Sons Co. v. Lattimer Foundry & Machine Co., C.A.3d, 1956, 239 F.2d 815.

31. Averhart v. Arrendondo, C.A.7th, 1985, 773 F.2d 919, 920.

32. Griggs v. Provident Consumer Discount Co., 1982, 103 S.Ct. 400, 459 U.S. 56, 74 L.Ed.2d 225.

33. See the Advisory Committee Note to the 1993 amendment of Rule 4(a)(4), reprinted in 147 F.R.D. at 361–364.

34. Colautti v. Franklin, 1979, 99 S.Ct. 675, 686 n. 16, 439 U.S. 379, 397 n. 16, 58 L.Ed.2d 596; Massachusetts Mut. Life Ins. Co. v. Ludwig, 1976, 96 S.Ct. 2158, 426 U.S. 479, 48 L.Ed.2d 784; In re Robinson, C.A.10th, 1990, 921 F.2d 252, 253.

lessening the rights of its adversary unless it files a cross-appeal, whether what it seeks is to correct an error or to supplement the decree with respect to a matter not dealt with below.[35] Until 1966 the appellee was given no additional time in which to file notice of a cross-appeal and might be trapped if it did not learn of its opponent's appeal until the time for appeal had elapsed. The rule now provides that if one party files a timely notice of appeal, any other party may file a notice of appeal within 14 days of the filing of the first notice or within the time in which he might otherwise have given notice of appeal, whichever period last expires.[36]

Ordinarily the appellant cannot seek reversal upon a ground not raised in the trial court. This is only a rule of practice, however, and it may be relaxed if the public interest so requires.[37]

Appellate Rules 10 and 11 prescribe how the record on appeal is to be prepared and transmitted to the appellate court. The record on appeal is defined as being "the original papers and exhibits filed in the district court, the transcript of proceedings, if any, and a certified copy of the docket entries prepared by the clerk." [38] When the Civil Rules were originally adopted a certified copy of the record on file in the district court was made and sent to the appellate court. This was a wasteful burden and expense.[39] In 1948 the Civil Rules were amended to permit a court of appeals, if it wished, to provide by rule that the original district court record could be used as the record on appeal and by 1962 every circuit had exercised this sensible option.

In addition to the record, of which only a single copy is required, some provision must be made for putting into the hands of each of the judges who will hear the appeal those portions of the record that are of particular significance. This document, known as the appendix, "is exactly what its name implies: an addendum to the briefs for the convenience of the judges." [40] What is to go into it and how it is to be prepared is of great significance because it forms a large part of the cost of appellate review. Rule 32(a) makes an important contribution by permitting briefs and appendices to be produced "by standard typo-

35. Morley Constr. Co. v. Maryland Cas. Co., 1937, 57 S.Ct. 325, 327–328, 300 U.S. 185, 191–192, 81 L.Ed. 593; Alexander v. Cosden Pipe Line Co., 1934, 54 S.Ct. 292, 293–294, 290 U.S. 484, 487–488, 78 L.Ed. 452; Robicheaux v. Radcliff Material, Inc., C.A.5th, 1983, 697 F.2d 662, 667–668; Stern, When to Cross–Appeal or Cross–Petition—Certainty or Confusion?, 1974, 87 Harv.L.Rev. 763; 15A Wright, Miller & Cooper, Jurisdiction 2d § 3904.

36. Appellate Rule 4(a)(3). The rule reaches "any other party" and is not limited to a cross-appeal. Jackson Jordan, Inc. v. Plasser American Corp., C.A.Fed.1984, 725 F.2d 1373.

37. Gardiner v. A. H. Robins Co., C.A.8th, 1984, 747 F.2d 1180, 1190;

Wratchford v. S.J. Groves & Sons Co., C.A.4th, 1969, 405 F.2d 1061; New York, N.H. & H.R. Co. v. Reconstruction Fin. Corp., C.A.2d, 1950, 180 F.2d 241, 244; Dennerline, Pushing Aside the General Rule in Order to Raise New Issues on Appeal, 1989, 64 Ind.L.J. 985; Martineau, Considering New Issues on Appeal: The General Rules and the Gorilla Rule, 1987, 40 Vand.L.Rev. 1023.

38. Appellate Rule 10(a).

39. See Dean, Proposed Rule for Hearing of Appeals on Original Papers, 1948, 8 F.R.D. 143, 148.

40. Ward, note 1 above, at 108.

graphic printing or by any duplicating or copying process which produces a clear black image on white paper." Thus, modern copying methods may be used and the parties are no longer confined to printing or offset duplicating.[41]

The question of the contents and preparation of the appendix was more controversial than any other question in the preparation of the Appellate Rules and at one point three different drafts were distributed for consideration by the profession.[42] The rule finally adopted contemplates that there will be filed with the appellant's brief a single appendix, prepared by the appellant, and containing all the portions of the record to which either the appellant or the appellee wishes "to direct the particular attention of the court."[43] The rule makes it very clear that the parties and the court may rely on portions of the record that are not included in the appendix[44] and it cautions that "in designating parts of the record for inclusion in the appendix, the parties shall have regard for the fact that the entire record is always available to the court for reference and examination and shall not engage in unnecessary designation."[45]

Rule 30(c) also provides that in some circumstances the appendix may be deferred until after the briefs have been prepared and filed 21 days after the brief of the appellee. The thought is that if the appendix is not prepared until after the briefs are completed the parties will be able to see precisely what the issues are, and what parts of the record need to be reproduced, and that this will encourage smaller appendices. In large cases the deferred appendix will be advantageous though the procedure for preparing it and referring to the appendix in the briefs is quite complicated. The rule was amended in 1970 to provide that the deferred appendix may be used only if the court has provided by rule for classes of cases or by order in the specific case.[46]

Finally Rule 30(f) somewhat grudgingly provides that a court of appeals may dispense with the requirement of an appendix altogether and permit appeals to be heard on copies of the relevant parts of the original record. It has been estimated that such a procedure, taking advantage of inexpensive modern copying machines, can cut the cost of

---

41. "In 1964 the cost of a single page of the brief or of the reproduction of the record by standard letterpress printing was approaching $4.00 per page; the cost of a page by offset duplicating, the only other method generally permitted by the circuits, was approximately $2.80 per page." Ward, note 1 above, at 108. See also Wilcox, Karlen & Roemer, Justice Lost—By What Appellate Papers Cost, 1958, 33 N.Y.U.L.Rev. 934.

42. Drafts of Proposed Rule 30, Uniform Rules of Federal Appellate Procedure, December 1966, 41 F.R.D. 311.

43. Appellate Rule 30. See U.S. v. Friedman, C.A.2d, 1990, 909 F.2d 705, 708–

709; Coogan v. City of Wixom, C.A.6th, 1987, 820 F.2d 170, 176.

44. Appellate Rule 30(a).

45. Appellate Rule 30(b). For helpful advice on what to include, see Aldisert, Winning on Appeal § 6.07 (1992).

46. The deferred appendix is praised as "a splendid appellate tool" by Judge John C. Godbold in Twenty Pages and Twenty Minutes—Effective Advocacy on Appeal, 1976, 30 Sw.L.J. 801, 806. The Sixth Circuit requires for most cases what amounts to a deferred appendix, although it does not use that name. Rule 11, 6th Cir. Rules.

reproduction by two-thirds and also eliminate most of the lawyer time otherwise required for preparation of the record.[47] This has been standard procedure in the Ninth Circuit since 1962 [48] and a number of other circuits now permit use of the original record and two copies of it in many kinds of cases.

As other circuits obtain experience with the Ninth Circuit practice in limited classes of cases, they are likely to become aware of its usefulness and to make it applicable in all cases. Just as in 14 years every circuit exercised the option given it and elected to adopt the original papers as the record on appeal, so too the option provided in Rule 30(f) is likely in a short time to have been exercised universally. Although a distinguished authority had said flatly of the Ninth Circuit practice that "it is not workable as a practical matter," [49] the Advisory Committee Note to Rule 30(f) states that "the judges of the Court of Appeals for the Ninth Circuit have expressed complete satisfaction with the practice there in use and have suggested that attention be called to the advantages which it offers in terms of reducing cost." [50]

The major changes in appellate procedure in the last 25 years have been with regard to oral argument and publication of opinions. In the face of overwhelming caseloads, most courts of appeals have felt the need to institute screening procedures to decide which cases merit oral argument and how much time should be allowed for it. In addition, many cases are now disposed of by summary orders.[51] Even when an opinion is written, it is frequently designated as not for publication and these opinions are usually regarded as without precedential effect.[52] If these drastic reforms had not been instituted, the federal courts of appeals would have collapsed under the pressure of docket congestion.[53] Even

47. Joiner, Lawyer Attitudes Toward Law and Procedural Reform, 1966, 50 Judicature 23, 25.

48. This now appears as Rule 30–1, 9th Cir.Rules. See Tigar, note 1 above, § 7.04.

49. Prettyman, The New Federal Rules of Appellate Procedure, 1968, 28 Fed.B.J. 97, 99.

50. 1967, 43 F.R.D. 61, 150.

51. Appellate Rule 34(a); Commission on Revision of the Federal Court Appellate System, Structure and Internal Procedures: Recommendations for Change, 1975, 67 F.R.D. 195, 247–260; Wasby, Oral Argument in the Ninth Circuit: The View from Bench and Bar, 1981, 11 Golden Gate L.Rev. 21; Haworth, Screening and Summary Procedures in the United States Courts of Appeals, 1973 Wash.U.L.Q. 257.

52. Reynolds & Richman, An Evaluation of Limited Publication in the United States Courts of Appeals, 1981, 48 U.Chi. L.Rev. 573; Reynolds & Richman, The Non–Precedential Precedent—Limited Publication and No–Citation Rules in the Unit-

ed States Courts of Appeals, 1978, 78 Col. L.Rev. 1167; Newbern & Wilson, Rule 21: Unprecedent and the Disappearing Court, 1978, 32 Ark.L.Rev. 37; Stern, The Enigma of Unpublished Opinions, 1978, 64 A.B.A.J. 1191; Walther, The Noncitation Rule and the Concept of Stare Decisis, 1978, 61 Marq.L.Rev. 581; Gardner, Ninth Circuit's Unpublished Opinions: Denial of Equal Justice, 1975, 61 A.B.A.J. 1224; Note, Unreported Decisions in the United States Courts of Appeals, 1977, 63 Cornell L.Rev. 128.

It has been suggested that inexpensive database access and computerized search technologies may justify reconsidering policies of not publishing certain opinions. Report of the Federal Courts Study Committee, April 2, 1990, pp. 130–131.

53. For a grim picture of the workload in a court of appeals today, see King, A Matter of Conscience, 1991, 28 Hous.L.Rev. 955, 956.

so, there is concern for the implications these new devices may have for the quality of justice administered by the appellate courts.[54]

54. Compare Carrington, Ceremony and Realism: Demise of Appellate Procedure, 1980, 66 A.B.A.J. 860, with Godbold, Improvements in Appellate Procedure: Better Use of Available Facilities, 1980, 66 A.B.A.J. 863.

The extent to which screening procedures and dispositions without published opinions are being used in each circuit is examined by the Senate Judiciary Committee in S.Rep. No. 94–404, 1975, and concern expressed that "our concept of due process imposes limits on the nature and on the extent of permissible short-cuts in the appellate process * * *." Id. at 25.

The Federal Courts Study Committee said that the federal appellate courts have been able to deal with the climb in appellate workload "only through increases in productivity that seem to be approaching their limit. Further attempts to raise productivity by the most commonly suggested and employed means, such as increases in staff and reducing opportunity for oral argument, could threaten the integrity of the process." Report of the Federal Courts Study Committee, April 2, 1990, p. 109.

Chapter 12

THE APPELLATE JURISDICTION OF THE SUPREME COURT

Analysis

§ 105. Review of Decisions of the District Courts [1]

A principal purpose of the Evarts Act of 1891, which created the circuit court of appeals, of the Judicial Code of 1911, which abolished the old circuit courts, and of the Judges' Bill of 1925, limiting appeals to the Supreme Court and substituting the discretionary writ of certiorari,[2] was to lessen the burden on the Supreme Court and to put control of its docket in its hands by substituting an intermediate appellate court to which most appeals would go and that would, in most cases, speak the final word.

That goal is highly desirable, yet on various occasions in the first part of this century the view became accepted that there were particular classes of cases of great public moment that required prompt review as a matter of right in the highest court of the land. Responding to these pressures, Congress made provision in four classes of cases for direct review by appeal from a district court to the Supreme Court.

Experience demonstrated the unwisdom of those provisions. The Supreme Court was forced to decide these cases without the guidance of a decision from a court of appeals. The cases took up a disproportionate amount of the limited time the Court has for oral argument.[3] That burden would have been even greater if the Court had not disposed of

---

§ 105

1. 17 Wright, Miller & Cooper, Jurisdiction 2d §§ 4039–4040; Stern, Gressman, Shapiro & Geller, Supreme Court Practice, 7th ed. 1993, §§ 2.6–2.10.

2. See § 1 above.

3. In an average term, 22% of the cases argued orally in the Supreme Court were direct appeals from three-judge courts though these cases made up only 2.7% of the Court's docket. Report of the Study Group on the Caseload of the Supreme Court, 1972, 57 F.R.D. 573, 598. The virtual elimination of three-judge courts in 1976—see § 50 above—has remedied this unhappy situation.

many of them by summary orders, without full briefs or oral argument, but summary disposition increases the risk that the Court may act erroneously. Many of these cases came to the Court on an inadequate record. Uncertainty about when direct appeal would lie and what the scope of review was added wasteful complications to the process.

For all of these reasons direct appeal from district courts has been a failure. Where prompt decision by the Supreme Court is truly important, it is possible for the Supreme Court to bypass the courts of appeals by granting certiorari before judgment in those courts.[4] Even this is not always necessary, because a prompt determination can be had even though there is review in a court of appeals prior to Supreme Court review.[5] These arguments against direct review have come to be accepted,[6] and in the last 18 years there has been great progress toward eliminating direct appeal.

The earliest of the direct appeal statutes was the Expediting Act of 1903,[7] which was intended originally to provide expeditious determination of actions brought by the United States under the antitrust laws and the Interstate Commerce Act, but was extended also to cover actions under the common-carriers sections of the Communications Act.[8] The Expediting Act had two features. In any case falling within the act the Attorney General could certify that the case was of general public importance. Upon such certification, the case had to be heard at the earliest practicable date by a three-judge district court. The other feature of the Expediting Act was that an appeal from the final judgment of the district court would lie only to the Supreme Court. It must be noticed that these features were independent. Certification by the Attorney General, which required a three-judge court, was not much used in recent years. Direct appeal ran from the final judgment, however, even though the case was not so certified, and accordingly was heard by a single judge.

The intricacies of the Expediting Act—and they were many—need not be explored because it is now a matter of past history. Responding to criticisms from the Court itself that direct review had proven "unsatisfactory" in Expediting Act cases,[9] Congress responded in 1974 by

---

4. 28 U.S.C.A. § 1254(1).

The disadvantages in not having an opinion from the court of appeals are described in the separate opinion of Justices Burton and Frankfurter in Youngstown Sheet & Tube Co. v. Sawyer, 1952, 72 S.Ct. 775, 343 U.S. 937, 96 L.Ed. 1344.

5. See § 106 n. 13 below.

6. Report of the Study Group on the Caseload of the Supreme Court, 1972, 57 F.R.D. 573, 596–602; Boskey & Gressman, Recent Reforms in the Federal Judicial Structure—Three–Judge Courts and Appellate Review, 1975, 67 F.R.D. 135, 143–147.

7. Act of Feb. 11, 1903, c. 544, 32 Stat. 823.

8. Prior to their amendment or repeal by the Antitrust Procedures and Penalties Act of 1974, Pub.L. 93–528, 88 Stat. 1706, the relevant statutes were: 15 U.S.C.A. §§ 28, 29; 49 U.S.C.A. §§ 44, 45; 47 U.S.C.A. § 401(d).

9. U.S. v. Singer Mfg. Co., 1963, 83 S.Ct. 1773, 1774 n. 1, 374 U.S. 174, 175 n. 1, 10 L.Ed.2d 823. Most commentators agreed. E.g., ALI Study, p. 324; Gesell, A Much Needed Reform—Repeal the Expediting Act for Anti-trust Cases, 1961 N.Y.S.B.A. Antitrust Law Symposium 98.

substantially abolishing the Act.[10] The rarely used right of the Attorney General to require a three-judge court was ended and so, for the most part, was direct appeal to the Supreme Court.[11] The only direct appeal that remains is in civil actions brought by the United States seeking equitable relief for violation of the antitrust laws or to enforce certain provisions of the Interstate Commerce Act.[12] In these cases both appeals from final judgments and interlocutory appeals go to the courts of appeals, with one exception. An appeal from a final judgment may still go directly to the Supreme Court if, on application of any party, the district judge makes an order "stating that immediate consideration of the appeal by the Supreme Court is of general public importance in the administration of justice." Even when such an order is made, the Supreme Court is given discretion either to hear the appeal or to deny the direct appeal and remand the case to the court of appeals.[13]

The second class of direct appeals from district courts was under the Criminal Appeals Act of 1907, as amended over the years.[14] The Supreme Court had held in 1892 that the act creating the circuit courts of appeals, passed the preceding year, had left the United States without any right of review in criminal cases, even where the defendant had not been put in jeopardy.[15] For years successive attorneys general asked that this omission be rectified, but their appeals were unheeded. The impetus that led to adoption of the Act of 1907 came from the action of a single district judge who directed a verdict for the individual defendants in an antitrust case of importance to the Roosevelt administration.[16] President Theodore Roosevelt accordingly pressed successfully for passage of a law giving the government the right of appeal, and providing that such appeal would be to the Supreme Court. It is somewhat ironic that the Act of 1907 would not have provided relief in the case that led to the legislation, since in that case defendants had been put in jeopardy. As the Act was successively amended, it defined some kinds of appeals that could be taken to the Supreme Court and others that went to the courts of appeals, with provision for transfer if, as not infrequently happened, the government appealed to the wrong court.

In 1928 Professors Frankfurter and Landis wrote: "The reasons which impelled the enactment of the Act of 1907 remain. They will continue to be controlling. Congress is not apt to give the power of invalidating its legislation wholly to the inferior federal courts without

10. Antitrust Procedures and Penalties Act of 1974, Pub.L. 93–528, 88 Stat. 1706.

11. See Boskey & Gressman, note 6 above.

12. 15 U.S.C.A. § 29, 49 U.S.C.A. § 45.

13. 15 U.S.C.A. § 29(b).

An eminent authority has said that it is "highly unlikely" that there will be many such antitrust cases in which both the district judge and the Supreme Court will find that there should be immediate review by

the Supreme Court. 1A Boskey, West's Federal Forms, 4th ed. 1992, § 241, p. 8. Stern, Gressman, Shapiro & Geller, note 1 above, report at p. 54 that as of 1993 a direct appeal has been authorized in only two cases.

14. Act of March 2, 1907, c. 2564, 34 Stat. 1246; 18 U.S.C.A. § 3731.

15. U.S. v. Sanges, 1892, 12 S.Ct. 609, 144 U.S. 310, 36 L.Ed. 445.

16. U.S. v. Armour & Co., D.C.Ill.1906, 142 F. 808.

an appeal as of right to the Supreme Court, and Congress is still less likely to do this with regard to criminal legislation. The criminal law is increasingly resorted to, for the 'achievement of some social betterment rather than the punishment of the crimes as in cases of mala in se.' The defeat of these purposes is not likely to be entrusted to any tribunal other than the Supreme Court." [17] This view was not accepted by more recent commentators, who thought it undesirable to burden the Supreme Court with an obligatory appeal in these cases, many of them of little consequence save to the parties.[18] The narrow scope of review made such appeals quite artificial,[19] and the circumstances in which the statute allowed appeal were defined in archaic terms that made the right of appeal quite uncertain.[20] In 1970 the Supreme Court called the Criminal Appeals Act "a failure," [21] and Congress responded in less than a year with drastic revision. The language of the former statute was much simplified, the right of appeal by the government was extended to all cases in which the Constitution permits appeal, and all appeals now go to the courts of appeals rather than to the Supreme Court.[22]

A third class of cases in which there is direct review is from an order granting or denying, after notice and hearing, an interlocutory or permanent injunction in any civil action, suit or proceeding required by any Act of Congress to be heard and determined by a district court of three judges.[23] There had been such a three-judge court, with direct appeal to the Supreme Court, since 1903 in certain cases under the Expediting Act, since 1906 in cases to enjoin orders of the Interstate Commerce Commission, since 1910 in cases seeking to restrain enforcement of a state statute or administrative order, and since 1937 in cases seeking to restrain enforcement of a federal statute. The circumstances in which a three-judge court was required and the bewildering rules on when the orders of such a court were appealable directly to the Supreme Court and when they had to go to a court of appeals have been considered in an earlier section.[24] As indicated there, Congress responded in 1974 and

---

17. Frankfurter & Landis, The Business of the Supreme Court, 1928, p. 120. Justice Frankfurter took the same view as had Professor Frankfurter. In a letter to the present author on June 17, 1959, he said: "I have of course not been unmindful that some of the cases which automatically come here under the Criminal Appeals Act of 1907 don't belong here, but that reflection has always been checked by the considerations that led to direct review of the invalidation or misconstruction of an important criminal statute."

18. Kurland, The Mersky Case and the Criminal Appeals Act: A Suggestion for Amendment of the Statute, 1961, 28 U.Chi. L.Rev. 419; Friedenthal, Government Appeals in Federal Criminal Cases, 1959, 12 Stan.L.Rev. 71.

19. See U.S. v. Borden Co., 1939, 60 S.Ct. 182, 186, 308 U.S. 188, 193, 84 L.Ed.

181. See also U.S. v. Cores, 1958, 78 S.Ct. 875, 356 U.S. 405, 2 L.Ed.2d 873; U.S. v. Harriss, 1954, 74 S.Ct. 808, 347 U.S. 612, 98 L.Ed. 989.

20. E.g., U.S. v. Sisson, 1970, 90 S.Ct. 2117, 399 U.S. 267, 26 L.Ed.2d 608; U.S. v. Mersky, 1960, 80 S.Ct. 459, 361 U.S. 431, 4 L.Ed.2d 423.

21. U.S. v. Sisson, 1970, 90 S.Ct. 2117, 2139, 399 U.S. 267, 307, 26 L.Ed.2d 608.

22. 18 U.S.C.A. § 3731, as amended by Act of Jan. 2, 1971, Pub.L. 91–644, Title III, § 14(a), 84 Stat. 1890. See 15B Wright, Miller & Cooper, Jurisdiction 2d §§ 3919–3919.10.

23. 28 U.S.C.A. § 1253; 17 Wright, Miller & Cooper, Jurisdiction 2d § 4040.

24. See § 50 above.

1976 to the widespread dissatisfaction with three-judge courts by ending them for Expediting Act and ICC cases and by virtually eliminating them for constitutional cases.

The final class of cases in which direct appeal to the Supreme Court had been permitted was enacted as part of the Judiciary Act of 1937. It allowed appeal to the Supreme Court from an interlocutory or final judgment of any court of the United States holding an Act of Congress unconstitutional in any civil action, suit, or proceeding to which the United States or any of its agencies, or any officer or employee thereof, as such officer or employee, is a party.[25] Unlike the provision for review of three-judge courts, there was no requirement here of an injunction to restrain enforcement of the act in question. Instead it was enough that an Act of Congress had been held unconstitutional, even as a matter of defense in a proceeding to enforce the act.[26] Direct review was available even though the act was held unconstitutional only as applied to a particular person, with its constitutionality in general not questioned.[27] The statute applied only if the act was held unconstitutional. If the district court decided in favor of the act, review was in the court of appeals as in any other case. Nor could there be direct review if the lower court had construed a statute narrowly to avoid a possible constitutional question.[28] Direct appeal was not provided, though an Act of Congress was held unconstitutional, in purely private litigation.[29] When direct appeal was available under this statute, it brought the whole case before the Supreme Court, and permitted the Court to pass on all the questions in the case.[30]

This statute was finally repealed in 1988.[31] Even though in recent years appeals from district-court decisions under this statute had been coming to the Court with some frequency,[32] Congress correctly concluded that appeal by right is an anachronism and that the Supreme Court should have control over its own docket.[33]

---

25. Act of Aug. 24, 1937, c. 754, §§ 2, 5, 50 Stat. 752, 753, as amended; 28 U.S.C.A. § 1252.

26. Fleming v. Rhodes, 1947, 67 S.Ct. 1140, 331 U.S. 100, 91 L.Ed. 1368.

27. U.S. v. Darusmont, 1981, 101 S.Ct. 549, 449 U.S. 292, 66 L.Ed.2d 513.

28. U.S. v. Christian Echoes Nat. Ministry, Inc., 1972, 92 S.Ct. 663, 404 U.S. 561, 30 L.Ed.2d 716.

29. But this had to be read in the light of 28 U.S.C.A. § 2403, requiring certification to the Attorney General when a constitutional question is raised in a case to which the United States is not a party, and permitting intervention by the United States in such a case as a matter of right. If the United States chose to intervene and an Act of Congress was held unconstitutional, the United States could appeal though it was not a party originally. International Ladies' Garment Workers' Union v. Don-

nelly Garment Co., 1938, 58 S.Ct. 875, 304 U.S. 243, 82 L.Ed. 1316.

30. McLucas v. DeChamplain, 1975, 95 S.Ct. 1365, 421 U.S. 21, 43 L.Ed.2d 699; U.S. v. Raines, 1960, 80 S.Ct. 519, 362 U.S. 17, 4 L.Ed.2d 524.

31. Act of June 27, 1988, 100th Cong., 2d Sess., Pub.L. 100–352, § 1, 102 Stat. 682.

32. See 17 Wright, Miller & Cooper, Jurisdiction 2d § 4039 n. 30.

33. See Boskey & Gressman, The Supreme Court Bids Farewell to Mandatory Appeals, 1988, 121 F.R.D. 81; Gressman, Requiem for the Supreme Court's Obligatory Jurisdiction, 1979, 65 A.B.A.J. 1325; Report of the Study Group on the Caseload of the Supreme Court, 1972, 57 F.R.D. 573, 601–602.

The exception that proves the rule is the Flag Protection Act of 1989 providing for

It is conceivable—though it apparently has happened only once—that in a case where direct appeal to the Supreme Court is provided, that Court will be unable to muster six qualified judges to constitute a quorum. Though appeal is not constitutionally required, there is a strong tradition that a party should be able to obtain appellate review in at least one court. Accordingly in 1944 a statute was passed to meet this situation when the Supreme Court could not muster a quorum to hear an appeal under the Expediting Act in an important antitrust case.[34] In the 1948 revision of the Judicial Code this special statute was made applicable to all cases where there is direct appeal from a district court to the Supreme Court and a quorum is lacking.[35] It provides that in such cases the case may be remitted to the court of appeals for the circuit in which the case arose, to be considered either by the three senior judges of that court of appeals or by the court en banc. The decision of the court of appeals in such a case is final and conclusive.

§ 106. Review of Decisions of the Courts of Appeals [1]

Decisions of the courts of appeals can be reviewed in the Supreme Court only by the statutory writ of certiorari. The statute authorizing such review is sweeping. The Court, in its discretion, may issue the writ "upon the petition of any party to any civil or criminal case, before or after rendition of judgment or decree." [2] Review of decisions of state courts necessarily is more limited [3] for in most such cases there is no basis for federal jurisdiction. Cases in the courts of appeals, on the other hand, must involve at least a claim of federal jurisdiction to have reached those courts and thus are within the constitutional limits of the appellate jurisdiction of the Supreme Court. Thus, as the Court said of an earlier form of the present statute for review by certiorari to the courts of appeals, "the generality of this provision was not a mere matter of accident. It expressed the thought of Congress distinctly and clearly, and was intended to vest in this court a comprehensive and unlimited power." [4]

The Court may issue a writ of certiorari to a court of appeals regardless of the subject matter of the case, the citizenship of the parties,

direct appeal of district-court rulings on the constitutionality of that act. 18 U.S.C.A. § 700(d). The Supreme Court took two appeals from district courts under that Act and affirmed the holdings of invalidity. U.S. v. Eichman, 1990, 110 S.Ct. 2404, 2406–2407, 496 U.S. 310, 312–316, 110 L.Ed.2d 287.

34. Act of June 9, 1944, c. 239, 58 Stat. 272; U.S. v. Aluminum Co. of America, 1944, 64 S.Ct. 1281, 322 U.S. 716, 88 L.Ed. 1557. A later phase of the same proceeding is reported in U.S. v. United States Dist.

Court, 1948, 68 S.Ct. 1035, 334 U.S. 258, 92 L.Ed. 1351.

35. 28 U.S.C.A. § 2109.

§ 106

1. 17 Wright, Miller & Cooper, Jurisdiction 2d §§ 4035–4038; Stern, Gressman, Shapiro & Geller, Supreme Court Practice, 7th ed. 1993, §§ 2.1–2.5.

2. 28 U.S.C.A. § 1254(1).

3. See § 107 below.

4. Forsyth v. City of Hammond, 1897, 17 S.Ct. 665, 668, 166 U.S. 506, 513, 41 L.Ed. 1095.

or the amount in controversy.[5] It may issue such a writ although the decision of the court of appeals is not a final judgment. The lack of finality may be a factor that will induce the Court to deny certiorari. It has said that it should not review interlocutory orders of the courts of appeals "unless it is necessary to prevent extraordinary inconvenience and embarrassment to the conduct of the cause."[6] But in the very case in which it said this it did in fact review the order below, though it was not final, and this power to review interlocutory orders of the courts of appeals has been exercised in many cases.[7] A party is not required to petition for certiorari to review an interlocutory order, and the fact that it did not petition, or that its petition was denied, does not bar the Court from granting certiorari after final judgment in the case and then considering the supposedly erroneous interlocutory order.[8]

The Court has power under the statute to grant certiorari before judgment in the court of appeals, so long as the case has been docketed in a court of appeals,[9] but "this is a power not ordinarily to be exercised."[10] The Court has granted such writs where the case involved an important constitutional question, or some other matter of great national significance, on which a speedy decision from the Supreme Court was important.[11] Even in these situations, there have been protests from justices who felt that a considered opinion from the court of appeals would be of sufficient assistance to the Court to justify such delay as it would cause.[12] In other instances, it has been demonstrated

5. Whitney v. Dick, 1906, 26 S.Ct. 584, 202 U.S. 132, 50 L.Ed. 963.

6. American Constr. Co. v. Jacksonville, T. & K.W.R. Co., 1893, 13 S.Ct. 758, 763, 148 U.S. 372, 384, 37 L.Ed. 486.

See also Brotherhood of Locomotive Firemen and Enginemen v. Bangor & Aroostook R. Co., 1967, 88 S.Ct. 437, 438, 389 U.S. 327, 328, 19 L.Ed.2d 560, in which the Court, in denying certiorari, said that the fact that the court of appeals had remanded the case for further proceedings made the case "not yet ripe for review by this Court." And see the opinion of Justice Scalia respecting denial of certiorari in Virginia Military Institute v. U.S., 1993, 113 S.Ct. 2431, ___ U.S. ___, 124 L.Ed.2d 651.

7. 17 Wright, Miller & Cooper, Jurisdiction 2d § 4036, pp. 26–33. For an elaborate justification of the power of the Court to do so, see Forsyth v. Hammond, 1897, 17 S.Ct. 665, 166 U.S. 506, 41 L.Ed. 1095.

8. E.g., Washington v. Washington State Commercial Passenger Fishing Vessel Assn., 1979, 99 S.Ct. 3055, 3067 n. 19, 443 U.S. 658, 672 n. 19, 61 L.Ed.2d 823; Hughes Tool Co. v. Trans World Airlines, Inc., 1973, 93 S.Ct. 647, 650 n. 1, 409 U.S. 363, 365 n. 1, 34 L.Ed.2d 577; City of Indianapolis v. Chase Nat. Bank, 1941, 62 S.Ct. 15, 314 U.S. 63, 86 L.Ed. 47; Toledo

Scale Co. v. Computing Scale Co., 1923, 43 S.Ct. 458, 261 U.S. 399, 67 L.Ed. 719; Hamilton–Brown Shoe Co. v. Wolf Brothers & Co., 1916, 36 S.Ct. 269, 240 U.S. 251, 60 L.Ed. 629; Panama R. Co. v. Napier Shipping Co., 1897, 17 S.Ct. 572, 574, 166 U.S. 280, 284, 41 L.Ed. 1004.

9. Gay v. Ruff, 1934, 54 S.Ct. 608, 292 U.S. 25, 78 L.Ed. 1099.

10. The Three Friends, 1897, 17 S.Ct. 495, 497, 166 U.S. 1, 49, 41 L.Ed. 897.

11. E.g., Mistretta v. U.S., 1989, 109 S.Ct. 647, 654, 488 U.S. 361, 371, 102 L.Ed.2d 714; Dames & Moore v. Regan, 1981, 101 S.Ct. 2972, 453 U.S. 654, 69 L.Ed.2d 918; U.S. v. Nixon, 1974, 94 S.Ct. 3090, 418 U.S. 683, 41 L.Ed.2d 1039; Wilson v. Girard, 1957, 77 S.Ct. 1409, 354 U.S. 524, 1 L.Ed.2d 1544; Youngstown Sheet & Tube Co. v. Sawyer, 1952, 72 S.Ct. 863, 865, 343 U.S. 579, 584, 96 L.Ed. 1153; U.S. v. United Mine Workers, 1947, 67 S.Ct. 677, 684, 330 U.S. 258, 269, 91 L.Ed. 884; Ex parte Quirin, 1942, 63 S.Ct. 1, 6–7, 317 U.S. 1, 19–20, 87 L.Ed. 3; Carter v. Carter Coal Co., 1936, 56 S.Ct. 855, 298 U.S. 238, 80 L.Ed. 1160.

12. Youngstown Sheet & Tube Co. v. Sawyer, 1952, 72 S.Ct. 775, 343 U.S. 937, 96 L.Ed. 1344 (separate opinion of Justices Burton and Frankfurter).

that it need not delay a case unduly to await decision in the court of appeals before granting certiorari.[13] The power to grant certiorari before judgment is also used to bring up a case that involves an issue also presented by a case then pending before the Court.[14] There is some question, never yet resolved, whether the Court has power to grant certiorari before judgment below where the court of appeals is reviewing an administrative order. The argument is that, unless there has been some order by a court that the Supreme Court can affirm, reverse, or modify,[15] review of the administrative decision in the first instance by the Supreme Court would be an unconstitutional exercise of original jurisdiction.[16]

The Court may grant certiorari on petition of "any party." In some cases where certiorari has been granted prior to judgment in the court of appeals it has been the United States, which was successful in the district court, that has sought speedy review by petitioning for certiorari.[17] There seems to be no case in which the Court has granted certiorari at the instance of a party who has been successful in the court of appeals.[18]

Until 1988 there were a few instances in which review of decisions of a court of appeals was by appeal rather than by certiorari. This was true where the court had held an Act of Congress unconstitutional in a case to which the United States is a party.[19] There was specific provision for appeal to the Supreme Court when a court of appeals had held a state statute to be repugnant to the Constitution, laws, or treaties of the United States.[20] These statutes were repealed because of a general belief that the Supreme Court should have control of its docket and that cases

13. In an important case involving a nationwide steel strike, the judgment of the district court was entered October 21st. The appeal was argued before the Third Circuit on October 22nd and decided by that court on October 27th. The case was argued before the Supreme Court on November 3d and decided November 7th. United Steelworkers of America v. U.S., 1959, 80 S.Ct. 1, 361 U.S. 39, 4 L.Ed.2d 12. See also Aaron v. Cooper, 1958, 78 S.Ct. 1189, 357 U.S. 566, 2 L.Ed.2d 1544.

A less happy example of judicial speed, at least according to the dissenters, is New York Times Co. v. U.S., 1971, 91 S.Ct. 2140, 403 U.S. 713, 29 L.Ed.2d 822.

14. E.g., Taylor v. McElroy, 1959, 79 S.Ct. 1428, 1429, 360 U.S. 709, 710, 3 L.Ed.2d 1528; Brown v. Board of Educ., 1952, 73 S.Ct. 1, 2, 344 U.S. 1, 3, 97 L.Ed. 3; cf. Turner v. City of Memphis, 1962, 82 S.Ct. 805, 807, 369 U.S. 350, 353–354, 7 L.Ed.2d 762.

15. There was such an order in Ickes v. Associated Indus., 1943, 64 S.Ct. 74, 320 U.S. 707, 88 L.Ed. 414.

16. Cf. U.S. v. Rice, 1946, 66 S.Ct. 835, 837, 327 U.S. 742, 747, 90 L.Ed. 982.

This question was presented, but not decided, in Chandler v. Judicial Council of the Tenth Circuit, 1970, 90 S.Ct. 1648, 398 U.S. 74, 26 L.Ed.2d 100.

17. U.S. v. Nixon, 1974, 94 S.Ct. 3090, 418 U.S. 683, 41 L.Ed.2d 1039; Youngstown Sheet & Tube Co. v. Sawyer, 1952, 72 S.Ct. 863, 343 U.S. 579, 96 L.Ed. 1153; U.S. v. United Mine Workers, 1947, 67 S.Ct. 677, 330 U.S. 258, 91 L.Ed. 884; U.S. v. Bankers' Trust Co., 1935, 55 S.Ct. 407, 410, 294 U.S. 240, 294, 79 L.Ed. 885.

18. Cf. Public Serv. Comm. of Missouri v. Brashear Freight Lines, Inc., 1939, 59 S.Ct. 480, 482, 306 U.S. 204, 206, 83 L.Ed. 608.

19. The statute, repealed in 1988, was 28 U.S.C.A. § 1252. See 17 Wright, Miller & Cooper, Jurisdiction 2d § 4037.1.

20. The statute, repealed in 1988, was 28 U.S.C.A. § 1254(2). See 17 Wright, Miller & Cooper, Jurisdiction 2d § 4037.

should ordinarily come to it by the discretionary writ of certiorari rather than by appeal.[21]

The only method other than certiorari now available for taking cases from a court of appeals to the Supreme Court is by certificate. The court of appeals may certify at any time any question of law in any civil or criminal case for which instructions are desired.[22] The power is that of the court of appeals, and it has been said to be improper for the parties to move for certification.[23] Certification is limited to questions of law, and the questions must be distinct and definite.[24] The Court will dismiss a certificate in which the questions are so broad that in effect they bring up the whole case,[25] although when a case has been certified the Court may itself require that the entire record be sent up for decision of the entire matter in controversy.[26] The statute purports to make it obligatory for the Supreme Court to consider questions certified to it, but there are so many grounds on which the Court may find the certificate improper that its jurisdiction over certificates is in fact discretionary.[27]

Certification has a long history in federal practice. The old circuit courts could certify a case when the two judges before whom it was heard were divided in opinion, and frequently the judges would disagree deliberately in order to bring a question to the Supreme Court. This practice is no longer considered proper. The courts of appeals recognize that certificates should be granted only when they are actually in doubt on a question.[28] In recent years the practice has become even more restrictive. For many years the Second Circuit has refused to certify questions except in cases where the point was involved in another appeal, already pending in the Supreme Court.[29] The Supreme Court seems to have endorsed this policy, saying that it is "the task of a Court of Appeals to decide all properly presented cases coming before it, except in the rare instances, as for example the pendency of another case before

---

21. See § 105 n. 32 above. The repealing statute is Act of June 27, 1988, Pub.L. 100–352, § 2(a), 102 Stat. 662.

22. 28 U.S.C.A. § 1254(2). This had been § 1254(3), but was renumbered in 1988 when what had been § 1254(2) was repealed. On certification generally, see 17 Wright, Miller & Cooper, Jurisdiction 2d § 4038.

23. Louisville, N.A. & C. Ry. Co. v. Pope, C.C.A.7th, 1896, 74 F. 1; Cella v. Brown, C.C.A.8th, 1906, 144 F. 742; Rutherford v. American Medical Assn., C.A.7th, 1967, 379 F.2d 641.

24. U.S. v. Mayer, 1914, 35 S.Ct. 16, 235 U.S. 55, 59 L.Ed. 129; Warner v. City of New Orleans, 1897, 17 S.Ct. 892, 167 U.S. 467, 42 L.Ed. 239; U.S. v. Union Pac. Ry. Co., 1897, 18 S.Ct. 167, 168 U.S. 505, 42 L.Ed. 559.

25. News Syndicate Co. v. New York Cent. R. Co., 1927, 48 S.Ct. 39, 275 U.S.

179, 72 L.Ed. 225; Chicago, B. & Q. Ry. Co. v. Williams, 1907, 27 S.Ct. 559, 205 U.S. 444, 51 L.Ed. 875.

26. 28 U.S.C.A. § 1254(3); Loewe v. Lawlor, 1908, 28 S.Ct. 301, 208 U.S. 274, 52 L.Ed. 488.

27. E.g., In re Slagle, 1992, 112 S.Ct. 2296, ___ U.S. ___, 119 L.Ed.2d 220; National Labor Relations Bd. v. White Swan Co., 1941, 61 S.Ct. 751, 313 U.S. 23, 85 L.Ed. 1165; Busby v. Electric Utilities Employees Union, 1944, 65 S.Ct. 142, 323 U.S. 72, 89 L.Ed. 78. See also Rule 19.3, 1990 Sup.Ct.Rules.

28. Glynn v. Krippner, C.C.A.8th, 1932, 60 F.2d 406; Williams v. Order of Commercial Travelers of America, C.C.A. 6th, 1930, 41 F.2d 745, certiorari denied 51 S.Ct. 80, 282 U.S. 876, 75 L.Ed. 774.

29. Taylor v. Atlantic Maritime Co., C.A.2d, 1950, 181 F.2d 84, 85.

this Court raising the same issue, when certification may be advisable in the proper administration and expedition of judicial business." [30]

Although writers have detected value in the certification process, and urged its more frequent use,[31] there are two very strong arguments against certification. Certificates bring to the Court abstract questions of law, divorced from a complete factual setting in which they may be more carefully explored. Further, it should not be for the courts of appeals to decide what matters are of enough importance to require decision by the Supreme Court. The control of that Court's docket should rest exclusively in its own hands.[32] The power of the Court to grant certiorari before judgment in the court of appeals permits of expedition where this is required. For these reasons, the power to certify cases to the Supreme Court seems an anachronism that the courts of appeals should not use, and that Congress should repeal.[33] That it did not do so in 1988, when it was abolishing virtually all of the jurisdiction by appeal, hardly reflects an appreciation of the occasional virtues of this almost completely unused device. It is much more likely that the retention of certification was the result of a careless lack of concern about a provision of so little practical consequence.

§ 107. Review of State–Court Decisions [1]

The Constitution does not, in terms, authorize the Supreme Court to review decisions of state courts. It does, however, extend the judicial power of the United States to defined classes of cases, some of which are as likely to arise in the courts of a state as in a federal court, and it gives

---

30. Bernard, Certified Questions in the Supreme Court: In Defense of an Option, 1978, 83 Dick.L.Rev. 31; Moore & Vestal, Present and Potential Role of Certification in Federal Appellate Procedure, 1949, 35 Va.L.Rev. 1; Comment, 1958, 43 Iowa L.Rev. 432.

31. Wisniewski v. U.S., 1957, 77 S.Ct. 633, 634, 353 U.S. 901, 902, 1 L.Ed.2d 658, noted 1958, 43 Iowa L.Rev. 432.

32. See Taylor v. Atlantic Maritime Co., C.A.2d, 1950, 181 F.2d 84, 85.

33. See 17 Wright, Miller & Cooper, Jurisdiction 2d § 4038.

The only three instances in modern times in which the Supreme Court has accepted a certificate are highly exceptional cases that prove the rule. In U.S. v. Barnett, C.A.5th, 1963, 316 F.2d 236, the Fifth Circuit was sitting as a court of original jurisdiction, rather than as an appellate court, the members of that court were equally divided in opinion, and the question was one that had to be resolved before the proceedings could continue. The question was answered in U.S. v. Barnett, 1964, 84 S.Ct. 984, 376 U.S. 681, 12 L.Ed.2d 23.

In Moody v. Albemarle Paper Co., 1974, 94 S.Ct. 2513, 417 U.S. 622, 41 L.Ed.2d 358, the certified question was whether 28 U.S.C.A. § 46(c) permits a senior circuit judge who has participated in the decision of a panel to vote on whether the case should be heard by the court en banc. Whether a rehearing was granted or denied turned on whether votes of senior judges are to be counted and here, as in Barnett, the question was one that had to be resolved before the proceedings could continue.

In Iran National Airlines Corp. v. Marschalk Co., Inc., 1981, 101 S.Ct. 3154, 453 U.S. 919, 69 L.Ed.2d 1002, the questions decided on certificate involved issues that had been decided the same day on a petition for certiorari before judgment in the court of appeals in another case. Even so three justices dissented, urging that the certificate should have been dismissed.

§ 107

1. 16 Wright, Miller & Cooper, Jurisdiction §§ 4006–4033; Stern, Gressman, Shapiro & Geller, Supreme Court Practice, 7th ed. 1993, c. 3.

to the Supreme Court appellate jurisdiction over all such cases, other than those within the original jurisdiction of the Court, with such exceptions and under such regulations as the Congress shall make.[2] It is unusual for the court of one sovereign to have appellate jurisdiction over the courts of other sovereigns, but federalism itself is—or was when the Constitution was adopted—an unusual system, and the Supremacy Clause is a sufficient basis on which to rest the appellate jurisdiction over state-court decisions. The First Congress, in the famous section 25 of the Judiciary Act of 1789, authorized such review.[3] That it did so can hardly have been surprising at the time. At the Constitutional Convention, in the ratifying debates, and again in the debates over the Judiciary Act in the First Congress, the issue was not whether the Supreme Court should be allowed to review state-court decisions, but whether there need be any inferior federal courts. Those who were opposed to a strong federal government saw no need for such courts, and argued that the judicial power of the United States could be exercised sufficiently by the Supreme Court, which would review decisions of the state courts raising questions within the federal judicial competence.[4] In the earliest years of our history this jurisdiction of the Supreme Court was accepted without question.[5] Controversy first arose when the Virginia court refused to obey a mandate of the Supreme Court on the ground that the Supreme Court had no jurisdiction over it. Justice Story's opinion in 1816 in Martin v. Hunter's Lessee,[6] if no longer satisfactory in all its reasoning, was a full and forceful defense of the jurisdiction. It was not the final answer. Criticism of this appellate jurisdiction continued over the years [7]—indeed even today it is not entirely stilled—and famous opinions by Chief Justices Marshall and Taney [8] were required to restate the principles of Martin v. Hunter's Lessee.

From 1789 to 1914 the jurisdiction over state courts was limited to cases in which the state court had held some federal act invalid, or had upheld the validity of a state act against a claim based on the federal Constitution or laws. The Supreme Court could not review a state-court decision that upheld the federal claim and found a state act invalid. Indeed this was true even after an 1867 statute had in important ways

---

2. See Berger, Congress v. Supreme Court, 1969, pp. 225–296; Merry, Scope of the Supreme Court's Appellate Jurisdiction: Historical Basis, 1962, 47 Minn.L.Rev. 53.

3. Act of Sept. 24, 1789, § 25, 1 Stat. 73, 85.

4. See § 1 above.

5. Between 1790 and 1815, 17 cases from state courts had been before the Supreme Court. Frank, Historical Bases of the Federal Judicial System, 1948, 13 L. & Contemp.Probs. 3, 16.

6. 1816, 1 Wheat. 304, 4 L.Ed. 97. See 2 Crosskey, Politics and the Constitution in the History of the United States, 1953, 785–817.

7. See Warren, Legislative and Judicial Attacks on the Supreme Court of the United States—a History of the Twenty–Fifth Section of the Judiciary Act 1913, 47 Am. L.Rev. 1, 161.

8. Cohens v. Virginia, 1821, 6 Wheat, 264, 5 L.Ed. 257; Ableman v. Booth, 1859, 21 How. 506, 16 L.Ed. 169. The Ableman case, written on the eve of the Civil War and involving the constitutionality of the Fugitive Slave Act, is particularly dramatic. For a full account, see Swisher, History of the Supreme Court of the United States: The Taney Period, 1836–1864, 1974, pp. 653–675.

extended the jurisdiction.[9] The reason for such a distinction was clear enough. When the state court had yielded to the authority of the federal government, and had held its own statute invalid, appeal to the Supreme Court was thought unnecessary to protect the federal government in the exercise of its rightful powers.[10] Review was not broadened in this respect until 1914, when the Supreme Court was for the first time permitted to hear cases in which the state court has sustained the federal claim.[11] The impetus for the 1914 statute was an unpopular New York decision a few years earlier holding a state workmen's compensation statute invalid as violating both the state and federal constitutions.[12] Rather ironically, the 1914 amendment would have furnished no relief in the case that led to its enactment, since, on principles developed later in this section, the decision that it violated the New York constitution would have precluded review of the determination that it also violated the United States Constitution.[13]

The 1914 amendment, with only a little further refinement,[14] defined the scope of Supreme Court review of state-court decisions that still exists today. Under the present statute review is possible of the final judgment of the highest court of a state in which a decision could be had in any case where the validity of a treaty or statute of the United States is drawn in question or where the validity of a state statute is drawn in question on the ground of its being repugnant to the Constitution, treaties, or laws of the United States, or where any title, right, privilege, or immunity is specially set up or claimed under the Constitution, treaties, or statutes of, or commission held or authority exercised under, the United States.[15] The jurisdiction does not depend on the amount in controversy[16] or the citizenship of the parties.[17] It rests entirely on the existence of what is always referred to as a "federal question" in the case. The distinction that persisted from 1789 to 1914 between cases where the state court had rejected the federal claim and cases in which it had honored the claim remained for many more years in distinguishing those cases where an appeal could be taken from those

---

9. Act of Feb. 5, 1867, § 2, 14 Stat. 385, 386.

10. Commonwealth Bank of Kentucky v. Griffith, 1840, 14 Pet. 56, 58, 10 L.Ed. 352.

Justice Stevens argues today that in reviewing the decisions of state courts, the primary role of the Supreme Court is to make sure that persons who seek to vindicate federal rights have been fairly heard. Michigan v. Long, 1983, 103 S.Ct. 3469, 3491, 463 U.S. 1032, 1068, 77 L.Ed.2d 1201 (dissenting opinion); Delaware v. Van Arsdall, 1986, 106 S.Ct. 1431, 1443–1445, 475 U.S. 673, 694–698, 89 L.Ed.2d 674 (dissenting opinion).

11. Act of Dec. 23, 1914, c. 2, 38 Stat. 790.

12. Ives v. South Buffalo Ry., 1911, 94 N.E. 431, 201 N.Y. 271.

13. This is not unusual with jurisdictional reforms. Thus, the Criminal Appeals Act of 1907 would not—and could not—have permitted appeal from the directed verdict in the antitrust case that led to its enactment. See § 105 above.

14. Act of Feb. 13, 1925, c. 229, § 1, 43 Stat. 937.

15. 28 U.S.C.A. § 1257(a).

16. Buel v. Van Ness, 1823, 8 Wheat. 312, 5 L.Ed. 624.

17. French v. Hopkins, 1888, 8 S.Ct. 589, 124 U.S. 524, 31 L.Ed. 536.

that were reviewable only on petition for certiorari, but even that ended in 1988 when appeal from state courts was abolished.

The state-court decision to be reviewable must be that of the highest court of the state in which a decision could be had. This by no means restricts review to decisions of the highest state court. Even a trial-court decision is reviewable in the United States Supreme Court if there is no higher state court to which the party can resort. In a well-known case certiorari was granted to review a decision of the Police Court of Louisville, Kentucky, where the fines imposed were so small that no review was available in any Kentucky court.[18] If discretionary review is available in some higher state court, such review must be sought, no matter how unlikely it may seem that it will be granted.[19] The attempt to secure further review will extend the time in which to resort to the Supreme Court, but if discretionary further review is refused, the judgment is that of the court below that rendered it, and it is this that must be taken to the Supreme Court.[20] However, if the higher state court takes action that amounts to an affirmance of what has been done below, it is the judgment of the higher court that must be taken to the Supreme Court.[21]

Review can only be had of "final judgments or decrees." Obviously there can be no final judgment unless there has been a judgment. Here however the Court has been liberal, and has even been willing to regard a letter from the clerk of the state court to the appellant, refusing to docket an appeal, as being a judgment of the state court.[22] In some states the highest court sits in divisions. If, after decision by a division, the party may obtain review by the whole court as a matter of right, the decision of the division is not a final judgment of the court and is not reviewable.[23] But if reconsideration by the whole court is discretionary, the decision of the division will be regarded as a final judgment, and reviewable, even though the party did not seek reconsideration by the

18. Thompson v. City of Louisville, 1960, 80 S.Ct. 624, 362 U.S. 199, 4 L.Ed.2d 654. In Cohens v. Virginia, 1821, 6 Wheat. 264, 5 L.Ed. 257, the judgment reviewed was that of the Quarterly Session Court for the Borough of Norfolk, Virginia. Decision of a magistrate was reviewed in Stanford v. Texas, 1965, 85 S.Ct. 506, 379 U.S. 476, 13 L.Ed.2d 431. In Brown v. Texas, 1979, 99 S.Ct. 2637, 443 U.S. 47, 61 L.Ed.2d 357, the judgment was from the El Paso County Court and in Koon v. Aiken, 1987, 107 S.Ct. 1599, 480 U.S. 943, 94 L.Ed.2d 786 the judgment was from the Court of Common Pleas for Aiken County.

19. Costarelli v. Massachusetts, 1975, 95 S.Ct. 1534, 421 U.S. 193, 44 L.Ed.2d 76; Banks v. California, 1969, 89 S.Ct. 1901, 395 U.S. 708, 23 L.Ed.2d 653; Gotthilf v. Sills, 1963, 84 S.Ct. 187, 375 U.S. 79, 11 L.Ed.2d 159; Stratton v. Stratton, 1915, 36 S.Ct. 26, 239 U.S. 55, 60 L.Ed. 142.

20. Michigan–Wisconsin Pipe Line Co. v. Calvert, 1954, 74 S.Ct. 396, 347 U.S. 157, 98 L.Ed. 583; Minneapolis, St. P. & S.S.M. Ry. Co. v. Rock, 1929, 49 S.Ct. 363, 279 U.S. 410, 73 L.Ed. 766; Virginian Ry. Co. v. Mullens, 1926, 46 S.Ct. 526, 271 U.S. 220, 70 L.Ed. 915.

21. Tumey v. Ohio, 1926, 47 S.Ct. 437, 273 U.S. 510, 71 L.Ed. 749.

22. Burns v. Ohio, 1959, 79 S.Ct. 1164, 360 U.S. 252, 3 L.Ed.2d 1209. Orders characterized as "informal" were held reviewable in Smith v. Hooey, 1969, 89 S.Ct. 575, 576, 393 U.S. 374, 375, 21 L.Ed.2d 607, and in In re Summers, 1945, 65 S.Ct. 1307, 1309, 325 U.S. 561, 564, 89 L.Ed. 1795.

23. Gorman v. Washington Univ., 1942, 62 S.Ct. 962, 316 U.S. 98, 86 L.Ed. 1300.

whole court.[24]　On the same principle, a party need not petition for rehearing by a court in order to have a final judgment of that court,[25] though if he or she does so unsuccessfully the pendency of his petition extends the time in which to seek review in the Supreme Court of the original decision.[26]

The limitation of review to "final" judgments is consistent with the general aversion of the federal courts to piecemeal review.[27]　Thus, the same principles that determine what is a final judgment of a district court, reviewable in a court of appeals [28] or, in some instances, directly in the Supreme Court, are generally applied in determining what is a final judgment of a state court.[29]　Indeed, although decisions in one area cannot be binding in the other, quite commonly the precedents are cited interchangeably.[30]

It might be supposed that the requirement of finality would be given stricter application in reviewing state-court decisions, since they involve potential conflict between the courts of two different governments and thus, as the Court has several times said, the requirement "is not one of those technicalities to be easily scorned.　It is an important factor in the smooth working of our federal system." [31]　There is no evidence, however, of any significant difference of this sort.

The Court decides for itself whether the decision of the state court is a final judgment.　State law and state practice are of importance in determining what has been done and what may still be done within the state judicial system, but the Court will then make its own determination of whether under such circumstances the judgment has that finality requisite for Supreme Court review.[32]　Although the early practice was

---

24. Local 174, Teamsters, Chauffeurs, Warehousemen and Helpers of America v. Lucas Flour Co., 1962, 82 S.Ct. 571, 369 U.S. 95, 7 L.Ed.2d 593.

25. Southern Ry. Co. v. Clift, 1922, 43 S.Ct. 126, 260 U.S. 316, 67 L.Ed. 283; cf. Market St. Ry. Co. v. Railroad Comm. of California, 1945, 65 S.Ct. 770, 324 U.S. 548, 89 L.Ed. 1171.

26. Chicago G.W.R. Co. v. Basham, 1919, 39 S.Ct. 213, 249 U.S. 164, 63 L.Ed. 534.

But a motion to clarify the mandate by certifying that a federal question was decided does not extend the time. Department of Banking, State of Nebraska v. Pink, 1942, 63 S.Ct. 233, 317 U.S. 264, 87 L.Ed. 254.

27. See Crick, The Final Judgment as a Basis for Appeal, 1932, 41 Yale L.J. 539.

28. See § 101 above.

29. See generally 16 Wright, Miller & Cooper, Jurisdiction §§ 4008–4010; Note, The Finality Rule for Supreme Court Review of State Court Orders, 1978, 91 Harv. L.Rev. 1004.

30. See § 101 n. 48 above.

31. Radio Station WOW v. Johnson, 1945, 65 S.Ct. 1475, 1478, 326 U.S. 120, 124, 89 L.Ed. 2092; Montgomery Bldg. & Constr. Trades Council v. Ledbetter Erection Co., Inc., 1952, 73 S.Ct. 196, 197, 344 U.S. 178, 180, 97 L.Ed. 204.　See also Cox Broadcasting Corp. v. Cohn, 1975, 95 S.Ct. 1029, 1050–1951, 420 U.S. 469, 502, 503, 43 L.Ed.2d 328 (Rehnquist, J., dissenting); 16 Wright, Miller & Cooper, Jurisdiction § 3908.

But see Dyk, Supreme Court Review of Interlocutory State–Court Decisions: "The Twilight Zone of Finality," 1967, 19 Stan. L.Rev. 907, 939–946, arguing that the Court should have discretion to review interlocutory state judgments.

32. Cole v. Violette, 1943, 63 S.Ct. 1204, 319 U.S. 581, 87 L.Ed. 1599.　See also Cox Broadcasting Corp. v. Cohn, 1975, 95 S.Ct. 1029, 1038 n. 8, 420 U.S. 469, 479 n. 8, 43 L.Ed.2d 328; Department of Banking, State of Nebraska v. Pink, 1942, 63 S.Ct. 233, 317 U.S. 264, 87 L.Ed. 254.

contrary, and did not permit the Court even to consider the opinion of the state court in determining whether the state decision was final,[33] it is now quite settled that the Court may look not only to the opinion but also to any other relevant matter, in or out of the record, in determining finality.[34] The test, as in other instances where finality must be determined, is increasingly a pragmatic one. A judgment is final for purposes of review if it leaves only ministerial acts, such as entry of judgment accordingly in the lower court, to be done.[35] The traditional rule has been that a judgment is not final for purposes of review, though it settles the important issue in the case, if it leaves open something not merely ministerial that might itself raise a federal question.[36]

In recent years the Court has departed strikingly from this traditional view. It said in Cox Broadcasting Corp. v. Cohn [37] that "as the cases have unfolded, the Court has recurringly encountered situations in which the highest court of a State has finally determined the federal issue present in a particular case, but in which there are further proceedings in the lower state courts to come. There are now at least four categories of such cases in which the Court has treated the decision on the federal issue as a final judgment for the purposes of 28 U.S.C.A. § 1257 and has taken jurisdiction without awaiting the completion of the additional proceedings anticipated in the lower state courts."

The first of these categories, as defined by the Court in Cox, includes those cases in which there are further proceedings yet to occur in the state courts but for one reason or another the federal issue is conclusive or the outcome of further proceedings preordained.[38] The second catego-

---

33. E.g., Haseltine v. Central Nat. Bank, 1901, 22 S.Ct. 49, 183 U.S. 130, 46 L.Ed. 117. This rule was abandoned in Clark v. Williard, 1934, 54 S.Ct. 615, 292 U.S. 112, 78 L.Ed. 1160.

34. Gospel Army v. City of Los Angeles, 1947, 67 S.Ct. 1428, 1430, 331 U.S. 543, 547, 91 L.Ed. 1662; Local No. 438 Constr. & General Laborers' Union, AFL–CIO v. Curry, 1963, 83 S.Ct. 531, 537, 371 U.S. 542, 551, 9 L.Ed.2d 514.

35. Board of Commrs. of Tippecanoe County v. Lucas, 1876, 93 U.S. 108, 23 L.Ed. 822; Department of Banking, State of Nebraska v. Pink, 1942, 63 S.Ct. 233, 317 U.S. 264, 87 L.Ed. 254; Cole v. Violette, 1943, 63 S.Ct. 1204, 319 U.S. 581, 87 L.Ed. 1599.

A judgment that terminates original proceedings in a state appellate court, in which the only issue decided concerns the jurisdiction of a lower state court, is final even if further proceedings are to be had in the lower court. Fisher v. District Court of Sixteenth Judicial Dist., 1976, 96 S.Ct. 943, 424 U.S. 382, 47 L.Ed.2d 106. See 16 Wright, Miller & Cooper, Jurisdiction § 4009, pp. 578–581.

36. Republic Natural Gas Co. v. Oklahoma, 1948, 68 S.Ct. 972, 334 U.S. 62, 92 L.Ed. 1212; Washington ex rel. Grays Harbor Logging Co. v. Coats–Fordney Logging Co., 1917, 37 S.Ct. 295, 243 U.S. 251, 61 L.Ed. 702; Houston v. Moore, 1818, 3 Wheat. 433, 4 L.Ed. 428.

For recent applications of this rule, see, e.g., Ashland Oil, Inc. v. Rose, 1987, 107 S.Ct. 1949, 481 U.S. 1025, 95 L.Ed.2d 522; O'Dell v. Espinoza, 1982, 102 S.Ct. 1865, 456 U.S. 430, 72 L.Ed.2d 237; San Diego Gas & Elec. Co. v. City of San Diego, 1981, 101 S.Ct. 1287, 450 U.S. 621, 67 L.Ed.2d 551.

37. 1975, 95 S.Ct. 1029, 1037, 420 U.S. 469, 502–503, 43 L.Ed.2d 328.

38. 95 S.Ct. at 1038, 420 U.S. at 479. As examples the Court cited Organization for a Better Austin v. Keefe, 1971, 91 S.Ct. 1575, 1577 n. 1, 402 U.S. 415, 418 n. 1, 29 L.Ed.2d 1; Mills v. Alabama, 1966, 86 S.Ct. 1434, 384 U.S. 214, 16 L.Ed.2d 484; Local No. 438 v. Curry, 1963, 83 S.Ct. 531, 536–537, 371 U.S. 542, 550–551, 9 L.Ed.2d 514; Pope v. Atlantic C.L.R. Co., 1953, 73 S.Ct. 749, 750, 345 U.S. 379, 382, 97 L.Ed. 1094; Richfield Oil Corp. v. State Bd. of Equalizary is the cases in which the federal issue, finally decided by the highest court in the state, will survive and require decision regardless of the outcome of future state proceedings.[39] The third category is those situations in which the federal claim has been finally decided, with further proceedings on the merits in the state courts to come, but in which later review of the federal issue cannot be had, whatever the ultimate outcome of the case.[40]

The fourth of the Cox categories was described by the Court as "those situations where the federal issue has been finally decided in the state courts with further proceedings pending in which the party seeking review here might prevail on the merits on nonfederal grounds, thus rendering unnecessary review of the federal issue by this Court, and where reversal of the state court on the federal issue would be preclusive of any further litigation on the relevant cause of action rather than merely controlling the nature and character of, or determining the admissibility of evidence in, the state proceedings still to come. In these circumstances, if a refusal immediately to review the state-court decision might seriously erode federal policy, the Court has entertained and decided the federal issue, which itself has been finally determined by the state courts for purposes of the state litigation." [41]

tion, 1946, 67 S.Ct. 156, 158–159, 329 U.S. 69, 73–74, 91 L.Ed. 80.

See also Duquesne Light Co. v. Barasch, 1989, 109 S.Ct. 609, 614–615, 488 U.S. 299, 304, 102 L.Ed.2d 646; City of Philadelphia v. New Jersey, 1978, 98 S.Ct. 2531, 2533 n. 3, 437 U.S. 617, 620 n. 3, 57 L.Ed.2d 475.

But in Minnick v. California Dept. of Corrections, 1981, 101 S.Ct. 2211, 452 U.S. 105, 68 L.Ed.2d 706, the state judgment was held not final despite the argument of plaintiffs that all of the evidence they could produce was already in the record and the outcome of any further proceedings was preordained.

39. 95 S.Ct. at 1038–1039, 420 U.S. at 480–481. As examples the Court cited Brady v. Maryland, 1963, 83 S.Ct. 1194, 1195 n. 1, 373 U.S. 83, 85 n. 1, 10 L.Ed.2d 215; Radio Station WOW, Inc. v. Johnson, 1945, 65 S.Ct. 1475, 1479–1480, 326 U.S. 120, 126–127, 89 L.Ed. 2092; Carondelet Canal & Navigation Co. v. Louisiana, 1914, 34 S.Ct. 627, 233 U.S. 362, 58 L.Ed. 1001; Forgay v. Conrad, 1848, 6 How. 201, 47 U.S. 201, 12 L.Ed. 404.

See also NAACP v. Claiborne Hardware Co., 1982, 102 S.Ct. 3409, 3422 n. 42, 458 U.S. 886, 907 n. 42, 73 L.Ed.2d 1215; New York v. Cathedral Academy, 1977, 98 S.Ct. 340, 343 n. 4, 434 U.S. 125, 128 n. 4, 54 L.Ed.2d 346.

40. 95 S.Ct. at 1039–1040, 420 U.S. at 481–482. As examples the Court cited North Dakota State Bd. of Pharmacy v.

Snyder's Drug Stores, Inc., 1973, 94 S.Ct. 407, 414 U.S. 156, 38 L.Ed.2d 379; California v. Stewart, 1966, 86 S.Ct. 1602, 1640 n. 71, 384 U.S. 436, 498 n. 71, 16 L.Ed.2d 694 (decided sub nom. Miranda v. Arizona).

See also Pennsylvania v. Ritchie, 1987, 107 S.Ct. 989, 995–997, 480 U.S. 39, 47–50, 94 L.Ed.2d 40; New York v. Quarles, 104 S.Ct. 2626, 2629 n. 1, 467 U.S. 649, 651 n. 1, 81 L.Ed.2d 550; Florida v. Meyers, 1984, 104 S.Ct. 1852, 1853 n. *, 466 U.S. 380, 381 n. *, 80 L.Ed.2d 381; Southland Corp. v. Keating, 1984, 104 S.Ct. 852, 465 U.S. 1, 79 L.Ed.2d 1; South Dakota v. Neville, 1983, 103 S.Ct. 916, 920 n. 6, 459 U.S. 553, 558 n. 6, 74 L.Ed.2d 748.

41. 95 S.Ct. at 1041, 420 U.S. at 482–483. As examples the Court cited Miami Herald Pub. Co. v. Tornillo, 1974, 94 S.Ct. 2831, 2834 n. 6, 418 U.S. 241, 247 n. 6, 41 L.Ed.2d 730; Hudson Distributors v. Eli Lilly & Co., 1964, 84 S.Ct. 1273, 1276 n. 4, 377 U.S. 386, 389 n. 4, 12 L.Ed.2d 394; Local No. 438 v. Curry, 1963, 83 S.Ct. 531, 536, 371 U.S. 542, 550, 9 L.Ed.2d 514; Mercantile Nat. Bank v. Langdeau, 1963, 83 S.Ct. 520, 522, 371 U.S. 555, 558, 9 L.Ed.2d 523.

See also Fort Wayne Books v. Indiana, 1989, 109 S.Ct. 916, 922–924, 489 U.S. 46, 53–57, 103 L.Ed.2d 34; Goodyear Atomic Corp. v. Miller, 1988, 108 S.Ct. 1704, 1708–1709, 486 U.S. 174, 177–179, 100 L.Ed.2d 158; Belknap, Inc. v. Hale, 1983, 103 S.Ct. 3172, 3176 n. 5, 463 U.S. 491, 497 n. 5, 77

The Cox case itself was held reviewable as falling in the fourth category. The state court had rejected a federal constitutional challenge to a state law authorizing damage suits against the press for publishing the names of rape victims. The state court had sent the case back for trial. The defendants might win at trial on nonfederal grounds, but if the statute was unconstitutional there should be no trial at all. Even if defendants won at trial, this would leave on the books the unreviewed decision of the highest state court rejecting the constitutional challenge. Delaying final decision of the constitutional claim until after trial would leave unanswered an important question about freedom of the press, while if the Supreme Court took the case and sustained the constitutional claim—as it in fact did—the litigation would be at an end.

There is one unusual procedure required by the final-judgment rule in combination with the rule that only the decision of the highest state court in which review can be had is reviewable. Suppose, for example, that a defendant demurs to a complaint, arguing that some provision of federal law makes the claim improper. The trial court sustains the demurrer, but the state appellate court reverses, rejecting the federal claim and remanding the case for trial. This is not a final judgment— unless the circumstances of the particular case bring it within one of the four categories defined in Cox—since it leaves something more than merely ministerial to be done. After trial judgment is entered for plaintiff. This is not immediately reviewable by the Supreme Court since it is not the judgment of the highest state court in which decision can be had. It may be that defendant can claim no error except the earlier overruling of his demurrer. He is required, however, to appeal to the state appellate court, even though that court will refuse to consider his only claimed error on the ground that its earlier decision of the federal question is now law of the case. Only after the judgment has been affirmed on this useless appeal is review in the Supreme Court

L.Ed.2d 798; Shaffer v. Heitner, 1977, 97 S.Ct. 2569, 2575 n. 12, 433 U.S. 186, 195 n. 12, 53 L.Ed.2d 683.

But in Flynt v. Ohio, 1981, 101 S.Ct. 1958, 451 U.S. 619, 68 L.Ed.2d 489, a bare majority of the Court refused to review, as not final, a judgment of the highest state court that reversed dismissal of a criminal complaint on the ground of selective and discriminatory prosecution. Even a claim of selective prosecution for having exercised First Amendment rights did not present the kind of "identifiable federal statutory or constitutional rights which would * * * [be] undermined by the continuation of the litigation in the state courts" that would justify a finding of finality. 101 S.Ct. at 1960, 451 U.S. at 621.

In other recent cases the Court has found a state judgment sufficiently final for review though the judgment was hardly final

in any traditional sense and does not seem to fit into any of the four Cox categories. See National Socialist Party of America v. Village of Skokie, 1977, 97 S.Ct. 2205, 432 U.S. 43, 53 L.Ed.2d 96, and American Export Lines, Inc. v. Alvez, 1980, 100 S.Ct. 1673, 446 U.S. 274, 64 L.Ed.2d 284, discussed in 16 Wright, Miller & Cooper, Jurisdiction § 4010.

The Mercantile National Bank case above, cited by the Court as an example of the fourth Cox category, now is relied on for the proposition that a decision of a state court rejecting an argument that federal law makes the chosen venue improper is final for purposes of review. Burlington N. R. Co. v. Ford, 1992, 112 S.Ct. 2184, 2186 n. *, ___ U.S. ___, ___ n. *, 119 L.Ed.2d 432; American Motorists Ins. Co. v. Starnes, 1976, 96 S.Ct. 1800, 1803 n. 3, 425 U.S. 637, 642 n. 3, 48 L.Ed.2d 263.

possible.[42] However on review of this second judgment of the state appellate court the Supreme Court will consider the federal question raised and decided on the first appeal, even though the state court has refused to consider it on the second appeal, or appellant has not raised it on the second appeal.[43]

Under the statute there must be a federal question in order to invoke the jurisdiction of the Supreme Court. Whether there is such a question in the case is a matter that the Supreme Court must decide for itself.[44] The mere presence of a federal question will not permit review, however, unless that federal question is "substantial."[45] Even though a question of federal law has been raised, if it appears that the question is wholly formal, or is so absolutely devoid of merit as to be frivolous, or has been explicitly foreclosed by a decision or decisions of the Supreme Court so as to leave no room for real controversy, the Court will not hear the case.[46] Prior to 1988 it was not uncommon for the Court, without hearing oral argument, to dismiss an appeal from a state court for want of a substantial federal question. Now it need only deny certiorari.

The federal question must have been raised in a proper and timely manner in the state courts. "No particular form of words or phrases is essential, but only that the claim of invalidity and the ground therefor be brought to the attention of the state court with fair precision and in due time. And if the record as a whole shows either expressly or by clear intendment that this was done, the claim is to be regarded as having been adequately presented."[47] It must be clear from the record that a claim under a federal statute or the federal constitution was presented to the state courts[48] and the claim must have been specifically identified. "A party may not preserve a constitutional challenge by generally

---

42. Great Western Tel. Co. v. Burnham, 1896, 16 S.Ct. 850, 162 U.S. 339, 40 L.Ed. 991.

43. Barclay v. Florida, 1983, 103 S.Ct. 3418, 3423, 463 U.S. 939, 946, 77 L.Ed.2d 1134; Hathorn v. Lovorn, 1982, 102 S.Ct. 2421, 2426, 457 U.S. 255, 261–262, 72 L.Ed.2d 824; Reece v. Georgia, 1955, 76 S.Ct. 167, 169, 350 U.S. 85, 87, 100 L.Ed. 77; Urie v. Thompson, 1949, 69 S.Ct. 1018, 1025–1026, 337 U.S. 163, 171–173, 93 L.Ed. 1282.

44. Angel v. Bullington, 1947, 67 S.Ct. 657, 330 U.S. 183, 91 L.Ed. 832.

45. 16 Wright, Miller & Cooper, Jurisdiction § 4014; Note, The Supreme Court Dismissal of State Court Appeals for Want of Substantial Federal Question, 1982, 15 Creighton L.Rev. 749.

46. Equitable Life Assur. Socy. v. Brown, 1902, 23 S.Ct. 123, 187 U.S. 308, 47 L.Ed. 190; Zucht v. King, 1922, 43 S.Ct. 24, 260 U.S. 174, 67 L.Ed. 194.

47. New York ex rel. Bryant v. Zimmerman, 1928, 49 S.Ct. 61, 63, 278 U.S. 63, 67, 73 L.Ed. 184; Street v. New York, 1969, 89

S.Ct. 1354, 1360–1362, 394 U.S. 576, 581–585, 22 L.Ed.2d 572; PruneYard Shopping Center v. Robins, 1980, 100 S.Ct. 2035, 2043 n. 9, 447 U.S. 74, 85 n. 9, 64 L.Ed.2d 741.

Ordinarily the Court will not consider questions that were not raised at all in the state court. Tacon v. Arizona, 1973, 93 S.Ct. 998, 410 U.S. 351, 35 L.Ed.2d 346. But the Court has claimed a power to consider plain error though not raised below. Wood v. Georgia, 1981, 101 S.Ct. 1097, 1100 n. 5, 450 U.S. 261, 265 n. 5, 67 L.Ed.2d 220; Stern, Gressman, Shapiro & Geller, note 1 above, at p. 346.

48. Webb v. Webb, 1981, 101 S.Ct. 1889, 1894, 451 U.S. 493, 501, 68 L.Ed.2d 392. The Court held that it lacked jurisdiction to review a state judgment when the petitioner had used the phrase "full faith and credit" several times in the proceedings below, but had never cited the federal Constitution or any of the cases relying on it.

invoking the Constitution in state court and awaiting review in this Court to specify the constitutional provision it is relying upon." [49]

The timeliness with which the federal question is raised in the state court is critical. This is largely a matter for the state to regulate by its own procedural rules. Failure to raise the question at the stage of the proceedings required by state law will preclude review,[50] unless the state rule is regarded as an attempt to evade decision of the federal question or permits no fair opportunity to assert the question.[51] The course of safety is to raise the federal question at every step in the proceedings in the state courts.[52] Even if the question has been properly raised in the trial court, the party may be held to have waived it by failing to preserve it on appeal [53] or by appealing to the wrong court.[54] It is too late to raise a federal question by petition for rehearing to the state appellate court,[55] except where the decision of that court has unexpectedly given rise to a federal question that the party seeking review has had no previous opportunity to assert and could not fairly have anticipated.[56]

49. Bankers Life & Cas. Co. v. Crenshaw, 1988, 108 S.Ct. 1645, 1650, 486 U.S. 71, 77, 100 L.Ed.2d 62. As the Court pointed out in that case, it is not clear whether the rule that the "not pressed or passed upon below" rule is jurisdictional or only a prudential restriction on review. 108 S.Ct. at 1651, 486 U.S. at 79.

See also Illinois v. Gates, 1983, 103 S.Ct. 2317, 2321–2325, 462 U.S. 213, 217–224, 76 L.Ed.2d 527. After the case had been argued the Court requested the parties to brief an additional question. When the time came to decide, the Court ruled— "with apologies to all"—that this new question should not be decided because it had not been presented to the state court.

But the Court distinguishes between a claim and arguments supporting a claim. "Once a federal claim is properly presented, a party can make any argument in support of that claim; parties are not limited to the precise arguments they made below." Yee v. City of Escondido, 1992, 112 S.Ct. 1522, 1532, ___ U.S. ___, ___, 118 L.Ed.2d 153.

50. Edelman v. California, 1953, 73 S.Ct. 293, 344 U.S. 357, 97 L.Ed. 387; Barbour v. Georgia, 1919, 39 S.Ct. 316, 249 U.S. 454, 63 L.Ed. 704; Mutual Life Ins. Co. v. McGrew, 1903, 23 S.Ct. 375, 188 U.S. 291, 47 L.Ed. 480.

Whether the federal question has been sufficiently and timely raised in the state court is itself a federal question that the Supreme Court can decide for itself. Johnson v. Mississippi, 1988, 108 S.Ct. 1981, 1987, 486 U.S. 578, 586, 100 L.Ed.2d 575; Street v. New York, 1969, 89 S.Ct. 1354, 1361, 394 U.S. 576, 583, 22 L.Ed.2d 572; Carter v. Texas, 1900, 20 S.Ct. 687, 689, 177 U.S. 442, 447, 44 L.Ed. 839. See, e.g.,

Chambers v. Mississippi, 1973, 93 S.Ct. 1038, 1043 n. 3, 410 U.S. 284, 290 n. 3, 35 L.Ed.2d 297, holding that the federal question was timely raised on a motion for a new trial since the challenge—that the cumulative effect of several rulings on evidence denied fundamental fairness in the trial—was not one that was available until the evidence had been concluded.

See 16 Wright, Miller & Cooper, Jurisdiction § 4022.

51. National Mut. Bldg. & Loan Assn. v. Brahan, 1904, 24 S.Ct. 532, 193 U.S. 635, 48 L.Ed. 823; Reece v. Georgia, 1955, 76 S.Ct. 167, 350 U.S. 85, 100 L.Ed. 77. But cf. Michel v. Louisiana, 1955, 76 S.Ct. 158, 350 U.S. 91, 100 L.Ed. 83. See generally 16 Wright, Miller & Cooper, Jurisdiction §§ 4026–4028.

52. See Wiener, Wanna Make a Federal Case Out of It?, 1962, 48 A.B.A.J. 59.

53. Beck v. Washington, 1962, 82 S.Ct. 955, 960–962, 369 U.S. 541, 549–553, 8 L.Ed.2d 98.

54. Parker v. Illinois, 1948, 68 S.Ct. 708, 333 U.S. 571, 92 L.Ed. 886; Central Union Tel. Co. v. City of Edwardsville, 1925, 46 S.Ct. 90, 269 U.S. 190, 70 L.Ed. 229.

55. Herndon v. Georgia, 1935, 55 S.Ct. 794, 295 U.S. 441, 79 L.Ed. 1530; Bilby v. Stewart, 1918, 38 S.Ct. 264, 246 U.S. 255, 62 L.Ed. 701; Forbes v. Virginia State Council, 1910, 30 S.Ct. 295, 216 U.S. 396, 54 L.Ed. 534.

56. Missouri ex rel. Missouri Ins. Co. v. Gehner, 1930, 50 S.Ct. 326, 281 U.S. 313, 74 L.Ed. 870; Brinkerhoff–Faris Trust & Sav. Co. v. Hill, 1930, 50 S.Ct. 451, 281 U.S.

To all of these rules about when and how the federal question must be presented in the state court, there is a salutary and sensible exception. If the highest court of the state in which decision could be had actually decides the federal question, it is reviewable in the Supreme Court regardless of when it was first presented. "There can be no question as to the proper presentation of a federal claim when the highest state court passes on it." [57]

The most important, and most difficult, limitation on Supreme Court review of state-court decisions has been well stated by Justice Jackson: "This Court from the time of its foundation has adhered to the principle that it will not review judgments of state courts that rest on adequate and independent state grounds. * * * The reason is so obvious that it has rarely been thought to warrant statement. It is found in the partitioning of power between the state and federal judicial systems and in the limitations of our own jurisdiction. Our only power over state judgments is to correct them to the extent that they incorrectly adjudge federal rights. And our power is to correct wrong judgments, not to revise opinions. We are not permitted to render an advisory opinion, and if the same judgment would be rendered by the state court after we corrected its views of federal laws, our review could amount to nothing more than an advisory opinion." [58]

In the early years such a limitation was imposed on the Court by the proviso to section 25 of the Judiciary Act of 1789, which said: "But no other error shall be assigned or regarded as a ground of reversal in any such case as aforesaid, than such as appears on the face of the record, and immediately respects the before mentioned questions of validity or construction of the said constitution, treaties, statutes, commissions, or authorities in dispute." This proviso was eliminated when that section of the statute was amended in 1867.[59] It seems entirely plausible that

---

673, 74 L.Ed. 1107; cf. Saunders v. Shaw, 1917, 37 S.Ct. 638, 244 U.S. 317, 61 L.Ed. 1163.

57. Raley v. Ohio, 1959, 79 S.Ct. 1257, 1265, 360 U.S. 423, 436, 3 L.Ed.2d 1344. See also Cohen v. Cowles Media Co., 1991, 111 S.Ct. 2513, 2517, 501 U.S. 663, ___, 115 L.Ed.2d 586; Orr v. Orr, 1979, 99 S.Ct. 1102, 1109, 440 U.S. 268, 274–275, 59 L.Ed.2d 306; Cox Broadcasting Corp. v. Cohn, 1975, 95 S.Ct. 1029, 1036–1037, 420 U.S. 469, 502–503, 43 L.Ed.2d 328. Boykin v. Alabama, 1969, 89 S.Ct. 1709, 1711, 395 U.S. 238, 241–242, 23 L.Ed.2d 274; Manhattan Life Ins. Co. of New York v. Cohen, 1914, 34 S.Ct. 874, 877, 234 U.S. 123, 134, 58 L.Ed. 1245; Grannis v. Ordean, 1914, 34 S.Ct. 779, 234 U.S. 385, 58 L.Ed. 1363; San Jose Land & Water Co. v. San Jose Ranch Co., 1903, 23 S.Ct. 487, 189 U.S. 177, 47 L.Ed. 765.

It has also been held that the Court need not consider whether the federal question was properly raised in the state courts if the state, as a party to the case, states in the Supreme Court that it is prepared to meet the federal question on its merits. Gomez v. Perez, 1973, 93 S.Ct. 872, 874 n. 2, 409 U.S. 535, 537 n. 2, 35 L.Ed.2d 56.

58. Herb v. Pitcairn, 1945, 65 S.Ct. 459, 463, 324 U.S. 117, 125–126, 89 L.Ed. 789.

See 16 Wright, Miller & Cooper, Jurisdiction §§ 4019–4032.

Two scholars have argued that the presence of state grounds, adequate or not, should never preclude the Supreme Court from reaching federal issues in an appeal from a state court. Matasar & Bruch, Procedural Common Law, Federal Jurisdictional Policy, and Abandonment of the Adequate and Independent State Grounds Doctrine, 1986, 86 Col.L.Rev. 1291.

59. Act of Feb. 5, 1867, § 2, 14 Stat. 385, 386.

Congress intended by eliminating the proviso to open the whole case for review by the Supreme Court, if there is a federal question in the case sufficient to take the case to the Supreme Court. Such a broad review may well be constitutional. When cases are brought in a district court because they arise under the Constitution, laws, or treaties of the United States, the district court, and the Supreme Court in reviewing the judgment, decides all the issues in the case, and is not limited to the federal question that provides the basis for jurisdiction.[60] In normal understanding the amendment of a statute to remove a limitation on it suggests that such limitation is no longer to apply. Such a course seems wholly consistent with the temper of the times, and with the other purposes of the 1867 act.[61] The Supreme Court, however, took a different view. In the landmark case of Murdock v. Memphis [62] the Court held that no such drastic change in its jurisdiction had been accomplished by the 1867 revision. This case, and others that have built on it,[63] lay down two fundamental propositions. The Court will not review a case, even though it contains a federal question, if there is an adequate state ground that supports the decision of the state court. Further, the Court will accept as binding upon it the state court's decision of questions of state law.

There has been an elaborate argument made that the Framers of the Constitution intended that the Supreme Court would speak authoritatively on questions of state law as well as on questions of federal law.[64] The historical evidence for this proposition is unconvincing, and the uniform practice of the Court has been to the contrary. It has considered that the state courts speak with final authority on questions of state law.[65] The exceptions to this principle are very few. Decisions of the state court about state law are only persuasive, rather than controlling, where state law is incorporated by reference in a federal statute,[66]

60. Osborn v. Bank of United States, 1824, 9 Wheat. 738, 823, 6 L.Ed. 204; Siler v. Louisville & N.R. Co., 1909, 29 S.Ct. 451, 213 U.S. 175, 53 L.Ed. 753. See § 19 above.

61. Charles Warren thought it "highly probable" that Congress actually meant to provide that "every question passed on by the State Court should be open for reconsideration in the Supreme Court." 2 Warren, The Supreme Court in United States History, rev.ed.1926, p. 682.

62. 1875, 20 Wall. 590, 22 L.Ed. 429. See 16 Wright, Miller & Cooper, Jurisdiction § 4020, pp. 662–665.

63. Eustis v. Bolles, 1893, 14 S.Ct. 131, 150 U.S. 361, 37 L.Ed. 1111; Berea College v. Kentucky, 1908, 29 S.Ct. 33, 211 U.S. 45, 53 L.Ed. 81; Enterprise Irrigation Dist. v. Farmers' Mut. Canal Co., 1917, 37 S.Ct. 318, 243 U.S. 157, 61 L.Ed. 644; Fox Film Corp. v. Muller, 1935, 56 S.Ct. 183, 296 U.S. 207, 80 L.Ed. 158.

64. 2 Crosskey, Politics and the Constitution in the History of the United States, 1953, cc. 23–26.

65. E.g., Mullaney v. Wilbur, 1975, 95 S.Ct. 1881, 1885–1886, 421 U.S. 684, 689, 44 L.Ed.2d 508; Scripto, Inc. v. Carson, 1960, 80 S.Ct. 619, 362 U.S. 207, 4 L.Ed.2d 660; Sutter Butte Canal Co. v. Railroad Comm. of California, 1929, 49 S.Ct. 325, 279 U.S. 125, 73 L.Ed. 637; American Ry. Exp. Co. v. Kentucky, 1927, 47 S.Ct. 353, 273 U.S. 269, 71 L.Ed. 639; Murdock v. Memphis, 1875, 20 Wall. 590, 22 L.Ed. 429; cf. Caldarola v. Eckert, 1947, 67 S.Ct. 1569, 332 U.S. 155, 91 L.Ed. 1968. See 16 Wright, Miller & Cooper, Jurisdiction § 4021, pp. 687–692.

66. Reconstruction Fin. Corp. v. Beaver County, 1946, 66 S.Ct. 992, 328 U.S. 204, 90 L.Ed. 1172.

or where protection of a federal constitutional right would be thwarted if the state had the last word on state questions, as in determining whether there is a "contract" within the meaning of the clause of the Constitution prohibiting impairment of the obligation of contracts,[67] or where the state-court interpretation of state law appears to be an "obvious subterfuge to evade consideration of a federal issue." [68] And it has been held that while the Supreme Court is bound by a state court's construction of a state statute, it is not bound by the state court's characterization of the "practical effect" of the statute.[69]

The other aspect of the rule of Murdock v. Memphis is that the Supreme Court cannot review a state decision at all if that decision rests on an adequate state ground. Thus, there can be no review if the state court has decided the case exclusively on some ground of state law, and has never reached a federal question present in the case.[70] Nor can there be review where the state court has decided both the state and federal questions, if its decision of the federal question was unnecessary in the light of its disposition of the state question.[71] But if the state court has decided the case entirely on the federal question presented, the Supreme Court can review, even though there was a state question in the case that could have been the basis for decision.[72] In such a case, if the state court's resolution of the federal question is erroneous, the Supreme Court will remand the case to the state court, which can then pass on the state question.[73] And it is held, though on shaky theoretical

67. General Motors Corp. v. Romein, 1992, 112 S.Ct. 1105, 1110, ___ U.S. ___, ___, 117 L.Ed.2d 328; Indiana ex rel. Anderson v. Brand, 1938, 58 S.Ct. 443, 303 U.S. 95, 82 L.Ed. 685; 16 Wright, Miller & Cooper, Jurisdiction § 4030.

68. Radio Station WOW, Inc. v. Johnson, 1945, 65 S.Ct. 1475, 1480, 326 U.S. 120, 129, 89 L.Ed. 2092; Ward v. Board of County Commrs. of Love County, 1920, 40 S.Ct. 419, 253 U.S. 17, 64 L.Ed. 751; Terre Haute & I.R. Co. v. Indiana ex rel. Ketcham, 1904, 24 S.Ct. 767, 194 U.S. 579, 48 L.Ed. 1124.

This was held not to be the situation when the pronouncement of state law by the state court, even if novel, would not frustrate consideration of the federal issue. Mullaney v. Wilbur, 1975, 95 S.Ct. 1881, 1886 n. 11, 421 U.S. 684, 691 n. 11, 44 L.Ed.2d 508.

69. "Once any ambiguities as to the meaning of the statute are resolved, we may form our own judgment as to its operative effect." Wisconsin v. Mitchell, 1993, 113 S.Ct. 2194, 2196–2197, ___ U.S. ___, ___, 124 L.Ed.2d 436.

70. McCoy v. Shaw, 1928, 48 S.Ct. 519, 277 U.S. 302, 72 L.Ed. 891; Johnson v. New Jersey, 1966, 86 S.Ct. 1772, 1782, 384 U.S. 719, 735, 16 L.Ed.2d 882.

71. Fox Film Corp. v. Muller, 1935, 56 S.Ct. 183, 296 U.S. 207, 80 L.Ed. 158; Jankovich v. Indiana Toll Road Comm., 1965, 85 S.Ct. 493, 379 U.S. 487, 13 L.Ed.2d 439; Sochor v. Florida, 1992, 112 S.Ct. 2114, 2119–2120, ___ U.S. ___, ___, 119 L.Ed.2d 326. But see Sandalow, Henry v. Mississippi and the Adequate State Ground: Proposals for a Revised Doctrine, 1965 Sup.Ct.Rev. 187, 201–203.

72. Quinn v. Millsap, 1989, 109 S.Ct. 2324, 2328–2329, 491 U.S. 95, 100, 105 L.Ed.2d 74; United Air Lines, Inc. v. Mahin, 1973, 93 S.Ct. 1186, 410 U.S. 623, 35 L.Ed.2d 545; Beecher v. Alabama, 1967, 88 S.Ct. 189, 190 n. 3, 389 U.S. 35, 37 n. 3, 19 L.Ed.2d 35; International Steel & Iron Co. v. National Sur. Co., 1936, 56 S.Ct. 619, 297 U.S. 657, 89 L.Ed. 961; Red Cross Line v. Atlantic Fruit Co., 1924, 44 S.Ct. 274, 275–276, 264 U.S. 109, 120, 68 L.Ed. 582.

73. California v. Ramos, 1983, 103 S.Ct. 3446, 3451 n. 7, 463 U.S. 992, 997 n. 7, 77 L.Ed.2d 1171; Orr v. Orr, 1979, 99 S.Ct. 1102, 1109–1110, 1114, 440 U.S. 268, 275–277, 283–284, 59 L.Ed.2d 306; Indiana ex rel. Anderson v. Brand, 1938, 58 S.Ct. 443, 303 U.S. 95, 82 L.Ed. 685. See Evans v. Newton, 1966, 86 S.Ct. 486, 490, 382 U.S. 296, 303, 15 L.Ed.2d 373 (White, J., concurring). For the later history of that case, see ground, that where a state statute incorporates federal law by reference, the Supreme Court may review a state-court decision about that statute, pass on the federal question that is incorporated by reference, and remand for the state court to reconsider its interpretation of the statute in the light of the Supreme Court's interpretation of the underlying federal law.[74]

In order to bar Supreme Court review, the state ground must be "adequate."[75] The adequacy of the state-law ground is itself a federal question that the Supreme Court reviews de novo.[76] If there is no fair and substantial support in the facts for the state court's ruling on the state ground, the Supreme Court can disregard it.[77] A new state rule cannot be invented for the occasion in order to defeat the federal claim.[78] It has been said that if the state court's refusal to consider the merits of a case is based on a rule "more properly deemed discretionary than jurisdictional" this does not bar review in the Supreme Court.[79] Even a

Evans v. Abney, 1970, 90 S.Ct. 628, 396 U.S. 435, 24 L.Ed.2d 634.

Cf. Stanton v. Stanton, 1975, 95 S.Ct. 1373, 421 U.S. 7, 43 L.Ed.2d 688; United Air Lines, Inc. v. Mahin, 1973, 93 S.Ct. 1186, 1192, 410 U.S. 623, 632, 35 L.Ed.2d 545.

74. Standard Oil Co. of California v. Johnson, 1942, 62 S.Ct. 1168, 316 U.S. 481, 86 L.Ed. 1611; cf. St. Martin Evangelical Lutheran Church v. South Dakota, 1981, 101 S.Ct. 2142, 2147 n. 9, 451 U.S. 772, 780, 68 L.Ed.2d 612; State Tax Comm. v. Van Cott, 1939, 59 S.Ct. 605, 306 U.S. 511, 83 L.Ed. 950, criticized 1939, 39 Col.L.Rev. 1043. See 16 Wright, Miller & Cooper, Jurisdiction § 4031; Redish, Supreme Court Review of State Court "Federal" Decisions: A Study in Interactive Federalism, 1985, 19 Ga.L.Rev. 861; Greene, Hybrid State Law in the Federal Courts, 1970, 83 Harv.L.Rev. 289.

75. 16 Wright, Miller & Cooper, Jurisdiction §§ 4025–4028; Bice, Anderson and the Adequate State Ground, 1972, 45 S.Cal. L.Rev. 750; Hill, The Inadequate State Ground, 1965, 65 Col.L.Rev. 943; Sandalow, Henry v. Mississippi and the Adequate State Ground: Proposals for a Revised Doctrine, 1965 Sup.Ct.Rev. 187; Note, State Constitutional Guarantees as Adequate State Ground: Supreme Court Review and Problems of Federalism, 1976, 13 Am.Crim. L.Rev. 737.

76. Howlett by Howlett v. Rose, 1990, 110 S.Ct. 2430, 2437, 496 U.S. 356, 366, 110 L.Ed.2d 332; NAACP v. Alabama ex rel. Patterson, 1958, 78 S.Ct. 1163, 1168, 357 U.S. 449, 455, 2 L.Ed.2d 1488; Hill, note 75 above, at 954–957.

77. Ward v. Board of County Commrs. of Love County, 1920, 40 S.Ct. 419, 253

U.S. 17, 64 L.Ed. 751; Ancient Egyptian Arabic Order of Nobles of the Mystic Shrine v. Michaux, 1929, 49 S.Ct. 485, 279 U.S. 737, 73 L.Ed. 931; Creswill v. Grand Lodge Knights of Pythias of Georgia, 1912, 32 S.Ct. 822, 225 U.S. 246, 56 L.Ed. 1074; 16 Wright, Miller & Cooper, Jurisdiction § 4033.

78. Ford v. Georgia, 1991, 111 S.Ct. 850, 856–858, 498 U.S. 411, 420–425, 112 L.Ed.2d 935; James v. Kentucky, 1984, 104 S.Ct. 1830, 1835–1837, 466 U.S. 341, 348–351, 80 L.Ed.2d 346; NAACP v. Alabama ex rel. Flowers, 1964, 84 S.Ct. 1302, 1306–1311, 377 U.S. 288, 293–302, 12 L.Ed.2d 325; NAACP v. Alabama ex rel. Patterson, 1958, 78 S.Ct. 1163, 357 U.S. 449, 2 L.Ed.2d 1488; Staub v. City of Baxley, 1958, 78 S.Ct. 277, 355 U.S. 313, 2 L.Ed.2d 302; see Parrot v. City of Tallahassee, 1965, 85 S.Ct. 1322, 381 U.S. 129, 14 L.Ed.2d 263. See generally 16 Wright, Miller & Cooper, Jurisdiction § 4027.

79. Sullivan v. Little Hunting Park, Inc., 1969, 90 S.Ct. 400, 396 U.S. 229, 24 L.Ed.2d 386. This doctrine had been suggested in Justice Black's dissent in Henry v. Mississippi, 1965, 85 S.Ct. 564, 571–573, 379 U.S. 443, 455–457, 13 L.Ed.2d 408. In the Sullivan case three members of the Court agreed that there was no adequate state ground but relied on a ground very different from that announced by the majority.

It is argued that this possible implication in the Sullivan opinion is unwarranted. 16 Wright, Miller & Cooper, Jurisdiction § 4026, pp. 733–736.

In Hathorn v. Lovorn, 1982, 102 S.Ct. 2421, 457 U.S. 255, 72 L.Ed.2d 824, the state court arguably had refused to decide a state procedural rule of general applicability may be thought not an adequate state ground if it is so strict that it interferes unduly with the presentation of federal questions.[80]   In the familiar words of Justice Holmes, "whatever springes the State may set for those who are endeavoring to assert rights that the State confers, the assertion of Federal rights, when plainly and reasonably made, is not to be defeated under the name of local practice." [81]

To bar review the state ground must also be "independent." The Supreme Court can review if the state ground is "so interwoven with the other as not to be an independent matter." [82] The state ground is not independent if the state court appears to have believed that federal law compelled a particular interpretation of state law.[83] State procedural grounds may also be found not independent.[84]

Review will not be defeated by a state-court decision that a case that otherwise would turn on a federal question is moot or that the party lacked standing to raise the federal claim.[85] The Court considers that these are not state grounds at all but rather questions of federal law on which only it can pronounce final judgment.

The question of the adequate state ground seemed to have been

federal question because it found it untimely when it was first raised in a petition for rehearing. The Supreme Court held that even if this was the explanation for the state court's action, it was not a bar to review. The Court found that the state court does not consistently preclude consideration of issues raised for the first time on rehearing, and said: "State courts may not avoid deciding federal issues by invoking procedural rules that they do not apply evenhandedly to all similar claims." 102 S.Ct. at 2426, 457 U.S. at 262. For analysis of this confusing decision, which could mean a great deal but is better read as meaning very little, see 16 Wright, Miller & Cooper, Jurisdiction § 4028. But Hathorn was relied on in Johnson v. Mississippi, 1988, 108 S.Ct. 1981, 1987, 486 U.S. 578, 587, 100 L.Ed.2d 575, for the proposition that a state procedural ground is not adequate to bar review unless it has been consistently and regularly applied. See also James v. Kentucky, 1984, 104 S.Ct. 1830, 1835, 466 U.S. 341, 348–349, 80 L.Ed.2d 346.

80. Brown v. Western Ry. of Alabama, 1949, 70 S.Ct. 105, 338 U.S. 294, 94 L.Ed. 100; Douglas v. Alabama, 1965, 85 S.Ct. 1074, 1078–1079, 380 U.S. 415, 420–423, 13 L.Ed.2d 934. See 16 Wright, Miller & Cooper, Jurisdiction § 4023, pp. 708–713, § 4027, pp. 740–742.

Professor Hill, in the article cited note 75 above, at 971–977, argues that neither the

Brown case, nor any other, supports the proposition stated in the text.

81. Davis v. Wechsler, 1923, 44 S.Ct. 13, 14, 263 U.S. 22, 24, 68 L.Ed. 143.

82. Enterprise Irrigation Dist. v. Farmers Mut. Canal Co., 1917, 37 S.Ct. 318, 320–321, 243 U.S. 157, 164–165, 61 L.Ed. 644. See also Abie State Bank v. Weaver, 1931, 51 S.Ct. 252, 255–257, 282 U.S. 765, 773–777, 75 L.Ed. 690; 16 Wright, Miller & Cooper, Jurisdiction § 4029.

83. E.g., St. Martin Evangelical Lutheran Church v. South Dakota, 1981, 101 S.Ct. 2142, 2147 n. 9, 451 U.S. 772, 780 n.9, 68 L.Ed.2d 612; Zacchini v. Scripps–Howard Broadcasting Co., 1977, 97 S.Ct. 2849, 2852–2854, 433 U.S. 562, 566–568, 53 L.Ed.2d 965; State Tax Commn. of Utah v. Van Cott, 1939, 59 S.Ct. 605, 606, 306 U.S. 511, 514, 83 L.Ed. 950.

84. E.g., International Longshoremen's Assn. v. Davis, 1986, 106 S.Ct. 1904, 1910–1913, 476 U.S. 380, 387–393, 90 L.Ed.2d 389; Ake v. Oklahoma, 1985, 105 S.Ct. 1087, 1092, 470 U.S. 68, 75, 84 L.Ed.2d 53. See 16 Wright, Miller & Cooper, Jurisdiction § 4023.

85. Liner v. Jafco, Inc., 1964, 84 S.Ct. 391, 375 U.S. 301, 11 L.Ed.2d 347; Cramp v. Board of Public Instruction, 1961, 82 S.Ct. 275, 368 U.S. 278, 7 L.Ed.2d 285; Allied Stores of Ohio, Inc. v. Bowers, 1959, 79 S.Ct. 437, 358 U.S. 522, 3 L.Ed.2d 480.

much confused by the decision in Henry v. Mississippi.[86] Although the majority in that case spoke of applying "settled principles," [87] three of the dissenters thought that the decision "portends a severe dilution, if not complete abolition, of the concept of 'adequacy' as pertaining to state procedural grounds," [88] while a commentator suggested that "the implication that a change in doctrine is under consideration is manifest, yet the holding is sufficiently narrow that retreat is not foreclosed." [89]

Henry's conviction was affirmed by the Mississippi Supreme Court, despite the admission of evidence that arguably had been illegally obtained, on the ground that his counsel had failed to object to the evidence when it was introduced, as normally required by state procedure. The question was whether this procedural failure barred Supreme Court review.

The Court first recognized the adequate-state-ground rule but drew a distinction between state substantive grounds and state procedural grounds, and declared it to be settled that "a litigant's procedural defaults in state proceedings do not prevent vindication of his federal rights unless the State's insistence on compliance with its procedural rule serves a legitimate state interest." [90] This indicates that the Court could review the case if it found that the state rule served no legitimate state interest. The Court immediately agreed that the state requirement of a contemporaneous objection clearly serves a legitimate state interest, but it pointed out other ways in which Henry's counsel had made his position known at a time when corrective action was possible. In those circumstances, the Court said, the delay in making the objection could not have frustrated the state's interest in avoiding delay and waste of time. Thus, to enforce the contemporaneous objection rule would be to force resort to an arid ritual rather than to serve a substantial state interest.[91]

At this point it sounded as if the Court was prepared to declare the state ground inadequate and consider the merits, but it then expressly stated that it was not holding that the state ground was inadequate nor was it looking into the merits.[92] It saw some reason to think that counsel might have withheld objection to the evidence in question as a matter of strategy. If he had deliberately bypassed the opportunity to make timely objection, Henry would be deemed to have forfeited his

86. 1965, 85 S.Ct. 564, 379 U.S. 443, 13 L.Ed.2d 408. The case is extensively considered in the articles by Hill and Sandalow, note 75 above. See also 16 Wright, Miller & Cooper, Jurisdiction § 4020, pp. 671–675.

87. 85 S.Ct. at 568, 379 U.S. at 449.

88. 85 S.Ct. at 572, 379 U.S. at 457.

89. Sandalow, note 75 above, at 197.

90. 85 S.Ct. at 567, 379 U.S. at 447. One commentator thinks this proposition "amply supported by previous case law,"

Sandalow, note 75 above, at 229, while another can find "no suggestion" of it in the earlier cases, Hill, note 75 above, at 988. The distinction between substantive and procedural grounds is said to be insignificant in Wechsler, The Appellate Jurisdiction of the Supreme Court: Reflections on the Law and the Logistics of Direct Review, 1977, 34 Wash. & Lee L.Rev. 1043, 1054.

91. 85 S.Ct. at 568, 379 U.S. at 448–449.

92. 85 S.Ct. at 568, 379 U.S. at 449.

state-court remedies.[93] The case was, accordingly, remanded to the state court to determine whether there had been such a waiver.

If there had been a waiver, that would bar Henry from a decision on the merits of his federal claim either in state or federal court. But if the state court found no waiver, it was still free to insist on its procedural requirements and could, if it wished, again affirm the conviction. In that case, however, Henry "could have a federal court apply settled principles to test the effectiveness of the procedural default to foreclose consideration of his constitutional claim." [94] Whether the federal court referred to was the Supreme Court, on direct review, or a district court, on habeas corpus, was not made clear.

Subsequent developments in the Henry case shed no additional light. In the course of three more years of litigation, the state court found that there had been a deliberate waiver by Henry and his counsel, and it again affirmed his conviction.[95] The Supreme Court denied certiorari "without prejudice to the bringing of a proceeding for relief in federal habeas corpus." [96] The case clearly must be studied in any consideration of the doctrine of the adequate state ground but the few obscure cases in which it has since been invoked go in opposite directions [97] and suggest that Henry was not a significant break with the past but only an unusual case heavily influenced by its facts.[98]

It is often difficult to determine whether there is an adequate state ground that bars Supreme Court review because of failure of the state

---

93. 85 S.Ct. at 568–569, 379 U.S. at 450–452.

94. 85 S.Ct. at 570, 379 U.S. at 452.

95. Henry v. State, Miss.1967, 198 So.2d 213; id., 202 So.2d 40.

96. Henry v. Mississippi, 1968, 88 S.Ct. 2276, 392 U.S. 931, 20 L.Ed.2d 1389.

A federal court subsequently held that there had been no waiver and that Henry was entitled to relief on habeas corpus. Henry v. Williams, D.C.Miss.1969, 299 F.Supp. 36.

97. See Camp v. Arkansas, 1971, 92 S.Ct. 307, 404 U.S. 69, 30 L.Ed.2d 223, in which the Supreme Court reversed because of remarks by the prosecutor in his summation, though no objection had been made in the trial court. The state court refused to consider the point because of the lack of objection but the Supreme Court cited Henry for the proposition that "petitioner's alleged procedural default does not bar consideration of his constitutional claim in the circumstances of this case."

Compare Monger v. Florida, 1972, 92 S.Ct. 1163, 405 U.S. 958, 31 L.Ed.2d 236, where the state court's dismissal of an appeal because notice of appeal had been given after the oral entry of judgment but before the written order was expressly held

to be an adequate state ground, over the dissent of three justices who relied on Henry.

Henry was cited, in circumstances that did nothing to clarify its meaning, in Chambers v. Mississippi, 1973, 93 S.Ct. 1038, 1043 n. 3, 410 U.S. 284, 290–291 n. 3, 35 L.Ed.2d 297. Later cases have cited it occasionally, but only for propositions that are supported by a multitude of cases.

Professor Hill has observed that "Henry has never been overruled, but seems relatively moribund." Hill, The Forfeiture of Constitutional Rights in Criminal Cases, 1978, 78 Col.L.Rev. 1050, 1052.

98. "[E]ven though not mentioned by the Court, is it really immaterial that the petitioner was not merely a man charged with disturbing the peace, but Aaron Henry, a Negro resident of Clarksdale, Mississippi, and president of both the Coahoma County Branch of the National Association for the Advancement of Colored People and of its State Conference of Branches? Is it, moreover, immaterial that the prosecution was commenced in 1962 in Mississippi and not at another time and in another place?" Sandalow, note 75 above, at 190.

decision to indicate with sufficient clarity whether that court was relying on a federal ground or a state ground. This can occur either where the state court has not written an opinion or where its opinion is ambiguous. It is not surprising that there should be such ambiguous state decisions. The state courts have power to pass on both state and federal questions, and there is no need for them to draw a sharp distinction between the two. The matter is, of course, very different when review is sought in the Supreme Court.[99] One remedy in such a situation is for counsel to seek clarification from the state court, either by amendment of its judgment[100] or by a certificate from the court, or the presiding judge.[101] If the state court does give such clarification, and it appears from it that decision rested on the federal ground, review can then be had.

Where there is no such clarification from the state court, four different techniques had been used by the Court in the past, with no principled explanation of why the Court chose one technique rather than the other.[102] In 1983 in Michigan v. Long[103] the Court announced a new approach. "[W]hen, as in this case, a state court decision fairly appears to rest primarily on federal law, or to be interwoven with the federal law, and when the adequacy and independence of any possible state law ground is not clear from the face of the opinion, we will accept as the most reasonable explanation that the state court decided the case the way it did because it believed that federal law required it to do so. If a state court chooses merely to rely on federal precedents as it would on the precedent of all other jurisdictions, then it need only make clear by a plain statement in its judgment or opinion that the federal cases are being used only for the purpose of guidance, and do not themselves compel the result that the court has reached."[104]

99. See 16 Wright, Miller & Cooper, Jurisdiction § 4032.

100. E.g., Kedroff v. St. Nicholas Cathedral of Russian Orthodox Church in North America, 1952, 73 S.Ct. 143, 145, 344 U.S. 94, 97, 97 L.Ed. 120.

101. E.g., Allenberg Cotton Co., Inc. v. Pittman, 1974, 95 S.Ct. 260, 262 n. 2, 419 U.S. 20, 23 n. 2, 42 L.Ed.2d 195. Indiana ex rel. Anderson v. Brand, 1938, 58 S.Ct. 443, 445, 303 U.S. 95, 99, 82 L.Ed. 685; cf. Marvin v. Trout, 1905, 26 S.Ct. 31, 199 U.S. 212, 50 L.Ed. 157; Wolfson & Kurland, Certificates by State Courts of the Existence of a Federal Question, 1949, 63 Harv. L.Rev. 111. A letter from the clerk of the court is insufficient for this purpose. Dixon v. Duffy, 1952, 73 S.Ct. 193, 194, 344 U.S. 143, 145, 97 L.Ed. 153.

102. (1) It could dismiss if its jurisdiction was ambiguous. (2) It could vacate the judgment below and remand so that the state court could clarify its ruling. (3) It could continue the case to give the parties an opportunity to apply to the state court for clarification. (4) If it thought that the federal question necessarily was decided, it could take jurisdiction and decide the federal question. "[E]ach disposition resulted from an ad hoc decision by the Court to apply one dispositive technique or another." Note, Supreme Court Treatment of State Court Cases Exhibiting Ambiguous Grounds of Decision, 1962, 62 Col.L.Rev. 822, 847.

103. 983, 103 S.Ct. 3469, 463 U.S. 1032, 77 L.Ed.2d 1201.

104. 103 S.Ct. at 3476, 463 U.S. at 1040–1041.

The case has produced a large literature. It is favorably analyzed in Althouse, How To Build a Separate Sphere: Federal Courts and State Power, 1987, 100 Harv. L.Rev. 1485, 1490–1511, in Redish, note 74 above, in Baker, The Ambiguous Independent and Adequate State Ground in Criminal Cases: Federalism Along a Möbius Strip, 1985, 19 Ga.L.Rev. 799, and in Schlueter, Judicial Federalism and Supreme Court Review of State Court Decisions: A Sensible Balance Emerges, 1984, 59 Notre Dame L.Rev. 1079. It is criticized in Matasar & Bruch, note 58 above, at 1367–1382,

The Court recognized in Michigan v. Long that there might still be cases in which clarification of the state decision might be necessary or appropriate,[105] but in most cases it has applied the "plain statement" rule without difficulty.[106] The rule applies regardless of whether the disputed state-law ground is substantive or procedural.[107] But there is no need for a plain statement by the state court to bar Supreme Court review if the decision does not appear to rest primarily on, or to be interwoven with, federal law.[108]

Until 1988 the statute for review of state-court decisions in the Supreme Court permitted review by certiorari in any case within its terms, but also allowed review by appeal if the state court had held a statute or treaty of the United States invalid [109] or if the state court had held valid a statute of the state against a claim that it is repugnant to the Constitution, treaties, or laws of the United States.[110] That distinction is now ended. Since 1988 decisions of state courts can be reviewed in the Supreme Court only on writ of certiorari.[111]

§ 108. Procedures in the Supreme Court [1]

To bring a case to the Supreme Court it is necessary to make timely application. In civil cases, whether from state or federal courts, the application must be made within 90 days of the entry of the judgment sought to be reviewed, with 30 days for most direct appeals from district courts.[2] Ninety days is now the time allowed in criminal cases.[3] An

in Seid, Schizoid Federalism, Supreme Court Power and Inadequate State Ground Theory: Michigan v. Long, 1984, 18 Creighton L.Rev. 1, and in Welsh, Reconsidering the Constitutional Relationship Between State and Federal Courts: A Critique of Michigan v. Long, 1984, 59 Notre Dame L.Rev. 1118.

105. 103 S.Ct. at 3476 n. 6, 463 U.S. at 1041 n. 6. In Capital Cities Media, Inc. v. Toole, 1984, the Court vacated the judgment below and remanded for such further proceedings as the state court might deem appropriate to clarify the ground of its decision.

106. See cases collected in Harris v. Reed, 1989, 109 S.Ct. 1038, 1042 n. 7, 489 U.S. 255, 261 n. 7, 103 L.Ed.2d 308, noted 1989, 58 Fordham L.Rev. 493.

107. Id., 109 S.Ct. at 1042, 489 U.S. at 261.

108. Coleman v. Thompson, 1991, 111 S.Ct. 2546, 501 U.S. 722, 115 L.Ed.2d 640. Coleman is a habeas-corpus case. The Court had earlier held in Harris v. Reed, note i above, that the "plain statement" rule applies to federal habeas-corpus proceedings so that a procedural default will not bar consideration of a federal claim on habeas review unless the state court ren-

dering judgment in the case has clearly and expressly stated that the judgment rests on a state procedural bar.

109. This was formerly 28 U.S.C.A. § 1257(1).

110. This was formerly 28 U.S.C.A. § 1257(2).

111. 28 U.S.C.A. § 1257(a), as amended by Act of June 27, 1988, Pub.L. 100–352, § 3, 102 Stat. 662. That Act eliminated most provisions for appeal to the Supreme Court, because of a feeling that the Court should have discretion to control its docket. See § 105 n. 33 above.

§ 108

1. 16 Wright, Miller & Cooper, Jurisdiction §§ 4003–4005; Stern, Gressman, Shapiro & Geller, Supreme Court Practice, 7th ed. 1993, cc. 4–7; Boskey & Gressman, The Supreme Court's New Rules for the Nineties, 1990, 128 F.R.D. 295.

2. 90 days: 28 U.S.C.A. § 2101(c); Rule 13.1, 1990 Sup.Ct.Rules.

30 days: Rule 18.1, 1990 Sup.Ct.Rules. The Supreme Court apparently overlooked the statutory requirement that the notice of appeal be filed within 10 days for certain orders of a three-judge court under the Gramm–Rudman–Hollings Act, 2 U.S.C.A.

3. See note 3 on page 797.

extension of time for petitioning for certiorari can be obtained, for good cause, from a justice of the Supreme Court, but no extension is permissible in those rare cases coming to the Court by appeal from a district court.[4]

The time limits for seeking Supreme Court review in civil cases have commonly been thought to be jurisdictional[5] and the Court has rejected persuasive arguments that review should not be barred if the delay was wholly caused by circumstances entirely beyond the applicant's control.[6] The Court has also held that it has discretion to entertain an untimely petition for certiorari to a court of appeals in a criminal case,[7] on the theory that this time limit is imposed solely by a rule of the Court and not by statute. A similar argument can be made with regard to an application for review of a state-court judgment in a criminal case.[8]

Questions of procedure in the Supreme Court, other than in part the time in which to apply for review, are governed by the 1990 Supreme Court Rules.[9] Many former procedural distinctions no longer exist, thanks for the 1988 legislation[10] that, as the Court has noted, "eliminates substantially all of our appellate jurisdiction * * *."[11] The only appeals that remain are direct appeals from a few limited classes of orders by district courts[12] and a single rule is enough to spell out for those cases the requirements for a notice of appeal and a jurisdictional statement.[13]

If, as now will almost always be the case, the party is petitioning for certiorari, it must file with the Supreme Court a petition for certiorari,

§ 922(b). See Boskey & Gressman, note 1 above, at 300–301. A more important problem is that most direct appeals from district courts seem to fall within 28 U.S.C.A. § 2101(b), which allows 60 days. The statute authorizing the Supreme Court to make rules requires that the rules "be consistent with Acts of Congress." 28 U.S.C.A. § 2071(a). Nevertheless prudent counsel will file the notice of appeal within the 30 days allowed by the rule, even in instances where the statute appears to allow 60 days. See Stern, Gressman, Shapiro & Geller, note 1 above, at p. 387.

3. 28 U.S.C.A. § 2101(c), (d); Rule 13.1, 1990 Sup.Ct.Rules. Before the 1990 Rules were adopted, only 60 days had normally been allowed in criminal cases.

4. 28 U.S.C.A. § 2101(c); Rule 13.2, 1990 Sup.Ct.Rules.

5. E.g., Missouri v. Jenkins, 1990, 110 S.Ct. 1651, 1660, 495 U.S. 33, 45, 109 L.Ed.2d 31; Gibson Distributing Co. v. Downtown Development Assn., 1978, 99 S.Ct. 606, 439 U.S. 1000, 58 L.Ed.2d 674; Toledo Scale Co. v. Computing Scale Co., 1923, 43 S.Ct. 458, 261 U.S. 399, 67 L.Ed. 719. See Rule 13.3, 1990 Sup.Ct.Rules.

6. Deal v. Cincinnati Bd. of Educ., 1971, 91 S.Ct. 1630, 402 U.S. 962, 29 L.Ed.2d 128 (dissenting opinion); Teague v. Regional Commr. of Customs, 1969, 89 S.Ct. 1457, 1460–1463, 394 U.S. 977, 981, 984, 22 L.Ed.2d 756 (dissenting opinion).

7. Sanabria v. U.S., 1978, 98 S.Ct. 2170, 2177 n. 12, 437 U.S. 54, 62 n. 12, 57 L.Ed.2d 43; Schacht v. U.S., 1970, 90 S.Ct. 1555, 1559–1560, 398 U.S. 58, 63–65, 26 L.Ed.2d 44.

8. See 28 U.S.C.A. § 2101(d); Stone v. Powell, 1976, 96 S.Ct. 3037, 3060, 428 U.S. 465, 511, 49 L.Ed.2d 1067 (Brennan, J., dissenting); Stern, Gressman, Shapiro & Geller, note 1 above, at pp. 279–282.

9. See Boskey & Gressman, note 1 above. The text of the 1990 Rules appears at 127 F.R.D. 547.

10. Act of June 27, 1988, Pub.L. 100–352, 102 Stat. 662. See § 105 n. 34 above.

11. Duquesne Light Co. v. Barasch, 1989, 109 S.Ct. 609, 615 n. 7, 488 U.S. 299, 307 n. 7, 102 L.Ed.2d 646.

12. See § 105 above.

13. Rule 18, 1990 Sup.Ct.Rules.

accompanied by a docket fee, within the time permitted.[14]   It is then discretionary with the Court whether to grant the writ.   Rule 10.1 of the 1990 Rules states clearly that "a review on writ of certiorari is not a matter of right, but of judicial discretion.   A petition for a writ of certiorari will be granted only when there are special and important reasons therefor."   The rule then lists six factors that, among others, indicate the kind of reasons that may induce the Court to grant certiorari.[15]

When certiorari is granted, it almost always means either that the petitioner will get the relief it seeks, or that it will at least be heard by the Supreme Court in support of such relief.   It does not mean that petitioner will always be heard.   Despite trenchant criticism,[16] the Court in a number of cases summarily reverses the decision below on the basis of the petition for certiorari and brief in opposition thereto, without hearing oral argument.[17]   Though occasionally the Court will grant certiorari and affirm summarily,[18] this is less common.

Even in the past, when a substantial number of cases came to the

---

14. Rule 12.1, 1990 Sup.Ct.Rules. The procedure for seeking a stay of the decision below pending review in the Supreme Court is set out in Rule 23, 1990 Sup.Ct.Rules.

15. 16 Wright, Miller & Cooper, Jurisdiction § 4004.

The percentage of certiorari petitions that are granted has steadily declined. In the 1971 Term the Court granted 8.9% of the paid petitions and 3.3% of those from indigents. Report of the Study Group on the Caseload of the Supreme Court, 1972, 57 F.R.D. 573, 615.

In the 1992 Term the Court granted review in 3.98% of the paid cases and 0.33% of the indigent cases. Sturley, Filing and Responding to a Petition for Certiorari, 1993, 24 J.Mar.L. & Com. 595, 595 n.2.

16. See Hellman, Error Correction, Lawmaking, and the Supreme Court's Exercise of Discretionary Review, 1983, 44 U.Pitt.L.Rev. 795; Brown, Process of Law, 1958, 72 Harv.L.Rev. 77; Stern, Gressman, Shapiro & Geller, note 1 above, at pp. 250–256.

The practice has frequently been criticized from within the Court. See, e.g., the dissent of Justice Blackmun, in which Justices Brennan and Marshall joined, in U.S. v. Hollywood Motor Car Co., Inc., 1982, 102 S.Ct. 3081, 3085–3086, 458 U.S. 263, 271, 73 L.Ed.2d 754: "The Court, it seems to me, has shown a disturbing tendency of late to dispose of difficult cases by summary per curiam reversals. I must assume that this tendency is prompted, at least in part, by the growing pressures of the Court's calen-

dar and an ill-conceived conviction that we must stay ahead of the increasing workload whatever the costs may be. I regret this pattern, for I think it demeans the Court and its work and surely tends to lessen the quality of its legal product." See also the dissenting opinion of Justice Marshall in Rhodes v. Stewart, 1988, 109 S.Ct. 202, 204, 488 U.S. 1, 4–5, 102 L.Ed.2d 1. And Justice Stevens has objected that summary reversal on the petition of a warden or prosecutor suggests that the Court is "primarily concerned with vindicating the will of the majority and less interested in its role as a protector of the individual's constitutional rights." Florida v. Meyers, 1984, 104 S.Ct. 1852, 1855–1856, 466 U.S. 380, 385–386, 80 L.Ed.2d 381 (dissenting opinion). See Comment, Supreme Court Review of State Court Cases: Principled Federalism or Selective Bias?, 1987, 36 Emory L.J. 1277.

But see 16 Wright, Miller & Cooper, Jurisdiction § 4004, pp. 525–526.

17. E.g., Trevino v. Texas, 1992, 112 S.Ct. 1547, ___ U.S. ___, 118 L.Ed.2d 193; Stone v. Graham, 1980, 101 S.Ct. 192, 449 U.S. 39, 66 L.Ed.2d 199; Idaho Dept. of Employment v. Smith, 1977, 98 S.Ct. 327, 434 U.S. 100, 54 L.Ed.2d 324; Day and Zimmerman, Inc. v. Challoner, 1975, 96 S.Ct. 167, 423 U.S. 3, 46 L.Ed.2d 3. The fact that the Court may do this is now stated in Rule 16.1, 1990 Sup.Ct.Rules.

18. E.g., Donovan v. Penn Shipping Co., 1977, 97 S.Ct. 835, 429 U.S. 648, 51 L.Ed.2d 112; Fuller v. Alaska, 1968, 89 S.Ct. 61, 393 U.S. 80, 21 L.Ed.2d 212.

Court by appeal, oral argument was heard in only a small fraction.[19] The other cases brought to the Court by appeal were disposed of summarily. Some appeals were not heard because of procedural defects in taking the appeal, or because the case was not one in which appeal would lie, but in most cases the Court summarily affirmed, or dismissed the appeal for want of a substantial federal question. While such dispositions represented decisions on the merits, they were of scant comfort to the appellant who had obtained no relief.

Six justices constitute a quorum of the Court.[20] The decision to grant or deny certiorari, or to hear or make summary disposition of an appeal, is made by the whole Court. The Court does not function by committees, or by dividing applications for review among the justices. Each justice studies the application individually and casts his or her vote at conference on whether to hear the case.[21] Under the well-settled "rule of four", certiorari is granted whenever four justices vote for a grant, and the Court will then hear the case even though five justices consider the case not worthy of the attention of the Supreme Court.[22] A similar practice applies on appeals. The case will be heard, rather than summarily disposed of, if four justices so vote.[23] Plainly it is important that the petition for certiorari, or the jurisdictional statement in those few cases that still come by appeal, be carefully drafted in order to

19. In the 1971 Term the figure was 18%. Report of the Study Group on the Caseload of the Supreme Court 1972, 57 F.R.D. 573, 622. This figure seems to have remained fairly steady in later years. See Stern, Gressman, Shapiro & Geller, note 1 above, § 4.26.

20. 28 U.S.C.A. § 1. Disposition of a case in which a quorum of qualified justices cannot be mustered is governed by 28 U.S.C.A. § 2109. Ordinarily in this situation the judgment below is affirmed with the same effect as an affirmance by an equally divided court. Sloan v. Nixon, 1974, 95 S.Ct. 218, 419 U.S. 958, 42 L.Ed.2d 174. If the case has come to the Court on direct appeal from a district court, the case may be remitted to the court of appeals for the circuit including the district in which the case arose. See § 105 above at notes 34–35.

21. See Furness, Withy & Co. v. Yang–Tsze Ins. Assn., 1917, 37 S.Ct. 141, 142, 242 U.S. 430, 434, 61 L.Ed. 409; Brennan, State Court Decisions and the Supreme Court, 1960, 21 Pa.B.A.Q. 393, 400–406; Stern, Gressman, Shapiro & Geller, note 1 above, §§ 5.1–5.3.

For a comprehensive discussion of the context in which members of the Supreme Court decide which cases are worthy of plenary consideration, see Perry, Deciding to Decide: Agenda Setting in the United States Supreme Court, 1991. The book is insightfully discussed in Levinson, Strategy, Jurisprudence, and Certiorari, 1993, 79 Va. L.Rev. 717.

At one time the neologism "certworthy" appeared even in United States Reports, though only in dissenting opinions. Fortunately "the word has passed officially from the scene." Sharpe, The Maritime Origin of the Word "Certworthiness", 1993, 24 J.Mar.L. & Com. 667, 670.

22. Rogers v. Missouri Pac. R. Co., 1957, 77 S.Ct. 443, 352 U.S. 500, 1 L.Ed.2d 493. See Stevens, The Life Span of a Judge–Made Rule, 1983, 58 N.Y.U.L.Rev. 1; Leiman, The Rule of Four, 1957, 57 Col. L.Rev. 975; Note, 1957, 105 U.Pa.L.Rev. 1084. There have been cases that the Court has refused to hear over three dissents though only seven justices participated. See 16 Wright, Miller & Cooper, Jurisdiction § 4004, pp. 512–516. And the fact that four justices can bring about a hearing of a case does not mean that they can require the Court to decide it on the merits. See the concurring opinion of Justice Stevens in New York v. Uplinger, 1984, 104 S.Ct. 2332, 2334–2335, 467 U.S. 246, 249–251, 81 L.Ed.2d 201.

23. Ohio ex rel. Eaton v. Price, 1959, 79 S.Ct. 978, 360 U.S. 246, 3 L.Ed.2d 1200 (opinion of Brennan, J.).

attract the interest of at least four members of the Court.[24]

Denial of certiorari, as has frequently been explained, imports nothing about the merits of the case. All it means is that, for whatever reason, there were not four members of the Court who wished to hear the case.[25] Summary disposition of an appeal, however, either by affirmance or by dismissal for want of a substantial federal question, is a disposition on the merits.[26] An affirmance by an equally divided Court leaves the judgment below in effect but it is not of any precedential value.[27]

In cases coming from state courts review in the Supreme Court is limited, as has been seen, to the properly presented federal questions.[28] On direct appeals from district courts and on certiorari from a court of appeals, no such limitations apply. The writ brings the whole case before the Supreme Court [29] and it may consider all issues in the case that have been properly raised below.[30] But the Court will normally consider only those issues presented in the petition [31]—though on occa-

---

24. Despite its title, even experienced practitioners will benefit from the excellent article, Prettyman, Petitioning the United States Supreme Court—A Primer for Hopeful Neophytes, 1965, 51 Va.L.Rev. 582. See also the equally helpful article, Prettyman, Opposing Certiorari in the United States Supreme Court, 1975, 61 Va.L.Rev. 197. A more recent, and also excellent, discussion is Sturley, note 15 above.

25. Hughes Tool Co. v. Trans World Airlines, 1973, 93 S.Ct. 647, 650 n. 1, 409 U.S. 363, 365 n. 1, 34 L.Ed.2d 577; Brown v. Allen, 1953, 73 S.Ct. 397, 437–441, 344 U.S. 443, 489–497, 97 L.Ed. 469; Maryland v. Baltimore Radio Show, 1950, 70 S.Ct. 252, 338 U.S. 912, 94 L.Ed. 562 (opinion of Frankfurter, J.); Linzer, The Meaning of Certiorari Denials, 1979, 79 Col.L.Rev. 1227.

In recent years dissents from the denial of certiorari have become more common. That practice is criticized by Justice Stevens in his separate opinion in Singleton v. C.I.R., 1978, 99 S.Ct. 335, 337–339, 439 U.S. 940, 942–946, 58 L.Ed.2d 335.

26. As such it is binding on lower courts, Hicks v. Miranda, 1975, 95 S.Ct. 2281, 2289, 422 U.S. 332, 344–345, 45 L.Ed.2d 223, although for the Supreme Court itself "summary actions do not have the same authority" as decisions rendered after plenary consideration. Metromedia, Inc. v. City of San Diego, 1981, 101 S.Ct. 2882, 2888, 453 U.S. 490, 500, 69 L.Ed.2d 800. See Stern, Gressman, Shapiro & Geller, note 1 above, §§ 4.28, 4.29.

27. Neil v. Biggers, 1972, 93 S.Ct. 375, 378–379, 409 U.S. 188, 190–192, 34 L.Ed.2d

401. Thus, it is not an actual adjudication that would bar habeas corpus under 28 U.S.C.A. § 2244(c). Habeas corpus is barred on issues on which the Supreme Court has dismissed an appeal for want of a substantial federal question but not on issues on which certiorari has been denied. Howell v. Jones, C.A.5th, 1975, 516 F.2d 53.

If the Court is able to reach a decision, but no majority can agree on the reason, it is difficult for lower courts to know how to regard the decision as precedent. See Note, The Precedential Value of Supreme Court Plurality Decisions, 1980, 80 Col.L.Rev. 756.

28. See § 107 above.

29. Lutcher & Moore Lumber Co. v. Knight, 1910, 30 S.Ct. 505, 217 U.S. 257, 54 L.Ed. 757.

30. FTC v. Travelers Health Assn., 1960, 80 S.Ct. 717, 362 U.S. 293, 4 L.Ed.2d 724; Marconi Wireless Tel. Co. of America v. Simon, 1918, 38 S.Ct. 275, 277, 246 U.S. 46, 57, 62 L.Ed. 568.

Writ dismissed where question was not raised in state court. Cardinale v. Louisiana, 1969, 89 S.Ct. 1161, 394 U.S. 437, 22 L.Ed.2d 398.

31. Rule 14.1(a), 1990 Sup.Ct.Rules; Kaisha v. U.S. Phillips Corp., 1993, 114 S.Ct. 425, ___ U.S. ___, 126 L.Ed.2d 396.

The rules on when the winning party below must cross-petition or cross-appeal are the same as apply to appeals to the courts of appeals. See § 104 above at notes 34–35. See also Northwest Airlines, Inc. v. County of Kent, 1994, 114 S.Ct. 855, 862, ___ U.S. ___, ___, 127 L.Ed.2d 183.

sion it departs from that rule [32]—and it may limit review still further by granting certiorari only on some of the questions set out in the petition.[33] By the same token the Court may expand review by requesting the parties to brief and argue an issue forumulated by the Court in addition to, or instead of, some or all of the issues tendered in the petition for certiorari.[34]

The Supreme Court does not ordinarily sit to decide questions of fact. If the facts have been found by a jury, the Court is precluded from reexamination of them by the Seventh Amendment.[35] Even where there is no such constitutional bar, the Court usually should not decide fact questions for its special competence is in questions of law. Accordingly the Court follows rules of self-limitation with regard to questions of fact. In civil cases coming from a court of appeals, the so-called "two court rule" applies, and the Court will not review findings of fact concurred in by two courts below in the absence of a very obvious and exceptional showing of error.[36] On review of decisions of state courts, the stated rule is that "all those matters which are usually termed issues of fact are for conclusive determination by the State courts and are not open for reconsideration by this Court. Observance of this restriction in our

32. E.g., Vachon v. New Hampshire, 1974, 94 S.Ct. 664, 414 U.S. 478, 38 L.Ed.2d 666; Blonder–Tongue Laboratories, Inc. v. University of Illinois Foundation, 1971, 91 S.Ct. 1434, 1438 n. 6, 402 U.S. 313, 320 n. 6, 28 L.Ed.2d 788; Terminiello v. City of Chicago, 1949, 69 S.Ct. 894, 337 U.S. 1, 93 L.Ed. 1131. The Court has more freedom in going beyond the questions presented in the writ where review is of a federal-court decision. See Piper Aircraft Co. v. Reyno, 1981, 102 S.Ct. 252, 261 n. 12, 454 U.S. 235, 24 n. 12, 70 L.Ed.2d 419; McGoldrick v. Compagnie Generale Transatlantique, 1940, 60 S.Ct. 670, 672–673, 309 U.S. 430, 434, 84 L.Ed. 849. A famous example is Erie R. Co. v. Tompkins, 1938, 58 S.Ct. 817, 304 U.S. 64, 82 L.Ed. 1188, 114 A.L.R. 1487. See § 55 n. 4 above.

33. E.g., Dennis v. U.S., 1951, 71 S.Ct. 857, 871, 341 U.S. 494, 516, 95 L.Ed. 1137; Beck v. Washington, 1962, 82 S.Ct. 955, 962, 369 U.S. 541, 554, 8 L.Ed.2d 98. See Bice, The Limited Grant of Certiorari and the Justification of Judicial Review, 1975 Wis.L.Rev. 343; 16 Wright, Miller & Cooper, Jurisdiction § 4004, pp. 516–518.

34. E.g., Mississippi v. Louisiana, 1992, 112 S.Ct. 1472, ___ U.S. ___, 117 L.Ed.2d 616; Ankenbrandt v. Richards, 1992, 112 S.Ct. 855, ___ U.S. ___, 116 L.Ed.2d 764; Wright v. West, 1991, 112 S.Ct. 672, ___ U.S. ___, 116 L.Ed.2d 763.

35. Chicago, B. & Q. R. Co. v. Chicago, 1897, 17 S.Ct. 581, 166 U.S. 226, 41 L.Ed.

979. But it is not barred from determining whether there were sufficient facts to require submission to the jury. The Supreme Court's willingness to accept cases of this sort, particularly arising under the Federal Employers' Liability Act and the Jones Act, was the subject of debate within and without the Court. See e.g., Wilkerson v. McCarthy, 1949, 69 S.Ct. 413, 336 U.S. 53, 93 L.Ed. 497; Note, Supreme Court Certiorari Policy in Cases Arising Under the FELA, 1956, 69 Harv.L.Rev. 1441. Compare Hart, The Time Chart of the Justices, 1959, 73 Harv.L.Rev. 84, with Arnold, Professor Hart's Theology, 1960, 73 Harv. L.Rev. 1298.

36. Goodman v. Lukens Steel Co., 107 S.Ct. 2617, 2623, 482 U.S. 656, 665, 96 L.Ed.2d 572; Graver Tank & Mfg. Co. v. Linde Air Products Co., 1949, 69 S.Ct. 535, 538, 336 U.S. 271, 275, 93 L.Ed. 672; Pick Mfg. Co. v. General Motors Corp., 1936, 57 S.Ct. 1, 2, 299 U.S. 3, 4, 81 L.Ed. 4. But cf. Baumgartner v. U.S., 1944, 64 S.Ct. 1240, 322 U.S. 665, 88 L.Ed. 1525.

The Court has indicated that the "two court" rule does not apply in habeas-corpus cases where the dispute between the parties is not so much over the elemental facts as over the constitutional significance to be attached to them. Neil v. Biggers, 1972, 93 S.Ct. 375, 379 n. 3, 409 U.S. 188, 193 n. 3, 34 L.Ed.2d 401.

review of State courts calls for the utmost scruple." [37]   Perhaps this is so, but only by an ingenious redefinition of what constitutes a question of fact.[38]   Only a year before the statement just quoted a unanimous Court had said: "The duty of this Court to make its own independent examination of the record when federal constitutional deprivations are alleged is clear, resting, as it does, on our solemn responsibility for maintaining the Constitution inviolate." [39]   In making such an independent examination the Court recognizes that it is reviewing the facts.   It has said that "this Court will review the finding of facts by a State court where a Federal right has been denied as the result of a finding shown by the record to be without evidence to support it; or where a conclusion of law as to a Federal right and a finding of fact are so intermingled as to make it necessary, in order to pass upon the Federal question, to analyze the facts." [40]   Since cases do not come to the Supreme Court from the state courts unless they involve some claim of a federal right, the exceptions seem quite broad enough to swallow up the announced rule against review of state-court fact determinations.

When the Supreme Court has disposed of a case coming to it from a federal court, it ordinarily reverses with directions to enter a particular judgment or to follow a particular course of action.   Occasionally a lower federal court may prove recalcitrant, but the Court can issue a writ of mandamus to compel the action that it has previously held proper.[41]   It is more likely to be a state court that refuses to comply with the Supreme Court's judgment.[42]   The problem of evasion of Supreme Court mandates by state courts is as old as Martin v. Hunter's Lessee [43] and as

---

37. Watts v. Indiana, 1949, 69 S.Ct. 1347, 1348, 338 U.S. 49, 50, 93 L.Ed. 1801; Wolfe v. North Carolina, 1960, 80 S.Ct. 1482, 1492, 364 U.S. 177, 196, 4 L.Ed.2d 1650.

38. Such a redefinition is attempted in Comment, Supreme Court Review of State Findings of Fact in Fourteenth Amendment Cases, 1962, 14 Stan.L.Rev. 328.

39. Napue v. Illinois, 1959, 79 S.Ct. 1173, 1178, 360 U.S. 264, 271, 3 L.Ed.2d 1217.

40. Fiske v. Kansas, 1927, 47 S.Ct. 655, 656, 274 U.S. 380, 385–386, 71 L.Ed. 1108. See also Norris v. Alabama, 1935, 55 S.Ct. 579, 580, 294 U.S. 587, 590, 79 L.Ed. 1074; Niemotko v. Maryland, 1951, 71 S.Ct. 325, 327, 340 U.S. 268, 271, 95 L.Ed. 267; Kern–Limerick, Inc. v. Scurlock, 1954, 74 S.Ct. 403, 410, 347 U.S. 110, 121, 98 L.Ed. 546; Vachon v. New Hampshire, 1974, 94 S.Ct. 664, 414 U.S. 478, 38 L.Ed.2d 666; NAACP v. Claiborne Hardware Co., 1982, 102 S.Ct. 3409, 3427 n. 50, 458 U.S. 886, 915 n. 50, 73 L.Ed.2d 1215.

See 16 Wright, Miller & Cooper, Jurisdiction § 4033.

41. U.S. v. Haley, 1962, 83 S.Ct. 11, 371 U.S. 18, 9 L.Ed.2d 1. As is customary in such matters, the Court followed the nicety of holding that the party was entitled to mandamus but not actually issuing a formal writ on the assumption that the district court would now do what the Court thought should be done. That mandamus is the proper remedy is held in Vendo Co. v. Lektro–Vend Corp., 1978, 98 S.Ct. 702, 434 U.S. 425, 54 L.Ed.2d 659.

42. Beatty, State Court Evasion of United States Supreme Court Mandates during the Last Decade of the Warren Court, 1972, 6 Valp.L.Rev. 260; Schneider, State Court Evasion of United States Supreme Court Mandates: A Reconsideration of the Evidence, 1973, 7 Valp.L.Rev. 191; Note, Remand to State Courts and its Effect on the Dual–Sovereign System, 1962, 50 Geo.L.J. 819; Note, Evasion of Supreme Court Mandates in Cases Remanded to State Courts Since 1941, 1954, 67 Harv.L.Rev. 1251; Note, State Court Evasion of United States Supreme Court Mandates, 1947, 56 Yale L.J. 574.

43. 1816, 1 Wheat. 304, 4 L.Ed. 97.

current as NAACP v. Alabama.[44]   In cases coming from state courts the
Supreme Court normally does not issue a mandate calling for specific
action, but remands for proceedings not inconsistent with its opinion.
The state court is deliberately left free to pass on any state questions
that may still be open in the case.[45]   A litigant, however, may disagree on
whether the subsequent disposition of the case by the state court is in
fact consistent with the Supreme Court's opinion.   In such a case the
Supreme Court can review, by appeal or by certiorari as is appropriate,
the second judgment of the state court and reverse again.   This was the
course followed in both Martin v. Hunter's Lessee and NAACP v.
Alabama.[46]   If the state court should still refuse to conform, the Court
has statutory power to direct the entry of an appropriate judgment,
decree, or order, or require such further proceedings to be had as may be
just under the circumstances.[47]   It may send its mandate directly to the
state trial court,[48] or issue its own execution.[49]   It would even seem that
the judges of the state court might be punished for contempt for refusal
to obey a lawful order of the Supreme Court,[50] but fortunately no case
has arisen that has required such drastic action.[51]

The Supreme Court, like all other courts established by Congress, is
authorized to issue "all writs necessary or appropriate in aid of their
respective jurisdictions and agreeable to the usages and principles of
law." [52]   The Court cannot be given original jurisdiction to issue such
writs except in cases within its original jurisdiction as defined in the
Constitution.[53]   But where a case is within the appellate jurisdiction of
the Supreme Court, it may issue the common-law writs of mandamus,
prohibition, and certiorari in aid of the appellate jurisdiction that might
otherwise be defeated by the unauthorized action of the court below.[54]
The question is not one of power to issue the writ but of discretion about

44.   1959, 79 S.Ct. 1001, 360 U.S. 240, 3
L.Ed.2d 1205.   For a later stage in the
same proceeding, in which federal habeas
corpus was used to force compliance with
the 1958 and 1959 mandates, see NAACP v.
Gallion, 1961, 82 S.Ct. 4, 368 U.S. 16, 7
L.Ed.2d 85.   Even this was not the end.
The Supreme Court was compelled to act
again, in NAACP v. Alabama ex rel. Flowers, 1964, 84 S.Ct. 1302, 377 U.S. 288, 12
L.Ed.2d 325, before the state court finally
complied.   1964, 167 So.2d 171, 277 Ala. 89.

45.   E.g., Stanton v. Stanton, 1975, 95
S.Ct. 1373, 1379, 421 U.S. 7, 17, 43 L.Ed.2d
688.

46.   This course is not available where
the state court has simply failed to enter a
final judgment in response to the Supreme
Court's mandate.   Lavender v. Kurn, 1946,
67 S.Ct. 111, 329 U.S. 762, 91 L.Ed. 656.
In the same case leave to file a petition for
a writ of mandamus was denied.   Lavender
v. Clark, 1946, 67 S.Ct. 108, 329 U.S. 674,
91 L.Ed. 596.

47.   28 U.S.C.A. § 2106; e.g., Poindexter
v. Greenhow, 1885, 5 S.Ct. 903, 114 U.S.

270, 29 L.Ed. 185.   See NAACP v. Alabama
ex rel. Flowers, 1964, 84 S.Ct. 1302, 1315,
377 U.S. 288, 310, 12 L.Ed.2d 325.

48.   E.g., Williams v. Bruffy, 1880, 102
U.S. 248, 26 L.Ed. 135.

49.   E.g., Tyler v. Magwire, 1873, 17
Wall. 253, 21 L.Ed. 576.

50.   18 U.S.C.A. § 401(3).

51.   Cf. U.S. v. Shipp, 1909, 29 S.Ct. 637,
214 U.S. 386, 53 L.Ed. 1041; id., 1909, 30
S.Ct. 397, 215 U.S. 580, 54 L.Ed. 337 (sheriff imprisoned for contempt for complicity
in lynching of a prisoner after Supreme
Court had granted a stay of execution).

52.   28 U.S.C.A. § 1651(a).   See 16
Wright, Miller & Cooper, Jurisdiction
§ 4005.

53.   Marbury v. Madison, 1803, 1 Cranch
137, 2 L.Ed. 60.

54.   McClellan v. Carland, 1910, 30 S.Ct.
501, 503, 217 U.S. 268, 280, 54 L.Ed. 762.

when it should issue,[55] and the considerations that govern the exercise of this discretion are similar to those that control when a court of appeals is asked to issue an extraordinary writ to a district court.[56]

It was long unclear whether the Court may issue these writs to a state court, but recent cases seem to settle that controversy by holding that the writ can issue, at least where the case has actually been within the jurisdiction of the Supreme Court.[57] There is no doubt that to protect its appellate jurisdiction the Supreme Court can issue a writ, even before a case has come to it, to a court of appeals, or to a district court in a case that is reviewable directly in the Supreme Court,[58] although there may be sharp differences of view about the propriety of exercise of this power in a particular case.[59] Further it is agreed that in a case that a court of appeals has refused to review, and that has therefore never been "in" the court of appeals so as to permit the Supreme Court to grant a statutory writ of certiorari, the Court may issue a common-law writ of certiorari on which it can review the action of the court of appeals in refusing to allow appeal, and can even determine the merits of the case.[60] Finally, the Court has held that it has power to issue one of the extraordinary writs to a district court, in a case where appeal would be to the court of appeals, and that while ordinarily application for such a writ should be made first to the court of appeals, it can be made directly to the Supreme Court in a case of public importance and exceptional character.[61]

The Supreme Court, or any justice thereof, also has power to issue a writ of habeas corpus.[62] The statute, however, authorizes the applica-

55. Ex parte Republic of Peru, 1943, 63 S.Ct. 793, 318 U.S. 578, 87 L.Ed. 1014; Ex parte Fahey, 1947, 67 S.Ct. 1558, 332 U.S. 258, 91 L.Ed. 2041; Wolfson, Extraordinary Writs in the Supreme Court Since Ex parte Peru, 1951, 51 Col.L.Rev. 997.

See Chandler v. Judicial Council of the Tenth Circuit, 1970, 90 S.Ct. 1648, 1654–1656, 398 U.S. 74, 86–89, 26 L.Ed.2d 100.

56. See § 102 above.

57. Deen v. Hickman, 1958, 79 S.Ct. 1, 358 U.S. 57, 3 L.Ed.2d 28; Bucolo v. Adkins, 1976, 96 S.Ct. 1086, 424 U.S. 641, 47 L.Ed.2d 301; General Atomic Co. v. Felter, 1978, 98 S.Ct. 1939, 436 U.S. 493, 56 L.Ed.2d 480. See 16 Wright, Miller & Cooper, Jurisdiction § 4018.

58. Ex parte Northern Pac. Ry., 1929, 50 S.Ct. 70, 280 U.S. 142, 74 L.Ed. 233; United States Alkali Export Assn. v. U.S., 1945, 65 S.Ct. 1120, 325 U.S. 196, 89 L.Ed. 1554.

59. E.g., De Beers Consol. Mines v. U.S., 1945, 65 S.Ct. 1130, 325 U.S. 212, 89 L.Ed. 1566.

60. House v. Mayo, 1945, 65 S.Ct. 517, 324 U.S. 42, 89 L.Ed. 739; In re 620

Church Street Bldg. Corp., 1936, 57 S.Ct. 88, 299 U.S. 24, 81 L.Ed. 16.

There is lively controversy within the Court, however, on whether the common-law writ of certiorari remains available in a case in which a habeas-corpus petitioner has been denied a certificate of probable cause, so that the case was never "in" the court of appeals and could not be reviewed by the statutory writ of certiorari. Compare the concurring and dissenting opinions in Davis v. Jacobs, 1981, 102 S.Ct. 417, 454 U.S. 911, 70 L.Ed.2d 226. See 17 Wright, Miller & Cooper, Jurisdiction 2d § 4036 n. 21.

61. Ex parte Republic of Peru, 1943, 63 S.Ct. 793, 318 U.S. 578, 87 L.Ed. 1014. See Wolfson, note 55 above.

62. 28 U.S.C.A. § 2241. See Oaks, The "Original" Writ of Habeas Corpus in the Supreme Court, 1962 Sup.Ct.Rev. 153; Stern, Gressman, Shapiro & Geller, note 1 above, § 11.3. See also Locks v. Commanding General, Sixth Army, 1968, 89 S.Ct. 31, 21 L.Ed.2d 78 (opinion of Circuit Justice Douglas), raising question about the power of an individual justice to issue the writ.

tion to be transferred to the district court having jurisdiction to entertain it, and the practice of the Court is not to exercise its power to grant habeas corpus, save in exceptional circumstances,[63] if an adequate remedy may be had in a lower federal court or there are state remedies that have not been exhausted. The power is now rightly regarded as "an anachronism."[64]

An important, but little-noticed, part of practice in the Supreme Court involves applications to an individual justice for a stay or for other forms of interim action. An individual justice has no power to dispose of cases on the merits,[65] but may make a variety of interim orders, sometimes of literally life-and-death significance.[66]

63. Ex parte Hudgings, 1919, 39 S.Ct. 337, 249 U.S. 378, 63 L.Ed. 656; cf. Hirota v. MacArthur, 1948, 69 S.Ct. 157, 335 U.S. 876, 93 L.Ed. 418.

64. Oaks, note 62 above, at 206. Apparently the most recent case in which the writ was actually issued is Ex parte Grossman, 1925, 45 S.Ct. 332, 267 U.S. 87, 69 L.Ed. 527.

65. Locks v. Commanding General, Sixth Army, 1968, 89 S.Ct. 31, 32, 21 L.Ed.2d 78 (opinion of Circuit Justice Douglas).

66. Stern, Gressman, Shapiro & Geller, note 1 above, c. 17; Note, The Powers of the Supreme Court Justice Acting in an Individual Capacity, 1964, 112 U.Pa.L.Rev. 981; Boner, Index to Chambers Opinions of Supreme Court Justices, 1972, 65 L.Lib.J. 213; 16 Wright, Miller & Cooper, Jurisdiction § 4005 n. 55. The procedure is set out in Rules 22 and 23, 1990 Sup.Ct.Rules.

Chapter 13

THE ORIGINAL JURISDICTION
OF THE SUPREME COURT

Analysis

§ 109. Cases in Which a State Is a Party [1]

Article III, § 2, of the Constitution defines the judicial power of the United States. It then provides: "In all Cases affecting Ambassadors, other public Ministers and Consuls, and those in which a State shall be Party, the supreme Court shall have original Jurisdiction." It has always been understood that this provision is self-executing, and that it is itself a grant of jurisdiction to the Supreme Court [2] that Congress can neither restrict nor enlarge.[3] In fact ever since 1789 statutes have

§ 109

1. 17 Wright, Miller & Cooper, Jurisdiction 2d §§ 4042–4049, 4051–4054; Stern, Gressman, Shapiro & Geller, Supreme Court Practice, 7th ed. 1993, c. 10; McKusick, Discretionary Gatekeeping: The Supreme Court's Management of Its Original Jurisdiction Docket Since 1961, 1993, 45 Maine L.Rev. 185; Note, The Original Jurisdiction of the United States Supreme Court, 1959, 11 Stan.L.Rev. 665. An appendix to the Note just cited lists all of the cases in the original jurisdiction through 1959 in which an opinion was written. Appendices to the article by Chief Justice McKusick complement that Note by listing all original-jurisdiction cases from 1961 to 1993.

Cases within the original jurisdiction are not a statistically significant part of the work of the Court. "Prior to October 1, 1961, the start of the period this paper studies, the Court issued opinions in only 121 original jurisdiction cases. From October 1, 1961, to April 1, 1993, the Court has published proportionately more opinions in such cases—51 in total—but it still typically

issues opinions in only two or three original jurisdiction cases a year, a very small fraction of its opinion output." McKusick, above, at 187–188. See also id. at 206, 207 n. *.

2. Chisholm v. Georgia, 1793, 2 Dall. 419, 1 L.Ed. 440; Florida v. Georgia, 1854, 17 How. 478, 492, 15 L.Ed. 181; Kentucky v. Dennison, 1860, 24 How. 66, 16 L.Ed. 717.

3. Marbury v. Madison, 1803, 1 Cranch 137, 2 L.Ed. 60; Wisconsin v. Pelican Ins. Co., 1888, 8 S.Ct. 1370, 1379, 127 U.S. 265, 300, 32 L.Ed. 239; California v. Southern Pac. R. Co., 1895, 15 S.Ct. 591, 604, 157 U.S. 229, 261, 39 L.Ed. 683. See 17 Wright, Miller & Cooper, Jurisdiction 2d § 4043.

In California v. Arizona, 1979, 99 S.Ct. 919, 924, 440 U.S. 59, 66, 59 L.Ed.2d 144, the Court thought it "extremely doubtful" that Congress could limit original jurisdiction by waiving the sovereign's immunity to suit but limiting suit against it to district courts. It was able to avoid the question by finding that the statute was not intended to exclude Supreme Court jurisdiction.

purported to describe the original jurisdiction of the Supreme Court. The present statute [4] does not list all the cases to which the constitutional grant of jurisdiction extends, but in the unlikely event that a case were to be brought that is within the constitutional grant but not within the statute [5] it seems clear that the Court would have jurisdiction of the case.

Chief Justice Marshall thought that the jurisdiction of the Supreme Court was exclusive in cases within its original jurisdiction.[6] The statutes, from 1789 to the present, have proceeded on a different theory, and have distinguished between situations in which the Supreme Court is given exclusive jurisdiction and those in which its jurisdiction is concurrent with the lower federal courts. The validity of such a division is now settled.[7]

The provision for original jurisdiction does not extend the judicial power of the United States as defined in the preceding language of Article III, § 2. Instead the latter language merely distributes the judicial power as previously defined.[8] Thus, the original jurisdiction of the Supreme Court does not reach to all cases to which a state is party, but only to cases within the judicial power to which a state is party. A suit by the United States against a state is within the judicial power, since it is a "Controversy to which the United States shall be a party," and it is within the original jurisdiction, since it is one "in which a state shall be Party." On this analysis it was held that such a suit can be brought in the Supreme Court.[9] A suit by a state against one of its own citizens is not ordinarily within the judicial power at all, and thus cannot be brought in the Supreme Court even though the state is a party.[10] It would seem that a suit by a state against one of its citizens that arises under the Constitution, laws, or treaties of the United States would be within the judicial power, and that the presence of the state as a party would permit invoking the original jurisdiction. The Supreme Court held to the contrary, however, without reasoned discussion and on the basis of earlier cases in which it did not appear that a federal question was present.[11]

Since the case must be within the judicial power of the United States, the usual tests of case or controversy, standing, political ques-

---

4. 28 U.S.C.A. § 1251.

5. As for example, a suit by a foreign government against a state to which the state has consented.

6. Marbury v. Madison, 1803, 1 Cranch 137, 174, 2 L.Ed. 60.

7. Rhode Island v. Massachusetts, 1838, 12 Pet. 657, 722, 9 L.Ed. 1233; Ames v. Kansas ex rel. Johnston, 1884, 4 S.Ct. 437, 111 U.S. 449, 28 L.Ed. 482; Plaquemines Tropical Fruit Co. v. Henderson, 1898, 18 S.Ct. 685, 170 U.S. 511, 42 L.Ed. 1126.

8. Pennsylvania v. Quicksilver Mining Co., 1870, 10 Wall. 553, 19 L.Ed. 998;

Duhne v. New Jersey, 1920, 40 S.Ct. 154, 251 U.S. 311, 64 L.Ed. 280.

9. U.S. v. Texas, 1892, 12 S.Ct. 488, 143 U.S. 621, 36 L.Ed. 285. See 17 Wright, Miller & Cooper, Jurisdiction 2d § 4048.

10. California v. Southern Pac. R. Co., 1895, 15 S.Ct. 591, 157 U.S. 229, 39 L.Ed. 683; Minnesota v. Northern Securities Co., 1902, 22 S.Ct. 308, 184 U.S. 199, 46 L.Ed. 499.

11. Texas v. ICC, 1922, 42 S.Ct. 261, 258 U.S. 158, 66 L.Ed. 531.

tions, and the like,[12] are applicable.[13] The Court has also held that its original jurisdiction is limited to civil cases.[14] It will not hear a case by which a state seeks to enforce a judgment for a penalty, even though the case is not criminal in the usual sense.[15]

Under the statute suits by one state against another are within the original and exclusive jurisdiction of the Supreme Court.[16] Such suits are the most numerous class of suits heard by the Court in its original jurisdiction.[17] The need for the Supreme Court as a tribunal for such suits is apparent. The states of the union are not at liberty to wage war against each other. Controversies between them, which when they were independent would have been resolved by diplomatic negotiation or by force, are now peacefully settled by a neutral court. No consent of the state is required. It is deemed to have consented by accepting the Constitution, which grants jurisdiction of "Controversies between two or more States."[18] This jurisdiction has been especially useful in resolving disputes as to boundaries[19] or water rights,[20] but it has been used also to enforce a financial obligation of one state to another,[21] or to provide a forum where two or more states are claiming a right to tax or escheat a fund that is insufficient to satisfy all the claims against it.[22]

The Supreme Court has original but not exclusive jurisdiction of actions by the United States against a state.[23] Again consent of the state

---

12. See §§ 12–15 above.

13. E.g., Mississippi v. Johnson, 1867, 71 U.S. 475, 4 Wall. 475, 18 L.Ed. 437; Georgia v. Stanton, 1868, 6 Wall. 50, 18 L.Ed. 721; Massachusetts v. Mellon, 1923, 43 S.Ct. 597, 262 U.S. 447, 67 L.Ed. 1078; Wyoming v. Oklahoma, 1992, 112 S.Ct. 789, 796–798, ___ U.S. ___, ___-___, 117 L.Ed.2d 1. See 17 Wright, Miller & Cooper, Jurisdiction 2d § 4051.

14. See Chisholm v. Georgia, 1793, 2 Dall. 419, 431–432, 1 L.Ed. 440; Cohens v. Virginia, 1821, 6 Wheat. 264, 399, 5 L.Ed. 257.

15. Wisconsin v. Pelican Ins. Co., 1888, 8 S.Ct. 1370, 127 U.S. 265, 32 L.Ed. 239. But a suit on a judgment for taxes is not considered penal. Milwaukee County v. M.E. White Co., 1935, 56 S.Ct. 229, 296 U.S. 268, 80 L.Ed. 220.

16. 28 U.S.C.A. § 1251(a). A political subdivision of a state is not the state for purposes of this statute. Illinois v. City of Milwaukee, 1972, 92 S.Ct. 1385, 406 U.S. 91, 31 L.Ed.2d 712.

17. For a complete list of all such cases as of that time in which the Supreme Court had written an opinion, see Note, note 1 above, at 708–718. Later cases are listed in McKusick, note 1 above, at 207–211.

18. See New Jersey v. New York, 1831, 5 Pet. 284, 291, 8 L.Ed. 127.

19. E.g., Rhode Island v. Massachusetts, 1838, 12 Pet. 657, 9 L.Ed. 1233; Nebraska v. Iowa, 1972, 92 S.Ct. 1379, 406 U.S. 117, 31 L.Ed.2d 733; Louisiana v. Mississippi, 1984, 104 S.Ct. 1645, 466 U.S. 96, 80 L.Ed.2d 74.

20. E.g., Kansas v. Colorado, 1902, 22 S.Ct. 552, 185 U.S. 125, 46 L.Ed. 838; id., 1907, 27 S.Ct. 655, 206 U.S. 46, 51 L.Ed. 956; Idaho ex rel. Evans v. Oregon, 1983, 103 S.Ct. 2817, 462 U.S. 1017, 77 L.Ed.2d 387.

21. E.g., South Dakota v. North Carolina, 1904, 24 S.Ct. 269, 192 U.S. 286, 48 L.Ed. 448; Virginia v. West Virginia, 1907, 27 S.Ct. 732, 206 U.S. 290, 51 L.Ed. 1068.

22. Right to tax: Texas v. Florida, 1939, 59 S.Ct. 563, 306 U.S. 398, 83 L.Ed. 817; California v. Texas, 1982, 102 S.Ct. 2335, 457 U.S. 164, 72 L.Ed.2d 755. But cf. Massachusetts v. Missouri, 1939, 60 S.Ct. 39, 308 U.S. 1, 84 L.Ed. 3.

Escheat: Delaware v. New York, 1993, 113 S.Ct. 1550, ___ U.S. ___, 123 L.Ed.2d 211. Texas v. New Jersey, 1965, 85 S.Ct. 626, 379 U.S. 674, 13 L.Ed.2d 596; see Western Union Tel. Co. v. Pennsylvania, 1961, 82 S.Ct. 199, 202–204, 368 U.S. 71, 77–80, 7 L.Ed.2d 139.

23. 28 U.S.C.A. § 1251(b)(2). See 17 Wright, Miller & Cooper, Jurisdiction 2d § 4048. It is held that the jurisdiction can validly be conferred on a district court in is not required.[24] Here it is not so easy to find consent in the state's acceptance of the Constitution, since the literal words of the Constitution might seem to preclude such jurisdiction,[25] but the alternative is the unthinkable one that controversies between the United States and a state would have to be resolved by force. This is an argument, however, that has been allowed to run only one way. Suit by a state against the United States is not permitted,[26] except in those instances where the United States has consented to be sued.[27]

The Constitution purports to grant jurisdiction of controversies between a state and a foreign country. Such a suit could not be brought against the foreign country without its consent, which surely would not be given. It would seem, however, that the foreign government could bring suit in the Supreme Court against a state, on the same principle that permits a state to be made a defendant where a sister state or the United States is plaintiff. This was the prediction of a distinguished authority, at a time when the question was unresolved.[28] The Court later held, however, that such a suit cannot be brought against a state where it has not consented to be sued.[29] Presumably such a suit could be brought where the state consented—indeed unless this is permissible, the constitutional grant of jurisdiction over such cases is meaningless— but the present statute makes no mention of such a suit.[30]

In a very early case it was held that the Supreme Court had original jurisdiction of a suit against a state by a citizen of another state.[31] The Eleventh Amendment was immediately adopted to bar such a result.[32] As the Amendment has been construed, it prohibits suit against a state by a citizen of another state, a citizen of the state itself, or an alien,[33]

Case v. Bowles, 1946, 66 S.Ct. 438, 441, 327 U.S. 92, 97, 90 L.Ed. 552. In a suit by the United States against a state, citizens of the state may be joined as defendants. U.S. v. West Virginia, 1935, 55 S.Ct. 789, 295 U.S. 463, 79 L.Ed. 1546; U.S. v. Wyoming, 1947, 67 S.Ct. 1319, 331 U.S. 440, 91 L.Ed. 1590.

24. U.S. v. Texas, 1892, 12 S.Ct. 488, 143 U.S. 621, 36 L.Ed. 285; U.S. v. Louisiana, 1950, 70 S.Ct. 914, 915, 339 U.S. 699, 701–702, 94 L.Ed. 1216.

Nor is consent required if the suit is brought in a district court. Barrett v. U.S., C.A.2d, 1988, 853 F.2d 124, 126, certiorari denied 109 S.Ct. 866, 488 U.S. 1041, 102 L.Ed.2d 990; Parks v. U.S., C.A.1st, 1986, 784 F.2d 20, 23.

25. See Frankfurter, J., dissenting in Ex parte Republic of Peru, 1943, 63 S.Ct. 793, 804, 318 U.S. 578, 598, 87 L.Ed. 1014.

26. Oregon v. Hitchcock, 1906, 26 S.Ct. 568, 202 U.S. 60, 50 L.Ed. 935; Kansas v. U.S., 1907, 27 S.Ct. 388, 204 U.S. 331, 51 L.Ed. 510; Hawaii v. Gordon, 1963, 83 S.Ct. 1052, 373 U.S. 57, 10 L.Ed.2d 191.

27. Minnesota v. Hitchcock, 1902, 22 S.Ct. 650, 185 U.S. 373, 46 L.Ed. 954. See

also Utah v. U.S., 1969, 89 S.Ct. 761, 394 U.S. 89, 22 L.Ed.2d 99; California v. Arizona, 99 S.Ct. 919, 440 U.S. 59, 59 L.Ed.2d 144.

28. Dobie, Federal Procedure, 1928, pp. 526–528.

29. Principality of Monaco v. Mississippi, 1934, 54 S.Ct. 745, 292 U.S. 313, 78 L.Ed. 1282. See Lenoir, Suit by a Foreign State Against a State of the Union: Monaco v. Mississippi, 1934, 7 Miss.L.J. 134.

30. See 28 U.S.C.A. § 1251.

31. Chisholm v. Georgia, 1793, 2 Dall. 419, 1 L.Ed. 440.

32. Mathis, The Eleventh Amendment: Adoption and Interpretation, 1968, 2 Ga. L.Rev. 207; Jacobs, The Eleventh Amendment and Sovereign Immunity, 1972, pp. 55–67; 13 Wright, Miller & Cooper, Jurisdiction 2d § 3524.

33. Ex parte Ayers, 1887, 8 S.Ct. 164, 123 U.S. 443, 31 L.Ed. 216; Hans v. Louisiana, 1890, 10 S.Ct. 504, 134 U.S. 1, 33 L.Ed. 842; Ex parte New York, 1921, 41 S.Ct. 588, 256 U.S. 490, 65 L.Ed. 1057;

except where the state has consented to suit.[34] It is a different matter where the state is plaintiff. The Supreme Court has original but not exclusive jurisdiction of all actions by a state against the citizens of another state or against aliens.[35] There is no jurisdiction if a citizen of another state is joined as defendant with a citizen of the plaintiff state,[36] presumably because the case is no longer "between a State and Citizens of another State" as the Constitution requires. As has already been pointed out, it is held, with doubtful logic and no discussion, that the same result applies where the case arises under the federal law and there is thus another basis of jurisdiction.[37] Since the jurisdiction of the Supreme Court is not exclusive if a state is suing a citizen of another state, the action can be brought in a district court, rather than the Supreme Court, if there is a statutory basis for jurisdiction in the district court.[38] This may induce the Supreme Court to refuse to permit filing of an original action, leaving the state to its remedy in the district court or in a state court, but there is no fixed rule on this point and the Court has entertained original actions in cases that could have been brought in a district court.[39]

In Ohio v. Wyandotte Chemicals Corp.,[40] the Supreme Court held that it had jurisdiction of a suit by a state against citizens of other states and another country for abatement of a nuisance allegedly caused by dumping mercury into streams that ultimately run into Lake Erie. In the exercise of its discretion, however, it refused to entertain the case, holding that the complex scientific issues presented by the case were inappropriate for the Supreme Court to consider as an original matter. It said: "we may decline to entertain a complaint brought by a State against the citizens of another State or country only where we can say with assurance that (1) declination of jurisdiction would not disserve any of the principal policies underlying the Article III jurisdictional grant

Employees of Dept. of Public Health & Welfare v. Department of Public Health & Welfare, 1973, 93 S.Ct. 1614, 411 U.S. 279, 36 L.Ed.2d 251; Atascadero State Hospital v. Scanlon, 1985, 105 S.Ct. 3142, 473 U.S. 234, 87 L.Ed.2d 171.

34. See § 46 n. 6 above.

35. 28 U.S.C.A. § 1251(b)(3).

36. California v. Southern Pac. Co., 1895, 15 S.Ct. 591, 157 U.S. 229, 39 L.Ed. 683.

37. Texas v. ICC, 1922, 42 S.Ct. 261, 258 U.S. 158, 66 L.Ed. 531. Dean Dobie, who had apparently not noticed this case, thought that a different result would be reached in this situation. Dobie, Federal Procedure, 1928, p. 531.

38. 28 U.S.C.A. § 1251(b)(3) is not itself a grant of jurisdiction. Ohio v. Wyandotte Chemicals Corp., 1971, 91 S.Ct. 1005, 1009 n. 3, 401 U.S. 493, 498 n. 3, 28 L.Ed.2d 256. A state is not a citizen of a state within the grant of diversity jurisdiction. Ibid. Suits

to abate pollution of interstate waters had been held to be governed by federal common law and thus to come within federal question jurisdiction. Illinois v. City of Milwaukee, 1972, 92 S.Ct. 1385, 406 U.S. 91, 31 L.Ed.2d 712. It has been held, however, that an Act of Congress passed shortly after the decision just cited has preempted federal common law for this kind of case. City of Milwaukee v. Illinois and Michigan, 1981, 101 S.Ct. 1784, 451 U.S. 304, 68 L.Ed.2d 114.

39. Georgia v. Pennsylvania R. Co., 1945, 65 S.Ct. 716, 324 U.S. 439, 89 L.Ed. 1051.

40. 1971, 91 S.Ct. 1005, 401 U.S. 493, 28 L.Ed.2d 256. See Ficken, Wyandotte and Its Progeny, The Quest for Environmental Protection Through the Original Jurisdiction of the Supreme Court, 1974, 78 Dick.L.Rev. 429.

and (2) the reasons of practical wisdom that persuade us that this Court is an inappropriate forum are consistent with the proposition that our discretion is legitimated by its use to keep this aspect of the Court's functions attuned to its other responsibilities."[41] Since that decision the Court has exercised its discretion to deny leave to file not only in other actions brought by states against citizens of other states,[42] but also in actions between the United States and two states[43] and between two states.[44]

It is the last class of cases, in which the Court has declined jurisdiction of suits between two states, that has caused controversy, because the statute says that the Supreme Court has "original and exclusive jurisdiction" of all such cases.[45] A recent case suggests that the Court may have had second thoughts about its refusal to accept jurisdiction of cases in which its jurisdiction is exclusive. In 1988, by a 5–3 vote, the Court denied leave for Louisiana to file a bill of complaint in a boundary dispute with Mississippi. The dissenting Justices speculated that leave had been denied because Louisiana had intervened in private litigation in a federal district court. In that private litigation Louisiana filed a third-party complaint against Mississippi and in 1992 the Supreme Court granted certiorari to review a Fifth Circuit decision that the island in question was in Louisiana. It held that "exclusive" in the statute means what it says and that the district court lacked jurisdiction of Louisiana's third-party complaint against Mississippi. The district court could decide title to the land as between the private parties, but it could not make any decision binding on the states about the boundary between them.[46]

A state cannot sue unless it is the real party in interest. In one leading case New Hampshire attempted to avoid the limitations of the

41. 91 S.Ct. at 1010, 401 U.S. at 499. See 17 Wright, Miller & Cooper, Jurisdiction 2d § 4053. How the Court exercises its discretion is illuminatingly discussed in McKusick, note 1 above.

42. Illinois v. City of Milwaukee, 1972, 92 S.Ct. 1385, 406 U.S. 91, 31 L.Ed.2d 712; Washington v. General Motors Corp., 1972, 92 S.Ct. 1396, 406 U.S. 109, 31 L.Ed.2d 727.

43. U.S. v. Nevada, 1973, 93 S.Ct. 2763, 412 U.S. 534, 37 L.Ed.2d 132; cf. California v. Nevada, 1980, 100 S.Ct. 2064, 447 U.S. 125, 65 L.Ed.2d 1.

44. Arizona v. New Mexico, 1976, 96 S.Ct. 1845, 425 U.S. 794, 48 L.Ed.2d 376; California v. West Virginia, 1981, 102 S.Ct. 561, 454 U.S. 1027, 70 L.Ed.2d 470. Dissenting from denial of leave to file, Justice Stevens said that in Ohio v. Wyandotte Chemicals the Court had explained why it will decline to exercise its nonexclusive jurisdiction over cases in which only one of the parties is a state, but "that explanation is inapplicable to cases in which our jurisdic-

tion is exclusive." 102 S.Ct. at 562, 454 U.S. at 1028. See also the dissent of Justice Thomas, joined by Chief Justice Rehnquist and Justice Scalia, in Wyoming v. Oklahoma, 1992, 112 S.Ct. 789, 811 n. 1, ___ U.S. ___, ___ n. 1, 117 L.Ed.2d 1.

45. 28 U.S.C.A. § 1251(a).

See Shapiro, Jurisdiction and Discretion, 1985, 60 N.Y.U.L.Rev. 543, 561; Note, Exclusive Original Jurisdiction of the United States Supreme Court: Does It Still Exist?, 1982 B.Y.U.L.Rev. 727.

46. Mississippi v. Louisiana, 1992, 113 S.Ct. 549, ___ U.S. ___, 121 L.Ed.2d 466.

Subsequently the Court granted a motion by Louisiana for leave to file a bill of complaint raising the same issue about which the Court had refused leave to file five years earlier. Louisiana v. Mississippi, 1993, 114 S.Ct. 377, ___ U.S. ___, 126 L.Ed.2d 327.

Eleventh Amendment by providing by statute that it would bring suit in its name for the benefit of its citizens who held bonds of another state. This was not permitted.[47] Nor can a state invoke the original jurisdiction to prosecute claims on behalf of particular citizens of the state even where the debtor is a citizen of another state and the Eleventh Amendment is no bar.[48] But where a state has been given bonds of another state absolutely, and is suing for its own benefit rather than as an assignee for collection, suit in the original jurisdiction will lie.[49] Similarly a state can sue to protect its own property interests.[50]

Under some circumstances a state has been permitted to sue as parens patriae to restrain conduct injurious to the health or welfare of the state's population as a whole.[51] Thus, suit by Missouri to restrain Illinois from discharging the sewage of Chicago through a canal running into the Mississippi River was held to lie in the original jurisdiction.[52] Georgia was permitted to enjoin a private corporation in Tennessee from emitting noxious gases which drifted into Georgia.[53] Pennsylvania was allowed to sue West Virginia to enjoin it from distributing natural gas produced in that state in such a fashion as to diminish the supply available for Pennsylvania consumers.[54] In the most far-reaching case of this type, Georgia v. Pennsylvania Railroad Co.,[55] the state was permitted to file an action under the antitrust laws against 20 railroad companies that were alleged to have conspired to set rates that gave northern shippers an advantage over those in Georgia, and thus retarded the economic growth of that state.

47. New Hampshire v. Louisiana, 1883, 2 S.Ct. 176, 108 U.S. 76, 27 L.Ed. 656; cf. North Dakota v. Minnesota, 44 S.Ct. 138, 139, 263 U.S. 365, 374–376, 68 L.Ed. 342. See also Pennsylvania v. New Jersey, 1976, 96 S.Ct. 2333, 426 U.S. 660, 49 L.Ed.2d 124.

48. Oklahoma ex rel. Johnson v. Cook, 1938, 58 S.Ct. 954, 304 U.S. 387, 82 L.Ed. 1416; cf. Oklahoma v. Atchison, T. & S.F. R. Co., 1911, 31 S.Ct. 434, 220 U.S. 277, 55 L.Ed. 465.

49. South Dakota v. North Carolina, 1904, 24 S.Ct. 269, 192 U.S. 286, 48 L.Ed. 448.

50. Pennsylvania v. Wheeling & B. Bridge Co., 1852, 13 How. 518, 559, 14 L.Ed. 249.

51. 17 Wright, Miller & Cooper, Jurisdiction 2d § 4047; Note, note 1 above, at 671–678.

52. Missouri v. Illinois, 1901, 21 S.Ct. 331, 344, 180 U.S. 208, 241, 45 L.Ed. 497.

53. Georgia v. Tennessee Copper Co., 1907, 27 S.Ct. 618, 619, 206 U.S. 230, 237, 51 L.Ed. 1038.

54. Pennsylvania v. West Virginia, 1923, 43 S.Ct. 658, 663, 262 U.S. 553, 592, 67 L.Ed. 1117, 32 A.L.R. 300.

Pennsylvania v. West Virginia was relied upon to establish standing in Maryland v. Louisiana, 1981, 101 S.Ct. 2114, 451 U.S. 725, 68 L.Ed.2d 576. There eight states were allowed to sue to enjoin a tax imposed by Louisiana on natural gas. The incidence of the tax fell not on a small group of citizens but on a great many citizens, and there was no clear alternative remedy.

55. 1945, 65 S.Ct. 716, 722–723, 324 U.S. 439, 450–452, 89 L.Ed. 1051. The Court distinguished, with questionable success, Oklahoma v. Atchison, T. & S.F. R. Co., 1911, 31 S.Ct. 434, 220 U.S. 277, 55 L.Ed. 465, which had held that a state could not sue in the Supreme Court to enjoin carriers from charging unreasonable rates for transportation.

In Hawaii v. Standard Oil Co. of California, 1972, 92 S.Ct. 885, 405 U.S. 251, 31 L.Ed.2d 184, it was held that a claim by a state in a district court as parens patriae is not for an injury to its "business or property" as is required for a treble damage action under § 4 of the Clayton Act, 15 U.S.C.A. § 15. That result has since been changed by statute.

There had been thought to be one clear limitation on the parens-patriae doctrine. Although a state may in some circumstances be permitted to sue in this capacity to protect its citizens against harm threatened by another state or by private persons, it cannot represent them in this way in a challenge of federal action. The citizens of a state are also citizens of the United States, and it is the United States to which they must look as parens patriae where federal law is involved. This was the holding of the well-known case of Massachusetts v. Mellon,[56] in which the state was held not able to sue on behalf of its citizens to restrain the Secretary of the Treasury from carrying out an allegedly unconstitutional Act of Congress.

Doubt is cast on this proposition by the more recent case of South Carolina v. Katzenbach.[57] There a state was seeking to restrain the Attorney General from enforcing portions of the Voting Rights Act of 1965. The Court held that the state lacked standing to challenge the statute under the Due Process Clause of the Fifth Amendment or the Bill of Attainder Clause of Article I, citing Massachusetts v. Mellon.[58] But the Court did consider and reject the state's claim that the statute violated the Fifteenth Amendment. It said: "Original jurisdiction is founded on the presence of a controversy between a State and a citizen of another State under Art. III, § 2, of the Constitution."[59] For this proposition it cited Georgia v. Pennsylvania R. Co. That there was jurisdiction is hardly doubtful, but the Court's failure to explain why the state has standing to raise the Fifteenth Amendment objection but not the others is mystifying.[60]

Where a state is suing in a representative capacity on behalf of its citizens, individual citizens within the state will not ordinarily be permitted to intervene and advance a position contrary to that of the state.[61] They can do so only if they can show some compelling interest in their own right apart from the interest that they have in common with all citizens.[62]

Actions within the original jurisdiction are almost always equitable in nature. A statute purports to give a right to trial by jury in original

---

56. 1923, 43 S.Ct. 597, 262 U.S. 447, 67 L.Ed. 1078.

57. 1966, 86 S.Ct. 803, 383 U.S. 301, 15 L.Ed.2d 769.

58. 86 S.Ct. at 816, 383 U.S. at 323–324.

59. 86 S.Ct. at 807, 383 U.S. at 307.

60. See Bickel, The Voting Rights Cases, 1966 Sup.Ct.Rev. 79, 80–93.

The Court decided, without discussing jurisdiction or standing, a challenge by a state to a federal statute concerning voting in Oregon v. Mitchell, 1970, 91 S.Ct. 260, 400 U.S. 112, 27 L.Ed.2d 272. It said only: "No question has been raised concerning the standing of the parties or the jurisdiction of this Court." 91 S.Ct. at 261 n. 1,

400 U.S. at 117 n. 1. See also 91 S.Ct. at 279 n. 1, 400 U.S. 152 n. 1 (opinion of Harlan, J.). And jurisdiction has been taken in suits by a state against the Secretary of the Treasury questioning federal statutes. South Carolina v. Baker, 1988, 108 S.Ct. 1355, 485 U.S. 505, 99 L.Ed.2d 592; South Carolina v. Regan, 1984, 104 S.Ct. 1107, 465 U.S. 367, 79 L.Ed.2d 372.

61. Kentucky v. Indiana, 1930, 50 S.Ct. 275, 281 U.S. 163, 74 L.Ed. 784; New Jersey v. New York, 1953, 73 S.Ct. 689, 345 U.S. 369, 97 L.Ed. 1081.

62. Cases in which individuals have been allowed to intervene are cited in 17 Wright, Miller & Cooper, Jurisdiction 2d § 4054 n. 16.

actions in the Supreme Court against citizens of the United States,[63] but no such jury trial has been had since the 18th century.[64] The Supreme Court has held that the Seventh Amendment and the statute, if they extend to original jurisdiction cases at all, are applicable only to actions at law.[65] Normally cases within the original jurisdiction that cannot be resolved as a matter of law are referred to a master.[66] Pleadings and motions in original actions are governed by the Federal Rules of Civil Procedure, and those rules are "a guide" on other procedural questions that may arise,[67] but the procedure remains not very well defined.[68] Commonly such cases are protracted and expensive, but it is likely that the importance, and the technical nature, of the issues that typically arise in original cases to which a state is a party are such that no system of procedure could prevent such delay and expense.

In deciding suits between states—and apparently in all other cases to which a state is a party, though the matter is not clearly settled—the Court applies "federal common law."[69] The source of such law, and its precise content, have never been clearly specified. Sitting, as it were, as an international, as well as a domestic tribunal, the Court draws on federal law, state law, and international law, as the exigencies of the particular case may demand.[70] While the municipal law relating to like questions between individuals is taken into account, it is not deemed to have controlling effect.[71] In such cases, as in cases involving the validity or construction of interstate compacts, the Court is free to decide questions of local law for itself if need be.[72]

63. 28 U.S.C.A. § 1872. See 17 Wright, Miller & Cooper, Jurisdiction 2d § 4054, pp. 279–281.

64. There was a jury trial in Georgia v. Brailsford, 1794, 3 Dall. 1, 1 L.Ed. 483, and in two other unreported cases in 1795 and 1797. Carson, The Supreme Court of the United States: Its History, 1891, p. 169 n. 1.

65. U.S. v. Louisiana, 1950, 70 S.Ct. 914, 917, 339 U.S. 699, 706, 94 L.Ed. 1216.

66. In Maryland v. Louisiana, 1981, 101 S.Ct. 2114, 2122, 451 U.S. 725, 734, 68 L.Ed.2d 576, the Court noted that "as is usual, we appointed a Special Master to facilitate handling of the suit."

67. Rule 17.1, 1990 Sup.Ct.Rules. The Civil Rules are a guide only "where their application is appropriate." See Utah v. U.S., 1969, 89 S.Ct. 761, 765, 394 U.S. 89, 95, 22 L.Ed.2d 99. See also Nebraska v. Wyoming, 1993, 113 S.Ct. 1689, 1694, —— U.S. ——, ——, 123 L.Ed.2d 317.

68. 17 Wright, Miller & Cooper, Jurisdiction 2d § 4054; Stern, Gressman, Shapiro & Geller, note 1 above, §§ 10.7–10.13; Cohen, Wading Through the Procedural Marshes of Original Jurisdiction Guided by the Tidelands Case: A Trial Before the United States Supreme Court, 1987, 11 Am.J. Trial Advocacy 55; Note, note 1 above, at 685–690.

69. Hinderlider v. La Plata River & Cherry Creek Ditch Co., 1938, 58 S.Ct. 803, 811, 304 U.S. 92, 110, 82 L.Ed. 1202. See 17 Wright, Miller & Cooper, Jurisdiction 2d § 4052; Note, note 1 above, at 680–685.

70. Kansas v. Colorado, 1902, 22 S.Ct. 552, 560, 185 U.S. 125, 146, 46 L.Ed. 838; id., 1907, 27 S.Ct. 655, 206 U.S. 46, 51 L.Ed. 956. See Note, What Rule of Decision Should Control in Interstate Controversies, 1907, 21 Harv.L.Rev. 132.

71. Connecticut v. Massachusetts, 1931, 51 S.Ct. 286, 289, 282 U.S. 660, 670, 75 L.Ed. 602.

72. Kentucky v. Indiana, 1930, 50 S.Ct. 275, 281 U.S. 163, 74 L.Ed. 784; Petty v. Tennessee–Missouri Bridge Comm., 1959, 79 S.Ct. 785, 359 U.S. 275, 3 L.Ed.2d 804; Nebraska v. Iowa, 1972, 92 S.Ct. 1379, 1380 n. 1, 406 U.S. 117, 118 n. 1, 31 L.Ed.2d 733; Vermont v. New York, 1974, 94 S.Ct. 2248, 2252, 417 U.S. 270, 277, 41 L.Ed.2d 61; Texas v. New Mexico, 1983, 103 S.Ct. 2558, 462 U.S. 554, 77 L.Ed.2d 1.

It is not clear how a judgment against a state would be enforced if a state were to prove recalcitrant. In the lengthy litigation between Virginia and West Virginia over some 12 million dollars owed by the latter to the former, the Court at one point wrote a strong opinion saying that the judgment was enforceable but not deciding precisely how it might be enforced.[73] It did not have to solve that question because West Virginia ultimately paid the judgment.[74] In another case that was before the Court a number of times, Wyoming sought to have Colorado held in contempt for violation of an earlier decree, but the Court found room for misunderstanding in the earlier decree and clarified Colorado's duties, rather than punishing the state.[75] In a more recent case the Court made it clear that it has full remedial powers to award both specific and monetary relief and that it has "ample authority to appoint a master and to enforce a judgment."[76] It is good that that authority is there as a last resort, but patience by the Court, and the moral suasion of its decree, are likely to be more satisfactory in resolving these delicate interstate controversies than is a more coercive attitude.

§ 110. Cases Affecting Ambassadors, Other Public Ministers, and Consuls[1]

In addition to cases in which a state is a party, the Constitution provides for original jurisdiction in the Supreme Court "in all Cases affecting Ambassadors, other public Ministers and Consuls." From the time of the First Judiciary Act on, a distinction was drawn by statute. The Supreme Court was given original and exclusive jurisdiction of proceedings against ambassadors and other public ministers or their domestics, or domestic servants, and original but not exclusive jurisdiction of suits brought by ambassadors or other public ministers, or in which a consul or a vice consul was a party.[2] This ancient distinction was abandoned in 1978. The statute was amended in that year so that there is no longer exclusive original jurisdiction of suits against ambassadors. Instead the Supreme Court now has original but not exclusive jurisdiction of all actions or proceedings to which ambassadors, other

---

73. Virginia v. West Virginia, 1918, 38 S.Ct. 400, 246 U.S. 565, 59 L.Ed. 1272. See Coleman, The State as Defendant under the Federal Constitution: the Virginia–West Virginia Debt Controversy, 1917, 31 Harv. L.Rev. 210; Powell, Coercing a State to Pay a Judgment: Virginia v. West Virginia, 1918, 17 Mich.L.Rev. 1; Fischer, Enforcement of a Money Judgment against a State, 1927, 12 St. Louis L.Rev. 57; Note, note 1 above, at 690–694.

In South Dakota v. North Carolina, 1904, 24 S.Ct. 269, 277, 192 U.S. 286, 321–322, 48 L.Ed. 448, the bonds of the defendant state on which suit was brought were secured by certain railroad stock. The Court ordered the Supreme Court marshal to hold a public sale of the state's interest in the stock if the state failed to pay the judgment.

74. W.Va.Acts, 1919 Ext.Sess., c. 10, p. 19.

75. Wyoming v. Colorado, 1940, 60 S.Ct. 765, 769, 309 U.S. 572, 582, 84 L.Ed. 954.

76. Texas v. New Mexico, 1987, 107 S.Ct. 2279, 2287, 482 U.S. 124, 134, 96 L.Ed.2d 105. An injunction issued in that case the following year. 1988, 108 S.Ct. 1201, 485 U.S. 388, 99 L.Ed.2d 450.

§ 110

1. 17 Wright, Miller & Cooper, Jurisdiction 2d § 4050; Note, The Original Jurisdiction of the United States Supreme Court, 1959, 11 Stan.L.Rev. 665, 667–668.

2. Act of Sept. 24, 1789, c. 20, § 13, 1 Stat. 73, 80–81.

public ministers, consuls, or vice consuls of foreign states are parties.[3] Another statute gives the district courts jurisdiction, exclusive of the courts of the states, of all civil actions against consuls or vice consuls of foreign states or members of a mission or members of their families.[4]

It is reassuring to know that the Supreme Court is no longer required to hear all actions against ambassadors, but Congress hardly needed to bother changing the law. The grant of original jurisdiction in suits affecting ambassadors, ministers, and consuls has almost never been used. Only three cases have been decided by the Supreme Court in which it was sought to invoke that jurisdiction.[5] In one early case it was held that suit would not lie against a consul where the claim was against his government rather than against the consul individually.[6] In another case the Court held, as the statute now provides, that the original jurisdiction extends only to diplomatic and consular representatives accredited to the United States by foreign powers, and not to those who represent the United States in other countries.[7] Finally there is one case in which, without discussing any jurisdictional question, the Court heard an action in debt against a vice-consul and gave judgment for plaintiff.[8] The diplomatic immunity that attaches to ambassadors and other public ministers,[9] though not to consuls, probably explains why there has been so little use of this head of original jurisdiction. There have been a few cases in which the grant of original jurisdiction has been construed because of unsuccessful attempts of parties to claim that the case was one "affecting" a diplomat, though he was not a party, and thus not properly brought in the lower court.[10]

3. 28 U.S.C.A. § 1251(b)(1).

4. 28 U.S.C.A. § 1351. See also 28 U.S.C.A. § 1364, giving the district courts original and exclusive jurisdiction of direct actions against insurers of members of diplomatic missions and their families.

Under an earlier version of what is now 28 U.S.C.A. § 1351, it was held that a suit against a consul for divorce cannot be brought in district court, and must be brought in state court. Ohio ex rel. Popovici v. Agler, 1930, 50 S.Ct. 154, 280 U.S. 379, 74 L.Ed. 489. See § 25 above.

5. In the last 32 years the Supreme Court has summarily denied all five attempts to invoke its jurisdiction in this class of cases. McKusick, Discretionary Gatekeeping: The Supreme Court's Management of Its Original Jurisdiction Docket Since 1961, 1993, 45 Maine L.Rev. 185, 206.

6. Jones v. Le Tombe, 1798, 3 Dall. 384, 1 L.Ed. 647.

7. Ex parte Gruber, 1925, 46 S.Ct. 112, 269 U.S. 302, 70 L.Ed. 280.

8. Casey v. Galli, 1877, 94 U.S. 673, 24 L.Ed. 168.

9. 22 U.S.C.A. § 252. See Bergman v. De Sieyes, C.C.A.2d 1948, 170 F.2d 360; Pooley v. Luco, D.C.Cal.1896, 76 Fed. 146; Gittings v. Crawford, C.C.D.Md.1838, 10 Fed.Cas. 447, No. 5,465.

10. U.S. v. Ortega, 1826, 11 Wheat. 467, 6 L.Ed. 521; Ex parte Hitz, 1884, 4 S.Ct. 698, 111 U.S. 766, 28 L.Ed. 592; In re Baiz, 1890, 10 S.Ct. 854, 135 U.S. 403, 34 L.Ed. 222.

Appendix

RESEARCHING FEDERAL COURT JURISDICTION AND PRACTICE ON WESTLAW®

Analysis

Section 1. Introduction

Law of Federal Courts provides a strong base for analyzing even the most complex problem involving federal jurisdiction and practice. Whether your research requires examination of case law, statutes, administrative materials or expert commentary, West books and WEST-LAW® are excellent sources.

WESTLAW expands your library, giving you access to decisions from federal courts and documents from the U.S. Congress, as well as to articles and treatises by well-known commentators. To help keep you up-to-date with current developments, WESTLAW provides frequently updated federal databases. With WESTLAW, you have unparalleled legal research resources at your fingertips.

Additional Resources

If you have not used WESTLAW or have questions not covered in this appendix, see the *WESTLAW Reference Manual* or call the West Reference Attorneys at 1–800–REF–ATTY (1–800–733–2889). The West Reference Attorneys are trained, licensed attorneys, available throughout the workday and on weekends to assist you with your WESTLAW or West book research questions.

Section 2.   WESTLAW Federal Law Databases

Each database on WESTLAW is assigned an abbreviation called an *identifier*, which you use to access the database. You can find identifiers for all databases in the online WESTLAW Directory and in the *WESTLAW Database List*. When you need to know more detailed information about a database, use Scope. Scope contains coverage information, related databases and valuable search tips. To use Scope from the WESTLAW Directory, type **sc** and the database or service identifier, e.g., **sc allfeds.**

The following chart lists WESTLAW databases that contain information pertaining to federal law. For a complete list of federal law databases, see the WESTLAW Directory or the *WESTLAW Database List*. Because new information is continually being added to WESTLAW, you should also check the Welcome to WESTLAW screen and the WESTLAW Directory for new database information.

WESTLAW Federal Databases

Description	Database Identifier	Beginning Coverage (see Scope for more specific information)
Federal Case Law		
Combined Federal Cases (includes U.S. Supreme Court, courts of appeals, district courts, U.S. bankruptcy courts, U.S. Court of Federal Claims, U.S. Tax Court, former Tax Court of the United States, former U.S. Board of Tax Appeals, military courts, and other federal and territorial courts)	ALLFEDS, ALLFEDS–OLD	1789
U.S. Supreme Court	SCT, SCT–OLD	1790

U.S. Courts of Appeals	CTA, CTA–OLD	1891
Individual Courts of Appeals	CTAX—CTAX–OLD (X represents the circuit number) CTAF, CTAF–OLD CTADC, CTADC–OLD	Varies by individual database
Former Temporary Emergency Court of Appeals	CTA	1972–1993
Former U.S. Court of Customs Appeals	CTA–OLD	1910–1929
Former U.S. Court of Customs and Patent Appeals	CTA, CTA–OLD	1929–1982
U.S. District Courts (includes cases reported in West's® *Federal Rules Decisions*®)	DCT, DCT–OLD	1789
Federal Judicial Circuit Cases (includes all U.S. Supreme Court decisions, court of appeals decisions for a circuit, U.S. bankruptcy and district court decisions for each state within the circuit, and decisions of the Judicial Panel on Multidistrict Litigation)	FEDX–ALL (X represents the circuit number or abbreviation)	Varies by court
U.S. Court of Federal Claims	FEDCL	1992
U.S. Court of International Trade (Includes cases from the U.S. Court of International Trade and former U.S. Customs Court)	FINT–CIT	1954
Judicial Panel on Multidistrict Litigation	DCT	1968
Special Court, Regional Rail Reorganization Act	DCT	1974
U.S. Tax Court	FTX–TCT	1969
Former U.S. Circuit Courts	DCT–OLD	1789–1911
Former U.S. Commerce Court	DCT–OLD	1911–1913
Former U.S. Court of Claims	FEDCL, FEDCL–OLD	1863–1982
Former U.S. Customs Court	DCT	1955–1980
Former U.S. Claims Court	FEDCL	1982–1992
Former Tax Court of the United States	FTX–TCT, FTX–TCT–OLD	1942–1969
Former U.S. Board of Tax Appeals	FTX–TCT–OLD	1924–1942

Combined Federal and State Case Law

Federal & State Case Law	ALLCASES, ALLCASES–OLD	1789
Individual States' State and Federal Cases	XX–CS–ALL (XX represents the state's two-letter postal abbreviation)	Varies by court
Circuits' Federal and State Cases	CTAX–ALL (X represents the circuit number or abbreviation)	Varies by court

Federal Statutes, Regulations and Court Rules

United States Code Annotated®	USCA	Current data
Federal Register	FR	July 1980
Code of Federal Regulations	CFR	Current data
Congressional Record	CR	First Session of the 99th Congress (1985)
United States Public Laws (current)	US–PL	Current data
United States Public Laws (historical)	US–PLYY (YY represents the last two digits of a year)	1989
United States Code Legislative History	LH	1948
Federal Rules	US–RULES	Current data
Federal Orders	US–ORDERS	Current data
Congressional Quarterly's Text of Congressional Bills	CQ–BILLTXT	Current data
Congressional Quarterly's Congressional Bill Tracking	CQ–BILLTRK	Current data
Billcast	BC	Current data
Bill Tracking—Federal (Summaries)	US–BILLTRK	Current data
Regulation Tracking—Federal	US–REGTRK	Current data

News and Information

WESTLAW Bulletin—U.S. Supreme Court	WLB–SCT	Current data
WESTLAW Topical Highlights—Federal Practice and Procedure	WTH–FPP	Current data

Texts and Periodicals

Federal Bar News & Journal	FEDBNJ	1983
Federal Circuit Bar Journal	FEDCBJ	1991
Federal Judicial Center Publications	FJC	1978
Federal Litigator	FEDLIT	1993
Federal Rules Decisions (articles from the West reporter)	FEDRDTP	1986 (vol. 108)
Journals & Law Reviews	JLR	Varies by database

Section 3. Menu–Driven WESTLAW: EZ ACCESS®

EZ ACCESS is West Publishing's menu-driven research system. It is ideal for new or infrequent WESTLAW users because it requires no experience or training on WESTLAW.

To access EZ ACCESS, type **ez.** The EZ ACCESS main menu will be displayed. Whenever you are unsure of the next step, or if the choice you want is not listed, simply type **ez;** additional choices will be displayed. Once you retrieve documents with EZ ACCESS, use standard WESTLAW commands to browse your documents. For more information on browsing documents, see the *WESTLAW Reference Manual* or the *WESTLAW User Guide.*

Section 4. Retrieving a Document with a Citation: Find and Jump

4.1 Find

Find is a WESTLAW service that allows you to retrieve a document by entering its citation. Find allows you to retrieve documents from anywhere in WESTLAW without accessing or changing databases or losing your search result. Find is available for many documents, including case law (federal and state), the *United States Code Annotated,* the *Code of Federal Regulations,* the *Federal Register,* federal rules, federal public laws, and texts and periodicals.

To use Find, type **fi** followed by the document citation. Following is a list of examples:

To Find This Document	**Type**
28 U.S.C.A. § 1332	**fi 28 usca 1332**
Akins v. Rodriguez, 15 F.3d 883 (9th Cir.1994)	**fi 15 f3d 883**
Greenfield v. National Westminster Bank USA, 1994 WL 96776 (S.D.N.Y.1994)	**fi 1994 wl 96776**
Borcher, *The Origins Of Diversity Jurisdiction, The Rise Of Legal Positivism, And A Brave New World For Erie And Klaxon,* 72 Tex.L.Rev. 79 (1993).	**fi 72 tex.l.rev. 79**

4.2 Jump

Jump is a feature that allows you to move from one location to another on WESTLAW. For example, use Jump to go from a case or law review article to a cited case, USCA® section or article; from a headnote to the corresponding text in the opinion; or from an entry in a statute index database to the full text of the statute. To use Jump, press the **Tab** key until the cursor reaches the Jump marker (> or ▶) you want to select, then press **Enter.** You can also use a mouse to click or double-click the Jump marker.

Section 5. Natural Language Searching: WIN®—WESTLAW is Natural™

Overview: WIN (WESTLAW is Natural) is a Natural Language search method on WESTLAW. With WIN, you can retrieve documents by simply describing your issue in plain English. If you are a relatively new user, Natural Language searching makes it easier to retrieve cases on point. If you are an experienced user, Natural Language increases your research proficiency by giving you a valuable alternative search method.

When you enter a Natural Language description, WESTLAW automatically identifies legal phrases, removes common words and generates variations of terms in your description. WESTLAW then searches for the legal phrases and other concepts in your description. Concepts may include significant terms, phrases, legal citations or topic and key numbers. Based on the frequency with which each concept occurs in the database and in each document, WESTLAW retrieves the 20 documents that most closely match your description, beginning with the document most likely to match.

5.1 Natural Language Searching

To use Natural Language searching, access the database containing documents relevant to your issue. If your current search method is Terms and Connectors, type **nat** or select the *Natural Language* Jump marker to change to the Natural Language search method and display the Enter Description screen. Then enter a Natural Language description such as the following:

what is the political question doctrine

5.2 Concept Ranking

WESTLAW displays the 20 documents that most closely match your description, beginning with the document most likely to match. If you want to view additional documents, use the Next command. Type **next** to display the next 10 documents. To retrieve more than 10 documents, specify a multiple of 10, such as **next20** or **next30.** You can retrieve up to 100 documents in total.

5.3 Browsing a Natural Language Search Result

Best Mode: To display the best portion (the portion that most closely matches your description) of each document in your search result, type **b.**

Standard Browsing Commands: You can also browse your Natural Language search result using standard WESTLAW browsing commands, such as citations list (L), Locate (loc), page mode (p) and term mode (t). When you browse your Natural Language search result in term mode, the five portions of each document that are most likely to match your description are displayed.

Section 6. Terms and Connectors Searching

Overview: With standard Terms and Connectors searching, you enter a query, which consists of key terms from your research issue and connectors specifying the relationship between these terms.

Terms and Connectors searching is useful when you want to retrieve a document for which you have specific information, such as the title or the citation. Terms and Connectors searching is also useful when you want to retrieve documents relating to a specific issue. To change from Natural Language searching to Terms and Connectors searching, type **tc** or select the *Terms and Connectors* Jump marker at the Enter Description screen.

6.1 Terms

Plurals and Possessives: Plurals are automatically retrieved when you enter the singular form of a term. This is true for both regular and irregular plurals (e.g., **child** retrieves *children*). If you enter the plural form of a term, you will not retrieve the singular form.

If you enter the non-possessive form of a term, WESTLAW automatically retrieves the possessive form as well. However, if you enter the possessive form, only the possessive form is retrieved.

Automatic Equivalencies: Some terms have alternative forms or equivalencies; for example, *5* and *five* are equivalent terms. WESTLAW automatically retrieves equivalent terms. The *WESTLAW Reference Manual* contains a list of equivalent terms.

Compound Words and Acronyms: When a compound word is one of your search terms, use a hyphen to retrieve all forms of the word. For example, the term ***along-side*** retrieves *along-side, alongside* and *along side.*

When using an acronym as a search term, place a period after each of the letters in the acronym to retrieve any of its forms. For example, the term **f.t.c.** retrieves *ftc, f.t.c., f t c* and *f. t. c.* Note: The acronym *f.t.c.* does <u>not</u> retrieve *Federal Trade Commission,* so remember to add additional alternative terms to your query such as **"federal trade commission"**.

Root Expander and Universal Character: When you use the Terms and Connectors search method, placing a root expander (!) at the end of a root term generates all other terms with that root. For example, adding the ! symbol to the root *realign* in the query

realign! /5 party

instructs WESTLAW to retrieve such words as *realign, realigned, realignment* and *realigning.*

The universal character (*) stands for one character and can be inserted in the middle or at the end of a term. For example, the term

s**holder**

will retrieve *shareholder* and *stockholder.* Adding three asterisks to the root *elect* in the query

elect***

instructs WESTLAW to retrieve all forms of the root with up to three additional characters. Terms like *elected* or *election* are retrieved by this query. However, terms with more than three letters following the root, such as *electronic,* are not retrieved. Plurals are always retrieved, even if more than three letters follow the root.

Phrase Searching: To search for a phrase, place it within quotation marks. For example, to search for references to forum non conveniens, type **"forum non conveniens".** When you are using the Terms and Connectors search method, you should use phrase searching only if you are certain that the phrase will not appear in any other form.

6.2 Alternative Terms

After selecting the terms for your query, consider which alternative terms are necessary. For example, if you are searching for the term *resident,* you might also want to search for the term *non-resident.* You should consider both synonyms and antonyms as alternative terms. You can also use the WESTLAW thesaurus to add alternative terms to your query.

6.3 Connectors

After selecting terms and alternative terms for your query, use connectors to specify the relationship that should exist between search terms in your retrieved documents. The connectors you can use are described below:

Use:	To retrieve documents with:	Example:
& (and)	both terms	**diversity & counter-claim**
or (space)	either term or both terms	**abstention abstain***
/p	search terms in the same paragraph	**discovery /p order /3 protection**
/s	search terms in the same sentence	**indispensable /s party**
+s	one search term preceding the other within the same sentence, especially useful when searching in the title field (ti) where both parties have the same name	**ti(kurzman +s kurzman)**
/n	search terms within "n" terms of each other (where "n" is a number)	**choice /3 forum**
+n	one search term preceding the other by "n" terms (where "n" is a number)	**summary +3 judgment**

Use:	To exclude documents with:	Example:
% (but not)	search terms following the % symbol	**attorney lawyer /5 client /s privileg! % sy,di(work-product)**

6.4 Restricting Your Search by Field

Overview: Documents in each WESTLAW database consist of several segments, or fields. One field may contain the citation, another the title, another the synopsis, and so forth. Not all databases contain the same fields. Also, depending on the database, fields of the same name may contain different types of information.

To view the fields and field content for a specific database, see Scope or type **f** while in the database. Note that in some databases, not every field is available for every document.

To retrieve only those documents containing your search terms in a specific field, restrict your search to that field. To restrict your search to a specific field, type the field name or abbreviation followed by your search terms enclosed in parentheses. For example, to retrieve a case in the U.S. Court of Appeals for the Eighth Circuit Cases database (CTA8) entitled *Ringsred v. City of Duluth,* search for your terms in the title field:

ti(ringsred & duluth)

The fields discussed below are available in WESTLAW databases you might use for researching federal practice issues.

Digest and Synopsis Fields: The digest and synopsis fields, added to case law databases by West Publishing's attorney-editors, summarize the main points of a case. The synopsis field contains a brief description of a case. The digest field contains the topic, headnote, court and title fields and includes the complete hierarchy of concepts used to classify the point of law, including the West digest topic name and number and the key number. Restricting your search to these fields limits your result to cases in which your terms are related to a major issue in the case.

Consider restricting your search to one or both of these fields if

- you are searching for common terms or terms with more than one meaning, and you need to narrow your search; or

- you cannot narrow your search by moving to a smaller database.

For example, to retrieve cases that discuss the principal place of business of an unincorporated entity in relation to federal court jurisdiction, access the U.S. Courts of Appeals Cases database (CTA) and type:

sy,di(principal /s business /p unincorporated /p jurisdiction!)

Headnote Field: The headnote field is a part of the digest field, but does not contain the topic number, hierarchical classification information, key number or title. The headnote field contains only the one-sentence summary of the point of law and any supporting statutory citations given by the author of the opinion. A headnote field restriction is useful when you are searching for specific statutory sections or rule numbers. For example, to retrieve headnotes that cite 28 U.S.C.A. § 1441, type the following query:

he(28 +5 1441)

Topic Field: The topic field is also a part of the digest field. It contains hierarchical classification information, including the West digest topic name and number, and the key number. You should restrict search terms to the topic field in a case law database if

- a digest field search retrieves too many documents; or
- you want to retrieve cases with digest paragraphs classified under more than one topic.

For example, the topic Federal Courts has the topic number 170B. To retrieve United States district court cases that discuss the fraudulent joinder of parties to defeat diversity jurisdiction, access the U.S. District Courts Cases database (DCT) and type a query like the following:

to(170b) /p fraud! /s join! /s defeat! /s diversity

To retrieve West headnotes classified under more than one topic and key number, search for your terms in the topic field. For example, to search for cases discussing remittitur, which may be classified to 170A, Federal Civil Procedure, or 170B, Federal Courts, type a query like the following:

to(remittitur)

For a complete list of West digest topics and their corresponding topic numbers, access the Key Number service; type **key.**

> Be aware that slip opinions and cases from topical services do not contain the digest, headnote or topic fields.

Prelim and Caption Fields: When searching in a database containing statutes, rules or regulations, restrict your search to the prelim and caption fields to retrieve documents in which your terms are important enough to appear in a section name or heading. For example, to retrieve federal statutes relating to interpleader actions, access the United States Code Annotated database (USCA) and type the following:

pr,ca(interpleader)

6.5 Restricting Your Search by Date

You can instruct WESTLAW to retrieve documents decided or issued before, after, or on a specified date, as well as within a range of dates. The following are examples of queries that contain date restrictions:

da(aft 1992) & "erie doctrine"
da(1994) & pend*nt /3 jurisdiction
da(3/17/94) & "rule 11" /s violat!

You can also instruct WESTLAW to retrieve documents added to a database on or after a specified date, as well as within a range of dates. The following are examples of queries that contain added date restrictions:

ad(aft 1993) & di("class action" /p certif!)
ad(aft 1–1–94 & bef 4–1–94 & case /3 controversy /s standing

Section 7. Verifying Your Research with Citators

Overview: WESTLAW contains four citator services to assist you in checking the validity of cases you intend to rely on. These citator services—Insta–Cite®, Shepard's® Citations, Shepard's PreView® and QuickCite™—help you perform many valuable research tasks, saving you hours of manual research. Sections 7.1 through 7.4 provide further information on these services.

WESTLAW also contains Shepard's Citations for federal statutes, and Shepard's Citations for state statutes are being added on a state-by-state basis.

For citations not covered by the citator services, including persuasive secondary authority such as restatements, treatises and law review articles, use a technique called WESTLAW as a citator to retrieve cases that cite your authority (see Section 7.5).

7.1 Insta–Cite

Insta–Cite is West Publishing Company's case history and citation verification service. Use Insta–Cite to see whether your case is good law. Insta–Cite provides the following types of information about a citation:

Direct History. In addition to reversals and affirmances, Insta–Cite gives you the complete reported history of a litigated matter including any related cases. Insta–Cite provides the direct history of federal cases from 1754 and state cases from 1879. Related references (cases related to the litigation) are provided from 1983 to date. Direct case history is available within 24–36 hours of receipt of a case at West.

Negative Indirect History. Insta–Cite lists subsequent cases that may have a substantial negative impact on your case, including cases overruling your case or calling it into question. Insta–Cite provides negative indirect history from 1972 to date. To retrieve negative indirect history prior to 1972, use Shepard's Citations (see Section 7.2).

Secondary Source References. Insta–Cite also provides references to secondary sources that cite your case. These secondary sources include the legal encyclopedia *Corpus Juris Secundum*®.

Parallel Citations. Insta–Cite provides parallel citations for cases, including citations to *United States Law Week* and many topical reporters.

Citation Verification. Insta–Cite confirms that you have the correct volume and page number for a case, as well as the correct spelling of proper names. Citation verification information is available from 1754 for federal cases and from 1879 for state cases.

7.2 Shepard's Citations

For case law, Shepard's provides a comprehensive list of cases and other documents that have cited a particular case. Shepard's also includes explanatory analysis to indicate how the citing cases have treated the case, e.g., "followed," "explained."

For statutes, Shepard's Citations provides a comprehensive list of cases citing a particular statute, as well as information on subsequent legislative action. The federal court rule divisions for each of the statute citators currently available on WESTLAW provide a comprehensive list of cases citing a particular federal court rule.. Federal court rule divisions include:

Supreme Court Rules	Federal Rules of Criminal Procedure
Federal Rules of Evidence	Federal Rules of Civil Procedure
Bankruptcy Rules	Federal Rules of Appellate Procedure

In addition to citations from federal, state and regional citators, Shepard's on WESTLAW includes citations from specialized citators such as *Evidence Citations*.

7.3 Shepard's PreView

Shepard's PreView gives you a preview of citing references for case law from West's National Reporter System® that will appear in Shepard's Citations. Depending on the citation, Shepard's PreView provides citing information days, weeks or even months before the same information appears in Shepard's online. Use Shepard's PreView to update your Shepard's results.

7.4 Quick*Cite*

Quick*Cite* is a citator service that enables you to automatically retrieve the most recent citing cases on WESTLAW, including slip opinions.

There is a four- to six-week gap between a citing case's availability on WESTLAW and its listing in Shepard's PreView. This gap occurs because cases go through an editorial process at West Publishing Company before they are added to Shepard's PreView. To retrieve the most recent citing cases, therefore, you need to search case law databases on WESTLAW for references to your case.

Quick*Cite* formulates a query using the title, the case citation(s) and an added date restriction. Quick*Cite* then accesses the appropriate database, either ALLSTATES or ALLFEDS, and runs the query for you. Quick*Cite* also allows you to tailor the query to your specific research needs; you can choose a different date range or select another database.

Quick*Cite* is designed to retrieve documents that cite cases. To retrieve citing references to other documents, such as statutes and law review articles, use WESTLAW as a citator (see Section 7.5).

7.5 Using WESTLAW as a Citator

Using WESTLAW as a citator, you can search for documents citing a specific statute, regulation, rule, agency decision or other authority. For example, to retrieve documents citing Wright, *Law of Federal Courts* § 92, access the U.S. Courts of Appeals Cases database (CTA) and type a query like the following:

wright /5 "federal court" /5 92

To retrieve cases that cite a section of the *United States Code Annotated,* such as 28 U.S.C.A. § 1257(a), search for the citation:

28 +5 1257(a)

7.6 Selected Citator Commands

Command:	Definition:
ic xxx or **ic**	Retrieves an Insta–Cite result when followed by a case citation (where **xxx** is the citation), or when entered from a displayed case, Shepard's result or Shepard's PreView result.
sh xxx or **sh**	Retrieves a Shepard's result when followed by a case or statute citation (where **xxx** is the citation), or when entered from a displayed case or statute, Insta–Cite result or Shepard's PreView result.
sp xxx or **sp**	Retrieves a Shepard's PreView result when followed by a case citation (where **xxx** is the citation), or when entered from a displayed case, Insta–Cite result or Shepard's result.
qc xxx or **qc**	Retrieves a Quick*Cite* result when followed by a case citation (where **xxx** is the citation), or when entered from a displayed case, Insta–Cite result, Shepard's result or Shepard's PreView result.
sc	Retrieves the scope of coverage for Insta–Cite or Shepard's PreView when you are viewing a result from that service. From a Shepard's result, displays the scope of coverage for the publication.
sc xx	Retrieves the scope of coverage of a citator service (where **xx** is the citator service), e.g., **sc ic.**
sh sc xxx	Retrieves the scope of coverage for a specific publication in Shepard's, where **xxx** is the publication abbreviation (e.g., **sh sc f2d**).
xx pubs	Retrieves a list of publications available in the citator service and their abbreviations (where **xx** is the citator service abbreviation).
xx cmds	Retrieves a list of commands in the citator service (where **xx** is the citator service abbreviation).
sh analysis	Retrieves a list of Shepard's analysis codes, e.g., *extended, revised,* etc.
sh courts	Retrieves a list of courts and their abbreviations used in Shepard's Citations.
loc	Automatically restricts an Insta–Cite, Shepard's or Shepard's PreView result to selected categories.
loc auto	Restricts all subsequent Insta–Cite, Shepard's or Shepard's PreView results to selected categories.
xloc	Cancels a Locate request.
xloc auto	Cancels a Locate Auto request.

Section 8. Research Examples

8.1 Retrieving Law Review Articles

Recent law review articles are often the best place to begin researching a legal issue because law review articles serve 1) as an excellent
introduction to a new topic or review for a stale one, providing terminology to help in query formulation; 2) as a finding tool for pertinent
primary authority, such as cases and statutes; and 3) in some instances,
as persuasive secondary authority. For example, you need to gain more
background information on the factors the federal courts have considered in determining what is a justiciable case or controversy.

Solution

- To retrieve recent law review articles relevant to your issue, access
  the Journals & Law Reviews database (JLR) by typing **db jlr**; select
  Natural Language searching; then enter a description like the
  following:

what is a justiciable case or controversy

- If you have a citation to an article in a specific publication, use Find
  to retrieve it. (Note: For more information on Find, see Section 4.1
  of this appendix.) For example, to retrieve the article found at 86
  Northwestern University Law Review 143, type

fi 86 nw u l rev 143

- If you know the title of an article, but not which journal it appeared
  in, access the JLR database and search for key terms from the title
  in the title field (ti). For example, to retrieve the article "The
  Ideologies of Forum Shopping—Why Doesn't a Conservative Court
  Protect Defendants?", type the following Terms and Connectors
  query:

ti("forum shopping"   &   defendant)

8.2 Retrieving Federal Statutes

You need to retrieve federal statutes dealing with removal of cases
from state court to federal court.

Solution

- Access the United States Code Annotated database (USCA). Search
  for your terms in the prelim (pr) and caption (ca) fields using the
  Terms and Connectors search method:

pr,ca(remov!   &   case   &   "state court")

- When you know the citation for a specific section of a statute, use
  Find to retrieve the statute. For example, to retrieve 28 U.S.C.A.
  § 1443, type

fi 28 usca 1443

- To look at surrounding statutory sections, use the Documents in
  Sequence command. To retrieve the section preceding § 1443, type
  d–. To retrieve the section immediately following § 1443, type **d.**

- When you retrieve a statute on WESTLAW, it will contain an
  Update message if legislation amending or repealing it is available

online. To display this legislation, select the Jump marker in the Update message with the **Tab** key or your mouse or type **update.**

> Because slip copy versions of laws are added to WESTLAW before they contain full editorial enhancements, they are not retrieved with Update. To retrieve slip copy versions of laws, access the United States Public Laws database by typing **db us-pl,** then type **ci(slip)** and descriptive terms, e.g., **ci(slip) &** *[term].* Slip copy documents are replaced by the editorially enhanced versions within a few working days. Update also does not retrieve legislation that enacts a new statute or covers a topic that will not be incorporated into the statutes. To retrieve this legislation, access US–PL and enter a query containing terms that describe the new legislation.

8.3 Retrieving Court Rules

You've misplaced your rules pamphlet and you need to check the Federal Rules of Civil Procedure.

Solution

- Access the Federal Rules database (US–RULES) and search for the rule abbreviation in the citation field (ci) and key terms in the caption field (ca):

ci(frcp) & ca(discover! & sanction)

To determine the abbreviation for the Federal Rules of Civil Procedure, as well as the Federal Rules of Evidence, Rules of the U.S. Supreme Court, rules of the U.S. courts of appeals and other rules, use Scope; type **sc us-rules.**

Note: Local rules of the U.S. district courts and U.S. bankruptcy courts are contained in the state court rules database (XX–RULES, where XX is the state's two-letter postal abbreviation) for the state in which the court sits. Access the database and search for the rule abbreviation in the citation field, e.g., **ci(usdct).** To determine the rule abbreviation, use Scope, e.g., **sc ia-rules.**

- When you know the rule number, use Find to retrieve the rule. For example, to retrieve Rule 11 of the Federal Rules of Civil Procedure, type

fi frcp rule 11

- When you retrieve a court rule on WESTLAW, it will contain an Update message if documents amending or repealing it are available online. To display these documents, select the Jump marker in the Update message with the **Tab** key or your mouse. Note: Slip copy documents, legislation enacting a new statute or rule, and legislation covering a topic that will not be incorporated into the statutes cannot be retrieved with the Update service. To retrieve these materials, run a descriptive word search in the US–PL or US–ORDERS database.

8.4 Using the Citator Services

One of the cases you retrieve in your case law research is *Republic National Bank of Miami v. United States,* 113 S.Ct. 554 (1992). You want to see whether this case is good law and whether other cases have cited this case.

Solution

- Use Insta–Cite to retrieve the direct history and negative indirect history of *Republic National Bank*. While viewing the case, type **ic.**
- To Shepardize® *Republic National Bank* from the Insta–Cite display, select the *Shepard's* Jump marker or type **sh.**

  Limit your Shepard's result to decisions containing a reference to a specific headnote, such as headnote 4. Type **loc 4.**
- Check Shepard's PreView for more current cases citing *Republic National Bank*. From the Shepard's display, select the *Shepard's PreView* Jump marker or type **sp.**
- Check Quick*Cite* for the most current cases citing *Republic National Bank*. From the Shepard's PreView display, select the *QuickCite* Jump marker or type **qc.** Then follow the on-screen instructions.

8.5 Following Recent Developments

As the federal courts and procedure specialist in your firm, you are expected to keep up with and summarize recent legal developments in this area of the law. How can you do this efficiently?

Solution

- One of the easiest ways to stay abreast of recent developments in federal civil practice is by accessing the WESTLAW Topical Highlights—Federal Practice and Procedure database (WTH–FPP). The WTH–FPP database summarizes recent legal developments, including court decisions, legislation and changes to the federal rules.

  To access the database, type **db wth-fpp.** You will automatically retrieve a list of documents added to the database in the last two weeks.
- To read a summary of a document listed, type its corresponding number.
- To view the full text of a document, type **fi** while viewing the summary, or type **fi** followed by the document citation while viewing the list, e.g., **fi 1994 wl 121824.**
- To search this database, type **s** to display the Enter Query screen. At the Enter Query screen, type your query. For example, to retrieve references discussing federal removal jurisdiction, type a query like the following:

remov! /s jurisdiction

Table of Cases

G

I

J

V

X

*

Table of Statutes and Court Rules

Index

References are to Pages.

IMPLIED RIGHTS OF ACTION
Effect of 42 U.S.C.A. § 1983, p. 137.
When recognized, 417–418.

INDEPENDENT COUNSEL
Appointment of, 20.

INJUNCTIONS
Abstention doctrines, 332–350.
Anti–Injunction Act, 296–306.
Appeal,
    Interlocutory orders, 749–753.
    Preliminary injunction, 750–751.
    Temporary restraining order, 750–751.
Contempt where jurisdiction lacking, 95–99.
Exhaustion of state remedies, 313–315.
Federal proceedings, 296.
Johnson Act, 319–322.
Jurisdictional amount, 204–207.
"Our Federalism," 339–350.
Rate orders, 319–322.
State injunctions of federal proceedings, 296.
State officers, 306–312.
    Restrictions on enjoining, 319–350.
    Substitution, 559–560.
State proceedings, 296–306.
        See Anti–Injunction Act.
    Interpleader, 536–537.
    State law enforcement, 339–350.
Tax Injunction Act, 319–322.
Three-judge court, 315–319.

INSTRUCTIONS TO JURY
Comment on evidence, 672–673.
Objection required, 673–674.
"Plain error," 673–674.
State practice not controlling, 672–673.

INTEREST
Effect on jurisdictional amount, 207–209.
Judgment, 700.

INTERLOCUTORY REVIEW
See Appeals.

INTERPLEADER
    Generally, 531–539.
Attorneys' fees, 534.
Defendant may seek, 537–538.
Deposit in court, 536–537.
Effect of state law, 389–391, 533–534.
Equitable restrictions on, 532–533.
Injunction against state proceedings, 536.
Jurisdictional amount, 534–535.
Jurisdictional requirements, 39, 157–158, 534–535.
Jury trial, 538–539, 658.
Process, 535–536.
Rule 22 interpleader distinguished from statutory interpleader, 531–538.
State procedure not controlling, 533.
States, 538.
Statutory interpleader distinguished from interpleader under rule, 531–538.
Supplemental-jurisdiction statute, 39.

INTERPLEADER—Cont'd
United States, 538.
Venue, 535.
When authorized, 531–534.

INTERROGATORIES
See Discovery.

INTERSTATE COMMERCE COMMISSION ORDERS
Review of, 315, 758–760.

INTERVENTION
    Generally, 539–547.
Appellate review, 547.
Class actions, 513–514, 520.
Jurisdictional requirements, 39, 544–546.
Of right, 539–542.
Permissive intervention, 542–544.
Procedure for, 546.
State law not controlling, 539.
Stockholders' derivative actions, 529.
Supplemental-jurisdiction statute, 39, 544–546.
Timeliness of application, 543.

ISSUE PRECLUSION
See Res Judicata.

JOINDER OF CLAIMS
        See Counterclaims; Cross–Claims.
    Generally, 561–564.
Consolidation of actions, 695.
Distinction between jurisdictional and procedural limitations, 552.
Jurisdictional amount, 209–210, 562–563.
Jurisdictional requirements, 39, 562–563.
Jury trial, 655–658.
Multiparty cases, 563–564.
Not compulsory, 562.
Separate trials, 693–695.
State law not controlling, 562.

JOINDER OF PARTIES
        See Class Actions; Impleader; Interpleader; Intervention; Stockholders' Derivative Actions.
    Generally, 494–507.
Additional parties to counterclaims, 573–574.
Alternative, 505.
Common question of law or fact, 503–504, 563–564.
Complete diversity required, 156–158, 534–535.
Compulsory joinder, 494–501.
Consolidation of actions, 695.
Distinction between jurisdictional and procedural limitations, 552.
"Indispensable" parties, 495–501.
Involuntary plaintiff, 501–502.
Joint interest, 496–497.
Jurisdictional amount, 211–215.
Misjoinder, 506–507.
Multiclaim cases, 563–564.
"Necessary" parties, 495–501.

TRIALS—Cont'd

Sufficiency of evidence, 651–653, 672, 683–686.

Verdict,
    Attacks on, 676–687.
    Directed, 672, 682–686
        Terminology changed, 672.
    General, 674.
    Special, 674–676.

Voluntary dismissal, 695–696.

UNFAIR COMPETITION

Jurisdictional amount, 192, 200–201.

Pendent jurisdiction, 115, 116.

Statute, 116, 192.

UNINCORPORATED ASSOCIATIONS

Business trust, 170.

Capacity, 493.

Citizenship, 169–171.

Depositions of, 611–613, 617.

Limited partnership, 170–171.

Partnership, 170–172.

Service of process upon, 445–451.

Venue, 266–267.

UNITED STATES

Counterclaims against, 129, 572.

Criminal prosecutions, 124–126.

Defendant, 128–131.

Interpleader, 538.

Officers and agencies, 130–131.

Plaintiff, 126–128.

Statistics, 126.

Substitution of officers, 557–560.

Suit against state, 808–809.

UNITED STATES CLAIMS COURT

Business of, 17–18.

History, 17–18.

Name changed, 17–18.

UNITED STATES COURT OF FEDERAL CLAIMS

Name given in 1992, pp. 17–18.

VENUE

Admiralty, 268, 279–280.

Aliens, 263.

Ancillary matters, 39, 554.

Appeal, 285–286.

Change of,
    Civil cases, 277–286.
    Criminal cases, 275–277.

Civil cases, 256–271, 277–286.

Claim arose, 260–261.

Class actions, 521.

Corporations, 264–266.

Counterclaims, 573.

Criminal cases, 271–275.

Cross-claims, 577.

Distinguished from jurisdiction, 257.

Divisions, 258.

Federal agencies and officers, 131, 264, 270–271.

Federal law controls, 257.

Forum non conveniens, 278.

Forum-selection clauses, 271, 408–409.

History of venue statutes, 256–262.

Impleader, 554, 555.

Interpleader, 535.

Local actions, 257, 268–270.

Multiparty cases, 259, 262.

National banks, 267.

1990 statute, 261–262.

Patent infringement, 267–268.

Proposals for change, 270–271.

Public officials, 131, 264, 270–271.

Removed cases, 242.

Residence, 263.

Special venue statutes, 267–268, 279.

Stockholders' derivative actions, 530.

Unincorporated associations, 266–267.

Wrong venue, 277–278.

VERDICT

See Trials.

†